Scarne's ENCYCLOPEDIA OF GAMES

Other Books by John Scarne

Scarne's

1817

ENCYCLOPEDIA

OF GAMES

John Scarne

HARPER & ROW, PUBLISHERS

New York, Evanston, San Francisco, London

Contents

Publisher's Note

The world's game fans, young and old, will ever be grateful to John Scarne for his years of untiring effort in making this book available to them. It is the most complete, most authoritative, and most up-to-date reference book on modern games. Not only does it provide the mathematics, rules, playing tips and strategy for more than 1,000 games, at least 300 of which are not available elsewhere in book form but for the first time it presents a detailed analysis of the underlying mathematics of countless popular games.

John Scarne is recognized as the world's foremost authority on games of chance and skill. The once universal "According to Hoyle" has been replaced among smart-money players throughout the world with the phrase, "According to Scarne." "According to Scarne" among these knowledgeable players means "correctly played" or "played according to the universally accepted rules." Recognition as the top authority could only be achieved by a man like Scarne who has spent a lifetime in constant study and research into every phase of games and gaming.

Guesses never satisfy Scarne (his name incidentally is pronounced Scarney); he is a perfectionist. This quality explains why he is acknowledged as the magician's magician. His worldwide fame as a game authority dates from World War II when he acted as gaming advisor to the United States Armed Forces. During the war he gave hundreds of gambling demonstrations before thousands of members of the Armed Forces to show them how to avoid being cheated by crooked gamblers. He also has been called into consultation as an expert on games and gambling by the United States Senate, the Federal Bureau of Investigation, the British Home Office, the Puerto Rican Government, the Government of Panama, the Government of the Netherlands Antilles, the Hilton International Hotel chain and numerous other governmental and hotel agencies throughout the world. In addition John Scarne is game consultant to the Encyclopædia Britannica and the World Book Encyclopedia.

Games are never static; they continually evolve and change. But some game books continue to print out-of-date rules long after they have become obsolete. Scarne, unlike many other game authorities, is and always has been on the inside of the gambling business. In the professional gaming world he is considered the greatest authority on rules, odds, percentages, and the mathematical structure of games of skill and chance. Time after time he has calculated the precise mathematics of private club, banking and casino games when other game experts and mathematicians have failed.

Over the years, John Scarne has been instrumental in having the rules of many card games changed, including those for Black Jack, Poker, Gin Rummy, Canasta and numerous other skill and chance games. In 1967, he developed a new dice layout which has since been installed in many casinos throughout the world. He follows the changes and variations of all kinds of games be they skill or chance; he revises his official rules regularly and incorporates new variations; and he often recommends new rules of his own which bring the games up to date and make them mathematically sound.

As an inventor of games, he has more than 200 to his credit, some of which he markets through his own company, John Scarne Games, Inc. of North Bergen, New Jersey. Among them are such delightful skill board games as *Teeko, Scarney Solitaire, Follow the Arrow,* and such hit card games as *Skarney* and *Skarney Gin.* His latest casino game innovation is *Scarney Baccarat* which has been hailed by casino personnel as the first really new casino banking card game in fifty years and is being played in dozens of major casinos all over the world. Some time ago he developed a new set of dice known as Scarney Dice. With these dice he has developed more than 40 new games, including *Scarney Put and Take, Scarney 21 Up and Down, Scarney Duplicate Jackpots* and the hit dice game, *Scarney 3000.*

In order to make *Scarne's Encyclopedia of Games* the definitive work in this field for years to come, John Scarne has spared neither expense nor effort in organizing and clarifying his material. He has made sure that the treatment of all games is systematic and uniform. The description of each game begins with the apparatus and the players, and then follows the natural course of play, step by step, until the end. Each phase of the game is treated in a separate paragraph, and each is preceded by key words in heavy type. Thus specific information on any aspect of a game can be located quickly and easily.

Technical terms are fully defined in the glossary and a complete index lists all the games, their variations, and any other names they are known by.

All disputed points have been settled in an original manner. Instead of taking any one person as an authority, the history of each game has been traced from its source to its present status, and its rules have been carefully compared with those of other members of the same family of games. The times and the reasons for the various changes have been ascertained, and the rules given are not only in strict accord with the true spirit of the game, but are based upon common sense and equity. When official rules exist for any game they are given in full.

Mr. Scarne is the author of many successful books on games, magic and gambling, including the best seller, *Scarne's Complete Guide to Gambling,* and the standard reference books on card and dice games, *Scarne on Cards* and *Scarne on Dice.*

In addition to his extraordinary dexterity at manipulating cards and his many years' experience in games of skill and chance, he has the unique ability to explain clearly and simply the fundamentals of playing each game. The famed magazine writer and editor, Sidney Carroll, aptly wrote about John Scarne, "To call Scarne an outstanding expert on games of skill and chance is to praise him with a faint damn. He is by all odds the world's greatest." And the late John Lardner wrote, "Scarne is to games what Einstein is to physics."

Preface

Introduction to Games You Can Play

A game means any amusement or sport, any contest or play. Thus, games cover a wide range of activities. But in this *Encyclopedia of Games,* I have selected the largest number of games that all can play, regardless of age or sex. Many of these can be traced back to the earliest times of man.

In fact, most of our gaming implements can be traced back to man's early practice of divination by arrows and sticks. Actually, the divinatory throwing of sticks is the casting of the lots of biblical mention, and many ancient writers refer to the bundles of sacred tamarisk twigs used by the magi of Chaldea and Babylonia, the divining rods of Assyria, and the similar *baresma* of the Parsis of India.

The game of Jackstraws can be traced back to this divination by throwing sticks. In other cultures the divining sticks were shorter and thicker and bore a greater resemblance to dice. Anthropologists describe their use among the African tribes of Mashonaland. "They are common among all the Abantu races and closely bound up with their occult belief in witchcraft. . . . On the evening of the new moon the village witch-doctor will go around, tossing each man a set of *dollasses* in the air, and by the way they turn up he will divine the fortune of the individual for the month to come." Missionaries who noted similar customs among the Zambesi referred to the diviner as a *dice doctor*. He also functioned as a detective since another use for his dice was that of discovering thieves.

Gradually these primitive fortune-telling devices began to be used as fortune-gaming devices. The mystical significance of the numbers was lost, and the throw determined winning scores and decided the outcome of wagers. The liturgical rites became games.

As the arrow used in divination began to be used in gambling, three general types of games evolved—guessing games, games of chance, and games of skill. In the guessing games, the arrow shaft became an ornamented gambling stick marked to denote rank which, in Korea, evolved into a deck of slim strips of oiled paper cards whose backs still bore an arrow-feather design that indicated their origin. Later Chinese cards of the same shape, called *stick cards,* bear figures whose resemblance to those on our present court cards is remarkable. The world's oldest known playing card found in Chinese Turkestan is of this type and is dated at the eleventh century. They were introduced into Europe from China in the thirteenth century and may be traced to the bundle of engraved or painted arrow-derived slips used in divination.

In many of the early games such as the Korean Nyout, the Egyptian Tab, and the ancient Pachisi (Parcheesi) of India, the throw of the dice controlled the moves of counters upon a marked playing surface as in the Backgammon of today. Later, when the dice and the element of chance were omitted, the game of pure skill developed and the counters became the men of Checkers, Chess, the Chinese Wei-Kei, and the Japanese Go.

Sophocles reported that dice were invented by one Palamedes, a Greek, who taught the game to the G.I. Joes at the siege of Troy three thousand years ago, and Herodotus went to press with a claim that the galloping ivories were invented by the Lydians as a means of diverting themselves from a great famine in the days of King Atys. Both dates are several thousand years shy of the mark. Dice were old before Troy was founded and before the Lydians had a king.

Man's very earliest written records not only mention dice and dice games, but crooked dice as well. Dice of one sort or another have been found in the tombs of ancient Egypt and the Orient and in the prehistoric graves of both North and South America. Thus, many of the games and gaming implements have been with us for centuries. But never has

there been such a complete collection of the world's greatest games that you can play as there is in this encyclopedia. There are hundreds of games played with dice, boards, counters, numbers, words, and cards.

All the games described in this book are divided into three categories: games of chance, games of skill, and games which combine both chance and skill.

Games of chance are those in which there is no element of skill. They are called "mechanical games." These include dozens of banking games. They include most dice games (Craps, Chuck-a-Luck, High Dice, Hazard, Scarney Put and Take, etc.). They include casino games (Roulette, Bingo, Keno, etc.) and dozens of card games (Baccarat, Chemin de Fer Las Vegas style, Faro, Banker and Broker, etc.).

Games of skill are those in which the element of chance is completely or nearly nonexistent, such as Chess, Teeko, Checkers, Go, Scarney Solitaire, etc.

Games of chance and skill combine both elements and include most games played with cards, Poker, Rummy, Bridge, Pinochle, Scarney Baccarat, Blackjack, etc.

Let's start with the wide world of cards.

CHAPTER 1

General Rules
Applying to All Card Games

Certain customs of card play are so well established that it is unnecessary to repeat them as part of the rules for each and every game. The following rules can be assumed to apply to any game, in the absence of any law expressly stating a different rule.

The Pack or Deck

The standard deck or pack of 52 cards contains four suits each identified by its symbol, or pip; spades (♠), hearts (♡), diamonds (♢), clubs (♣), thirteen cards of each suit; ace (A), king (K), queen (Q), jack (J), 10, 9, 8, 7, 6, 5, 4, 3, 2. Wherever the pack used for a game is stated to be "52 cards," reference is to this standard pack.

Packs of less than 52 cards are usually formed by stripping cards out of the standard pack. The various depleted packs may then be defined by the total of cards remaining, for example:

40 cards (five is the lowest remaining rank)
36 cards (six is the lowest remaining rank)
32 cards (seven is the lowest remaining rank)
24 cards (nine is the lowest remaining rank)

The 48-card Spanish deck still bears the old suits of Cups, Swords, Coeur, and Batons. The 40-card Italian deck, which is used in several of the games in this book, is made by stripping out eights, nines, and tens from a regular 52-card deck. The 32-card deck is made up of stripping out sixes, fives, fours, threes, twos.

A double deck is formed by mixing two 52-card packs together, and so has 104 cards (plus one or more joker, in some games). A triple-deck packet is formed by mixing three 52-card packs together. Some card packets used in banking games make use of four, five, six, and eight decks shuffled together. In some of the Canasta games that are described in Chapter 6 as many as four standard decks plus eight jokers (216 cards) are used in play. A Pinochle deck of 48 cards consists of two cards in the four familiar suits (spades, hearts, diamonds, and clubs) in each of the following denominations: ace (high), king, queen, jack, ten, nine (low). In assembling any multi-packs it is usually desirable to use cards of identical back design and color.

Various other kinds of card decks have been marketed in the past half century, such as circle (round) decks and cards marked with additional symbols, but they have all fallen by the wayside and do not merit inclusion in these pages.

How to Select Partnerships

Partnerships are determined by prearrangement or by cutting. Rules to determine partnerships by cutting follow:

1. The four players seat themselves at any four places around the table; where they sit is for the moment irrelevant.

2. Any player may shuffle the pack and offer the pack to any other player for a cut.

3. For the purpose of cutting for partners and seating positions, the cards rank ace (high)–K–Q–J–10–9–8–7–6–5–4–3–2 (low). When cutting for partners, jokers are excluded from the deck.

4. Each player cuts a group of cards from the pack immediately exposing to the others the bottom card of his group. Players cutting the two low cards become partners. So do the players cutting the two high cards. Although it may be agreed to keep the same partnership throughout several games, any player may nevertheless at the end of the game demand a new draw for partners and seating position.

5. If two, three, or four players cut cards of equal rank, the suits then rank spades (highest), hearts, diamonds, clubs (lowest).

6. If in cutting, a player exposes more than one card or cuts one of five cards resting either at the top or bottom of the pack, he must cut again.

7. The player who has cut the highest card may choose any seat. His partner sits opposite him. The opposing partnership takes the remaining seats.

Rotation of Play

In all the card games described in this book, the right to deal, the turn to bid, and the turn to play all rotate clockwise, that is, from each player to his left-hand neighbor. True, many of the native games—South American, Italian, Spanish, etc.—if played in their home land, would rotate counterclockwise, or to the right. But, to reduce confusion, I have changed the rules of these games to agree with the American clockwise rotation of card games.

The Shuffle

Any player at the table has the right to shuffle the pack (and as a matter of common law this right remains even where special rules of a game designate one player responsible for shuffling). In most games, the dealer has the right to shuffle last, and this is the rule when no different provision is stated.

The proper method of shuffling cards is fully described in Chapter 22.

The Cut

Cutting is the act of dividing the pack into two packets and transposing the bottom packet to the top. Custom is for the dealer to present the pack, after shuffling, to his right-hand neighbor, who lifts a packet from the top and sets it down beside the bottom packet. Dealer completes the cut by placing the bottom packet on top of the other. If that player refuses to cut, any player may cut. If all the players refuse to cut, the dealer must cut the cards. He cannot refuse. At least five cards must be in one portion of the cut deck. However, in high stake games I recommend the use of the Scarne cut described on page 433.

The Deal

In most games the first card dealt goes to the player at the dealer's left, and the cards, as previously stated, are distributed in clockwise rotation. There is variance in the number of cards dealt at one time, so that this number is expressly stated in connection with every game. The rule may be "one at a time" or "two at a time" or more at a time, but the same number of cards is dealt to every player in any one round. Sometimes the quota varies from round to round; for example, the rule to "deal three–two" means to deal a round of three cards at a time, then a round of two cards at a time.

Unless otherwise noted, all cards must be dealt face down so that no player can see the face of the card dealt to another. The finding of a card face up in the pack is usually valid cause for declaring a misdeal.

Dealer is required generally to hold the entire deck in his hand while dealing. He may not deal from a cut portion. In some games, however, where multiple decks are used—particularly banking games—dealer is permitted, after the deck has been cut, to take a portion of the deck from the top and deal from it. He then lifts the other portions as needed.

It is customary for players to wait until the deal is completed before touching any of their cards. This permits all players including dealer to begin arranging cards at the same time. It also prevents any confusion in case there is a mistake in the deal.

Misdealing

Most games have rules governing misdeals. But, it is a universal rule that on demand of any player there must be a new deal by the same dealer if the customary or prescribed rules of shuffling, cutting, and dealing are breached in any way. Usually, the demand may no longer be made by a player who has looked at any of the cards dealt him, or by any player after the last card has been dealt (or the prescribed deal has been completed).

In addition, it is the principle of most misdealing rules that if the deal is an advantage, a misdealer loses the deal; if the deal is a disadvantage, the dealer must deal again in case of a misdeal.

Imperfect Deck

A pack or deck is incorrect if it does not comprise exactly the number, rank, and suits of cards prescribed by the rules of the particular game. A pack may be incorrect by reason of the fact that some cards have been dropped on the floor, or have been gathered up in another pack, or by reason of the fact that it contains some cards belonging to another pack. The term *imperfect* is used in a narrower sense, to mean an incorrect pack which cannot be rectified by the simple act of removing foreign cards or restoring to it cards which originally were included in it. The only frequent imperfection is that the cards have become so worn and defaced that some are identifiable from the back.

When it is discovered that the pack is incorrect (and presumably was incorrect at the beginning of the current deal), the current deal is at once abandoned, even though it may have progressed through various stages of bidding or play. All scores made before the deal, however, stand without change. When it is discovered that a pack is imperfect, but only through having an identifiable card, the current deal usually stands if dealing has been completed, but the pack is then replaced.

Arranging Cards

Most players arrange their cards in suits in alternating colors, black, red, etc., or red, black, etc., to prevent confusion of suits of the same color. Most experienced players, however, vary the order in which they arrange their suits in their hands. Observant opponents can tell a lot about the distribution of cards in the hand of a player who makes a habit of arranging his suits in a certain way every time. They note from what part of his hand he made his plays.

The Bidding

The turn to bid begins with some designated player, usually the dealer or the player at his left, and continues to the left, each player waiting until the one at his right has made some declaration. The standard declaration when unable or unwilling to make a bid is to say distinctly "I pass" or "Pass." Gestures or other declarations, such as "By me," "By," "No bid," or "No," often cause misunderstandings of the players' intentions.

In partnership games where there is bidding, a player should be careful to make his bid without inflection or emphasis that might convey illegal information to his partner.

Bids once made may not be withdrawn and may be changed only if they are insufficient to overcall someone else's bid. The player is then required to make the bid sufficient. This general rule is particularly important in a partnership game where a bid once made gives important information to a partner.

The Play

All important games have strict rules governing play which should be carefully observed by the players, not only because they put everyone on an equal footing, but because they make for a better and far more enjoyable game.

Most games if played with too much informality lose their interest after a few minutes of play. If a player finds the rules of the game too strict and confining for him, he should either observe them in the interests of fair play or suggest that some other game be played instead, where the rules are less strict.

The bane of most card games is the play out of turn. Players should exercise special care to make their plays only in their turns to do so. If a player leads a card when it is not his turn, he may be giving valuable but illegal information to his partner; and if two are teamed against one in a three-handed game, this information is often important enough to determine the fate of a closely bid contract.

Plays should be made without gestures or undue emphasis which are likely to convey information beyond that given by the card itself.

Trumps

A player who has never played a game in which trumps are used is likely to have some difficulty at first in comprehending their function. The word "trump" is a corruption of "triumph," which means "to conquer." Trumps are therefore literally conquering cards, winning over nontrump cards because of special powers given to them in play. Usually the cards of some entire suit may be trumps, but sometimes only certain cards. Trumps are chosen in different ways according to the game. In many the right to name the trump suit is bid for competitively. In others the trump suit is decided by turning up a certain card. In either of the foregoing methods, the particular suit named trump holds that rank only for that deal.

Another way is to establish some suit or certain cards as permanent trumps, in which case trump for the game is the same deal after deal. In some games, Euchre, Skat, and Spoil Five (to name three), cards of other suits beside the trump suit also are trumps. In the last two games certain cards are permanent trumps, regardless of which suit is the trump suit in the deal. Or, finally, suits may become trumps in an arbitrary order of rotation. This last method is rare.

When a suit has been given special rank as a trump suit, it means that the lowest-ranking card in it will beat in play the highest-ranking card of any other (nontrump) suit, usually called a *plain* suit. *Example:* In a game where ace is the highest-ranking card in a suit and deuce (two) the lowest, a deuce of trumps will beat an ace in a plain suit, but will be beaten in turn, of course, by a three, four, or other higher trump.

Consequently, because of the power of trumps, even the smallest ones, players in bidding will naturally try—all things being equal—to establish as trump the suit in which they have the most cards.

Scoring

The scoring in most games can be done simply with a pencil and a sheet of pad paper. Each player's score is noted in a separate column under his name or initials.

In poker, most banking games, and some others, it is convenient to use chips or checks. These are small disks made of ivory or plastic and are usually colored, white, red, blue, and sometimes yellow. The value of the chips is discussed on page 11. If no chips are available, other counters may be used—beans, buttons, matchsticks, etc.

In games where scoring runs into the hundreds, it is customary to use the unit method of scoring. The total for a game is brought to the nearest even hundred, the terminal zeros canceled, and the remaining digit set down as the score. *Example:* The score is 890. This becomes 900, which is reduced to 9.

Settlement

When the time for settlement comes at the end of the session, scores are compared.

The Difference in Two Scores. If two are playing, the one with the better score collects according to the difference between his total and opponent's. Thus if player A has a score of 360 and opponent a total of 220, A's winning margin is 140. A value is usually set per point beforehand, and settlement is made on that basis.

In partnership games the same principle is used as above with each member of the winning side collecting from one opponent, not both, that is, one collects from one opponent and his partner collects from the other.

The Difference in All Scores. When three or more play each for himself, settlement may be made on the difference in all scores. Here is the way it works: Suppose four are playing. A has 980 points; B 720 points; C 420; D 390. A wins 260 points from B, 560 from C, and 590 from D. B wins 300 from C and 330 from D. C wins 30 from D.

Pie. In sociable round and banking games, many players favor the "pie" procedure of keeping in the game a player who loses his table stake. Generally, this is done by everyone's chipping in equally to provide the player with a new stake.

Some play that when any player loses a certain sum, he may continue in the game without a further stake until the end of play. If he wins anything, he may keep it and use it in play. If he loses, he does not have to pay.

Duration of Play

To avoid disputes it is advisable, generally, to set a specified time limit for a session of cards, at the expiration of which any player who chooses to may feel at liberty to leave the game. The others, if they so desire, may continue play after setting a new time limit.

Instead of a time limit, players may agree beforehand to play a certain number of rounds of dealing, games, hands, or points. The matter of setting a time limit for play is especially important in stake games where much hard feeling can thus be avoided.

Condonement of an Irregularity

The laws of different games vary widely in the penalties applied to irregularities and in the extent to which they may be rectified to allow play to continue. But in all there is limitation of the time during which an allegation of error and claim to a penalty is valid. Thereafter, the failure to draw attention to the error is deemed to have condoned it, to have accepted it as regular.

Custom has fortified at least the following "statute of limitations."

Procedural error in shuffling, cutting, or dealing (not resulting in wrong numbers of cards in any hand): Stands after all players look at their hands. If a hand has too many or too few cards, a misdeal may be called until the cards have been mixed together; thereafter the deal and the score for it stand.

Error in bidding, declaring, making trump, etc.: Stands after the opening lead of the play.

Error in playing out the hands: Stands after the score for the deal is agreed upon.

Error in recording scores or in arithmetical computations: Stands after payment has been offered and accepted in settlement of the score. Many games place a greater limitation upon the time available for penalization (and

rectification) of an irregularity. But none extends the time beyond this "natural statute," which may therefore be accepted as the law in any case for which the rules of a game do not make specific provision.

In *Encyclopedia of Games,* I have taken a modern approach and use the language of today. Many present-day game compilers, still copying from the old Hoyles, dating back as far as 1845—over a hundred years ago—still call, for instance, the leadoff man—the player who plays first after the deal—the *Age,* or refer to his cards as the *Eldest Hand.* Try, in your next card game, referring to this player as "the Age" and see if he knows what you're talking about. In *John Scarne's Encyclopedia of Games,* the player who makes the first play in any card game is known as the *leader* or the *player to the dealer's left.*

Of course, ever since Americans decided to play Poker, Bridge, Gin Rummy, Canasta, and the many other games that have become our favorites, unsuspecting players have considered Hoyle to be the ultimate authority on the play. I'm no iconoclast, I don't believe in making it tough for any man to make a living; but we'd better, at the outset, face the facts about this venerable myth. You can't play most of the card games today according to Hoyle simply because Hoyle (*a*) never played these games, (*b*) never uttered a ruling on them, and (*c*) never even heard of them. Edmund Hoyle was an English barrister who wrote a short treatise on such games as Piquet, Whist, Backgammon, Quadrille, and a few other games which are not now even played or if played, have been vastly changed. In fact, most of the card games we play today were not heard of until decades after Hoyle's death in 1769.

The rules of the games set forth in the *Encyclopedia of Games* are not according to Hoyle, but ACCORDING TO SCARNE. They are based on modern conventions and conditions of play. They have been devised for players who understand and love the game. They are based on exhaustive investigation of current practice. They have been tested in clubs, casinos, and private games throughout the world, and they have stood the test. They are mathematically sound, they recognize the realities of the play, and they are authoritative.

CHAPTER 2

Draw Poker

Poker is by far the most popular card game throughout the world today, measured both by the amount of money that changes hands daily and by the number of players. Thirty years ago Poker was almost exclusively a man's game; today more women than men play the game largely because so many interesting new Poker variations have sprung up during the past twenty years.

It is impossible to say that any specific earlier card game is the direct ancestor of Poker; it seems to have borrowed elements from many games. The basic principle of Poker is such an obvious one that its use must be very old. When my son John Teeko was about three years old, I gave him 20 shuffled cards, all the aces, kings, queens, jacks, and tens, and without any prompting on my part he separated them into those five groups. The first Poker in this country was played with just such a deck.

The first reference in print to Poker which I have found is one by Jonathan H. Green, published in 1834. He gives the rules for what he calls a "cheating game" which was then being played on the Mississippi riverboats. He stated that this was the first time the rules had been published; he noted that the *American Hoyle* then current did not mention the game; and he called it Poker. The game he described was played with 20 cards—aces, kings, queens, jacks, and tens. Two, three, or four players could play, and each was dealt five cards. Most dictionaries and game historians say that the word "poker" comes from an early eighteenth-century French game, Poque. Others say it is derived from an old German game, Pochspiel, in which the element of bluffing played a part and the players indicated whether they would pass or open by rapping the table and saying "Ich poche!" A few historians have tried to trace the word to poche, the French word for pocket, and I have even heard it argued that Poker derives from the Hindu pukka. I doubt all these theories. I believe it was originally underworld slang and came from the pickpocket's term for pocketbook or wallet: poke.

The Mississippi River sharpers who first called the game Poker may have gotten their original inspiration in New Orleans from sailors who played a very old Persian game called As-Nas, whose basic structure is the same. Twenty cards were used, five being dealt to each player. Pairs and such combinations and sequences as form the melds at Rummy were winning combinations, and bluffing was an important factor. As-Nas may also have been the father of the Italian game of Primero and the French Gilet which, during the reign of Charles IX (1560–74), became Brelan and fathered its variants Bouillotte and Ambigu. In Le Poker Américain, as the French play it today, brelan-carré means four of a kind. The early published poker rules in this country also hinted at French antecedents; the 32-card piquet pack was used; it was cut to the left; the cards were dealt from the bottom of the deck, and certain combinations of cards bore French names. The draw feature of Poker is found in Ambigu, and the blind, straddles, raise, table stakes, and freeze-out in the pre-Revolutionary Bouillotte. Bluffing and the use of wild cards were important features in the English game of Brag. In all these European games, however, a hand consisted of only three cards. The credit for the use of a five-card hand and also the bluff must go to the Persian As-Nas, from which our word Ace may also have come.

In 1845 an early American edition of Hoyle included Twenty-Card Poker and also "Poker or Bluff." Twenty years later the *American Hoyle* added the game, calling it simply "Bluff." Perhaps a few players who may have confused it with the English Brag also called it that, but most players have always called it Poker. Game-book editors who do their research in previous game books sometimes still call it "Poker" or "Bluff," although no player has used the latter term for nearly a century.

There are countless ways to play Poker. All have some features in common, such as the rank of the hands and the basic fact that most Poker games eventually possess five cards on the showdown. But all have their points of difference that affect not only the playing rules but also the skill of the game. The selection of a game is not entirely a matter of taste or place. Some games are definitely more suitable to a particular group or a particular place (such as home, club, or casino) than other games. I will list the main subdivisions of Poker and make some observations on their suitability for particular groups and places.

For all practical purposes, there are two main divisions or forms of Poker: (1) Draw, or closed, poker, in which all of the players' cards are unknown to his opponents until the showdown; and (2) stud, or open, poker, in which some of the players' cards are exposed to all players as the play of the hands progresses. The Poker rules set forth in this chapter and the next one are not according to Hoyle, but *according to Scarne*. They are based on modern conventions and conditions of play; have been devised for players who understand and love the game; and are based on exhaustive investigation of current practice. They have been tested in clubs, casinos, and private games throughout the world; are mathematically sound; recognize the realities of the play; and are authoritative.

GENERAL RULES FOR POKER

To play the standard games of the Poker family a standard 52-card deck is used. In some variations jokers and wild cards are added. It is not unusual to strip from the deck some low-ranking cards such as deuces and treys. In Poker each player is on his own; there is no such thing as partnership play in any kind of legitimate game.

The Pack. The Poker deck consists of four 13-card suits; spades, hearts, diamonds, and clubs. The suits have no relative superiority to each other. The ace is the highest-ranking card, and in order of descending value the rest of the cards are the king, queen, jack, ten, down to two, or deuce. But the ace may be used at either end of a sequence, as the highest or the lowest card in a straight. Thus in the straight flush ten–jack–queen–king–ace, the ace is high; in the straight ace–two–three–four–five the ace is low.

I recommend the use of two packs of cards having backs of sharply contrasting design or color. This is to enable a change of packs at the request of any player. In two-pack play a contestant can ask for a change at any time, and the change takes place immediately after the showdown of the current hand.

Object of the Game. To win the pool (pot) by holding, at the showdown, a hand of higher rank than that of any other player—as evaluated by the rules of the game being played; or to win by forcing the other players to drop out of the competition. The winner (or winners) collects the pot.

Tied Hands. When two or more players hold hands of equal rank, they divide the pot equally. If a pot is not equally divisible by the number of winners, the odd sum left after division—breakage, as horse bettors call it—goes to the player who was called. In High-Low Poker the indivisible odd amount goes to the player of the high hand.

Standard Rank of Poker Hands with a 52-Card Deck. It must be specified for clarity's sake that in the following list of Poker hands in ten categories called ranks, any hand listed in a superior rank beats any hand listed in an inferior rank. The royal flush, listed in Rank 1, beats any hand listed in Rank 2. Any hand listed in Rank 6 beats any hand in Rank 7, 8, 9, or 10, and loses to any hand in Rank 5, 4, 3, 2, or 1.

Rank 1 (*The Supreme Rank*), *The Royal Flush:* the five highest cards, namely, ace–king–queen–jack–ten of any one of the four suits. The suits have equal rank. Royal flushes tie for winner.

Rank 2, The Straight Flush: any five cards of the same suit in numerical sequence, such as the ten–nine–eight–seven–six of spades. This flush is called a *ten high.* If there are two or more straight flushes in competition for the pot, that one whose top card is of the highest denomination wins; a *ten high* beats a *nine*

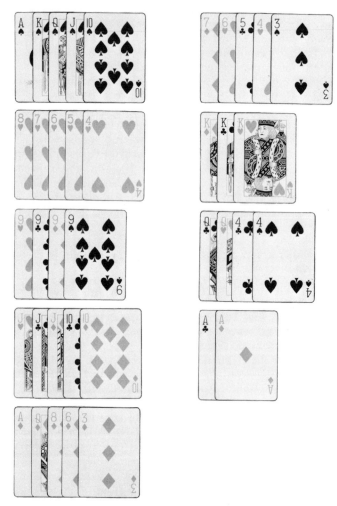

Ranking hands of Poker without wild cards: (left) A royal flush (top) is the highest-ranking natural hand. The next highest is a straight flush, then comes four of a kind, then a full house, then a flush. (Right) Ranking after a flush is a straight (top). Next is three of a kind; two pair; one pair.

high, etc. If two or more players hold a straight flush whose top card is of the same denomination, the hand is a tie.

Rank 3, Four of a Kind: any four cards of the same denomination (ace, ace, ace, ace, and two, for example). The odd card is irrelevant and does not affect the rank of the hand.

Rank 4, The Full House: three of one kind and two of another (three, three, three, two, and two, for example). In evaluating two or more competing full houses, the hand with the highest three-of-a-kind wins, regardless of the rank of the pair. *Example:* A full house including three aces beats a full house including three kings, regardless of the pairs.

Rank 5, The Flush: any five cards of the same suit but not in sequence (ten, seven, five, four, and three of spades, for example). In evaluating two or more flushes, the winner is determined by the rank of the highest card in the hand. If the highest cards in contesting hands are of the same rank, then the next highest cards determine the winner. And if these are of the same rank, then the winning hand is determined by the third highest cards. If all the cards of the players are equal, then the hands are tied.

Rank 6, The Straight: five cards in consecutive sequences but not of the same suit (three, four, five, six, seven). In competing straights, the winner is decided by the rank of the highest card. Straights of the same denomination are equal, and tie.

Rank 7, Three of a Kind: three cards of the same numerical value plus two different and irrelevant cards that are not paired (king, king, king, five, and four, for example). The hand having the highest three of a kind wins, regardless of the value of the unmatched cards.

Rank 8, Two Pairs: two different pairs of cards plus one odd card (ten, ten, five, five, and four, for example; this example is called *tens up*). In evaluating two or more two-pair hands, the winner is the player holding the highest pair. If the highest pairs are tied, the rank of the second pair in the hands determines the winner; if the second pairs also are tied, then the higher card of the odd cards determines the winner. If all cards of the competing hands are of matching value, the hands are tied.

Rank 9, One Pair: two cards of the same denomination plus three indifferent (unmatched) cards (ten, ten, nine, seven, and three, for example). In evaluating two or more hands each including a pair, the player who holds the highest pair wins. If the pairs are of equal value, the hand with the highest indifferent card wins. If these are of equal value, the hand with the next highest card is the winner, etc. If all the cards in the competing hands match, the hands tie and the winnings are divided.

Rank 10, High Card: a hand which contains five indifferent cards not of the same suit, not in sequence, and falling into none of the above combinations. Ace, ten, seven, five, and three, of two or more suits, for example, would be called an *ace high* hand. If the highest card of two such hands is the same, the next highest card determines the winner; if these tie, the determinant is the next, then the next, etc. If all cards in more than one hand are of matching value, the hands tie, and the pot is divided.

THE STANDARD RANKS OF POKER HANDS WITH A 52-CARD DECK

In order of their value: Rank 1 being highest and Rank 10 being lowest

1	Royal flush
2	Straight flush
3	Four of a kind
4	Full house
5	Flush
6	Straight
7	Three of a kind
8	Two pairs
9	One pair
10	High card

Wild Cards. By mutual prior agreement certain cards are designated as wild. The wild card can be used to represent any card of any suit and any denomination, even as a duplicate of a card already held by the player. Here are some wild-card combinations:

1. The joker, which when added to a standard pack makes it a 53-card deck. Often more than one joker is introduced into the play. If no joker is handy, any fifty-third card can be marked joker and added to the deck, as wild.

2. Deuces are the most popular wild cards next to the joker. Any one of the deuces, or the two black deuces, or the two red, or all

four deuces may by mutual consent be declared wild.

3. In combination with one or more of the above variations, threes are occasionally declared wild cards.

4. It is not unusual for players to declare wild the low card of a five-card hand, the one-eyed jacks, the jacks with mustaches, the black sevens, or the profile kings. For that matter, any card or group of cards may be arbitrarily designated as wild.

The following are the rank of Poker hands with one or more wild cards (in order of their value, *Rank 1* being the highest and *Rank 12* lowest):

RANK OF POKER HANDS WITH ONE OR MORE WILD CARDS

1　Five of a kind (the highest-ranking hand)
2　Royal flush
3　Straight flush
4　Four of a kind
5　Full house
6　Double-ace flush
7　Flush
8　Straight
9　Three of a kind
10　Two pairs
11　One pair
12　High card (but of course this can occur only when none of active players has a wild card).

Rank of Low Poker Hands. Low or High-Low Poker differs from other forms of the game in that either low or both high and low hands bid for the pot. This one variation in Poker rules has such a great effect on the play of a hand, and provides so many unusual and interesting situations and strategies, that it has replaced many other forms of Poker. The rank or value of high hands is the same as in any Poker game; however, low hands are the reverse. Originally, aces were only treated as a high card when declaring low. Thus the best low hand was seven, five, four, three, and deuce of mixed suits. The Scarne rule that follows is to count the aces as both high and low. Therefore the "perfect" low hand is six, four, three, two, and ace of mixed suits. If they are all of the same suit, it counts as a flush. If you announce low, it is still counted as a flush. Similarly ace–two–three–four–five is a straight. Second best low hand is six, five, three, two, and ace. Treating the aces as either high or low adds extra zip and skill to the game.

The Low Poker hand is evaluated by the rank of its highest card; if there is a tie between highest cards, by the rank of its second card, etc. The value of the lowest card is irrelevant to the hand's value except when on the showdown the four higher cards are exactly matched by another player's. *Example:* A mixed-suit hand such as nine, seven, six, five, and three, being a nine low, would beat a mixed suit nine low with nine, eight, six, five, and three. To repeat, the lowest-ranking perfect hand at High-Low Poker is the six, four, three, two, and ace in mixed suits.

Here in categories called ranks, I list the best hands at High-Low Poker. These are mixed suits, of course. Any hand in a superior rank beats any hand listed below it.

6–4–3–2–A
6–5–3–2–A
6–5–4–2–A
6–5–4–3–A
7–4–3–2–A
7–5–3–2–A
7–5–4–2–A
7–5–4–3–A
7–5–4–3–2
and so on

How to Declare in High-Low Poker. There are two basic methods of declaring (announcing) high or low, or both high-low, before the showdown in all High-Low Poker games. They are: (1) simultaneous declaration, which is recommended for high-limit games, and (2) consecutive declaration, which is recommended for low-limit games.

The Simultaneous Declaration. Prior to the showdown, each player takes two chips and moves both hands under the table. He returns one clenched fist to the center of the table. Now, when all the active players have their hands above the table, the dealer calls "Open." All players must open their hands immediately. The absence of a chip indicates a low call, the presence of one chip indicates a high call. The presence of two chips indicates the player is going for both high and low. If chips are not available, coins can be used.

The Consecutive Declaration. Prior to the showdown in all High-Low games, the player who made the last aggressive move (raised or bet first on the final betting round) declares first. If everyone checked on the final round, the high hand showing must declare first. Declarations then proceed in clockwise rotation from one active player to another. In all the High-Low Draw Poker games, should all players check on the last round, the last aggressive player in the preceding round or rounds must declare first.

It is a sad but true fact that in this consecutive method, it is a great advantage to call last, or near the end of the declaration, because very often a player with good position is able to win half of the pot with a very weak hand because all others have declared in one direction. Such a position is called being *in the driver's seat*.

How Winners Are Determined in High-Low Poker. A winner in High-Low Poker games is determined as follows:

1. When playing High-Low Poker variations the player holding the highest-ranking hand, provided he has declared for high, and the player holding the lowest-ranking hand, provided he has declared for low, share the pot equally.

2. If a player declares his hand incorrectly and the pot has not yet been collected, he may correct the error; but if the pot has been collected the error must stand.

3. The rank of a low hand is inverse to the rank of a high hand. If the hand contains less than a pair, its determinant is its highest-ranking card; if two players are tied as to highest-ranking card, the next highest-ranking card decides the winner, etc. See rank of High-Low Poker hands (page 10).

4. When a player announces for low, he no longer has any interest in high.

5. When a player announces for high, he no longer has any interest in low.

6. When a player announces high-low both, he must win both high and low to collect the pot. Should he lose either way or tie for either high or low, he loses the entire pot.

7. If two or more players are tied for low, half the pot is equally divided among the winners tied for low. The other half of the pot goes to the winner, or winners, with the high hand. If there is an indivisible amount left over and a lone player has bid either high or low, he gets it. Otherwise, it goes into the next pot.

8. If there are two or more players in at the showdown and they all declare high, the higher of the hand takes the entire pot. If they all declare low, the lower of the hand takes the pot.

Preparation for the Play: The Banker and His Duties. One of the players is selected by mutual or majority consent to be the banker for that session of play. If cash is to be used in the betting, the banker must make change and see that players bet or ante properly. As a rule it is he who takes the cut out of certain pots (which pots and how much cut are determined by the players) and puts that cash into a kitty—used to buy cards, food, drinks, or to help pay the rent. Under the common usage, all other players help the banker with these chores during the play. If chips are used the banker keeps the supply, sells them to the players, and redeems them to settle accounts at the end of the game.

Professional Poker, or the House Game. In a house, club, or casino game, the management:

1. Supplies all the essentials for Poker playing, namely, the gaming room, a special kind of Poker table, the chips, and the cards, and a dealer or lookout man or both.

2. Takes a cut (charge) in return for these goods and services.

The amount of the cut is just exactly what the traffic will bear then and there, in that ward of the city, in that month of the year. Some houses, perhaps a majority, impose a direct charge of 25 to 50 cents on the winner of each pot.

3. Many Poker clubs, including the licensed California Poker clubs, rent tables at hourly rates and supervise the honesty of play.

Value of the Chips. Nationwide, this is the most common evaluation of Poker chips:

   White—1 unit
   Red—5 units
   Blue—10 units
   Yellow—25 units

The value of cash for each of the units is entirely up to the players. It may range from 1 to 5 cents, 10 to 30 cents, 25 cents to $1, $1 to $4, $2 to $8, etc.

Optional Rules Better Discussed Before the Start of the Game. The following points should be covered before any Poker game is started:

1. There must be common agreement on

the kind of game to be played. Local conventions on such things as royalties and bonuses must be talked over before the game, and reduced to writing on a pad. These conventions or rulings must be thoroughly understood by all players.

2. Although any player has the right to quit whenever he wants to, a time limit must be decided on before the start of the game.

3. Before play starts, there must be common agreement as to the amount of the ante if any, and the minimum and maximum amount of money or chips that can be bet at any one time.

Freezing a Raise or Possible Raises. The following rule is recommended to Poker players who do not want restrictions on their raises but at the same time desire some protection against sandbagging. How often have you been sandwiched between two players who are raising and reraising each other with no consideration for you, and you had to cough up enough money to match their raises just to stay in till the decision? You had made up your mind to stay to the bitter end even if you lost all your money, and there were times when you did exactly that. The author counted 30 raises one night between two reckless high rollers in one round of Draw Poker, and one player who never raised had to match the 30 raises to stay in the pot. Then and there I decided something must be done to protect a player from being sandbagged or whipsawed between two confederates, two cheaters, or two reckless players with no regard for the other men in the game. I give all Poker players a rule that eliminates this hazard from Poker without putting a limit on the number of raises permitted. Here it is—a *freezer*.

A freezer is a special bet that can be used at any time and puts an end to all raises for that particular betting round. When a player bets the freezer, all other active players may drop out or stay by putting into the pot the amount of the freezer bet plus all previous bet amounts, if any. The amount of the freezer bet must be agreed on by mutual consent before the start of the game. I would suggest it to be equal to the maximum bet or four times the minimum bet permitted at the game in play.

Royalties or Bonuses. Some players elect to pay a royalty to any player holding an excep-

tionally high-ranking hand, such as a royal flush, straight flush, or four of a kind. This is not incorporated in my rules, and is optional with players. I mention it just to make this chapter definitive and complete. Royalties and bonuses on a royal flush or any other kind of bonus hand are optional, but as a rule are from three to five times the amount of the maximum permitted bet. Each player, whether active or not, must pay the player holding the bonus hand the amount agreed on at the start of the game.

Selecting the Dealer and Establishing Seating Positions at the Table. As a rule at the start of the game players may sit wherever they like. A new player may take any vacant seat he chooses unless the game is Dealer's Edge or Ante, in which case he must wait until it becomes his turn to deal before he can have cards. Just to avoid any possible dispute about seating positions, the start of the game, the seating of new players, and the selection of the dealer, it might be well to incorporate the following rules into the game:

1. Any player shall by mutual or majority consent shuffle the cards, and the player to his right shall cut the deck.

2. The player acting as dealer shall deal one card to each player face up, starting with the player at his left, dealing clockwise around the table, and ending with himself.

3. The player dealt the highest card shall become the first dealer and select any seat he wants.

4. The player with the next highest card selects any remaining seat, the player with the third highest any remaining seat, etc.

5. In case of ties, each of the tied players shall be dealt a new card face up until the tie is broken.

6. At the completion of each hand the deal shall pass to the player at the immediate left of the player who dealt that round.

The Shuffle. The dealer shuffles the cards. Any player may call for a shuffle at any time before the cut, although the dealer has the privilege of shuffling the cards last.

The Cut. After the cards have been shuffled, the dealer presents the pack to the player at his right to be cut. If he refuses to cut the cards, the player to that player's right has the privilege of cutting, etc. If all other players refuse to cut, the dealer must cut. *It is mandatory.*

At least five cards must be in each of the cut packets should a player use a regular cut. Should he desire, a player may use the *Scarne Cut* (see page 433) or cut the deck more than once. After the cut, the cut portions must be squared or reunited and dealt as a complete pack. It is not permissible to pick up one cut portion of the pack and start dealing from it. A player can demand to have the cards cut again before a deal has started, but no player has the right to demand a cut after the deal has started, or at any other time.

Asking for a New Cut. If a player does not like the way the cards have been cut before the start of the deal, doubting legitimacy of the cut or for any other reason, he may call for another cut; and any other player but the player calling for the new cut may cut the cards.

The Deal. The dealer deals one card at a time to each player, starting with the leader (player to the dealer's left) and continuing clockwise until each player in the game has the required number of cards. The cards are dealt face up or face down according to the rules of the game being played.

Misdeal. In case of a misdeal there must be a new shuffle and cut. The same dealer deals again.

Illegal Cutting of Cards. Under no circumstances may a player ask to cut the cards after a bet has been made. I must stress particularly that cards cannot be cut *after* the deal has started or for that matter at any other time except *before* the start of the deal unless some overt crookedness has been suspected.

Five-Minute Time Period for a Play. If an active player is taking too much time to decide how to play his hand, any other active player may call time, and if the hesitant player fails to complete his play within 5 minutes, after time is called, his hand is dead: he is forced to drop out. *Note:* This situation happens often in a high-limit game; the author has seen players take a half hour or more to decide on a play.

Changing Positions at the Table. At the completion of any hour of play, players may demand a new deal for a change in their seating positions. The procedure is the same as in establishing places at the table at the start of a game. The player whose turn it is to deal (1) deals for seating positions and (2)

deals the next hand in play.

Tapping Out. When a player has put all his money into the pot and no longer can bet, it is called a *tap-out*. That player is permitted to play for the size of the pot up until the time he no longer has money. If the other players keep betting they put their bets to one side, as the tapping-out player has no legal interest in that side pot. The tapping-out player receives cards until the hand is completed, and should he have the highest-ranking hand on the showdown, he wins only the original pot, not the side pot. That is won by the player having the highest ranking cards among the remaining bettors. Except in table stakes and freeze-out, when a player taps out and loses, he is out of the game. He cannot continue playing. However, if he wins on the tap-out and therefore has money, he may continue to play as before. A player is permitted only one tap-out during a Poker session.

When tapping out, a player may raise only if he still possesses an amount equal to the maximum limit so that in case of a reraise he can call the bet. A player cannot tap out with money on the table.

Going Through the Discards. In no circumstances is a player permitted to look at the discards before or after the showdown. Nor is a player permitted to look at another player's hand even though he is out of the pot. Looking through the undealt cards is forbidden. The above rules should be strictly enforced.

Loaning Money or Chips. Under no circumstances is a player allowed to borrow money or chips from another player during the play. If a player desires to borrow money from another player, it must be done before the cards are dealt. Passing money or chips from one player to another during the play is not permitted.

Betting for Another Player. Under no circumstances is a player permitted to ante or bet for another player.

Angling. Angling is positively prohibited. For example, discussion among two or more players to split the pot regardless of the winner, or to give back part of the money, or ask for a free ride or call, or any violation of the Poker rules is prohibited.

Overs in the Pot. No money or chips may be taken out of the pot except when the stakes are cash, under which circumstances a player may take out his proper change after placing a bet at his turn of play. It must be observed by all the players that the proper change is taken.

Should a player ante or put into the pot an amount larger than required and thereafter should another player make a bet, the overage cannot be taken out of the pot.

Exposed Hands on Showdown. All players, active or nonactive, are entitled to see all active player's hands on the showdown, provided a bet has been called. Therefore, on the showdown all the players in their proper turn must spread their cards face up on the table.

Criticism. A player is not permitted under any circumstances to criticize another player's methods. Poker is a game in which each man plays his own hand as he elects. No consideration should be expected by one player from another.

BASIC DRAW POKER RULES

Draw Poker, also known as Closed Poker, Poker Jack's or Better, and Five-Card Draw Poker, is the forerunner of all other kinds of Poker, including Stud Poker and its variants.

Draw Poker (and its countless variations) is one of the more popular games at women's weekly Poker sessions. Big-money gamblers prefer Stud to Draw Poker. Every adult and teenager has probably played penny-ante Draw Poker at least once during his or her lifetime; children usually learn to play it before any other game. It is probably the world's most popular family card game.

Requirements

1. Two to six players make the best game, although up to ten players may play—with the following added rule: Should the pack become exhausted and there are players who still must draw cards to complete their hands, the discards are assembled, shuffled, and cut, and the draw is continued. But when playing for high stakes, the maximum number of players is six.

2. A standard pack of 52 cards is used. It is best to have two packs available of different backs and colors, so a player may call for a change of decks upon completion of any deal.

The Object of the Game. For a player at the showdown to hold a higher-ranking five-card hand than any of the other players. The player (or players) having the best hand is declared the winner (or winners), and collects the pot.

Preliminaries Before the Deal. All the preparations before the start of the actual play are as described under the basic *General Rules for Poker:* selecting the banker, his duties, rank of hands, royalties, time limit, betting limits, preparations before play, select-ing the dealer and seating positions at the table, irregularities in cutting the cards, the shuffle and cut.

The Ante. Two types of antes are used in Draw Poker, as follows:

1. Each player, before the cards are dealt, antes an equal amount into the pot. All players must ante in turn, starting with the player to the dealer's left and rotating clockwise.

2. Dealer's Edge. The player whose turn it is to deal antes an amount into the pot. In dealer's edge a new player entering the game must wait until it is his turn to deal before he is permitted to play.

The Deal. Dealing clockwise, starting with the player on the dealer's left, the dealer deals a card to each player until each has five cards. The dealer gets the last card. The remaining cards are put to one side in front of the dealer for future use in drawing.

Openers. The player who opens the pot must hold in his hand a pair of jacks or a higher-ranking hand. It is essential for the stability of the game that a player have jacks or better when opening. If this rule is not enforced and a player opens the pot any time he feels like it, one of the greatest factors of skill in the game is automatically eliminated —which depends on knowing that the opener holds at least a pair of jacks.

Splitting Openers. The player who opened the pot has the right to discard his openers or part of his openers, but he must announce that he is doing so and place his openers or the discarded part of his openers to one side to verify at the showdown the fact that he had them.

Player's Turn of Play. The leader (player

to the dealer's left) has the first privilege of play. After examining his cards and determining that he holds a pair of jacks or a hand of higher rank, he must do one of two things:

1. He may open by putting a bet into the pot.

2. He may pass, which indicates that he does not desire to start the betting. Should he fail to hold a pair of jacks or a hand of a higher rank, he is compelled to pass.

If all the players pass, they must ante again, and the new dealer deals another hand to each player; and, if playing dealer's edge, the new dealer must ante.

When a player opens by putting an amount within the limit into the pot, each succeeding player in turn can do one of these three things:

1. He may pass; and, should he pass when the pot has been opened, he merely folds his cards and puts them in the center of the table. This is folding up.

2. Should he decide to play, he must put up an amount equal to the bet of the player who opened the pot.

3. If he wants to raise, he merely says "Raise" and puts into the pot an amount equal to that put into the pot by the opening player, plus an amount for the raise.

All the other players may now either play by putting into the pot an amount equal to the total amount of the raiser or, should they already have put the opening bet into the pot, merely put into the pot an amount equal to the raise. Or a player may reraise by putting into the pot an amount equal to the raiser plus an amount for the reraiser. Or he may drop out by folding his cards and throwing them into the discard pile on the table. This procedure of dropping out, playing, raising, and reraising is continued until the players stop raising. If all the players drop out but one, he wins the pot. Should he be the player who opened the pot, he must show his openers to the rest of the players. If he is not, he does not have to expose his hand.

The Draw. When all the players have either dropped out or put into the pot an equal amount and there are no uncovered bets in the pot, and when the active players number two or more, these remaining players may, if they desire, draw either, one, two, or three cards in an attempt to improve their hands or stand pat. This procedure is called the draw, and it is played as follows:

The dealer must ask each player (starting with the nearest active player to his left and rotating to the left, clockwise) at his proper turn of play how many cards he wants to draw, if any; to each player he says "How many?" The player either says he's standing pat or tells the dealer how many cards he wants to draw. The dealer must wait until the player discards a like number before dealing the new cards; or he passes the player by should the latter say "I stand pat."

In Draw, every player must take the cards he asked for if the dealer has dealt them off the deck. If too many, player must discard to make a legitimate hand. If too few, he has fouled his hand, as he has fewer than required for a playing hand. Dealer must take the exact number of cards laid off the deck for himself. Cards once discarded cannot be taken back. If a player does not get the correct number of cards he asked for, the dealer must rectify the mistake, provided no one at the player's left has drawn cards.

The Betting after the Draw. The player who opened the pot has the first turn of play after the draw, and the play goes on to each active player, starting with the player to the opener's left and moving clockwise. A turn of play now consists of either checking, betting, calling, dropping out, raising, or reraising. But a player cannot check at his turn of play after a bet has been made. The play continues around the table until one of the following situations develops:

1. A player has made a bet and is not called by any player, in which case he wins the pot and does not have to expose his hand, unless he was the opener. Then he is compelled to show his openers only.

2. All players have passed; and now the opener must be the first player to expose his hand for the showdown. This is done by announcing the rank of his hand and turning his five cards face up on the table. The same holds for all the remaining players, continuing with the first remaining player to the opener's left and rotating clockwise.

3. Or, an equal amount has been put into the pot by betting on the part of two or more active players. In this case the biggest bettor is being called, and he must be the first to

announce the rank of his hand and turn it face up on the table for the showdown. The first active player to his left does the same, the showdown rotating clockwise. The player holding the highest-ranking hand as described under General Rules for Poker wins the pot. In case of ties, the tied players split the pot equally. (See rules for "Tied Hands," page 7.)

Showdown. In Draw Poker the cards in the showdown speak for themselves. If a player calls a lower- or higher-ranking hand than he holds and this error is noticed before the pot has been collected, the error can be rectified. But if it is noticed after the pot has been collected, the error cannot be rectified. The same rule regarding the showdown holds true should all the players pass after the draw.

Misdeals. Whenever a misdeal occurs there must be a new shuffle and cut. The same dealer deals again, but should the dealer make two misdeals in a row the deal passes to the player at his left. The following will determine if a misdeal has occurred or not:

1. If one or more cards are exposed in cutting or reuniting the cut packets, there is a misdeal.

2. If the pack has not been offered to the proper player to cut, and the pot has not been opened yet, there is a misdeal. If the pot has already been opened, and the irregularity has not been discovered, the deal stands, there is no misdeal.

3. If the pack has not been cut and the betting has not started, there is a misdeal.

4. If one or more cards are observed face up in the pack before each player has received his five cards or the betting has not yet started, there is a misdeal.

5. If a player's card is exposed by the dealer before the draw, there is a misdeal.

6. If the dealer exposes one or more of his own cards at any time, the deal stands. There is no misdeal.

7. Should a player expose one or more of his own cards at any time, the deal stands. There is no misdeal.

8. If an imperfect pack is being used with fewer cards than the standard pack or with duplicate cards and it is discovered before the pot has been collected, there is a misdeal. Play immediately stops when the imperfect pack is discovered, and all the players get back the amounts they put into the pot.

9. If the cards have been improperly dealt —for example, more than one card at a time—or another player has received improper cards and it is noticed before the pot is opened, there is a misdeal.

10. If too few or too many hands have been dealt, there is a misdeal.

11. If too few or too many cards have been dealt to one or more players and it is discovered before the pot is opened, there is a misdeal unless it can be properly corrected before any one player has looked at his hand.

12. If the wrong player is dealing and it is discovered before the pot has been opened, there is a misdeal.

Passing the Deal. A dealer cannot pass his turn to deal unless he is incompetent to deal the cards.

Exposed Cards on the Draw. The following will cover situations involving an exposed card on the draw:

1. Should a dealer expose one or more of a player's cards on the draw, the player is not permitted to take the exposed cards. They must be put into the center of the table face up, and are out of play. The dealer deals the player whose card has been exposed another card in place of it.

2. Should a player expose one or more of his drawn cards, he must take them.

3. Should a dealer expose one or more cards on his own draw or if they are found face up on the draw, the dealer must take them.

Betting. A bet once placed in the pot, regardless of whether it's a player's proper turn or not, must stand. It cannot be taken out of the pot. If a player should put into the pot an amount less than the amount of the previous bettor, he must add the required sum so that his bet is equal to the previous bet. Should he fail to do so, his hand is dead, and the amount he bet must remain in the pot.

Betting Out of Turn. The following rules apply to playing, calling, or raising out of turn. A player making a bet out of turn must leave the bet in the pot. He cannot take it back, and the play reverts to the proper player. When it is the proper turn of the player who bet out of turn he must do one of the following:

1. If no bet has been made by any preced-

ing player, the bet stands as is.

2. If a bet has been made by a previous player smaller than the bet made out of turn, it stands as a raise.

3. If a bet has been made by a previous player equal to the bet out of turn, it stands as a play or call.

4. If a previous bet was raised by another player and the bet is in excess of the amount bet by the out-of-turn player, the out-of-turn player may either drop out of the pot, play, or call by equaling the bet made by the previous bettors, or reraise the pot after equaling the raised bet.

Verbal Betting. If a player in his turn of play announces he is making a bet, he must abide by the announcement. He cannot increase or decrease the oral bet. Should a player make an announcement at an improper turn of play and has not placed any money into the pot, it should be disregarded and considered a joke or an attempted bluff.

Passing or Checking Out of Turn. If a player passes out of turn before the draw and still holds his cards in his hand, there is no penalty. He just waits for his proper turn of play, but he is not permitted to raise should a preceding player make a bet. The same holds true for passing or checking after the draw, provided no previous bet has been made.

False Openers

1. Player opening a pot with false openers forfeits his right to the pot, and his hand is dead. Remaining players in the pot, if any, will play the pot out as though it had been opened legitimately. If no one stays, the opening bet remains in the pot, and a new deal is declared.

2. If opener bets with false openers and his bet is not called, the amount of bet shall be withdrawn, but any ante remains in the pot.

3. If bet is called, the false opener loses the entire pot to the best legitimate hand.

Foul or Dead Hand

1. If a player holds more or fewer than five cards on the showdown, that player's hand is declared foul or dead, and he has no interest in the pot. But if the irregularity is discovered after the pot is collected, the hand must stand as legitimate.

2. If a player forgets to draw cards or permits another player to draw cards at his turn of play, he must play his hand as is. If he has

discarded and failed to draw, his hand is dead.

Improper Fold-Up. If a player decides to drop out of the pot or fold up, he cannot give an indication, verbal or otherwise, until it is his proper turn of play. Strict observance of this rule makes for a better game. But should he fold up out of turn, his hand is dead.

Optional Betting Limits at Draw Poker. The most popular betting limits are as follows:

1. Penny to 5 cents, 5 to 10 cents, 10 to 25 cents, 10 to 50 cents, 25 cents to $1, 25 cents to $2, etc. Only two amounts are specified, the minimum and the maximum permitted; which means at a player's turn of play a player must conform with one of the following rules:

(*a*) A player cannot bet an amount less than the minimum limit.

(*b*) A player cannot bet an amount larger than the maximum limit.

(*c*) A player may bet any amount between both limits.

(*d*) The ante is usually the amount of the minimum bet.

2. Variation in betting limit. Often three figures are mentioned, such as 5 cents, 10 cents, and 15 cents, or $1, $2, and $4, which indicates the ante and opening bets are the low amount and after the draw a bet must be either the middle or highest amount. The same holds true for any other three-figure limit, regardless of the amount.

3. Jack Pot. Should all the players pass on the first deal, the amount of the opening bet on the second deal can be any amount not higher than the ante already in the pot, provided the limit bet is less than the amount in the pot before the opening. Thereafter each bet after the draw can also be the amount of the possible opening bet. The dealer must announce the Jack Pot limit to the opening player and that amount cannot be exceeded in betting, except if it be lower than the maximum limit.

4. Pot Limit. Undoubtedly the fastest betting limit of all the limits played today at Poker. A player at his betting turn is permitted to bet any amount up to the total amount in the pot.

5. Table Stakes or Freeze-Out. Each player puts up a certain amount of money on the

table, but not less than a minimum agreed on beforehand. The maximum amount is often agreed on also, but as a rule it isn't. A player may increase or decrease the amount he has on the table, but only after a showdown and before the next deal. He may not take any money off the table before he leaves the game. On any bet a player is permitted to bet any or all of the amount he has in front of him. (See Tapping Out under General Rules for Poker.) But, after the tapping-out hand, the player may continue playing by putting more money on the table.

The above variation is not as popular as it used to be about twenty years ago, and "sky's the limit" games have almost vanished completely in this modern Poker era.

For additional betting methods see the basic Betting Rules for Friendly or Social Poker, page 52.

Draw Poker Strategy. You should always open the pot when you have an opportunity to do so. If the pot is opened ahead of you and there are two or more players, stay in with queens or better. If you are the dealer or anchor man (player to the dealer's right) and hold aces or better, and there are only two active players remaining, raise immediately. If there has been but one raise before your turn to speak, stay with a pair of kings or better. If there have been two raises, you must have at least a pair of aces or a four-flush (four-card flush) to stay.

Most of the above tips and many of those listed under General Poker Strategy (pages 7 to 14) go out the window in Draw or Stud Poker variations that make use of wild cards because chance is so much more a determining factor. The Poker tables on page 48 to 52 are given as an aid to better Poker playing. Try especially in Draw Poker to memorize the chances of improving certain hands, such as a pair, four-card straight, and four-card flush.

DRAW POKER VARIATIONS

There comes a time in every Poker player's life when he or she tires of the old game. Not known by many Poker players are the countless number of great games that bear a relationship, close or otherwise, to Draw Poker. Here then, are the greatest number and the most popular variations of Draw Poker games ever collected by one author from years of watching and analyzing all kinds of Draw Poker being played here and abroad.

I have divided the best-known Draw or Closed Poker-style games into four categories: (1) Basic Variants of Draw Poker; (2) Low and High-Low Poker Variants; (3) Spit-Card Variants; and (4) Miscellaneous Draw Poker Variants. Specific Poker games can be found in the index. However, you may know certain games under other names. In this case, determine the type of game you are interested in and look through the relevant category. You should find either the game itself or a close cousin.

BASIC VARIANTS OF DRAW POKER

The player will find the rules governing these games under General Rules for Poker and Basic Draw Poker Rules and in the text that follows.

Dealer's Choice

Many weekly Poker games played in private homes throughout the United States favor this variation. Dealer's Choice is exactly what the name implies. When it is your turn to deal, you have the privilege of naming the Poker variant to be played, and it is often necessary to give a little lesson in playing your version of the game. The dealer may deal any game he knows how to play and he is not limited to the common forms of Poker. He may select non-Poker games such as Blackjack or Yablon or In Between, or even a game of his own invention or knowledge which can be easily explained to the other players without too much loss of time.

Draw Poker—Deuces Wild

This variant of Draw Poker is played exactly as is Draw Poker, and all the rules that apply to Draw Poker apply to Deuces Wild, with the exception that a deuce is counted as any card a player desires to call it. It may even be counted as a duplicate of a card already held by a player. Therefore the highest-ranking hand a player can hold is five aces. A player should take extreme care in calling the rank of his hand, because the rank called must stand, contrary to the practice in Draw Poker, where the cards speak for themselves. Take, for example, a hand like this: two of clubs, two of diamonds, two of spades, six of hearts, ten of hearts. The average player very often calls four tens instead of a ten-high straight flush. Deuces and natural cards have the same value. Rank of hands in Deuces Wild is described under "Rank of Poker Hands with One or More Wild Cards," page 10.

English Draw Poker

The English version of Draw Poker is played exactly as is Draw Poker, with this exception: that the leader is permitted to draw up to four cards, whereas all other players are permitted to draw up to three cards only.

Draw Poker—Joker Wild

When one or more jokers are added to a standard pack of 52 cards the game is called Joker Wild. The amount of skill required to play Joker Wild is reduced immeasurably, more and more with the addition of each extra joker. The more jokers added, the less strategy to the game. Rank of hands is described on page 10.

Draw Poker with a Blind Ante

This variant of Draw Poker, which is also called Blind Tiger, and Blind and Straddle, is recommended to the boys who like fast and furious action. The game is played exactly as is Draw Poker, with the following exceptions:

1. No players ante into the pot.

2. The players are not permitted to pick up their cards and look at them.

3. The leader must make the first blind bet, without looking at his hand.

4. The players in proper rotation, as in Draw Poker, may either drop out, stay, raise, or reraise.

5. After the blind betting has ended and two or more active players remain in the pot,

the active players are permitted to look at their cards.

6. The privilege of playing first goes to the player to the left of the player who made the last blind raise.

7. If no player raised blind, the privilege passes to the player to the dealer's left.

8. The betting now proceeds as in Draw Poker, except that a player is not permitted to pass, or check. He must drop out, call the bet, play or stay by putting into the pot an amount equal to the bettor's raise, or reraise.

Progressive Draw Poker

In this variation of Draw Poker, all the rules that apply to Draw Poker are binding, with the following additional rules:

1. Should all the players pass (not open the pot) on the first deal, the requirement for openers on the second deal becomes a pair of queens or better. If the pot is not opened on the second deal, a pair of kings or better is required as openers for the third deal, and a pair of aces or better for the fourth deal.

2. The requirement for the fifth deal is kings or better; for the sixth, queens; and for the seventh, jacks; and then back up to aces and back to kings, etc.

3. Once the pot has been opened by a player, the game reverts back to Draw Poker, jacks or better as openers, etc.

Draw Poker High Spades

This is a side bet between two or more players that one will hold a higher-ranking spade card than any of the other players in his first five cards dealt. Players announce the approximate value of their hands—for example, a player says "I have a low spade." The other player says "I have a high spade," then shows it to all the players betting on spades. The reason for this is not to expose too many cards. Although spades is a popular bet at Draw Poker, it often exposes a hand of a player, and gives other players, not betting on spades, a slight advantage in the game.

Showdown Straight Poker

In this variation of Draw Poker, which is also called Cold Hands, the only betting is done before the cards are dealt, as if anteing into the pot. Then five cards are dealt each player, one at a time face up, starting with the leader and rotating to the left clockwise. The player holding the highest hand wins the pot. There is no draw. All other rules are identical to those for Draw Poker.

Pass-Out

Also known as Bet or Drop, the play is the same as in Draw Poker, except that a player may not check. He must either bet or drop out of the game.

Straight Poker

Each player antes a set amount and is given five cards face down. There are betting intervals and then there is a showdown. There is no draw.

Straight Draw Poker

The game is played exactly as in Draw Poker with the following two exceptions:
1. A player may open the pot on any hand he desires.
2. A player may draw up to five cards on the draw.

Draw Poker with a Five-Card Buy

The game is played exactly as is the standard game of Draw Poker. All the rules that apply to the standard game apply to this variant, with the following exception: that a player is permitted to draw one, two, three, four, or five cards on the draw.

Draw Poker—Blind Openers

If you think Draw Poker is too slow, then this is your game—that is, if you can get enough players who feel as you do. All the rules that apply to standard Draw Poker apply to this game, with the following exception: that you can open the pot on the blind; that is, you do not have to hold jacks or better to open. Or, if you like, the leader must open the pot regardless of the value of his hand.

Canadian Draw Poker

Canadian Draw Poker is played exactly as is the standard game of Draw Poker with the following exceptions: A player may open on a four-card straight or a four-card flush and, on the showdown a four-card straight or flush beats a pair, and a four-card flush beats a four-card straight.

Spanish Draw Poker

This variant of Draw Poker is played the same as ours, and all the rules that apply to Draw Poker apply to European, or Spanish, Draw Poker, with the following exceptions:
1. From two to five players; four makes the best game.
2. A 32-card deck is used, made by stripping out twos, threes, fours, fives, and sixes.
3. If there are not sufficient cards to satisfy each player's draw, the discards are picked up, shuffled, and cut, and the draw continues.

Fives and Tens

Also called St. Louis Draw or Woolworth Draw, this game is played as regular Draw Poker except that *all* fives and tens are wild cards. But, to open the first round of betting, a player must hold at least one five and one ten in his hand as openers. (The game cannot be opened if a player holds all four five spots, but does not have a ten.) If no player has the minimum openers—a five and ten—the deal passes, the players ante again, and new hands of five cards are dealt. This procedure is repeated until someone has the necessary openers. While the obtaining of the necessary openers may appear difficult to achieve, in reality, there are no more passes in this game than in standard jack pots. Once the pot is opened standard draw rules are followed. Since there are possibly eight wild cards in the game, a high four-of-a-kind is the average winning hand, but straight flushes and five-of-a-kind occur frequently.

LOW AND HIGH-LOW POKER VARIANTS

Here are the more popular Low and High-Low Poker variants.

Lowball

This game, especially popular in the Western States, is Draw Poker in reverse. In the legal games of California Poker clubs, Lowball is probably played as much as Five-Card Draw Poker. Incidentally, Stud Poker is prohibited by law in California licensed Poker clubs.

There are no minimum requirements for opening the pot and in the showdown the lowest hand wins the pot. Flushes and straights do not count. In other words if a hand consists of one suit or five cards in sequence, that does not affect it. The ace ranks low, counting as a 1. If all players pair and stay until the showdown, one pair of aces wins the pot since they are lower than one pair of deuces or any other pair. The lowest possible hand is five, four, three, two, ace, and is called a wheel, or bicycle.

The addition of a wild joker, commonly called *the Bug,* is used frequently in Lowball games. The joker occupies a unique position. If there is a natural ace in the hand the joker does not pair that ace—it simply ranks as the missing card next higher than the ace. Examples: an ace–two–three–four–five hand cannot be beaten by joker–ace–two–three–five. These hands tie, but ace–two–three–five–six loses to ace–joker–three–four–six because the joker can be designated as the missing deuce. Some Lowball clubs have instituted what is known as *the sevens rule.* This means that after the draw if a player checks with a seven-low or better, he forfeits any further profits from the pot. He may still win the pot of course, but should another player bet and the player with a seven-low calls and wins the pot, the player who made the bet is entitled to remove it from the pot.

The player should realize that when playing Lowball, a pair, particularly a high pair (from nine up), is almost worthless. It is foolish to play a hand after an opening bet on the strength of having three low cards with the hope of getting two low cards on the draw. This is one of the most foolish draws at Lowball. Players do not seem to realize that the probability of drawing two low cards is almost as remote as the probability of filling a three-card straight at Draw Poker. If you draw two low cards, you have the possibility of pairing your other three low cards; and you now hold a pair or probably two pairs. So, as an overall tip, the best hand at Lowball is a good pat hand, but you don't always get good pat hands; therefore I suggest you draw only one card to a four-card no-pair at this unique game.

Hands such as six-high are equal to a straight flush in Draw Poker, and a seven-high is equal to four of a kind. These hands usually will win the pot.

Double-Barrel Draw

This game is a combination of Draw Poker and Lowball. The author highly recommends this game to a player who considers Draw Poker too slow and Lowball too fast. Double-Barrel Draw is played exactly as in Draw Poker, except that if openers do not happen to be dealt and everyone has passed, the game is continued on the basis of Lowball and the leader has the option of opening or passing, and each player has a turn in the same rotating order as the previously played Draw Poker hand. Should all players pass, a new deal is dealt as in Draw Poker and the game continues as described above.

Leg Poker

This fascinating addition to Draw Poker or any of its variants is sometimes called Leg in a Pot. In Leg Poker the pot stays on the table until one player has won two legs (won it twice); then it is his to keep. The legs need not be won consecutively. *Warning:* If you are in a five-, six-, or seven-handed game, don't play this near quitting time because it might be several hours before one player does win two legs.

Speedy High-Low Leg Poker

This is a fast variation of Leg Poker with these added rules. If no one has a pair of aces or better on the first round, the hand is played as Lowball, described above. If no one opens, the same dealer keeps dealing until a leg (hand) is won. However, the pot stays in the center of the table until a player has won two legs (won it twice) which wins the pot for keeps.

The same dealer must keep dealing until a player has won a leg. Players must ante on each new dealt hand. To avoid arguments, and confusion, use a score pad to record winning games.

High-Low Draw

This is simply Draw Poker in which the highest hand and the lowest hand split the pot. However, unlike Draw Poker, a player can open on any hand (jacks or better are not required) and no high or low announcement is required. Cards decide at the showdown.

In playing for high I recommend that you play any hand that you would play in regular Draw Poker, and, in addition, remember that any possible low four-card flush or straight may turn out to be a low hand. The majority of players usually draw for low rather than for high. The high hands may run slightly higher than those in Draw Poker, and the low hands not much worse than the low hands in Lowball. As a rule it is better to draw to a good high possibility than to a good low one. See the basic General Rules for Poker (page 10) for rank of low hands.

Nine-Handed High-Low Draw Poker

Played exactly as standard Draw Poker except for the following: Up to nine players can play at the same time. After each player has been dealt five face-down cards, betting starts with the player to the dealer's left—he must open the pot and make a bet, but on the draw he can check if he so wishes. Only three raises are permitted on this betting round and other betting rounds. Players may choose to stand pat or discard one or two cards. After the discard turn of play has been completed the dealer places the two top cards of the deck in the center of the table face up, placing a coin on the first dealt card for identification. If a player discarded one card he makes use of the upturned card with the coin on top for his fifth card. If a player discarded two cards, he makes use of both upturned cards. If he failed to discard, he cannot make use of the center cards. Straights and flushes may be considered both high and low hands. *Example.* A hand comprised of ace, two, three, four, and five may be declared high or

low, or both high and low. A deuce, three, four, seven, eight flush also may be declared as high or low, or both high and low.

Seven-Card High-Low Draw Poker

This is a variation of Draw Poker with the following exceptions: After the ante has been made each player is dealt seven cards face down one at a time in rotation to the left. This is followed by a betting interval in which any amount up to the maximum limit can be wagered. After the first betting interval, each remaining player passes three cards to the player at his left, and in turn, receives three cards from the player at his right. Each active player next discards two cards, making his best five-card high hand or his best five-card low hand. Then starting with the leader each player, in rotation to the left, *rolls* a card (turns it face up and places it on the table in front of him) and a betting interval takes place. Each player may turn up any four of his five cards, but he must, of course, always have one card face down. Three additional cards are rolled, each followed by a betting interval. After the last betting interval, the declaration for high, low, or high and low follows.

Rockleigh

In this fascinating High-Low variation, four cards are dealt to each player as in Draw Poker. After the dealer receives his fourth card, he then deals four groups of two cards each in a row face down in the center of the table. After the players look at their four cards and a betting round takes place, the dealer turns face up any two-card group he wishes. Another betting round and another two-card group is turned face up. Continue betting and turning of a two-card group until the last two-card group from the center of the table has been turned face up, followed by the fifth and final betting round. On the showdown a player, announcing high, is permitted to select the best five cards for his hand, using either one or two cards from only one of the four groups. The same holds true when announcing low. Players on the showdown must stipulate and point to the two-card group they wish to incorporate in their high or low hand.

When announcing both high and low, a player may make use of one two-card group for high and another two-card group for low. Or, if desirable, make use of one two-card group for both high and low.

Jersey High-Low

One of the Poker creations of the author, this game is played the same as High-Low Draw Poker except for the following:

1. Five cards are dealt to each player as in Draw Poker. After the dealer receives his fifth card, he now deals four groups of three face-down cards on to the center of the table in a horizontal row.

2. After the players pick up their cards and look at them, the first betting round takes place.

3. Next, the dealer turns face up the first three-card group to the dealer's left, and a second betting round takes place. He continues turning a group of three cards face up followed with a betting round, as each row is face up until the last row of three cards has been turned face up and the fifth and final betting round has been completed.

4. A player must make use of three cards from his hand and two cards from one of the four three-card groups resting on the table. However, if a player calls "high-low," he may use two cards from one group to help form his high hand and two cards from another group to help form his low hand. Straights and flushes are not considered as low.

SPIT-CARD VARIANTS

The following are the most popular spit-card variants I have been able to find.

Spit in the Ocean

There are numerous variants of this game, which are themselves always being changed by one player or another. The author has seen at least 25 different variations played throughout the country. I include only the most popular versions.

In Spit in the Ocean itself, each player is dealt four cards instead of the usual five as in Draw Poker. After each has received his four cards, the next card is turned face up on the table. After a betting round, the players draw cards as in Draw Poker. Each of the players must consider the upturned card his own fifth card. The player to the dealer's left must open the pot regardless of the value of his hand.

On the showdown each player must hold only four cards in his hand, and is compelled to include the upturned card on the table as his fifth card.

Pig in the Poke

A variation of Spit in the Ocean is to call a wild card any of the three other cards of the same denomination as the upturned card, but not to call wild the upturned card in the center of the table. Another variation is to call the upturned card in the center of the table wild—plus the three cards of the same denomination.

Wild Widow

In this variation of Draw Poker, four cards are dealt face down to each player. Then one card is dealt face up in the center of the table. The deal is continued for the players until each player has a hand of five cards. Any cards of the same denomination as the one in the center of the table are considered wild. The card in the center of the table is not used in play but remains there until the end of the game.

The procedure for play otherwise is as in Draw Poker, and there is a draw. The general rules and those for wild cards apply.

Twin Beds

In this variation of Spit in the Ocean, each player is dealt four cards. After the dealer has received his fourth card, two horizontal rows of five cards each are dealt face down on the table. The betting round takes place, and the dealer turns up one card from each row. Another betting round, and another card is turned up from each row. Continue betting and turning a card from each row until the last card in each row has been turned face up and the betting round has been completed.

The last card to be turned up from each row is wild, and so are the three cards of the same denomination as the wild card. The player may use up to five cards from either row to complete his hand, but he cannot use cards from both rows to help his hand.

Twin Beds High-Low

Countless high-low games have developed from Draw Poker. However, Twin Beds High-Low is probably the most exciting. The game is played exactly like Twin Beds with the following exceptions:

After the ten center cards are turned face up and the fifth betting interval is completed, each player, starting with the leader, selects one of his five closed cards; when all are ready the card is turned face up and placed on the table directly in front of each player. This is known as *rolling*. Once the rolling begins, the high man bets first. The game continues in this fashion until four cards have been rolled over by each active player. The final betting interval is followed by the declaration of high or low or both ways. The last raiser declares first; if no raise has taken place, the player who started the last betting round declares first. The player may use up to five cards from either row to make the best high or low hand. However, if you call both ways, you are permitted to make the high hand from one row and your low hand from the other row. I repeat, in no instance are you allowed to use cards from both rows to create a high or low hand. For further information see Seven-Card High-Low Stud (pages 41 to 42).

Laino or Roll 'em

This game combines many of the features of both Draw and Stud Poker. The cards are dealt as in five-card draw. The player to the dealer's left must open the pot regardless of the value of his hand. Players can stand pat or discard one or two cards. After the draw players arrange their cards face down on the table as they see fit. Each player then selects one of his five face-down cards and when all players are ready, dealer calls "Roll 'em" and each player faces up a card and the betting takes place. The game continues in this manner until four cards have been rolled by each player. The last round of betting is followed by the declaration of high or low or both high

and low. Straights and flushes count both high and low.

Laino with a Spit

This game is played exactly as Roll 'em except that after the draw and betting round a spit card is dealt face up in the center of the table and another round of betting takes place followed by the rolling of four cards, each followed by a round of betting. The spit card is a common card available to all players. The sixth card (spit) permits more two-way hands since a low hand and a straight or a low hand and a flush appear more often in this variation.

Stormy Weather

This version of Spit in the Ocean is a variation of Draw Poker with extra draws. Each player is dealt four cards, singly, face down, as in Draw Poker; only, after the dealer has received his second card, he deals a card face down in the center of the table, another card onto the center of the table after receiving his third card, and a third card face down in the center of the table after dealing himself the fourth and last card of the deal.

The betting round and the drawing of cards is as in Draw Poker, except that a player may open the pot on any hand he desires (jacks or better are not required), and a player may draw up to four cards if he desires. If all the players pass, a new hand is dealt, and all the players ante again, as in Draw Poker. If the pot is opened and the active players have completed their draw, there is no betting at this time, instead:

The dealer now turns up the first card dealt of the three cards in the center of the table, and a betting round begins, the opener making the first bet. When all bets have been met, the dealer turns up the second card dealt in the center of the table and another betting round ensues, with the opener having the first turn. The same holds with the facing up of the third card in the center of the table.

On the showdown, a player is permitted to use for his fifth card any one of the three cards turned up in the center of the table. Player must indicate verbally, at his proper turn of play, which of the three upturned cards in the center of the table he is using for his fifth card. No mistakes may be rectified by a player after his proper turn of play has passed.

Lame Brain

In this variation of Spit in the Ocean, which is also called Cincinnati and Confusion, five cards are dealt each player and five cards are dealt face down in a row in the center of the table. The dealer, after dealing himself a card on each round, deals one face down in the center of the table. There is no draw in this game as in Draw Poker. After each player has looked at his five cards, the dealer turns face up the first card dealt in the center of the table. The betting now starts. The player to the dealer's left has the first turn of play. Betting and the rotation of play are as in Draw Poker.

On completion of the betting round, the dealer turns the second card dealt face up in the center of the table, and another betting round takes place. This procedure is followed until the five cards in the center of the table are face up and five betting rounds have taken place. On the showdown, a player may make use of any or all the five cards shown face up in the center of the table. In other words, he selects the best hand of five cards out of a total of ten—five in his hand and five face up in the center of the table.

Round the World

This game is played as is Cincinnati or Lame Brain, except that each player is dealt only four cards, and the odd hand also has only four cards. The game is usually played for high at the showdown but may be played for high-low also.

Lame Brain Pete

In this variation of Cincinnati or Lame Brain, the lowest-ranking card in the center of the table and three cards of the same denomination are wild.

Lame Brain High and Low

Played exactly as is Cincinnati or Lame Brain, with the added feature of high and low. In this game of High-Low, it is not uncommon for a player to win both the high and the low, nor is it uncommon to find two players tying for low.

Klondike

This game, which is known also as Tennessee, is played like Lame Brain or Cincinnati, except for a slight dealing variation. Five cards are dealt to each player, face down; then the dealer turns up five cards from off the top of the pack, one at a time, with a betting interval after each. In the showdown, each player selects the best hand from his five plus the exposed five cards.

Many times a Klondike game is played with progressive betting. That is, each betting unit is increased one unit on each round and a raise must be double. For example, if the betting unit is one chip, the first interval would require a bet of one chip; the second round a bet of two chips; the third, three, and so on. If you wish to raise, say in the fourth round, you would have to double the bet, or put eight chips in the pot; a reraise of an original bet would cost twelve chips. In this system of betting, there is no checking—you must bet, call, or drop. The betting position progresses, too. In other words, the first position—at the left of the dealer—must bet first on the first round; the second position—the second player to the left of dealer—bets first on the second interval; the third position first on the third round; and so on.

Klondike Bob

Played like Klondike except that one of the center cards is designated as being wild. It can be either the lowest exposed card, or the fourth, or the fifth card that is turned up. It is played in all three ways. But regardless of the designation of the card, it and all of the same denomination are wild.

Criss Cross

This game, which is also called Cross Widow, X Marks the Spot, and Crossover, is the same as Cincinnati or Lame Brain except that the center cards are dealt out after each player has received a five-card hand and are laid out in the shape of a cross.

$$1$$
$$4 \quad 5 \quad 2$$
$$3$$

The top card of the cross is rolled (turned up) first. Each adjacent card is turned up in clockwise fashion. The card in the center of the cross is turned up last. This last card is wild and so is any other card of the same rank, which includes the cards in the player's hand or the laid-out cards on the table. As each card is rolled a betting round follows. Each player must select his Poker hand from among his own five cards plus either one, two, or three cards from the cross on the table, but the cards selected must be in the same row (either in a horizontal or vertical row).

Shotgun or Pig Poker

Played the same as Draw Poker, except as follows: After each player has been dealt three original cards, the deal is suspended for a betting interval. Then each player is dealt another face-down card (fourth) and another betting interval takes place. Then, each player receives a fifth card face down and another betting interval takes place. Then, there is a draw of one, two, or three cards, as in Draw Poker, followed by a final betting interval. At the end of the final betting interval, high hand of active player wins.

Butcher Boy

Each player is dealt an open card. Dealer then continues dealing open cards in turn until a card comes up that matches in denomination some card in any player's hand. The dealer then gives this card to that player's hand. Every time a matching card is dealt, there is a round of betting. Play continues in this fashion until some player has been dealt four of a kind. He wins the pot. This can also be played high-low.

Omaha

Each player receives two cards face down. Five cards are dealt to the center, face down.

There is a betting interval. Then the center cards are turned up one by one, with a betting interval after each. Each player makes his hand from his own two cards plus the five in the center.

Hold 'em

The same as Omaha, but after the first betting interval three cards are turned up in the center. The last two cards are turned up one at a time.

Bull

Each player receives three cards face down. He arranges them in any order he wishes, but may not thereafter change the order. There is a betting interval. Then each player receives four face-up cards, with a betting interval after each. Then each player turns up his first face-down card, followed by a betting interval, and his second face-down card, followed by the final betting interval. The last cards are then turned up for the showdown. The game is usually played high-low and a player may win both high and low.

Bing-O-Draw

This game is played the same as Criss Cross except for the fact that nine cards are placed in the center of the table in the shape of a square.

$$1 \quad 2 \quad 3$$
$$4 \quad 5 \quad 6$$
$$7 \quad 8 \quad 9$$

The four corner cards of the square are dealt face up and the remaining five cards face down. This is followed by a three-raise maximum betting interval. Thereafter the remaining five cards are faced one at a time, with the center card reserved for the last turn. This last card is wild and so is any other card of the same rank, which includes the cards in the player's hand or the cards laid out on the table. The player then proceeds by rolling and betting as in Criss Cross. A low or high hand is made by using a set of three cards from the square on the table (running horizontally, vertically, or diagonally) with the five dealt cards.

Double-Barrel Shotgun

Also known as Texas Tech, this game is played high and low. Each player is dealt five cards, as in Draw Poker. There is no opening or drawing card. The leader turns up one card, and each active player in his proper turn of play, as in Draw Poker, does likewise. A round of betting takes place. The leader turns up a second card, and each active player does the same, then there is a second betting round. This procedure is followed until the five cards have been turned face up. There are four rounds of betting.

Scarney Poker

This game creation of the author's is one of the most bizarre, exciting and charmingly exasperating of all Poker variations. Scarney Poker combines the principles of High-Low Draw Poker, Spit-in-the-Ocean, plus an entirely new Poker game lay-off principle reminiscent of Rummy-type games. The Poker purist can, and will, find holes through which he can drive a truck in the architecture of this game. Its compulsory method of getting rid of cards in hand, for instance, makes a farce out of Poker skill, but the stark fact remains that when Poker players like a game, as many seem to like this variation, the game fills the bill. All the rules for High-Low Draw Poker hold true for Scarney Poker with the following exceptions and additional rules.

Requirements

1. A standard pack of 52 cards.

2. Three to eight players. Six, seven, or eight players make for the best game.

Object of the Game. For a player at the showdown to hold a higher-ranking Poker hand or to hold fewer total points, or both at the same time, than any other active player.

The Deal. The dealer deals five cards to each player, one at a time clockwise, starting with the player at his left. After the dealer has received his fifth card, two horizontal rows of five cards each are dealt face down on the table. The row farthest from the dealer is known as the "Poker row," and the row closest to the dealer is known as the "lay-off row." Poker row cards may be used to help form Poker hands; the lay-off row is used only to lay off matching cards.

Winners on Showdown. When playing Scarney Poker, the player holding the highest-ranking five-card hand, provided he has declared for high, and the player holding the lowest total point count with 0, 1, 2, 3, 4, or 5 cards, provided he has declared for low, share the pot equally. If a player calls "high-low," he must win both high and low to be declared the winner, see page 11. When declaring high, the player may select the best five cards out of his hand and Poker row. Lay-off row cards cannot be used as part of a hand. The point value of cards when calling low are as follows: The ace is the lowest ranking card having a value of 1; the king, queen, and jack are valued at 10 points each. All other cards have their numerical face value. To repeat, standard Poker hands do not count when announcing low. When cards are used from the Poker row to fill in a hand, the player must state the value of his hand. If a player declares his hand incorrectly and the pot has not yet been collected, he may correct the error; but if the pot has been collected the error must stand.

If the low hand is comprised of 0, 1, 2, 3, 4, or 5 cards, the rank of low is determined by the total number of points of the cards held by the player. *Example:* a player holds five cards, four aces, and a two spot, the low point count is 6. A player holds four cards, four aces, the low point count is 4. A player holds three cards, three aces, the low point count is 3; a player holds two cards, two aces, the low point count is 2; a player holds one card, one ace, the low point count is 1; a player holds no cards, the low point count is zero, which is the best possible low-count hand.

For the rules for announcing high or low or both on the showdown, see page 10.

Preliminaries Before the Deal. All the preparations before the start of the actual play are as described under General Rules for Poker, including rank of hands, betting limits, preparations before play, selecting the dealer and seating positions at the table, irregularities in cutting the cards, the shuffle, the cut, and the ante.

The Play. After each player has picked up and studied his hand, the first betting round takes place. Next the dealer turns up (faces) the first card to his left of each row and a second betting round takes place. The second card is turned face up from each row and a third betting round takes place. The dealer continues turning up a card from each row followed by a betting round until the last card from each row has been turned face up and the sixth and final betting round takes place.

The Play of the Poker and Lay-Off Row

1. The Poker row: The player may, if he chooses, use from one to five cards of the Poker row to complete his hand.

2. The lay-off row: As each card is turned face up in the lay-off row, a player holding one or more cards of the same rank *must* immediately place these cards face up on top of the matching card or cards of the lay-off row. *Example:* A player holds the ace of clubs and the ace of spades; the dealer turns the ace of hearts face up in the lay-off row, the player must lay-off his two aces on top of the ace of hearts of the lay-off row, leaving him with a three card hand. As other cards are turned face up in the lay-off row, all matching cards held by players must be placed on the lay-off row. If a player lays off his five cards, he has zero points. If a player fails to lay-off a playable card onto a card of the lay-off row and this irregularity is discovered after the next betting round has begun, the player's hand is dead and he must throw in his cards.

MISCELLANEOUS DRAW POKER VARIANTS

There are many miscellaneous Draw Poker variants but the following are the most commonly played:

Three-Card Poker

Played the same as Draw Poker, except that any hand may open the pot, and each player is dealt only three cards on the first round and must draw two cards on the draw. Betting is exactly as described under Draw Poker. There may be three-card straights or flushes, and the cards rank as in standard poker. But some players consider three of a kind as the highest hand.

Three-Card Monte or Three-Toed Pete

This three-card Poker game should not be confused with the Three-Card Monte game described in Chapter 16. In this Poker game, one card is dealt to each player face down and two cards face up, with a round of betting following the dealing of each card. The rank of Poker value is the same as Three-Card Poker.

Two-Card Poker or Frustration

A variation of Draw Poker on a reduced scale. Each player is dealt two cards, singly, as in Draw Poker. On the draw a player must do one of the following:

1. Stand pat.

2. Draw one or two cards. The highest-ranking hand in this game is a pair of aces.

Two-Card Poker, Deuces Wild

Played exactly as is Two-Card Poker, plus this: The deuces are wild, and the game is played as is High-Low, with the ace ranking high in the high hand and low in the low hand.

Hurricane

Each player receives two cards as in Two-Card Poker, but in this game, one is face down and one is face up. There is usually a previous ante as in all Two-Card Poker games. Wild cards may be used. The play may also be for high-low. This game is also known as Dynamite, Gruesome Two-Some, and Double Trouble.

One-Card Poker

In this game, which is sometimes called Lazy Edna or Lazy Mary, each player is given one face-down card. This is the complete hand. The betting is for high-low. Tie cards divide the pot high or low. If a joker is used, it holds rank equal to an ace for high or to a deuce for low. The ace is played only as high.

Show Five Cards

Seven cards are dealt face down to each player, and each player looks at his cards. At a signal from the dealer, each player turns up one of his cards on the table. Before giving the signal, the dealer should inquire whether everyone is ready. After the cards are exposed, there is a round of betting. After the betting is completed, the dealer gives the signal for the exposure of the second cards. All these second cards must be exposed at the same time. The process continues until all players in the game have five cards exposed before them for the showdown. The game is usually played high-low. It is not unusual for a player to change his mind during the game and try for a low hand rather than a high one, according to the cards exposed by the other players.

Big Sol

In this game, which is also called T.N.T. and Snookie, each player receives three cards face down dealt in rotation one at a time. Then follows a round of betting. Then each player is dealt another closed card, followed by another round of betting. This continues until every active player has seven down cards, with betting after each round of cards has been dealt.

Each player now discards any two cards from his hand, leaving him with five cards. Every player, beginning with the man at the dealer's left, then turns one card face up. This is followed by a round of betting. In like manner, three more cards are turned up, one by one, with a round of betting each time. The fifth card is kept face down and is not exposed. The players then declare for high-low, and there is a showdown.

Draw Your Own

Each player is given five cards face down, dealt in rotation, one at a time. Then also in rotation and one at a time, each player is dealt three additional cards face down to form an individual stock from which to draw later.

There is a round of betting. Then each player discards a card from his hand and draws a card from his individual stock of three cards. He may not look at any of the cards from his individual stock. He may look only at the card he draws. There is another round of betting, and then another card is discarded and a second one drawn from the individual stock. This continues until all the players have exhausted the cards in their stock. The game is high-low.

Whiskey Poker

This game is the ancestor of all the Poker games, but is seldom played today. But since this book is an *encyclopedia,* I include the following brief description of how the game was played:

The dealer gives five cards face down to each player and an extra hand ("widow") of five cards face down in the middle of the table. He must deal to each player in turn around to the left, one card at a time, then to the widow, then to himself last. Each player, beginning at the dealer's left, has the option of exchanging his hand for the widow, or keeping it as it is. If he takes up the widow, he places his five cards face up on the table and they become the new widow. Each player in turn has the option of taking up one card or all of the new widow and replacing it with cards from his hand. If a player wishes to play his original hand, he signals by knocking on the table, but he cannot draw and knock at the same time.

The process of exchanging cards continues around the table until some player knocks. A knock means that this player will show his present hand when it is his next turn around the table, and that thus each player has only one more chance to exchange cards. No player may draw after he has once knocked. A player may knock before the widow is exposed, if he wishes to.

If no one takes the widow until it comes around to the dealer, the dealer must either take up the widow for himself, or turn it face up on the table. Even if the dealer knocks, and does not take up the widow, he must spread it on the table for each player to see and draw once more. A player may pass in any turn—decline either to exchange or to knock—but he may not pass in two consecutive turns. Having passed on the previous round, he must either exchange or knock.

After the knock and the final round of draws, all hands are shown to the table. The highest takes the pot. The lowest pays the forfeit agreed upon beforehand. Some players have a round of betting before the showdown.

Knock Poker

Knock, or Rap, Poker is the direct survivor of Whiskey Poker. This fascinating game for three to five players is designed not only for Draw Poker fans but Rummy players as well. At the start of the game, each player antes one chip into the pot, and is dealt a hand of five cards (as in Draw Poker) from a regular 52-card deck. The remaining undealt cards are then placed face down in the center of the table to form a stock from which players will draw (as in Rummy—see Chapter 5). The top card of the stock is turned face up on the center of the table to begin a discard pile, as in most Rummy games. Then each player in turn, starting with the leader (or nondealer if there are only two players), may take either the last discard or the top card of the stock, after which he must discard a card to reduce his hand to a legal five-card Draw Poker hand. As in Gin Rummy, a player may not discard a card he picked up from the discard pile until his next turn of play.

Each player tries to build up the best possible five-card Poker hand from the cards he was previously dealt and the cards he takes from the discard pile and stock. The hands rank as in Draw Poker.

Whenever a player believes he has a good enough Poker hand, providing he holds jacks or better, he *knocks* (he merely says "Knock"), but he may do so only after having made his discard to the discard pile. The knock means that the game will end after one more round. Each player has one more turn in which he may pick up the last discard or draw from the stock and then discard, until it comes to the knocker again, at which time a player may decide either to drop out (fold) or stay. A player who drops out must immediately pay one chip to the knocker regardless of the outcome of the hand. The knocker does not have another play. He is stuck with the hand he had when he knocked, or as soon as any player knocks. The betting in this game is unlike usual Draw Poker betting. There is no betting during play. The pot consists of the antes plus an additional charge of 1 chip to the knocker from each of the players who dropped out.

At the end of the hand, the showdown takes place. If the knocker has the high hand he takes the pot, and in addition, all active players pay him two chips. However, if anyone beats the knocker, then the knocker must pay two chips to each active player and the winner takes the pot.

If the stock has been exhausted and no one has knocked, high hand wins on the showdown. At the showdown, if the winning player's hand is comprised of four of a kind or a straight flush, he receives a bonus award of 4 chips from each player. If he holds a royal flush he receives a bonus award of 8 chips from each player. Only the winning player is entitled to a bonus award.

Knock Poker—Deuces Wild

All the rules that apply to Knock Poker apply to Knock Poker—Deuces Wild, with the following exception. A deuce may be counted as any card a player desires to call it. It may even be counted as a duplicate of a card already held by a player.

Bonus awards: Winning player holding five of a kind, a straight flush, or a royal flush receives a bonus award of 4 chips. There are no bonus awards for four of a kind.

Brag

Great Britain's three-card representative of the poker family. The rules of Draw Poker apply except as noted:

1. There are three wild cards, ace of diamonds, jack of clubs, and nine of diamonds, ranking in that order and called *braggers.*

2. The dealer antes an agreed amount into the pot (dealer's edge) and this ante is considered as an opening blind bet.

3. The dealer deals three cards face down to each player. This is followed by a betting round as in Draw Poker. Then each player in turn, beginning with the leader, may call the dealer's blind bet, raise, or drop out. If all players drop out, the dealer then retrieves his blind bet and the deal rotates to the player on his left.

4. After the betting round, if two or more active players remain, there is a showdown in which the highest-ranking hand—three of a kind, pair, or a high card—wins. In hands of equal rank, natural cards beat hands including wild cards. As between two hands both possessing wild cards, the highest-ranking wild card wins. If two players hold pairs of equal value, the highest-ranking odd card wins. If the odd cards are of the same value, high suit wins. The suits rank: spades (high), hearts, diamonds, and clubs (low).

There are many Brag variants, but the one just described is a good example of the basic game.

Pokino

This variant of Draw Poker is also known as Poke.

Requirements
1. Two players only.
2. A standard 52-card deck.

Object of the Game. To score as many points as possible. Each hand is divided into two stages. First stage is played as in Five-Card Draw Poker, and in the second stage the cards are played out in the form of tricks.

The Play of the Hand. The players cut for high card. The player cutting the highest card becomes the first dealer. The deal alternates in subsequent hands.

The First Stage of Play. Five cards are dealt to each player as in Draw Poker. The nondealer plays first. He may stand pat or discard and draw from one to three cards. By drawing cards he doubles himself, that is, he is penalized double for each trick he loses in the play-out period. If, after his draw, he is still not satisfied, he may discard and draw a second time. This automatically *redoubles* him and he is penalized quadruple for each lost trick.

The dealer may stand pat or has the option (minus the penalty) of one free draw of one, two, or three cards. This free draw may be followed by a double and a redouble, making three possible draws in all.

Second Stage of Play. The second stage of play begins with the nondealer making the opening lead. The hands (five cards each) are played out in tricks, one card by each player. High card takes the trick regardless of suit, and a player does not have to follow suit. In case of two like-valued cards being played to

the same trick, the first led wins. The winner of a trick leads to the next. Each player retrieves his own card and faces it up to indicate a trick won, or down to indicate a trick lost.

A player may lead to two tricks at the same time by playing a pair (two of a kind). The opponent can only win both tricks by playing a larger pair. However, he does not have to respond with a larger or smaller pair; he may discard any two cards to the pair leads. In the same manner three or four of a kind can be played.

Scoring. In Pokino as in Bridge, the score is kept in columns divided in the middle by a heavy line. Trick scores are entered below the line, while bonuses and honors are marked above the line. A player receives one point for each trick he wins, if opponent is not under penalty. If opponent is doubled, each trick is valued at 2 points, and if redoubled, 4 points.

After the last trick has been played and the score recorded, players show their Poker hands; the winning Poker hand in accordance with standard values of Poker hands receives an honor score as shown in the table that follows. Both players may score trick points in the same hand, but only the winning hand gets an honor score.

If a player wins all five tricks, which is known as a *sweep,* he receives a bonus of 250 points.

A game consists of 20 points below the line. The player making game receives a 100-point bonus above the line and all partial trick scores of opponent below the line are canceled. If the same player wins his second game, he receives the 100-point bonus plus a rubber bonus of 750 points providing his opponent has not won a game, or 500 points if his opponent has won a game.

Upon completion of a rubber, the player with the highest score is the winner.

Table of Honors

Pair	50 points
Two pair	100 points
Three of a kind	200 points
Straight	300 points
Flush	400 points
Full house	500 points
Four of a kind	600 points
Straight flush	750 points
Royal flush	1,000 points

Table of Bonus Values

Game bonus	100 points
Two-game rubber bonus	750 points
Three-game rubber bonus	500 points
Sweep bonus	250 points

Red and Black

In this game the cards of the deck are assigned an arbitrary numerical value as follows: king, queen, jack, ten, 10 points each; 1 point for the ace; and all other cards, their face or pip value. In figuring the value of the hand, the point counts of the cards are totaled. All cards in a red suit count their real value, but all cards in a black suit count a minus value. In a hand containing both red and black suits, one is subtracted from the other. *Example:* The point total for a hand containing king of clubs, jack of hearts, seven of spades, three of clubs, and two of diamonds would be a minus 8.

In actual play, after an agreed ante has been made by all players, each receives five cards, face down, one by one, in a clockwise rotation. There is an opening round of betting, followed by the draw. All active players have the option of taking one to three cards or not taking any cards at all. There is then a final round of betting and the showdown. The highest point count and the lowest point count divide the pot. It often happens that nobody in the game has a minus count, the smallest number of plus points wins low, while the largest number of plus points wins high. Conversely, if nobody has a plus count, the smallest number of minus points wins high, and the largest minus figure is low.

CHAPTER 3

Stud Poker

Stud Poker, also known as Open Poker, is the most scientific and fastest gambling game in the Poker family. Rich and poor play it for cash ranging from penny ante to table stakes in the thousands. Although Draw Poker (and its variants) is the favorite family game, "money players" prefer Stud.

Stud Poker in all its variations allows for more strategy than Draw Poker, and the most popular forms of Stud, such as Five-Card Stud Poker and Seven-Card Stud Poker, have four and five betting rounds, while straight Draw Poker has only two. The pots are, therefore, much greater in Stud than in Draw.

In Stud Poker the average rank of winning hands is lower than in Draw Poker, because the maximum number of cards anyone is dealt in Stud is either five or seven depending on the variation being played. However, with the introduction of spit cards, center cards, and substitutions in Stud and Draw variants, this situation changes completely.

FIVE-CARD STUD POKER RULES

Five-Card Stud Poker is the basic game of the Stud Poker group, and since each player receives a maximum of five cards, it is possible to have as many as ten players.

Requirements

1. Two to ten players; seven players make the best game.

2. A standard 52-card deck. (Usually at hand are two packs of different backs or colors so a player may call for a change of packs upon completion of any deal.)

Object of the Game. For a player at the showdown to hold a higher-ranking hand than any of the other players. The player (or players) having the best hand is declared the winner (or winners) and collects the pot.

Preliminaries Before the Deal. All the pre-liminaries before the actual play are as described under General Rules for Poker, Chapter 2, such as the pack of cards, rank of cards, rank of hands, preparations for play, betting limit, time limit, royalties, selecting the dealer and establishing seating positions at the table, the shuffle and cut, irregularities in cutting the cards, etc.

The Beginning of the Deal. The dealer deals each player face down one card (which is known as the hole card), starting with the player to the dealer's left and rotating clockwise, dealing the last card to himself (the dealer), then one card face up to each player in the same order. Then he places the pack face down on the table in front of himself so that the cards are handy for the following part of the deal. The hole card is very carefully protected by each player to keep it hidden from his opponents. The hole card is the only card in Stud Poker that is unknown to the other players, and on the rank of this card depends the betting and the outcome of the hand. Each card that is face up on the table shall be known as an *upcard,* after the expression I coined for Rummy games.

First Round of Betting. The players having carefully examined their hole cards, the player holding the highest-ranking upcard must make the opening bet (first bet). It may be a specified amount agreed on or any amount within the limit. (Some players, to speed the betting, rule that the lowest ranking card must make the opening bet.) Should two or more players hold matching high-ranking or low-ranking cards (whichever rule is adopted), the one nearest to the dealer's left must make the opening bet. Thereafter each player in turn, starting with the player to the bettor's left and rotating clockwise, must

In Five-Card Stud (left) the first card is dealt face down, the rest up. In Seven-Card Stud (right) the first two and last are dealt face down, the middle four, up.

make one of the following plays:

1. He may fold up, or drop out, which means he does not want to continue playing his hand. This is indicated by his saying "Out," and putting his two cards on the discard pile on the table.

2. Or he accepts the bet, and says "I'll play," or "Stay," and puts into the pot an amount of money equal to the opening bettor's.

3. Or he raises the pot, by putting into the pot an amount of money equal to the previous bet plus an additional amount within the limit.

4. Or he reraises (if a previous player has raised) by putting into the pot an amount equal to the raiser's plus an additional amount. Any active player can reraise the reraiser by putting into the pot an amount equal to the reraiser's plus an additional amount, etc. Each player in proper turn must follow this procedure until:

   (*a*) Only one player remains in the game; he wins the pot. Should all the other players drop out and only one player remains, he does not have to expose his hole card.

   (*b*) Or until two or more players have put an equal amount of money into the pot, which means the opening bet, raise, or reraise if any has been met by all the active players.

If two or more active players are still in the game and all bets have been met by these players, the dealer continues the deal by dealing each player one card (the third card) face up in the same rotation as before, except that from now until each active player has been dealt a complete hand, or until only one player is active, the cards must be dealt in the following manner: The dealer cannot pick up the remaining stock, but must leave the stock resting on the table. Dealing must be done with one hand, picking one card at a time off the top of the stock. This rule is highly recommended to minimize dealer mistakes and to help eliminate cheating on the deal. This method of dealing is used in most of the high-stake games the author has witnessed.

Second Round of Betting. The player holding the highest-ranking hand with the two up cards has the option of making the first play, which consists of:

1. Dropping out of the pot. This he signifies

by saying, "Out," and throwing his hand face down into the discard pile.

2. Checking, which he signifies by saying, "Check." Which means he desires to play but does not desire to make a bet at present.

3. Betting, which he signifies by putting an amount of money into the pot, within the limit.

If the player who has the option of betting does not bet, the turn to check, bet, or drop out passes to the player on his left. This procedure continues until all players have had their turn of play. Should all the players fail to bet and there are two or more remaining players in the game, which means they have checked, the dealer deals each player one card (his fourth card) face up in the same rotation as before. But should a player make a bet, each player in turn starting with the player to that player's left must:

1. Play or stay, by putting into the pot an amount equal to the previous bettor's.

2. Drop, fold up, or go out, by throwing the three cards he is holding face down into the discard pile.

3. Raise, by putting into the pot an amount equal to the previous bettor's plus an additional amount within the limit.

4. Reraise, provided a previous player has raised. This is done by putting into the pot an amount to equal the raiser's, plus an additional amount. Any active player can reraise the reraiser by putting into the pot an amount equal to the reraiser's plus an additional amount, etc.

A player cannot check after a bet has been made. Any player who had previously checked must abide by the above four rules. This procedure is followed until only one player is left in the game and he wins the pot, or two or more active players remain in the game and all bets have been met by the remaining players.

The dealer then deals each player another card face up in the proper rotation for a total of three upcards plus a hole card, and the third round of betting takes place under the same rules as for the second round. On completion of that betting round, if there are still active players, the dealer deals each player one upcard in proper turn for a total of five cards to each player.

Fourth and Final Round of Betting. This is the final round of betting. The same rules

govern this play as are stipulated for the second round of betting, except that a play hand is now called a *call* hand. If at any time before the hand is called, only one player remains in the game, he wins the pot and does not have to expose his hole card. The only time the players must expose their hole cards is when a call is made after each player has been dealt five cards.

A call is similar to a play or stay in the second round, only it completes the hand. The dealer must call attention, by announcing orally, to the highest-ranking hand at each turn of play. Should any player hold a hand comprised of a pair or better, he must call it so that all players can hear. He must also call possible flushes or straights, and must announce the last round of cards being dealt.

Showdown. When the final betting round is over, all active players, starting with the player who is being called and rotating to the left clockwise, must turn their hole cards face up on the table for all the players to see. The player holding the highest-ranking hand wins the pot. For further rules on tied hands see page 7 under General Rules for Poker. On completion of each showdown the game continues in the same manner with a new deal.

Additional Rules at Five-Card Stud Poker

Misdeals. Whenever a misdeal occurs there must be a new shuffle and cut. The same dealer deals again. Should the same dealer make a second misdeal, the deal passes to the player to the dealer's left. The following errors determine if a misdeal has occurred:

1. If one or more cards is exposed in cutting or reuniting the cut packets, there is a misdeal.

2. If the pack has not been offered to the proper player to cut and the betting has not started, there is a misdeal.

3. If the pack has not been cut and the betting has not started, there is a misdeal.

4. If one or more cards is observed face up in the pack and the betting has not started, there is a misdeal.

5. If the dealer exposes his own or a player's hole card while dealing it, or a card is found face up while dealing a player a hole card, there is a misdeal.

6. If an imperfect pack is found, containing fewer cards than the standard pack or

duplicate cards, the play must stop immediately on its discovery, and the players take out of the pot the money they put into it. If it is discovered after a pot has been collected, the previous hands stand, and are legitimate.

7. If any player has been dealt out, or an extra hand has been dealt in, there is a misdeal.

8. If a player (or players) has been dealt too many or too few cards before the betting has started, there is a misdeal.

9. If the dealer has dealt a player a hole card out of turn and that player has looked at it, there is a misdeal.

Passing the Deal. A dealer cannot pass his deal in his turn to deal unless incompetent to deal the cards.

Dead Hands. If a player holds too few or too many cards during the betting interval or at the showdown, his hand is foul, or dead. But should this be discovered after that player has collected the pot, it stands as a legitimate hand.

On Being Dealt an Exposed Card. If a card is found face up in the pack and the betting has started, the player must take that card in his turn of play, except if it is the first card to be dealt of a new round. That card is immediately burned (put to the bottom of the pack, out of play), and after the betting has been completed on that round, the dealer must burn enough other cards from the top of the pack so that the total number of burned cards equals the active number of players in the game.

Dealing in More or Fewer Players. If a dealer deals a player out or deals an extra hand in, and it is discovered before the players have looked at their hole cards, and if the error can be corrected so that each player receives his proper cards (by shifting a card from one player to another and placing the extra card or cards back on top of the pack or dealing one or more cards from the pack without any of the cards being exposed to any player), there is not a misdeal.

Exposing the First Card of a Round. If the dealer exposes the top card of the pack before the betting has been completed on the previous round, he leaves the card face up on the pack until the betting on that round, then the dealer must burn or bury from the top of the pack as many cards (including the exposed card) as there are active players left in the game. Under no conditions are the players permitted to look at the burned cards. Then the play continues according to the rules.

Improper dealing. A dealer is not permitted to deal the first card face up and the second card face down. The first card must be dealt face down, becoming the player's hole card.

Protecting a Hole Card. A player must protect his hole card at all times. Protecting a hole card means permitting no other player to know its identity, regardless of whether the player is active or dead.

A player is not permitted at any time to turn up his hole card and call for his next card face down. A player, when folding up, is not permitted to expose his hole card to any of the players or to mention its identity.

Checking on the Last Round. If a player checks on the last round, each other player, in order to check too, must be able to beat the checking player's four open cards. Otherwise a check is not permitted. For example, a player who has checked has a pair of open aces. The next and following players cannot check unless they can beat the open pair, although they may bet if the situation permits. This rule is incorporated to protect a player's hand against another player who calls an impossible hand, although there is no penalty that could be imposed on a player for failure to comply.

Dealer Errs in Calling Highest Open Hand. When the dealer errs in calling the highest open hand and as a result the wrong player bets (if it is discovered before the betting is completed on that round), the dealer must correct the play by giving back out of the pot the money that was improperly bet. This is the only time a player is permitted to take money out of the pot.

Going Through the Discards. In no circumstances is a player permitted to look at the discards either before or after the showdown. Nor is a nonactive player permitted to look at an active player's hole card before or after the showdown, unless a bet has been called and the player is compelled to expose his hole card.

Looking at Undealt Cards. Looking at the top card or any of the undealt cards while a hand is in progress, regardless of whether or not the player is out of that pot, is not permitted. Other additional rules are the same as those on pages 16 to 18.

Optional Betting Limits at Stud Poker

There are numerous types of betting limits at Five-Card Stud Poker (and its variants). We give here the most popular and most commonly used. Whatever the limits, the minimum and the maximum must be specified before the start of the game.

Betting Variation I

1. Players do not ante, nor does the dealer edge.

2. A minimum amount and a maximum amount are specified before the start of the game: for example, a penny and two, 5 and 10, 5 to 25 cents, 50 cents to $1, 25 cents to $2, $1 to $4, or any two specified amounts.

A player may bet the minimum, the maximum, or any amount between limits at his turn.

Betting Variation II. In this betting variation only two different amounts may legally be wagered, no amount between limits. For example, 10 and 20 cents means a player cannot bet 15 cents, which would be between limits. Other limits: 5 and 10 cents, 25 and 50 cents, $1 and $2. The maximum amount may be bet only on the following conditions:

1. If a player holds an open pair or better.

2. On the betting round prior to a player's being dealt his fifth or last card, and on the final betting round before the showdown.

Betting Variation III. Often three figures are mentioned in the limits—such as 5, 10, and 25 cents—meaning the player is permitted to bet the minimum amount or up to the second amount until the third and fourth betting round or until an open pair shows. Then he is permitted to bet up to the maximum.

Betting Variation IV. See Betting Rules for Friendly or Social Poker, page 52.

Betting Variation V (Dealer's Edge). Before the deal starts the dealer edges into the pot an amount agreed upon, usually equal to the amount of the minimum limit.

Betting Variation VI (Player's Ante). Each player antes into the pot an amount equal to the minimum bet, or a larger amount agreed upon by mutual consent.

Jack Pot. The following additional betting feature may be added to any of the above variations except Variations V and VI. When the opening bettor fails to have an active opponent on his first bet—that is, all the other players have dropped out—the next deal is called a *jack pot*. All the players must ante into the pot an amount equal to the bet made by the lone active player in the previous hand. After all the players have anted and a new hand is dealt, the opening bettor (in Jack Pot, high or low card can check on the opening bet or thereafter as governed by the Stud Poker rules) is permitted to bet an amount equal to the total amount anted into the pot. In other words, if that amount is in excess of the maximum limit, the new maximum limit for that Jack Pot is the amount anted into the pot prior to the opening bet.

Table Stakes or Freeze-Out. Each player puts up on the table a certain amount of money, but not less than a minimum amount agreed upon beforehand. The maximum amount is sometimes agreed on also, but as a rule it is not. Upon the completion of each showdown, a player is permitted to increase or decrease the amount on the table, and on any bet a player is permitted to bet any amount or the entire amount that a player has on the table—excepting that a player may continue playing by putting more money on the table. Should a player fail to have as much money as the previous bettor, he is permitted to play for the pot. (See Tapping Out, under General Rules for Poker, page 13.) The above variation is not as popular as it was twenty-five years ago.

Pot Limit. Undoubtedly the fastest betting limit of all the limits played today is pot limit. A player in his betting turn may bet any amount up to the total of the pot.

Strategy of Five-Card Stud Poker

Let us assume you have been dealt a hole card and your first upcard. This is the most important phase of any stud game. You must decide the value of those two cards, and you do it by considering the value of both your cards and the value of every other player's upcard. No general rule will cover this situation.

First, if your hole card is lower than a ten-spot, you fold (provided you do not hold a pair back to back), regardless of the value of your upcard. If it is an ace or a high card and you are compelled to make the opening bet, bet the minimum amount permitted.

So much for the first two cards. Now the first betting round has ended, and each player has received his second upcard. If you see any other player's two upcards paired, and if you fail to hold a pair, fold up. This is the traditional theory of Stud Poker and a sound one: "Never play a hand at the start which you know is lower than your opponents'." In other words, don't chase a pair or a higher hand when the pot is small; because if you did pay for the third upcard, you might be tempted to chase the money which you have in the pot. That is not good Poker playing. It boils down to this: Play them tight, at least until you receive your third upcard. For further information on how to better your Poker playing, see General Poker Strategy and the Poker tables later in this chapter.

FIVE-CARD STUD POKER VARIATIONS

In the following selection of the most popular variations of Stud Poker are many which appear in print for the first time. These are Five-Card Stud Poker unless otherwise specified. These games have been collected from years of watching various kinds of Stud Poker being played in card rooms, Poker clubs, and casinos here and abroad. I have divided the Stud, or Open, Poker variants into two general categories: Basic Variations of Stud Poker and Miscellaneous Stud Poker Variants. The player will find the rules governing these games under General Rules for Poker (page 7), under Five-Card Stud Poker Rules (page 33), and in the text that follows.

BASIC VARIATIONS OF STUD POKER

Five-Card Stud—Deuces Wild

Played exactly as is Five-Card Stud, except that the deuces are wild, and on the showdown cards do not speak for themselves; a player must announce the value of his hand in his proper turn of play. Announcement cannot be changed after a player's turn of play has passed on the showdown. Often a joker is added as an extra wild card.

Five-Card Stud—Last Card Down

This variation is played the same as Five-Card Stud except that the last card is dealt face down, thus giving each active player two hole cards.

Five-Card Stud—Five Bets

This game, which is also known as Pistol Pete, Hole-Card Stud, and John's Poker, is played as is Five-Card Stud Poker, except that there is an extra betting round that occurs after the hole cards have been dealt to each player and before any upcards are dealt.

Low-Hand Stud Poker—Ace Low

In this variation of Low-Hand Stud Poker the ace ranks only as a one, and the best hand is ace, two, three, four, and six of mixed suits.

Lowball Stud Poker

This game, which is also called Low-Hand Stud, is played like Five-Card Stud with the following exceptions:

1. The lowest-ranking hand wins the pot.
2. The player with the lowest-ranking card or cards showing has the option of making the first bet in each betting round. For ranking low-valued hands see Lowball, page 21.

Double-Handed High-Low

In this game, which is also called Bimbo High-Low, the play is the same as Five-Card Stud except for the following:

1. Each player is dealt two hands of five cards each. Each hand is dealt separately in turn and is bet as a different hand.
2. When a player bets on one of his hands, his other hand must call the bet along with the opponents or fold.
3. A player may fold one hand at any time and stay with the other.
4. Before showdown, each player announces what he is going to do with each hand—go low, or high, or high-low.

Skeets with Spit Cards

Played exactly the same as Five-Card Stud Poker except that at the dealer's option after each round of betting the dealer calls "skeets" and deals a spit card in the center, which may be used by all players in making their best hand. This is followed by a round of betting. The dealer has the option of refusing to deal a spit card in the center—whenever he chooses. This game slightly favors the dealer because, should he hold a valuable hand, he may not spit. However, with each player having a turn at dealing the odds are equalized.

Five-Card High-Low Stud

Five-Card High-Low Stud has been gaining popularity with millions of Stud players. However, in recent years Seven-Card High-Low Stud has outdistanced Five-Card High-Low Stud in popularity (see page 41 for Seven-Card High-Low Stud). Most of the rules that apply to Five-Card Stud apply to this High-Low variation with the following addition: at the showdown, the highest and lowest hands divide the pot equally (see page 10 for rank of high and low hands).

Another High-Low variation is to call straights and flushes high or low, or both high and low.

Three-Card Substitution

Also known as Three-Card Buy, this game is a high-low variation of Five-Card Stud, but after each player's fifth card has been dealt and its betting round is completed, the dealer calls "Buy one," or "Substitution one." Then, each player in turn is permitted to discard and draw a card. Players may discard an upcard or a hole card. If an upcard is discarded the player receives an upcard. If a hole card is discarded the player receives a face-down card. After the first substitution, or "buy-in," there is a round of betting. Dealer then calls "Substitution two" and there is another substitution followed by another round of betting. Then, the dealer calls "Substitution three," followed by a discard and draw and a final betting round. A player may reject the opportunity to substitute any time he wishes. The substitutions, or buy-ins, are not free; they must be paid for. In a one-, two-, and three-unit limit game, the first buy-in costs 3 units, the second costs 6 units, and the third buy-in costs 9 units.

Both variations detailed under Five-Card High-Low Stud apply equally to Three-Card Substitution.

Two-Card Buy or Substitution

Played the same as Three-Card Substitution except that only two substitutions, or buy-ins, are permitted.

One-Card Buy or Substitution

Played the same as Three-Card Substitution except that only one buy-in is permitted.

Crazy Five-Card High-Low Stud

This unusual type of Stud Poker, also called Shove 'em Along, Forward Pass, Take It or Leave It, Push, or Rothschild, is played the same as Five-Card Stud Poker with the following exceptions and additional rules:

1. Crazy Five-Card High-Low Stud begins with each player receiving a hole card. The dealer then deals an upcard to the leader (player at his left). The leader has two alternatives: he may keep the upcard or pass it on to the player on his left. If he passes it on, he receives another dealt upcard which he must keep. However, if he decides to keep the original dealt card, the dealer deals an upcard for the next player in turn. This player also has the option of keeping the upcard or passing it to the next rightful player.

2. The procedure continues clockwise around the table with each player either accepting a passed upcard or passing it on to the player on his left and having the dealer deal him an upcard in its place, which he must keep; or if he has not been passed a card, the dealer must deal him an upcard and he has the option of keeping the upcard or passing it to the player on his left, in which case he will be dealt a second upcard which he must keep. In any event a player is not permitted to accept a passed card and have an upcard dealt to him too.

3. The above procedure continues until the dealer's turn of play, when he is bound by the following rules: He may accept a passed card or refuse it and burn it (place it face up) on the bottom of the deck. If he refuses it, he deals himself an upcard which he must keep. If a passed card has not been offered to him, he may keep this first dealt upcard or burn it and deal himself a second upcard which he must keep.

4. When each player has received a hole

card and his first upcard, a betting interval takes place. After the betting, the dealer deals a second round of upcards and the play continues as before. This deal is again followed by a betting interval, and this procedure of play and betting continues until each remaining player has a hole card and four upcards and the fourth betting interval takes place.

5. And now comes another unusual aspect of this fascinating game: a delayed showdown. Each remaining player in turn may discard his hole card or any upcard and be dealt another card in its place. If a hole card is discarded, a face down card is dealt in its place. If an upcard is discarded, a face up card is dealt in its place.

6. The fifth and final round of betting then takes place, followed by a high-low showdown. At the showdown, the highest and the lowest hands divide the pot equally (see page 10 for rank of high and low cards).

Five-Card Turn-Up Stud

This game is also known as Mexican Stud, Peep-and-Turn, and Flip Poker, and is played the same as Five-Card Stud, with the following exceptions and additional rules:

The first two cards are dealt face down to each player, and he has the option of turning up whichever one he chooses. This is followed by a betting interval in which high hand bets first. The third card is also dealt face down, and again the player has the option of turning up either card. This is followed by another betting interval. Each player's fourth and fifth (last) cards are also dealt face down and another betting interval takes place after each player turns up his optional card. A player may turn up either his previous hole card or the one just dealt, but he must always have only one card in the hole.

Shifting Sands

This game is played the same as Five-Card Turn-Up Stud except that the first card that a player turns up and every other card of the same rank in his hand at the showdown are wild.

Monterey

Played like Five-Card Turn-Up Stud, except that in this game, which has been called

Rickey de Laet by some, every player's hole card and every other card of the same rank in his hand are wild.

Blind Five-Card Stud Poker

Played like Five-Card Stud with the following exceptions and additional rules:

One card is dealt each player face down followed by a betting round started by the leader. A second face-down card is dealt each player followed by a second betting round. The leader starts the betting each time a card is dealt. The same procedure of being dealt face-down cards and betting is followed until five cards have been dealt face down. No player may check; he must either bet, raise, or get out. This game may also be played with deuces wild or with the added joker as wild card.

New York Stud

In this Five-Card Stud game, a four flush (a four-card flush) beats a single pair but loses to two pairs or higher. In the final betting round, a player with a four flush showing bets first as compared to a player with any single pair showing.

Canadian Stud Poker

Canadian Stud Poker is played the same as Five-Card Stud, except that a four-card straight or flush beats a pair, and four-card flush beats a four-card straight. Skill is even more important here than in Five-Card Stud.

Spanish Stud Poker

This variation is played the same as is Five-Card Stud Poker, and all the rules that apply to Five-Card Stud apply to this game, with the following exception. A 32-card deck is used, made up by stripping out all the twos, threes, fours, fives, and sixes.

Pig Stud Poker

This is a variation of Five-Card Stud and Five-Card Draw Poker combined. The rules are as follows:

1. The player whose turn it is to deal antes an agreed amount into the pot.
2. Each player is dealt three face-down cards one at a time in rotation.

3. The leader, as in Stud Poker, makes the first bet, followed by each player in rotation, and each player at his turn of play may check, bet, raise, or drop out.

4. After this betting round is completed, a fourth card face up is dealt to each player and another betting round takes place with high card betting first. The fifth card dealt, also an upcard, is followed by a betting interval.

5. The player now has five cards, three face down and two face up. He picks up the two upcards and places them face down among the three face-down cards; he then plays it out as in Five-Card Draw Poker by discarding and drawing to his hand, or standing pat.

Pig Stud Poker is considerably more interesting, incidentally, when played deuces wild and joker wild.

Six-Card Stud

Played the same as Five-Card Stud Poker with the following additional rules:

1. A player is dealt his sixth card face down to give him two hole cards.

2. The best five cards out of six may be used to form a Poker hand.

Six-Card High-Low Stud

Played the same as Six-Card Stud with the following additional rule: Any player may go for high or low, or both, according to rules governing high-low declarations as found under General Rules for Poker, page 10.

Seven-Card Stud Poker

In the past few years Seven-Card Poker, also known as Down the River, Seven-Toed Pete, and Peek Poker, has replaced Five-Card Stud as the most popular form of straight Stud Poker played in the United States. It is played the same as Five-Card Stud with the following exceptions and additional rules:

Each player is dealt two hole cards singly in proper rotation, as described under dealing in General Rules for Poker. The third card is dealt face up for each player, then a round of betting takes place, as in Stud Poker. The fourth card is dealt face up to each active player, and another round of betting takes place. The fifth and sixth cards are dealt and similarly followed by betting rounds. The

seventh card is dealt face down, giving each active player his third hole card, and the last betting round takes place. In the showdown, each player selects for his hand the best five cards of his seven. One should be especially cautious in sorting a five-card hand from the seven cards dealt.

Seven-Card Stud—Deuces Wild Plus the Joker

Played exactly as is Seven-Card Stud, except that a joker is added as a wild card and the deuces are wild. In this variation of Stud, cards shown do not speak; player must call or announce his hand. Once called, hand must stand; it cannot be changed.

English Seven-Card Stud

This game is played like the American version except as follows: After each active player has received his two cards face down and three face up, and the appropriate betting intervals have taken place, he may then discard one card and draw a replacement as in Draw Poker, the replacement being dealt face up or down depending on the card discarded. There is then another betting round, followed by each player discarding and drawing one more card. The game is completed after a final betting interval and a showdown. A player may stand pat instead of drawing, but should he stand pat for the first draw, he must remain pat for the second.

Low-Hole-Card Stud

Also known as Low-Hole-Card Wild, this variation, which can be used in any variety of six- or seven-card stud, is played exactly as Seven-Card Stud except that the lowest-ranking card in the hole is wild, and all cards of the same denomination are also wild. Anything can happen, such as four and five of a kind, and even royal flushes.

Seven-Card High-Low Stud Poker

Because of the heavy betting I have recently witnessed at Seven-Card High-Low Stud by American gamblers from New York to California, I predict that it soon will be the nation's most popular Stud Poker game. I know dozens of illegally operating high-rolling Seven-Card High-Low Stud Poker games situated in various sections of the

United States in which thousands of dollars change hands nightly.

The game is played the same as Seven-Card Stud Poker (see page 41) with the following exceptions and additional rules: In this variant, each active player is required to declare, after the last betting interval but before the hole cards are exposed, whether he is going for high, for low, or for both. At the showdown, each player's best five cards out of his seven may be used to form either a high or a low Poker hand, or he may also use his two best groups of five cards out of his seven to form both a high and a low Poker hand. For detailed information on high-low declarations before the showdown and high-low betting restrictions see General Rules for Poker, page 10.

By far the soundest method of play at Seven-Card High-Low Stud is to play for low with the first three cards dealt. If you start with low cards, you have a chance to wind up with a straight or possibly a flush or a straight flush which will win high for you, and at the same time your low cards may give you the best low hand and you may win the entire pot. Playing for high at the start, you may win high, but it is almost a foregone conclusion that you will never win low as well.

Seven-Card High-Low Progressive Stud

Played the same as Seven-Card High-Low Stud with the following exceptions and additional progressive betting rules: The first player to the dealer's left starts the first round of betting, and he must bet one unit (10 cents) or drop out. On the second round of betting the second player on the dealer's left must start the betting with two units (20 cents) or drop out. On the third round of betting the third player to the dealer's left starts the betting with three units (30 cents) or drops out. The fourth player on the dealer's left starts the fourth round of betting with four units (40 cents). On the fifth and final round the fifth player on the dealer's left starts the betting with five units (50 cents) or drops out. Should a player whose turn it is to bet drop out, the turn to bet rotates to the next active player and so on.

Seven-Card High-Low Stud with a Joker

This game is played exactly as Seven-Card High-Low Stud described previously. But it is played with 52 cards plus a joker. The joker, called *the bug,* may be used as an ace or as a wild card in a straight or flush.

Fairview High-Low Stud

This game is a two-card high-low stud game that has three buy-ins, or substitutions. Each player is dealt a down card after which a three-raise-limit betting round takes place. Then an upcard is dealt and another betting round takes place. This is followed by three separate buy-ins with a betting round after each trade. Ace is a high card only. A pair of aces is a perfect high hand and a three and a deuce is a perfect low. However, a pair of sevens always takes the whole pot.

Eight-Card Stud

The same as Seven-Card Stud except that each active player receives an eighth card, dealt either up or down, as the dealer may decide in advance.

MISCELLANEOUS STUD POKER VARIANTS

Five and Ten Stud Poker

In this variation which can be used in any type of five-, six-, or seven-card stud, mixed fives and tens are wild, but you must have at least one of each. *Example:* If you hold one five or more and no ten, the fives are not wild. The same holds true if you hold one or more tens and no five. However, if you hold one or more fives and one or more tens, all fives and tens are wild. Deuces and threes may be used instead of fives and tens if desired. Four of a kind are common in this variation.

Two-Leg Stud

In this variation, which can be used in any stud game, no player may rake in the pot until he has won two hands. These need not be won consecutively. This is an exciting and thrilling gimmick for building big pots.

Baseball Stud

This is dealt like Seven-Card Stud with the

first two and the last card dealt face down. A three-spot upcard strikes a player out, and out he goes—no matter how much he has contributed to the pot, and regardless of how good his hand may be. The nines are wild, whether face up or face down, and a four dealt face up to a player gives him an extra face-up card. The holder of the four-spot receives his extra card after all the players have been dealt their upcards for that round. A three or a four in the hole has no special significance; it is played the same as other nonvalued cards. The betting is the same as any seven-card stud variation. After the first upcard is dealt a betting round takes place and every round thereafter. It usually takes a flush or better to win a pot, but a straight will occasionally stand up.

Football

This game is the same as Baseball except that all sixes and fours are wild, a four requires a player to match the pot or drop out, and a deuce entitles a player to an extra hole card.

Woolworth

In this Seven-Card Stud game, fives and tens are wild. A player dealt a five face up must pay 5 chips to the pot or drop out, and a player dealt a ten face up must pay 10 chips to the pot or drop out. *Note:* Woolworth is sometimes played so that a player is knocked out (must drop from the game) if a ten is dealt face up. In this version, the holder of the five does not have to ante extra chips to the pot.

Heinz

This Seven-Card Stud game is played with fives and sevens wild but a player dealt one of these cards face up must match the pot or drop.

Dr. Pepper

This Seven-Card Stud game is played with all tens, fours, and twos wild. There is no penalty or extra chips required when they are exposed. *Note:* Some play that when a deuce is exposed as upcard the player must put two chips in the pot or drop; if a four is dealt up,

four chips must be put in the pot or the player must drop; and when a ten is exposed, the player must pay ten chips to pot or drop.

Four Forty-Four

This is an Eight-Card Stud game in which four cards are dealt face down, one at a time in a clockwise rotation. Then one card is dealt face up and there is a betting round. Then three more upcards are given, with a betting interval after each. All fours are wild.

Three Forty-Five

Similar to Four Forty-Four except that only three cards are dealt face down at the start. There is a betting round after each of the next four upcards is dealt. Then the eighth card is dealt face down and there is a final betting interval. All fives are wild.

Seven-Card Flip

In this variation of Seven-Card Stud Poker, four face-down cards are dealt to each player. After examining them he may turn up any two of them. There is a betting interval, then play proceeds as in regular Seven-Card Stud, with three more cards dealt, two up and one down, a betting interval following each.

In another variation, each player first receives two cards, one up and one down, followed by a betting interval; then another two cards, one up and one down, and another betting interval; then two cards a third time and a betting interval; then a seventh card face down. Each player then discards one of his face-down cards and one of his face-up cards, leaving himself with three concealed cards and two exposed cards. The final betting interval and showdown follow.

Kankakee or Albemarle

In this Seven-Card Stud variation, there is a betting round after two hole cards are dealt, beginning with the player at the dealer's left. Then, the first face-up card to each player is wild and all like it are wild to that player only. After the wild cards are given there is a betting interval, starting with the player at dealer's left. Three more face-up cards and one final face-down card are then dealt to each active player, with a betting interval after each.

Rollover

This game, which is also called Beat Your Neighbor, Beat It, No Peekie, and No Lookie, is similar to Seven-Card Stud except for the following:

1. Seven face-down cards are dealt, one at a time, to each player, moving clockwise from the dealer's left. Keeping their hands concealed, even to themselves, the players arrange them into a pack, which is placed face down on the table. Then the player to the left of the dealer rolls over (turns face up) one card and bets on it. After the betting round, the player to the leader's left rolls over cards until he beats the card turned over by the leader. There is another betting round.

2. This procedure of rolling over cards until he beats the card turned over by the player before him, followed by a betting round, continues around the table.

3. When a player runs out of cards without beating the preceding player, he is out of the game.

4. Play continues around the table until one player presents an unbeatable hand and he wins the pot.

Night Baseball

This game, which is also called No-Peekie Baseball, is a combination of Rollover and Baseball Stud. That is, the threes and nines are wild, but when a three comes up, the player must drop or pay a penalty. See page 43. Any four rolled up entitles the recipient to an additional card, which the dealer immediately gives him, face up, from the top of the pack. In the play of the game, each player in rotation turns up his cards, one by one, until his showing combination beats any cards previously turned, after which there is a betting interval. Remember that no one can look at his cards until they are exposed to all. The penalty for peeking should be stiff, say five chips for each card that is face down or at the beginning of the game twenty-five chips.

Pass the Garbage

This game, which is also called Screw Your Neighbor, is a stud game in which seven cards

are dealt to each player face down. This is followed by a round of betting. After the bet, each player passes three cards to the individual on his left. After another betting round, each player discards two cards, making his best high hand, or his best low hand, if high-low is played. Then four cards are turned up, one at a time, with a bet after each card. After the final betting interval, there is a showdown.

Basketball

To add more activity to Pass the Garbage, some players add an extra passing round. After the first betting interval, each player passes three cards to the player on his left. There is a betting period, after which each player passes two cards to the person on his left. (The game can also be played where the players first pass three cards to the right and then on the next round they pass two to the left.) Then each player discards two cards, and after a final betting round, there is a showdown at which the high hand takes the pot. This game can also be played high-low.

Anaconda

This game is played like Seven-Card Stud except for the following:

1. Seven cards are dealt, face down, one at a time to each player. A single betting round follows—beginning with the person on the dealer's left.

2. After the close of the betting round, each player passes three cards of his choosing, face down, to the player on his left. The pass is made simultaneously by all players on a signal from the dealer. Following the pass, a betting round commences with the player to the dealer's left.

3. On completion of the second betting round, each player passes two cards, face down, to the player on his left and a betting round follows in the same manner as before.

4. After the third betting round, each player passes one card, face down, to the player on his left and a betting round follows in the same manner as 2.

5. After the betting has stopped, each player selects his best five cards and places them, face down, in a pack before him on the table.

6. On signal from the dealer, each player

rolls the top card of his pack. When everyone has one card exposed on the table, a betting round opens—starting with the player exhibiting the highest card. Then another card is simultaneously rolled over by all active players, and another round of betting follows, and so forth. The game can be played as a high game only or as a high-low game. In the latter case players must declare low or high hands at the end of the betting round when only one card remains, face down, in front of each player. This last card is then rolled for the showdown, and low and high hands divide the pot.

Note: Frequently, Anaconda is played with only one passing phase. That is, rules 3 and 4 are omitted.

Screwy Louie

This game is played the same as Anaconda, except that each player passes his two discards to the active player nearest his left. On receipt of these discards the player may use either or both of the cards in his hand. But, before the game rolling begins, he must place two discards in the center of the table, face down.

In a variation of Screwy Louie, instead of passing two cards, you pass three to your left and discard two from your new seven cards. This feature of one additional card to pass can be most frustrating especially when you have to break up a ready-made straight, flush, or full house.

Follow the Queen

In this game, which is also called Follow the Lady, the card and all of the same rank following the *last* queen turned face up on the table is wild. If the last card turned up to an active player is a queen, then *nothing* is wild. The cards may be dealt as in seven-card stud: three down, four up; or the first two cards may be dealt down and the remaining five may be turned face up. The latter method is usually preferred, and there is a betting interval after each face up card round. This game is most interesting since the wild card may change several times during the game—each time a queen is turned up—and there is always a possibility that nothing will be wild, should a queen be exposed on the last card dealt. In this game there can never be more than four wild cards in play.

Follow the King

Also called Follow the Cowboy, this game is played in the same manner as Follow the Queen, except that the card, and all of the same rank, following the last exposed king is wild. If the last card exposed to an active player is a king, then nothing is wild.

Follow Mary

This game is played like Follow the Queen, except that all queens are wild cards. In other words, the queen, whether in hole or face up, is always wild; also, the card, and all cards of the same denomination following the last-exposed queen, are wild. This means that there could be a total of eight wild cards in play. Of course, if the last card exposed to an active player is a queen, then only queens are wild.

Curaçao Stud

Curaçao Stud, or Dutch Stud, is a very unusual form of Stud which is most popular in the Netherlands and the Dutch West Indies. It is played as follows:

Each player is dealt a face-up card. If two or more players receive cards of the same denomination, the cards are dead and placed at the bottom of the deck by the dealer. The dealer continues dealing a card to each player until each has a card of a different denomination. When this occurs, the dealer reshuffles the remainder of the deck, and, after the cut, continues dealing cards face up onto the center of the table until a card is dealt whose denomination matches a card in a player's hand. The player whose card it matches, says "Give it to me." Each time a matching card is dealt, a round of betting takes place, and the player who has received that matched card starts the betting. As in Five-Card Stud, a player at his turn of play may check, raise, call, or fold. When a betting interval is ended, the deal continues. Play continues in this manner until some player has been dealt four of a kind, whereupon he takes half the pot. The other half goes to the low hand. Since not all players have the same number of cards, low hand is ranked as follows: low single card, low pair, and low three-of-a-kind.

Put-and-Take Stud Poker

Put-and-Take Stud is one of the best banking games in the poker family. As in most banking games, the dealer banks the game and players bet against the dealer. Two to eight players may participate but five or six makes the best game. The game is played like Five-Card Stud with the following exceptions and additional rules:

1. Each player except the dealer antes a chip into the pot.

2. The dealer deals each player (except himself) five face-up cards, one at a time, in Stud Poker fashion.

3. The dealer then deals himself five face-up cards (called *put* cards) one at a time. As the first put card is turned up, any player who has a card or cards of the same denomination antes to the pot one chip. For the second put card, the rate goes up to two chips, four if it is the third, eight if it is the fourth, and sixteen chips if the player matches the fifth put card. After the dealer's fifth upcard has been dealt and the holders of matching cards have contributed to the pot, the dealer places his five face-up cards on the bottom of the deck.

4. Now comes the payoff to the players by way of a second deal of cards, and these cards are called *take* cards. The dealer again deals himself five cards one at a time, but this time the holders of matching take cards collect from the pot at the same rate that governed the put-card contributions.

5. If there are any chips left after the dealer's fifth take card has been turned up, the dealer takes them. But if the pot does not have enough chips to pay the winners, the dealer must make good.

The dealer has a chip advantage equal to the original antes. However, with a rotating deal, this advantage is equalized.

Acey-Deucey

This is a form of two-card poker popular in the United States Army. Each player is dealt two cards, one up and one down. He may stand on the cards he is dealt, or at any later time, or he may draw by discarding one of his cards and being dealt a replacement (when his turn comes). If he discards a face-down card, the replacement is dealt face-down; if he discards a face-up card, the replacement is face-up. If he draws one card he pays the pot one chip; for a second card he pays two chips, and for a third card five chips. Betting begins when all hands have stood. High card bets, as in Stud Poker. The game is usually played high-low. Only pairs and high cards count. Highest hand is two aces; lowest hand is ace and deuce, since the ace is treated as low when the player tries for low (but a pair of aces is never a low pair). Winners split the total pot, including bets and chips paid to draw cards.

GENERAL POKER STRATEGY

Card players who want to become excellent poker players have much to learn. If they have played other card games, they also have much to forget because poker is totally different from most other games. Bridge, for instance, is mathematics and analysis, plus signals. Poker is mathematics, analysis, psychology, and personalities, plus money management.

Before the introduction of high-low hands, wild cards, rolling cards, six- and seven-card poker, and dozens of other such variations, it was a simple matter to formulate a set of rules for improving one's poker game. The odds and chances of being dealt and improving a five-card poker hand could be figured exactly and most subsequent developments were easily calculable. Since poker today has

countless variations and playing gimmicks, it would take a book this size to cover thoroughly all the strategic aspects of the game.

There are 20 fundamental rules, however, which a player should remember. They are general rules, many of which apply not only to Poker but to many other card games as well. Here they are:

1. The first rule is: don't try to beat the other players; let them try to beat you. This isn't just an introductory sentence; it is probably more important than all the tips and hints that follow. Do yourself a favor by memorizing it.

2. Be sure you know the rules of the game. The player who knows the rules has a decided advantage in any game against players who are vague about them.

3. Study the Poker probability tables that follow this section. A player who knows the Poker probabilities in drawing and improving hands has a decided edge over the player who only thinks he knows. But, don't become a slave to Poker probabilities. They are probabilities, not laws; and they do not supply a sure-fire recipe for winning.

4. Observe your opponents; learn their Poker mannerisms. Are they loose or tight players? And avoid giveaway mannerisms of your own.

5. Play as often as possible; experience is the best teacher.

6. Always remember that in a Poker game the average hand becomes less valuable the more players there are.

7. Treat every round of betting as though it were the first. Forget the previous betting rounds and the money you have contributed to the pot.

8. When you hold a cinch hand, wait till the last round to raise.

9. Fold a doubtful hand at the start rather than in the middle or at the end.

10. Call your opponent or opponents when you believe your hand is good enough to win, not merely because you suspect a bluff.

11. As a general rule, don't try to steal a pot by trying to bluff a poor player, a heavy winner, or a heavy loser.

12. When you're in a losing streak, don't let yourself get panicky. The more reckless you feel, the wiser it is to get away from the table at once. An excited player or a player plunging to recoup losses is a player at his worst.

13. You must expect to lose the pot unless you believe you have the best hand going in.

14. Most Draw Poker players would win instead of lose if they never tried to outdraw the opener.

15. Bet your big hands to the hilt and make every active player pay to see your hand.

16. Vary your playing strategy. The player whose game is always the same becomes an easy mark for smart Poker players.

17. Try to keep a Poker face. Don't complain when losing or show elation when winning. The emotional aftermath will prohibit clear thinking and proper evaluation of succeeding hands.

18. Try to sit with your back to the wall and try to avoid kibitzers who watch your hand. Many good hands are tipped off by onlookers who don't keep Poker faces.

19. Trust no one at Poker; it is a game for blood. If you want to play a good game you must forget friendship and bet your hand for what it's worth. Top-money winners do.

20. When you play Poker, give the game all you've got, or get out. That is not only the best way to win at Poker; it's the only way you and the rest of the players can get any fun at all out of what ought to be fun.

Poker Probabilities

The relative values of Poker hands were not just conjured up by some rule maker nor arbitrarily assigned by the first Poker players. They were discovered by finding out, through the use of permutation and combinations of formulas, the exact number of possible five-card Poker hands in a 52-card deck, a total of 2,598,960.

These hands were divided into groups or ranks such as no pair, pair, three of a kind, straight, flush, full house, four of a kind, straight flush, and royal flush. The ranks were then arranged in relative value according to the frequency of their occurrence. The hands which can be expected to appear most often have the lowest rank; those which appear least often, the highest rank. A good Poker player must have a fair idea of Poker odds and probabilities. Without such knowledge he has no good way of deciding on his course of action in the various situations which arise, no way of making any mathematical analysis on which to base a decision. This information is given in the Poker tables in this chapter. These same tables can also be used to prove the relative value of Poker hands and to settle disputes that arise regarding the chances of drawing certain valuable hands in Five-Card Draw Poker, Five- or Seven-Card Stud Poker, or in the first five cards dealt in any other form of Poker.

It would be simple if all one had to do to become a winning player was to memorize the following Poker tables. But knowing the exact strength of your hand or the exact chances of bettering your hand on the draw will not always help you, because the playing habits of your opponents will often throw a monkey wrench into your best-laid mathematical plans. *Example:* A big raise from a habitually tight player means quite a different thing from the same big raise from a drunk who has already been caught trying to steal (bluff) the last half-dozen pots.

Although Poker is a game of skill, the judgments and decisions to be made by even the average Poker player involve a general knowledge of the game's probabilities. The chances of being dealt any certain pat hand are the same, regardless of the number of players in the game. The same holds true in drawing cards to try to improve a hand.

The following pages contain the most informative and comprehensive tables of Poker mathematics found in any card book. They apply to Draw Poker, Five-Card Stud Poker, Seven-Card High-Low Poker, and many of the Poker variants found in this book. The tables list the names of each different possible hand in order of rank starting from the top, the possible number of ways each can be made, and the chance of being dealt such a hand in the first five cards dealt, such as the original five cards dealt in Five-Card Stud or in Five-Card Draw Poker before the draw.

POSSIBLE POKER HANDS IN A 52-CARD DECK

Ranking Order of Hands	Number of Possible Ways Hand Can Be Made	Chance of Being Dealt in Original 5 Cards
Royal flush	4	1 in 649,740
Straight flush	36	1 in 72,193
Four of a kind	624	1 in 4,165
Full house	3,744	1 in 694
Flush	5,108	1 in 509
Straight	10,200	1 in 255
Three of a kind	54,912	1 In 47
Two pairs	123,552	1 in 21
One pair	1,098,240	1 in 2⅖
No-pair hand	1,302,540	1 in 2
Total	2,598,960	

In the Chance column above, fractional figures have been rounded out to the nearest 2/5 or whole number. The probability of being dealt a pair or better in the first five cards dealt is almost even—and the probability of being dealt a no-pair hand is practically the same. So it's almost a three-to-one chance, when playing against two opponents, that one of them will hold a pair or better in the first five dealt cards. The probabilities vary slightly depending on what you hold.

The 1,302,540 possible five-card no-pair hands are divided as follows:

POSSIBLE POKER HANDS OF LESS VALUE THAN ONE PAIR IN A 52-CARD DECK

Ace Counting High	King Counting High, Ace Low	Number of Possible No-Pair Hands
Ace high	King high	502,860
King high	Queen high	335,580
Queen high	Jack high	213,180
Jack high	Ten high	127,500
Ten high	Nine high	70,380
Nine high	Eight high	34,680
Eight high	Seven high	14,280
Seven high	Six high	4,080
		1,302,540

CHANCES OF HOLDING ANY PARTICULAR HAND OR BETTER IN FIRST FIVE CARDS DEALT

	Approximately Once in
Any pair or better	2 deals
Pair of jacks or better	5 deals
Pair of queens or better	6 deals
Pair of kings or better	7 deals
Pair of aces or better	9 deals
Two pairs or better	13 deals
Three of a kind or better	35 deals
Straight or better	132 deals
Flush or better	273 deals
Full house or better	590 deals
Four of a kind or better	3,914 deals
Straight flush or better	64,974 deals
Royal flush	649,740 deals

CHANCES OF BEING HIGH WITH THE FIRST FIVE CARDS DEALT, PERCENT

	Number of Opponents							
Player's Hand	1	2	3	4	5	6	7	8
Three of a kind	98	94	92	89	87	84	82	80
Two pairs	93	86	80	74	68	63	59	53
Pairs:								
Aces	89	79	70	62	55	49	43	39
Kings	88	78	69	61	54	48	42	36
Queens	83	68	56	46	38	32	26	20
Jacks	79	63	50	40	32	25	20	15
Tens	76	58	44					
Nines	73	53	38					
Eights	70	49						
Sevens	66	43						
Sixes	63	40						
Fives	60	36						
Fours	57	32						
Threes	53	28						
Twos	51	25						

The above table presents the chance of a specific hand being high at Five-Card Draw Poker against one to eight opponents. This is expressed in percent; thus 98 means 98 percent, or this will happen 98 times out of 100.

The lowest-ranking regular five-card Poker hand when an ace is both high and low is comprised of six, four, three, two, ace in mixed suits. The above table is particularly helpful to players who play high-low variants of Poker. In the short run each additional active player in the game increases the odds against you on any particular hand. But in the long run, since all players have to put an equal sum into the pot, thus increasing the size of the pot in direct ratio to the increased odds, it doesn't make much difference, as far as odds are concerned, if you are bucking one or seven players. To simplify matters, the figures in the following tables have been rounded out when necessary to the nearest 1/10 or whole number.

ODDS AGAINST IMPROVING THE HAND IN DRAW POKER WHEN DRAWING THREE CARDS TO ONE PAIR

Odds against any improvement	2½ to 1
Odds against making two pairs	5 to 1
Odds against making three of a kind	8 to 1
Odds against making a full house	97 to 1
Odds against making four of a kind	359 to 1

ODDS AGAINST IMPROVING THE HAND IN DRAW POKER WHEN DRAWING TWO CARDS TO A PAIR AND A KICKER*

Odds against any improvement	3 to 1
Odds against making two pairs	5 to 1
Odds against making three of a kind	12 to 1
Odds against making a full house	119 to 1
Odds against making four of a kind	1,080 to 1

* An unmatched card held in the hand when drawing.

Note that your chances of making four of a kind are three times as great when drawing to a pair minus a kicker than when holding a kicker. In fact, you have a better chance of improving your hand when drawing three cards to a pair than when drawing two cards to a pair plus a kicker. The tables above give ample proof of that. However, good Poker playing demands that a player occasionally hold a kicker with a pair so as to keep your opponents in doubt as to your playing habits. The chances of making a full house by drawing one card to two pairs are about 11 to 1.

ODDS AGAINST CHANCES OF IMPROVING THE HAND IN DRAW POKER WHEN DRAWING TWO CARDS TO THREE OF A KIND

Odds against any improvement	8½ to 1
Odds against making a full house	15½ to 1
Odds against making four of a kind	22½ to 1

CHANCES OF IMPROVING THE HAND IN DRAW POKER WHEN DRAWING ONE CARD TO THREE OF A KIND PLUS A KICKER

Odds against any improvement	11 to 1
Odds against making a full house	15 to 1
Odds against making four of a kind	46 to 1

The two tables above show that the best chance for improvement with three of a kind is to draw two cards and not hold a kicker. Holding a kicker increases the odds against the player for any improvement.

ODDS AGAINST FILLING IN A FOUR-CARD STRAIGHT IN DRAW POKER WHEN DRAWING ONE CARD

Odds against filling a straight open at one end	11 to 1
Odds against filling a straight open in the middle	11 to 1
Odds against filling a straight open at both ends	5 to 1

ODDS AGAINST FILLING A FOUR-CARD FLUSH IN DRAW POKER

The odds against making a flush by drawing one card of the same suit are about 4½ to 1. If you insist on drawing to a three-card flush, the odds against your catching two cards of the same suit are approximately 23 to 1.

ODDS AGAINST MAKING A STRAIGHT FLUSH IN DRAW POKER WHEN DRAWING ONE CARD

Odds against making a straight flush open at one end	46 to 1
Odds against making a straight flush open in the middle	46 to 1
Odds against making a straight flush open on both ends	22 to 1

CHANCES OF HOLDING VARIOUS POKER HANDS IN THE FIRST FIVE CARDS DEALT WHEN THE FOUR DEUCES ARE WILD

Rank of Hand	Number of Each	Chance
Five of a kind	672	1 in 3,868
Royal flush	484	1 in 5,370
Straight flush	4,072	1 in 638
Four of a kind	30,816	1 in 84
Full house	12,672	1 in 205
Flush	13,204	1 in 197
Straight	66,236	1 in 39
Three of a kind	355,056	1 in 7
Two pairs	95,040	1 in 27
One pair	1,222,048	1 in 2 1/10
No-pair hand	798,660	1 in 3 1/4
Total	2,598,960	

CHANCES OF HOLDING VARIOUS POKER HANDS IN THE FIRST FIVE CARDS DEALT WHEN THE JOKER IS WILD (53-CARD PACK)

Rank of Hand	Number of Each	Chance
Five of a kind	13	1 in 220,745
Royal flush	24	1 in 119,570
Straight flush	216	1 in 13,286
Four of a kind	3,120	1 in 920
Full house	6,552	1 in 438
Flush	7,768	1 in 369
Straight	20,532	1 in 140
Three of a kind	137,280	1 in 21
Two pairs	123,552	1 in 23
One pair	1,268,088	1 in 2½
No-pair hand	1,302,540	1 in 2
Total	2,869,685	

A very unusual mathematical situation arises in Deuces Wild and also in a 53-card deck with the joker wild regarding the relative value of three of a kind and two pairs. In Deuces Wild, as detailed in the table, the chances of drawing three of a kind are one in 7 deals and the chances of drawing two pairs are one in 27 deals. In Joker Wild, you see that the chances of drawing three of a kind are one in 21 deals and the chances of drawing two pairs are one in 23 deals. This peculiar situation is caused by the fact that in one-pair hands the player holding a wild card will naturally call three of a kind instead of the lower-ranking two-pair hand.

Five-Card Stud Poker Probabilities

The chances against holding a given hand in Five-Card Stud are the same as in Five-Card Draw. However, it must be noted that players will drop out before receiving their fifth card if they have potentially weak hands. Therefore, the player who stays until the showdown in Five-Card Stud has a higher average winning potential than those who remain until the showdown in Five-Card Draw.

The following table gives the chances that a certain card (ace, king, queen, jack) is the high-hole (down) card depending on the number of players. This table is expressed in percent.

CHANCES OF HOLDING VARIOUS HIGH-HOLE CARDS IN FIVE-CARD STUD

Player's Hole Card	Number of Opponents							
	1	2	3	4	5	6	7	8
Ace	95	89	83	79	74	70	66	63
King	86	74	63	55	47	40	35	30
Queen	78	61	48	37	29	23	18	14
Jack	69	49	34	24	16	12	08	05

The following table gives the chances of pairing your hole card at Five-Card Stud when each player has gotten two cards (one down and one up).

PAIRING YOUR HOLE CARD AT FIVE-CARD STUD, THREE CARDS COMING

Number of Players	Approximate Chances of Pairing if Your Hole Card Is Unmatched on the Table	Approximate Chances of Pairing if Your Hole Card Is Matched Once on the Table
Five	Once in 6 deals	Once in 8 deals
Six	Once in 6 deals	Once in 8 deals
Seven	Once in 5 deals	Once in 7 deals
Eight	Once in 5 deals	Once in 7 deals
Nine	Once in 4 deals	Once in 6 deals
Ten	Once in 4 deals	Once in 6 deals

With your hole card matched twice in the upcards the chance of catching that last hole-card match is about half that with one hole-card match showing. After being dealt your third card your chance of pairing your hole card on the last two cards is as follows:

PAIRING YOUR HOLE CARD AT FIVE-CARD STUD, TWO CARDS COMING

Number of Players	Approximate Chances of Pairing if Your Hole Card Is Unmatched on the Table	Approximate Chances of Pairing if Your Hole Card Is Matched on the Table
Five	Once in 7 deals	Once in 11 deals
Six	Once in 7 deals	Once in 11 deals
Seven	Once in 6 deals	Once in 10 deals
Eight	Once in 6 deals	Once in 10 deals
Nine	Once in 5 deals	Once in 9 deals
Ten	Once in 5 deals	Once in 9 deals

Seven-Card Stud Poker

The following tables give the approximate odds against making a straight, flush, and full house when holding three or four particular cards in Seven-Card Stud.

CHANCES AGAINST MAKING A STRAIGHT IN SEVEN-CARD STUD POKER

Player's Hand	Chances Against Making a Straight
J 10 9	4 1/5 to 1
J 10 9 4	8 to 1
J 10 9 4 3	21 to 1
Q J 10 9	1 3/10 to 1
Q J 10 9 2 (or A Q J 10 8)	2 1/4 to 1
Q J 10 9 3 2 (or A Q J 10 8 3)	2 1/10 to 1
Q J 10 8	2 7/10 to 1
Q, J, 10, 8, 3	4 1/2 to 1
Q J 10 8 3 4	10 1/2 to 1
K Q J (or 4 3 2)	6 3/10 to 1
K Q J 2 (or Q 4 3 2)	12 to 1
A K Q (or A 2 3)	12 6/7 to 1
A K Q 3 (or 3 2 A 8)	24 to 1

CHANCES AGAINST MAKING A FLUSH IN SEVEN-CARD STUD POKER

Player's Hand	Chances Against Making a Flush
Three cards of the same suit	5 1/2 to 1
Three cards of the same suit plus one odd card	9 2/5 to 1
Three cards of the same suit plus two odd cards	23 to 1
Four cards of the same suit	1 1/8 to 1
Four cards of the same suit plus one odd card	1 4/5 to 1
Four cards of the same suit plus two odd cards	4 1/10 to 1

CHANCES AGAINST MAKING A FULL HOUSE IN SEVEN-CARD STUD POKER

Player's Hand	Chances Against Making a Full House
One pair and one odd card	13 to 1
One pair and two odd cards	19 to 1
One pair and three odd cards	39 to 1
Two pairs	4 to 1
Two pairs and one odd card	7 to 1
Two pairs and two odd cards	10 to 1

Player's Hand	Chances Against Making a Full House
Three of a kind	1½ to 1
Three of a kind and one odd card	1½ to 1
Three of a kind and two odd cards	2 to 1
Three of a kind and three odd cards	4 to 1

Seven-Card High-Low Stud Poker

The following table gives the approximate chances against filling in various low hands in Seven-Card High-Low Stud governed by Scarne rules that state aces count both low and high and straights and flushes count only high. A cinch low hand is six, four, three, two, ace.

CHANCES OF MAKING A LOW HAND IN SEVEN-CARD HIGH-LOW STUD POKER

Hand	Chances Against Making a Six Low	Chances Against Making No Worse Than a Seven Low	Chances Against Making No Worse Than an Eight Low
6 2 A	4 to 1	2 to 1	Even
6 2 A J	8 to 1	4 to 1	2 to 1
6 2 A J K	22 to 1	10 to 1	6 to 1
6 3 2 A	1⅓ to 1	2 to 3	1 to 3
6 3 2 A J	2 to 1	1¼ to 1	2 to 3
6 3 2 A J K	5 to 1	3 to 1	2 to 1
3 2 A	6⅗ to 1	2¾ to 1	Even
3 2 A J	12 to 1	5 to 1	2¼ to 1
4 3 2	12 to 1	3¼ to 1	1¼ to 1
4 3 2 J	24 to 1	6 to 1	2⅗ to 1

POSSIBLE POKER HANDS IN AN ITALIAN 40-CARD PACK (stripped of eights, nines, and tens)

Ranking Order of Hands	Number of Possible Ways Hand Can Be Made	Chance of Being Dealt in Original 5 Cards
Straight flush	28	1 in 23,500
Four of a kind	360	1 in 1,828
Full house	2,160	1 in 305
Flush	980	1 in 670
Straight	7,140	1 in 92
Three of a kind	23,040	1 in 29
Two pairs	51,840	1 in 13
One pair	322,560	1 in 2⅓
No pair	249,900	1 in 2½
Total	658,008	

**POSSIBLE POKER HANDS IN A
FRENCH 32-CARD PACK
(stripped of twos, threes, fours, fives, and sixes)**

Ranking Order of Hands	Number of Possible Ways Hand Can Be Made	Chance of Being Dealt in Original 5 Cards
Royal flush	4	1 in 50,344
Straight flush	16	1 in 12,586
Four of a kind	224	1 in 899
Full house	1,334	1 In 151
Flush	204	1 in 987
Straight	5,100	1 in 40
Three of a kind	10,752	1 in 19
Two pairs	24,192	1 in 8
One pair	107,520	1 in 2
No pair	52,020	1 In 4
Total	201,376	

BETTING RULES FOR FRIENDLY OR SOCIAL POKER

Personally I feel that when playing Poker for money, friendships should be left behind and a player may do anything to try and fool his opponents so long as he does not cheat. I frown on a game where the betting is restricted by rules and a player must bet a specific amount at certain times. I consider it part of the skill of the game to vary the amounts of my bets in certain situations. I also consider it scientific Poker to check on a good hand in the hopes that someone else will bet and then I can raise or reraise as the situation dictates. I also consider it good Poker playing to make a first big limit bet in an attempt to steal the pot ante. However, I do know that the girls that play Poker together once a week don't care much for my style of Poker—and prefer the Poker playing rules where sandbagging is prohibited and a more social form of Poker playing prevails. Twenty years ago a Poker club in my home town made up of both women and men asked me to formulate a set of Poker rules for them to correct the following conditions: (*a*) to discourage the so-called "Poker professionals" and Poker hustlers from joining their group; (*b*) to simplify the play of the game and to minimize the betting skill factor in Poker for the benefit of the poorer players; and (*c*) to avoid sandbagging, which

is the number one factor in breaking up a friendly Poker game.

I did formulate their club rules and this same group still meets regularly and no one has really been hurt financially over the years. I have revised these rules slightly to agree with the changing times and offer them as my social or friendly Poker playing rules.

All the basic preliminaries before actual play and those of actual play that are discussed under previously stated rules in Chapters 1, 2, and 3 hold good, except for the following betting regulations:

1. Three units must constitute the betting limits: such as 1, 2, and 4 cents—or 5, 10, and 15 cents—or $1, $2, and $4—or any other three-figure limit, regardless of the amount. Players are permitted to bet only the three specified figures, as dictated by the rules previously established before the start of the game.

2. *Draw Poker and Its Variants.* The player who opens the pot is permitted to bet only one unit. After the draw, the opener must bet two units. He is not permitted to check nor can he bet other than two units.

3. *Stud Poker and Its Variants.* The player who holds high card on the first betting round must bet one unit; he cannot check or drop out. During each succeeding round of betting,

the high hand must bet one unit. But, if the high hand shows a pair or better, the holder may bet two units. He may, however, check or drop out.

4. After the first bettor of a particular round has made a legal bet as described here, other players may raise either one, two, or three units.

5. If a player checks he is not permitted to raise in the same betting round. In other words, sandbagging is illegal in a friendly or social Poker game.

6. The maximum number of raises during any given betting round cannot exceed three.

CHAPTER 4

Rummy Games

Rummy is, after Poker, the second most popular card game in the United States. It is, contrary to what most other game authorities say, a direct descendant of Whiskey Poker, a truly American game which first appeared in the Midwest about 1850. It was called Whiskey Poker, says the 1864 *American Hoyle,* because it was played for drinks. Card playing at that time was seldom permitted in the home; most women looked on cards as "the Devil's pasteboards," and nearly all the card playing took place in gambling halls and saloons. By the late 1890's three of the most popular barfly varieties of Poker played in America were Whiskey Poker, Rum Poker, and Gin Poker. Then, about 1905 a name change took place. Rum Poker became known as Rum or Rummy, Whiskey Poker and Knock Poker as Knock Rummy, and Gin Poker as Gin Rummy.

The name of the game changed from Poker to Rummy because by the time of the first years of this century the Poker family had more variations than any other family of games. Here are just a few, a very few, of the games that bore the name Poker at that period: Draw Poker, Stud Poker, Freezeout, Gin Poker, Jackpot, Rum Poker, Whiskey Poker, Tigers, Blazer, Bluff, Double Up, Mistigris, and Patience Poker. That's what I said: Patience Poker. You've played it often, probably within the last week, always with yourself. More than a hundred games of the Patience family are played today. It's Solitaire

too, as you'll see if you'll reexamine its basic structure and principles.

Card games are tribes that break off from the main body and drift away into separate existences of their own, devising their own laws, bearing new generations, hammering out their own morals and language and atmosphere. Rum Poker, in the course of its pilgrimage up through the strata of society, must first have dropped its tawdry family name; and then, I suppose, people fell to calling it by the affectionate diminutive Rummy so as to make it clear that they weren't talking about—or playing sweatily for—vulgar rum. And so it bore its young, and it gave them its name, and they prospered, every one. But none has prospered like the variation called Gin Rummy. From 1905 to 1938 the growth of Rummy was gradual, with Straight Rummy, Knock Rummy, and 500 Rummy being the favorite variants.

Then, in 1939, Hollywood Gin Rummy became a fad in the motion-picture colony and spread on ripples of nationwide publicity in newspapers, magazines, and on radio until not only millions of players were conscious of Hollywood Gin but Gin Rummy (the sleeper) became the most-played two-handed game in America—a distinction it still holds at the present time. In 1949 a Rummy importation from South America called Canasta came north, and from then until 1952 was the biggest fad in the history of card games.

There are countless forms of Rummy being

played today but they all follow the same basic principles and differ only in details. The main differences are:

1. The use of one or multiple decks of cards.

2. Various ways of scoring a hand or game.

3. Restricted melds.

4. Different ways of discarding and picking upcards.

5. Wild cards and bonus cards.

The single-deck category includes Straight, Knock, 500 Rummy, and Gin Rummy. The multiple-deck division includes Canasta, Samba, Contract, and Chicago Rummy. Al-though the basic principles of these Rummy games are identical, many of the games have mathematical defects because the rules, like Topsy, just grew and have never been properly formulated and codified. This lack of good, tight rules very often causes bitter dissension among players, and many friendships have been severed because of such arguments. In the rules which follow, I have tried to eliminate these flaws as far as possible without changing the structure of the games themselves. Unless otherwise stipulated under each game, the following general rules apply to all games of Rummy described in this chapter.

GENERAL RULES FOR RUMMY GAMES

The Object of Rummy. The object of all Rummy games is to form matched sets, groups, and sequences called melds, or lays, the deduction of which from the hand will bring the value of the unmatched cards to a lower total than the unmatched cards of all other players, or to meld, or lay, an entire specified hand of cards in matched sets, which is called *rummy*.

A matched set may be either a sequence of three or more cards in the same suit—for example, four, five, and six of spades (in games where the player's hand is comprised of ten or fewer cards, it is possible to meld all the cards in the hand in a single sequence); or three or four of a kind, for example, the queen of clubs, queen of diamonds, queen of hearts, and queen of spades.

Rank of Cards. One or more standard packs of 52 playing cards are used, from ace to king in four suits. Unless otherwise stipulated the ace is the lowest-ranking card, having a value of 1. The king, queen, and jack are valued at 10 points each. All other cards have their numerical face value. The suits have no value.

Selecting the Dealer and Establishing Seating Positions at the Table

1. Any player (preferably chosen by mutual consent) shall shuffle the cards. Player to the dealer's right shall cut the cards.

2. Player acting as dealer shall deal one card to each player face up, starting with the player to his left and continuing clockwise.

3. Player dealt lowest-rank card becomes the first dealer, and may select any seat he wants.

4. Player dealt the second-lowest card selects any remaining seat; player with third-lowest, any remaining seat, etc.

5. In case of ties, each of the tied players shall be dealt another card face up, this to go on until the tie is broken.

6. On completion of each hand, the deal passes to the player to the left of the dealer of that hand.

The Shuffle and Cut

1. Dealer shuffles the cards. Any player may call for and shuffle the pack any time before the cut, although the dealer has the privilege of shuffling the pack last.

2. Dealer puts the pack of cards face down on the table to his right. The player to his right has first privilege of cutting the cards. If that player refuses to cut, any other player may cut. If all the other players refuse to cut, the dealer must cut the cards. He cannot refuse. At least five cards must be in each portion of the cut deck.

The Deal. The dealer deals one card at a time to each player, starting with the leader (player to the dealer's left) and continuing clockwise until each player in the game has the required number of cards. Then, when the rules of the game require it, the next card is placed face up on the table and is known as the upcard. The remainder of the deck is placed face down on the table, forming the stock. On completion of each hand, the deal passes to the player at the dealer's left.

Changing Seats. Some players like to change seats after a certain time or number of hands, but rarely do players agree on when. Therefore, let us establish that at the end of each hour of play a new deal is in order as prescribed under the rules for Selecting the Dealer and Establishing Seating Positions. This ruling will make for a better all-around game of Rummy.

Note: Unless otherwise detailed, the rules for selecting the dealer and establishing seating positions at the table, the shuffle and cut, and changing seats hold good for all the Rummy games in this chapter.

Irregular Pack or Irregular Hand. An irregular pack of cards or an irregular hand is:

1. One that has more or less cards than are required by the rules of the game being played.

2. Or, one that has one or more cards of a design different from the deck's, cards which are not specified as permissible under the rules of the game being played.

No-Game

1. If it is established during or at the completion of a hand that the pack is irregular, that hand is void. If any scores have been previously entered toward a game, the entire game of which that hand is a part shall be void, and the game is no-game.

2. If a game is completed and it then is discovered that an irregular pack has been used, that game and all previous games are valid.

Misdeals. The following determines whether a misdeal has occurred:

1. If a dealer or player accidentally turns up a card belonging to another player during the deal, that deal is void, a misdeal is declared, and the same dealer deals again.

2. If the dealer or a player accidentally turns up a card or cards belonging to himself, that deal stands.

3. If a card is found face up in the pack during the deal, there is a misdeal.

4. If a card is found face up in the stock during the play, the card is righted and the stock is shuffled by the dealer of that hand and cut by the player to his right, and the play continues.

5. If one player or more has an irregular hand and it is discovered before the leader has completed his first play, the deal is a misdeal.

6. If more than one player has an irregular hand and it is discovered during the play, that hand is a misdeal.

Dead Hand. If it is discovered that one player has an irregular hand during the play (after the leader has completed his first play), that player's hand is dead. He must put the

cards aside, face down, and be adjudged a loser of that hand.

On Drawing from the Discard Pile

1. When a play has been made from the discard pile—for instance, if an upcard or group of cards or the entire pile has been picked up as the rules of that game stipulate—and the card or cards have left the table or the top of the discard pile, that play cannot be changed. That play must be completed. A player cannot change his mind. He cannot put the card or cards back into the discard.

2. A player cannot discard an upcard he has just taken until his next turn of play.

Drawing from the Stock

1. If a player picks a card off the stock, it is a play, regardless of whether the player looks at the card's face or not.

2. But if a player merely touches the top card of the stock, he does not have to take that card.

3. If a player in the act of drawing the top card sees any other card in the stock, or any other player has reason to believe that he has done so, then the first player must show his card to the rest of the players.

Playing Out of Turn

1. If a player takes an upcard or cards from the discard pile out of turn and it is discovered while he still has the card or cards in his hand, he simply puts the card or cards back on the discard.

2. If a player out of turn has taken a card off the stock and has not looked at it, he replaces it on top of the stock.

3. If a player has taken a card from the stock and looked at it, it is put back on the stock, and the stock is shuffled and cut. There is no penalty.

4. If a player has played out of turn and it is not discovered until after that player has completed his play, the play stands as if it were a proper turn of play, and the player whose turn it was to play loses that turn. It is up to the player to protect his own interests at all times.

Miscount. If a player errs in counting his points, he may correct the error—if the correction is made before the next player starts his play.

Rearranging Melds. A player may rearrange his melds in any manner he likes, providing he does so before the next player starts his play.

Errors in Scoring. If an error has been

made in entering or adding scores, it may be corrected, but not if another game has been

completed following the hand in which the error was made.

SIX- AND SEVEN-CARD STRAIGHT RUMMY

One of the most widely played games of the Rummy family; a favorite with gamblers, cops, athletes, children, ministers, and old ladies. A game in which the stakes are a penny or a dollar per hand. This is Straight Rummy, one of the humble offsprings of Whiskey Poker.

Requirements

1. Two to six people, each playing for himself.

2. A regular 52-card deck.

Note: The variation called Seven-Card Straight Rummy is favored by expert players, because it affords more latitude for strategy. Six-Card Straight Rummy is recommended for two to five players, the most interesting game being constituted of four or five. Six may play, but the element of skill is minimized because the number of draws from stock by each player is reduced. Seven-Card Straight is played by two to five players, the ideal game being constituted by four players.

Beginning of the Game. Selection of the dealer, seating positions, changing seats, shuffle, and cut are as described under General Rules for Rummy Games (page 55).

Object of the Game

1. To go rummy by laying down the entire hand at one time in melds of three or four cards of the same rank (kind) or three or more cards of the same suit in sequence, like the melds in Gin Rummy.

2. Or, to have the lowest total of points in unmatched cards at the end of the game.

Value of Cards. For scoring, the ace is low, counting one point; kings, queens, and jacks count 10 points; all other cards have their face value.

The Deal. Dealing one card to each player clockwise starting with the player at his left, the dealer gives to each the correct number of cards (six or seven, as agreed). The dealer gets the last card dealt. (At this point it is the practice of some players to turn the next card face up on the table, making it the first upcard. I do not recommend that this card be faced up. It gives the leader an unearned and unfair advantage.) The rest of the cards, the remainder of the deck, are placed face down

on the table, forming the stock. On completion of each hand, the deal passes to the player at the dealer's left.

The Play of the Hand. The leader makes the first play by picking the top card of the stock. He then must discard one card. From that point on, each player in his turn of play, which goes clockwise, may take either the upcard or the top card of the stock, discarding one card to complete his play. Play continues until a player goes rummy and is declared the winner or until the break.

The Break. Should the players fail to go rummy and should cards in the stock be reduced to the number of players in the game, we arrive at a phase of the game called the *break*. The player whose turn it is to pick the top card of the stock is called the breaker. After the break has begun, a player cannot in his turn pick the top card of the discard pile (upcard) unless that card can be used in an immediate meld.

When the cards are broke (i.e., when fewer cards remain in the stock than there are players in the game), the player breaking must put down all his melds on the table in separate sets and hold covered in his hand his unmatched cards. The next player does likewise, but may lay off cards if he can on any exposed melds. He also holds covered his unmatched cards. All the players do likewise in rotation. When the last player has completed his play:

1. He announces the total value of the unmatched cards still in his possession, and shows the cards.

2. Rotating clockwise, each player in turn does the same until all the players have laid their unmatched cards on the table.

3. The player having the lowest score in unmatched cards is the winner.

Players cannot show their unmatched cards until the last play has been completed. If two or more players have an equal number of points at the end of the game and the breaker is one of those players, the breaker wins. If neither of the tied players is the breaker, the winner is the one closest to the breaker's left.

The Payoff

1. Should a player be declared the winner

after the break, either by having a lower card count or by going rummy, he receives one unit from each other player.

2. Should a player go rummy before the break, he receives two units from each player.

3. Should a player (a) go rummy on his first pick or (b) go rummy by melding his hand in a sequence of the same suit before the break, he receives four units from each player.

The unit may be any amount agreed upon. Some players choose to pay off in multiples of the point value of unmatched cards. In such cases the principles enunciated above hold good. Each player pays the winner on the difference in points between their scores.

Additional Rules. Violations and infractions of the rules are covered under General Rules for Rummy Games (see pages 55 to 57).

Strategy. The most important thing to keep in mind is to save cards that give you a maximum chance to fill a set. Unlss you are so lucky as to be dealt a complete hand, you have to build up one or more matched sets, starting with combinations. A combination is two cards that will become a matched set if a specific third card is added. *Example:* Eights of hearts and spades become a group; three and four of clubs may become a sequence.

Not all combinations are of the same value. The best has two places open, that is, it can be filled to a set by either of two cards. The above examples are two-way combinations, if none of the filler cards respectively (eights of diamonds and clubs, and two and five of clubs) is dead. A skip sequence such as king and jack of hearts is inferior, since it can be filled only by one card, the queen of hearts. Any two-way combination becomes demoted to a one-way if one of the filler cards is dead; for example, if the eight of clubs is buried in the discards, a pair of eights is no better than a skip sequence.

So long as all cards are live, a sequence combination is preferable to a pair, for it has better chance to be enlarged to a set of four. After a pair is filled, the group has only one chance to become a set of four, but after a sequence is filled it still has a two-way chance to grow, provided that it is not at the top or bottom of the ranking. Thus, queen and jack of hearts if filled by the ten of hearts remains two-way, but if filled by the king of hearts becomes one-way.

In reckoning what cards to keep, figure in terms of the specific cards you need to fill. Combinations sometimes interlock, and when they do they are inferior to wholly separated combinations. For example, eights of hearts and clubs and nine and ten of spades are both two-way combinations, but if you hold both of them you have only three chances to fill, not four. The eight of spades is wanted by both, and if you get it you cannot use it both ways. Don't confuse this situation with a double combination, which is the ideal holding because it is the most economical. *Example:* With eights of hearts and spades and nine of hearts, you have four chances to fill. It is true that when you fill either a sequence or a group, you will be left with one useless card. But until that time, you keep four places open by holding only three cards.

As a general rule, don't pick up a discard merely to make a combination. Take potluck on a draw from the stock instead—you may fill a set. But a possible exception can arise when you have few or no combinations, and taking the discard will make a double combination. One drawback of this play, however, is that you warn your opponent not to discard another card of the same rank, or near in rank in the same suit. You will probably have to rely for a filler, if you ever get one, on the stock.

It is normal to discard high cards rather than low ones, for high cards in the hand are costlier if an opponent goes out. This being the case, you may expect your right-hand opponent to feed you high cards, and a high one-way combination may be worth saving for two or three rounds—but not too long.

Sometimes you are stuck with a card you know your neighbor wants. For example, he has picked up an eight, and later you draw another eight for which you have no use. Yet you do not dare discard it, especially if you are sure he has a group of eights rather than a sequence. As a general rule, if stuck with one or more such cards, meld what you can as soon as you can. The idea is to encourage everybody to meld, and so give you a chance to lay off your "players."

Skip Rummy

Skip Rummy is a fascinating variation of Straight Rummy in which each player is dealt five cards. This game introduced a restricted form of melding and is responsible for modern Rummy games which prescribe an initial specific meld or melds for each new dealt hand.

Requirements

1. Two to six players, each playing for himself.

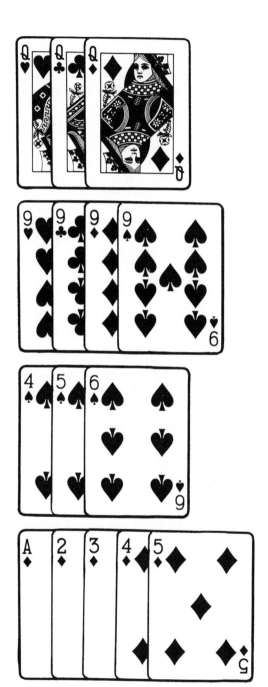

Typical Rummy combinations—three or four of a kind and numerical sequences by suit.

2. A regular 52-card deck. For scoring, the value of the cards follows: Ace is low, counting one point; jacks, queens, and kings count 10 points, all other cards count their numerical value.

Object of the Game. To go rummy by melding or laying off a five-card hand at two or more turns of play, or to score the least number of points in unmatched cards at the end of the game.

The Deal. The dealer, starting with the leader, deals five cards to each player one at a time clockwise. The remainder of the cards are placed face down, forming the stock.

The Play. Same as in Straight Rummy. The leader makes the first play by picking the top card of the stock. He then must discard one card. Then each player in his turn of play, which goes clockwise, may take either the upcard of the discard pile or the top card of the stock, discarding one card to complete the play. Play continues until a player goes rummy and is declared the winner or the game ends when the cards in the stock are reduced to the number of players in the game and the player having the lowest card count is declared the winner.

Melding. A player at his turn of play can meld either (a) a three-card meld which may be either three cards of the same rank, or three cards of the same suit in sequence, or (b) he may lay off only one card on any exposed meld resting on the table. If by picking the top card of the stock, the player makes a three-card meld that gives him rummy, he is not required to discard a card.

All other melds or layoffs at one time are prohibited, such as melding a set of four matched cards, or any combination of two matched sets, or the laying off of more than one card. Nor can a player meld a matched set and lay off a card on the same turn of play.

End of Hand. When a player goes rummy, he receives two units from each player. If the players fail to go rummy and the cards in the stock are reduced to the number of players in the game, the game ends and the player having the lowest unmatched card count receives one unit from each player.

The unit may be any amount agreed upon. Some players choose to pay off in multiples of the point value of unmatched cards. In such cases, each player pays the winner a unit on the difference between their scores.

Round-the-Corner Rummy

Round-the-Corner Rummy, also known as Boat House Rummy and Dizzy Rummy, is a novel variation of Straight Rummy, with a one- and two-card draw and a one-card discard. Also the ace may be used in high, low, and round-the-corner sequence melds. This game is the same as Straight Rummy, except for the following:

1. Two to four players, although four make the best game.

2. The ace does not have to begin a sequence meld, but may be used high, low, or round-the-corner. *Example:* ace–king–queen, ace–two–three, or king–ace–deuce.

3. To determine the number of cards to be dealt to each player, subtract the number of players from nine. Thus, in a four-handed game, each of the players, starting with the leader, will be dealt five cards, one at a time in rotation to the left. The remainder of the undealt cards are placed face down on the table to form a stock, and the top card of the stock is turned up alongside it as the starter for the discard pile.

4. The actual play begins with the player at the dealer's left, and each player in turn clockwise may take cards in any one of the following ways:

(*a*) Pick the top card of the discard pile, plus the top card of the stock.

(*b*) Pick only the top card of the stock.

(*c*) Pick the two top cards of the discard pile whenever two are available.

(*d*) A player may not pick up a card from the discard pile after having picked the top card of the stock. In this instance, he is only entitled to one card (the top card of the stock). Whenever a player picks a card from the discard pile, he is compelled to draw one more card either from the top of the stock or from the discard pile.

(*e*) After completing his draw play, the player is permitted to discard only one card. This method of play rotates to the left from player to player until some player goes rummy (melds his entire hand). If no player has gone rummy and the stock is exhausted, the cards in the discard pile except the top one, which is used as a discard pile starter, are shuffled by the same dealer,

and cut by a player. Then they are placed face down on the table forming a new stock and the game continues as described under rules (*a*) through (*e*) as detailed above. This procedure continues until some player goes rummy and collects the agreed stake from each player.

Block Rummy

This game is played in the same manner as Straight Rummy except for the following:

1. The player who goes out must make a final discard; therefore his cards must constitute valid sets and still have a card for discard.

2. After the stock is exhausted, play continues only so long as each successive player takes the discard. When any discard is refused, play ends. The player with the lowest total count wins the difference from each of the other hands. If two or more hands tie for low, they share the winning equally.

Queen City Rummy

This game, which is sometimes called Cincinnati Rummy, is the same as Straight Rummy except for the following:

1. Seven cards are dealt to each player. A player may not meld until he can go rummy. When he goes out he may meld seven or eight cards. He does not require a discard.

2. The player going rummy collects the point value of his own hand (not the value of his opponent's hand, and not double) from each of the other players.

Carousel

This is a fairly popular and interesting form of Rummy.

Requirements

1. Two to five players.

2. With two players, one regular 52-card deck plus a joker. With three or more players, two 52-card decks are shuffled together, plus two jokers.

3. The cards rank: king (high), queen, jack, ten, down to two, ace (low).

Beginning of the Game. Selection of the dealer, seating positions, changing seats, shuffle, and cut are as described under General Rules for Rummy Games (page 55).

The Deal. Each player receives ten cards. The rest of the pack is put face down in the center of the table to form the stock.

The Play. Each player in turn, beginning with player to the dealer's left, must draw at least one card from the stock. He may then meld and lay off all the cards he wishes. Failing to meld any card, he must draw a second card from the stock. Again he has a chance to meld. If he does not do so, he must draw a third card. Thereupon his turn ends; he may not meld after drawing the third card. If he melds after one or two draws, his turn ends after he has stated that he is finished melding.

Object of Play. Each player strives to reduce the count of cards left in his hand. A player may knock if this count is 5 or less. Face cards count 10, aces 1, other cards their index value, and jokers 25. A knock must be made in the player's turn, after he has drawn one or two cards.

Melds. Both sequences and groups are valid melds. A group may never be extended to more than four cards, and there must be no duplication of suits. All melds are common property. A player may lay off additional cards on any matched sets on the table; he may also rearrange any number of cards on the table to enable him to lay off to form new sets. *Example:* On the table: the sevens of spades, hearts, and clubs. The player may lay off the seven of diamonds, then borrow any one of the other sevens to form a sequence. On the table: king, queen, jack, ten, nine of clubs. The player breaks the sequence in two to allow melding of the jack of clubs. Elaborate rearrangements are often feasible; for example, with groups of eights, sevens, and sixes on the table, the player may be able to arrange them as sequences to allow laying off of nines and fives. If he commences to rearrange melds on the table, the player must in that turn meld at least one new card from his hand. (Rearrangement cannot be used as a subterfuge to avoid melding or drawing extra cards.) Before the player finally states that he is finished, he must leave every set on the table correct.

A joker is wild. In melding it, the player must state its intended rank and suit, and subsequent melding is bound by that statement. *Example:* If a joker is melded as the king of hearts with the natural queen and jack of hearts, it may not be moved to the other end to become the ten of hearts and so permit layoff of the nine of hearts. However,

a player holding the natural card represented by the joker may exchange it for the joker, then name the joker to be what he pleases to assist further melding. The joker may likewise be captured in exchange for a card already on the table, if the player can satisfy all the foregoing rules as to melding and rearranging melds. Once melded, a joker may never be taken back into any hand, but must be left on the table, available to all players. Even though able to meld after one draw, a player need not do so; if he prefers, he may draw one or two additional cards.

Scoring. Play ends when any player knocks, having a count of 5 or less in his hand. There is no laying off after the knock. All hands are counted, and lowest hand is the winner. The winner alone scores; he is credited with the difference of his count from each of the other hands. If another party ties the knocker or has a lower count, he wins and scores a bonus of 10 for undercut. If two or more players other than the knocker tie for low count, each wins the difference of his count from each of the other hands, plus 10 for undercut. If the knocker gets rid of all his cards, he scores a bonus of 25.

If the player who draws the last card of the stock does not knock, each player in turn has one more chance to meld and lay off, but there is (of course) no more drawing. All hands are then counted, and lowest count wins the deal; if two or more tie for low, each wins what any alone would have scored.

A running total is kept of each player's score, and the first to reach 150 wins a game. He scores a game bonus of 100. Each player is then credited with 25 points for each deal he has won, and each settles with every other according to the difference of their scores. A player who has scored not a single point pays the winner of the game double (but each other opponent singly).

Strategy. In your first several turns, you should usually draw three cards even though able to meld. The more cards you get initially, the better your chances of having a joker, or a card you can exchange for someone else's joker, and the better your chances of melding and rearranging melds to suit your purpose. In fact, the more cards you start with, the better your chances of reducing the deadwood to 5 or less. This fact is so patent that in a game among "sharps" there is often no melding at all until the stock is completely exhausted.

You need not go to this extreme, however, and certainly should not when any player ahead of you "cracks" by starting the melding. Then play your hand on its merits. Meld after one draw if you have real prospects of reducing your hand solely by laying off. Otherwise, take two cards, and then decide— the extra card taken may be helpful, and one card more or less does not hurt, so long as you can still meld if you wish.

Always study the table to see what you can lay off by various rearrangements. If you fail to do so, you may actually overlook an opportunity to go out with zero count. (The only drawback of this otherwise excellent game is the delay due to the necessity of studying the cards on the table. Carousel fans cure this ill by putting a time limit of two minutes on the turn of each player; if a player exceeds the time limit, he must withdraw from that deal.)

Double Rummy

This game is the same as Straight Rummy, except for the following:

Two full decks plus two jokers are shuffled together. Each player receives ten cards. (The best game is four to six players.) A joker is wild; it may be designated by the owner to be of any suit and rank in order to complete a matched set. Once melded, a joker may not be recaptured, but it may be moved in a sequence to make way for additional cards to be laid off. *Example:* In nine–joker–seven sequence, the joker may be moved to the end to make way for a natural eight-spot; in joker–three–four sequence, the joker may be moved to the other end as a five, to make way for a natural two. In settlement, a joker left in the hand counts 15. An ace counts 11. The ace may be used either high or low, so that queen–king–ace and ace–two–three are sequences, but king–ace–two is not. A group consists of any three or more cards of the same rank, regardless of suit.

Java Rummy

This game, which is also called Elimination Rummy and Freeze Out, is played as in Straight Rummy with the following differ-

ences:

1. Each player is dealt seven cards one at a time.

2. Any deuce is wild, which means that the holder may call it any card that he wishes. One or two jokers may also be added to the deck, and they are also wild.

3. If a player wishes to meld in his turn, he must do so before drawing a card. If he does meld, he may not discard.

4. A player may either meld all of his seven cards in one turn, that is, go rummy, or meld six cards if his seventh card counts 5 or less. He may not make his melds in installments. If the player melds six cards, he shows the seventh to verify that its count is 5 or less. The player who first melds either all seven cards or six cards according to the rules is the winner.

5. Ace counts one point; a deuce or joker 25; all other cards as Straight Rummy. Each player totals his unmatched cards, and their point count is added to his previous score (including the winner if he goes down with only six cards). If the winner goes rummy with all seven cards, 25 points are subtracted from his previous tally even if this gives him a minus score. As soon as a player's score reaches 100, he is eliminated from the game and must put a chip into a pool. When only one player remains in the game, he collects the pool. If two players remaining in the game go over 100 points on one hand, the one with the lower score wins.

Rummy Poker

In this variation of Java Rummy, two decks are shuffled together and used as one, and four jokers are added. Each player is dealt ten cards. A player may either meld all his cards at once or go down with nine if the tenth card has a count of 3 or less.

An ace counts 10. If his hand is a complete sequence—straight—the winner receives a bonus of 25. A flush, that is, all cards in the same suit, scores a bonus of 25. A flush in sequence—straight flush—scores a bonus of 50. Flushes or sequences may be made with wild cards. Any player who first scores 100 is the winner. There is no elimination.

PIF-PAF

This game (pronounced *peef-poff*) is a combination of Rummy play and Poker. It started

at the beginning of World War II and was very popular in the United States until the advent of Canasta. It is still played a great deal in South America, especially in Brazil.

Requirements

1. Four to eight players.

2. Two regular 52-card decks, shuffled together and used as one.

3. The cards rank in sequence as in Straight Rummy but do not have point value.

The Deal. Players cut for deal, low cut dealing.

Beginning with the player at dealer's left, each is dealt a hand of nine cards, one at a time per round. The remainder of the deck—stock—is placed face down in the center of the table.

The turn to deal in subsequent hands goes to the left or clockwise rotation.

Object of the Game. To be the first to match up the entire hand in sets and sequences. Sequences may be of three or more cards in the same suit. Ace is low only and may not follow a king in a sequence. Sets may be of three or more cards of the same denomination; however, they must contain at least three different suits.

The Betting. All players chip in equally to a pot (pool). Dealer must then put in an amount equal to the pot; he has no option. The leader may then raise "blind," that is, increase the betting without looking at any of the cards of his hand. If he does raise blind, he must put into the pot an amount double the dealer's. The next player to the left (second player after dealer) may then raise again, also without looking at his hand. His raise must be double that of the previous player's.

Players in following turn may not raise the betting. They may, however, look at their hands and decide whether they wish to remain in the game—stay—or drop out. If they wish to stay, they must meet the bets made by the blind bettors, and each player in turn must equalize bets. *Example:* A, B, C, and D are playing. Player A, the dealer, must put in 4 chips after all have anted 1 chip apiece at the beginning. Player B raises blind, putting in 8 chips, and player C also raises blind, putting in 16 chips. Player D may not raise, but he must put in 16 chips if he wishes to stay. Player A had originally put in 4 chips,

so he must now add 12 if he wishes to stay. Player B put in 8 chips on his first raise, so he must now add 8 more if he wishes to stay.

If either player following dealer looks at his hand, he may not raise but must meet the previous bet to stay in the game. In the example above, if player B looks at his hand, he bets only 4 chips to stay in the game. Player C, however, may still raise blind, and all others are required to meet that bet to stay. That is, if player B should raise blind and player C looks at his hand, he and the others must meet player B's raise to stay in the game.

On the next round of betting the last raiser may raise higher if he chooses. In this case, any other player still in the game may also reraise. The betting then continues until no one will raise further and all bets are equalized. Play then begins. Thus, if player C was the last raiser, he may reraise when his turn comes again. If player B raised blind, but player C did not, player B may reraise. If neither player B nor player C raised blind, then player A may raise.

The Play. After all bets have been met, the first active player at the dealer's left turns up the top card of the stock. He may keep it or discard it. If he discards it, any player who needs it to go rummy may pick it up and make a discard in its place. When the first discard is not taken by some other player, the leader may draw another card and must make any discard face up to begin a discard pile, alongside of the stock or the top card of the discard pile as in Straight Rummy. But at any time that a player requires a discard to go out—and only in that case—he may take it out of turn. If more than one player needs a discard, it goes to the one closest to discarder's left. The player who goes rummy collects the pot.

Additional Rules

1. The betting is governed by applicable Poker rules (see Chapter 2).

2. Irregularities are governed by applicable rules, pages 55 to 57.

3. If a player draws a discard out of turn but cannot use it to go rummy, he simply returns it to discard pile without penalty.

RAMINO

This modern Italian development of Rummy incorporates three basic features of Draw

Poker: (1) the ante, (2) a betting round, and (3) melds which include three-, four-, or more card poker straights. I was introduced to Ramino in the Municipal Casino in San Remo, Italy, a few years ago and feel that its popularity among Italian gamblers justifies its inclusion here.

Requirements

1. Up to seven players.

2. Two regular 52-card decks plus four jokers, shuffled together and used as one. All four jokers are wild. That is, a joker may be used to represent any card.

Beginning of the Game. Selection of the dealer, seating positions, changing seats, shuffle, and cut are as described under General Rules for Rummy Games (page 55).

Ante. Prior to a hand being dealt, each player antes a chip into the center forming a pot.

The Deal. Starting with the leader, the dealer distributes ten cards to each player one at a time clockwise. The next card is faced up on the table as the upcard, and the stock is placed face down beside it.

Betting Round. Players study their hands and a betting round similar to Poker takes place. The leader (player at dealer's left) has the first privilege of play. After examining his cards and establishing the strength or weakness of his hand, he must do one of three things:

1. He may pass, which indicates he does not desire to start the betting.

2. He may bet by putting any amount into the pot within the *limit* (an amount agreed upon by players before the start of the game).

3. Or, he may *fold* (throw in his hand because he has no desire to bet or play out the hand).

If all players pass, the hand is played out in Rummy fashion, winner of the hand taking the pot. Once a player bets by putting an amount within the limit into the pot, each succeeding player at his turn of play can do one of three things:

1. He may throw in his hand and retire from the game.

2. If he decides to play, he must put up an amount equal to the bet of the player who made the first bet.

3. If he wants to raise, he merely says "Raise," and puts into the pot an amount equal to that put in by the first bettor plus an amount for the raise.

All the other players may now either play by putting into the pot an amount equal to the total amount of the raiser or, if they already have put the opening bet into the pot, merely put into the pot an amount equal to the raise. Or a player may reraise by putting into the pot an amount equal to the raiser plus an amount for the reraiser. Or he may drop out by folding his cards and throwing them into the discard pile on the table. This procedure of dropping out, playing, raising, and reraising is continued until the players stop raising, or, if agreed upon beforehand, until each player has raised or reraised either two or three times.

If all the players drop out but one, he wins the pot and the new dealer deals another hand. If two or more active players remain in the hand, the hand is played to a finish in Rummy fashion.

The Rummy Play of the Hand. The leader (player to the dealer's left) makes the first play—he picks a card from the stock and then discards one, as in Straight Rummy. The second player may pick up the first player's discard or take a card from the stock. This method of play, going clockwise from player to player, continues until a player goes ramino (wins the game) by melding his entire hand (all ten cards) at one time. When this occurs, he wins the pot, the hand is over and a new deal takes place. If no player has gone ramino and the stock is exhausted, the hand ends and all players, starting with the leader, show their hands and the player with the least points in unmatched cards is declared the winner. The value of unmatched cards is as follows: king, queen, and jack, 10 points each; all other cards, their face value; ace, 1 point.

Bonuses. In Ramino, as in many Poker games, certain valuable hands such as four of a kind and straight flushes carry a bonus value to the holder. They are as follows:

1. If a player goes ramino by melding a ten-card straight flush (ten cards in sequence of the same suit) he receives a bonus award of an amount equal to four times his ante from each player, including any player who has dropped out of the hand.

2. If a player goes ramino and his hand possesses two groups of four of a kind not including jokers, he receives a bonus of twice the amount of his ante.

3. If a player goes ramino and his hand possesses a ten-card straight (ten cards in sequence of mixed suits) he receives a bonus equal to his ante.

BANKERS' RUMMY

The most avaricious dream of any gambler or casino operator is to turn a people's game into a so-called banking game. It took years to develop the game of Indian Craps—which is what at the end of the nineteenth century they called "craps vulgaris"—into the casino game of Bank Craps. It took years to develop Bankers' Rummy. The game was created by Harry J. Dorey about 1935. Its popularity is greatest in the East, particularly in northern New Jersey.

Requirements

1. This is a regular six-card Straight Rummy game. There may be from two to six players, including the banker who is called the *book*. The game's terminology derives from Craps and the horse-race track.

2. The game is played with a regular 52-card deck of playing cards. Two decks are kept on hand to allow change of decks at any player's demand.

3. The operator—another name for the banker or book—sits in the game, and deals the first hand. Deal moves to the left clockwise.

The Play

1. Before any deal, the banker shuffles the deck, then hands it to the dealer to be shuffled again. This is, bluntly, to minimize the chance of cheating. The rules of Straight Rummy apply.

2. Before the cards are dealt, players may make two different kinds of bets against the banker:

(*a*) They may bet any amount within the limit on spades. That means they may bet that in the first round of cards dealt the player will hold a spade higher in rank than any spade dealt the banker. Nonplayers around the table, or kibitzers if you insist, can bet on any player's hand against the banker too. First bet is a free bet. No charge is made against it. But all bets over $2 after the first deal are taxed.

Any $2 bet by any player is a free bet. But if a player bets any amount over $2 that his spade will be higher than the banker's, he must pay a 5 percent charge on the amount over the $2 limit. *Example:* A player decides to bet $10 that he will get a higher spade than the banker in the first six cards dealt. He puts his $10 on the table before him, and throws

the banker 40 cents for the privilege of making the bet. The 40 cents is 5 percent of the amount over the $2 free-bet limit. This is a game with plenty of what the boys call action. That betting charge gives the banker a considerable edge in what is otherwise a nicely balanced game.

The house limit usually runs from 25 cents to $75 on any one player's spade in any one play.

(*b*) A player may bet that he will call correctly the rank and suit of two cards out of the first six dealt before he picks from the stock or discard pile. The limit on this bet is from 5 cents to $1 and the bank pays off at 70 for 1. Gamblers call this a combination bet. It gets action, because players like to get their odd nickels, dimes, and quarters into play at these odds.

The banker will generally stipulate that only pairs can be called, because pairs are easier to remember than random cards. It is almost impossible to recall accurately twenty to thirty different combinations; so most players will call two black aces or red aces, black or red kings, the ace and king of spades, or something of that sort. Players get to ride some favorite combination. Bankers get to know them by heart.

The money wagered on combinations is put on the table in front of the spade bets, and the banker usually turns the wagered coin or bill face up to indicate that a red combination was called, tail up to indicate a black combination. Ordinarily when the play is heavy the banker will keep a lookout standing beside him to prevent players from calling a combination they have drawn instead of one they bet. The lookout can refresh the memory of a green banker or steady the nerves of a confused one. Often players will bet the four of a kind. This bet is called a *round robin*. The player is paid off on the basis of one combination if he catches two aces (for instance), on three combinations if he catches three, on six combinations if he catches all four. Aces is used here only as an example. The player may bet any four of a kind. The bet costs him six units, because the cards can fall into six different two-way combinations. While the banker pays off at 70 to 1 for one combination and while that payoff is actually 69 to 1, the correct odds are 87.4 to 1 against getting a combination dealt in six cards. It is a pretty substantial percentage margin, but the banker wouldn't be in there without an edge, would he?

Thereafter the play continues as in regular six-card Straight Rummy.

Additional Rules. Violations and infractions of the rules are covered on pages 56 to 57.

SIX- AND SEVEN-CARD KNOCK RUMMY

This variation of Straight Rummy was one of the most widely played games of the Rummy family prior to the advent of multiple-deck Rummies. In recent years it is showing signs of a comeback.

The game is played by two to six players. As in Straight Rummy, six or seven cards are dealt each player. It is generally conceded that the seven-card variety requires more skill. In seven-card Knock Rummy, a four-handed game is more fun; in six-card Knock, the five-handed game is likely to be found the more interesting. But whether played with six or seven cards, a standard deck of 52 cards is used.

Object of the Game

1. To go rummy by melding the entire hand at one time in melds of three or four of a kind or three or more in sequences of the same suit.

2. Or, to knock and terminate the hand at any stage.

Value of the Cards. Ace is low, counting 1 point; kings, queens, and jacks count 10 points; all other cards have their face value.

Start of the Play. After each player has been dealt his cards, the leader may elect to knock. This he does by rapping his knuckles on the table or just uttering the word "Knock." That means he proposes to end the game then and there. He must place on the table his melds, if any (it is not necessary to have any melds in the hand as a requisite to knock), and, separately, his unmatched cards, announcing his total of the latter. Players in rotation from the dealer's left must do likewise. The player with the lowest total in unmatched cards is the winner.

Continuation of the Play. If the leader does not elect to knock, he must pick a card off the stock and then discard one. Each player to his left in rotation may pick up either the top card of the discard pile or the top card of the stock and then discard one. A player cannot pick up an upcard and discard it immedi-

ately. He must wait until his next turn of play to discard it.

A player cannot knock after he has taken a card from the discard pile or the stock. If he wants to knock, he must decline to pick a card at his turn to play. Instead, he must knock and expose his hand face up, melds and unmatched cards separately, on the table. If he picks a card and with that picked card completes a Rummy hand, he then discards one card and lays the hand face up on the table. But this rule applies only to a Rummy hand.

The Break. No player can knock after the break (see the rule on this under Straight Rummy, page 57). When it is a player's turn to break, he cannot pick the upcard unless he can use it in a meld, and other players are privileged to ask him whether he can so use it. If not, he must not take it, and must pick the top card of the remaining stock. This restriction applies to all players after the break.

There is no laying off of cards on other players' melds in Knock Rummy; each player must hold his own cards in his hand. Players must discard their highest unmatched card after the break.

When the stock is exhausted, the player with the lowest total of unmatched cards is the winner. In case of ties the breaker or the player nearest to the breaker's left is the winner.

Knockers and Winners. Even if another player can tie the knocker's count (total of unmatched cards), the knocker is still the winner. If another player or other players have a count lower than the knocker's, the player who has the lowest count wins. In case of ties, the player nearest the knocker's left wins.

The Payoff

1. The player who wins by a knock is paid one unit by each other player.

2. The knocker who loses to another player having fewer points in unmatched

cards than he (which is an underknock) must pay the underknocker two units. Each of the other players pays the underknocker one unit.

3. When a player knocks and melds all his cards, he has gone rummy, and must be paid three units by each of the other players.

4. If a player goes rummy without making a pick or by melding his entire hand in a sequence of the same suit before the break, he must be paid six units by each of the other players.

Additional Rules. See pages 55 to 57.

Strategy. Be quick on the trigger in knocking. Any hand of Knock Rummy that lasts more than about six draws is probably misplayed by some or all. Knock on your first turn (in two-hand) if your deadwood (unmatched cards in the hand) totals 60 or less. After one draw, 40 is a good knock; after two draws, 30; after three draws, 20; at any later time, knock on 10 or less. You may well knock with more at any of these later turns, if the play convinces you that your opponent has not bettered his hand appreciably.

In three-hand play, the average requirements are: for a knock on first turn, 35 or less; on second turn, 20; thereafter, 10. These figures are conservative; you will win many times by knocking with considerably more.

Poker Rummy

This game is the same as Knock Rummy, except for the following:

1. With four or more players, using only one deck, only six cards are dealt to each. A preferable alternative is to shuffle two full packs together and deal ten cards to each player. With the double deck, there is no limitation or requirement as to the number of suits in a group.

2. A player may knock only if the count of his deadwood is 15 or less.

3. An ace may be used as either high or low, so that queen–king–ace and ace–two–three are valid sequences but king–ace–two is not. An ace counts 10 as deadwood.

One Hundred and One Rummy

A Knock Rummy variation with certain additional, exciting, negative scores to be aimed for. It is a favorite in the United States wherever gamblers congregate.

Requirements

1. A standard deck of 52 cards.

2. From two to six players, four making the best game.

Beginning of the Game. Selection of the dealer, seating positions, changing seats, shuffle, and cut are described under General Rules for Rummy Games (page 55).

Object of the Game. This game resembles an elimination tournament. When a player's score reaches 101 or more points, he is barred from further play. One by one the contestants are eliminated until only one is left. The player who hasn't reached 101 wins.

Play of the Hand. Starting with the player at his left and dealing clockwise, the dealer deals each player seven cards one at a time. The remaining cards are put in the center of the table, constituting the stock. The leader makes the first play by picking the top card of the stock, then discarding. Other players, starting with the player at the leader's left, may take the top card of the stock or the upcard, then discarding. This goes on clockwise until a player knocks.

Knocking. If a player's score is 91 or fewer points, he may knock with a count of 9 or fewer points in unmatched cards in his hand. If his score reads 92, he must have a count of 8 points or fewer to knock. If his score reads 93, his knocking count must be 7 points or less. And so on up to 99, when he must have a count of exactly 1 point to knock. If he has a score of 100 points, he cannot knock at all. He must go rummy. If a player knocks with more points than this law allows, he is eliminated from the game immediately as his penalty, and the hand is no-game for the other players. An underknock does not affect the scoring.

When a player goes rummy he gets a score of zero. All other players must add to their cumulative score their total amount of unmatched cards. They cannot lay off cards, but can lay down melds.

A knocker must enter his total knocking count on the score sheet. Scoring and melding for the other players is the same as prescribed for Straight Rummy.

The Break. Should a player fail to knock or go rummy and should cards in the stock be reduced to the number of players in the game, we arrive at a phase of the game called the break. The player whose turn it is to pick the top card of the stock is called the *breaker*. After the break has begun, a player cannot in his turn pick the top card of the discard pile (upcard) unless that card can be used in an immediate meld.

When the cards are broke (i.e., when fewer cards remain in the stock than there are players in the game), the player breaking must put down all his melds on the table in separate sets and hold covered in his hand his unmatched cards. The next player does likewise, but may lay off cards if he can on any exposed melds. He also holds covered his unmatched cards. All the players do likewise in rotation. When the last player has completed his play:

1. He announces the total value of the unmatched cards still in his possession, and shows the cards.

2. Each player in turn, clockwise, does the same until all the players have laid their unmatched cards on the table, and the total is entered on the score sheet.

Buying into the Game. This game is generally played for a stipulated amount, say, $1 a game per player, which is put into the kitty beforehand. The winner gets the kitty. It can grow to a pretty respectable size, that kitty, because a player can buy his way back into the game after he has scored his fatal 101.

1. It costs an eliminated player $1 to get back into the game. That dollar goes into the kitty.

2. And he must start now with a score equal to the highest surviving player's.

Now, if he should be eliminated a second time he can still get back into the game. Only this time his reentry costs him $2. Out again? He can buy back into the proceedings, this time for $4. The cost of returning doubles every time a player does it.

Chicago Rummy

This is an exciting double-deck variation of One Hundred and One Rummy which permits up to eight players. Chicago Rummy follows the rules of One Hundred and One Rummy except as noted:

1. Two identical standard packs of 52 cards, shuffled together and used as one. All eight deuces are wild. Any deuce may be used to represent any card a player likes.

2. From two to eight players, six making for the best game.

3. When a player goes rummy and his meld is comprised of seven cards of the same rank (wild deuces may be included), such as seven five's, seven six's, etc., the game automatically ends and the holder is declared the winner.

COON CAN

The only game of the Rummy family played before the turn of the twentieth century that is still popular throughout the country. The reason for its long sovereignty is its provision of reward for fine strategy. It's as generous in this respect as any modern game of the family. The greatest popularity of this game, with its picturesque idiom, is in the South, but wherever Blacks congregate, a round of Coon Can is likely to get under way.

Requirements

1. Two players.

2. A 40-card deck (a regular pack stripped of all tens, nines, and eights). Jack and seven are in sequence. Ace counts low, and is used only in melds of three or four aces or in sequence: ace, 2, 3, of the same suit.

Object of the Game. To go coon can, which is to lay down your entire hand plus the card which ordinarily would be the dis-

card. The total must be eleven cards. A player may have ten cards melded and discard a card, but—even though he has no cards in his hand—he is not coon can, and continues to play. He must have eleven cards in melds on the table in front of him before he can call coon can and be the winner.

Glossary. Coon Can is distinguished by (among other things) its own vocabulary, which is characteristically salty and economic in the use of words. Here are the common ones:

To overlook a play is to *sleep it*.

Laying off a card on a meld is a *hit* (noun) or *to hit* (verb).

A lay or meld of the same rank is a *short spread*.

A lay or meld of three or more cards in sequence of the same suit is a *long spread*.

A draw game is a *tab game*.

To pick or take a card from the stock is to *pluck* it.

To take a card from one lay in order to form another is to *switch*.

A hand you can't go coon can with is a *hole*.

Selecting the Dealer. Players cut for the deal. Low man deals. Loser of the previous game deals the next game. In case of a tab (draw game), player other than the previous dealer deals.

The Shuffle and Cut. The dealer shuffles the deck. Nondealer may call for a shuffle at any time before the deal starts, though dealer retains the right to shuffle last. After the shuffle, cards are offered to the nondealer for the cut. If he refuses, dealer must himself cut before starting the deal. Dealer deals himself and his opponent ten cards each, one at a time, starting with the opponent. Dealer places the remainder of the cards on the table, forming the stock.

Start of the Play. The nondealer plucks the top card of the stock, exposes the card by holding it so that the dealer can see its face, and decides what to do with it. If he decides to take it, he must use it immediately as part of a spread and lay the spread down, or he may discard it. Mark this well: a plucked card cannot be placed in the player's hand among his other cards. It must be used as part of a spread or must be discarded.

The dealer may now either pick up the discarded card (upcard) or pluck the top card of the stock. But if he plucks the upcard he must use it immediately in a spread and put the spread on the board. The play alternates until the end of the game.

A player may lay off (hit) any number of cards on his own melds. Also he may hit his opponent's melds with one card at each turn of play. But when a player hits an opponent's melds, that card is considered his discard. He cannot discard from his hand after a hit. And the player who has been hit cannot pluck a card after the hit but must just discard one card. This peculiarity of Coon Can, hitting the opponent, leads naturally to another noteworthy feature.

A player will deliberately discard a card which can be used to extend a spread of his opponent's. He calls the opponent's attention to it. The opponent picks it up, adds it to a spread, and then discards. The purpose of this is to lure an opponent into discarding from his hand. That's called *breaking the hand*. By getting an adversary to shorten his hand you put him into a ten-card hole, which precludes his going coon can. A man with a spread ranging from ace to king of the same suit is a man with a ten-card hole on his hands; and since the game requires an eleven-card lay-down, including the discard card, that man can't go coon can.

A player may lay as many spreads as possible at any turn of play. Should a player discard a card he can use as a hit, his opponent may call his attention to it and compel him to hit it. The attempt to make such a discard is called trying to *sleep it*.

A player having on the table before him a spread of more than three cards may remove or switch one of them to help form another spread—provided the removal doesn't interrupt the sequence of a long spread. Suppose a player has before him a short spread consisting of four fives and has in his hand the six and seven of hearts. He can switch the five of hearts from the short spread and meld the six and seven on it, forming a long spread or sequence. If the upcard plus a switched card added to any card in his hand will form a spread, the player is entitled to pluck the top discard, lay his card, and switch the third card. But bear in mind that whenever a card has been switched from a spread, that spread must still consist of three cards having the same numerical value or at least three cards in sequence of the same suit. Otherwise the switch is barred.

End of the Game. When a player has laid down eleven cards in spread, he calls coon can, and the game ends. He wins. If the entire stock is exhausted without either player going coon can, the game is a tab. The amount of the agreed stake is added to the kitty for every tab game until one player wins. He gets the whole kitty.

TONK

Popular with the Blacks in the United States and quite a betting game. It combines some interesting features of Knock Rummy and Coon Can.

Requirements

1. Two to six players, four or five making for the best game.

2. A regular 52-card deck.

Object of the Game. To go tonk by going rummy or by tonking (knocking) and having the lowest points in unmatched cards.

Beginning of the Game. Selection of the dealer, seating positions, changing seats, shuffle, and cut are as described under General Rules for Rummy Games (page 55).

The Deal. After the cards have been shuffled and cut, the dealer, starting with the player at his left and dealing clockwise, deals each player seven cards, one at a time. He then faces up the next card as the first upcard, and puts the rest of the cards face down beside it as the stock.

Value of Cards. Aces count 1 point; jacks, queens, and kings, 10 points; all other cards their pip or face value.

The Play. After the deal and before the leader makes his play, a player may call tonk if he holds any seven of the following cards: tens, jacks, queens, and kings.

He may tonk whether these cards occur in a spread (meld) or not, and is the winner and collects from each of the other players whatever stakes have been agreed on. But if a play has been made and a player calls tonk, this rule does not apply. If no player calls tonk, the leader makes the first play. He may either pluck (colloquial for pick, or take) the up-card or take the top card of the stock. If he plucks the upcard, he cannot place that card in his hand, but must make use of it immediately in a spread (meld) and put that spread on the table. If the card can't be used in an immediate spread he must discard it, and play goes on.

A player may call tonk any time he thinks he has the low hand, just as in Knock Rummy, but if he tonks and some other player has a lower hand, the tonker must pay each of the other players double the amount stipulated as stakes.

A player may hit (lay off) one card only from his hand at each turn of play, if possible; but when he lays off a card he cannot then discard. He must always have seven cards, no more and no less, either melded before him or in his hand.

Breaker. No player may tonk or knock after the break (when the stock has been reduced to one card less than the number of players), but should a player go tonk (rummy) after the break, the game is ended and that player is a winner. In the absence of a tonk after the break, the player ending with the lowest total points is the winner. In case of ties, the breaker (player who plucks the first card from the stock when it is reduced to the number of players in the game), or the player nearest to the breaker's left, is the winner.

FIVE HUNDRED RUMMY

Five Hundred Rummy, also known as Pinochle Rummy, was one of the earliest Rummy games to give scoring values to melds. The game is a favorite with experienced Rummy players. It is for two to four players, each of whom plays and scores for himself.

Requirements

1. A standard deck of 52 cards.

Beginning of the Game. Selection of the dealer, seating positions, changing seats, shuffle, and cut are described under General Rules for Rummy Games (page 55).

Object of the Game. To lay down melds totaling 500 or more points. The player so melding ends the game and wins it.

If two or more players meld 500 or more points the *highest* score wins.

Hand. A hand is completed when any player has no more cards in his hand or the cards in the stock are exhausted. Then each player is given credit for all the cards he has melded, and is penalized for the points he still holds in his hand. When one player goes rummy (or out), each other player is penalized for the count he holds, whether or not they are melds. Ace counts 15 points, except when used with the deuce–trey of the same suit.

The Deal. Seven cards are dealt each player in turn one at a time starting with the leader, and rotating clockwise. Then the next card is faced up to begin the discard pile, and the remaining cards are put face down beside it, constituting the stock.

The Play. Start with the leader and play in

turn clockwise. Each player may draw either a card from the top of the stock or as many cards from the discard pile as he pleases; but if he draws from the discard he must use the bottom card drawn immediately as part of a meld. Thus he must have at least two cards of a meld before he draws from the discards. The cards in the discard pile are fanned out so that the players can see them clearly. In discarding, the card must be placed tidily on the last discard so that all other discards are visible. In his proper turn of play a player may lay down as many melds as he can and will.

The ace may be laid as either the high or the low card of a sequence: ace–two–three or queen–king–ace; but it cannot be used around the corner, that is, king–ace–deuce. Cards may be laid off both on the player's own and on opponents' melds. But in laying off on opponents, the player may place in front of himself the laid-off card so that it can be scored for him.

Let me suggest that you'd better watch sequence melds most carefully and stay aware of whether other players' layoffs have extended sequences on the board. Player A melds the ace–two–three of hearts; player B lays the four in front of himself; player C lays the five. A little later you find in your hand a six of hearts, which is doing you no good at all. Glancing around the board, you see the ace–two–three meld; but if you don't watch the other layoffs diligently you may discard that six instead of laying it off to your profit.

To most experienced Rummy players the following may seem rudimentary, but I'd better point it out to have it on record. When a card can be laid off on either of two melds, the player must specify which meld. Let's hypothesize that two melds are on the board. One is three treys. The other is the four–five–six of diamonds. You hold the three of diamonds. Now, melding your three, you must specify whether it goes on the three of a kind or the sequence. If you meld it on the treys, that meld is dead, and the lower end of the sequence is closed off; no more cards can be melded on it in that direction. But if you meld on the sequence, it remains open to further extension. The point is worth bearing in mind, especially if you have in your hand the diamond ace and suspect someone else might hold the diamond deuce to lay off on

the sequence and afford you the chance to down your card.

Value of the Cards. The ace counts 15 points—except when used in a meld of the ace–two–three of the same suit, in which case it is valued at 1 point. Jacks, queens, and kings count 10 points each; all other cards, their pip or numerical face value.

End of the Game. It is convenient to keep score cumulatively. But some players prefer to run a score sheet for each contestant, entering melds as laid, and some others prefer to add up the totals at the end of each hand. The game is ended when any player scores 500 or more points. Player with the highest score wins. Five Hundred is usually played for so much per game or so much per point, the payoff being based on difference in points.

Streamlined Scoring. This scoring method is suggested for players who like a faster game and abhor bookkeeping. As in Fortune Rummy, count all cards from two to seven as being worth 5 points, all from eight to king as being worth 10. The ace when laid in a meld with the deuce–trey counts 5 points, otherwise 10.

Strategy. The real object of play is to get "the tempo" in taking the discard pile. The player who first takes the pile, if it amounts to, say, six cards or more, is likely to have gained an advantage that lasts throughout the play. The method of prolonging this advantage is to refrain from melding low sets; instead sacrifice one card from the set. This so-called "bait" enables the player to take the pile at any later time, after sufficient riches have accumulated, always provided that it has not been captured by another player.

A player could not wish for better fortune than to be dealt some such holding as deuces of spades, diamonds, and hearts, and three of hearts. He can then discard the two of hearts with positive assurance that no other player can dig down to this card in taking the discard pile. Lacking deuces of spades and diamonds and the three of hearts, no other player could use the two of hearts in a meld.

The early discards should be used, when possible, to "salt" the discard pile in this way. Make your first discard one of a low set or a low pair. The points to be gained by melding, say, three sixes are trifling, compared with the potential advantage to be gained by using such a set to salt the discard pile. Also as a matter of course, try to avoid discarding high cards (say, eights or higher) until you are forced to do so, or until you see that such discards are fairly safe. Even letting another player take the first discard pile (say, through a pair of deuces) is not so mortal a blow as giving him 30 in 10-point cards or 45 in aces.

When the stock is low, and no one has gone out—the normal condition of affairs—the question sometimes arises whether to take the discard pile for a middling meld (as three sevens) at the cost of taking a larger count of nondescript cards into the hand. More mistakes are made through failing to "dig" than through digging. Apart from the cash points involved—the actual meld as against the additional deadwood—there is also an equity to be weighed: whatever you take from the discard pile decreases the chances of another player to increase his score or to go out before you have had another opportunity to unload.

You must tacitly conspire with other players not to help a player who nears a 500-point score. As a general rule, do not meld at all from your hand (apart from establishing the right to dig into the discard pile) unless you thereby go out or unless you see that such a meld will not add to the chances of other hands to lay off.

Partnership Five Hundred Rummy

This is a partnership game—two players against two, facing each other across the table—which is played exactly the same as Five Hundred Rummy, except that partners try to help each other to form matched sets and to go out. When any player goes out, play ends and the score of each partnership is figured as a unit. The game is over when either side reaches 500.

Michigan Rummy

The game is played exactly as Five Hundred Rummy, with the following exceptions:
1. Each hand is a completed game.
2. Should a player discard a card that can

be laid off on a meld, the first player to call stop may use this card, then discard one. The turn of play then reverts to its proper place.
3. Winner of the game is the first to go Michigan (rummy).

Polish Rummy

This game is played exactly as Michigan Rummy, except that a player may pick up the entire discard pile at any time.

Wildcat Rummy

This game is the same as Michigan Rummy, except for the following:
1. Deuces are wild. One or two jokers may be added to the deck, as wild cards, if desired. Wild cards left in the hand count 15; melded, they have the value of the cards they represent. A melded wild card may be captured by any player in exchange for a natural card.
2. Round-the-corner sequences are permitted, so that king–ace–two as well as queen–king–ace and ace–two–three are valid sequences. Aces count one in all circumstances.
3. The same card may be used to complete both a sequence and a group. Thus a player may meld, for example, eight, seven, and six of spades, and the sixes of hearts and diamonds as two valid sets. When melded sets can be made to interlock in this way, but need not do so to contain the minimum of three cards each, the melder must state his intention, and following players are bound by the statement.
4. *Variation:* Players often agree on the following special rules: (*a*) It is forbidden to discard a card that is of the same rank, or same suit and in sequence with, the top card of the discard pile; (*b*) for going out after drawing only one card, a player wins double; for going out without drawing any card (and so without discarding), a player wins triple; (*c*) an unmatched queen of spades held in the hand counts 40 points.

CONTINENTAL RUMMY

Continental Rummy was the forerunner of the whole family of Rummy games using multiple packs of cards as one. It is also a big betting game.

Requirements
1. The game can be played by two to six persons. The four- or five-handed games are best.

2. Two standard packs of 52 playing cards are used as one. The packs may be of the same design or of different design and even color.

Beginning of the Game. Selection of the dealer, seating positions, changing seats, shuffle, and cut are as described under General Rules for Rummy Games (page 55).

The Deal. The dealer deals 15 cards three at a time to each player, starting with the player at the dealer's left (leader) and going clockwise. The rest of the cards are placed face down on the table, forming the stock. On completion of the hand, the deal passes to the player at the dealer's left.

Object of the Game. To go rummy by melding the entire 15 cards in matched sets of three or four of a kind or in sequences of three or more in the same suit. (Sequences of five or six are not uncommon, and sequences have been built up from ace to king in the same suit.)

Value of the Cards. The ace is scored low, counting 1 point; kings, queens, and jacks count 10 points each; all other cards have their numerical values.

The Play

1. The first player to the dealer's left picks a card off the stock and discards a card, placing it face up next to the stock. Each player in turn, clockwise, picks the upcard from stock, then discards. This goes on until a player goes rummy.

2. If the entire stock is exhausted without any player going rummy, the discards are picked up by the dealer of the hand and reshuffled; then they are cut by the player at the dealer's right, and go back to the center of the table to constitute a new stock. And the play goes on until someone goes rummy.

3. When a player goes rummy, he places all his cards face up on the table in melds, separating each from the others so that all hands can certify the rummy. The rest of the players then lay their own melds, holding their unmatched cards. The scorekeeper, who may be one of the players or a kibitzer, now verifies the count of the player to the left of the winner, and enters this amount as a credit to the winner, at the same time subtracting it from the player's score. This computation is made for each player around the table, going clockwise.

4. A game is four completed deals or hands.

5. Or, arbitrarily, a game can be played to a time limit. Thus we may set a two-hour limit for the game. At the expiration of that time, or at the completion of any hand which reaches beyond the agreed time, the game is over.

The Payoff. A player's plus points and minus points are canceled against each other, and the payoff is at so much per point on the remainder. It is not uncommon to pay a prearranged amount to the player with the highest number of points for the game. A cent a point makes for a nice game, in which nobody will lose too much.

Specimen Score. The score card at the completion of two hands should look something like the following:

A	B	C	D
+69	−15	−19	−35
+59	+40	−39	−60

Observe that losing and winning points, the plus and minus points, must be exactly equal. In the above score A has gone rummy on the first hand; B was caught, or stuck, with 15 points, C with 19, D with 35. In the second game which B won, A was caught for 10 points, C for 20, D for 25. While some players prefer the simplicity of jotting down the scores per game and adding them at the end (see page 87), I keep a cumulative score. This minimizes the possibility of error and trouble, and at the end the penny-a-point payoff is exactly what the last entry on the sheet shows for each player.

Additional Rules. All violations and infractions are covered under the rules on pages 56 and 57.

Strategy. Despite the holding of 15 cards, the limitation of melds to sequences alone makes it rather more difficult than might be imagined to collect a sufficiency of combinations in a hurry. A hand without, say, four combinations to start with is desperately weak. If saddled with such a hand (not compensated by wild cards), give consideration to picking up early discards merely to make combinations. Part of the reason for so doing is that your right-hand neighbor is apt to commit himself by his early discards to letting go other cards of the same suit and near rank; scope for defensive play by holding back cards wanted by the left neighbor is very limited. Taking discards to make combinations is the more advisable if the pack contains only a few wild cards (jokers); if deuces are wild also, the policy is dubious, but less so than in most other Rummy variants.

Generally it is better to go out as soon as possible rather than play on in the hope that

a lucky draw will complete a bonus hand. An exception is found when there are three or four places open to fill a hand without a wild card.

MISSISSIPPI RUMMY

At one time this was one of the most popular forms of Rummy in women's afternoon games, but in 1950 it lost out to Canasta. It is akin to One Hundred and One Rummy in requiring that one by one the contestants are eliminated until only one is left. Rules of the game prevent losing more than a sum stipulated before play starts. I know a group of eight women who played Mississippi for hours a day every day through a solid month's vacation a number of years ago. Not one of them had lost more than $5 at the end of the month. I strongly recommend this game to women since they seem to relish its weird complications.

Requirements

1. Two standard packs of playing cards shuffled and used as one. Color and design don't matter.

2. From two to eight players, five to eight making for the best game.

Aces and Deuces. The deuces are wild, and may be used for any card in any suit.

Aces may be melded only in a group of three or four or in the queen–king–ace sequence. The ace–two–three sequence is barred.

Beginning of the Game. Selection of the dealer, seating positions, changing seats, shuffle, and cut are as described under General Rules for Rummy Games (page 55).

Object of the Game. To score as few points as possible. Any player scoring 102 points or more is out of the game for its duration. The game continues until only one player remains. He—or rather, she—wins and takes the kitty.

Sharing the Wealth. Often the kitty is divided between the last two players, who are both declared winners. If, this being the case, any odd cash is left over, it goes into the kitty for the next game.

Value of the Cards. In scoring, aces count 15 points; face cards, 10; spot cards, their face value.

Stipulations. Before starting play, it is agreed by open democratic vote what is the maximum amount any player may lose in the

course of the evening—say $1. Commonly a time limit on the play is stipulated. It is entered on a corner of the score sheet.

If chips are available, one of the players is elected cashier, and collects $1 from each player for her supply of chips. After that no player may buy any more chips either from the cashier or from any other player. Should she lose all her chips, she keeps right on playing anyway, as follows:

Should she continue to lose, she owes no penalties to the winners. But should she resume winning after her losing streak (during which she has not paid penalties), the other players—unless they happen to be broke in turn—must pay her. Play continues until expiration of the agreed time limit.

The Kitty. To begin, each player drops in a cup to start the kitty a chip equal in value to a nickel. Should a player hold ten cards of the same suit, whether or not in sequence, that's a ten-card meld and is called Mississippi, and the melder gets a 20-cent bonus from each other player; but she must put 20 cents in the kitty, which goes on growing for the winner. Should a player go rummy without picking a card, that's a *dream,* and each other player pays the player 20 cents, whereupon she must put 20 cents in the kitty. Should a player go rummy, she gets 10 cents from each other player, and must put 10 cents in the kitty. Should a player score an underknock (having fewer points than the knocker), the knocker must pay the underknocker 20 cents and the underknocker collects 5 cents from each other player. Underknocker then must put 10 cents in the kitty. Should a player knock with 5 points or fewer, she collects 5 cents from each other player and puts 5 cents in the kitty. These bonuses have nothing to do with the scoring of the game. They're extras. They are there for the sheer thrill of it.

The Deal. The dealer gives herself the first card, then deals to the left, clockwise, one at a time, ten cards to each player except the dealer, who gets eleven cards. The rest of the cards are put face down on the table to constitute the stock. If the entire stock is exhausted without any player's knocking or going rummy, the discards are shuffled and cut, the top card is faced up to start the new discard pile, and the rest of the cards become the new stock.

Start of the Play. The dealer makes the first play, discarding one of her eleven cards. Then each player in turn clockwise, starting with the player at the dealer's left, may pick either the upcard or the top card of the stock, discarding one card. This goes on until a player goes rummy or knocks with less than 5 points in unmatched cards in her hand. To go rummy a player must lay the whole ten cards in melds, then discard her last card.

With the above stipulated exceptions, the melds in Mississippi are the same as the melds in any other Rummy game.

Knock. When a player knocks she must table her melds separately, announce her count, and put her unmatched cards on the table face up so the other players can check them. The count for a knock must be 5 or fewer in unmatched cards. Players cannot lay off cards after another player has either knocked or gone rummy. But they may meld their lays after a rummy or knock, then hold their unmatched cards until the total is entered on the score sheet. Players are scored as being plus the total of their unmatched cards at the rate of 15 for aces, 10 for face cards, and spot value for the other cards.

Underknock. When another player has fewer points than a player who has knocked, that's an underknock. There is no extra penalty for the knocker other than the cash penalty stated under Stipulations above. Both knocker and underknocker are scored as plus their points in unmatched cards.

Buy. A player eliminated from the game after the second hand may buy herself back into the game. She puts 10 cents in the kitty, and starts again with a score equal to the surviving player with the second lowest score.

Courtesy Buy. If a player has a score of 81 or more, she may make a courtesy buy. She puts 10 cents in the kitty, and starts the next hand with a score equal in points to the second lowest score then in the game. A player may make only two courtesy buys per game.

Scoring. A score card like the one shown in Continental Rummy is used. When a player goes rummy, she gets a minus 10. When a player knocks and wins, she gets a plus in the number of cards she knocked with. All other players must add up their unmatched cards, and the total count of each player is entered against her as a plus.

The score is balanced cumulatively and kept running. Should a player have ten cards in the same suit (Mississippi), she gets a minus 20 points. Should a player go rummy without a pick (the *dream*), she gets a minus 20 points.

FORTUNE RUMMY

Fortune Rummy was very popular in Midwestern clubs during the late forties. It has many remarkable features found in no other Rummy game. Try it as a family game.

Requirements

1. Any two standard 52-card decks, shuffled and used as one. All eight deuces are wild. Any deuce may be used to represent any card a player likes.

2. Two to eight players. A four- or five-handed game is most fun.

Beginning of the Game. Selection of the dealer, seating positions, changing seats, shuffle, and cut are as described under General Rules for Rummy Games (page 55).

The Deal

1. Starting with the leader, the dealer deals 11 cards to each player one at a time clockwise.

2. The next card is face up on the table as the upcard, and the stock goes face down beside it.

Object of the Game

1. To form melds or lays of three or more cards.

2. And to get the melds down on the board so as to receive credit for them, because—

3. A meld in the hand is a liability; a meld is worth points only when it is down on the table.

4. On the completion of each hand, each player is credited with his total points.

5. Play continues until a player runs up a score of 500 or more points.

6. Players are credited for the points they have melded. The scorekeeper subtracts points in the hand from points on the board, and enters the resultant sum against the

player's name. If he has more points in his hand unmelded than points on the board melded, he owes his score the difference. If he has not previously scored, the difference goes against his name with a minus before it. If he has a score, the difference is subtracted from it.

Value of Cards. Kings, queens, jacks, tens, nines, and eights count 10 points; threes, fours, fives, sixes, and sevens count 5 points. Aces count 10 points when used in a high-sequence meld, to wit, the queen–king–ace. Used in the low sequence (ace–deuce–trey) or in a meld of three or four aces, each ace counts 5 points. But an ace in the hand at the conclusion of play, whether unmatched or in an unused meld, counts 10 points against that player. The queen of spades is the highest-ranking card. It has a value of 50 points regardless of when or how used. A wild deuce may be used as a queen of spades, but its value then is 10 points.

Deuces Wild. *Example:* You have the queen and ten of spades and the deuce of clubs. You meld that sequence, and it is worth 70 points, because you are using the wild deuce to represent the jack of spades. If a deuce is used to represent any card below the eight, it may be counted as only 5 points in a meld. If a player has a deuce in his hand at the completion of the hand, he is penalized 10 points for it.

The Play

1. The leader may either pick the upcard, in which case he must forthwith lay down a meld including that card.

2. Or, take the top card of the stock, after which he may (if he is able) put down any melds he pleases.

3. After either of which he discards one card.

Certain Peculiar Features. A player may pick the upcard only when he has in hand at least two cards of the meld into which it will go. The player taking the upcard must take the entire discard pile. But immediately he must put down a meld in which the upcard is embodied. A player may put down as many melds as possible or as he wishes at any play. After his melds have been laid down, player discards.

A player cannot lay off cards on his opponent's melds, as in other Rummy games; his cards may be laid off only on his own melds. Discards must always be neatly squared up so

that no card below the upcard is visible, and players are not allowed to spread the discards. If the entire stock is exhausted before any player is clean (rummy), the discards are turned over (with the exception of the upcard, the cards are not shuffled but merely turned over), and the game continues with those cards as the new stock.

End of Hand. The hand ends when any player has melded his entire hand, whereupon the other players, holding cards in their hands whether they are perfected melds or unmatched cards, are penalized for the total number of points they represent.

End of Game. When any player (or players) reaches 500 points or more the game ends, and the player with the highest score wins. In a four-handed game, the two highest players may by previous agreement be declared winners; in a six-handed game, the three highest, etc.

These stipulations must be made before starting the game, and all players must be clearly acquainted with the method to be used in ending the contest.

The Speedup. Players in a five-, six-, seven-, or eight-handed game who want a faster decision may agree that 300 points is the winning score; or players may decide that three or four hands will constitute a complete game. In this case, the player with the highest score wins, or else (as above) the two highest in a four-handed game, the three highest in a six-handed game, and so on.

Oklahoma Rummy

This variation of Fortune Rummy is also called Arlington. Its popularity, like that of its forerunner, is due to its interesting point scoring system and its ruling on discards.

Requirements

1. Two standard 52-card packs are used, shuffled together and treated as a single deck. Packs of different colors may be used.

2. From two to six persons may play, but the game goes best with four.

3. The eight deuces are wild.

Object of the Game. To score 1,000 or more points by laying down melds. If two or more players score 1,000 or more points, the winner is the player with the highest score.

Beginning of the Game. Selection of the dealer, seating positions, changing seats, shuffle, and cut are as described under General Rules for Rummy Games (page 55).

The Deal. After the cards have been shuffled and cut, the dealer deals each player thirteen cards at a time in turn, starting with the player to his left and dealing clockwise. He then turns up the next card, and places it on the table face up. That's the upcard. He puts the remaining stack of cards face down beside the upcard. This pile is the stock.

Play of the Hand. The player to the dealer's left makes the first play, and the turn to play rotates clockwise. Each player in his turn may do either of the following:

1. Pick the top card of the stock, then meld if he can and wants to, and then discard.

2. Or, pick the upcard (top card of the discard pile)—if he can use that card immediately in a meld.

But note: If he chooses to pick the upcard, the player must also take into his hand the rest of the cards in the discard pile. Then he can lay down whatever melds he can and will. Then he discards a card.

Laying Off Cards. Players may lay off cards only in their proper turn of play and only on their own melds.

Exhausted Stock. If the stock is exhausted without any player having gone rummy, the discards are managed in the following manner:

1. The upcard stays on the table as the start of the new discard pile.

2. The remaining discards are picked up by the dealer of that hand and shuffled by him, cut by the player to the dealer's right, and put back on the table, constituting a new stock.

3. Play continues from the point where it was interrupted.

If all the cards are exhausted including the discard pile, which rarely happens, and no player has gone rummy, then each player's unmatched cards are scored against him with a minus sign.

Value of Melded Cards. Aces count 15 points each; tens, jacks, queens, and kings, 10 points each with the exception of the queen of spades, which counts 50 points; threes, fours, fives, sixes, sevens, eights, and nines count 5 points each.

Deuces count as the card they represent in the laid meld, unless used in a meld as deuces. They then count 25 points each.

For a wild deuce to count as the queen of spades, it must be used to represent the natural queen in a spade meld; for example, a meld consisting of the jack of spades, wild deuce, and king of spades. The author urges that the above rules be strictly enforced. To let a player meld three deuces and claim credit for three spade queens with a value of 150 points is to corrupt the game. A deuce used naturally in kinds of sequences is worth 25 points, no more.

Value of Cards in the Hand. Cards retained by a player in his hand after an opponent has gone rummy count the same as when used in a meld—with the exception of the queen of spades. It counts 100 points.

Scoring. The dealer is the scorekeeper. The player who has gone rummy is credited with a plus amounting to the points of his melds. Each of the other players is credited with the difference between his meld points and the point value of the cards left in his hand. Melds left in a player's hand are charged against him. Just to prevent any ambiguity, an *example:* A player's melds total 70 points. The cards in his hand total 50 points. Under his name on the score sheet is entered a net plus score of 20 points: +20. *Another example:* A player's melds total 50 points, the cards in his hand total 70; so he is marked for a net minus score of 20 points, or −20.

The player who goes rummy and wins gets a bonus of 100 points, which is entered to his credit on the score sheet.

Winner of the Game. The first player to score 1,000 or more points is the winner. If two or more players score 1,000 or more points at the same time, the player with the highest score wins, and takes whatever stakes have been stipulated, say, 25 or 50 cents a game. Or the winner may be paid on the basis of the difference in points between his score and the other players'. The rate can be one-tenth of a cent per point—or whatever you think is feasible and fun, not that these two are always compatible.

Strategy. Don't meld too early in the play; after four or five draws your hand may form other combinations that will use more cards. Usually hold a pair rather than a two-card sequence, as there is a better chance to improve the pair.

Save an odd queen or a high spade—king, jack, or ten—even when it is unmatched with other cards. If you draw the queen of spades you cannot discard it, and a matching card will improve your chance of melding it.

When you take the discard pile, before mixing it with your hand count back to remember which cards each other player has thrown. It is both ethical and proper to throw a card that will put the next player out, if there is a danger that otherwise another player will go out concealed.

Prefer to meld three of a kind rather than four of a kind, using the fourth card in another meld.

CONTRACT RUMMY

Also played under such names as Zioncheck, Liverpool Rummy, Progressive Rummy, King Rummy, Joker Rummy, Shanghai Rummy, Hollywood Rummy, and Combination Rummy. There are a dozen variations. Some of them are mere confusion. Some of them are intolerably unsound or complicated. I've developed here rules for an eminently playable standard version of an exciting Rummy.

Requirements

1. Two standard packs of 52 playing cards, shuffled together and used as one.

2. Any number of players from two to eight, although four or five make for the best game.

Stipulation. Deuces are wild, and count for any rank and suit their holder dictates.

Beginning of the Game. Selection of the dealer, seating positions, changing seats, shuffle, and cut are as described under General Rules for Rummy Games (page 55).

The Deal. Starting with the leader and dealing clockwise, the dealer deals each player ten cards one at a time face down. He faces the next card up, and puts the stock beside it in the middle of the table.

Object of the Game. Each game consists of six deals. It is suggested that the rules on the different hands be copied out and kept handy to avoid what Liverpudlians call a social error, which is playing one's hand by somebody else's rules. Each deal ends when some player has laid down melds as prescribed by the rules.

We shall call a meld of three or more cards having the same numerical rank a *group*.

We shall call a run of three or more cards of the same suit a *sequence,* and the sequences are as follows:

A *red sequence* is a sequence of hearts or diamonds.

A *black sequence* is a sequence of spades or clubs.

A *high group* is a meld of three or four or more eights, nines, tens, jacks, queens, or kings of the same rank.

A *low group* is such a meld of aces, threes, fours, fives, sixes, or sevens. Deuces being wild, they may be assigned any rank in any suit.

Chart of Legal Plays. For reference at the table, copy out this chart of permissible melds:

First Hand: One high and one low group.

Second Hand: One red and one black sequence.

Third Hand: One high group and one red sequence.

Fourth Hand: One low group and one black sequence.

Fifth Hand: Three sequences.

Sixth Hand: Three groups.

Start of the Play. Starting with the dealer and playing clockwise, each player in turn may pick either the upcard or the top card of the stock, then discard one card. Before discarding, the player may lay down any meld or group of melds as prescribed by the rule for each hand, and he may lay off any cards on his own melds or any other player's.

End of the Hand. When a player has laid his melds according to the rules and has no more cards in his hand after discarding, the hand ends. He may lay off cards on his own or other players' melds, as set forth above, but these are the only conditions under which he can win the hand:

He must have before him the melds prescribed for his hand.

He must get rid of all his cards.

If the stock is exhausted before any player has gone rummy, the discard pile (except the upcard, which is left on the board as the start of a new discard pile) is shuffled by the dealer of that hand (see page 77), and is thereafter used as the stock in the continuing game. On a player's going rummy, he is credited with the total points of all unmelded cards held by the players, that is, held in the others' hands, regardless of whether they are groups, sequences, or unmatched cards.

Scoring. Aces, deuces, threes, fours, fives, sixes, and sevens count 5 points each; eights, nines, tens, jacks, queens, and kings count 10 points each. On the score sheet the winner's score is marked with a plus sign, and each loser is marked minus the amount with which he was caught. It is best to keep a cumulative score.

End and Payoff. The game ends when six hands have been completed. Players having minus scores must pay on the table at so much per point, as previously stipulated. Players having plus scores get paid at so much per point. It is usual to establish a premium for the player with the highest score, payable by each other player. I suggest a 25-cent-per-man premium, and a penny a point seems about right.

KALOOKI (CALOOCHI)

A fascinating double-deck form of Rummy which is a favorite among women in card rooms from New York to Florida. Kalooki is also played in sporting clubs, casinos, and homes in Great Britain. Last year when I visited England as a Gambling Consultant to the British Home Office, I stopped off at the Victoria Sporting Club in London and witnessed a half dozen Kalooki games in action.

Requirements

1. Two, three, or four players; the game is best suited to four-handed competition.

2. Two standard 52-card decks and four jokers, shuffled and used as one pack, a total of 108 cards. Jokers are wild.

Beginning of the Game. Selection of the dealer, seating positions, changing seats, shuffle, and cut are as described under General Rules for Rummy Games (page 55).

Value of the Cards. All cards bear their pip value except the ace, which counts 11, and the joker, which bears the value indicated by its use in the meld. A meld of three or four jokers gives them an arbitrary value of 15 points each. It had better be added that it is rarely if ever advisable to lay down three or four jokers. There's generally more useful work for them to do.

Shuffle and Cut. Dealer shuffles cards, then offers pack to player at his right for the cut. That player must cut the cards, showing the bottom card of the cut portion of the stock by turning the cut portion face up. Should the bottom card be a joker, the player cutting the cards takes it as his first card, and the cut is carried (completed). If it is not a joker, it remains where it is in the pack when the cut is completed. When the cutter takes the joker, the dealer skips that player on the first round in the deal.

Fifteen cards are dealt each player face down one at a time in turn, starting with the player at the dealer's left and going clockwise. The next card is faced up, becoming the upcard. The dealer may take that card if he wants it, discarding one card if he does claim it.

The Play. After the dealer takes the upcard or declines it, play passes to the player at his left, and thereafter clockwise. The dealer cannot take the top card of the stock if he declines the upcard. Succeeding players may take the top card of the stock, or may take the upcard only if it can be used in a meld immediately.

A player cannot meld unless the initial meld totals 51 or more points. If he takes the top card of the stock he may embody it in his hand and discard one card. Remember: no meld may be laid unless it counts 51 or more points! A card laid off on other melds may be counted toward this total, but a player may lay off only when melding himself. If a player goes rummy by melding and/or laying off his 15 cards in the single play, that play is Kalooki and the player is paid doubled stakes by each other player. If he melds or lays off all his cards in more than one down, he is rummy and wins the game.

Each losing player is penalized 1 cent for each card he still holds in his hand at game's end. With one exception, the cards have this 1-cent value. The exception is the joker. It counts as two cards and 2 cents in penalties. A player going Kalooki gets doubled stakes from each other player, plus the kitty. Generally in a-cent-a-card game, each player antes a nickel for the kitty. When a joker is one card of a meld and a player holds the natural card for which that joker is stand-in, he can swap his natural card for the joker. Suppose a meld of diamond eight, joker, and diamond ten are on the board. Suppose you hold the nine of diamonds. In your turn of play you may exchange the natural nine for the joker, and use the joker for your own dark purposes.

Strategy. More than half the time, a player finds enough in his original hand to make an initial meld of 51 or more. The meld should be made at once, so that the player can draw from the discard pile when he wishes. The great opportunities for melding, enhanced by laying off on the initial melds (two or three sets each), give a strong chance to go out within a few rounds. With four or more players, it is a fact that some hand goes out usually within six rounds. Consequently there can be no thought of holding up melds to avoid letting other players lay off on them. The chances are too great of being caught. Even jokers can rarely be hoarded safely.

PERSIAN RUMMY

One of the few games in the Rummy family played in partnership; two players team and play against two other partners.

Requirements

1. A standard 52-card deck plus four jokers, making a 56-card pack. The jokers must be of the same design and color as the pack.

Selecting Partners and Seating Positions

1. The four players seat themselves at any four places around the table; where they sit is for the moment irrelevant.

2. Any player may shuffle the pack and offer the pack to any other player for a cut.

3. When cutting for partners the jokers are excluded from the deck.

4. Each player cuts a group of cards from the pack, immediately exposing to the others the bottom card of his group. Players drawing the two low cards become partners. So do the players drawing the two high cards.

5. If players draw three or four cards of the same rank, a new deal must take place. Upon deciding which two are high and which low, partners seat themselves opposite each other.

6. To avoid controversy as to positions the several partners take, one player for each team cuts the pack and exposes the bottom card of his cut. If it is a black card, partners remain in the positions they have taken. If it is a red card, they must exchange seats.

7. The player who cut low card in the cut for partner positions starts the game by dealing the first hand. From then on the deal moves to the dealer's left, clockwise.

Object of the Game. For a team of two partners to score more points than the other team at the conclusion of three hands or deals. Points are scored by putting down melds of three or four cards of the same numerical rank or three or more cards in sequences of the same suit. The ace may be used with two or three other aces, with the king and queen of the same suit, or with the deuce and trey of the same suit. It cannot be used in the around-the-corner combination of king–ace–deuce. The jokers are not wild. They may be used only in a meld of three or four jokers. They cannot be used in a sequence.

Face cards count 10 points; all other cards have their numerical values except the ace. It counts 15 points—except when melded with a deuce and trey, in which case it counts but 1 point. The joker counts 20 points either in a meld or when caught in a player's hand, except in case a player melds the four jokers at one time, in which one case he is credited with 160 points for them, twice their normal value.

All cards melded four at a time count twice their normal value. The ace counts 15 points except when laid in a meld with the ace–deuce–trey of the same suit. It then counts but 1. A player laying down a meld of the three aces would get a point credit of 45 points, and if in a later play he laid the fourth ace on that meld, its points value would become 60 points. But if a player melds the four aces at the one time, they score 120 points for the melder.

The Deal. Beginning with the player at his left, the dealer deals each player seven cards one at a time. The twenty-ninth card is faced up, constituting the upcard, and the rest of the cards are turned face down beside it to become the stock.

The Play. Each player in his turn may (*a*) either take the top card of the stock or (*b*) take any card of the discard pile, *provided:*

1. That he takes all cards in the discard pile above the card he wants.

2. That he uses this card in a meld im-

mediately with at least two other cards already in his hand.

A player may lay down as many melds as he likes at his turn of play, and may lay off cards on his own melds or his partner's melds, keeping his layoff cards in front of him. Then he discards.

End of the Hand

1. The deal or hand ends whenever a player melds all his cards, either in proper melds or in layoffs. The player must discard his last card; he cannot meld it.

2. If the stock is exhausted without any player having gone rummy, the upcard is set aside to start the new discard pile, and the discard pile is turned over to form the new stock. This goes on until a player goes out.

3. When a player goes out, his team goes out.

Scoring

1. At the end of each hand, each player counts the value of the cards he has melded, and subtracts the value of the cards remaining in his hand.

2. Partners consolidate their credits and subtract their consolidated minuses, because partners' scores are entered as a unit on the score sheet.

3. The player who goes out (rummy) gets a 25-point bonus.

End of Game. The game ends on the completion of three hands. The side having the highest score wins.

Bonuses. The winning side gets credit for the difference between the consolidated team scores. The winning side gets a game bonus of 100 points. The game is played for so much per point. Winning partners divide their winnings evenly.

Strategy. This is a game of jokers, aces, and other high cards. Lesser melds are of trifling value. Persian Rummy fans have devised a "system" comparable with Bridge systems—e.g., the discard of an ace shows that the player has two or three jokers and the discard of a face card shows two or three aces. (These conventional meanings do not obtain if the discard is made in the same turn when a player melds.) All lower melds are used so far as possible to capture the discard pile, and to enable one partner to transfer useful cards to the other.

PAN

This gambling game, popular in the Nevada casinos and Western states, was originally called Panguinge but is now commonly known as Pan. A favorite of Filipinos in California, it is in fact an adaptation of Coon Can. Pan is a house game, though not a banking game. Substantial cash flows to and fro in the play, and the house takes a charge (a chip or so) out of each pot. The pot in Pan, as in Poker, is the sum of the antes put up by all the players, and it is taken by the player winning the hand.

Requirements

1. From six to eleven 52-card packs, used as one.

2. The eights, nines, and tens are stripped from each pack, as in Coon Can.

3. Any number of players; the more players, the more packs are used; seven to nine players make for the best game.

4. Many houses add to the pack certain extra payoff cards, such as threes, fives, and sevens. Usually the extras are spades.

5. But when extra cards are used it is essential that the operator tell the players so

and tell them how many payoff extras are in play.

Object of the Game. To go pan (rummy) by the player's melding his entire hand (ten cards) in spreads of three cards or more of the same denomination or sequences of three cards or more of the same suit.

The Deal. After the players have put up their antes the cards are shuffled by the gamekeeper, who when playing usually deals the first hand, or by the player who was low man in the cut for the deal. (In case of ties in this cut, players cut again until one man is low.) All the players help shuffle the cards, each taking a group of cards and shuffling. Then they are all put together face down on the table, and the player to the dealer's right cuts the cards.

Now the dealer takes a handful of cards from the top of the pile, and deals to each player, starting with the player at the dealer's left and going clockwise, ten cards, one at a time. If he hasn't taken off enough cards to go around ten times, he just grabs another handful and keeps dealing. If he has some left over after the deal, they go back on top of the pack. The deal moves clockwise, to the left.

After any player has gone pan (rummy), only the cards that have been used are shuffled and cut; then these are put on the bottom of the other cards which haven't been used.

Payoff Spreads. Two peculiarities of this game:

1. Players ante some amount, a chip or more, in the center of the table before the cards are dealt.

2. Only certain spreads pay off. A player can meld any spread he likes, as in Coon Can, but only the following pay off:

Ace–two–three of the same suit collects a chip from each player. If it is in spades, the sequence collects double. Any other card which extends that sequence collects an extra chip. If that other card is a spade in a spade sequence, it collects two chips.

Jack–queen–king of the same suit collects one chip. If it is in spades it collects two chips.

Threes, fives, and sevens are the only cards which, melded in the same rank, pay off.

Three of a kind in these ranks will pay off two chips except in spades, in which case they pay off three chips.

The player is paid an extra chip for each card added to the spread of the same suit and rank. For example, if a player spreads four diamond fives, he is paid off three chips. Three diamond fives (see the three-of-a-kind rule above) are worth but two chips. If the spread is in spades, two chips are collected for each extra card melded. Suppose you spread six spade sevens: then you collect three chips for the first three-card spread and two extra chips for every seven over three. You'd get nine chips for that spread. Please note well that up to this time we have been discussing spreads of cards having the same rank and the same suit. Melds mixing the suits come under a different heading.

A payoff spread using three cards of equal rank in three different suits pays off one chip. A payoff spread of four of a kind in different suits pays two chips. A three-card spread using payoff cards but having two of these cards in the same suit does not pay off, and the *aficionados* call it *Kamokee*.

When a player goes pan he (*a*) gets one

chip from each other player, (*b*) takes the pot, and (*c*) collects from each player for the points he has melded. In a word, he collects twice for spreads he melds before going rummy.

The Play. Before the leader makes his first play, each player is entitled to play his hand or drop out. If he drops, he loses the chip he has anted. It is often excellent economics, as in Poker, to drop out if the hand looks unpromising. After the dealer, who is last to decide, says whether he is in or out of the hand, the leader makes his first play. From then on no player may drop out of the game.

The leader may take either the upcard or the top card of the stock, the play rotating to the left of the leader. He then melds any spreads he can or wants to, collects from each other player if they are payoff spreads, and then discards one card.

A player may hit a player to his left, as in Coon Can (we'll remind you about hitting in just a second), thereby forcing that player to discard a card and lose his pick at his turn of play. The reminder: let's say a player to your left has before him a meld of three sixes. You have a six, and you decide to lay it off on his meld, which is hitting. That card is considered your discard. But now witness the condition in which you have left your opponent.

The rules provide that no player may have more than ten cards, counting cards melded and cards in hand. But your hit has given your opponent a total of eleven cards on the board and in his hand. With these eleven, he cannot draw a twelfth; he must reduce his holdings to ten; he is compelled to discard without picking a card of his own.

Additional Rules. A player having melded a spread of more than three nonpaying cards may remove one of those cards (which is called *switching*) to form another spread— provided the switch does not break the sequence of a long spread. You've melded four deuces. You have the ace and three of spades in your hand. Now you may switch the two of spades from the melded spread and with it form an ace–two–three spread. But, a payoff spread cannot be broken up. A player cannot borrow or switch a card from a spread on which he has already collected.

Strategy. A player should stay if he has one

matched set, or five or more combinations that would be two-way with one pack (a pair or two cards of the same suit in sequence). Four combinations are a good hand with no more than four players, but dubious with five or more. However, the game is so far a matter of pure luck that many inveterate Pan players will stay with three combinations in an eight-hand house game.

CHAPTER 5

Gin Rummy

Gin Rummy is the most popular two-handed card game of all time. Except for Poker, more money changes hands at Gin Rummy than at any other game. It is one of the finest two-handed games, and is also an excellent game for three, four, or six players. I believe its popularity is due to three main reasons: (*a*) it is easy to learn and simple to play; (*b*) every other player believes he's a champ at the game; and (*c*) the game is fast with plenty of action.

Gin Poker, the father of Gin Rummy, first made its appearance in saloons and gambling joints throughout the country back in 1899. Most present-day bridge writers and game authors erroneously credit a New York bridge expert in 1909 with the invention of Gin Rummy. It doesn't make sense, because when we compare the 1899 rules of Gin Poker with those of early Gin Rummy, we find them the same with the exception of the name of the game and several expressions used. The rules for Gin Poker are as follows: A standard pack of 52 cards is used. The game is for two players. Game is 100 points. Each player is dealt ten cards, one to each alternately. The twenty-first card is turned face up. Each player can pick off the top card of the discard pile or take a card off the top of the stock, then discard a card. The object of the game is to get sequences of three or more in a suit, or three or four of a kind. As soon as deadwood (unmatched cards) total ten or less the player can call for a showdown, and has to announce the amount of his deadwood and show his hand, laying the combinations aside. If an opponent has less deadwood than the caller (the present game's "knocker"), he and not the caller gets paid. Not only that, he gets a 10-point penalty from the caller.

Since Gin Rummy surged to the front early in 1939, many changes have taken place in the game. I've seen hundreds of games of Gin Rummy played in the United States and abroad, and except when played in the same local area, rarely have I seen the game played under the same rules. Gin Rummy, like all other card games, has had to live through an awkward age, pending the establishment of a standard practice and standard laws universally acceptable.

In my opinion there's only one practical way to evolve a set of rules for Gin Rummy, and that's the hard way—by playing hundreds and hundreds of games, identifying the bugs as they come up, rewriting laws to eliminate them, and ascertaining from the best Gin Rummy players throughout the country why they use a specific rule or scoring method. These things and others I have accomplished over the past thirty years. The end result of these efforts is the following modern method of playing Gin Rummy. I've taken the legislator's privilege of giving a name to this improved game. I call it Standard Gin Rummy.

STANDARD GIN RUMMY RULES

Requirements for Play

1. Gin Rummy is strictly a two-handed game.

   (a) Only two persons may play against each other at a time.

   (b) Although the game may involve three, four, or more players, only two of these may be in play against each other simultaneously.

2. A standard pack of 52 playing cards is used: from ace to king in the four suits. The ace is the lowest-ranking card, having a value of 1; the king, queen, and jack are valued at 10 points each. All other cards have their numerical face value. The suits have no value. Usually at hand are two decks of different back designs or colors so that a change of decks may be made upon completion of each hand.

3. Pencil and pad to keep score.

Object of the Game. The object of the game is to form matched sets, called *lays,* or *melds,* the deduction of which from the hand will bring the value of the remaining unmatched cards to a total (called a *count*) as indicated by the numerical value of the first upcard, or to meld, or lay down, all the ten cards in matched sets, which is called *Gin.*

A matched set may be either a sequence of three or more cards in the same suit—for example, the five, six, and seven of hearts, or three or four cards of the same rank, for example, the ace of diamonds, ace of clubs, and ace of spades and ace of hearts. The ace may only be used in a low sequence, for example: ace, two, and three of spades, etc. Incidentally, it is possible to meld the entire hand (ten cards) in a single sequence.

Selecting Dealer and Starting Position. By mutual consent either player may shuffle the deck.

1. Each player cuts a group of cards from the deck. Player cutting the low card deals. In case of a tie, players cut again.

2. If players want to cut for seat position, the player cutting high card takes his choice of seat.

3. The loser of a hand deals the next hand.

The Shuffle and Cut. The dealer shuffles the deck. His opponent may call for a shuffle at any time he likes prior to the cut, though the dealer retains the privilege of shuffling last. Then dealer must offer the deck to opponent for cut. If opponent refuses to cut, dealer must cut his own cards before starting the deal. When cutting, at least five cards must be in each cut portion of the deck.

The Deal

1. The dealer deals his opponent ten cards and himself ten cards, one at a time, alternately, the opponent being dealt the first card off the top of the deck and so on down until the dealer gets the last, twentieth card.

2. The twenty-first card is dealt on the table face up—the *upcard;* the remainder of the deck is placed face down beside the upcard to form the *stock.* The upcard determines the maximum number of points in unmatched cards with which a player may knock. For example, if the dealer turns up a six-spot, the player who proposes to knock must have in his hand 6 points or less in unmatched cards. It is suggested that when playing this game, you note on the score sheet, at the moment it is turned, the numerical value of the twenty-first card, the upcard. If the twenty-first dealt card is an ace, a player is not permitted to knock. He has no choice but to play for gin. This eliminates arguments. If the twenty-first card is a spade, the points won in that hand are doubled. *Note:* This double-spade rule may be waived if mutually agreed upon at the start of the game.

3. The remainder of the deck, called the stock, is placed on the table and is spread slightly to the right by the dealer. This is done to minimize the possibility of accidentally picking up or seeing the two top cards of the stock when drawing a card.

Optional Deal. An extra deck of cards must be made available for this optional deal. Any participant shuffles the deck. Any other participant cuts and places the face-down deck halfway into its card case. Then, the dealer deals out the two gin hands, but instead of facing the twenty-first card dealt in the center of the table to form the upcard (first card of discard pile), he deals it face down to the nondealer, giving him eleven cards in all. His first play will be a discard.

Next the top card of the pack inside the card case is turned face up for all to see. This card replaces the dealt upcard (in the original deal) and determines the maximum number of points or less in unmatched cards with which each contestant may knock. After the first hand is finished, the faced card of this extra deck is placed on the bottom of the deck and the second card from the top is turned face up to denote the maximum number of points or less in unmatched cards with which a player may knock for his second dealt hand. And so it goes, hand after hand, until the end of the game, when this extra deck is reshuffled and placed halfway into the card case, and the above procedure is repeated.

This optional deal is highly recommended when playing multiple partnerships in which the knock number for all contestants is determined by the same faced card in the card case.

The Play

1. The nondealer begins the play either by taking the upcard into his hand or by declining it.

2. If he declines it, the dealer in his turn has the option of taking it or declining it.

3. If the dealer declines the upcard, the nondealer must take the top card of the stock.

4. After taking the first card (either the upcard or the top card of the stock), that player must discard one card from his hand onto the discard pile. Play continues with each player in turn having the option of either picking his opponent's discard (upcard) or drawing the top card from the stock. After a player has picked the upcard or the top card of the stock and has discarded, his turn of play is completed, and he must wait for the completion of his opponent's play before he can make his next play. The rules in play apply alike to dealer and nondealer, and the play continues thus alternately until a decision or no-game has been attained.

5. If a player has gin—i.e., if he can meld all ten of his cards—he turns his discard face down on the table, and announces "Gin!" Then he places all his melds, separate from each other, face up on the table. The opponent then must face all his melds separately on the table, placing his unmatched cards face up to one side. He then counts the total of his unmatched cards.

6. If a player wants to knock, he turns his discard face down on the table and announces "Knock!" or "Down!" He places his melds face up on the table separate from each other, and places his unmatched cards face up to one side. Then he adds the numerical values of the unmatched cards, and announces the count.

When a Player May Knock. When a player holds enough melds to bring the total count of his unmatched cards down to the point value or less as shown by the first upcard, he may either knock or, as he elects, continue playing. Should he decide to knock, he must first put his discard face down on the discard pile and announce his knock as described above, meld his combinations, and set aside his unmatched cards. After he has announced his count, his opponent must then expose his hand, and is permitted to discard in any of the following ways:

1. He may place on the table, separate from each other, any melds he holds.

2. He may lay off any cards which can be added to the knocker's melds.

3. He now places on the knocker's unmatched cards an equal value of his own unmatched cards.

4. The knocker now gets credit for the value of unmatched cards still in the possession of his opponent.

This is called a *box,* or *line*. It is the score of that hand.

The Underknock. Should the opponent have a total of unmatched cards less than the knocker's total or count after melding and laying off cards, the opponent wins the box, and is credited, moreover, with the difference in points between the knocker's hand and his own hand, plus a bonus of 25 points for scoring an underknock. If the knocker and opponent are tied in unmatched cards, the opponent wins the hand and scores a bonus of 25 points.

To Go Gin. If a player lays down his ten cards in melds, he has gone Gin. In this event his opponent may put down only his own melds, and is not allowed to lay off cards on the other player's melds. The player who went Gin gets credit for all his opponent's unmatched cards plus a 25-point bonus.

No-Game. Should the hand be played down to the fiftieth card, leaving two cards face down in the stock, the player whose turn it is to draw may pick up the last discard and knock or go Gin, but he cannot pick up either of the last two down cards. Should he fail to knock or go Gin with the upturned card, the deal is considered at an end, and a no-game is declared. Neither player receives any credits.

If the deck is found to have less or more than 52 cards, the game in play automatically becomes void, regardless of what the scores may be, the moment the discovery is made (though all previous completed games and hands stand and are valid).

End of Game. The game ends when one of the players scores 150 points or more.

1. Winner of the game scores the difference between the two totals.

2. An extra 25 points is added to each player's score for each box won.

3. Winner of the game gets a game bonus of 150 points for winning.

In the following sample Standard Gin game, John Scarne's new game-scoring method is employed. The hand score for each player is written down at the left, then a dash followed by the cumulative game score to the right. This makes it known to each player at all times how far ahead or behind he is.

(Top) A gin is worth 25 points. It shows all cards in runs of at least three of the same denomination or in numerical sequence by suit. (Bottom) A player "knocks"—here with three odd points: an ace and deuce.

SAMPLE SCORING FOR A STANDARD GIN RUMMY GAME

	You	*He*
First hand	11—11	
Second hand		45—45
Third hand		5—50
Fourth hand	40—51	
Fifth hand	25—76	
Sixth hand	19—95	
Seventh hand	27—122	
Eighth hand	40—162	
Game scores	162	50
Box bonuses	150	50
Game bonus	150	
Total score	462	100
		—100 Minus loser's
		(He) score
		362 Your net winnings

First hand: You knock with 8. He has 19. You score 11.

Second hand: He goes Gin. You have 20. He scores 20 + 25 points Gin bonus, 45 in all. He scores 45.

Third hand: He knocks with 3. You have 8. He scores 5, giving him a total of 50.

Fourth hand: You knock with 9. He has 49. You score 40 and your new total is 51.

Fifth hand: He knocks with 3. You also

have 3. You score 25, the underknock bonus. Now your score is 76.

Sixth hand: You knock with 7. He has 26. You score 19 and your new total is 95.

Seventh hand: You go Gin. He has 2, you score 2 + 25 points Gin bonus, adding 27 to your score. Your new total is 122.

Eighth hand: You knock with 5. He has 45, adding 40 to your score. This puts you over the 150-point game mark with a total of 162 points and gives you game. You won six boxes, 150 points at 25 points each. He won two boxes, worth 50 points to him. Then you add 150 points for winning the game. Your total score is 462, his is 100. So your winnings for the game are the difference in score, or 362 points net. At 1 cent a point you collect $3.62 for your win.

Shutout, Skunked, Schneidered, Blitzed

1. If a player scores 150 points or more

before his opponent scores any points at all, the winner gets the 150-point game bonus plus a 150-point shutout bonus—plus all other credits.

2. *Variations in Scoring.* A very popular variation is to double everything for a shutout —point total, box bonuses, and game bonus. It's popular because it's exciting, especially thrilling to get that big score when you schneider your opponent. But of course it does throw the game off balance. A whole evening's play may be decided by one lucky shutout game. If you don't mind that sort of thing, go ahead and use this hopped-up scoring system.

Optional Standard Gin Rummy Game Ending Variants. For the player who prefers a longer game, the author recommends 200 or 250 points as a completed game. In that case the Gin, underknock, and box bonuses remain at 25 points each. But the game bonus

and shutout bonus are each 200 points for a 200-point game and are each 250 points for a 250-point game. Some Gin clubs now play 200-point games.

Unit Scoring. This is a streamlined method of scoring. At the completion of a game and before the final tally, the right-hand digit of each entry on the score sheet is canceled off. Thus, you have won a game with the following credits:

22 points' difference in scores
60 points for boxes
100 points for game

It adds up to 182 points, but in unit scoring you give yourself:

2 points for difference in scores
6 points for boxes
10 points for game

It adds up to 18 points. Some players like this method because it's fast and easy.

STANDARD HOLLYWOOD GIN RUMMY

Standard Hollywood Gin is played exactly as is Standard Gin Rummy. The only difference is that in Standard Hollywood Gin, three games are played at the same time.

The scoring is not so complicated as it may sound.

1. When a player wins the first hand he scores in Game 1.

2. The second hand he wins is scored under Game 1 and Game 2.

3. The third hand he wins is scored under Game 1, Game 2, and Game 3.

4. Every hand he wins thereafter is scored under all three games.

5. If a player scores 150 or more points under Game 1 and has lesser scores under Game 2 and Game 3, he thereafter enters his scores under Game 2 and Game 3.

6. If a player scores 150 or more points in Game 1 and Game 2, he thereafter enters his scores under Game 3.

7. A game ends when a player has reached 150 or more points in all three games.

Here's how it works, in a sample game between Players A and B.

Sample Game Scoring for Standard Hollywood Gin Rummy

First Hand. The first step is to enter A and B names alternately across six sections of a

score sheet. Player A wins the first hand by 25 points. This score is entered to A's credit in Game 1, but nothing is written on any of the other game scores.

Game 1		Game 2		Game 3	
A	B	A	B	A	B
25—25					

The Score Sheet after the First Hand

Second Hand. A wins the second hand by 18 points. He adds this to his score in Game 1 for a total of 43 points. Then he enters 18 points to his credit as his first score in Game 2. Nothing is entered on the score of Game 3.

Game 1		Game 2		Game 3	
A	B	A	B	A	B
25—25		18—18			
18—43					

The Score Sheet after the Second Hand

Third Hand. A wins the third hand by 36 points. He adds this to his score in Game 1 for a total of 79 points. He adds those 36 points to his score in Game 2 for a total of 54 points. Finally he scores 36 points as his first entry in Game 3.

Game 1		Game 2		Game 3	
A	B	A	B	A	B
25—25		18—18		36—36	
18—43		36—54			
36—79					

The Score Sheet after the Third Hand

Fourth Hand. B wins the fourth hand by 39 points and it is entered on the score sheet to his credit under Game 1.

Game 1		Game 2		Game 3	
A	B	A	B	A	B
25—25	39—39	18—18		36—36	
18—43		36—54			
36—79					

Fifth Hand. B wins the fifth hand by 19 points. He adds this to his score in Game 1 and enters 19 points in Game 2.

Game 1		Game 2		Game 3	
A	B	A	B	A	B
25—25	39—39	18—18	19—19	36—36	
18—43	19—58	36—54			
36—79					

The Score Sheet after the Fifth Hand

Sixth Hand. A wins the sixth hand by 50 points, adding this to his score in Game 1, Game 2, and Game 3.

Game 1		Game 2		Game 3	
A	B	A	B	A	B
25—25	39—39	18—18	19—19	36—36	
18—43	19—58	36—54		50—86	
36—79		50—104			
50—129					

The Score Sheet after the Sixth Hand

Seventh Hand. A wins the seventh hand by 53 points and these are added to his score in all three games. By passing 150 points, A has won the first and second games. Since A and B are playing a series of three games, they must continue to play until Game 3 is finished. Whatever happens from now on, Game 1 and Game 2 are over.

Game 1		Game 2		Game 3	
A	B	A	B	A	B
25—25	39—39	18—18	19—19	36—36	
18—43	19—58	36—54		50—86	
36—79		50—104		53—139	
50—129		53—157			
53—182					

The Score Sheet after the Seventh Hand

Eighth Hand. A wins the eighth hand by 22 points and it is entered on the score sheet to his credit under Game 3. By passing 150 points in the third game, the three games

Game 1		Game 2		Game 3	
A	B	A	B	A	B
25—25	39—39	18—18	19—19	36—36	
18—43	19—58	36—54		50—86	
36—79		50—104		53—139	
50—129		53—157		22—161	
53—182					

The Score Sheet at the End of Three Games

have been finished. Since three games have been completed, the game series ends and A is the winner in all three. The score of each game is totaled exactly as if only one game was played (see page 87). The box bonuses of 25 points a hand and the game bonus of 150 points apply. A has scored a schneider in the third game. A wins the first game by 349 points, the second game by 363 points, and the third by 561 points, for a grand total of 1,273 points.

Standard Gin Rummy for Three Players

Gamblers call this game *Round Robin Gin Rummy*. The name comes from a horse-racing idiom. Although three players take part, only two are in play against each other simultaneously. To determine which two shall start, any player, by consent of the others, shuffles and three cards are cut. Low man—he whose exposed card is of lowest rank—sits out the first hand. The other two play a game of Gin Rummy.

The score of the first hand is credited to the winner, and the loser drops out. The winner proceeds to play the next hand against the third man. (Generally the nonplayer keeps the score.) So it goes, loser giving way to nonplayer hand by hand, until one of the three scores 150 points or more.

The winner is paid off in the amount of his credit over each opponent. The player with the second-highest score collects from low man. A player scoring a shutout can collect his shutout bonus only from the player who scored zero. For example, A scores 160 points; B, 90; and C, none. A gets credit for a shutout over C but not over B. Value of credits and bonuses is the same as in two-handed Standard Gin Rummy. In three-handed Gin Rummy a player may collect from two players, lose to two players, or win from one and lose to one.

Captains

This is a variation of Standard Gin for three players, borrowed from Backgammon, where it is called *Chouette* or "in the box." A plays the first game as captain against B and C, B playing the first hand and continuing to play as long as he wins. When he loses, C takes his place and continues to play until he loses, when B comes back again, and so on until the game ends. The captain keeps playing to the end of the game, regardless of whether he wins or loses. A single score is kept and totaled at the end of the game. The captain wins or loses the net total from or to each of the opponents. Then B becomes the captain playing against A and C, and so on. This principle can be extended to five or seven or any other odd number of players as explained under Partnership Gin.

Standard Partnership Gin Rummy

This is four-handed Standard Gin Rummy. Two players are teamed against the other two. Two games of two-handed Gin Rummy are played simultaneously and the partners enter their score as one. The players cut for partners, holders of the two highest exposed cards being teamed against the holders of the two lowest. The rules of Standard Gin Rummy apply. The only variation is in the scoring.

Team scores, not players' scores, are entered. Example: A and B are partners playing against C and D. A, playing the first hand against his opponent C, wins by 28 points. D, playing against B, wins by 20 points. Team A-B wins the box by 8 points. That is the only score entered on the sheet. Mind you, for it is crucial, the score is not entered in Partnership Gin Rummy until both hands have been played, counted, and balanced off against each other.

In each succeeding hand teammates compete against alternate opponents. In this way each player has the opportunity of playing against a different opponent on each alternate hand. Example: As before, A and B are partners playing against C and D. A plays the first hand against C. B plays the first hand against D. At the end of the hand, A twists around in his chair and plays against D, while B turns around to play against C. At the end of the second hand, all players shift back to the original position. This alternation continues with each hand until the game ends. When any two players end their hand, they may relax until the other players finish. Then all the scores for that hand (as stated before) are computed together and credited as a single score.

Game is 250 points, game bonus 250, shutout bonus 250, and all other scoring is as in two-handed Standard Gin Rummy.

Standard Multiple-Partnership Gin Rummy

Team play can be extended beyond four hands. There can be three on each side, and I have seen as many as eight men play in two teams of four each. Game should be increased 50 points for each extra pair above the 250-point game of four-handed partnership. Otherwise the principles of four-handed Standard Partnership Gin prevail. The arrangement of players can be made to suit convenience; either team A on one side of a long table with team B on the opposite side; or in groupings of four, two from each team at each table.

Standard Hollywood Partnership Gin Rummy

Standard Hollywood Partnership Gin Rummy follows the rules of Standard Hollywood Gin Rummy except as noted:

1. This is a four-handed partnership game. Two players are teamed against the other two. Two games of two-handed Standard Hollywood Gin Rummy are played simultaneously and partners enter their score as one.

2. Game is 250 points, shutout bonus 250 points. All other bonuses remain the same. For further information about Partnership and Multiple Partnership Play, see pages 95 to 97.

Old-Fashioned Gin Rummy

The Old-Fashioned, or Turn-up, Gin Rummy version is played under the Standard Gin Rummy Rules, except for the following:

1. The game ends when one of the players scores 100 or more points.

2. A player may knock whenever the total of his unmatched cards is 10 or less. The rank of the first upcard (the twenty-first dealt card) is disregarded.

3. Knock bonus is 10 points, gin bonus 20 points, box bonus 25 points, game and shutout bonuses each 100 points.

4. *Optional rule:* The dealer deals eleven cards to the nondealer and ten to himself. The nondealer for his first play must discard one of his eleven cards. Thereafter the play of the hand remains the same as in Standard Gin Rummy.

Spades Double Turn-Up Gin

If the twenty-first card is a spade, the points won in that hand are doubled. Because of this feature, game is 150 instead of 100.

Oklahoma Gin

In this variation of Old-Fashioned Gin, which was first called Cedarhurst Gin, the twenty-first card, which the dealer has faced and made the upcard, determines the maximum number of points in unmatched cards with which a player may knock. For example, if the dealer turns up a six-spot (suit does not matter), then the player who proposes to knock must have in his hand 6 points or less in unmatched cards—as compared with the regulation 10 points or less of Old-Fashioned Gin Rummy. It is suggested that when playing this game you note on the score sheet, at the moment it is turned, the numerical value

of the twenty-first card, the upcard. It avoids debate.

Game is 200 points. Penalty for underknock is 20 points, gin bonus 25 points, boxes 25 points. If the upcard is an ace, there is no knock—players must go for gin. Oklahoma usually incorporates the spades double feature: when the upcard is a spade, the count of boxes and bonuses is doubled.

Oklahoma Gin with Extra Bonuses (Kisses)

The same as Oklahoma Gin except that besides the usual bonuses for gin and underknock, two extra boxes (50 points) are given for gin and one extra box (25 points) is given for underknock. However, in Partnership Gin, only the winning team gets the extra boxes. If A is ginned by X for 37 points but his partner B gins Y for 40 points, A-B gets 3 points plus 2 boxes and X-Y gets nothing. If spades are double, bonus boxes are doubled, 2 for underknock, 4 for gin. *A vital point in Oklahoma strategy:* the fact that only the team winning the hand can get extra boxes is a crucial factor in the play of the hand. If your partner has been ginned for 67 points and it appears that you can't get it back, even with gin, don't try for gin unless the game is involved and then only if you think that going gin may save the game. Here's why: you can't get extra boxes by going gin whereas your opponent can get extras by ginning you. The odds are far and away against you. On the other hand, if your partner has given you a comfortable lead so that even if you are ginned you will not lose the box, it's worth trying for gin even with unlikely (but not practically impossible) chances. The odds favor it. You can get extra boxes; your opponent can't.

Schneider Doubles Everything. Most Oklahoma players and many regular Gin Rummy players double points, game, and box bonuses in the case of a shutout or schneider. This is rather high flying and makes for terrific swings, but some like it that way.

Layoff Gin Rummy

The game is played exactly like Old-Fashioned Gin Rummy, with the following exceptions:

1. A player is permitted to lay off cards on gin.

2. A player who scores an underknock gets a bonus of 15 points instead of the 10-point bonus of Old-Fashioned Gin Rummy.

3. The gin bonus is 25 points.

4. And, should a player go gin by laying off cards after his opponent has knocked, he wins the hand and receives a 30-point bonus plus the difference in points between players.

Super Gin

This is Layoff Gin with two added features:

1. *Gin on Gin.* Laying off all unmatched cards on an opponent's gin to go gin yourself is worth 50 points.

2. *Eleven-card Gin.* Going gin with all eleven cards matched (not requiring the discard of the eleventh card) is worth 50 points.

Straight Gin Rummy

Straight Gin Rummy is not much different from Old-Fashioned Gin Rummy itself. Well, it *is* Old-Fashioned Gin Rummy, but the scoring is drastically simplified. As you will note from the following, the saving on bookkeeping is the main reason for its popularity:

1. Players decide at the start of game the amount of the game stake and the amount each box shall be worth. For instance, they may decide to play $1 a game and 25 cents a box. *Note:* As a rule, boxes are assigned a value of one-fourth, or thereabouts, the value of the game.

2. The player who first scores 100 or more points is the winner. The difference in count

between winner and loser is irrelevant.

3. If a player scores a shutout, that winning player is paid double the amount of the agreed game stake and double the amount of extra boxes won, if any.

Round-the-Corner Gin

The rules of Old-Fashioned Gin Rummy, of which this is a variation, apply with the following exceptions:

1. The ace may be played in either the high or the low sequence of the same suit—hence the name Round-the-Corner. *Example:* ace–two–three; ace–king–queen; or king–ace–two, or of course these sequences may be extended.

2. Aces instead of counting 1 point when unmatched count 15 points. This latter rule makes it harder for a player to hold a count of 10 or less, and cuts down knocks and underknocks. Since the ace may be used in three sequences, making it easier to go gin in Round-the-Corner than in Gin Rummy, the 20-point bonus for Old-Fashioned Gin is reduced to 10 points in Round-the-Corner. Regardless of the difference in the gin bonus, the box scores tend to run higher in this variation, because players tend to get caught with high unmatched cards in their hands. They try to organize round-the-corner sequences, which are high-card sequences; and the ace, remember, counts 15 instead of 1.

3. Game is 150 points.

4. Partnership (four-handed) game is 175 points.

JERSEY GIN

How often do you wish you could have a three-handed game of Gin, all three persons playing at the same time? Here it is. A Jersey politician brought it into my life and yours; he told me that three-handed Gin was being played at several political clubs in Jersey City. I drifted over and investigated it, and found first of all that the game in that form was full of mathematical bugs. I've undertaken to correct these defects, and the result is the following great game, which I've taken the discoverer's liberty of naming Jersey Gin. It's a combination of Old-Fashioned Gin and Six- and Seven-card Knock Rummy. (See pages 57 to 58.)

Requirements. A standard pack of 52 playing cards.

Selection of Dealer and Seating Positions. Any player shuffles the deck, which is then cut by any other player. Three cards are dealt face up, one to each player. The two players drawing in low cards sit opposite each other. The player drawing the high card chooses his seat; in other words, he decides who he prefers to have throwing to him or, in other words, which opponent's discards he would rather play.

Player drawing the high card becomes the first dealer.

Value of the Cards. Same as in all forms of

Gin Rummy; ace, 1 point; jack, queen, and king, 10 points; all other cards, their face value.

The Deal

1. Dealer shuffles the pack, and offers it to the player on his right to be cut; if that player declines to cut, the third player may do so; if he declines, the dealer must cut the cards himself before dealing.

2. On the completion of each hand, which is called a box, the deal passes to the player on the previous dealer's left, and continues clockwise.

3. Dealer deals ten cards to each player one at a time clockwise, starting with the player at his left.

4. The rest of the cards are placed in the center of the table face down. They are the stock.

Play of the Hand. The rules of Old-Fashioned Gin Rummy govern this game, with the following exceptions:

When a player knocks, the score entered to his credit is the total reached by adding the difference between his score and one opponent's to the difference between his score and the other opponent's.

Let's have an example. Only the winner of the box can get any credits in the scoring. Now, A knocks with a count of 5 points. B has a count of 15 after melding and laying off on A's melds. C has a count of 13 after melding and laying off on A's and B's melds. Now, subtract A's 5 from B's 15. That leaves a difference of 10. Subtract A's 5 from C's 13. The difference is 8. Add up the two differences. A, the knocker, is credited on the score sheet for 18 points. The counts of B and C have been canceled out in the calculation of the two differences; each gets zero for the box. Should a player underknock the knocker, that player gets the difference in points between his score and that of the knocker, plus the difference in points between his score and that of the third player, plus a 10-point bonus for the underknock. Should two players score an underknock, only one can be legally declared the underknocker. That one is the player with the lowest point total. Should two underknockers have the same number of points, the player to the knocker's left is declared the underknocker and winner.

A player going gin gets the total point difference of both opponents, as described above, plus a bonus of 20 points for gin from each opponent, a total bonus of 40 points.

Break. The game does not end in a no-game, as in Old-Fashioned Gin Rummy, when the stock gets down to its last three cards. Instead:

Should any player fail to knock or go gin before only three cards are left in the stock, the player whose turn it is to pick the top card of the stock becomes the breaker (the man who puts his meld down first). That player must pick that top card, unless the upcard (top card on the discard pile) can be used in a meld. After the break, after the stock is reduced to less than three cards, players cannot knock.

The breaker must lay down his melds separately and hold his own unmatched cards in his hand. The player to the breaker's left must pick a card (top card or upcard) and do likewise—and he may lay off cards on the breaker's melds. The third player also picks a card and must lay down his melds, and may lay off on both other players. If, because of picking an upcard for use in a meld, there remain cards in the stock after that round, the play continues and players may continue laying off on any meld on the table. Should a player go gin after the break, the rules of Gin Rummy apply: the hand is completed, and no layoffs are permitted; but the player does not get a bonus for going gin; he is credited only for the opponents' unmatched cards.

When the last card of the stock has been picked and the last player has discarded, the player with the lowest count becomes winner of that box, and he is credited with points as set forth for the knocker on page 86.

If the breaker is one of two players to tie in total of unmatched cards, he is the winner. If two players other than the breaker tie for low, the player to the breaker's left is the winner of that box. He gets credit for point difference only from the player with the higher total points. At the break and after the break, a player cannot pick an upcard unless it can be used in a meld.

Additional Rules for Gin Rummy

Misdeals. A misdeal is declared, and the dealer of the hand immediately starts a new deal, whenever any of the following improprieties are discovered (there are no penalties for the dealer or the responsible player):

1. If a card is turned over during the deal.

2. If either player or both players have been dealt an incorrect number of cards.

3. If, during the play of the hand, either player or both players are found to be holding an incorrect number of cards.

4. If a player deals out of turn and the error is discovered before a play has been completed.

5. If a player looks at an opponent's card or cards during the deal.

6. If a card is found face up in the stock either during the deal or during the play.

False Knocks and Sundry Errors. The following are some irregularities that often come up in a game:

1. A player who inadvertently knocks with a count of more than the required number of points in unmatched cards indicated on the first upcard must place his entire hand face up on the table and continue to play it thus exposed.

2. If while holding a gin hand a player fails to knock and his opponent thereupon knocks with 10 points or less, the player does not get credit for a gin hand, but instead gets credit only for an underknock.

3. Once a player has laid down his hand and announced his total and it is entered on the score sheet, he cannot call for rectification of some mistake he has made. An opponent is not required to inform a player that he has committed an error or failed to lay off a card or failed to meld his holding to his best advantage, nor is he required to notify a player that he is calling an incorrect count to his disadvantage.

4. In melding, a player may rearrange his melds in any way he likes, but not (*a*) if the final count has been entered on the score sheet; or (*b*) if an opponent has laid off one or more cards on the player's melds as first arranged.

For Money Players: One More Rule. It is recommended that two packs of cards, with backs of different colors, be used in the play. While the dealer is shuffling for the deal, the nondealer is giving the other pack a preliminary shuffle, after which it is set to one side. It is shuffled again by the loser of this hand before he deals the next hand. Reasoning:

1. Many players shuffle so badly that one or more of the melds of the previous hand are undisturbed in the shuffle. Their recurrence in due order in the stock pile makes the game a mere memory test, and a dull one.

2. This rule insures two shuffles for the pack and doubles the troubles of the cheater.

3. Even if neither player shuffles skillfully, it is harder to remember the melds of two hands ago.

Discards. The following covers irregularities in discarding:

1. A card is not discarded until it has been placed on top of the discard pile. Once it touches the discard pile it completes a play and cannot be recaptured by the player.

2. When a knock or gin is announced the discarded card must be placed face down on the top of the discard pile. But if the player accidentally discards the wrong card when knocking or going gin, that card may be retrieved and the error corrected without penalty.

3. A player cannot touch or pick a card either from the stock or from the discard pile until his opponent has discarded and completed his play.

4. A player cannot discard a card before taking his pick.

5. A player cannot discard the upcard he just picked until his next turn of play.

6. Once a player touches an upcard in his turn of play, he is compelled to take that card.

7. If at the start of play a player should refuse the first discard (the upcard) by stating his decision verbally, he cannot then decide to take it. His refusal to accept it is his final decision on that card.

8. If at the start of the play the nondealer should take the top card of the stock without granting the dealer a chance to take or refuse the upcard, then that play stands; but in his own turn of play the dealer may now take either one of the two discards or take the top card of the stock.

9. No player is permitted to spread the discards to see what cards have been played.

Picking from the Stock Pile. Here are the rules for covering picking from the pile:

1. Once a player has taken the top card of the stock in his correct turn of play, he cannot replace it and decide to take the upcard instead. And this ruling holds even though the player may not have looked at the card.

2. If a player inadvertently picks off the stock two cards instead of one, or inadvertently sees the face of the card below the one he has just taken, or his opponent has reason to believe that he has seen it, then his oppo-

nent may, if he likes, ask to see the face of the card the player has just drawn. If this demand is made the player must comply.

3. If a player plays out of turn, taking the top card of the stock for the second time in a row, then he must discard the last card picked and his opponent may now pick either of the two top discards or the top card of the stock.

Coaching in Partnership or Multiple-Hand Gin. Gin, as I have said, is essentially a two-handed game and therefore coaching or advising a partner is not permitted. Not only is it against the rules for one partner to advise or consult with another partner as to the wisdom of a play, or the wisdom of going down, but no guiding remarks are permitted, not even a reference to the score, except that it is permissible for a partner who has finished his hand to bring to the attention of a still-playing partner the result of his game. But otherwise a partner is not permitted to volunteer information as to the current state of the score. He must not say, "Partner, I lost 47 and that gives our opponents 130 total, so play to save the game." However, if the playing partner says, "How do we stand? What is the total score at the present moment?" the information may be given to him.

Looking at Partner's Hand. When the layout of the game is such that partners sit next to each other, it is perfectly legitimate to look at your partner's hand. In fact, it is wise to do so, and act in accordance with the information thus gained. Whether your partner has a bad hand and is likely to lose or a good hand likely to win should be taken into consideration, especially in relation to the current score.

You are permitted in the play of your own hand to benefit all you can from your observation of your partner's hand. But you must not give him any advantage as a result of your watching his play of his hand. This is specially important in the case of errors.

Errors. A basic rule in cards is that the cards stand for themselves. Therefore, if you see an opponent making a miscount—calling a six, seven, and four as 15, for instance—you are privileged to point out the error. You are obligated to do so if your partner makes that error or if the opponent has made a miscount in your favor. Of course, you are also privileged to point out the error when your partner has made a miscount against you. But if you are watching your partner's hand and see that he is about to make a mistake—going

down with more than 10 through miscounting, or calling gin when he doesn't have gin—you must not prevent the error. You must not give him any benefit as a result of your watching the hand.

Gin Rummy Strategy and Mathematics

I'm not going to try to calculate the exact percentage of influence exerted by chance and skill in any specific Gin Rummy situation, because (a) there are 15,820,024 possible ten-card hands in Gin Rummy, (b) no two players will play the same kind of game consistently, and (c) the variations in the way a gin player uses the cards he catches are the crucial factors. But, I can assure you that skill is a more powerful factor in Gin Rummy than in the Rummy games involving more than two players, and if you will take time out to study the Gin Rummy strategy tips that follow, you'll win many more Gin games than before.

In the game of Gin Rummy there are 52 three-card melds of three of a kind, i.e., cards of the same rank: Three aces, three deuces, and so on. There are 44 melds of three cards of the same suit in sequence, i.e., three–four–five of hearts, nine–ten–jack of spades, and the like. After you have formed a three-card meld it is twice as hard to extend three of a kind into four of a kind as it is to extend a sequence. A sequence meld can be extended at either end (except ace–two–three and jack–queen–king), whereas three of a kind can be bettered only one way. Besides, a sequence meld of four cards can be extended into five, and one of five into one of six; but four cards of equal rank have no further possibilities. They're dead.

Early in the game—and whenever possible —it is advisable to discard a card ranking one or two away (preferably one away) and in a different suit to the one previously discarded by your opponent. *Example:* Your opponent's first discard is the nine of clubs, which is probably a bait card. Hence, bait or no bait, your safest discard is either the eight or ten of diamonds, eight or ten of hearts, or eight or ten of spades, or the seven or jack in spades, hearts, or diamonds.

If you do not hold such a card, your next best bet is to discard a card of rank equal to one which your opponent has previously discarded. There are only four possible ways in which an equal-rank card can be used against you. Any card can be used six ways in a meld. That is, unless you're holding *stoppers* —cards which will prevent a discard from being used in a meld by your opponent.

The Gin Rummy player, however, prior to his first play, must be able to visualize and memorize all the possible melds in a hand the instant he picks it up. He must be able to calculate at sight the probabilities for his two-of-a-kind sequences; and he must not overlook any melds he may hold.

There is a way of cultivating this knack of forming mental pictures and avoiding fatal plays in the early stages of the game. It lies in a way of picking up cards which have just been dealt. Never pick up all your ten cards at once. It is impossible to impress them on your mind when they are seen in their natural confusion. Pick them up one at a time, sorting them as you go, impressing them on your mind, and marshaling them for your first play. Moving thus deliberately, you can appraise the odds on every possible combination of your cards; and at the very least, you have them in orderly array when the time comes to make your first draw. This is the secret. More players make their bad play at the start of the hand than at any other time. Never forget it—pick up your hand slowly and arrange it carefully. Think—first about your own resources and strategy, then about your opponent's.

Gin Rummy is a game of deduction and counterdeduction. You must try to figure what is in your opponent's hand so that (1) you won't give him any useful cards, and (2) you won't be holding cards for an impossible or unlikely meld.

In Gin Rummy, the seven is the most valuable card in the deck as far as forming melds is concerned, just as the seven is the crucial number at dice because it occurs most often. The seven can be used to extend melds more than any other card. The seven can be used in seven different seven-card-sequence melds, whereas the most valuable of the 12 other cards can be used only to form six-card sequences.

In conclusion, I submit the following five rules of play every winning Gin Rummy player must know:

1. Try to get on the score as quickly as possible.

2. Expect your opponent's first two discards to be bait.

3. When tempted to speculate, do so with a poor hand; don't with a good hand.

4. It's usually smart to knock as soon as possible.

5. Toward the end of the game, play the score or try to keep under and prevent your opponent from winning the game that hand.

Protection Against Gin Rummy Cheats

The best Gin player in the country doesn't stand a winning chance against even the average Gin cheat. So if you want to play winning Gin you must first learn to protect yourself from the sharks. Here's what to watch out for:

Bottom Stack. After a hand has been played and it is the cheater's turn to deal, he scoops up the cards and leaves an entire meld, usually four of a kind, on the bottom of the pack. Then he gives the pack a riffle shuffle that does not disturb the bottom four cards. He cuts about one-third of the pack off the top, puts it on the bottom, and offers the pack to be cut. Most players cut at about the center. This puts the wanted meld near the top, and each player in the deal receives two of these four of a kinds.

The cheat knows two of the cards in your hand, and you don't know that he has two of the same value. Later in the play you will usually discard one of those cards, giving him his meld. Or he will throw you one, proceeding to underknock your knock by laying off that fourth card on your meld. This is one of the most common of all cheating devices in Gin, and one of the most effective, because it is impossible to accuse anyone of resorting to it. An honest player might even shuffle and cut the cards the same way without intending anything crooked.

You can protect yourself against the bottom stack by shuffling the cards before the dealer shuffles.

51-Card Deck. This may seem amateurish, but it is one of the most common and least hazardous cheating devices. When detected it can be made to look like an honest error. When he removes the new deck from the case, the cheat leaves one card behind. He knows what card that is.

The advantage appears trivial. But is it? Let's see. Suppose the card left unnoticed in the box is the eight of diamonds. What can it do for him? First, he will rarely try to make a meld of eights, because he knows that the chances are only 25 percent of normal. Second, he knows—and you don't—that the chance of getting a meld in a sequence involving the eight of diamonds is zero. There are three such melds: the six–seven–eight, the seven–eight–nine, and the eight–nine–ten. With the three melds of eights in which the diamond would figure, this makes six dead melds out of a total of 96 melds in the game. This is a terrific advantage.

There is also a psychological throw-off. If, during the play, you find the missing card in the box, the cheat promptly blames you. "Why," he asks, if he knows his business, "didn't you take them all out when we started?"

The chances are that, having forgotten by this time who did remove the deck, you will mumble your apologies. You can protect yourself against this ruse by counting the cards before you start to play. Better yet, look in the box.

No Cut. Some cheats will keep a certain group of cards at the top of the pack, shuffle some cards over them and then deal without offering the deck for the cut. The effect on the game is the same as in the bottom stack. If you ask for a cut, they blandly murmur "Sorry." If you don't you're a dead duck.

When the cards have been cut into two blocks, but the cut has not yet been completed, some sharpers will lean back, light a cigarette, then simply pick up the cards and put them back as they were before. The lapse of time and the intervening stage business may make you forget which block should go on which. If caught at it, they apologize for the error. Don't take your eye off your game.

Dealing from Half the Deck. When the cheat knows what the top cards are, he shuffles, you cut, and instead of completing the cut he picks up the lower portion of the deck and deals from it. Then he completes the cut by putting the remaining cards of the lower pile on the top.

It is a casual little informality, but the cheat now knows precisely what cards are going to appear. Don't allow anyone to deal from half the pack. Insist on the completion of the cut before the deal begins.

Signaling. He may look like an authentic kibitzer. But when you're playing for money, watch him. Satisfy yourself that no onlooker with access to your hand is signaling.

Signaling is often done, both amateurishly and expertly. It is easy and deadly effective in Gin Rummy because all that your opponent needs to find out is whether you have a high or low count in unmatched cards. A well-conceived signal system is hard to detect. If you entertain the slightest suspicion that signals are being passed, play your next few hands too close to your vest for the kibitzer to see.

Peeking at Two Cards. This is one of the most flagrant violations in the game. Reaching for his draw from the stack, the cheat affects to fumble and lifts two cards instead of one. At a critical stage of the play, that glance at your next card is all he needs to know.

To protect players against this violation, whether by design or by accident, I suggest that you spread the stack fanwise. This may not completely eradicate the danger, but it will minimize it. And if the violation does occur, the rules of Gin Rummy provide that the player who has committed it must show to his opponent the card he just picked. By thus canceling his advantage, this will temporarily make an honest man of the cheat.

Recognizable Cards. Some amateur cheats will bend the corner of certain cards so as to be able to spot them in play. This is not a marked card in the professional sense of the term; it is a cheating device of, by, and for the cheat and against the decent player. Don't play with an old or defaced pack of playing cards.

Cheating on the Count. The practitioners of this crude larceny will keep a fair score sheet—until the count gets too close for comfort. Then, knowing that one point is often the difference between winning and losing a game with its big-money bonuses, they will miscall their points in unmatched cards and, holding them in their hands, fan them casually before you.

They will then toss them back onto the deck. To prevent this, insist on the rule that unmatched cards be placed face up on the table, separate from the melds—and count them yourself. Also, check the addition of points, not only at the end of the game but also when each hand's score is entered: 87 plus 26 might be entered as 103 instead of 113. And it's easy to be an even 100 points out of the way when adding up a long score. Added wrong? Oops, sorry!

The Counterfeit. Do you examine your

opponent's meld closely? If not, you tempt him to slip in the queen of clubs between the king, jack, and ten of spades. He'll put them down close together, with a little hocus-pocus about his other cards and "How many did I get you for?"

His purpose is to distract your attention and get away with it. How many times have you made a similar error yourself when first glancing at your cards? Watch it.

Protection Against a Crooked Gin Deal. Whenever you play Gin Rummy make it a habit to reshuffle the deck when it is offered to you for a cut. However, it must be understood, of course, that the dealer is entitled to the last shuffle if he so desires. Such extra precautionary measures on your part may be construed as a mistrusting gesture by some players, but it pays off in the long run by preventing a great deal of manipulative skulduggery.

How to Beat a Gin Rummy Hustler. Now let's look at the Gin hustler, the character who only plays with opponents who know less about the game than he does. He wins because he possesses a superior knowledge of Gin and knows it. A hustler who gambles with friends who know little or nothing about the finer points of the game cannot really be called an honest player, even though he does not resort to cheating. He gets the same end result as the cheat: his opponent always loses. There are two ways to beat a Gin hustler: stop playing with him or improve your skill to equal or surpass him. For further information on cheating at card games, see Chapter 22.

CHAPTER 6

Canasta

Canasta, a game of the rummy family, originated in Uruguay, was developed in Argentina, and reached the United States in 1949. From 1951 through 1953 it became the rage, perhaps the greatest in card history. (Its popularity exceeded that of Mah-Jongg in the twenties and the craze for Contract Bridge in the thirties.) In the early fifties it displaced Contract Bridge as the most-played American partnership card game. Its popularity fell off after 1953 but it still has millions of players, mostly women. It's an enjoyable game, especially for mixed partnerships; and, like Spanish, it's easy to learn but hard to master.

The rules that follow are the original partnership Canasta rules that made the game the great hit of the early fifties. Today, however, every hamlet, town, city, state, and country seems to have its own variation of play, many of which are described in later pages.

REGULAR PARTNERSHIP CANASTA

Requirements
1. Four players, two against two, as partners.
2. Two standard packs of 52 cards each, shuffled together and used as one, plus four jokers, totaling 108 cards dealt and played as a single deck. The jokers and the eight deuces are wild. As in Poker, any wild card may be used to represent, in the play, any other card. Most card packs sold in the United States contain two jokers. Actually, any two regular decks will do for Canasta; the color of the pattern on the back and its design do not matter.
3. Pencil and paper to keep score. A player is elected to keep score; better still, when possible, a nonplayer is scorekeeper.

Object of the Game. A partnership must score 5,000 or more points before the opposing partnership does so—by laying down melds of three or more cards in the same numerical rank; sequence melds are *not* allowed.

Point Value of the Cards in Scoring. The following are the point value of the cards in scoring:

Jokers	50 points each
Deuces	20 points each
Aces	20 points each
Eights, nines, tens, jacks, queens, kings	10 points each
Fours, fives, sixes, sevens	5 points each
Black threes (clubs and spades)	5 points each
Red threes (diamonds and hearts)	100 points each

(But, if a partnership holds four red three's, on the board, their value becomes 800 points, the combination of all four red three's giving a value of 200 points to each.)

Bonuses are given for a red three, four red threes, natural Canasta (second from bottom), and mixed Canasta (bottom).

To receive a plus credit for red three's, a partnership must have laid down at least one meld. In the event of failure to meld, the red three's become a penalty against the partnership: 100 points for each red three, or 800 points if the nonmelding partnership holds four red three's. (It must be interpolated that the possibility of holding four red three's without making a meld is remote.) If upon the completion of the hand a player is caught with a red three in the hand, having neglected to put it down, he is penalized 200 points.

Natural and Mixed Canastas: What the Terms Mean. This is a *natural canasta:*

4444444

or

KKKKKKK

or any seven cards of the same rank *regardless* of suit.

Wild cards cannot be used in a natural canasta. A natural canasta has a value of 500 points.

This is a *mixed canasta:*

6666 plus three wild cards

or

66666 plus two wild cards

or

666666 plus one wild card

A mixed canasta is a combination of seven cards having the same rank, at least four of which must be natural cards; a maximum of three cards may be wild. A mixed canasta has a value of 300 points.

When a player melds a canasta—or forms a canasta by adding to cards already melded on the table—the canasta is folded together and tagged for identification. When it is a natural canasta, any red card, when possible, is placed on top of it to designate its nature. When it is a mixed canasta, its identifying top card is a black or a wild card. Once the cards have been folded, the meld is a *closed canasta.*

In the subsequent play a player may meld (lay off) additional cards on a canasta. Cards of corresponding rank or wild cards may be added to any canasta, natural or mixed—but adding a wild card to a natural canasta transforms this canasta into a mixed one, with a consequent change in its value from 500 points to 300 points. Wild cards cannot be added to a mixed canasta which already embodies three wild cards.

Penalties. When a contestant goes rummy or goes out, any cards still held by *any* player in his hand are totaled and assessed against the player as a penalty. Even when one member of a partnership goes rummy, the cards left in the other partner's hand are counted against the partnership. And these penalty cards have the same value as they would have if melded, except the red three's. The penalty for holding a red three at the completion of a hand is 200 points; as a penalty card its value is twice its value when laid on the board.

Selecting Partners and Seating Positions

1. The four players take places at the four sides of the table.

2. Any player by mutual consent shuffles the deck and offers it to any other player for the cut.

3. From the cut deck each player now cuts a block of cards, turning his block and exposing the bottom card. The players drawing the two lowest cards become partners, as do the players drawing the two highest cards. Rank of cards for cutting purpose: two (low), three, four, on up to ace (high).

If three- or four-way ties occur on the cut for partners, a new deal and cut must take place.

When cutting for partners, the jokers are excluded from the deck. The partners now seat themselves opposite each other. To avoid any possibility of controversy as to seating position, one player for each team cuts the deck and exposes his card. If it is a black card, partners remain in the seats they have taken. If it is a red card, they must exchange seats. The player who cut low card in cutting for the partner's seat positions starts the game by dealing the first hand. Thereafter, on the completion of each hand, the deal passes to the player at the previous dealer's left, clockwise. On the completion of each game, players may change partners, or may cut for new partnerships and seat positions.

The Shuffle and Cut. These are governed by General Rules for Rummy Games, page 55.

The Deal. Each player is dealt 11 cards, one at a time, starting with the player at the dealer's left and dealing clockwise. The dealer then faces up the forty-fifth card in the center of the table (this card becoming the first upcard). The rest of the deck is placed face down next to the upcard and is now the stock. If the upcard is a wild card (deuce or joker) or a red three, the top card of the stock is turned up and placed on top of the first upcard. This procedure is followed until some card other than a wild card or a red three is the upcard.

Important Rule at Canasta. At a player's proper turn of play, should he hold any red threes, he places them on the table face up as if they were a meld, and for each red three he lays down he picks a card from the stock. If this drawn card is a red three, that too is laid on the table, and the player draws another card from the stock. This procedure is continued until the player fails to draw a red three. This rule holds true for each player at each turn of play.

The Actual Play. The player to the dealer's left has the first turn of play. Thereafter the turn of play rotates to the left, clockwise, from player to player until the completion of the hand.

First Player. The player to the dealer's left plays as follows:

1. The player may pick the top card from the stock. He may then meld if he can, if he wants to do so. Then he must discard one card. His first (initial) meld or melds must total 50 or more points. He may make up the 50 points by laying off as many or as few melds as will suffice.

2. Or, the player may pick up the entire discard pile—if the upcard can be used with two other natural cards of its numerical rank to form a meld. Again, his meld or melds must total 50 or more points. Before taking the upcard the player must lay down from his hand the cards to be melded with it; of the discard pile, only the upcard can be used to help form the required meld. After the cards are melded, the remainder of the discard pile is incorporated into the player's hand. The player may now put down any other meld he elects. Having melded, he must discard one card.

Second Player. The rules for the first player, as just stated, govern the play of the second.

Third and Fourth Players (partners of the first and second). If the partner has not melded cards, the rules as stated above apply to these players. If the partner has melded, two new elements come into play:

1. The player may take up the discard pile with only one natural card matching the upcard plus one wild card, instead of needing two matching natural cards.

2. He may take the discard pile when the upcard can be added to his or his partner's meld, except if the discard pile is a frozen pile. However, the upcard can never be taken up to be melded with two or more wild cards.

Upon the completion of the first hand, should a partnership fail to meld the required minimum of 50 points and find itself in the minus column, this partnership is required to meld only 15 points for its first meld of the next hand. If, upon the completion of a hand, this partnership has attained a scoring in the plus column, the minimum meld of 50 or more points is required for the first meld of the next hand.

Once a partnership has scored the minimum meld of 50 or more points, a player or his partner may put down legal melds of any value until their partnership's score reaches 1,500 or more at the end of a hand. Then the next initial meld requirement must total 90 points or more. Then, when a partnership has scored 3,000 or more points at the end of a hand, the next initial meld must be 120 or more points. When a score of 5,000 points is reached, that's game.

Bonus cards, such as red three's, cannot be counted in amassing the required 50-, 90-, or 120-point melds.

To emphasize: The initial meld requirement must have a minimum count that depends upon the accumulated total score of that partnership at the beginning of the current deal. These are shown below in tabular form.

Accumulated Score at the Beginning of the Deal	Minimum Meld Count Requirement
Minus	15 points
0 to 1,495	50 points
1,500 to 2,995	90 points
3,000 or more	120 points

The count of a meld is the total point value of the cards in it. To meet the minimum, a player may make two or more different melds. If he takes the discard pile, he may count the top card (but no other) toward the requirement. Bonuses for red threes and canastas do not count toward the minimum. After a partnership has made its initial meld, either partner may make any legal meld without reference to any minimum count.

Frozen Pile. The discard pile becomes a *frozen pile* whenever it contains a wild card or a red three. The frozen pile, also called the *prize pile,* may be taken up only when the player holds two natural cards matching the upcard. It cannot be taken up to play off the upcard on a meld.

Stop Card. When the upcard of the discard pile is a wild card or a *black three,* it is a *stop card;* the next player cannot take the discard pile but must draw from stock. Sometimes it is wise to freeze the pile by discarding a wild card to make it difficult for the opponent to pick up the pile.

Black Threes. Black three's can be melded to go rummy only when a player holds three or more black three's in his hand. Black three's cannot be melded at any other time, and they cannot be melded with wild cards.

Exhausting the Stock. If no one goes rummy and the entire stock is exhausted, the player picking the last card from the stock must discard one card. If the upcard of the discard pile can then be laid off on one of the melds of the player whose turn it is or of his partner, then the player must take the entire discard pile and lay off the card. Then he must discard one card. If the discard pile contains only one card (upcard) and that upcard can be laid off on a meld of the player whose turn it is or of his partner, he must take that card, lay it off, and then discard a card. This pattern of play continues until the upcard cannot be laid off by the player whose turn it is.

By this time, if no one has gone rummy, the game ends and no one gets the rummy bonus of 100 points. If the last card of the stock pile is a red three, the hand ends, and the scores are totaled. The player who draws this red three does not get credit for it. (This summary end of the hand takes place because the red three cannot be replaced.)

End of the Game. At the end of each hand, new hands are dealt until one partnership reaches a score of 5,000 points. But the partnership reaching the winning score cannot call out; the hand must be completed. If both partnerships have 5,000 or more points, the partnership with the higher score wins. If the teams tie at 5,000 or more points, new hands are played until the tie is broken. There is no game bonus for scoring 5,000 points.

Additional Rules. The rules that govern irregularities are designed to define the offense and to provide an adequate remedy in all cases where a player accidentally, carelessly, or inadvertently violates a rule of the game and gains an unintentional but nevertheless unfair advantage. An offending player should be ready to pay a prescribed penalty graciously. The rules governing irregularities follow:

1. In Canasta, the meld or lay consists of three or more cards in the same numerical rank: three four's, four four's, five four's, six four's, etc. A meld once laid down cannot be changed.

2. The sequence meld, permitted in most Rummy games, is *not* a legal meld in Canasta. The five–six–seven of spades, for instance, is no meld at all in Canasta; the cards

have no legal relationship to each other; they cannot be laid.

3. "Laying off" means to extend an existent meld. A player may lay off cards on either his own or his partner's melds. *Example:* A player has melded three queens on the table before him. His partner has a queen or a wild card. He can lay this card on the three melded queens—but, of course, only in his proper turn of play.

4. After a player has drawn a card from the stock he may meld if he wants to and if he has the points required to meld.

5. After a player has drawn the upcard of the discard pile, he must meld at least the number of points required at that stage of the game.

6. A player may also meld cards taken in the discard pile immediately on taking up the discards. But points melded from the discard pile cannot be used to help make up the number of points required with each first meld.

Improper Melding. If a player melds fewer than the number of points required under the rules for the game at that stage, he may rectify the error if he has additional cards or melds in his hand—enough cards to satisfy or exceed the stipulated necessary amount. If he lacks such cards, he must discard the exposed cards he has laid on the table, one for each discard, in his proper turn of play. These penalty cards cannot be used in any accounting for scoring purposes. He must continue to discard so until either he or his partner has melded the amount required.

After the player or his partner has melded the amount required, the offending player may pick up any remaining penalty cards in his correct turn of play. He may incorporate them again into his hand, and may meld them if possible in due time. When an improper meld is made after the upcard has been taken, this card must be returned to the top of the discard pile. And if the discard pile has been taken up, it too must be returned to the table. But the penalty meld may remain on the table, being governed by the above rules.

Seeking Information. During the game, any player may ask any other player how many cards he has left in his hand. The other player, whether opponent or partner, is not obligated to answer unless he is reduced to a single card, in which case he must answer, "I hold only one." If, holding but one card, he answers that he holds more than one, on discovery that he has misstated his holding, that player shall be penalized 50 points.

When holding more than one card, it is required of the player to whom the query is put only that he reply, "I hold more than one." This is the minimum legal response. It is perhaps more conducive to affable relations in the play to give an accurate answer; but that is not obligatory.

At his proper turn to play, and before melding or laying off cards or indicating he had the necessary melds to go out, a player may ask, "Partner, may I go out?" It is strongly recommended that only this phrase be used. The partner must reply either "Yes" or "No" (nothing more), and the answer is binding. If the player fails to abide by the answer, his side is penalized 100 points. A player, however, may go out without asking this question.

Discarding. After a player has drawn a card and has melded (if he can and wants to), he *must* discard one card. If a player goes rummy he may meld his discard, and is entitled to the extra points at which it is valued.

Additional Irregularities. Misdeals and other irregularities are governed by the General Rules for Rummy Games on pages 55 to 57.

How to Go Rummy. To go rummy, a player must meld or lay down all the cards in his hand, melding or laying them off on his own or his partner's melds—if there are any. But, a player is not permitted to meld or to lay off all of his cards unless a canasta has been formed from his or his partner's melds. A player must hold at least one card in his hand if neither he nor his partner has melded or formed a canasta.

Rummy Bonus of 100 Points. If a player has laid down a meld—remembering that red threes laid on the board are not admissible as a meld—and then goes rummy, he receives a bonus of 100 points, provided his partnership has melded at least one canasta.

Going Out Concealed: Rummy Bonus of 200 Points. If a player goes out without previously having melded (remember: red threes on the board are not a meld), he receives a special bonus of 200 points—provided the going-out hand contains a canasta or the player's partner has melded or formed a canasta.

Scoring. At the completion of each hand, the values of the melded cards and bonuses of each partnership are added together and entered on the score sheet for the partnership as a unit total. To minimize the possibility of errors in scoring, the following procedures may be useful:

1. List:
    (*a*) the total value of the red threes.
    (*b*) the values of the canastas.
    (*c*) the bonus (if any) for going rummy.
    (*d*) the total count of all the cards melded.
2. Add these totals together, and mark the total at one side of the score sheet.
3. Deduct from this amount:
    (*a*) the value of cards held by the partners in their hands at the end of play. (At the completion of a hand all the cards in a player's holding count against his partnership, whether they are melds or not.)
    (*b*) any penalties incurred during the play.

Each partnership is privileged to check the opponent's count.

The plus and minus scores are canceled against each other. The adjusted score is entered on the sheet as the total for that game.

Additional Penalties

1. For failing to expose a red three, the penalty is 200 points.

2. For seeing more than one card when drawing a card from the stock, the player must show the drawn card to the other players.

Players are not permitted to inform their partners of the value of any cards in their hands.

Six-Hand Canasta

There are several ways to play this variation. The rules of Regular Partnership Canasta apply, except as follows:

1. There are two partnerships of three players each, seated A B A B A B (each player is seated between two opponents). Or, there are three partnerships of two players each, seated A B C A B C.

2. A triple deck is used: three 52-card decks plus six jokers, all shuffled together. Thirteen cards are dealt to each player. Game is 10,000; when a side reaches 7,000, it needs 150 for its initial meld. Four red threes count only 100 each; five red threes count 1,000 in all; six red threes count 1,200. A side needs two canastas to go out.

Two-Hand Canasta

The rules for Regular Partnership Canasta hold true in this two-handed variant with the following exceptions:

1. The dealer deals himself and his opponent 15 cards each, one at a time, starting with his opponent.

2. When a player, at his turn of play, draws from the stock, he must take the two top cards; but when he discards, he discards only one card.

3. A player must meld two canastas to go out.

Cutthroat (Three-Hand) Canasta

Three may play Canasta under the rules for Regular Partnership Canasta, with the sole difference that each plays for himself. However, a speedier and more interesting game is obtained by modifying the foregoing rules as follows:

1. Three players participate, each scoring for himself. But, during the play, they form sides of two against one. The player who first takes the discard pile becomes the *lone hand*. The other two join in a partnership against the lone hand, combining their melds and otherwise aiding each other. If a player goes out before the discard pile is ever taken, he becomes the lone hand and the other two score as partners. Each player receives a hand of 11 cards.

2. When drawing from the stock, a player takes two cards, but then discards only one card.

3. The initial meld requirement for a player depends on his own score. Hence, it may happen that one partner has a higher requirement than the other.

4. If no one goes out, play ends with the discard of the player who drew the last card of the stock.

5. A red three counts only for the owner, plus or minus, according to whether or not his side has made any meld. Therefore, the base scores of the partners may differ if they have not drawn an equal number of red threes. All other scores made by the partnership are totaled, and each partner receives the total, plus or minus his own red threes. Game is 7,500 points.

Five-Hand Canasta

One side has three players, who take turns sitting out while the other two play the deal against the opponents. Regular Partnership Canasta is played. The player sitting out may not give any advice to his teammates, and may not call attention to irregularities, except in scoring after the play is completed.

VARIATIONS OF CANASTA

During the early 1950's as Canasta's popularity spread throughout the United States and abroad, many variants of Canasta cropped up in various countries and in some cases the variations have become just as popular as the original game. But, in my opinion, none of them is as good as the standard two-deck partnership game. However, for the player who likes novelty and variety, I have selected the following Canasta variants as the ones that I believe to be most worthy of inclusion in these pages.

Uruguay Canasta

Uruguay Canasta, the forerunner of Regular Partnership Canasta, is played the same, except for the following:

1. From three to seven wild cards form a valid meld. A canasta (seven cards) of wild cards counts 2,000 points.

2. The discard pile is always frozen—the discard pile may be taken up only when the player holds two natural cards matching the upcard.

Bolivian Canasta

Bolivian Canasta is played the same as is regular Canasta. The points on which Bolivia differs from Regular Partnership Canasta are as follows:

1. Three standard decks of 52 cards plus six jokers are used, making a 162-card deck.

2. Game is 15,000 points.

3. Each player is dealt 15 cards.

4. A draw from the stock is two cards, but only one card is discarded.

5. *Wild Cards.* From three to seven wild cards form a valid meld. A canasta of seven wild cards is a *Bolivia* and counts 2,500 points.

6. A sequence meld of three or more cards in the same suit forms a valid meld—for example, the four–five–six of hearts. A suit ranks from ace (high) to four (low)—wild cards and threes are not involved. A seven-card sequence in the same suit (containing no wild cards) is called an *Escalera* and counts 1,500 points.

7. *Contract Melds.* Here are the requirements for the initial meld: A minus score needs 15 points; zero to 1,495 needs 50 points; 1,500 to 2,995 needs 90 points; 3,000 to 6,995 needs 120 points; 7,000 or more needs 150 points.

8. Two canastas are required to go out, and at least one of them must be an Escalera. A black three left in the hand counts 100 minus. A black three melded counts only 5 points.

9. Red threes count 100 points each; all six count 1,000. They count plus if the partnership has melded two canastas of any kind, otherwise they count minus.

Brazilian Canasta

Brazilian Canasta is played the same as is Bolivia, except as follows:

1. Game is 10,000 points. Initial meld requirements are:

Total Score	Minimum Count
Minus	15
0 to 1,495	50
1,500 to 2,995	90
3,000 to 4,995	120
5,000 to 6,995	150
7,000 to 7,995	200
8,000 to 8,995	Any canasta
9,000 or more	Natural canasta

2. A wild-card canasta counts 2,000 points. Red threes count 100 points each, five red threes count 1,000 points, and all six count 1,200 points. They count plus if the partnership has melded two canastas of any kind, otherwise they count minus. If a partnership has a melded sequence of less than five cards when the hand ends, 1,000 points are deducted from its score.

Cuban Canasta

This game is the same as Regular Partnership Canasta, except for the following:

1. Thirteen cards are dealt to each player. Draw one card in each turn.

2. The pack is always frozen (may be taken only by a natural matching pair) and canastas may not contain more than seven cards.

3. Game is 7,500. From 5,000 up, initial meld must be 150.

4. One canasta is required before a side may score for its melds, or go out. It is necessary to have a discard when going out. You may not start a second meld of the same rank as a previous meld, unless the first meld is a completed canasta.

5. Red threes count 100 for one, 300 for two, 500 for three, 1,000 for all four. They count minus unless a side has at least one canasta.

6. Black threes may not be discarded on the first round. Any black threes in the pack when they are taken are discarded and out of play, counting 5 each for the side that took them. All four black threes, discarded or melded, count 100.

7. Wild cards may be melded and a canasta of wild cards counts as follows: 4,000 for seven deuces; 3,000 for four jokers and three deuces; 2,000 for any other combination of seven wild cards. Sequences may not be melded. A discard pile topped by a wild card may not be taken.

8. Going out earns the 100-point bonus.

Mexicana

The basic rules of Regular Partnership Canasta apply except for the following:

1. A triple deck is used, with six jokers (162 cards).

2. Each player is dealt 13 cards. When a player makes the *initial* meld for his side, he draws the top 13 cards of the stock and adds them to his hand.

3. The discard pile may not be taken when topped by a seven. But sevens may be melded as usual, and a canasta of sevens (natural or mixed) counts 1,000.

4. To go out, a side must have two canastas, plus at least as many red threes as it has canastas.

Joker Canasta

Joker Canasta is played the same as Regular Partnership Canasta with the following exceptions:

1. Thirteen cards are dealt to each player.

2. The discard pile is always frozen (it may be taken only by a natural pair from the hand).

3. The game is 8,500 points. The initial minimum meld is 100 points for a score under 3,000; a meld of 130 points is needed from 3,000 to 4,995; and a meld of 150 points is needed from 5,000 to the end of the game.

4. No canasta may contain more than seven cards.

5. A partnership needs two canastas to go out.

6. Wild cards may be melded. A canasta of seven deuces counts 4,000 points; a wild-card canasta counts 3,000 points if it includes all four jokers; any other wild-card canasta counts 2,000 points.

7. Black threes are played and scored the same as red threes—but points for black threes and red threes are counted separately. A partnership's first three in a color counts 100 points, two in that color count 300 points, three in that color count 500 points, and all four in that color count 1,000 points. The black and red threes are counted minus against a partnership that fails to complete a canasta.

Italian Canasta

This is the same as Regular Partnership Canasta, except for the following:

1. A triple deck is used with six jokers (162 cards). Each hand is dealt 15 cards and the draw from the stock is two cards (each player discards one card).

2. After the deal and before a card is turned, each player replaces his red threes. Then the top card is turned. A number of cards equal to its rank (counting jack 11, queen 12, king 13, ace or joker 20) are counted off the stock to begin the discard pile. They are turned face down, and the upcard is placed face up on them.

3. The discard pile is always frozen.

4. Deuces may be melded as an independent rank, with or without the aid of jokers as

wild cards. A side that has melded deuces may not meld deuces as wild cards elsewhere until the canasta of deuces is completed.

5. The game is 12,000 and the initial meld must meet the required count without aid of any wild card. The requirements are:

Total Score	Minimum Count
0 to 1,495	50
1,500 to 2,995	90
3,000 to 4,995	120
5,000 to 7,495	160
7,500 to 9,995	180
10,000 or more	200

6. A wild-card canasta does not count as one of the two canastas required to go out. The bonus for going out is 300.

7. When a side has no more than three red threes, they count 100 each; four or more, 200 each.

8. Seven deuces count 3,000; a mixed canasta of deuces and jokers counts 2,000. But, these bonuses go only to the side that goes out; opponents having deuce melds score only the point value of the cards. Extra bonuses: for five pure canastas, 2,000; for five canastas including a mixed one, 1,000; for ten canastas of any kind, 2,000.

Pennies from Heaven

While there are several variations of Canasta called by this name, it usually means the game for six players, in two partnerships of three players each. The rules of Regular Partnership Canasta apply with the following exceptions:

1. Use four decks plus eight jokers (216 cards). Deal 13 cards to each player, then deal each player a packet of 11 cards, face down which he may add to his hand when he has completed his first canasta. Draw two cards from the stock and discard one card per turn.

2. No canasta may contain more than seven cards.

3. Sevens may not be discarded until each side has completed a canasta of sevens (natural or mixed), which counts 1,500 points. A seven may not be discarded in going out.

4. Wild cards may be melded (jokers and deuces together) and a wild-card canasta counts 1,000 points. But the discard pile may not be taken when topped by a wild card.

5. Red threes count 100 each; if all eight are held by one side, they count 1,000. They count minus for a side that has not completed a canasta of sevens.

6. Requirements for initial meld are:

Minus	15
0 to 495	50
500 to 995	90
1,000 to 1,495	120
1,500 or more	150

7. To go out, a side must have a canasta of sevens, one of wild cards, one natural, and one mixed.

8. Game is 20,000 points.

Race Horse Canasta

The rules of Pennies from Heaven apply except for the following:

1. With four players, each receives 15 cards; with six players, each receives 13 cards.

2. The first player to complete any canasta gets a bonus of 11 cards from the top of the stock. These 11 cards are placed in the player's hand and may not be melded until his next turn. There is only one such bonus in each deal.

3. A mixed canasta of sevens counts only 1,000 points.

4. The discard pile is always frozen—it may be taken only with a natural pair from the hand.

5. The initial meld requirements are as follows:

0 to 2,995	50
3,000 to 5,995	90
6,000 to 9,995	120
10,000 or more	150

Samba

This game is played in the same manner as Regular Partnership Canasta except for the following rule changes:

1. Three standard 52-card decks plus six jokers are combined, making 162 cards in all. Each player of the two partnerships (four players) is dealt 15 cards. A draw from the stock (when not picking up a discard or discards) is two cards, but only one card is discarded.

2. A *samba* is seven cards of the same suit

in sequence and ranks as a canasta (seven cards of the same rank) for purposes of going out. Three or more cards of the same suit in consecutive rank (as in Gin Rummy) are a valid meld. A suit ranks from ace (high) to four (low), with wild deuces and threes not involved. Such a meld may be increased by sequential cards up to a total of seven, when it becomes a samba and is turned face down; no more cards may be added to it. No wild cards may be used in a sequence. The bonus award for a samba is 1,500 points.

3. No more than two wild cards may be used in a group meld. Natural cards from a player's hand may be layed off (added) to a canasta, but the discard pile may not be taken to add its upcard to a completed canasta.

4. A partnership may meld two or more groups of the same rank. Either partner at his turn of play may combine such groups for canasta-building. Separate partnership sequence melds may be joined if they do not exceed a seven-card sequence meld.

5. The discard pile may be taken only by melding its upcard with a natural pair from the hand, or (if frozen) to lay off the upcard on a sequence or group meld of less than seven cards.

6. Game is 10,000 points, the winning partnership getting credit for the difference between their count and their opponent's. The initial meld requirements are:

Minus	15
0 to 1,495	50
1,500 to 2,995	90
3,000 to 6,995	120
7,000 or more	150

7. In order to go out, a partnership must have at least two canastas or two sambas or one of each. A side must go out to count its melds of red threes. If all six red threes are melded by one partnership, they count 1,000 points. The bonus award for going out is 200 points. Concealed hands receive no bonus.

Note: The arrangements for playing Samba with two, three, five, or six players are the same as given in the rules for playing Regular Canasta in these forms (see pages 99 to 104), except that with three players it is possible to deal 15 cards to each player. (In six-hand play, however, 13 cards may be dealt to each player, if all agree.) The standard Samba rules, of course, apply.

Chilean Canasta

Chilean Canasta is played the same as Samba except for the following rules:

1. The game makes use of four standard 52-card decks plus four jokers, making 212 cards in all. Each player is dealt 11 cards. A seven-card sequence counts as a canasta, but is not closed; sequential cards up to a total of 11 (ace down to four) may be added.

2. Three or more wild cards of the same rank may be melded and built into canastas.

3. The discard pile may be taken if the upcard may be laid off on a sequence meld, or on a group of wild cards. It may also be taken with a wild-card pair or a natural pair from the hand to initiate a meld.

4. A partnership must have melded two canastas to go out, but its red threes count plus if the partners have melded one canasta.

5. The minimum initial meld is 50 points for scores up to 2,995; it is 90 points from 3,000 to 4,995; and it is 120 points thereafter.

6. As in Samba, game is 10,000 points. A joker counts 30 points, a wild-card canasta counts 2,000 points, a sequence canasta (seven to ten cards) counts 2,000 points, and an 11-card canasta counts 3,000 points.

Hollywood Canasta

Hollywood Canasta is the same as Samba, except for the following:

1. Wild cards may be melded in groups apart from natural cards. A canasta of wild cards counts 2,000 points.

2. Each group or sequence meld must commence with at least three natural cards. One wild card may be used in a sequence canasta, and two may be used in a group canasta. A mixed sequence canasta counts 1,000 points, a pure sequence counts 1,500 points. Additional cards (wild or otherwise) may be added to completed canastas.

3. When the top card is natural, the discard pile may be taken by a matching pair or by two cards in suit and sequence. When the top card is a two, it may be taken by a pair of twos; when it is a joker, by a pair of jokers. When the pile is not frozen, the top card may be taken to lay off on any minor meld (less than seven cards). A one-card pile may never be taken.

4. Red threes count plus if the side has made its initial meld. (But, as in Samba, two canastas are required to go out.)

Quinella

This game is the same as Samba, except for the following:

1. Four decks of 52 cards plus four jokers are combined, making 212 cards in all.

2. Each player receives 11 cards.

3. A sequence of seven counts as a canasta, but is not closed—additional cards may be laid off on it, up to the total of 11 cards (ace down to four).

4. Wild cards may be melded and built into canastas.

5. The discard pile may be taken to lay off the top card on a sequence already melded or on a group of wild cards. It may be taken with a natural or wild-card pair from hand to initiate a meld.

6. A side must have two canastas to go out, but its red threes count plus after it has one canasta.

7. The minimum initial meld requirement is 50 points up to a score of 3,000; then 90 up to 6,000; and 120 thereafter.

8. A joker counts 30. The bonus for a wild-card canasta is 2,000. A sequence canasta of less than 11 cards counts 2,000; a sequence canasta of 11 cards counts 3,000.

Tampa

This game is the same as Samba, except for the following:

1. Sequences may not be melded. But wild cards may be melded in groups apart from natural cards. A wild-card canasta counts 2,000.

2. A red three counts minus 200 against a side that has not melded when the other side goes out. Otherwise, a side with one to four red threes scores 100 plus for each; it scores 1,000 for five threes and 1,200 for all six.

3. A black three left in hand counts 200 minus, but counts only 5 when melded in going out.

4. The discard pile may be taken only by a natural pair (not wild) matching the top card. Thus it is always "frozen."

5. The minimum initial meld requirement is 50 points up to 3,000; then 90 up to 5,000;

then 120 up to 7,000; and 150 thereafter. As in Samba, game is 10,000.

6. To go out, a side must have two "red" canastas. Wild-card canastas and natural (not mixed) canastas are "red."

Combo-Canasta

This is one of the most exciting and highest scoring games of the Canasta family.

Requirements

1. Four players, two against two, as partners.

2. Three 52-card decks, plus six jokers; all 162 cards are shuffled together.

Selecting Partners and Seating Positions. See page 100.

The Deal. The shuffle and cut are governed by General Rules for Rummy Games, page 55.

The dealer gives 15 cards to each player, one at a time, clockwise, beginning with the opponent at his left and ending with himself. The undealt remainder of the deck is placed face down in the center of the table, becoming the stock. The top card of the stock is turned face up beside the stock, forming the upcard. If the upcard is a joker, a two, or a black or red three, one or more additional cards must be turned up on it until a natural card of rank ace to four appears.

Wild Cards. The jokers and deuces are wild. Wild cards may be melded with natural cards (maximum of two wild cards to each meld), or by themselves in a set of from three to seven cards.

Red Threes. A player finding a red three in his hand must, at his first turn, put it face up on the table and draw a replacement from the stock. When drawing a red three from the stock he must immediately place it face up on the table and draw a replacement from the stock. In addition, if a player takes a discard pile that contains a red three, or picks up a red three when taking bonus cards from the stock, he must place the red three up on the table but does not draw a replacement.

Each red three has a bonus value of 100 points. A side that acquires all six red threes scores 2,000 points (1,400 additional). If a side, at the end of a deal, has not completed a Bolivia, an Escalera, or a natural canasta of sevens, they score 100 points minus for each red three.

Black Threes. A side, after having met their initial meld requirements, may meld a set of three or four black threes as a group in any proper turn of play, but no additional black threes may be added to the meld. No wild cards may be melded with black threes. When a player discards a black three, the next player may not take the discard pile at that turn.

If at the end of a deal a player has one or more black threes left in his hand, his side is penalized 200 points for each black three.

Sevens. A natural canasta of sevens scores 1,500 points and a mixed canasta of sevens scores 1,000 points. If a player, at the end of a deal, has one or more sevens left in his hand, his side is penalized 500 points for each seven. Sevens may be melded and discarded the same as other natural cards.

Order of Play. The opponent at the left of the dealer plays first. Thereafter the turn to play rotates clockwise, to the left. In each turn a player must first draw (two cards), then meld (optional), and then discard (one card).

The player in turn is always entitled to draw two cards from the top of the stock. He may instead take the top card of the discard pile to use in a meld; having done so, he must take the rest of the discard pile. But, in Combo-Canasta, the discard pile is always frozen; it may only be taken by a player in turn who has a natural pair in his hand, ace down to four inclusive, that matches the top discard. When taking the discard pile the player should, before touching the discard pile, show his pair, together with such additional cards as may be necessary to meet the minimum count for the initial meld. Having taken and melded the top discard legally, the player takes the rest of the discard pile into his hand, and may then meld any such additional cards as he pleases. The discard pile may not be taken when it is topped by a wild card or a black three.

Melds. The principal object of play is to form melds. The possible melds are group melds of natural cards (with or without the help of wild cards), sequence melds, and group melds of wild cards. No meld is valid unless it contains at least three cards and no more than seven cards. In addition to the point-count values of the cards, a canasta earns a bonus as follows:

Bolivia (wild-card canasta)	2,000
Escalera (sequence canasta)	1,500
Sevens (natural, no wild cards)	1,500
Sevens (mixed with wild cards)	1,000
Red canasta (natural, no wild cards)	500
Black canasta (mixed with wild cards)	300

To count plus, a meld must be laid face up on the table, in a proper turn of the player. All cards left in the hand when play ends, even though they form melds, count minus. In his turn, a player may meld as many cards as he pleases, of one rank or of different ranks, forming new melds and adding to previous melds. But, he must keep one card in his hand so he will be able to discard. (*Exception:* a discard is not necessary when the stock is exhausted and a player melds his last card.) All melds of a partnership are placed in front of one member thereof. A partnership may make as many different melds as they care to, even if they or their opponents have made previous melds of the same rank. It is legal to combine melds, or to add to melds, provided they do not exceed seven cards. A player may not add cards to his opponents' melds.

Minimum Count. As in Regular Partnership Canasta, all cards have a point-count value as follows:

Jokers	50 points each
Deuces	20 points each
Aces	20 points each
Kings, queens, jacks, tens, nines, eights	10 points each
Sixes, fives, fours, melded sevens, melded black threes	5 points each

The point count for all cards left in the hand when the deal is over is the same as above, except that a seven counts 500 points and a black three counts 200 points against the holder.

The first meld made by a side (its initial meld) must meet a minimum count requirement that depends on the accumulated total score of that side at the beginning of that deal, as follows:

Accumulated Score	Minimum Count
0 to 3,495	60
3,500 to 6,995	100
7,000 to 10,495	140
10,500 or over	180

The count of a meld is the total point value

of its component cards. To meet the minimum, a player may make melds of two or more different ranks. If he takes the discard pile, he may count its top card (but no other) toward the requirement. Bonuses for red threes and canastas do not count toward the minimum.

After a side has made its initial meld, either partner may make any valid melds without reference to any minimum count.

Special Bonus. The individual player who completes the first canasta (of any kind) in a deal, gets a bonus of eleven cards from the top of the stock; the cards become part of his hand and he may meld any or all of the bonus cards in the same turn of play. There is only one such bonus in each deal.

End of Deal. Each deal is played until the last card has been drawn from the stock; and, if the player who drew the last card melds his entire hand, the game ends. If the player who drew the last card discards, the next player may if he chooses take the discard. Play continues until a player melds his entire hand or until a discard is refused.

If the last player to draw picks a red three from a one-card stock, or two red threes from a two-card stock, he faces each red three on the table and scores it; but the deal is then ended and he may not make any further melds or a discard.

Scoring a Deal. The base score of a side for a deal is determined by totaling all applicable items previously mentioned. That is, the point score of a side is the total point values of all cards melded, less the point values of the cards left in both hands.

End of Game. A game consists of four complete deals. The side with the higher score wins the difference between the two scores from its opponents. There is no going out; every deal is played until the stock is exhausted.

Additional Rules. The following are additional rules that come into play during a game of Combo-Canasta:

New Deal. There must be a new deal by the same dealer (*a*) if he departs in any respect from the laws of correct procedure in dealing, (*b*) if he exposes a card other than the correct upcard, (*c*) if it is discovered during the deal that the cut was omitted. There must be a new deal if it is discovered, before every player has completed his first turn, that (*a*) any hand was dealt an incorrect number of cards, (*b*) a card is faced in the stock, (*c*) the deck contains a foreign card (a card from another deck). (If the error is discovered too late for a new deal: A short hand continues short; an exposed card is turned face down and shuffled into the stock; a foreign card is discarded from the deck and, if it was in a hand, the player draws a replacement.)

Drawing Too Many. If a player draws too many cards from the stock and if they are not placed in his hand, he must show the excess cards to all players and replace them on the stock. The next player to draw from the stock may, if he wishes, shuffle it before drawing. If excess cards drawn are placed in the hand, the player must forgo drawing in enough successive turns to reduce his hand to the correct number, discarding one card in each turn. Until his hand is correct, he may not meld.

Exposed Card. If a player exposes a card from his hand, except as a meld or discard, such card becomes a penalty card and must be left face up on the table. A penalty card counts as part of the hand, and may be duly melded. If not melded, it must be discarded at the first opportunity. With two or more penalty cards, the owner may choose which to discard.

Insufficient Count. If a player puts down an insufficient count for an initial meld, he may correct the error by melding additional cards and may then rearrange the cards melded. If he chooses (or is compelled) to retract all the cards, then the minimum count requirements for his side (for that hand only) is increased by 10 points.

Illegal Meld. Cards melded illegally or excess wild cards in a meld must be retracted. The side is penalized 100 points for the offense. The same penalty applies if a player, having put down insufficient count for an initial meld, makes it sufficient with additional cards but retracts one or more of those already exposed.

Failure to Declare a Red Three. If at the end of play a hand is found to contain an undeclared red three, the side is penalized 500 points.

Condonement. If a player makes an illegal meld and the error is not called until the next player has drawn or has indicated his intention to take the pack, the two previous rules do not apply. An initial meld of insufficient count stands as sufficient; an incorrect combination is retracted without penalty. However, excess wild cards in a meld remain and are debited against the side. (The debit is 50 points each if there is question as to which was the fifth wild card added.)

Taking Pack Illegally. A player attempting to take the discard pile without having established his right to do so should be stopped at once. There is no penalty if he can then show a valid claim. But if he has taken the pile into his hand before doing so, the opponents may face his whole hand and reconstruct the pile from it. The offender then picks up his cards, draws from the stock, and his side is penalized 100 points.

Information. A player may (*a*) examine the discard pile before he has made his first discard, (*b*) call attention to the correct minimum count requirement if his partner is in the act of making an initial meld, (*c*) remind his partner to declare red threes or draw replacements, (*d*) turn the sixth card of a meld crosswise to indicate that one more card is needed to complete a canasta.

In his own turn to play, a player is entitled to be informed of (*a*) the minimum count requirements or score of either side, (*b*) the number of cards held by any player, (*c*) the number of cards remaining in the stock.

Two-Hand Combo-Canasta

Follow the rules of the four-handed partnership game, with the following exceptions:

1. Use only two 52-card decks, plus four jokers.

2. Score 1,000 points (instead of 2,000 points) for all four red threes.

3. In the Additional Rules, the penalties for exposed cards and insufficient count do not apply.

Three-Hand Combo-Canasta

Follow the rules of the four-handed partner-

ship game, with the following exceptions:

1. There are three players, each scoring for himself. During the play sides form of two against one.

2. The first player to take the discard pile or to complete any canasta becomes the lone hand. The other two join in partnership against the lone hand, combining their melds and otherwise aiding each other as much as possible.

3. The initial meld requirement for a player depends on his own score. Hence it may happen that one partner has a higher requirement than the other.

4. A red three counts only for the owner, plus or minus according to whether or not his side has melded the necessary canasta of sevens, the Bolivia or the Escalera. The base scores of the partners therefore differ if they have not drawn an equal number of red threes. All other scores made by the partnership are totaled, and each partner receives credit for the total, plus or minus his own red threes.

5. A game consists of three complete deals.

Five-Hand Combo-Canasta

Follow the rules of the four-handed partnership game, with the following exceptions:

1. One side has three players who take turns sitting out a deal while the other two play against the opponents. A regular four-handed game is played. The player sitting out may not give advice of any kind to his teammates, and may not call attention to any irregularities, except in scoring after the play is completed.

Six-Hand Combo-Canasta

Follow the rules of the four-handed partnership game, with the following exceptions:

1. There are two partnerships of three players each, seated A B A B A B (each player seated between two opponents).

2. Each player is dealt 13 cards.

INTERNATIONAL CANASTA

I first learned to play Canasta in Panama, back in 1946. Shortly thereafter, I wrote a small booklet on the rules of the game and

added my own observations on how to improve the game. These rules later appeared in the first edition of *Scarne on Cards,* in 1949.

It was obvious to me then that Canasta needed considerable improvement to survive. After more than twenty years of globe-trotting and Canasta playing in Panama, Cuba, England, France, Italy, South America, and the Caribbean Islands, I have learned the many different variations of the game, most of which appear on the preceding pages. Many of these variations, which were meant to improve the original game, did the opposite—they made it less interesting. However, each of these variations had one or two good rules that, if applied by themselves to the original Canasta, might have improved the game. I studied every possible method of playing Canasta that came to my attention, took a rule from one game and a rule from another, then created and added several new rules of my own. My new rules include the elimination of stop cards and the first dealt upcard, the addition of initial meld bonuses, schneider bonuses, and blitz bonuses, plus others. After formulating these rules I presented them to a number of my friends who played the game for several months while I watched. During this time I removed the bugs, added some new rules, and improved the old rules. So, after years of Canasta research, I have come up with a set of Canasta rules that encompasses the best of all Canasta variations. I'm sure that Canasta players the world over, who have been playing their local variations for years, will welcome this new Canasta game which I have taken the inventor's liberty of naming "International Canasta." Why did I create International Canasta? It was to give Canasta players the world over a game that combined a lot of special features they have proved they liked, but weren't permitted under the Canasta variation they played. In addition, I want to codify a set of Canasta rules for all players throughout the world.

Requirements

1. Four players, two against two, as partners.

2. Two regular 52-card decks with four added jokers, shuffled together, and used as one 108-card deck.

Object of the Game. For a partnership to score 10,000 or more points before the opposing partnership does so—by laying down melds of three or more cards in the same numerical rank; sequence melds are not allowed.

Game Opening Preliminaries. The game opening preliminaries of selecting partners and seating positions, shuffling and cutting are the same as for Regular Partnership Canasta, page 100.

The Deal. The dealer, starting with the player on his left, deals each player (including himself) 13 face-down cards, one at a time, in clockwise fashion. The remainder of the undealt cards are placed face down in the center of the table forming the stock.

If the 108-card deck is too bulky to hold for the deal, the dealer may lift off a portion from the top of the deck, as close to 52 cards as he can estimate, and deal from this portion. If he holds any cards after the deal, they are replaced on top of the deck. If the dealer took less than 52 cards to begin with, he takes additional cards from the top of the deck to complete the deal and any leftover cards are replaced on top of the deck. A player may not look at or pick up his cards until the deal has been completed. The deal begins with the completion of the cut and ends when the dealer has dealt the fifty-second card and has placed the stock in the center of the table.

Order of Play. Each player at his turn, starting with the player on the dealer's left and continuing clockwise around the table, does the following: Each turn comprises first a one-card draw from the stock, then a meld (optional), and then a discard. The player in turn is always entitled to draw the top card of the stock, subject to restrictions given in the following text. He may instead take the top card of the discard pile and immediately use it in a natural meld (no wild card). Having so taken the last discard, he must take the entire discard pile and add it to his hand or to his melds; he may lay down other melds. A discard must always be made from the hand, never from a meld. A player is not permitted to discard a wild card unless he fails to hold a natural card. Only then may he discard a wild card. The act of discarding ends a player's turn at play.

In brief, the order of play is as follows:

(*a*) the draw
(*b*) the meld (optional)
(*c*) the discard

A player draws when he raises the top card of the stock or discard pile from its former position. The choice is fixed: A player commits himself to draw as soon as he touches either card, unless accidentally or obviously for the purpose of straightening out cards in disordered arrangement. The choice is fixed if he puts cards down on the table for the apparent purpose of taking the discard pile. During his turn of play, however, either before or after the draw, a player has the privilege of moving and looking at the three top cards of the discard pile.

When a player has established his right to take the top card of the discard pile, the remaining cards in the pile become part of his hand, except as provided here. If a player should forget to take all of the pile, it is the duty of all other players to call attention to the oversight. He retains his right to those cards until the next player has drawn, whereupon they become part of the new discard pile.

The Meld. At his turn of play, a player may place three, four, five, six, or seven cards of the same rank face up on the table; or he may lay off cards (add cards to groups already placed on the table) in front of himself or his partner. These groups are known as *melds* and the act of placing them on the table or adding to them is known as *melding*.

A meld comprises a minimum of three cards and a maximum of seven cards—including at least five natural cards and never more than two wild cards. Exceptions may take place (*a*) when putting down an initial meld or when putting down red and black threes and (*b*) when melding wild cards in groups of three to seven, apart from natural cards. A side may not meld more than one set of the same rank. After a player has melded a set, all additional cards of the same rank melded by him or his partner must be laid on (added to) this set until a meld is made up of seven cards. It is called a canasta. A player may in turn lay off one, two, three, or four cards on a set or sets melded by his partnership. All melds of a partnership are kept in front of one of the partners and no distinction is drawn between those made by one partner and those made by the other. A player is not permitted to lay off on opponents' melds. A player may not lay off a wild card on a natural meld until the partnership has a base of five natural cards. Point value of the cards in scoring is the same as given on page 99.

All unmelded cards caught in a player's hand (partner's or opponent's) at the end of a hand, even though they form melds, are referred to as penalty cards and are deducted at amounts equivalent to their melding value, except threes.

(Card Left in a Player's Hand at the End of a Hand)

Jokers	50 points each
Deuces	20 points each
Aces	20 points each
Eights, nines, tens, jacks, queens, kings	10 points each
Fours, fives, sixes, sevens	5 points each
Threes	100 points each

Canastas. A partnership must have melded at least two canastas (with the exception of a schneider or a blitz) to go out. No canasta may contain more than seven cards. A natural canasta counts 500 points. A mixed canasta counts 300 points. Wild cards may also be melded: A canasta of seven deuces counts 4,000 points. A canasta of wild cards which includes all four jokers counts 3,000. Any other wild-card canasta counts 2,000 points. A partnership needs two canastas to go out (go rummy).

Natural and Mixed Canastas and Their Scoring Values. This is a natural canasta:

5-5-5-5-5-5-5

or

K-K-K-K-K-K-K

or any seven cards of the same rank regardless of suit. A natural canasta has a value of 500 points. However, a canasta made up of seven 7's or seven aces has a value of 2,500 points each, such as,

7-7-7-7-7-7-7

or

A-A-A-A-A-A-A

There is no mixed seven (7) canasta because wild cards cannot be used with sevens in a canasta. If a player goes out and a player is caught with four or more seven's or four or more aces in his hand, he is penalized 1,500 points for the sevens and 1,500 points for the aces.

This is a Mixed Canasta:

A-A-A-A-A plus two wild cards

or

8-8-8-8-8 plus one wild card

A mixed canasta is a combination of seven cards regardless of suit having the same rank (7's excepted), at least five of which must be natural cards and a maximum of two which may be wild. A mixed canasta has a value of 300 points.

This is a Seven Deuce Canasta:

2-2-2-2-2-2-2

A Seven Deuce canasta is a combination of seven wild deuces and has a value of 4,000 points.

This is a Four Joker Canasta:

joker-joker-joker-joker-2-2-2

A Four Joker canasta contains four jokers and three deuces and counts 3,000 points.

This is a Mixed Wild Canasta:

joker-joker-joker-2-2-2-2

A Mixed Wild Canasta contains one, two, or three jokers plus enough deuces to form a canasta and counts 2,000 points.

Red and Black Threes. At a player's proper turn of play, should he hold any threes, he places them on the table as if they were a meld (black and red threes must be melded separately). For each three he lays down, he picks a card from the stock. If this drawn card is a three, it is laid on the table and the player draws another card from the stock. This procedure is continued until the player fails to draw a three. This rule holds true for each player at each turn of play. At the end of a hand, if a partnership has placed four same-colored threes (reds or blacks) on the board, their total value becomes 1,000 points. The melding value of either red threes or black threes is progressive: 100 points for one red three, 300 for two red threes, 500 for three red threes, and 1,000 points for all four red threes. The same progressive melding value procedure holds true for the black threes. Red and black threes cannot be combined into one meld. They are melded and scored separately.

To receive credit for threes, a partnership must have laid down at least one canasta. In the event of failure to meld one or more canastas, the threes become a penalty against the partnership of 100 points for each three. Upon the completion of a hand, if a player is caught with one or more threes in his hand, having failed to put it or them down, he is penalized 100 points for each three.

The Actual Play

First Player. He may pick the top card from the stock. He may then meld if he can and if he wants to do so. Then he must discard one card. His first or initial meld or melds must total 90 or more points. He may make up the 90 points by laying as many or as few melds from his hand as will suffice.

Or the player may pick up the entire dis-card pile—if the upcard can be used with two other natural cards of its numerical rank to form a meld. Again, a player's initial meld or melds must total 90 or more points from the hand. Before taking the upcard or the discard pile, the player must lay down from his hand melds totaling 90 points or more. An initial meld must contain at least one natural meld made up of three natural cards.

After the cards are melded, the remainder of the discard pile is incorporated into the player's hand. The player may now put down any other meld he elects. Having melded, he must discard one card.

Second Player. The rules for the first player as just stated govern the play of the second.

Third and Fourth Players (partners of the first and second). If the partner has not melded cards, the rules as stated above apply to these players.

Once the partnership has melded 90 or more points for its first initial meld, a player or his partner may meld cards of any value until their partnership's score reaches 2,500 or more points at the end of a hand. Then the next initial meld required must total 120 points or more. Then when a partnership's score has reached 5,000 or more points at the end of any hand, the following initial meld must total 150 points or more. When a partnership's score has reached 7,500 or more points at the end of any hand, the next initial meld must total 180 points or more. After that, melds of any value are in order until a score of 10,000 or more is reached at the end of a hand and the game is ended. There are no further complications. That's game. Bonus cards, such as black and red threes, cannot be counted in amassing the initial required 90, 120, 150, or 180 or more point melds.

To Emphasize: The initial meld must have a minimum count that depends upon the accumulated total score of that partnership at the beginning of the current deal. These are shown below in tabular form:

Accumulated Score at the Beginning of the Deal	Minimum Meld Count Requirement
Minus to 2,495	90 points
2,500 to 4,995	120 points
5,000 to 7,495	150 points
7,500 or more	180 points

The initial meld may be made as follows:

1. A meld of three or more wild cards.

2. A meld of three or more natural cards.

3. One or more melds of two or more natural cards plus a wild card. Such an initial meld must contain at least one meld of three or more natural cards to be valid.

Going Out. A player goes out (goes rummy) when he (legally) gets rid of the last card of his hand by meld or discard. When a player goes out, play ends for that hand and the hands are scored. A player may go out only if his partnership has melded at least two canastas. Failing this requirement, he must retain at least one card in his hand. A player need not discard a card in going out, he may lay off or meld all cards in hand. A player going out receives a 100 going-out (rummy) bonus. If a player legally goes out by melding his entire hand (13 or 14 cards) in one turn, having made no previous meld, he receives a "once-out bonus" of 200 points plus any other bonuses attributed to the hand.

Initial Meld Bonus. Immediately after putting down an initial meld and before discarding, a player has the privilege (optional) of taking three cards off the top of the stock and adding them to his hand. This is known as an "initial-meld bonus," or "three-card bonus," a reward for fulfilling the initial count requirement. If the player for reasons of his own refuses to accept the three cards, he simply says "I refuse." After the acceptance or refusal, the player discards and ends his turn of play.

Schneider and Blitz Going-Out Hands

Schneider Hand. If a player for his first meld of a deal puts down his entire hand of 14 cards and it is made up of seven pairs of different rank cards (no wild cards), he calls "Schneider." This ends the hand and the player receives a 2,000-point *schneider bonus*. In such an instance, the two-canasta rule requirement to go out is waived.

Blitz Hand. If a player for his first meld of the deal puts down his entire hand of 14 cards and it is made up of 13 cards in sequence plus a joker, he calls "Blitz." He goes out, receiving a *blitz bonus* of 2,500 points. A blitz hand is as follows: ace, deuce, three, four, five, six, seven, eight, nine, ten, jack, queen, king, and joker. Deuces and jokers are not wild in a blitz hand. In such an instance, the two-canasta rule requirement to go out is waived. If partners score any points, they are deducted.

Exhausting the Stock. If no one goes out and the entire stock pile is exhausted, the player picking the last card from the stock must discard one card. If the next player does not hold a pair to match the upcard of the discard pile, the hand ends then and there. If the player holds a matching pair and the partnership has put down their initial meld, he takes the entire discard pile and lays down his melds and lay-off, if any. He discards a card and the hand ends.

End of the Game. At the end of each hand, new hands are dealt until one partnership reaches a score of 10,000 or more points. But the partnership reaching the winning score cannot call out; the hand must be completed. If both partnerships have 10,000 or more points, that partnership with the highest score wins. If the teams tie at 10,000 or more points, new hands are played until the tie is broken. There is no game bonus for winning the game.

The Score. At the end of a hand, each partnership's score is counted as follows: The partnership is credited with bonuses for canastas, for red and black threes, and for going out. Then the total value of all cards melded is counted. These points are added, and from that sum is subtracted the total point values of the cards remaining in the partners' hands. The net balance is the partnership score at the end of the hand, and this may occasionally be a minus score. Note that all cards left in the hand count against the player, regardless of whether or not they could have been melded.

The scores are entered on a score sheet in "We" and "They" columns (see below), after which the next hand is dealt. A cumulative total score is kept of each hand scored.

TYPICAL FOUR-HANDED SCORE SHEET

We	They	
800	1,000	Base score (bonuses) for the first hand
170	270	Net point values for the first hand
970	1,270	Total score at end of the first hand
600	3,200	Base score (bonuses) for the second hand
90	565	Net point value for the second hand
1,660	5,035	Total score at end of the second hand
900	1,800	Base score (bonuses) for the third hand
230	385	Net point values for the third hand
2,790	7,220	Total score at end of the third hand
1,800	3,200	Base score (bonuses) for the fourth hand

We	They	
125	340	Net point value for the fourth hand
4,715	10,760	Total score for game
	−4,715	Score of *We*
	5,945	Points *They* won by

At one-fiftieth of a cent a point, partnership They collects $1.18 from partnership We. When the game (not a hand) ends, the score is usually figured in even hundreds—50 or more counting 100, and less than 50 counting zero. In the game above, the final score would read: We, 4,700; They, 10,800. They won by 6,100 points. At one-fiftieth of a penny a point, They receive $1.22 from the We partnership (6,100 ÷ 50 = 122 cents = $1.22).

Additional Rules. The additional rules governing irregularities in International Canasta are basically the same as those governing Canasta. See page 104.

Canasta Strategy

The basic approach to Canasta strategy applies in general to all variations described in the preceding pages, though, of course, each game gives rise to some specific bits of strategy. Actually, the skill of Canasta centers around the effort to get the discard pile and to do a lot of melding. The partnership that takes the first discard pile has every prospect of keeping control to the end of the hand and of increasing its margin of victory at every draw. The beginner's worst mistake is putting down his initial meld fast and reducing his hand to a few cards. Then he will probably never get the discard pile during that hand, minimizing the chances of completing canastas and of going out. A good rule to follow is this: When you need 50 for the initial meld, do not meld without taking the pack. When you need 90, expend no more than four cards from your hand for the initial meld; when you need 120 no more than six cards. This basic theory, of course, changes with the variations of Canasta.

Make mixed canastas fast rather than wait for natural canastas. Don't be in a hurry to go out if your partnership has a better chance of further scoring. Also, don't pay too much attention to the bonus for a concealed hand.

If you have some wild cards to build up your count for an initial meld, build up a hand of pairs. Don't meld from your hand when the discard pile is big—wait until you can take the pile. Safest late discards are those that match your left-hand opponent's earliest discards or his side's melded cards. When melding, try to keep at least one wild card in your hand.

Before your partnership has put down its initial meld, know at all times the meld count you have in your hand and what discards might allow you to take the pile and meld.

Forget about extra bonuses for natural canastas and for special going-out hands. Think twice about saying "No" to "May I go out?" It pays to keep your score at the end of a hand just under the next initial meld count, even at the sacrifice of a couple of hundred points you might have scored. In this way you avoid increasing the minimum initial count you need for the next hand.

More mistakes are made by hoarding than by squandering wild cards. Usually try to keep even with the opposition in the number of canastas, using wild cards when necessary to complete your own. It is especially important to be first to complete your canasta requirement. The partnership that does this puts added pressure on the opposition.

CHAPTER 7

Bridge: Contract and Auction

The principle of Bridge goes back more than 400 years in England. Whist, the basic game, developed into Bridge (1896), then Auction Bridge (1904), and finally Contract Bridge (1925). Whist and Auction Bridge still have many followers, but since about 1930 Contract Bridge has been most popular.

CONTRACT BRIDGE

Contract Bridge is the "hobby" game of more millions of people than is any other card game played in the English-speaking countries and throughout the world. It is first in the affections of the ultrafashionable circles that frequent Palm Beach, Newport, and other famous resorts; and it is equally the property of all walks of life, all sections of the United States, and all types of card players, from those who play seriously in clubs and tournaments to those who play casually in their homes.

Contract Bridge is an ideal game for the entertainment of guests, especially when married couples get together, because it is a partnership game and husband and wife do not have to play against each other. It is as ideally adapted for play by clubs which meet weekly in groups of eight, twelve, or more; for large card parties; and for tournament play, in clubs or homes, among serious players. But the most fascinating feature of Contract Bridge is that it is equally enjoyable to the casual player who does not want to take any game too seriously and to the scien-

tific player who wishes to study and master the intricacies of the game.

The following pages describe the fundamentals of the game, together with its rules, ethics, and proprieties. For those who wish to learn the game well, there are hundreds of books, and thousands of professional teachers who give lessons in Bridge; but the best and quickest way to learn is to play in actual Bridge games as often as possible.

The Laws of Contract Bridge

The following rules of Contract Bridge are condensed from the Laws of Contract Bridge and reprinted here by permission of the American Contract Bridge League.

Preliminaries

Number of Players. Four, two against two as partners. Five or six may take part in the same game, but only four play at a time.

The Deck. 52 cards. Two packs, of contrasting back designs, are invariably used. While one pack is being dealt, dealer's partner shuffles the other pack for the next deal.

Rank of Cards. Ace (high), king, queen, jack, ten, nine, eight, seven, six, five, four, three, two.

The Draw. A shuffled pack is spread face down on the table and each player draws one card, but not one of the four cards at either end. A player who exposes more than one card must draw again. No player should expose his card before all have drawn.

The player drawing the highest card deals first. He chooses his seat and the pack with which he will deal; next highest is his partner and sits across the table from him; the two others take the other two seats. If two players draw cards of the same rank, as ♡6 and ♣6, the rank of the suits determines the higher card.

Precedence. When five wish to play, the draw establishes order of precedence. *Example:* North draws ♣A, South ♠K, East ♣5, West ♡2 and a fifth player draws ◊2. North and South play as partners against East and West. After the first rubber the fifth player plays and West sits out; after the next rubber West reenters the game and East sits out, and so on until North has sat out a rubber, after which the fifth player sits out again. The procedure is the same with six players, except that two sit out each rubber.

The Shuffle. The player on dealer's left shuffles the cards and places them at the dealer's left. The dealer (after shuffling again, if he wishes) sets the cards down at his right to be cut.

The Cut. The player at dealer's right must lift off a portion of the pack (not fewer than four cards nor more than 48) and set it down toward dealer. Dealer completes the cut.

The Dealer. Dealer deals 13 cards to each player, one card at a time face down, in clockwise rotation beginning with the player at his left.

Rotation. The turn to deal, to bid, and to play always passes from player to player to the left.

The Auction

Calls. After looking at his cards, each player in turn beginning with dealer must make a call (pass, bid, double, or redouble). If all four pass in the first round, the deal is passed out and there is a new deal by the next dealer in turn. If any player makes a bid in the first round, the bidding is opened.

Passing. When a player does not wish to bid, to double, or to redouble, he says "Pass."

Bidding. Each bid must name a certain number of tricks in excess of six (called *odd tricks*) which the bidder agrees to win, and a suit which will become the trump suit, if the bid becomes the contract; thus "One spade" is a bid to win seven tricks (6 +1) with spades as trumps. A bid may be made in no-trump, meaning that there will be no trump suit. The lowest possible bid is one, and the highest possible bid is seven.

Each bid must name a greater number of odd tricks than the last preceding bid, or an equal number of a higher denomination. No-trump is the highest denomination, outranking spades. Thus, a bid of two no-trump will overcall a bid of two hearts, and a bid of four diamonds is required to overcall a bid of three hearts.

Doubling and Redoubling. Any player in turn may double the last preceding bid if it was made by an opponent. The effect of a double is to increase the value of odd tricks, overtricks, and undertrick penalties (see Scoring Table 123) if the doubled bid becomes the contract.

Any player in turn may redouble the last preceding bid if it was made by his side and doubled by an opponent. A redouble again increases the scoring values.

A doubled or redoubled contract may be overcalled by any bid which would be sufficient to overcall the same contract undoubled: thus, if a bid of two diamonds is doubled and redoubled, it may still be overcalled by a bid of two in hearts, spades, or no-trump and by a bid of three clubs, or by any higher bid.

Information as to Previous Calls. Any player in turn may ask to have all previous calls made in the auction restated, in the order in which they were made.

Final Bid and the Declarer. When a bid, double, or redouble is followed by three consecutive passes in rotation, the auction is closed. The final bid in the auction becomes the *contract.* The player who, for his side, first bid the denomination named in the contract becomes the *declarer.* If the contract names a trump suit, every card of that suit becomes a *trump.* Declarer's partner becomes *dummy,* and the other side become *defenders.*

The Play

Leads and Plays. A play consists of taking a card from one's hand and placing it, face up, in the center of the table. Four cards so

According to Contract Bridge rules, this trick consists of a card from each player; declarer (bottom) also plays partner's hand—the dummy (top).

played, one from each hand in rotation, constitute a trick. The first card played to a trick is a *lead*.

The leader to a trick may lead any card. The other three hands must follow suit if they can, but, if unable to follow suit, may play any card.

Opening Lead; Facing the Dummy Hand. The defender on declarer's left makes the first lead. Dummy then spreads his hand in front of him, face up, grouped in suits with the trumps at his right.

Winning of Tricks. A trick containing a trump is won by the hand playing the highest

In Contract Bridge the first six tricks (bottom) make up the "book," and the remaining four score toward the contract.

trump. A trick not containing a trump is won by the hand playing the highest card of the suit led. The winner of each trick leads to the next.

Dummy. Declarer plays both his and dummy's cards, but each in proper turn. Dummy may reply to a proper question but may not comment or take an active part in the play; except that he may call attention to an irregularity and may warn declarer (or any other player) against infringing a law of the game; as by saying "It's not your lead," or asking "No spades?" when a player fails to follow suit to a spade lead. See Dummy's Rights, page 126.

Played Card. Declarer *plays* a card from his own hand when he places it on the table or names it as an intended play; and from dummy when he touches it (except to arrange dummy's cards) or names it. A defender plays a card when he exposes it, with apparent intent to play, so that his partner can see its face. A card once played may not be withdrawn, except to correct a revoke or in the course of correcting an irregularity.

Taking in Tricks Won. A completed trick is gathered and turned face down on the table. The declarer and the partner of the defender winning the first trick for his side should keep all tricks won by his side in front of him, so arranged that it is apparent how many tricks each side has won, and the sequence in which they were won.

Claim or Concession of Tricks by Declarer. If declarer claims or concedes one or more of the remaining tricks, or otherwise suggests that play be curtailed, play should cease, and declarer, with his hand face up on the table, should forthwith make any statement necessary to indicate his intended line of play. A defender may face his hand and may suggest a play to his partner. If both defenders concede, play ceases and declarer is considered to have won the tricks claimed. If a defender disputes declarer's claim—see page 127.

Trick Conceded in Error. The concession of a trick which cannot be lost by any play of the cards is void.

Inspecting Tricks During Play. Declarer or either defender may, until his side has led or played to the next trick, inspect a trick and inquire which hand played any card to it.

The Scoring. When the last (thirteenth) trick has been played, the tricks taken by the respective sides are counted and their number agreed upon. The points earned by each side in that deal are then entered to the credit of that side on the score sheet. See the Scoring Table on page 123 for the point values.

Any player may keep score. If only one player keeps score, both sides are equally responsible to see that the score for each deal is correctly entered.

Each side has a *trick score* and a *premium score*.

Trick Score. If declarer made his contract, the trick-point value of the odd tricks he bid for is entered to the credit of his side in its trick score (called *below the line;* see page 123).

Premium Score. Odd tricks won by declarer in excess of his contract are *overtricks* and are scored to the credit of his side in its premium score (called *above the line;* see page 123). Honors held in one hand and premiums for slams bid and made, for winning the rubber, and for undertricks are scored to the credit of the side earning them, in its premium score.

Undertricks. When declarer wins fewer odd tricks than he bids for, his opponents score, in their premium score, the undertrick premium for each trick by which he fell short of his contract.

Slams. If a side bids and makes a contract of six odd tricks (all but one trick), it receives the premium for a *little slam;* seven odd tricks (all the tricks), the premium for a *grand slam.*

Vulnerable. A side which has won its first game toward the rubber becomes *vulnerable.* It is exposed to increased undertrick penalties if it fails to make a contract, but receives increased premiums for slams, and for overtricks made in doubled or redoubled contracts.

Honors. When there is a trump suit, the ace, king, queen, jack, and ten of that suit are honors. If a player holds four trump honors in his hand, his side receives a 100-point premium whether he is declarer, dummy, or a defender; five trump honors in one hand, or all four aces at a no-trump contract, 150-point premium.

Game. When a side amasses 100 or more points *in trick points* (whether these points are scored in one or more hands), it wins a game. Both sides then start at zero trick score on the next.

Rubber. When a side has won two games, it receives the premium for the rubber—500 points if the other side has won one game, 700 points if the other side has not won a game. The scores of the two sides are then totaled, including both trick points and premium points, and the side which has scored the most points has won the rubber. The players then draw again for partners and seats (page 119) and a new rubber is begun. (Or they may *pivot*—see page 145.)

Back Score. After each rubber, each player's standing, plus (+) or minus (−), in even hundreds of points, is entered on a separate score called the back score. An odd 50 points or more counts 100, so if a player wins a rubber by 950 he is +10, if he wins it by 940 he is +9.

Four-Deal Bridge, or Chicago, or Club Bridge. In a cut-in game, a player who is cut out often has a long wait till the rubber ends and he can get back in. Playing Four-Deal Bridge, a player seldom has to wait more than 15 or 20 minutes. The game is often called Chicago because it originated in the Standard Club of Chicago.

A round consists of four deals, one by each player in turn. Vulnerability is automatic, as follows:

First Deal: Neither side vulnerable.

Second and Third Deals: Dealer's side vulnerable, opponents not vulnerable (even if they previously made game).

Fourth Deal: Both sides vulnerable.

A passed-out deal is redealt by the same dealer. There is a bonus of 300 for making game when not vulnerable and 500 when vulnerable. A part score carries over as in rubber Bridge and can help to make game in the next deal or deals, but is canceled by any game. There is a bonus of 100 for making a part score on the fourth deal. After four deals have been played, the scores are totaled and entered on the back score, as in rubber Bridge, and there is a new cut for partners, seats, and deal.

Some play that on the second and third deals the dealer's side is *not* vulnerable and the opposing side *is* vulnerable.

More points are usually scored in Four-Deal Bridge than in the same number of deals at rubber Bridge—estimates vary from 15 to 50 percent more. This is chiefly because at least one side is vulnerable in three deals out of four.

Illustration of Contract Bridge Scoring

(*a*) We bid two hearts and win nine tricks, scoring 60 points below the line (trick score) for two tricks at hearts bid and made (30 each), and 30 points above the line (honor score) for one overtrick at hearts. We now have a part score of 60 toward game.

(*b*) We bid two clubs and make four odd, scoring 40 points trick score for two tricks bid and made (20 each), completing our game (100 points), so a line is drawn across both columns to show end of first game of rubber. We also score 40 points for two overtricks at clubs (20 each), and 100 points for four honors in one hand (one of us held ♣ A K J 10). *We are now vulnerable.*

WE	THEY
500	50
150	500
300	100
120	70
	180
100	
1170	900

Typical Contract Bridge pad. Points for holding honors, winning overtricks, making little slam or grand slam, penalties, etc., go *above the line*. Points for tricks over six, bid in contract, go *below the line*; amount of each side's score toward game.

(*c*) We bid four hearts and are doubled and set one trick. They score 200 for defeating our contract because we are vulnerable.

(*d*) They bid four spades but take only nine tricks, being set one. We score 50 points, for they are not vulnerable and we did not double. One of them held ♠ A Q J 10, so they score 100 points for honors even though they did not make their contract.

(*e*) We bid and make one no-trump. This scores 40 points for us below the line. We need only 60 points more to make a game.

(*f*) They bid and make three no-trump, scoring 40 for the first, 30 for the second, and 30 for the third trick over six (100 points below the line), a game. Another horizontal line is drawn across both columns, marking end of second game. Our part score no longer can count toward a game. *Now both sides are vulnerable.*

(*g*) We bid two spades and are doubled. We are set three tricks and the opponents

held 100 honors as well. They score 800 for the set and 100 for the honors.

(*h*) We bid and make six diamonds, a small slam, scoring 120 points trick score, 750 for a little slam, and 500 for winning the rubber.

Adding the score for both sides, we have 1,730 points, they 1,300; we win the rubber by 430. This gives us a 4-point rubber (see Back Score, page 122).

CONTRACT BRIDGE SCORING TABLE

GAME: 100 points.
Each trick over six:
♣ 20   ◇ 20   ♡ 30   ♠ 30
No Trump: First Trick—40; Each subsequent trick—30

As in the Table:

TRICK VALUES

Tricks over six	One	Two	Three	Four	Five	Six	Seven
Clubs	20	40	60	80	100	120	140
Diamonds	20	40	60	80	100	120	140
Hearts	30	60	90	120	150	180	210
Spades	30	60	90	120	150	180	210
No-trump	40	70	100	130	160	190	220

Doubling multiplies each of these values by 2.
Redoubling multiplies them by 4.
Vulnerability does not affect trick values.

PREMIUMS

Overtricks	Not Vulnerable	Vulnerable
Undoubled, each	Trick Value	Trick Value
Doubled, each	100	200
Redoubled, each	200	400
Making doubled or redoubled contract	50	50

Slams		
Little Slam	500	750
Grand Slam	1,000	1,500

RUBBER		HONORS (in one hand)	
Won in 2 games	700	Four	100
Won in 3 games	500	Five	150
Unfinished 1 game	300	4 Aces, No-trump	150
Unfinished, if only one side has part score on unfinished game	50		

Doubling and redoubling do not affect honor, slam, or rubber points.

PENALTIES FOR UNDERTRICKS
(scored by defenders)

Number of Tricks	Not Vulnerable		Vulnerable	
	Un-doubled	Doubled	Un-doubled	Doubled
1 Down	50	100	100	200
2 Down	100	300	200	500
3 Down	150	500	300	800
4 Down	200	700	400	1,100
5 Down	250	900	500	1,400
6 Down	300	1,100	600	1,700
7 Down	350	1,300	700	2,000

If redoubled, the penalties are twice those for doubled

Revoke: Penalty for first revoke in each suit, two tricks won after the revoke. No penalty for a subsequent revoke in same suit by same player.

Irregularities in Contract Bridge

The Scope of the Laws. The laws are designed to define correct procedure and to provide an adequate remedy where a player, by irregularity, gains an unintentional but unfair advantage. The laws are not designed to prevent dishonorable practices. Ostracism is the ultimate remedy for intentional offenses.

New Shuffle and Cut. Before the first card is dealt, any player may demand a new shuffle and cut. There must be a new shuffle and cut if a card is faced in shuffling or cutting.

Changing the Pack. A pack containing a distinguishable damaged card must be replaced. The pack originally belonging to a side must be restored if reclaimed.

Redeal. There must be a redeal if, before the last card is dealt, a redeal is demanded because a player is dealing out of turn or with an uncut deck. There must be a redeal if the cards are not dealt correctly, if a card is faced in the pack or elsewhere, if a player picks up the wrong hand and looks at it, or if at any time (until the end of play) one hand is found to have too many cards and another too few (and the discrepancy is not caused by errors in play).

When there is a redeal, the same dealer deals (unless the deal was out of turn) with the same pack, after a new shuffle and cut.

Missing Card. If a missing card is found, it is deemed to belong to the deficient hand, which may then be answerable for exposing the card and for revoke through failure to play the card in a previous trick. But if a missing card is found in another hand, there must be a redeal; or in a trick, the law on defective trick (page 127) applies. If a missing card is not found, there must be a redeal.

Surplus Card. If a player has a surplus card owing to an incorrect pack or incorrect deal, there must be a redeal. If the surplus is due to omission to play to a trick, the law on defective trick (page 127) applies.

Drawing Attention to an Irregularity. Any player (except dummy if he has forfeited his rights) may draw attention to an irregularity. Any player may give or obtain information as to the law covering it. The fact that the offending side draws attention to its own irregularity does not affect the rights of the opponents.

Enforcing a Penalty. Either opponent (but not dummy) may select or enforce a penalty. If partners consult as to selection of enforcement, the right to penalize is canceled.

Improper Remarks and Gestures. If by remark or unmistakable gesture a player other than declarer discloses his intentions, desires, or the nature of an unfaced hand, or the presence or absence of a card in an unfaced hand, or improperly suggests a lead, play, or plan of play, the offender's side is subject to penalty as follows:

1. If the offense occurred during the auction, either opponent may require the offending side to pass at every subsequent turn; and if that side becomes the defenders, declarer may require or forbid the opening lead of a specified suit by the offender's partner, for as long as he retains the lead.

2. If the offense occurred during the play, declarer or either defender (as the case may be) may require the offender's partner, on any one subsequent trick, to withdraw a lead or play suggested by the improper remark or gesture and substitute a card not so suggested.

Cards Exposed During the Auction. If during the auction a player exposes a single card lower than a ten there is no penalty. If a player exposes an ace, king, queen, jack, or ten, or a lower card prematurely led, or more than one card, such cards must be left face up on the table and become penalty cards (see page 126) if the owner becomes a defender; and the partner of the offender must pass at his next turn.

Improper Call Overcalled. If the offender's left-hand opponent calls before the penalty for an illegal call has been enforced, the auction proceeds as though the illegal call had been a legal call, except that it becomes a pass if it was a bid of more than seven, a call after the auction is closed, a double or redouble when the only proper call was a pass or bid.

Changing a Call. A player may change an inadvertent call without penalty if he does so without pause. Any other attempted change of call is void. If the first call was illegal, it is subject to the appropriate law. If it was a legal call, the offender may either (*a*) allow his first call to stand, whereupon his partner must pass at his next turn; or (*b*) substitute any other legal call, whereupon his partner must pass at every subsequent turn.

Insufficient Bid. If a player makes an insufficient bid, he must substitute either a sufficient bid or a pass. If he substitutes (*a*) the lowest sufficient bid in the same denomination, there is no penalty; (*b*) any other sufficient bid, his partner must pass at every subsequent turn; (*c*) a pass (or a double or redouble, which is treated as a pass), his partner must pass at every subsequent turn, and if the offending side becomes the defenders, declarer may impose a lead penalty (see next paragraph) on the opening lead.

Lead Penalty. When declarer may impose a lead penalty, he may specify a suit and either require the lead of that suit or forbid the lead of that suit for as long as the opponent retains the lead. When in the following pages only a "lead penalty" is cited, declarer has these rights. There are some other cases in which declarer has some control over a defender's lead, but not so much. In such cases, the exact penalty will be specified.

Information Given in Changing Call. A denomination named and then canceled in making or correcting an illegal call is subject to penalty if an opponent becomes declarer: if a suit was named, declarer may impose a lead penalty (see above); if no trump was named, declarer may call a suit, if the offender's partner has the opening lead; if a double or redouble was canceled, the penalties are the same as when a pass is substituted for an insufficient bid.

Barred Player. A player who is barred once, or for one round, must pass the next time it is his turn to bid; a player who is barred throughout must pass in every turn until the auction of the current deal is completed.

Waiver of Penalty. When a player calls or plays over an illegal call or play by his right-hand opponent, he accepts the illegal call or play and waives a penalty. The game continues as though no irregularity had occurred.

Retention of the Right to Call. A player cannot lose his only chance to call by the fact that an illegal pass by his partner has been accepted by an opponent. The auction must continue until the player has had at least one chance to call.

Call Out of Rotation (or "out of turn"). Any call out of rotation is canceled when attention is drawn to it. The auction reverts to the player whose turn it was. Rectification and penalty depend on whether it was a pass, a bid, or a double or redouble, as follows:

A call is not out of rotation if made without waiting for the right-hand opponent to pass if that opponent is legally obliged to pass; nor if it would have been in rotation had not the left-hand opponent called out of rotation. A call made simultaneously with another player's call in rotation is deemed to be subsequent to it.

Pass Out of Turn. If it occurs (*a*) before any player has bid, or when it was the turn of the offender's right-hand opponent, the offender must pass when his regular turn comes; (*b*) after there has been a bid and when it was the turn of the offender's partner, the offender is barred throughout; the offender's partner may not double or redouble at that turn; and if the offender's partner passes and the opponents play the hand, declarer may impose a lead penalty.

Bid Out of Turn. If it occurs (*a*) before any player has called, the offender's partner is barred throughout; (*b*) after any player has called and when it was the turn of the offender's partner, the offender's partner is barred throughout and is subject to a lead penalty (this page), if he has the opening lead; (*c*) after any player has called and when it was the turn of the offender's right-hand opponent, the offender must repeat his bid without penalty if that opponent passes, but if that opponent bids the offender may make any call and his partner is barred once.

Double or Redouble Out of Turn. If it occurs (*a*) when it was the turn of the offender's partner, the offender's partner is barred throughout and is subject to a lead penalty (this page) if he has the opening lead, and the offender may not in turn double or redouble the same bid; (*b*) when it was the turn of the offender's right-hand opponent, the offender must repeat his double or re-double without penalty if that opponent passes but may make any legal call if that opponent bids, in which case the offender's partner is barred once.

Impossible Doubles and Redoubles. If a player doubles or redoubles a bid that his side has already doubled or redoubled, his call is canceled; he must substitute (*a*) any legal bid, in which case his partner is barred throughout and if he becomes the opening leader declarer may prohibit the lead of the doubled suit; or (*b*) a pass, in which case either opponent may cancel all previous doubles and redoubles, the offender's partner is barred throughout, and if he becomes the opening leader he is subject to a lead penalty (page 125).

Other Inadmissible Calls. If a player bids more than seven, or makes another call when legally required to pass, he is deemed to have passed and the offending side must pass at every subsequent turn; if they become the defenders, declarer may impose a lead penalty (page 125) on the opening leader.

Call After the Auction Is Closed. A call made after the auction is closed is canceled. If it is a pass by a defender, or any call by declarer or dummy, there is no penalty. If it is a bid, double, or redouble by a defender, declarer may impose a lead penalty at the offender's partner's first turn to lead.

Dummy's Rights. Dummy may give or obtain information regarding fact or law, ask if a play constitutes a revoke, draw attention to an irregularity, and warn any player against infringing a law. Dummy forfeits these rights if he looks at a card in another player's hand.

If dummy has forfeited his rights and thereafter (*a*) is the first to draw attention to a defender's irregularity, declarer may not enforce any penalty for the offense; (*b*) warns declarer not to lead from the wrong hand, either defender may choose the hand from which declarer shall lead; (*c*) is the first to ask declarer if a play from declarer's hand is a revoke, declarer must correct a revoke if able but the revoke penalty still applies.

Exposed Cards. Declarer is never subject to penalty for exposure of a card, but inten-tional exposure of declarer's hand is treated as a claim or concession of tricks.

A defender's card is exposed if it is faced on the table or held so that the other defender may see its face before he is entitled to do so. Such a card must be left face up on the table until played, and becomes a penalty card.

Penalty Cards. A penalty card must be played at the first legal opportunity, subject to the obligation to follow suit or to comply with another penalty.

If a defender has two or more penalty cards that he can legally play, declarer may designate which one is to be played.

Declarer may require or forbid a defender to lead a suit in which his partner has a penalty card, but if declarer does so, the penalty card may be picked up and ceases to be a penalty card.

Failure to play a penalty card is not subject to penalty, but declarer may require the penalty card to be played, and any defender's card exposed in the process becomes a penalty card.

Lead Out of Turn. If declarer is required by a defender to retract a lead from the wrong hand, he must lead from the correct hand (if he can) a card of the same suit; if it was a defender's turn to lead, or if there is no card of that suit in the correct hand, there is no penalty.

If a defender is required to retract a lead out of turn, declarer may either treat the card so led as a penalty card, or impose a lead penalty on the offender's partner when next he is to lead after the offense.

Premature Play. If a defender leads to the next trick before his partner has played to the current trick, or plays out of rotation before his partner has played, declarer may require the offender's partner to play his highest card of the suit led, his lowest card of the suit led, or a card of another specified suit. Declarer must select one of these options and if the defender cannot comply, he may play any card. When declarer has played from both his hand and dummy, a defender is not subject to penalty for playing before his partner.

Inability to Play as Required. If a player is unable to lead or play as required to comply with a penalty (for lack of a card of a re-quired suit, or because of the prior obligation to follow suit), he may play any card. The penalty is deemed satisfied, except in the case of a penalty card.

Revoke. A revoke is the act of playing a card of another suit, when able to follow suit to a lead. Any player, including dummy, may ask whether a play constitutes a revoke and may demand that an opponent correct a revoke. A claim of revoke does not warrant inspection of turned tricks, prior to the end of play, except by consent of both sides.

Correcting a Revoke. A player must correct his revoke if aware of it before it becomes established. A revoke card withdrawn by a defender becomes a penalty card. The nonoffending side may withdraw any cards played after the revoke but before attention was drawn to it.

Established Revoke. A revoke becomes established when a member of the offending side leads or plays to a subsequent trick (or terminates play by a claim or concession). When a revoke becomes established, the revoke trick stands as played (unless it is the twelfth trick—see below).

Revoke Penalty. The penalty for an established revoke is two tricks (if available), transferred at the end of play from the revoking side to the opponents. This penalty can be paid only from tricks won by the revoking side after its first revoke, including the revoke trick. If only one trick is available, the penalty is satisfied by transferring one trick; if no trick is available, there is no penalty.

There is no penalty for a subsequent established revoke in the same suit by the same player.

A transferred trick ranks for all scoring purposes as a trick won in play by the side receiving it. It never affects the contract. *Example:* If the contract is two and declarer wins eight tricks plus two tricks as a revoke penalty, total ten tricks, he can score only 60 points below the line and the other 60 points go above the line.

Revokes Not Subject to Penalty. A revoke made in the twelfth trick must be corrected, without penalty, if discovered before the cards have been mixed together. The nonoffending side may require the offender's partner to play either of two cards he could legally have played. A revoke not discovered until the cards have ueen mixed is not subject to penalty, nor is a revoke by any faced hand (dummy, or a defender's hand when faced in consequence of a claim by declarer). A revoke by failure to play a penalty card is not subject to the penalty for an established revoke.

Defective Trick. A defective trick may not be corrected after a player of each side has played to the next trick. If a player has failed to play to a trick, he must correct his error when it is discovered by adding a card to the trick (if possible, one he could legally have played to it). If a player has played more than one card to a trick, he does not play to the last trick or tricks and if he wins a trick with his last card, the turn to lead passes to the player at his left.

Declarer Claiming or Conceding Tricks. If declarer claims or concedes one or more of the remaining tricks (verbally or by spreading his hand), he must leave his hand face up on the table and immediately state his intended plan of play.

If a defender disputes declarer's claim, declarer must play on, adhering to any statement he has made, and in the absence of a specific statement he may not exercise freedom of choice in making any play the success of which depends on finding either opponent with or without a particular unplayed card.

Following curtailment of play by declarer, it is permissible for a defender to expose his hand and to suggest a play to his partner.

Defender Claiming or Conceding Tricks. A defender may show any or all of his cards to declarer to establish a claim or concession. He may not expose his hand to his partner, and if he does, declarer may treat his partner's cards as penalty cards.

Correcting the Score. A proved or admitted error in any score may be corrected at any time before the rubber score is agreed to, except as follows. An error made in entering or failing to enter a part score, or in omitting a game or in awarding one, may not be corrected after the last card of the second succeeding correct deal has been dealt (unless a majority of the players consent).

Effect of Incorrect Deck. Scores made as a result of hands played with an incorrect deck are not affected by the discovery of the imperfection.

Concession of a Trick That Cannot Be Lost. The concession of a trick that cannot be lost by any play of the cards is void if attention is drawn to the error before the cards have been mixed together. If a player concedes a trick he has in fact won (as by claiming nine tricks when his side has already won ten) the concession is void, and if the score has been entered it may be corrected as provided above.

Illustrations of Most Frequent Irregularities and Penalties. In all the following examples, the four players at the bridge table are designated as South, *declarer;* North, *dummy;* West and East, *defenders.* Their relative positions are:

NORTH (*Dummy*)

WEST   EAST

SOUTH (*Declarer*)

Lead Out of Turn. West should make the opening lead, but East leads the ◇7. South may say to West "Lead anything but a diamond." West may lead any spade, heart, or club; and East picks up the ◇7 and puts it in his hand. Or South may say to West "Lead a diamond." West may lead any diamond in his hand and East may pick up the ◇7 and play either it or any other diamond he may hold. Or South may permit West to make any lead he pleases, but in this case ◇7 becomes a penalty card; East must place it face up on the table in front of him and leave it there. The first time he can legally lead or play it he must do so, subject only to his duty to follow suit. Or, South may accept the ◇7 as a correct lead. In this case dummy exposes his hand and then South plays to the trick. West plays next and dummy last. If, after East's out-of-turn opening lead, South had inadvertently exposed his hand, the lead would have stood, South's hand would have become the dummy, and North would have become the declarer.

In another case, North makes an opening lead, thinking that West has won the contract. But South is the actual declarer. North's card is put back in his hand. There is no penalty against the declaring side for exposing cards, since the information so given can be utilized only by the opponents.

Declarer Leads from Wrong Hand. North (dummy) won the last trick, but South (declarer) leads the ♠K. West says "The lead is in dummy," South replaces the ♠K in his own hand and must lead a spade from dummy. When South plays to that trick, he does not have to play the ♠K if he has another spade he prefers to play. (If dummy had not held a spade, South could have led any card from dummy.)

West could accept the out-of-turn lead of the ♠K, if he wished, by following to it at once, before either he or East made any remark about its irregularity.

Revoke Corrected. South leads ◇6. West has some diamonds, but he plays ♣9. Dummy plays ◇K and East plays ◇3. At this juncture West says "Wait, I have a diamond."

There is time for West to correct his revoke, because it is not established—neither West nor East has led or played to the next trick. West must leave the ♣9 face up on the table as a penalty card. He may play any diamond he wishes and he elects to play ◇A. Now declarer may retract dummy's play of the ◇K and substitute a small diamond. But East may not change his card.

In another case, South (the declarer) revokes and notices his error in time for correction. He replaces the revoke card in his hand, without penalty, and follows suit with any card he chooses.

Revoke Established. South leads ♠K. West has a spade, but plays ♡7. East wins the trick with the ♠A and leads a heart.

It is now too late for West to correct his revoke. East, a "member of the offending side," has led to the next trick and the revoke is established. Play proceeds normally, and let us suppose that East-West win one more trick.

South's contract was two spades, and when play is ended he has won eight tricks. But, as the revoke penalty, he may take two of East-West's tricks and transfer them to his pile. That gives him ten tricks in all. He scores 60 below the line for making two spades, and 60 above the line for two overtricks. Note that South does not get game for making ten tricks at spades. He bid only two spades, and that is all he can score toward game. Tricks transferred as the result of a revoke penalty are scored exactly as though won in play. If South, having bid two spades, had won ten tricks without the revoke, he could not have made game; therefore he cannot make game as a result of the revoke penalty.

Finally, take a case in which West revokes and East, who wins the trick, establishes the revoke by leading to the next trick; play continues, but East-West do not win another trick.

After the play is completed, South may take only one trick as the revoke penalty—the trick on which the revoke occurred. He is not entitled to any trick the defenders won before the revoke occurred, because obviously the revoke could have had nothing to do with how such tricks were won.

Proprieties in Bridge. The dealer should

refrain from looking at the bottom card before completing the deal. The other players should refrain from touching or looking at their cards until the deal is completed.

A player should refrain from: calling with special emphasis, inflection or intonation; making a call with undue delay which may result in conveying improper information to partner; indicating in any way approval or disapproval of partner's call or play; making a remark or gesture or asking a question from which an inference may be drawn; attracting attention to the number of tricks needed to complete or defeat the contract; preparing to gather a trick before all four hands have played to it; detaching a card from his hand before it is his turn to lead or play; watching the place in a player's hand from which he draws a card.

Do not allow partner's hesitation or mannerism to influence a call, lead, or play. It is proper to draw inferences from an opponent's gratuitous acts, but at one's own risk.

It is proper to keep silent in regard to irregularities committed by one's own side, but it is improper to infringe any law of the game deliberately.

It is improper to employ any convention whose significance is known to partner but has not been announced to the opponents.

Contract Bridge Strategy

The main object in Bridge is to score as many points as possible. This can be done in one of two ways: by securing the contract for your side and fulfilling it successfully, scoring points for tricks, overtricks, and premiums; or by keeping your opponents from fulfilling their contract and so score for your side points for penalties.

Often more points can be scored for your side by catching opponents in overbids and doubling them than by taking the bid yourself. Bear in mind that the winner of the rubber is the side that scores the most points and that may not necessarily be the side that played the most contracts.

In life the fellow who always knows the score holds a definite advantage. The same is true in Bridge. Become thoroughly familiar with the tables of scoring values. Develop the habit of checking your side's score after every hand. Bids and play are affected by the score.

Evaluating the Hand. To get some idea of the strength of a hand, the following table of quick tricks may be used in making an estimate. A quick trick is a card or combination of cards which will usually win a trick, regardless of what suit is eventually trump and regardless of who wins the contract. Learn this table by heart if you can. (*x* refers to a low card, usually lower than ten.)

QUICK TRICKS

	Quick Tricks
Ace and king of the same suit	2
Ace and queen of the same suit	1½
Any ace	1
King and queen of the same suit	1
Any king and *x* of the same suit	½

Queen, jack, and *x* of the same suit, or queen and *x* of one suit plus jack and *x* of another suit are considered by many to have 1/2-quick-trick value. Others consider these simply as plus values but give them no definite numerical weight. Any jack added to any of the values in the table is also a plus value. *Note:* Do not count any one suit for more than two quick tricks. Thus, ace, king, and queen or ace, king, queen, and jack are only counted as two quick tricks each—the values of their ace–kings.

The Point Count. In recent years there has been a popular revival of the point-count method of evaluating hands for bidding. The point count goes back to Milton Work, who is credited with having originated it some decades ago.

The most useful application of the point count in its modern form seems to be in no-trump bidding, where it has proven itself a precise and scientific instrument. Most good players use both the quick-trick and point-count methods in evaluating the strength of a hand, as circumstances warrant, and rely on neither exclusively. This should be borne in mind when reading the following summary of the highlights of the point count as it is used today.

The Point-Count Table: Any ace, four; king, three; queen, two; jack, one.

A combined count of approximately 26 points in the two hands of a partnership normally will produce game in no-trump or a major, 29 points in a minor. A total of approximately 33 points will produce a small slam and 37 a grand slam.

In opening bids of one in a suit the count

of the hand is arrived at by combining the point value of high cards and the following: 3 points for a void, 2 for a singleton, 1 for a doubleton. A hand of 14 points should usually be opened, but hands with lesser count may be opened as convenient.

One No-Trump and Responses: Only high cards are valued when bidding no-trump and no points are assigned for distribution. To open with one no-trump the hand must be of no-trump pattern with at least three suits stopped. The count should be between 16 and 19—some prefer 16 to 18. It is not a forcing bid and may be passed.

If the responding hand is of no-trump type, raise to two no-trump with 8 or 9 points or 7 points and a five-card minor. Raise to three no-trump with 10 to 14, or four no-trump with 15 to 16, to six no-trump with 17 or 18, to seven no-trump with 21.

A response of two in a minor indicates a long suit but less than 7 points; two in a major shows a five-card suit with perhaps as many as 8 or 9 points in the hand and an unbalanced distribution. A response of three in a suit shows an unbalanced hand and 10 or more points. A response of four in a major shows a fairly long suit, an unbalanced hand and less than 10 points in high cards.

The Stayman Convention: In a modification known as the Stayman convention a response of two clubs to one no-trump is artificial. It suggests the responder has one or two major suits of four cards or more and 8 or 9 points. It asks the original no-trumper to name, if he can, a major suit of four cards headed by at least a queen. It looks toward a safer contract in a major.

If original no-trumper has no four-card major, he makes the artificial rebid of two diamonds with a hand of minimum point count. This permits responder to rebid two or three no-trump according to the strength of his hand.

If responder bids a major suit over declarer's two diamonds, he is guaranteeing five cards in the suit.

If responder rebids his clubs a second time, he indicates he wants to play the hand in clubs only, since his holding is insufficient to have the hand play in no-trump.

Two and Three No-Trump and Responses: Open two no-trump with 22 to 24 and all suits stopped; three no-trump with 25 to 27. An opening two no-trump is not a demand bid and may be passed; an opening three no-trump is not a shutout.

In responding to two no-trump: Raise to three with 4 to 8 points and to four no-trump with 9. With 10 points go to three of a suit and then rebid four no-trump. Jump to six no-trump with 11 or 12 points. Bid three of a suit and then rebid six no-trump with 13 or 14. Jump to seven no-trump with 15. Show any six-card major regardless of how low the point count.

In responding to three no-trump: Raise to four no-trump with 7 points; to six no-trump with 8 or 9. Bid four diamonds and rebid six no-trump with 10 or 11 points; raise to seven no-trump with 12. Show a five-card suit with 5 points in the hand.

Responding to a Suit Bid of One: Holding 5 to 9 points, a suit may be shown at the level of one; otherwise the response is one no-trump. A suit may be shown at the level of two with 10 points, or with fewer points if the suit is fairly long.

With no-trump distribution jump to two no-trump holding 13 to 15 points; to three no-trump with 16 to 18. Jump to three in partner's suit with 13 to 15; to three of another suit with 13 to 16.

Bidding Inferences. The player should think of the bidding as a kind of special language in which he tries to convey to his partner, or receive from him, information that will help both partners to gauge correctly the possibilities in their combined holdings and so enable them to reach the best contract. He should also pay attention to the bidding of opponents. He can learn things from their bidding that may prove useful in playing a contract or defending against it.

Biddable Suits. Generally a suit should have four or more cards to be originally biddable. For safety's sake a four-card suit should have at least ace, king or queen, and ten—though this is not a must—and a five-card suit, queen or jack, and ten. A six-card suit or longer needs no honor card.

More Than One Biddable Suit: With two biddable suits, bid them as follows: If the suits are equal in length and touch in rank—for example, spades and hearts, hearts and diamonds—bid the higher-ranking one first *regardless* of which suit has the higher cards. Later the lower-ranking suit is bid. *Example:* If a player holds two four-card biddable suits in spades and hearts, he should bid spades first; then bid the heart suit when his next turn to bid comes.

If both suits are of five-card length, bid the higher-ranking suit first, even if it is weaker than the other suit; then bid the lower-ranking suit. If the two biddable suits are of unequal length, bid the longer suit first, even if the other has higher cards.

Rebiddable Suits. A suit is considered rebiddable—it may be bid again—if it is at least of five-card length. Generally, a five-card suit should have at least a king and a lower honor card or be headed by queen-jack-nine to qualify as a rebiddable suit. Any suit of six cards is rebiddable, regardless of whether it has any honor cards. If there are two five-card rebiddable suits, the lower-ranking one is rebid, not the higher-ranking one. This indicates to the partner that the player holds two five-card suits.

MINIMUM BIDDABLE SUITS

For an Opening Bid

Four-Card Suits must contain four high-card points
(example: K-J-x-x, A-x-x-x)

Five-Card Suits: Any Five-Card Suit (x-x-x-x-x)

For a Response or Rebid

Q-10-x-x or better (example: Q-10-x-x, K-x-x-x, A-x-x-x)

Any Five-Card Suit (x-x-x-x-x)

REBIDDABLE SUITS

Four-Card Suits	No four-card suit is rebiddable
Five-Card Suits	Must be Q-J-9-x-x or better
Six-Card Suits	Any six-card suit is rebiddable (x-x-x-x-x-x)

Opening Bids. An opening bid is the first bid made in the deal. There are basic requirements of the opening bid, as shown in the list below.

One of a suit	(*a*) 14-point hands must be opened.
	(*b*) 13-point hands may be opened if a good rebid is available (a rebiddable suit or a second rebiddable suit).
	(*c*) All openings must contain two quick tricks.
	(*d*) A third-position opening is permitted with 11 points if hand contains a good suit.
Two of a suit (*forcing to game*)	(*a*) 25 points with a good five-card suit (1 point less with a second good five-card suit).
	(*b*) 23 points with a good six-card suit.
	(*c*) 21 points with a good seven-card suit.
Three, four, or five of a suit (*preemptive bids*)	Preemptive bids show less than 10 points in high cards and the ability to win within two tricks of the contract vulnerable and within three tricks not vulnerable. They should usually be based on a good seven-card or longer suit.
One no-trump	16 to 18 points (in no-trump bidding only high-card points are counted) and 4-3-3-3, 4-4-3-2, or 5-3-3-2 distribution with Q-x or better in any doubleton.
Two no-trump	22 to 24 points and all suits stopped (J-x-x-x; Q-x-x; K-x; or better).
Three no-trump	25 to 27 points and all suits stopped.
Choice of suits	Generally speaking, bid your longest suit first.

With two five-card suits bid the higher-ranking first. With two or more four-card suits, bid the suit immediately lower in rank to your short suit (doubleton, singleton, or void).

General Principles. Any bid of a new suit by the responding hand is forcing on the opening bidder for one round. Thus, each time the responder bids a new suit, the opener must bid again. If responder should jump, his bid is forcing to game.

With less than 10 points, responder should prefer to raise partner if partner has opened in a major suit, and to bid a new suit himself at the one level in preference to raising a minor-suit opening bid. With 11 or 12 points, responder can make two bids but should not force game. With 13 points or more he should see that the bidding is not dropped before a game contract is reached. With 19 points he should make a strong effort to reach a slam.

Responses to Suit Bids of One. Raise. To raise partner's suit responder must have adequate trump support. This consists of J-x-x, Q-x-x, x-x-x-x, or better for a non-rebid suit; and Q-x, K-x, A-x, or x-x-x for a rebid suit.

Raise partner's suit to two with 7 to 10 points and adequate trump support.

Raise to three with 13 to 16 points and at least four trumps.

Raise to four with no more than nine high-card points plus at least five trumps and a short suit (singleton or void).

Bid a New Suit. At one level requires 6 points or more. This response may be made on anything ranging from a weak hand, where responder is just trying to keep the bidding open, to a very powerful one, when he is not sure where the hand should be played.

At two level requires 10 points or more.

Jump in a new suit requires 19 points or more. (The jump shift is reserved for hands where a slam is very likely. Responder should hold either a strong suit or strong support for opener's suit.)

No-Trump Responses (made on balanced hands). One no-trump requires 6 to 9 points in high cards. (This bid is often made on an unbalanced hand if responder's suit is lower in rank than the opening bidder's and responder lacks the 10 points required to take the bidding into the two level.)

Two no-trump requires 13 to 15 points in high cards, all unbid suits stopped, and a balanced hand.

Three no-trump requires 16 to 18 points in high cards, all unbid suits stopped, and 4–3–3–3 distribution.

Responses to Suit Bids of Two. An opening bid of two in a suit is unconditionally forcing to game and responder may not pass until game is reached. With 6 points or less he bids two no-trump regardless of his distribution. With 7 points and one quick trick, he may show a new suit or raise the opener's suit. With eight or nine high-card points and a balanced hand, responder bids three no-trump.

Responses to Preemptive Bids. Since the opener has overbid his hand by two or three tricks, aces, kings, and potential ruffing

(trumping) values are the key factors to be considered when responder is contemplating a raise. One or two trumps constitute sufficient support.

Responses to a One No-Trump Bid. Balanced Hands. Raise to two-no-trump with 8 or 9 points, or with 7 points and a good five-card suit. Raise to three no-trump with 10 to 14 points. Raise to four no-trump with 15 or 16 points. Raise to six no-trump with 17 or 18 points. Raise to seven no-trump with 21 points.

Unbalanced Hands. With less than 8 points plus a five-card suit, bid two diamonds, two hearts, or two spades. (Do not bid two clubs on a five-card club suit.) With 8 points or more and a four-card major suit, bid two clubs. (This is an artificial bid asking opener to show a four-card major if he has one. See section on rebids by opening one no-trump bidder.) With 10 points and a good suit, bid three of that suit. With a six-card major suit and less than 10 points in high cards, jump to game in the suit.

Responses to a Two No-Trump Opening. Balanced hands. Raise to three no-trump with 4 to 8 points. Raise to four no-trump with 9 to 10 points. Raise to six no-trump with 11 or 12 points. Raise to seven no-trump with 15 points.

Unbalanced Hands. With a five-card major suit headed by an honor plus 4 points, bid the suit at the three level. Show any six-card major suit.

Responses to a Three No-Trump Opening. Show any five-card suit if the hand contains 5 points in high cards. Raise to four no-trump with 7 points. Raise to six no-trump with 8 or 9 points. Raise to seven no-trump with 12 points.

Rebid

Rebids by Opening Bidder. The opener's rebid is frequently the most important call of the auction, as he now has the opportunity to reveal the exact strength of his opening bid and therefore whether game or slam is in contemplation. His opening is valued according to the following:

13 to 16 points	Minimum hand
16 to 19 points	Good hand
19 to 21 points	Very good hand

13 to 16 points. *Minimum hand.* If partner has made a limit response (one no-trump or a single raise), opener should pass, as game is

impossible. If partner bids a new suit at the one level, opener may make a single raise with good trump support, rebid one no-trump with a balanced hand, or, with an unbalanced hand, rebid his own suit or a new suit (if he does not go past the level of two in the suit of his original bid).

16 to 19 points. *Good hand.* If partner has made a limit response (one no-trump or a single raise), opener should bid again, as game is possible if responder has maximum values. If responder has bid a new suit, opener may make a jump raise with four trumps, or jump in his own suit if he has a six-card suit, or bid a new suit.

19 to 21 points. *Very good hand.* If partner has made a limit response (one no-trump or a single raise), opener may jump to game in either denomination, according to his distribution. If responder has bid a new suit, opener may make a jump raise to game with four trumps, or jump to game in his own suit if it is solid. With a balanced hand and 19 or 20 points, opener should jump to two no-trump. With 21 points he should jump to three no-trump. With 22 points and up he should jump in a new suit (forcing to game and suggesting a slam).

Rebids by Opening No-Trump Bidder. Two-Club Convention. When the responder bids two clubs, the opening bidder must show a four-card biddable major suit if he has one: with four spades, he bids two spades; with four hearts, he bids two hearts; with four cards in each major, he bids two spades; with no four-card major suit, he bids two diamonds.

Opening no-trump bidder must pass: When responder raises to two no-trump and opener has a minimum (16 points); when responder bids two diamonds, two hearts, or two spades, and opener has only 16 or 17 points and no good fit for responder's suit; when responder bids three no-trump, four spades, or four hearts.

Defensive Bidding

Overcalls. An overcall is a defensive bid (made after the other side has opened the bidding). Prospects for game are not as good as they are for the opening bidder, in view of the announced adverse strength, and safety becomes a prime consideration. Overcalls are therefore based not on a specified number of points but rather on a good suit. Generally speaking the overcaller should employ the

same standards as a preemptor; he should be able to win in his own hand within two tricks of his bid if vulnerable and within three tricks if not vulnerable.

One No-Trump Overcall. An overcall of one no-trump is similar to a one no-trump opening bid and shows 16 to 18 points with a balanced hand and the opening bidder's suit well stopped.

Jump Overcall. Any jump overcall, whether it is a single, double, or triple jump, is preemptive in nature and shows a hand weak in high cards but with a good suit that will produce within three tricks of the bid if not vulnerable and within two tricks if vulnerable.

Takeout Doubles (also called *negative* or *informatory* doubles). When a defender doubles and all the following conditions are present: (*a*) his partner has made no bid; (*b*) the double was made at the doubler's first opportunity; (*c*) the double is of one, two, or three of a suit—it is intended for a takeout and asks partner to bid his best (longest) suit. This defensive bid is employed on either of two types of hand: (1) a hand of opening-bid strength where the doubler has no good or long suit of his own but has good support for any of the unbid suits; and (2) where the doubler has a good suit and so much high-card strength that he fears a mere overcall might be passed out and a possible game missed.

Overcall in Opponent's Suit (cue bid). The immediate cue bid (*example:* opponent opens one heart; defender bids two hearts) is the strongest of all defensive bids. It is unconditionally forcing to game and shows approximately the equivalent of an opening forcing bid. It normally announces first-round control of the opening bid suit and is usually based on a void with fine support in all unbid suits.

Action by Partner of Overcaller. The overcaller's bid is based on a good suit; therefore less than normal trump support is required to raise (Q-x or x-x-x). A raise should be preferred by the partner to bidding a suit of his own, particularly if the overcaller has bid a major. The partner of the overcaller should not bid for the sole purpose of keeping the bidding open. A single raise of a one no-trump response should be made only in an effort to reach game. If appropriate values are held, a leap to game is in order, since a jump raise is not forcing.

Action by Partner of Takeout Doubler. In this situation, the weaker the hand the more important it is to bid. The only holding that would justify a pass would be one that contained four defensive tricks, three in the trump suit. The response should be made in the longest suit, though preference is normally given to a major over a minor.

The doubler's partner should value his hand as follows: 6 points, fair hand; 9 points, good hand; 11 points, probable game. Doubler's partner should indicate a probable game by jumping in his best suit, even if it is only four cards in length.

Since the partner of a doubler may be responding on nothing, it is a good policy for the doubler subsequently to underbid, while doubler's partner should overbid.

Action by Partner of the Opening Bidder (when the opening bid has been overcalled or doubled). When the opener's bid has been overcalled, the responder is no longer under obligation to keep the bidding open; so a bid of one no-trump or a raise should be based on a hand of at least average strength. Over a takeout double, the responder has only one way to show a good hand—a redouble. This bid does not promise support for opener's suit but merely announces a better-than-average holding. Any other bid, while not indicative of weakness, shows only mediocre high-card strength.

Slam Bidding. When the two partners have been able to determine that they have the assets for a slam (33 points between the combined hands plus an adequate trump suit), the only thing that remains is to make certain that the opponents are unable to cash two quick tricks. Various control-asking and control-showing bids have been employed through the years, but only three have stood the test of time—Blackwood, Gerber, and cue bids (individual ace showing).

Blackwood Convention (Invented by Easley Blackwood). After a trump suit has been agreed upon, a bid of four no-trump asks partner to show his total number of aces. A response of five clubs shows either no aces or all four aces; five diamonds shows one ace; five hearts shows two aces; five spades shows three aces. After aces have been shown, the four no-trump bidder may ask for kings by now bidding five no-trump. The responder to the five no-trump bid now shows kings: by bidding six clubs if he has no king, six

diamonds if he has one king, etc., but six no-trump if he has all four kings.

Gerber Convention (Invented by John Gerber). This convention is similar to Blackwood in that it asks for the number of aces. Its advantage lies in the fact that it initiates the response at a lower level. A sudden bid of four clubs where it could not possibly have a natural meaning (*example:* opener, one no-trump; responder, four clubs) is Gerber and asks partner to show the number of his aces. If he bids four diamonds, he shows no aces; four hearts, one ace, etc. If the asking hand desires information about kings he bids the next-higher suit over his partner's ace-showing response. Thus, if the responding hand has bid four hearts over four clubs to show one ace, a bid of four spades would now ask him for kings and he would now reply four no-trump to show no king, five clubs to show one king, etc.

Cue bidding (individual ace showing). The Blackwood and Gerber conventions are designed to cover only a small number of potential slam hands. Many slams depend on possession of a specific ace, rather than a wholesale number of aces. Cue bids are employed in such cases. *Example:* Opener bids two spades, responder bids three spades, opener now bids four clubs; the four-club bid shows the ace of clubs and invites responder to show an ace if he has one. The responder "signs off" by bidding the agreed trump suit.

Other Contract Bridge Conventions

Club Convention. This method of bidding was devised by Harold S. Vanderbilt, who invented the modern game of Contract Bridge, and for that reason it is often called "the Vanderbilt Club." It is very popular in Europe. An opening bid of one club is artificial—it does not necessarily show a club suit but it shows a strong hand with 3 1/2 or more quick tricks. The opener's partner must respond one diamond if he has less than two quick tricks. Any other response shows at least two quick tricks. After the opening bid and response the partners show their suits naturally.

Two-Club Convention. This convention, used by many expert players, is usually combined with "weak two-bids." An opening bid of two clubs is artificial, not necessarily showing a club suit but showing a very powerful hand. It is forcing to game. The opener's partner must respond two diamonds if he has a weak hand. Any other response shows strength, usually at least 1 1/2 quick tricks. An opening bid of two diamonds, two hearts, or two spades is a preemptive bid, made on a fairly weak hand that includes a good five- or six-card suit but does not have 13 or more points. After a two-club opening bid, the opener will show his powerful suit on his next chance to bid.

Unusual No-Trump. If a player bids two no-trump after the opposing side has opened the bidding, and when his partner has not bid, the two no-trump bid is a convention showing a two-suited hand (usually with five or more cards in each of the two minor suits). The partner of the two no-trump bidder is required to respond in his best minor suit, even if it is a three-card or shorter suit.

Defender's Play. In leading against a contract, a defender should consider carefully which card to play. The fate of the contract often hinges on the very first card led. Proficiency in the technique of choosing the proper lead comes only with experience, but below are some suggestions that are helpful as generalizations.

CONVENTIONAL LEADS

Holding in Suit	Lead at Suit Bids	Lead at No-Trump
A-K-Q alone or with others	K, then Q	K, then Q
A-K-J-x-x-x-x	K, then A	A*, then K
A-K-J-x-x or A-K-x-x(-x)	K, then A	Fourth best
A-Q-J-x-x	A†	Q
A-Q-10-9	A†	10‡
A-Q-x-x(-x)	A	Fourth best
A-J-10-x	A†	J
A-10-9-x	A	10
A-x-x-x(-x)	A	Fourth best
A-K-x	K	K
A-K alone	A	K†
K-Q-J alone or with others	K, then J	K, then Q
K-Q-10 alone or with others	K	K
K-Q-x-x(-x-x)	K	Fourth best
K-Q alone	K	K
K-J-10 alone or with others	J	J
K-10-9-x	10	10
Q-J-10 or Q-J-9 alone or with others	Q	Q
Q-J-x or Q-J	Q	Q
Q-J-8-x (four or more)	Q	Fourth best
Q-10-9 alone or with others	10	10
J-10-9 or J-10-8 alone or with others	J	J
J-10-x or J-10	J	J
J-10-x-x or more	J	Fourth best
10-9-8 or 10-9-7 alone or with others	10	10
10-9-x-x(-x)	10	Fourth best
K-J-x-x(-x-x)	Fourth best	Fourth best

Holding in Suit	Lead at Suit Bids	Lead at No-Trump
Any other four-card or longer suit not listed above		Fourth best Fourth best

* The lead of the ace of an unbid suit at a no-trump contract requests partner to play his highest card of the suit led, even the king or queen, unless dummy reveals that such a play might risk losing a trick.
† Usually not a good lead at this contract.
‡ When dummy seems likely to have the king, the queen is a better lead.

LEADS IN PARTNER'S BID SUIT

Holding in Suit	Lead at Suit Bids	Lead at No-Trump
A-x, K-x, Q-x, J-x, 10-x, or any other doubleton	High card	High card
J-10-x or x-x-x	Highest	Highest
A-J-x or A-x-x	Ace	Lowest
K-J-x, K-x-x, Q-10-x, Q-x-x, J-x-x	Lowest	Lowest
Q-J-x(-x)	Q	Q
A-x-x-x or better	A	Fourth best
A-K-x(-x) or K-Q-x(-x)	K	K
Any other four or more cards	Fourth best	Fourth best

More Information on Making Leads. As a general guide to making leads, the following principles should be observed by the defenders. They are especially helpful when a defender has no good suit of his own to play and there is no indication from partner what his best suit is.

1. Lead through dummy's strong suit other than trump. "Leading through" means that dummy is the second hand to play to the trick and declarer last. This suit is often indicated by declarer's and dummy's bidding. After the dummy goes down, this kind of lead should not be made if it helps declarer establish a long suit that will give him the contract before the setting tricks have been taken.

2. Lead up to the weak suit in dummy. This lead is made by the defender at dummy's left, and it means that dummy is the last hand to play to the trick and declarer is the second hand.

3. Do not lead up to a tenace; that is, do not make a lead that will permit the dummy or declarer's hand to play last to a trick when they hold a tenace in the led suit (see The Finesse, page 137, for description of tenaces).

The Play after the Opening Lead.

1. *The Rule of Eleven.* When a defender

makes an opening lead which is probably his *fourth* highest card in that suit, his partner can get useful information by applying the "rule of eleven." Here is the way it works: Subtract the denomination of the led card from 11. The resulting number will tell how many cards *higher* in denomination than the lead are outside of the leader's hand. Since the cards in dummy and in his own hand can be counted, leader's partner knows how many higher cards remain in declarer's hand.

2. *Third-Hand High.* A defender is generally required to play his highest card on the lead of a low card by partner. This is known as "third-hand high," as the player is the third hand to play to the trick. The principle is that a still higher card must be played from declarer's hand, or dummy's as the case may be. This play helps establish cards in partner's hand, since it is assumed he led from his best suit. However, if leader's partner holds a sequence of high cards, he plays the lowest card of the sequence on the lead of his partner's low card. *Example:* If a player holds king–queen–*jack* or queen–jack–*ten* or jack–ten–*nine,* he plays the *lowest* card of the three. This gives partner valuable information, as declarer in order to take the trick must play a card higher than the top card of the sequence.

Another exception to third-hand high would be as in the following example: Defender A leads a six. Dummy shows queen–ten–nine of that suit. Defender B holds king–jack–x. If dummy plays the nine or ten, B should play the jack, not the king, since the jack in this case is as good as the king and it will take an ace to beat it.

3. *Second-Hand Low.* When a low card is led from dummy or declarer's hand and defender is the second one to play to the trick, he should not, as a rule, play his highest card. He plays a low card, because declarer generally intends playing a high card anyway, since he has led the suit. There are, of course, exceptions, such as when a defender as second hand holds a winning card which will set the contract; or when he wants to have the lead for some reason and the playing of a winning card will obtain it for him right away.

4. *Come-on Signal.* When a defender wishes to encourage his partner to continue a suit, he plays high then low, that is, a lower card to the second trick in that suit than he

played to the first trick. This is known as a "come-on," "high-low," or "echo." In general, the play of a seven or better on partner's lead of a card which promises to take a trick is a signal that the suit should be continued. The high-low may be also used in leading to indicate a doubleton.

5. *Discouraging Signal.* When a player wishes to discourage his partner from continuing a suit, he should play the lowest card he has. This is a signal that partner should consider shifting to another suit unless he has very good reason to continue in the suit led.

6. *Returning a Lead.* When a player's partner has led a suit, the player should try to lead that suit again at his earliest opportunity, returning his highest card in it, unless there is a very clear indication that partner was leading from a weak suit.

Declarer's Play

Planning the Play. Declarer's first step after the opening lead has been made and the dummy hand laid down is to take stock of the two hands. He should figure out a basic line of attack which promises to give him the needed tricks for his contract. Any bids that the opponents have made may provide clues to the location of key defensive cards or the distribution of adverse strength.

As the game progresses, he may be forced to modify his plan, but it is better to give some thought to the matter at the beginning than to play along haphazardly, hoping that enough tricks will be made somehow. Experienced players usually plan alternate lines of play that they can switch to if the basic one does not prove feasible.

Playing at a Trump Declaration. In playing a contract where there is a trump suit, it is generally best to draw opponent's trumps at the first opportunity. This should be done even though the opponents will take a trick or tricks in trump in the process. Trumps are drawn to protect declarer's good nontrump suits and prevent them from being trumped—ruffed—by opponents.

There are occasions, however, when the drawing of opponent's trumps should be postponed or avoided entirely. This is usually the case when declarer is short-suited in nontrump suits in one hand or the other, or in both, and wishes to make some or all pieces of trump individually.

Playing at a No-Trump Declaration. In playing a no-trump contract, declarer should

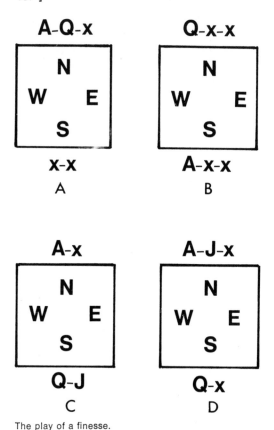

The play of a finesse.

first work out a simple problem in arithmetic. He should count the tricks he definitely is sure of, then subtract them from the number he needs for the contract. He should then plan how he can make the needed tricks. These are usually to be made in the suits in which his hand and dummy's are longest. This generally involves surrendering a trick or two in that suit to the opponents. But it does not matter since declarer can usually afford to lose a certain number of tricks in the hand and still make his contract. Giving up a trick or tricks in a suit so that the remainder of the cards will be winners is known as "establishing a suit."

Experienced players when holding no high card but the ace of a strong suit led by opponents will often refuse to take the trick until the suit is led a second or third time. This is done in the hope of breaking the connection between the opponent's hands in that suit so that one player will have none of the suit to play when he is next in the lead. This type of play is known as "a holdup."

The Finesse. The finesse is an attempt to establish a card as a winner while some higher card held by opponents in that suit has not yet been played. The combination of cards where an extra trick or tricks may be won by means of a finesse is known as a *tenace.* Thus, ace–queen is a tenace, and other illustrations will be found in the following examples. In each of the following cases, the finesse described is the one generally used. A good way of fixing these finesses in mind is actually to make the plays indicated with cards.

A. Lead a small card from South and, assuming that West plays a low card, his normal play, put on the queen from North. If West has the king of the suit, the queen will win to provide another trick besides the ace.

B. Lead the ace from South for the first trick. For the second trick, lead a small card from South toward North. If West has the king, the queen will be established as a trick to be taken later. Do not lead the queen from North for the first trick since that play will produce only one trick out of the two honors regardless of which opponent holds the king.

C. Lead the queen from South. If West does not play the king, put on the small card from North. This is known as letting the queen *ride.* The lead of the queen in this situation offers a chance to win two tricks if West had the king.

D. The same principle as C applies.

E. Lead a small card from North and play the jack from South to the first trick. The next time, lead a small card from North again and play the ten for a second finesse. If West and East each have one of the two missing honors, or if East has both of them, this line of play is sure to win two tricks.

F. The same principle as E applies.

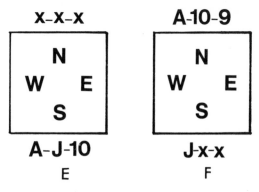

Examples of "double" finesses.

Lead the jack to the first trick and later finesse again by playing a small card from South and putting on the ten from North.

These plays in E and F are known as *double finesses.*

Unblocking. When a suit is longer in one hand than in the other, care should be taken to play the cards in such a way that the player does not prevent himself from continuing to lead that suit without interruption.

In the following example, South is declarer and North is dummy hand.

K-Q-x-x-x

A-x-x

An example of unblocking.

If declarer leads his king to trick one and his queen to trick two, he will find himself in the South hand after playing trick three. This will prevent him from continuing the suit without getting back into the North hand in some other way.

But if he first leads his ace from South and then continues with a small card from South on the next trick, he will find himself able to play the suit uninterruptedly. The principle to remember is that the high card or cards should first be played from the shorter holding.

The End Play. This is a stratagem by which declarer gives opponents a trick, which they must win in any case, at a time when it will be to declarer's advantage to have the opponents in the lead. In the following example seven tricks have already been played, leaving this situation:

North, the declarer, must win five out of the remaining six tricks to fulfill his contract. Spades are trump.

His first lead is the ace of trumps from dummy, exhausting West of trump. He then leads the four of clubs, which he trumps with one of the two remaining trumps in North. This play strips South of clubs.

North's next play is the ten of hearts, giving up a trick that he would have to lose in any case. This play is known as the *throw-in.*

West is now in the lead. He must lead a club or a diamond. If he leads a club, declarer can trump in his own hand and discard the losing jack of diamonds from dummy. But if West chooses to lead a diamond instead of the club, declarer will win two tricks in diamonds. Thus, two apparent losers have been reduced to one.

The Squeeze. This is a stratagem by which declarer squeezes an opponent out of an apparent winner by giving him a choice of plays.

In the following example, after ten tricks have been played, this is the situation:

South, the declarer, must win all three tricks to fulfill his contract. Hearts are trump.

South's first lead is the ten of trumps. East is in trouble no matter which card he discards to the lead. If he discards one of the spades, South's next lead is the four of spades and he wins both spades in North. On the other hand, if East discards the nine of diamonds on the lead of the ten of hearts, that makes South's eight of diamonds a good card, on which he will discard the losing three of spades.

Other Notes on General Play

Splitting Honors. When holding two touching honors, such as king–queen or queen–jack, it is generally wise to play one of them on the lead of a low card by opponent. This is known as *splitting honors.* It forces opponent to play a higher honor, thus promoting the other honor in the hand to a winner or near winner.

Covering an Honor with an Honor. When an opponent leads an honor, it is generally wise for a player to put a higher honor on it if he has one. This is known as *covering an honor with an honor.* It forces declarer to play a still higher honor if he wishes to win the trick, that is, two honors for one. This

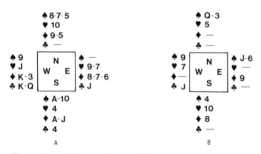

Examples of the end play (A) and the squeeze (B).

play may also promote a lesser honor or an intermediate card in partner's hand.

Trump and Discard. When a player knows that both opponents are void of the same suit and that both have trump cards, he should not lead that suit since it provides an opportunity for discarding a losing card in one hand and trumping in the other. This is also known as a *sluff and ruff.*

Correct Bridge Odds

The reason Bridge surpasses most other card games in strategy is due to the fact that in dealing out bridge hands, unlike most other card games, all fifty-two cards are first dealt out, thirteen to each of four players to start the game. Therefore, the number of different card combinations that face each player is virtually infinite, to be specific the astronomical figure is 635,013,599,600. Because of this factor there is no such thing as 100 percent accuracy in bidding. Two partners of expert ability are doing well if they bid and get a contract which appears makeable when the dummy hand is exposed. But the contract in question may stand up or fall on the way the opponents' twenty-six cards (half the deck) are divided. Let's take a simple example: Players A and B are partners, and they bid four hearts on cards they hold. The dummy is exposed and it seems certain that the contract will be made if one particular opponent holds the jack of trump; but A and B will be set one trick if the other opponent holds that jack of hearts. The above is true of most hands with the exception of a laydown hand. No one can predict with certainty how many tricks he can win because the declarer cannot know the exact distribution of cards held by the opposing team. All that is expected of any good bridge player is to make the bid which has the highest expectation. Following is a list of tables that will help improve your bridge playing:

Possible Point Counts. Almost all bridge writers agree that the point-count bidding method (see page 129) has improved the bidding accuracy of the average bridge player. The total number of high-card points in a thirteen-card hand is 37 (out of a possible 40). The following table gives the chance of being dealt any exact number of points from 0 to 37. The chances are expressed in terms of percentages. In other words, the number of

times in 100 dealt hands you can expect to hold a specific number of points.

CHANCES OF HOLDING VARIOUS POINT COUNTS

Total Number of Point Counts	Expected Appearance in 100 Deals	Total Number of Point Counts	Expected Appearance in 100 Deals
0	0.364	19	1.036
1	0.788	20	0.643
2	1.356	21	0.378
3	2.462	22	0.210
4	3.846	23	0.112
5	5.186	24	0.056
6	6.554	25	0.026
7	8.028	26	0.012
8	8.892	27	0.005
9	9.356	28	0.002
10	9.405	29	0.0007
11	8.945	30	0.0002
12	8.027	31	0.0001
13	6.914	32	0.000017
14	5.693	33	0.0000035
15	4.424	34	0.00000077
16	3.311	35	0.000000099
17	2.362	36	0.0000000023
18	1.605	37	0.00000000015

Possible Suit Splits Held by Opponents. The table depicts the percentage probability of finding all possible splits of cards held by the opponents. The number in the left-hand column is the combined total of cards held by both opponents in the suit in question. The numbers in the center column depict all possible split hands held by the opponents. The percentage figures shown in the right-hand column is the chance possibility of each suit split. These values are shown in terms of percentages; in other words, the number of times in 100 dealt hands you can expect your opponents to hold the suit split in question.

CHANCES OF VARIOUS SUIT SPLITS HELD BY OPPONENTS

Cards Held by Opponents	Split of Suit in Opponents' Hands	Percentage Chance
1	1—0	100.000
2	1—1	52.000
	2—0	48.000
3	2—1	78.000
	3—0	22.000
4	1—3	49.739
	2—2	40.696
	4—0	9.565

Cards Held by Opponents	Split of Suit in Opponents' Hands	Percentage Chance
5	1—4	28.261
	2—3	67.826
	5—0	3.913
6	2—4	48.447
	3—3	35.528
	5—1	14.534
	6—0	1.491
7	3—4	62.174
	5—2	30.522
	6—1	6.783
	7—0	0.522
8	3—5	47.121
	4—4	32.723
	6—2	17.135
	7—1	2.856
	8—0	0.165
9	3—6	31.414
	5—4	58.902
	7—2	8.568
	8—1	1.071
	9—0	0.046
10	5—5	31.414
	6—4	46.197
	7—3	18.479
	8—2	3.780
	9—1	0.350
	10—0	0.011
11	6—5	57.169
	7—4	31.760
	8—3	9.528
	9—2	1.444
	10—1	0.096
	11—0	0.002
12	6—6	30.490
	7—5	45.735
	8—4	19.056
	9—3	4.235
	10—2	0.462
	11—1	0.021
	12—0	0.0003
13	7—6	56.6250
	8—5	31.8510
	9—4	9.8310
	10—3	1.5730
	11—2	0.1170
	12—1	0.0030
	13—0	0.0001

The general percentages on suit splits listed above apply mostly when the opposing side has not bid. Usually when a player bids a specific suit, he shows strength in that particular suit and indicates a shortness in other suits.

Finesses. The table of finesses coupled with the table of suit splits become very useful when a player has a choice of plays. To illustrate, let's suppose that you can make your contract if you win a finesse in spades or if the hearts split favorably. You try for the heart split first, and if the heart suit fails to split favorably, you play the spade finesse later on. If your hand forces you to make one of the two possible plays, you then compare the odds (for the heart split with the 1 to 1 odds or a successful spade finesse) and then you make the best odds play in your favor.

The following table depicts the chance of winning one or more finesses from a given number of attempts. The chance is given in terms of percentages; in other words, the number of times in 100 dealt hands you can expect to win one or more finesses in a given situation. The percentage figures on finesses are as follows:

To attempt 1 finesse and win 1	50.00%
To attempt 2 finesses and win 2	25.00%
To attempt 3 finesses and win 3	12.50%
To attempt 2 finesses and win exactly 1	50.00%
To attempt 2 finesses and win 1 or 2	75.00%
To attempt 3 finesses and win exactly 1	37.50%
To attempt 3 finesses and win exactly 2	37.50%
To attempt 3 finesses and win 2 or 3	50.00%
To attempt 3 finesses and win 1, 2, or 3	87.50%

Possible Long Suits in Player's Hand. Every now and then some practical joker gets the bright idea to switch a "cooler" (stacked deck) into a bridge game so that his buddy Joe Blow gets thirteen spades. If the ruse is executed skillfully, Joe gives the hand the silent treatment for a few seconds, then in a fit of excitement spreads his hand face up on the table and gleefully shouts, "Boys, look at them, thirteen beautiful spades from ace to king, how about that?" Within a few minutes Joe calls the local newspapers and by that time it's too late for the joker to admit it was a gag. It would infuriate Joe to learn he was victim of such a prank.

Since the chances of holding any thirteen-card suit with an honest shuffle and deal is one in 158,753,389,899 deals, you should look with suspicion upon the honesty of the deal if you pick up a complete suit hand.

If you play bridge regularly, you probably

remember getting a seven-card suit now and then, but an eight-card suit is rather a rare animal. This experience conforms to the expected probabilities. About four hands in every 100 dealt hands has a seven-card suit but only one in about 200 hands has an eight-card suit. A nine or longer suit appears about once in a minimum of every 2,500 dealt hands. Although I play bridge occasionally, I don't remember ever holding an honestly dealt eight-card or longer suit in my lifetime. For those who are interested in long suits, the following table gives the chance of being dealt exactly, at most or at least a specified number of cards in a specified suit.

THE CHANCES OF BEING DEALT VARIOUS LONG SUITS

Longest Suit in Your Hand	Odds Against Holding Such a Suit
Any four (4) card suit	About 2 to 1
Any five (5) card suit	About 1 to 1
Any six (6) card suit	About 5 to 1
Any seven (7) card suit	About 27 to 1
Any eight (8) card suit	About 213 to 1
Any nine (9) card suit or longer	About 2,580 to 1
Any ten (10) card suit or longer	About 59,448 to 1
Any eleven (11) card suit or longer	About 2,722,719 to 1
Any twelve (12) card suit and longer	About 312,506,671 to 1
Any thirteen (13) card suit	Exactly 158,753,389,898 to 1

Possible Hand Distribution. Very often a hand that does not contain a long suit is exciting because it contains an unusual four-suit distribution. Hands with two long suits usually have great playing potential and are fun to play out. The table that follows lists the chances of holding each possible suit distribution made up of thirteen cards.

CHANCES OF HOLDING VARIOUS SUIT DISTRIBUTIONS

Distribution in Your Hand	Odds Against Being Dealt	Distribution in Your Hand	Odds Against Being Dealt
4-4-3-2	3.7 to 1	5-4-4-0	79.2 to 1
4-3-3-3	8.3 to 1	5-5-3-0	110.7 to 1
4-4-4-1	32.4 to 1	6-3-2-2	16.7 to 1
5-3-3-2	5.3 to 1	6-4-2-1	20.2 to 1
5-4-3-1	6.7 to 1	6-3-3-1	28.1 to 1
5-4-2-2	8.4 to 1	6-4-3-0	74.4 to 1
5-5-2-1	31.5 to 1	6-5-1-1	140.8 to 1

Distribution in Your Hand	Odds Against Being Dealt	Distribution in Your Hand	Odds Against Being Dealt
6-5-2-0	150.4 to 1	10-3-0-0	647,957.4 to 1
6-6-1-0	1,381.4 to 1	11-1-1-0	4,014,397.1 to 1
7-3-2-1	52.2 to 1	11-2-0-0	8,697,861.7 to 1
7-2-2-2	195.2 to 1	12-1-0-0	313,123,055.9 to 1
7-4-1-1	254.2 to 1	13-0-0-0	158,753,389,898 to 1
7-4-2-0	275.5 to 1		
7-3-3-0	376.1 to 1	8-5-0-0	31,947.0 to 1
7-5-1-0	920.7 to 1	9-2-1-1	5,612.6 to 1
7-6-0-0	17,970.2 to 1	9-2-2-0	12,164.8 to 1
8-2-2-1	519.0 to 1	9-3-1-0	9,952.1 to 1
8-3-1-1	850.2 to 1	9-4-0-0	103,510.9 to 1
8-3-2-0	920.6 to 1	10-1-1-1	252,653.4 to 1
8-4-1-0	2,211.6 to 1	10-2-1-0	91,235.3 to 1

Cheating at Bridge

In August, 1961, as gambling advisor to the United States Senate Permanent Subcommittee on investigating gambling and crime in the United States, I watched as an electronic device used to cheat at Bridge, called a radio cue prompter, was demonstrated to the committee. Read into the Congressional Record at the time was an ad from a crooked gambling supply house which described this radio cue prompter as follows: "Not to be confused with many inferior units now on the market. This item is the ultimate in precision electronics and enables two people to cue each other, such as actors on a stage, mental reading, etc. Using these two miniature units and a dot-dash system, you can carry on a conversation with your partner in any card game. No wires, all self-contained, card-pack size. Full instructions with every order. Guaranteed the best. Longer distance than many." Senate testimony further revealed that the electronic company alone in question had sold several hundreds of these gadgets during 1960. Since that time, it's anybody's guess how many thousands have been sold by various electronic companies, and how many of them are in use today.

In August of 1949 I was hired by one of Hollywood's biggest movie moguls to check out a swank west coast bridge club where he said he had lost a quarter of a million dollars playing bridge in a one year period. My investigation later revealed that the bridge club was as crooked as an electronic corkscrew, and its yearly take from Hollywood celebrities ran into the millions. The club was owned and operated by several Las Vegas gamblers who employed a former movie actor as host. The bridge club harbored ten tables and no matter at which table the bridge player sat, he was sure to be clipped with a radio cue prompter.

The swindle was accomplished as follows: Two player card cheats were aided by a third unseen confederate who operated a radio cue prompter from the room above the club. The bridge club was rigged up as follows: Ten small camouflaged holes had been drilled from the floor above and through the club's ceiling; each hole was situated directly above each bridge table. Each hole known as a "Peek joint" contained the eye of a stationary telescope that when looked through by the confederate above revealed each player's hand. In addition, a secret listening device made it possible for the crook above to hear the bidding conversation of the players below. The additional equipment involved a radio cue prompter comprised of three miniature electronic units: one a transmitter and two receivers. Each player cheat had a receiver strapped to his bare leg hidden by his trousers. The cheat confederate above scanned the player's hand through the telescope and directed the cheat's play below by making use of the transmitter which sent the desired information by transmitting a small electric shock to the leg of each player cheat. I had not as yet completed my investigation when a three-page picture story showing five pictures of me appeared in *Life* magazine describing various cheating methods at bridge, poker, and gin rummy. It was apparent that the operators of the bridge club also read the article and recognized me by my pictures in *Life* because when I arrived at the club several days later, the only cheating evidence that remained was the holes in the ceiling. The crooks had left in a hurry.

In the late 1960's the American team entry in the World's Duplicate Bridge Championship Tournament held in Buenos Aires, Argentina, accused the British team of cheating by making use of a series of hand signals. Do you know what? The signals mentioned were identical to the hand signals I exposed in the August 9, 1949, issue of *Life* magazine.

The late Nick "the Greek" Dandolos, the most famous gambler of the past thirty years,

was once cheated of $500,000 with the same above-described device, the radio cue prompter, at a two week session of gin rummy. The game took place at the poolside of the famous Flamingo Hotel Casino on the Las Vegas strip. Nick and the gin-rummy cheat who fleeced him were attired in bathing suits and the cheat's accomplice with telescope and radio cue prompter operated from a hotel room overlooking the pool. The player cheat's radio receiver was hidden under his bathing suit. Incidentally, the table and chairs were fastened to the pool's concrete floor so as to prevent Nick the Greek from moving his gin rummy hand out of range of the telescope.

The most publicized radio cue prompter cheating incident of all times came to light in the middle 1960's, when the court testimony of several Hollywood celebrities described how they were fleeced of hundreds of thousands of dollars playing bridge and gin rummy at a famous club in Los Angeles, California. This cheating episode made newspaper headlines across the country for weeks. The hole in the ceiling incident and the radio cue prompter explained earlier were again put to work by a number of Las Vegas gamblers. Several perpetrators of this swindle were later convicted and received long jail sentences.

Bridge and Gin Rummy cheats who operate in hotel rooms build their "peek joints" by cutting out a small square from the top of a door of a closet or adjoining room and replacing the missing square with a two-way mirror which to the unsuspecting victim appears as a hanging glass painting. The player cheat's confederate hides in a closet or room, sees through the two-way glass peek joint and transmits the cheating information by a radio cue prompter to his accomplice who is wearing a hidden receiver. When a peek joint is not available many bridge cheats armed with radio cue prompter receivers receive signals describing their opponents' hands from a confederate cheat in the room armed with a transmitter. This confederate usually acts as a nonplayer waiting for a seat.

Just to illustrate that a top notch sleight-of-hand card cheat can do just about as he pleases in the bridge game the following is an excerpt from my autobiography *The Odds Against Me*. I discuss a performance of mine attended by two hundred persons including President Franklin D. Roosevelt, Governor A. Harry Moore of New Jersey, and Mayor Frank Hague of Jersey City.

I ended my performance that evening by playing two Bridge hands against Governor Moore and Mayor Hague—while President Roosevelt and the assembled guests watched in silence. Two regulation fifty-two card Bridge decks were produced by Mayor Hague. I shuffled the blue-backed deck and the governor shuffled the red-backed deck. After several shuffles I offered the blue-backed deck to Mayor Hague to cut, which he did. I then instructed the governor to deal out four Bridge hands, first hand to me, second to the mayor, third to my dummy, and the fourth and last hand to himself. When I exposed my hand it was found to contain thirteen Spades—a cinch grand slam.

For the second Bridge hand the Mayor handed me the red-backed deck to deal. The deck had previously been shuffled by the governor and cut by the mayor. While I was dealing out the four Bridge hands I bid seven no trumps. The hand was played to a finish and I made my bid—another grand slam.

Party Bridge

The host or hostess should make all decisions as to what form of Bridge is to be played. She should tell her guests at what table they are to play and what form of Bridge (regular Rubber Bridge, Pivot Bridge, Progressive Bridge, etc.) is to be played. She should consider the probable desires of her guests, but should not consult them. Leaving such decisions to the guests usually serves only to make them uncomfortable and may even cause arguments and disagreements among them.

The Casual Game. When a Bridge game or party is not planned in advance, there are seldom more guests than will make up a single table, or at most two tables (eight players).

Four, five, or six players may play a cut-in game at one table. The host or hostess should play in the game; the guests will not mind sitting out in their proper turns, and it is embarrassing to them if the hostess insists on sitting out.

If the group includes a husband and wife who may not wish to play against each other, the hostess may suggest a "set match" in which the couple are always partners; in a five- or six-hand game, there may be a "semi-set match" in which the couples are partners

whenever they are both in the game at the same time. The hostess should not make this suggestion, however, if the married couple are better players than the other guests, or if they are thought to be.

If one player is better than the others, Pivot Bridge (page 145) should be suggested, so that everyone will have equal opportunity to play with the better player.

With six players, it is advisable to set up a second card table and provide cards so that the two players who are sitting out may amuse themselves by playing a two-hand game such as Gin Rummy, Russian Bank, Canasta, or Samba while waiting for the rubber to end.

Seven players are the most inconvenient number. They cannot very well all play in the same Bridge game. It may be best to try to arrange some game in which all seven can play at once, instead of Bridge. Otherwise the hostess must sit out and let six play.

Eight players make two tables of Bridge. The hostess should arrange the placing of the players at the respective tables. If all are married couples, it is usually wiser to split them up than to have any couple at the same table. If four of the players are quite good and the other four weaker, the four good players should be put together; but the reason for the grouping should not be mentioned.

The Laws of Progressive Contract Bridge

The following are reprinted thanks to National Laws Commission of the American Contract Bridge League:

1. *Arrangement of Tables.* The game is played by two or more tables of four players each. The tables are numbered consecutively from Table 1 to the highest number.

Comment: It is customary to provide each table with two decks of cards having different backs. The tables should be numbered conspicuously for the convenience of the players, and each one should be provided with one or more pencils and a score pad showing contract scoring.

2. *Tally Cards.* Prior to the beginning of play, the game director or committee prepares individual tally cards, one for each player. Each tally card bears a table number and designates a position (North, South, East, or West) at the table.

The tally cards may be drawn at random by the players or assigned by the game director, as he prefers. When play is called, each player takes the position assigned by his tally card.

Comment: At mixed parties it is customary to arrange the tallies and seat assignments so that a gentleman will always have a lady as a partner and vice versa. This is accomplished by having tallies of two different kinds or colors, one for the ladies and the other for the gentlemen.

3. *A Round.* A round consists of four deals, one by each player. When all tables are through play, the game director gives a signal and the players move to their positions for the next round according to the type of progression used.

4. *A Deal Passed Out.* Only four hands are dealt at each table, one by each player. If a deal is passed out (that is, if all four players pass at their first opportunity to declare), the deal passes to the left and both sides score zero for that deal.

5. *Method of Progression.* At the conclusion of each round, the winning pair at Table 1 remain and the losing pair move to the last table. At all tables except Table 1, the losers remain and the winners move up one table toward Table 1.

Comment: The above is the standard method of progression, but this may be waived or altered to suit the wishes of the game director or the players. Special tallies may be arranged or obtained, assigning positions for each round in such a way as to give each player as wide a variety of partners as possible. Another method is to have the ladies progress one way and the gentlemen the other way.

6. *Selection of Partners.* At mixed parties, it is customary but not essential for a gentleman to play with a lady partner and vice versa. If the standard method of progression is used, the visiting lady at each table becomes partner of the gentleman who remains.

If the players are all of the same sex, the four players at each table draw cards to determine partners at the start of each round. The two new arrivals at each table draw first, and the one drawing higher has choice of seats and is the first dealer. The one drawing lower sits at the left of the first dealer. The two players who remain at the table from the preceding round then draw, the higher becomes the partner of the dealer. Thus all players change partners after each round.

Comment: Since the chief function of Progressive Bridge is social, it is preferable to change partners at each round. However, if for some reason a pair contest is desired, the same partnerships may be retained throughout by simply progressing as described in paragraph 5 without changing partners at the next table. Another method is to have the original North-South pairs remain in the same positions throughout the game, and to have the East-West pairs progress one table at a time until they reach Table 1, and then go to the last table. In this case, the progression is followed automatically, regardless of which pair wins at each table.

7. *Draw for Deal.* Unless the dealer is already determined under paragraph 6, the four players at a table draw for first deal. The player who draws highest is the first dealer and may select either deck.

Progressive Bridge Scoring. With the exceptions specifically mentioned below, the scoring for Progressive Bridge is exactly the same as for Rubber Bridge:

Each deal is scored and recorded separately, and no trick points are carried over from one deal to the next.

Game is 100 points for tricks bid and made in one deal. The game premium is 300 points if not vulnerable and 500 points if vulnerable, and it is allowed only when game is bid and made in one deal.

A premium of 50 points is scored for making any contract less than game. This premium is in addition to the value of the tricks made. Premiums for a small and grand slam are allowed only if bid for.

8. *Scoring Limits.* A side may not score more than 1,000 points in a single deal except in the case of a slam contract fulfilled.

Comment: It is not correct to prohibit doubles or redoubles. The limitation of penalties avoids the necessity of this restriction.

9. *Vulnerability.* The first deal of each round shall be played and scored as if neither side were vulnerable.

The second and third deals of each round shall be played and scored as if the dealer's side were vulnerable and the other side not vulnerable.

The fourth deal of each round shall be played and scored as if both sides were vulnerable.

Comment: This is the most desirable

method of determining vulnerability in Progressive Bridge, but if preferred all deals may be played as though neither side were vulnerable, or all deals as though both sides were vulnerable. In any event, the method should be announced before play starts.

10. *Recording the Score.* One of the four players at each table is appointed to record the score. He enters the result of each deal on the score pad separately and, at the end of the round, totals all the points made by each side.

He enters on the individual tally of each player the points made by that player's side and also the points made by the opponents.

Comment: Correctly designed tallies provide spaces to record both *My score* and *Opponent's score.* It is important that both be entered on the tally, for otherwise the record would be meaningless.

11. *Computing Total Scores.* At the conclusion of the game, each player totals his score. He also totals the scores of his opponents, as recorded on his tally, and subtracts his opponents' total from his own. The difference, plus or minus as the case may be, is recorded in the space provided at the bottom of his tally.

Comment: Let us suppose that a player scores 2,460 points, and the opponents score 1,520 points against him. This makes his net score +940 for the entire session. On the other hand, if a player scores only 1,650 points, and the opponents score 1,940 points against him, then his net score for the session is −290 points. Do not make the mistake of recording only plus scores, for that method gives false results, and is likely to lead to improper doubling and redoubling.

12. *Determining the Winner.* The player with the largest plus score is the winner. Other players with plus scores rank in descending order followed by the players with minus scores, the one with the largest minus being last.

Comment: The method of awarding prizes is left to the discretion of the game director. At mixed parties it is usual to award one or more prizes to the highest ladies and one or more prizes to the highest gentlemen.

Progressive Rubber Bridge

Progressive Rubber Bridge is a variation of the usual progressive game. It has proved in-

creasingly popular, and may in time supplant the usual form. It follows the methods of progression and change of partners described in the preceding laws, but the scoring is somewhat different.

Under this arrangement it is preferable to play six or eight deals to a round, or to fix the length of a round by a definite time limit—say 30 minutes. If the length of a round is determined by a time limit, any deal which has been started before time is up may be completed, but no new hand may be dealt.

Rubber scoring is used. (See the scoring instructions on page 122.) As many rubbers as possible are completed during the time allotted. A rubber completed in two games carries a bonus of 700 points. A three-game rubber carries a bonus of 500 points. If a side has won one game toward a rubber and the other side has not won a game, 300 points are allowed for the single game won. If a rubber is unfinished and one side has made one or more part-score contracts in an unfinished game, but the other side has made no part score in that game, the side with the part score(s) adds 50 points to its score.

Vulnerability is determined by the state of the score and not according to paragraph 9 in the Progressive Code. A side is vulnerable when it has won a game and remains vulnerable until the conclusion of that rubber. However, vulnerability lapses at the conclusion of a round and a new rubber is started at the beginning of each new round.

At the end of a round each player enters on his tally only his net gain or loss—not his total score. At the end of the session these net gains and losses are totaled and the player's final score, plus or minus as the case may be, is entered at the bottom of this tally. (If each side is permitted to enter all the points it has scored, without subtracting its opponents' score; and if each side has scored a game toward an unfinished rubber, then each side adds 300 points to its score; and if each side has a part score in an unfinished game of an unfinished rubber, then each side adds 50 points to its score.)

The Laws of Pivot Contract Bridge

Pivot bridge is played by four (or five) players at a table. This form may be used for a single table or for large gatherings in which it is desirable to have each table play as a separate unit without progression by the players.

The game is so arranged that each player plays with each other player at his table both as partner and opponent. There are two methods of play; first, four deals may be played to a round, one deal by each player, and the players change partners at the end of each four deals; second, rubbers may be played, and the players change partners at the end of each rubber.

If four deals to a round are played, the scoring is exactly the same as in Progressive Bridge; if rubbers are played, the scoring is exactly the same as in Rubber Bridge. The laws given below explain only the method of rotation in changing partners, not scoring vulnerability, etc., which are covered elsewhere.

1. *Draw for Partners.* The players draw cards for partners and deal and for a choice of seats and deck. The player who draws highest is the first pivot, and he deals first and has the choice of seats and decks. The player who draws second highest is the pivot's first partner; the player who draws third highest sits at the pivot's left during the first round; the player who draws fourth sits at the pivot's right; and if a fifth player is present, he does not participate in the first round or rubber.

2. *Changing Partners (For Four Players).* During the first three rounds or rubbers, the players change positions as indicated in the following diagram:

The diagram for changing partners for four players.

After the third round or rubber, the players again cut for position and partners.

3. *Changing Partners (For Five Players).* If five players desire to play at the same table, they may be accommodated in this manner:

For the first round or rubber, the players take the positions indicated by their draw for position under paragraph 1. For rounds of one to five, they take the positions indicated in the following diagram:

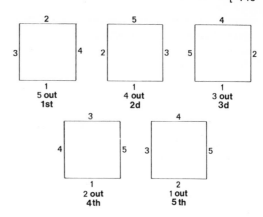

The diagram for changing partners for five players.

At the end of each five rounds, the players again draw for positions and partners.

Comment: This arrangement permits each player to play with each other player once as partner and twice as opponent, and each player sits out one round in turn.

4. *Determining the Winner.* At the completion of each round or rubber, the player enters on his tally both his own score and that of his opponents. Each player totals his own and his opponents' scores separately and records the difference, plus or minus as the case may be, at the bottom of his tally. The player having the highest plus score is the winner and the others rank in descending order according to their scores.

The Laws of Duplicate Contract Bridge

Duplicate Bridge is the only form of the game played in tournaments, but is equally adapted to play in homes and clubs. It is considered the supreme test of skill among card games. The following description and the laws of the game are condensed, by permission, from the National Laws Commission of the American Contract Bridge League.

Number of Players. Four players in two partnerships may play Replay Duplicate. Eight or more players may play a pair game, an individual game, or a team-of-four match.

Equipment. A set of duplicate boards, or trays, and one pack of cards for each board. Each board has four pockets, corresponding to the compass points, for holding the hands of the respective players. The face of each board is marked with an arrow pointing toward the North pocket, and with an indication of the dealer and vulnerability. There should be at least 16 boards to a set, numbered consecutively, with dealer and vulnerability as follows:

Dealer	Vulnerability	
N 1, 5, 9, 13	Neither	1, 8, 11, 14
E 2, 6, 10, 14	N-S only	2, 5, 12, 15
S 3, 7, 11, 15	E-W only	3, 6, 9, 16
W 4, 8, 12, 16	Both	4, 7, 10, 13

Boards numbered 17 to 32, if used, correspond to boards 1 to 16 respectively except in their identifying numbers.

Shuffle and Deal. Any player, in the presence of an opponent or of the tournament director, prepares a board by shuffling the pack of cards and dealing it, one card at a time face down, into four packets, each of which he inserts in a pocket of the duplicate board.

The Auction. The arrow on the board is pointed in the direction of the room designated as North. Each player takes the hand from the pocket nearest him, and counts his cards to make sure he has 13. The player designated as dealer calls first, and the auction proceeds as described on page 119 until the contract is determined. There is no redeal when a hand is passed out.

The Play. The opening lead, exposure of dummy, and subsequent play are as described on page 119, except: After a trick is completed, each player retains possession of his card and places it face down on the table directly in front of him, pointed lengthwise toward the partners who won the trick. Declarer plays dummy's cards by naming or touching them, and then dummy turns them and keeps them in front of him.

Scoring. The score of each board is independent of the scores of the other boards, and trick points scored on one board cannot count toward game on a subsequent board. No rubber premium is scored. Instead the following premiums are scored:

	Declarer's Side	
	Vulnerable	Not Vulnerable
For bidding and making a game contract	500	300
For making a contract of less than game	50	50

If match-point scoring is used to determine the winner of the game, there is no premium for holding honors in one hand.

In other respects the scoring of each board follows the schedule shown on page 123.

Determining the Winner. Match-point scoring is always used in individual games, is most often used in pair games, and may be used in team-of-four games or replay games. Cumulative (or "total point") scoring may be used in pair and team-of-four games.

Irregularities in Duplicate Bridge. Rubber Bridge and Duplicate Bridge are governed by the same laws so far as the nature of the two games makes it possible. The procedure described on pages 124 to 127, and the penalties and rectifications of irregularities described on pages 127 to 128, govern in Duplicate Bridge except as provided below.

Tournament Director. One person, who may be a player, must be appointed to conduct and supervise the game or tournament. His duties include: listing the entries; selecting suitable movements and conditions of play; maintaining discipline; administering the laws; assessing penalties and assigning adjusted scores; collecting and tabulating results.

Drawing Attention to an Irregularity. The director must be summoned as soon as attention is drawn to an irregularity. Players do not have the right to assess or waive penalties on their own initiative.

Adjusted Score. The director may assign an adjusted score when the laws provide no penalty which will fully indemnify a nonoffending contestant for an opponent's irregularity, or when no rectification can be made that will permit normal play of the board; but may not assign an adjusted score on the ground that the penalty provided by the laws is unduly severe or unduly advantageous to the nonoffending side. An adjusted score may be assigned by altering the total-point score on the board, or by the assignment of zero or more match points. Penalty points may be assessed against the offending side, indemnity points given to the nonoffending side; these need not balance.

Bidding and Playing Conventions. A player may make any call or play (including an intentionally misleading call such as a "psychic" bid) except that he may not make a call or play based on a partnership understanding unless the opposing pair may reasonably be expected to understand its meaning, or unless his side has announced its use before either member has looked at his hand. If the director decides that a pair has been damaged through its opponents' failure to make such announcement, he may assign an adjusted score.

The director, on a player's request, may require the player who made a call or play to leave the table and his partner to explain its meaning.

The director (or other authority) may forbid the use of such conventions as might place other contestants at a disadvantage or take too long to explain.

Dummy's Rights. In addition to the rights stated on page 126 dummy may: notify the director of any matter that may affect the legal rights of his side; keep count of the tricks won and lost; draw attention to another player's card played to the preceding trick and pointed in the wrong direction. He may play the cards of the dummy hand as directed by declarer; if he places in the played position a card that declarer did not name, the error may be corrected before a card has been led to the next trick and a defender may withdraw a card played after the error but before attention was drawn to it. If dummy (in the director's opinion) suggests a play, the director may require or forbid declarer to play that card or its equivalent.

Error in Play from Dummy. Declarer may change his designation of a card to be played from dummy if he does so practically in the same breath, or if he designated a card that is not there.

Improper Information. If a player receives improper information about a board, he should notify the director, who shall require that the board be played and scored normally if that seems feasible, and otherwise shall assign an adjusted score. Examples of improper information: looking at the wrong hand; seeing another player's card before the auction begins; overhearing calls or remarks; partner's improper remark or gesture.

Revoke Time Limits. A revoke made in the twelfth trick must be corrected if discovered before all four hands have been returned to the board. An established revoke is not subject to penalty if attention is first drawn to it after the round has ended and the board has been moved. In all other respects the provisions stated on page 126 apply.

Claims and Concessions. The concession of a trick which cannot be lost by any play of the cards is void, provided the error is brought to an opponent's attention before the round has ended and the board has been moved. The concession of a trick the player has in fact won is void, provided the error is brought to the director's attention within 30 minutes after the end of the session.

If a claim or concession is disputed, the director must be summoned and no action should be taken without him. The director determines the result on the board, awarding any doubtful trick to the claimant's opponents.

Correction of Scoring Errors. A time limit should be established for the correction of errors in recording scores; it should be no less than 30 minutes nor more than 24 hours after the posting of the official score. To change a score because an opponent has received improper information, a contestant must notify the director within 30 minutes after the end of the session.

Wrong Number of Cards. If the director decides that one or more pockets of the board contained an incorrect number of cards, he should correct it if possible, and should then require that the board be played normally unless a player gained information of sufficient importance to warrant assigning an adjusted score.

Interchanged Cards. If the cards or hands in a board become interchanged during a session, the director rates separately each group that played identical boards, as follows: Each pair receives 1 match point for each lower score in the same group, 1/2 match point for each identical score in the same group, and 1/2 match point for each pair in the other group(s).

Disciplinary Penalties. For an error in procedure (failure to count cards, playing the wrong board, etc.) which requires an adjusted score for any contestant, the director may assess a penalty against the offender (10 percent of the maximum match-point score on one board is recommended). A similar indemnity may be awarded to a contestant who is required to take an adjusted score through no fault of his own. The director may increase the penalties for flagrant or repeated violations. In total-point play, 100 total points are equivalent to 1 match point.

Appeals. If there is a tournament or club committee in charge, appeal may be made to it from any ruling of the director on a question of disputed fact or an exercise of discretionary power. Appeals from the director's

rulings on points of law may be made only to the National Laws Commission, 33 West 60th Street, New York, N.Y. 10023.

AUCTION BRIDGE

There is no difference whatsoever between Auction Bridge and Contract Bridge except in the scoring. Pages 118 to 124 cover the procedure in Auction Bridge and pages 124 to 128 cover the irregularities. But whereas in Contract Bridge declarer's tricks count toward game or slam only if he bid for them, in Auction Bridge declarer's overtricks count toward game or slam just as do the tricks he bid for. Auction Bridge scoring is as follows:

Scoring. Provided declarer wins at least the number of odd tricks named in his contract, declarer's scores for each odd trick won:

	Un-doubled	Doubled	Re-doubled
With no trump	10	20	40
With spades trump	9	18	36
With hearts trump	8	16	32
With diamonds trump	7	14	28
With clubs trump	6	12	24

Game and Rubber. When a side scores, in one or more hands, 30 points or more for odd tricks, it has won a game and both sides start fresh on the next game. When a side has won two games it wins the rubber and adds to its score 250 points.

Doubles and Redoubles. If a doubled contract is fulfilled, declarer's side scores 50 points bonus plus 50 points for each odd trick in excess of his contract. If a redoubled con-

tract is fulfilled, declarer's side scores 100 points bonus plus 100 points for each odd trick in excess of his contract. These bonuses are additional to the score for odd tricks, but do not count toward game.

Undertricks. For every trick by which declarer falls short of his contract, his opponents score 50 points; if the contract is doubled, 100 points; if it is redoubled, 200 points.

Honors. The side which holds the majority of the trump honors (ace, king, queen, jack, ten), or of the aces at no-trump, scores:

For three honors (or aces)	30
For four honors (or aces), divided	40
For five honors, divided	50
For four trump honors in one hand	80
For four trump honors in one hand, fifth in partner's hand	90
For four aces in one hand at no-trump	100
For five honors in one hand	100

Slams. A side which wins 12 of the 13 tricks, regardless of the contract, scores 50 points for a small slam. A side which wins all 13 tricks, regardless of the contract, scores 100 points for grand slam.

Points for overtricks, undertricks, honors, and slams do not count toward game. Only odd tricks count toward game, and only when declarer fulfills his contract.

GAMES BASED ON BRIDGE

Here are a few games which are based on the play of Contract Bridge.

Honeymoon Bridge (Two-Hand Bridge)

Number of Players. Two.

The Pack, 52 cards.

Rank of Cards and Suits, as in Contract Bridge (page 119).

The Shuffle, Cut, and Deal. Each draws; the player drawing the higher card deals first. Each player may shuffle, dealer last, and dealer's opponent must cut. Dealer gives each

player 13 cards, one at a time, and places the remaining cards face down in the center as the *stock.*

The Play. Nondealer leads first. It is necessary to follow suit to the lead if able. Play is at no-trump, as in Contract Bridge. After each trick, each player draws a card from the stock, the winner of the previous trick drawing first and then leading to the next trick. Tricks won during this period have no scoring value.

Bidding and Final Play. When the last card of the stock has been drawn, dealer may bid or pass. Bidding then proceeds as in Contract Bridge until a bid, double, or redouble is followed by a pass. The player who does not make the final bid leads first and 13 tricks are played with or without a trump suit as determined by the final contract.

Scoring. Auction or Contract Bridge scoring may be used.

Additional Rules. If a player revokes during the first 13 tricks, or draws out of turn from the stock, or in drawing sees the face of more than one card; his opponent, when next he draws, may look at the two top cards of the stock and select either.

Double-Dummy Bridge (Two-Hands)

Four hands are dealt. Each player receives one hand, and two remain face down. Each bids, seeing only his own hand. When the bidding is over, both players turn up the face-down hands opposite them so that the hands are in this order: declarer, opponent's dummy, declarer's dummy, opponent.

Opponent's dummy makes the opening lead, and play proceeds as in regular bridge. Scoring is also as in regular bridge. The deal alternates.

Double-Dummy Bridge with a Widow (Two-Hands)

In this game, 12 cards are dealt to each player and two dummy hands. Four cards are dealt separately face down to a widow. The players look at their own hands and their own dummies and bid. After the bidding is over, declarer takes the cards of the widow which are face down and, without looking at them, deals two to himself and two to opponent. Each player, after looking at these cards, places one in his hand and one in the dummy; both doing so at the same time. Declarer then specifies which of the opponents' hands makes the opening lead. Play and scoring are otherwise as in regular bridge.

Partially Exposed Dummy Bridge (Two-Hands)

In this game, also called Chinese Bridge, four hands are dealt. Players receive their own hands face down. But the cards to the dummies are dealt in the following fashion: the first six cards in a row face down; the next seven cards face up on top of these, one on

one—the seventh card alongside. Or the first seven cards may be dealt face down and the next six face up on them, one on one, leaving one card uncovered.

The bidding is as in regular bridge. After the bidding, the lead comes from the hand at declarer's left so that he plays last.

After an exposed card from dummy has been played, the card underneath it may be turned up. Only exposed cards may be played to tricks.

The play and scoring are otherwise as in regular bridge.

Single Exposed Dummy Bridge (Two-Hands)

In this game, also called Single Dummy Bridge, four hands are dealt, one to each player and two as dummies. One of the dummy hands is exposed. The players then bid. After the bidding is over, the declarer chooses which dummy he will take—the exposed one or the one face down. Whichever one he chooses is placed opposite him; if it is the face-down one, it is turned up. Once declarer has made his choice, he may not change his mind.

Play then proceeds with the lead coming from the hand at declarer's left. The play and scoring are otherwise as in regular bridge.

Strip or Draw Bridge (Two-Hands)

In this game, also known as Domino Bridge, each player is dealt a hand of 13 cards. The remaining 26 cards are placed between the players as a stock from which cards are to be drawn in play. The cards of the stock are face down.

There is no bidding until later. Nondealer leads to the first trick, and opponent also plays a card to complete the trick. The play is at no-trump. There are two ways of playing, and players decide on the method before the game begins. One way is to allow a player to follow suit or not, as he chooses. The other is to require that a player follow suit when able to.

When a player wins a trick, he places it in a discard pile. He then draws the top card from the stock into his hand, and opponent draws the card under it. The winner of a trick leads to the next trick. Play continues in this fashion until the stock is exhausted.

Each player is then left with a hand of 13

cards. Now there is bidding, beginning with the dealer. The bidding proceeds as in regular bridge until some player passes. Doubles and redoubles are allowed.

Opponent of the declarer leads to the first trick. Play then continues as in regular bridge with players required to follow suit if they can. Tricks taken in play now are kept by the winners and not placed in the discard pile. The scoring is as in regular Bridge—either Contract or Auction.

Exposed Stock. In this version, the twenty-seventh card after the hands are dealt is turned face up on top of the stock. The player winning a trick takes the top card of the stock, and the loser takes the card under it which is not exposed. But a player finding the exposed card undesirable, may of course deliberately lose a trick to avoid taking that card and so get the next card underneath it.

After both players have played to a trick and drawn their cards, the next card of the stock is turned face up. This process of always turning up the top card of the stock after a trick has been won continues until the stock is exhausted.

Draw and Discard Bridge (Two-Hands)

In this game, no cards are dealt. Instead, the deck is placed face down between the two players.

One player (it does not matter which one) draws the top card of the stock and looks at it without showing it to opponent. If he wishes to keep it, the turn to draw passes to opponent. But if the player does not wish to keep the card drawn, he discards it but *must* take the next one in the deck.

Players draw alternately in this fashion until each has a hand of 13 cards. Each player in turn has the option of keeping the first card he draws or discarding it and taking the next one. When each has a hand of 13 cards, they bid against each other. Bidding is as in regular bridge, as is the scoring.

If the player who made the last pass in round one also passes in round two, opponent may make one more bid, as high as he likes. *Example:* Here is the bidding in rounds one and two. Player A is the dealer and bids one spade: player B passes. After two cards are dealt to each and arranged, player B has the first bid. Since he passed in round one, he must bid at least game. He bids four hearts,

let us say, and player A overcalls with four spades. B passes. That ends the bidding and A is declarer at four spades.

When the final bid has been made, the remaining four cards of the stock are distributed two and two, and the players reduce their hands again and build up their dummies as described above. But this time, the two cards that go into dummy are placed *face down* and are not turned up for play until all of dummy's exposed cards are exhausted.

Defending hand may not place trumps in the closed cards. Declarer may, provided he tells how many, but he need not identify them.

The play is as in regular bridge with the hand at the left of declarer making the opening lead so that declarer plays last to the trick. Seats are changed after every rubber to equalize any advantage of position. Scoring is as in regular bridge with this important exception: A player collects a double score if he plays and makes the contract at a suit he bid in the first round. He does not incur double penalties, however, if he fails to make the contract in that suit.

Money Bridge (Two-Hands)

In this game, 13 cards are dealt to each player, and the remaining stock of 26 cards is laid aside face down.

Each player picks up his hand, and the game begins with nondealer making the first lead. Each trick consists of two cards. The play is at no-trump. When the hands have been played out, the one with the most tricks gets a score for one no-trump and a premium of 100 points.

The remaining 26 cards of the stock are now dealt, 13 to each player. Dealer begins the bidding in any suit and opponent may overcall, the bidding continuing until there is a pass. Doubles and redoubles are allowed. Opponent of the successful bidder leads to the first trick. The result is scored as in Contract or Auction Bridge. Remembering what cards were played in the first deal, of course, is very important.

Three-Hand (Cutthroat) Bridge

Number of Players. Three.

The Pack. 52 cards. Two packs are used as in Contract Bridge.

The Draw. Draw for deal and seats only. High deals.

The Shuffle and Cut. Player at dealer's left shuffles (dealer may shuffle last) and player at dealer's right cuts.

The Deal. Four hands are dealt as in Contract Bridge, a dummy hand being dealt between the players at dealer's left and right.

The Bidding. Dealer bids first and bidding proceeds until any call is followed by two passes.

The Play. The highest bidder becomes declarer; the other two players become defenders, and the defender at declarer's left makes the opening lead. The dummy is then spread out between the two defenders and play proceeds as in Contract Bridge.

Scoring. Either the Auction Bridge or Contract Bridge scoring table may be used. A separate score is kept for each player. If declarer makes his contract, the points are scored to his credit; if he is defeated, each of his opponents scores the undertrick penalties. If the defenders or either of them hold honors, both defenders score for them. In three-hand Auction Bridge, the first player to win two games receives 250 points bonus; in three-hand Contract Bridge, he receives 700 points if neither opponent has a game, 500 points if either opponent has a game.

Settlement. Each player settles separately with each other player, paying or collecting the difference in their scores to the nearest 100 points, 50 or more counting as 100.

Irregularities. During the auction, an improper double may be canceled by the player who is doubled and thereafter neither opponent may double him at any contract. There is no penalty for any other improper call, which may be canceled by either opponent or condoned by agreement of both opponents. If a player improperly looks at any card in the dummy, he is barred from the auction thereafter. *During the play,* the laws of Contract Bridge (page 119) apply.

Trio (Contract Bridge for Three)

Players. The three players are designated as South, North, and East, seated in those compass positions. South and North are partners against East and the dummy, which is in the West position.

Preliminaries. As in Three-Hand Bridge. After the deal the entire dummy hand is faced and is seen by all players during the bidding.

Bidding. South always bids first, then North, then East, and so on in rotation. Any player may become declarer, though East always plays the dummy.

Play. The player (which may be dummy) at declarer's left makes the opening lead and play proceeds as in Bridge.

Scoring. Score is kept as in Contract Bridge, with East and dummy constituting one side and North-South the other. Hence, East wins or loses doubly, North and South each singly.

Towie (for Three or More)

Players. Only three play at a time, but there may be as many as seven in the game.

Preliminaries. Four hands are dealt, then the dealer turns up six cards of the dummy (hand opposite him).

Bidding and Play. The three players bid. High bidder becomes declarer and after the opening lead (by the player at his left) he turns up the rest of the dummy and places it opposite him. Play proceeds as in Bridge.

Scoring. Contract Bridge scoring may be used, but most players use special scoring in which down three, vulnerable and doubled, counts 1,000 (called *towie*). A separate scoring column is used for each player. If declarer makes his contract he scores the trick score plus 500 for his first game and 1,000 for his second (rubber) game. If declarer is defeated, every player (active or inactive) scores the undertrick penalties.

Goulash. If a contract worth at least 100 trick points is not reached, each player sorts his hand into suits, these hands are stacked, and the pack is cut, and the same dealer redeals them in three rounds—five, five, and three cards at a time. Six of dummy's cards are turned up and bidding begins again.

Retirement. When there are more than three in the game, each player becomes inactive after being declarer. Players reenter in the order in which they went out, except that vulnerable player may not reenter as long as any player is not vulnerable.

Cutthroat Contract (for Four Players)

Players. Four, but with no fixed partnerships.

Bidding. As in Contract Bridge, except:

(a) the opening bidder must have at least 13 high-card points or 3 quick tricks (see page 129) and if he does not he pays a penalty of 300 points to each other player; (b) after an opening bid of one club to four spades, the next player must bid at least four no-trump; (c) if no one opens the bidding, a goulash (see below) is dealt by the same dealer.

Partnerships. The high bidder selects any player to be his partner. That player may accept and score with declarer, or reject and score with the opponents, but in any case his hand is dummy and the players change seats if necessary to put it opposite declarer. After this, declarer's left-hand opponent may double; if he does not, declarer's right-hand opponent may double; and if either doubles, declarer (or then dummy, if he has accepted) may redouble. Play proceeds as in Contract Bridge.

Scoring. A separate score is kept for each player. The first player to win two games scores 700 for rubber if neither defender is vulnerable and 500 if either defender is vulnerable. A dummy who has acccepted gets only 300 for game if he is not vulnerable. Both defenders, plus dummy if he has rejected high bidder's invitation, score undertrick penalties. The value of undertrick penalties depends solely on whether declarer is vulnerable or not vulnerable.

Goulash

This variant, which is also called by such names as Hollandaise and Mayonnaise, is played like regular Contract or Auction Bridge, except that when a deal is passed out, or in Contract Bridge, when the contract if fulfilled will not produce a game, there is a redeal by the same dealer in the following manner: Each player arranges his cards into suits; the order of the cards in each suit, however, is up to him. The four hands are then stacked face down, the player to the dealer's left being at the bottom, the dealer's partner's hand next, and so on with the dealer's hand on top. The pack is cut (but not shuffled) and dealer deals the cards in three rounds of five, five and three cards at a time. Then bidding and play continues in the normal manner.

Passing Goulashes

In this variant, play is the same as Goulash except that after the completion of the goulash deal each player passes three cards to his partners. After looking at these cards, he passes two cards to his partners and finally, in the same way, passes one card. Then bidding and play follows.

Super Contract Bridge

This variant is based on the rules of Contract Bridge except as follows:

1. A 53-card pack is used, the standard deck plus the addition of a joker.

2. The joker may be named as the highest-ranking card of any suit, at the time it is played. This includes the trump suit. But the joker may not be named as part of any suit to which the holder has previously discarded. If this should occur, it is considered a revoke.

3. Each player receives 13 cards, the last card being placed face up on the table.

4. After the opening lead is made and the dummy goes down, the declarer may exchange the face-up card for any card in his hand or the dummy, always showing the card for which it is exchanged.

5. The scoring is as in Contract Bridge except that the joker may be counted as a trump honor, or as an ace at no-trump, in which case six trump honors score 300; five aces at no-trump score 300.

Plafond

One of the earliest forms of Contract Bridge, Plafond is a French game. It is played the same as Contract Bridge except that scoring is done as follows:

1. The trick score is the same as in Auction Bridge (see page 149) except that only the value of odd tricks bid for and made can be scored below the line, as in Contract Bridge. Any trick won in excess of the contract scores 50 points.

2. Fulfilling any contract, whether or not it is doubled, scores 50 points in addition to the trick score and overtricks, if any. If the contract is doubled, the bonus is 100; if redoubled, 200. Each undertrick counts 100 points undoubled, 200 doubled, 400 redoubled; there is no vulnerability.

3. Four honors in one hand count 100, or 150 if partner holds the fifth; five honors in one hand or four aces at no-trump count 200.

4. It is not necessary to bid a little slam (which counts 100) or grand slam (which

counts 200) in order to score for it.

5. Each side receives a bonus of 100 points when it wins its first game. The side which wins the rubber receives 400 points. If the rubber is unfinished, a side having the only game receives a bonus of 150.

Nullo Bridge

This variant of bridge, which is sometimes called Spanish Bridge, permits the holder of a bad hand to bid and score as a declarer. Either the rules of Contract or Auction Bridge are used, except for the following:

1. There is an added denomination ranking called *nullo,* which falls between spades and no-trump. That is, nullo ranks above spades, but below no-trumps.

2. A nullo contract is played without a trump suit and is scored the same as no-trump except that every trick the declarer loses counts for him and every trick he wins counts against him. *Example:* If a player bids three nullos and wins four tricks, he makes his contract, and game (if contract), for the nine tricks won by his opponents counts for him. Doubling and redoubling rules hold good in this game.

Antibridge or Reverse Bridge

This game is played like Nullo Bridge except that it extends the same principle to trump-suit contracts. That is, a minus or negative bid ranks just lower than the regular or positive bid. *Example:* Minus four spades ranks above four hearts but below a regular or positive four spades. The bid, in this case, would be made if the declarer takes no more than three tricks with spades trumps.

CHAPTER 8

Other Games in the Whist Family

Until the turn of this century Whist was considered the king of the socially acceptable card games in both the United States and Great Britain. Today, however, while it and its many variants have been almost completely overshadowed by its more complex offshoots, Contract and Auction Bridge, it has still kept some of its earlier popularity.

AMERICAN WHIST

Here is a description of the basic game as it is generally played in the United States.

Requirements

1. Four players, two against two as partners.

2. A standard 52-card deck is used. Two decks of contrasting back designs should be used, one being shuffled while the other is dealt, as in Bridge.

3. Rank of cards: *in play*, ace (high), king, queen, jack, ten, nine, eight, seven, six, five, four, three, two. All suits are of *equal* rank. *In drawing for partners and deal, ace is low.*

The Shuffle, Cut, and Deal. Any player may shuffle, the dealer last; the player at the dealer's right cuts. The dealer gives one card at a time, face down, to each player, in clockwise rotation beginning with the player on his left, until he comes to the last card, which is the trump card.

The Trump Card. The dealer must play the last card of the pack face up on the table before him, and every card of its suit becomes a trump. When it is the dealer's turn to play to the first trick, he picks up the trump card and it becomes part of his hand.

Object of Play. To win at least seven tricks out of 13 in play.

The Play. The turn to play is from player to player in clockwise rotation. The player at the dealer's left makes the first lead, and may lead any card. Each player in turn thereafter must play a card, following suit if able. If not able to follow suit, a player may play any card. Four cards so played (including the card led) constitute a trick. A trick containing any trump is won by the player of the highest trump; a trick not containing a trump is won by the player of the highest card of the suit led. The winner of each trick leads to the next.

Scoring. Each odd trick (trick in excess of six) counts 1 point for the side winning it.

The Laws of Whist

The following rules are condensed from the Laws of the American Whist Congress:

The Game. A game consists of 7 points,

each trick above six counting 1. The value of the hand is determined by deducting the loser's score from seven.

Cutting. The dealer must present the deck to his right-hand adversary to be cut; the adversary must take a portion from the top of the deck and place it toward the dealer. At least four cards must be left in each packet. The dealer must reunite the packets by placing the one not removed in cutting upon the other. If, in cutting or reuniting the separate packets, a card is exposed, the deck must be reshuffled by the dealer and cut again. If the dealer reshuffles the deck after it has been properly cut, he loses his deal.

Dealing. When the deck has been properly cut and reunited, the dealer must distribute the cards, one at a time, to each player in regular rotation starting at his left. The last, which is the trump card, must be turned up before the dealer. At the end of the hand, or when the deal is lost, the deal passes to the player next to the dealer on his left, and so on to each in turn. There must be a new deal by the same dealer (a) if any card except the last is faced in the pack; or (b) if, during the deal or during the play of the hand, the pack is proved incorrect or imperfect. (However, any prior score made with that pack shall stand.) If a card is exposed during the deal, the side not at fault may demand a new deal, provided neither member of that side has touched a card. If a new deal does not take place, the exposed card is not liable to be called.

Anyone dealing out of turn, or with the wrong deck, may be stopped before the trump card is turned. If the trump card is turned, the deal is valid and the deck, if changed, is kept.

Misdealing. It is a misdeal if the dealer:

(a) Omits to have the deck cut, and his adversaries discover the error before the trump card is turned and before looking at any of their cards.

(b) Deals a card incorrectly and fails to correct the error before dealing another.

(c) Counts the cards on the table or in the remainder of the pack.

(d) Having a perfect deck, does not deal to each player the proper number of cards and the error is discovered before all have played the first trick.

(e) Looks at the trump card before the deal is completed.

(f) Places the trump card face downward upon his own or any other player's cards.

A misdeal loses the deal unless, during the deal, either of the adversaries touches a card, or in any other manner interrupts the dealer.

The Trump Card. The dealer must leave the trump card face up on the table until it is his turn to play to the first trick. If it is left on the table until after the *second* trick has been turned and quitted (a quitted trick is a trick that has been turned face down), it is liable to be called (taken). After it has been lawfully taken up it must not be named; any player naming it is liable to have his highest or his lowest trump called by either adversary. A player may, however, ask what the trump suit is.

Irregularities in the Hands. At any time after all have played to the first trick (the pack being perfect): If a player is found to have either more or less than his correct number of cards, and if his adversaries have the right number, then the latter, upon the discovery of such surplus or deficiency, may consult and may choose (a) to have a new deal; or (b) to have the hand played out, in which case the surplus or missing cards are not taken into account.

If either of the adversaries also has more or less than his correct number, there must be a new deal. If any player has a surplus card by reason of an omission to play to a trick, his adversaries can exercise the foregoing privilege only after he has played to the trick following the one in which the omission occurred.

Cards Liable to Be Called. The following cards are liable to be called by either adversary:

(a) Every card faced upon the table other than in the regular course of play, but not including a card led out of turn.

(b) Every card thrown with the one led or played to the current trick. The player must indicate the one led or played.

(c) Every card so held by a player that his partner sees any portion of its face.

(d) All the cards in a hand lowered or shown by a player so that his partner sees more than one card of it.

(e) Every card named by the player holding it.

All cards liable to be called must be placed and left face upward on the table. A player must lead or play them when they are called, providing he can do so without revoking. The call may be repeated at each trick until the card is played. A player cannot be prevented from leading or playing a card liable to be called; if he can get rid of it in the course of play, no penalty remains. If a player leads a card better than any that his adversaries hold of the suit, and then leads one or more other cards without waiting for his partner to play, the latter may be called upon by either adversary to take the first trick. The other cards thus improperly played are liable to be called; it makes no difference whether he plays them one after the other or throws them all on the table together. A player having a card liable to be called must not play another until the adversaries have stated whether or not they wish to call the card liable to the penalty. If he plays another card without waiting the decision of the adversaries, this other card also is liable to be called.

Leading Out of Turn. If any player leads out of turn, a suit may be called from him or his partner the first time it is the turn of either of them to lead. The penalty can be enforced only by the adversary on the right of the player being penalized.

If a player so called on to lead a suit has none of it, or if all have played to the false lead, no penalty can be enforced. If all have not played to the trick, the cards erroneously played to such false lead are not liable to be called, and must be taken back.

Playing Out of Turn. If the third hand plays before the second, the fourth hand may also play before the second. If the third hand has not played, and the fourth hand plays before the second, the latter may be called upon by the third hand to play his highest or lowest card of the suit led; or, if he has none, to trump or not to trump the trick.

Abandoned Hands. If all four players throw their cards on the table, face upward, no further play of that hand is permitted. The result of the hand, as then claimed or admitted, is established; provided that, if a revoke is discovered, the revoke penalty attaches.

Revoking. A revoke may be corrected by the player making it, before the trick in which it occurs has been turned and quitted, unless (*a*) either he or his partner, whether in his right turn or otherwise, has led or played to the following trick; or (*b*) his partner has asked whether or not he has any of the suit renounced.

If a player corrects his mistake in time to save a revoke, the card improperly played by him is liable to be called.

The penalty for revoking is the transfer of at least two tricks, from the revoking side to their adversaries. It can be enforced for as many revokes as occur during the hand. The revoking side cannot win the game in that hand. If both sides revoke, neither side can win the game in that hand. The revoking player and his partner may require the hand in which the revoke has been made to be played out, and score all points made by them up to score of 6. The revoke can be claimed at any time before the cards have been presented and cut for the following deal, but not thereafter.

Miscellaneous. During the play of a trick, and before the cards have been touched for the purpose of gathering them together, any one may demand that the players draw their cards (expose the cards to that trick).

If any player says "I can win the rest," "The rest are ours," "We have the game," or words to that effect, his partner's cards must be laid upon the table, and are liable to be called.

If a player is lawfully called upon to play the highest or lowest of a suit, or to trump or not to trump a trick, or to lead a suit, and unnecessarily fails to comply, then he is liable to the same penalty as if he had revoked. In all cases where a penalty has been incurred, the offender must await the decision of the adversaries. If either demands a penalty to which they are entitled, such decision is final.

English Whist

This variant is played the same as American Whist, except for the following differences in scoring:

1. A score for honors is made for the ace, king, queen, and jack of trumps. The side holding three such honors scores 2 points; the side holding all four scores 4. But, a side cannot win game on an honor count alone. It must also win at least one odd trick in that deal. Tricks are counted before honors; this is important in deciding who has reached game first. After game has been reached, a losing side's honors are not counted, but the winning one's are.

2. Game is 5 points, rather than 7. Rubbers are generally played—two games out of three. If a side reaches game before their

opponents have scored anything, it receives 3 rubber points. If a side reaches game before their opponents have won 3 game points, it gets 2 rubber points. If the opponents have won 3 or more game points, the side reaching game is given 1 rubber point. For winning rubber, a side scores 2 additional points. The highest winning margin possible after rubber is over is 8, known as a *bumper*. The lowest winning margin is one. The rubber score of the losers is subtracted from that of the winners to establish the winning margin.

3. Revokes are handled in one of three following ways:

    (*a*) 3 points are deducted from offending side's score.

    (*b*) 3 points are deducted from offending side's score and added to nonoffenders.

    (*c*) 3 points are added to nonoffender's score.

Prussian Whist

This variant is played like American Whist except that, instead of turning up the last card for trump, the player to the dealer's left cuts a trump from the deck not in use.

Favorite Whist

Favorite Whist is American Whist with this variation: Whenever the suit first cut for trumps reappears as trumps during the rubber, tricks and honors count double. A favorite suit must be cut for afresh at the beginning of each rubber.

Suit-Value Whist

In this variant of American Whist, each trick over six is worth 1 when spades are trumps; 2, when clubs; 3, when diamonds; and 4, when hearts. There is no count for honors, and 10 points is game. The rubber bonus is 10 points. The difference between the score of the winners and that of the losers is the value of the rubber.

Duplicate Whist, Progressive Whist, Progressive Rubber Whist, and Pivot Whist

These are all played the same as in Contract or Auction Bridge (Chapter 7), except that Whist scoring and play is used. Each deal is a unit in Duplicate and Progressive Whist, and a bonus of 2 is added for game on a deal.

Dummy Whist

This variant of English Whist, called *Mort* by the French, is for three players. Before the play begins the players cut, and lowest wins dummy for the first rubber; next to lowest wins dummy for the second; highest wins dummy for the third. It is regarded as compulsory to play three rubbers. After the opening lead, the dummy's hand is placed face up, arranged in suits, and thereafter dummy's partner plays dummy's cards one by one. Dummy is not allowed to revoke and its position is always between the opponents.

Double Dummy Whist

Double Dummy Whist is played by two players. Lower in the cut deals, dealing to his dummy first. The dealer has the privilege of sitting to the right or to left of the other player. The seat to the right is regarded as preferable, as it permits leading through the concealed hand. This variant is scored as in English Whist.

Humbug Whist

In this variation of Double Dummy, the two players sit opposite each other. Four hands of 13 cards each are dealt, and the last card is faced for the trump. Either or both players, after examining the hands dealt to them, have the privilege of exchanging the hands dealt to them for the hands respectively to their right, facing down the hand they have examined. If the dealer exchanges his, the trump suit remains the same, but he naturally loses the faced trump card. The face-down hands are not used in the play. The nondealer makes the first lead and, except that each trick consists of only two cards, the rules for play are as in American Whist; however, the scoring counts as in English Whist.

Trump Humbug Whist

This variant is played the same way as Humbug Whist, except that no trump is turned. Instead, the dealer names the trump after looking at his hand, but he may not exchange it. His opponent then has the privilege of playing the hand dealt to him, or exchanging it for the hand to his right.

Chinese Whist

In this game for four hands, each player is dealt six cards, one at a time, in a face-down row. Then six more cards are dealt to each player, one at a time, face up. The face-up cards cover the six face-down cards. Then one "playing" card is dealt to each player, face down. The "playing" cards are held in the hands of the players until the dealer names one suit as trump. The player to the dealer's left then leads his "playing" card or one of the face-up cards, and the other players in rotation play to it from their face-up cards. It is required to follow suit if possible; if not, players may trump or discard. As soon as a card faced up is played, the concealed card beneath it must be faced up. The rules of play and scoring are as in American Whist.

BID WHIST

Requirements

1. Four players, two against two in partnership.

2. A standard 52-card deck. Cards rank same as in American Whist.

The Deal and Bidding. The dealer gives each player 13 cards, one at a time, in rotation, left to right. No trump is turned. Instead, each player, beginning with the player to the dealer's left, bids or passes. When a player bids, he names number of points his side will win in tricks and honors if he is allowed to make the trump, but he does not disclose the suit. Each bid must be for a higher number than the preceding one; low bid is 1 point and high bid is 11—seven odd tricks and four more for honors (ace, king, queen, and jack of trumps). Some players do not count the honors in bidding and thus 7 points would be high. Before play, the successful bidder names trump suit.

The Play. The highest bidder leads to the first trick, and the winner of each trick leads to the next. A suit must be followed when possible; otherwise players can trump or discard. The honors count to the side that wins them in tricks, not to the original holders.

Scoring. If the bidder's side fulfills its contract, it scores for all odd tricks and honors that it makes. If it fails, the amount of the bid is deducted from the previous score, even if it means going minus. Opponents score for any odd tricks above six and honors that they win in defeating the bid.

NORWEGIAN WHIST

Requirements

1. Four players, two against two as partners.

2. A standard 52-card deck.

The Deal and Bid. The deal is as in American Whist, except that no trump is turned or named; every hand must be played at *no trumps*. But there are two declarations which a player may make: *nullo,* in which case the object of the game is for his side to lose as many tricks as possible; or *grand,* in which case the object is to win as many tricks as possible. The player to the left of the dealer has the first opportunity to bid one of these declarations, or to pass. If he passes, the opportunity goes to the player on his left, and so on, in a clockwise rotation. Whatever bid is named first must be played. If all pass, the hand is automatically played at nullo, with the dealer acting as the bidder.

The Play. If the declaration is grand, the player at the bidder's right makes the opening lead. If the bid is nullo, the player at the bidder's left makes the opening lead. In any case play continues to the left, and each player must follow suit, if able. The highest card of the suit led wins the trick. The winner of a trick leads to the next, and play continues in this fashion until all 13 tricks have been played.

Scoring. The game is 50 points. There are two methods of scoring. In a bid of grand, each trick over the book of six counts 4 points for the side that declared. If the bid is not made, each trick over the book of six taken by the opponents counts double, or 8. If nullo is bid, the side making the bid is penalized 2 points for each trick taken over the book while the opponents score 2 points for each trick the bidders make over six. In nullo, the value of each trick over the book is always 2 points.

A simpler scoring system is to count every trick. In this system, every trick at grand is scored at 4 when the bid is made; when the bid is not made, the opponents score 6 for each trick they take. At nullo, the side taking the smaller number of tricks scores 2 for each trick taken by their opponents. This scoring system permits a game to be completed in one hand when a grand slam (all 13 tricks) is made at grand (13 times 4, or 52). The opponents could go game in one hand by setting a grand bid by at least three tricks, in which case they would take nine tricks and score 9 times 6, or 54.

Additional Rules. The additional rules for American Whist hold good except that the revoke penalty is to give up three tricks in grand or to take three tricks in nullo, if the other side has that number; if not, to take what they have. A call out of turn forfeits 20 points to the other side, and loses the player's right to bid on that hand.

Dutch Whist

This Whist partnership game consists of five deals played in the following order:

1. *First Deal.* This hand is played exactly as American Whist, in that the last card turned up determines trump. Scoring is the same.

2. *Second Deal.* This hand is played without any trump at all. Play and scoring in all the five deals is as in American Whist.

3. *Third Deal.* No trump is turned, but the player at the dealer's left chooses the suit to be trump and announces it as he makes his lead.

4. *Fourth Deal.* This is a nullo hand, played at no-trumps, in which the object of the game is to give opponents tricks. Each partnership scores for tricks taken by opponents.

5. *Fifth Deal.* The dealer cuts a card to determine trump, then immediately places it somewhere in the deck. No one may ask what trump is after that; if anyone revokes, his side is penalized according to the rules of American Whist.

After the five deals are concluded and the scores totaled, the partners holding the highest number of points are the winners.

BRIDGE-WHIST

Bridge-whist was the most popular card game of its type from the 1890's to about 1908. It was supplanted by Auction Bridge and is not played too often today.

Requirements

1. Four players, two against two as partners.

2. A standard 52-card deck.

3. Rank of cards; ace (high), king, queen, jack, down to two (low).

4. Rank of suits are equal, except in scoring.

The Deal and Bidding. The dealer deals 13 cards, one at a time, in rotation, left to right, to each player. No trump is turned. After looking at his hand, the dealer is permitted to name a trump suit, or to name no-trumps. He may pass this privilege to his partner, who then has to name a trump suit or no-trumps. After the trump suit or no-trump has been determined, the player on the dealer's left either doubles or says "May I lead?" In the latter case, his partner may double or tell him to lead. If either opponent doubles, the dealer and his partner, in turn, have the right to

redouble as in Contract Bridge, page 119.

The Play. Once the bidding phase has ended, the player to the dealer's left leads any card he desires. The dealer's partner then lays down his hand and play continues as in Contract Bridge, page 124.

Scoring. Whichever side wins, the odd tricks are scored as follows: If spades were trumps, 2 points per trick; if clubs, 4; if diamonds, 6; if hearts, 8; if no-trumps, 12. These values are increased by any doubling (two times) and redoubling (four times). The first partnership to score 30 points in its trick-score makes game; the first side to win two games wins the rubber and gets a bonus of 100.

Additional points, which count in the total score but not in the trick score, are as follows: little slam counts 20 points, grand slam counts 40 points, and *chicane* (being void of trumps) counts twice the value of an undoubled odd trick. All these scores go above the line, together with the following scores for trump honors or for the aces at no-trumps:

If Trumps Were:	Spades	Clubs	Diamonds	Hearts	No-Trumps
3 honors in one hand	4	8	12	16	30
4 honors in one hand	16	32	48	64	100
5 honors, divided	10	20	30	40	
5 honors, 4 in one hand	18	36	54	72	
5 honors in one hand	20	40	60	80	

Additional Rules. The laws for irregularities are the same as those for American Whist (page 156) and Contract Bridge (page 124).

VINT

This Whist variation, which is also called Russian Whist, is quite popular in parts of the United States and Europe.

Requirements

1. Four players, two against two as partners.

2. A standard 52-card deck.

3. Rank of cards: ace (high), king, queen, jack, ten, down to two (low).

4. Rank of suits: no-trumps (high), hearts, diamonds, clubs, and spades (low).

The Deal and Bidding. The dealer gives 13 face down cards, one at a time, in clockwise rotation, to each player. No trump is turned. Beginning with the dealer, each player must bid or pass. The minimum bid is to win the odd trick (seven out of thirteen) with spades as trumps. This bid is stated "One, in spades." Each player in rotation, to the left, can overbid by bidding in a higher suit or in no-trumps. Or, a player can overbid by a bid for a greater number of tricks, such as "Three, in diamonds" (meaning a bid to take nine tricks), etc. A bid of an identical number in a higher ranking suit or in no-trumps overcalls a bid of the same number in a lower ranking suit. The highest possible bid, of course, is "Seven, no-trumps." A player cannot overcall himself after three passes. If a player is overcalled, he can bid higher, and partners can overcall each other without an intervening bid by opponents, as in Contract Bridge.

The Play. The player on the left of the successful bidder leads for the first trick, and each player in rotation must follow suit if he can. If not, he must trump or discard. The winner of each trick leads to the next.

The Scoring of the Game. The game score, which is entered below the line, depends on the tricks taken. Both sides score for each trick taken, whether the bid is made or not. But the value of each trick depends upon the number of tricks bid, not the suit rank. That is, if there is a one-bid, each trick counts 10 for the side winning it; if a two-bid, 20; and so on. At a seven-bid, each trick counts 70.

The game is won by the first partnership to reach a game score or trick score of 500, even if it is in the middle of a hand. Contrary to most bidding games, the first side to score 500 wins the game, regardless of which partnership won the bidding.

Honor Scoring. Points called *honor points,* counted above the line, are also given as bonuses. For winning a game, for example, 1,000 honor points are given. For winning a rubber, the first two games, there is an honor score of 2,000 whether opponents have won a game or not.

All honor scores are above the line. The honors are the ace, king, queen, jack, and ten, all of trumps, and also the three aces. At no-trumps, the aces are the only honors. When there is a trump suit, the ace counts twice, both as an honor and as an ace. Each honor is worth ten times as much as a trick, so its value varies with the final bid. Thus, if the bid is four, the tricks are worth 40 each, and each honor is worth ten times 40, or 400. The side that has the majority of either aces or honors or both scores honor points. *Example:* If one side holds four aces and two honors (which may include the ace), and the other side holds three honors, the majority of honors (three) is deducted from the number of aces (four) and the ace-holding side scores one honor only—worth ten times the value of the trick, according to the number of tricks bid. If one side has two honors and three aces, and the other side has three honors and one ace, neither side scores because the three honors cancel out the three aces. If each side holds two aces, only the side that wins the majority of the tricks can score them.

At no-trumps, the value of each ace is 25 times the value of a trick. If aces are *easy* (two for each side) neither side scores. If not, the side having the majority of aces scores for each ace it holds.

In the hand of a single player, sequences of three cards or more headed by an ace, in any suit, are called *coronets,* no matter whether the declaration be of trumps or no-trumps. Also, three or four aces in one hand rank as a coronet, which is worth 500 points. In a declared trump, the ace, king, and queen of a plain suit (not trumps), or three aces, are worth 500. Each additional card in the sequence adds 500. A sequence from the ace to the seven in a plain suit would count 3,000. In the trump suit, or in any suit when the declaration is no-trumps, these sequences are worth double. Thus, the ace, king, and queen are worth 1,000; a sequence from the ace

through the nine in a trump suit, or in any suit in no-trumps, is worth 4,000 points.

If the declaring side fails to make its bid, the penalty for each undertrick is 100 times the value of each trick, scored above the line. In a bid of four no-trumps, each trick is worth 40. Thus, failing by three tricks would cost a penalty of three times 40 times 100, or 12,000. In addition, the opponents would score six tricks won at 40 each, or 240, below the line, toward game. At the same time, the bidders would score for the seven tricks they took: seven times 40, or 280. This again differs from most other bidding games, in which unsuccessful bidders do not score below the line.

Other honor score bonuses are:

Little slam, 12 tricks, made but not bid	1,000
Grand slam, 13 tricks, made but not bid	2,000
Little slam bid and made	6,000
Litlle slam bid, grand slam made	7,000
Grand slam bid and made	12,000

Additional Rules. The laws for irregularities are the same as those for American Whist.

CAYENNE

Requirements

1. Four players, two against two, as partners.

2. Two standard 52-card decks; one is used for play, the other names cayenne.

The Deal and Bid. The dealer gives 13 cards to each player at a rate of four, four, and five, in a rotation, left to right, beginning with the dealer's left. Then the player at the dealer's left cuts the unused or *still deck* to expose a card that is known as *cayenne.* The suit of the same color as cayenne is known as the *second color.*

After examining his hand, the dealer may make one of three declarations. He may name (*a*) cayenne or any other suit trumps; (*b*) grand, which means his side will try to win as many tricks as possible with no trump suit named for the deal; (*c*) nullo, which is played with no trumps. If the dealer cannot decide, he may pass the turn to his partner who must select a trump suit, grand, or nullo. But one or the other must make the declaration.

The Play. The player at the dealer's left leads to the first trick. If there is a trump suit,

the rules for play are as described for American Whist. If the bid is in grand or nullo, the rules of play for Norwegian Whist should be followed.

Scoring. Each trick above the book of six counts 1. There is also a count for honors—ace, king, queen, jack, and ten of trumps. If either side holds three of these honors between them, it is worth a count of 2; four honors count 4; and all five honors count 5. These points, made by honors and tricks, are *multiplied* at the end of the hand, according to the value of the trump suit. In grand or nullo, the multiplier is always eight, and only applies to tricks. Otherwise, the multiplier depends on which suit is trumps and on its relation to the suit which has been cut for cayenne on that deal. Here is the table of values:

Cayenne	Second Color	Third Color	Fourth Color
Hearts	Diamonds	Clubs	Spades
Diamonds	Hearts	Clubs	Spades
Clubs	Spades	Hearts	Diamonds
Spades	Clubs	Hearts	Diamonds

If the cayenne is trumps, the multiplier is four; if the second color is trumps, the points are multiplied by three; if the third color, multiplied by two; if the fourth color, multiplied by one. In nullos, every trick over the book counts to the other side. There is no honor count in grand or nullo.

The side that first reaches 10 points wins the game, but all games are played to completion. Any points over 10 won in one game are credited toward the next game or games. When the opponents have not scored at all, the winners of the game earn a bonus of 4 rubber points; if the opponents fail to reach a game score of 4, then 3 rubber points are given to the winners of the game; if the opponents have not reached 7, the winners earn 2 rubber points; if the opponents have 8

or more points, the victory is worth 1 rubber point. The side that first wins four games of 10 points each receives a bonus of 8 rubber points, in addition to the other rubber points already scored. The side with the most rubber points scored wins by the difference between its score and the opponents'. Tricks count before honors, and players cannot go game on honors alone, but must stop at 9 points if they have no trick score on that hand.

Additional Rules. Irregularities are handled in the same manner as American Whist except that a revoke carries with it a penalty of three tricks, and the side in error cannot go game on that deal; but they may play the game out and may score as high as 9, if they can.

SOLO WHIST

This game is also known as Whist de Grand.

Requirements

1. Four or five players, each playing himself. With five players, the dealer takes no cards.

2. A standard 52-card deck.

The Deal and Bid. Each player receives 13 cards, four rounds of three cards each, and a final single card to each. The last card is turned up for the trump, and belongs to the dealer. In a five-handed game, the turned trump belongs to the player at the dealer's right.

The bidding begins with the player to the left of the dealer and rotates clockwise. Each player makes one of the following declarations of what he proposes to do—or passes. He may try:

1. To win eight tricks, playing with a partner and the turned-up suit as trump. This is called *proposal* (lowest bid).

2. To win five tricks, alone against the others, with the turned-up suit as trump. This is called *solo*.

3. To win no tricks, alone against the others, at no-trump. This is called *misère* or *nullo*.

4. To win nine, alone against the others, if allowed to name any suit but the turned one as trump. This is called *abundance*.

5. To win nine, alone against the others, with the turned suit as trump. This is called *abundance in trumps*.

6. To win no tricks, alone against the others, at no-trump, the bidder's hand being exposed on the table after the first trick. This is called *spread* or *open misère*.

7. To win all 13 tricks, alone against the others, at no-trump. This is called *misère* or lead. This is called *abundance déclarée* or *slam* (highest bid).

To bid proposal, bidder says "I propose." Any succeeding player, in turn, may propose to become his partner by saying "I accept." The seating at the table remains unaltered. The proposer and acceptor must take eight tricks, if no higher bid is made. No player may bid after once passing; however, the player to the left of the dealer, who opened the bidding, may accept a proposal, even if he has previously passed. The bidding continues in clockwise rotation until no one will make a higher bid. A player who has made one bid may change it to a higher-ranking one, in turn, if some other player has bid higher than he. If all pass, the hands are thrown in and the deal goes to the left.

The Play. The player at the dealer's left leads, except in the case of a slam bid when the bidder leads. Each player must follow suit, if able; if not, he must discard or trump as in American Whist. (In misère bids, of course, there are no trumps.) The highest card of the suit led wins a trick, unless it is trumped; then the highest trump wins. The winner of each trick leads for the next.

Scoring. Chips may be used for settlement or a pencil-and-paper score may be kept. With the former, each player begins with the same number of chips. In proposal, the bidder and his partner, if successful, win one chip each from each adversary; if unsuccessful, they pay one chip to each opponent. A bidder playing alone against the others wins from or pays to each other player the following, depending on whether he succeeds or not:

	Number of Chips
Solo	2
Misère or nullo	3
Abundance	4
Abundance in trumps	4
Open misère or spread	6
Abundance déclarée or slam	8

In addition to the above: For each trick under or above the amount bid, one whole counter is paid by the bidder or by each adversary. Misères and slams pay no odd tricks. The moment a misère player takes a trick, or a slam player loses one, the hands are abandoned, and the stakes are paid.

Additional Rules. Irregularities are handled in the same manner as American Whist, except that the revoking side or player cannot win the hand; at the end of the play, the side or player must forfeit three tricks to the opponents. After this, the overtricks and undertricks are computed and paid for.

Three-Handed Solo Whist

This game is played like four-handed Solo Whist except for the following:

1. A 40-card pack is made by stripping the twos, threes, and fours from a standard 52-card deck.

2. Each player receives 13 cards and the fortieth card is turned for trumps and belongs to no one.

3. The proposal bid is not employed.

BOSTON

Requirements

1. Four players, each playing for himself.

2. Two standard 52-card decks; one is used for play, the other names the trump suit.

The Deal and Bid. Each player receives 13 cards: four rounds of three cards, and a final single card to all. The player opposite the dealer cuts the unused cards and the top card of the bottom portion is turned up for trump or "preference." The other suit of the same color is known as "color." The remaining two suits are plain suits.

Bidding begins with the player at the dealer's left, and each player, in turn to the left, bids or passes. The bids rank (from lowest to highest) as follows:

1. To win five tricks playing alone in a plain suit. This is called *Boston*.

2. To win six tricks.

3. To win seven tricks.

4. To lose 12 tricks after each player discards one card not shown to others. This is known as *little misery*.

5. To win eight tricks.

6. To win nine tricks.

7. To lose every trick. This is known as *grand misery*.

8. To win ten tricks.

9. To win 11 tricks.

10. To play little misery with all the cards in one's hand exposed. This is known as *little spread*.

11. To win twelve tricks.

12. To play grand misery with all the cards in one's hand exposed. This is known as *grand spread*.

13. To win all 13 tricks. This is known as a *grand slam*.

In bids number 1, 2, 3, 5, 6, 8, 9, 11, and 13, the calls rank as follows: in plain suits (low), in color, in preference (high).

The Play. The same as in American Whist.

Scoring. If the bidder fulfills his bid, he collects from each player according to the following table. The bidder is paid by each of the others just what he bid and made, by this scale:

Tricks bid	5	6	7	8	9	10	11	12	13
Payment	2	3	4	5	7	9	13	21	34

When the bidder fails, he is said to be "put in for" so many tricks, and he pays as follows:

Tricks Bid	Number of Bid Put in For												
	1	2	3	4	5	6	7	8	9	10	11	12	13
5	2	4	6	8	10								
6	3	5	7	9	11	13							
7	4	6	8	10	12	14	16						
8	5	7	9	11	14	17	20	23					
9	7	9	11	13	16	19	22	25	28				
10	9	11	14	16	19	22	25	28	31	34			
11	14	16	19	22	25	28	31	34	37	40	44		
12	24	26	29	32	26	40	44	48	52	56	60	64	
13	36	40	44	48	52	56	60	64	68	72	78	84	90

Bidder collects or pays four chips for little misery, eight for grand misery, 16 for little spread, and 32 for grand spread. Each puts up two chips for the pot at the beginning; the player winning on a bid of seven tricks or better collects the pot, in addition to the regular payments. If any opponent will not concede a bid under seven and forces the bidder to play out the hand, the bidder must play; but he gets the pot besides the regular payments if he makes seven tricks or more. If a pot goes over 50 chips, the excess is put into the next pot.

If all pass a deal, each chips in to the pot or they play general misery (no-trumps), the player taking the most tricks paying each other player ten chips for each trick difference between them. A misdeal loses the deal, and the dealer places one chip in the pot as penalty. A revoker pays eight chips into the pot, besides losing the hand. Losing on a bid of seven or more requires the loser to double the pot.

Boston de Fontainbleau

This variant is played the same as Boston, except as follows:

1. There is no cut for "preference," the suits ranking diamonds (highest), hearts, clubs, spades (lowest).

2. The bids rank (from low to high): (a) Boston, to win five tricks; (b) to win six tricks; (c) little misery; (d) to win seven tricks; (e) to win exactly one trick at no trump after having discarded a card that no one sees, called *piccolissimo;* (f) to win eight tricks; (g) grand misery; (h) to win nine tricks; (i) little spread; (j) to win ten tricks; (k) grand spread; (l) to win 11 tricks; (m) to win 12 tricks; (n) grand slam; (o) to win all 13 tricks playing with all cards exposed, called *spread slam.* The payments are the same whether the bidder wins or loses. Overtricks are paid for at the rate of one chip per trick.

TABLE OF PAYMENTS

	Clubs or Spades	Hearts	Diamonds	No-Trumps
Boston, five tricks	2	4	6	
Six tricks	6	8	10	
Little misery				15
Seven tricks	10	12	14	
Piccolissimo				20
Eight tricks	14	16	18	
Grand misery				30
Nine tricks	18	20	22	
Little spread				40
Ten tricks	22	24	26	
Eleven tricks	26	28	30	
Twelve tricks	30	32	34	
Grand slam				50
Slam, thirteen tricks	50	60	70	
Spread slam	70	80	90	

3. A player who has once passed cannot bid later; nor can he increase his own bid, unless he is overcalled. The suits must be named in the bidding: diamonds rank highest, then hearts, clubs, and spades. The successful bidder may ask for a partner, and if one accepts him, their joint score must be three tricks more than the bid.

4. A general misery gives the pot to the player who takes the least number of tricks. In case of a tie, the pot is divided. There are no other payments. The pot is made up by one chip from each dealer in turn, plus such penalties as increase it. There is no limit to its size. Any successful bid wins the pot; any call that fails requires the caller to pay into the pot the amount he pays to each opponent. Partners whose bid succeeds divide the pot equally; partners whose bid fails each pay one opponent, and put half that amount into the pot. If the opponents agree to pay before playing to the second trick, this does not save the pot; but it prevents the chance of overtricks.

Russian Boston

In this variation of Boston de Fontainbleau, a player who does not hold any trumps may declare *Chicane* before play begins and collect two chips from each of the other players.

CHAPTER 9

Pinochle with Its Many Variations

Pinochle, in spite of its decline in the past two decades, still ranks as the fourth most popular card game in the United States. It is only surpassed in popularity by Poker, Rummy, and Bridge. Two-handed Pinochle, once the most popular head-to-head money game in the country, has lost a great deal of favor since the advent of Gin Rummy.

Most card historians seem to agree that Pinochle was originally an improved form of the card game Bezique. But the history of Bezique itself is very much in question. Some experts claim that it was a descendant of Cinq Cents (or Five Hundred), itself a descendant of an ancient showdown card game called Matrimony, which was introduced in the early 1700's. Some historians even trace Bezique all the way back to a French card game called Piquet, which is said to have been first played during the reign of Charles VII (1422–61).

However, I tend to go along with the 1864 *American Hoyle* (and the majority of card historians), which claims that Bezique was invented—just as I've invented the card games of Skarney, Scarney Baccarat, and Skarney Gin, and the skill board games of Teeko, Scarney, and Follow the Arrow—by a Swedish schoolmaster named Gustav Flaker, who presented the game under the name Flakernuble to the King of Sweden as an entry in a national contest during the early 1800's. It spread to other countries, turned up with certain sea changes in Germany as Binochle or Penuchle, and later appeared in the United States as an American adaptation of a French adaptation of the Swedish-German game which is now called Pinochle. The game came to this country with the Germans and Irish who immigrated during the Civil War.

GENERAL RULES FOR PINOCHLE

In the early days Pinochle was played with two or three Euchre decks (see Chapter 14), but today most of the games of this family are played with a standard Pinochle deck (although in some variations two or three standard Pinochle decks are shuffled together and used as one). The Pinochle deck is composed of 48 cards—two cards in the four familiar suits (hearts, diamonds, spades, and clubs) in each of the following denominations: ace, king, queen, jack, ten, nine.

If no packaged Pinochle deck is at hand, players can make up their own deck by stripping all cards below the nine-spot from two standard 52-card packs and combining the remainder into a deck consisting of eight aces (two of each suit), eight kings (two of each suit), eight queens (ditto), eight jacks (ditto), eight tens (ditto), and eight nines (also ditto). It's best to combine two decks having identical patterns on the backs.

Rank of Cards and Suits. The cards in Pinochle rank in the following order: ace (high), ten, king, queen, jack, nine (low). Except for the suit designated as trumps, the suits have identical value. When a suit is designated as trumps (either by the turn of a card or by bidder's choice), that suit outranks the three others. A card of the trump suit wins over a card of any other suit regardless of face value. *Example:* If clubs are trumps, the nine of clubs (that suit's lowest-ranking card) wins over the ace of hearts (that suit's highest-ranking card).

When two cards of the same suit and rank are played, the first played has precedence; this card is construed as having the higher rank.

Object of the Game

1. To score the points necessary to win the game (usually 1,000 points is game), a player adds together the value of his *melded* cards and the value of the cards taken by his winning tricks. In some variations each hand is a separate game.

2. The bidder, in a version involving bidding, tries to score the number of points he has bid.

Standard Values of Melded Cards. Irrespective of the brand of Pinochle, the following score values for melds are standard in the United States. Only the names commonly used throughout the country are used; local expressions, signifying nothing anywhere else, are not discussed.

1. In trumps, the ace, ten, king, queen, and jack are commonly called a *flush*, a *run*, a *yard and a half*, or a *royal sequence*. *Scoring value: 150 points.*

2. The nine of trumps will be called the *deece* (after American usage) rather than the affected and confusing *dix* of some outdated game books. *Scoring value: 10 points.*

3. The king and queen of trumps are commonly called the *marriage in trumps* or the *royal marriage. Scoring value: 40 points.*

4. The king and queen of any suit, not trumps, are generally called a *marriage* or a *common marriage. Scoring value: 20 points.*

5. The queen of spades and jack of diamonds are called *Pinochle. Scoring value: 40 points.*

6. The four aces of different suits are called a *hundred aces. Scoring value: 100 points.*

7. The four kings of different suits are called *80 kings. Scoring value: 80 points.*

8. The four queens of different suits are called *60 queens. Scoring value: 60 points.*

9. The four jacks of different suits are called *40 jacks. Scoring value: 40 points.*

10. The king and queen of each suit are commonly called a *roundhouse,* a *round trip,* or *around the world. Scoring value: 240 points.*

If a player holds duplicates of the above melds, each meld has the value set forth.

The Rules of Melding

1. Melds may be laid down (melded) at one time only: before the start of play. This rule holds for all Pinochle games except two-handed Pinochle.

2. To score his melds, a player must win at least one trick with his playing hand. Failure to win a trick loses for that player the score of all the cards he melds in that hand.

3. When playing a partnership game, each partner must meld for himself. But, in a partnership game, only one of the players need win a trick in order to score the melds of both partners.

A player cannot meld a flush (royal sequence) and claim credit for a marriage in trump to boot. He can have a credit of 150 points for the flush only; the marriage does not count. Nor can a player use a party of one marriage to help form another marriage. *Example:* A player melds the marriage of the king and queen of hearts, and retains in his hand the other king of hearts. He cannot meld the second king with the queen already melded; to meld another marriage he must have the other queen of the suit.

The rule holds for all marriages, including the marriage in trumps; marriages once melded cannot be altered. However, three queens of suits other than hearts can be added to a melded queen of hearts to make up a meld of 60 queens. Or three kings of suits other than hearts can be added to the heart king in the above example to make a meld of 80 kings. And provided hearts are trumps, the ace, ten, and jack of hearts can be added to the hearts marriage to make a flush meld. But, if a player holds four kings and four queens of different suits, he should meld a roundhouse and get credit of 240 points all at one time.

In Pinochle these various card combinations called melds carry special point bonuses. For instance, a king-queen of the same suit, a marriage, is worth 20 points, the jack of diamonds–queen of spades, or Pinochle, 30 points. Full scoring of the three classes of melds is explained in the text.

If a player melds Pinochle (the queen of spades and the jack of diamonds), he may use that queen of spades with the king of spades for a marriage. Or he may use it to help make 60 queens. The queen can also be used to help make a flush; but in that case the marriage is void. The jack of diamonds, from the Pinochle meld, may be used simultaneously to help form a flush and 40 jacks.

If a player melds a flush, he can use the king and queen involved to help meld a roundhouse; however, he gets only 200 points for the roundhouse (40 points less than the usual scoring value of 240). This makes a total of 350 points for the roundhouse and the flush together. But, if the player melds a flush in diamonds plus a roundhouse, he gets credit for 390 po nts—the extra 40 points being contributed by the Pinochle meld.

Standard Bonus Melds—Triple and Quadruple Melds. Many players like to incorporate bonus melds into their game. If you choose to do this, use the following standard bonus melds, triple melds, and quadruple melds. These melds may be adopted *in toto* or in part, but it must be stipulated and reemphasized that these meld values are valid and binding only if they have been agreed upon by all players before the start of the game. When such a prior agreement is made, the scorekeeper must make on the score sheet a record of the melds to be honored and their value in points. The standard bonus melds are as follows:

1. Two flushes in one hand are usually called a *double flush. Scoring value: 1,500 points.*

2. Eight aces in one hand (two in each suit) are usually called *double aces. Scoring value: 1,000 points.*

3. Eight kings in one hand (two in each suit) are usually called *double kings. Scoring value: 800 points.*

4. Eight queens in one hand (two in each suit) are usually called *double queens. Scoring value: 600 points.*

5. Eight jacks in one hand (two in each suit) are usually called *double jacks. Scoring value: 400 points.*

6. Two jacks of diamonds plus two queens of spades in one hand are usually called *double Pinochle. Scoring value: 300 points.*

7. Two kings and two queens of the same suit in trumps are usually called a *double marriage in trumps. Scoring value: 300 points.*

8. Two kings and two queens of the same suit (not trumps) in one hand are usually called a *double marriage. Scoring value: 150 points.*

When playing with two or three decks of Pinochle cards consolidated as one deck, players may, in conjunction with the above standard bonus melds, incorporate into their game and scoring the following triple bonus melds.

1. Three flushes in one hand are called a *triple flush. Scoring value: 3,000 points.*

2. Twelve aces in one hand (three in each suit) are called *triple aces. Scoring value: 2,000 points.*

3. Twelve kings in one hand (three in each suit) are called *triple kings. Scoring value: 1,600 points.*

4. Twelve queens in one hand (three in each suit) are called *triple queens. Scoring value: 1,200 points.*

5. Twelve jacks in one hand (three in each suit) are called *triple jacks. Scoring value: 800 points.*

6. Three jacks of diamonds plus three queens of spades in one hand are called *triple Pinochle. Scoring value: 600 points.*

7. In trumps, three kings and three queens in one hand are commonly called a *triple marriage in trumps. Scoring value: 600 points.*

8. Three kings and three queens of the same suit (not trumps) in one hand are commonly called a *triple marriage. Scoring value: 300 points.*

A *quadruple bonus meld* is what its name sounds like: It is a triple meld plus an additional, fourth meld of the same kind. It scores double the value of the corresponding triple bonus meld.

Value of Cards Won in Tricks. There are three radically different methods of scoring cards won in tricks:

1. The old-timers' count. This gives the widest latitude for strategy in play and is generally favored by the Pinochle expert.

2. The simplified count.

3. The streamlined count.

Whatever count is used, it must be mutually agreed upon by all the players before the start of actual play. *Note:* Although these are three different methods of scoring, the total count under each method adds up to the same figure, which is 240 in cards plus 10 for the last trick, won. Under any system there is an invariable total of 250 points.

OLD-TIMERS' COUNT

Ace counts	11 points
Ten counts	10 points
King counts	4 points
Queen counts	3 points
Jack counts	2 points
Nine counts	0 (zero, nothing)

SIMPLIFIED COUNT

Ace counts	10 points
Ten counts	10 points
King counts	5 points
Queen counts	5 points
Jack and nine count	0 (zero, nothing)

STREAMLINED COUNT

Ace counts	10 points
Ten counts	10 points
King counts	10 points
Queen, jack, nine count	0 (zero, nothing)

Number of Players. Although some variations involving the use of double and triple decks allow up to eight persons to play at a time, the most popular forms of Pinochle are played two-, three-, and four-handed. These include the partnership games.

Selecting the Dealer and Establishing Seating Positions at the Table. Two methods are feasible, as follows:

1. By mutual consent any player may shuffle the cards. Then he puts the deck on the table for any other player to cut. The player completing the cut squares the deck. Now each player, starting with the leader (the player to the left of the player who shuffled), and going clockwise around the table, cuts a group of cards. After each has cut, the players turn over their group, exposing their bottom card. The player cutting the highest-ranking Pinochle card becomes the first dealer. If two or more players tie for high card, the tied players cut again until the deal is determined. Under this method the player cutting the highest card (the dealer) has the first choice of seating position. The player cutting the next highest has second choice, and so on until all players are seated.

2. Any player by mutual consent shuffles the cards. Any other player cuts them. The acting dealer deals the cards face up one at a time to all the players, starting with the

player at his left and dealing clockwise, until a player is dealt an ace. That player becomes the first dealer. Now the acting dealer proceeds to deal until a second ace has been dealt. The dealer gets first choice of seating position. The player getting the second ace has second choice. The process goes on until all the players have been seated. Any player dealt an ace is dealt out on the succeeding rounds.

Selecting Partners and Seating Positions. Generally, Pinochle players come to the table with a pretty clear idea of how they want to team off into partnerships. However, if four players prefer to establish partnerships by impartial chance, the following two methods are recommended:

1. Each player cuts a group of cards, as described under rule No. 1 for selecting the dealer. Players cutting the two highest-ranking Pinochle cards form one partnership. The partner cutting the highest of the four cards has the choice of seats. His partner must sit opposite him. The player cutting the lowest-ranking card has his choice of the other two seats, and his partner must of course sit opposite him. If three players tie for high or low, all players must cut again until no tie exists.

2. The acting dealer deals cards face up one at a time until two players have been dealt an ace (omitting from subsequent rounds of the deal any player who has been dealt an ace). These two players become partners. The first player dealt an ace has his choice of seats. Partners must always sit opposite each other.

Changing Partnerships or Seating Positions. Any player may, on the completion of any hour of play, ask for a new cut or deal to try changing partnerships, seating positions, or both. The cut or new deal becomes operative immediately on the conclusion of the hand or game being played. The dealer whose turn it is next to deal becomes the acting dealer, or shuffles for the cut, and the rules set forth immediately above apply to the new deal or cut. The same rules are observed if a player quits the game and another player wants to come into it.

Discussion Before the Play

1. There must be clear and common agreement and understanding among all players as to what type of game is to be played.

2. When the play is for money, the amount involved must be amply discussed and must be agreeable to all players.

3. Players must agree on penalties for infractions such as *holes* and *reneges*.

4. Players must agree on extra bonuses for certain hands; for example, double on spades, triple on hearts, the kitty, etc. Bonuses for special extra-high hands must be agreed upon, and the scorekeeper must record—in writing—the specific point value of special hands.

5. Bonuses for special melds must be agreed upon. The point or cash value of bonus melds must be expressly understood by all.

6. If it is a bidding game, players must agree on the minimum bid.

7. If a kitty is being played for, the amount of money to be put into the kitty and the amount of the minimum bid that can win the kitty must be established.

The Shuffle. The cards are shuffled by the dealer. Any player may call for a shuffle before the cards are cut. The dealer, however, always retains his right to shuffle the cards last.

The Cut. The shuffle completed, the dealer places the cards before the player to his immediate right to be cut. If that player declines to cut, any other player may cut the deck. If no other player cuts, it becomes mandatory that the dealer himself cut the cards before starting to deal. For the cut to be legal there must be at least five cards in each cut block of the deck.

Two-Handed Pinochle (Turn-Up Trump)

Although not played as often as three- and four-handed versions of the game, two-handed Pinochle is in my opinion the one game of the family demanding of the player the most in skill. No, I'll go further than that: In this game there is more room and need for strategy than in any other two-handed game currently being played. In most two-handed games, including Gin Rummy, a lucky beginner can occasionally hold his own against an expert in a session lasting over several hours. In two-handed Pinochle the element of skill is decisive, over the short or the long run.

Requirements

1. Two players.

2. A standard Pinochle deck. For descrip-

tion of the Pinochle deck, rank of cards and suits, value of melded cards, rules for melding, and value of cards won in tricks see General Rules for Pinochle (page 167).

Object of the Game. To score 1,000 or more points before one's opponent and thus to win the game. The value of melded cards and the value of cards taken by winning tricks in successive hands or deals are added until the winning score has been accumulated.

The Stakes, if Desired. *X* being what you think you can afford, the game is played for *X* cents or *X* dollars per 1,000 points, which is game. Most players let the stakes range from 25 cents to $1 a game.

Scorekeeper. Selection of the scorekeeper is by mutual consent. If there's a kibitzer, he usually keeps score. It's best to use a pencil and paper; memory is not entirely trustworthy in a fast-running game. The scorekeeper enters under each player's name on the sheet his scores as they are made. Player A wins a trick and melds 20 points. The 20 is entered immediately under his name on the sheet. Player B wins a trick and melds 40 points. His 40 is forthwith posted to his credit. Totals are computed at the completion of each hand, and the play proceeds until one column or the other totals 1,000 points or more and a winner is declared. *Note:* Some players in scoring drop the last digit from their running account. For example, a 40 meld, is entered as 4, a 20 as 2, etc. Under this system, of course, the winning score is 100.

And here's another way to score, using poker chips. Each player gets the following stack:

Nine blue chips, each valued at 100 points;

Four red chips, each valued at 20 points;

Two white chips, each valued at 10 points. Each player keeps his chips at his right. When he makes a meld he switches to his left side chips equal in point value to that meld. Likewise, when he counts his points won in tricks, he switches chips from his right-hand stack to his left-hand stack equal in value to the points won. When the chips on his right side are exhausted he has scored 1,000 points.

The Deal. After the cards are shuffled by the dealer and cut by the nondealer, they are dealt four at a time, alternately, first to the dealer's opponent and then to himself, until each has 12 cards. The next card dealt from the top of the deck, which is the twenty-fifth

card, is placed on the table face up. The rest of the stock goes down next to the upturned card, but the stock is fanned out to facilitate drawing from it. Players alternate, hand by hand, in dealing.

How Trump Is Determined. The trump suit in two-handed Pinochle is determined by the suit of the upcard, the twenty-fifth card. If this card, face up on the table, is a club, the trumps for this hand is clubs . . . and so on. If the twenty-fifth card is a nine, it's called the *deece of trumps* and the dealer is immediately credited in the scoring with 10 points.

Beginning the Play

1. The nondealer plays first. He may lead off (start the game) by taking any card he elects from his hand and playing it face up on the table.

2. The dealer plays next. He may play any card he elects on his opponent's face-up lead-off card.

In this phase of the game, the player is not required to follow the same suit as his opponent; nor is he required to trump should he fail to have a card of the suit led by his opponent. But it must be borne in mind that, in order to gain points, a player must win tricks because: (*a*) he can meld only after winning a trick; (*b*) points won in tricks are tallied at the end of the hand.

To win a trick means: (*a*) to play to a trick a higher-ranking card of the same suit as your opponent's card, be it a trump or a nontrump suit; (*b*) if your opponent has led a card of a nontrump suit, to play a card of higher rank in the same suit or to play a trump card; (*c*) if two cards of the same rank and suit are played, to win the trick by having played the first card.

3. The player who wins a trick gathers the cards won and puts them *face down* in front of himself. In no circumstances during the play may a player look through the cards he has won in tricks.

4. The winner of the first trick is thereafter entitled to meld—if he has a meld in his hand and chooses to meld. It is not compulsory that he meld if he doesn't elect to do so. He is allowed only one meld for each trick won. A meld is a combination of cards (see Standard Values of Melded Cards, page 168), having special scoring values, that are played face up on the table.

5. If the winner of the first trick has the deece in his hand, he may exchange it for the

face-up trump card; doing this counts as a meld. However, he may make any other meld simultaneously with this exchange. When he exchanges the deece for the upcard he is credited with 10 points on his score. A deece can be melded any time after a player wins a trick, with or without another meld. *Note:* If the deece was not turned up by the dealer and was not used in exchange by the winner of the first trick, then the upcard may be taken at any time by the winner of any trick for a score of 10 points if he holds the deece in his hand.

6. After the first-trick winner has picked up the trick and has melded (or not melded), he now picks a card from the stock. The meld must be down before the card is picked; melds cannot be laid down after picking from the stock.

7. A card that has been melded may be put into play at any time. It is still considered part of the player's hand, although exposed.

8. The first-trick winner's opponent now takes a card from the stock. Each has played one card to the trick. Each has drawn a fresh card. Each still holds 12 cards.

9. The winner of the first trick leads off for the next trick. Play continues as described above. To summarize: nondealer plays a card, opponent plays a card, winner takes the trick and is entitled to meld; winner picks a card from the stock, opponent takes a card from the stock, winner leads off anew. This goes on until the stock is exhausted.

10. The winner of the last trick takes the last card from the stock. The loser takes the upcard—by this time the deece, or nine of trump—but no score is credited now for this deece as it has already been scored for one player or the other.

11. Now each player picks up his melds, and holds them in his hand. Once again each player has 12 cards.

Special Rules for Melding. The following are special rules for melding that are usually enforced:

1. Only the winner of a trick may meld.

2. Only one meld may be made at a time, *except* that a deece may be melded alone or with any other meld.

3. No meld may be made after a card has been taken from the stock.

4. After the stock is exhausted and the last stock card and upcard have been taken, no melds may be made.

5. A card used in one marriage meld cannot be used in another marriage meld.

6. A player may meld a roundhouse in two-handed Pinochle *only* by melding it all at once. He may meld kings separately, three marriages separately and then queens (in any order); but that is not a roundhouse, totaling at most only 220 points.

7. If dealer turns up a nine (deece) as the twenty-fifth card he gets score credit for 10 points.

8. The winner of any trick, holding the deece, may exchange it for the upturned trump card, and is credited with 10 points.

9. The holder of the second deece (nine of trump suit) is also credited with 10 points *if* he melds the deece.

10. Loser of the last trick, who automatically draws the deece, is credited with no points for it.

Rules for Drawing from the Stock. The following are rules for drawing from the stock:

1. If a player fails in his turn to draw a card, the deal is void because that player now has one less than the legal number of cards in his hands.

2. If a player draws two cards instead of one, he may replace the second card on the stock—if he hasn't seen it. If he has seen it he must show his own card to his opponent.

3. If a player has drawn out of turn, the drawn card must be returned to the pack. If that card properly belongs to his opponent, the player must show his next drawn card to the opponent.

4. A player is permitted to count the number of cards left in stock—but in no circumstances may he alter their order.

Second Turn in Playing the Hand. When the stock is exhausted and the players have picked up their melds, play is continued. But there is a change, as follows, in the play of tricks:

1. The winner of the last trick before the stock ran out leads off any card.

2. His opponent is obliged, if he has it, to play a card of the same suit as the leadoff. If he does not have such a card, he *must* play a trump card. (A trump card wins the trick against any card of any other suit.) If a trump is led, the opponent must play a higher-ranking trump, if possible; if he cannot do so, he still must play a trump card if he has one. Only when he has no trumps at all may he play a card of another suit. When two trump

cards are played, the one having the higher value wins the trick. When two cards of the same suit and value are played, the first card played wins the trick.

3. If the opponent does not have a card of the same suit as the leadoff card and does not have a trump card, he may play any other card in his hand.

Play continues in accordance with these rules until all the tricks are played and each player has exhausted the cards in his hand. Winner of the last trick is credited with 10 points added to his score.

Renege. After the stock has run out and play for the tricks is in progress, a *renege* takes place if a player (*a*) fails to follow the suit of the card led when he can; (*b*) fails to trump when he has a trump and does not have any cards of the suit led; (*c*) fails to play a higher trump when he can, trump being led. His opponent can call attention to any of these failures and, at any time during or after the hand is played, can claim a renege. In any case the *reneger*—the player who failed to follow the rules—loses his entire count of cards made in tricks and his opponent gets credit for 250 points, the total count of cards won in tricks. The player who *reneged,* however, retains his melds and their scoring values.

Declaring the Winner. Successive hands are dealt until one or both players score 1,000 or more points. The player who reaches 1,000 or more points is the winner, and the game is over. If (as occasionally happens) both players reach 1,000 points, the one with the higher score wins. If (as more rarely happens) the players are tied at some score higher than 1,000 points, one or more extra hands are dealt until the tie is broken; then the player with the higher score wins.

As long as neither player has 1,000 points, the game continues and a new hand is dealt. The deal changes with each new hand, the player who dealt the last hand becoming the next nondealer.

Variation in Declaring the Winner: The Call-Out. The *call-out* is legal *only* if it has been mutually agreed upon before the game starts. If, at any time before all the cards have been played, a player thinks he has scored 1,000 points or more, he may call. When he calls, the game ends forthwith, immediately. Then, if that player can prove he was right in calling (i.e., that his score is 1,000 or more),

he wins the game. But if he is wrong—if his score is less than 1,000—he loses the game, no matter what his opponent's score is. A player may call at any time during the game.

Other Ways to Win. Although a score of 1,000 points or more is the accepted criterion for winning at two-handed Pinochle, some players prefer one of these alternatives. (*Note:* For a variation in scoring to be used legally it must be agreed upon before the start of the game.)

1. One hand is dealt and the player scoring the most points in that hand wins. In case of a tie score, a new hand (or hands) is dealt until the tie is broken. Under this scoring system, players either keep a running score with pencil and paper or tally the score mentally. *Example:* Player A melds 20 points. Player B melds 40 points. Player B doesn't announce his 40; he merely says, "I have 20, right?" Players add and subtract as the hand develops until the last card of the stock has been picked. The player who has the plus credit then adds the points to his count in cards.

2. It may be decided before play starts that the winning total shall be not 1,000 but 1,250 or 1,500 or 2,000 points. When the winning total runs into such high numbers as these, it is usual and wise to keep score with pencil and paper.

Additional Rules for Two-Handed Pinochle

Misdeals. There must be a new shuffle and cut whenever a misdeal occurs. The same dealer deals again. Here is how to determine whether or not a misdeal has occurred:

1. If one or more cards are exposed in cutting or reuniting cut cards, there is a misdeal.

2. If the pack has not been offered to the nondealer to be cut and the nondealer has not yet picked a card from the stock, there is a misdeal. But, if the nondealer has picked a card from the stock, there is *not* a misdeal: The deal stands.

3. If one or more cards are exposed face up in the pack and the nondealer has not yet picked a card from stock, there is a misdeal.

4. But if the nondealer has picked a card from the stock and one or more cards are observed face up in the pack, there is *not* a misdeal, and the player whose turn it is must take the face-up card.

5. If the dealer exposes one or more of his own cards on the deal, there is not a misdeal. If the dealer exposes one or more of the non-

dealer's cards, there is a misdeal.

6. If the nondealer exposes one or more of his own cards on the deal, there is *not* a misdeal.

7. If either player exposes one or more of his own cards during the game, there is *not* a misdeal.

8. If it is found that an imperfect pack is being used, a pack containing insufficient or duplicate (extra) cards, in violation of the rules on the Pinochle deck, play must stop immediately on the discovery. That hand is a dead hand and does *not* count, although all the previous hands are legal.

9. If either dealer or nondealer has been dealt fewer or more than 12 cards on the deal or if the cards have been dealt in any manner other than stipulated under the rules of the game, there is a misdeal.

Incorrect Melds. If a player lays down an improper meld or credits himself when melding with more or less points than is proper, he may correct the error, and there is no penalty. An incorrect meld or a credit for more or less points than correct on a legal meld may be corrected at any time before the last card is drawn from stock. After that the error cannot be rectified.

If a player lays an improper meld, he is allowed to replace the cards involved in his hand. A player cannot meld if he has too few or too many cards in his hand.

Leading Out of Turn. If, before the trick has been completed, it is established that a player has led out of turn, players merely pick up their cards and correct the error. If the trick is completed and stacked with the completed tricks, the play stands, and the player who won the trick makes the next lead.

Drawing a Card from the Stock. The following rules cover slips of the hand when drawing a card from the stock:

1. If in his turn of play a player fails to draw a card and his opponent has already picked a card from stock and put it in his hand, then the former draws two cards in his next legal turn of play to give himself a legitimate hand of twelve cards.

2. If a player draws two or more cards instead of the legal one, he puts the extra cards back on the stock in their proper order. If he has looked at the cards he picked by mistake, he must show them to his opponent, and in addition must show his legally drawn card to his opponent. After the cards have

been shown, they go back on the stock in their original order.

3. If a player has too many cards in his hand, he draws no more until his hand is reduced to the legal number by discarding.

4. If a player has too few cards in his hand, he draws enough cards in his next turn to bring his hand up to the legal number.

5. If a player draws a card out of turn he may put it back on the stock—provided he has not looked at it. If he has looked at it, he gives the card to his opponent, but must then show the card he draws properly. If both players draw the wrong card, the play stands; it is a legal play.

6. If on the last draw three cards are left instead of two—that is, two face-down cards and the upturned trump card—the winner of the trick must draw the top card of the stock. The loser must take the turned trump card. The extra card is taken by the player who has a hand with one card missing. There is no penalty when this occurs, nor is a misdeal declared.

Looking Through Cards Taken in Tricks. If he has not yet played his card for the following trick, a player may look at the last trick gathered in; this rule holds regardless of which player won the last trick. In no other circumstances is looking through the cards permitted, except when looking through tricks to determine whether a player has reneged. There is no enforceable penalty for an infraction of this rule. Crooked players, when they want to look through the cards, will simply allege that their opponent has reneged. To prevent this, it may be agreed upon before the play begins that examination of the tricks for a renege shall be allowed only on completion of the play of the hand. Further, any player who violates the above rule by looking through his tricks shall (by prior agreement) lose his count in cards.

Strategy at Two-Handed Pinochle. The well-trained memory plays a vital role in two-handed Pinochle. Accurate card memory is important in any game involving the play of cards to successive tricks; thus it is important in any Pinochle game. But the two-handed version is especially demanding because, during any one hand, each player must handle 24 cards—many more than at any other variant. Playing accurately and intelligently to 24 tricks puts a high premium on the disciplined memory.

Card Memory. There is no shortcut to the development of a vivid and dependable card memory. Because I've practiced hours a day for many years, I can remember just about where every card in the deck is through successive shuffles and cuts; but this is regarded as unusual. Yet I know several players with no marked intellectual talents who can remember virtually all the cards played at Pinochle up to the time the stock is exhausted; whereupon, after due consideration of their own hand, they know exactly what 12 cards their opponent holds.

How is it done? Well, how do you know, when riding in a bus or railroad train and reading a paper or just dozing along, when you've reached your corner? What is the mental machinery that, quite independently of any conscious effort on your part, ticks off the corners and stations and jogs you when the total is your number? The human mind is a remarkable adding machine. All it requires is housebreaking.

Psychologists tell us that a normal memory notices and marks down everything the senses perceive. You don't have to think to have a remarkable memory. All you have to do is start trying. Let me suggest ways to start:

1. At first, try to concentrate on remembering only trump and the play of the eight aces.

2. If you can't remember the number of trumps up to the time the stock is exhausted, let me suggest you try practicing with a game I invented called *Teeko*. In this game the pieces played are out in the open, so that it is possible to check on your memory of what's happened.

3. Don't count the trump cards you hold; just the trumps played.

4. And don't count your aces; just the aces played to tricks.

5. After you've learned to run an accurate count on these cards, you're over the hump: Your memory knows what you expect of it. Now add another suit to the cards you're trying to remember.

6. Don't get discouraged if a card or so slips your memory in actual play. Some of the world's greatest Bridge players confess they've muffed hands because they simply couldn't count up to thirteen. The job you've assigned yourself is harder than that.

7. But don't take the easy way out and say this is too hard for any mortal man. I know a little girl five years old who can remember every card played at Gin Rummy. She's no genius; she just taught herself that this is one of the things people do.

8. Keep trying. One of these days you'll find that of course you remember the cards. "Doesn't everybody?" you'll add, surprised.

Melding. One of the most important aspects of two-handed Pinochle is knowing when and how to meld. *Example:* If a player holds a flush in trump early in the game, it is obviously advisable to meld the marriage in trump first. Upon winning a later trick, the ace, jack, and ten of trumps are laid down for a flush. Thus the player runs up credit for 190 points. But, let's consider a later stage of the game. Let's assume the stock has only about six cards left and that the player doesn't hold the extra ace and ten of trumps. Now it is advisable to lay the flush at once and get credit for the 150 points forthwith. Otherwise, the player may not be able to meld the flush if his opponent prevents him from taking another trick.

Experience is the best guide as to when and what to meld. A consistently profitable strategy which I cannot emphasize too strongly is sacrificing (as cheaply as possible) the first few tricks to one's opponent and then trying to win the last few tricks. The possibilities of melding are enhanced toward the end of a hand, because the player has had access to more cards. But the value of this line of play is variable too, and must be judged hand by hand after careful assessment of the possibilities in the particular holding. Also, in the later stages of the hand, it becomes important that the player try to prevent his opponent from melding, particularly if his observation of the cards played indicates the possibility of the opponent's making a flush, 100 aces, or some other high-value meld.

Counting. Keep a count of the points made in tricks, as you go. This is very important in the later stages of the play of the hand. It is a crucial factor when you play the variety of two-handed Pinochle that scores each hand as a separate game.

What to Save. Nobody can state a rule on this point. The judgment in each case depends on the particular hand. But remember this: You can't save everything. You can't hold possibilities for aces, kings, a flush, and so on. Consider the chances and the relative advantages as the hand develops. If you have a lot to meld in your hand, it may be better for you to break up your three aces and take tricks with them, rather than risk being unable to complete all the melds you already have. This is especially true when you take your opponent's tens with your aces.

Some Finer Points. Sound card play consists of handling intelligently the cards you're most apt to get. You learn that play not from made-up problems or erudite puzzles but from practice, from experience—from playing. However, here are a few tips that might help almost anyone:

1. Try to hold back a few high trump cards to be used, if necessary, when the stock runs low.

2. If you hold duplicate cards and have melded one of them, always play to the trick the card that has been melded. *Example:* You have melded a marriage in hearts. You have the other queen of hearts in your hand. Now, if you play a heart queen to a trick, play the one from the melded marriage on the board.

3. If you have 100 aces, meld them at your first opportunity. Melded, they are much more potent in the play than they would be in your hand. You'd hesitate to play an unmelded ace to a trick. This reluctance, with its inevitable effect on your timing, might be crucial in the development of the hand. Meld 'em and use 'em!

4. When leading to a trick, it is generally sound to play a card from your long suit—provided that isn't your trump suit. Ordinarily the ten-spot of the long suit is the soundest lead, because rarely will your opponent play on it the ace of that suit if he has it. And even if he does play his ace (unless he holds the duplicate, paired ace), he has sacrificed a chance of melding 100 aces. If he trumps your ten with a trump card whose duplicate you hold, he has thrown away his chance of making a flush. If your opponent does play an ace on your ten, you'd better assume he has the other ace—unless it's in your own hand.

Two-Handed Pinochle:
Doubling and Redoubling

This is the same as regular two-handed Pinochle with this exception: At any time a player may call "Double!" His opponent then has to decide whether to accept the double, in which case the stakes for that hand are doubled, or to concede the hand, in which case only the normal stakes are paid. If the double is accepted, the acceptor has the option to redouble at any time. When a hand is redoubled, the original doubler must decide whether to play for redoubled stakes or to concede the doubled stakes. The privilege of redoubling passes to the original doubler if he accepts the redouble. And so on.

Almost invariably this variation is played on an each-game-a-separate-game basis, not on the 1,000-point game basis.

Two-Handed Pinochle, Turn-Up Trump, with a 64-Card Deck

This is played exactly as is two-handed Pinochle (see page 171), with the following exceptions:

1. To the standard Pinochle deck are added eight eights and eight sevens (two cards in these ranks of each suit), to constitute a 64-card deck.

2. The eight and the seven are ranked below the nine, the seven being the lowest-ranking card.

3. The deece is the seven of trump instead of the nine of trump.

4. Excepting only the deece, the sevens and eights have no value in the count.

5. Instead of the usual 12-card hands, as in standard two-handed Pinochle, 16 cards are dealt each player, four at a time.

6. The thirty-third card is turned face up to identify the trump suit.

Three- or Four-Handed Pinochle, Individual Play, Turn-Up Trump

This is a three- or four-player Pinochle game that is played with a standard Pinochle deck. Under basic General Rules for Pinochle (page 167) are set forth the laws governing selection of the dealer and establishment of seating positions at the table, changing seats, the shuffle, and the cut. The determination of stakes and scorekeeper are the same as in two-handed Pinochle (turn-up trump).

Object of the Game. To win the game by scoring 1,000 or more points before any of one's opponents does so.

The Deal. *When the game is three-handed:* The dealer deals to each player 16 cards, four at a time, starting with the leader (the player to the dealer's left) and dealing clockwise until the dealer has four cards left in his deck stock. The top one of these four cards is turned face up and placed on the table, in the middle. (It's the forty-fifth card from the top of the original deck.) He takes the three remaining cards for himself.

When the game is four-handed: Each player, in the manner described above, is dealt 11 cards. Again, the forty-fifth card is placed face up on the table. Again, the dealer takes the last three cards for himself.

How Trump Is Determined. The suit of the face-up card in the center of the table, the forty-fifth card dealt from the deck, establishes the trump suit. If the upturned card happens to be a nine-spot (deece), the dealer is immediately credited in the scoring with 10 points.

If the face-up card is not a deece, the privilege of exchanging the upturned card for a deece passes to the player to the dealer's left. If he lacks a deece, or chooses not to exchange it for the upturned card, the privilege moves to his left. This privilege rotates clockwise until the face-up card has been ex-. changed for a deece. The player exchanging the upcard for the deece gets credit for a 10-point meld. The holder of the other deece (nine of trumps) may meld it and get credit for 10 points.

If all players except the dealer fail or decline to exchange the upcard for a deece, the dealer may take the upcard as part of his hand. If the upcard has been previously exchanged for a deece, the dealer must take the deece to complete his hand. However, he is not credited with 10 points for that deece; the exchanger gets the 10-point credit.

The players now meld. The card which had been the upcard may be used by the holder in his melding.

Melding. All the players lay down their melds, and the scorekeeper enters each player's total under his name on the score sheet. After the scores have been recorded, the players pick up their melds and put them back into their hands; they are now ready for the play of the hand.

The Play. The dealer leads off. He may play any card he elects. Turn of play then rotates to the left, clockwise. After the first card has been led, each player in his turn of play (which, remember, moves to the left)

must observe the following rules:

1. Each player, if he has it, must play a card of the suit led. *Example:* A diamond is the first card led; therefore, all players must follow with diamonds if they have any in their hands.

2. If the player does not have a card of the suit led, he must play a trump card.

3. If he does not have a card of the suit led or a trump card, he may play any other card in his hand.

4. When a trump card is led, each other player must play a higher trump card than any previously played, if he has one.

5. But if a nontrump card is led and a player trumps that card, succeeding players, if compelled to trump, are not obliged to play a trump card higher than the one already played.

6. The highest-ranking card played to it wins the trick. When two cards of the same value tie for the trick, the winner is the first one played.

7. The winner of the trick leads off again, and play rotates to the left under the rules set forth above.

8. Winner of the last trick is credited with 10 points more on his score.

This routine of play continues until all cards in the players' hands have run out and all cards have been played to tricks. Then the score for melds and points taken in tricks is totaled; a new deal takes place and play continues until one of the players has scored 1,000 points and has won the game.

Additional Rules

Misdeals. Here is how to determine whether or not a misdeal has occurred:

1. If one or more cards are exposed in cutting or reuniting the pack, there is a misdeal.

2. If the pack has not been offered to the player at the dealer's right to be cut, there is a misdeal if the trump card has not been turned up. But, there is *not* a misdeal if the trump card has been turned up: The deal is legal.

3. If one or more cards are observed face up in the pack during the deal, there is a misdeal.

4. If on the deal the dealer exposes one or more of any other player's cards, there is a misdeal. But if the dealer exposes one or more of his own cards on the deal, there is *not* a misdeal.

5. If a player exposes one or more of his own cards during the deal or the play, there is *not* a misdeal.

6. If any player including the dealer has been dealt fewer or more cards than constitute a legal hand, there is a misdeal.

7. If it is discovered that an imperfect deck is in use, that is, a deck containing fewer or more cards than required under the rules for the game, play must stop immediately on the discovery. The hand in progress is a dead hand and does *not* count. All previous hands are legal and do count.

8. If when the last trick is played it is found that one or more players have an incorrect number of cards, there is a misdeal.

Looking Through Cards Taken in Tricks. If a player insists that a renege has been committed, he may ask to examine any cards he or any other player has won in tricks. But he can look at another player's last trick or his own only before playing his card to the following trick. The rules of Pinochle provide that cards taken in tricks must not be looked through on an allegation of reneging. But no penalty is provided for infraction of the rule, since any player determined to violate its spirit can still comply with its letter by charging a renege before examining the cards at the end of the hand.

Leading and Playing Out of Turn. If a player leads or plays a card out of turn and this is discovered before the trick has been covered and a card has been played to the next trick, the card played in error must be taken back by the offending player and the error must be corrected. But if play to the trick has been completed and the player who won the trick has led a card to the next trick, the play is legalized *de facto,* and cannot be corrected.

No Angling. It is not feasible to define a penalty when any player instructs another player as to what card to play. This can be done verbally, by grimace, by gesture, or by flashing a tip-off card. Such *angling* is often indefinable. The player who consistently resorts to devices inimical to decent sportsmanship and fair play is a crook. The only enforceable penalty against him is refusing to play with him.

Renege Rules. Any of the following violations shall be construed as a renege, providing the offender's card has been covered by a card played by the next succeeding player or (if there is no further play to that trick) the trick has been taken and a card has been led to the following trick. A renege may be corrected if the error is noted before the next proper play in the game has been made. There is a renege:

1. If a player able to do so fails to follow the suit led when the laws of the game require him to do so.

2. If a player able to do so fails to trump when required.

3. If a player able to do so fails to play a higher trump card when the laws of the game he is playing require that he do so.

The following are the recommended penalties for reneges:

1. If the bidder reneges, the amount of the penalty against him shall be the same as if he had played the hand and failed to make his bid.

2. If a player reneges, the amount of the penalty he must pay the bidder shall be the same as if the bidder played the hand and made his bid.

3. When any player defending against a bidder reneges, his renege is binding upon any other defending player. The amount of the penalty each other player must pay the bidder shall be exactly as if he himself committed the renege.

Partnership Pinochle, Turn-Up Trump

This game is played exactly as is three- or four-handed Pinochle (individual play, turn-up trump), with the following exceptions:

1. Four players, two against two, play as partners.

2. Selection of partnerships is governed under basic General Rules for Pinochle (see page 167).

3. *Table talk is forbidden.* Partners are not permitted to cue their teammates as to what card it would be desirable to play, nor are they permitted to comment by word or sign on the play of the hand. For instance, to observe that the previous play, or any previous play, was good or bad is absolutely banned.

4. The scores of the two players forming a partnership are totaled as a single score.

AUCTION PINOCHLE WITH WIDOW: EACH HAND A COMPLETE GAME

Favored by money players because of its speed and its prompt and straightforward pay-off, this version of the game is probably the biggest gambling variant of the Pinochle family. You can play it for stakes ranging from a penny a hundred points to X dollars a hundred, and write your own ticket. The most popular scale of betting is five or ten cents a hundred.

Requirements

1. Three or four players. (When three are playing, each is dealt a Pinochle hand, and each is an active player. When there are four players, the dealer stays out of the play, dealing a hand only to each of the three others. In a four-handed game the deal rotates and each player takes his turn at dealing and staying out; hence, in an extended session, this feature will work mathematically to the disadvantage of no one. But I do recommend the three-handed version.)

2. A standard Pinochle deck. (For rules on the deck, rank of cards and suits, value of melded cards, bonus melds, and value of cards won in tricks, see basic General Rules for Pinochle, page 167.)

Object of the Game. To make a winning bid and then to score a number of points equal to or greater than the number bid. In this competition, where every hand dealt is a game complete in itself, the objective of the opponents is to prevent the bidder from making his bid. The maximum points a bidder can make at Auction Pinochle (holding a legal hand of 15 cards plus the three cards buried, and disregarding such special circumstances as bonus melds, reneges, and bad play) is 721 points. This total is arrived at by making use of the oldtimers' card count. The use of the simplified card count gives us a count of 720. The use of the so-called streamlined count would reduce these totals to 710 points. Since I've encountered some players who don't understand how to calculate this maximum, here's the way the cards can be distributed to pile up a 721-point total:

In the Bidder's Hand:

1. Double flush in diamonds (ten cards).
2. Ace of clubs, ace of spades, and ace of hearts (three cards).

3. Two queens of spades (two cards).
4. Bidder buries the widow which holds the ace and two tens of spades (three cards).

Held by the Opponents:

1. Opponent No. 1 holds two kings of spades. Distribution of other cards in his hand does not affect the score.

2. Opponent No. 2 holds two jacks of spades and two nines of spades. Distribution of other cards in his hand has no effect on the scoring.

Stipulating the above distribution, the bidder would meld 480 points (300 in trump, 100 aces, and 80 Pinochle), and the bidder's count in valuable cards won in tricks would total 241 points, for a grand total of 721 points. It is possible for the bidder to make 730 points, providing the bidder's opponents played the hand incorrectly.

The Kitty. The kitty is *not* a compulsory feature of Auction Pinochle. To be legal it must be agreed upon by all players at the start of the game. It is simply a pot, additional to other routine settlements among the players, to be put aside and collected by the player who bids and makes a 350-point hand. Since the kitty is optional, the rules for paying and collecting from it are also optional and subject to wide variation. However, here are the rules I suggest for the kitty:

1. Before the game starts each player antes into the kitty an amount equal to the stipulated settlement for a 250-point bid.

2. Whenever all contestants pass, or fail to bid, each player must ante into the kitty an amount equal to the first ante. (By mutual consent, players may stop anteing whenever they choose.)

3. To collect the kitty a player must bid *and make* a minimum of 350 points.

4. If a player bids 350 or more, irrespective of suits, and then concedes the hand he must ante into the kitty an amount equal to the sum already in the kitty.

5. Moreover, if a player bids 350 or more, irrespective of suit, and plays the hand and fails to make his bid he must ante into the kitty an amount *double* the sum already in the kitty.

I do not recommend compelling the unsuccessful bidder to ante into the kitty an amount four times its value for failure to make a spade hand, or six times its value for failure to make a heart hand. This arrangement is grossly inequitable. No matter what he bids, the player can win only the total amount in the kitty. That is, the kitty doesn't pay off any more if spades or hearts are trump; it offers the player no advantage for the risk he assumes, so why should his contract with the kitty impose all the hardship on him? That's a personal credo. But certain players will insist on a maximum of excitement and a minimum of logic. For them I append the following two rules, with this admonition: They cannot be binding unless they are mutually and unanimously understood and agreed upon before the start of the game.

1. If a player bids 350 or more points in spades, plays the hand, and fails to make the bid, he must ante into the kitty an amount triple the sum already in the kitty.

2. If it has been agreed that hearts are payable at triple value and a player bids 350 or more points in hearts and fails to make his bid, he must ante into the kitty an amount four times the sum already in the kitty.

These rules, as stated above, are optional. The following are compulsory:

1. If a player goes broke he is entitled to take out of the kitty an amount determined by the number of players in the game. If there are three players he may take out one-third of the kitty's total cash value. If there are four players he may take out one-fourth of the kitty's total cash value. But taking money from the kitty signifies the player has quit the game. He cannot resume play with the money he takes from the kitty.

2. If the kitty gets unusually big, the players may by mutual consent divide it among themselves in equal portions.

3. If the game ends and a kitty survives, it is split equally among the players.

4. If, when a new player enters the game, there is an existent kitty, that player must put into the kitty an amount determined by the number of other players. If he is the fourth player, he must ante an amount equal to one-third of the sum in the kitty.

5. A bidder cannot play for the kitty unless he has on the table enough money to cover the kitty in the event he fails to make his bid. Lacking enough cash on the table, he

may play for as much of the kitty as his means will cover—after deducting the amount he must pay the other players for an unsuccessful bid.

The Stakes. The amount of cash bet, collected, and paid at this game depends on the number of points bid by the highest bidder. But, be it the minimum 250 or the maximum 700 plus, there is a standard ratio determining the cash worth of any hand. Although players before the start of the game solemnly agree that they'll play for so much per hundred—a cent or 5 or 10 or 25 or 50 cents, and on up to X dollars—it doesn't work out in that per-hundred ratio. *Example:* Suppose you are playing for the minimum bid of 250 at 5 cents a hundred. On any bid up to 290 points, the settlement is 10 cents—which isn't anywhere near a nickel a hundred. If you increase the bid by 50 points, making it from 300 to 340 points, the settlement becomes 15 cents. An increase of 50 points over that, making the bid from 350 to 390 points, calls for a settlement of 20 cents . . . and so on up in successive units of 50 points and 5 cents.

The following chart has been set up to specify the payoff in a game played for a nickel a hundred; but the last column will indicate the settlement at any stakes. To get the settlement on any bid in column I, multiply your stakes-per-hundred by the corresponding unit in column III.

STANDARD TABLE OF BETTING LIMITS AND UNITS

Column I Amount Bid in Points	Column II Amount to Be Paid at 5 Cents a Hundred	Column III Units by Which to Multiply Your Stakes per Hundred
250 to 290	10 cents	2
300 to 340	15 cents	3
350 to 390	20 cents	4
400 to 440	25 cents	5
450 to 490	30 cents	6
500 to 540	35 cents	7
550 to 590	40 cents	8
600 to 640	45 cents	9
650 to 690	50 cents	10
700 or over	55 cents	11

Special Bonus Betting Limits. Many players like to pay off at certain special bonus rates for high bids. While any scale of bonuses is permissible, the most common rates are set forth below; to be legal, however, such special arrangements must be made before the start of the game and must be entered in writing on the score sheet.

Amount Bid in Points	Amount Paid Off in Units
250 to 290	2
300 to 340	3
350 to 390	5
400 to 440	7
450 to 490	10
500 to 540	13
550 to 590	17
600 to 640	21
650 to 690	25
700 and over	30

The Settlement or Payoff. The terms of settlement in this game are customarily cash. Chips are often used, but since—except in most unusual circumstances—the chips are negotiable for cash in the house, it amounts to the same thing. The amount of settlement on each hand is established by the betting-limit scale and the number of points a player bids. The extra points he may score above his bid are irrelevant to the payoff.

1. If the bidder plays the hand and makes his bid or his opponents concede the hand to him, and if hearts, clubs, or diamonds were trump, he collects a single unit amount from each player. *Example:* If the betting limit is 5 cents a hundred and the bid is 250 points, the winning bidder collects 10 cents from each of the other two players.

2. If, playing the hand, the bidder fails to make his bid or if after playing one or more cards he concedes the hand, and if hearts, clubs, or diamonds were trump, he must pay each other player a double amount. *Example:* If the betting limit is 5 cents a hundred and the bid is 250 points, the losing bidder must pay each other player 20 cents.

3. If the bidder concedes he cannot make his bid and throws in his cards without playing a card, he pays a single amount to each other player. *Example:* If the limit is 5 cents a hundred and the bid is 250 points, the losing bidder must pay each other player 10 cents as settlement.

4. If the bidder makes *spades* trump and makes his bid or his opponents concede the hand, he collects double the amount from each other player. With the betting limit 5 cents a hundred and the bid 250 points, the winning bidder collects 20 cents from each other player.

5. If, making spades trump and playing the hand, the bidder fails to make his bid or if he plays one or more cards and then concedes the hand by throwing in his cards, he must pay each other player double-double. *Example:* The betting limit is the same 5 cents a hundred and the bid is 250 points; in this circumstance the losing bidder must pay each other player 40 cents.

A player who makes spades trump and throws in his hand without playing a card pays only a single amount to each other player. My ruling here is dictated by my respect for realism. If opponents insist on their right to collect double on a spade-trump hand, the losing bidder would coolly reply—and well within his rights to do so—that in fact one of the other three suits was trump. (He can change the trump suit any time before he leads his first card.) *Note:* This rule, giving spades a special doubled value, is incorporated into my rules for the game, but players may agree that spades shall pay single value only. When this exception is played, however, it must be agreed upon before the start of the game to be legal.

6. In a four-handed game, even though the dealer stays out of the play of the hand, he is included in the cash settlement. When the bidder wins, the dealer must pay him as do the active players in the game. When the bidder loses, he must pay the dealer the same as he pays the active players.

Hearts Triple. The hearts-triple rule is optional, and is not incorporated into my standard rules. Choosing to play this rule is within the players' discretion; however, it must be agreed upon by all the players before the start of the game.

1. If the bidder makes hearts trump and makes his bid or his opponents concede the hand, the winning bidder collects a triple amount from each other player. In our familiar example, the betting limit is 5 cents a hundred and the bid is 250 points. The bidder, when he wins, collects 30 cents from each other player.

2. If, making hearts trump, the bidder plays the hand and fails to make the bid or concedes the hand after playing one or more cards, he must pay each other player an amount called "triple-triple" (two times triple), which is six times the single amount. At 5 cents a hundred and a bid of 250 points, the losing bidder must pay each other player

60 cents. *Note:* For the realistic reasons cited above (when referring to spades), a player who makes hearts trump and then throws in his cards without playing the hand is liable to pay each other player only the single amount. The triple-triple or any other special penalty here is unenforceable; the bidder would simply state that trump was clubs or diamonds.

Agreements Before the Game Starts. The following must be marked on the score sheet by a scorekeeper, mutually chosen: (*a*) amount of the stakes; (*b*) rules governing the kitty, if any; and (*c*) special bonus payoffs for high hands, if any.

Before the Deal. For selection of the dealer, establishment of positions at the table, and the shuffle and cut, see basic General Rules for Pinochle, page 167.

The Deal. Starting with the leader, the dealer deals one round of cards clockwise, three at a time, until each player has three cards. Then he deals one card face down in the center of the table to start the *widow* or *blind*. (The first widow card is the tenth card dealt from the pack.) He repeats this deal. (The second widow card is the twentieth card dealt from the pack.) The third round is dealt the same way. (Third widow card is thirtieth card off the deck.) Now, starting with the leader again and going clockwise, three cards at a time are dealt each player until the deck is exhausted and each player has 15 cards in his hand. *Note:* A method of dealing preferred by some players is to give each player in turn four cards and then to deal one into the widow. This method is continued for three rounds, after which each player is dealt cards three at a time until the whole deck has been dealt.

The Bidding. The bidding starts with the leader and rotates to the left, clockwise, until all or all but one player have passed. At his bidding turn, a player may elect:

1. *To pass.* When a player announces a pass, he indicates that he doesn't want to bid and no longer has any interest in bidding. Once he has passed, a player cannot bid again on that hand.

2. *To bid.* When a player calls out a certain total of points, he commits himself to make those points with the hand he holds and the widow, if he wins the bid.

If the first bid is made by the leader or the player to the leader's immediate left, it must be 250 or more. Should the leader and the

man at his left pass, the last active player may bid—but he must bid at least 290 or 310 points. Just as 250 is the minimum bid for the first and second players, 290 or 310 is the minimum bid for the third. This last player cannot bid 300 flat; but he may bid any amount he likes over 310. If all three active players pass, their hands are thrown in, and a new hand is dealt by the next dealer.

If a player opens the bidding by stating a legal bid, and the other two players pass or have passed, the bidding player is the winner of that bid. If, the bidding being opened, one or both of the other active players want to enter the auction, the bids must be higher than the previous bidder's by at least 10 points. Bidding is permitted in multiples of 10 only.

Bidding rotates around the table to the left until at last two players have passed and only one bidder remains. That player has won the bid.

The Widow, the Blind, or the Buy. In no circumstances may a player, be he active or inactive, look at the three cards in the widow while the bidding is still under way. The *widow,* the *blind,* or the *buy* is the name given the three cards face down on the table during the deal. The bidder—the player who won the auction—takes these three cards and may use them in an attempt to improve his hand. But before putting them into his hand, he must turn them face up on the table to let the other players see them. Now, having incorporated them into his holding, he may do one of two things: He may concede the hand and throw in his cards; or, he may decide to play the hand.

Conceding the Hand. Having considered the potentials of his hand plus the widow, and before leading a card to the first trick, the bidder may concede that he cannot with his melds and prospective tricks make his bid. It is his right to throw in his cards and pay the other players a single amount—as well as the kitty, if there is one. (See The Kitty, page 180.)

The concession may work the other way. The bidder, holding a hand, may show a part of it plus his meld (equaling or nearly equaling the amount of his bid), and the opponents may concede and make their cash settlement with him. Also, the opponents may concede defeat at any time during the play by throwing in their cards. *Note:* If only one of the opponents concedes the hand, the game must be played out to a formal decision.

The bidder may concede defeat at any time during the play of the hand by throwing in his cards, but if he has led a card to start the play, he must pay each other player a double amount, just as if he had finished the hand and had failed to make the bid. This is unless the trump was spades, in which case he must pay each other player four times the single amount. If neither the bidder nor the opponents concede the hand, it must be played out. Before actual play begins, the bidder must discard and meld.

Discarding or Burying Three Cards. To reduce his hand to the legal 15 cards for the play, the bidder must bury three cards after picking up the widow. These three cards are put face down in front of the bidder, and are counted as tricks taken or won by the bidder, although he must win a trick from his opponents to validate them.

Discards. The following rules on discarding must be observed:

1. The bidder cannot bury (discard) any card he has used to form a meld, that is, a melded card for which he has already received credit in points. If he should bury such a card and his attention is called to the fact any time after the first card has been led in the play of the hand (but not after payment for the hand has been made), then that bidder has reneged and he loses the hand. His opponents collect on the same basis as if the bidder had failed to make his bid.

2. The bidder may change his melds, exchange the buried cards, or change his trump suit at any time before he leads his first card in actual play.

3. A bidder may, if he elects, bury a trump card (that is, one not used in a meld), but he *must* announce the fact that it is a trump card he is burying. It is not mandatory that he reveal the denomination of that card. Failure to announce the burial of a trump card is to be construed as a renege, and loses the hand for the bidder; the penalty is the same as if he failed to make his bid in play.

4. A bidder is not required to announce the burying of an ace or any other denomination of card.

5. When starting the play of the hand, if the bidder leads a card and it is found that he has buried too few or too many cards or has failed to bury any cards, and his attention is

called to that fact, this constitutes a renege. The penalty is the same as if the bidder played the hand and failed to make his bid.

Melding. As he sees fit, a bidder may meld before or after discarding, providing he adheres to the rules for discarding or burying. The bidder, that is, the player who won the auction, is the only player permitted to put down melds. For the rules governing the meld, see basic General Rules for Pinochle.

The Play of the Hand. After a bidder has discarded and picked up his melds, actual play for tricks begins under the following rules:

1. The bidder may lead any card he selects from among the 15 in his hand, putting it face up on the table to start the trick.

After a card has been led, no changes in melds may be made.

2. Each other player must follow the suit of the card led, if he has a card of such a suit.

3. If another player does not have a card of the suit led, he must trump.

4. If he does not have a card of the suit led or a trump, the opposing player may play to the trick any card he chooses.

5. Only when a trump card is led must a player play a higher-ranking card if he has one.

6. If a nontrump card is led, the second player trumps it, and the third player is then compelled to trump because he does not have a card of the suit led, then this third player is not compelled to play a trump card of rank higher than the previous player's

7. Winner of a trick leads off to the next trick.

To win a trick, a player must (*a*) play a higher-ranking card in the suit led than any other player, be it a trump or a nontrump suit; or (*b*) in trumping a trick, play a higher-ranking trump card than any other player.

When two cards of the same value are played and are tied to win the trick, the first card played wins the trick. Play continues thus until all the cards in the players' hands are exhausted, fifteen tricks in all.

Counting Valuable Cards in Tricks. To the value of the three cards he has buried, the bidder adds the value of the cards he has won in tricks. He adds this total to the points he has scored in melds. If the resulting grand total equals or surpasses the amount of his bid, he has made his bid and wins the hand, collecting from each player the amount at stake. If the grand total is less than his bid, the bidder has lost the hand and must pay each opponent the amount at stake.

The bidder's opponents count their valuable cards in tricks won to certify that the bidder's count is correct.

Additional Rules

Reneges. Any of the following violations shall be construed as a renege, providing the offender's card has been covered by a card played by the next succeeding player or (if there is no further play to that trick) the trick has been taken and a card has been led to the following trick. A renege may be corrected if the error is noted before the next proper play in the game has been made. A renege takes place if:

1. A player able to do so fails to follow the suit led when the laws of the game require him to do so.

2. A player able to do so fails to trump when required.

3. A player able to do so fails to play a higher trump card when the laws of the game require him to do so.

Following are the penalties for reneges:

1. If the bidder reneges, the amount of the penalty against him shall be the same as if he had played the hand and failed to make his bid.

2. If a nonbidder reneges, the amount of the penalty he must pay the bidder shall be the same as if the bidder played the hand and made his bid.

3. When any player defending against a bidder reneges, his renege is binding upon any other defending player. The amount of the penalty the other player must pay the bidder shall be exactly as if he himself committed the renege.

Improper Bidding. If a player bids or passes out of turn, or bids an incorrect amount, or bids after passing, there is *no* penalty. He may correct his error. If a player in his proper turn bids an amount equal to, or lower than, the previous player's bid, he *must* correct his bid; he must make a bid sufficiently higher to be legal.

The additional playing rules given on page 174 regarding misdeals, looking at cards in tricks, leading and playing out of turn, etc., should be followed in Auction Pinochle with Widow.

Strategy at Auction Pinochle with Widow

My assumption, based on my own observation of how people behave at the card table, is that when you play three- or four-handed Pinochle with widow (each hand a complete game), you play for money. This is the most popular game in the Pinochle family. It is played oftener and for more cash than all the other variants combined.

One owes it to himself and to other people, I hold, to play any game as well as one can. I can't abide the ham who, duly butchering the hand, explains in a wheedling way that he's just a social player—as if a reasonable skill at cards were antisocial. The game just discussed is well worth playing for all it's worth; and it's worth a lot. In it is enough of the scientific to arrest the interest of the most serious student of cards. In it, too, is more than enough of the chance element to fascinate the most reckless of gamblers. Understand it; learn it; enjoy it. Its scientific side may be divided into three big parts:

1. The evaluation of the hand; that is, deciding what the hand is worth for bidding purposes.

2. How, after the melding, to play the cards to their maximum advantage.

3. How to discard, or bury, properly and profitably.

Chance plays its dominant role in these two phases of the game:

1. Bidding in hope of finding one or more cards in the widow—cards whose addition to your dealt holding will give you a cinch hand.

2. Doggedly playing out a boderline hand and hoping that certain crucial cards held by your opponents will fall on the tricks as you want them to.

Unquestionably the best way to improve your Pinochle game is to play and play and then play some more. But there are thousands of Pinochle addicts who've been playing for years, decades, all their lives, and still play very bad games. If experience is the best teacher, why hasn't it taught them anything? Simply because they have stubbornly refused to learn. To play a good game of Pinochle requires native intelligence, a certain humility, and an awareness that one doesn't know all the answers, not by a long shot.

Some players evaluate their hands very

accurately before the bidding starts, and then bid like fools. They're a little like the fishermen who cast flies like angels, who know all there is to know about tackle and water and trout, but never catch a fish. Once the bidding gets under way, the Pinochle professor loses his head or his nerve, gets angry or stubborn, lets a wily opponent needle him, and winds up by overbidding his cards to an impossible level. The gymnasium fighter is a commonplace in every kind of competition: the sound theoretician, the flawless stylist, the perfect critic. The only thing wrong with him is that he can't perform when the chips are down. That's one kind of Pinochle player.

There's another. There's the hard-headed realist who bids like an angel—never too much, never too little; he never loses his nerve; he never loses his temper; and he winds up broke. He has never noticed that the play of the cards at Pinochle is as much a test of a man's nerve and skill as is the bidding. He has never bothered to learn the subtleties in the play of the hand. All he has missed—if you don't count $300 or $400 a year in cash he's dropped to more observant comrades—is half the fun of the game. Learn, as a fine Bridge player learns, to enjoy the play of the hand. I have no formula, no short cut, to guarantee you'll win at your next Friday night Pinochle session. Successful Pinochle is, I guess, a little like successful writing: It's a matter of keying yourself up to a certain level and sweating to sustain that level. Every step of the game must be a new problem to be solved. That's what makes Pinochle—or gardening, or music, or living—the fun it is. Don't ask me for formulas. But you do have a right to ask me for tips. And it's a pleasure to share with you certain general truths I've learned.

First: Study the rules. The player who knows the Pinochle rules has a decided advantage over the player who's never quite sure what happens next. Knowing the rules enables you to defend yourself. It prevents your acceding to an unfair or inequitable decision against you. It saves you money.

Second: The Pinochle player must be alert at all times. If you're tired or have had a bad day at the office or plant, don't sit in on that Pinochle game. Order a beer, get a sandwich, lean back, and watch.

Third: Make it a matter of principle never to let another player exasperate you, whether on purpose or with unconscious mannerisms.

Few players—the exceptions being the geniuses of the game—play a cool, sound game when they're angry. That's why professional gamblers try to get amateur opponents roiled up. There's an old gambler's saying: "Lose your head," it goes, "and lose your money."

Bidding. In Auction Pinochle there are three kinds of bidding available to the accomplished player. They are:

The Safe Bid. This bid never exceeds the total of visible points in melds plus the points certain to be won in tricks.

The Risk Bid. Depending on how far it exceeds the certainties, this may be either a brilliant gamble or sheer recklessness. It is the bid surpassing in total points the points in meld plus points certain to be won in tricks.

The Fake Bid. This corresponds, approximately, to the blind psychic bid at Bridge. It is an attempt to push an opponent's bid past the safe-bid level and thus to trap him in an unmakable contract.

It may be noted that the fake bid not uncommonly boomerangs on the fake bidder. I advise you to use it, if at all, at a very low level of bidding. And I further advise that, if you find you've gotten a reputation for fake bidding, you abandon it; wait until you have a rock-crushing hand, then make a bid that sounds like a fake, and let your opponents topple into that deadfall. It is obvious that, if a player sticks to the safe bid as defined above, he will rarely if ever go into the hole. But it must also be clear that safe bidding is by no means the best bidding. The really fine player must use all three kinds of bid. How? When? This is to a degree a psychological problem, a matter of timing and card sense and the other almost telepathic conditions around the table. The player must judge for himself. But you have to start somewhere. So I'd suggest using the risk bid. Overbid your visible hand with this in mind: Do not expect the widow to improve your holding more than 30 points with the improved meld and the improved playing hand.

I'm not going to yield to the temptation to tell you when to throw in a fake bid. It depends on who you're playing against, what time of night it is, what's happened so far, the looks on your opponents' faces, and the distribution of your cards. Psychology, as it's called, is crucial in any game involving competitive bidding. Psychology is a very unstandardized variable. If I tell you to fake with such-and-such a hand on the assumption you're playing Caspar Milquetoast, you may fake against a Russian diplomat next time you're out, and you may get your ears pinned back. People react differently.

Help from the Widow. Most of the grave errors made in the bidding are traceable to the fact that unreasoning players insist on bidding in the hope of finding in the widow enough valuable cards to justify their excesses. It is a queer fact that if there's one reckless player at the table the other players will bid badly. If that guy can expect so much from the widow, goes the reasoning (if any), then why can't I? But if a player understands the rudiments of sound bidding and can keep his skull screwed on, he need seldom have a losing session at Auction Pinochle. But, to bid well, a player must have some acquaintance with probability and reasonable expectations; he must have some general knowledge of the chances for finding a wanted card in the widow or of at least finding a valuable card affording him an extra meld or a stronger hand.

In the following chart you'll find the bidder's chances of buying one wanted card in the widow. I haven't calculated the chances of finding more than one wanted card. I'd like to insist that a bidder should never bid a hand in the hope of finding more than one needed card. So that we shall understand each other, the reader will bear in mind that a Pinochle deck consists of 24 cards each duplicated once, making 48 cards in all. Thus each card twin (the two aces of clubs, the two kings of hearts, etc.) must be considered as one chance, since it is not necessary for our purposes to find both in the widow; all we need do is find one of the twins. Right? If a player holding one of the twin cards of a given rank was seeking the other, he would have only half the tabulated chance; but the appended chart and analysis will not cover half-chances.

CHANCES THAT A WANTED CARD WILL BE FOUND IN THE WIDOW

Wanted Cards Out of Number in the Widow	Chances of Finding It in the Widow	Odds on Finding That Card
1 of 1	961 in 5,456	1 in 5.67
1 of 2	1,802 in 5,456	1 in 3.02
1 of 3	2,531 in 5,456	1 in 2.11
1 of 4	3,156 in 5,456	1 in 1.72
1 of 5	3,685 in 5,456	1 in 1.47
1 of 6	4,125 in 5,456	1 in 1.31

In a word, a player has a better than even chance of finding in the widow a valuable card that will help him *only* when he has four or more openings in the hand. I concede cheerfully that in every player's experience there has occurred the widow that gave him two or three cards he needed and a cinch hand; but the Pinochle player who consistently relies on this fantastic improbability is *not* a good player. The sound bidder rarely expects to find an additional meld in the widow. He anticipates improving his playing hand with the three widow cards, but that's all. A player who says the widow ruined his hand is not telling the truth. The widow can't, under the rules of the game, hurt your hand. You can always bury the three widow cards and still have the same (unruined) hand with which you started. The best Pinochle players I know calculate the average value of the widow at 30 points. This means melds and additional points won in tricks by using the widow cards. I agree with them. If in your bidding you give a tentative value of 30 to the widow you'll have a soundly conservative bidding technique.

When to Play or Concede the Hand. Having examined the widow and decided he can't meld enough points to make his bid a cinch hand, the bidder must make up his mind then whether to concede the hand or play it out. If he plays and wins, all very well! If he concedes and throws in the cards, he must pay his opponents but a single unit each. But if he elects to play the hand and then fails to make his bid he must pay each opponent at least two units. It is not uncommon (see page 171) that he is compelled to pay each four units if spades were trump and six units if hearts were trump. Hence the hesitant bidder, calculating the tricks he may lose (which is the right way to estimate a hand for the play—not tricks it may win!), is confronted with a situation not quite comparable to anything else in cards.

He must reckon the number of trump cards held by his opponents (and the cards in the other suits) and he must decide under what distributional conditions it's possible for him to make them break favorably. It is quite a delicate calculation. If some crucial suit breaks unfavorably (that is, if the cards in one opponent's hand total more than the cards in the other's), then he can't break the suit, and he can't possibly make the bid.

Master Contract Bridge players have been through some of this, but theirs is quite a different kettle of fish. Our Pinochle bidder, for example, holds six trump cards. Six trumps are out against him in the other hands. If those six are distributed between his opponents evenly, three and three, he can break the suit, control the other suits, and bring home his bid. If they're five to one or four to two or six to zero he hasn't a chance.

It is impossible to decide on this problem by reliance on card sense. Card sense is too variable, if it is really anything at all. The player who depends on what he thinks is some abstruse instinct at cards is a player generally headed straight for the cleaners! You need something more tangible, something based more on demonstrable reality, to estimate the probable distribution of cards between your opponents. Again, since it's your bank account, I must petition you to stay with me. Let's say a player has to decide on the distribution of the missing ace and ten of diamonds. If he's an average player, he concludes there are four ways in which these cards can fall:

1. Opponent A holds the ace of diamonds, opponent B holds the ten of diamonds.

2. Opponent A holds the ten of diamonds, opponent B holds the ace of diamonds.

3. Opponent A holds the ace and ten, opponent B holds neither.

4. Opponent A holds neither, opponent B holds both ace and ten.

Hence, our average player decides, the ace and the ten can be divided two ways so as to fall on a single lead; also, they can be divided two ways so that they won't fall on a single lead. There are two ways either can happen. Thus the chances that either will happen are exactly even. But it doesn't work out that way. As you'll note below, the correct percentages are 48 percent in favor of the 2–0 distribution and 52 percent in favor of the 1–1 distribution. The mistake our average

player made was to consider only the two crucial cards, whereas he should have taken also into consideration the 28 other cards that made up the hands. Here's a table of suit distribution that will help any player:

POSSIBLE DISTRIBUTION IN SUITS

Bidder Holds	Distribution of Missing Cards	Approximate Probability (percent)
10 of one suit	1-1	52
	2-0	48
9 of one suit	2-1	78
	3-0	22
8 of one suit	3-1	50
	2-2	40
	4-0	10
7 of one suit	3-2	67
	4-1	29
	5-0	04
6 of one suit	4-2	48
	3-3	35
	5-1	15
	6-0	02
5 of one suit	4-3	61
	5-2	31
	6-1	07
	7-0	01
4 of one suit	5-3	467
	4-4	318
	6-2	180
	7-1	033
	8-0	002

Be Sure You're Right, Then Don't Go Ahead. Conceding the hand, unless it is a cinch, is in the long run a costly habit. How you manage yourself at this critical stage of the game is decisive as to whether you can win or must lose. Before deciding whether to play it out or throw it in, the bidder of any hand should refer mentally to the above table of suit distribution. If the probability is 33.3 percent or more that the suits will fall in the bidder's favor, he should play out the hand. Another way of saying it: He should not concede unless the probability is 66.7 percent that the cards will fall adversely. I select the 33.3 percent figure since at that level the bidder has the same mathematical case whether he concedes or plays; in the act of deciding to play it out he neither gains nor loses; he is no worse off playing than he is conceding. Let's break down three theoretical hands:

1. If the bidder concedes all three hands he must pay each opponent three units, one for each hand.

2. If he plays out the three hands and the

probabilities turn out as predicted by the mathematics, he must lose two hands and pay each opponent four units, two for each hand. Meanwhile, the bidder wins one hand and collects one unit from each opponent. So far our man's even: He loses three units by conceding; he loses three by playing.

Thus, if the probabilities are any better than 33.3 percent in the bidder's favor, he *must* play out the hand, and he *must* win in the long run. *Example:* The bid is 470 points. You have melded 220 points. There are two trumps out against you: the ace and the ten. You need 250 points to make your bid. If the ace and ten are divided between your opponents, you make all the tricks and win the hand. If one opponent holds both ace and ten, you lose a trick and fail to make the hand. *Question:* Should you elect to play the hand? *Answer:* Absolutely yes; you must play it out. You have a 48 percent chance to win, which is much higher than the 33.3 percent chance that is our minimum. *But note this well:* When spades are double or hearts are triple, this 33.3 percent rule is out. I recommend that you do not play out a spade hand unless you have at least a 50 percent chance to break your suit and that you do not play a heart hand without a 56 percent chance.

Cash Value of Your Opponent's Incompetence. It is not generally sound to assume that one of your opponents will make a feebleminded mistake favorable to you, and to then play out a squeaker hand. You can't build a good game of any kind on the assumption that the adversary will drop the ball or will consistently behave himself like a fool. It is obviously better—so obviously that I hesitate to state it—to build up your game in the expectation that your opponent will play or defend his hand like a master. But . . .

There is always a "but." If you know your opponent's game, if you are sure he's bound to make a mistake and you know what kind of mistake it's apt to be, and if you can maneuver the play so as to enhance the odds he'll make it, then you're entitled to take account of that consistent margin of error in your bidding and play. Don't forget, though, that for every weakness in your opponent's game there's very likely to be one in yours. Maybe you have little consistent flaws of which other people are aware. Maybe you regularly overbid or underbid; maybe you play the hand like a butcher; maybe you lose

track of trumps and make a practice of trying to break unbreakable suits. When you undertake to play mistakes for profit, you're assuming risks.

Count Tricks as They Are Won. The most common fault I find in the majority of Pinochle players is a peculiar hoggishness. The player isn't satisfied to make his bid and rack it up. He takes it for granted, at a certain stage of the game, that he'll of course make his bid, and he proceeds to concentrate on running up a count higher than his contract.

Don't do it. Make your bid. The player who does this is not a losing player. But the player who concentrates all his faculties on amassing a high count is almost invariably a loser. The play of the hand for a high count is radically different from the play for a low or modest count. It is necessary to take long chances, to risk adverse suit breaks, to neglect safety plays. It is even sometimes necessary to set up good tricks for the opponent in side suits. The risks are never commensurate with the potential gain. They are a bad bet. Play for your bid.

The player should always count, as they are made, the points taken in tricks so that he will have an accurate calculation on his hand as it goes along. Often a player neglects an opportunity to put on a trick a high-ranking card that would win the hand for him; not having counted his points, he thinks he needs more points than he in fact does need. By failing to play the high-ranking card at the right time, he never gets another chance to take a trick.

Count your valuable cards won in tricks, whether you're the bidder or his opponent. It pays off. And—while I've said this before, it's worth repeating—by all means train yourself to count the trump cards as they're played. Once you've mastered that, you'll find it's not so hard to keep track of the cards played in the side suits, too.

New England Pinochle

This game, also known as Hartford Pinochle, is played in the same manner as Auction Pinochle with Widow: each hand a complete game, except as follows:

1. When and if the bidding reaches 300, one card of the widow is exposed to all players as the bidding continues. The choice of this card is left to the dealer.

2. When and if the bidding reaches 350, another card of the widow is exposed by the dealer. The third card of the widow is *not* exposed until the bidding has stopped. The three cards of widow, of course, belong to the highest bidder as in all Auction Pinochle games.

Auction Pinochle with Widow: Game—1,000 Points

This game is essentially the same as the one just described (Auction Pinochle with Widow: Each Hand a Complete Game), except that the object is to score, before any other player does so, 1,000 points by totaling the value of melded cards and of cards taken in tricks during successive hands.

Basically, the difference in this game lies in the counting of tricks and in the fact that all hands, when there is a bid, must be played to completion. (There is no conceding of a hand.) In counting tricks, remember:

1. The bidder counts his tricks. If he has scored enough points in his melds and tricks to equal or exceed his bid, he enters the total on his score. The other player's points in tricks and melds are scored for each, in his own respective column. (In this game, after the bidder has announced trump, the other two players put down their melds.) A player must win at least one trick to score his melds.

2. If the bidder fails to make his bid he loses the melds previously credited to him on his hand, gets no credit for the number of points won in tricks, and he is holed for the amount of the bid. This amount is subtracted from his total score. If that (his total score) is less than the amount he is holed for, his deficit is entered on the score sheet with a minus sign. The other players get credit for their tricks scored.

This scoring goes on until one—or more—player scores 1,000 points or more. If one player alone scores 1,000 points, he is the winner. If two players have 1,000 points or more and *neither* is the bidder, the player with the higher score wins. If two players, excepting the bidder, are tied with 1,000 or more points, they both are declared winners and share equally in the stakes. If the player who won the bidding is one of two players to score 1,000 or more points, he wins the game, even if another player (or players) has a higher score.

Optional Rule for Holed Payoff. Often players collect an amount (in addition to the penalty detailed above) from a bidder who is holed. Generally, the additional penalty is one-fourth of the stakes for the game. If, for example, it is stipulated that each loser shall pay the winner $1 per game, a player going into the hole would have to pay each opponent one-fourth of $1, or 25 cents. But this rule must be expressly agreed upon before the start of the game.

Partnership Auction Pinochle with Widow

Requirements

1. Two partnerships of two players each—four players in all.

2. The standard Pinochle deck. (For rules on the deck, rank of cards and suits, value of melded cards, bonus melds, and value of cards won in tricks, see page 168.)

Object of the Game. For one partnership, by scoring 1,000 points or more before the other partnership does, to win the game.

Details Before the Actual Deal. Selecting partnerships, choosing the dealer, establishing seat positions, changing partnerships and seat positions, the shuffle, and the cut, are governed by basic General Rules for Pinochle.

The Deal. Eleven cards are dealt to each player and four cards are dealt to the widow. Starting with the leader and dealing clockwise, one card is dealt face down to each player and the fifth card is dealt face down in the center of the table for the widow. This deal is repeated three more times. Thus the fifth, tenth, fifteenth, and twentieth cards off the deck are dealt to the widow. After the last card is dealt to the widow, the fifth and succeeding rounds are dealt to the players only until the deck is exhausted and each player has 11 cards.

The Bidding. The leader may pass, indicating that he doesn't want to bid. Or, he may make a bid. However, the player who makes the first bid is not required to bid any stipulated number of points; he may bid any amount he likes.

Each player in his turn, starting with the leader and rotating clockwise, passes or bids. But if one player bids, the following bidder's bid must be higher by at least 10 points; bids can be raised only in multiples of 10. This bidding continues until only one bidder remains unchallenged. He has won the bid for his partnership. Once a player has passed, he cannot bid later in the same hand. If all players pass, the cards are thrown in and a new hand is dealt by the player to the left of that hand's dealer.

The Widow, the Blind, or the Buy. The four cards dealt face down on the table during the deal of the hand are called the *widow,* the *blind,* or the *buy.* It must be reemphasized that under no circumstances may a player, be he active or inactive, look at the four cards in the widow while the bidding is going on. The bidder—the player who has won the bid—takes these four cards in an attempt to improve his holding; but before placing them in his hand, the bidder must expose the widow cards and let the other players see them. The bidder may either put the widow cards in his hand with his other 11 cards, or he may leave them on the table and use them in a meld. The bidder may announce his trump suit either before or after melding.

Discarding or Burying Four Cards. Now, to give himself the legal 11 cards, the bidder must discard four cards. These four are placed down in front of him and are counted as tricks he has won—although his partnership must win a trick from the oponents to make his meld good. Any points among these four cards are counted in the bidder's favor as points won in tricks. These rules on the discard must be observed:

1. The bidder cannot bury (discard) any card he has used to form a meld for which he has received point credits. If he buries such a card, and if his attention is called to the misplay, he has reneged and loses the hand. The partnership that reneges is holed for the number of points bid.

2. The bidder may bury a trump card (one not used in a meld), but he must announce the fact that it is a trump he's burying. He does not have to reveal its denomination, but failure to announce burying a trump card is considered a reneg* by the bidder and loses the hand for him. The penalty is the same as if he failed to make his bid in play.

3. The bidder is not required to announce the burying of an ace or any other card that is not a trump card.

4. If the bidder leads a card in starting the play of the hand, and his attention is drawn to the fact that he has neglected to bury four cards or has buried too few or too many cards, he has reneged; the penalty is the same

as if the partnership played the hand and failed to make the bid.

The Play. This game is governed by the rules for Auction Pinochle with Widow: Each Hand a Complete Game (see page 180).

Counting Valuable Cards Won in Tricks. Each partnership counts its tricks, adding up the total of valuable cards won in tricks. The partnership that won the bid also adds the four cards buried by the bidder. If the bidding partnership makes the bid, the total points won in tricks are added to its credit on the score sheet. The other partnership adds to its credit its own total, whether the bidding partnership did or did not make its bid. If the bidding partnership fails to make its bid, it loses the melds previously credited to it on that hand, and loses its points won in tricks. Also, the partnership is holed for the amount of the bid. This latter amount is subtracted from its running score. If the total of this score, which does *not* include the lost melds and points, is less than the amount of the holed bid, a minus sign is used to indicate the deficit. The partnership must cancel this deficit before it can enter any score as a plus.

Melding. After the bidder announces his trump, all the other players may meld. Once the bidder has named trump and one or more other players have melded, he cannot change his trump suit. The melds of each partnership are added and each total is entered on the score sheet. After the melds have been entered in the score, each player picks up his melds, restores the cards to his hand, and goes on with the play.

Determining the Winning Partnership. Play continues until one partnership has scored 1,000 or more points and has won the game.

If both partnerships score 1,000 or more points, the team that won the last bid wins the game, even if the other has a higher score. Since the bidder is considered to be the first to count cards, his team is thus legally first over the finish line.

Optional Payoff. To be legal, this rule must mutually be agreed upon before the start of the game. An additional sum in cash is often collected from one partnership by the other for the former's failure to make its bid. The holed partnership's payoff is usually one-fourth of the agreed stakes of the game.

Standard Bonus Melds. Under mutual agreement, before the start of the game, players may make use of the standard bonus melds. (See this table under basic General Rules for Pinochle, page 168.) It may be stipulated, when using this table of melds, that game shall be 1,000, 1,500, or 2,000 points.

Cutthroat Pinochle

This is played exactly as is Partnership Auction Pinochle with Widow—with the following single exception: The game is played four-handed; there are no partnerships; it is every man for himself.

Double-Deck Auction Pinochle with Widow: Individual Play

This is played exactly as is Auction Pinochle with Widow (game 1,000 points) with the following differences:

Requirements

1. Two Pinochle decks are used, from which all the nines have been removed. These are shuffled together and used as one; decks of contrasting color or design may be used. The consolidated deck adds up to a total of 80 cards.

2. There are four players, each playing for himself.

The Deal. Nineteen cards are dealt to each player and four cards are dealt into the widow. The first round of cards, starting with the leader and going clockwise, is dealt four at a time. The next four cards are dealt into the widow. Thereafter each player is dealt five cards at a time until the deck is exhausted.

The Scoring

1. The winner of the last trick is credited with 20 points instead of ten points as in Pinochle with a single deck.

2. For special bonus melds, which are often used in Double-Deck Auction Pinochle, see basic General Rules for Pinochle under standard bonus melds and triple and quadruple melds.

3. When using standard bonus melds, game is 3,000 points.

4. When using triple or quadruple melds, game is 10,000 points.

Double-Deck Partnership Pinochle with Widow

This is played exactly as is Double-Deck Auction Pinochle with Widow, Individual Play,

except that the four players play as partners, two against two.

Wipe-Off

This is Double-Deck Partnership Pinochle with the proviso that a side must score 200 or more in cards to count either its meld or its cards.

Six- and Eight-Handed Auction Pinochle with Widow

Auction Pinochle, either six- or eight-handed, is played exactly as is the four-handed partnership game described above, with these exceptions:

The Six-Handed Game

1. Partnerships may be formed of (a) three teams of two players each, or (b) two teams of three players each.

2. Two full decks of Pinochle cards are combined as a single deck. There are 96 cards in all.

3. The partnership that wins the last trick of the hand gets credit for 20 points.

The Deal. Each player is dealt 15 cards and the widow is dealt six cards. The cards are dealt clockwise, starting with the leader and including the dealer, three at a time to each player. Then three cards are dealt into the widow, these being the nineteenth, twentieth, and twenty-first cards off the deck. A second round of three cards is dealt to each player, and the fortieth, forty-first, and forty-second cards off the deck are dealt into the widow, which now has a total of six cards. No more cards are dealt into the widow. The remaining cards are dealt to each player in turn, three at a time, until the deck is exhausted.

The Eight-Handed Game

1. Partnerships may be formed of (a) four teams of two players each, or (b) two teams of four players each.

2. Three decks of Pinochle cards, 144 cards in all, are combined as one deck.

3. The partnership that wins the last trick of the hand gets 30 points.

The Deal. Each player is dealt 17 cards, and eight cards are dealt into the widow. Starting with the player to his left, rotating clockwise, and including himself, the dealer gives each player five cards. Then he deals the next four cards into the widow. On the second round, each player is dealt four cards, and the next four cards off the deck go into the widow, which now has eight cards. No more cards are dealt into the widow. The remaining cards are dealt the players four at a time, in rotation, until the deck is exhausted. *Note:* Very often, in these two variations of Auction Pinochle, players use standard bonus melds, triple melds, and quadruple melds.

AUCTION PINOCHLE WITHOUT WIDOW, INDIVIDUAL PLAY: GAME—1,000 POINTS

The object of this version of Auction Pinochle is to win the game by scoring 1,000 or more points before any one of your opponents. When you are the bidder, you try to score enough points to cover your bid and thus avoid going into the hole. Actually, the play and rules are the same as for Auction Pinochle with Widow: Game—1,000 Points (page 190), except for the following:

The Deal. Whether there are three or four players in the game, the deal goes the same. If four, each is dealt 12 cards, four at a time, starting with the leader (the player to the dealer's left) and rotating clockwise, the dealer including himself in the deal. If three, each player is dealt 16 cards, four at a time, in the same way.

The Bidding. The leader may (*a*) pass, or (*b*) bid any amount he thinks he can make with the hand just dealt to him.

In this version of Pinochle there is no stipulated minimum bid. The first bidder may make any bid he elects. Thereafter, each successive bidder (the bid going to the left, clockwise) must bid at least 10 points higher than the previous bidder; bidding can be done only in multiples of 10. A player who has passed cannot bid again during the same hand. A bidder cannot alter the amount of his uttered bid. If all players pass, the deal moves on to the player at the left of the one who dealt that hand.

Naming Trump and Melding. The highest bidder, that is, the player who won the auction, has the right to name as trump any suit he chooses. After the bidder has named the trump suit, all players including him lay down their melds; the scorekeeper, after verifying the claims, enters each player's melds on the sheet under each name. The number of points bid is also noted on the score sheet.

The Play. After the melds have been recorded, the cards are restored to the player's hands and the play begins as described on page 184.

Failure to Make the Bid. If the total in melds and points won in tricks does not contain enough points to equal the bid or to exceed it, the bidder loses. The hand, his melds for that hand already scored, and the amount that he bid are all subtracted from his score. He may find himself in the hole for the amount bid if he had no previous score; or he may be holed for the difference between his losing bid and his previous score if the former exceeds the latter. His deficit is indicated by a minus sign on his score. An additional sum may be assessed against the bidder for failure to make his bid, collectible by each other player—if the penalty is mutually agreed upon before the start of the game. The penalty is usually one-quarter of the amount staked by the player on the game.

Partnership Auction Pinochle without Widow: Game—1,000 Points

Like other 1,000-point partnership Pinochle games, the object of this contest is for one partnership to win the game by scoring 1,000 or more points before the other partnership does. If both partnerships score 1,000 or more points on the same hand, the partnership that won the game-going bid on the last hand is the winner. Requirements for play and the steps taken before the actual deal are the same as in other partnership Pinochle games.

The Deal. To each player, including himself, the dealer deals 12 cards, three at a time, starting with the leader and dealing clockwise until the entire pack has been distributed.

Informatory Bidding. It is permissible to make *informatory bids* in this game, although all bidding must be in multiples of 10. Thus, a player cannot bid 105 to notify his partner he has five aces. Here are sample informatory bids:

1. The first bidder says 120. He is notifying his partner he holds a 20 meld.

2. The bidder says 200. He means he has 100 points in meld.

In comparison with the delicate and ornate Contract Bridge conventions, this is, of course, fairly rudimentary. The only informatory bid absolutely prohibited is one that instructs one's partner (*a*) what suit to make trump if the team wins the bid, or (*b*) the number of cards one holds in a certain suit. As in Bridge, the leader is in the best position to bid informatively, because at his stage of the first round the bidding has not yet reached a forbidding point total.

Partners may at the start of the game discuss what kind of informatory bids they propose to use; but it is not compulsory that they use such bids, nor, if such bids are used, is it compulsory that they mean what has been agreed. Such bids are to be liberally construed, and are used at the player's risk.

The leader is the first bidder. For the subsequent play—that is, bidding, naming trump, melding, the play, failure to make the bid, winning the game, in-the-hole payoffs, additional rules, and all else—apply rules as set forth on pages 190 to 192.

Firehouse Pinochle

Rules for Partnership Auction Pinochle without Widow: Game—1,000 Points (see page 193) govern this game, with the following exceptions:

Rules for Bidding

1. Starting with the leader and rotating clockwise, each player is allowed but one bid. If all pass, there is a new deal.

2. The highest bidder names the trump suit.

Army and Navy Pinochle

This game is similar to Firehouse Pinochle—only one round of bidding—but a double pinochle deck is used in the Army and Navy variety with all nines stripped out so that a deck of 80 cards remains. Also, there is a widow, which goes to the highest bidder. The actual play rules, except for bidding, are the same as Double-Deck Partnership Pinochle with Widow. The lowest bid is 500, and bids must be raised by multiples of 50. If the quadruple system of melds is used, as on page 170, the minimum bid is 200 and successive bids must rise by 100.

Partnership Aeroplane Pinochle

The spelling of "aeroplane" looks a little old-fashioned in this day of airplanes, or planes; but this is what they call it. Incidentally, in some sections of the country, this game is called Racehorse Pinochle.

Rules, as set forth on page 193, govern this game—with the following additional rules:

1. Each player is allowed to make only two bids.

2. The minimum permissible bid is 250 points.

3. The highest bidder names the trump suit.

4. After naming the trump suit, the bidder may pass any four cards from his hand face down to his partner.

5. In return, this partner must pass to the bidder four cards in exchange, from his own hand. He must select these four cards before looking at the cards passed to him by the bidder.

Check Pinochle

This is a partnership auction Pinochle game in which there are special bonuses, paid in *checks* (chips), for unusual melds and for making or defeating the bid. While this variety has been ballyhooed lately as a new game, I remember having seen it played twenty-five years ago in a half-dozen Midwestern states. Games do not move as rapidly across a country or a culture as some *ex post facto* historians would like to believe. Requirements are the same as in other partnership Pinochle games.

Requirements

1. Four players; two against two in partnership.

2. The standard Pinochle deck. (For description of the deck, rank of cards and suits, value of melded cards, rules for melding, and value of cards won in tricks, see General Rules for Pinochle, page 168.)

Object of the Game. For a partnership, on the completion of a 1,000-point game, to have scored more checks than the opposing partnership. A *check award* is a unit of value given for a specified meld, for fulfilling a bid, for winning the game, etc.

The Stakes and the Scorekeeper. The scorekeeper shall be selected by mutual consent. The score is kept with paper and pencil, and the scorekeeper must in a separate column record the check awards won by each partnership. The game may be played for any stakes, but 5 cents per check is a reasonable sum.

Rules Prevailing Before the Actual Deal. Under rules on page 170 are described selection of partners and dealer, establishment of seating positions, changing seats and partners, the shuffle, and the cut.

The Deal. Each player, including the dealer, is dealt 12 cards. The cards are dealt three at a time, starting with the leader and going clockwise, until the entire pack has been exhausted. On the completion of each hand, the deal rotates to the player at the previous dealer's left.

The Bidding. The leader, who has the first opportunity to compete in the auction, may either bid or pass. The turn to bid rotates from player to player, clockwise, to the left.

1. To qualify as a bidder, the player must have in his hand a marriage ((king and queen in the same suit); regardless of the strength of his hand in melds, he cannot bid unless he holds a marriage. But see rule No. 4.

2. The minimum bid, no matter what the position of the player, is 200 points. Each succeeding bid must be at least 10 points higher than the current bid, the bids being raised in multiples of 10.

3. A player, having once passed, cannot bid again.

4. If the first three players pass, the dealer must bid whether he holds a marriage or not. If he holds no marriage he can bid only the minimum 200 points. If he holds a marriage he can put in whatever bid he likes.

5. The player bidding the highest amount becomes the bidder. (The highest bidder is the only bidder remaining in competition, the other players having passed.) Winning the bid, the bidder commits himself and his partner to win the hand by scoring the number of points stated in the bid.

Naming Trump. The player who won the bid names the suit which is trump for the hand. The bidder must choose the trump himself; he cannot consult his partner.

Informatory Bidding. In this game, informatory bidding is permitted. In contrast to the rigid conventions of Bridge and even of some Pinochle games, the bidding may be whatever the players agree to make it. But it must be in multiples of 10, and the information must be conveyed by the amount of the bid and in no other manner. A player cannot tell his partner the strength of any special suit he holds. Because his bid is put in first, before the auction has reached forbidding levels, the leader can best make an informatory bid.

Sample bid: The leader says 220. He means to tell his partner that he holds 80 meld. Their convention gives each 10 points bid above the minimum of 200 a meld value of 40. A bid of 210 (10 points above the minimum) would mean he has 40 meld. A bid of 230 (30 above the minimum) would mean 120 meld.

Melding. After the bidder has named trump, all the players put their melds face up on the table to be recorded by the scorekeeper. No melds may be put down by any player before the trump is named. Melds are entered on the score sheet under the partnership to which they belong. A partnership's total melds are added together as a single score for that team. Although melds are laid down by individual players for the common benefit of the partnership, no player may use his partner's cards to help form a meld of his own.

The Play. After the melds are recorded, the cards are taken back into the players' hands, and the play begins.

1. The bidder leads the first card. He may lead any card he likes.

2. After the first card has been led, each player in his turn must obey the following rules, the turn of play rotating around the table clockwise to the left:

   (*a*) Each player must play a card of the suit led, if he has one.

   (*b*) If he does not have a card of the suit led, he must play a trump card.

   (*c*) If he lacks a card of the suit led and a trump card, he may play any other card in his hand.

   (*d*) If a trump is led, each player must play to the trick a higher trump if he has one. If he hasn't a higher trump, he must still play a trump card if there's one in his hand. Only if he has no trump at all may he play a card of another suit.

   (*e*) Once a card is led it cannot be taken back into the hand.

   (*f*) If a nontrump card is led, the next player trumps it, and one or both of the following players are compelled to trump because they do not have a card of the suit led, it is not compulsory that they play a trump card higher than that of the previous player who trumped.

3. The trick is won by the highest-ranking card played. When two cards of equal value

tie for the trick, first card played wins.

4. The winner of the trick leads off to the next trick, and play rotates to the left under the rules just described.

5. The winner of the last trick scores an additional 10 points.

This pattern of play is followed until all the cards in all hands have been played. Then the score for melds and points in tricks is totaled. After this a new deal starts, and play continues until one of the partnerships totals 1,000 points or more. (But note well the following passage.)

Check Scoring. Check Pinochle differs from other games in the family because of its distribution of check awards. There is some disagreement, generally based on a faulty conception of the mathematics, among modern writers on the scoring of checks. I've decided to make official the following system, which is both sound and is popular among experienced players throughout the Midwestern states. Players may, of course, increase the value of check awards as they see fit, but the increase should be in ratio to the scale here set forth.

Checks to which a partnership is entitled are entered on the score sheet under the check column. At the completion of the game, the partnership with the highest total in checks wins the game, and is paid off for the difference between its check total and the losing partnership's total. It is not uncommon for one partnership to score 1,000 or more points and still lose after the computation of checks, which determines the final result.

CHECK AWARDS FOR MELDING

Melds	Checks Awarded
Flush (ace, ten, king, queen, jack of trump)	4
100 aces (four aces, one in each suit)	2
80 kings (four kings, one in each suit)	1
60 queens (four queens, one in each suit)	1
40 jacks (four jacks, one in each suit)	1
Double Pinochle (two jacks of diamonds, two queens of spades)	1
Roundhouse (four kings and four queens in different suits)	4

CHECK AWARDS FOR BID

Number of Points Bid	For Partnership Making Its Bid, Checks	For Defeating the Opponents' Bid, Checks
200 to 240	2	4
250 to 290	4	8
300 to 340	7	14
350 to 390	10	20
400 to 440	13	26
450 to 490	16	32
500 to 540	19	38
550 to 590	22	44

For each series of 50 points above 590 the bidding partnership is credited with three additional checks; the partnership defeating such a bid gets six additional checks.

Additional Check Awards

1. For winning the game in play—scoring 1,000 or more points before the opponents do—the partnership gets seven checks.

2. For winning all 12 tricks in a hand, the partnership gets five checks.

3. For holding all the valuable cards in one hand (scoring a count of 250 points in one hand, not necessarily all the tricks), a partnership gets four checks.

Failure to Make the Bid. If the bidding partnership fails to make its bid, it loses both its meld points and points won in valuable cards taken in tricks on that hand, and goes in the hole for the number of points bid. This deficit is subtracted from the partnership's total score; if the score is not sufficient to cover the deficiency, a minus sign is entered to indicate the amount for which the partnership is in the hole.

The bidding partnership can score nothing on a holed hand. Melds and checks already entered on the score sheet for that hand are canceled, and the opposing partnership scores its melds and cards won in tricks. In addition, the bidders' opponents score their own checks plus double the value in checks of the defeated bid.

Winning the Game

1. If a partnership scores 1,000 or more points, it is declared the winner of the game.

2. If both partnerships score 1,000 or more points, the winner is the partnership which won the bid on the hand, even if the other partnership's score is actually higher.

Contract Pinochle

This diverting variation uses several bids and rules adapted from Pinochle's cousin, Bridge.

Requirements

1. Four players; two against two in partnership.

2. The standard Pinochle deck. (For description of the deck rank of cards and suits, see General Rules for Pinochle, page 168.)

Object of the Game. For a partnership to win by scoring 3,000 or more points before the other partnership does.

Rules Prevailing Before the Actual Deal. Beginning on page 170 rules are described for selecting partners, establishing seat positions, choosing the dealer, changing seats and partnerships, and the shuffle and the cut.

The Deal. Twelve cards, three at a time, are dealt to each player, including the dealer, starting with the one at the dealer's immediate left and going clockwise. Four rounds of dealing exhaust the pack.

The Bidding. The first turn to bid is the dealer's. He may either pass or bid at least 100. The turn to bid rotates clockwise around the table. Once a player has bid, the next bidder must bid at least 10 points more; that is, bids must be raised in multiples of 10. If all players pass, there is a new deal and the player to the dealer's left becomes the next dealer. In the bidding, the trump suit must be declared along with the point total. That is, the bidder says "200 spades" or "200 clubs."

The suits are equal in rank. A player may bid a suit previously bid by another player, or he may bid any other suit. A player may reenter the bidding after having passed. The bidding continues until three successive passes have occurred. A player may double an opponent's bid, or he may redouble an opponent's double, with the following results:

1. Doubling multiplies by two the value of all points scored.

2. Redoubling, which doubles the doubled values, results in multiplying by four the value of all points scored.

The double and redouble may be used only against opponents' bids. Players cannot double and redouble their own partnership's bids.

Melding. After three players in succession have passed, the partnership that won the auction and took the bid lays down its melds. The opposing partnership is not permitted to lay down melds. (For value of melded cards and the rules for melding see rules on pages 168 to 169.) The following are exceptions to the general rules:

Combination Melds. By adding a card or cards to his partner's melds, a player may make combination melds. If, for example, his partner has melded the king and queen of spades, then the player may lay down a jack of diamonds which, in conjunction with partner's spade queen, makes a combination meld of Pinochle; or he may lay down three queens of suits other than his partner's spade queen to make a combination meld of 60 queens; likewise, he may lay down kings or queens to combine for a roundhouse.

Calling for Melds. After these melds have been laid down, the bidder may call on his partner to produce a card to enable him to form another meld. *Example:* The bidder holds the ace, ten, king, and jack, of trump. He may now call on his partner for the queen of trump to form a flush.

If the partner can produce the demanded card, the bidder lays down the new meld; thereupon, he is entitled to ask for still another card to help form another meld. Only one card may be called for at one time. If the bidder calls for a card and the partner cannot produce it, the turn to call for a card passes to the partner. When the partner calls on the bidder for a card and the bidder fails to produce it, this phase of the game ends; neither of the partners may call for any more cards.

Combination melds may be laid down on melds developed in calling for cards, and this play does not affect the player's right to call for cards. If the partnership that won the bid melds points enough to equal or exceed the amount of its bid, it is not required that it play out the hand. In Contract Pinochle it is not necessary to win a trick to make the melds good.

The scorekeeper notes the bidding partnership's melds, but he does not enter them on the score sheet. If the bidding partnership fails to make its bid, then its melds are not entered on the score sheet.

Conceding the Hand. Either the bidding partnership or the opposing partnership may concede the hand before the start of play or at any time during play.

1. If the bidding partnership concedes before a card is led in play, the opponents score one-half the value of the bid—but they score the full value if the bid was doubled and twice the bid's value if it was redoubled.

2. If the bidding partnership concedes after a card has been played, the opponents score the full value of the bid—but they score double the value of the bid if it was doubled and four times its value if it was redoubled.

3. If the opponents concede the hand at any time before or during the play, the bidding partnership scores the full value of its bid—with the relevant gains if it was doubled or redoubled.

In order for a concession to be legal and binding, both players of a partnership must agree to concede. If only one is willing to concede, the hand must be played out.

The Play. The bidding partners pick up their melds, and each player restores his own melded cards to his playing hand.

1. The bidder leads any card he chooses, playing it face up on the table to start the trick. After a card has been led, no changes in melds may be made.

2. Succeeding players must follow the suit of the card led if they have a card of that suit.

3. If a player does not have a card of the suit led, he must trump.

4. If he does not have a card of the suit led or a trump, he may play any card.

5. Only when a trump is led must a player having a higher-ranking trump card play that card.

6. If a nontrump card is led, the second player trumps it, and the third player is forced to trump because he does not have a card of the suit led, then the third player doesn't have to play a trump card of higher rank than the previous player's.

7. The winner of the trick leads off to the next trick. To win a trick a player must (*a*) play a higher-ranking card than his opponent's in the suit led, be it a trump or a nontrump suit, or (*b*) when trumping, play a higher-ranking trump card than his opponents.

When two cards of the same value are played and are tied to win the trick, the first played to the trick wins it. This pattern of play is followed until all the cards in the player's hands are exhausted.

Scoring the Hand. If the bidding partnership's total score in melds and valuable cards won in tricks totals an amount equal to or higher than its bid, then the value of the bid is entered to that partnership's credit on the score sheet. If the bid was doubled, the scorekeeper doubles the value of the bid scored; if it was redoubled, the score entered is the bid multiplied by four. If the bidding partnership fails to make its bid, the opposing partnership is credited in the scoring with the full amount

of the bid, double its value if doubled, four times its value if redoubled.

Winning the Game. The partnership first scoring 3,000 points wins the game.

Radio Partnership Pinochle

One of the most fascinating partnership games of the whole Pinochle family is Radio Partnership Pinochle. This game originated in Union City, New Jersey, where it has been played since 1933. Basically it's Double-Deck Partnership Pinochle. But its unique feature is an informatory exchange, in certain arbitrary and authorized bidding terms, that is made orally between partners before the bidding begins. This discussion, which is *not* bidding, is done with cues that must be explained to and understood by all the players. Secret conventions are barred.

A cue is not a binding contract. It need not even be an accurate description of what it purports to describe, namely, the card values in the player's hand. Players will often give their partners inaccurate cues—and thus lead their opponents, duly eavesdropping, to disaster. This table talk is capable of being used with infinite subtlety and it is, of course, fraught with risk. A misinformed opponent is a wonderful asset in any game. A misinformed partner, inspired by some harmless little cue of yours, can turn into a runaway and rush off into a beautiful accident.

Requirements

1. Two standard Pinochle decks from which all the nines have been removed, making one deck of 80 cards. The decks may be of contrasting color or pattern.

2. Four players, two against two as partners.

Object of the Game. For a partnership to run up at the end of four hands a higher score than its opponents. If at the completion of four hands the score is tied, a fifth tiebreaking hand is played. There is no bidder's choice.

Rules Prevailing Before the Actual Deal. Basic General Rules for Pinochle govern selection of partnerships, choosing the dealer, establishing seat positions, changing seats and partners, the shuffle, and the cut.

The Stakes. At the North Hudson Men's Club, where the game originated, and the only source of a criterion, the stakes are generally $1 a game, plus a 25-cent additional penalty when a partnership goes in the hole.

The Deal. Each player including the dealer is dealt 20 cards face down, five at a time, starting with the leader and rotating to the left, clockwise. The dealer gets the last five cards.

The Informatory Discussion. Before the bidding starts the partners try, using terms familiar to all hands, to impart to each other an idea of each hand's strength. In no circumstances may a player tell his partner in what *suit* his strength lies. *Example:* Holding a flush in diamonds, he may say "I have a flush"; he is *absolutely* forbidden to say "I've a diamond flush." Suits cannot be mentioned in the cueing.

Let's start: A player looks at his partner and says "Sing!" Now the partner must respond—not necessarily telling the truth—in certain conventional terms, a sort of shorthand familiar to everyone at the table.

INFORMATORY TERMS

The Term	*Its Meaning*
A ten	A flush
Twenty	A long suit—seven or more cards in the same suit, but not comprising a flush
A five	100 aces
One	An ace
Two	Two aces
Three	Three aces
Four	Four aces, but not 100 aces

Any meld other than a flush or 100 aces is stated in precise terms. A player holding a 140 meld says "A hundred forty." Holding 200 meld, he says "Two hundred." The player states his holding in a series of spoken numbers; this may seem complicated at first but, as you'll see, these numbers break down into readily understandable units. What the players do is to put informatory sentences together with numbers rather than with words alone. Here are some examples:

1. A player holds 100 in meld, 100 aces, and three other aces with the 100 aces. "Sing," says his partner. "One hundred, three, and a five," the player responds.

2. A player holds 160 in meld (not a flush), 100 aces, and an ace besides. "Sing!" And the player calls that hand thus: "No ten, one hundred sixty-one, and a five."

3. A player holds a double flush (300 points) and 40 meld, plus three aces (not 100 aces). "Sing!" And the player calls the hand thus: "Double ten, and forty-three."

4. A player holds a roundhouse (240 points) and no aces. The player would call "A weak two hundred forty." After this informatory exchange has ended, the bidding proper begins.

The Bidding. The leader starts the bidding, and the turn to bid rotates to the left around the table until three successive players have passed; the last bidder wins the auction for his partnership. There is no minimum bid. A player may bid any amount he elects, but the amount bid must end with a zero—200, 300, 320, 400, and so on. The average bid that wins the auction in this game is 600. Every bid after the first must be a raise in some multiple of 10, as in all other Pinochle games. When the final bid is passed by the other three players, this bid is entered on the score sheet.

Naming Trump and Melding. The bidder has the privilege of naming the trump suit. After trump is declared, the players lay down their melds. After verifying each player's count, the scorekeeper enters the total meld score for each partnership as a unit to its credit on the sheet. Then, players restore their melded cards to their holding in their hand, and they are ready for the play.

The Play

1. The bidder, playing any card he elects, leads off to the first trick. Turn to play rotates to the left, clockwise.

2. Each player must play a card of the suit led, if he has one.

3. If the player does not have a card of the suit led, he must play a trump card.

4. If a player does not have a card of the suit led or a trump card, he may play any other card in his hand.

5. When a trump card is led to the trick, each succeeding player must play a higher trump card than the leadoff card if he has one.

6. If a nontrump card is led and one player trumps that card, the succeeding player (or players), if compelled to trump, need not play a card of higher rank than the trump already played.

7. The highest-ranking card played wins the trick. When two cards of the same value tie to win the trick, the trick is won by the first one played.

8. The winner of that trick leads off to the

next, and play continues, rotating to the left, as in the above pattern.

9. Play continues thus until the hands are exhausted and all cards have been played in tricks.

10. The partnership winning the last trick scores 20 points for it.

Counting Valuable Cards Won in Tricks: The Hole. The value of cards won in tricks is totaled for each partnership and entered as a unit on the score sheet. If a partnership fails to make its bid, it is holed (penalized) for the amount of the bid. It loses its melds previously scored, and the amount by which it is holed is subtracted from its recorded score— or a minus sign is used to indicate its deficit. The bidding partnership scores nothing on a holed hand. The opposing partnership, however, scores its melds and valuable cards won in tricks.

Cash for Going in the Hole. A cash settlement must be paid by a partnership going in the hole. The amount is commonly reckoned as one-quarter of the total stakes for the game. In a game being played for $1, the penalty for a hole is 25 cents. This penalty must be agreed upon before the start of the game. Here is an optional way of paying off a hole penalty at the end of the game: If a partnership has gone into the hole, but still goes ahead and wins the game, it is not penalized for having gone into the hole. But if the holed partnership loses the game, it must pay a doubled penalty on the holed hand or hands.

Completion of the Game. After four hands have been dealt and played out, the partnership with the highest score at that point wins the game, which is thereupon completed. In case of a tie, a new hand is dealt to break the tie and decide the winner.

CHAPTER 10

Other Members of the Bezique Family

Bezique is the forerunner of Pinochle and has been eclipsed by the popularity of the latter game and some of its more modern variations. That is, some forms of Bezique (Rubicon, Chinese, or Sixty-Six) are still popular, but the original game invented, as most experts agree, by the Swedish schoolmaster, Gustav Flaker, is played little today.

TWO-HANDED BEZIQUE

The card game that was most popular in Europe in the 1850's and came to the United States in the early 1860's was Two-Handed Bezique. While it isn't played very much in America today, it's still fairly popular in certain sections of Europe.

Requirements

1. Two players.

2. A 64-card deck made of two standard 52-card decks with the twos, threes, fours, fives, and sixes stripped out.

3. Rank of cards is as follows: ace (high), ten, king, queen, jack, nine, eight, seven (low).

Object of the Game. For a player to score a number of points mutually agreed upon before the start of the game, such as 1,000, 1,500, or 2,000. The total point score is arrived at by adding points scored in melds and tricks won by each player.

Each ace or ten (called a *brisque*) taken in a trick counts 10 points. Dealer receives 10 points if he turns a seven as a trump card, and thereafter either player, upon winning a trick, may exchange a seven of trumps for the trump card that is face up on the table, or he merely shows a seven of trumps and scores 10 points for it. Winning the last trick counts 10 points.

The Deal. Players cut for the deal and the high card deals. Each player is dealt eight cards: first three at a time, then two at a time, and finally three. The next card (seventeenth) is turned face up on the table and its suit determines the trump for that hand. After this, the deal alternates from player to player.

STANDARD VALUE OF MELDED CARDS

	Points
Trump marriage (king and queen of trump)	40
Nontrump marriage: (king and queen of any suit not trump)	20
A sequence comprised of ace–ten–king–queen–jack of trump	250
Queen of spades and jack of diamonds (called *bezique*)	40
Two queens of spades and two jacks of diamonds made as a single meld (called *double bezique*)	500

SCORING

	Points
Any four aces	100
Any four kings	80
Any four queens	60
Any four jacks	40

The Play of the Hand. The nondealer plays first. He may lead off by taking any card he elects from his hand and playing it face up on the table. The dealer plays next. He may play any card he elects on his opponent's face-up leadoff card. This constitutes a trick and is taken by the higher card of the suit led, or by a higher trump. When identical cards are played to the same trick, the card led first wins the trick. The winner of a trick leads to the next after melding and drawing one card from the stock, the winner of the trick drawing first and his opponent next. This procedure of play is continued until the stock is exhausted.

A meld is made after winning a trick and before drawing a card from the stock, by placing the melds on the table. Once melded, the cards remain there until the stock is exhausted, unless the holder wishes to lead or play them, which he may do as though they were in his hand. Only one meld may be scored in each turn. A card may be used in different melds, but not twice in the same meld.

Example: Queen of spades may be used in a marriage, sequence, bezique, and four queens; but if four queens have been melded and one of the queens has been played, another queen may not be added for an additional 60-point meld. Four different queens would be required to score an additional 60-point meld. A king or queen of trumps which has been melded in a sequence may not be later melded in a royal marriage.

Bezique may be melded as 40 points, and a second bezique added for 500 points for a total of 540 points, but if double bezique is melded at the same time, it counts only 500 points.

End of Hand. When only one face-down card and the trump card remain in the stock, there may be no more melding. The winner of the next trick takes the face-down card, and his opponent the trump card; each picks up all melded cards he has on the table, and the last eight tricks are played. In this final stage of play, a player is required to follow suit to the card led, and to win the trick, if he is able to do so.

End of Game. As a player wins a brisque he scores for it at once instead of waiting until the end of the hand to score for it. As soon as a player reaches 1,000 or more points (or 1,500 or 2,000 as agreed), the game ends and he is declared the winner.

Additional Rules. Irregularities are handled as in Two-Handed Pinochle; see Renege (page 174) and Additional Rules (pages 174 and 175).

First Melded Marriage Determines Trump

This variation is played exactly the same as the regular Two-Handed Bezique, except that no trump card is turned face up. Instead, the first marriage melded and scored by any player decides the trump suit for the hand. There is no score for the seven of trump.

Five Hundred Bezique

This variation of Two-Handed Bezique (also called One-Deck Bezique and French Pinochle) comes closer to regular Two-Handed Bezique as played today than any other form of Bezique. The rules for Two-Handed Bezique apply with the following exceptions:

1. A 32-card deck is used, with all the twos, threes, fours, fives, and sixes stripped out.

2. In addition to the melds of Two-Handed Bezique, there is this special: ace–king–queen–jack–ten of any no-trump suit. Value: 120 points.

3. The queen of spades and jack of diamonds are called *binage*. There is no double binage, of course.

4. A card used in one meld may not be used to help form any other meld.

5. The values of cards taken in tricks are:

Aces	11 points
Tens	10 points
Kings	4 points
Queens	3 points
Jacks	2 points

Points are counted when play is over. Each player scores cards taken in tricks. Game is 500 points. As in Two-Handed Pinochle, players keep a running record of their melds.

When a player believes he has scored 500

(or more) points he announces it. If the count verifies his claim he is the winner even if the other player has more points. If the count is less than 500, the opponent wins even though he has the lesser score. If neither player calls out and if both players are found to have scores of 500 or more after a hand has been completed, the game is continued and 600 points is game. If only one player at the end of a hand is found to have scored 500 or more points, he is the winner.

Polish Bezique

This game is played exactly the same as Two-Handed Bezique except that the winner of a trick takes any picture cards it contains and any ten of trumps and places these cards face up but apart from any of his melds. He may employ these cards to form separate melds, combining with them any cards in his hand or won in tricks thereafter. But they may not be played to tricks again and may not be picked up for play after the stock is exhausted.

Three-Handed Bezique

A three-handed game using a 96-card deck, made from three standard 52-card decks from which the twos, threes, fours, fives, and sixes have been stripped out. First deal is decided by cutting high card. The dealer, starting with the player to his left, deals each player eight cards as in the two-handed game, the twenty-fifth card is turned for trump, and the rest of the undealt cards are placed face down on the table to form the stock.

The turn to play begins with the player at the dealer's left and goes clockwise. A trick consists of three cards, one from each player. Before the stock is exhausted, a player may or may not follow suit, as he pleases. After the stock is exhausted, a player must follow suit if he is able to and must trump if he

cannot follow suit when a nontrump lead is made. Winner of a trick leads to the next.

In addition to the melds used in the two-handed game, there is also a single meld of triple bezique which is valued at 1,500 points. Each player scores for himself. Game is either 2,000 or 2,500 points.

Four-Handed Bezique

The 128-card deck used in this four-player variation is made up of four standard 52-card decks with all the twos, threes, fours, fives, and sixes stripped out. The rules for Two-Handed Bezique apply with the following exceptions:

1. Starting with the leader (player to the dealer's left) and dealing clockwise, dealer gives each player eight cards as in the two-handed game, and the thirty-third card is turned face up on the table for trump. The turn to play begins with the leader and goes to the left. A trick consists of four played cards, one by each player, and the rules governing play are as in the three-handed game. If two play against two as partners, each team scores as a side.

2. Only the player who wins a trick may lay down a meld, and only one meld is permitted at each turn of play. However, a player may lay down as many melds as possible although he may score for only one meld at each turn of play. A player is permitted to lay down a meld by combining one or more cards from his hand to a previous meld put down by his partner.

3. Game is 2,000 points. A triple bezique (three queens of spades and three jacks of diamonds) counts 1,500 points. If a player melds a quadruple bezique (all four beziques —four queens of spades and four jacks of diamonds), it counts only 1,500 points, the same as a triple bezique.

4. Irregularities are handled as in three- and four-handed Pinochle.

RUBICON BEZIQUE

Rubicon Bezique is, today, probably the most played game of the Bezique family.

Requirements. A two-player game played with a deck of 128 cards made up by stripping the twos, threes, fours, fives, and sixes from four standard 52-card decks.

The Deal. The dealer deals the nondealer and then himself nine cards, one at a time alternately. The rest of the undealt cards are placed face down on the table, forming the stock. The winner of the previous hand deals the next hand.

The Play. The nondealer makes the opening play after drawing one card from the stock. The hand is played out in tricks, the same as in Two-Handed Pinochle (page 172) until the stock is exhausted. The second player to a trick need not follow suit; he may play any card. Play begins without a trump suit. But when the first marriage or sequence is melded, its suit becomes trumps until the hand is ended.

A trick is won by the higher trump or by the higher card of the suit led. If identical cards are played, the one led takes the trick. The winner of a trick leads to the next, but must first draw the top card of the stock and his opponent takes the next card, so that the cards belonging to each player remain at nine cards each until the stock is exhausted. Cards won in tricks prior to trump being named have no scoring value.

A meld in Rubicon Bezique is the same as a meld in Pinochle: a group of cards that score points when legally laid out on the table.

Scoring. In addition to the Bezique melds described in Two-Handed Bezique (page 202), there are the following:

A *backdoor* (ace, king, queen, jack, and ten of trumps) valued at 150 points.

Triple Bezique (three queens of spades and three jacks of diamonds laid down as a single meld). Value: 1,500 points.

Quadruple Bezique (four queens of spades and four jacks of diamonds laid down as a single meld). Value: 4,500 points.

Carte Blanche (an originally dealt hand that contains no picture cards—ace, king, queen, jack). Value: 50 points. This hand must be shown to the opponent. Also, each time thereafter that the player fails to draw a picture card he scores another 50 points, and this continues until he draws a picture card. There is a big difference in the method of scoring from that of Two-Handed Bezique.

A player is permitted to break up a meld (play a card) by playing one or more cards from it and then adding one or more cards to this same partial meld to complete it and score again. It is usual for players not to gather tricks they have won which do not contain point-valued cards (aces or tens, called brisques) until a brisque is played, then the winner of that trick takes in all the previously played cards (upcards). If a player fails to take in a trick containing a brisque, his opponent, if he next wins a trick containing brisques, may also take in those overlooked by his opponent, scoring them for himself.

The Game. Each deal constitutes a game, the player with the higher score wins and scores the difference between both scores. In addition, the winner receives a game bonus of 500 points. All fractions of 100 points are disregarded, unless they are necessary to determine the winner of the game. Brisques are not usually counted in the scoring of a game unless a player can prevent himself from being rubiconed by counting brisques. If one player counts brisques, the other may also do so. The only score counted from the play, usually, is 50 points for last trick. But brisques are also counted when there is a question of winning the game or escaping rubicon.

If the losing player has scored fewer than 1,000 points, he is said to be *rubiconed,* and gets no score at all. The winner receives a bonus of 1,000 points instead of 500; plus all his own points, plus all the loser's points, plus 320 points for all brisques.

Six-Deck or Chinese Bezique

This two-handed variation was one of the most popular games of the fashionable in the early 1900's before the advent of Bridge. It is played like Rubicon Bezique except for the following rules:

1. A 192-card deck is used, made up from six standard 52-card decks from which the twos, threes, fours, fives, and sixes have been stripped out.

2. The dealer, starting with the nondealer, deals 12 cards to each, one at a time alternately.

3. In addition to the melds used in Rubicon Bezique, the following are also used:

	Points
4 aces of trump	1,000
4 tens of trump	900
4 kings of trump	800
4 queens of trump	600
4 jacks of trump	400
Carte blanche	250
For winning last trick	250

4. Brisques do not enter into the scoring, and all played cards (upcards) accumulate in the center of the table.

5. It is permissible for a player to count

the cards remaining in the stock and to look through the upcards, by spreading the cards a bit.

6. Each played hand constitutes a game. Game bonus to the winner of the hand is 1,000 points. If the loser's total score is less than 3,000 points, he is rubiconed and the winner scores the total points of both players.

7. As in Rubicon Bezique, fractions of 100 points are ignored except to determine the winner of the game.

Six-Deck Bezique Variation

After the cards have been shuffled and cut, the dealer cuts off part of the 192-card packet. If the portion contains exactly 24 cards, dealer scores 250 points. But before the cards are dealt, the nondealer estimates the number of cards cut off the top of the deck. If his estimate is correct he scores 150 points. The remainder of the cards are turned face down on the table and form the stock.

Eight-Deck Bezique

Eight-Deck Bezique is played exactly the same as Six-Deck Bezique except for the following:

1. A 256-card deck is used, which is made up by stripping out all the twos, threes, fours, fives, and sixes from eight standard 52-card decks.

2. Each player starting with the dealer is dealt 15 cards alternately.

3. Scoring:

	Points
Single bezique	50
Double bezique	500
Triple bezique	1,500
Quadruple bezique	4,500
Quintuple bezique	9,000
5 aces of trumps	2,000
5 tens of trumps	1,800
5 kings of trumps	1,600
5 queens of trumps	1,200
5 jacks of trumps	800

If the loser fails to score 5,000 points he is rubiconed.

Strategy of Bezique

The strategy of Bezique is dominated by the importance of meld. For this reason, every effort must be made to save cards that may be turned into declarations. Tens, nines, eights, and sevens have little value in the matter of meld. By far the most important cards are the queens and jacks that make bezique. Never, so long as any hope remains of making the double bezique, does one play a queen of spades or jack of diamonds. Also, if a four of a kind is scored, make haste to play one of them so that the same declaration can be scored again.

Leads should be made to force the opponent to give up cards which might form declarations in the future if retained.

TWO-HANDED SIXTY-SIX

Sixty-Six is one of the simplest forms of Bezique and is still popular in its homeland of Germany.

Requirements

1. Two players.

2. Twenty-four cards (ace, king, queen, jack, ten, and nine of each suit). (In Germany, the 48-card Pinochle deck was called a *double Sixty-Six pack.*) Rank of cards: ace (high), ten, king, queen, jack, nine (low).

The Deal. After being shuffled and cut, the dealer gives six cards to each, three at a time, beginning with his opponent. The thirteenth card is turned up for trump and laid beside the stock (undealt cards).

The Play of the Hand. The nondealer leads any card. It is not necessary to follow suit if

the player chooses not to, but he may trump at will. He need not follow suit even if a trump is led. A trick is won by the highest card of the suit led. But if a trick contains one trump, that trump wins. If a trick contains two trumps, the higher trump wins. Winner of a trick places it face down in front of him. Then he draws the top card of the stock (his opponent the next card) and leads for the next trick.

In his turn to play and provided that he has won at least one trick, the player holding the nine of trumps may exchange it for a turned-up trump card. But, if the nine of trumps happens to be the last card of the stock, the player drawing it may not exchange. His opponent gets the trump card.

In his turn to lead, and provided that he has taken at least one trick, a player having a marriage (a king and queen of the same suit) may meld it by showing the two cards and leading one of them. The nondealer may declare a marriage on his first lead, and score it when he wins a trick. Marriages may be announced only in leading them unless a player by showing a marriage makes his score 66 or more.

When the stock is exhausted, a player must follow suit if able, but he is still not required to win a trick. A player may trump if holding none of the suit led, or he may play some other card. Marriages may still be scored during this play.

Closing. A unique phase of Sixty-Six is the process known as *closing*. Either player, when it is his turn to lead, may announce that the game is closed before leading. (A player may close before or after drawing a card, but if he draws a card and then closes, his opponent may also draw a card.) This is done by turning down the trump card, and thereafter no cards will be drawn from the stock and play continues in the same manner as for an exhausted pack, except that the last trick does not score 10.

Object of Play. To score 66 points as follows:

Marriage in trumps (king and queen announced)	40 points
Marriage in any other suit (king and queen announced)	20 points
Each ace (taken in on tricks)	11 points
Each ten (taken in on tricks)	10 points
Each king (taken in on tricks)	4 points
Each queen (taken in on tricks)	3 points
Each jack (taken in on tricks)	2 points
Winning last trick	10 points

The player who first reaches 66 scores 1 game point. If he reaches 66 before his opponent gets 33 (*schneider*) he scores 2 game points; if before his opponent gets a trick (*schwarz*), he scores 3 game points. If neither player scores 66, or each has scored 66 or more without announcing it, neither scores in that hand, 1 game point being added to the score of the winner of the next hand.

If a player closing gets 66 or more, he scores the same as if the game had been played out. If he fails, his opponent scores 2 points. Should a player close before his opponent has taken a trick, and fails to score 66,

his opponent scores 3 points.

If either player announces, during play, that his score is 66 or more, the play immediately stops and the hand is closed.

End of Game. The game ends when one player obtains seven game points.

Additional Rules. Irregularities are handled in the same manner as in Pinochle (see page 174).

Three-Handed Sixty-Six

This game is played the same as Two-Handed Sixty-Six except that the dealer takes no cards, and scores as many game points as are won on his deal by either of the players. If neither scores 66, or both score 66 or more but fail to announce it, dealer scores 1 game point and active players nothing. Game is 7 game points. A dealer cannot score enough to win game. His seventh point must be won when he is an active player.

Four-Handed Sixty-Six

This is a partnership game, but the basic rules for Two-Handed Sixty-Six are enforced except for the following:

1. Use the 32-card deck (ace, ten, king, queen, jack, nine, eight, and seven of each suit).

2. Eight cards are dealt to each player— three, then two, then three, in rotation to the left, beginning with the player next to the dealer. Last card is turned for trump and belongs to dealer.

3. The player on the dealer's left leads, and each succeeding player in turn must not only follow suit, but must win the trick if possible. Having no card of the suit led, a player must trump or overtrump if he can.

4. Scoring is the same as in the two-hand game, except that there are no marriages. A side counting 66 or more, but less than 100, scores 1 game point; over 100 and less than 130, 2 points; if it takes every trick (130), 3 points. If each side has 65, neither scores and 1 game point is added to the score of the winners of next hand.

5. Game is 7 game points. In some localities the ten of trumps counts 1 game point for the side winning it in addition to its value as a scoring card. If one side has 6 game points and wins the ten of trumps on a trick, that side scores game immediately.

Gaigel

Gaigel is the name given to the most interesting form of partnership Sixty-Six.

Requirements

1. Two to eight players can play, each scoring for himself, but the best game is four-handed, two partners against the other two.

2. A 48-card deck is used, made up by combining two standard 52-card decks and stripping out nines, eights, sixes, fives, fours, threes, and deuces.

3. Rank of cards: ace (high), ten, king, queen, jack, seven (low). If two cards of the same denomination and suit are led to a trick, the one played first is considered to be of higher rank.

The Deal. Each player receives a hand of five cards. These are dealt three at a time in a clockwise rotation, then two at a time, or first two, then three. The next card is turned up and determines the trump suit for the deal. The remainder of the deck—the stock—is placed face down on the table for the players to draw from.

Object of Play. To score 101 points as follows:

Common marriage	
(king and queen of plain suit)	20 points
Double common marriage	
(2 kings and 2 queens of plain suit)	40 points
Royal marriage	
(king and queen of trumps)	40 points
Double royal marriage	
(2 kings and 2 queens of trumps)	80 points
Any five sevens (drawn or	
held by one player at one time)	101 points
Each ace (taken in on tricks)	11 points
Each ten (taken in on tricks)	10 points
Each king (taken in on tricks)	4 points
Each queen (taken in on tricks)	3 points
Each jack (taken in on tricks)	2 points

The Play. The player to the left of the dealer leads any card. In clockwise rotation, each player plays any card, not being required to follow suit or trump. The highest card of the suit led wins, unless the trick is trumped, in which case the highest trump wins. Partners keep their tricks won face down in a common pile in front of one player or the other.

After winning a trick and before drawing from the stock, the player who won may declare one marriage, exposing it so that all the players can see it. Two single marriages cannot be declared in the same suit, even at different times. The second marriage, after one has been scored, counts nothing. After declaring a marriage or not, the winner of the trick takes the top card from the stock, and each player in a clockwise rotation takes one. The winner of each trick leads to the next trick.

After he takes a trick and before drawing from the stock, a player holding a seven of trumps—*dix*—may exchange it for the turned-up trump card and score 10 points for it. The holder of the other seven of trumps then also scores 10 for it by merely showing it after he has taken a trick.

When all the cards have been drawn from stock, all melding ceases, and thereafter each player must not only follow suit, but must try to win the trick in the suit led if possible. If he cannot follow suit, the player must trump; and if the trick has been trumped, he must beat the trump, if possible. Failure to do either of these forfeits the game to the opponents. If unable to follow suit or trump, a player must discard.

Scoring. The players must keep a mental count of points made by cards taken in tricks and are not permitted to record them in any way. They enter the melds on the score sheet as they make them, however. When a player believes his side has reached 101 points, he must cease playing and knock on the table, signifying that he has won the game. If incorrect, he forfeits the game. Before game is claimed, no player is allowed to examine any trick except the last trick taken, under penalty of forfeiting the game to the opponents. If a claim of game is questioned by an opponent, the disputed player's or side's tricks are turned over at once, and the points counted. In counting for going out, marriages take precedence over all other scores.

A *gaigel,* or bonus, is for double game (2 game points) and is worth 202 points. It may be scored in one of the following ways:

1. Scoring 101 before opponents have won a trick.

2. Holding five sevens in one hand, before opponents have won a trick.

3. When an opponent claims to be out, and is proved to be in error.

4. When the opponents play again, after reaching 101.

5. When the opponents refuse the privilege

of counting the current trick again, or mix the cards before the count is settled.

6. When an error is claimed and the claim is proved to be baseless, the disputing players score a gaigel for their opponents.

End of Game. The game ends when one partnership scores 7 game points.

Auction Sixty-Six

In this game of Sixty-Six, trump is bid for—not turned.

Requirements

1. Four players, two against two as partners.

2. Either a 24-card deck or 32-card deck, which includes eights and sevens, may be used.

The Deal. The entire deck is dealt out evenly. Each player, beginning with the one at dealer's left, gets a six-card hand dealt three at a time with the 24-card deck. With the 32-card deck, each player receives a hand of eight cards, dealt three, then two, then three.

Bidding. The player at dealer's left may make the first bid or pass. He bids the number of points his side will take at a minimum if he may name the trump suit. He does not mention the suit. He must bid a minimum of 60 but may start as high as he likes. Each player in turn to the left then bids or passes. Each succeeding bid must be higher than the preceding one and must raise by 6 or any multiple of 6. However, some play that a bid must be raised by 10 or any multiple of 10. The bidding continues around the table until no player will raise a bid. A player who passed during his first turn may reenter the bidding only if partner has bid. Highest pos-

sible bid is 130, known as the *grand bid*.

A hand *cannot* be passed out. If the first three players pass, the dealer must become the bidder on the hand, though he need not make any actual bid. He simply names the trump for the deal and play begins.

The Play. The successful bidder names the suit to be trump for the deal and leads any card to the first trick. Each player in turn to the left then plays a card to complete the trick. A player must follow suit if able to. Otherwise he may play a trump or any other card.

The highest card of a led suit wins the trick. But in a trick containing one trump, that trump is the winning card. If a trick contains more than one trump, the highest trump wins. A player need not go over a trump if he does not choose to. The winner of a trick leads to the next. Partners keep their tricks together, face down in one pile.

Scoring. After all tricks have been played, both sides total their points won in play according to the schedule used in Two-Handed Sixty-Six. If the successful bidder's side has made at least the number of points it bid, it scores for all the points that it made in play. If the successful bidder's side fails to fulfill the bid, opposing side scores whatever it has won in play *plus* the amount of the bid by the unsuccessful side. The latter scores nothing.

If the bid is 130, the side fulfilling it scores 260. But if it fails, opposing side scores 260. If the dealer has named the trump after the others passed, each side simply scores for what it makes. There is no contract to fulfill. First side to reach 666 points wins.

Additional Rules. Additional rules are the same as in Partnership Auction Pinochle (page 179).

TWO-HANDED PIQUET

As we stated in Chapter 9, a few card historians claim that the Bezique family beginnings can be traced to Piquet. This card game was introduced in France in the middle of the fifteenth century. Its French pronunciation is *pee-kay,* but English-speaking card players usually refer to it as *picket.*

Requirements

1. Two players.

2. A Piquet or 32-card deck; two packs are usually used alternately.

3. Rank of cards: ace (high), king, queen, jack, ten, nine, eight, seven.

The Deal. Each player receives 12 cards, dealt two at a time. The remaining eight cards are spread face down on the table, forming the stock. (In former times, the first five cards of the stock were distinctly separated from the last three, but now that formality is usually omitted.)

Discarding. After picking up his hand, nondealer must discard at least one card, and may discard up to five, then take an equal number of cards from the top of the stock. If he leaves any of the first five, he may look at them without showing them to dealer.

Dealer is entitled to take all of the stock left by nondealer, after first discarding an equal number of cards. Dealer is not obliged to take any cards from the stock. If he chooses to leave any or all, he may decide whether they shall be turned up to view of both players or set aside unseen.

The object in discarding is to form certain scoring combinations as follows:

Carte Blanche: A hand with no king, queen, or jack is *carte blanche.* If dealt such a hand, nondealer may expose it before his discard and score 10 points. If dealer picks up carte blanche, he may wait until nondealer has discarded, then show it and score 10. (English rules require either player holding carte blanche to announce it before nondealer discards.)

Point: The greatest number of cards in any suit scores for *point* as many cards as are held. As between two holdings of the same length, the one with the greater pip or index total scores, counting ace 11, king, queen, jack and ten at 10 each; lower cards at pip value. If the players tie in point, neither scores.

Sequence: A *sequence* of three cards in the same suit (*tierce*) counts 3; a sequence of four (*quart*) counts 4; a sequence of five or more counts 10 plus the number of cards. Only the player holding the highest sequence can score in this class; having established that he has the best sequence, he may score for all additional sequences he holds. Any sequence is higher than one of lesser length; as between sequences of equal length, the one headed by the higher card scores. If the players tie for best sequence, neither scores in this class.

Sets: A *set* comprises three or four cards of the same rank, higher than nine. The player holding the highest set scores it and any additional sets he may hold. Four of a kind, counting 14, are higher than three of a kind, counting 3. As between sets of an equal number of cards, the set higher in rank of cards scores.

Declaring. The discarding completed, the players declare their holdings to determine the scores for point, sequence, and sets, in that order. But the player who does *not* score in a class need give no more information than is necessary to establish the other's superiority. The declaration therefore proceeds as

in the following example (nondealer being obliged to make the first declaration for each class):

Nondealer. Four. (Naming length of suit for point.)

Dealer. How much. (With five or more cards of a suit, dealer would state "Five," etc. With no suit as long as four, dealer would say "Good.")

Nondealer. Thirty-seven.

Dealer. Not good. Thirty-nine. (Dealer scores 4 for point.)

Nondealer. Sequence of three. (Or tierce.)

Dealer. How high? (He also holds a tierce.)

Nondealer. Ace.

Dealer. Good.

Nondealer. And another tierce. I score 6. I have three kings.

Dealer. Not good. 14 tens. I start with 18.

Nondealer. I start with 6.

On demand a player must show any combinations of cards for which he has scored. Proving of scores is usually unnecessary, the player being able to infer the suit of his opponent's point, etc.

A player is not obliged to declare any combination. *Example:* Nondealer may say "No set" although he holds three queens, believing that dealer holds three kings. But if a player thus sinks a combination, he may not later declare it when he finds that it would have been high.

The Play of the Hand. The declaring completed, nondealer leads to the first trick. The other must follow suit to a lead when able. A trick is won by the higher card of the suit led. The winner of a trick leads to the next.

The player scores 1 point for each card he leads higher than a nine, and 1 point each time he wins his opponent's lead with a card higher than a nine. The winner of the last trick gets one extra point for it. (In America it is usual to count one for each lead and one for each trick taken, regardless of the rank of cards.) Each, as he plays his card, announces his cumulative score up to that juncture, including the initial count for combinations. To continue the preceding example: Nondealer scored 6 for two sequences. On his first lead (an ace) he announces "Seven." Dealer scored 18 for combinations; on winning his first trick (with a king) he says "Nineteen."

Tricks. The winner of seven or more of the twelve tricks scores 10. If the tricks are split six to six, neither scores. If one player wins all twelve tricks, he scores 40 for *capot* (nothing extra for majority or for the last trick).

A player who reaches a score of 30 or more in declarations, before his opponent scores anything and before a card is led, adds 60 for *repique*. A player who reaches 30 or more in declarations and play, before his opponent scores anything, adds 30 for *pique*.

Once the play is completed, the total points won by each player during the hand are recorded on paper.

The Game. There are three variants as to how the winner of the game is decided, as follows:

1. *Piquet au Cent.* The player who first obtains a total score of 100 or more is declared the winner. Settlement is made on the difference of the final scores. (Double the amount is usually given if the loser fails to reach 50 points.) The last deal of a game is played out; there is no "counting out" during the play.

2. *Rubicon Piquet.* A game comprises six deals. The player with the higher cumulative score at the end of the game wins the difference of the totals plus 100 for game, provided that the loser reached at least 100. If the loser failed to reach 100, he is said to be rubiconed, and the winner scores the sum of the totals plus 100 for game. (The loser is rubiconed even if the winner, also, failed to reach 100.)

3. *Club Piquet.* The game is four deals, the scores of the first and last being doubled.

Additional Rules

New Deal (by the same dealer). A compulsory new deal is required if a card is exposed in dealing, or if either player receives the wrong number of cards.

Erroneous Discard. If a player discards more or fewer cards than he intended, he may not change his discard after touching the stock. If there are not enough cards available to him in the stock to replace all his discards, he must play with a short hand.

Erroneous Draw from Stock. If a player draws too many cards from the stock, he may replace the excess if he has not looked at them and if the correct order of the cards is determinable; otherwise the following rules apply. If nondealer draws more than five cards from the stock he loses the game. If he draws fewer than five he should so announce; if he fails to do so, the dealer is entitled to draw all that are left, even should dealer discard three and then touch the stock. If dealer draws any card from the stock before nondealer has made his draw, dealer loses the game.

Concession. Once a player concedes an adverse combination to be good, he may not claim a superior combination.

False Declaration. If a player claims and scores for a combination that he does not hold, he may announce his error before playing a card, and the scoring in that class is corrected. Should a player play a card before announcing his error, he may not score at all in that deal.

Piquet Normand (Three-Handed Piquet)

This game is played in the same manner as Two-Handed Piquet, except for the following:

1. Each player receives ten cards in the deal. The remaining two are placed face down on the table as a widow. Dealer may exchange two of his cards for the widow, but no other player may do so.

2. Player at dealer's left makes the first announcement, and each player in turn also announces. He may also score a bonus of 90 for repique if he reaches 20 in announcements before the others have made anything. He gets 60 for pique if reaching 20 before both opponents have any score. Majority of tricks scores 10 points; but if all tie, each gets 5 points.

3. If one player scores capot, he gets 40 points. If two players take all the tricks together, each scores 20 points. A pot (pool) formed by equal antes for each hand is won by the player just to reach a total 100 points. Or the players settle up by each lower score paying to the winner of 100 points the difference of their scores.

Piquet Voleur (Four-Handed Piquet)

This variant is for four players, two playing as partners against the other two. It is played the same way as Two-Handed Piquet, except for the following:

1. The whole pack is dealt out, each player receiving eight cards.

2. The player to the left of the dealer declares whatever he holds in combinations. Then he leads a card to the first trick. If the player at his left has no better combinations,

he plays to the trick and says nothing. If he has any better combinations, he announces them. Play proceeds in this manner around the table to the left. If a player's partner has announced a combination that is good, the player may also score for any combination he holds of the same kind.

3. The side which scores 20 before tricks are played while opponents have nothing scores a 90-point bonus for repique. If a side scores 20 in announcements and play before the other side has scored a point, it gets a bonus of 60 points for pique. In this game, carte blanche counts toward pique or repique, so that a double carte blanche between partners would be a certain repique. Only one partner of a side may score for point made in leading to a trick.

4. A game may be scored by any of the three methods used in Two-Handed Piquet.

Piquet à Ecrire

Any number from three to seven may play this game, which is also known as Round-

Table Piquet. The game is played like Two-Handed Piquet, except for the following:

1. Each player plays a hand first with the player at his right and then with the player at his left.

2. The deal passes to the left, and after each player has played as described above, the players settle up. Each lower score pays to the holder of the higher score the difference of their scores.

Strategy of Piquet

The basic strategy of Piquet, as in most card games where all or most of cards are in play, is:

1. Establish a long, strong suit by driving out your opponent's stoppers.

2. If a long suit can't be established, lose the lead only after making your opponent play his top cards, rather than low stoppers.

3. Watch the fall of the cards.

In Piquet, a great deal of information about the play of the hand can be learned in the declaring portions of the game.

IMPERIAL

Imperial is often called *Piquet with a Trump.*
Requirements
1. Two players.
2. A Piquet or 32-card deck.
3. The cards rank: king, queen, jack, ace, ten, nine, eight, seven. The king, queen, jack, ace, and seven of trumps are honors.
4. For scoring purposes, a common pool or pot of 12 white chips and nine reds is placed in the center of the table. A red chip is worth six whites.

The Deal. The cards are dealt 12 to each player in batches of three at a time. The twenty-fifth card is turned to decide trump for the deal. There is no discarding and drawing.

Declaring. Announcing is as in Two-Handed Piquet, except that nondealer scores for all equals. That is, nondealer commences by showing any *imperials* he may have. Imperials are the following: carte blanche; a sequence of king–queen–jack–ace, in one suit; four kings, four queens, four jacks, four aces, or four sevens. Sets of three of a kind do not count. Dealer may use the turned trump to complete a sequence or four of a

kind, but otherwise that card is not used in play. He next announces his point, as below; then makes the opening lead.

Dealer, before playing to the lead, shows his own imperials, shows a superior point, or concedes that nondealer's point is good. In the last case, nondealer must show his point, the rule being that every combination scored must be exposed to inspection by opponent. (Point is the numerical total of the best suit in the player's hand, counting the ace 11, each face card 10, lower cards their index value. *Example:* king, jack, ace, eight, seven has a "point of forty-six.") This order of announcing or declaring must be observed strictly. A player loses claim to his imperials if he refers to point first, or loses the point if he fails to announce it before leading or playing to the opening lead.

The Play. The nondealer may lead any card for the opening lead. The second player must follow a lead with a higher card in the same suit or he must play trump if out of the suit, that is, he must try to win the trick. Points in play are made by winning a trick containing a trump honor or honors. Cards are not gathered in tricks; each puts his own cards face up before himself, and may examine them at any time. The winner of a trick leads to the next.

Scoring. For every imperial that a player scores during the declaring phase, he takes a red chip from the common pool. The player with the highest point takes one white chip from this pool. Also, if the turned-up trump is an honor, the dealer takes one white chip.

During play, for catching the jack and ace of trump by leading the king and queen, a player takes a red chip. For each honor won in a trick the winner takes a white chip. If one player wins more tricks than his opponent, he takes a white chip for each trick in excess of opponent's. Capot entitles a player to take two red chips.

When a player has taken six white chips, he returns them to the pool and takes one red chip. Whenever a player takes a red chip in exchange for whites or in direct payment of a capot, etc., his opponent must put back into the pool all the white chips—not the red ones—he has at the moment.

The first player to win five red chips wins a game, and the hand in progress is abandoned.

KLOB OR KLABERJASS

Klaberjass, known also as Kolobiosh, Kabababrious, Kalabriasz, Clobberyash, Kob, Klab, Club, Clabber, Clobber, Indiana Clobber, and Clubby, is one of the best of all two-handed games. Prior to the advent of Gin Rummy, Klaberjass was the most popular two-handed money game among the gentry who liked to put their money up to prove their skill at the game. It is the famous two-hand game played by the Broadway characters in Damon Runyon's stories. Its origin has been variously claimed by the Dutch, Swiss, French, and Hungarians, but the fact that the game first became popular in Jewish goulash joints (card rooms) causes me to lean toward the Hungarian claim.

Requirements

1. Two players.

2. A 32-card deck is used, made up by removing all cards ranked below seven. In other words, the 32-card deck is comprised of aces, kings, queens, jacks, tens, nines, eights, and sevens.

Rank of Cards. In a trump suit the cards rank as follows: jack (high), nine, ace, ten, king, queen, eight, seven (low). The jack of trumps is known as the *boss* or *jass* (pronounced "yass"). The nine of trumps is known as *menel*. The seven of trumps is known as *dix* (pronounced *"deece"*). In a nontrump suit they rank as follows: ace (high), ten, king, queen, jack, nine, eight, seven (low).

The Shuffle, Cut, and Deal. Players cut for the deal and low card deals the first hand. Thereafter, the deal alternates. The dealer shuffles the cards and offers them to his opponent to cut. The dealer deals three cards at a time to his opponent, then three cards to himself. Then three more cards to his opponent and three more cards to himself. Each player now holds six cards.

The next card (thirteenth) is placed face up on the table and the remaining stock (undealt cards) is placed partially over this face-up card in such a manner that the face-up can be seen and identified at all times.

Object of the Game. To try and score 300 or 500 points, as may be agreed, before your opponent, which takes into consideration the following factors:

1. To try to establish one's best suit as trump.

2. To meld certain combinations which have the highest-counting values.

3. To score points by taking tricks which contain certain cards possessing point value.

Making the Trump. The nondealer has the first say in naming trump. He may accept the suit of the turned-up card as trump by merely calling the name of the suit of the turned-up card and saying that specific suit is trump, or he may pass. If he accepts the suit of the turned-up card, it becomes trump and the deal continues. If the nondealer refuses the suit of the upturned card as trump, he says "Pass." Then it is the dealer's turn to accept the suit of the turned-up card as trump, and the deal continues. If he also passes, the hands are considered void and thrown in, and the cards are shuffled and cut and two new hands are dealt.

Instead of committing himself on the suit of the upturned card or passing, a player may say *"Schmeiss"* (pronounced "shmice") or *"Throw them in."* This is an offer to throw in the hands and have a new shuffle, cut, and deal. If the player's opponent agrees, both hands are thrown in and a new deal is effected. But if the opponent says "No," which means he has refused the offer, the player who called "Schmeiss" or "Throw them in" must name the trump suit.

If schmeiss was called in the first round, the suit of the turned-up card is trump. If it was called in the second round, the caller of schmeiss may name the suit he desires as trump.

The Continued Deal. After trump has been named, the dealer deals to each player three additional cards from the top of the stock (the undealt cards) beginning with three to the nondealer and then three to himself. He then indicates the end of the deal by taking the bottom card of the remaining stock and placing it face up on the stock. However, this card does not enter into play, nor do any of the cards in the remaining stock. Before play begins, the holder of the dix (seven of trumps) may exchange it for the card originally turned up for trump. The exchange must be made before players declare their melds prior to the play of the hand.

Melds. Players compare matched sets called *melds,* or *lays,* for the right to score them. The melds may be a sequence of three, four, or more cards in the same suit. For example, the seven, eight, and nine of hearts; or the ace, king, queen, and jack of spades. It is possible to meld eight cards in a single sequence. A three-card meld is valued at 20 points; a meld of four cards or more is valued at 50 points.

How to Score Melds. Only one player may score a meld or melds. The method of establishing which player scores his meld or melds is as follows: The nondealer has the first say. If the nondealer possesses a meld he announces its point value. For example, if he holds a three-card meld, he calls "Twenty"; if he holds a meld of four or more cards he calls "Fifty." A player holding a meld of five or more cards may show only four cards of the meld. The extra cards carry no additional value or significance with reference to scoring or deciding the highest meld. If the dealer has a meld of a lower point value or no meld at all, he replies "Good." If the dealer has a meld of a higher point value, he replies "No good," shows his meld, and scores his meld. If the dealer has a meld of equal point value, he replies "Same" or "How high?" In this instance the nondealer names the highest-

ranking card of his meld. The dealer then replies "Same," "Good," or "No good," depending on what the highest-ranking card of his own meld happens to be.

If players hold melds that are equal in point value and highest-ranking card, neither of which is in trump, the meld belonging to the nondealer is considered the best and is scored. The dealer's meld is considered void. As between melds of the same point value and the same highest-ranking card, a trump meld is considered the best. If nondealer has no melds, he says "No melds," and the dealer then calls out the point value of any meld or melds he wishes to score points for.

The player who claims the best meld receives credit for its point value after showing the meld to his opponent, and the player holding the best meld may also receive credit for other melds he shows. The opponent who held the inferior meld scores nothing, but he does not have to show his meld; nor is a player required to show a meld he does not wish to receive point credits for.

Following is an example of meld comparing and the conversation involved:

Nondealer holds a meld comprised of ace–king–queen–jack in one suit and queen–jack–ten in another suit. The dealer holds king–queen–jack–ten in a third suit.

The *nondealer* calls "Fifty" (the point value of his ranking four-card meld).

The *dealer* replies "How high?" (since he has a meld of equal point value).

Nondealer responds "Ace high."

Dealer acknowledges "Good" (since his highest-ranking card is a king).

Nondealer shows his 50-point meld and his 20-point meld, and scores 70 points.

Dealer does not show his meld because it is valueless and cannot be scored.

There is another meld which carries a value of 20 points. It is the king and queen of trumps and is known as *bella.* It scores automatically and does not have to be announced until the game is completed and the cards taken in by each player are being counted for scoring.

The Play of the Hand. Regardless of who made the trump, the nondealer plays first. He may play any card he chooses. The dealer then plays a card. If the lead card is of a nontrump suit and the dealer has no cards of the led suit, he must play a trump if he is able to do so. Otherwise, he may play any card he desires. If the lead card is a trump, the dealer must play a higher trump if he is able to do so, but he must follow suit in any case.

A trick is comprised of two cards and is won by the highest-ranking card of the suit led. But if a trick involves one trump card, that trump card wins. If a trick involves two trumps, the highest-ranking trump wins. The winner of the trick takes the two cards and places them face down in front of himself. The winner of a trick leads the first card of the next trick, and so it goes until all nine tricks have been played and the hand is ended.

When all the nine tricks have been played, each player takes point credit for the valuable cards among his gathered cards. The point values of the valuable cards are as follows: jack of trumps, 20 points; nine of trumps (menel), 14 points; ace of any suit, 11 points; ten of any suit, 10 points; king of any suit, 4 points; queen of any suit, 3 points; jack of any suit except trump, 2 points.

Winner of the last trick is credited with 10 points more on his score. There is a total of 162 points in the game. This includes the 10 points for the last trick. However, because only 18 of the 32 cards are in play, the greatest possible total of points scored in any single hand is 156.

Scoring the Hand. If the total score of the bidder (the player who made trump), which includes melds and points scored in tricks won, is greater than the nonbidder's (opponent's), each player receives credit for his own score. But if the nonbidder's total score is equal to or greater than the bidder's score, the nonbidder receives credit for his own scored points plus the total points the bidder scored. These are comprised of points scored in tricks and melds, including bella, be it announced or unannounced. The bidder in this instance scores zero and is said to have *gone bate.*

End of Game or Match. The first player to reach 300 (or 500) points wins the game. If both players score 300 points or more in the same deal, the player with the highest score is declared the winner.

Additional Rules

Misdeals. The following will determine whether or not a misdeal has occurred:

1. If the dealer or nondealer turns up a card belonging to his opponent, that deal is void, a misdeal is declared, and the same dealer deals again. If the dealer or nondealer turns up a card or cards belonging to himself, the opponent may let the deal stand or call for a new deal.

2. If either player is dealt too many cards and this is discovered before a trick is played, opponent removes the excess cards from player's hand and has the right to look at them before they are placed at the bottom of the undealt cards. If a player is dealt too few cards and this is discovered before a trick is played, the deficiency is made up from the top of the deck.

Reneges. If, when play for tricks is in progress, (a) a player fails to follow the suit of the card led when he can, (b) fails to trump when he has a trump and does not have any cards of suit led, or (c) trump being led, he fails to play a higher trump when he can, then his opponent can call attention to this failure, and, at any time during play or after the hand is completed, can claim a renege.

In each case the reneger (the player who failed to follow the rules) loses all his scored points and the opponent receives credit for the reneger's total points plus his own scored points.

Improperly Called Melds. If a player is found to have made a call that has undervalued or overvalued a meld, his opponent can call attention to this irregularity at any time during play or after the hand is completed and claim a renege. The offender loses all his scored points and his opponent receives credit for the offender's total points plus his own scored points.

Irregular Hands. If a player possesses fewer or more than the allotted nine cards and one or more tricks have been played, the player possessing the irregular hand is declared to have reneged and loses all his scored points. His opponent receives credit for the offender's total points plus his own scored points.

Leading Out of Turn. If, before a trick has been picked up by a player, it is established that a player has led out of turn, players merely pick up their cards and correct the error. If the trick has been completed and stacked with the completed tricks, the play stands and the player who won the trick makes the next lead.

Looking Through Cards Taken in Tricks. If he has played his card for the following trick, a player may look at the last trick gathered in, and this rule holds regardless of which player won the last trick.

In no other instance is it permitted to look through the gathered cards, except when looking through tricks to determine whether a player has reneged. There is no enforceable penalty for an infraction of this rule.

Three-Handed Klaberjass

The rules of Two-Handed Klaberjass apply except as follows:

1. The player at the dealer's left is dealt to first and after that the procedure for the deals is as in the two-handed game.

2. The turn to bid, meld, and play begins with the player at the dealer's left and goes in a clockwise rotation.

3. The bidder must score more than both opponents together or he is beaten or goes bate. Each player scores his own melds and points won in play, but the opponents share the bidder's points equally if he gets beaten.

Four-Handed Klaberjass

Four-Handed Klaberjass can be played in either of two ways:

1. It may be played as in the three-handed game, with all cards being dealt out and last card turned for trump leaving dealer with a hand of seven cards. The other players have eight cards each. The player holding the dix exchanges it for the turned-up card, and dealer takes the dix to complete his hand.

2. It may be played two against two as partners. The turn to deal, bid, meld, and play passes to the left, beginning with the player at dealer's left. When one player establishes the best sequence, partner may also show and score for sequences. Partners keep their tricks together and score as a side. Otherwise, the rules for Two-Handed Klaberjass apply.

Belotte

This popular two-handed game of France is almost identical with Klaberjass, except the schmeiss is called *valse* (waltz). The highest-ranking melds are four of a kind, counting 200 for four jacks and 100 for four nines, aces, tens, kings, or queens, the groups rank-

ing in that order. A five-card sequence is worth 50, a four-card sequence 40, a three-card sequence 20. The player having the highest-ranking group scores all groups in his hand; the player having the highest-ranking sequence scores all sequences in his hand. If the maker of trump does not score more points than his opponent, he loses his own points but the opponent does not score the combined totals of both players.

Darda

The rules of this game are the same as in Klaberjass with the following exceptions.

1. Two, three, or four may play; if four play, the dealer scores against the maker (the player who names the trump suit).

2. The rank of cards in trumps is queen, nine, ace, ten, king, jack, eight, seven; and the queen (not the jack as in Klaberjass) counts 20, the jack only 2. If nontrump, the suits rank as follows: ace, ten, king, queen, jack, nine, eight, seven. There is no schmeiss.

3. After trump has been named and three more cards have been dealt to each player, the undealt cards are turned face up, squared so that only the top card shows, which becomes the widow. A player may exchange the trump seven for the turned-up card (the trump eight may be exchanged if the seven was turned), then may successively take the exposed card of the widow as long as it is a trump, discarding a card from his hand each time.

4. The maker then leads. Each player announces his meld on his first play; thereafter it does not count, including trump king and queen (bella). After the first trick is completed, players with melds of the same length ask and decide which is highest.

5. *Scoring.* The maker succeeds if neither opponent has as high a score as his. If he succeeds, he scores 1 if his score is less than 100; 2 if it is 100–149; 3 if it is 150–199; 4 if it is 200 or more. Game is 10.

6. *Four of a Kind.* If four of a kind are held, there is no play; the highest four of a kind wins the hand, scoring: 4 for four queens, 3 for four nines, 2 for four aces, kings, jacks, or tens.

7. *Irregularities.* Any irregularity stops play, and every player except the offender scores 2.

Alsös

This popular Hungarian game is played exactly the same as Three-Handed Klaberjass, except that the bidder may increase his score by selecting any of the following "side" declarations:

Casa. To win the majority of points including a bella.

Csalad. To win ace, king, queen of trumps.

Tous les trois. To win jack, nine, seven of trumps.

All the Trumps. To win ace, king, queen, jack, ten, nine of trumps.

Volata. To win all nine tricks.

Bettli. To win no tricks.

Absolute. To win 82 points at a trump, 62 points at no trump.

One-hundred. To win 100 points at a trump, 80 points at no trump.

Two-hundred. To win 200 points at a trump, 180 points at no trump (but melds may be included).

Forty-four. To win all four aces.

Uhu. To win the next-to-last trick with the ace of diamonds (or if diamonds are trumps, with the ace of hearts).

Ultimo. To win the last trick with the seven of trumps. Some play that these side declarations are worth a bonus of 75 points, while others play that all the trump, 244, carry an extra bonus of 75 points, making a total 150 points. An opponent of the bidder may double his declaration. If he wins, he receives the bonuses, but should he lose, the bidder gets double the bonus score.

Felsös

This game is played the same as Alsös except that rank of cards in trumps is queen, nine, ace, ten, king, jack, eight, seven.

Strategy of Klaberjass

The total points at stake per deal average about 110. When taking on the obligation of trump maker, a player should reasonably expect to score 60 points with his nine cards, or 40 with his first six cards. But the state of the score and the particular hand often justifies a take on 35 or 30. Remember that in Klaberjass, length in the trump suit is not so vital as strength. Actually, the most important factor is the presence or absence of jass. A singleton jass plus a side ace and ten is the "classic take," whereas many four-trump hands not containing jass and nine will be beaten. Jass alone is often enough in trumps to warrant taking.

The dealer, of course, should stay at a minimum for a take when the nondealer passes, rather than allowing his opponent a new suit. Sometimes, however, it is wise, with an especially good defensive hand of several cards in jacks and nines, to permit the opponent to name trump.

Under most conditions, the nondealer should not schmeiss on the first round, since he may be forced to become trump maker against a strong hand. But the nondealer can use the schmeiss to advantage on the second round, to prevent dealer from naming his own suit. Of course, the schmeiss is a powerful tool for the dealer in the event the nondealer starts by passing. Remember, however, that the schmeiss is a psychological weapon and it should be used wisely.

Don't count on draw (the three extra) after the bidding to furnish a specific high card. True, these cards do add to the strength of the hand (20 points on the average), and often give protection to a singleton nine or ten. But remember that your opponent has a good chance to improve, too.

JASS

This interesting card game is related more to the Pinochle-Bezique side of the family than to the game of Klaberjass, which it is often confused with and only resembles in the rank of the cards in trump. It also is called Yass.

Requirements

1. Three or four players, each for himself.

2. A 36-card deck made by stripping out all cards below the six from a regular 52-card deck.

3. Rank of cards: In nontrump, they are as follows: ace (high), king, queen, jack, ten, nine, eight, seven, six (low). In a trump suit, they rank: jack (high), nine, ace, king,

queen, ten, eight, seven, six (low).

The Deal. Players cut for deal, and high cut is dealer. Each player, beginning at dealer's left, receives a hand of nine cards, dealt three at a time per round. If four are playing, the last card is turned up to determine the trump suit. If three are playing, the twenty-eighth card is turned up for trump, and the remainder of the deck is put aside.

The turn to deal in subsequent hands passes to the left.

Exchanging Hands and Trump

1. If three are playing, dealer has the first privilege of exchanging his hand for the nine cards left in the deck, which he does not see. But he must first wait until the player who holds the six of trumps exchanges it for the turned trump (unless, of course, dealer holds it himself). If dealer does not wish to exchange his hand for the face-down cards, any player in turn may then do so. But a player must exchange his entire hand, and once the exchange is made, no further exchanges are allowed. Rotation of choice of the exchange is to the left.

2. If four play, there can, of course, be no exchange of hands, but the player who holds the six of trumps exchanges it for the turned trump. Dealer picks up the card after the exchange to complete his hand.

The Play. The player at dealer's left may lead any card. Each player in turn must follow suit and try to win the trick if possible. If a player cannot follow suit, he must trump if able to and must trump higher if a trick already has been trumped. But the holder of the jass may trump with it even when able to follow suit.

After a player has played to the first trick, all hands may expose any melds for which they wish to score. The values of melds are as follows:

	Points
Four jacks	200
Four aces, kings, queens, or tens	100
Five cards in consecutive sequence in the same suit	100
Four cards in consecutive sequence in the same suit	50
Three cards in consecutive sequence in the same suit	20
King and queen of trumps	20

A sequence must be adjacent in rank, and rank for this purpose only being: ace (high),

king, queen, jack, ten, nine, eight, seven, six. This ranking of sequence holds for trumps, too. But, a player loses the score of his meld if he fails to win at least one trick in the play.

The winner of a trick leads to the next, and play proceeds until all tricks have been played.

Scoring. At the end of play, each player is credited with what he won. These are the counting cards and their value: jack of trumps (jass), 20 points; nine of trumps, 14; any ace, 11; any ten, 10; any king, 4; any queen, 3; any jack except jass, 2. For winning last trick, the player scores 5 points in addition to any others he may win in the trick.

A player who does not win at least 21 points is set back 100 points, which is subtracted from his score.

The Game. The first player to reach 1,000 points announces it. If his claim is verified, he is the winner, if not, he loses. If a player or players is found to have 1,000 points at the end of play in a deal, game is set at 1,250 or 1,500. A player may win only by announcing that he has scored enough for game.

Variations. Here are two variants that are often injected into the game.

1. Some play that, as in Pinochle, a player must undertrump if unable to overtrump when playing to a suit in which he cannot follow.

2. Some play that in a four-handed game, a player who thinks his hand cannot score at least 21 points may drop out of play. The turn to do so begins with the player at dealer's left and passes to the left. Only one player may drop out.

Two-Handed Jass

This follows the same procedure of play as Two-Handed Pinochle (page 172), but the rules are that of Jass. That is, each player is dealt nine cards at the start, and after each trick the winner takes the top card of the stock, his opponent drawing the next. Melds may be made, only one per turn, by the winner of a trick before leading to the next. Until the stock is exhausted, there is no obligation to follow suit to a lead. But once the stock is gone, it is obligatory to follow suit if able, as well as to win any tricks.

JULEPE

A fascinating Spanish game which combines the basic features of both Poker and Pinochle. I first saw it played at the Curaçao Club in Curaçao, Netherlands Antilles, where its members play Julepe and Chemin de Fer at the same time.

Requirements

1. Two to nine players; six and seven make for the best game.

2. A standard deck of 52 cards plus a joker, whose suit is wild and is valued at 10½. However, when it is turned face up on the table to denote trump it becomes the 10½ of spades. Cards rank as in poker, two (low), three, four, five, six, seven, eight, nine, ten, joker (10½), jack, queen, king, and ace (high).

Start of the Game. Each player antes a chip into the center of the table, forming the pot.

Object of the Game. To win the game by scoring two or three tricks out of five played. If one player wins two tricks and another two or three tricks, they divide the winnings.

The Deal. Any player by mutual consent becomes the first dealer. From then on the deal moves to the dealer's left, clockwise. (Deal rotates counterclockwise in Latin America.) After the dealer shuffles the cards, he offers them to the player on his right to cut.

In a six- or seven-handed game, dealer deals each player five cards, three at a time, then two at a time in clockwise fashion. Player to the dealer's left, known as the leader, receives the first three cards and the dealer the last two cards. In a seven-, eight-, or nine-handed game each player is dealt five cards. In a five- or six-handed game each player is dealt six cards, three at a time. In a two-, three-, or four-handed game, each player is dealt nine cards in groups of threes.

After each player has been dealt the proper number of cards, the next card is faced up on the table and denotes the trump suit. The stock (remainder of the undealt cards) is placed alongside the trump card.

The First Play of the Hand. The first play at Julepe is played the same as Draw Poker. The leader has the first privilege of play.

After examining his cards, he must do one of three things.

1. He may *open,* which indicates he plays.

2. He may *pass* (drop out), which indicates he doesn't desire to play the hand.

3. He may *reserve,* which indicates he reserves the privilege to play or pass after all the other players have had their turn to play or pass. Should one or more players play, the leader may either play or pass. But, should all the players pass, he must also pass.

After the leader has decided, each player in turn, starting with the player to the leader's left, may do one of two things: play or pass. They cannot reserve. This privilege is only valid for the leader. If all the players pass but one, he wins the pot. If they all pass, a new hand is dealt with the same ante.

Should one player play and the player who reserved plays (the leader), the former may *vira*—throw in his entire hand and take the trump upcard from the table and draw four cards. Otherwise the trump upcard cannot be taken by a player. But, should a player hold a six of trumps, he can exchange that six of trumps for the trump upcard resting on the table before the said player viras.

When the active players number two or more, these remaining players may if they desire draw cards in an attempt to improve their hands, or stand pat. This procedure is called the *draw,* and is played as follows:

The dealer must ask each player (starting with the nearest active player to his left and rotating clockwise) at his proper turn of play how many cards he wants to draw, if any. This he indicates to the player by saying "How many?" The player either says none or tells the dealer how many cards he wants to draw, which number cannot exceed five. The dealer must wait until the player discards. In a two-handed game in which a player is dealt nine cards, should he stand pat, he must discard four cards to make a playing hand of five cards. Should he want to draw cards he discards six cards plus the number of cards he wants to draw. *Example:* Player holds eleven cards, he discards eight cards and has three cards left in his hand; he is permitted to draw two cards to make his five-card hand. The same procedure of discarding and drawing holds true be it a two-handed game or a nine-handed game. In short, a player must have only five cards in his hand after the draw. If the stock runs out, discards are shuffled and dealt to complete the draw.

The Second Play of the Hand. The second play of Julepe is similar to the play of Pinochle in which players play out their hands in the form of tricks. The first player who opened plays first. He may lead off (start the play) by taking any one of the five cards he holds from his hand and playing it face up on the table. Turn of play then rotates to the left, clockwise. After the first card has been led, each active player in turn of play (which remember moves to the left) must observe the following rules:

1. Each player, if he has it, must play a card of the suit led. *Example:* A diamond is the first card led, therefore all players must follow suit with a diamond.

2. If the player does not have a card of the suit led, he must play a trump card (same suit as the trump upcard).

3. If he does not have a card of the suit led or a trump card, he may play any other card in his hand.

4. When a trump card is led (is the first card played to the trick), each player must play a higher trump card than any previously played if he has one.

5. But if a nontrump card is led and the player trumps that card, succeeding players are not required to trump or play a trump card higher than the one that has been previously played.

This routine of play continues until all five cards in the players' hands have run out and all cards have been played to tricks.

How to Score the Hand. A player who wins two or more tricks wins the hand. If one player wins two tricks and another two or three tricks, they divide the pot. Should an active player fail to win two or more tricks, he must pay the winner or winners an amount equal to the pot. *Example:* If the pot contained six chips, each active player who failed to score two or more tricks must pay the winner or winners six chips.

BOO-RAY OR BOURÉ

This is another game that combines the features of Draw Poker and the playing of tricks as in Pinochle. The game is most popular in Louisiana and in areas where French-Canadians live.

Requirements

1. Two to seven players, each playing for himself.

2. A regular 52-card pack. The cards rank: ace (high), king, queen, jack, ten, nine, eight, seven, six, five, four, three, two (low).

3. Players ante an agreed amount into the pot. There is no further betting, but a losing player may be subject to additional losses.

Object of the Game. To win the most tricks and thus the pot.

The Deal. Five cards are dealt to each player in Draw Poker fashion, starting with the player at the dealer's left and continuing in a clockwise direction. Then the dealer turns the next card face up in the center of the table. This card denotes the trump suit.

After looking at his hand and the trump card, each player—starting with the leader and moving in clockwise rotation—may

throw in his hand and drop out of the game, or may stay in and have a chance to win the pot but also be subject to additional losses. Each active player in turn to dealer's left may then discard and draw one to four cards, as in Draw Poker. Or he may stand pat.

The Play. Once the draw is completed, the player at dealer's left leads and the cards are played out in tricks (one card from each player in turn). The leader must lead his highest trump if he has the ace, king, or queen. To each trick a player in turn must follow suit, if able, "play over" (play a higher card than any previously played), if able, and play a trump if unable to follow suit; but a player unable to follow suit need not overtrump, and if unable to follow suit or trump, a player may play any card. A trick is won by the highest card of the suit led unless a trump is played, in which case the highest trump wins. The winner of a trick leads to the next trick and may lead any card in his hand, except that if he holds the ace, king, or queen of trumps he must lead his highest trump.

Scoring. The player who wins the most

tricks takes the pot. If two players win two tricks each, or if five players win one trick each, they divide the pot equally. A player who fails to win a trick must pay an amount equal to the pot ante which, however, is added to the next pot and not to the current pot.

Three-Card Boo-Ray

This game, for seven to ten players, is played like Bouré, except for the following:

1. Three cards are dealt face down to each player, plus several blind hands. (Four to six is the usual number of blind hands dealt.)

2. After the trump card has been turned face up from the remaining stock, play begins. There is no exchange of cards as in Bouré. The winner of the hand and the penalty for no-tricks is the same.

3. A player with a poor hand may either drop out or take one of the extra blind hands, which he then must play.

CHAPTER 11

Cribbage and How It Is Played

Cribbage, known as *Noddy* in its original form, is one of the oldest card games in existence today. Its invention has been popularly accredited to the English poet and soldier Sir John Suckling, who lived from 1609 to 1642.

The game is simple to learn. The mechanics of Cribbage can be thoroughly mastered after 15 minutes' study. A few hours of play, and you believe you have mastered everything there is to know about the strategy of the game. Then, after becoming an inveterate Cribbage player, you learn that although memory counts for little in the strategy of the game, there are many real possibilities for skillful play and you begin to see its potential. Modern six-card Cribbage is basically a two-handed game, but it can be played three-handed, and also four-handed—partnership style.

TWO-HANDED CRIBBAGE

Requirements
1. Two players.
2. A standard 52-card deck.
3. A Cribbage board. As the scoring in

Cribbage players keep score on this special board by moving pegs; first along the outside row of holes, then back along the inner row.

Cribbage is practically one continuous operation, pencil and paper are seldom used. The Cribbage board keeps track of the score unerringly. The illustration here shows what it looks like. The board is usually made of wood and is about 12 inches by 3 inches. Holes are recessed into the board, and two pegs are provided for each player. There are thirty holes in each long row, and these allow the players to go up and down and across the finish line for a count of 61 points. Each group of five holes is marked off to facilitate the tally. Once around completes a 61-point game, twice around a 121-point game. Players score by each making use of two pegs, advancing the rear peg one hole for each point scored, beginning in the outer row and then coming back on the inner row. For example, a player scores (a) 2, then (b) 3, then (c) 6. At (a) he moves one peg to hole 2, outer row. At (b) he moves the rear peg to hole 5, outer row. At (c) he moves the new rear peg (originally the forward peg) to hole 11, outer row. Thus at all times the forward peg shows the player's total score; the difference between forward and rear pegs shows the player's last score.

If a Cribbage board is not available, each player may use a piece of paper or cardboard, marked thus:

Units: 1 2 3 4 5 6 7 8 9 10
Tens: 1 2 3 4 5 6

Two small markers are used (as small chips or coins) for counting in each row.

The Object of the Game. To be the first to reach game, which may be either 61 or 121 points (as agreed upon before the start of the game), which sum total is made by combined play and meld.

The Rank of Cards. The ace counts 1, the two 2, the three 3, and so on up to the ten-spot. The king, queen, and jack also count 10. For purpose of scoring a sequence, the cards rank in their natural order—king, queen, jack, ten, down to ace, or the reverse.

The Shuffle, Cut, and Deal. The players cut cards to determine who deals first; the player cutting low becomes first dealer. The dealer shuffles the cards, the nondealer cuts, and the dealer then deals six cards alternately to the nondealer and himself, the first card being dealt to the nondealer.

The Crib. When each player has been dealt six cards, the remainder of the cards are put aside for the time being. Each player selects two of his six cards and discards them face down to the dealer's right. These four cards are known as the *crib*, which is actually an extra hand and is credited to the dealer's score upon completion of play. The turn to deal alternates, as does the advantage of the crib.

The Starter. After the crib has been formed and laid away, the nondealer cuts the undealt cards. The dealer places the top card of the bottom section face up on the undealt packet. This face-up card is known as the *starter*. If the starter is a jack, the dealer scores 2 points immediately, the nondealer getting nothing. The dealer announces "Two for his heels," and pegs 2 points. That is, on his side of the Cribbage board he advances a peg 2 holes.

The Play

1. After the starter has been determined,

the nondealer places (plays) face up on the table on his side any one of the four cards he holds, announcing its pip value. For example, if a card is a five-spot, he announces "Five," if it is a four, he announces "Four," and so on.

2. The dealer plays next on his side of the table adding the pips on his card to that of the card played by his opponent and calling the sum total of the two cards.

3. The nondealer then plays his second card on his side of the table and calls the sum total of the three cards played so far. For example, the nondealer begins by playing a four, announcing "Four"; the dealer plays an eight, calling "Twelve"; the nondealer plays a six, calling "Eighteen," and so on, until one of the players finds that each of his cards will, if played, carry the score to 31. (During this procedure of alternate play, each player keeps his exposed cards on his side of the table, separate from those of his opponent, and each one already played must be visible. Cards played are not stacked together as in other games.)

The Go. If a player at his turn of play cannot play a card within the limit of 31, he calls "Go." If the opponent also is unable to lay down a card within the 31-count, he too calls "Go," and a bonus of 1 point is pegged by the first player. But if the second player holds a card or cards that will keep the score under 31, they must be played, and that player pegs one point if the sum total is less than 31 and two points when it is exactly 31.

The final go may occur at any point between 22 and 31. To avoid confusion, when a final go or 31 has been reached, each player turns his previously played cards face down and continues to play the cards remaining in his hand. The player whose turn it is to play starts a new count toward 31.

Scoring During the Play. In addition to the points scored for go and 31, there are numerous other scoring factors in the play of Cribbage, as follows:

1. Each sum total of cards played that brings the score to 15 earns 2 points. *Example:* The nondealer plays a four, calling "Four." Dealer plays a jack, calling "Fourteen." Nondealer plays an ace, and calls "Fifteen–two," and scores 2 points immediately.

2. Pairs. Two successively played cards of the same denomination score 2 points. *Ex-*

ample: Dealer plays a six, calling "Six." Non-dealer also plays a six and calls "Twelve and a pair," scoring 2 points.

3. Triplets—three of a kind. Scores 6 points. *Example:* If a player plays a card that is of the same denomination as the previously played pair, he scores 6 points.

4. Four—four of a kind. Scores 12 points. *Example:* If a player extends previously played three of a kind into four of a kind on his play, he immediately pegs 12 points.

5. Three-card run or sequence. Scores 3 points. *Example:* If a player plays a card that forms a run of three cards with the two previously played cards, he says "Run of three," and pegs 3 points. The cards do not necessarily have to be played in numerical order, but they must form an unbroken run, such as two–ace–three; ace–three–two, three–two–ace, ace–two–three, and so on. The ace cannot be used to form a run with the king and queen. It can be used only to form a run with the two and three or an extended run.

6. Four-card run or sequence. Scores 4 points.

7. Five-, six-, or seven-card run or sequence. Scores 5, 6, or 7 points.

8. Double runs. *Example:* 10-10-9-8, a double three-card run using the nine and eight with each 10, scores 8 points. A 10-10-9-8-7 holding is a double four-card run and scores 10 points. A 10-10-10-9-8 holding is a triple run and scores 15 points. A 10-10-9-9-8 holding is a quadruple run and scores 16 points.

9. Flush. Four cards of the same suit in the hand (but not in the crib) without the starter scores 4 points. Five cards of the same suit in the hand or the crib with the starter scores 5 points.

10. The limit of play. 31 scores 2 points. The final card played is considered a go and scores 1 point.

The Meld. In Auction Pinochle and other games, the meld occurs before the hand is played, but in Cribbage, the meld is scored after the play of the hand. The nondealer scores his melds first. This is important (counting is known as *showing*) because if he counts out enough points to peg the game (61 or 121 points or more), he wins, even though the dealer may have scored an equal or higher total score.

If the nondealer fails to score enough points to win the game, the dealer first scores his melds and then the crib. The melded cards

must always consist of five cards—the four cards held by each player plus the starter, the turned-up card. When showing, the scoring is the same as in the actual play of the game. Each combination of 15 scores 2 points.

Scored Points When Showing. The scoring combinations are as follows:

	Points
One pair	2
Three of a kind	6
Four of a kind	12
Runs of three cards or more	1 for each card
Double three-card run	8
Double four-card run	10
Triple run	15
Quadruple run	16
Flush, four cards of a suit	4
Flush, five cards of a suit	5
Jack of the same suit as the starter (called His Nobs)	1

In scoring 2 points for a fifteen combination, it should be noted that each time an additional card is used to total 15, an additional 2 points is scored. Thus, king–king–five–five invokes four fifteens and is scored as 8 points. In short, four combinations of fifteen can be formed with four such cards. By adding 2 points for the pair of kings and 2 for the pair of fives, the total sum is 12 points. If the starter happens to be a third king, your count jumps to 22 points, 6 points for the three kings and 4 more for the extra two 15's.

Tabulations, or the Showing. Because the melding combinations that are possible at Cribbage are varied and some of them well hidden, a beginner is excused for missing a few points now and then. The highest scoring that can be made with any five cards is 29 points. This 29-point score can only be attained when holding a jack and three fives with the starter a five of the same suit as the held jack. The four fives total 12 points, and the eight ways of forming 15 are worth 16 points, with 1 point for His Nobs.

It would be quite a task to list all the different possible scoring combinations, but selecting one combination in each category running from 12 to 29 points should prove helpful to the reader. The scoring totals of 19, 25, 26, and 27 do not appear in the following chart, and for a very good reason. They cannot be made. Whenever a player claims one of those four scores, something is wrong with his count. Some of the tabulated scores listed in the following chart include 1 point for His Nobs. Flushes seldom achieve a high score. The five, six, seven, eight, and nine of a suit score only 14 points.

TOTAL SCORES WITH FIVE CARDS INCLUDING STARTER

Five Cards	Total Points	Five Cards	Total Points
1-1-6-7-7	12	6-9-9-9-9	20
1-1-7-7-8	12	7-8-8-8-8	20
1-4-4-4-10	12	7-8-8-9-9	20
2-2-4-9-9	12	3-3-6-6-6	20
2-6-6-7-7	12	4-4-4-7-7	20
1-1-6-7-8	13	3-3-4-5-5	20
1-4-4-4-J	13	1-1-7-7-7	20
3-3-6-6-9	14	3-4-4-4-4	20
4-4-7-7-7	14	4-5-6-6-6	21
1-2-2-2-3	15	7-7-7-8-9	21
J-Q-Q-Q-K	15	5-5-J-J-J	21
1-1-2-3-3	16	3-3-3-4-5	21
2-2-3-3-4	16	5-5-5-K-K	22
2-6-7-7-8	16	5-5-5-J-J	23
6-7-8-9-9	16	4-5-5-5-6	23
2-3-4-4-4	17	3-6-6-6-6	24
2-3-3-3-4	17	4-4-5-6-6	24
3-4-4-4-5	17	4-5-5-6-6	24
3-3-3-6-6	18	7-7-8-8-9	24
5-5-J-Q-K	18	3-3-3-3-9	24
6-6-9-9-9	20	4-4-4-4-7	24
6-6-7-7-8	20	6-7-7-8-8	24
3-3-4-4-5	20	5-5-5-5-10	28
7-7-7-8-8	20	5-5-5-5-J	29

The italicized jack designates it as the same suit as the starter, and 1 point is allowed for His Nobs.

Fifteen may be formed with as many as five cards and as few as two: one–two–three–four–five totals 15, as does ten and five. The high scores are usually made when holding triple and quadruple runs, which are augmented when fifteens are included. In counting melds, it will help matters to remember that all three-card double runs score 8 points, triple runs 15 points, and quadruple runs 16 points. A four-card double run scores 10 points. These total counts include the pair or three of a kind, but not the fifteens. They must be added. The ace can be used in a low run only, it cannot join the king and queen. All other cards may extend at both ends (except the king).

Muggins Optional. Some Cribbage players still abide by the old rule of muggins, which simply states that if a player overlooks a meld, his opponent may announce "Muggins," point out the overlooked meld, and

credit to his own score the total number of points overlooked by the other player.

Dealing New Hands and Games. At the completion of the hand, after the meld is counted, the next deal takes place. All the cards are shuffled together as at the start. If two decks are used, the second hand is dealt from the second deck, the third from the first, and so on. After the first hand has been dealt, the deal alternates between player and player. The loser of each game deals first in the next game.

Additional Rules. The following covers the major irregularities in Cribbage:

Misdeal. A new deal by the same dealer is required: (*a*) when any hand receives the wrong number of cards; (*b*) when the cards are not dealt one at a time; (*c*) when a card is exposed in dealing; (*d*) when a card is found face up in the pack; and (*e*) when the deck is found to be imperfect.

Wrong Number of Cards. When one hand (not crib) is found to have an incorrect number of cards after laying away for the crib and the other hand and crib are correct, the opponent has the right to either demand a new deal or peg 2 and correct the hand by drawing out the excess cards or dealing additional cards from the pack to supply a deficiency. If the crib is incorrect, both hands being correct, nondealer pegs 2 and the crib is corrected by drawing out excess cards or dealing additional cards from the pack. If more than one hand (including crib) is found incorrect and there must be a new deal, the nondealer pegs 2.

Erroneous Announcement. There is no penalty for announcing a wrong total of cards or a wrong count, but the error must be corrected on demand. If an error in announcing the total is not noticed until the next card is played, it stands as announced. If an error in counting a hand is not noticed until the opponent commences counting, or until the cut for the next deal, it stands. No player is entitled to help from another or from a bystander in counting his hand. Scores overlooked may not be taken by the opponent unless there has been previous agreement to enforce muggins.

Failure to Play. A player who calls "Go" when able to play may not correct his error after the next card is played. A player who gains a go and fails to play additional cards when able may not correct his error after the next card is played. In either case, the card or cards erroneously withheld are dead as soon as seen by the opponent, and the offender may not play them or peg them, and the opponent of the offender pegs 2 for the error.

Error in Scoring. Should a player place a peg short of the amount to which he is entitled, he may not correct his error after he has played the next card or after the cut for the next deal. If he pegs more than his announced score, the error must be corrected on demand at any time before the cut for the next deal and his opponent pegs 2.

Strategy at Cribbage

Here are some of the fine points of Cribbage play:

Discarding to the Crib. The most important decision the player must make at the game of Cribbage is the discarding of two cards from his hand to the crib. Skillful play demands careful consideration be given to three different discarding situations:

1. Discarding to the dealer's own crib.
2. Discarding to the opponent's crib.
3. Discarding to the score.

A large proportion of hands offers no problem in finding the proper two cards to discard to the crib, especially when you are the dealer and the crib is yours. However, even then the discarder requires good judgment to take full advantage of his opportunities.

It is simple wisdom for the dealer to put good cards into the crib—that is, if he can—and conversely, the nondealer should not feed the crib with cards that are likely to assist the dealer's crib to a large score. The most valuable card is the five-spot. Its chances of helping to make a fifteen with two cards are four times greater than those of any other card. This is because it can be combined with the sixteen 10-count cards. Two cards in sequence are fine to discard into your own crib, but may prove costly if discarded to your opponent's crib. The seven- and eight-spot are fine cards for your crib. The six and eight are also good because you have your opponent's two discards and the starter to help find a seven, which counts 5 points (3 for a run of 3 cards and 2 for the seven and

eight). When holding a five and a single 10-count card, don't hesitate to discard them into your own crib. Even a pair of fives that don't fit well in the dealer's hand should be discarded into his crib.

What to discard into your opponent's crib presents the most difficult problem of Cribbage. The nondealer often finds himself in a tough spot. He must often decide to split a good hand or contribute valuable cards to the dealer's crib that are likely to help him run up a big score. If the nondealer discards a pair (other than fives) or a fifteen to the enemy's crib, that isn't too harmful, but a pair of fives would be suicidal. The ideal discard for the nondealer to give to his opponent's crib is one high and one low card, such as a nine- and a two-spot.

When a game is nearing its end, mathematics and restriction in discarding are often disregarded. This is especially true when the opponent is practically certain to go out by the counting of the hand and the crib. The chance must be taken that a favorable starter will turn up to win the game for the nondealer before his opponent is afforded the opportunity to meld. Even though the opponent is stopped short of game, it must be considered that, on the next deal, the first meld goes to the adversary, so the only hope to win rides on the current hand. As a general rule, it is smart to play conservatively when in the lead and play boldly when behind, because one good hand may turn the losing tide into a winning streak. When another hand is not likely, discarding even a pair of fives for the opposing crib may pull the chestnuts out of the fire.

It should be borne in mind that the nondealer plays first and at times may not be able to score even a single point. But the dealer is assured of at least 1 point. The dealer cannot be prevented from scoring a go—as a result of playing the last card—and this point may be the deciding factor in many close games.

Strategy of Play. The 1's and 2's pegged during the play of the hand may seem to be a small reward when compared to the counts of 20 or more that may be scored by melds. Nevertheless, the majority of Cribbage games are actually won by skillful play of the hands. The initial play is most important, and when certain cards are held, the first card played gives you a basis for analyzing your opponent's three-card hand.

After the opening play, the dealer and nondealer can score only 2 points, by making a fifteen and by pairing. Any played card can be paired, but fifteen must be comprised of two cards above 4. Because the five-spot and any one of the sixteen 10-count cards add up to 15, there are four times as many chances for your adversary to score a fifteen by the initial play of a five-spot than of any other card. Therefore, the five is out as an opening play. A good opening is a four-spot, because it cannot be combined with another card to total 15. Opening with a four-spot when holding a pair is good strategy, because if the opponent is able to score 2 points on a pair, the opener can later score 6 points for three of a kind.

Not having a four to lead, play the card that gives you the best prospect of making a score if your opponent makes a score. Leading from a pair is always sound strategy. When forced to lead an odd card, if possible lead one that will let you score a run if your opponent makes a fifteen.

The lead of a 10-count card is not as bad as it is proclaimed to be. The argument against it has been that the opponent makes a fifteen by playing a five. Since there are sixteen cards with a 10-count value and only four fives, the argument isn't too sound.

It is not always sound to pair the opponent's card. The type of hand and the scores must be taken into consideration. You might score 2 points and then possibly lose 6 points on three of a kind.

When the opponent leads a high card, extra care must be taken to avoid playing cards in sequence, or even irregular sequence. If the opening lead is a ten, a queen, jack, eight, or nine may open the way for a run of three. With low cards there is the possibility of a comeback with a run of four, but with high cards there is no further chance of scoring but a possible go or 31.

Auction Cribbage

This variant is played in the same manner as standard Two-Handed Cribbage except for the following:

1. After the cards are dealt the dealer has the right to say the number of points he will bid for the right of holding the crib. The nondealer can then overbid him if he desires. The dealer can again increase the bid, and then the nondealer, each bidding in turn until one of the players declines to bid any higher. The points so bid are deducted from the score of the player immediately. If a player has bid for and won the crib at the beginning of the game, it will be found convenient to backmark on the board the number of points so bid; that is to say, if a player bids 5 points, he places his peg 5 points from the start on the inner line of holes.

2. The winner of the crib plays first and has the first meld. (In standard Two-Handed Cribbage, the nondealer has the first meld.) It follows that when the game is nearing its end the advantage of holding the crib is such that it is worth bidding high for it, but the advantage is counteracted by having to deduct from the score the number of points bid for the crib.

3. The game is 121 points.

Three-Handed Cribbage

The game is played the same as Two-Handed Cribbage with the following additional rules:

1. Players cut for deal, high card dealing the first hand. Thereafter each new deal passes to the left. Each player is dealt five cards. The next card is put aside for the crib. Each player puts one card in the crib.

2. The player to the left of dealer plays first, the player to his left plays next, and the dealer last.

3. When one player scores game, the game ends; however, in some sections of the country, the two remaining players finish their game to determine the loser.

4. Cribbage boards with three series of holes to tally the points are available.

Four-Handed Cribbage

The game is played the same as Two-Handed Cribbage with the following exceptions:

1. Four-Handed Cribbage is played in partnership style. It affords many opportunities for skillful partnership play. Players cut

for partnership. The two low men are partners; the two high are the opposing partners. The four players cut for deal, high card dealing the first hand. The play rotates clockwise, the player left of the dealer making the first play and becoming the next dealer.

2. Each player is dealt five cards alternately, each putting one card in the crib. The cards are cut and the dealer turns up the starter card. One player of the partnership keeps score.

Five-Card Cribbage

In this, the original form of Cribbage, each player is dealt five cards and two are laid away to the crib. This means that each hand (with starter) is comprised of four cards, the crib five. Play ends at 31 or go. Otherwise, this old form is much like the modern six-card game, which has superseded it as the standard form of Cribbage.

CHAPTER 12

Casino

Casino (sometimes misspelled Cassino) is a hardy, perennial two-handed game that can trace its beginning back to the Italian game of Scopa (see page 232). It had its greatest popularity prior to the advent of Gin Rummy.

Although Casino is easy to learn, it is a game that can be played *very* scientifically, and the best Casino two-handed players are very expert, at least as expert as the best Gin Rummy players are at their game. For this very reason the average player when pitted against an expert is bound to lose unless he knows some of the scientific aspects of the game. If you lose constantly against a certain player, it is because you are not as good as the other fellow, not because of the bad cards you are dealt. Although Casino is sometimes played with three or four players, I do not recommend either method for expert play since more than two players reduce the strategical possibilities of the game. But, for family play, the following variations are recommended: Three- and Four-Handed Casino, Royal Casino, Draw Casino, and Spade Casino.

REGULAR CASINO

Requirements

1. A standard deck of 52 cards.
2. Two players.

Number Values of the Cards. The play of the game requires that the cards be given number values; ace counts 1, two 2, three 3, and so on, through ten. The jack, queen, and king have no given point values. Rank of cards does not enter into the game.

Object of the Game. To win the hand or game by scoring more points than your opponent. Six or more points win a hand.

Point-Scoring Values

1. Each ace taken in counts 1 point.
2. Two of spades (known as *little casino*) taken in counts 1 point.
3. Ten of diamonds (known as *big casino*) taken in counts 2 points.

4. Seven or more spades (known as *spades*) taken in counts 1 point.

5. Twenty-seven or more cards of any suits (known as *cards*) taken in count 3 points. If both players take in 26 cards there is no score for cards.

All told there are 11 points to be scored in each hand.

The Shuffle, Cut, and Deal

1. Players cut for deal, and low card deals the first hand. Thereafter, the deal alternates between players.

2. The dealer shuffles the cards and offers them to his opponent to cut.

3. The dealer deals his opponent two cards face down, then turns two cards face up on the center of the table. He then deals two cards to himself face down. Two more face-

(Right) The player holding this Casino hand (fanned cards) against the four cards dealt to the table used his six to take the four and two. (Left) With this hand (fanned), the Casino player may place his four upon the table's six, announcing that he is "building tens."

down cards are dealt to his opponent, two more face up on the table, and two more cards face down to himself. In brief, each player now holds four cards, and four face-up cards are resting on the table.

The Play of the Hand. Beginning with the nondealer, each player alternately may play any card he wishes from his hand. A player may make any of the following possible plays at each turn of play:

A player possessing a card of the same number value as any on the table removes the card from his hand and places it face down on the matched card, picks up the matched pair, and places them face down in a pile in

front of him. One card or several can be paired in this way. In addition to this, a player also may take in any group of cards resting on the table whose total numerical value adds up to the number value of the card he plays.

Example 1: Suppose that a player at his turn of play has a ten-spot card in his hand, and exposed on the table are three ten-spot cards and an ace, a six, and a three. The player can take in the three tens, and also the ace, six and three, which total 10. All seven cards (which include the player's ten-spot) are taken on the play and placed face down in a pile in front of him.

Example 2: Suppose that there are three deuces on the table and a player holds both a deuce and a six-spot. He can play either the deuce or the six from his hand to take in the three deuces: he can play his deuce because it is a card of the same number value as the cards on the table, since the three deuces add up to 6. Or if there were three deuces and a six on the table the player could play the six from his hand, call "Six," and take in the three deuces and the six-spot with his lone six, thereby cleaning the board.

A player may take in only one picture card (jack, queen, or king) on the table with a matching picture card from his hand, unless he holds the fourth to a set of three on the table. *Example:* If a player holds a king in his hand and two kings are exposed on the table, he may take in only one of the exposed kings at his proper turn of play. But if there are three kings, or three queens, or three jacks, on the table and a player holds the matching fourth card, he is permitted to take in all three picture cards exposed on the table, plus the one card in his hand, making a total of four picture cards.

A player may play a card from his hand onto a card on the table, leave it there, and announce he is *building,* simply by naming the number value (from 1 to 10) he is building. There are a number of ways of making builds. Suppose there are a six and a deuce on the table, and the player possesses an ace and a nine in his hand. He places the ace together with the six and deuce in a group and announces "Building nine," which statement indicates that the player holds a nine-spot in his hand with which he can take the nine build. This type of build is known as a *single build.* Either player may change any single build resting on the table to a higher number value at his proper turn of play by adding a card from his hand to the existing single build. *Example:* Suppose a player has made a single build of five. His opponent at his proper turn of play adds an ace to it and calls a new build of six. Only a six can take this build. Naturally, the player who increases the five build to a six build holds a six in his hand. This six build can be increased to a seven, eight, nine, or ten build providing the player abides by the above single-build rules.

A player may not make use of a card on the table to change the number value of a single build. He must play a fresh card from his hand.

A player may take in an opponent's build when it is his proper turn of play only if he holds a card of the same number value as the build. Once a player has made a build he must, on his next play, either take a trick, make another build, increase a single build to a higher number, make a single build into a multiple build, or add to a multiple build.

A *multiple build* is a build in which more than one unit of the number is built. For example, a build of nine made of six plus three and a duplicate made of eight plus ace. A player may add to a single build and make it a multiple build at his next turn by adding a card from his hand, with or without another card, or cards, from the table.

Example 1. A player has built nine at his previous turn of play. He has two nines in his hand. He puts one of them on his single build of nine, making it a multiple nine ready to be taken with the second nine in his hand.

Example 2. A player has a single build of nine. In addition to holding a nine he holds a four and a six. If there is a five on the table he can add his four-spot to it, call "Nine," and place both cards on his build pile of nines, making a multiple build which he must take on his next turn of play, unless he can add another nine build or his opponent takes the build with a nine-spot.

A player may not change the number value of a multiple build.

Example 1. A multiple build of sevens has been made consisting of a seven and a four and a three. No player may add a card to this build and call a higher build.

Example 2. A player has played a four from his hand, placed it atop another four on the table, and called "Fours" (a multiple build). No player is permitted to take this build with an eight.

When a player does not take a trick or make or contribute to a build, he must discard a card from his hand face up onto the table. This is known as *trailing.* A player may discard at any time he pleases providing he does not have a build of his own on the board.

Continued Deals. After both players have played their first four cards one at a time, the dealer picks up the stock (the undealt ones) and deals four more cards to the nondealer and himself in the same manner as in the original deal. However, he does not deal any cards face up on the table at any time for the rest of the deal.

Play continues until all the cards in the deck have been exhausted (dealt). When each player is dealt his last four cards, the dealer must announce the fact by saying "Last" or "Deals up."

Taking In the Last Trick. The player who takes in the last trick also takes in any other cards that may be left on the table.

End of Game. When the hand is over, the players look through their piles of cards (the tricks they have taken) and score as described under "Point-Scoring Values." The player scoring the greatest number of points is declared the winner of the game. The lower score is deducted from the higher score, and the difference is the winning margin.

Casino Match Style. Instead of considering each deal a separate game, the players may decide to make the goal of the game a point total, in which case the deals continue until the goal is reached. For example, the player first to reach the goal of 11 or 21 points wins the match. If both players score the required number of 11 or 21 points or more in the same hand, the player with the higher score is declared the winner. The reward for the winner is usually stipulated before play starts.

Additional Rules

Misdeals. The following determines whether or not a misdeal has occurred:

1. If a player accidentally turns up a card or cards belonging to his opponent and this occurs with the first 12 dealt cards, that deal is void, a misdeal is declared, and the same dealer deals again.

2. If a player accidentally turns up a card or cards belonging to his opponent and this occurs after the first 12 cards have been dealt, the previous dealt hands stand. However, the current dealt hand is retrieved and shuffled back into the stock and a new hand is dealt.

3. If a player turns up a card or cards belonging to himself, he must play that hand. No new deal or shuffle takes place.

4. If a card, or cards, is found face up in the deck during a deal, the play stands. However, the player receiving the face-up card or cards is permitted to remove the same number of cards from his opponent's hand, look at them, and return them to the opponent.

5. If a player has too few or too many cards and this is discovered before the first trick is completed, a misdeal is declared and the same dealer deals again.

6. If a player has too few or too many cards after the first trick, and this is discovered after one or more cards of the hand have been played, he loses the deal and his opponent is credited with 11 points.

Announcing the Last Deal. If the dealer fails to announce "Last deal" when the last eight cards of the deck are dealt and a trick is played from the last eight cards of the deck, he loses the game and his opponent is credited with 11 points.

Faulty Builds. If a player makes a build and does not have a proper card to take it in, he loses the game and his opponent is credited with 11 points. If a player trails (plays a card without taking a trick) and he has a build already lying on the table, he loses the game and his opponent scores 11 points.

Looking Through Cards Taken In. If a player takes in a trick, his opponent may ask to see the trick even though the cards have been gathered and placed in the taker's pile. This is the case only if the opponent has not played after the taker of the trick under consideration. If a player makes a play after the opponent has committed an error, the incorrect play is considered condoned. In no other instance is it permitted to look through gathered cards. The penalty for such infraction is loss of game and a score to the opponent of 11 points.

Strategy at Casino

The important thing is to keep a mental count of the cards, spades, and points you have taken in. This count can make all the difference between winning and losing by indicating which is the best play. For example, on the board there is an ace, a three, a five, and an eight. You have already taken in 23 cards and 3 points. You have in your hand an ace, a seven, an eight, and a queen. If you take the three, five, and eight with your eight, you will have 27 cards, and the 3 points this wins will, with the 3 points already in, give you 6 points on the game. If you take the aces you will have a total of only 5 points and will lose if, as is possible, you don't take another card.

Royal Casino

This variant is recommended for children and family play merely because it is less strategic than regular Two-Handed Casino. Follow all the rules of regular Casino except:

1. Jacks count 11, queens 12, kings 13, aces either one or 14 as the holder wishes; all these cards may be used to take in builds and may be built in triplets and quadruplets (an optional rule is to count little casino as 2 or 15, big casino as 10 or 16).

2. If a player makes a sweep—takes in all cards remaining on the table—he scores 1, but this score ranks last in order of precedence when the cards taken in are counted. A sweep is noted by turning one card face up among the cards taken in. The award of cards finally remaining on the table, to the player last to take in, does not count as a sweep.

Draw Casino

Either the rules of regular Casino or Royal Casino apply, as the players prefer, except for the following:

Four cards are dealt to each player and four to the table. The remainder of the deck is placed face downward on the table, and each player, after playing a card from his hand, draws the top card from the stock, thus restoring his hand to four. After the stock is exhausted, the remaining cards are played out without drawing, and the count is made in the regular manner. Incidentally, if a player fails to draw in proper turn he cannot correct the error until his next turn to draw, when he must draw two cards.

Spade Casino

Either regular or Royal Casino is played, but (in addition to the count for cards, spades, big casino, and aces other than the spade ace), the ace, jack, and deuce of spades count 2 points each and other spades count one point each; 25 points may be scored in each deal, exclusive of sweeps, if played. Game is 61 points and the margin of victory is the difference between the winning score and the losing score; this is doubled if the losing score is less than 31. Spade Casino can most conveniently be scored on a cribbage board (see page 221) with every point being recorded as the card is taken in.

Three-Handed Casino

In Three-Handed Casino, each plays for himself and is dealt four cards, as in Two-Handed Casino. Also four are dealt to the table on the first round, but no cards thereafter. The player at the dealer's left plays first and the turn to play passes in clockwise rotation. Should a tie exist for the most spades or cards, the respective points do not count for any player. A game of 11 is usually played; if it is attempted to make each deal a game, there are too many ties.

Four-Hand or Partnership Casino

Two play against two as partners in this game and the partners sit opposite each other. Cards taken in by each partnership are combined and counted together, and partners attempt to help each other at all times, but each player must observe the rules of regular Casino. *Example:* Should a five be on the table and one player knows that his partner holds a nine and he holds a four but no nine in his hand, he cannot build a nine, even though he knows that his partner could take it in.

This type of partnership Casino may be played for a 21-point game, or each deal may represent a game.

Scopa or Italian Casino

In this parent game variation of Casino, which is also called Scoop or Diamond Casino, an Italian or European deck of 40 cards (tens, nines, and eights are stripped from the deck) is used. Each king counts 10, each queen 9, each jack 8, each ace 1, each other card its numerical value.

While this game can be played by two, it is best as a four-hand partnership or by six players in two partnerships of three.

The Deal. Three cards are dealt to each player, instead of four, but fourth cards are exposed on the table. After the cards have been played, using any of the dealing methods in regular Casino, three more cards are dealt to each player; and so on until all of the cards have been dealt and played. The rotation in dealing is counterclockwise or to the right.

The Play. Playing in counterclockwise rotation, each player must play one card starting with the player at dealer's right. In turn, a player may take in one card from the table with a card of the same rank played from his hand. Also he may take in two or more cards from the table whose sum equals the count of the card played from his hand. (A build may not be duplicated as in regular Casino.) If a player has a choice between taking a single card or a combination of cards from the table, he must take the single card. Cards taken in are placed face down before the player who took them. Cards remaining on the table after the last card has been played go to the player who last took any cards.

The Scoring. When play is completed, the points are scored as follows:

	Points
Cards (greatest number taken in)	1
Diamonds (greatest number taken in)	1
The seven of diamonds	1
Sweep or scoop (taking in all cards on the table)	1
Settanta	1

A *settanta* is scored for the highest-counting four cards, one of each of the four suits, taken in by a player (or side). This four-card grouping is called a *primiera,* and to determine the highest-ranking primiera, each seven counts 21, each six 18, each ace 16, each five 15, each four 14, each three 13, each two 12, and each face card 10. Thus the four sevens would constitute the highest primiera. However, in a primiera, it is not necessary to have four of a kind or even a pair so long as every suit is represented.

The Game. The game consists of 11 points. A player (or partnership) may declare himself out during play and if he has 11 points he wins; if he does not, the opponent wins. If both players (or partnerships) reach 11 or more points, the first to claim the game wins.

Scopone

This is a partnership form of Scopa in which the entire deck of 40 cards is dealt out, ten cards to each player, none to the table. Each player in counterclockwise rotation, beginning with the player at the dealer's right, plays one card at a time until all are played. Taking in and scoring are the same as for Scopa, but the game is 15 points.

CHAPTER 13

The Big Euchre Family

The Euchre or Trumps family of card games is one of the largest. With its many variations, this game has long been considered eminently respectable and has held its place as the leading family game until Whist and its popular offspring, Bridge, began to overshadow it during the early part of the twentieth century. Most card historians believe that it is a direct descendant of the old Spanish game of Triomphe, mentioned in the earliest writings on card games as far back as 1520. In France, Triomphe was modified slightly and became known as Ruff. This game underwent a few changes in the early eighteenth century and was given the new name of Euchre. Incidentally, Euchre was probably introduced into America by the French in Louisiana.

PARTNERSHIP EUCHRE

The description that follows is of the standard partnership game, which is the popular form of Euchre.

Requirements

1. Four players, two against two as partners.

2. A standard Euchre 32-card deck is used, made up by stripping out all cards below the seven from a standard 52-card deck.

3. In a suit that is not trump the cards rank as follows: ace (high), king, queen, jack, ten, nine, eight, seven (low).

4. In a suit that is trump the ranking is as follows: jack of trumps, highest; jack of the other suit of the same color, next highest; then follow ace, king, queen, ten, nine, eight, seven. *Example:* If hearts were the trump suit, the rank of trumps would be heart jack, diamond jack, heart ace, heart king, heart queen, heart ten, heart nine, heart eight, heart seven. In the diamond suit (the same color), the ten would follow the queen. The other suits would retain their rank.

5. The jack of trumps is known as the *right bower,* and the jack of the other suit of the same color is known as the *left bower.*

Variant. Some players strip out all cards below the nine, leaving a 24-card deck for play. The rank of the remaining cards is the same as described previously, and there is usually no change in the number of cards dealt.

Beginning of the Game. The selection of the dealer, seating positions, changing seats, selecting partners, shuffle and cut are as provided under the General Rules for Card Games, chapter 1.

The Deal. The dealer deals each player five cards in two rounds beginning with the player at his left and going in clockwise rotation. He deals three cards at a time per round to each player and then two at a time per round, to give each a hand of five cards. Or, he may deal two cards around the first time and then three around. The next card (twenty-first) is turned face up on top of the remainder of the deck. Should the turn-up be accepted as trump, regardless of by whom, dealer has the right to exchange the turn-up for any card in his hand. In practice, the turn-up is not taken into his hand but is left on the deck until played; dealer signifies his exchange by placing his discard face down underneath the deck.

The deal passes in a clockwise rotation.

Making the Trump. Commencing with player to dealer's left, each player in turn has the option of passing or of accepting the turn-up for trump. An opponent of dealer accepts by saying "I order it up." Partner of dealer accepts by saying "I assist." Dealer accepts by making his discard; his acceptance is called *taking it up.*

Dealer signifies refusal of the turn-up by removing the card from the top and placing it (face up) partially underneath the pack; this is called *turning it down.* When all four players pass in the first round, each hand in turn, commencing with the player at the dealer's left, has the option of passing again or of naming the trump suit. The rejected suit may not be named. Declaring the other suit of the same color as the rejected suit is called *making it next:* declaring a suit of opposite color is called *crossing it.* If all four players pass in the second round, the cards are bunched (mixed together for the shuffle) and the next dealer in turn deals.

Once the trump is fixed, either by acceptance of the turn-up or declaration after it is rejected, the bidding ends and play begins.

Playing Alone. The player who fixes the trump suit has the option of playing alone, without help of his partner's cards. If he wishes to exercise this option, he must declare "Alone" distinctly at the time he makes the trump. His partner then turns his cards face down and does not participate in the play.

The Play. The opening lead is made by player to the left of dealer, or if a player is alone, opening is made by opponent to his left. Each hand must follow suit to a lead if able; if unable, the hand may trump or discard at will. A trick is won by the highest card of the suit led, or, if it contains trumps, by the highest trump. The winner of a trick leads to the next.

Object of the Play. To win at least three tricks. If the side that made the trump fails to get three tricks, it is said to be *euchred.* Winning all five tricks is called a *march.*

Scoring. The following table shows all scoring situations:

Partnership making trump wins 3 or 4 tricks	1
Partnership making trump wins 5 tricks	2
Lone hand wins 3 or 4 tricks	1
Lone hand wins 5 tricks	4
Partnership or lone hand is euchred, opponents score	2

The Game. Five, seven, or ten points, as agreed. In 5-point game a side is said to be *at the bridge* when it has scored 4 and opponents have scored 2 or less.

Markers. A widespread method of keeping score is by use of small cards lower than those in play. When game is 5 points, each side uses a three-spot and a four-spot as markers. To indicate score of 1, place the four face down on the three, leaving one pip exposed; score of 2, place the three face down on the four, leaving two pips exposed; score of 3, place the three face up on the four; score of 4, place the four face up on the three. In higher-point games a four-spot and a three-spot or a five-spot and two-spot are frequently used as markers to keep score.

Rubbers. Many Euchre games are scored by rubber points, as in Whist. The first side to win two games wins the rubber. Each game counts for the side winning it: 3 rubber points if the losers' score in that game was nothing; 2 rubber points if the losers' score was 1 or 2; and 1 rubber point if the losers scored 3 or more. The winners' margin in the rubber is 2 points bonus, plus the winners' rubber points, minus the losers' rubber points.

Additional Rules

Misdeal. There may be a new deal by the same dealer if a card is exposed in dealing; if a card is faced in the pack; or if the pack is found imperfect. When a pack is found imperfect, previous scores stand.

A deal by the wrong player may be stopped before a card is turned up; if the error is not noticed until later, the deal stands.

Error in Bidding. A player who *orders it up* when he is partner of dealer, or *assists* when he is an opponent of dealer, is deemed to have accepted the turn-up for trump. If a player names for trump the suit of the turn-up after it has been turned down, his declaration is void and his side may not make the trump.

Euchre scoring by using small value cards.

Declaration Out of Turn. If a player makes a declaration (or turn-down) other than a pass, out of turn, it is void and his side may not make the trump.

Incorrect Number of Cards. If any hand is found to have too many or too few cards, and the error is discovered before the first trick is quitted, there must be a new deal; if the error is not noticed until later, play continues and the side holding the erroneous hand may not score for that deal. If dealer has accepted the turn-up and plays to the first trick before discarding, he must play with the five cards dealt him and the turn-up card is out of play.

Lone Hand. A hand playing alone does not incur penalty for lead or play out of turn or exposing a card, but must correct the error on demand if it is noticed in time.

Lead Out of Turn. If a hand leads out of turn and all other hands play to the trick before the error is noticed, the trick stands. But if any hand has not played, the false lead must be taken back on demand of any player and becomes an exposed card. Any cards played to the incorrect lead may be retracted without penalty. An opponent of the incorrect leader may name the suit to be led at the first opportunity thereafter for the offender or his partner to lead; such call must be made by the hand that will play last to the trick.

Exposed Cards. A card is deemed exposed if it is led or played out of turn; dropped face up on the table except as a regular play in turn; played with another card intended to be played; or named by a player as being in his hand. An exposed card must be left face up on the table and must be played at the first legal opportunity.

Quitted Tricks. Each trick as gathered must be turned face down, and the tricks must be kept separate so that the identity of each can be determined. Quitted tricks may not be ex-amined for any purpose until the end of play. If a player turns up a quitted trick at any previous time, the opponents may call a lead from his side.

Revoke. Failure to follow suit to a lead when able is a revoke. A revoke may be corrected before the trick is quitted, and if it is corrected any opponent who played after the revoke may retract his card and substitute another. If a player so mixes the tricks that a claim of revoke against his side cannot be proved, the claim must be considered proved.

Upon proof of established revoke, the nonrevoking side has the option of scoring the hand as played or of taking the revoke penalty. The revoke penalty is 2 points, which may be either added to the score of the nonrevoking side or subtracted from the score of its opponents. If the revoke was made by the opponents of a lone hand, the penalty is 4 points.

Strategy of Euchre

As to the number of trumps in play, it is fairly safe to assume that there will be about six. Of these, the maker of trump will generally hold three, leaving an average of one for each other player. But if trump is ordered up, there is a very good chance that the dealer will have at least two trumps. The odds are approximately 7 to 3 against any hand's being dealt a card of each suit, but roughly 2 to 1 against the opening side's being able to trump the first lead of a side suit.

With two fairly "sure" tricks in the hand, a player is usually justified in taking action. It is safe to assume that your partner will give you at least one trick. Any three trumps are a "take," and ace + or king + is worth a try. At 0–0 score, however, neither opponent of the dealer will have little interest in ordering it up, for if it is turned down their side will have first chance to name a new suit. Actually, the only reason for ordering it up is a hand of three fairly sure tricks, including at least two good trump cards. Of course, the dealer should order it up if he can, even at some risk, at the beginning of a game.

Advanced scores sometimes require different strategy. For instance, with the score 4 to 2, or 4 to 1, the side at the bridge (having 4 points) will frequently accept the turn-up regardless of its cards, for even if they suffer euchre, the 2 points will not give the opponents the game. But if an opponent becomes the maker, he might play alone, make march, and thus win the game.

Another common situation arises when one side has 3 points. Here a conservative strategy is called for by the opponents, since if it makes the trump the side with the 3 points needs to take only three tricks to win, whereas if the opponents make the trump they require all five tricks.

The determining factor of playing alone should be based on one of the two following situations: (1) a sure winning hand, such as two bowers and the ace of trumps, or every card either an ace or a trump; or (2) a hand having a reasonably good chance of three tricks when your opponents are at the bridge and your side has 1 or 2 points.

The best move for the opening leader, if he holds two or more trumps, is to lead one of them. Otherwise, he should generally open a plain suit in which he has no high card, rather than one in which he has. In following to a lead, always attempt to win the trick (or let your partner win). Holding up a high card for a possible later trick in a suit once led is poor strategy.

Call-Ace Euchre

This is a variant in the matter of determining partnerships, with four, five, or six players. Trump is made as in Partnership Euchre, by acceptance of the turn-up or declaration after it is rejected. The maker of trump calls a suit, and the holder of the best card in that suit becomes his partner, but must not reveal the fact until the card is duly played. As certain cards are not in play, the best card may turn out to be a king, queen, or even a jack; or the caller may hold it himself, in which case he has no partner. The maker of the trump may

also say "Alone," or call on a suit of which he holds the ace.

If the maker of the trump and his partner take three tricks, they score 1 point each; for a march, 3. If they are euchred, each opponent scores 2. A lone hand scores 1 for three tricks; for a march, 1 for each player, including himself (4, 5, or 6, depending on the number playing).

Two-Handed Euchre

The rules of Partnership Euchre apply except as follows:

1. The deck is reduced to 24 cards by discarding the sevens and eights.

2. The declaration "Alone" does not exist and the score for march is 2 points.

3. Laws on irregularities omit penalties for errors that do not damage the opponent, for example, exposure of cards, lead out of turn.

Three-Handed or Cutthroat Euchre

The rules of Partnership Euchre apply except as follows:

1. Each player plays for himself and there is no assisting.

2. In play, the player who makes trump plays against the other two, who keep their tricks together as partners. The scoring is as follows:

Maker of trump wins 3 or 4 tricks	1
Maker of trump wins 5 tricks	3
Maker of trump is euchred, each opponent	2

3. In applying rules on irregularities, the maker of trump is deemed a lone hand and the other two a partnership.

Railroad Euchre

This very popular variant (also called Joker Euchre) is a partnership game (two players as partners against two) which is played with a 24-card deck to which a joker is added. The joker is the highest trump, ranking ahead of the right bower. The suit of the joker, if it should happen to be the turned-up card, may be agreed on beforehand, but it is usually set as spades.

The rules of Partnership Euchre hold good except in the manner of playing alone as given here:

1. When a player declares that he will play alone he may "call for his partner's best." He does this by passing any card from his hand face down across the table to his partner and receiving a card in exchange, also face down. Neither he nor his partner may look at the other's passed card before passing his own. The lone player cannot recall the exchange or make another.

2. When the dealer is playing alone, he has a chance to make another discard after receiving partner's card, exchanging a card for the turned-up trump. If he so wishes, the card he exchanges may be the one just passed to him by partner.

3. A lone player may be opposed by either one of his opponents, also playing alone against him. The lone opponent must make the announcement. After he does so, he calls for partner's best, and the exchange is made in the manner described in 1 above.

4. The opponents of a lone hand that is euchred score 4 points.

Railroad Euchre Variations. Any or all of the following variations may be employed to increase the interest in Railroad Euchre or any other Euchre game:

Laps. Points in excess of those required to win a game are carried over and counted as part of the next game. The effect of this rule is to preserve the incentive of playing alone, regardless of the score.

Slams. If a side reaches game with the other side having no score, the winners score for two games. Thus, a single can often be a rubber.

Pat Hand. If a player decides to play a lone hand "pat," that is, without exchanging with his partner or exchanging for the turned-up card if he is dealer, he scores 5 points if he wins all five tricks. Should he fail to win all five tricks, his opponents score 1 point. Should he be euchred, the opponents score 3 points. When a player announces that he is playing a pat hand, neither opponent is permitted to play alone against him.

Jambone. If a lone-hand player announces "Jambone," he exposes his entire hand face up on the table. Whenever his turn to lead comes, the opponent at his left may call the card for him to play. Whenever it is lone

hand's turn to play a trick, opponent at his right may call the card for him to play. Opponents, however, may not consult with each other, nor may they force the lone-hand player to make an illegal play. Opposing jambone alone is not permitted. If the lone-hand player succeeds in taking all five tricks, he scores 8 points. If he wins three or four tricks, he scores 1 point. If he is euchred, opponents score 2 points.

Jamboree. Should the player who made trump hold the five highest trumps ("jamboree"), he may show them immediately and score 16 points (which includes the score for march). The hand is not played out. This royalty rule applies only to the player who made trump. If the dealer was the maker of trump, he may use the turned-up card to complete a jamboree. The needed card may also be received in an exchange with partner, but in this case, most players score the jamboree as only 12 points.

Jackpot Euchre

This variation, which is sometimes called Buck Euchre, may be played by four, five, or six players, each playing for himself. If four play, the 24-card deck is used; the 28-card deck is used for five players, the 32-card deck for six players. The joker is added to the deck and ranks as the highest trump ahead of the right bower as in Railroad Euchre. However, making the trump and the play are as in Partnership Euchre. The differences are as follows:

1. Each player must put a chip into the pot before the deal.

2. The player who makes trump is not required to take 3 tricks. He simply has the advantage of deciding a favorable trump suit. But any player must take in at least one trick or pay a chip to the pot. Each player scores 1 point for each trick he takes in play.

3. The player who first reaches a score of 12 wins all the chips that are in the pot. Should at any time a player take all five tricks, however, he collects the entire pot, regardless of what his score is at the time. A new game is then begun.

AUCTION EUCHRE

Requirements

1. Five, six, or seven players.
2. The deck: five-hand, 32-cards, as in

four-hand; six-hand, 36 cards, the usual pack with sixes added; and seven-hand, 52 cards. In each instance, the joker may be added if desired, ranking as the highest trump.

3. Rank of cards: same as Partnership Euchre (page 234).

The Deal

Five-Hand and Six-Hand. Same as in four-hand, but after the first-round deal two cards face down for a widow. *Seven-hand:* Give each hand seven cards, a round of three cards at a time, then a round of four, or vice versa. After the first round, deal three cards face down for a widow (or four cards if the joker is used).

The Bidding. Each player in turn, commencing with the player to the left of the dealer, may make a bid or pass. There is only one round of bidding. Highest bidder names trump suit. Each bid names a number of points, and must be higher than the preceding bid.

The Widow. Maker of trump may take the widow in his hand and discard an equal number of cards, unless he has contracted to play without the widow.

Partners

Five-Hand. Maker of trump chooses his partners after seeing the widow. Bid of three tricks entitles him to one partner; bid of four or five tricks, two partners. He may choose any he pleases, regardless of where he sits. *Six-hand:* usually played by set partnerships of three against three, partners sitting alternately. *Seven-hand:* maker of trump chooses his partners after seeing widow. Bid of four or five tricks entitles him to one partner; bid of six or seven, to two partners.

Scoring. The play is the same as for Partnership Euchre, but the following tables show the various numbers that may be bid and the obligation of each bid.

FIVE-HAND

3 maker must win 3 tricks with help of one partner
4 maker must win four tricks with help of two partners

5 maker must win 5 tricks with help of two partners
8 maker must play alone and win 5 tricks, using widow
15 maker must play alone and win 5 tricks, without widow

SIX-HAND

3, 4, 5 side making trump must win number of tricks named (widow taken by maker of trump)
8 maker must play alone and win 5 tricks, using widow
15 maker must play alone and win 5 tricks, without widow

SEVEN-HAND

4, 5 maker must win number of tricks named with help of one partner
6, 7 maker must win number of tricks named with help of two partners
10 maker must play alone and win 7 tricks, using widow
20 maker must play alone and win 7 tricks, without widow

If the side making trump wins the number of tricks bid, it scores the value given in the table. There is no credit for winning more tricks than necessary. If the side making trump is euchred, the opponents score the value of the bid. In six-hand partnership play, only two accounts need be kept, one for each side. But with five or seven players, the full amount to which a side is entitled is credited to each member individually.

Additional rules are the same as in partnership play.

Progressive Euchre

Progressive Euchre is, as Progressive Bridge, a method of determining an overall winner when a number of players are playing at various tables. Any of the partnership forms of Euchre mentioned may be played at all tables, and the method of progression is the same as described in Progressive Bridge, page 143.

FIVE HUNDRED

The game of Five Hundred, while considered basically a member of the Euchre family and even sometimes called Bid Euchre, has some points in common with Bridge and Whist. It also includes an important feature similar to one in Auction Pinochle—a three-card widow for the successful bidder. The game for three hands is the most popular form.

Three-Hand Five Hundred

Requirements

1. Three players.

2. The 32-card Euchre deck, made up by stripping out all cards below the seven from the standard 52-card deck, is generally used.

A joker is added and is the highest trump of the deck. It is also known as the *best bower*. The function of the joker is described later. If no joker is available, the deuce of spades may be used instead.

3. The rank of the other cards is exactly as described in Partnership Euchre, except that bowers are not used in no-trump bids.

Beginning of the Game. The selection of the dealer, seating positions, changing seats, shuffle, and cut are as provided under the General Rules for Card Games, chapter 1.

The Deal. After the cards have been shuffled by dealer and cut by the player at his right, dealer serves cards beginning with the player at his left. He deals three cards to each player at a time, then three cards face down on the table for a widow or blind to be used later in play. He then completes the deal, dealing two cards at a time, then three and finally two until each has a hand of ten cards. Or, he may deal four cards at a time after the first round and finally three, or any other variation. Thus the entire 33-card deck is dealt out.

Object of the Game. The object is to be the highest bidder and win at least enough tricks in play to fulfill the contract, scoring points thereby. The opponents of the highest bidder try to win enough tricks in play to defeat the contract.

Bidding. Each player in turn, beginning with the player at dealer's left, has one opportunity to bid. He may pass or bid; if there has been a previous bid, his bid must be higher than any previous bid. Each bid must name a number of tricks, from six to ten, together with a denomination, which will establish the trump suit (as, "Six spades"). To overcall a previous bid, a player must bid more tricks or the same number of tricks in a higher-ranking denomination (see Schedules, page 241).

Optional Rule: If the Original or Inverted Schedule is used, as shown on page 241, a bid overcalls the preceding bid if its scoring value is higher or if it requires a greater number of tricks for the same scoring value.

Nullo Bid: Some permit the bid "Nullo," which is a contract to lose all the tricks at no-trump. The nullo bid has a scoring value of 250; on the Avondale Schedule it overcalls eight spades or lower and is overcalled by eight clubs or higher. If nullo becomes the contract, in a partnership game the contractor's partner or partners abandon their hands and the contractor plays alone against the others. If he wins a trick he (or his side) is set back the 250 points and each opponent scores 10 for each trick the contractor takes.

If all players pass, the deal is abandoned without a score.

Optional Rule: A passed deal is played at no-trump, each player for himself. The player at the dealer's left leads first. Each trick won counts 10 points. As there is no contract, there is no setting back.

The Play. The high bid becomes the contract. In this three-hand play, the two other players combine in temporary partnership against the contractor.

The contractor takes the widow into his hand, without showing it, and then discards any three cards face down, without showing them.

The contractor makes the first lead. The leader at any time may lead any card. Each other hand must follow suit if able; if unable to follow suit, the hand may play any card. A trick is won by the highest trump, or, if it contains no trump, by the highest card of the suit led. The winner of a trick leads to the next. Each of the contractor's opponents takes in and keeps the tricks he wins.

The Joker. When there is a trump suit, the joker is the highest trump; it belongs to the trump suit, must be played if necessary to follow suit, and may be played only when a card of the trump suit can legally be played. At no-trump contracts (or nullo, if played), the joker is a suit by itself but also is the highest card of any suit and wins any trick to which it is legally played. The holder of the joker may not play it when he can follow suit to the suit led, but if he cannot follow suit and plays the joker he wins the trick. If a player leads the joker at a no-trump (or nullo) contract, he must specify the suit others must play to follow suit, but the joker wins the trick.

Scoring. If the contractor wins as many tricks as he bid, he scores the number of points called for in whichever scoring table is being used. There is no credit for extra tricks over the contract, except that if the contractor wins all ten tricks he scores a minimum of 250 (more, if his bid was for more).

If the contractor fails to make the contract, the value of his bid is deducted from his score. It is possible for a player to be set back until he has a minus score; he is then said to be *in the hole* (from the common practice of drawing a ring around a minus score).

Whether the contract is made or defeated, each opponent of the contractor scores 10 for each trick he himself has taken.

TABLE OF SCORING POINTS: AVONDALE SCHEDULE

When Trumps Are In	Point Values				
	6 Tricks	7 Tricks	8 Tricks	9 Tricks	10 Tricks
Spades	40	140	240	340	440
Clubs	60	160	260	360	460
Diamonds	80	180	280	380	480
Hearts	100	200	300	400	500
No-trump	120	220	320	420	520

ORIGINAL SCHEDULE

When Trumps Are In	Point Values				
	6 Tricks	7 Tricks	8 Tricks	9 Tricks	10 Tricks
Spades	40	80	120	160	200
Clubs	60	120	180	240	300
Diamonds	80	160	240	320	400
Hearts	100	200	300	400	500
No-trump	120	240	360	480	600

Note: In this table, for instance, eight clubs is a higher bid than nine spades; seven hearts is higher than nine spades; seven no-trump is higher than eight clubs, etc.

INVERTED SCHEDULE

In this method of scoring, the suits run clubs (lowest), spades, hearts, diamonds and no-trump, in that order upward.

When Trumps Are In	Point Values				
	6 Tricks	7 Tricks	8 Tricks	9 Tricks	10 Tricks
Clubs	40	80	120	160	200
Spades	60	120	180	240	300
Hearts	80	160	240	320	400
Diamonds	100	200	300	400	500
No-trump	120	240	360	480	600

The Game. The player or side first to reach a total of 500 points wins the game. A player or side that goes 500 in the hole loses the game; if one player in a three-hand game becomes minus 500 he cannot win the game but continues play until the game is won, and if he is first to reach 500 no one wins the game. If the contractor and an opponent reach 500 on the same deal, the contractor wins.

In a three-hand game, if the contractor does not reach 500 but both his opponents do, the first opponent to reach 500 wins. If the contractor could not reach 500 by making his bid, the opponent first to reach 500 may claim the game as soon as the tricks he has won bring him to 500. At the time of making the claim he must show his remaining cards. If he does not have the 500 he claimed, play continues; all his remaining cards become exposed cards. (An optional alternative is to require 1,000 or 1,500 for game. The scoring is speeded up by awarding points for cards won in tricks; 1 for each ace, 10 for each face card or ten, the pip value for each lower card, nothing for the joker. These points do not affect the question of whether the contractor makes his bid, which depends on the number of tricks won. He scores his points, extra, if he makes his bid; the opponents always score them.)

Additional Rules

New Deal. There must be a new deal by the same dealer if a card is found exposed in the pack; if the dealer gives the wrong number of cards to any hand; or if, before the last card is dealt, attention is called to the fact that the cut was omitted or that the dealer departed in any way from the prescribed method of dealing (as by dealing batches of three-three-four or four-three-three, or laying out the widow at any time but after the first round).

Bid Out of Turn. In three-hand play, there is no penalty for a pass or bid out of turn; the call is void, and the player may make any legal call in his proper turn. In partnership play, a bid (not a pass) out of turn is bid and that side may make no further bid (though a bid made previously by partner of the offender is not canceled).

Wrong Number of Cards. If, during the bidding, two hands (excluding the widow) are found to have the wrong number of cards, there must be a new deal by the same dealer. If the widow and one hand are incorrect, the incorrect hand loses the right to bid; any other player draws a sufficient number of cards from the excess and gives them to the deficient hand. If, during the play, the contractor and an opponent are found to have incorrect hands, or if there is one incorrect hand due to an incorrect pack, there must be a new deal by the same dealer. If two opponents have incorrect hands, the contractor's being correct, the bid is deemed to have been made and the opponents may not score. The contractor may continue in an effort to win all the tricks, and he is deemed to win all the final tricks to which the short hand cannot play. If the opponents' hands are correct, the contractor's hand and his discard incorrect, the bid is lost, but the deal is played out to determine how many tricks are to be credited to each opponent.

Exposed Card. A card is deemed exposed if it is dropped face up on the table, held so that a partner sees its face, or named by the owner as being in his hand. An exposed card must be left face up on the table and played at the first legal opportunity thereafter. But there is no penalty against a contractor playing alone for exposing cards, except in case of a corrected revoke.

Lead or Play Out of Turn. A lead out of turn must be retracted on demand of an opponent, if the demand is made before the trick is completed; and cards played to it may be retracted without penalty. The card led in error is treated as an exposed card; and if it was the offender's partner's turn to lead, an opponent may require him to lead a named suit, or not to lead the suit of the exposed card. If a player plays out of turn, not as leader, his card is deemed exposed. If an error in leading or playing out of turn is not noticed until the trick is gathered, the trick stands as regular.

Revoke. Failure to follow suit to a lead when able is a revoke. A revoke may be corrected at any time before the next ensuing lead, otherwise it stands as established. When a revoke is corrected, the incorrect card is deemed exposed, including a case where it belongs to a contractor playing alone. If an established revoke is claimed and proved before the cut for the next deal, and the revoking hand was on the contracting side, the contract is scored as lost; if the revoking hand was an opponent, the contract is scored as made, and the opponents score nothing.

Illegal Information. If a player gives information illegally to his partner, or looks at a trick after it is gathered and quitted, or if the contractor's discards are looked at by him after the opening lead, or by another player at any time, the opponent at the right of the leader may name the suit to be led the next time the offender or his partner has the lead.

Error in Score. A proved error in recording scores must be corrected on demand made before the first bid (not pass) of the next deal after that to which the error pertains. In any other case, recorded scores may not be changed.

Strategy of Five Hundred. Since there are only ten trumps, the normal minimum trump length for any bid is four including two or three of the higher ones. Actually, most contracts go to hands with five or more trumps.

CHANCES OF FINDING AT LEAST ONE TRUMP IN WIDOW

If you hold 4 trumps the chances are 1,091 in 1,771 or 1.00 to .62 for.
If you hold 5 trumps the chances are 955 in 1,771 or 1.00 to .85 for.

CHANCES OF FINDING ONE WANTED CARD IN THE WIDOW

Wanted Cards Out of Number in the Widow	Chances of Finding It in the Widow	Odds on Finding That Card
1 of 1	231 in 1,771 or	6.66 to 1 against
1 of 2	441 in 1,771 or	3.01 to 1 against
1 of 3	631 in 1,771 or	1.81 to 1 against
1 of 4	802 in 1,771 or	1.21 to 1 against
1 of 5	955 in 1,771 or	1.00 to .85 for

A simple but rough method of figuring how many tricks a hand will win is to count one trick for each trump in excess of three, and one trick for each side ace and king.

For a no-trump bid, it is usually necessary to have stoppers in all four suits. (Minimum stoppers are ace, king +, queen ++.) Of course, with a joker, it is possible to bid no-trump with a stopperless suit provided the rest of the hand is fairly solid in top cards. The best hand for no-trumps is a long solid or nearly solid suit. The opening lead gives the contractor the advantage of starting with his long suit before the opponents have a chance to go after his stoppers in their long suits.

It's not wise to bid in hopes of buying a specific card in the widow. But, usually some help can be expected to improve the hand by adding a trump or an extra card to a long suit. Since only one chance of bidding is allowed, it must be the highest safe bid that can be made. You may have to stretch the bid slightly and count on some help from the widow.

After taking the widow, try, through your discards, to establish a short suit, but keep all long suits intact. At no-trump, save your longest suit intact and discard whatever is possible without exposing your stoppers. In other words, the discards are almost invariably worthless low cards.

With five or more trumps, the bidder should lead trumps at once in order to pull two adverse trumps to his one. Even with only four trumps it is wise to lead to the opening trick with trump, especially if you have stoppers in every suit. Your only long suit, even if not solid, should be led early in the effort to establish it. High cards in short suits should be used only for reentries. At no-trump, the bidder should usually open his longest suit (regardless of its top strength) and continue to play that suit at every opportunity. With no really long suit (five or more cards), he should attempt to drive out the adverse aces and kings that stand in the way of his lower-card tricks.

As an opponent of the bidder, do not help him by opening new suits. If possible develop your own strong suit and if you can find what he is void in, force this suit at every chance.

Two-Hand Five Hundred

The pack and the deal are the same as in the three-hand game, except that the hand at dealer's left is dealt face down on the table and is dead. With these ten cards out of play, the bidding is largely guesswork. Not to be left "at home" by a bold opponent, a player is bound to be forward in bidding and to speculate on buying just what he needs from the widow. If one player's score reaches minus 500, the other wins the game.

The two-hand game may also be played with a 24-card pack, nine-spot low; the widow is four cards, no extra hand is dealt, and the rules otherwise are as in three-hand.

Four-Hand Five Hundred

The four-hand game is played with fixed partnerships, partners sitting opposite each other. The pack is 42 or 43 cards, made by discarding the twos, threes, and black fours from a 52-card pack, and adding a joker if desired; often it is not. Each player receives ten cards and the remaining cards go to the widow. If one side's score reaches minus 500, its opponents win the game. All other rules are as in the three-hand game, except that two always play against two.

Five-Hand Five Hundred

Five players use the regular 52-card pack, usually with the joker added, so that each player receives ten cards and there is a three-card widow as in three-hand. After the bidding, the high bidder may select any other player to be his partner; if he bid for eight or more tricks, he may name any two partners. (Some play that the high bidder selects his partner by naming a card, as in Call-Ace Euchre, page 237.)

Six-Hand Five Hundred

For six players there is available a 62-card pack that includes spot cards numbered 11 and 12 in each suit and 13 in each of two suits; the joker may be added, making a 63-card pack and permitting a deal of ten cards to each player and three to the widow. There are two sides of three partners each, the partners being seated alternatively so that each has an opponent on his right and left.

NAPOLEON

This game, more commonly called *Nap*, is another relative of Euchre and one of the easiest to learn and play. It is particularly popular in England.

Requirements

1. Two to six players, but four make the best game. Each plays for himself. A standard 52-card deck may be used, but the game is much more interesting when enough cards are stripped from the deck so that only six cards remain after the deal. For four players, that would mean a deck of 26 cards containing aces, kings, queens, jacks, tens, nines, and two eights.

2. Cards rank as follows: ace (high), king, queen, jack, ten, nine, eight, seven, six, five, four, three, two (low).

Beginning of the Game. The selection of the dealer, seating positions, changing seats, shuffle, and cut are as provided under the General Rules for Card Games, chapter 1.

The Deal. After the shuffle and the cut by the player at his right, the dealer gives five cards to each player, beginning with the one at his left. He deals two cards at a time, then three, or the other way around. (If five or six are playing, dealer takes no cards, but he takes part in the payoff.)

The Bidding. There is only one round of bidding. Each player in turn, beginning on the dealer's left, must make a bid higher than any preceding bid, or pass. Each bid is the number of tricks, out of five, the bidder will take playing alone against all the others, if allowed to name the trump. When bidding, he does not name the suit he intends to name as trumps. If no one bids, the dealer must bid at least one.

Variants. (1) Sometimes a bid of three no-trumps (called *Misère*) is allowed and it ranks above three with trumps and below four with trumps. Actually a bid of Misère is a contract to lose every trick, without naming any trump suit. It scores as a bid of three. (2) Some also play that two bids (Wellington and Blücher) are permitted, which successively outrank Nap (ordinarily the highest-possible bid). Blücher is then the highest bid. Each of these contracts and Nap must take five tricks and they differ only in scoring.

Object of Play. *For the high bidder,* to take number of tricks bid; for the other players, who are combined in a temporary partnership, to defeat the bid.

The Play. The high bidder makes the opening lead, and the suit of this lead becomes trump. Each player, in turn, must follow suit, if possible; if not, he may trump or discard as he desires. The winner of each trick leads to the next. Tricks taken should be quitted face down, in such arrangement that they may be easily counted, but they may not thereafter be examined. The highest card of the suit led takes the trick; unless it is trumped, in which case the highest trump wins. It is only required to lead trumps to the first trick.

Scoring. There is no credit for extra tricks won by the bidder or by his opponents beyond what are needed to make or defeat the bid. If the bidder makes his bid, he collects

from each other player; if he is defeated, he pays every other player.

Bid	Bidder Wins	Bidder Loses
Less than 5	1 for each trick	1 for each trick
Nap	10 for each trick	5 for each trick
Wellington	10 for each trick	10 for each trick
Blücher	10 for each trick	20 for each trick

The usual way of scoring is to distribute an equal number of chips to all players before the game and then settle in chips after each deal.

Additional Rules

Misdeal. When a misdeal occurs, the cards are redealt by the same player.

Wrong Number of Cards. If a player is dealt the wrong number of cards, he must demand a new deal before bidding or passing; otherwise he must play with an incorrect hand. If the bidder has the correct number of cards, but another hand is defective, he must be paid, if he succeeds; if he fails, he need not pay. If the bidder has too many cards, he scores nothing for making his contract; if less, he must pay or be paid as he loses or wins. He loses any tricks upon which he has no card to play.

Play Out of Turn. A bidder leading out of turn must take back the card, unless all have played to it; in the latter event it stands. An opponent leading out of turn pays three chips to the bidder, and is not paid if the bidder loses.

Revoke. When a revoke is detected, the hands are abandoned. If the bidder revoked, he pays each player the same amount as if he lost. When an opponent revokes, he must pay the amount of the bid to the bidder and also to the other players.

Widow Nap

This variation, often called Sir Garnet, has an extra hand of five cards which is dealt and placed on the table. Any player in turn may pick up the widow. When he does so, he commits himself to a bid of Nap. He must then discard any five cards. If he uses the widow and is successful in play, he collects ten chips from each player; but if he is unsuccessful, he pays out ten chips to each player. If a player does not use the widow, the regular Nap payoffs prevail.

Pool Nap

In this variation, in which the rules of regular Nap prevail, a pool or pot is formed by ante of two chips from each player. This pot goes to the first player who bids a Nap and makes it. A player who bids Nap and fails to make it, must pay in an amount equal to the pool. So long as the pot is not won, each successive dealer antes two more chips. In addition a revoking player contributes five extra chips to the pot, and a player making a lead out of turn contributes three extra chips.

Peep Nap

This is a variety of Pool Nap. A widow of one card is dealt. Each player in turn may look at it, by paying one chip to the pot. The successful bidder gets the widow (whether he has peeped or not) and discards one card, to bring his hand down to five. Even after Nap (or Wellington or Blücher) has been bid, later players in turn may pay their counter and peep at the widow.

Purchase Nap

This game, also called Ecarte Nap, is another Pool game. After the deal, but before any bids are made, a player may discard as many cards as he pleases and the dealer gives him the proper number of cards from the stock to replace them. For each card the player discards, he must pay a chip into the pot. Each player in turn to the left has one chance to make the exchange, but he is not required to do so if he does not wish to. The player who first bids and wins a Nap hand wins the pool.

SPOIL FIVE

One of the oldest card games, Spoil Five (also called Five Cards or Five Fingers) is a particular favorite of the Irish.

Requirements

1. Two to ten players, but the best game is with five to seven, each playing for himself.

2. A standard 52-card deck.

3. Rank of cards: In trumps, the ace of hearts is always the third-best trump, no matter the suit. Of the trump suit, the five is high, the jack second highest, the ace of hearts third, then the ace, king, queen in order. The rank of the spot or index cards, trump or not, is expressed "highest in red, lowest in black." In plain suits (that is, suits not trumps) the king, queen, jack are high in that order; followed by the spot cards, as above. In plain suits, the diamond ace is lowest of all; the black aces come between the jack and the deuce. When hearts are trumps, there are 13 trumps; five, jack, ace, king, queen, ten, nine, eight, seven, six, four, three, two. When diamonds are trumps, there are 14, the ace of hearts ranking third highest and two lowest. When spades or clubs are trumps, there are 14, ranking five, jack, ace of hearts, ace, king, queen, two, three, four, six, seven, eight, nine, ten (low).

The Deal. There is no cutting for the deal. Any player deals cards one at a time and face up to each player until a jack is turned. The player who gets the jack is the dealer for the first hand. The turn to deal then goes to the left for subsequent hands.

After shuffling the deck and having it cut by the player at his right, dealer gives each player a hand of five cards beginning with the player at his left. He deals first three at a time around, then two at a time. The next card is turned up, and that card determines the trump suit for that deal.

Robbing the Trump. Should the turned trump card be an ace, the dealer may discard any card in his hand face down for it, and his card does not have to be a trump card. He can either discard when playing to the first trick, or he can leave the ace there until ready to play it. The dealer, however, does not have to take the ace if he does not desire it. But he must declare whether or not he is exchanging for the ace. It is customary for the leader (the player at the dealer's left) when making the first play to ask dealer whether he wishes to exchange for the ace. If dealer has made no declaration by then, he must do so before playing.

If the turned trump card is any card other than an ace, a player who does hold the ace of that suit may exchange any card in his hand for the turned-up card when it is his turn to play. If he does not wish to rob the trump, he does not have to do so. But in that case, he must tell the dealer to turn the trump face down, thus identifying himself as the holder of the ace. If the holder of the ace of trumps makes a play without exchanging or identifying himself, his ace becomes the lowest trump in play. And if it should happen to be the ace of hearts, it loses the privilege previously described for that card.

Object of the Game. To win three of the five tricks played; or, as opponents to defeat any one player's chance of taking three tricks.

The Play. Player at dealer's left leads any card to the first trick. Each player in turn must follow suit, or he may play a trump even if able to follow suit. If he cannot follow suit, he may play a trump or throw off any card, as he pleases. A player must follow suit to a trump if able to, but the following three cards are exempt from this rule: five and jack of trumps or ace of hearts. That is, he need not follow suit with such a card if the card led is a trump card of lower rank. But he must follow suit with such a card if the lead was a trump card of higher rank. The highest-ranking card of a led suit wins the trick if there are no trump cards in the trick. A trump card wins a trick, but if the trick contains more than one trump card, the highest-ranking trump wins. The winner of a trick leads to the next until all five tricks have been played. Each player keeps tricks that he won face down in front of him.

Scoring. Each player puts one chip in the pool. The pool may be taken by the first player to win three tricks in any deal. If a player continues to play after winning three tricks, he must win all five (in which case he gets the pool plus one chip from each other player); if he does not win all five tricks, he does not get the pool. After any hand in which the pool is not won, each player puts in another chip for the next deal.

Additional Rules

Misdeals. If too many or too few cards are dealt on any round; if dealer exposes a card in dealing; if the deal is commenced with an uncut pack (provided a new deal is demanded before the deal is completed); or if dealer counts the cards on the table or in the pack, a misdeal is declared.

Irregular Hand. A hand with an incorrect number of cards is dead, and the other players continue play; but if a player has won three tricks with an irregular hand before it is discovered, he wins the pool.

Revoke. (*Illegal exposure of a card after any player has won two tricks; robbing the trump when not holding the ace.*) The offender's hand is dead and he does not receive cards until the pool in progress is won; but he must still add to the pool when other players do.

Forty-Five

Variation of Spoil Five, for two, four (two against two), or six (three against three) players. Game is scored by points; side taking three or four tricks scores 5 points; five tricks, 10 points. Sometimes each trick counts 5 points, and score of side taking fewest tricks is deducted from that of side taking most tricks. Thus three tricks count 5; four tricks, 15; five tricks, 25 points; 45 points is game.

Twenty-Five

In some areas, the game is played for 25 points; otherwise it is played in the same manner as Forty-Five.

Auction Forty-Five

This form of Spoil Five and Forty-Five is the national game of Nova Scotia. It is played in the same manner as Spoil Five except for the following:

1. Four players, two against two as partners, or six, three against three as partners, seated alternately.

2. When bidding, the player to the left of dealer does so first and the turn passes to the left. Bids are in multiples of 5 points and the highest bid is 30. Each bid must be higher than the preceding bid, except that dealer may beat the previous bid without going over, by saying "I hold"; if he does, each player who did not previously pass gets another turn and dealer again may take the bid without going over. A side having 100 points or more may not bid less than 20.

3. When discarding and drawing, the high bidder names the trump, then each player discards as many cards as he wishes and dealer restores his hand to five cards from the top of the pack. The player at the left of the high bidder leads first.

4. When scoring, each trick won counts 5 and the highest trump in play counts an additional 5, making 10 in all for the trick it wins. If the high bidder's side makes its bid, it scores all it makes; if it fails, the amount of the bid is subtracted from its score. The opposing side always scores whatever it wins in tricks. A bid of 30 (for all five tricks) is worth 60 if it is made and loses 30 if it fails. Game is won by the first side to reach 120.

SINGLE HASENPFEFFER

This old game is another offshoot of Euchre. Its name means hare or rabbit stew in German and it is a fast-moving game.

Requirements

1. Four players, two against two as partners.

2. A 25-card deck consisting of the ace, king, queen, jack, ten, nine of each suit plus a joker.

3. The joker is the highest trump. The rank of the other cards is exactly as described in Partnership Euchre, page 234.

Beginning of the Game. The selection of the dealer, partners, seating positions, changing seats, shuffle, and cut are as provided under the General Rules for Card Games, chapter 1.

The Deal. Dealer gives three cards at a time to each player until all have hands of six cards. The last card is turned face down in the center of the table and is not looked at by any player.

Object of Game. The object of the game is to win 10 points in tricks, each trick counting 1 point.

The Bidding. Beginning with the player at dealer's left, each in his turn bids the number of tricks that he believes his side will take, or he passes. A bidder names only the number of tricks, but not the suit. A bid may begin as low as a player chooses. Every succeeding bid must be for a higher number. A player has only one bid and may not bid after passing. If all players pass, the player holding the joker must bid three and name which suit is to be trump. If no one holds the joker, there is a new deal by the same dealer.

The Play. The successful bidder picks up the face-down card and places it in his hand without exposing it to the other players. He then names the suit for that deal. After this, he discards any one card to bring his hand to six cards. Then he leads any card he wishes for the first trick.

Playing turn goes to the left. A player must follow suit if able to do so; if he cannot follow suit, he may play a trump or any other card. The highest card in a trick wins the trick, except when a trump is played. Then the highest trump card takes the trick. The winner of a trick turns it face down in a common trick pile kept by his side, that is, all tricks won by himself and his partner. The winner of a trick leads any card to the next trick, and play continues in this fashion until all tricks have been played. A player may not play the joker as long as he can follow to a nontrump suit led.

Scoring. If the bidder's side fulfills the contract, it scores 1 point for each trick it won in play. If the bidder's side does not make its contract, it is "set back." In such a case the amount of the bid is deducted from any previous score, even if it means going minus or in the hole. Whether bidder's side fulfills the contract or not, opponents score 1 point for each trick they win during the play. The side first reaching 10 points is winner. If both sides reach 10 points in the same deal, the bidding side wins.

Additional Rules. If irregularities occur, follow the additional rules for Partnership Euchre, page 235.

Double Hasenpfeffer

This game is played in the same manner as Single Hasenpfeffer except for the following:

1. Four or six players, in two partnerships.

2. A 48-card Pinochle deck is used, ranking as in Partnership Euchre, with no joker. Each player is dealt four cards at a time, until the whole deck is distributed.

3. In bidding, the lowest bid is 6. If the bidder thinks he can win all the tricks, he may, after naming the trump suit, discard two cards and ask his partner (or partners, if any) for his two best; thereafter he plays alone.

4. If the game is four-handed, his side scores 24 if he wins, but is set 12 if he fails. In six-handed, his side scores 16 if he wins, or is set 8. If all pass without a bid, the dealer must bid 6 and play the hand. Each trick counts 1, except in lone hands, which count double; and 62 makes the game.

Variation. The game may also be played by two to six players as individuals. In a five-hand game the three nines are removed from the deck and each player is dealt nine cards.

RAMS

This easily learned, lively game is today comparatively little played but deserves to be better known.

Requirements

1. Three to six players, each scoring for himself. If six play, dealer does not take a hand.

2. A 32-card deck is used, made up by stripping out all cards below the seven from a standard 52-card deck.

3. The cards rank: ace (high), king, queen, jack, ten, nine, eight, seven (low). Some old-time players, however, rank the ace below the jack.

Beginning of the Game. The selection of the dealer, seating positions, changing seats, shuffle, and cut are as provided under the General Rules for Card Games, chapter 1.

The Deal. After the shuffle and the cut, dealer gives each player a hand of five cards, beginning with the player at the left and going in clockwise rotation. He deals two cards to each for the first round and then three, or first three and then two. He deals an extra hand, or widow, to the table just before dealing cards to himself. The next card, after the deal, is turned up and its suit is trump.

Object of the Game. To win as many as possible of the five tricks to be played for.

The Play. The player to the left of the dealer has three choices: he may (1) play with his original hand; (2) discard his hand face down on the table and take the widow; or (3) pass. Actually, any player may discard his hand for the widow, as long as no other preceding player has done so. In fact, each player in turn must decide to play; or exchange for the widow, if this has not been done; or pass. The hands of those who have passed must not be discarded until every player has said whether he will play or pass. Of course hands, once discarded, should not be examined thereafter. If all have passed except the player to the dealer's right, he must play with the dealer. If all but one have passed, the dealer must play with him. If two or more declare to play, the dealer may play or pass, as he chooses. The dealer is allowed to discard one card and take the turned trump into his hand in its place. Each player who

plays must take at least one trick, or forfeit five chips to the next pot.

Any player may declare a *general rams*. He then has the lead, and must win all five tricks. Each other player must play in a general rams, even if he has already passed. Except when a general rams is announced, the active player to the left of the dealer leads a card of any suit he wishes. Each player in turn must follow suit, and must play a higher card than the one led if he can. If he cannot win or head the trick, he may play a card of the suit led. If he cannot follow suit, he must trump (or overtrump, if trumps have already been played). Even though he cannot overtrump, he must still play trump if he can. If he can neither follow suit nor trump, he may discard. The highest card played of the suit led wins, unless the trick is trumped; in which case the highest trump wins. The winner of the first trick leads to the second, and so until the hand is played out.

Scoring. Each dealer in his turn contributes five chips to the pot. As previously stated, any player who does not pass and who fails to take a trick puts five counters in the next pot. At the end of each hand, each player takes one-fifth of the pot for each trick he has taken. A pot containing only the dealer's five chips is called a *simple pot,* and all players must play. If it contains more than the five chips, it is called a *double pot,* and players can pass or play. If a player declaring general rams takes all five tricks, he takes the pot, and each other player pays him five chips. If he fails, he must pay each player five chips, and double the pot.

Bierspiel

This variant of Rams, also called Beer Play, is played like the parent game except for the following:

1. The seven of diamonds is always the second highest trump, regardless of which suit is trump. If the seven of diamonds should be the one turned up for trump, another card is dealt from the stack and the card beneath it determines the trump suit and dealer may use both cards, discarding two others in their

place. If dealer passes, the first active player at his left may exchange for the trump and the seven of diamonds.

2. Players must not look at their hands until the dealer has turned up the trump card.

3. If there are four or more active players in the play, the first three leads must be in trump; for three active players there must be two initial trump leads; for two active players only the opening lead must be in trump.

4. If a leader to a trick in which a trump lead is required holds no trump, he may play any card but place it on the table face down. The other players, however, must play trumps.

5. Each player begins with 15 points. For each trick he takes he cancels 1 point. The first to cancel all his points is declared the winner. Penalties are added to a player's score.

Rounce

This game is played the same as Rams, except for the following:

1. A standard 52-card deck is used and the cards rank ace (high), king, queen, jack, ten, down to two (low).

2. The widow is dealt six cards, one of which is discarded by the player taking the widow.

3. A player is not required to win a trick, and he need not trump a trick if he chooses not to. But, the winner of the first trick must lead trumps for the second trick. Thereafter, any suit may be led. There is no general rams.

THREE-CARD LOO

This relative of Euchre, whose real name is Lanterloo or Lanterley, and is sometimes called Limited Loo, was at one time the most popular of all social games of cards in Europe. Today it has given way to several other games.

Requirements

1. Three to 17 players, but the best is with five to eight.

2. A standard 52-card deck.

3. Cards rank from ace (high), king, queen, jack, ten down to two (low).

Beginning of the Game. The selection of the dealer, seating positions, changing seats, shuffle, and cut are as provided under the General Rules for Card Games, chapter 1.

The Deal. After the cards are shuffled and cut, the dealer puts three chips in the pot and deals three cards to each player, in rotation left to right, one at a time. No trump is turned when there are only three chips or counters in the pot, which is called a *simple pool* or *pot*. This deal is called a *bold stand,* since everyone must play the hand dealt him.

Player at the dealer's left leads any card he pleases. Other players in turn must follow suit to a lead and try to win it if they can. The cards are not gathered into tricks, but are left face up before each player. If everyone can follow suit, the winner of the trick leads for the next, and so on. But if one or more players are unable to follow suit to any trick,

the dealer turns up the top card of the stock for a trump before play to the next trick. If any trump has been played, the highest trump wins the trick. When a trump is turned, the winner of a trick must lead a trump to the next trick if able to.

For each trick a player wins, he takes one-third of the pot. A player who takes no tricks is *looed* and must put up three chips for the next pot. The dealer of the next round adds his three chips, and the pot, now containing more than three chips, is known as a *double pool* or *pot*.

When the double pot is played, the dealer deals as before, but also deals a hand just before his own for a widow. Then he turns up a trump. Beginning with the player at the dealer's left, each player in turn has the choice of standing on the cards dealt him, exchanging his hand for the widow if it has not been taken up, or passing. If he passes, he drops out of the deal. But remember that any player standing or exchanging will be looed, unless he wins a trick. If all pass but the player to the right of the dealer, he must play the hand, take the widow, or give up the pool to the dealer.

If all but one player pass, and if he has no exchange for the widow, the dealer must stand or defend with the widow. If he takes any tricks, his winnings are left in the pool. If he is looed, he does not pay. If the one player standing has taken the widow, the pool is his, unless the dealer will play against him on his own account.

All having declared, the active player to the left of the dealer must lead a trump if he has one, and he must lead the top of two or more. The winner of the trick must lead a trump if he has one. Each player in turn must follow suit, and must try to win the trick if he can. Players must trump if they cannot follow suit and must overtrump if they are able to, but need not undertrump. The winners of the three tricks divide the pool proportionately. All who are looed put up three chips each for the next pool. If no one is looed, the next will be a simple pot.

Additional Rules

Misdeal. If a dealer deals a wrong number of cards or hands, he loses the deal, forfeits three chips to the pool, and the next pool is a double.

Revokes. If a player revokes, by failing to follow suit, or to head a trick, or to lead a trump when required, the pot is divided equally among the rest who hold cards; and the offender antes up six chips for the next pot.

Unlimited Loo

This is the same as Three-Card Loo except that every player who is looed must double the amount in the current pot, as a foundation for the next pot.

Loo with Flushes

In this variation, which is played like Three-Card Loo except that if any player in a double pot holds three trumps, either dealt to him or found in the widow, he waits until all the players (including dealer) have declared or passed. He then shows his flush in trumps, and takes the pot without playing for it; all who have not passed pay three chips to the pot. If two players hold trump flushes, the one on the left of the dealer wins the pot, regardless of the rank of the cards; but the other flush is not looed.

Pam-Loo

This game is played like Three-Card Loo except that the jack of clubs (known as *pam*) is the highest trump, regardless of the suit that is trump. When the ace of trumps is led, however, pam must not be played unless its holder has no other trump.

Irish Loo

This variation is played like Three-Card Loo except for the following:

1. There is no difference between single and double pots in that no extra hand is dealt and the trump card is always turned up before the opening lead.

2. If a player who stands or stays in the game wishes to exchange any cards, the dealer gives him replacements from the top of the stock.

Five-Card Loo

This variant is played like Three-Card Loo except for the following:

1. Each player receives a hand of five cards.

2. The dealer antes five chips into the pot.

3. A flush of five trumps wins the pot without playing.

Everyone at the table, whether playing the hand or not, is looed if he does not take a trick, and must contribute five chips to the next pot. Forfeits for irregularities are in multiples of five, so that the pot can be distributed equally for the five tricks won.

ECARTE

Once a leading stake game for two hands in France and England, Ecarte has suffered a steady decline. But it has attractive elements and a pace that make it a potential candidate for revived popularity.

Requirements

1. Two players.

2. A 32-card deck, made up by stripping out all cards below the seven.

3. The cards rank: king (high), queen, jack, ace, ten, nine, eight, seven (low).

Beginning of the Game. The selection of the dealer, seating positions, changing seats, shuffle, and cut are as provided under the

General Rules for Card Games, chapter 1.

The Deal. Each player is dealt a hand of five cards; three at a time, then two at a time; or the other way around, alternately, beginning with nondealer. The eleventh card is turned up, and its suit is trump for the entire deal. If it is a king, the dealer scores a point immediately. The remainder of the deck may be used for further play, but the trump card is not used and is kept face up during the play.

Object of the Game. To win at least three out of five tricks.

Drawing. If the nondealer wishes to play his original hand, he says "I play." If he wishes to strengthen his hand by discarding and drawing to it from the stock, a privilege the dealer then shares, he says "I propose." The dealer may refuse this privilege, by saying "Play"; or he may accept it, dealing the opponent as many cards from the top of the stock as he discards. The dealer may then discard and draw to fill his own hand. This process may be repeated alternately until one of the players announces that he is ready to play. (With the deck exhausted, the hands must be played.) Each time, the number drawn must be the same as the number discarded. Discards are made face down, and may not be examined thereafter.

Declaration of King. If the king of trumps is not turned up as the eleventh card, the player holding the king may score 1 point provided the holding is announced before a card is led. If the player holding the king does not wish to declare it, he does not have to do so. But he may not score for it in that case.

The Play. The nondealer leads any card he pleases to the first trick. Before he does so, he should say "I play." It is customary to announce the suit that he is leading but not the denomination of the card. The dealer must follow suit, if able; and is compelled to take the trick with a higher card, if he can. If he cannot follow suit, he must play a trump, if able; if not possible, he discards any card. The higher card of the suit led takes the trick, unless it is trumped; in the latter case the trump or the highest trump wins. The winner of each trick leads to the next, announcing the suit of the card led. If this is announced incorrectly, the other player may demand that the card be taken back and one of the announced suit led; or that the card led remain.

If the leader has no card of the suit he announced and failed to lead, the other player may name a suit for him to lead. The winner of a trick turns the trick face down in a trick pile in front of him, and play continues in this way until all five tricks have been played.

Scoring. The nondealer who stands, or dealer who refuses, or either player who finally elects to play, scores 1 point for three tricks; 2 points for *vole,* or five tricks. If a player stands or refuses, and fails to take three or more tricks, the other player scores 2 points. The game may be scored with pencil and paper.

Additional Rules

Misdeal. A misdeal loses the deal. Any faced card except the eleventh causes a misdeal. If either hand has too few or too many cards, the opponent may claim a misdeal, or may have the correct number arrived at by adding from the stock or drawing. If more than one card is faced for trump, the opponent, if he has not examined his hand, may claim a misdeal, or select the trump; or if he has seen his hand, he may claim a misdeal, or declare the eleventh card to be the trump.

Renounce. If a player does not follow suit or win a trick when possible, or if he trumps when he could follow suit, it is a *renounce.* The cards are taken up, the hand is played over, and if the renouncer takes less than five tricks on the replay, he does not score. If he takes five tricks, he scores 1 point only. A player leading out of turn must take back the card unless the opponent has played to it, in which case it stands. Tricks must be turned down and quitted as soon as taken, and may not be reexamined under any circumstances until the end of the hand, on penalty of playing the balance of the hand exposed, though not subject to call.

Strategy of Ecarte. The play of Ecarte is almost completely mechanical, with little chance of showing any great skill. Practically the entire game is a matter of when to stand and when to propose. There are certain hands, called *jeux de regle,* on which the opponent should play without proposing, and on which dealer should refuse. These are:

1. Any hand with three trumps in it.

2. Any hand with two trumps and three cards of one suit; or two cards of one suit as high as queen; or two cards of one suit and king of another suit; or three cards of differ-

ent suits, as good as king and jack.

3. One trump and three winning cards in another suit; or a four-card suit to a king; or three cards of one suit, with two kings in hand.

SKAT

Skat, the most popular game of Germany, has been carried by German emigrants to other countries, where they have won many converts to it. Many rate it among the most scientific of all games.

Requirements

1. Three, four, or five players, but only three play at a time.

2. A 32-card deck made of the standard 52-card deck with the two's, three's, four's, five's, and six's stripped out.

3. Rank of cards: When there is a trump suit, the four jacks are always the four highest trumps, ranking as follows regardless of which suit is trump: club jack (high), spade jack, heart jack, diamond jack. The remainder of the trump suit, and also non-trump suits, rank in order: ace (high), ten, king, queen, nine, eight, seven (low). When there is no trump suit the cards in every suit rank: ace (high), king, queen, jack, ten, nine, eight, seven (low).

4. In home play, the selection of the dealer, seating positions, changing seats, shuffle, and cut are provided under General Rules for Card Games, chapter 1.

The Deal. The cards are dealt only to three players. With four at the table, the dealer does not give cards to himself. With five at the table, the dealer omits himself and the third player to his left. In any event, the first packet of cards is dealt to the player adjacent to dealer at his left.

The rule of the deal is "three-skat-four-three." That is, a round of three cards at a time is dealt. Then two cards are dealt face down in the center of the table, constituting a *skat,* or *blind.* Then a round is dealt four at a time, and finally a round three at a time.

Designation of Players. The player adjacent to the dealer at his left is called the *forehand,* or *leader,* the other two players in order being the *middlehand* and the *rearhand* (or *endhand*). He who finally wins the right to name the trump is then called the *player,* and the other two become the *opponents.*

Bidding. The leader is entitled to name the trump unless another player makes a bid which the leader is unwilling to equal. The leader does not specify how high he is willing

to bid. The middlehand begins by making a bid. If the leader is willing to bid the same amount, he says "I hold," or "Yes." To win the right to name trump, the middlehand must increase his bid to an amount that the leader is unwilling to meet. When a player wishes to drop out of the bidding he says "Pass," or "No." When the survivor is determined as between the leader and middlehand, the rearhand may if he wishes try to buy the privilege by the same procedure of bidding against the survivor. If the middlehand and rearhand pass without making any bid, the leader may name his "game" (without bidding any specific number of points) or may pass. In the latter case, the hand must be played at *ramsch.*

Each bid names merely a number of points, without specification of the intended trump or game. The lowest possible bid is 10. It is customary to bid up by increases of two—10, 12. 14, and so on. On conclusion of the bidding, the winning bidder, now called the *player,* must declare his "game."

The "Games." Following is the list of the 15 possible games that may be declared by the player, together with the base value of each.

Game	Base Value
Tournee	
with diamonds as trumps	5
with hearts as trumps	6
with spades as trumps	7
with clubs as trumps	8
Solo	
with diamonds as trumps	9
with hearts as trumps	10
with spades as trumps	11
with clubs as trumps	12
Grand	
tournee	12
guckser	16
solo	20
ouvert	24
ramsch	10
Null	
simple	20
ouvert	40

Tournee. On declaring tournee, the *player* picks up the top skat card. He may accept it as fixing the trump suit, in which case it must be shown to the others, or he may reject it without exposure (this privilege is called "Passt mir nicht"—"It does not suit me"). If the first skat card is rejected, the second is turned face up and fixes the trump suit. The game is then known as "second turn." If the card turned is a jack, the player may select either the suit of the jack as trump, or may decide that only the jacks will be trumps, in which case the game becomes grand tournee. When trump was fixed by the first or second card, the player is entitled to put both skat cards in his hand and then discard any two cards face down.

Solo. On declaring solo, the player must also name the trump suit. The two skat cards (blind) are left face down and the hands are played out as dealt.

Grand. In all grand games the only trumps are the jacks. Grand solo is played without the use of the skat. On announcing guckser, the player picks up the skat cards without showing them, then discards face down any two cards to reduce his hand to ten. Grand ouvert is a contract to win all of the tricks, with the player's hand exposed on the table before the opening lead. Grand tournee can arise only through the chance that a jack is turned up from the skat, following announcement of tournee. The player then has the option of declaring only jacks trumps, for a grand tournee.

Null. At null, there are no trumps, and the cards in each suit rank: ace (high), king, queen, jack, ten, nine, eight, seven. Announcement of null is a contract not to win a single trick. The skat cards are set aside unused. At null ouvert the player must expose his whole hand face up on the table before the opening lead.

Ramsch. Played only when all three participants refuse to make a bid or name another game. Ramsch is a grand game, with only the jacks trumps. Each plays for himself and tries to take in as few points as possible.

The Skat. The two cards set aside from the play, whether they are the skat originally dealt or discards from the player's hand, are added to the player's tricks at the termination of play. Any counting cards found in the skat are reckoned in his score. At ramsch, the skat is added to the winner of the last trick.

Values of the Games. The point value of each game has to be computed for scoring as well as bidding purposes. The point value of null games is invariable, as gi en in the table

under section The "Games." The point value of every other type of game is found by multiplying the base value, as given in the table, by the *sum* of all applicable multipliers. Following is the list of possible multipliers:

Matadors (each)	1
Game	1
Schneider	1
Schneider announced	1
Schwarz	1
Schwarz announced	1

Matadors. The term matadors refers to the holding of top trumps in unbroken sequence from the jack of clubs down. A hand holding the jack of clubs is said to be "with" a specified number of matadors. A hand lacking the jack of clubs is said to be "against" as many matadors as there are trumps higher than the highest in the hand. *Examples:* A trump suit headed by club jack, spade jack, diamond jack is "with two," because the jack of hearts is missing. A trump suit headed by jack, ace, ten of diamonds is "against three."

The first item in the total of multipliers applicable to a trump declaration is the number of matadors which the hand is either "with" or "against." The skat cards, whether used or not during play, are reckoned as part of the player's hand in counting matadors. If the hand is "with," the skat may increase but cannot decrease the value of the player's game. But if the hand is "against," a matador found in the skat may decrease the value. *Example:* A player has bid 30 and declares heart solo. His trumps are headed by jack of hearts. Thus he is "against two," and expects to make contract through "matadors 2, game 1, total multipliers 3; 3 times 10 is 30." But jack of clubs is found in the skat. The hand is thus "with one," the multipliers are reduced by one, and the player is set unless in the play he manages to make schneider.

Game. In declaring any trump game, the player contracts to win in tricks (plus whatever is in the skat) at least a majority of the 120 points in the pack, reckoned on this count:

Each ace counts	11
Each ten	10
Each king	4
Each queen	3
Each jack	2

For gathering in trick cards that total 61 points or more, the player earns one multiplier, called the point for game.

Schneider. The player strives to reach 61 points in cards, while the opponents strive to reach 60. Failure by either side to reach the half-total, that is, 31 for the player, 30 for opponents, constitutes schneider, and adds one multiplier.

The player may add one multiplier by predicting, before the opening lead, that he will make schneider, that is, gather at least 91 points in cards. Such announcement is allowed only in games where the skat cards are set aside untouched.

Schwarz. The winning of all ten tricks by one side constitutes *schwarz,* and it adds one multiplier. The player may announce schwarz before the opening lead, that is, he may contract to win every trick, and thereby gain one additional multiplier. Schwarz may be so announced only in games where the skat is not used.

Computing the Game. The table of multipliers above shows the order in which the total must be computed, for all points beyond the count of matadors are cumulative. That is, having earned any of the subsequent multipliers, the player is entitled to all preceding it. *Example:* If he earns the point for schwarz, the player also gets the points for schneider and schneider predicted.

The player is not permitted to announce a game which cannot possibly score the value of his bid. That means that he may not declare null if the bid is more than 20, nor null ouvert if the bid is more than 40.

The Play of the Hand. The opening lead is invariably made by the hand at the left of the dealer. The leader may lead any card he holds. Each other hand must follow suit to the lead, if able, remembering that at any trump declaration all four jacks are trumps. If unable to follow suit, a hand may trump or discard as he pleases. There is no compulsion to try to win tricks in any suit if able. A trick is won by the highest trump played if it contains a trump, otherwise by the highest card of the suit led. The winner of each trick leads to the next.

Object of Play. At all trump declarations, the primary object of play is to win counting cards to the total of 61, the secondary objects are to win 91 points or win all the tricks. If the game is null or schwarz announced, the object of the player is to lose or to win all the tricks. At ramsch the object is to gather as few counting cards as possible. It must be

emphasized that the player cannot score at all, but loses the value of his game, if he fails to take in tricks the minimum number of points guaranteed by that game—61, 91, all the tricks, or none of the tricks, as the case may be.

Scoring. The score sheet contains one column for each participant in the game. At the end of a hand, the value of the game is computed, as described in the foregoing sections. This value is entered as a plus quantity in the column of the player, provided that it is at least as large as his winning bid, and provided that he has taken the minimum of points or tricks called for by his game. If the player fails in either respect, the value of his game is entered in his column as a minus quantity. But the loss is doubled if the game was guckser or second turn in a tournee.

The multipliers for game, schneider, schwarz are duly applied to determine the value of the game, even when the player fails to catch 61 points. In this case, the multipliers are deemed to accrue to the opponents. Therefore, on catching 60 points the opponents need not cease play, but may demand that it continue so that they may try to earn the multipliers for schneider or schwarz.

The value of the game may fall short of the bid by reason of an unlucky skat when the player is "against." But the amount of his loss must be at least equal to his bid. In this case, his debit is the lowest multiple of the base value of his game that equals or exceeds his bid. *Example:* The player bid 24 and announced *spade solo.* He was originally "against two," but skat held jack of spades. Although the player made 61 points in cards, his game was worth only $2 \times 11 = 22$. His loss is 33, the lowest multiple of the base value 11 that exceeds 24.

Scoring of Ramsch. Ramsch is the only game in which each plays for himself. The player who gathers the least points in tricks is credited with 10 for winning the game, or 20 if he takes no tricks at all, the others scoring nothing. If all three tie in points taken in tricks, the leader is deemed the winner and scores 10 points. If two players tie for low score, the one who did not take the last trick as between these two is deemed the winner and scores 10. If one player takes all the tricks, he is considered to have lost the game and has 30 points subtracted from his score.

Settlement. The scoring column is kept as a

running total of the points scored (or lost) by each player. When play terminates and settlement is to be made, each participant pays or receives according to the amount by which his final score falls below or above the average of all the scores. *Example:*

Final scores:

A	B	C	D
28	−75	137	82

It is convenient first to eliminate the minus signs by adding to all scores the numerical value of the largest minus score. Add 75 to each score above:

A	B	C	D
103	0	212	157

The total of the scores is now 472. Divide by 4, the number of players, to find the average, 118. Then the differences from average are:

A	B	C	D
−15	−118	+94	+39

The final pluses and minuses must of course balance.

Additional Rules. The following excerpts from the Official Rules of the North American Skat League cover the major irregularities.

DEALING. *Section 1*. After the cards have been properly shuffled by the dealer, they must be cut once (by the player to his right, taking off three or more, so as to leave at least three cards in each packet), and dealt in the following order: three-skat-four-three. The full deck of 32 cards must be taken up and dealt.

Section 2. If all cards are dealt, and bidding has commenced, the game must be played, even if the dealing was done out of turn; in such case the next deal must be made by the one who sh⋅uld have dealt before, and then proceed as if no misdeal had been made, omitting, however, the one who had dealt out of turn. Thus each player deals but once during one round.

Section 3. In case a card is served face up, a new deal must be made.

Section 4. A dealer misdealing (or turning a card face up) must deal again. If in the course of a game it develops that one or more

players has either too many or not enough cards, then the player loses the game if he does not have the right number of cards, even if the same thing occurred with one of the opponents. But if the player has the right number of cards and one or both of the opponents has too many or not enough, then the player wins, even if he would have lost the game otherwise. Each player should make sure before beginning the game that he has ten cards, neither more nor less. (The dealer is no longer fined 10 points for misdealing.)

Section 5. The dealer has the right, and it is his duty, to call attention to any error in the play.

BIDDING. *Section 1*. Bids must be made only in numbers, the value of which occur in some possible game.

Section 2. He who bids and is awarded the play must play some hand that will score an equal amount of his bid or more.

OVERBIDDING. *Section 1*. If a player has overbid his hand, the next higher value of the respective game is counted and charged against the player; except in second turn and guckser, where the charge is doubled.

Section 2. If the player has overbid his game and one of the opponents makes an error, he wins the value of the game, being the amount he might have lost had no error occurred, and the same value shall be charged against the opponent making such error. Both scored within a circle.

The "next higher value" in an overbid hand, mentioned above, is charged against a player if he bids over the multiple. *Example:* If he bids 40, having DJ in a heart solo and makes 61 points or more, he loses only 40 points if a black jack is in the blind.

THE SKAT. *Section 1*. If before a game is announced, it is discovered that one or both of the skat cards are in the hand or amongst the cards of any participant, the dealer shall draw out of the hand of the person having the skat card or cards sufficient cards to leave said player 10 cards, after which the bidding shall proceed as if no mistake had been made, but the player causing this proceeding shall be fined 25 points and is forbidden to participate in the bidding and denied the opportunity to play any game during this particular deal.

Section 2. If any player by mistake has looked at either of the skat cards, he shall be barred from playing and fined 10 points. If he exposed one or both skat cards to another player, dealer shall mix the two skat cards, and he who plays a tournee must turn the top card (second turn is barred), or he can play any other play.

Section 3. A dealer looking at the skat during play is charged with 100 points (encircled).

Section 4. If a player, when turning, accidentally sees both cards without having announced second turn, he shall be compelled to turn the top card and loses the right to play second turn or grand.

Section 5. The skat must not be looked at by any participant before the end of the game, except by the player when playing a game with the aid of the skat. The two skat cards, except when the player plays a hand with the aid of the skat cards, shall remain with the dealer until the end of the game—and then turned face up on the table.

Section 6. If the player who plays a solo looks at the skat, he loses his game, but opponents may insist on his continuing for the purpose of increasing his loss.

Section 7. If either opponent examines the skat, the player wins. He has the same privilege as in Section 6, and the one who looks at the skat loses the number of points the player wins.

Section 8. Whoever discards more or less than two cards loses his game.

TRICKS. *Section 1.* All participants must keep their respective tricks in the order in which the cards were played so that each trick can be traced at the end of the game.

Section 2. The player has the privilege to throw his game after the first trick and claim schneider. He loses this privilege after two cards of the second trick are on the table.

Section 3. Participants have the privilege to examine the last trick made. This must, however, be done before the next card is played.

Section 4. Examining tricks taken, except the last, or recounting is not permitted. Should this be done the opposing side may claim the game.

Section 5. If a player throws down his cards and declares his game won, he cannot claim another trick.

REVOKES AND MISPLAYS. *Section 1.* If the player misleads or neglects to follow suit, he loses the game, even though he already has 61 or more points. Anyone of the opponents,

however, has the privilege to have such error corrected and proceed with the game to its end for the purpose of increasing the player's loss. If, then, one of the opponents makes one of these errors, the player wins his game, and the full value scored by the player is charged, within a circle, against the opponent making the error.

Section 2. If either of the opponents leads wrongly, plays out of turn, or neglects to follow suit, the error must immediately be corrected if possible. The play then must proceed to the end. If the player then makes one of the errors above mentioned, he loses the game and the first error is fully condoned. If the game proceeds at the insistence of either of the opponents, and again one of the opponents makes one of the errors referred to above, all previous errors are condoned. The player must get 61 or more points to enable him to get a bona fide game. (The meaning of this section is that no player can win a bona fide hand on a misplay by an opponent. In such case the hand must be played to the end to determine if the player could win his hand, or had a possible chance had the misplay by an opponent not occurred. The skatmeister must be called to decide if the player had a possible chance to win, and if so, he may so rule. He must okay the play if won. If the skatmeister rules that the player could not win, he then, nevertheless, receives credit for points, within a circle. The one making the error also loses the full value of the hand, within a circle.)

Section 3. If, during the progress of a game, the player places his cards upon the table or exposes them, this shall be construed as his claiming the remaining tricks, and if he fails to make them all, he loses the full value of the game unless he already has 61.

Section 4. If, during the progress of the game, any one of the opponents places his cards upon the table or exposes them, this shall be construed as his declaring thereby to have defeated the player's game; all the remaining cards belong to the player, and should this make 61 or more points for the player, he wins and the opponent who erred shall be charged with the full value of the game within a circle.

Strategy of Skat. For a trump bid the hand should usually hold a minimum of five trumps. Actually, the normal conservative minimum for a handplay bid is eight cards that are trumps, aces, or tens. But many experienced players will bid with a count of seven, or six, if the player wishes to use the skat. But it is not wise to bid in the hope that the skat will furnish a trump or other specific card, but proper to expect the skat to strengthen the hand by one trick. The following tables show why:

CHANCES OF BUYING ONE CARD IN THE SKAT

To Find	Approximate Odds
Any one card	10 to 1 against
Either of two cards	5 to 1 against
Any one of three cards	3 to 1 against
Any one of four cards	2 to 1 against
Any one of five cards	3 to 2 against
Any one of six cards	even
Any one of seven cards	6 to 5 for
Any one of eight cards	3 to 2 for
Any one of nine cards	2 to 1 for

After obtaining skat, make the discard as in Five Hundred (page 239). That is, it is best to keep long suits intact and reduce short suits. Sometimes a ten not guarded with the ace must be discarded in order to save it.

The player should usually lead trumps. By pulling two trumps for one, he will protect his side cards. But, don't overlook the possibility to discard unwanted cards, rather than trumping, when an opponent leads a suit of which the player is void.

The opponent should attempt to keep the player "in the middle," that is, throw the lead to the opponent on the right so that he can lead through the player. The opponents should try to smear (discard) to each other the aces and tens that they could not otherwise win against the player's trump tricks. To forestall a smear by one opponent on the other's trump tricks, the player should give up tricks to adverse trump stoppers on early rounds rather than later.

Räuber Skat

In this variant of regular Skat, the tournee game is eliminated, and the player has the option of *handplay*—playing without the skat —or of picking up the skat and then naming his game. In either case he has a choice between naming a suit or only the jacks as trumps. The increased use of the skat leads to livelier bidding and to some spectacular possibilities. Suppose that forehand wins the bid, picks up the skat, and then holds

> ♣ none
> ♠ A 9 8 7
> ♡ A 10 8 7
> ◇ A 10 8 7

If he wishes to risk the chance of finding a void in the hand of an opponent, the player may try for maximum score by declaring clubs trump. He lays away the two red aces, then leads his remaining ace and the two tens. If he can win these three tricks, he must catch at least 7 additional points in spades and 3 each in the red suits. The opponents catch only 54 points. The player, being "against eleven," scores 12 times 12, or 144 points.

SCHAFSKOPF

Schafskopf (also called Schafkopf or Sheepshead) is at least 200 years old, being one of the precursors of Skat.

Requirements

1. Three, four, or five players, but only three play at a time.

2. A 32-card deck.

3. Rank of cards: All queens, jacks, and diamonds are trumps ranking in order: club queen (high), spade queen, heart queen, diamond queen, club jack, spade jack, heart jack, diamond jack, diamond ace, diamond ten, diamond king, diamond nine, diamond eight, diamond seven. In each of the three other side suits the cards rank: ace (high), ten, king, nine, eight, seven.

Beginning of the Game. The selection of the dealer, seating positions, changing seats, shuffle, and cut are as provided under the General Rules for Card Games, chapter 1.

The Deal. Dealer gives three cards at a time to each of the three players, then two cards face down for the blind, then a round of four at a time, finally a round of three at a time. Each player thus receives 10 cards.

Determine the Player. The player on the

left of the dealer has first right to pick up the blind. If he refuses, the privilege passes to the two others in turn. Whoever picks up the blind assumes a contract to win a majority of the points for cards, and plays alone against the other two. The player after picking up the blind must discard two cards face down to restore his hand to ten cards. If all three pass, the hand must be played at "least," as described below.

Card Point Values. For purposes of determining game, the cards have point values as follows (whether trump or plain):

Each ace	11
Each ten	10
Each king	4
Each queen	3
Each jack	2
(No count for lower cards)	

The total points in the pack are 120, and the player wins *game* if he takes 61 or more in tricks won in play. If he gathers 91 points or more, he wins *schneider,* and if he takes all the tricks he wins *schwarz.*

If all three players pass, the hand is played for "least." Each plays for himself, the object being to take as few of the points for cards as possible. The blind is left untouched until play is completed, when it is added to the last trick and goes to the winner thereof.

The Play of the Hand. The hand at dealer's left invariably makes the opening lead. The winner of each trick leads for the next. Other hands must follow suit to the lead if able. If unable to follow suit, a hand may trump or discard at will. There is no compulsion to win any trick if able. The highest trump played, or the highest card of the suit led if no trump is played, wins the trick. It is important to remember that all queens, jacks, and diamonds are of the same "suit."

Scoring. Individual accounts are kept, a running total of the items won or lost by each participant. If the blind is picked up, the scoring values are:

Game	2
Schneider	4
Schwarz	6

If the player catches 61 points or more, he is credited with the appropriate figure. If he fails to make 61, he is debited the appropriate figure. (Four if he fails to catch 31 points or 6 if he loses all the tricks.)

At the game *least,* the player who gathers the fewest points scores plus 2, or plus 4 if he wins no tricks at all. If one player takes all the tricks, he is debited 4. If two players tie for low, the winner is he who did not take the last trick as between these two, and he gets 2 points. If each player gets 40 points in cards (triple tie), the winner is the hand that passed third, and he scores 2.

Additional Rules

Misdeal. If a card is dealt face up there must be a new deal. If the wrong player deals, and the error is not discovered before the deal is complete, the hand is played; the deal then reverts to the player whose rightful turn it was, and continues in rotation, except that the player who dealt out of turn is skipped at his next turn in rotation. If any hand is dealt the wrong number of cards, there must be a new deal if the error is discovered before the opening lead; if the error is discovered later, play ends and the player wins if his hand was correct, or loses if it was incorrect.

Wrong Discard. If after the opening lead the player is found to have discarded more or less than two cards, he loses.

Looking at the Blind. No participant (including dealer) may look at the cards in the blind, except the player. Penalty, 4 points.

Misplay. If either opponent leads or plays out of turn, fails to follow suit when able, exposes a card except in his rightful turn to play, indicates his holding of any card by word or act, or examines any quitted trick but the last, the player wins and the opponent in error is charged with the full loss. If the player leads or plays out of turn, fails to follow suit when able, or examines any quitted trick but the last, he loses.

Claims and Concessions. If either side claims to have won game, all remaining unplayed cards belong to the other side. An opponent who makes an erroneous claim is charged with the entire loss. If the player concedes loss of game, the concession must stand.

Auction Schafskopf

This variant is played the same as regular Schafskopf except for the following:

1. Four players, two against two as partners.

2. The cards are dealt out four at a time, each hand receiving eight cards. The player at dealer's left makes first bid or pass, and each other hand in turn is allowed one bid. Bidding is by the number of points over 60 that the bidder (with help of his partner) guarantees

to win in play.

3. The only permanent trumps are club jack (high), spade jack, heart jack, diamond jack. The winning bidder names the trump and player at the dealer's left makes the first lead.

SIX-BID SOLO

Many local variants of Skat are played, under such names as Solo, Slough, Sluff, Salt Lake Solo, and Six-Bid Slough. All have in common that the point value of the cards and the object of play are the same as in Skat. They differ mainly in the number and types of "games" or declarations that may be bid. One of the most popular variants is Six-Bid Solo. (The name Solo has also been given to certain variants of Whist, Bridge, and to the modern version of Ombre, as described on pages 163 and 374.)

Requirements

1. Three or four players, but only three play at a time.

2. A 36-card deck. The cards in each suit rank: ace (high), ten, king, queen, jack, nine, eight, seven, and six.

Point Value of Cards. The point value of the high cards is as in Skat:

Each ace counts	11
Each ten counts	10
Each king counts	4
Each queen counts	3
Each jack counts	2

Beginning of the Game. The selection of the dealer, seating positions, changing seats, shuffle, and cut are as provided under the General Rules for Card Games, chapter 1.

The Deal. If four play, the dealer does not give cards to himself. The rule of the deal is "four-three-widow-four." That is, dealer first deals a round of four at a time, beginning with the player at his left; then a round of three at a time, then three cards face down for a widow or blind; finally a round of four at a time. Each hand thus receives 11 cards.

Bidding. The hand to the left of the dealer makes the first bid or pass. Each bid consists in naming one of the six games. If he bids and the next hand bids more (names a higher-ranking game), these two first settle who can make the higher bid. Once a player passes, he is out of the bidding. Third player settles with

survivor of first two as to which can make the higher bid. Player who wins the bidding is called the *bidder*. If all pass, there is a new deal by the next dealer in turn.

The Games (Bids). There are six possible bids, ranking as follows:

Call solo (high)
Spread misere
Guarantee solo
Misere
Heart solo
Solo

Call Solo. The bidder undertakes to win all 120 points. The widow is not used in play but is added to the bidder's tricks at the end. Before the opening lead, the bidder calls for any card not in his hand, and the holder of this card must give it to him in exchange for any that the bidder chooses to give in return. If the called card is in the widow, there is no exchange of cards.

Spread Misere. Same as misere with two additions: the bidder exposes his whole hand face up after the opening lead, and opening lead is made by the player at left of bidder.

Guarantee Solo. The bidder guarantees to win a certain minimum of the counting cards: 74 points if he names hearts as trumps, or 80 if he names another suit. The widow is not used during play but is added to the bidder's cards afterward.

Misere. There are no trumps, and the bidder undertakes to avoid taking any counting card. The widow is set aside and is not used during play or counted afterward.

Heart Solo. Same as simple solo in all respects, but hearts are trumps.

Solo. At simple solo, the bidder names any suit other than hearts as trumps. The widow is set aside untouched, but is added to bidder's cards at the end of play. The bidder does not name his trump unless and until his bid proves to be the high one.

The Play of the Hand. Except in spread misere, the opening lead is invariably made by the player at left of dealer. Each hand must follow suit to the lead, if able, and if unable to follow suit must trump, if able. But there is no compulsion to trump high or low. The object in play (if there is a trump) is to win counting cards. The object in both misere games is to avoid taking any cards that count. The two other players combine against the bidder.

Scoring. It is most convenient to use counters or chips and settle after every deal. The bidder, if he makes the required number of points in play, collects the value of his game from each of the other players; if he fails, he pays a like amount to each other player. If there are four players, all share in the gains or losses, except that if the bidder makes simple solo or heart solo he collects only from the two other active players.

Game	Bidder Must Take	Value in Chips
Call Solo	120 points	
Hearts trumps		150
Another trump		100
Spread misere	no points	60
Guarantee solo		40
Hearts trumps	74 points	
Another trump	80 points	
Misere	no points	30
Heart solo	60 points	3 for each point over or under 60
Simple solo	60 points	2 for each point over or under 60

In simple solo and heart solo, if each side wins 60 points there is no score for the deal.

Additional Rules. The rules of Skat (page 252) should be used to govern irregularities in play.

Frog

This variant, very popular in Mexico, where it is called Rana, and the Southwestern portion of the United States, where it's called Sixty Solo or Heart Solo, makes an excellent introduction to Six-Bid Solo and Skat. It is played the same as Six-Bid Solo, except that there are only three possible bids:

Frog (*lowest*). Hearts are trumps. The bidder picks up the widow and then discards any three cards face down. He collects or pays for every point he takes in play over or under 60.

Chico has the same meaning as simple solo in Six-Bid Solo.

Grand (*highest*) has the same meaning as *heart solo* in Six-Bid Solo.

Coeur D'Alene Solo

This variation is played the same as Six-Bid Solo except for the following:

1. Each hand constitutes a complete game, 61 points being needed to win; excess points are not considered. If a bidder makes 60 points, it is rated a tie, and the deal passes to the left.

2. The settlements for wins and losses are computed as follows: 1 chip for a frog; 2 chips for a simple solo; 3 chips for a heart solo.

Progressive Solo

Also called Denver Solo, this game is played like Six-Bid Solo except for the following:

1. There are five standard bids, which rank upward: frog, spade solo, club solo, diamond solo, heart solo. The bidding continues around and around, until all players but one have passed. Once a player passes, he may not reenter the bidding.

2. Only a frog bidder may take the widow and discard in its place, the discards counting for him in play. Other bidders do not use the widow, but the cards in it count for them.

3. In addition to passing or making some higher bid, any player in his turn may double a bid. If the doubled bid is passed and not made, the bidder loses twice the usual amount to the other players; if he makes his bid, doubling player pays the bidder twice the usual amount, while the others pay the usual amount. A doubled player may redouble, and the payoffs are then figured at four times the usual amount, according to the plan described immediately above. A double or redouble does not end the bidding. The doubled or redoubled bid may be overcalled by anyone making a higher bid in turn.

4. For every point under or over 60, the scoring is: frog, 1 chip; spade solo, 2 chips; club solo, 3 chips; diamond solo, 4 chips; heart solo, 5 chips. If both sides make 60, it is rated a tie.

5. In addition, each player contributes equally to a frog pot and a solo pot. If a bidder succeeds, he takes the appropriate pot; if he fails, he doubles the value of the pot. This is in addition to the usual payments for points.

CHAPTER 14

The Heart Group

Hearts is one of the foremost of the nonpartnership games that provides an opportunity for skill in the play of cards. In fact, Hearts and its many variants, in which the object is to avoid taking certain cards and tricks, is the answer to people who always complain they hold poor cards and very few trumps. Actually, in Hearts and its allied games, the premium is on holding poor cards.

REGULAR HEARTS

This is the basic and simplest form of Hearts, but it is not played as often today as my own Heart game and the many other variations and related games.

Requirements

1. A standard deck of 52 cards.

2. Four hands make the best game, but as few as two and any number more than four may play. If more than six play, a double deck should be used. Each person plays for himself, although partnerships may be arranged in the four-handed game.

Rank of Cards. Ace (high), king, queen, jack, ten, nine, eight, seven, six, five, four, three, two (low). The suits have no relative rank although the play revolves about the hearts.

The Object of the Game. To win the game by scoring fewer points than any of your opponents. In short, to try to avoid taking hearts.

Selecting Dealer and Seating Positions

1. The players seat themselves at any place around the table. Where they sit at the beginning is not important.

2. Any player may shuffle the pack and offer the pack to any other player to cut.

3. Each of the players is dealt a card face up. The player drawing the highest card selects his seating position, then the drawer of the second highest, and so forth. In case of ties, each tied player receives another card until the tie is broken. On the first draw, should two players receive high card, each receives another card to decide the order of seat selection.

4. The player who was dealt low card starts the game by dealing the first hand. From then on, the deal moves to the dealer's left, clockwise.

Shuffle and Cut. Any player may shuffle, the dealer last. The player at the dealer's right cuts the cards.

The Deal. The cards are dealt one at a time as far as they can be dealt, equally. The remaining cards are placed on the table face down, forming a widow or blind. The player who wins the first trick takes the blind; no one may look at these cards during play.

The Pass. Right after each deal and before

the start of the play, after looking at his hand, each player selects any three cards in his hand and passes them face down to the player at his left without exposing them to the others. Each player must pass three cards before looking at the three cards he receives from his right. In six- and seven-handed play, only two cards are passed to the left.,

The Play. The leader (the player to the dealer's left) makes the opening lead. Each player must follow suit to a lead if able; if unable, a player may discard any card he wishes. Highest-ranking card of the suit led wins the trick.

Each heart counts 1 point. When Hearts is being played as a match, five hands constitute a match. At the end of each hand the points taken in tricks by each player are totaled and entered under his name on the score sheet. When a single hand is played as a game, the player who scored the fewest points is declared the winner and he collects the difference in points between his score and that of each of the other players. In brief, he collects 1 point for each heart held by the losing players. If two or more players tie for the fewest points taken, they divide the winnings, and if there are odd units left over, they cut or draw high card to determine who shall receive the odd units.

The player who scores the fewest total points for the five games is declared the winner and gets credit for the difference between his score and that of each of the losers.

Settlement. When play is completed, there are several ways of settling, of which the following methods of using chips are the most popular:

1. Each player begins with a specific number, say 50 or 100 chips. For every heart he takes in play he puts a chip into the pot or kitty. The player who has taken the fewest hearts wins the pot. If two or more players tie for lowest number of hearts, they divide the pot equally, and if there are odd chips, they are carried over to the next pot.

2. Another method, which emphasizes the element of chance, is known as "jackpots," or "sweepstakes." After each hand is over, the players put one chip into the pot for each heart that they took. If any player took no hearts, he collects the entire pot; if two or more players took no hearts, they divide the pot equally; and if there are any odd chips,

they are carried over to the next pot. If no player is free of hearts, the pot accumulates until some players or player takes no hearts. Some play that a jackpot may be won only when one player is clear of hearts, while others play that a jackpot is carried over to the next deal if any one player takes all 13 hearts.

3. Possibly the best-known way of Hearts settling is the Howell method. In it, each player, after a hand is over, puts as many chips into the pot for each heart that he has taken as there are *other* players in the game. He then subtracts the hearts that he took from the number 13, and the difference represents the chips he may take back from the pot. *Example:* A player has taken four hearts in a four-handed game. He puts 12 chips into the pot (4 times 3). He takes back 9 chips (13 minus 4). Altogether, he has paid in 3 chips (12 minus 9). If, as in some variants, where a double deck is used, the number to subtract from is 26 instead of 13.

4. If a pencil-and-paper score is kept, each player is charged 1 point for every heart that he took. When any player reaches 50 or 100 points, the player with the lowest score is the winner. This method is called *cumulative scoring.*

Additional Rules

Misdeals. The following determines whether or not a misdeal has occurred:

1. If a dealer or player turns up a card or cards belonging to another player during the deal, that deal is void, a misdeal is declared, and the same dealer deals again.

2. If a dealer or player turns up a card or cards belonging to himself, the deal stands.

3. If a card is found face up in the deck during the deal, a misdeal is declared and the same dealer deals again.

4. If one or more players have too few or too many cards and this is discovered before the first trick is completed, a misdeal is declared and the same dealer deals again.

5. If a player has too few cards and this is discovered during the play of the final trick, he must take the last trick. If he is more than one card short, he must take in every trick which he cannot play.

Play Out of Turn. A lead or play out of turn must be retracted if demand is made by a player before all have played to the trick; however, if all have played, the play out of turn stands as a regular turn of play without penalty.

Reneges. Failure to follow suit when able constitutes a renege. A renege may be corrected before the trick is picked up from the table and turned face down. If it is not discovered until later, the renege is established, play immediately ceases, and the reneger must pay each player 10 units. In match-style play, 10 points for each of the other participants is added to the offender's score sheet. For example, in a four-handed game the offender adds 30 points to his score sheet. The other players jot down a zero for their scores.

Strategy in Regular Hearts. The basis of play is to win no tricks, or only harmless tricks. It is best to get rid of high cards as soon as possible. That is, high cards that can be forced to take tricks in three leads of a suit should be played early rather than late in the game. Aces and high cards accompanied by some low cards are not dangerous as a rule, but middle cards (eight, nine, ten) without low cards are very dangerous, especially after the first round of a suit has been led. Middle cards should be discarded whenever chance permits, so long as any lower cards of the suit remain unplayed.

A good lead at any time is in a short suit. This play often will lead to the opportunity for early discarding on leads by other players in that suit.

When playing under cumulative or Howell method scoring, it frequently is wise to take a few hearts in the early going rather than be stuck with a greater number later in the hand.

Spot Hearts

This is just a scoring variation of Regular Hearts in which each heart has a certain minus count: Ace −14; king −13; queen −12; jack −11, and all other hearts their face value. Thus, there are 104 points, and each hand is settled as an individual game. Incidentally, this scoring variation may also be employed in some other Heart games, if desired.

Hearts with a Widow

In this variant of Regular Hearts, which is also called Heartsette, three to six can play. When three or four play, omit the deuce of spades; when more than four, use the complete deck. Deal as in Regular Hearts; in three-handed, each player receives 16 cards; four-handed, 12; five-handed, 10; six-handed, 8. The remaining cards are placed face down on the table for a widow.

The winner of the first trick must take the widow in with this trick, and all hearts in it count against him. While the player who wins the widow may look at it, it should not be shown to the other players. Otherwise, the play is as in Regular Hearts.

Joker Hearts

In this variant, which is best played three-handed, the deuce of hearts is omitted from the deck, and the joker is added. (If no joker is available, the deuce of hearts is retained as a joker.) The joker ranks between the ten and jack of hearts, and wins any trick unless the jack of hearts or a higher heart is played, in which case the higher heart wins, regardless of the suit led. The holder of the joker must follow suit to hearts. In scoring the joker counts 5 points against the player taking it. (Some play that the joker counts 20 points.)

Domino Hearts

In Domino Hearts, each player is dealt six cards, in rotation left to right, one at a time. The remainder of the deck is placed face down as a stock from which players will draw.

The rules of play are the same as for Regular Hearts, except that a player unable to follow suit must draw cards from the top of the stock until he can follow. After the stock is exhausted, a player who cannot follow suit may discard. The highest card played of the suit led wins the trick. A player who plays out all the cards in his hand drops from the play for the remainder of the hand. If a player wins a trick with his last card, the next active player to his left leads for the next trick. If all except one player play out their hands before the stock is exhausted, the hearts remaining in his hand and in the stock are counted against him. If all of the active players play out the same trick, any hearts remaining in the stock count against the player of the last card. When any player reaches 31 points, the player with the lowest score is considered the winner.

Draw Hearts

This game is for two players. Each player is dealt 13 cards and the remainder of the deck is placed face down as a stock from which the players will draw.

The rules of play are as in Regular Hearts, but after each trick, which consists of two cards, the winner draws the top card of the stock, and opponent takes the one under it, so that the hands are maintained at 13 cards. After the stock is exhausted, the hands are played out without drawing. The player taking fewer hearts is the winner by the difference between his count and his opponent's. If the play is for game, then the difference between the scores for each hand is put down under the loser's name. When either player reaches 50 (or 100), the player with the lower score wins. If both reach game in the same deal, the player with the lower score wins.

Auction Hearts

In this game each player makes a bid to name the suit of penalty cards; it may be hearts or any other suit. That is, bidder states the number of chips that he is willing to put into the pot or pool if he is permitted to name the suit of penalty cards. Bidding begins with the player at the dealer's left and rotates to the left, each player being allowed one bid only. Each player must bid higher than the preceding bid or must pass.

When the bidding is over, the highest bidder places the chips that he bid into the pot and then names the penalty suit. (It is not named during the bidding.) He leads first, and then play proceeds as in Regular Hearts.

When the hands are played out, each player adds one counter to the pot or kitty for each card he has taken of the penalty suit. The player taking no card of the penalty suit wins the pot; if two players take no cards of penalty suit, they divide the pot, leaving an odd counter, if any, for the next pot. If more than two players take no card of the suit or one player takes all thirteen or each player takes at least one, no player wins. The deal passes, and the successful bidder on the original deal names the suit to be avoided, without bidding. The play proceeds as before, and at the end of play of the hand each player puts up a chip for each card of penalty suit he has taken. If no player wins on this deal, a new deal ensues, and so on, until the pot or kitty is won.

HEARTS ACCORDING TO SCARNE

Hearts According to Scarne retains a secure hold on the affections of its numerous devotees. Hearts is a real cutthroat game when played this way, a deceptively simple game that never fails to provide much amusement, arguments, and conversation after the play of each hand or game. It offers more opportunities than are found in Regular Hearts to apply skill and deduction in analyzing the meanings of your opponent's play and in planning your own strategy so as to make the most of what you deduce about the other players' hands when compared with the strength of your own hand.

The requirements of play and rank of cards are the same as for Regular Hearts.

Value of Cards. As in Regular Hearts, the play of the game revolves about the 13 hearts and, in addition, the queen of spades, which is referred to as the *Black Queen, Black Lady, Black Maria, Calamity Jane,* and the *Slippery* *Bitch.* Each heart card counts 1 point. The queen of spades counts 5 points, making a total of 18 points per hand or game.

Object of the Game. Either to score the least number of points and at the same time to try to load each opponent with 1 or more points, or to score all 18 points.

The Shuffle, Cut, and Deal. After the dealer and seating positions have been determined as suggested on page 261 the first dealer shuffles the cards and offers the pack to the player to his right to cut. Then the dealer serves each player one card at a time until all the cards have been equally distributed—13 to each player.

The Play. The leader (the player at the dealer's left) makes the opening lead. He may play any card he desires. Each player in turn must play a card in the same suit, if he is able to do so. If he is unable to follow suit, he may play a card of any other suit. A trick is constituted when each player has played a card to the lead, and it is taken by the highest card of the suit led by the first player.

The winner of the trick leads the next play of the hand. This manner of play continues until 13 tricks or all cards have been played out.

Settlement of Hand or Game. After 13 tricks have been played, each player looks through his cards (won tricks) to determine how many points he has scored. These include 1 point for each heart and 5 points for the queen of spades. The player who has taken the fewest points wins the hand and collects from each player the difference in points between his own total and the other player's total. For example, A has 2 points, B has 4 points, C has 4 points, D has 8 points. A wins 2 from B, 2 from C, 6 from D. However, if a player has scored all 18 points he is said to have made a *step* and he collects 18 units (points) from each of the three losing players. If two or more players tie for the fewest points taken, they divide the winnings, and if there are odd units left over, they cut or draw high card to determine who shall receive the odd units.

Additional Rules. The additional rules of play for Regular Hearts are given on page 262 under Misdeals and Play Out of Turn and apply to Hearts According to Scarne, together with the following rule:

Reneges. Failure to follow suit when able constitutes a renege. If two or more players renege they divide the penalty. A renege may be corrected before the trick is picked up from the table and turned face down. If not discovered until later, play immediately ceases when the renege is established, and the reneger must pay each player 18 units if the game is played as a single hand. In match-style play the units are multiplied by the number of opponents, and this total is entered in the offender's column on the score sheet. For example, in a four-handed game the points penalty is computed as follows: $18 \times 3 = 54$ points. Other players jot down zero for each of their scores.

Hearts—Match Style

For the players who prefer their games to run longer and their scores higher, this match-game variation is highly recommended. The rules of play are the same as in Hearts According to Scarne, described in the foregoing text, with the following exceptions:

1. *End of Match.* The match ends when five hands or games have been played.

2. *Deciding the Winner.* The player who scores the fewest number of points is declared the winner of the match and receives the difference in units between his points and those of each of his three opponents.

The Scoring. As each hand or game is completed, each player's score is recorded on the score sheet. If a player stops and collects 18 points, he receives a zero (0) on his score sheet. Each losing player is penalized with 18 points. Losers of the match each receive a penalty bonus of 50 points, which is added to their five-game total.

Below is an example of Hearts match scoring:

POINTS SCORED BY EACH PLAYER

Games	A	B	C	D
First game	18	0	18	18
Second game	2	2	6	8
Third game	1	5	3	9
Fourth game	9	1	4	4
Fifth game	8	5	2	3
Total five-game score	38	13	33	42
Penalty-point bonuses	50	–	50	50
Total match scores	88	13	83	92
Minus winner B's score	−13	–	−13	−13
B wins by	75 pts		70 pts	79 pts

At a penny a point, B receives 75 cents from A, 70 cents from C, and 79 cents from D, for a total of $2.24.

Black Widow Hearts

This game, which is also called Black Lady, Black Maria, Slippery Anne, and Discard Hearts, is played in the same manner as Hearts According to Scarne except that the queen of spades counts a minus 13 and cards are passed as in Regular Hearts. In addition, if one player takes all penalty cards (queen of spades and all hearts), he receives a bonus of 26 points for the "take-all." Thus, the object of Black Widow Hearts is to avoid taking any hearts or the queen of spades; or to win all these cards. A game is generally deemed won by the player with the best score (least minus) when another player reaches minus 100.

Strategy in Hearts According to Scarne and Black Widow Hearts. The basic strategy in Regular Hearts holds true in these games, too. In addition, remember that the ace and king of spades are dangerous in Hearts According to Scarne and Black Widow Hearts. It is often better to discard these in the early stages of play than to throw hearts. High hearts, of course, should be discarded as soon as possible, but low ones are not too dangerous and often can be used as leads to force players with high hearts to win these tricks.

Actually, spades should be led whenever possible until the queen of spades has been played. Never lead a king or ace of spades on which the queen may be possibly dropped, or lead the spade suit if you hold the queen inadequately protected.

When a player appears to be maneuvering for a take-all or sweepstakes, at least one of his opponents should take a trick containing penalty cards, even if it is a trick he would normally not take. To recognize when you have an opportunity for a take-all requires experience, of course. As a rule, it is not a good idea to attempt a take-all unless the hand shapes up as an *almost* absolute certainty that it can be done since the penalty score is great if it is not accomplished.

Black Jack Hearts

This is a variant in which the jack of spades is the penalty card instead of the queen. Otherwise the game is played like Black Widow Hearts.

Cancellation Hearts

From seven to ten players can participate in this variant. Two decks of 52 cards are used, shuffled together. The cards are dealt one at a time as far as they will go evenly, and any odd cards are left in a widow, which goes to the winner of the first trick. The play is as in Black Widow Hearts, except that when two identical cards fall on the same trick they cancel each other; neither can win the trick. It is thus possible for the two of spades to win both queens, all other cards being likewise

paired. If all cards played of the suit led are paired, the trick is held in abeyance and goes to the winner of the next trick. The leader of a trick so held in abeyance leads again.

The counting cards are the hearts, 1 each, and queen of spades, 13. Use cumulative scoring, as given under Regular Hearts. A game ends when one player reaches a prefixed total, usually 100.

Omnibus Hearts

Omnibus Hearts, which is also called Pass-On Hearts, New York Hearts, and Hooligan Hearts, is played the same as Black Widow Hearts, except that there is a 10-point bonus for the player winning the ten of diamonds in a trick. Therefore, the object of this game is to avoid taking hearts and the queen of spades, while taking the bonus card (ten of diamonds). Or, alternately, to try to take all the penalty cards and the bonus card. This bonus card retains its rank as a diamond, and the holder of it must follow a diamond lead with it, unless he has some other diamond he prefers to play.

Red Jack Hearts

This variation is played the same as Omnibus Hearts, except that the jack of diamonds fills the role of bonus card rather than the ten.

Greek Hearts

Greek Hearts is the high-scoring game of the Hearts family. The general play of the game is the same as Black Widow Hearts except passing is to the right and scoring is as follows:

	Debited Points
From deuce to ten of hearts	Face value
Jack, queen, and king of hearts	10
Ace of hearts	15
Queen of spades	50

If, however, a player takes all the hearts and the queen of spades, 150 points is added to all the other players' scores. He receives zero count for that hand.

Sometimes the jack of diamonds is counted a ten bonus card as in Red Jack Hearts.

Another rule often imposed in Greek Hearts is that the first lead of the game may not be a heart.

Progressive Hearts

This is managed generally as in Progressive Euchre (page 239). Only one deal is played to a table. The winner of the fewest hearts between the two ladies and the winner of the fewest hearts between the two gentlemen progress.

Polignac

Also known as Four Jacks, Quatre-Valets, Stay Away, No-Jacks, and Four Valets, this game is the French form of Hearts and it is played with a 32-card pack, running in value from ace down to seven. The ace is high both in cutting and play.

From four to seven players make the best game. The deck must be dealt out evenly, and if it will not do so, sevens are stripped out as necessary, the seven of hearts last. The cards are dealt out two at a time; or three at a time; or two, then three.

The object of the game is to avoid taking any jacks. The jack of spades (polignac) counts 2 points against the player taking it, other jacks counting 1 each against. In addition, before the opening lead, any player may announce capot (that he attempts to win all the tricks). If the capot is successful, he gets no score but 5 points are added to the score of each other player. He does not receive any penalty count for the jack, either. If he fails, the penalty of 5 points is charged against his score as well as any jacks in the tricks he has taken.

Game may be set at 10 points. When a player reaches that score, the one with the lowest score is the winner. Each player collects according to the difference between his score and that of any player with a higher score.

Slobberhannes

The object of the game is to avoid taking the first trick, the last trick, and the trick containing the queen of clubs. The player winning any of these tricks has one point scored

against him for each trick; for taking all three, he loses an extra point, 4 in all. The first player to have a score of 10 against him pays the other players the difference between 10 and their score.

The players, deck, and deal are as in Polignac. The play is as in Regular Hearts.

Knaves

Knaves, or Jacks, like most games in the Heart family, admirably combines the elements of skill and chance.

Requirements
1. Three players.
2. Standard 52-card deck.

Beginning of the Game. The selection of the dealer, seating positions, changing seats, shuffle, and cut are as provided under the General Rules for Card Games, chapter 1.

The Deal. Players cut for deal, the dealer giving 17 cards to each player. The remaining card is turned face upward on the table; the suit of this card is the trump suit.

The Play. The object of the game is to take as many tricks as possible (players following suit if they can do so, but otherwise discarding or trumping as they like), but penalties are incurred if any trick taken includes a jack.

The Game. The first player to obtain 20 points is the winner. Each trick counts one point, while points for collecting jacks are deducted as follows:

For taking the jack of hearts	4 points
For taking the jack of diamonds	3 points
For taking the jack of clubs	2 points
For taking the jack of spades	1 point

Thus, if a player makes six tricks which include the jacks of hearts and spades, his net score for the deal is 1 point. A trick with the jack of spades only in it cancels itself out. A trick may, of course, include two or even three jacks. The aggregate score for the deal (unless the card indicating the trump suit happens to be a jack) is 17 points for tricks, minus 10 for the jacks, or 7 points in all.

Two-Ten-Jack

The object of this popular two-handed game is to win tricks containing certain cards of counting value and to avoid taking tricks containing cards which count against the winner.

In Two-Ten-Jack, hearts are always trumps. The cards rank as follows: ace (high), king, queen, jack, ten, nine, eight, seven, six, five, four, three, two (low). But the ace of spades is always the highest card, ranking ahead of the ace of hearts, and may be used as a trump. The ace of spades is also known as speculation.

The Deal. After shuffle and cut, the dealer deals six cards to each player, one at a time, beginning with his opponent. The remainder of the deck, the stock, is placed face up on the table.

The Play. The nondealer leads any card, and the dealer then plays to the trick. A player must follow suit or trump, except in one instance; when trumps are led, it is optional with the holder of speculation whether to play it or not. But if the holder of speculation holds no other spade, speculation must be played to a spade lead. If a player cannot follow suit or trump, he may play any card. The highest card of the suit led wins a trick, unless it is trumped, in which case the trump wins.

The winner of the first trick takes the top card of the stock into his hand and the loser takes the second. The winner of each trick leads to the next. This continues until the stock is exhausted and the hands played out. Points made are then recorded, and the deal passes.

The Scoring. Players score as follows for certain cards won in tricks:

For heart two, ten, jack, each	+10 points
For heart ace, king, queen, each	+ 5 points
For diamond six and club ace, king, queen, jack, each	+ 1 point
For spade two, ten, jack, each	−10 points
For spade ace, king, queen, each	− 5 points

At the end of each hand, each player totals his plus points, then his minus points, and deducts the lesser total from the greater. If the greater score is plus, it is scored plus; if minus, as minus.

The Game. The game may be set at 30, or more, with the player first reaching the agreed total considered the winner.

Three-Handed Two-Ten-Jack

When playing this variant, the three of clubs is removed from the deck. Each player receives six cards in the deal, beginning at the dealer's left. The winner takes the first card of the stock, and the two others draw the next cards in a left to right rotation. The deal passes to the left. The play, scoring, and game is the same as for Two-Handed Two-Ten-Jack.

Four-Handed Two-Ten-Jack

In this game, which is played with a full 52-card deck, each player receives four cards, dealt in rotation left to right, beginning with the player left of the dealer. The play is the same as Three-Handed Two-Ten-Jack, the winner of each trick drawing the top card from the stock and the others drawing a card each in rotation, left to right. Scoring is as in the two-handed game.

CHAPTER 15

The All-Fours Group

The All-Fours family of games can trace its history back for at least three hundred years. Of English origin, the name "All-Fours" refers to the four major points that players try for in play. While some variants give other points in which it is possible to score, the all-fours original feature still persists in all members of this closely related family.

SEVEN-UP

Seven-Up was possibly the first of the All-Fours family to migrate to America from England in the early 1700's. Also known as High-Low-Jack and Old Sledge, it is a true form of All-Fours (it is still called by that name in some parts of the world) and remains popular today. It receives its name from the fact that it takes 7 points to win.

Requirements

1. Two or three play individually. With four players, it is a partnership game, two against two.

2. A regular 52-card deck. In each suit the cards rank: ace (high), king, queen, jack, ten, nine, eight, seven, six, five, four, three, two (low), in descending order.

The Object of the Game. To be the first player to score 7 points and win the game.

Beginning of the Game. The selection of the dealer, seating positions, changing seats, shuffle, and cut are as provided under the General Rules for Card Games, chapter 1.

The Deal. After the deck has been shuffled and cut, dealer gives each player a hand of six cards. He deals three at a time, beginning with the player at his left and going in clockwise rotation. The next card is then turned up and proposes the trump suit. It is placed on top of the remainder of the deck (stock). If this card is a jack, dealer scores one point.

The turn to deal in subsequent hands rotates clockwise.

Determining the Trump. The player at the left of the dealer, after looking at his hand, has the first right to "stand" or "beg." To stand means that he is satisfied with the turn-up card as trump and play begins immediately. To beg is to pass the decision to the dealer. The latter must either give the player who begged 1 point as a gift to let the trump stand, or deal three new cards to each player, plus a face-up card as a proposed new trump. The original trump card remains face up on the table. If this trump is the same suit as the one first turned, the same process is repeated, until a different suit is reached. The last card of the deck cannot be turned for trumps. If the whole deck is exhausted, without arriving at a different suit for trumps, the cards are gathered, shuffled, and redealt by the same dealer. No player but the dealer and the player to his left may look at his cards until the first trump turned has been decided upon. If a jack is turned for the new suit, the dealer scores 1. But the dealer never scores for the turn of a jack in the suit of the first rejected turn-up.

The Play. Once the trump has been set, each player reduces his hand (if necessary) to six cards, by discarding superfluous cards face down. Then the player to the dealer's left leads any card. If this is a trump, the other players must follow suit if possible; if not a trump, they also must follow suit, but if unable to do so, they may trump or discard. The highest card of the suit led wins, unless the trick is trumped, in which case the highest trump wins. The winner of each trick leads to the next.

Scoring. The object of play is to win points in tricks. There are at the maximum 4 points, as follows:

High: highest trump in play; player to whom dealt.

Low: lowest trump in play; player to whom dealt.

Jack: jack of trumps, to dealer turning it for trump, or player taking it in a trick.

Game: highest total of point values of cards taken in tricks in which the count is as follows: each ace, 4; each king, 3; each queen, 2; each jack, 1; and each ten, 10 (lower cards have no value).

If there is only one trump in play, it scores 2 as both high and low (or 3 if it is the jack). The 1 for game is not scored if there is a tie for the highest count.

The Game. The player or side first to reach a total of 7 points wins the game. If more than one secure points to win the game in a single hand, the points are scored in this order, to determine the winner: high; low; jack; game. The player who first scores out wins. If the dealer needs but one point to win game, and on the deal turns up the jack for trumps, he wins.

Additional Rules

Misdeal. If the dealer gives any player an incorrect number of cards, he loses the deal, which passes to the next player in turn. If the dealer exposes a card, the player to whom it is dealt may decide to let the deal stand or to have a new deal by the same dealer. If a card is faced in the pack, there is a new deal by the same dealer.

Revoke. Failure to follow suit (or trump) when able is a revoke. It may be corrected before the lead to the next trick, but each player in turn after the revoker may withdraw his card and substitute another. If not corrected in time, the revoke trick stands and the offender cannot score for jack or game, and each opponent scores 1 point if the jack is not in play; 2 points if the jack is in play.

Exposed Card. In partnership play only, a card exposed except in legal play must be left face up on the table and must be played on demand of either opponent (provided that its play is legal).

All Fives

Follows the rules of Seven-Up except that points are also scored by a player winning any of the following trumps in a trick: for the ten, 10 points; five, 5; ace, 4; king, 3; queen, 2; jack, 1. The count for game is as in Seven-Up. The player first to reach a total of 61 wins the game. For convenience in scoring some players peg points on a cribbage board (see page 221).

California Jack

In this two-handed variation, which is sometimes called California Loo or Draw Seven-Up, each player receives six cards, dealt face down one at a time, and the remainder of the deck—the stock—is placed face up on the table. The top card of the stock indicates the trump suit; or the trump suit may be established by cutting before the deal. The non-dealer makes the first lead. The winner of the first trick takes the top card from the stock and his opponent takes the card underneath. The winner of each trick leads to the next, and play proceeds as described until all cards in the stock and hand have been exhausted. A trick consists of two cards, one from each player, and rules of tricks in Seven-Up apply.

At the end of play, each player goes through his trick pile and scores 1 point for having high (ace of trumps), 1 point for low (deuce of trumps), 1 point for jack of trumps, and 1 point for game, which is figured exactly as in Seven-Up. (Note: "Low" scores for the player taking it, not the player holding it.) Game consists of either 7 or 10 points, and should both players go out in the same deal, the order of precedence is handled as in Seven-Up.

Variation. California Jack can also be played three- and four-handed. For three hands, remove any deuce from the deck, while for four hands, play with a full 52-card deck. Each player draws from the stock in turn—both play and draw go to the left.

Otherwise, three- and four-hand variations are the same as two-hand California Jack.

Shasta Sam

Shasta Sam is played in the same manner as California Jack except that the stock is kept face down so that the winner of each trick does not know what card he will draw. Before the deal, a card is cut or turned from the pack to determine the trump suit for that deal.

AUCTION PITCH OR SET-BACK

The most popular All-Fours game today in the United States is Auction Pitch. There are many varieties and the rules have changed greatly over the years, but the essential feature of Pitch, as in all All-Fours games, is always the scoring of high, low, jack, and the game. I have selected the most popular present-day variation to include in this chapter.

Requirements

1. Two to seven players. Four make the best game. Each player plays for himself.

2. A standard 52-card deck is used. The card values rank as follows: ace (high), king, queen, jack, ten, nine, eight, seven, six, five, four, three, deuce (low) in descending order. Suits have no rank.

Beginning of the Game. The selection of the dealer, seating positions, changing seats, shuffle, and cut are as provided under the General Rules for Card Games, chapter 1.

The Deal. After the cards are shuffled and cut, each player, beginning with the player to the dealer's left and going clockwise, is dealt three cards at a time until each has been dealt six cards. The remainder of the deck is not used.

The Object of the Game. To become the first player to score 11 points (or 7, 9, or 21, as agreed upon). The points are counted after the hand has been played and as in Seven-Up are as follows:

1. *High.* One point for the original player holding the highest trump showing during play of the hand.

2. *Low.* One point for the original player

holding the lowest trump showing during the play of the hand.

3. *Jack.* One point to the player who wins the jack of trumps during play. Naturally, if it is not in play, no one scores it.

4. *Game.* One point to the player scoring the most number of points. Cards are valued in game count exactly as in Seven-Up.

The Bidding. The player to the dealer's left bids first. Each player, in turn clockwise, has one chance to bid or pass. He may bid 1, 2, 3, or 4. Suits have no value, hence are not named. Each bid must be higher in numerical value than the preceding bid, and the highest possible is four, which is known as a *slam, smudge,* or *shoot the moon*. If all the players pass, the hand is declared dead and the same dealer deals again.

The Play of the Game. The highest bidder, sometimes called the *pitcher,* leads to the first trick, and the suit of that card establishes the trump suit for the deal. On a trump lead, each player must follow suit when able; when any other suit (but trumps) is played, a player must follow suit, play a trump card, or, if unable to follow suit or trump, throw off any card he pleases. The highest card of a suit wins the trick if no trumps are played to the trick. When only one trump card is played to a trick, the trump wins. But if more than one trump is played, the highest trump takes the trick.

The winner of a trick leads a card to the next trick. The play of each trick continues as described above until all six cards have been played.

Scoring. When the six cards have been played, each player receives credit for the points he scores, except that if the player who took the bid fails to score as many points as he bid for, he is *set back* the same number of points as he bid. The full total of his bid is deducted from his previous score. If his setback is greater than his previous or plus score, a minus score is recorded for the difference. A circle is usually drawn around a minus score and the holder is said to be *in the hole*.

End of Game. The first player to reach 11 points (or 7, 10, or 21, as agreed on) wins the game. In the event the bidder of the last hand and any other player or players have scored 11 or more points (or 7, 9, or 21 points as agreed on) the bidder is declared the winner of the game. If two players other than the last bidder should reach 11 points with the last hand, the points are counted in the following order: high, low, jack, and game.

The winner receives from each player the difference in points between his score and each player's score.

Scoring Variant: In some sections of the country, it is customary for every player to start with a score of 7. When a player is set back, the points he bid are added to his score; points he makes are subtracted from his score; and the first player to reach zero is the winner of the game.

Additional Rules

Misdeal. The following are cause for a misdeal:

1. If the dealer does not offer the deck to be cut.

2. If an ace, deuce, or jack is exposed during the deal by the dealer. Because the deal carries an advantage, a misdeal by dealer loses him the right to deal, and it passes to the player on his left.

Irregularities in Bidding. The following can occur during the bidding:

1. A bid out of turn or a bid lower or equal to the previous bid loses the bidding privilege for the offender. He must pass. A card once played cannot be taken back.

2. If a player plays out of turn, the bidder reserves the right to force the offender at his proper turn of play to play his highest or lowest card of the suit led, or to trump or not to trump.

3. If the bidder has played to an incorrect lead, he cannot take back his played card. However, he is permitted to name the proper trump and must then lead it at his first opportunity, that is immediately after winning his first trick.

Revokes. When a player fails to follow suit when able to do so, a revoke is committed. If the bidder revokes, he is set back the amount of his bid. Each of the other players scores the points he makes. If a player other than the bidder revokes, an amount equal to the bid is deducted from his score and the same amount is added to the score of all other players, including the bidder, even if the latter scores fewer points than he bid.

Strategy of Auction Pitch. Since the dealer has the chance to bid last he has an advantage and should take full advantage of it by taking risks to win it. The first two players to dealer's left, on the other hand, should be rather conservative.

It is usually safe to make a bid of one when holding three trumps since you can usually capture the game point, if nothing else. The jack once guarded is also worth a bid of one, and the two-spot even once guarded has a fairly good chance of being saved. In addition, it is sometimes worth the chance to bid in the hope that a king in hand will prove to be high, or a three-spot low. Side aces and tens strengthen the hand but cannot be counted upon to win the game point. Remember that bidding is generally based on trump length. Since a player isn't required to follow suit if he can trump, the bidder can't consider aces as winning tricks unless he has first drawn trumps. Because all the cards are not dealt in Auction Pitch, the odds are usually good that all the outstanding trumps can be pulled in two rounds and almost invariably in three.

It is important that the player conspire to beat the bidder, or pitcher. For example, when playing for game, all opponents should try to throw their tens to some one opponent who has a good chance of costing the bidder that point for game.

Smudge

One of the more popular forms of Auction Pitch is Smudge, and it is usually considered the easiest to play. This variant is played the same as Auction Pitch, except that winning all four points in one hand constitutes a *smudge* by any player, whether he won the bid or not, and wins the game immediately regardless of that player's previous score. (In certain areas, a smudge wins the game provided its player is not "in the hole." If he has a minus score at the time of making a smudge, the minus count is dropped and his score becomes plus 4.)

Auction Pitch with a Joker

Also called Joker Pitch, this variant has a joker added to the pack so that there is a 53-card deck. The joker is a trump but ranks below the lowest trump in the play, but does not score for *low*, that point going to the holder of the lowest natural trump card. The joker makes a fifth point in play, counting one to the player who wins it in a trick. In counting points to determine the winner of the game if there is a tie, they count in order: high, low, jack, joker, game. However, the pitcher's points are always counted first. While the game is won by the first player to reach 10 points, the play of the game is the same as Auction Pitch.

Low Pitch

In this variation, as in California Jack, low can be scored only by the player winning it in a trick.

Racehorse Pitch

This variant of Auction Pitch is played with a 32-card deck, ace high to seven low. Points are scored for high, low, jack, and game, in the order named.

Sell-Out or Commercial Pitch

While this game uses one of earliest popular methods of bidding in Pitch, it is seldom employed today. In it, the player to the left of the dealer has the choice of making the trump or selling the right to do so. If he makes the trump, he does so without bidding. He simply leads a card, whereupon the suit of that lead is trump for the deal, and he obligates himself to make all 4 points or be set back. Otherwise, if he offers to sell the right to make

trump, the other players in turn (clockwise rotation) may make a bid or pass. He then has the right to sell to the highest bidder, or to name the trump himself under obligation to make as many points as the highest bidder's declaration or to be set back. If he sells to the highest bidder, the latter makes the trump and plays at that contract, but the former adds the points of the bid to his score. If player with the right to sell does not do so to the highest bidder, the latter adds the points of the bid to his score. If there are no bids, the deal is considered passed and the same dealer redeals. Under no circumstances is a bid permitted that will automatically give the player at the dealer's left enough points for game, and he must sell if by declining to he would give the highest bidder enough points for game. Thus, no player is permitted to make a declaration which will automatically present another player with enough points for game. The play, the hands, and other rules are the same as for Auction Pitch.

Pedro

Pedro is a collective name for a number of elaborations of Auction Pitch. It is also the name given to one of the simplest forms of these elaborations.

Pedro. In this game there is one extra point card, the five of trumps (called *Pedro*), which gives the taker 5 points. Each hand, therefore, has a potential of 9 points. The player who first reaches 21 is the winner.

Pedro Sancho. In this game the nine of trumps (called *Sancho*) is also a point card, worth 9 itself. Thus each hand has a potential of 18 points. Scoring is as follows: high, low, jack, ten of trumps (which takes the place of game), Pedro, and Sancho, scoring in the order named. First to reach 50 (or 100) points is the winner.

Dom Pedro or Snoozer. This variant of Auction Pitch with a joker is the same as Pedro Sancho with the addition of two more counting cards: the three of trumps (called *Dom*), which is worth 3 points when taken in play, and the joker (called *Snoozer*), worth 15 points to the taker, bringing the total per deal up to 36 maximum. (Remember that if a point card fails to appear during play, it is not scored in that hand.) Dom counts after the ten (game), and the Snoozer counts after

Sancho. Snoozer is the lowest trump, ranking below the deuce, but it is not considered as low. The player first reaching 100 is the winner.

CINCH

Once the most popular game of the All-Fours family, Cinch (also called High Five, or Double Pedro) eventually gave way to Auction Bridge and finally to Contract Bridge among serious card players.

Requirements

1. Four players make the best game, two against two as partners, or each player may play for himself.

2. The regular 52-card deck is used. In suits that are not trumps, the cards rank as in Seven-Up. But in the trump suit there is an extra trump, the five of the same color as the trump suit. This five is known as *left pedro* and ranks right below the five of trumps, known as *right pedro*. Thus the trump suit would rank as follows: ace (high), king, queen, jack, ten, nine, eight, seven, six, right pedro, left pedro, four, three, two (low).

Beginning of the Game. The selection of the dealer, seating positions, changing seats, shuffle, and cut are as provided under the General Rules for Card Games, chapter 1.

The Deal. After the deck has been shuffled and cut by player at dealer's right, the deal begins. Dealer serves each player three cards at a time, starting with player at his left and continuing in that direction until each has a hand of nine cards.

The deal rotates to the left.

The Bidding. Player at dealer's left has the first opportunity to bid, after which the bidding continues to the left. Each player in turn may make only one bid, or he must pass. In bidding the player states the number of points that he and his side will contract to win if he is given the privilege of naming his own trump suit, but he does not mention the trump suit until after the bidding has ceased. Bids may range from 1 to 14; every succeeding bid must be higher in numerical value than the preceding one. If all players pass to dealer, he may name trump suit without making a bid, or he may also pass. If all pass, there is a new deal by the next dealer in turn.

Drawing and Discarding. The successful bidder names the trump suit, at which time all the players except the dealer discard from their hands any cards they don't want to hold. The usual discards are in nontrump suits. But in any case, a player must not hold more than six cards in his hand. Then each player in turn is dealt enough cards from the remainder of the deck to fill his hand out to six cards, unless, of course, he already holds six cards.

The dealer then may select from the remainder of the plack and his original hand any six cards he chooses, placing the discards from his hand face up on the table. If the remainder of the deck contains any trumps that the dealer does not take into his hand, they must be placed face up on the table. (Variation: Some play that dealer makes this discard before looking through the deck.)

The Play. When all players have had their hands restored to six cards, the high bidder leads any card he pleases. (It does not have to be a trump.) Each player in turn to the left also plays a card to this trick.

A player may either follow suit or he may play a trump even if able to follow suit. If he cannot follow suit, he may play a trump or throw off any card, as he desires. However, a player must follow suit to a trump lead if able to. The highest card of a led suit wins the trick if there are no trump cards in the trick. A trump card wins the trick, but if the trick contains more than one trump card, the highest trump wins. The winner of a trick leads to the next and play continues as described until all six cards have been played.

Scoring. If the bidding player or side wins at least as many points as it bids, the side with the higher count scores the difference between the two counts; thus, either the bidding or the nonbidding side may score. If the bidding side does not make its contract, the nonbidding side scores 14 plus the number of points by which the bidding side fell short. *Examples:* The bid is 6, bidding side wins 6 points, opponents win 8 points; opponents score 2 points for the hand. The bid is 8, bidding side wins 7 points, opponents win 7 points, opponents score 15 points.

Game is won by the first player or side to reach 51 points.

Additional Rules

New Deal by the Same Dealer. If a card is found faced in the pack; or, on demand of an adversary, if a card is faced in dealing; or if the shuffle or cut was improper, provided attention is called to it before the deal is completed, the dealer must deal again.

Misdeal. If dealer gives too many or too few cards to any player in any round, and the fact is discovered before the first bid is made, the hand is declared dead and the deal passes to the left.

Incorrect Hand. A player with too few cards must play on; a player with too many cards must offer his hand, face down, and an opponent draws out the excess, which are shuffled into the stock.

Bidding Out of Turn. Neither member of the offending side may bid thereafter, but any bid previously made stands.

Lead or Play Out of Turn. The card must be withdrawn upon demand of an opponent if neither opponent has played to the trick. The card played in error is subject to call. If the lead out of turn was made when it was the offender's partner's turn to lead, the offender's right-hand opponent may require the offender's partner to lead or not to lead a trump.

Revoke. Play continues, but the offending side may not score in that hand, and, if the offender is an opponent of the bidder, the bidder cannot be set.

Razzle-Dazzle or Auction Cinch

This is a variation for five or six players, each for himself. Only six cards are dealt to each player, three at a time. Bidding is exactly the same as in Cinch; the highest bidder has the privilege of naming the trump. All cards that are not trumps or sure winners are discarded, and the dealer gives cards from the deck to restore each hand to six. The highest bidder then names a card he needs (generally a trump); the holder of that card must acknowledge it, and thereby becomes bidder's partner, but the players do not change seats.

Cinch with a Widow

Cinch is occasionally played with a widow of four cards dealt face down in front of each player, after the first round of three cards apiece has been dealt. Subsequent deals give each player six additional cards, as in Cinch. After the bidding is completed, but before the trump suit is named, each player picks up his widow. Then after the trump is named, each player discards all but six cards and play proceeds as a Cinch.

Progressive Cinch

The tables are made up as in a Progressive Euchre (see Chapter 13). Each table is provided with a bell, and as soon as any side scores 32 points, they ring it. Play stops at once at all tables, and totals are added up, as of the last hand scored. The winning teams progress, as in Progressive Euchre. Ties may cut to decide who progresses and scores, or a half game may be scored for each side, cutting to progress only.

Sixty-Three

In this modification of Cinch, nine cards are dealt to each player; and after discarding, the hands are filled out to six cards, as in Cinch. A game is made up of 152 points. The trump cards count as follows: ace (high), 1; king, 25; trey (3), 15; nine, 9; ten, 1; five (right pedro), 5; five of same color (left pedro), 5; two (low), 1. All of these count to the player taking them in play. Bidding continues in rotation until no one will bid higher. The highest possible bid is 63.

In Progressive Sixty-Three, teams change tables after four hands are played. Except for this, the rules of Progressive Cinch hold.

CHAPTER 16

Banking Card Games

Properly speaking, so-called banking games are games in which the gambling establishment or one player is continually opposed to all other players. There are two distinct classes of banking games: casino games and private games. Casino games are those that require special apparatus, have a mathematical advantage for the bank, and as a rule are played mostly in gambling casinos and sporting clubs. Among these games the best known are probably Black Jack Casino Style, Chemin de Fer, Baccarat–Chemin de Fer, Baccarat, Scarney Baccarat, Trente et Quarante, Monte, and Faro. Private banking games are those that require no apparatus but a pack of cards and some checks (chips) or money. Among these we find Black Jack, Farmer, Red Dog, Banker and Broker, Yablon, and Slogger. Some of these banking or showdown games are good for sociable group participation. Stakes need not be high for full enjoyment of such games. Many people have an excellent time playing for the fun of it with chips, matchsticks, or tokens—the main satisfaction coming from being the winner.

BLACK JACK, B.J., OR TWENTY-ONE

It is a matter of record that this game is the most widely played banking card game in the world. Black Jack is played in every casino, private card room, and gambling club from California to New England and from New York to Panama. Every major casino in Nevada, Puerto Rico, Netherlands Antilles, Grand Bahamas, England, North Africa, Macao, Yugoslavia, France, Italy, Turkey, Monte Carlo, and elsewhere harbors at least five Black Jack tables.

There is almost as tense a scholarly dispute over the origin of the game as there is over Coon Can. Italy and France have claimed it as their own, the French alleging a blood relationship with their Ferme and Chemin de Fer (Shimmy), the Italians insisting that it is a vulgarization of their Seven and a Half. These games are obviously similar, structurally. To identify who first played Black Jack, and when and where, is obviously outside the purview of the present work; I should as soon undertake to arbitrate when and where the first blackjack was bounced off the first human skull.

The etymology of the game seems to have escaped the attention of the professors, although it might be a rewarding inquiry. *The American Hoyle* of 1875 calls it *Vingt-Un.* Foster's *Hoyle,* thirty years later, lists it as *Vingt-et-Un.* Now see what happens to French in a half century of abrasion in everyday speech. Today a substantial minority of Americans call the game Van John or Pontoon. From Vingt-et-Un to Pontoon; from Chemin de Fer to Shimmy! A man with a sensitive ear can have a lot of fun at a gambling table and never lose a dime. . . .

Let me stipulate at the outset a distinction which I shall have to emphasize later. There are two kinds of Black Jack:

1. The private, sociable, reasonably equitable game, in which every player has a right and chance to become dealer and banker.

2. The professional or casino game, in which the house man does all the dealing and all the banking.

First, let's talk about the private game.

Private Game of Black Jack

Requirements

1. Two to seven players constitute the best game.

2. Onlookers (kibitzers) may bet on the hand of any player except the dealer.

3. The standard 52-card pack plus joker is used.

Value of Cards

1. Any ace counts either 1 or 11 according to the discretion of its possessor.

2. Kings, queens, and jacks count 10 each.

3. All other cards count their face value, two 2, three 3, four 4, etc.

4. The joker has no value, and does not enter into the play; it is used only as a locater in the deck.

Object of the Game. To get a higher count (total value of cards in hand) than the dealer up to but not over 21. Should the player draw cards forcing his total over 21, he must immediately pay the dealer-banker and he sacrifices any chance to beat or tie the dealer. The player may demand and draw any number of cards until he reaches or exceeds a count of 21.

Selecting the Dealer. The first dealer shall be selected as follows *and in no other manner:*

1. Any player by mutual consent shuffles the deck.

2. Any other player may cut it.

3. The player acting as dealer pro tem deals cards one each, face up, to each player clockwise until an ace is dealt.

4. The player dealt the first ace becomes the dealer-banker.

Losing the Deal and Bank. Ordinarily, I don't think the lawmaker on games should build variations into the basic structure of the game, but for reasons to be stated below Black Jack is an extremely special case. Herewith are specified two alternative rules under which the bank may be lost. Either is legal. I recommend that the second be adopted for the private social game. I must emphasize that before play starts all players must be acquainted with the rule under which they are playing.

1. The first player dealt a *natural* (two cards totaling 21) shall become dealer and banker at the completion of that deal. If that player refuses the deal, the player holding the natural nearest to that player's left wins the deal. If all players holding a natural refuse the deal, it remains in possession of the present dealer. Should he refuse to continue dealing, the deal passes to the player at his immediate left. If that player refuses, it passes to his left. If all players refuse it, a new dealer is selected by the means stated above under Selecting the Dealer.

2. This rule is added to stabilize the situation, too often encountered in Black Jack, in which one player gets the bank for a single deal, then loses it to another player who through sheer luck holds it for eight or ten deals. After the first dealer has been selected by the procedure set forth under Selecting the Dealer, he shall deal (bank) five complete deals. On completion of these five deals, the deal and bank shall pass to the player at the dealer's left; and, each five deals thereafter, shall move to the left, clockwise. When using this alternate rule, a natural 21 does not win the bank, although the player drawing it shall still be paid two to one on his bet.

The Betting Limit. The dealer establishes arbitrarily his own betting limits. Should a dealer after suffering losses have less money in the bank than the players want to bet, he is privileged to lower his limits. As a result of a winning streak, he can increase them.

A dealer deciding he no longer wants the bank is privileged to put the bank and deal up for auction and sell it to the highest bidder. He may auction the deal at any time—provided there are no uncompleted hands on the board. If the dealer offers the bank at auction and no player bids, it passes to the player at the dealer's left. If he rejects it, the deal passes clockwise around the table until it is accepted or a new deal for selecting the dealer is compelled.

The Shuffle and Cut. The dealer shuffles the cards and puts them in the center of the table to be cut. Any player may call for the right to shuffle any time he likes, but the dealer has the right to shuffle last. Any player may cut the cards. If more than one player wants to cut, he or they must be allowed to do so. After the cut has been completed, and the cards are squared, the deck is placed on the upturned joker, which has been left resting before the dealer. This face-up card is used as a locater in the deck.

If a joker is not handy, the dealer removes the top card of the deck, shows it to all other players, then puts it on the bottom of the deck, face up. (This is called *burning a card*.)

Payoffs. All bets are paid off at even money by both dealer and players, *except* when a player is dealt a natural, when he is paid two to one.

Betting. Before any cards are dealt, each player must put the sum he proposes to bet (within the limit) in front of himself within full view of the dealer.

The Deal. To each player, beginning with the player at his left and going clockwise, the dealer gives one card face down, dealing himself the last card face up. Then a second card is dealt to each player face down, the second card being dealt to the dealer face down. (I suggest facing the dealer's first card instead of his second, because, by giving the players more time to study the dealer's upcard and possibilities, it tends to speed the game.)

The Play. If the dealer's face-up card is a 10 count (picture card or a 10 spot) or an ace, he must look at his hole (face-down) card. If he has caught a natural—a ten or picture card plus an ace, totaling a count of 21—he immediately faces his cards and announces a natural black jack or twenty-one. The players now announce whether they have a natural. If anyone does, that sets up a *standoff,* or *push.* The dealer collects the bets of all players not holding a natural. The payoff is at even money, except in a standoff when no bets are paid.

If the dealer has not caught a natural, the player to his left plays first. If that player has 21 he calls a natural, turns over his two cards, and the dealer pays the bet off at 2 to 1 odds. Then the dealer puts them on the bottom of the deck, face up. If the player's two

cards total less than 21, the player can elect within his discretion to *stay* or get *hit.*

If he is satisfied that his count is closer than the dealer's to a total of 21, the player may stay by declining another card. He signifies this intention by putting his bet on top of his cards and/or saying "Good," "I stand," or "I have enough." If he is not satisfied with his count and elects to draw more cards he says "Hit me," and the dealer gives him another card face up. The player may draw one or as many more cards as he likes, as long as his count does not exceed 21, or *bust.* When the player is satisfied with his count, he says "I stay," and puts his bet on his cards. Should a player draw a card forcing his total count over 21, he must call "Bust," and turn over all his cards. The dealer collects the bet, and turns that player's cards face up at the bottom of the deck. And the player is out of competition until a new hand starts.

Play as here described moves around the table to the left, clockwise, a man at a time.

The Dealer's Play. The dealer plays last. He may, like the players, elect to stay or draw. He turns his down card face up, and announces "Stay" or "Draw."

If he draws one or more cards and goes over 21, he must pay all players still in the game. If, staying or drawing, he remains below 21 on completing his play, he collects bets from players who have a lower count than he, and pays all surviving players having a higher count. When dealer and player have the same count it's a standoff, and neither wins.

Additional Rules. The above rules will suffice for a private game, but there's nothing sacrosanct about them. Players may by agreement incorporate into their private play as many rules as they like out of Scarne's Rules for Black Jack, Casino Play.

Black Jack, Casino Style

The basic rules of Black Jack, as played in legal casinos the world over, are the same except for some minor "dealing" and "doubling down" variations. Some casinos deal Black Jack with a single deck from the hand, dealing the players' initial two cards face down. Others deal two or four decks out of a shoe, and deal the players' first two cards face down or face up as the case may be. Some

European and Caribbean casinos, in order to prevent their Black Jack dealers from tipping off (signaling) their hole cards to agents (player cheats), do not permit their dealer to look at his face-down card until all the players have played out their hands. For the same reason, some casinos do not allow the dealer to deal his face-down card until all the players' hands have been completed.

I have selected for analysis the Black Jack rules that I have formulated—which are now in use in Nevada, Puerto Rico, Netherlands Antilles, Europe, and countless other casinos the world over. They have been chosen because they are the best of all casino rules—not only for the player's protection, but for the casino's as well. I predict that, within a few years, Scarne's Black Jack Casino rules, which follow, will be standard throughout the world.

Scarne's Rules for Black Jack, Casino Play

Requirements

1. A regulation Black Jack table with six or seven betting spaces on its layout.

2. A check rack filled with betting chips.

3. A card-dealing box called a *shoe,* and a discard receiver.

4. Four standard packs of 52 cards each, shuffled together and used as one, a total of 208 cards dealt as a single deck.

5. Two indicator cards (advertising cards). One is used by players to cut the deck

and the other indicator card is used to determine the end of the deal.

6. A dealer (house man) who deals the game and functions as the banker, collecting player's losing bets and paying off player's winning bets.

7. A pit boss, or supervisor, who is a casino inspector and who stands alongside the dealer, observing every action of play. He sees to it that no mistakes are made by the dealer or the players. He is in complete charge; he rules on all disagreements and his decisions are final. All players and the dealer must abide by them, provided they are within the laws set down by the governing powers.

Number of Players

1. The house man, who is the steady dealer and the banker. He never surrenders the deal or bank.

2. One to six or seven active players, each of whom may bet on several hands depending on the betting spaces available.

Values of Cards. The cards have the following values:

1. Aces count either 1 or 11 at the discretion of the player–holder. However, the dealer must value the ace as set down by the casino rules (see The Dealer's Turn at Play, page 281).

2. Kings, queens, and jacks each have a count of 10.

3. All other cards are counted at their face value; such as ten 10, nine 9, eight 8, etc.

The Object of the Game. A player tries to

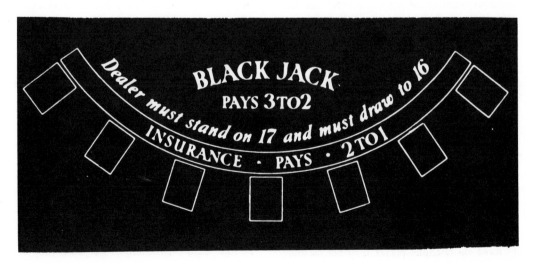

The most common Blackjack layout.

obtain a higher total card count than the dealer by reaching 21, or as close to 21 as possible without exceeding that count. If the player's total count exceeds 21, he has busted and must turn his cards face up at once. He has lost his bet, and the dealer immediately scoops it up. The player, at his proper turn of play and at his own discretion, may stand or draw one or more cards in an attempt to better his count.

The Betting Limits. The casino sets its own limit, and the minimum and maximum bet must be announced to the players. The minimum bet limit in the Las Vegas Strip casinos is usually one silver dollar. The maximum limit is $100 in some; in others it is $200, $300, or $500. The operators will often raise the maximum to $1,000 or more at the sight of a high roller. If you like your Black Jack action small and can't stand the silver-dollar minimum, you can go to the downtown Las Vegas tables, where the minimum may be as little as 10 cents. This also holds true in Reno and other Nevada towns. The above limits in one form or another also hold true for most casinos the world over.

The Shuffle and Cut. The cards are shuffled by the dealer who then hands a player an indicator card and says "Cut, please." The player inserts the indicator card into the deck to show where he wants the cards cut. The dealer cuts the cards at this position, putting the indicator and all the cards above it on the bottom. The indicator goes to the bottom of the deck. The dealer then inserts the second indicator card about 40 cards from the bottom of the deck, and places all the cards into the dealing box face down. The dealer next deals three cards from the shoe and puts them to one side, out of play. The shoe is now ready to be dealt by the dealer. When the indicator card inserted by the dealer makes its appearance, and enough cards have been dealt to complete the round in progress, the deal ends. The dealer must begin a new shuffle and must again repeat the procedure described above.

Betting. Before the deal begins each player must place his bet in cash or chips in the betting space, which is indicated as a rectangle or circle painted on the playing layout, directly before him in full view of the dealer. In most casinos, one player may bet as many hands as there are available holes (betting spaces). Regulation Black Jack tables bear

six or seven betting spaces. When a player plays more than one hand at a time, he must play the hand farthest to his right to completion before being permitted to look at his next hand or hands.

The dealer may check the amount of the player's bet to see that it is not greater than the maximum limit. If a player desires a higher limit, he may ask the pit boss, who will either grant or refuse his request.

The Deal. After all players' bets are down, the dealer, starting with the player on his extreme left, begins dealing clockwise, giving one card face up to each player and one face up to himself. He next deals each player one card face up and one face-down card to himself.

The Play. If the dealer's face-up card is a 10-count or an ace, he must look at his hole (face-down) card. If he has a natural 21 (a count of 21, with two cards), he must face it and announce "Twenty-one," or "Black Jack."

Any player with a natural 21 also announces it, and the dealer declares this to be a standoff, or push. There is no action on this hand, and no payoff is made. The dealer wins and collects bets from players not having a natural 21.

When the dealer does not hold a natural 21, the player at his left plays first. If the player holds a natural 21, he announces it and faces his cards so that the dealer can verify the count. The dealer pays off the winning natural at 3 to 2 odds. This means that if the player has bet $2, he collects $5—his own $2 plus an additional $3. The dealer then burns (buries) the two played cards.

If the player's two cards total less than 21 he may elect:

1. *To stay.* Either he is satisfied with his count or he fears that a third card may make his count go above 21. He says "Good," or "I have enough," or "I stand." Or he signifies that he is staying simply by sliding his cards under the chips he has bet.

2. *To draw a card or cards.* When the player is not satisfied with his count, he says "Hit me," or makes a beckoning motion by closing and opening his hand, or a come-on motion with a finger. The dealer then deals another card off the top of the deck face up before the player, next to his original two cards. Although the cards are dealt one at a

time, the player may continue to draw as many as he likes. When he believes that his count is the best he can get, he stays. If he draws a card that puts his count above 21, he must turn his cards up and announce a bust. The dealer scoops up the player's bet and cards, and places the cards in the discard receiver.

The play moves to the player's left, clockwise, around the table, until all players have played out their hands.

The Dealer's Turn at Play. If all players have busted, the dealer merely places his own cards in the discard receiver and deals a new hand. If any active player or players are left, the dealer plays his hand.

He turns up his hole card so that all his cards are exposed. If his count is 17, 18, 19, or 20, the dealer must stay. If his count is 16 or less, he must draw a card and continue to draw until his count reaches 17 or more—at which point he must stay. If the dealer holds a *soft* 17, that is, a 17-count that includes an ace, he must also stay. This also applies to a soft 18, 19, or 20.

It is important to note here that the Black Jack dealer has no choice as to whether he should stay or draw. His decisions are predetermined and known to the players. Since all the dealer's cards are exposed at his turn of play, he has no opportunity for any departure from these rules. The rule requiring the dealer to hit on 16 or less and to stay on 17, 18, 19, 20, and 21 is standard today in all casinos here and abroad.

Final Settlement. At the end of his play, the dealer starts with the first active player on his extreme right and moves around the table counterclockwise, paying off players who have a higher count than his with an amount equal to the bet they placed, and collecting the bets placed by players showing a lesser count. If player and dealer have the same count, it is a standoff or tie, and no one collects or loses. If the dealer busts, he pays off each surviving active player with an amount equal to his bet. As each player's bet is settled, the dealer scoops up the cards. When all the cards have been scooped up, including the dealer's, they are placed in the discard receiver and a new round is dealt.

Splitting Pairs. Any two cards that are identical except for suit may be treated as a pair. Also, any two cards each having a value of 10 may be treated as pairs, such as a ten and jack, jack and queen, queen and king, etc. A player who receives two cards forming a pair or considered to be a pair on the initial round may, if he chooses, turn them face up and treat each card as the first card dealt in two separate hands. This is called *splitting pairs*. When pairs are split, the player's original bet is placed on one of these cards and an equal amount must be bet on the other.

The player is then dealt one face-up card on the face-up card on his right, and he must play this hand out. If, in drawing to the first face-up card, he forms a pair again, he may again split pairs, betting an amount equal to his first card on this third hand. He may continue to split any further pairs. The first hand on the player's extreme right must be played to completion before the adjacent split hand is dealt a second card. Each split hand must be played out in its proper order from the player's right to his left.

When a player splits a pair of aces, he is only permitted to draw one card to each split ace, giving him two cards in all. If a paint (picture card) or ten or ace are part of a split hand, and the players make a two-card count of 21, this is not a natural and the player is paid off at even money.

The Double Down. After looking at his two face-up cards, the player may elect to double his bet and draw one additional card only. This is known as a *double down* or *double for double*. A player before calling "down for double" or "double down" must place an amount equal to his original bet on the betting space. The player is then dealt a third and final face-down card on the two face-up cards. Player is not permitted to look at his face-down card until the dealer turns it face-up after the deal has been completed.

Insurance Betting. In many casinos, when the dealer's face-up card is an ace, players may make an insurance bet against losing to the banker's possible natural. The dealer, before looking at his down card, inquires if any player wants insurance. A player who desires insurance places an amount equal to half his present wager on his own hand. When this bet is made, the dealer looks at his down card. If it is a 10-count, he turns it face up and announces a natural. The insurance bettor is paid off at the rate of 2 to 1 for every unit wagered. If the dealer's down card is not a 10-count card, the player loses his insurance bet.

Why Scarne's Casino Rules Are Used. Back in 1957, while acting as gaming consultant to the Havana Hilton Hotel Casino in Cuba, I developed the present four-deck Black Jack dealing box and ruled that all cards be dealt face up except the dealer's hole card and players' double-down cards. Shortly thereafter, I also devised the ruling that 40 or more bottom cards of the four-pack deck should never come into actual play. This was achieved by having the dealer insert an indicator card 40 or more cards from the bottom of the 208-card deck and ending the hand when the indicator card makes its appearance. These innovations achieve the following advantages:

1. The card box eliminates 95 percent of the cheating methods employed by both crooked house dealers and players alike.

2. When the players' cards are dealt face up, it helps the dealer to correct any errors that a player may have made when totaling the numbered value of his playing hand. And, owing to the fact that the dealer (house) does not have any discretionary powers on when to hit or stand, it doesn't matter if the dealer sees a player's cards or not. In addition this prevents any card-cheat player from switching one or both of his face down cards for others that he may have secretly palmed.

3. The purpose of inserting the indicator card toward the bottom of the 208-card deck is to prevent the cutoff cards from coming into actual play. This, in turn, prevents casedown or count players from memorizing or clocking the cards as they are being dealt; by so doing, such players learn the identity of the last few undealt cards, thereby gaining an advantage over the house.

Although this last ruling was devised by me back in 1957, it did not gain popularity until shortly after the publication of *Scarne's Complete Guide to Gambling* in 1961. At that time, hundreds of Black Jack players learned from its pages that the more aces and tens remaining in an undealt portion of a single 52-card deck, the greater were their chances of beating the house. So, hundreds of these players began casing the deck, and it seemed at that time that every other player seated at a Black Jack table in Nevada and elsewhere was clocking aces and tens. Las Vegas Casino operators became so alarmed that they changed a number of rules. They ruled that

players could not double down on a count of 11, nor could players split aces; but to no avail. Then came my four-deck deal with its indicator cut, and Black Jack play was restored to normal.

Black Jack Strategy

In the following pages I shall show you exactly where the house extracts its advantage, and how you can shave that percentage to a minimum. But, more important, if you adhere to my strategy, you will certainly improve your game, and become as Black Jack sharp as most professional gamblers in Las Vegas or, for that matter, anywhere else in the world.

In Black Jack, the house advantage is the result of the dealer playing last. When you bust by going over the mathematical deadline of 21, the dealer doesn't bother to wait to play his hand. He rakes in your bet; and, as far as you are concerned, the transaction is closed. You are through. All you can do is sit around and wait until the hand is completed and a new deal takes place. This is the crux of the hidden percentage that works in the house's favor; this is the real reason why gambling-house operators get richer and players get poorer. However, this isn't as unfair as it may appear, because the dealer has five disadvantages going against him. These disadvantages will help to reduce the dealer's advantage of playing last—providing the player knows what to do at the proper time.

1. Despite the fact that the dealer sees the player's hand (and knows the player is standing with a count of 12, 13, 14, or 15) and he holds a 16 count, he (the dealer) must hit. On the other hand, if the player holds a count of 18, 19, 20, or 21, and the dealer has a count of 17, he must stand.

2. The player is paid off at 3 to 2 odds on a black jack (or natural). This happens about once in 21 deals. The dealer, therefore, pays out one additional unit as a bonus every 42 deals for a player advantage of 2.37 percent. (The standoff that occurs when both dealer and player hold a natural 21 happens once in 441 deals. It affects the percentage figure so very little that we can forget about it.)

3. The player may call double down and double the amount of his original bet in favorable circumstances.

4. The player may split a pair and double the amount of his bet by playing two hands instead of one in favorable circumstances.

5. The player sees one of the dealer's cards (the upcard) and may use this information in deciding how to play his hand. This, combined with the dealer's predetermined rules of drawing to 16 or less and standing on 17 or more, is going to figure prominently in the strategy I have outlined in the following pages.

To set the record straight, I repeat what I first claimed in *Scarne's Complete Guide to Gambling* in 1961 and what is now accepted as fact, namely: The dealer's bust advantage is 8.27 percent when the player adheres to the dealer's fixed strategy by hitting a count of 16 or less. Then, by subtracting a player's 2.37 percent advantage when paid 3 to 2 odds when holding a natural, the dealer's advantage comes to 5.90 percent. The author was also first to calculate the dealer's advantage at 8.72 percent when the player refuses to hit a possible bust count and stands on a count of 12, 13, 14, 15, or 16. Subtracting the player's bonus of 2.37 percent for a natural black jack, the dealer's advantage is 6.35 percent. These results have been proven to be correct over the years; without this information, any mathematical analysis of the game of Black Jack would be meaningless. The player can cut down the bank's overall edge of 5.90 percent or 6.35 percent considerably if he follows the Scarne Black Jack strategy that follows. The bank's edge is cut:

1. About 2 1/2 percent for proper hitting or standing on both "hard" and "soft" hands.

2. About 2 1/2 percent for proper doubling down when the casino permits a double down on any two cards. About 1/4 percent for proper doubling down when the casino permits a double down on a count of 9, 10 or 11; the same holds true for doubling down when the casino permits a double down only on 11.

3. About 1/2 percent for proper splitting of pairs.

To emphasize, these figures apply only when the Scarne strategy is used intelligently. All the mathematical analysis contained in this chapter is based on the use of a single 52-card deck. However, I would like to point out that the bank's favorable single-deck advantage of 5.90 percent or 6.35 percent increases to a mere 6.00 percent or 6.45 percent when four decks are in use. The Scarne strategy as depicted in this text equally applies to single-deck and double-deck Black Jack. However, my strategy does not guarantee that you will win—it simply cuts down the bank's percentage to its lowest possible level and gives you a better opportunity to win than any other method of Black Jack play, including those of the many so-called computerized systems making the rounds.

Scarne's Basic Strategy for Black Jack

Hitting and Standing on Hard Counts

1. Always stand on a count of 17 or more.

2. Always draw to a count of 2 to 11.

3. When the dealer's upcard is a 5-spot or 6-spot, the player should stand on a count of 12 or more, draw to a count of 11 or lower.

4. When the dealer's upcard is a 2-, 3-, or 4-spot, the player should stand on a count of 13 or more, draw to a count of 12 or lower.

5. When the dealer's upcard is an ace or 10-count card, the player should stand on a count of 16 or more, draw to a count of 15 or lower.

6. When the dealer's upcard is a 7-, 8-, or 9-spot, the player should hit a count of 16 or less.

Soft-Hard Strategy. When a player holds a hand that contains an ace, there are sometimes two possible counts, neither of which exceeds 21. A hand containing an ace and a six may have a count, or value, of either 7 or 17, because an ace can be valued as either 1 or 11. This ambiguous type of hand is known to Black Jack dealers as a soft count or as a two-way hand. Playing it correctly requires special strategic considerations, as follows:

1. When the dealer's upcard is an eight, nine, ten, or ace, the player should stand on a soft count of 19 or higher, and draw to a soft count of 18 or lower.

2. When the dealer's upcard is a two, three, four, five, six, or seven, the player should stand only on a soft count of 18 or higher, and draw to a soft count of 17 or lower.

Note that the holder of a soft hand should never stand until his total count is at least 18. He should continue to draw to his soft count, and stand as indicated above. If, when the player draws one or more cards, his soft count exceeds 21 (this occurs often, since a high soft count is being hit), the player should revert to the standard hard count hit-and-stand strategy, because he no longer holds a soft hand. *Example:* The dealer's upcard is a 6-spot; the player hits a soft 14 and draws a 9-spot. His total count is now 13. If he counts the ace as 11, he has a count of 23. The hand is no longer soft, so the player reverts to his standard strategy, and stands on 13.

Soft hands are advantageous to the player because, if he uses the right strategy, he gets two chances: First, he tries for a high count by hitting a soft count; and if that fails, he reverts to the standard hard count hit-and-stand strategy.

Splitting Pairs

1. Always split aces, even when the casino rules permit only a one-card draw to a split ace.

2. Never split fours, fives, sixes, or tens.

3. Always split eights unless the dealer's upcard is a nine or ten.

4. Split sevens when the dealer's upcard is a two, three, four, five, six, seven, or eight.

5. Never split nines when the dealer's upcard is a seven, ten, or ace.

6. Always split twos and threes when the dealer's upcard is an eight, nine, ten or ace.

Doubling Down

1. Always double down on a count of 11, no matter what the value of the dealer's upcard is.

2. Double down on a count of 10 when the dealer's upcard is anything but an ace or 10-count.

3. Double down on a count of nine when the dealer's upcard is a two, three, four, five, or six.

4. Double down on a soft 12, 13, 14, 15, 16, or 17, when the dealer's upcard is a six.

The strategy rules shown above take into consideration all the Black Jack bets permitted in all the casinos the world over. However, rarely will you find a casino in which you can put into play all strategy rules described above. *Example:* Casinos in Puerto Rico permit a double down on 11 only. Casinos in Curaçao, Aruba, and St. Maarten permit a double down on 10 and 11 only. Most casinos in Nevada permit a double down on any two cards. And so it goes, from country to country. However, the hit-and-stand strategy rules on both the hard and soft counts are usable in all casinos, and will be of greater help in cutting down the house's advantage than all the other strategies combined. So, memorize them first.

Insurance Betting. As previously mentioned, some casinos allow players to make a so-called insurance bet against losing to a natural whenever the dealer shows an ace as his upcard. Since the insurance bet pays off at 2 to 1 odds, the player must win one-third of the time to get a dead-even proposition. If the dealer's upcard is an ace, and you have no knowledge of any other cards, then the dealer's down card may be considered drawn at random from 51 cards that remain unseen. But under such conditions the 51-card deck contains 16 10-count cards, and the player can win this bet only when the dealer has a 10-count card in the hole. In the long run he will win only 16 of his bets, losing 35. Since insurance bets are paid off at 2 to 1, or 32 to 16, against an expectation of 35 to 16, the player is shorted 3/51, or approximately 6 percent; or, to be exact, 5 15/17 percent.

Most gamblers unwisely insist on buying insurance whenever they hold black jack on the grounds that they want to be sure of a win. The odds are 34 to 15 that the dealer doesn't have a natural, and you will not collect the 2 to 1 insurance bet. Your expectation is minus 4/49, for a house edge of about 8 percent. The casual card caser (counter) can use the insurance bet advantageously if he has kept track of the 10-count cards dealt in previous hands. For example, suppose half the deck (26 cards) has been dealt and the card caser recalls that only three 10-count cards have been dealt. If an insurance bet could be made on the next deal, it would be wise to take out insurance. Under these circumstances the player will win 13/26, or 50 percent, of his bets. Since the bank pays insurance bets off at 2 to 1, the player has an edge of 33 1/3 percent over the bank on this bet.

For the above reason, banks permit players to bet only half the amount of their initial wager when making an insurance bet, and for the same reason several small casinos no longer permit any insurance bets. But don't think for a moment that card casing and the memorizing of previously dealt cards will put the Black Jack percentages in your favor—not with the present-day method of dealing casino Black Jack. I have known only six professional gamblers in my entire gambling history who ever beat the game of Black Jack by putting the percentages in their favor through "card casing," or, as it is more commonly known, "counting down the deck." I was the first person to beat the game with a countdown, and the first to be barred from playing Black Jack in Las Vegas, back in 1947. I was barred because I told Benjamin (Bugsy) Siegal, builder of the swank Flamingo Hotel Casino, that I could beat the game with a countdown. He challenged me to prove it. I did, by beating every casino on the Las Vegas Strip. The result—I was barred from the casino Black Jack tables throughout Nevada and the rest of the country.

Though card casing, or counting down the deck, has been a lost gimmick since 1963, now and then you'll spot a Johnny Come Lately trying it on some casino boss. If the boss doesn't know his business, the card caser may get away with it. The machinations of a modern-day card caser stand out like a bright light in a moonless night. First, he seeks a casino that deals single-deck, then he takes a vacant Black Jack table for himself. Then his confederate, who is a partial card caser, takes his position beside him—sometimes the caser makes use of two confederates. At the beginning of each new deal, his bets are usually the house minimum of each of the six or seven betting spaces. This type of betting continues until near the end of each deal, when a whispered consultation takes place between the card caser and his assistants. If they agree that the remaining undealt cards appear disadvantageous to the house, they increase the size of their bets to the maximum house limit. A smart house man counters this Black Jack chicanery by reshuffling the entire deck, including the undealt cards. The card caser

complains a bit, calls off his bets, exits from the casino, and shops around seeking a casino whose boss is stupid enough to stand for such nonsense. That's the life of a professional card caser. Most of these casers haven't got a dime. Therefore my advice is: Don't try to be a card caser.

However, I should like to emphasize an important practice to follow at the Black Jack tables: When your luck is running good, and you're winning money, by all means increase the size of your bets and try to win as much as possible in the shortest space of time. However, if your luck is running bad, decrease the size of your bets. Better yet, seek the nearest exit.

Protection Against Black Jack Cheats. More cheating takes place at the Black Jack tables than in any other casino banking game because Black Jack offers more opportunities for cheating. Many complaints about cheating usually come from players, but very often it is the casino operators themselves who have been cheated. Actually, casino operators lose millions of dollars annually by crooked Black Jack dealers tipping off (signaling) their face-down or hole card to player cheats (when the dealer's upcard is an ace or ten). I don't intend to explain all the cheating methods used to beat the operators because I don't want to aid and abet the Black Jack cheats. But because I am interested in protecting the public, I will explain how some dishonest casinos fleece the honest player.

The most common cheating method used in crooked casinos when making use of four

Cheating at Blackjack. Scarne demonstrates (left) how a dishonest dealer can, under cover of looking at his hole card, get a peek at the top card of the deck held in his left hand. If the top card is one the dealer wants to retain, he deals the second card instead (right), but you can't stop the action as the photographer did here; the move is undetectable when it is fast and smooth.

Hole-card switch. Cheat looks at his hole card (left) as right hand approaches with ace palmed. Ace slides in under king (center), and is left on table (right) as right hand goes away with the king palmed. The whole action takes only a second or two.

decks (208 cards) is to remove a number of 10-count cards and to replace them with 5-count cards. Because the dealer must hit a count of 16, the substitution of fives for tens avoids many a normal dealer bust and supplants these with additional dealer twenty-ones. To protect yourself against such cheating subterfuges, count the 5-counts and 10-counts as the hands are played. If you count less than sixty-four 10-count cards or more than sixteen 5-count cards—seek the nearest exit. For your own safety, don't make a scene. A thief caught red-handed is always a dangerous thief.

More cheating takes place when the game is dealt single-deck from the hand than in any other phase of the game. For additional information on card cheating, see Protection Against Card Cheats, page 423. The best assurance you can have that the game is honest is to see that the players' cards are dealt face up, out of a shoe (card box) containing four decks, instead of one or two decks being dealt from the hand.

Pontoon

Pontoon, an English variant of the American game of private Black Jack, is also referred to as Van John in Australia. Its basic rules, as played throughout the British Empire, are the same except for the doubling, redoubling, and bonus variations that have been included in this text. The rules of the Private Game of Black Jack apply, with the following exceptions and additional rules:

1. *First Round of Dealing.* Dealer gives one face-down card to each player in rotation, including himself.

2. *Betting.* After looking at his card, each player places a bet, which must be not less than the minimum bet nor more than the maximum bet designated by the dealer (banker). After all players have placed their bets, the dealer has the option to have each player's bet doubled, providing it does not exceed the maximum limit. Any player may thus redouble his bet. *Example:* A player bets one unit, dealer doubles, requiring that player to put up one more unit. Any player refusing to double loses the bet already put up and is out of the game for that hand. The player redoubles, putting up two units making his total bet four units.

3. *Completion of the Deal.* Dealer then gives one card face up to each other in rotation, including himself.

4. *Natural.* If the dealer has a natural (ace and 10-count), every player pays him double the amount of his bet; however, a player holding a natural pays the dealer only the amount of his bet. If a player holds a natural and the dealer does not, the dealer pays that player double the amount of his bet.

5. *Dealer Takes Ties.* If the dealer and a player have the same count, the dealer wins the bet.

Bonus Payments. Any player who possesses one of the following combinations collects immediately from the dealer and cannot lose his bet even if the dealer has a higher count:

1. If a player has five cards and his total is 21 or under, he collects double his bet; with six cards totaling 21 or under, four times his bet; and so on, doubling for each additional card.

2. A player who makes 21 with three sevens receives triple the amount of his bet.

3. A player who makes 21 with eight, seven, and six is paid double the size of his bet.

The dealer is not entitled to any of the above bonuses.

Farmer

This game is a rather sophisticated country cousin of Private Black Jack.

Requirements

1. A regular pack of playing cards out of which have been stripped the eights and all the sixes except the six of hearts, making a 45-card deck.

2. Two to eight players.

Value of the Cards. The cards take the same value and count as the cards at Black Jack, except that aces count 1 only.

Object of the Game. To draw cards for a total of 16 or as close to 16 as possible without exceeding 16.

Selecting the Farmer. Any player may shuffle. Any player may cut. The acting dealer deals each player one card face up, starting with the player to his left and continuing clockwise. The player to whom the six of hearts is first dealt becomes the *farmer*.

The Ante. Each player antes one unit in cash to form a pool known collectively as the farm.

The Shuffle and Cut. The farmer shuffles. While any other player may call for and have the right to shuffle before the cards are cut, the farmer has the right to shuffle last. The deck is then squared and presented to the player at the farmer's right for the cut. He may decline, and any other player may cut the cards; but if all other players decline to cut, it is compulsory that the farmer himself cut.

The Deal. Starting with the player at his left and dealing clockwise, the farmer deals each player one card face down, the last card to himself.

The Play. The player at the farmer's left plays first, and thereafter the turn of play rotates one man at a time, clockwise, the farmer playing last. A turn of play consists of a player's drawing at least one card. This is mandatory. The player may draw as many cards as he chooses, as long as his total count does not exceed 16. A player may stay—that is, decline to draw more cards—after drawing one or more. Should a player's count exceed 16, he does not (as in Black Jack) turn up his face-down card and announce that he is over. He merely says "I stay."

After all players including the farmer have

had a turn of play, each player—starting with the one at the farmer's left—face their cards, and announce their count.

1. Any player holding a count of 16 wins the farm and becomes the next farmer.

2. If more than one player hold a count of 16, and one of those players has the six of hearts, he is the winner.

3. If more than one player have a count of 16 without the six of hearts, the player having the fewest cards is the winner.

4. Should there be ties and should the farmer be one of the tied players, the farmer is the winner.

5. In case of ties, if the farmer is not involved, the tied player closest to the farmer's left is the winner. The winner, in any case, becomes the new farmer or dealer.

6. If no one holds a count of 16 the farm (pool) remains on the table, and the same farmer deals a new hand; and each of the players must ante again.

Payoff. On the completion of each deal, whether or not the farm has been won, each player who has gone over 16 must pay one unit to the farmer who dealt the bust hand. Should the farmer bust, he does not have to pay a unit to anyone. If no one holds a count of 16, the player with a count nearest to 16 gets one unit from each player holding a lesser count—but not from players who have gone over the limit of 16. In case of ties on counts nearest 16, the tied players divide the payoff units equally.

Fifteen

One of the names by which this variation is known, Quince, suggests *quinze* and a French genealogy. It's also known as Ace Low, and Cans. Fifteen is Black Jack for two players; otherwise all the Black Jack rules apply except for the following:

1. The count which dealer and nondealer are trying to approach but not exceed is 15.

2. The value of the cards is the same as at Black Jack, except that aces count 1 only.

3. Before the cards are dealt, dealer and nondealer put up an equal amount in the pool.

4. The dealer gives his opponent one card face down, then one face down to himself.

5. The nondealer may draw cards (face up) or stay as in Black Jack. If, when draw-

ing, he should bust (go over 15), he does not announce that fact; he says simply "I stay."

6. Now, as he sees fit, the dealer may either draw cards or stay. In either event, at the completion of his play, both players face their down card, and announce their count.

7. The contestant holding a count of 15, or a count closer than his opponent's to 15 without exceeding 15, collects the bets. If the players tie on the same count, or both players hold a count of 16 or more, it is a standoff. Neither wins or loses and bets are carried over to the new deal, when new bets may be laid if it is desired.

8. The loser of the hand deals next hand.

Where the Dealer's Advantage Lies. Although the dealer does not automatically collect his opponent's bet when the opponent busts at fifteen, he nevertheless enjoys a tactical advantage in that the nondealer's bust may be clear from his face-up cards. The dealer, observing that the player must have a count of 16 or better, simply stays—stands pat—and wins. Although this situation is uncommon, it occurs often enough to give the dealer an impressive percentage.

Seven and a Half

This is the game Italians say is the forerunner of Black Jack. I've seen it come into rather modest vogue in the last 25 years. Although casinos won't run it, Seven and a Half has its public in the little political clubhouses you find in the back streets of every big industrial city that has a high concentration of foreign-born people.

Requirements

1. A standard pack of cards from which the eights, nines, and tens have been removed, making a 40-card deck.

2. A banker and as many players as can crowd around an ordinary table. Onlookers may bet on the players' hands.

Value of the Cards. The court cards, kings, queens, and jacks, count 1/2. All other cards count their numerical face value: ace, 1; deuce, 2; trey, 3; and so on. The king of diamonds is designated as the joker, and is wild. A player may assign it any value he pleases from 1/2 to 7.

Object of the Game. To get a card count of 7 1/2 or as close to 7 1/2 as possible without exceeding 7 1/2.

Selecting the Dealer. Any player may, by mutual consent, shuffle the deck. Then he puts it in the center of the table. Any player may cut. The acting dealer squares the cut and, starting with the player at his left and going clockwise, deals to each player including himself, one card face up until the king of diamonds has been dealt. The player receiving it becomes the first dealer and banker.

The Betting Limit. The dealer may establish for his deal the minimum and maximum bet any player may make. He may raise or lower his limits as he sees fit.

The Shuffle and Cut. The dealer shuffles the cards; any player may call for a shuffle at any time before the cut, but the dealer has the right to shuffle last. He then puts the cards on the table, and any player may cut; if more than one wants to cut, he or they must be allowed to do so. *Note:* If the dealer does not like the way in which a cut is made, he may designate a player to make a new cut, and that cut is final.

The Betting and Deal. Before the deal begins:

1. Each player, announcing the amount to the dealer, must place on the table before him the money he proposes to bet,

2. Or, if a player doesn't want to bet on that hand, he must say to the dealer, "Deal me out." He is skipped in the ensuing deal.

Thereupon one card is dealt face down to each player who has placed a bet. The player cannot alter his bet after a card is dealt.

Each round of play requires a new shuffle and a new deal.

The Play. The player at the dealer's left has the first turn to play. He may do one of two things, as in Black Jack. He may:

1. Stay, which he signifies by saying, "I have enough," or "I pass."

2. Draw, at his discretion, one or more cards—provided such cards and his down card do not add up to a count of 8 or more.

The play moves clockwise around the table. If any player draws one card giving him a total of 7½ he must immediately face his down card and announce his count. This is paid off at premium rates.

The Bust. Should a player, drawing cards, run his total to 8 or more, he has busted, and must forthwith pay the dealer the amount of his bet. The dealer picks up the cards with which the player went bust, and puts them to one side. All players who have not busted leave their cards in full view of the banker.

The Banker's Turn of Play. The dealer's turn of play comes last. He may, of course, either stay or draw. If he draws and busts, he must pay all players surviving in the game an amount equal to their bet, and must pay off at two to one to players holding a count of 7½ with two cards. If he stays, he collects bets from players having a lower count than he, and pays off players having a higher count. All ties are stand-offs; no one wins or loses.

Note: Although some club games are played in which the dealer arbitrarily wins ties, I do not countenance this rule; it is manifestly unfair to the player, and further reduces his already very meager chance of getting home solvent.

A player holding a two-card 7 1/2 wins the bank on completion of the deal as well as winning his bet at two to one; but if the dealer also catches a 7 1/2 with two cards, he retains the bank. Should more than one player hold a count of 7 1/2 with two cards, the player nearest the dealer's left becomes the next dealer. A count of 7 1/2 with two cards always beats a 7 1/2 with more than two cards.

The Dealer's Advantage. Unlike Black Jack, the dealer at his turn of play and at his own discretion, may stand, or draw one or more cards in an attempt to better his count and beat the player or players. Under such conditions, the dealer's advantage due to players busting first may be increased or decreased due to the dealer's skill. A skilled dealer may increase his bust advantage; a poor dealer may even put the percentage factor in favor of the player by poor drawing and standing on certain counts. In Seven and a Half it is wise for the dealer to play against the big money hands and ignore the small money hands. However, the only way to give yourself anything like an even chance of winning at this game is to bank it whenever you get the chance. Some players have a superstitious reluctance to handle the deck as dealer. That is a sure-fire, never-fail, foolproof way of going broke. The bank is a privilege. Use it.

Ten and a Half

This is the Dutch version of the Italian game of Seven and a Half. It is known as Satan Pong in Holland and its possessions. Unlike the rules of Black Jack and Seven and a Half,

the rules of Ten and a Half give the banker-dealer less of an advantage if any at all.

Requirements

1. Two to seven players constitute the best game, although standers by may bet on the hand of any player except the dealer.

2. A standard pack of 52 cards which are valued as follows: Court cards, kings, queens, and jacks count one-half. All other cards count their face value, aces 1, twos 2, threes 3, and so on up to ten which counts 10.

Object of the Game. To get a higher count (total value of cards in hand) than the dealer (banker) up to but not over 10½. Should the player draw cards forcing his total over 10½, he must immediately pay the dealer-banker, and he sacrifices any chance to beat or tie the dealer. The player may demand and draw any number of cards until he reaches or exceeds a count of 10½.

The Rules Governing the Game Such as the Following. The selection of the first dealer-banker, the betting limit, shuffle, and cut are the same as those governing Seven and a Half.

The Betting and the Deal. Before the deal begins:

1. Each player except the dealer-banker must place on the table before him the money (within the betting limit) he proposes to bet. Thereupon one card is dealt face down to each player including the dealer-banker. The player cannot alter his bet after a card is dealt.

2. When all cards are dealt out the deal (bank) passes to the player on the left of previous dealer-banker. If, however, the banker-dealer is in the midst of a deal and there are not enough undealt cards remaining in the deck, he is permitted to reshuffle the dealt cards and complete the last hand.

The Player. The player to the dealer-banker's left has the first turn of play. He may do one or two things. He may:

1. Stay, which he signifies by saying, "No cards" or "I have enough."

2. Draw, at his discretion, one or more cards, provided they and his down card do not add up to a count of eleven or more. The play moves clockwise around the table. If any player draws one card giving him a total of 10½ he must immediately turn up his down card and announce his count. The dealer-banker immediately pays this natural 10½ count off at 2 to 1 odds. If the player makes a count of 10½ with three or more cards, he

announces the fact, turns up his face-down card and is paid off at even money (1 to 1).

3. Bust. Should a player drawing cards run his total to eleven or more, he has busted and must forthwith turn up his down card and announce his bust count. The dealer-banker takes the bet and picks up the cards which the player went bust with and puts them face up on the bottom of the deck.

4. All players who have not busted leave their cards in full view of the dealer-banker.

The Dealer-Banker's Turn. The dealer-banker's turn of play comes last. He may, of course, either stay or draw. If he draws and busts, he must pay all active players an amount equal to their bets. If he stays or draws and does not bust, he collects from players having a lower count than he, and pays off players having a higher count. All ties are stand-offs, no one wins or loses.

Macao

This Black Jack variation, which is also called Three Naturals, was popular in the twenties and the thirties, but isn't played too frequently today. It is played in the same manner as Black Jack except for the following:

1. There is no count for the picture cards or the tens, and the aces count 1 only.

2. The object of the game is to obtain 9 in one or more cards.

3. Each player makes a bet and receives one card face down. The dealer also receives one card face down.

4. If the player has a nine, he is paid three times the amount bet; if it is an eight, he is paid twice; if it is a seven, he is paid singly. However, the dealer ties a nine with a nine, beats an eight with a nine, beats a seven with an eight or nine, and ties if he has the same number.

5. If the dealer has no seven, eight, or nine, the bets involving those cards are settled. Then each player in turn, starting at the dealer's left, may draw one or more cards as in Black Jack. The object is to reach 9 or as close thereto as possible without going bust (over 9). As in Black Jack, when a player and dealer tie, there is a standoff.

CHEMIN DE FER

Chemin de Fer and its cousins Baccarat, Baccarat–Chemin de Fer, and Baccarat Banque, are the most popular private banking card games to be found in European and Latin American sporting clubs and gambling casinos. The present-day forms of Baccarat and Chemin de Fer are the French variations of the Italian game of Baccara, which was first introduced into France about 1490 during the reign of Charles VIII. Outside of the United States, Baccarat is known as Baccara.

The vocabulary of Chemin de Fer as used in the United States is partly French (banco, la grande, la petite), partly Black Jack lingo (hit me!), and partly from Craps (next shooter, the bank's faded). Unlike the Baccara games in French casinos, checks (chips) are seldom used in Shimmy games in the United States; the green stuff (money) makes for a more interesting game. During the 1950's Chemin de Fer, usually called Shimmy or Chemmy by American gamblers, was the type of Baccarat most often played in Nevada casinos; but its popularity was to be short lived. In 1958 Baccarat (or Baccarat–

Chemin de Fer, as it is known in the state of Nevada) made its debut at the Sands Hotel Casino in Las Vegas, Nevada, to be followed later by other Las Vegas casinos. This soon resulted in the demise of Shimmy in Nevada casinos.

There is only a slight difference in the playing rules of Shimmy and Baccarat. In Baccarat, as it is played in Monte Carlo and other European casinos, the game is banked by the casino operators or by concessionaires. Players who bet the bank to win are charged 5 percent of their winnings on each bet. Players who bet the bank to lose do not pay a direct charge, but they do pay a hidden percentage.

Chemin de Fer is played exactly the same as Baccarat, with the exception that the casino operators take no risk, since the players bet against each other. The house acts as a *cutter,* the same as the operator of a poker game. For a standard *cut* (charge) of 5 percent taken out of the player banker's winning *coup* bet), the house rents out the Shimmy equipment and supplies three croupiers to operate the game. In return for the 5 percent charge, the croupiers run the game, manage the banker's money, collect winning bets, and pay out losing bets. Some operators charge each player a fixed hourly fee for their supervision of the game.

The Chemin de Fer equipment is bulky. The game requires a heavy kidney-shaped table, its surface padded and covered with a fancy green-baize layout divided into numbered sections for nine or twelve players. Other requirements are six or eight decks of cards and a mahogany *sabot* or shoe (card-dealing box). A money box in the table holds the casino's gambling revenue. The croupier who handles the dealt cards sits in the concavity of the kidney-shaped table and uses a wooden *palette* to slide the cards, cash, or chips around to the players.

The two croupiers who sit opposite the operator also have palettes to facilitate handling the bets. A lookout sits on a stand overlooking the Shimmy table. Although Shimmy and Baccarat are as fair percentage-wise as any other banking game, many American gamblers didn't realize this until recently, and rarely sat down to play the game.

Requirements

1. From two to as many players as there are player spaces available on the layout. Some tables have nine, others twelve. The banker plays against only one player at a time, but any or all the other players may bet on that one player's hand against the bank, provided the bank possesses enough money to cover the wagers.

2. A regulation Chemin de Fer table with a discard box into which the player's discards are dropped and the money box to receive the casino's 5 percent charge.

3. A card-dealing box called a sabot or shoe.

4. Eight standard packs of 52 cards, four red-backed decks and four blue-backed decks, plus two advertising cards, which are used as indicators. (In some casinos only six decks are used.)

5. Three Chemin de Fer palettes, long thin paddles which enable the seated croupiers to transact business at the far reaches of the table.

Object of the Game. To win a coup by holding a combination of two or three cards totaling 9 or as close as possible to 9, or to a two-digit number ending in 9. When the total of the cards is a two-digit number, only the latter digit has any value. *Examples:* A count of 19 has a value of 9, a count of 23 has a value of 3, and so forth.

Value of the Cards. The ace is the lowest ranking card and has a point value of 1. Kings, queens, and jacks have a value of 10 each. All other cards have their numerical face value, tens have a point count of 10, nines 9, eights 8, etc. The suits have no comparative value.

The Shuffle and Cut. At the start of the game, the dealer-croupier spreads the eight packs of cards face up on the table and all the players and croupiers are permitted to take groups of cards and to shuffle them. On later deals, when the discard receiver is emptied onto the layout and some cards are face up and some face down, the croupiers and players turn the face-up cards down and shuffle them.

After the players have shuffled groups of cards, the croupier gathers all the cards and shuffles them together, usually shuffling about two packs at a time and ending up by weaving one group of cards into another. Finally, the croupier assembles all eight packs into one deck, and after several cuts, hands a player an indicator card, and says "Cut, please." The player inserts the indicator card into the deck to show where he wants the cards cut. The croupier cuts the cards at this position, putting the indicator and all the cards above it on the bottom. He then inserts the second indicator card seven, eight, or ten cards from the bottom of the packet and places all the cards into the shoe face down. The croupier next deals three cards from the shoe and drops them through a slot in the table into the discard receiver. This is called burning the top cards. (Some operators burn five or six cards instead of three.) The shoe is now ready to be dealt by the first banker-player.

Selecting the First Banker. The first player on the croupier's right has the privilege of being first banker. If the first player declines the bank, the privilege passes to the player to his right, and so on, counterclockwise. (Or, the bank may be auctioned to the highest bidder.) The banker-dealer at Chemin de Fer continues to deal until he misses a pass (loses a bet). When the active player wins a bet, the croupier passes the shoe to the player on the dealer's right. It always moves on to the right, counterclockwise. In mid game, as at the start, the bank may be declined.

When the first advertising card shows, the croupier announces "One more hand, please." Upon completion of this last hand, a reshuffle takes place which is governed by the rules for the original shuffle and cut.

Preparation for the Play. The croupier slides the shoe to the first designated banker, who places on the table an amount of money within the house betting limits. This amount may be from a low of $100 to a high of $5,000, $10,000, or more, all depending on the banker's gambling spirit. A lucky bank may at times hold several hundred thousand dollars, and a player can bet all or any part of it, as he wishes.

The Betting. Before any cards are dealt, the players make their bets (called fading). If a player wants to fade the bank for its total worth, he calls "Banco." A *banco* bet has precedence over any other. The player to the right of the dealer has the first privilege to banco. If he does not banco, the privilege passes to the next man on the right, and so on around the table. Then, any watcher or former nonplayer may call banco.

If no one bancos, then partial bets are accepted. The first man on the right places his bet, for whatever amount he chooses, on the table before him. Then the player on his right bets, and so on, around the able until the bank is partly or completely *faded*. If the bank is not completely faded, the amount which has not been faded is set aside for the banker.

Anyone who bancos, whatever his position around the table, has the right of *banco suivi* (following banco) if he loses. His right to call banco on the next deal has precedence over all others; if he fails to call banco, and more than one person calls banco, the player nearest the dealer starting from the right has precedence, even though he may call banco after another player has done so. This right is known as *banco prime*. The player who bancos becomes the active player. If no one has chosen to banco, and there are partial bets, the player who has bet the most money is designated by the croupier as the active player. Because the rules of Chemin de Fer are so many and so complicated, each player is supplied with a card, as illustrated at the bottom of this page, describing the player's and the banker's rules.

CHEMIN DE FER

Game Must Be Played According to Rules

PLAYER

HAVING		
	0 - 1 - 2 - 3 - 4	Always *Draws* a Card
	5	Optional—*Stand or Draw*
	6 - 7	Never Draws—*Stands*
	8 - 9	*Turn* Cards Face Up

BANKER

HAVING		Draws When Giving	Does Not Draw When Giving		OPTIONAL
	3	1 - 2 - 3 - 4 - 5 - 6 - 7 - 10	8	9	
	4	2 - 3 - 4 - 5 - 6 - 7	1 - 8 - 9 - 10		
	5	5 - 6 - 7	1 - 2 - 3 - 8 - 9 - 10	4	
	6	6 - 7	1 - 2 - 3 - 4 - 5 - 8 - 9 - 10		

Banker Always Draws When Having   0, 1, 2
Banker Never Draws When Having   7
Banker Faces   8, 9
If Player Takes No Card, Banker Stands Only on   6, 7

—NO MISTAKES ARE ALLOWED—
IF ANY ARE MADE IT IS COMPULSORY
for the DEALER to Reconstruct the COUP

The Coup, or Play. The banker slides one card out of the shoe and deals it to the active player; then he deals one card for himself, a second card to the player, and finally a second card to himself. All four cards are dealt face down.

The First Turn of Play.

1. The active player now examines his cards. If they total a count of 8 or 9, he turns them face up on the table. If the count is 8, he calls "La petite!" If it is 9, he calls "La grande!" The croupier verifies the count. The banker must now turn his two cards face up.

2. If the active player's count is higher than the banker's, the croupier pays off all the winning players. If the active player's count is lower than the banker's, the banker wins, and the croupier collects all the bets for him.

3. If the active player holds a count of less than 8, he says "Pass," and the banker now examines his own cards. If they total 8 or 9, he turns them face up, and the croupier collects all the bets for him. If the banker does not hold a count of 8 or 9, play reverts to the active player.

4. If the banker's count is the same as the player's count, it is a legal tie, or standoff, and neither banker nor player wins or loses.

The above four rules also apply with equal force to the player's and banker's second turn of play.

Active Player's Second Turn of Play. If the active player holds a count of 1, 2, 3, 4, or 0, he must draw a card. If the active player has a count of 5, the draw is optional; he may elect either to get hit (draw) or to stay (not draw). This is the only discretionary play the active player has in Chemin de Fer. If the active player has a count of 6 or 7, he *must* stay.

Banker's Second Turn of Play. If the banker holds a count of 0, 1, or 2, he must draw a card. If the active player stays and the banker holds a count of 4 or 5, he *must* draw. If the active player stays and the banker holds a count of 6 or 7, he must stay.

Rules for the Banker When the Active Player Draws a Card. If the active player draws a card valued 1, 2, 3, 4, 5, 6, 7, or 10, the banker must draw. If the active player draws an 8, the banker must stay. If the active player draws a 9, the banker's play is optional; he may either draw or stay.

The preceding paragraph contains the basic rules for the banker's play. As shown on the card describing the player's and banker's rules, the banker must play as follows when holding a count of 3, 4, 5, 6, or 7:

Banker Holds a Count of 3. If the banker holds a count of 3 and the active player, in his turn of play, has drawn a card valued at 1, 2, 3, 4, 5, 6, 7, or 10, then the banker must draw. If the active player has drawn an 8, the banker must stay. If the active player has drawn a 9, the banker's play is optional; he may draw or stay.

Banker Holds a Count of 4. If the active player fails to draw a card, the banker (holding a count of 4) must draw. If the active player draws a card valued 2, 3, 4, 5, 6, or 7, the banker must draw. If the active player draws a card valued 1, 8, 9, or 10, the banker must stay.

Banker Holds a Count of 5. If the active player did not draw a card on his turn of play, the banker (holding a count of 5) must draw. If the active player draws a card valued 5, 6, or 7, the banker must draw. If the active player draws a card valued 1, 2, 3, 8, 9, or 10, the banker must stay. If the active player draws a 4, the banker's play is optional; he may either stay or draw.

Banker Holds a Count of 6. If the active player fails to draw, the banker (holding a count of 6) must stay. If the active player draws a 6 or 7, the banker must draw. If the active player draws a card valued 1, 2, 3, 4, 5, 8, 9, or 10, the banker must stay.

Banker Holds a Count of 7. Regardless of the active player's draw, the banker (holding a count of 7) must stay.

Rules Governing the Bank. If the bank loses a coup, the deal passes. If the bank wins, the same player holds the bank and all the money in the bank is now at stake—the banker's original bet and his winnings, less the 5 percent charge (in some casinos the 5 percent is not collected from the first win by the bank). The banker does not have the privilege of dragging down or reducing his bank. It is all or nothing. He may, of course, pass the bank at any time; but if he wants to retain the bank, he risks the entire bank, except when the bank exceeds the house limit or the bettors have not faded the full amount of the bank. In either case, the excess is put aside for the banker by the croupier.

A typical Baccarat table layout for 12 players and three dealers.

When the banker passes, the croupier holds an informal auction of the bank, and gives it to the player who will put up a bank equal to the one that has just been passed. If the high bidder happened to be the player to the right of the banker, that player now gets the bank, in his regular turn. The bank can pass at any time up to the actual dealing of the cards.

Baccarat, Las Vegas Style

Baccarat, called *Baccarat–Chemin de Fer* in Nevada, is the most popular European and South American casino game. Several Latin American casinos have 40 or more Baccarat tables in action at one time. The reason Nevada casinos have replaced Shimmy with Baccarat is that Baccarat receives more action (play) than Chemin de Fer, and thus earns more money.

The game's equipment and playing rules for Baccarat–Chemin de Fer, Las Vegas style, are similar to those of Chemin de Fer with the following exceptions:

1. The Baccarat–Chemin de Fer layout has two betting spaces at each end of the table, one marked *Bank* and the other marked *Player*. There are spaces for 12 players at the table, numbered from 1 to 12. A bet placed on the space of the layout marked Bank indicates the player is wagering that the bank (often called the shooter) will win (pass) the bet. The Bank hand is the one that remains at or next to the shoe (dealing box). A bet

placed on the layout marked Player is against the house and called a loss bet. The hand away from the shoe is the player's hand. A count of 0 in Baccarat is known as *baccarat,* and a count of 9 is known as a natural. Several shills are used at a baccarat table to stimulate action. In European and Latin American casinos, checks or chips are used in the game, and they run from a low of 50 cents to a high of $100. The 50-cent chips are used to facilitate the croupiers' taking of the 5 percent house charge from winning players who have bet on the bank. In the Nevada casinos, money rather than chips is used. The bank hand is paid off at even money, and a marker is charged to the customer to the tune of 5 percent or in the amount of 5 cents for each $1 won. This amount is collected from the players by the house at the end of each dealt shoe.

2. Because the house banks the game of Baccarat, one lone player can play, whereas at Chemin de Fer players may sit around for hours (as in Poker), waiting for enough players to arrive to get the game started.

3. Baccarat has the advantage that a player can bet two ways: on the bank, or on the player's hand. Hence, players often switch their betting from the bank to the player's hand or vice versa.

4. Baccarat has a bigger draw for the big-time player than Chemin de Fer: the player knows that if he gets lucky he can win big, because the casino's entire bankroll is at

stake. At Chemin de Fer, the amount a player can win is limited by how much, the other players are willing to lose. The betting limits for Baccarat in Nevada casinos run from a low of $5 to $20, depending on the casino policy, to a maximum of $2,000. There are, of course, special betting limits for well-known high rollers.

5. The game is strictly mechanical. The player's only optional play is that he may bet either the bank's hand or the player's. The croupier directs and coaches everyone at the table, following the posted rules of play.

6. The playing rules for Baccarat–Chemin de Fer are the same as for Chemin de Fer except that the optional plays—such as when

the banker holding a count of 3 deals the player a 9, or when the banker holding a 5 deals the player a 4—are compulsory draws. The same holds true for the player when holding a count of 5. The abolishment of these optional rules at Baccarat makes the game mechanical; all a player can do is follow the rules. It does, however, eliminate those arguments that arise in Chemin de Fer caused by a player's hitting or staying against the wishes of another player. The rules of Baccarat, like those of Chemin de Fer, are so many and so complicated that each player is given a card like the one that is shown below which describes the rules for players and banker:

BACCARAT

Game Must Be Played According to Rules

PLAYER

HAVING		
	1 - 2 - 3 - 4 - 5 - 10	Draws a Card
	6 - 7	Stands
	8 - 9	Turns Cards Over

BANKER

HAVING		Draws When Giving	Does Not Draw When Giving
	3	1 - 2 - 3 - 4 - 5 - 6 - 7 - 9 - 10	8
	4	2 - 3 - 4 - 5 - 6 - 7	1 - 8 - 9 - 10
	5	4 - 5 - 6 - 7	1 - 2 - 3 - 8 - 9 - 10
	6	6 - 7	1 - 2 - 3 - 4 - 5 - 8 - 9 - 10
	7	Stands	
	8 - 9	Turns Cards Over	

PICTURES AND TENS DO NOT COUNT

Percentages Against the Player at Baccarat and Chemin de Fer. The rules governing Chemin de Fer and Baccarat seem unnecessarily complicated, but before we blend our voices in with the Shimmy and Baccarat addict's immemorial complaint "Why don't they simplify the laws?" let's reexamine one of the inner secrets of all banking games.

That secret may be stated as follows: Nothing in gambling is unreasonably complicated. If it's complicated, there's a reason. The reason for the strange and apparently unnatural statutes governing the play at Chemin de Fer or Baccarat is that in their complication lies

the hidden percentage against the player at the game. Before giving a mathematical analysis of the game, I would like to point out to the reader that the source of the banker's advantage is the fact that, as in Black Jack, the player must always play first. Although the Baccarat or Chemin de Fer player cannot bust his hand as in Black Jack, he does expose his possible card count to the banker by his decision of play. From there on, the rules of the game do the rest. They are devised so as to give the bank or dealer a percentage edge over the player. In short, the player's hand is penalized by the rules that permit the banker-player to win 50 67/100 percent of the time, for a banker-player advantage of 1.34 percent. The thought then comes that the Bank space is the place to put your money. No. Because of the 5 percent commission charged against the bank when it wins, the banker-player is faced with a 1.19 percent disadvantage.

If you still insist on casino gambling after having read this book, and you find yourself in a casino that harbors all the standard casino games including Chemin de Fer and Baccarat, and you would like to give yourself the best possible chance to win, then sit yourself down at the Shimmy or Baccarat table. The low house percentage that the player or banker-player must buck in these games makes the 1.34 percent and the 1.19 percent bets the best available at any casino banking game, with the exception of two bets permitted at Bank Craps: a "front-line or come bet plus the front-line odds" and a "back-line or don't come bet plus the back-line odds." However, I must remind the reader that any gambler must lose in the end if he *repeatedly* takes the worst percentages in any game, whether his disadvantage is a low of 1 percent or a high of 10 percent or more. I'll add again that the higher the house percentage, the faster the player is sent to the cleaners.

Baccarat Banque

Baccarat Banque (bank), also called Baccarat à Deux Tableaux (double table), is an old-time cousin of Chemin de Fer played mostly in France. The game is usually banked by the casino operators or by concessionaires (usually from a Greek syndicate), who pay the casino operators 50 percent of their monthly winnings for the banking privilege. Unlike Baccarat or Chemin de Fer, there is a permanent bank and three hands are dealt instead of two. There is one hand for the bank and two player hands, one at each side of the table. The table layout is divided at the center by a heavy line.

Players may wager on either player hand, right or left; or they may wager on both by placing their money, *à cheval,* that is, across the line. If one side wins and the other loses, a bet placed in this manner is a standoff and no one wins or loses. If both sides lose, the bet is lost; if both sides win, the bet is won.

When all wagers have been placed, the croupier deals one face-down card to the player on his right, one to the player on his left, and one to himself. He repeats this procedure and, when each has two cards, the hands are checked. If any of the three persons has a count of 8 or 9, it must be turned face up and the other two hands are exposed ending the play. Bets are paid off as in Chemin de Fer. When either player holds an 8 or 9, the player on the dealer's right acts first. He draws or stands, according to the Chemin de Fer rules, and has the option to draw or stand with a 5. Then the player on the left acts and is guided by the same rules.

When the players have completed their hands, it becomes the bank's turn to play. Here is where considerable judgment and skill on the banker's part comes into play. In this version of Baccarat Banque, the banker does not have any restrictions, he may stand or draw a card as he pleases; he is really the only one that has any opportunity to exercise any judgment in the play of his hand. It must be remembered that the banker will mentally total the amount wagered on each side of the table, and will draw or stand to try and beat the side betting the most money. *Example:* The banker has 5, the player on his left has drawn a 10, and the player on his right did not draw. The banker would stand or draw depending on which side had the most money wagered. If the left-side hand had the most money wagered, the bank would stand on 5. The reasoning is that the player on the left, having drawn a 10, has a count of 0, 1, 2, 3, 4, or 5. The banker would feel it's about 5 to 1 to win the most money. If the right side had the biggest wager, the banker would calculate the difference in money on both bets and then decide whether to draw or stay.

One of the reasons this game has not made any headway in the United States is the fact that it is open to all sorts of cheating practices—especially player cheats who signal their card count to a banker cheat so that, in a short time, the bank must win all the money in sight. The cheats split the take later, and the honest player hasn't a chance.

Slogger

This simplified and demechanized version of Chemin de Fer first appeared in print in *Scarne on Cards*. The special virtue of Slogger, or Schlager, as it is sometimes called, is that it's dead even for the banker and the player. With the following exceptions, the game is played exactly like Chemin de Fer:

1. The standard 52-card deck used alone.

2. (*Selecting the first banker.*) The players may sit anywhere they like. By mutual consent any player may shuffle the cards and any player may cut the cards. The acting dealer deals each player one card at a time, starting with the player at his left and dealing clockwise, until some player is dealt an ace. That player becomes the first banker.

3. (*The shuffle and cut.*) The banker shuffles. Any player may ask for the right to shuffle at any time, but the banker has the right to shuffle last. After the shuffle, the banker-dealer puts the cards on the table to be cut. Any player may cut. More than one

player may cut. If no other player cuts, banker must.

4. Dead cards (cards which have been played) are burned (placed upside down) on the bottom of the deck.

5. When the deck is exhausted or it is a new dealer's turn to bank, a new shuffle must be made.

6. There is no restriction in this game—as there is in Chemin de Fer—on any player drawing or staying on any count below 8. This includes the banker. Regardless of his count on the first two cards, the banker or the player may draw or stay at his own discretion.

7. The count of 9 with two cards is called *big slogger,* and is immediately turned up by the holder. The same holds true for the count of 8, called *little slogger.*

SCARNEY BACCARAT®

Scarney Baccarat is the first really new casino banking card game in the past century. This new game, which I invented, combines the principles of the great casino game of Baccarat, Chemin de Fer, Baccarat–Banque, Bank Craps, and Black Jack, plus several entirely new game principles. Scarney Baccarat was first introduced at the Curaçao

® Copyright © John Scarne Games, Inc. The design and name are trade-marked and its contents copyrighted and no part of this game can be reproduced in any form without written permission from its owner and distributor: John Scarne Games, Inc., 4319 Meadowview Avenue, North Bergen, New Jersey 07047.

The layout for Scarney Baccarat.

Hilton Hotel Casino in Curaçao, Netherlands Antilles, and spread rapidly to Nevada, England, Turkey, France, Italy, Yugoslavia, North Africa, and then around the world.

Requirements

1. A regulation Scarney Baccarat table with six betting spaces on its layout.

2. One to seven players, each of whom may bet on one to three hands, depending on the betting spaces available.

3. A card-dealing box called a shoe.

4. Four standard packs of 52 cards each, shuffled together and used as one, a total of 208 cards dealt as a single deck.

5. Two indicator cards. One is used by players to cut the deck and the other indicator card is used to determine the end of the deal.

Value of Cards. The ace is the lowest-ranking card and has a point value of 1. Kings, queens, and jacks have a value of 10 each. All other cards have their numerical face value. The deuce is counted as 2, the three is counted as 3, the four is counted as 4, etc. The suits have no value.

Object of the Game. Each player tries to obtain a higher total card count than the dealer by holding a combination of two or three cards totaling 9 or as close as possible to 9, or to a two-digit number ending in 9. *Examples:* $1 + 8$ gives point 9; $2 + 5$ gives point 7; $3 + 1$ gives point 4; and so forth. When the total of the cards is a two-digit number, only the last digit has any value. *Examples:* $10 + 9$ gives point 9; $9 + 3 + 1$ gives point 3; $1 + 3 + 10$ gives point 4; $6 + 7 + 9$ gives point 2; and so forth.

A player, at his proper turn of play and at his own discretion, regardless of the value of his two-card count, may stand or may draw a third card in an attempt to better his card count.

The Shuffle and Cut. The cards are shuffled by the dealer who then hands a player an indicator card and says "Cut please." The player inserts the indicator card into the deck to show where he wants the cards cut.

The dealer cuts the cards at this position, putting the indicator and all the cards above it on the bottom. The indicator goes to the bottom of the packet. The dealer then inserts the second indicator card sixty cards or thereabout from the bottom of the deck and places all the cards into the dealing box face down. The dealer next deals three cards from the shoe and puts them to one side out of play.

The shoe is now ready to be dealt by the dealer. When the indicator card inserted by the dealer makes its appearance, and enough cards from below the indicator card have been dealt to complete the round in progress, the deal ends. The dealer must begin a new shuffle and must again repeat the above procedure.

Betting. Before the deal begins, each player must place his bet, in chips, in one of the rectangular betting spaces that are painted on the playing surface; all bets are in full view of the dealer. I repeat, players may place bets on one to three betting spaces providing there are available holes (betting spaces). When a player places bets on more than one betting space at a time, he must play the hand farthest to his right to completion before being permitted to play his next hand or hands.

The Deal. After all players' bets are down, the dealer, starting with the player on his extreme left, begins dealing clockwise. He gives one card face up to each player and one face up to himself. He next deals each player, starting with the player on his extreme left, a second face-up card and one face-down card to himself.

Player's Turn at Play. The player to the dealer's extreme left makes the first play of the hand. He may elect to stay or draw.

1. To stay: Either he is satisfied with his two-card count or he fears that a third and final card may reduce his count. He says "No card," "I have enough," "I stand," or "Good."

2. To draw the third and final card: When a player is not satisfied with his count, he says "Hit me," "Give me a card," makes a beckoning motion by closing his hand, or makes a come-on motion with a finger. The dealer then deals a third and final card from the shoe face up before the player and next to his original two face-up cards. A player is not permitted to draw more than one card. Each dealt hand remains in front of the player or players.

The play moves to the player's left, clockwise, around the table until all players have played out their hands. At this time it becomes the dealer's turn.

The Dealer's Turn at Play. After all the players have played out their hand or hands, the dealer must play his hand and abide by the following rules:

1. He turns up his hole card so that his two cards are exposed.

2. If his count is 5, 6, 7, 8, or 9, the dealer must stay. He is not permitted to draw a third card.

3. If his count is 0, 1, 2, 3, or 4, he must draw a third and final card, after which he must stay. However, if a dealer's three-card count totals zero (0), and is made up of three 10-count cards, he must continue to draw cards until his total count is anything except zero (0). This is called the *Scarney Baccarat* or *Baccarat*. With the above exception, every Scarney Baccarat hand is made up of either two or three cards.

Final Settlement. At the end of his play, the dealer starts with the first active player on his extreme right and moves around the table to the left; he pays off players who have a higher count than his with an amount equal to the bet they placed, and collects the placed bets from players showing a lesser count. If a player and the dealer have the same count, it is standoff or tie, and no one collects or loses. A total three-card count has the same value as a similar total two-card count. *Example:* A 9-count made with three cards ties a 9-count made with two cards, etc. (The same holds true for a Scarney Baccarat hand comprised of 3, 4, 5, or more cards.)

Splitting Pairs. Any two aces, cards that are identical, regardless of their suits, may be treated as a pair. Also, any two cards each having a count of 10 (totaling zero) may be treated as a pair, such as two tens, two jacks, two queens, two kings, or a combination of any of the two above 10-count cards; such a combination is called baccarat. Each of the above pairs, at the discretion of the player, may be treated as the first card dealt of two separate hands.

A player being dealt two cards forming a pair on the initial round may, if he chooses, separate one from another and treat each card as the first card dealt in two separate hands.

When the pairs are split, the player's original bet is placed on one of these cards and an equal amount must be bet on the other card. The player is then dealt a second and final card face down on the face-up card on his right and then a second and final card face down on the other face-up card. When splitting pairs, at no time is a player permitted to draw a third card on any hand.

Players are not permitted to look at a face-down card until the dealer turns it face up after the deal has been completed.

The Double-Down Bet. A player after being dealt his first two cards (which may be any two cards) may elect to double his original bet before drawing his third card. This is known as a double down or *down for double*. A player at his turn of play, and before calling "down for double" or "double down," must place an amount equal to the original bet on the betting space. The player is then dealt a third and final face-down card on the two face-up cards. The player is not permitted to look at his face-down card until the dealer turns it face up after the deal has been completed.

The Scarney Insurance Bet. If the dealer's face-up card is a 9-count, players (at the dealer's turn of play) may elect to make an insurance bet against a loss or standoff to the dealer's possible two-card 9-count (9 + 10), called *Scarney*. The dealer, before turning his hole card face up, inquires if any player wants *Scarney insurance*. A player who desires insurance places an amount equal to half his present wager towards the center of the table.

After the dealer faces his hole card, and it is a 10-count, he calls "Scarney" and each insurance bettor is paid off at the rate of 2 to 1 for every unit wagered. If the card is not a 10-count, the dealer collects the player's insurance bet and the dealer continues to play out his hand.

The Scarney Baccarat Insurance Bet. After the dealer faces his hole card (at dealer's turn of play) and his initial two dealt cards are both 10-counts, players may elect to make the Scarney Baccarat insurance bet. The dealer, before drawing his third card, inquires if any player wants Scarney Baccarat insurance. A player who desires the Scarney Baccarat insurance places an amount equal to half his present wager towards the center of the table.

After the dealer draws his third card, and it is a 10-count, he calls "Scarney Baccarat" and each insurance bettor is paid off at the rate of 2 to 1 for every unit wagered; the dealer continues to play out his hand. If the card is not a 10-count, the dealer collects the players' insurance bets and the hand is played out. If the dealer's third dealt card is a 10-count, a second Scarney Baccarat insurance bet is permitted. Should the dealer's fourth dealt card be a 10-count, a third Scarney Baccarat insurance bet is allowed; and so it goes, insurance bet after insurance bet, until the dealer fails to draw a 10-count card and the hand ends.

The Side Bets. Scarney Baccarat layouts

have betting spaces marked 5—6—7—8—9, and above these numbers appears the phrase "Each Pays 10 for 1." Before a new deal begins, the player places his side bet by betting on a specified number or numbers, betting that on the next round of play the dealer's first two dealt cards will total the same count. The dealer pays off such winning bets at odds of 10 for 1. These wagers are also called *propositions*.

Field Bets. The field bears the numbers 5, 6, 7, 8, 9. When a player puts his bet on the space of the layout marked "Field," he is betting that on the next round of play, the combined total of the dealer's first two dealt cards will be 5, 6, 7, 8, or 9 as shown on the layout. The dealer pays off winning bets at even money. If the dealer's first two dealt cards total 0, 1, 2, 3, 4, the players lose their Field bets.

A dealer's two-card nine count comprised of a 9 and 10 is known as "Scarney." A count of zero with two or three cards is known as "baccarat." A dealer's count of zero with three or more ten-count cards is known as "Scarney Baccarat."

A player is not permitted to double down on a split pair.

Scarney Baccarat Strategy. Before giving a mathematical analysis of the game, I would like to point out that, in Scarney Baccarat, a player cannot bust his hand as in Black Jack. A player's cards are always in play until the dealer completes his play and the payoff takes place. In Scarney Baccarat the house advantage is the result of the dealer's special play of the game called Scarney Baccarat. In Scarney Baccarat, if the dealer's three-card total is zero (0) and is made up of three 10-count cards, the dealer continues to draw cards until his final count is different from zero. This is the only time a Scarney Baccarat hand is made up of more than three cards. It is not feasible, of course, to figure the exact percentage against individual players because their playing differs so much. Some players will stay on a count of 5 or more; some will draw on 5 and 6; others stay on 4 or more; and there's always the hero who will hit a 7 and an 8. However, since the dealer has no choice as to whether he stays or draws, because the rules predetermine this, he must draw to a count of 4 or less and stay on a count of 5 or more. We can calculate the

exact percentage for the house by having a player adhere to the dealer's fixed strategy of drawing to a count of 4 or less and standing on a count of 5 or more and not permitting a player to split pairs or to double down.

If the player adheres to the dealer's fixed strategy, and does not split pairs or double down, the house percentage in which a hand consists of a play of the game which terminates in a win, loss, or tie, is a low 2.44 percent. If a tie is not counted as a trial, then the house advantage is 2.71 percent. In other words, Scarney Baccarat will appear on the average of about once in 37 deals. I must reemphasize one fact you should not forget: The only positive advantage in favor of the bank is the 2.44 percent that it gains through a Scarney Baccarat.

There are several situations which, played properly, give the player an opportunity to cut down this house percentage. Most players handle these situations so inexpertly that, instead of reducing the percentage they are bucking, they add to it. Here are the playing factors which can be utilized to the player's advantage:

1. The player actually knows a little more than the dealer because one of the dealer's two initial cards is dealt face up; this gives the player important information about his possible card count. The rules governing the dealer's play prevent him from making use of similar information about the player's hand, even if the latter's first two cards were dealt face up.

2. Unlike the dealer, the player can stay or draw on any count he wants. At one turn of play he may draw to a count of 3, 4, 5, or more; and at other times he may stand on the same count. In some situations this is advantageous to the player.

3. The player can decide whether or not he wants to double down or split pairs, a strategy denied to the dealer.

4. The player may play one to three hands when there are available betting spaces; the dealer can only play one hand.

5. The player is the one who decides the amount of the bet and can raise or lower it at will within the prescribed betting limits.

6. The player may case the deck. If he can remember the cards previously dealt or exposed, this knowledge will greatly improve his chances of winning.

If you adhere to the strategy that I shall outline for you in the following pages, I promise that you can cut down the house 2.44 percent considerably. The strategy utilizes these factors: The dealer must hit a 4 or less and stand on 5 or more; the knowledge of the dealer's face-up (exposed) card; the player's total count; when it is to your advantage to stand, to draw, to split pairs, and to double down.

Playing according to the table below will assure you that you are fighting an average house advantage of considerably less than 2 percent. However, my strategy does not guarantee that you will win—it simply cuts down the house percentage to its lowest possible level and gives you a much better opportunity to win than any other method of Scarney Baccarat play.

Scarney Baccarat Strategy Table

Hit-and-Stand Strategy:

1. When the dealer's upcard is anything, stand on a count of 6, 7, 8, or 9.

2. When the dealer's upcard is anything, draw to a count of 0, 1, 2, 3, or 4.

3. When the dealer's upcard is 0, 1, 5, 6, 8, or 9, draw to a count of 5.

Splitting Pairs

1. Split threes when the dealer's upcard is 7, 8, or 9.

2. Split fives when the dealer's upcard is 1, 2, 3, 4, or 5.

3. Split sixes when the dealer's upcard is 0, 1, 2, 3, 4, 5, or 6.

4. Split sevens when the dealer's upcard is 0, 1, 2, 3, 4, 5, 6, or 7.

5. Split eights when the dealer's upcard is 7.

Doubling Down

Double down on a count of 4 when the dealer's upcard is 0, 1, 2, 3, or 4.

Double down on a count of 3 when the dealer's upcard is 0, 1, 2, 3, 4, or 5.

Double down on a count of 2 when the dealer's upcard is 0, 1, or 2.

Scarney Insurance Bet. Whenever the dealer shows a nine as his up-card, he will invite you to place an additional wager (called Scarney insurance) equal to half the amount already bet, which will pay you 2 to 1 if the dealer's downcard is a 10-count card, and which you will lose if it is not. In this optional bet, you are thus "insur-

ing" your hand against the possibility of a loss to a dealer Scarney. In order for this bet to be a profitable bet, more than one-third of the undealt cards must be 10-count cards. This is not very often the case, so let's take a look at the usual odds. If the dealer's upcard is a nine, and you have no knowledge of any other cards, the quadruple deck would contain 64 10-count cards.

Suppose you do not look at your own cards, nor do you see any of the other player's cards, prior to taking the insurance. Then the dealer's downcard may be considered drawn at random from the 207 cards that remain unseen. Clearly, 64 of these cards are 10-counts and the other 143 are not 10-counts. The odds are 143 to 64 against the dealer having a 10-count in the hole. The payoff is 128 to 64, approximately 7 percent. As a general rule, I don't recommend insurance betting. However, the casual card caser (counter) can use the insurance bet advantageously if he has been keeping track of 10-count cards in previous hands. *Example:* Suppose half the deck (104 cards) has been dealt and the casual card caser recalls that only 12 10-count cards have been dealt. If an insurance bet could be made on the next deal, it would be wise to take insurance because the player has an edge of more than 33 percent over the house on this bet.

Scarney Baccarat Insurance. The house advantage in Scarney insurance also holds true when placing a Scarney Baccarat insurance bet.

Proposition on Side Bets. In addition to the preceding wagers, Scarney Baccarat layouts have spaces marked 5, 6, 7, 8, or 9, and above these numbers appears the phrase, "Each Pays 10 for 1." A bet placed on a 5 means that the player is betting that the dealer, on the next turn of play, will hold a count of 5 with his first two dealt cards. The dealer pays off such winning bets at 10 for 1 and since the correct odds are 9 23/64 to 1, the house enjoys an advantage of 3.46 percent. The same house percentage holds true for the numbers 7 and 9.

When a player places a bet on the 6 (same rules apply as on the 9), he is again paid off at 10 for 1. But since the correct odds on being dealt a count of 6 in the first two cards are 9 43/62 to 1, the house enjoys an advantage of 6.48 percent. The same holds true for number 8.

Field Bet. When a player places a bet on the space of the layout marked "Field" he is betting that the dealer's first two dealt cards on the next round will total a count of 5, 6, 7, 8, or 9. The dealer pays such winning bets at even money. The dealer may be dealt 1,326 different two-card counts of which 632 comprise the field (5, 6, 7, 8, and 9) and 694 comprise the losing numbers (0, 1, 2, 3, and 4). When we subtract 632 winning two-card counts from the 694 losing two-card counts, we find the field bettor has a disadvantage of 62 two-card counts for a dealer's edge of 4.67 percent.

FARO OR FAROBANK

Since the advent of the casino games of Bank Craps and Black Jack, Faro is no longer widely played. Many people believe that the game has now disappeared, but at the time of writing there are about seven Faro games in operation in Nevada. But once—when Mark Twain was roughing it—this was perhaps the most celebrated and popular game in the United States. It may be the oldest banking game in the world, and seems to have been of Italian extraction originally; but it got its vogue and name in the court of Louis XIV. "Faro" is the English version of Pharaon; Louis' royal gamblers called the game Pharaon because one of the honor cards bore the face of an Egyptian Pharaoh. Maybe it doesn't really matter, but the game's language is a matter of legitimate interest; it has given us such ineradicable phrases as "coppering the bet" and "calling the turn." And will some etymologist tell me why the first card in the box is called *soda* and the last is called *hoc* or *hock?* Faro was introduced into this country by way of New Orleans, moved up river on the Mississippi steamboats, and spread across the country like a prairie fire. Many a plantation, many a slave, and many a poke of gold were won and lost on Faro tables. To advertise that a Faro game was available, Western houses used to display a big sign bearing the likeness of a tiger, that's all; that's where the game got its alias, "Bucking the Tiger."

Requirements

1. A Faro table. This is a big table covered with green felt on which is painted a layout of 13 cards, running from ace to king of spades. The spades suit is conventionally used for the layout, but the suit of the cards in actual play has no bearing on the game.

2. A Faro dealing box. This, like all other dealing boxes, is open at the top. Only one card at a time is available, appearing to be framed by wood on all four sides. The box has a narrow slit at one side through which one card at a time can be slid out. A spring in the bottom of the box holds the deck firmly against the top frame.

3. A device called the *casekeeper,* which resembles a counting rack, having pictures of the thirteen cards painted across its middle. Running from each card to the outside frame of the rack is a metal spindle. On each spindle are four sliding wooden markers like the big beads on an abacus or a child's toy. Each marker represents one of the four cards of that rank. Their use and usefulness will be developed presently.

4. A rack of chips, generally kept to the right of the dealer, about a foot from his right hand.

5. Markers, used to denote bets—not to be confused with the markers on the casekeeper described above. The bet-denoting markers are flat oblong ivory or plastic chips, about the size of half a piece of chewing gum.

6. Faro coppers. In the Gold Rush days, pennies were used to *copper* a lose bet. But today a black or red hexagonal chip is placed on top of a pile of chips when they are bet that a certain card will lose.

7. Betting chips. Their value runs generally as follows:

    White—valued from 25 cents to $1

    Red—valued at either $1 or $5

    Blue—valued at either $5 or $10

    Yellow—valued at either $25 or $50

    Note: Color and value of chips are discretionary with the casino.

8. A standard deck of 52 playing cards. The suits have no relative value, the only thing that matters being the rank of the cards.

9. One dealer, who keeps the deal and banks the game; one casekeeper; and one lookout, who manages the markers and sees that bets are paid and collected.

10. As many players as can comfortably sit or stand around a Faro table. About ten is average.

Object of the Game. To win money by betting correctly on the rank of cards as they are dealt from the box and on whether they will be winning or losing cards. This is strictly a gambling game. There is very little, if any, latitude for skill and strategy.

Betting Limits. The betting limits in the seven Faro games being played in Nevada vary, ranging from $1 up to $100 and sometimes $5 up to $200, with special exceptions over and above for some high-rolling customers. The lower limits are most common and in some games the minimum bet is 25¢ and the maximum $25.

The Shuffle and Deal. The house banker shuffles the deck, cuts it, and places it in the box face up. The first card of the deck, exposed in this act, is called the soda card, or just soda, and is dead as far as betting action is concerned.

After the bets have been placed, the dealer then removes soda to the far right of the table, commonly putting it to rest in contact with the rack of chips just off his right hand; then he removes the next card from the box and puts it immediately next to the box at its right. This action exposes two new cards. The card which has been drawn out and put on the table beside the box is the loser card. The card which remains in the box but is also visible is the winner card. Now the bets on the two exposed cards are won or lost. Then the dealer proceeds to slide the winner card out of the box and to discard it on the soda stack. Thereupon the action is repeated. The next card is put on the loser stack, and the exposed card remaining in the box is the winner. The entire deck is dealt like that. The card that comes out of the box is the loser, and the exposed card remaining in the box is the winner. All bets remain on the painted layout until a decision is reached through the appearance of the bet card as one of the two dealt cards that have action.

Players may change or remove a bet between actions. But if a bet remains on the layout, it must win or lose. Every time the dealer removes two cards from the box it is called a *turn*. The entire deck is dealt—down to the last card to complete a deal. Then, after reshuffling the deck, the action starts again. The last card is called the hoc or hock card; and, like the soda card, it is arbitrarily dead as far as betting action is concerned.

The Casekeeper. As the dealer proceeds to make the turns, the casekeeper with his peculiar gadget keeps a record of each card that has received action and whether it was a winner or loser. For instance, if the first seven dealt is a loser, the first button or marker on the spindle of the seven is slid down to touch the other end of the frame. Should it be a winner, the marker is moved down the spindle, but not until it touches the frame; a space of about a half-inch is left between frame and marker. If the next seven is a loser, the next marker is moved down to touch the first. If the next seven is a winner, the same small space is left between the two. This goes on until all four of that kind are dealt from the box, whereupon all four markers are pushed down together to touch the frame, signifying to the players that there will be no more action on that number in that deal.

From the casekeeper's record, the player can tell at all times how many cards are left in the box awaiting their turn, what their denomination is, and whether preceding cards of that rank won or lost. On the basis of this record, many players develop and constantly play occult "systems."

Cases. When three cards of a kind have received action, the remaining card bearing that number, the card still in the box, is referred to as *cases*. The idiom is "Cases on the King!" Many smart players will bet only the cases on any deal. The reason is that the house does not have any percentage in its favor on this bet, due to the fact that splits cannot occur. However, Faro banks today compel a player to make at least one possible split bet before he can bet on cases.

Calling the Turn. After 24 successive turns of two cards each have been dealt, there remain in the box three cards. This stage of the game is called the *last turn*. (The last card in the box, the hoc or hock card, is dead for betting action.)

When the last turn comes up, the player may either bet any one of the cards as an individual bet or call the turn—that is, bet that he can enumerate the next cards dealt in the order of their appearance. *Example:* The three cards remaining to be played are a deuce, a jack, and a king. The player may bet that the three will come out as follows:

Deuce first to lose
King second to win
Jack to be the hoc card

Now the dealer pulls out and tables the loser, exposing the winner. But he also moves the winner halfway out of the box, so that the players can see the hoc card at the same time.

A player may call the last turn any way he chooses. In the instance here cited, a player would say he was calling it deuce–king. On the painted layout before him he would place his bet on the loser card's edge facing his winner card, and would tilt his wagered chips on the edge of the bottom chip. In this case the player, having perhaps six chips to bet, would place one chip on the edge or corner of the deuce nearest the king and would tilt the other five on that chip so that they would tilt toward the king. If the player wants to call a last turn on two cards separated on the layout by the third card, he must tilt his bet toward the outside edge of the layout, signifying that his call goes around the middle card. *Example:* The last turn is comprised of the king, queen, and eight. The player wants to call the turn as king–eight; so he must tilt his bet on the outside (lower) edge of the king. But this convention for placing last-turn bets by tilting them on the bottom chip is valid only for a bet of two or more chips, of course. If a player means to bet only one chip, the bet must be placed differently (see page 305).

Last-Turn Payoffs. Should the player call the turn correctly, the payoff is four to one. If he does not call it in exact sequence, he loses his bet. There are six ways for the last turn to show up. Should the last turn include two of a kind in the box, this is called a *cat-hop.* Obviously it is much easier to call this turn; so the payoff is two to one. There are three ways for the cat-hop to show up.

Should the last turn be comprised of three of a kind, then players bet on the colors at the same odds as govern a cat-hop. *Example:* The last turn has come up with three queens in the box, two red and one black. The players bet on red or black to win or lose. Bets are placed in front of the dealer and called as to color.

In Case of Error. If the casekeeper is wrong as the last turn comes up, and does not show there are three cards in the box, then the dealer must check back through the winning and losing discard piles to correct the mistake. If the dealer has made a mistake and the last turn shows only two cards instead of three, then the turn is void, and no bets have action.

The Betting Apparatus. The majority of all betting is done with chips of different colors. Most modern houses assign a different color to each player, thus eliminating any possibility of dispute between players as to ownership of a bet. For each color category of chips there is a smaller matching chip, which is placed atop all chips of that color in the rack to designate the price per stack of twenty chips. By extension, of course, this indicates the price per chip.

The Lookout. The lookout man sits to the right of the dealer on a high chair and watches the game. His duties are to see that all bets are paid correctly and that the game proceeds in an orderly way. His job is comparable to that of a pit boss in the common casino.

The Routine Payoff. To place a bet on a card to win, the player puts his money on the table's painted or enameled representation of the card he wants. If the number he bets is the exposed card which remains in the box, he wins the bet. All bets except those on calling the last turn are paid at even money.

The House Percentage. If any turn comes up two of a kind, the turn is called a *split,* and the house takes half the bet forthwith. The split and the payoff on calling the last turn are the only percentages in favor of the house. The percentage in favor of the house on splits amounts to approximately 2 percent. On the last turn, the payoff is at four to one, the correct odds are five to one; therefore, the house gets a favorable percentage on this bet of 16.66 percent.

Betting on the Loser. If a player wishes to bet on a card to lose, he still places his money on the layout of his choice, but must also place on top of his money a small marker, generally black and hexagonal, made for just this purpose. This marker is called a *copper.* The move is called coppering the bet.

Other Bets. As to straight bets on the last turn, the same action applies as during the entire deal. First card out is the loser, second is the winner; and if the bet is made on the card which remains as the hoc card there is no action; the bet is a standoff.

Another bet may be made: on odd or even. This bet applies to the whole 13 cards. Only one bet is necessary, and it takes action on every turn. The bet is that the winning (or losing) card will be an even number (or odd; it's your bet). If a split occurs and both winning and losing cards are even or odd, the bet is a standoff. The money is usually placed in front of the dealer on the table between the represented deuce and the edge of the layout to signify even; behind the five to signify odd.

Systems. Three main types of systems are played, plus another kind of betting on the high card to win or lose, which is itself in reality a kind of system. As for the latter, the player betting the high card puts his money on the proper space on the layout. It signifies that, of the two cards in the next turn, the higher-numbered of them will win (or lose, according to the bet placed). In the event of a split, the bet is a standoff. The three most common systems may be classified as follows:

1. *Double Out.* After the first of a kind has received action, the player bets the other three of the same kind to follow the same pattern of win or lose as the first. *Example:* If the first king dealt is a loser, the player bets the other three too will be losers; and the reverse prevails if the first king were a winner.

2. *Single Out.* After the first card of a kind is played, the player bets the next of that kind to come out the opposite, the third to revert to the first's character, and the fourth to be the same as the second. *Example:* If the first deuce is a winner, the player bets the second deuce to lose, the third to win, and the fourth to lose. (*Note:* Most players bet the above systems on the cases only.)

3. *Three–One.* After the first three of a kind have taken action and if the action was alike, the player bets the last card to be opposite to the first three. *Example:* The first three eights were winners; so, the player bets the last eight to be a loser.

When a player bets one card to lose and another to win and loses both bets on the same turn, he is said to have been *whipsawed*.

Betting More Than One Card. Most players have more than one bet on the layout at the same time; and so there are alternate methods of placing a bet so that one gamble can cover more than one card at a time. But should any of his designated cards lose, the player loses the entire amount of his bet on the layout, and must cover his remaining bets again if he still wants to play them. *Example:* The player has placed $5 in such a position as to cover the ace–deuce–king. This indicates that he has $5 bet on each of these cards. Now should the ace turn up a loser, the dealer takes the $5; and the player must bet again if he still wants to cover the deuce and king. But should the turn come up with the ace a loser and the king a winner, the bet is obviously a standoff.

How Bets Are Placed. In the illustration here, the various ways of placing a bet are indicated by the position of the chip on the card. Each bet is numbered. Now for the explanations:

1. Bets the four only. This position is used on every card.

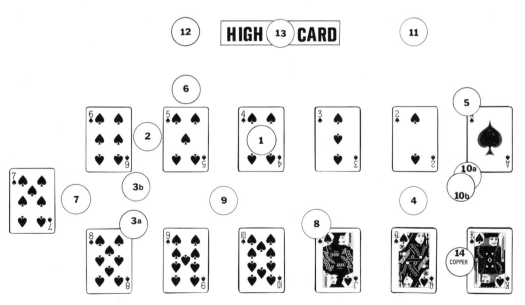

The Faro layout.

2. Bets the five and six. This position may be used between any two cards. Between six and seven, and between eight and seven, the chip would be slightly off center from the seven.

3a. Bets the eight and five. This may be used wherever two cards are diagonal to each other. It cannot be used on a seven. This is called a *heeled bet.* The top chips are tilted on the bottom chip toward the other card included in the bet. This is the usual position for bets of two or more chips. If the player wishes to bet both to lose, he coppers the top chip only. If he wishes to bet one to lose and the other to win, he places the bet as in example 10. For one chip, see the example below:

3b. Bets the six and nine. This is the same bet as example 3a, except that this is the position for one chip only. It may also be used for a bet of more than one chip, but that is not customary. If the player wants to bet one card to lose and the other to win, he places a copper on the corner of the to-lose card, and heels the other chip toward the winner. The copper is underneath the chip.

4. Bets the deuce and queen. This may be used between any two cards opposite each other.

5. Bets the ace and three, skipping the deuce. This may be used on any outside corner which will skip one card and bet the following one. It cannot be used on the upper left corner of the six, lower left corner of the eight, upper right corner of the ace and deuce, lower right corner of the queen and king, or the seven.

6. Bets the four, five, and six. This may be used anywhere if three cards are included in the bet; it cannot be used on the outside of the ace or king, or on the seven.

7. Bets the six, seven, and eight. This position is used only on the one shown and on no other.

8. Bets the three, jack, and ten. This may be used anywhere possible to include a triangle of which the card holding the chip is the center card. It cannot be used on the lower right corner of the ace, the upper right corner of the king, the lower left corner of the six, the upper left corner of the eight or the seven.

9. Bets the four, five, nine, and ten. This may be used to include any four cards forming a square.

10a, 10b. This bet is the same as example 3a, with the copper on the bottom chip and the other chip heeled. It bets the ace to lose and the queen to win. Bets are always placed on the card bet to lose and heeled toward the card bet to win.

11. This is the position of a chip when betting even.

12. This is the position of a chip when betting odd.

13. This is the position of a chip when betting high card.

14. This is the method of placing one chip to call a last turn. The player must place a copper on the edge of the card, then tilt the chip on it and place another copper on top of the chip. This is to make certain, doubly certain, that the player is calling the turn and not just heeling his bet as shown in example 3b. It is meant to eliminate all doubts as to the bet made.

Stuss

This is a Faro variant, sometimes called Jewish Faro. It is much more popular than Faro because it lacks the intricate props and is much easier for a player to learn to play. Also, gambling houses prefer it to Faro because it has a greater percentage in favor of the bank. The game is played exactly as Faro, with the following exceptions:

1. The 13 spades on the layout are designed differently from the Faro layout.

2. A Stuss card box is similar to a Faro box, except that the Stuss box prevents the last four cards from being dealt out. They are held at the bottom of the box, in a recess called a *pocket,* and are out of play.

3. The pack is put into the box face down and dealt from that position.

4. The first card placed face up to the right of the Stuss box is the house card, and if a player has a bet on that card, he loses to the house. However, if the card turned up is not covered by a bet, then the dealer deals the next card, turns it face up, and places it to the left of the Stuss box. A bet on this card wins for the player. If there is no bet on either the house or the player card, the next turn or deal of two cards takes place.

5. Also, in Stuss, there is no coppering of bets as in Faro; in other words, the players cannot bet on any cards to lose. Every bet must be to win.

6. There is no calling the turn on the last

four cards left in the box—no pocket bets are permitted.

7. After 48 cards have been dealt, the Stuss box automatically holds out four cards in the box. Then the dealer takes the four cards out of the box and turns them over. If there are any bets on the layout corresponding to the cards showing on this turnover, all of these bets are won by the house or dealer.

8. *Splits.* In case of splits or ties, where two cards of the same denomination appear on one turn, the house takes the entire bet instead of half the bet as in Faro.

9. In some smaller casinos, Stuss is dealt from the hand, entirely eliminating both the Stuss box and the layout. In some casinos, second bets (a bet on a card after a card of that rank has been dealt) are not permitted. When second bets are not permitted, the house does not pocket the last four cards.

The Bank's Percentage at Stuss. The bank enjoys its biggest percentage at Stuss from the four last cards left in the pocket of the card box, which is calculated as an advantage of 3 11/13 percent. (Four cards out of a total of fifty-two gives a percentage of 7 9/13, but since, on the average, two of these would be house winnings anyway, half of this percentage—3 11/13 percent—may be considered extra.)

The bets on splits figure the same as in Faro, approximately 2 percent. Whereas the house takes the entire bet on splits at Stuss but only half of the bet at Faro, it comes to the same thing because there are no lose bets in Stuss. In Faro, the house takes half of two bets, win or lose. In Stuss, the house takes all of only win bets. Adding these two figures together, we get a total of approximately 6 percent in favor of the bank at Stuss.

ZIGINETTE

This is a betting game popular among Americans of Italian extraction, and is the biggest money card game in Italy. As you read this line, hundreds of Ziginette games are going on in smoky little clubrooms throughout the nation; thousands of dollars are changing hands; the yearly turnover is in the millions. Although it is a banking game, the house never banks Ziginette; it just runs the game, and cuts itself 10 percent of the dealer's winnings per game.

Requirements

1. A 40-card deck—a standard pack from which have been removed the eights, nines, and tens.

2. A metal card box, like a Faro box, permitting the removal of only one card at a time.

3. A houseman, called the *cutter,* who collects and pays bets for the dealer (as does the croupier in Chemin de Fer), and who extracts the house's cut.

4. A dealer who is the banker. One or more players, eight constituting the average game.

Object of the Game. For the player to guess which card of his will not be matched before the dealer matches his (the dealer's) card. To *match* means to deal from the box a card of the same denomination as the player's or dealer's card in action. Whenever a card is matched from the box, the player or dealer holding that card loses his bet.

Selecting the Dealer. The houseman shuffles the cards, allows any player to cut them, and squares the cut. He deals to each player, starting with the player at his left and dealing clockwise, one card at a time face up until a player is dealt an ace. That player becomes the first banker or dealer.

Thereafter, on the completion of each deal, the bank rotates to the player immediately to the right of the dealer—providing the dealer has matched his card. Should the deal run out before the dealer has matched his card, the bank remains in his possession until he does so. But even though his card has not been matched, the dealer may, if he likes, pass the bank at the completion of a deal; and he may also pass the deal if the table is barren of unsettled bets.

The Betting Limit. The dealer-banker may establish his own limit by specifying the smallest and largest amount anyone may bet on any card. He may increase or decrease his limits at will. The cutter collects winning bets for the dealer. He pays off his losing bets. If the dealer wins, he must pay the house its cut of 10 percent of his winnings on that deal.

Shuffle and Cut. The dealer shuffles the cards. Any player may demand the right to shuffle, but the dealer may shuffle last. He then puts the cards in the center of the table to be cut by any player who wants to cut them. Then the pack is squared and deposited in the card box face upward. The dealer does this.

The Betting. The first two cards are dealt onto the table face up, and any player may lay a bet on either card. The third card, now visible on the top of the boxed deck, is the dealer's card. He does not remove it from the box until bets, if any, are made on the cards on the table. By putting his money on a faced card, the player bets that this card will not be matched before the dealer's card is matched. *Example:* Should the first two cards be an ace and a deuce, and the dealer's card a three, the player's bets are laid on the ace and deuce; only then does the dealer take his three out of the box. He puts it under the box, its surface protruding so that perhaps four-fifths of it is visible. If the top card now is another three, matching the dealer's, he loses; he must pay off the two players who have bet on the table cards; he loses the bank. If the top card is an ace or deuce, the player who has bet on the table deuce or ace loses; the dealer collects from him.

The same procedure is followed with each fresh card (i.e., a card that has not been matched). When a fresh card appears on top of the pack, it goes onto the table face up, and the players bet on it. This goes on until the dealer matches and pays off all remaining bets. Whenever a player matches, the dealer wins the bet.

When two cards of the same denomination are dealt in the first three cards, it's called a *playette.* Most houses call it *no play,* and the

cards are reshuffled and redealt until the first three cards are of different denominations. But some houses insist that when two or three cards of the same denomination appear for the first three cards, they must be doubled or tripled. *Example:* If three aces appear on the first three cards, they are put on top of each other representing a single card; the fourth card is placed on the table face up and the fifth card becomes the dealer's card. But before the dealer can lose, he must draw three cards of the same denomination as his card. In other words, a player loses a bet when all four cards of the same denomination are dealt before all four of the dealer's. If two of the first three cards were of the same denomination, three cards of any denomination would have to be dealt before a decision is effected.

The house assigns a lookout to the game. His job is to see that no monkey business takes place, that all players who win get their money, that all players who lose pay off, and to guard against dead cards getting into the play. (A dead card is a card that has been matched in that round of play.) The holder of that card has already lost a bet on it. Whenever a card has been matched, it and the matching card are picked up by the lookout and put aside; they—as well as the two remaining cards of that kind—cannot have action again for the remainder of that deal.

As to the Odds. Ziginette is dead even; that is, there is no advantage to either player or dealer. Thus, in the long run, the only consistent winner will be the house, because its 10 percent deal cuts into the dealer's winnings.

THE SKIN GAME

In my opinion, Skin, Skinball, or Skinning is the fastest gambling game played with cards. If you like to bet big and often, this is for you. It seems to be of Negro origin, is played mainly in the South and Midwestern states, and probably gets its name from its high incidence of bald cheating. However, it is so similar to Ziginette that Skin may merely be short for zigin (-ette). Although it is a banking game, the houses don't bank it; they just run it, and collect a fixed charge.

Requirements

1. A deck of 52 cards.
2. A card box.

3. A houseman, who acts as lookout and cutter.
4. A banker and two or more players up to six, which is best.

Value of Cards. The cards have no relative value; neither do the suits.

Object of the Game. To win a bet that the dealer's card or another player's card will be matched before your card. A card is matched when another card of its kind is dealt from the box. *Example:* Your card is the ace of spades. The dealer draws one of the three remaining aces from the deck in the box. Your card has been matched. You lose.

Selecting the Dealer. By mutual consent, any player may shuffle the deck. He puts it in the center of the table, and any player may cut. The acting dealer squares the cut and deals each player, including himself, one card face up, starting with the player at his left and continuing clockwise until a player is dealt the first ace. That player becomes banker-dealer. When the pack is exhausted on the banker's deal, the bank passes to the player at his right; and so on, counterclockwise.

The Shuffle and Cut. The banker-dealer shuffles. Any player may demand the right to shuffle, the dealer shuffles last, and the player to his right cuts. If he declines, any other player may cut. The dealer then squares the deck and puts it into the card box face down.

The Deal and the Betting. The banker slides the top card out of the box and deals it to the player on his right, turning the card face up.

The player may do one of two things: He may accept the card, or he may refuse it. Some players entertain the belief that certain cards are unlucky for them; others believe certain cards are so lucky they can be taken down to the bank and put up as collateral on a substantial loan. For any reason, a player may decline a card. But if he refuses the first card dealt to him, the player is out of the game for that turn of play. He must wait until it comes his turn to make a bet.

Should the first player refuse the card, the right to take it passes to the player at the first player's right, and so on. The right to the card moves counterclockwise around the table.

After the first card has been accepted by a player, the dealer gives himself the second card out of the box. The player now states his bet. He may bet any amount up to the limit, but the dealer is not compelled to accept the entire bet, even within the limit; the dealer has the right to reduce the bet to any amount he chooses, and the player must adhere to the dealer's rulings. He (the dealer) cannot withdraw his bet after making it. In accepting the player's bet, the dealer puts an amount of money equal to the bet directly on the center of the player's card. The player covers the bet by putting his money on the dealer's money.

The player is betting that the dealer's card will be matched before his own card is matched. Should he also bet against another player, the bet is that the other player's will

be matched before his card is. *Example:* The dealer's card is the ace of diamonds, and the player holds the ten of diamonds. If the next card dealt is one of the other three aces, the dealer has been matched, and loses all bets on the board. If it is one of the other three tens, the player has been matched and loses his bet.

Should the third card dealt not match either the dealer's or the player's card, it is dealt to the next player whose turn it is. The player makes a bet in the manner described above against the dealer. But he may, if the first player accedes, make a bet against that player. And, in turn, he may make a bet against any other. The same rules prevail as between dealer and player.

This goes on until each player has had his turn. Often a player will be betting against every other player in the game, plus the dealer. But note that the first bet a player makes must be with the dealer. If the player refuses to bet against the dealer, he has refused the card and cannot bet with any other player. When players bet against each other, the money is stacked to one side to avoid confusion with the dealer's stakes.

The house assigns a lookout to the game. His job it is to see that no monkey business takes place, that all players who win get their money, that all players who lose pay off, and to guard against dead cards getting into the play. (A dead card is a card that has been matched in that round of play.) The holder of that card has already lost a bet on it. Whenever a card has been matched, it and the matching card are picked up by the lookout and put aside; they—as well as the two remaining cards of that kind—cannot have action again for the remainder of that deal.

A player who has refused a card or has lost his bet may, after each other player has had a turn of play, take a fresh card (that is, a card that has not been matched); and the betting continues as before. If, with all players holding a card already, a fresh card is dealt, it is placed in the center of the table. Whenever a player has been matched, so that he does not hold a card, he may take any of the fresh cards he wants.

Whenever the dealer's card is matched, he must pay off all the players. Should the players have bets riding against each other when the dealer loses his bets, the dealer may (*a*) complete dealing for the players or (*b*) take the first fresh card dealt off the pack.

Players still in the game are not obliged to bet against the dealer once the dealer's card has been matched, but may do so if they choose.

As to the Odds. The game of Skin is dead even; that is, dealer and player have exactly equal chances of winning. For that reason—since there is no percentage in the dealer's favor—the house runs the game instead of banking it. In return for supplying a place and the equipment—plus a lookout—it extracts a 25 percent charge from the player or dealer winning the last bet of the deal. (*Variation:* Some houses charge a flat 2 percent on each bet won by a player from the dealer and 2 percent of the dealer's winnings on any deal—if there are any winnings.)

MONTE

This game is also called Spanish Monte and Monte Bank. Due to its big money-making feature and its lack of bulky equipment, which minimizes police raids and arrests, Monte has replaced Bank Craps as the number one banking game in most illegal gambling clubs operating in the big cities of the United States.

Requirements

1. A standard deck of 52 cards from which the eights, nines, and tens have been removed, making a 40-card deck.

2. A banker chosen from two or more players. As a rule, the admissible maximum is the number that can crowd around the card table.

3. A houseman, called a cutter, whose official duty is to aid the player-banker in his dealing chores, including the payoff, the collection of losing and winning bets, and the collection of a 25 percent charge from each player's door or gate winnings. This 25 percent charge is known as a "cut" and is divided equally between the banker and the house at the end of a player's banking role.

Object of the Game. To win a bet that one or more face-up cards on the table layouts will be matched before one or more of the remaining face-up cards of the Monte layout.

Value of the Cards. The cards have no special value relative to each other, and neither do the suits.

Selecting the Banker. By mutual consent any player shuffles the pack, then puts it in the center of the table. Each player cuts a group of cards off the pack. The player cutting the low card is the first dealer and banker. In case of a tie for low card, the tied players cut until one is low. On completion of the banker's deal, the deck and the deal pass to the player on the dealer's left; thereafter, it rotates to the left, clockwise. At any time, the dealer may pass the bank (i.e., decline to bank the game)—if there are no unsettled bets on the table. To announce that he means to pass the bank, the dealer utters the word "Aces!"

Betting Limit. The dealer is privileged to place as much money in the bank as he chooses. If a player wagers more money than is in the bank, and the bank loses the bet, the largest wager is paid off first; the second largest is paid off next; etc. Other bets are called off. The banker is only responsible for money in the bank. The wagers are always in cash.

The Shuffle and Cut. The dealer shuffles the pack. Any player may call for a shuffle before the cut, but the dealer is entitled to shuffle last. After the shuffle, the dealer puts the cards before the player at his right to be cut. That player must cut, although the other players may also call for the right to cut before the player to the dealer's right completes his own cut.

Start of the Deal. After the cut the banker, holding the pack face down, deals two cards off the bottom of the deck, facing these two cards and putting them in the center of the table two or three inches apart. This is known as the *top layout*. Then the dealer takes two cards off the top of the deck, and puts them face up two or three inches below the first two cards, about the same distance apart, forming the *bottom layout*.

Should the two dealt cards of the bottom layout be of the same rank, there is no play and a new deal is in order. If the two dealt cards of the top layout are of the same rank, the dealer places one card on top of the other and then deals a third card alongside it. Bets placed on a pair indicate that a player is betting against two same rank cards of the opposite color of the other card in the top layout. *Example:* If the other card is red, the player is betting against a black card (spades or clubs) of the same rank; or vice versa. Should three cards of the same rank appear in the top layout, they are grouped in threes and a bet on a triple means that the player is betting against the same color of the other card. The above bets are all paid off at even money.

Types of Bets

Crisscross Bet. To bet that a selected one of four face-up cards on the table will be matched before a designated card of the remaining other three cards. (A card is matched whenever one of three remaining cards of the same denomination is dealt from the pack.) *Example:* Face up on the table are the ace, two, three, and four of clubs. The player puts his bet on the ace, placing his cash in such a way that it points or just touches the deuce as well. He is now betting that one of the three remaining aces will be dealt from the pack before one of the three remaining deuces.

Doubler or Doubler Bet. To win a bet that a card in the top layout will be matched before a card is matched in the bottom layout, or vice versa; or that one of the two cards resting on the dealer's left will be matched before one of the two cards on his right, or vice versa. This bet is paid off at even money.

Circle Bet or Circling a Card. To win a bet that a specific (one) card will be matched before any one of the three other cards. This bet is paid off at 3 to 1 odds.

Monte Carlo Bet. To make a combination of the three listed bets at one time. The payoff of such bets is determined by the sum wagered on each. All Monte Carlo wagers are indicated by the placement of the money (bills) as described under the crisscross bet. Bets can be placed any time during a deal.

The Play. After the bets have been placed, the cutter tells the dealer "That's all," which formally terminates that phase of the game, and the dealer turns the deck face up in his hand. From then on the cards will be dealt from the pack face up one at a time. Some gambling joints insist that, after each decision, the deck be turned face down and future bets must be placed before the deck is turned face up.

If the top card of the deck matches one of the four faced cards, either the dealer or a player (or players) wins; and the dealer keeps taking cards off the pack (*a*) until all the cards bet on are matched or (*b*) the cards the

players are betting against have been matched. As a card is matched, it is removed from the board. When all bets are won or lost the deal is completed and a new deal starts.

The House Take. When a player places a bet (any time during the game) and the next (first) dealt card matches his winning card, the cutter takes a 25 percent cut from the player's winnings. This is called the *door* or *gate.* This cut is put aside and is divided equally by the banker and house at the end of the player's banking session. Percentagewise, this 25 percent cut amounts to an overall advantage of about 3 percent.

Three-Card Monte

Three-Card Monte was the most popular con game of the Old West. Countless Monte operators plied their trade on the steamboats of the Ohio and Mississippi, and throughout the West in the 1850's. The most notorious Monte operator, "Canada Bill" Jones, summed up the whole philosophy of the Three-Card cheat in one sentence: "Suckers have no business with money, anyway."

In recent years, however, the Monte operators have returned, apparently figuring that there is a new generation of suckers with cash in their pockets who don't know that it is a swindle, not a game. I have spotted some 15 Monte men working in various parts of the country within the last year or two.

Three-Card Monte operators and their confederates work the big cities during the winter months, pitching their confidence game in alleys, subway stations, doorways, with the lookout half a block away to give them the *office* (signal) when he spots a cop. The operator of this swindle, usually a clever card sharp, shows three cards slightly bent lengthwise, so as to be more easily picked up by the ends—which in turn facilitates the deceptive flipping of the cards. The three cards most commonly used are the two red aces and the queen of spades.

To illustrate the working of a Monte operator and his confederates, let me relate the following: One day, several years ago, I was in New England giving a carnival the once-over as part of one of my gambling surveys. As I was leaving the carnival grounds, I spotted several men gathered around a rusty oil drum whose top was covered with a newspaper. One man was throwing three cards out on the paper. I joined the group and listened to the *broad tosser's* (Monte thrower's) spiel, the standard one: "Men, I have here three little cards, two red aces and the black queen of spades. The idea is for you to find the queen. If you find it you win; if you turn up an ace you lose. It's as simple as that. And remember, I take no bets from paupers, cripples, or pregnant women. I show you all three cards, then throw them face down— fast, like this. If your eye is faster than my hand and you find the queen, I pay you the same amount you bet. I'll accept bets of five, ten, twenty, fifty, or a hundred that you can't find the lady. Remember, men, if you don't speculate you can't accumulate. Money in hand or no bet. Let's go."

There are numerous ways that a confederate marks the so-called winning card, notably by a bent corner, so that it seems to be known by the back; but the operator skillfully shifts the mark during the throwing of the cards.

A final word of caution: Don't think, now that you know how the Monte swindle is worked, that you can outsmart the operator at his own game. Because, even should you place your hand on the winning card, the Monte man takes the money from a confederate who is betting on another card—and since the operator's spiel informs you that "money in the hand or no bet," you just don't have a bet when the operator knows you picked the winning card.

CHINESE FAN-TAN

This Faro-type banking card game, once popular in Western gambling establishments, is no longer played today. But I think it's worth mentioning how it was played.

The house acts as the banker; the layout for Chinese Fan-Tan consists of a joker face up in the center of a table. The corners of the

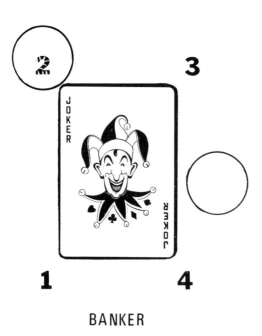

The Chinese Fantan layout.

joker are assigned numbers as follows: The left-hand corner nearest the banker is 1; the left-hand corner above that is 2; the right-hand corner away from the banker is 3; and the right-hand corner nearest the banker is 4.

Players place their bets, as many of them as the house agrees to cover. If a player places his bet exactly at a corner of the card, he bets on that number to win. If a player places his bet between two corners of the card, he bets on *either* number to win. In the illustration, one bet is on 2 and one is on both 3 and 4. A player does not have to place all his bets on one place, but can scatter them over the card.

Any player then shuffles the deck thoroughly and the banker cuts a large packet off the deck. He then begins to count off the cards in the packet in groups of four. When he can no longer count a complete set of four cards, the cards remaining determine the winning number. But, if he can count the cards exactly by fours, the winning number is four. *Example:* A packet of 21 cards leaves a winning number of 1; 22 cards, 2; 23 cards, 3; 24 cards, 4.

On bets placed exactly on a corner (on a single number), the banker pays 3 to 1. On bets placed between two numbers, the banker pays even money if either number wins. I think you can see why the game isn't played today in casinos; but it makes a good game for a large group at home.

YABLON

Also known as In-Between and Ace–Deuce, this is one of the fastest-betting private card games played today. It is a game that usually has only one winner at the end of a game session. If you value your card-playing cronies' friendship, make the minimum and maximum betting limits real small. Play it and you'll see the wisdom in this advice.

Requirements

1. A standard pack of 52 playing cards.

2. From two to eight (or more) players.

3. The deuce (two) is the lowest-ranking card and, in order of ascending value, the rest of the cards are the three, four, five, six, seven, eight, nine, ten, jack, queen, king, and ace (highest). The suits have no value.

Object of the Game. To win by being dealt one card from the pack on the draw whose rank will be in between two cards previously dealt to him. *Example:* The player holds a deuce and a four; only a three on the draw will win for the player. Should a player hold a three and ten, winning draw cards are four, five, six, seven, eight, and nine. There is no sure-win hand in Yablon. The best possible hand to hold in Yablon is a deuce and an ace—drawing a three, four, five, six, seven, eight, nine, ten, jack, queen, or king wins for the player; but being dealt a deuce or an ace loses for the player.

Selecting the Dealer. By mutual consent, any player may shuffle the pack; then he places it in the center of the table and any player may cut. The acting dealer squares the cut and deals one card face up to each player including himself, starting with the player at his left and rotating to the left, clockwise. This goes on until an ace is dealt; the player receiving it becomes the dealer.

On completion of each deal the deal rotates to the player at the dealer's left, and moves clockwise on the completion of each deal.

The Ante. Each player puts in the center of the table a like amount of money, forming a pool called the pot.

The Shuffle and Cut. The dealer shuffles the cards. Any player may call for the right to shuffle, but the dealer retains the privilege of shuffling last. The player to the dealer's right cuts, and at least three cards must be left to constitute each cut group of cards. Should the first player to the dealer's right decline the cut, the cards may be cut by any other player.

The Deal. After the cards have been cut the dealer, starting with the player at his left and dealing clockwise, deals each player including himself two cards face down one at a time.

The Betting. The player to the dealer's left has the first turn of play; thereafter, the turn moves to the left, clockwise, with the dealer playing last. Any player may bet (*a*) at least the amount of his ante, (*b*) the entire amount of the pot, or (*c*) any part thereof. *A note as to responsibility at Yablon:* It is up to the dealer to keep track of the bets.

The Draw. When a player, having examined his cards judiciously, has placed his bet—which he does by placing the amount bet, in cash, up close to the pot—the dealer deals the top card off the pack, and turns it face up on the table before the bettor whose turn of play it is. The player now turns his two cards face up on the table. If the numerical value of the dealt card falls in between the player's low and high card, he wins the bet and removes from the pot an amount equal to his bet. But, if the value of the dealt card does not fall in between the player's two cards, he loses his bet and puts his bet into the pot.

When all players including the dealer have had their turn of play, the deal passes to the player at the dealer's left. If any money remains in the pot at that point, there it stays—only now the players ante again to make it bigger. If the pot gets so big that the players are financially or morally unable to bet it, they may by mutual consent split it among them. Following the splitting of the pot, they ante anew.

Variation Applying to the Banker. The banker may put any amount of money he pleases into a pot before the deal, and each player in his turn may bet the pot or any part of it. If the pot is exhausted before the deal is completed, the deal passes to the player at the dealer's left. The players do not ante under this variation.

FINISH LINE

The layout for the Horse Race Game.

HORSE RACE

Rarely booked by casino management, this game is a favorite with card hustlers who like a muscular percentage on their side. The basic principle of the game has been pirated by some of the big game companies and adapted to board amusements for the general market. Horse fanciers get a special belt out of it, but it is fun for almost anybody—provided the stakes aren't allowed to get too big.

Requirements

1. A standard pack of 52 playing cards.
2. A banker and any number of players.

Value of Cards. Reversing the usual situation, the denomination of the cards has no relative merit at Horse Race; the values depend on suit only.

Selecting the Dealer. By mutual consent, any player shuffles the pack and puts it on the table to be cut by any other player. The acting dealer then deals each player, starting with the one at his immediate left and going clockwise, one card face up until a player is dealt an ace; that player becomes the first dealer and banker. Thereafter, on the completion of each deal (called a *race*), the deal and bank pass to the player at the dealer's left.

Object of the Game. To win the race—and your bet on it—by having six cards of your selected suit dealt from the pack before six cards of any other suit.

The Betting Limit. The banker establishes his own betting limits—the highest and lowest amount of cash any player can lay on the four suits. He may raise or lower the limits if he holds the bank more than one deal.

Preparation for Play. The banker-dealer extracts the four aces from the deck and puts them in front of him side by side in a straight starting line.

Shuffle and Cut. The dealer shuffles the deck. Any player may call for and must be allowed the right to shuffle at any time before the cut, but the dealer retains the privilege of shuffling last. After the shuffle the dealer puts the pack in the center of the table for any player to cut. If the players decline to cut, it is mandatory that the dealer do so.

The Deal. Now, in a straight line perpendicular to the edge of the table, the banker deals six cards, one at a time face up, about an inch apart. The line in which they lie is at right angles to the four lined-up aces, which are below and to one side of the six cards that indicate the distance of the race.

The Betting. It is up to the banker to declare his own odds depending on the suits of the six track cards—and here is where a little knowledge of arithmetic is handy. *Example:* Suppose the six cards are of one suit—clubs, let's say. Now there remain in the pack only six clubs as against twelve cards of each of the other suits. The six cards may be three spades and three diamonds—or any of fifteen different combinations. If one suit dominates the six cards, the banker may quote five to one on the ace horse of that suit and even money on the other three suits. It is absolutely within the banker's power to fix his own odds and, if any player doesn't like them, he just doesn't bet. Each player's bet is placed below the aces.

A banker may get six cards from *another* deck to place on the course as guides. Then he transfers four aces from that other deck to the deck in play. He is now dealing from a full 52-card deck, and the odds are corrected to 3 to 1 on any suit.

The Play. After the bets have been placed the banker then deals the cards from his hand one at a time face up. The ace of whatever suit he turns up is advanced one card length. When an ace reaches the finish line it wins, and the bets are paid off on that suit at the quoted odds.

BANKER AND BROKER

This game, which is also known as Dutch Bank and Blind Hookey, is a fast way to win or lose money.

Requirements

1. A standard pack of 52 playing cards.
2. Two or more players.

Rank of the Cards. Same as in Poker: ace (high), king, queen, jack, ten, nine, eight, seven, six, five, four, three, and deuce (low). The suits have no comparative value.

Object of the Game. To win a bet on a card that will turn out to have a higher value than the banker's card.

Selecting the Banker. The pack having been shuffled by any player by mutual consent, it is placed on the table and each player cuts a group of cards and exposes his bottom card. The player with the highest card becomes first banker. In case of a tie, the tied players cut again—and, if necessary, again, etc.

When, during play, a player has an ace he has bet on, that player becomes the next banker unless the banker also has an ace; in which case the banker retains possession of the bank. If more than one player has an ace, the tied players cut for the bank; the highest card cut wins the bank.

The Play. The banker establishes minimum and maximum betting limits. He then shuffles the cards. Any other player may claim and have the right to shuffle, but the banker can shuffle last.

The banker puts the deck in the center of the table to be cut by any player who wants to cut it. Having squared the cut deck, the banker removes the bottom card, and puts it to one side. (This card is dead, out of play; the move is precautionary, to safeguard

against any players seeing the bottom card.) The banker now cuts the deck into as many groups of cards as there are players in the game, plus one more group, provided the players do not exceed six. If they exceed six, the banker cuts seven groups of cards regardless. The groups are called *piles*.

After the piles are formed the bets are laid. Players may bet on one or more piles, but one pile must remain open (without a player's bet) and the open pile is designated the banker's. To make a bet, players put their money on or near the pile they have selected. All bets having been made, the banker then turns over his pile so that the bottom card is exposed. The rank of that card is the banker's score. If he turns an ace he collects all bets without turning over the players' cards; in this game the banker wins ties, and the top-ranking ace can't be beaten.

If the banker's card is any card other than the ace, he now turns over the first player's pile. Should the exposed card in that pile rank higher than the banker's card, the banker pays off at even money. Should the player's card rank even with or lower than the banker's, the banker wins and collects the bet. So it goes, pile by pile, around the table.

Advice to Players. Because the bank collects on ties at Banker and Broker, the percentage in its favor is 5 15/17. The player can reduce the odds against him by banking the game at his every opportunity.

ACE–DEUCE–JACK

This is strictly a card hustler's dream, which offers the player little or no chance of beating the game in the long run because of its high take of 10 10/17 percent for the operator. Card hustlers usually operate this game around race tracks and fair grounds.

Requirements

1. A standard pack of 52 playing cards. (The only cards having any value are the aces, deuces, and jacks. These 12 are the winning and losing cards. The other 40 have no value whatever, either as to rank or suit.)

2. A banker and one or more players.

Object of the Game. The banker or the players cut three piles of cards, as in Banker and Broker. The players then place bets that an ace, a deuce, or a jack will not appear at the bottom of any pile.

The Limit. The banker hustler establishes betting limits. I should say the average runs from a minimum of $5 to a maximum of $200. But the banker is boss.

The Shuffle and Deal. The banker shuffles the deck. Any player may call for a shuffle at any time before the cut, but the banker retains the right to shuffle last. The banker then puts the deck in the center of the table to be cut by any player.

After the cut has been carried, the banker removes three cards from the bottom of the deck, and puts them to one side. He must take scrupulous care that these cards are not seen by any player. These three are dead cards; they cannot enter into the play of the hand.

The Play. The banker now cuts two groups

of cards from the squared deck, making in all three piles of cards. Each player may now lay, within the limits, a bet that the bottom card of any of the three piles is not an ace, deuce, or jack.

After the bets have been placed the banker proceeds to turn up the piles so that the bottom card of each is exposed. If no ace, deuce, or jack shows as a bottom card of any pile, the bank loses, and must pay off all bets. If the bottom card of any of the three piles does happen to be an ace, deuce, or jack, the bank wins all bets. No bonuses are paid. It is important to remember that even when more than one winning card turns up, the payoff is one for one, even.

RED DOG

Red Dog or High Card Pool was one of the most popular fast-action card games played by servicemen during World War II, surpassed only by Black Jack. It is an occupational disease with newspapermen, the origin of some great city-room anecdotes, and at least a sure-fire short story plot.

Requirements

1. From two to eight players.
2. A standard pack of 52 playing cards.

Rank of the Cards. Exactly as in Poker: deuce (low) three, four, five, six, seven, eight, nine, ten, jack, queen, king, and ace (high). The suits have no value relative to each other.

Object of the Game. To win by holding in the hand a card of the same suit but higher in rank than the card dealt from the pack on the draw.

Selecting the Dealer. By mutual consent any player may shuffle the pack; then he places it in the center of the table and any player may cut. The acting dealer squares the cut, and deals one card face up to each player including himself, starting with the player at his left and rotating to the left, clockwise. This goes on until the ace is dealt; the player receiving it becomes the dealer. On the completion of each deal, the deal rotates to the player at the dealer's left; it moves clockwise on the completion of each deal.

The Ante. Each player puts in the center of the table a like amount of money, forming a pool called the pot.

The Shuffle and Cut. The dealer shuffles the cards. Any player may call for the right to shuffle, but the dealer retains the privilege of shuffling last. The player to the dealer's right cuts, and at least three cards must be left to constitute each cut group of cards. Should the first player to the dealer's right decline the cut, the cards may be cut by any other player.

The Deal. After the cards have been cut, the dealer, starting with the player at the left and dealing clockwise, deals each player four cards face down one at a time.

The Betting. The player to the dealer's left has the first turn of play; thereafter the turn moves to the left, clockwise. Any player may bet (a) at least the amount of his ante, (b) the entire amount of the pot, or (c) any part thereof. *A note as to responsibility:* It is up to the dealer to keep track of the bets.

The Draw. When a player, having examined his cards judiciously, has placed his bet—which he does by placing the amount bet, in cash, up close to the pot—the dealer deals the top card off the pack, and turns it face up on the table before the bettor whose turn of play it is. Now, if the bettor holds a card of the same suit as the dealt card but of higher numerical value or rank, he wins the bet; the dealer removes from the pot for him an amount equivalent to that player's bet.

But if he does not hold a higher card of the same suit as the dealt card, he loses the bet, and the dealer sweeps his bet into the pot.

When all players, including the dealer, have had their turn of play, the deal passes to the player at the dealer's left. If any money remains in the pot at that point, there it stays—only now the players ante again to make it bigger. If the pot gets so big that the players are financially or morally unable to bet it, they may by mutual consent split it among them. Thereupon they ante anew.

Variation Applying to the Banker. The banker may put any amount of money he pleases into a pot before the deal, and each player in his turn may bet the pot or any part of it. If the pot is exhausted before the deal is completed, the deal passes to the player at the dealer's left. The players do not ante under this variation.

The Percentage at Red Dog. Because he plays last and gets the last card, the percentage favors the dealer at Red Dog. He has seen several exposed cards played, and this factor is a great advantage. To take a rather extreme example—but an example familiar to every experienced Red Dog fancier—let's say the dealer holds the aces of spades, diamonds, and clubs, plus the king of hearts. Only one card in the deck can beat him. That card is the ace of hearts. Any other player in the game holding this hand—say, the first player —knows that his hand is almost certain to win if he bets the pot, even though that pot totals the entire United States public debt. But he can't be sure. On the other hand, the dealer, having seen a fairly wide assortment of faced cards, plus a few discarded hands, has had a fair chance to see the ace of hearts actually exposed and out of the way. He can bet the whole pot with absolute certainty that he can't be beaten. As mentioned, this is a rather extreme example. But it applies consistently. Holding a hand of jacks, a dealer who has seen a batch of higher court cards exposed can take and win hazards that would be foolhardy for any other player.

Strategy at Red Dog. The only decision you have to make is how much to bet. This depends almost entirely on how good your hand is. Add up the value of the cards in your hand. Count the ace as 14, king as 13, queen, 12, jack, 11, and the spot cards as their numerical value; count only the highest card in any one suit. If you hold four deuces, your total is 8. With such a hand you cannot win. If you held four aces your count would be 56 and you couldn't lose. If your hand adds to 32 you have an even chance of winning. Upon this calculation a player may decide how much he desires to bet.

Six-Spot Red Dog

This fine variation of Red Dog, which is also called Slippery Sam, is popular in Fort Wayne and various other sections of Indiana. The rules for Red Dog apply with the following exceptions:

The Pot. The dealer, also called the banker, puts into the center of the table any amount (pot) he alone decides. Or at least a minimum amount agreed upon by the players at the start of game. Players do not ante.

The Deal. The banker deals three cards face down to each player, beginning on his

left. Then he turns one card face up on the table in front of himself.

The Betting. The player, before looking at his hand (three cards), may bet the entire pot or any part thereof. Or, he may refuse to bet against the banker's upturned card and may say "Deal me another card," which is a request that the dealer discard the upturned card and deal a second card from the top of the deck onto the table face up. For this privilege the player must ante into the pot an amount equal to one-fifth the sum in the pot—or an amount agreed upon by all players at the start of the game. The player is limited to three such cards, naturally paying for the privilege each time. After paying for the third upcard, the player may either bet or pass his turn of betting. The same procedure takes place between banker and player in a clockwise fashion around the table.

After each player has had his turn of play or the pot is exhausted, the bank and deal moves to the player at the dealer's left.

Polish Red Dog

This game, which is also known as Stitch and Polski Rachuck, is generally believed to be of Polish origin. The basic rules of Red Dog apply with the following exceptions:

The Pot. The dealer, also called the banker, puts into the center of the table any amount (pot) he alone decides. Or at least a minimum amount agreed upon by the players at the start of game. Players do not ante.

The Deal. The banker deals three cards face down to each player—one at a time per round—beginning on his left. He takes no cards for himself.

The Betting and Play. Beginning with the player at his left, the banker asks what that player will bet. The player may bet any sum up to one-half the bank. Banker then burns the top card of the deck—places it face up on the bottom of the deck—and turns up the next card of the deck. The player then turns up his own cards. If any one of them is higher and in the same suit as the turned-up card of the deck, he collects twice the amount of his bet from the bank. If he has no higher card in the same suit, he puts his bet into the bank.

This process is repeated for each player in turn, the player always being permitted to make a bet up to one-half the amount in the bank. This amount, of course, varies in size from player to player. But the banker *must* always burn a card before turning up one for a player.

After the round has been completed, if the bank has not been busted (cleaned out by a player), the same banker continues to deal. But if at any time the bank is busted, the turn to be banker passes to the next player at the left. If, at the end of a round, the bank has increased to at least three times its original size, the banker declares what is known as a *stitch round*. That means he will deal just one more round—at the expiration of which he will collect whatever the bank contains, if it has not been exhausted. The turn to be banker will then pass to the next player at the left. The banker may not pass the turn to be banker until a stitch round has been declared and completed. The banker must continue play until either the bank is busted or a stitch round has been completed.

CARD CRAPS

The creation of Card Craps was the answer to the prayers of gamblers and operators in towns where crapshooting is forbidden by the local police, although card games are not molested. This game is crapshooting with playing cards. I know the gamblers who created the game; indeed I was a witness to the first Card Craps game ever operated, in the Horseshoe district of craps-banning Jersey City early in the spring of 1945. At that time the professionals couldn't calculate the correct percentage on the bets they were handling; so they came to me for advice on the odds. I wrote and published a small monograph on the game. It appears to have had some esteem in the trade; at least now, early in 1972, gambling establishments are featuring Card Craps in cities where local moralities and police will positively not let a low dice game run.

The present game has been so evolved that if the specified rules, methods of play, and betting odds are scrupulously followed, the *right* and *wrong* bettors each will have an equal chance of winning. There is one exception: The *center* bet has a 1.21 percent advantage for the fader. This is perceptible improvement on the 1.41 percent for this bet at craps with dice; the shooter's and the fader's chances at Card Craps are .20 percent nearer even on this bet. In the long run such a factor, infinitesimal as it may seem on paper, can add up to a good pocketful of cash.

Requirements

1. A special deck of dice cards consisting of 48 cards. There are two each in all four suits of the aces, deuces, threes, fours, fives, and sixes. That is, there must be eight cards of each denomination. A complete deck must be used at all times.

2. A set of chips or other objects to be used as markers. Each player at the start of the game gets—by buying them, of course—an equal number of markers. The winner is the player who, at the game's end, has the most chips.

Players

1. Any number may play.

2. The player who deals the cards is called the *shooter*.

3. Any player may, by consent of the others or by any method of choice they elect, start the game by becoming the shooter. A new player may enter the game any time there is an opening at the table. The deal moves around the table to the left, clockwise.

Shuffle and Cut. The shooter shuffles the pack. Any other player may call for the shuffle at any time before the cards are cut. The shooter has the right to shuffle last. The cards are then offered to the player at the shooter's left to be cut. Any other player may demand and have the right to cut, but the player at the shooter's left retains the right to cut last if he wants to. If he declines to cut, then some other player must cut.

The Play or Deal. The shooter deals off the top of the deck two cards face up onto the playing surface, one at a time. The numerical values of these two cards are added to form a deciding number (just as the top-surface numbers on two dice are added). Any combination of two cards dealt by the shooter is called a *throw*.

The first throw of the cards starting any new decision is called a *come-out*. The two cards of each come-out throw must be returned to the pack for the new deal, regardless of whether the come-out throw is a crap (2, 3, or 12), a natural (7 or 11), or a point number (4, 5, 6, 8, 9, or 10). *Note:* It is critically important that the above rule be faithfully obeyed. Failure to obey it will corrupt the mathematical possibilities and derange the betting odds.

If on the first throw the shooter deals a natural 7 or 11, it is a winning decision called a *pass*. If he deals a crap 2, 3, or 12, it is a losing decision called a *miss-out*. If he deals a 4, 5, 6, 8, 9, or 10, then that number becomes the shooter's point. The two dealt cards are then shuffled back into the pack, which then must be cut, and the shooter continues dealing the cards in pairs until he (*a*) throws his point, which is a winning decision (pass); (*b*) throws a 7, which is a losing decision (miss-out); or (*c*) exhausts the entire pack without getting a decision; in which case the pack is reshuffled and cut and the shooter continues dealing.

When by throwing a 7 the shooter misses out on the point, the cards pass to the player at the shooter's left, and it becomes his turn to shoot. The shooter may, if he likes, pass the cards to the next player on completion of any winning decision, without waiting to miss out on the point. Any player may, if he wishes, refuse to shoot in his turn, and may pass the cards to the player next to his own left.

When two decks are available, players may call for and have a change of packs, the exchange taking place immediately before the next succeeding deal.

Betting. The contribution of markers to a pool by the players is called betting. Here are various bets available:

1. *Right bet.* This is a bet that the shooter will pass (win either by throwing a natural on the come-out, or by throwing a point on the come-out and then repeating the point before throwing a 7).

2. *Wrong Bet.* This is a bet that the shooter won't pass.

3. *Center Bet.* Before the come-out, the shooter may (but he is not required to) bet that he will pass. Players who cover this bet by betting an equal amount against the shooter *fade* the shooter, and are known as *faders*. Their bets, placed in the center of the playing surface, are *center bets*.

4. *No Bet.* If only a part of the shooter's center bet is covered, he may shoot for that amount; or he may call off the bet by saying "No bet!"

5. *Side Bet.* Any bet not a center bet is a side bet. The player may make any side bet, including the following:

6. *Flat Bet.* This is a side bet made before the come-out that the shooter does pass (wins) or doesn't pass (loses). It is the same as a center bet, except that the shooter is not being faded and the bet is being placed at the side.

7. *Point Bet.* A bet made by a right bettor, after the shooter has thrown a point on the come-out, that the shooter makes his point is a *right-point bet*. A bet by a wrong bettor that the shooter misses his point is a *wrong-point bet*. The right bettor takes the odds on that point; the wrong bettor lays the odds on that point.

8. *Double Hardway.* Making a point the double hardway consists in making any of the even point numbers (4, 6, 8, or 10) with duplicate or paired cards. For example, making the point 4 with two deuces of spades, or with any two deuces of the same suit is making 4 the double hardway.

The Betting Odds. The odds against passing on the center or flat bet are even money, one to one.

ODDS AGAINST PASSING ON THE POINTS

Point	Correct Odds	Exceptions
4	2 to 1	(Except when thrown the double hardway, in which case the wrong bettor must pay off at four to one)
10	2 to 1	
5	3 to 2	
9	3 to 2	
6	6 to 5	(Except when thrown the double hardway, in which case the wrong bettor must pay off at twelve to five)
8	6 to 5	

The double payoff on the point numbers 4, 6, 8, and 10, when made the double hardway, serves to equalize the right and wrong bettors' chances of winning a point bet on the even point numbers.

For Larger Groups. When a relatively large number of players want to get into the game, I recommend that a deck of 72 cards be used. This deck is made up of three each in all four suits of the aces, deuces, threes, fours, fives, and sixes. The odds remain the same as with the 48-card deck, except for the payoff on the double hardway. The point 4 or the point 10 made the double hardway pays off at three to one on point bets in the 72-card deck. The point 6 or the point 8 made the double hard-way pays off at nine to five.

The Book at Card Craps. The *book,* who is a man, not a bound document, works the same at Card Craps as at Open Craps. That is, he takes win or lose bets, accommodating all comers, and for this banking service he collects a charge called *vigorish.* Some books charge more than others, but we shall deal here with the average nation-wide practice. As a general rule, most books charge 5 percent of the bet; while some charge 3 percent of the bet and pick it up on right and wrong action alike.

Following in tabular form are the correct percentages against the players for both 5 percent and 3 percent charges.

A word of advice: Any man playing in a private game of Card Craps—that is, a game without benefit of book—by accepting the correct odds and shooting no more often than the other players, has as healthy a chance of winning as anybody else at the table. Temperament and the degree of understanding of the game's nature will, of course, make some difference; but, granted these are equal, the chances are equal. But if you play in a good game and consistently bet the book, you must and will go broke eventually. No system, no lucky streak, can beat the percentages.

1. CORRECT VIGORISH ON THE ODDS WAGERS WHEN THE BOOK PICKS UP THE 5 PERCENT CHARGE BOTH WAYS

Right Bettor Pays — 4.761+percent, or about 25¢ when taking $5 worth of odds on any point number.

Wrong Bettor Pays — 2.439+percent, or about 12¢ when laying odds of $10 to $5 on point number 4 or 10.
3.225+percent, or about 15¢ when laying odds of $7.50 to $5 on point number 5 or 9.
4.000+percent, or 20¢ when laying odds of $6 to $5 on point number 6 or 8.

2. CORRECT VIGORISH WHEN THE BOOK PICKS UP THE 3 PERCENT CHARGE BOTH WAYS

Right Bettor Pays — 2.912+percent, or about 15¢ when taking $5 worth of odds on any point number.

Wrong Bettor Pays — 1.477+percent, or about 7¢ when laying odds of $10 to $5 on point number 4 or 10.
1.960+percent, or about 10¢ when laying odds of $7.50 to $5 on point number 5 or 9.
2.439+percent, or about 12¢ when laying odds of $6 to $5 on point number 6 or 8.

PUT AND TAKE

This game is a fascinating combination of Red Dog and the kind of Put and Take normally played with a spinning top or with dice. In some parts of the country, this game is called Up and Down the River.

Requirements
1. A standard pack of 52 playing cards.
2. From two to eight players.

Selecting the Banker. The player cutting high card becomes the banker (dealer). On completion of a deal, the bank rotates to the player at the dealer's left.

The Deal. The banker deals each player excluding himself five cards, one at a time, starting with the player to his left and rotating clockwise.

The Betting Limit. The value of the betting unit is fixed by mutual consent. Bets consist of from one to 16 units, as prescribed by the rules of the game.

Putting and Taking
1. *Putting units into the pot.* The banker gives himself five cards, as described below, and the players ante into the pot as specified, card by card:
   a. The banker gives himself one card face up on the table. Each player holding a card of the same denomination as that card must put one betting unit into the pot—one for each card he has of that rank.
   b. The banker's second card calls for two units from each player for each card he has of that rank.
   c. The banker's third card calls for four units.
   d. The fourth requires eight units.
   e. The fifth requires 16 units.
2. *Taking units out of the pot.* The banker now picks up his five cards, places them face

up on the bottom of the pack, and deals himself, off the top of the pack, five more cards, one at a time. But this time, each player *takes* on the first card one unit from the pot for each card he holds of the same denomination as the banker's. And he gets two on the second card, four on the third, eight on the fourth, and 16 on the fifth. Any units remaining in the pot at the end of the play go outright to the banker. If the pot owes any player or players money, the banker must cover its deficit out of his pocket.

Red and Black Variation. Some players have speeded up the game with this variation: Any player holding three or more cards the same color as the dealer's (first) card must put one unit into the pot. On the second card the three-card holder's ante is two units; on the third, three; on the fourth, four; and on the fifth, five. They take out at the same rate on the dealer's second (take) turn of play.

THIRTY-FIVE

This is one of the more popular private banking games in which the deal rotates from player to player. It is a modern adoption of the old Italian game of Trenta-Cinque.

Requirements

1. A standard pack of 52 playing cards.
2. From two to five players.

Value of the Cards. The court cards—kings, queens, and jacks—count 10 points; all other cards have their face value: ace, 1; deuce, 2; and so on.

Object of the Game. To win by having in the hand a card count of 35 or more in one suit. *Example:* Among the cards in his hand the player holds the following clubs: ace, queen, jack, ten, and five. These cards' value totals 36. The player wins his bet.

Selecting the First Dealer. Any player by mutual consent having shuffled the cards and put the deck face down on the table, each player cuts a group of cards. That player cutting the highest-ranking card becomes first dealer. In case of a tie for high, the tied players cut again, and again, to a decision. Thereafter, the deal passes to the player on the dealer's left; on the completion of each deal, it moves to the left around the table, clockwise.

The Ante. Each player antes in the center of the table a sum of chips mutually agreed upon; this becomes the pot.

The Shuffle. The dealer shuffles the cards. Any player may ask for and have the right to shuffle, but the dealer can shuffle last. The player to the dealer's right should cut the cards; but, if he declines, the player to *his* right may cut them. If all other players refuse to cut, the dealer must cut. The cut must be such that there are at least five cards in each cut group.

The Deal. To each player including himself the dealer gives one card face down, starting with the player to his left and dealing clockwise. He deals the next card face down in the center of the table. This he repeats, until each player has four cards and there are four cards face down on the table. The latter four cards are called the *buy.* Thereafter, each player is dealt a face-down card in turn until all hands have nine cards each; but no more cards are dealt onto the table; and the rest of the cards are set aside. They are dead. They do not enter into the subsequent play.

Taking the Buy. The bidding starts now. The player to the dealer's left makes his bid for the buy. The bid may be any part or the whole amount of the pot. The man to the first player's left now has his turn to bid. He may:

1. Decline to make a higher bid than the first player, in which case he passes by throwing his nine cards aside. They're dead.
2. Raise the bid. That's all there is to this; he just bids more money for the buy.

So it goes, around the table, until one player is identified as the highest bidder. This player discards four cards from his hand, and takes the four cards in the buy.

The Payoff. The Payoff is as follows:

1. If this player holds a card count of 35 or more in one suit, he takes out of the pot an amount of cash equal to his bid. (*Note:* If the bid is more than the amount in the pot, he takes the pot only; there is no assessment against the other players.)
2. Should he hold a count of 34 or less, he must put the amount of his bid into the pot.
3. If a player at the very outset is dealt a count of 35 or more, he announces it then and there, and takes the pot. If more than one player is dealt a count of 35 or more, the tied players divide the pot equally.

The players may, at the start of the game,

establish a maximum tolerable limit on the pot. If during play the pot is swollen beyond that maximum, it is divided equally among all players.

LOTTERY

This is one of the real old-time banking games, but it is still played by many, and is very well suited to large groups.

Requirements

1. Any number from five up.

2. Two regular 52-card decks.

Value of the Cards. The cards and suits have no comparative rank.

Selecting the Dealer. By mutual consent any player may shuffle the pack; then he places it in the center of the table and any player may cut. The acting dealer squares the cut and deals one card face up to each player including himself, starting with the player at his left, and rotating to the left, clockwise. This goes on until an ace is dealt; the player receiving it becomes the dealer. On completion of each deal the deal rotates to the player at the dealer's left, and moves clockwise on the completion of each deal.

The Ante. Each player antes in the center of the table a sum of chips mutually agreed upon; this becomes the pot.

The Deal and Play. The two decks are kept separated at all times. After both decks have been shuffled and cut, the dealer selects one of them and deals each player a card face down. Then, from the second deck, he deals one card to each player face up. Each player then turns up his downcard, and if it matches any face-up card on the table in denomi-

nation, he collects the chips in the pot. (If there are two or more winners on one card, they divide the chips equally.) If his card also matches some face-up card in color as well as denomination, he collects an extra chip from the player who has that card. If a player's downcard matches his own upcard, he collects his own stake as well as the stake in front of any other face-up card he matches; besides that, each player in the game pays him an extra chip. The chips are then gathered for another deal. Any stake in front of a player, which has not been collected, remains there for the next deal. But each player must ante a new stake for the next deal.

Variations. Here are two variations of Lottery:

1. In one variation, each player may be dealt two, three, or even more cards face down. Each player is then dealt two, three, or more cards face up. He places an ante on each card separately. The downcards are then turned up, and the players collect on matching cards as in regular Lottery.

2. The game also may be played with a single deck when there are but a few players. The deck is divided into two 24-card sections, each containing one red and one black suit. First one section is dealt for downcards, then the other section is dealt for upcards.

BANGO

A little like Bingo, a little like the old poker-solitaire game of Lotto, this one has always been an attractive pastime. I've taken some bugs out of the rules to make the game mathematically sound.

Requirements

1. Two ordinary 52-card decks having different backs.

2. From two to ten players.

Object of the Game. To go *bango* by—in accordance with the rules—turning five face-up cards face down.

Selecting the Dealer. By mutual consent any player shuffles one pack of cards, which

is cut by any other player. The acting dealer gives each player one card at a time face up, starting to the player at his left and dealing clockwise, until a player is dealt an ace. This player becomes the first dealer; on the completion of each deal the deal passes, clockwise, to the player at the dealer's immediate left.

The Deal. The dealer and the player at his left each shuffles one pack of cards and the dealer offers his deck to the player at his right for the cut. (If that player declines the cut, the dealer must cut.) Then to each player the dealer deals five cards one at a time, starting with the man at his left and dealing clockwise. The remainder of the cards are set aside, dead, out of play. The players turn their five cards face up in front of them. The dealer takes the pack that the player to his left has shuffled, cuts them, and is ready for the play.

Play of the Hand. Each player antes into the pot an equal amount of chips previously agreed upon. Then the dealer turns face up on the table the top card of the deck, announcing its numerical value and suit. Any player having before him a card of the same denomination and suit turns that card face down.

The dealer goes on exposing and announcing the cards until some player has turned his five cards face down. That is bango, the player says so, and he wins the pot. After a player has declared himself bango, it is conventional in this game—and no reflection on the player's integrity—for the dealer to examine first the player's cards and then the face-up stack of dealt cards to certify the correctness of the claim.

THIRTY-ONE

This game is often called Schnautz.

Requirements

1. Any number may play, but four or more make the best game.

2. A regular 52-card deck is used.

Rank of the Cards. Cards rank as follows: ace (high), king, queen, jack, ten, nine, eight, seven, six, five, four, three, two (low). Cards count: ace, 11; king, queen, jack, 10; all other cards, their face value.

Beginning of the Game. The selection of the dealer, seating positions, changing seats, shuffle, and cut are as provided under the General Rules for Card Games, chapter 1.

The Deal. The players cut and low cut deals. Each player is dealt three cards, one at a time, per round. Three cards are also dealt face up, one after each round. These cards are dealt in the middle of the table and constitute an open widow or blind. The turn to deal in subsequent hands goes to the left.

Object of the Game. To obtain a hand whose count totals 31 in cards of one suit. Or to have a hand at the showdown whose count in one suit is higher than any other player's.

The Ante and Play. Before play begins, each player antes an equal amount into the pot.

Play begins with the player at the dealer's left. He may exchange a card from his hand for any card in the widow, leaving his own card face up in its stead. Some players permit the exchange of two cards or even three. The turn to exchange in similar fashion goes around the table to the left. This procedure continues in clockwise rotation until some player knocks to indicate that he is satisfied. Then all hands are shown and compared, and the player with the highest count in cards of the same suit is the winner of the pot. If there is a tie in the count between two or more players, the player with the highest-ranking card wins. If there is a tie in the highest cards, the next highest are compared and so on.

A player may knock at any time, even before the exchanging of cards begins. If a player knocks after exchanging has begun, the other players following him in turn are allowed to exchange cards. At any time that a player holds 31, he simply exposes his hand and collects the pot without further delay.

TRENTE ET QUARANTE

Also known as Rouge et Noir (red and black), this game is a standard European casino banking card game and is most popular in French and Italian casinos including the world famous Monte Carlo Casino. Actually, its popularity is only surpassed by Baccarat and Roulette. The name Trente et Quarante (thirty and forty) is derived from

the fact that the winning point always lies between these two numbers.

Requirements

1. A regulation Trente et Quarante table with a double layout. See the illustration showing one-half of the Trente et Quarante layout.

2. Any number of persons can play against

the bank, as many as can be accommodated at the gaming table.

3. Five croupiers. Four serve as banker and one as dealer (tailleur) and count caller. A supervisor sits on a stand overlooking the Trente et Quarante table to see that no errors are committed.

4. Six standard packs of 52-cards each, shuffled together and used as one, a total of 312 cards dealt as a single deck.

Value of Cards. The ace is the lowest-ranking card and has a point value of 1. Kings, queens, and jacks have a value of 10 each. All other cards have their numerical face value. Deuce is counted 2, three is counted 3, etc. Suits have no value. Only colors count; hearts and diamonds are called red; spades and clubs are called black.

The Shuffle and Cut. At the start of each round of play, the dealer (croupier) spreads the six packs of cards on the table and all players and croupiers are permitted to take a group of cards and shuffle them. On later deals, when the discard receivers are emptied onto the layout and some cards are face up and some are face down, the croupier and players turn the face-up cards down and shuffle them.

After the players have shuffled groups of cards, the croupier then gathers all the cards and shuffles them together, usually shuffling about two packs at a time. Finally, the croupier assembles all six packs together and then hands a player an indicator card and says "Cut, please." The player inserts the indicator card into the packet to show where he wants the cards cut. The dealer cuts the cards at this position, putting the indicator and all the cards above it on the bottom.

Object of the Game. To bet that a specific color (black or red) will produce a count of 31 or a total nearer to 31 than the opposite color. The player may also place his bet on *rouge* (red), *noir* (black), couleur, or inverse.

The Play. All betting is done against the casino or bank. Before the deal begins, the players place their bets. The dealer takes about 50 cards off the top of the pack and deals out the first card face upward onto the noir (black). He then deals a second, a third, etc., which he places in the same row, right and left, announcing the cumulative total of the spots with each card dealt. The dealing stops with the card which causes the total to reach or exceed 31. The second row, rouge (red) is dealt below the first and in the same manner.

The row with the total nearer to 31 is the winning row. For example, a bet on noir wins if the count of the first or noir row is 34 while the rouge row totals 36. A bet on *couleur* wins if the very first card dealt is the same color as that designating the winning row. If this card is of the opposite color, a bet on *inverse* wins. The dealer traditionally announces the result for red and color only, calling "rouge gagne" (wins) or "rouge perd" (loses) or "couleur perd." All bets are paid off at even money (1 to 1).

If both rows total the same count (tie), it is called a *refait* and all bets are called off. If there is a refait at 31—refait de trente et un—the bank takes half of all bets. In such

Diagram showing half of Trente-et-Quarante table layout. N = Noire; C = Couleur; R = Rouge; I = Inverse; D = Dealer; CR = Croupier; and P = Prison.

cases, however, the player has the option of leaving his bet in *prison,* where it remains for the next game or coup. If he wins on this coup, he withdraws his bet; but if he loses, he loses the whole.

As bets are settled, the cards dealt for that coup are brushed into the discard receiver. When there are insufficient cards for the next coup all the cards are reshuffled.

Refait Insurance Bet. Before the cards are dealt, players may insure their bets against a possible loss of half their bets when a refait at 31 takes place. The insurance charge is 5 percent of the amount wagered.

Probabilities. Of the ten numbers that fall from 31 to 40, the number 31 appears more often than any other number.

Number	Times	Number	Times
31	13	36	8
32	12	37	7
33	11	38	6
34	10	39	5
35	9	40	4

Our mathematics informs us that a refait (tie) of 31 will happen about once in 41 dealt hands of play, which is about 1 1/2 percent when the bank takes 50 percent of each player's bet when a standoff of 31 occurs.

Thirty and Forty

This is an adaptation of Trente et Quarante for private use.

Requirements

1. Any number can play.

2. Three regular 52-card decks, shuffled together. An ace of spades and an ace of diamonds are removed from the decks and are placed face up in the middle of the table—well separated from each other.

Card Count. The cards of the deck have the following count: picture cards, 10; ace, 1; other cards, their face value.

The Deal and Play. A banker is selected by cut or by some other suitable method. The banker, after a shuffle and a cut, places the deck face down in front of him. Players then make their bets. They bet on the ace of diamonds (red) or on the ace of spades (black), the limits of the bets being determined by the banker.

The banker then turns up cards one by one. The first color he turns up is for *black.* He counts the total value of the cards aloud. When he reaches exactly 31, or passes it, he stops. He then begins to turn up new cards for *red,* again stopping when he reaches 31, or passes it. Whichever is closest to 31, red or black, is the winner; the banker pays off even money for bets placed on the ace of the winning color. Ties are handled the same way as in Trente et Quarante—casino style.

The cards counted off are put aside face down. The next deal is then continued from the remainder of the deck without a shuffle. When an insufficient number of cards are left for counting off, all cards are reshuffled. The method of passing the bank must be decided on by the players before the start of the game.

Red and Black

This is a very simple variation of Thirty and Forty in which each player makes a bet of any size, up to the limit established by the banker, on red or black. After the bets are placed, the banker deals each player five cards face up, one at a time, beginning with the player on his left. The payoff is at even money; the player wins if he named black and has three or more black cards; he wins if he named red and has three or more red cards; he loses if he fails to name the dominant color. If his first four cards are two black and two red, he may double his bet before receiving his final (fifth) card.

Other variations include a provision that four of the color named collect double for the player; four of the opposite color pay double to the banker; five either way collect or pay quadruple.

CHAPTER 17

The Stops Games

Stops is the name given to a whole family of games, grouped together because they are based on the following principles: A player holding specified eligible card or cards, when his turn comes, may play. Otherwise, he is "stopped" and the turn to play passes to the next player. The first to play off all his cards is the winner.

MICHIGAN

This game, which is also called Newmarket, Chicago, Michigan Boodle, and Saratoga, is the most popular of the Stops family and is ideal for groups in which there is no acceptable game known to all members; a novice can play the game after a brief explanation.

Requirements

1. Three to eight players.

2. A regular 52-card deck. The cards rank in this order; ace (high), king, queen, jack, ten, nine, eight, seven, six, five, four, three, two (low).

3. From another pack the following four cards are removed: ace of hearts, king of clubs, queen of diamonds, and jack of spades. These, known as "boodle" or money cards, are placed face up in the center of the table where they remain throughout the entire session.

4. Each player receives an equal number of chips or counters, and before every deal each player places one chip on each money card.

Object of the Game. To play a card corresponding to a money card and so collect the chips on it; to be the first player to play all of his cards.

The Deal. Players cut for the deal; the highest card cut deals the first hand. Thereafter the deal rotates to the left.

All cards are dealt out, one at a time in a clockwise rotation (left) and as though an extra hand were in the game. *Example:* If five are playing, six card hands are dealt out. The extra hand, or widow, is at the dealer's left and is the first hand dealt to. It does not matter if, owing to the number of players, the pack does not divide evenly.

Beginning of the Game. The selection of the dealer, seating positions, changing seats, shuffle, and cut are as provided under the General Rules for Card Games, chapter 1.

Exchanging for the Widow or Extra Hand. After dealer looks at his hand, he may exchange it for the widow if he desires. If he makes the exchange, he places his original hand face down on the table without showing it to the other players and picks up the widow. If he decides to keep his original hand, he must auction off the right to exchange the widow to the highest bidder among the other players. Dealer collects the amount of the chips of the highest bid. In either case, once an exchange has been made for the widow, there can be no further exchanges. That is, once having made an exchange, a player may not take back his original hand. The face-down hand is not used in play.

The Play. Player at dealer's left begins by putting face up on the table his lowest card of any suit he chooses. It need not be any particular suit, but it must be the lowest card he holds in that suit. If he holds any card, or cards, in next higher rank, he may continue to play. When he can no longer play, the turn passes to any player who can continue to build up on the suit, playing one card or more. *Example:* If the first card played is the four of clubs, the next card played is the five of clubs, then the six of clubs, etc.

As a player plays a card, he announces its denomination and suit. When the ace is reached in building up a suit, or when no one can play an eligible card on a suit (because the missing card happens to be in the face-down hand), it is a "stop." The one who played the last card may now lead the lowest card he holds in some other suit, announcing the suit and denomination of the new card. If he cannot change the suit, the turn to play passes to his left. If it should happen that no player can begin a new suit, the turn comes back to the original passer, who then may play the lowest card in his hand. Each player plays his cards in a pile before himself. It is not permitted to spread a pile to inspect played cards.

When a player plays a card that duplicates a money card, he takes all the chips on that card. If a money card is not cleared in one deal, the chips remain on it until duly won. But before the next deal the players must put new chips on the money cards as previously described.

Play ends when any player goes out by getting rid of all his cards. The winner collects a chip from each other player for every card that player has left in his hand.

Additional Rules. For failing to play properly in his turn, the player pays a penalty of one chip to each of the others. If in not playing properly in his turn a player keeps someone from winning boodle chips, the offender must make good the loss, but the chips on the boodle card are carried over to the following deal.

Strategy. Whether to take or bid for the widow or extra hand depends, to a great extent, on whether or not your hand contains a money card and if it contains a better-than-average number of face cards and aces. Remember that a hand with high cards has a good chance of going out.

In addition to giving the possibility of a better hand and money cards, the purchase of the widow gives a player complete knowledge of the stops in the dead hand. This can be used to great advantage during play.

In early play, always lead the longest suit in the hand. Of course, if you have a money card, it is sometimes best to lead its suit at every opportunity.

Cross-Color Michigan

Follow the rules of Michigan except as follows:

When a stop has occurred, a player may only start a new suit in a different color from the last one played. *Example:* Only a spade or club may follow a heart; a diamond may not because it is the same color as the heart.

Sequence Michigan

Follow the rules of Michigan except as follows:

There is an extra money-card sequence consisting of the nine, ten, and jack of hearts. A player who holds and plays two cards of this sequence in consecutive order, for example, ten then jack, collects all the chips on the sequence. New chips are added in each deal, whether the boodle chips are won or not.

Jackpot Michigan

Follow the rules of Michigan except as follows:

A jackpot is established by having each player ante one chip to a special pool on each hand of a complete round of dealing. When the deal returns to dealer, who started the round, the winner of that hand receives the extra bonus of the jackpot. In other words, the dealer who started the jackpot is the one who deals it off.

Boodle

Follow the rules of Michigan except as follows:

1. The money or boodle cards are: ace of

hearts, king of diamonds, queen of spades, and jack of clubs.

2. Before the deal, each player may place his four chips on the money cards as he pleases, all on one card or some on all, etc.

3. The deck is dealt in equal hands to the players, leaving three or more cards for a widow in the following manner:

Players	Each Receives	Widow
3	15	7
4	12	4
5	9	7
6	8	4
7	7	3
8	6	4

4. The widow cannot be exchanged or purchased, and it is set aside, face down, as a dead hand to create stops.

Spinade or Spin

Follow all the rules of Boodle except that a player who holds the ace of diamonds may stop any sequence when his turn comes by playing it and announcing "Spin." He then plays his lowest card in some other suit. It is important to note that he must, however, play an eligible card before playing the ace of diamonds.

Pope Joan

Follow all the rules of Boodle except for the following:

1. Boodle or money cards: nine and ten of diamonds, jack of clubs, queen of spades, and king of hearts.

2. Only the dealer puts the chips on the money cards, usually one on the ten of diamonds, two on the jack of clubs, three on the queen of spades, four on the king of hearts, and five on the nine of diamonds.

3. A player who is caught at the end of the play with the duplicate of a money card in his hand must double the chips on that card for the next deal in addition to what the dealer puts on.

FAN-TAN

This game, which is also known as Parliament, Card Dominoes, Sevens, and several other names, should not be confused with Chinese Fan-Tan (see page 312), which is purely a banking game and is played in an entirely different manner.

Requirements

1. Two to eight players, but four makes the best game.

2. A regular 52-card deck. The cards rank in this order; ace (low), two, three, four, five, six, seven, eight, nine, ten, jack, queen, king (high).

3. Each player puts one or more chips in a pool before each deal.

Beginning of the Game. The selection of the dealer, seating positions, changing seats, shuffle and cut are as provided under the General Rules for Card Games, chapter 1.

The Deal. Players cut for the deal, lowest card dealing the first hand. In subsequent hands the turn to deal rotates in a clockwise direction.

Each player, beginning at dealer's left and going clockwise, is dealt one card at a time per round until the complete pack is exhausted. It does not matter if, owing to the number of players, some receive one card more than the others.

The Play. The player at dealer's left makes the first play. If he holds any seven, he may lay it face up in the center of the table. If he has no seven, he passes his turn. The player

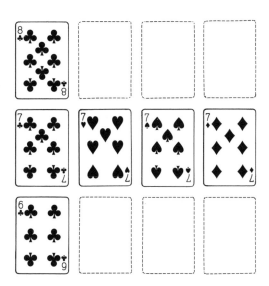

The layout for Fantan after a 6 or 8 are played.

at his left then may play a seven if he holds it, and so on around the table, the turn to play always clockwise.

Any player in turn may play a seven; or, he may play a six or eight of the same suit as a seven already on the table. A six goes to the one side of the seven and an eight to the other side. As soon as an eligible eight or six has been played, any player when his turn comes may play a card in next higher rank on the eight pile or a card in next lower rank on the six pile. The ace is the last card played on the six pile, going on the two; the king is the last card played on the eight pile, going on the queen. If a player has no eligible card to play, he passes his turn and must put one chip into a pool.

The first player to get rid of all his cards is the winner and takes the pot. Other players also pay him one chip for each card that they have left in their hands, no one being permitted to play after the winner has put down his last card.

Additional Rules. A player who passes when he holds an eligible card must pay three chips as penalty to the pot. If he passes when he could play a seven, he must pay not only the three-chip penalty but an additional five chips to the holder of the eight of the same suit and five chips to the holder of the six. If he holds the seven and the next card (or cards in sequence to it, up or down), but does not play the seven, he pays the five-chip penalty to the player who holds the next card in sequence.

Around-the-Corner

This game, which is sometimes called Play or Pay, is played the same as Fan-Tan except for the following:

1. The player at dealer's left begins with any card, not necessarily a seven. The players

following in turn must build higher in sequence on that card. If a player cannot play a card, he pays a chip to the pot. If a player holds more than one card in sequence, he continues to play, collecting a chip from each other player for each card played.

2. Cards may be played "around the corner." That is, in sequence past the king (queen, king, ace, deuce). The player who plays the last card of a suit is then privileged to play a card to begin a new suit. The player who gets rid of his cards first collects the pool and a chip for each card other players hold.

Five or Nine

The play of this game, which is often called Domino Whist, is the same as Fan-Tan except that the first card played must be a five or a nine. The first card played determines rank or layout for that deal. If it is a five, the six or four may be played on either side of it. If it is a nine, the eight or ten may be played on either side of it. In any case, the set cards (five or nine) must be built up and down in suit to the limits of king and ace respectively.

Domino Fan-Tan

This is a two-handed game which is played in the same way as Fan-Tan except for the following:

1. Each player is dealt 17 cards, and the rest of the pack is placed face down to form a stock.

2. If a player cannot play in his turn, he puts a chip into the pot and draws the top card of the stock. If he still cannot play, he puts another chip into the pot and draws the next card of the stock. This continues until he is able to play. When the stock is exhausted the hands are played out.

SNIP–SNAP–SNOREM

This is a very simple game which is also known as Earl of Coventry.

Requirements

1. Three to eight players.

2. A regular 52-card deck.

3. All players are supplied with an equal number of chips, from which they each ante

one chip to form a pot, which is increased by payments during the play.

Beginning of the Game. The selection of the dealer, seating positions, changing seats, shuffle, and cut are as provided under the General Rules for Card Games, chapter 1.

The Deal. After the shuffle and cut, the

cards are dealt out one at a time. It does not matter if the deck does not divide evenly.

The Play. The player at dealer's left (called the leader) leads any card, calling out its denomination. The next player to the left leads a card of the same denomination, if he has it. If not, he passes and the turn goes to the next player. *Example:* If a queen were led, the second player must also lead a queen or pass. There is no payment forfeit, since the player is penalized by the loss of the opportunity to get rid of a card.

Whenever two consecutive hands play, the first of the two is snipped if he was the leader, or snapped if he played the second card of the rank, or snoremed if he played the third card of the rank. For being snipped player pays one chip to the pot; for being snapped, two chips; for being snoremed, three chips. Anyone who plays after a pass by his right-hand opponent escapes payment. Incidentally, some like to follow the old tradition of having the player of the second card of a set say "Snip," the player of the third card say "Snap," and the player of the fourth and last card say "Snorem."

The one who plays the fourth card of a set leads a new card to begin another set. In any one turn a player may not play more than one card. He must give the other players a chance to play, unless he holds all the remaining cards of denomination.

The Game. The first player to get rid of all his cards is the winner. Each loser must pay one chip for each card remaining in his hand, and the winner takes the entire pot.

Jig

This is a variation of Snip-Snap-Snorem in which cards are played in consecutive sequence in the same suit until a set of four has been played. The one who plays the fourth card of the set may lead any card for the next set. *Example:* If someone plays a queen of spades, the next player may put on a king of spades, the next an ace, and the player of the deuce of spades completes the set and leads any card to the next set.

EIGHTS

The game of Eights, which is also known as Crazy Eights, Snooker, and Swedish Rummy, offers more opportunity than any other member of the Stops family to overcome poor cards by skillful play.

Requirement

1. From two to eight players; best for two, three, or four with partnerships.

2. The regular 52-card deck is used, except when five or more play. In that case, two decks are used. The cards and suits have no rank.

Beginning of the Game. The selection of the dealer, seating positions, changing seats, shuffle, and cut are as provided under the General Rules for Card Games, chapter 1.

The Deal. Players cut for deal, lowest card deals. If four are playing, two highest cuts play against two lowest. The turn to deal in subsequent hands passes to the left.

Each player is dealt a hand of seven cards, one at a time per round in clockwise rotation. The remainder of the deck is placed face down on the table to form a stock. Its top card is turned face up beside it as the *starter.*

The Play. Beginning with the player at the dealer's left, each player in turn must place one card face up on the starter pile which must match the previous play in either rank or suit. *Example:* On the five of spades, any spade or any five may be played. If unable to play, a player must draw cards from the top of the stock until he can, or until the stock is exhausted. If unable to play and the stock is exhausted, a player passes his turn. A player may draw from the stock if he wishes, even though able to play.

Each card played (other than an eight) must match the card showing on the starter pile, either in suit or in denomination. Thus, any club may be played on any club; any queen on any queen. The eights are wild; that is, an eight may be played at any time in turn, and the player specifies a suit for which it calls (never a denomination). The following player must play either a card of the specified suit or an eight.

Object of Play. As in most Stop games, the

object is to get rid of all cards in the hand. The player who first succeeds wins the game, and collects from each other player the value of his remaining cards computed on this count:

Each eight	50
Each king, queen, jack, or ten	10
Each ace	1
Each other card	face value

If the game ends in a block, no hand being able to play and the stock being exhausted, the player with the lowest count in his remaining cards collects from each other player the difference of the counts. Players who tie divide the points. Generally, score is kept on paper. Each deal may be settled as a separate game, but when two play, it is usual to award the game to the one who first reaches 100 points or more.

A four-handed partnership game does not end until both partners on a side go out. When the first hand goes out, the other three continue to play. If the game ends in a block, the total counts of the two sides are compared to determine the winner.

Additional Rules. If the dealer gives any hand more than the correct number of cards, any other player draws the excess cards from the hand and restores them to the middle of the pack. If the dealer gives a player less than the correct number of cards, this player must draw a sufficient number of additional cards from the top of the stock. After the stock is exhausted, a player who is able to play must play. If the score of a game ending in a block has been agreed upon, it stands even though the discovery is made that a hand could have continued play.

Wild Jacks

In Wild Jacks or Crazy Jacks, jacks are wild instead of eights. All other rules of Eights are the same.

Go Boom

This variation is played like Eights except there are no wild cards of any kind.

Hollywood Eights

This variant is two-hand Eights with scoring like that of Hollywood Gin Rummy (see page 90). The cards count: each eight, 20; ace, 15; face cards, 10; lower cards, face value. The player who first amasses 100 points wins the game. The scoresheet is set up for three simultaneous games. The first hand won by each player is scored only in game 1. The second hand won is scored in games 1 and 2. The third and all subsequent wins are scored in all three games. When any of these games ends, game 4 may be opened up, and so on.

COMET

Most card historians consider this the oldest of all Stops games. There is reason to believe that the invention of the game was inspired by the return, in 1759, of the comet whose advent had been predicted by Edmund Halley fifty years previous. The fulfillment of this prophecy made a profound impression on the social as well as the scientific world.

Requirements

1. Two to five players but two to four make the best game.

2. Two separate decks are used. All the aces are stripped out. The black suits (clubs and spades) are put together to make up one deck. The red suits (diamonds and hearts) are put together to make up the other deck. But one nine of diamonds is placed in the black deck and one nine of clubs is placed in the red deck. These nines are known as *comets*.

3. The cards rank from king (highest), queen, jack, ten, down to two (lowest) in regular order.

The Deal. Low cut deals, and each player is dealt one card at a time per round in clockwise rotation. Or, the deal may be three cards at a time, except when there are four players, at which time two cards may be dealt at a time. The entire deck is not dealt out; the undealt portion varies with the number of players in the game as follows:

Number of Players	Each Player Receives	Number of Undealt Cards
2	18	12
3	12	12
4	10	8
5	9	3

The undealt or dead cards are put aside face down and are not used in play.

The turn to deal goes to the left in subsequent hands. It does not matter which deck is used first, but the decks must then be alternated.

The Play. Player at dealer's left plays any card face up. He may continue to play any other cards on it face up in consecutive upward sequence, but they do not have to be in the same suit. When he is no longer able to play an eligible card or does not wish to, he passes and the next player on left may continue to build up in sequence. *Example:* If a four is played, then a five, six, seven, eight, etc., may be built up on it, regardless of suit.

When a sequence is ended either because the king is played or because the next eligible card is in the dead pack, a stop is created. The player who created the stop begins a new sequence with any card he wishes, and play continues. Any player in his turn may play as many cards of an eligible denomination as he desires. *Example:* If the sequence can be continued with a jack and a player holds three jacks, he may play all of them in one turn.

In his turn a player may play a comet, designating it as any card he likes. The first player to play all his cards is the winner, or if no one can play further, the game is considered blocked and scored as described below.

Scoring. There are two basic ways of calculating the score. In one method, the cards are given point values as follows: any king, queen, or jack, 10 points each; other cards, their face value. If a player gets rid of all his cards, he collects from each of the others according to the point count of the cards they have left. When a game is blocked, the player with the lowest point count collects from each player according to the differences in point counts. If two or more players tie for low, they divide the winnings equally.

The second method, which is much easier, is for the winner to collect according to the number of cards the other players have left in their hands, using no point count whatsoever. But in either way of scoring, the player caught with a comet in his hand after play is over pays double. If the last card played by the winner is a comet, he collects double; and if it is played as a nine, he wins quadruple. Some play that if a player makes an *opera* (being able to play all his cards and go out in only one turn) all collections mentioned

above are doubled. Another optional payment is sometimes given on the paying; the holder of opera immediately collects one or two chips from each other player.

Commit

This is a variation of Comet, which began in the mid 1800's.

The Requirements

1. Three to seven players.

2. A regular 52-card deck with eight of diamonds removed. The cards rank ace (low), two, three, four, five, six, seven, eight, nine, ten, jack, queen, king (high).

Beginning of the Game. The selection of the dealer, seating positions, changing seats, shuffle, and cut are as provided under the General Rules for Card Games, chapter 1.

The Deal. Low cut deals first. The cards are dealt out one at a time in a clockwise rotation as far as they will go evenly, setting aside the extra cards left over as a dead hand.

In subsequent hands, the turn to deal goes to the left.

The Play. Player at dealer's left plays any card he desires face up. He may continue to play any additional cards on it face up in consecutive upward sequence, but they must be in the same suit. When no longer able to play an eligible card or should he not wish to do so, any other player, in or out of turn, may continue to build up on the sequence. When the sequence is stopped and no one can play further to it, the player who caused the stop may begin a new sequence with any card he wishes.

The nine of diamonds may be played when its holder cannot continue a sequence that he has been playing to, or when all players are stopped and no one can continue. The nine of diamonds may not be called any card the holder designates. But the sequence it was played to may be continued by any player in turn who holds the next eligible card. Or the ten of diamonds may be played on the nine of diamonds to build a diamond sequence. The option goes to the holder of the nine of diamonds.

The first player to get rid of all his cards is the winner.

Scoring. Each player chips in equally to the pot before each hand, and the winner takes all. The one who plays the nine of diamonds collects two chips from every other player immediately on playing it. But if a player is caught with the nine of diamonds in his hand when play is completed, he must pay two chips to every other player. As an optional payment, some play that for each king a player is caught with after the play is over he pays one chip to every other player.

ENFLÉ

This game, also known as Schwellen and Rolling Stone, is another old time Stops.

Requirements

1. Four to six players.

2. From a standard 52-card deck strip out enough cards so that there remain eight for each player in the game. The cards in each suit rank ace (high), king, queen, jack, ten, and so on down. The cards deleted should be from the deuces up, an equal number from each suit.

3. Prior to each deal, every player antes one or more chips to a pot.

The Deal. Cards are drawn for the first deal; highest card deals. The entire deck is dealt out into hands of eight cards, either one or two at a time.

The turn to deal goes to the left in subsequent hands.

The Play. The player on the dealer's left leads any card he wishes. A lead calls upon each other player to follow suit if able; if all follow, the trick is won by the highest card. The winner of a trick leads to the next. Since the tricks are of no value in themselves, they are discarded face down in a common pile.

When a player is unable to follow suit, he must pick up and put into his hand all cards already played to the trick, and then lead to the next trick. He may, if he wishes, lead the suit which he just renounced. Normal policy is always to lead from the longest suit in the hand, so as to keep some cards of each suit as long as possible.

The first player to get rid of all his cards wins the game and takes the pot.

MAU-MAU

Mau-Mau is considered the newest and most scientific of the Stops family, a favorite second game among many bridge players. Whereas most of the Stops games are best for four or more players, Mau-Mau is strictly a two-handed game.

Requirements

1. Two players.

2. A regular 52-card deck and the cards are point valued as follows: jack, 20; eight, 20; seven, 15; ace, 15; queen and king, each 10; and other numerical cards their face value, such as two, 2; three, 3; four, 4; etc.

Object of the Game. To try and win the game by scoring 500 or more points, which may involve one or more dealt hands. The purpose of each hand is to try to get rid of all your cards and receive point credits for all cards held by your opponent.

The Deal. To determine first dealer, players cut for deal. Ace is high, low man deals. Thereafter the deal alternates.

The dealer starting with the nondealer deals each player seven cards one at a time in alternate fashion. The rest of the pack is placed face down in the center of the table to form the stock. The dealer then takes the top card of the stock and places it face up beside it as the starter for the discard pile.

The Play. Beginning with the nondealer, the turn of play passes from player to player. A play consists of discarding one card face up on the discard pile begun by the starter. Each card played must match the previous discard (called the *upcard*) in either suit or rank. *Example:* On the five of diamonds, any diamond or any five may be played. If in turn a player is unable to play such a card, he must pick a card from the top of the stock and add it to his hand until able to play. If a player holds one or more playable discards, he must discard.

A 50-point penalty is charged to the offender for failure to abide by this rule. If a player discards a seven, his opponent must take one card from the top of the stock, but is not permitted to discard under any circumstances. If a player discards an eight, his opponent must draw three cards from the top of the stock and again as before is not permitted to discard.

If a player discards a jack, the same player has the right, if he so desires, to call a change of suit. *Example:* If a jack of spades has just been discarded, the player may call either clubs, diamonds, or hearts, and the opponent must follow with that suit or with another jack. If, however, the discarder of the jack fails to call a change of suit, the opponent does not have to follow suit or rank, and he may discard any card from his hand. If the upcard is either a jack, seven, or eight, and the player whose turn it is to play cannot follow suit, he has the option of discarding the same rank card or holding it and taking a card from the top of the stock.

The moment a player has discarded and has only one card left in his hand, he must announce to the opponent "One card." Should he fail to make this announcement, he is not permitted to discard his last card; instead he must take a card from the top of the stock.

Scoring. Play ends when any player gets rid of the last card in his hand and he is declared the winner and scores the total points of the cards remaining in his opponent's hand: 20 for each jack, 20 for each eight, 15 for each seven, 15 for each ace, 10 for each queen or king, the numerical face value for each other card, 2 for two, 3 for three, etc. If the starter (first upcard) of the discard pile is a spade, the winner's total point score is doubled. If a player goes out and his last discard is a jack, his total point score is doubled. If a player has two jacks (a player may discard two jacks at one time at his turn of play) his total point score is quadrupled (double-double).

Score is kept on a paper. Each deal may be settled as a separate game, but the most interesting game is to award the game to the one who first reaches 500 points or more. The winner is usually paid off on the difference between both scores.

Strategy of Mau-Mau. One's long suit is most often the best to play, as is any suit that the opponent has failed to respond to. As a rule sevens and eights should be saved for the end of the hand so that they can be played consecutively, thereby denying your opponent a discard and forcing him to increase the number of cards his hand has by one or three cards at a time, while you go out or decrease the number of cards in your hand.

CHAPTER 18

Skarney® and How It Is Played

Skarney, the first really new card game concept of this century, can be played in more than 30 different ways. However, due to limited space the rules of play for only Skarney Partnership and Skarney Singles appear in this chapter. Skarney Partnership is one of the most bizarre, exciting, and charmingly exasperating partnership card games in history. It has bluff as in Poker, scores big like Canasta, and is played like no other game. It has the flavor of Pinochle, the partnership understanding of Contract Bridge, and the suspense of Gin Rummy. And withal, it has an inner world and logic of its own, taxing the capacity of the most inveterate card player. I am especially proud of Skarney because the games are my own invention, which I've taken the creator's liberty of naming Skarney. The complete Skarney set can be purchased at most gift and game stores.

SKARNEY PARTNERSHIP

Requirements
1. Four players, two against two as partners.
2. Two standard 52-card decks, with four added jokers shuffled together and used as one, a total of 108 cards.

The Game. A game consists of seven deals or hands and terminates at the end of the seventh deal, in which a final score is attained by each partnership. The partnership with the higher score wins the game. The winners of the game score the difference between their total game and that of the losers. Should both partnerships have identical scores, the game is a tie. The four jokers and the eight deuces are wild and can be used to represent any card of any denomination or any card of any denomination and suit their holders dictate.

Melds. The whole game of Skarney pivots around the combinations of three or more cards of the same rank and three or more cards of the same suit in consecutive order, which players singly or in partnership seek to form in order to score points and special bonuses for their side. The four jokers and the eight deuces (twos) are wild and can be used to represent any card the holder dictates. For instance, three or more cards of the same denomination (such as three queens or two queens and a wild card) or three or more cards of the same suit in consecutive order (such as three of hearts, four of hearts, and five of hearts, or the three of hearts, wild card, and five of hearts) when legally placed face up in front of a player are called a *meld*. That is, cards are melded as soon as they are placed face up on the table with the evident intent to meld. If the exact location of a melded card is in doubt, any player may ask that the meld be clarified.

There are two basic kinds of Skarney melds: a *group* and a *sequence*. Each basic meld is subdivided as follows:

1. *A natural group meld* is a combination of three or more cards of the same rank.

2. *A mixed group meld* is a combination of only one wild card (deuce or joker) with two or more cards of the same rank. But only one wild card can be used in a mixed group meld.

3. *An independent deuce group meld* is a combination of three or more deuces. An independent deuce group meld of three or more deuces is commonly referred to as a *deuce spread,* or a *silver spread.*

4. *An independent joker group meld* is a group of three or four jokers. An independent joker group meld is commonly referred to as a *joker spread,* or *gold spread.*

5. *A natural sequence meld* is a combination of three or more cards of the same suit in consecutive order. An ace can be used only to form a high sequence meld such as ace, king, queen of the same suit. It cannot be used to form a low sequence meld such as ace, deuce, three of the same suit.

6. *A mixed sequence meld* is a combination of only one wild card (deuce or joker) with two or more natural cards of the same suit in consecutive order. When a mixed sequence meld is placed on the table, the exact position of the wild card indicates the natural card it is meant to represent. It should be noted that a joker or a deuce can be used as a king of any suit in a sequence meld such as ace, wild card, queen. It cannot be used to form a low sequence such as ace, deuce, three of the same suit.

It is possible to meld 13 cards of the same suit in a natural or mixed sequence (two, three, four, five, six, seven, eight, nine, ten, jack, queen, king, and ace) with or without one wild card. To emphasize, at no time can more than one wild card be part of a Skarney meld—except when deuces or jokers are melded separately to form an independent deuce group meld or an independent joker group meld.

Laying Off Cards. As in Rummy the addition of one or two cards to a meld already placed on the table is known as a *layoff* and the act of adding one or two matching cards to a meld already placed on the table is known as *laying off.*

After the partnership has fulfilled its initial meld contract, a player at each turn of play, in addition to placing legal melds on the table, may extend his or his partner's previous meld or melds by laying off (adding) one or two matching cards or a matching card and a wild card to a specific melded group or sequence. Players are not permitted to lay off on melds of the opposing partnership. Detailed rules governing natural and wild card layoffs are as follows:

1. *A natural group meld* comprised of the king of spades, king of diamonds, and king of clubs is lying on the table. The melder of this group or his partner holds three or more kings. At his turn, he is permitted to lay off only one or two of these kings on the king group meld. However, the three kings he holds can be melded as a separate group meld and must be placed in front of the melder. They cannot be placed in front of his partner.

2. *A mixed group meld* comprised of the king of spades, king of diamonds, and a wild card (deuce or joker) is lying on the table. The melder of this group or his partner holds two kings. At his turn, he is permitted to lay off one or both of the kings on the mixed group meld.

3. *A natural sequence meld* comprised of the five of hearts, six of hearts, and the seven of hearts is lying on the table. The melder of this sequence or his partner holds the four of hearts, eight of hearts, and the nine of hearts. At his turn of play, he is permitted to lay off only one or two of these cards. He can extend the sequence meld on one or both ends by laying off a single card, such as the four of hearts or the eight of hearts or both—or he can lay off the eight of hearts and the nine of hearts —but never is he permitted to lay off more than two cards on any one meld at any one turn of play.

4. *A mixed sequence meld* comprised of the five of hearts, wild card (deuce or joker), and the seven of hearts is lying on the table. The melder of this sequence or his partner holds the four of hearts, eight of hearts, and the nine of hearts. At his turn of play, he is permitted to lay off only one or two of these cards. He can extend the sequence meld on one or both ends by laying off a single card such as the four of hearts or the eight of

hearts or both—or he can lay off the eight of hearts and the nine of hearts—but never is he permitted to lay off more than two cards on any one meld at any one turn of play.

Wild Card Layoff. A player at his turn is permitted to lay off a wild card (deuce or joker) on either a natural group or natural sequence meld belonging to his partner providing the wild card is accompanied by a natural matching card that will extend the meld, and the meld does not already contain a wild card such as a mixed group or mixed sequence meld. In addition, a player is permitted to lay off one or two deuces on an independent deuce group meld, and one joker on an independent joker group meld.

Swapping a Wild Card. One of the many fascinating features of Skarney is the often present possibility of the holder of a natural card exchanging it for a wild card (deuce or joker) that is part of a mixed meld belonging to his opponents. A player under no conditions is permitted to exchange or swap a wild card for a natural card from either his own or his partner's meld. Rules governing the swapping of a wild card for a natural card are as follows:

1. If a partnership has a mixed group of three or more cards resting on the table which includes a wild card, an opponent at his turn may swap the wild card for a same rank card of a missing suit.

2. If a partnership has a mixed sequence meld of three or more cards resting on the table which includes a wild card, an opponent at his turn may swap the wild card for a natural card that the wild card is meant to represent.

3. A player is permitted to swap a wild card in an opponent's meld or melds at any time during the play of the hand but only at his proper turn of play. Failure of the partnership to fulfill its initial contract meld does not alter this ruling.

4. To reiterate, a player under no condition is permitted to swap or exchange a wild card for a natural card from either his or his partner's melds.

5. A player at his turn of play and before melding or laying off can swap from as many mixed melds as possible and from one or both of his opponents at the same turn of play.

Note: Whenever a wild card is swapped from a mixed group or a mixed sequence meld, that meld becomes a natural meld.

Whenever a wild card and a matching natural card are laid off on a natural group or sequence meld, that meld becomes a mixed meld. It is not unusual to see the same meld change from a mixed meld to a natural meld or vice versa several times during a hand.

Contract Melds. The first meld by each partnership in each of the seven deals must meet the exact initial meld requirement as described by contract. Only one player of each partnership is required to fulfill the initial meld contract.

To simplify matters we shall call an initial basic group meld (natural group meld, mixed group meld, deuce spread, and joker spread) made up of only three cards a "group." We shall call an initial basic sequence meld (natural sequence meld and a mixed sequence meld) made up of only three cards a "sequence." To reiterate, no part of a contract meld can have more than three cards when first placed on the table. Nor can the contract melds be made up of a combination of *groups* and *sequences*. They must be either all groups or all sequences.

CONTRACT REQUIREMENTS FOR FIRST MELD

1st Deal:	3 Three card groups or	3 Three card sequences
2nd Deal:	3 Three card groups or	3 Three card sequences
3rd Deal:	3 Three card groups or	3 Three card sequences
4th Deal:	4 Three card groups or	4 Three card sequences
5th Deal:	4 Three card groups or	4 Three card sequences
6th Deal:	4 Three card groups or	4 Three card sequences
7th Deal:	4 Three card groups or	4 Three card sequences

Skarney or Hand Bonuses. When a player melds or lays off his last card or cards in his hand, he calls "Skarney," ending the hand. This is also known as Rummy, or Going Out. The partnership going Skarney receives the following designated Skarney bonus for each of the seven hands or deals that follow:

BONUSES FOR GOING SKARNEY

First hand	100 points
Second hand	100 points
Third hand	100 points
Fourth hand	200 points
Fifth hand	300 points
Sixth hand	400 points
Seventh hand	500 points

When a player draws the last card of the stock and does not go Skarney, the hand ends without that player offering a potential discard, and the partnership scoring the higher number of points wins the hand and receives a *hand bonus* equal in point value to the Skarney bonus designated for the specific hand. In case each partnership scores the same number of points, the hand does not count and the same dealer deals again.

Skarney Shutout Bonuses. Should a player go Skarney (on the fourth, fifth, sixth, or seventh hand) when putting down his partnership's contract meld (four three-card melds) and the opposing partnership has not put down their contract meld, his partnership receives a Skarney *shutout bonus* (also referred to as a Skarney blitz, or a skunked bonus) of 200 points in addition to the Skarney bonus for the specific hand. When a player is trying for a shutout bonus, it is said that "He's blitzing."

Point Count of Each Skarney Card. At the end of each hand, cards melded on table are credited as follows: tens, jacks, queens, and kings are referred to as high cards and each counts 10 points. Threes, fours, fives, sixes, sevens, eights, and nines are referred to as low cards and each counts 5 points. Aces known as stop cards count 15 points each. Deuces and jokers known as wild cards count as follows:

An independent joker group meld of three or four jokers also known as a joker spread or gold spread counts 100 points for each joker. When a single joker known as a lone joker is part of a mixed group or a mixed sequence meld, it counts 50 points. Each unmelded joker caught in a player's hand is referred to as a penalty card or disaster card and counts 100 points against the holder. An independent deuce group meld of three or more deuces also known as a deuce spread or silver spread counts 50 points for each deuce. When a single deuce known as a lone deuce is part of a mixed group or mixed sequence meld, it counts 25 points. Each unmelded deuce caught in a player's hand is referred to as a penalty card or calamity card, and counts 50 points against the holder. All other unmelded cards (threes to aces) caught in a player's hand, even though they may form melds, are also referred to as penalty cards and are deducted at amounts equivalent to their melding values. So that the reader can see the card counts at a glance, they have been placed in tabular form.

Joker (part of a mixed group meld or a mixed sequence meld)	50 points
Jokers (3 or 4 forming an independent joker group meld)	each 100 points
Deuce (part of a mixed group meld or a mixed sequence meld)	25 points
Deuces (3 or more forming an independent deuce group meld)	each 50 points
Ace	15 points
10, jack, queen, and king	each 10 points
3, 4, 5, 6, 7, 8, and 9	each 5 points

POINT SCORING FOR PENALTY CARDS

Cards Left in Player's Hand at the End of a Hand

Joker	minus 100 points
Deuce	minus 50 points
Ace	minus 15 points
10, jack, queen, and king	each minus 10 points
3, 4, 5, 6, 7, 8, and 9	each minus 5 points

Beginning of the Game. The selection of partnerships, seating positions, changing seats, dealer, shuffle, and cut are provided under General Rules for Card Games, chapter 1.

The Deal. Dealer gives each player including himself 11 face-down cards, starting with the player on his left, one at a time in clockwise fashion. The remainder of the undealt cards are placed face down in the center of the table, forming the stock.

The Actual Play of the Hand. Each player, at his turn, starting with the player on the dealer's left and continuing clockwise around the table, does as follows:

1. He draws the top card of the stock.

2. He may, if he chooses, exchange a natural card for a wild card from each of his opponent's melds.

3. After his partnership has fulfilled its initial meld requirement, he may, if he chooses, place on the table before him any possible melds and lay off, either two or one cards, on each of his and his partner's previous melds.

4. He removes a potential discard from the cards he is holding, turns it face up, and offers it to the player on his left by extending it toward him and asking "Do you want this card?" The player may do either of two things, accept or refuse the potential discard. If he refuses it, he replies "I don't want it," and the potential discard is then offered to the next player, and so it goes from player to player in a clockwise fashion. Should one of

the players accept the potential discard, he must say "I'll take it." This action ends the turn of play for the player who offered the card. Or, if each player in turn refuses the potential discard, the player who offered it must keep the card and return it to his hand, and his turn of play is ended. If however, a player's potential discard is either a wild card or an ace, it may be offered only to the player's opponent on his immediate left—and if the opponent accepts it, he loses his turn to pick the top card of the stock. If he refuses it, the player who offered it must keep it. He is not permitted to offer it to the other players. An ace or wild card offered as a potential discard is referred to as a *stop card*.

A player cannot offer his last accepted potential discard (nor an identical card) immediately but must wait until his next turn of play. *Example:* If his last accepted potential discard was the six of hearts, he cannot offer it until he has offered one other card first. Moreover, if he has another six of hearts in his hand, the same restriction applies.

If a player has one card left in his hand after either melding or laying off or doing both, he is not permitted to offer it as a potential discard. He simply says "Last card," and retains it in his hand. And so it goes, from player to player until the end of the hand.

Giving and Receiving Information. A player during his turn and at no other time may:

1. Ask any other player how many cards he holds. The question must be answered correctly. However, a player must announce when he has only one card in his hand.

2. Ask the scorekeeper what hand is being played or to announce the cumulative score. He may also ask the point value of the Skarney bonus for the hand being played.

3. Call attention to the correct contract meld requirement if his partner is in the act of making an initial meld.

4. Before melding or indicating by word or action that he holds a Skarney hand ask, "Partner, may I go Skarney?" It is strongly recommended that only this phrase be used. Partner must reply "Yes," or "No" (nothing more), and the answer is binding. However, a player may go Skarney without asking permission of his partner. For further information, see Irregularities in Asking Permission to go Skarney, page 344.

End of Hand. When a player melds or lays off the last card or cards in his hand, he calls "Skarney," ending the hand. This is also known as rummy, or going out. The partnership going Skarney receives the designated Skarney bonuses for each of the seven hands as shown on page 338. Should the cards in the stock be exhausted before any player has gone Skarney, the hand ends and the partnership scoring the higher number of points wins the hand and receives a hand bonus equal in point value to the Skarney bonus designated for the specific hand. In case each partnership scores the same number of points, the hand does not count and the same dealer deals again.

When the number of cards in the stock is low (ten or less cards), any player is permitted to count the number of cards remaining so as to know the number of rounds left.

How to Score a Hand. The following steps are used to determine the score. The partnership is credited with the total value of all cards melded. These points are added, and from this sum is subtracted the total penalty point values of the cards remaining in the partner's hands. The net balance is the partnership's score at the end of the hand and this may occasionally be a minus score. Note that all cards left in the hand count against the player regardless of whether or not they could have been melded. Should a player commit a rule violation during the hand and a penalty has been assessed, then penalty points for such offense are charged to the offender and deducted from the partnership's total hand score.

The partnership that went Skarney or won the hand with a higher number of scored points is credited with either a Skarney bonus or a hand bonus for the designated hand as stipulated under Skarney or Hand Bonuses (page 338) and this figure is entered on the score sheet. The scores for each hand are then added to (or subtracted from, as the case may be) each previous cumulative score, if any. In this manner, players can not only check the score and Skarney bonus for each hand but also have a cumulative total at the end of each hand.

To speed up the arithmetic in scoring, first group together your partnership's penalty cards. Second, remove enough cards, if possible, from yours and your partner's melds whose point values equal those of the penalty cards. These and the penalty cards are put aside as they no longer enter into the scoring.

Third, add up the point values of yours and your partner's melded cards still left on the table, and from this amount deduct any penalties assessed for irregularities. The balance is the partnership's hand score. The counting process will be further speeded up if the melds are stacked in separate piles of 100 points whenever possible.

End of Game. The game ends upon completion of the seventh hand and the partnership with the higher total score wins the game and gets credit for the point difference between both scores. See the sample scoring game that follows:

Score Sheet	They	We
First hand scores	130	65
Skarney bonus	100	
Total scores 1 hand	230	65
Second hand scores	195	50
Skarney bonus	100	
Total scores 2 hands	525	115
Third hand scores	295	345
Skarney bonus		100
Total scores 3 hands	820	560
Fourth hand scores	180	230
Skarney bonus		200
Total scores 4 hands	1,000	990
Fifth hand scores	160	375
Skarney bonus		300
Total scores 5 hands	1,160	1,665
Sixth hand scores	265	15
Skarney bonus	400	
Total scores 6 hands	1,825	1,680
Seventh hand scores	195	−280
Skarney bonus	500	
Total game scores	They 2,520	We 1,400
	−1,400 We's score	
They wins by	1,120 Points	

First Hand: They go Skarney, scoring 130 points + 100 points Skarney bonus. We score 65 points. The score at the end of the first hand is 230 to 65 in favor of They.

Second Hand: They go Skarney, scoring 195 points + 100 points Skarney bonus. We score 50 points. These scores are added to the score of the first hand, showing They leading We at the end of the second hand by 525 to 115.

Third Hand: We go Skarney, scoring 345 points + 100 points Skarney bonus. They score 295 points. These scores added to the previous cumulative scores show They with 820 points and We with 560.

Fourth Hand: We go Skarney, scoring 230 points + 200 points Skarney bonus. They score 180 points. The scores at the end of the fourth hand are 1,000 to 990 in favor of They.

Fifth Hand: We go Skarney, scoring 375 + 300 points Skarney bonus. They score 160 points. At the end of the fifth hand We is leading They 1,665 to 1,160.

Sixth Hand: They go Skarney, scoring 265 points + 400 points Skarney bonus. We score 15 points. The score at the end of the sixth hand is They 1,825, We 1,680.

Seventh Hand: They go Skarney, scoring 195 points + 500 points Skarney bonus. We score minus 280 points. They's game total is 2,520 points. We's game total is 1,400 points. So, They's winnings for the game are the difference in scores or 1,120 points. At one-tenth of a cent a point, partnership They collects $1.12 from partnership We.

Alternate Skarney

This is a most fascinating variation of Skarney and my favorite. It is highly recommended to the experienced Skarney player who wants his Skarney game to have greater scope leading to more possibilities for skilled card maneuvers and more opportunities for error. This is all due to the fact that Alternate Skarney possesses two sensational progressive game features, such as (1) Each of the seven initial (contract) meld requirements becomes a bit more difficult to attain with each succeeding deal. (2) The point value of each of the seven succeeding Skarney or Hand Bonuses increases by 100 points in direct relation to the attainment of the contract meld—thereby making for a more balanced scoring game. The rules governing Skarney apply in full for Alternate Skarney, except as follows:

**CONTRACT REQUIREMENTS FOR FIRST MELD
PLUS POINT SCORE FOR EACH SKARNEY
AND HAND BONUSES**

Deals		Bonuses for Winning the Hand
1st Deal	Any 3 three card melds comprised of 3 groups, 3 sequences or a combination of both	100 points
2nd Deal	3 three card groups	200 points

CONTRACT REQUIREMENTS FOR ALTERNATE SKARNEY (*cont.*)

Deals		Bonuses for Winning the Hand
3rd Deal	3 three card sequences	300 points
4th Deal	Any 4 three card melds comprised of 4 groups, 4 sequences or a combination of both	400 points
5th Deal	2 three card groups and 2 three card sequences	500 points
6th Deal	4 three card groups	600 points
7th Deal	4 three card sequences	700 points

Additional Rules

The rules that govern irregularities are designed to define the offense and provide adequate remedy in all cases where a player accidentally, carelessly, or inadvertently violates a rule of the game and gains an unintentional but nevertheless unfair advantage. An offending player should be ready to pay a prescribed penalty graciously. The general rules governing irregularities follow:

1. When an irregularity has been committed, a player may draw attention to it and give or obtain information as to the penalty applicable to it. The fact that a player draws attention to an irregularity committed by his partnership does not affect the rights of the opposing partnership.

2. After attention has been drawn to an irregularity, play shall stop and not be resumed until all questions in regard to rectification and to the assessment of a penalty have been determined. Either player of the offended partnership has the right to impose a penalty without consulting his partner.

3. A penalty may not be imposed until the nature of the offense has been clearly stated; however, a penalty once paid, or any decision agreed and acted upon by the players stands, even though it may later be adjudged wrong.

4. The right to penalize an offense or irregularity is forfeited if a player of the offended partnership (*a*) waives the penalty, (*b*) consults with his partner as to the imposition of a penalty before a penalty has been imposed, (*c*) calls attention to an opponent's irregularity after he or his partner has drawn a card from the stock.

5. Rectification or validation proceeds as provided in the following irregularities applicable to the specific offense. When these irregularities are appreciated and the penalties invoked, arguments are avoided and the pleasure and enjoyment which the game offers are materially enhanced.

First Hand: They go Skarney scoring 130 points + a 100 point Skarney Bonus. We score 65 points. The score at the end of the first hand is 230 to 65 in favor of They.

Second Hand: They go Skarney scoring 195 points + 200 points bonus for Skarney. We score 50 points. These scores are added to the score of the first hand showing They leading We at the end of the second hand by 625 to 115.

Third Hand: We go Skarney scoring 345 points + 300 points Skarney Bonus. They score 295 points. These scores added to the previous cumulative scores show They with 920 points and We with 760.

Fourth Hand: We go Skarney scoring 230 points + a 400 point Skarney Bonus. They score 180 points. The scores at the end of the fourth hand are 1,390 to 1,100 in favor of We.

Fifth Hand: We go Skarney scoring 375 points + a 500 point Skarney Bonus. They score 160 points. At the end of the fifth hand We is leading They 2,265 to 1,260.

Sixth Hand: They go Skarney scoring 265 points + a 600 point Skarney Bonus. We score 15 points. The score at the end of the sixth hand is We 2,280, They 2,125.

Seventh Hand: They go Skarney scoring 195 points + a Skarney Bonus of 700 points. We score minus 280 points. They's game total is 3,020 points. We's game total is 2,000. So, They's winnings for the game are the difference in scores or 1,020 points. At one-tenth of a cent a point, partnership, They collect $1.02 from partnership We.

SAMPLE SCORING OF AN ALTERNATE SKARNEY PARTNERSHIP GAME

Score Sheet	They	We
First Hand Scores	130	65
Skarney Bonus	100	
Total Scores 1 Hand	230	65
Second Hand Scores	195	50
Skarney Bonus	200	
Total Scores 2 hands	625	115
Third Hand Scores	295	345
Skarney Bonus		300

Score Sheet	They	We
Total Scores 3 Hands	920	760
Fourth Hand Scores	180	230
Skarney Bonus		400
Total Scores 4 Hands	1,100	1,390
Fifth Hand Scores	160	375
Skarney Bonus		500
Total Scores 5 Hands	1,260	2,265
Sixth Hand Scores	265	15
Skarney Bonus	600	
Total Scores 6 Hands	2,125	2,280
Seventh Hand Scores	195	—280
Skarney Bonus	700	
Total game scores	They 3,020	We 2,000
	—2,000	We's score
They wins by	1,020	Points

Dealing Out of Turn. Should a deal out of turn be discovered before the first play, the deal stands and the first play is made by the player whose turn it would have been if no irregularity had occurred. In this case, the deal passes as though the cards had been dealt by the correct player. But should a deal out of turn be discovered after the beginning of the first play, the deal stands and play continues from that point. In this case, the deal passes as though the irregular deal had been correct.

Misdeals. There must be a new deal if:

1. It is discovered during the deal that the cut was omitted.

2. During the deal the dealer exposes any card other than his own.

3. Before each player has made his first play, it is discovered that any player was dealt an incorrect number of cards. If such discovery is made after each player has made his first play, the play continues without correction.

4. Before each player has made his first play, a card is found faced up in the stock, or a foreign card is found in the pack or in a player's hand, or it is discovered that a card is missing from the pack.

Irregularities in the Draw from the Stock. The following rules cover irregularities in the draw:

1. If a player draws the top card of the stock and sees or exposes another card or cards of the stock in the process, he must show the card or cards so seen or exposed to all the players and replace them. In addition, he must show his drawn card to all the players before placing it with the cards in his hand. The player whose turn it is to play next

may either take the top card of the stock or shuffle the stock and cut before drawing from the stock.

2. If a player draws two or more cards from the stock and puts them in his hand, he must forgo his draw for as many turns as the number of extra cards he has drawn. He must offer a potential discard at each turn and may not meld, lay off, or swap wild cards until after his next legal draw.

3. If a player draws from the stock before the preceding player has offered a potential discard, the draw stands, and the player loses his turn to accept the potential discard and the offender is not permitted to meld or lay off until his next turn of play.

4. If a player draws from the stock when it is not his turn, he must show the card erroneously drawn to all players and replace it on the stock. The player whose turn it was to play may either take it as his draw or shuffle the stock and cut before drawing.

Irregular Deck During Play. An irregular deck during play is one in which:

1. A card is found face up in the stock. It must be turned and shuffled with the rest of the stock and cut.

2. A foreign card is found in the pack. It must be removed. If it is in a player's hand, it is removed and replaced immediately by the top card of the stock.

3. One or more missing cards are found and no player admits to their ownership. They should be shown to all players, then put into the pack, which is shuffled and cut.

Stop-Card Irregularity. If a player's potential discard is a stop card (joker, deuce, or ace) it may be offered only to the player on his immediate left, and if that player accepts the stop card, he loses his turn to pick the top card of the stock. If he refuses the stop card, the player who offered it must keep it. He is not permitted to offer the stop card to the other players. If, however, the player accepts the stop card and draws from the stock inadvertently, he must show the card erroneously drawn to all the players and replace it on the stock. The next player may, if he chooses, take the card as his draw or shuffle the stock and cut before drawing. There is no penalty for this infraction.

Last-Card Irregularity. When a player holds only one card in his hand, he cannot offer it as a potential discard. When holding only one card, a player must announce "Last card," in a voice that all can hear. Second, he must hold the card so that its value is hidden from the other players' views. If, however, a player inadvertently exposes the value of his last card, there is no penalty, but the player may be reprimanded. If the player repeats the infraction, his partnership is penalized 50 points for each new offense.

Potential Discard Irregularities. The following covers potential discard irregularities:

1. If a player offers a potential discard without drawing, he must draw the top card of the stock if attention is called to the irregularity before the next player has drawn. If the next player draws before attention is called, the offending player must take the next top card of the stock and play reverts to the other player.

2. If a player at his turn has refused the potential discard either by word or action, the decision stands. He cannot accept the refused potential discard under any conditions.

3. If a player at his turn has accepted a potential discard either by word or action, the decision stands. He cannot refuse the potential discard under any conditions.

Illegal Contract Melds. If it is discovered during a player's turn to play that he has:

1. Placed on the table as a contract meld an insufficient or illegal meld, (*a*) he may correct the irregularity by putting down sufficient melds from his hand, in which case he may rearrange the cards put down in error providing he makes use of all melded cards; or (*b*) he may return to his hand one or more cards put down in error and rearrange all his melds from melded cards and cards in his hand, in which case his partnership is penalized 100 points.

2. Placed on the table an illegal or insufficient contract meld and cannot remedy the situation, he is permitted to return the cards to his hand and the penalty to his partnership is 100 points.

Irregularities in Melding and Laying Off. After a partnership's contract meld has been fulfilled and a player has laid down a meld or melds, he cannot pick them up and replace them in his hand. Nor is he permitted to rearrange them in any other kind of meld. Cards once melded and laid down on the table remain as legal melds. The same ruling holds true for a one- or two-card layoff on either partner's melds. If a player lays down an illegal meld or layoff and attention is brought to it, he is permitted to correct the irregularity or replace the cards in his hand

and the penalty for the infraction is 50 points. If, after an illegal meld or layoff, the next player draws a card from the stock before attention is called to the error, the illegal meld or layoff stands as a legal play.

Irregularities in Asking Permission to Go Skarney. The following cover irregularities in asking to go Skarney:

1. At his proper turn of play and before melding or laying off cards, or indicating he has the necessary melds to go Skarney, a player may ask, "Partner, may I go Skarney?" It is strongly recommended that only this phrase be used. Partner must reply either "Yes," or "No" (nothing more), and the answer is binding. If the player fails to abide by the answer, his side is penalized 100 points.

2. If a player calls "Skarney" without asking his partner's permission and finds he cannot go Skarney, his partnership is penalized 100 points and the cards (if any) that the player may have exposed in attempting to go Skarney are returned to his hand.

3. If the player after asking the question, but before receiving a reply, melds or lays off, indicates a meld or layoff, withdraws the question, or gives any other information; or if the partner, in giving a negative answer, transmits information, either opponent may demand that the player go Skarney (if he possibly can) or not go Skarney.

4. If after asking his partner's permission to go Skarney and receiving an affirmative answer to the question, a player states he cannot go out, his partnership is penalized 100 points and the cards (if any) that the player may have exposed in attempting to go Skarney are returned to his hand.

5. If a player who receives a negative answer to the question "Partner, may I go out?" proceeds to attempt to meld all of his cards, he must rearrange these melds so that at least two cards will remain unmelded. The two cards or more remaining unmelded are returned to his hand and offender must offer a potential discard and the partnership is penalized 100 points.

Score Corrections. Here are the important points of rules of scoring:

1. When a score is agreed upon and written down, it may not later be set aside. Proven mistakes in addition or subtraction on the score sheet may be corrected at any time prior to the start of a new game. If the error is proven after the first draw of any hand, the

hand must be completed before the error can be corrected.

2. Once a partnership has counted its cards and announced its total score and the score is entered on the score sheet and a new hand has started, the partners cannot call for rectification of some previous mistake they have made. Players are not required to inform their opposition that they have committed an error or failed to lay off a card or failed to meld to their best advantage, nor are they required to notify the opposition that they are calling an incorrect count to their disadvantage.

3. A player who inadvertently mixes his melds with the rest of the cards before counting them forfeits their count.

4. A player who inadvertently mixes an opponent's melds with the rest of the cards before they are counted may not dispute that opponent's claim to their point value.

Skarney Singles

Double-Deck Skarney Singles is just like Skarney Four-Handed Partnership except that everyone plays for himself. You can use all your knowledge in Skarney Four-Handed Partnership to good advantage except that the partnership factor is missing. Yet it is different enough to create novel and exciting situations that could never arise in partnership play. The official rules for Skarney Four-Handed Partnership apply with the following exceptions and additional rules:

1. Two, three, or four players, each playing for himself.

2. Each player is required to fulfill his initial contract meld.

3. A player at each turn of play may swap (if possible) a wild card (deuce or joker) from one or more melds of each and every opponent.

4. A player is only permitted to lay off cards on his own melds. To emphasize, a player is not permitted to lay off cards on opponent's melds.

5. When a singles player goes Skarney by putting down his contract meld, he receives the Skarney shutout bonus only if each and every opponent has failed to put down a contract meld.

Skarney Strategy

The following are the 20 basic points of Skarney strategy:

1. Learn the rules of the game so that you can recall them at a moment's notice.

2. Pick up your 11 dealt cards one at a time.

3. Take time out to arrange your hand in ranks and suits.

4. Don't give the strength of your hand away by saying you have a weak hand, or no wild cards, or a strong hand and many wild cards.

5. When putting down a contract meld, do not expend vulnerable wild cards in mixed melds too freely when no great urgency presses.

6. Think twice before offering a stop card (ace, deuce, or joker) to your left-hand opponent—especially when he holds only a few cards.

7. When holding a weak hand, accept all matching potential discards. When holding a strong hand, think twice before accepting a nonmatching potential discard.

8. Before melding and laying off, study your opponent's mixed melds for possible wild-card swaps.

9. Study your natural and mixed melds and your partner's for possible layoffs and lock-ups.

10. When melding and laying off, try to keep one wild card in your hand to help a possible Skarney hand.

11. The safest potential discard to offer your opponents is a card of the same rank they have previously refused.

12. Remember the potential discards taken by your partner and try to feed him the like—or hold same for possible layoffs on partner's melds.

13. Try not to leave yourself with just one wild card as your last card.

14. Wild cards without natural pairs near the end of a hand are expendable—too many may be a handicap.

15. Try to put down your mixed meld so that the wild card will be as safe as possible.

16. It's mathematically best to meld groups rather than sequences, better for laying off cards.

17. Think twice before saying "No" to the question, "May I go Skarney?"

18. You should play for Skarney whenever it appears that the prolongation of the hand will benefit your opponents more than yourselves.

19. Don't discuss or criticize your partner's play during the play of the hand.

20. Study the score at the end of each hand.

Probabilities in a Skarney Hand. In Skarney, as in all card games of skill, there is a mathematical basis for many correct plays. But mathematics plays only a minor part of Skarney strategy. You do not have to be a mathematician to play well, nor do you have to memorize mathematical rules laid down by anyone. There are, of course, some probability factors in Skarney, which are apparent even to the beginner. It should be obvious that you have a better chance of making a 3-card natural group meld than a 3-card natural sequence meld when you hold a pair of kings than if you hold a king and queen of spades. In fact the odds are 3 to 2 in favor of the natural group. The reason, there are six kings to draw from and there are only four cards (two aces of spades and two jacks of spades) to draw from to make a 3-card natural sequence.

The number of ways that 11 cards can be dealt to a player out of a total of 108 cards is a figure with 15 digits—approximately 344,985,000,000,000. But this does not represent the number of different Skarney hands because a ten of hearts, for instance, in a group meld is not different from a ten of diamonds or a wild card. The number of significantly different hands that can be dealt in Skarney is very much smaller—approximately 3,500,000.

On the average, you will be dealt one or more wild cards per hand (11 cards) and you are better than a 3 to 1 favorite to be dealt at least one wild card. Your whole hand, on the average, in approximate figures will be:

Wild cards	1 (plus)
Aces	1 (minus)
High cards	3 (plus)
Low cards	6 (minus)
Total	11 cards

Your hand will have two natural pairs (or longer sets) and will for example be: deuce, ace, 3-3, queen-queen, jack, 9, 8, 6 and 5. The most disconnected hand in Skarney is one containing no matched cards and no wild cards, but you will be dealt a hand of this type about once in 3,000 deals.

Techniques in Playing for Skarney. The principle of mobility is a general principle common to most card games of skill. In Skarney to keep your hand fluid and to be prepared for most contingencies is of utmost importance. In playing for Skarney, the desired flexibility can be maintained by forming as many two-way melds incorporating the same cards in both groups and sequences as you possibly can. For instance, among your cards you hold three three-card sequences, the seven, eight, nine of diamonds; seven, eight, nine of spades; and the seven, eight, nine of clubs. These same three three-card sequence melds can be switched to three three-card groups, such as 3 sevens, 3 eights, and 3 nines. It becomes quite a problem to some players when holding twenty or more cards to segregate the melds in their proper manner. I have seen many players holding a Skarney hand but unaware of it and never going Skarney simply because the hand was not arranged properly. This is especially true when a few wild cards are among the large number of cards a player is holding. The best advice that can be given is to take your time when sorting out melds in your hand, because who knows, a simple rearrangement of melds may spell Skarney for you.

Tactics When You Need a Contract Meld. A contract meld of three three-card groups or three three-card sequences is fairly easy to obtain. Possession of one or two wild cards, for instance, practically assures it. But don't rush to put down mixed melds (melds possessing a wild card) unless they are fairly safe from being stolen (swapped for a natural card) by your opponents. Otherwise it is best to wait even several rounds in order to put down natural melds or closed mixed melds. That is, providing your opponents have not as yet put down their contract meld.

If your opponents have fulfilled their contract meld and your side has not, by all means get down on the board (if possible). It is best to gamble a stolen wild card (deuce or joker) than to be caught with a 50- or 100-point penalty card in your hand. As play progresses, the urgency for putting down a contract meld increases to the point where its desirability can no longer be weighed too delicately.

A contract meld of either four three-card groups or four three-card sequences is difficult to get unless you happen to be dealt two or three wild cards. With no wild cards, it is really tough. The general principles as to when you should put down your four three-card contract melds are simple. You should almost always go down as soon as you can.

Only very seldom may you indulge in the luxury of waiting for a more desirable contract meld. Always remember Skarney Four-Handed Partnership is a partnership game and partners must cooperate in putting down a contract meld. Some players holding a contract meld wait for their partners to meld, hoping to go Skarney after their partners fulfill the contract meld. Skarney Partnership, like Contract Bridge, is a partnership game and to win at Skarney, as at bridge, partnership cooperation is required. So when you have an opportunity to fulfill a four three-card contract meld in the early part of a hand, do so and try for a big scoring hand. The 200, 300, 400, 500, 600, or 700 points for Skarney bonus is big—but so are the penalty cards your opponents may be caught with.

Getting your contract meld down has obvious advantages. It is your race toward going Skarney. It gives your partner a chance to meld groups and sequences, plus laying off on your melds, and vice versa. It also relieves your partner of the pressure of trying to attain the contract meld. Last but not least, it puts the pressure on your opponents, and at times causes them to put down mixed melds with vulnerable wild cards. But as you may already have discovered, it may be to your disadvantage to put down either a natural or mixed contract meld during the early stages of the hand. It makes it easier for your opponents to choose safe potential discards and reduces the flexibility of your own hand. Therefore, you will have to weigh the advantages against the disadvantages such as being left with four or five disconnected cards in your hand, after fulfilling your contract meld.

The necessity for making such decisions arises frequently in Skarney, and the player who consistently uses good judgment will win many more games than his opponents.

To succeed in blitzing, some luck and considerable psychological bluffing on your part and your partner's are required. You both must keep poker faces and play it cool so as not to alert your opponents to the fact that you are attempting a blitz. And, always remember: When you have a good reason to fear that your opponents may go Skarney quickly—it is wise for you, if possible, to unload—put down all your melds and layoffs be they natural or mixed melds.

The Subtle Art of Potential Discarding. Skarney is a game of deduction and counter deduction. (1) You must try to figure out what cards each opponent is holding in his hand so that (a) you won't give them any useful cards and (b) you won't be holding cards for an impossible or unlikely meld. (2) You must try to figure out what cards your partner is holding in his hand so that (a) you'll be holding cards you can lay off on his possible melds and (b) you'll be offering potential discards that are useful to your partner. Therefore, good potential discarding is both offensive and defensive. Offensively, you want to build up or maintain a hand that will give you a contract meld and a fair chance to go Skarney. Defensively, you want to make the attainment of these objectives as difficult as possible for your opponents.

At the very beginning of the hand the question of what is and what is not a safe potential discard is not too important. On the first few rounds any potential discard is usually accepted by one of your opponents or partner. You should not worry at this point because more often than not some one will take almost every card coming his way, if he needs it or not. Such a player is referred to as a "garbage picker." What you should do at the beginning of the hand is to concentrate on building your own hand and keeping your opponents in the dark regarding the strength of your hand. However, during the middle of the hand, prior to your opponents' fulfillment of their contract meld, you cannot do better than to match your opponents' previous potential discard with a similar rank card. If one of your opponents offers a five, you should retaliate and offer a five if you have one and can spare it. The presumption is that he does not have a pair left in a rank that he has offered so early. Sometimes you will be wrong, but more often you will be right.

If you hold a lone ace (stop card) it is usually wise to offer it to your left-hand opponent. Again the presumption is that he will not accept it for fear of losing a pick from the top of the stock. Think twice, however, before offering an ace or a wild card in the later phase of the hand.

The foregoing advice on potential discards is intended to apply in any situation where the two partnerships are on equal or near-equal terms. The partnership trailing by several hundred points is bound to accept nearly every potential discard that might come its way hoping to net hundreds of points more than you could make by going Skarney quickly.

Once your opponents have put down their contract meld, each of your potential discard plays must be thoroughly analyzed, more so if one of your opponents holds his last card. You must be ultrasafe in offering a potential discard. Study your opponents' and your own melds (if any) very carefully and then think twice before making the play. Owing to the luck (chance) aspect of Skarney, the most skillful potential discarding cannot guarantee success every time.

Acceptance and Refusal of Potential Discards. Prior to either side having fulfilled its contract meld, there is no need to consider taking a potential discard when it matches a card in your hand or gives you a meld: just take it with a feeling of gratitude to the giver. But, when the offered card does not give you a match or a meld, the problem of taking it poses a dilemma. It frequently happens that an opponent tries to pass his partner a card of the same rank as previously taken. When such a condition prevails, it may be good tactics to take it even though it doesn't help your hand. You can always offer it back later on if you must.

An important question that often arises at the beginning of a hand is whether to try for a big score and take almost every card that comes your way or to accept fewer valuable cards and try for Skarney. However, not every hand is suitable for a big score. Often a player is dealt 11 cards which are better adapted for a fast contract meld and a quick Skarney—providing the player gets an assist from his partner. Such a decision depends on the score. If your partnership is far ahead, you should play for Skarney, only accepting a potential discard that gives you a meld or extends a meld. If your partnership is far behind—and all other things being even—try for the big score. The necessity for making such decisions arises frequently in Skarney and the player who consistently uses good judgment will be the winner. Should you be offered an ace (stop card) in the early stages of the game and you are bent on trying for a big score—accept it when first offered. It very often is part of the opponent's meld or matched aces and he is offering it as bluff card so as not to break up any of his other matched sets or melds. If you have what you consider a possible Skarney hand, don't take it, because a disconnected ace is a difficult card to get rid of when your opponents have put down their contract meld.

When both partnerships are down with melds, you should be extra cautious in accepting an opponent's potential discard. Take a careful look before accepting or offering a potential discard. Observe all melds on the table. At this stage, it is fairly easy to tell what card is good or bad for your side or your opponents'.

Most beginners at this stage of the game are tempted to accept an opponent's potential discard merely to extend one of their own melds. By all means, do not accept an opponent's potential discard that he cannot get rid of by laying it off on one of his own melds.

Should you have no quick chance of going Skarney, and your partner holds very few cards in his hand, accept all potential discards from your partner, thereby giving him the opportunity to go Skarney. And last but not least, think twice before offering or accepting an ace or wild card when both partnerships are down to their last few cards.

Defense Against Opponents Who Have Many Cards. Going Skarney? Should the opponent be the ones who are holding big hands of 20 or more cards by taking every potential discard that comes their way, your best defense is, of course, to go Skarney and catch them with a boodle of penalty cards. Partners should cooperate in this situation. For instance, it may easily be that both partners would be in good position to go Skarney if their side puts down its contract meld. In this situation, one of the two partners may have to injure his own Skarney hand by using a couple of wild cards to fulfill his partnership's contract meld. The question arises, which partner should it be? Obviously the one who can best spare the wild cards—but how can one tell? One good indication that the partner has an excellent chance to go Skarney and is merely waiting for his partner to put down the initial meld is that he is not trying to further build up his hand and is refusing most potential discards, and usually offering the drawn card as his potential discard. Consequently, this player's partner should be the one to make the sacrifice and put down the contract meld.

Protecting Your Jokers and Deuces. One of the most important factors in skillful Skarney playing is the use of a wild card. Do you hold it in your hand and wait until you can deploy it in a safe (locked) mixed meld but by so doing take a chance of getting caught with it in your hand? Or do you meld it in an open mixed meld and hope your opponents don't steal it? I can't help you on this one because there are billions of possible hands in Skarney and each requires a different strategy, so you'll have to use your best judgment on how to deploy the wild card. But, whenever you are faced with a decision on whether to use a joker or a deuce in a locked (safe) mixed meld, consider the fact that the joker counts 50 points and the deuce 25. The penalty against you if you are caught with a joker in your hand is 100 points, a deuce 50 points. Hence, there are times when you should use a joker in an open mixed meld, other times a deuce. It all depends on whether your opponents are trying for a contract meld or going for Skarney. Also to be taken into consideration are the opponents' chances of stealing (swapping) the wild card. At times, too many wild cards pose a question. For instance, you hold three jokers. If melded as a joker spread they count 300 points. You wonder if the 300 points are better than a try at the Skarney bonus by using the jokers in mixed melds where they are worth only 150 points, plus the chance of being caught with them in your hand for a disaster penalty of 300 points. Such decisions can only be appraised at the time of happening. There is no cut and dried rule that fits wild cards.

Asking Permission to Go Skarney. When you are ready to go Skarney, you may, according to the rules, ask permission of your partner. But, remember you are not obliged to ask that question. Ask it only if there is a reason for you to do so.

You should not ask permission whenever your hand clearly indicates what to do. *Example:* If you are able to go Skarney on the seventh hand and win the game at the same time, you should not ask the question. Your partner does not know your hand and it is conceivable that he may give a negative reply. Neither should you ask permission if you are sure that you shouldn't go Skarney because you don't want to risk the possibility of an affirmative reply.

You should ask permission of your partner any time you are really interested in his opinion. For instance, you suspect that the handful of cards your partner is holding contains a number of wild cards whose penalty point values could possibly reduce your hand score to a minus score, but of course you cannot be sure about it. By putting the question to him, you are giving him the opportunity to say "No," if he actually has the hand you suspect. In that case, he will put down all possible melds at his next turn and you may or may not go Skarney on the next round. But, if his is not the type of hand you expected, he will say "Yes."

Expert Skarney players will also sometimes ask permission with the definite expectation of getting a negative reply. For instance, if a partner has just stolen a joker or two from his opponent's melds and has a great many cards in his hand and has not melded any cards as yet, it is obvious that he does not want the hand to end at this stage. By asking him, you simply advise him of the strength of your own hand. He will surely answer "No," and will have acquired the knowledge that as soon as he puts down his melds you will try to go Skarney. If he judges, however, that prolongation of the hand would be more profitable, or by chance he cannot meld as he would wish, he will still not meld, and at your next turn, you should ask again, etc.

For more detailed information and strategy of winning play for all 30 Skarney variants, read *Skarney,* a 145-page book which I wrote several years ago.

SKARNEY GIN®

"What card players the world over need is a great two-handed card game." I have said this for many years, and now it seems Skarney Gin fills the bill. It is truly the most fascinat-

ing and exciting two-handed card game in history. Regular Gin Rummy, unlike Skarney Gin, is basically a gambling game. Leave the stakes out of Gin Rummy and it falls flat on its face as a nongambling game. Skarney Gin, however, is a great family pastime. For the millions of married couples Skarney Gin is the ideal two-handed game.

Skarney Gin is the game that I honestly believe will soon displace regular Gin Rummy as America's favorite two-handed card game.

It outclasses regular Gin Rummy not only in fun and excitement but in strategic planning. The reasons for the above statements are: (1) Skarney Gin makes use of three melds, groups, sequences, and poker straights—whereas regular Gin Rummy employs only groups and sequences. This factor alone gives Skarney Gin greater scope and flexibility, causing the player to commit more errors than he would in regular Gin Rummy. (2) The ten-card initially dealt hand in regular Gin Rummy always remains the same during play. In Skarney Gin the ten dealt cards held by a player fluctuate. They may increase to twenty or more cards, decrease to one, increase to ten or more, remain the same, or dwindle to zero when a player goes Skarney or gin. This unusual and fascinating scientific aspect of Skarney Gin makes the game much more interesting and requires greater player concentration than regular Gin Rummy. (3) Although Skarney Gin is a scientific game, poor players win occasionally, so that everyone becomes convinced that he plays well. In no other card game do you find so many self-proclaimed local champs.

Ten Things Every Winning Skarney Gin Player Must Know

1. Learn the rules so thoroughly you can recall them instantly and correctly.

2. Minimize mechanical errors by picking up your dealt cards singly.

3. Don't break up a possible meld at the start of the hand to withhold a doubtful card from your opponent.

4. Study your contract meld before putting it down. However, it usually pays to put down poker straights rather than groups or sequences.

5. Risk adding to opponent's meld rather than offer a live potential discard.

6. Late in the hand, think twice before offering an ace (stop card) as your potential discard.

7. It usually doesn't pay to accept a potential discard only for its layoff value.

8. When purposely holding back your contract meld, make sure to study the score.

9. When putting down poker straights, it is best to meld them in sets of threes rather than sets of fours, fives, or sixes—the reason is, there are more opportunities for layoffs.

10. Don't play hunches—play the odds.

Standard Rules for Skarney Gin

Requirements

1. Two players—although the game may involve three or four players, only two of these may be in play against each other simultaneously.

2. A standard 52-card deck. It is recommended that two packs of cards with backs of different colors be used in the play. While the dealer is shuffling for the deal, the non-dealer is giving the other pack a preliminary shuffle, after which it is set to one side. It is shuffled again by the loser of this hand before he deals the next hand.

Point Scoring for Penalty Cards. Melded cards resting on the table at the end of a hand count zero. Only the cards left in a player's hand at the end of a hand are scored. Even though they form melds they are counted as penalty cards against the holder. The ace is the highest-ranking penalty card, having a value of 15 points. The king, queen, and jack are valued at 10 points each. All other cards have their numerical face value, such as deuce 2 points, three 3 points, four 4 points, etc. The suits have no value.

So that the reader can see the penalty card counts at a glance, they have been placed in tabular form.

POINT SCORING FOR PENALTY CARDS LEFT IN HAND AT END OF HAND

Cards	Points
Aces	Minus 15 each
Kings	Minus 10 each
Queens	Minus 10 each
Jacks	Minus 10 each
Tens	Minus 10 each
Nines	Minus 9 each
Eights	Minus 8 each
Sevens	Minus 7 each
Sixes	Minus 6 each
Fives	Minus 5 each
Fours	Minus 4 each
Threes	Minus 3 each
Twos	Minus 2 each

Melds. The following three types of melds are permitted in Skarney Gin.

1. *Group Melds.* Three or four cards of the same rank such as three or four eights, three or four kings, etc.

2. *Sequence Melds.* Three or more cards of the same suit in consecutive order. *Examples:* three, four, five of hearts; or eight, nine, ten, and jack of spades. Aces, however, may be used in both low and high card sequences. *Examples:* ace, deuce, three of spades; queen, king, ace of clubs. Aces, however, cannot be used in a round-the-corner sequence such as king, ace, deuce of diamonds.

3. *Poker-Straight Melds.* Three or more cards of various suits in consecutive order. *Examples:* poker straights such as the three of clubs, four of diamonds, five of spades; or ten of diamonds, jack of hearts, queen of clubs, and king of diamonds, etc. Aces, as in sequence melds, may be used in both a low or high card run or straight. *Examples:* ace of hearts, deuce of diamonds, three of clubs; or queen of spades, king of hearts, ace of clubs, etc. Aces cannot be used in a round-the-corner straight such as king, ace, deuce.

Contract Melds. The first meld made by each player in each and every deal (hand) until the completion of the game must meet the exact initial contract meld requirement of three three-card melds, a total of nine cards. The three three-card melds may be comprised of any of the following: (*a*) three three-card group melds; (*b*) three three-card sequence melds; (*c*) three three-card poker-straight melds; (*d*) any three three-card meld combinations made up of groups, sequences, and poker straights. *Examples:* (1) one three-card group, one three-card sequence, and one three-card poker straight; (2) one three-card group and two three-card sequences; (3) one three-card group and two three-card poker straights, etc. To emphasize, no part of a contract meld can have more than three cards when first placed on the table, nor can the contract meld be comprised of more or less than three three-card melds.

Selecting Dealer and Starting Position. By mutual consent either player may shuffle the deck of cards. Each player cuts a group of cards from the deck. Player cutting the low-faced card deals first. In case of a tie, players cut again. The loser of a hand deals the next hand.

If players want to cut for seat position, the player cutting low takes his choice of seat.

The Shuffle and Cut. Dealer shuffles the deck. Opponent may call for a shuffle at any time he likes prior to the cut, though the dealer retains the privilege of shuffling last. Dealer must offer the deck to opponent for cut. If opponent refuses to cut, the dealer must cut his own cards before starting the deal. When cutting, at least ten cards must be in each cut portion of the deck.

The Deal. Dealer deals the opponent ten cards and himself ten cards, the opponent being dealt the first card off the top of the deck and so on alternately, until the dealer gets the last, twentieth card. The remainder of the deck, called the stock, is placed face down on the table between both players. It is advisable to spread the stock out fan-shaped on the table to minimize the chances of inadvertently drawing and seeing any cards other than the one to which the player is entitled.

The Actual Play of the Hand. Each of the two players in turn, starting with the non-dealer, does as follows:

First, he takes (draws) the top card of the stock (the remainder of the undealt cards which are face down on the table).

Second, once a player has fulfilled his contract meld, he may, if he chooses, place on the table before him any possible melds and any possible one- or two-card layoffs on each of his previous melds. A player at each turn of play is not permitted to lay off more than two cards on each previous meld. Nor is a player permitted to lay off cards on his opponent's melds.

Third, he removes a potential discard (remember, I said "potential discard") from the cards he is holding, turns it face up in his hand and offers it to his opponent by extending it toward him, asking, "Do you want this card?" The opponent may either accept or refuse the potential discard. If he accepts it, he replies, "I'll take it." This action ends the turn of play for the player who offered the card. If the opponent refuses the potential discard, the player who offered it must keep the card and return it to his hand, and his turn of play is ended. A player cannot offer the same potential discard he just accepted from his opponent at his subsequent turn of play. *Example:* A player accepts his opponent's potential discard, which is the six of spades. He cannot offer the six of spades to his opponent until he has offered another card first.

Fourth, if a player's potential discard is an ace, and the opponent accepts it, the opponent loses his turn to pick the top card of the stock.

Fifth and last, should a player hold one card in his hand, he is not permitted to offer it as a potential discard. He merely says "Last card" and keeps it.

A player during his turn and at no other time may ask his opponent how many cards he holds. The question must be answered correctly. And, so it goes from player to player until the hand ends by a player getting rid of all the cards in his hand by going Skarney—or two cards remain in the stock. When a player draws the fiftieth card from the stock and puts down his melds and lay-offs, if any, the hand ends then and there without the player offering a potential discard.

To reemphasize, a player at each turn of play after having put down his contract meld may meld and lay off one or two cards on each previous meld as he wishes. A player is not permitted to lay off cards on his opponent's melds.

Note: In Skarney Gin, to minimize the chances of not picking from the stock at a player's turn of play, the following rule should be enforced. Once a player has refused a potential discard, he must immediately pick a card from the top of the stock. The strict observance of this rule will avoid many arguments between players as to whether a player at his turn of play has or has not taken a card from the stock.

How to Score a Hand

1. When a player, after having laid down his contract meld gets rid of every card in his hand, he calls "Skarney," ending the hand. This is also known as *gin,* or *going out.* The player who goes Skarney receives a 20-point Skarney bonus plus a total point count of all the cards that his opponent holds in his hand at the end of the hand even though they form melds. *Example:* A player goes Skarney. His opponent holds seven cards comprised of four tens, two fives, and one ace. The player who Skarneyed scores 65 points. The penalty value of his opponent's seven unmelded cards, plus 20 points for going Skarney, makes a total of 85 points. His opponent does not score.

2. When a player goes Skarney or gin, and his opponent has failed to put down his con-

tract meld, the 20-point Skarney bonus for the hand is doubled to 40 points and is known as *double Skarney,* or *double gin.*

3. When a player has drawn the fiftieth card (the last card, leaving two in the stock), the hand ends without that player offering a potential discard—and the player holding the lower penalty point total in unmelded cards in his hand wins the hand and gets credit for the point difference between both totals. *Example:* The hand ends and player A is caught with 15 points in unmelded cards in his hand. Player B has 36 points in unmelded cards in his hand. Player A is the winner of the hand and scores 21 points, the difference between both totals. Should both players tie, a no-hand is declared and the same dealer deals again.

End of Game. A game terminates at the end of any hand in which a total of 200 or more points is scored by either player.

How to Score a Game

1. Winner of the game scores the difference between both totals.

2. Winner of the game gets a *game bonus* of 200 points for winning.

3. An extra 25 points known as a *box bonus* is added to each player's score for each hand won.

4. Should a player score 200 points or more before his opponent scores any points at all, winner gets a 200-point game bonus plus a 200-point shutout bonus—plus all other credits. Following is a sample scoring of a Skarney Gin game, using my new game scoring method. The hand score for each player is written down at the left, then a dash followed by the cumulative game score to the right. This makes it known to each player at all times how far ahead or behind he is.

First Hand: You go Skarney. Your oppo-

SAMPLE SCORING OF A SKARNEY GIN GAME

	You	Opponent
	44-44	
		64-64
	36-80	
	40-120	
	27-147	
		70-134
	120-267	
Game scores	267	134
Box bonuses	125	50
Game bonuses	200	
Total scores	592	184
Minus loser's score	−184	
Your net winnings	408 points	

nent is caught with 24 points in unmelded cards (penalty cards). You score 24 points plus a 20-point Skarney bonus—a total of 44 points.

Second Hand: Your opponent goes Skarney. You are caught with 44 penalty points. Opponent scores 44 points plus a 20-point Skarney bonus. A total of 64 points. At the end of the second hand your opponent leads by 64 to 44.

Third Hand: Two cards are left in the stock. No one goes Skarney. You hold 9 penalty points, your opponent 45. You score the difference, 36 points. At the end of the third hand, you lead 80 to 64.

Fourth Hand: You go Skarney. Your opponent is caught with 20 points in unmelded cards (penalty points). You score 20 plus a 20-point Skarney bonus for a total fourth-hand score of 40 points. The cumulative game score at the end of the fourth hand is 120 to 64 in your favor.

Fifth Hand: You go Skarney. Your opponent holds 7 penalty points. You score 7 plus a 20-point Skarney bonus for a fifth-hand total of 27 points. The score at the end of the fifth hand is 147 to 64 in your favor.

Sixth Hand: Your opponent goes Skarney. You are caught with 50 penalty points. Your opponent scores 50 plus a 20-point Skarney bonus, or 70 points in all. At the end of the sixth hand the score reads 147 to 134 with you in the lead.

Seventh Hand: You go double Skarney. Your opponent holds 80 points in unmelded cards (penalty points). You score 80 plus a 40-point double-Skarney bonus for a total seventh-hand score of 120 points. The 120 points puts you well over the 200 mark with a total of 267 and gives you game. You have five boxes, a total of 125 points at 25 points each, your opponent has two boxes worth 50 points; these are added to the scores. You add a game bonus of 200 points for winning the game. Your grand total is 592. Your opponent's is 184. So your point winnings for the game are the difference in scores, or 408 points net. At one-tenth of a cent a point, you collect 41 cents from your opponent.

Additional Rules for Skarney Gin

If a player accidentally, inadvertently, or purposely violates a rule of the game he must pay a prescribed penalty. The right to penal-

ize an offense or irregularity is forfeited if the offended player (*a*) waives the penalty, or (*b*) calls attention to an opponent's irregularity after he has drawn a card from the stock.

Misdeals. A misdeal is declared, and the dealer of the hand immediately starts a new deal, whenever any of the following improprieties are discovered (there are no penalties for the dealer or the responsible player):

1. If a card is turned over any time during the deal.

2. If either player or both players have been dealt an incorrect number of cards.

3. If a player deals out of turn and the error is discovered before a play has been completed.

4. If a player looks at an opponent's card or cards during the deal.

5. If a card is found face up during the deal.

6. If, however, a card is found face up in the stock, it must be properly turned, the stock shuffled and cut, and play continues.

Irregularities in the Draw. Here are problems that may arise when drawing:

1. If a player inadvertently picks off the stock two cards instead of one or inadvertently sees the face of the card below the one he has just taken, or his opponent has reason to believe that he has seen it, then his opponent at his turn of play, may, if he likes, look at the face of the top card of the stock and take it or shuffle the stock and cut before drawing from the stock.

2. If a player draws from the stock before his opponent has offered a potential discard, he loses his turn to accept the potential discard. Furthermore, he cannot meld or lay off until his next turn of play and the penalty to the offender is 25 points.

Imperfect Deck During the Play. The following are the rules when a faulty deck is discovered:

1. There must be a new deal by the same dealer:

   (*a*) If it is discovered that the deck has one or more duplicate cards.

   (*b*) If a foreign card (not from either deck) is found in the deck during the deal or in the stock at any time before a player goes Skarney.

   (*c*) If it is discovered while the hand is still in play that the deck has fewer or more than the standard 52 cards.

2. If, however, a card of the other deck, when two decks are being used, is found in

the stock, it shall be eliminated and play continues.

3. If it is discovered after a player goes Skarney or the hand is over that the deck has fewer or more cards, it has no bearing on that or previous hands.

Irregularities in the Potential Discard. Here are rules covering discards:

1. If a player offers a potential discard without drawing, he must draw the top card of the stock if attention is called to the irregularity before his opponent has drawn. If the opponent draws before attention is called, the offending player must take the next top card of the stock and the play refers back to the opponent, and the offender on his next turn to play may not meld or lay off until his subsequent turn to play.

2. If during the play a player should refuse a potential discard either by word or action, he cannot then decide to take it. His refusal to accept it is his final decision on that card.

3. If a player at his turn has accepted his opponent's potential discard either by word or action, the decision stands. He cannot refuse the potential discard under any condition.

4. A potential discard once offered cannot be returned to the player's hand and another potential discard substituted; the play stands.

Illegal Contract Melds. If it is discovered during a player's turn to play that he has placed on the table as a contract meld an insufficient or illegal meld, the following can be done:

1. He may correct the irregularity by putting down sufficient melds from his hand, in which case he may rearrange the cards put down in error providing he makes use of all melded cards. The offender is penalized 25 points.

2. He may return to his hand one or more cards put down in error and rearrange all his melds from melded cards and cards in his hand, in which case he is penalized 25 points.

3. If a player errs by placing on the table an illegal or insufficient contract meld and he cannot remedy the situation, he is permitted to return the cards to his hand and he is penalized 25 points.

4. If a player errs by placing on the table more than nine cards (3 three-card melds) as his contract meld, he may correct the irregularity by returning the extra cards to his

hand. There is no penalty for the infraction providing no cards from the hand are used to help achieve the contract meld.

Irregularities in Melding and Laying Off. The following details rule melding and laying-off irregularities:

1. After a player's contract meld has been fulfilled, and he puts down an additional meld or melds, he cannot pick them up and replace them in his hand. Nor is he permitted to rearrange them in any other kind of meld. Cards once melded and laid down on the table remain as legal melds. The same ruling holds true for a one- to two-card layoff.

2. If a player lays down an illegal meld or layoff and attention is brought to it, he is permitted to correct the irregularity and replace the card or cards in his hand. The penalty for this infraction of the rules is 25 points.

3. If after an illegal meld or layoff, the opponent draws a card from the stock before attention is called to the error, the illegal meld or layoff stands as a legal play.

4. If a player melds or lays off cards before drawing a card from the stock, and attention is called to the error, the player must draw a card from the stock and return the illegal melds and layoffs to his hand, and he cannot meld or lay off until his next turn of play.

Stop-Card Irregularity. If a player's potential discard is an ace, commonly known as a *stop card,* and if the opponent accepts the ace, he loses his turn to pick the top card of the stock. If the opponent refuses the ace, the player who offered it must keep it. If, however, the opponent accepts the stop card and draws from the stock inadvertently, he must show the card erroneously drawn to his opponent and replace it on the stock. The opponent may, if he chooses, take the card as his draw or shuffle the stock and cut before drawing. There is no penalty for this infraction.

A Last-Card Irregularity. When a player holds only one card in his hand, he cannot offer it as a potential discard. When holding only one card, a player must announce "Last card," in a voice that his opponent can hear. If, however, a player inadvertently does offer his last card, there is no penalty, but the player may be reprimanded. If the player repeats the infraction, he is penalized 25 points for each new offense.

Score Correction. If a scoring error is made, the following rules prevail:

1. When a score is agreed upon and written down, it may not later be set aside. Proven mistakes in addition or subtraction on the score sheet may be corrected at any time prior to the start of a new game. If the error is proven after the first draw of any hand, the hand must be completed before the error can be corrected.

2. Once the winner of the hand has verified his point count for the hand and entered it on the score sheet and a new hand has started, players cannot call for rectification of some previous mistake they all have made. A player is not required to inform his opponent that he has committed an error or failed to lay off a card or failed to meld to his best advantage, nor is he required to notify the opposition that he is calling an incorrect count to his disadvantage.

3. A player who at the completion of a hand inadvertently mixes his or his opponent's penalty cards with the rest of the cards before they are counted may not dispute that opponent's claim to their point value.

Skarney Gin Doubles

This exciting and scientific variation of Skarney Gin is recommended to the Skarney Gin players who want their game to have greater scope plus a reward for skillful preplay card analysis and psychological bluff. The addition of these two scientific maneuvers leads to a more strategic and greater point scoring game. This feat is accomplished by simply adding a pass, double, and redouble bidding system to Skarney Gin. This bidding system corresponds roughly to the passing, doubling, and redoubling elements of Contract Bridge.

Skarney Gin Doubles is played and scored the same as you play Skarney Gin with the following exceptions and additional rules.

1. A game terminates at the end of any hand in which a total of 300 or more points is scored by either player.

2. *How and When to Bid.* The bidding begins when each player has been dealt his initial ten-card hand and before either player has drawn a card from the stock. The non-

dealer makes the first bid, his opponent the second, the nondealer the third if necessary. Following is a description of each of the five possible bids that can be made in Skarney Gin Doubles.

(a) The nondealer calls "Pass," and the dealer calls "Pass." The winner of the hand scores the actual penalty point count.

(b) The nondealer calls "Pass," the dealer "Double," the nondealer "Pass." The winner of the hand scores double the penalty point count.

(c) The nondealer calls "Pass," the dealer "Double," the nondealer "Redouble." The winner of the hand scores quadruple the penalty point count.

(d) The nondealer calls "Double," the dealer "Pass." The winner of the hand scores double the penalty point count.

(e) The nondealer calls "Double," the dealer "Redouble." The winner of the hand scores quadruple the penalty point count.

3. *How to Score a Bid Hand.* In Skarney Gin Doubles the penalty point score of a pass bid hand remains the same as in regular Skarney Gin, the penalty point score of a double-bid hand is multiplied by two, and the penalty point score of a redouble-bid hand is multiplied by four. *Examples:* (a) The winner of a pass hand goes Skarney and catches his opponent with 16 penalty points in his hand. The winner is credited with 16 points plus the 20-point Skarney bonus for a final hand score of 36 points, the same scoring as if he were playing regular Skarney Gin. (b) The winner of a double hand goes Skarney and catches his opponent with 16 penalty points in his hand. The winner is credited with 16 twice, or 32 points, plus the 20-point Skarney bonus for a final hand score of 52 points. (c) The winner of a redouble hand goes Skarney and catches his opponent with 16 penalty points in his hand. The winner is credited with 16 four times, or 64 points, plus the 20-point Skarney bonus for a final hand score of 84 points.

The above-described method of calculating the penalty point score of the loser also holds true when a player goes double Skarney. Should a player win the hand with a lesser number of penalty points, only the winning difference in points is doubled, redoubled, or remains the same. The pass, double, or redouble bid affects only the specific hand. It does not have anything at all to do with the score of other hands.

Note: Skarney Gin Doubles may be played in all the multiple game and partnership variants described in the following pages.

Round-the-Corner Skarney Gin

This fascinating variation of Skarney Gin is recommended to the nonserious players who like variety and prefer their game to possess more luck and a quicker ending. All the rules governing Skarney Gin apply with the following additional rule:

An ace, in addition to being used in high and low sequences, or poker straights, such as ace–two–three, or ace–king–queen, can also be used to go round the corner, such as king–ace–two; or two–ace–king. These round-the-corner sequence and poker-straight melds may be extended of course. *Examples:* (*a*) king–ace–two–three; (*b*) queen–king–ace two–three; (*c*) two–ace–king–queen–jack; (*d*) three–two–ace–king–queen–jack–ten, and so on.

Skarney Gin Triples

This variation is played exactly like Skarney Gin except that the scoring system used in regular Hollywood Gin Rummy (see page 88) is employed.

Skarney Gin for Three Players

Skarney Gin, though primarily for two players, makes an enjoyable game for three players. Although three players take part, only two are in play against each other simultaneously, as in captain play (page 90).

To determine which two shall start, any player, by consent of the others, shuffles, and the three cut cards. Low man—that man whose exposed card is of lowest rank—sits out the first hand. The other two play a game of Skarney Gin.

The score of the first hand is credited to the winner, and the loser drops out. The winner proceeds to play the next hand against the third man. (Generally the nonplayer

keeps the score.) So it goes, loser giving way to nonplayer hand by hand, until one of the three scores 200 points or more.

The winner is paid off in the amount of his credit over each opponent. The player with the second highest score collects from low man. A player scoring a shutout can collect his shutout bonus only from the player who scored zero. For example, A scores 205 points; B, 90; and C, none. A gets credit for a shutout over C but not over B. Value of credits and bonuses is the same as in two-handed Skarney Gin. In three-handed Skarney Gin a player may collect from two players, lose to two players, or win from one and lose to one.

Skarney Gin Captains

This is a variation of Skarney Gin for three players, borrowed from Backgammon where it is called chouette or "in the box." A plays the first game as captain against B and C; B playing the first hand and continuing to play as long as he wins. But when he loses, C takes his place and continues to play until he loses, when B comes back again, and so on until the game ends. The captain keeps playing to the end of the game, regardless of whether he wins or loses. A single score is kept and totaled at the end of the game. The captain wins or loses the net total from or to each of the opponents. Then B becomes the captain playing against A and C, and so on.

Skarney Partnership Gin

This is four-handed Skarney Gin. Two players are teamed against the other two. Two games of two-handed Skarney Gin are played simultaneously and the partners enter their score as one. The players cut for partners, holders of the two highest exposed cards being teamed against the holders of the two lowest. All the rules of Skarney Gin apply to this variation. The only variation is in the scoring.

Team scores, not players' scores, are entered. *Example:* (*a*) A and B are partners playing against C and D. A, playing the first hand against his opponent C, wins by 68 points. D, playing against B, wins by 20 points. Team A-B wins the box by 48 points.

That is the only score entered on the score sheet. (*b*) As before, A and B are partners against C and D. At the end of the first hand A switches seats with B and plays against D, while B plays against C. At the end of the second hand, A and B shift back to the original positions. This alternation continues with each hand until the game ends.

Note: Due to the great number of cards melded, it is suggested that two tables be used, one for each two contestants. Game is 300 points. Game bonus remains at 200, shutout bonus 200, and all other scoring is as in two-handed Skarney Gin.

Skarney Gin Strategy

Skarney Gin becomes a considerably more scientific game than regular Gin Rummy, owing to the lack of a discard pile. However, like regular Gin, it is a game of deduction and counterdeduction: (1) You must try to figure out what cards your opponent is holding so that you won't offer him vital cards; (2) you must try to build up your hand for a possible contract meld.

In Skarney Gin, as in most card games of skill and chance, there is a mathematical basis for many correct plays. There are, of course, some probability factors in Skarney Gin which are apparent even to the beginner. It should be obvious that you have a better chance of making a three-card poker straight than a three-card group when you hold a five and six (any suits) than if you hold a pair of sixes. In fact, the odds are 4 to 1 in favor of the poker straight. The reason is there are eight cards (four fours and four sevens) to draw from to make a poker straight and only two sixes to draw from to make a group meld.

At the very beginning of the hand, what is and what is not a safe potential discard is not too important. On the first few rounds any discard with the possible exception of an ace (stop card) is usually accepted. You should not worry at this point because more often than not, your opponent will take it. Therefore, what you should do at the beginning of the hand is to offer potential discards that you wish to get rid of and at the same time concentrate on building up your hand.

While concentrating on building your own hand you should try to keep your opponent in the dark regarding the strength of your hand. An initial meld of three three-card melds is fairly easy to obtain toward the middle of the hand. Even possession of three three-card melds at the beginning of the hand occurs quite frequently in Skarney Gin. But, what to do with such a hand requires some analytical reasoning. Sure, you can go down with your contract meld and put the pressure on your opponent. Great, but what about the one or more cards that will remain in your hand— are they unmatched cards? How about the next potential discard of yours? Is it a part of a matched set or a possible layoff card? Or, is it a useless card to your hand? Do you believe your opponent will take it? All the above factors are vital in playing a good game of Skarney Gin. And such deductions must be studied carefully.

I've seen many a player put down his initial meld after his first pick off the stock—and see his hand grow from two cards to eight or more cards, and his opponent goes Skarney and catches him with a hundred or more points. This upward movement of the number of cards held by a player is caused by his opponent's refusal to accept said player's potential discard, something the player has no control over.

Study your contract meld before putting it down—study it from one angle—then switch your melds around and study it from another angle. You'll be surprised what you'll see that passed unobserved a moment ago. As mentioned earlier, there are more opportunities to lay off on poker straights than group melds. However, don't rule out group melds—they play a vital part in preventing your opponent from getting such cards. The principle of mobility is a general principle in Skarney Gin. To keep your hand fluid at all times and be prepared for most contingencies is of the utmost importance. There can be no definite instruction at this point without ifs, ands, and buts.

In preparing to fulfill your initial meld or in playing for Skarney, try to form as many two-way melds incorporating the same cards in groups and poker straights. For instance, you hold three sixes, three sevens, and three eights. These same three-card groups can and should be switched to three three-card poker straights. It becomes quite a problem to some players when holding 15 or more cards to segregate the melds to their best advantage. The best advice that can be given to achieve this aim is to take your time when sorting out melds in your hand because a simple re-arrangement of melds may spell an eventual Skarney for you. In fact, more games are lost by an early improper arrangement of cards in the hand than by all other erroneous plays.

As a rule, it is best to wait several rounds before putting down your contract meld. That is, providing your opponent has not as yet put down his contract meld. If your opponent has fulfilled his contract meld and you have not, by all means get down on the board (if possible) with any kinds of melds you can muster together.

Once your opponent has put down his contract meld, each of your potential discard plays must be thoroughly analyzed. You must be ultra-safe in offering a potential discard. Think twice before offering an ace (stop card) in the later phase of the hand. Study your opponent's and your own melds (if any) very carefully and think twice before playing.

When your opponent's point total is close to game, you must be extra careful about the point total (of melds or unmatched cards or both) in your hand. You must try to "keep under." That means that you must reduce your point total so that, if possible, even if your opponent goes Skarney, you will still be under going out. Just being aware of the necessity of keeping under will improve your chances of winning the game by 25 to 33 1/3 percent. Except for expert play, my observation is that every third or fourth final hand of a game is lost because of the avoidable failure to keep under.

It is, I take it, the author's privilege to point out—and the player's privilege to ig-nore—the fact that there are 15,820,024,220 possible ten-card hands in Skarney Gin. In every game there occurs a certain incidence of useless statistics. I don't expect you to remember how often in how many billion hands your present holding will occur. I shouldn't be surprised if you fail to remember that the odds of the dealer's being dealt one or more three-card melds in his first ten cards is about 15 to 1 in your favor—although remembering that will improve your game. To attempt to tell the player whether to hold pos-sible layoffs in his hand or lay them off seems to me unsound without knowledge of (*a*) the cards he holds, (*b*) the melds he sees (if any), (*c*) the cards still alive, and (*d*) the potential discards taken by one's opponent. As to this play, you must use your own judgment—as, in fact, you must learn to do in any hand at Skarney Gin.

CHAPTER 19

Children and Family Card Games

In this chapter, I have grouped a collection of card games that are easy to play and simple to learn. But despite their simplicity, these games are most entertaining and they provide a fine medium through which card players of all ages may meet for mutual enjoyment.

I DOUBT IT

Requirements

1. Up to 12 players.

2. For five or fewer players, use a standard single 52-card deck; for six or more players, use a double pack, two standard 52-card decks shuffled together.

3. Rank of cards: ace (high), king, queen, jack, ten, nine, eight, seven, six, five, four, three, two (low).

The players cut for deal, and highest card deals. The cards are dealt out one at a time per round, beginning at dealers' left and going in clockwise rotation until all cards are given out. It does not matter if some players receive more cards than others.

The Play. The player at dealer's left must place on the table in front of him, face down, any number of cards from one to eight (four with a single deck); as he puts them down, he must announce that he is putting down as many aces as the number of cards. Thus, he may put down three cards, saying "Three aces." But the cards need not be aces; the player is not compelled to tell the truth.

Any player at the table may then say "I doubt it," in which event the cards are turned up. If the player's statement was true (if, in the case cited, the three cards were actually aces), the doubter must take them and all other cards which have been played on the table into his hand; if the announcement was false in any respect, the player himself must take all the cards on the table, including his own, into his hand. If two or more players doubt the announcement, the one who speaks first is the official doubter; if two players doubt simultaneously, the one nearer the player's left is the official doubter.

When an announcement is not doubted, the cards played remain on the table in front of the player until, by the rules of the game, some player is compelled to pick them up and add them to his hand.

After the first player's announcement has been doubted or accepted, the player on his left must put down one to four cards and announce that he is putting down so many kings; next, the player at his left must put down and announce so many queens; and so on around the table, so that when a player in turn has announced deuces, the next player must start with aces again.

When the double pack is being used, the player is permitted to put down any number of cards from one to eight. The principle is that a player must be permitted to put down every card of a group if he holds it; four of a kind with a single pack, eight of a kind with a double pack.

When a player puts his last card down on the table and either is not doubted, or, upon being doubted, is shown to have announced correctly, the game ends and each other player pays him one point (one chip). *Variant:* Some play that each other player must give him one chip for every card remaining in his hand.

1. If a player doubts any player's announcement before it is made, his doubt is void and he may not doubt that player's announcement when it is made.

2. There is no misdeal; any irregularity in dealing must be corrected as well as possible by adjusting the cards in the respective hands even if the players have looked at them.

3. It is quite ethical to make false statements, such as saying, when in turn to play sevens, "I haven't any sevens," when in fact the player has one or more sevens in his hand.

Three-Card I Doubt It

In one popular variant of I Doubt It, the cards are dealt around only as far as they will go equally and any remaining cards are put face down in the center of the table. Each player in turn puts down exactly three cards in front of him, and the first player may choose what denomination of cards he will announce; that is, he may say "Three sevens" or "Three kings" or anything else he chooses. Each player in turn thereafter, in putting down his three cards, must name the next higher denomination from the player preceding him. When a player has only one or two cards left, he must draw enough cards from the stock in the center of the table to be able to put down three cards. The game ends when a player gets rid of his last three cards.

Cheat

Cheat is an interesting variant of I Doubt It.

Requirement

1. Four to 12 players.

2. Two standard 52-card decks. (If there are more than eight at the table, use three decks.)

The Play. The cards are dealt out as far as they will go. The player to the dealer's left leads off. He takes any card he likes from his hand and places it face downward on the table, at the same time naming its denomination. Thus, if his card is a four, he says "Four." He does not, however, show it. The next player must now play a five on top of the four, again face downward; if he has no five (as, of course, may well be the case), he must still play a card, at the same time saying "Five"; and must do his best to look as if there is nothing wrong. So the play goes on. Six follows five, eight follows seven, and so on. King is followed by ace, then deuce, and so on. Thus, the pile of cards in the center of the table keeps building up as play goes on.

After any player has played his card, he may be challenged by anyone else at the table. The challenge takes the form of a cry of "Cheat," and quite likely more than one player will challenge, especially toward the end of the game, so it is advisable to appoint someone as referee. Generally it is best to let each player, in turn, stand out for one round so that all his energies can be devoted to refereeing. As soon as "Cheat" is called, the card last played must be turned up. If the challenge is successful (i.e., if the player actually has cheated) he has to take into his hand all the cards on the table. If, however, the challenge is unsuccessful, the player who has first called "Cheat" is awarded the stock of cards. And it is from this point of view that a referee's services are needed.

After a challenge, the player next to the one challenged plays a card to the table. He can play any card he likes.

It is legitimate to cheat not only by playing a card not of the denomination named, but also by playing two cards at once if one can get away with it. But here, again, of course, one is liable to be challenged. Of course, the first player to get rid of all his cards is the winner.

WAR

The game is also known as Beggar-Your-Neighbor.

1. Two players.
2. A standard 52-card deck.

3. Cards rank: king (high), queen, jack, ten, nine, eight, seven, six, five, four, three, two, ace (low).

After a shuffle and cut, the cards are dealt out one at a time, alternately; each player being dealt 26 cards.

The object is to win all the cards.

Each player turns up his top card and places it face up in front of his face-down pile. The higher card wins the other and both cards are placed face down beneath the winner's packet.

When the turned-up cards are the same rank, "war" begins. These two cards are put in the center, and each player adds an additional card from his packet. Then each player turns up another card, and the higher card of these two wins all six cards. If these third cards are a pair, they also go in the center, and each player adds another card. This continues until one of the turned-up cards is higher than the other and its owner wins the whole group of cards.

The object is to capture all 52 cards, but since this seldom happens, it is usually agreed that the first player to win three wars wins the game.

Persian Pasha

This game is played in the same manner as War, except for the following:

1. The two players keep turning up cards, each on a single pile in front of himself, until both players turn up cards of the same suit. The player with the higher-ranking card then captures all of the other player's cards in the face-up pile.

2. When two cards of the same suit cannot be turned up at the same time, the game ends, and the player with the majority of cards is the winner.

OLD MAID

Requirements

1. Two to five players.

2. The standard 52-card deck is used, but the queen of clubs (or any one other queen) is taken out and put aside so that only 51 cards remain for play.

Any player may deal the first hand. The turn to deal then passes to the left in subsequent hands.

Beginning at the dealer's left, each player is dealt, face down, one card at a time until all cards have been given out. It has no bearing on the game if the cards do not deal out evenly.

Object. To get rid of all of one's cards by putting them into pairs of the same denomination.

Each player spreads his cards face up, picks out and discards all pairs, putting them face up in the center of the table. Each player shuffles his hand out of sight of the other players, usually behind his back. If no queens have been paired and discarded, three remain in play and the player on the dealer's left draws one card from the dealer's hand. If only one queen remains in play, the first draw is made from the hand holding it.

The player who gives the first draw holds his face-down cards toward the player on his left, and the latter draws out one card. If this card pairs with one in his hand, he discards the pair. In any case, he then shuffles his hand and allows the player on his left to draw one card. The play continues in rotation with each pair formed being discarded until all the cards have been paired except the odd queen. The player who is stuck with this is the "Old Maid" and loses the hand.

Play is continued until one player is the "Old Maid" a certain number of times. This player is considered the loser of the game while the one with the fewest "Old Maids" is the winner. It is advisable to keep the score on paper.

AUTHORS

Authors was originally played with special cards bearing the pictures of famous writers. These cards are still available, but regular playing cards can be used.

1. Three to six players; four or five is best.

2. A standard 52-card deck.

The 52 cards are dealt out, one at a time, as far as they will go. It does not matter if some players receive one more card than the others. When there are fewer than six players, some ranks may be discarded in order to reduce the size of the hands.

Each player in clockwise rotation (starting at the dealer's left) calls any other by name and asks for a specific card by suit and rank. The asker must have at least one card of the same rank in his hand, but he may not ask for a card he already holds. If the person asked has the card, he must give it up; if not, he says "No." The same player continues to ask various players for particular cards by suit and rank as long as he is successful in obtaining them; when he fails, the turn passes to the left.

As soon as a player gets four cards of the same rank, he must show them, and place them on the table in front of himself. These four cards are called a book. The player who collects the most books is the winner of the game.

When Authors is played for a stake, chips are used, and when a player completes a book he collects one chip from each other player, but he must put down the book before calling for another card in order to collect. For any violation of procedure, such as asking for a card he already holds or asking for a card when he does not hold another of the same rank, a player must pay one chip to each other player. If a player asks out of turn, or fails to surrender a card when it is requested, he may not score for making a book of that rank.

Go Fish or Fish

A simplified form of Authors.
1. Two to five players.
2. A standard 52-card deck.

Cards are dealt one at a time. If there are two players, each gets seven cards; if more than two players, each gets five. The remaining cards comprise the stock.

Each player in turn asks any other player for all the cards he holds of a specified rank, for example, "Give me your nines." The asking player must have one or more cards of the asked-for rank in his own hand. The person asked must give up all the cards he has of that rank. The first player's turn continues as long as he succeeds in getting cards from any other player. If that player asked has no cards of the rank requested, he replies "Go Fish." The asker then takes the top card of the stock, and the turn moves to the left.

Whenever a player gets four cards of the same rank, he must show them and put them down in front of himself. The winner is the player who first matches up all his cards and has none left in his hand. Or, the play continues until the stock is exhausted, in which case the player having the most books wins.

Optional Rules. The asker's turn continues if (*a*) the card drawn from the stock is of the rank asked for, or (*b*) if it is of another rank but completes a book.

DONKEY

Requirements
1. Three to 13 players.
2. A standard 52-card deck that has been stripped so that for each player in the game there is a complete set of four cards of the same denomination: four kings, four queens, etc. When six are playing, the deck would contain 24 cards. The remainder of the cards are placed aside and not used in play.
3. One chip is placed in the center of the table for each player in the game less one. *Example:* If there are five players in the game, only four chips are placed on the table.

Object of the Game. To make a group of four of a kind in the player's hand, or not to be the last to notice when someone else accomplishes this.

The Deal. Any player shuffles the pack thoroughly and deals four cards, one at a time, to each player.

The Play. Once all the cards have been dealt, the dealer announces "Go." At that time, every player passes a card to the player at his left simultaneously. The passing continues until one player matches his four cards. He then quickly picks up a chip from the table, attempting to do so unnoticed. As soon as this is observed, every other player grabs for a chip. One player, of course, will not be able to obtain a counter and he is the "donkey" for that hand. The winning player must be prepared to show that his hand contained the required set, otherwise he becomes the donkey.

Each time a player loses a game, he receives a different letter in the word "donkey" in the order that the name is spelled. First player to score D-O-N-K-E-Y loses. The score is kept on paper.

Pig

This game is similar to Donkey, except:

1. When a player has in his hand four cards of one denomination, as four kings, he stops passing or picking up cards and puts his finger to his nose. The other players must immediately stop passing and each must put his finger to his nose. The last to do this is the "Pig."

2. The first player to become a pig ten times is the "prize pig" and must "oink-oink" for the others.

My Ship Sails

A variation of Pig for older children.

Requirements

1. Three to seven players, each for himself.

2. A standard 52-card deck. (When only three or four are playing, use 21- or 28-card decks, respectively, comprising any seven cards of each of three or four suits. With five to seven players, use the full deck.)

Object of the Game. To be the first player to get a hand of cards all in the same suit.

The Deal. Anyone may deal. Each player is dealt a hand of seven cards, one at a time, beginning with one at dealer's left and going in clockwise rotation. The remainder of the deck is put aside.

The Play. Each player puts any one card face down at his left; then at the same time all players pick up the cards at their right. This continues until one player has collected seven cards of the same suit. He shows his hand, announces "My ship sails!" and wins the deal.

Variation. Some play that the first player to get a hand of all cards in the same suit announces "My Bird Sings."

SLAP JACK

Requirement

1. Three to eight players, each for himself.
2. A regular 52-card deck.

Object. To win all the cards, by being the first to slap each jack as it is played to the center.

Any player may deal first. The cards are shuffled and dealt out, one at a time to each player in clockwise rotation until all have been dealt; they do not have to come out even. Each player without looking at any of his cards squares up his hand into a neat pile in front of him, face down.

Each player in turn, beginning at the dealer's left, must lift one card from the pile in front of him and place it face up in the center of the table; in doing this, he must turn up the card away from him, not toward him, so that he may not see it any sooner than any other player. Accordingly, he should try to make the play with a very quick movement so that other players may not see the denomination of the card before he does.

When the card played to the center is a jack, the first player to slap his hand down on it takes it, and with it, all cards below it in the

center of the table. The player winning these cards turns them face down and shuffles them with the cards in his hand still remaining on the table in front of him, to form his new hand.

When several players slap at once, the one whose hand is nearest the jack wins the pile. If a player slaps a card that is not a jack, he must give one card from the top of his pile, face down, to each of the other players.

Snap

This game is similar to Slap Jack except for the following:

1. Each faces up his cards one at a time on a pile in front of his face-down hand; the cards being faced up one at a time in rotation. When a card is faced up which is the same in denomination as a card already faced up on some other pile, the first player to call out "Snap" wins both piles, and adds them to his pack.

2. The player remaining in the game the longest and holding all the cards is the winner.

ANIMALS OR MENAGERIE

Requirements

1. Three to six, playing for themselves.

2. A standard 52-card deck.

Object of the Game. To win all of the cards, by being the first to make the proper call, when matching cards are faced up.

Before Play. Each player chooses the name of an animal—dog, cat, cow, lion, etc. Then he imitates the sound of that animal so that other players know how to call him.

The Deal. Anyone can deal. Beginning at the dealer's left, each player is dealt one card at a time until all cards have been given out. It does not matter if the cards do not deal out evenly. The hands are placed faced-down in packs as in Slap Jack.

The Play. Beginning at the dealer's left, each player, in clockwise rotation, plays one card face up to an exposed pile in front of his face-down pack. Whenever a card so faced up matches a card faced up on the pile of any other player, each tries to give the proper call of the other player. The one who gives the correct call first wins the other's up pile, and places it below his own pile. If both give the calls correctly, the one starting it first wins. An incorrect call, or a call given at the wrong time, costs a penalty of the top card of the pile (or of the pack, if there is no pile) to the other player. After each call, the player who loses leads. When a hand has been played out, the pile is reversed, and becomes a pack, as at the beginning of the game. The player who takes all of the cards is the winner.

Variant. In a simpler variation of this hilarious game, the names of the animals are called out, instead of their calls.

CONCENTRATION

This game is also known as Memory or Pelmanism.

Requirement

1. Two to six players, but the best game is two.

2. A standard 52-card deck is used.

The Deal and Play. The deck is shuffled and then either dealt face down into any number of rows so that no two cards overlap, or the face-down cards may be mixed, some of them overlapping (this takes less space and makes the game a bit harder to play).

Each player turns one card face up, and the player turning the highest card is the first player. (In case of ties, the tieing players each turn up one more card.) Then the cards are all turned face down again in exactly the same positions.

The first player then turns up two cards, one at a time. If they form a pair (two cards of the same denomination), they are a *set* and the player puts them face down in front of himself and gets another turn. If the cards are not a pair, they are turned face down again in exactly the same positions, and the next player on the left takes his turn.

Players try to remember the denominations and positions of cards previously exposed so that they can form pairs. If a player turns up a king as his first card and can remember the location of a king previously exposed, he can turn it up as his second card. The game is a test of memory. When all the cards have been paired and collected, the player who has the most sets wins the game.

The game can also be played using chips or counters and is then scored as follows:

1. The player who collects the greatest number of sets takes one chip from each of the other players.

2. Or each player collects one chip from each other player for every pair he has collected.

Variant. A more difficult variation is to turn up four cards at a time and collect sets of four-of-a-kind.

CUCKOO

This game is also known as Ranter Go Round.

Requirements

1. Six to approximately 20 players.

2. A standard 52-card deck. Rank of cards: king (high), queen, jack, ten, nine, eight, seven, six, five, four, three, two, ace (low).

3. Each player is given three chips.

The Deal and Play. One card is dealt to each player. Then beginning with the player at the dealer's left, each in turn must say "Stand" (keeping his card) or "Change" (in which case he exchanges with the player at his left). A player must exchange when requested except when he holds a king. In such a case, he responds to the demand "Change" by showing the king, and the turn passes to his left. When play reaches the dealer, he may either stand on his original card or exchange it for one drawn at random from the undealt remainder of the deck.

After all the players have had a chance to stand or change, the cards are exposed and the holder of the lowest card must pay a chip to the pot or pool in the center of the table. If the dealer, however, obtains a king by exchange, he is the only one to put a chip into the pot. If two or more players tie for the lowest, each must pay a chip.

On losing all three chips, a player must drop out of the game and others continue until there is just one survivor. He is the winner.

STEALING THE OLD MAN'S BUNDLE

This game is also known as Old Man's Bundle and Stealing Bundles.

Requirements

1. Two players.
2. A standard 52-card deck.

The Deal. Each player is dealt four cards, one at a time, and then four cards are placed face up on the table. Thereafter, each time the hands are played out, four more cards go to each player, but none are placed on the table. The game ends when the pack is exhausted.

The Play. The nondealer leads first, and from then in, the play alternates. The player may either *take* in a card from the table with a card of the same rank from the hand or *trail* by placing a card face up on the table. Cards taken in must be placed in a pile face up, forming the bundle. A player may steal his opponent's bundle by taking it in with a card of the same rank as its top card.

The player who has the greater number of cards in his bundle by the time the pack is exhausted wins the game.

DIG

Requirements

1. Two to five players.
2. A standard 52-card deck.

The Deal. Each player is dealt seven cards one at a time. The remaining cards are the stock which is placed face down in the center except for its top card which is put to one side face up.

The Play. The first player to the dealer's left tries to play from his hand a card of either the same suit or the same rank as the upcard. It is played face up on the upcard. If he has no card that matches in either suit or rank, he must dig by taking the next card from the stock, and he continues to dig until he gets a playable card. Eights are wild and may be played on the upcard at any time, and this changes the suit to any suit or rank the player names.

The first player to get rid of all the cards in his hand is the winner.

FROGS IN THE POND

This game is also called Frogpond.

Requirements

1. Two to five players, but the best game is playing as partners, two against two.
2. A standard 52-card deck. When there are four players, remove two deuces from the deck.
3. Rank of cards: ace (high), king, queen, jack, ten, nine, eight, seven, six, five, four, three, two (low).

The Deal. The dealer deals the cards two at a time until each player has ten cards. He then deals the next ten cards face down to make a pile, and puts this pile in the center of the table. These are the "Frogs in the Pond."

When there are three players, use the whole pack and deal 13 cards to each player and 13 cards to the frogs pile. When five people play, remove the four deuces, and deal eight cards to each player and eight cards to the frogs pile. Each player must always have the same number of cards as the Frogs in the Pond.

The Object of the Game. To be the first to score 100 points by winning cards that count in the scoring.

Each ten	10 points
Each five	5 points
Each ace	4 points
Each king	3 points
Each queen	2 points
Each jack	1 point

Variant. Some play that the jack of spades (called the *tadpole*) counts a minus 10 points against the player (or side) taking it.

The Play. The player to the left of the dealer starts the game by leading a card, placing it face up in the center of the table. (The best strategy, when you are playing partners, is to lead an ace. Then, if your partner has a ten or a five or some other scoring card, he can put it on your ace and your side will win both cards.) Each trick is won by the highest card of the suit led. The players must follow suit if they can. If a player "revokes," or fails to follow suit when he can, he loses 10 points from his score. When a player cannot follow suit, he may play any card he desires.

The winner of each trick picks up the cards won and, at the same time, takes the top card of the frogs pile. He looks at this card, but he must take care that no one else, not even his partner, sees it. He does not add it to his hand, but puts it face down with the cards he has just won. If it is a scoring card, it will count for him. He then leads for the next trick.

Each winner of a trick always does the same thing—takes a frog to add to the cards won. When all the cards have been played, each side adds up its score and writes it down. The cards are then shuffled and dealt again, the new dealer being the player to the left of the previous dealer.

The first side to score 100 points wins the game. If players are playing independently, each for himself, the first one to score 100 points is the winner.

TWENTY-ONE

Requirements

1. Four to seven players.
2. A standard 52-card deck.

The Deal. The cards are dealt to each player, one at a time, as far as they will go evenly. Any remaining cards are laid aside face up and not used in that deal.

The player on the dealer's left begins by playing one card face up in the center, announcing its value. Aces and face cards count one each; other cards count their index value. Each player in rotation places a card to the center and announces the total it makes with the preceding cards. If, for instance, the first player began with a six and the next player added a queen, the latter announces "Seven."

No player may exceed a total count of 21. Each must play if he can, but if unable to add a card without going over 21, a player says "Stop." The player on his right then wins all the center cards. The one who called stop begins a new series of plays, starting the count again from zero. Play continues in this way until all the cards have been won.

It is sometimes agreed that each deal is a game, and the player who captures the most cards wins. But it is better to keep score on paper, crediting each player with the number of cards he wins, and the first to reach a total of 50 wins the game.

TWENTY-NINE

Requirements

1. Four players, playing as partners, two against two.
2. A standard 52-card deck.

The Deal and Play. Thirteen cards are dealt to each player from a standard deck. Aces and face cards count one each, other cards their index value. The player at the dealer's left plays a card and announces its value. Each player in turn plays a card, adds its value, and announces the new total, until 29 is reached. The player who makes the total

29 takes the trick, and the player at his left starts the count again at zero. There are eight possible tricks, and the object is to win more cards in tricks than one's opponents.

Whenever a player is unable to play without exceeding a total of 29, the play ends and the cards won in tricks are counted to deter-mine the winner of the deal. The deal passes in a clockwise rotation.

In addition to card games in this chapter, many of those mentioned in the earlier chapters are suitable for play by children and beginners.

CHAPTER 20

Miscellaneous Card Games

In this chapter I have included various games which are rather difficult to place in any particular category. Many of them are of foreign origin.

PARTNERSHIP TRESSETTE

Tressette derives its name from the fact that it has both seven- and three-card melds. It is the most popular partnership game among the working and middle classes in Italy. (Bridge is the favorite card game of Italy's upper classes.) Tressette is often played for big stakes, small stakes, and for refreshments (most often wine). It has countless devotees in the United States, particularly in the small political and social clubhouses in every big town and city with a high concentration of foreign-born Italians. Tressette retains a secure hold on the affections of its millions of adherents as a deceptively simple game that seldom fails to provide much amusement, arguments, and conversation after the play of each hand or game. It is a most strategic card game.

Requirements

1. Four players, two against two, as partners.

2. A 40-card Italian deck, that is, a standard 52-card deck from which the eights, nines, and tens have been removed.

3. The cards rank as follows: three (high), two, ace, king, queen, jack, seven, six, five, and four (low). The suits have no relative rank.

Object of the Game. For a partnership to win the game by scoring 31 points or more before the other partnership does. The side which first scores 31 points or more announces "Game" and the hand in play ends immediately. The reward for winning is stipulated before the start of the game.

Point Value of Cards Won in Tricks. Aces, 1 point each; threes, twos, kings, jacks, and queens, 1/3 point each. Eleven is the maximum number of card points that can be scored in a hand. If a partnership's odd trick is valued at 2/3 point, the side is credited with 1 point. If a partnership's odd trick is valued at 1/3 point, the side is credited with zero (0).

Melds or Napoletanas. After each player has played to the first trick, the winner announces his meld or melds. Then, each player, in a clockwise rotation starting at the dealer's left, must do likewise. Each player or partner must announce for himself. These matched sets are not melded or placed on the table. They are announced, shown to all players, and returned to the hand. The sequence melds called *napoletana* are four in number: ace, two, and three of each of the four suits, valued at 3 points for each meld.

Example: When a player announces a sequence group which is comprised of ace of diamonds, two of diamonds, and three of diamonds, he calls "Diamond napoletana," or "Diamond sequence," etc. In addition to the napoletana, there are three valuable group melds, which are aces, deuces, and threes. Three aces are valued at 3 points, four aces 4 points, three threes are valued at 3 points, four threes 4 points, three twos are valued at 3 points, four twos 4 points. If a player holds one or two (aces, deuces, or threes) they do not count as points.

If a player holds *three* sequence melds (napoletana)—ace, two, and three all diamonds; ace, two, and three all spades; and ace, two and three all hearts—he scores 3 points for each napoletana for a total of 9 points. In addition he gets 9 points for the three group melds, three aces, three twos, and three threes, for a total of 18 points. If the tenth card were an ace, two, or three, the player would score 19 points, the highest possible number of points in one hand. Twenty-one points is the maximum number of possible points in all hands.

How to Select Partnerships. Partnerships are determined by prearrangement or by cutting. Rules to determine cards by cutting are as follows:

1. The four players seat themselves at four places around the table. Where they sit is for the moment irrelevant.

2. Any player may shuffle the deck and offer the deck to any other player for a cut.

3. For the purpose of cutting for partners and seating positions, the cards rank as stated earlier for this game.

4. Each player cuts a portion of cards from the deck, immediately exposing to the others the bottom card of his group. Players cutting the two high cards become partners. So do the players cutting the two low-ranking cards.

6. Players (partners) who cut low cards have the privilege of seating themselves at any side of the table, providing they sit opposite each other. The other two players take the remaining seats.

7. Either player of the partnership which cut the high cards starts the game by dealing the first hand. Thereafter on the completion of each hand, the deal passes to the player at the previous dealer's left.

The Shuffle, Cut, and Deal. The dealer shuffles the cards. Any player may call for the right to shuffle, but the dealer retains the privilege of shuffling last. The player to the dealer's right cuts, and at least three cards must be left to constitute each cut group of cards. Should the first player to the dealer's right decline the cut, the cards may be cut by any other player.

After the cards have been cut, the dealer deals each player ten cards face down, five at a time, starting with the player at his left and dealing clockwise.

The Play of the Hand. The leader (the player at the dealer's left) makes the opening lead. He may play any card he desires. Each player in turn must play a card in the same suit if he is able to do so. If he is unable to follow suit, he may play a card of any other suit. A trick is constituted when each player has played a card to the lead and it is won by the highest card of the suit led by the first player. The winner of the trick leads the next play of the hand. This manner of play continues until ten tricks or all cards have been played out.

How to Score Melds or Lays. After the first trick has been played, the winner of the trick announces his meld or melds. For example, if he holds ace of diamonds, two of diamonds, and three of diamonds, he announces a diamond napoletana or sequence. If he holds four aces, he announces four aces and 4 points. If he fails to hold a meld, he says "No meld." Each player in turn announces his meld or melds and enters the melds on the score sheet under his partnership's name. Each player who has announced a meld must show his melds before play continues. Many Tressette players do not require the showing of melds—they just remember them.

Scoring the Hand. At the end of each hand, the score for each partnership is recorded on the score sheet. Only one player of a side calculates the score while the other verifies the count of the other side's score. To speed up the arithmetic in scoring, count 1 point for every three cards having a value of 1/3 point.

The partnership that wins the last trick (tenth) receives 1 point.

End of Game. The game ends when a partnership announces game, or 31 points. Should a partnership announce game and their game score is less than 31 points, the opponents are declared the winners. If a player, able to do so, fails to follow the suit led, it is a "renege," and the penalty to the offending partnership is the loss of the game.

SAMPLE SCORING OF A
TRESSETTE PARTNERSHIP GAME

Score Sheet	They	We
Melds	6	3
First hand scores	4	7
Total scores, 1 hand	10	10
Melds	3	—
Second hand scores	11	—
Total scores, 2 hands	24	10
Melds	—	3
Third hand scores	2	9
Total scores, 3 hands	26	22
Melds	3	3
Fourth hand scores	5	—
Total Game Score	34	25

They by passing 31 points wins the game and receives the reward due the winners—which in Italy is often a glass or bottle of wine.

Tressette Low Hand

I first witnessed this fine variation of Tressette being played in Naples many years ago. As a matter of record, all the Tressette rules of play were written by me while visiting Naples. Low Hand Tressette strategy is just the opposite of that of Tressette and it is played exactly as Tressette with the following exception. The object of the game is for a partnership to score less points than the opposing partnership. When a partnership scores 31 points or more, the game ends and the partnership with the lower score wins the game.

Three-Handed Tressette

This game is played exactly as is Partnership Tressette (or Tressette Low Hand) with the following exceptions:

1. There are three players each playing for himself.

2. The game is won by scoring 31 or more points before any opponent does.

3. The dealer deals four hands as in Partnership Tressette except that one hand is pushed aside as a dead hand and does not come into play.

Two-Handed Tressette

This game is played the same as Partnership Tressette except for the following:

1. Only two players, each playing for himself, are required.

2. The dealer deals each player ten cards and places the remaining 20 cards in the center of the table to form the stock.

3. After the first trick is completed, the players announce their melds and score them. Then the winner of the trick picks the top card of the stock, while his opponent takes the next one. This continues after each trick until the stock has been exhausted. Then the last ten tricks are played out to complete the game.

Mediatore

This game is a form of Partnership Tressette in which there is no melding and the partnerships are not fixed, but are determined by the bidding. The other major differences between Tressette and Mediatore are as follows:

1. Each player antes a set number of chips into the pot, usually five.

2. Nine cards are dealt to each player and the four remaining ones are set aside as the widow.

3. The player to the dealer's left has the chance to be the *mediator* (which is an undertaking to win six of the 11 possible points), or he may pass. If he does the latter, the privilege of becoming mediator moves to the player on his left. This procedure continues until a mediator is selected or all the players pass. If all pass, there is a new deal by the same dealer.

4. When a player becomes the mediator, he may decide to play alone, or he may call for a specified card the holder of which becomes his partner. The mediator then takes the widow into his hand and discards four cards. If he called for a card and it is in the widow, he must play alone.

5. When the mediator decides to play by himself, he must match the pot, putting in 20 chips. Should he have a partner, they put in ten chips apiece.

6. Playing and scoring (except for melds) are as in Partnership Tressette. Incidentally, the mediator's discard counts as a trick for him. Should the mediator, or his side, win the

majority of the 11 possible points, he takes the pot; if he does not, there is no penalty. But the pot remains and there is another deal without additional contributions from the players. However, a player who becomes mediator must always match the pot, so on the next deal there will be 40 chips in the pot for the mediator (and his partner, if any) to match.

BRISCOLA

This is one of the truly great Italian partnership games which is played extensively in the United States by Americans of Italian extraction.

Requirements

1. A standard 52-card deck from which the eights, nines, and tens have been removed, making a 40-card deck.

2. Partners, two players against two.

3. The cards rank in descending order as follows: ace (high), three, king, queen, jack, seven, six, five, and four and two (low), the ace being highest and the four lowest both in cutting and in play.

Point Scoring Values of Cards Won in Tricks. Aces count 11 points, threes 10 points, kings 4 points, queens 3 points, and jacks 2 points. Sevens, sixes, fives, fours, and twos have no point values. The maximum number of points that can be scored in one hand by a partnership is 120.

Object of the Game. For a team of two partners to first score 121 or more points in two or more hands or deals, or score 61 points or more in one hand. When the hand is over, each partnership looks through its pile of cards (the tricks they have taken) and scores as described under Point Scoring Values.

How to Select Partnerships. Partnerships are determined by prearrangement or by cutting. Rules to determine partnerships by cutting the cards is the same as in Partnership Tressette. This also holds true for the shuffle and the cut.

The Deal. Dealer, starting with the player on his right, deals each player including himself three face-down cards, one at a time in counterclockwise fashion. The next card from the top of the deck, which is the thirteenth card, is placed on the table face up and the rest of the stock goes face down next to the upturned card.

How Trump Is Determined. The trump in Briscola is determined by the suit of the upcard, the thirteenth card. If the card faced in the center of the table is a club, the trump for this hand is clubs, and so on.

Beginning the Play. The player to the dealer's right leads the first card. It may be any one of the three cards he holds. Thereupon, the turn of play passes to the right. Each player in his turn can play any card he wishes, he does not have to follow suit. A trick which contains one trump is won by the trump. A trick which contains more than one trump is won by the higher trump card. Any other trick is won by the highest card of the suit led.

The Stock. The winner of a trick draws the top card of the stock to restore his hand to three cards. The player on the winner's right draws the next card, and so it rotates counterclockwise until each player has three cards. When all four hands have been restored to three cards, the winner of the previous trick must lead to the new trick, and play rotates to the right according to the rules set forth. The routine of play continues until all cards have been played to tricks. Then the score for points taken in tricks is totaled, and a second deal takes place and play continues until one partnership has scored 121 points and wins the game. The upturned trump card is considered the last card of the stock. Immediately upon the picking up of the last card of the stock (trump upcard), partners are permitted to exchange hands and after studying such hands return them to their rightful owner; then the last hand is played to a finish. *Note:* If partners believe they have scored a total of 121 points, they may throw in their hands to their opponents. However if such is not the case, the opponents are declared the winners.

Briscola and Tressette both have a unique feature of an informatory exchange in certain arbitrary and authorized facial and verbal cues which inform the partner as to what good or bad cards each is holding. This discussion and cueing is sort of a secret convention and is not a binding contract and cannot take place until the first trick has been taken. It need not even be an accurate description of what it purports to describe, namely the card values in a partner's hand.

Players will often give their partners inaccurate cues with the thought in mind of misleading their eavesdropping opponents.

CALABRASELLA

This is another game of Italian origin. While it has a rather unique rank of cards, it's not too difficult to learn and is simple in its bidding and in its play, which never has a trump suit.

Requirements

1. Three players, but four may play with the dealer taking no cards.

2. The 40-card Italian deck.

3. The cards rank as follows: three (high), two, ace, king, queen, jack, seven, six, five, four (low). Suits have no comparative rank.

Beginning of the Game. The selection of the dealer, seating positions, changing seats, shuffle, and cut are as provided under the General Rules for Card Games, chapter 1.

The Deal. Players cut and low card deals. Dealer gives each player a hand of 12 cards, dealt four at a time per round, beginning at dealer's left. The remaining four cards are placed face down in the center of the table as a widow. The turn to deal in subsequent hands passes to the left.

Object of the Game. To win in tricks as many as possible of the 35 points that can be made in counting cards.

Points to Be Won in Play. Certain cards have counting value as follows: ace, 3 points; three, deuce, king, queen, and jack, 1 point each—a total of 8 points per unit. Winning the last trick is worth 3 points. Thus a total of 35 points can be scored on a hand.

The Bidding. Player at dealer's left has first turn. He may say "I play" or "Pass." If he says "I play" he proposes to play alone against the other two, who combine as partners against him. If he passes the turn goes to the player at his left. But as soon as any player announces he will play, there is no further bidding by the others. If no one proposes to play, the deal goes to the player at the left.

The Play. The single player discards face down from one to four cards as he pleases. He then turns up the widow and takes from it as many cards as he discarded. The cards left over from his discards and the widow are placed together in a single pile face down and

will go to the winner of the last trick. Player at dealer's left leads any card to the first trick. Each other player in turn must follow suit if able to but may play a card of any rank. If a player cannot follow suit, he may play any card. There is *never* any trump.

A trick, which consists of three cards, one from each player, is won by the highest card of the suit led. Winner of the last trick also takes the cards in the discard pile and adds them to his trick pile. Opponents of the single player keep their cards together in a common trick pile. Winner of a trick leads to the next, and play proceeds until all 12 tricks have been played.

Scoring. Players count the points in their trick piles as previously described. Lower score is deducted from higher score and the difference represents the winning margin for the player or side with the higher score. If either side takes in all 35 points, the winning score becomes 70.

If the single player is the loser, he pays to each opponent in chips or points. If he is the winner, each opponent pays him. Game may be set at 100 points if a pencil and paper score is kept. Or the game may end, if chips are used, when any player loses all his chips.

Additional Rules. The following will cover the various irregularities of Calabrasella:

1. In case of a misdeal, the same player deals again.

2. If a player looks at any cards of the widow before there has been a proposal to play, the hands are thrown in and offender pays 35 to each opponent. The same is true if the single player looks at the widow cards before he discards.

3. If an opponent of the single player looks at any cards of the widow after there has been a proposal to play, there is no penalty. But the single player may look at the widow cards before discarding.

4. If an opponent of the single player exposes a card, except for the purpose of playing it, or leads out of turn, the single player may demand that the hands be thrown in. Opponents then score only for points that

they won before the offense and single player scores for all points that he took plus 3 for last trick.

5. If a player fails to follow suit when able to, it is a revoke and 9 points are subtracted from his score and added to the score of opponent or opponents. The hand is played out.

PRIMIERA

This is another popular game in both Italy and the United States.

Requirements

1. Three to six players.
2. A 40-card Italian deck.
3. Each player antes to form a pot.

Beginning of the Game. The selection of the dealer, seating positions, changing seats, shuffle, and cut are as provided under the General Rules for Card Games, chapter 1.

The Deal. Each player is dealt four cards; the remaining cards are to be used as stock. The rotation of the dealing and play is clockwise.

Rank of the Hand. The ranking of hands is as follows:

Primiera: One card of each suit; highest ranking.

Flush: Four cards of one suit; next highest.

Fifty-Five: Ace, seven, six of one suit.

As between combinations of the same rankings, the winning hand is determined by the point values of the cards: Each seven counts 21, six 18, ace 16, five 15, four 14, three 13, two 12, face cards 10 each.

The Play. The object of the play is to make either primiera, flush or fifty-five combinations. Each player in turn, beginning with player at the dealer's left, may discard any number of their four cards and receive replacements from the stock to keep their hands at four. This procedure continues until any player knocks. When this occurs, there is a showdown and the highest-ranking hand wins the pot. If hands are otherwise tied, the player at the dealer's left has precedence, and after him each player in rotation to his left. If no one knocks when the stock is exhausted, the discards are shuffled and play continues as before.

DOCTOR VIDETTI

An interesting and strategic game of card elimination created by the author, Doctor Videtti is played unlike any other card game. The rules are few and simple; however, considerable skill can be employed to play winning Doctor Videtti.

Requirements

1. A standard deck of 52 playing cards.
2. From two to six players, four making for the best game.

Object of the Game. This game resembles an elimination tournament. When a player gets rid of the last card in his hand by playing it to a losing trick, he is out of the game. One by one the players are eliminated until only one is left and he is the winner.

Rank of Cards. Cards in descending order rank as follows: ace (high), king, queen, jack, ten, nine, eight, seven, six, five, four, three, and two (low). Suits have no value except trump which is high.

Preliminaries Before the Start of the Game. Players select any vacant seat they desire. Any player may shuffle the cards and become the first dealer. Doctor Videtti is usually played for so much a game. However, it is best to play so much for each card held by the winner at the end of the game.

The Shuffle and Cut. Dealer shuffles the deck. Player to his right must cut the cards. At the completion of each hand the deal shall pass to the player at the immediate left of the player who dealt the previous hand.

The Deal. The dealer deals one face-down card at a time to each player, starting with the player to the dealer's left and continuing clockwise until each player in the game has the required number of cards—two-handed, ten cards each; three-handed, eight cards each; four-handed, seven cards each; five-handed, five cards each; six-handed, four cards each. The next card dealt from the top of the deck, which is the dealer's last card, is placed on the table face up. The rest of the cards (stock) goes face down next to the up-turned card, but the stock is fanned out to facilitate drawing from it.

The trump is determined by the suit of the

upcard in the center of the table. If this card is a club, the trump for the hand is clubs, and so on.

Beginning the Play. The player to the dealer's left leads off for the first trick. He may play any card he selects. Turn of play then rotates to the left, clockwise. After the first card has been led, each player in turn of play, which remember moves to the left, must observe the following rules:

1. Each player may play any card he chooses to any suit led. He does not have to follow suit nor trump when a trump is led, nor does he have to trump when not holding a suit led. In short, a player can do as he wishes when leading or playing to a hand (suit led).

2. The highest ranking card of the suit led wins the trick, providing no trump has been played.

3. The highest ranking trump wins the trick when two or more trump comprise a trick.

4. The winner of the trick *must take one card* from the top of the stock and place it in his hand with other cards, if any, and then lead off again, and the play rotates to the left under the rules set forth above. When the last trick of the game is played and no cards are left in any player's hand, the winner of the trick is the winner of the game by taking the top card of the stock.

5. This method of play continues until all cards in all but one player's hand have run out and all such cards have been played to tricks. *Example:* A, B, C, and D are engaged in a game of Doctor Videtti. Each player has been dealt seven cards, A and B each win three tricks. C and D have been eliminated from the game because they no longer hold any cards. A and B each possess six cards in hand. The game continues between A and B. Finally B has no cards left in his hand and A has three cards. A is declared the winner and receives so much for each game or so much for each of the three cards held by the winner as previously agreed on. *Note:* If all active players hold but one last card, the winner of the trick still must draw a card from the stock.

6. If the stock is exhausted and more than one player still remains in the game, all the cards taken in tricks by all players are gathered together, shuffled, and cut by the active players and placed into the center of the table to form a new stock.

GERMAN SOLO

This game, a development of an old Spanish game known as Ombre, or Hombre, should not be confused with the variants of Skat (page 258) and Whist (page 163) known by the same name.

Requirements

1. Four players, each playing for himself.

2. A 32-card deck, made by stripping out sixes, fives, fours, threes, and twos from a regular 52-card deck.

3. Rank of cards: The black queens are permanent trumps. The queen of clubs, called *spadilla,* is the highest trump, and the queen of spades, called *basta,* is the third-highest trump. The second-highest trump, called *manilla,* is the seven of the trump suit. The cards in each suit, trump or plain, rank as follows: ace (high), king, jack, queen (in red suits), ten, nine, eight, seven (unless promoted to *manilla*).

Beginning of the Game. The selection of the dealer, seating positions, changing seats, shuffle, and cut are as provided under the General Rules for Card Games, chapter 1.

The Deal. Each player is dealt a hand of eight cards, three, then two, then three. Every dealer, when his turn comes, antes an agreed number of chips to a pot. This pot goes to the first player making and fulfilling any one of certain three bids, or "games" (see below).

Object of Play. To win at least five tricks, or to win all eight tricks, dependent on the bid.

The Color. One suit is fixed as the color by agreement before play commences. In the absence of agreement, clubs is the color. (*Variant:* Some play that the game commences without a color, and the suit of the first game won becomes the color thereafter.) A bid is in color when it names this prefixed suit as trump; a bid is in suit if it names any other suit. Bids in color rank higher than bids in suit.

The "Games." The possible games that may be declared rank in bidding precedence as follows:

Simple game in suit
Simple game (frog) in color
Solo in suit
Solo in color
Tout in suit
Tout in color (high)

Simple Game (Frog). Player names the trump suit and then calls an ace which he does not hold himself. The holder of the called ace becomes his partner, but must say nothing to reveal the fact. The partnerships become evident when the called ace is played. Player and his partner must win at least five tricks. If a player holds both spadilla and basta (the black queens), he may not allow the hand to be played at simple game. If no higher bid has been made ahead of him, he must declare solo or tout. (This compulsion is called *forcée.*)

Solo. Player names the trump suit and then plays alone against the other three. He must win at least five tricks.

Tout. This game is a solo in which the player undertakes to win all eight tricks.

Spadilla. If all four players pass without a bid, the holder of spadilla (queen of clubs) must announce it and must undertake a simple game.

The Bidding. The player to the dealer's left has the first turn to bid. He first settles with the next hand as to which will bid higher; the survivor settles with the third hand, and so on. Once a player has passed he is out of the bidding. The winning bidder is entitled to hold to the bid that won, or to name any higher declaration. Each bidder therefore conceals his real intention so far as possible, bidding only high enough to overcall the previous bid.

The player to the dealer's left has the first turn to bid, and if he does not pass he says "I ask" (German, *ich frage,* whence the term *frog*). This is equivalent to a bid of simple game. If the next hand wishes to overcall he asks, "Is it in color?" If the answer is "Yes," the other may continue, "Is it a solo?" and so on. When the bidder whose intentions are so asked passes, the questioner stands committed to play a game at least as good as the last he named.

The winning bidder becomes the player,

and must at once announce his game and the trump suit.

The Play. The opening lead is invariably made by the player at dealer's left. Each other hand must follow suit to the lead if able; if unable, the hand may discard or trump at will. A trick is won by the highest card of the suit led, or by the highest trump if it contains a trump. Winner of a trick leads for the next.

Scoring. The basic values of the games are as follows:

Simple game in suit	2
Simple game in color	4
Solo in suit	4
Solo in color	8
Tout in suit	16
Tout in color	32

At simple game, the player and his partner each win 2 or lose 2. (If settlement is by chips, four chips thus change hands.) At color or tout, the value of the game is paid by each opponent to, or collected by each opponent from, the player. (*Variant:* In addition to this settlement for each hand, dealer puts 2 chips into a pool, and the pool accumulates until it is won by the first player who makes a solo in color or a tout.)

Additional Rules. A player who fails to follow suit when able loses the game and must pay the entire loss for his side. If an opponent of the player leads or plays out of turn, or exposes a card, his side loses and the offender must pay the entire loss. There is no penalty against the player for similar errors; the error must be corrected if possible and play continued. (*Variant:* Where there is a pool, if a penalizable error is made in a simple game the offender also pays a *bete* to the pool. The bete is 16 chips, or as many as are needed to double the amount already in the pool.)

Variants. There are many of these, because Solo has been played for so many generations. Among the principal variants still played are:

1. The player may not call the ace of a suit of which he is void.

2. The player may not call the ace of a suit of which he is void unless he also puts a card face down on the table; that card must be played to the first trump lead but cannot win a trick.

3. In a declared simple game or solo, either side may win a double (in suit) or quadruple

(in color) game by taking eight tricks; provided that if the side plays on after winning the first five tricks, and then loses a trick, it must pay the double or quadruple value of the game.

Three-Handed German Solo

This game is played as the name implies—by three players—and employs a 24-card deck,

made up by stripping out the eight of hearts and all diamonds except the seven from the 32-card deck. Diamonds are color, and the spadilla, manilla, and basta are the only other trumps, except the seven in color. The only bids are solos. If there is no bid, the hand is played with diamonds as trump, the winner of the last trick losing the equivalent of a solo in diamonds.

SCOTCH WHIST

This game, which is often called Catch the Ten, is very unlike Whist, although named as a whist.

Requirements

1. From two to six, each playing himself; four players may play in partnerships, two against two.

2. A 36-card deck is used. This is made up by stripping out all cards below the six from a standard 52-card deck.

3. In a suit that is trump the cards rank as follows: jack (high), ace, king, queen, ten, nine, eight, seven, six (low). In a nontrump suit the cards rank as follows: ace (high), king, queen, jack, ten, nine, eight, seven, six (low).

Beginning of the Game. The selection of the dealer, seating positions, changing seats, shuffle, and cut are as provided under the General Rules for Card Games, chapter 1.

The Deal. If two or three play, each receives a hand of ten cards dealt one at a time per round, beginning at dealer's left and going in rotation to the left. If four or more play, all the cards are dealt out as far as they will go. It does not matter if the cards do not come out even. The last card, which belongs to dealer's hand, is turned up to determine the trump suit for the deal.

The turn to deal in subsequent hands goes to the left.

Object of the Game. The object of the game is to win certain valuable trump cards in tricks; to win as many tricks as possible.

The Play. The player at dealer's left leads any card he chooses. The others in turn to the

left must follow suit if able to. If a player cannot follow suit, he may or may not play a trump. If a player can neither follow suit nor play a trump, he may play any card. The highest card of a led suit wins the trick unless a trump is played, in which case the trump wins. If more than one trump is played to a trick, highest trump wins. The winner of one trick leads to the next, and play proceeds as described until all tricks have been played.

Scoring. Certain trump cards have a counting value. These are jack, 11 points; ten, 10; ace, 4; king, 3; queen, 2. Players holding any of these cards score for them. Each player also scores 1 point for every card he takes that exceeds the number of cards he originally held in his hand. *Example:* If a player was dealt 10 cards and takes 15 cards in tricks, he scores 5 points (15−10).

The first to reach 41 points is the winner. If more than one player reaches 41 points in the same deal, the winner is decided by scoring the points in this order: ten of trumps, card points, ace, king, queen, and jack of trumps.

Additional Rules. Any player who breaks a rule of play may not score in that deal, and 10 points are deducted from his score.

French Whist

This is a variation of Scotch Whist in which the ten of diamonds always scores 10 points if it is not a trump. Otherwise the game is played the same as Scotch Whist.

TABLANETTE

Tablanette is said to have come originally from Russia. It is one of the best of the lesser-

known games for two. It is a game of skill, but not at all difficult to learn.

Requirements

1. Two players.

2. Standard 52-card deck.

3. Value of cards: king counts 14; queen, 13; jack, 12; ace, either 1 or 11. The pack is treated differently as detailed later.

Beginning of the Game. The selection of the dealer, seating positions, changing seats, shuffle, and cut are as provided under the General Rules for Card Games, chapter 1.

The Deal and the Play. The cards are cut for deal, the lower card taking the deal. Six cards are then dealt to each player, and four cards are turned face up on the table. When the dealer has exposed the four cards, his opponent has to play. If he plays a card of the same denomination as any of the four cards on the table, then he takes such card. Or, if there are any two or three cards on the table whose card values added together make a total equal to that of any one card, then he takes such cards. He may be able to do both. *Example:* If the four exposed cards are the king, nine, four, and three, and the opponent plays a king he takes the king; if he plays a queen he takes the nine and four (13); if a seven, the three and four. These cards are put in a pile on one side, each player having his own pile. Should either player, now or at any time, be able to take with one card *all* the cards on the table (sometimes there is only one) then he calls "Tablanette," and scores the total face value of all such cards, including that of the card he himself plays.

The opponent having played, the dealer, in his turn, plays a card. This continues in turn until each player has played his six cards. If either player makes tablanette, then the opponent must play a card onto the table. In doing so he will play either a card of the lowest denomination possible (in order to give his opponent the minimum score in case he can again make tablanette), or else a card which he thinks it improbable or impossible for his opponent to match. *Example:* If a player has two fours in his hand and one four has previously been played, the chances are against his opponent holding the remaining four. When each player has played his six cards, the dealer deals a further six to each player (any cards on the table remaining face up), and the game continues until these cards are also played. Then a third six, and finally the last six.

When the last six cards have been played, any cards left on the table are taken by the player last taking a card from the board. That is to say, if neither player can take a card from the board for the last three times, then the player who before that matched a card or cards takes the remaining cards. Each player then counts from his pile one point for every ace, king, queen, jack, and 10, and one for the two of clubs. The ten of diamonds counts two.

The player with the greater *number* of cards counts three extra. The cards are then shuffled and the deal passes, and the next hand is played as before. The player who first makes 251 wins.

BLACKOUT

This game, also called Oh Hell or Oh Pshaw, is based on many of the principles of Bridge.

Requirements

1. Three to six players, but best for four or five. Each player plays for himself.

2. A standard 52-card deck.

Object of Play. The object of play is to win exactly the number of tricks bid, neither more nor less.

Beginning of the Game. The selection of the dealer, seating positions, changing seats, shuffle, and cut are as provided under the General Rules for Card Games, chapter 1.

The Deal. Each game is comprised of a series of deals; in the first deal, each hand receives one card; in the second deal, two cards; and so on to the limit. With four players, there are 13 deals; with five players, 10 deals; with three players it is advisable to limit the game to 15 deals.

The Turn-up. Having completed the deal, the dealer turns up the next card of the pack. The turn-up fixes the trump suit for that deal. When the last deal leaves no odd card to turn up, the deal is played at no-trump.

The Bidding. Beginning with dealer, each player in turn bids exactly the number of tricks that he thinks he can win. Thus, on the first deal the possible bids are one and zero. The total of all bids need not be equal to the number of tricks in play. It is a duty of the scorekeeper to announce, after the dealer has bid, "Over" or "Under" or "Even" according to how the total of bids compares with the number of tricks.

The Play. The player to left of bidder makes the opening lead. Each hand must follow suit to a lead if able; if unable, the hand may trump or discard at will. A trick is won by the highest card of the suit led, or, if it contains trumps, by the highest trump. The winner of a trick leads to the next.

Scoring. A player who takes more or fewer tricks than his bid scores nothing for the hand and loses nothing. For making his bid exactly, a player scores 10 points plus the amount of his bid. (Practice is not standardized as to the scoring of zero bids. In different localities the score is 10, 5, or 5 plus the number of tricks in the deal.) A running account is kept of each individual's cumulative score.

The player with the highest cumulative score at the end of the game wins. Each player settles with every other player on the difference in their final scores. (*Variant:* The winner gets a bonus of 10 points.)

Additional Rules. There is no penalty for a bid out of turn, but such a bid must stand. The turn to bid reverts to the right player. A player may change his bid without penalty before the player at his left bids.

A lead or play out of turn must be retracted on demand of any player, and the card played in error must be left face up on the table and played at the first legal opportunity. A card exposed in any way but by legal play in turn becomes exposed and is treated in the same way.

A player is entitled to be informed at any time how much any other player has bid, and how many tricks each player has won. Each player should keep his tricks arranged in an orderly fashion so that they may be counted by inspection.

LIFT SMOKE

This is one of the favorites of British card players.

Requirements

1. Four to six players, each playing for himself.

2. The standard deck of 52 cards. The cards in each suit rank: ace (high), king, queen, jack, ten, down to two (low).

3. Each player usually antes a certain number of chips to form a pot.

The Deal. Cards are dealt one at a time beginning with the player to the dealer's left. Each player receives as many cards as there are players in the game. The last card dealt to the dealer is turned up to establish the trump suit. The remaining cards in the deck are placed face down on the table to form the stock.

The Play. The player to the left of the dealer leads any card he desires. The other players must follow suit, if able; if unable, the hand may play any card. A trick is won by the highest trump, or by the highest card of the suit led. Winner of a trick draws the top card of the stock and leads to the next trick.

When a player's cards are exhausted, he drops out of the deal and the other players continue. The last survivor to have any cards left wins the pot. If several hands are exhausted by the last trick, the winner of that trick wins the pot. The winner of the pot deals for the next game.

TAROK

This ancient card game, also called Tarock, Tarocchini, Taroky, and Trappola, is still a leading game in Central Europe, especially Czechoslovakia.

Requirements

1. Three players. Four may participate; the dealer receives no cards, but shares in the winnings and losses of the opponents.

2. A special 54-card Tarok deck. This deck, available from major card suppliers, is comprised of the following:

    (*a*) 32 plain cards, eight each in spades, hearts, diamonds, clubs. In each of these are four court cards: king, queen, cavalier, and jack.

    (*b*) 22 trump cards. The skus or joker may

bear a picture or simply the number XXII. The other trump cards are numbered XI to I.

3. The rank of cards: In trumps, joker (high), XXI, XX, and so on in order to I. In the red suits, king (high), queen, cavalier, jack, ace, two, three, and four. In the black suits, king (high), queen, cavalier, jack, ten, nine, eight, seven.

Count Value. Nineteen cards of the Tarok deck have count or point value as follows:

Joker	5
XXI (called *mond*)	5
I (called the pagat)	5
Each king	5
Each queen	4
Each cavalier	3
Each jack	3

The 35 cards that have no count or point value are called *nulls*.

Trick Value. The following are the point values which are given to tricks containing:

Three nulls	1 point
Two nulls and one counter	Value of counter
One null and two counters	Total value of counters less one
Three counters	Total value of counters less two

Beginning of the Game. The selection of the dealer, seating positions, changing seats, shuffle, and cut are as provided under the General Rules for Card Games, chapter 1.

The Deal. The three active players (including or excluding the dealer, depending on the numbers of players) are called in clockwise rotation *forehand* (at left of dealer), *middlehand*, and *endhand*. Each player receives 16 cards, dealt in batches of eight cards at a time. On completion of the first round of the deal, six cards are placed face down upon the table as a widow. Then the second round is dealt in the same clockwise rotation.

The Bidding. There are only two possible bids: threesome and solo. A bid of solo overcalls a bid of threesome.

The forehand bids first and the bidding continues in clockwise rotation until the winning bidder is decided. Of course, a solo bid by the forehand ends the bidding immediately, since this is the highest and there is no higher overcall bid. If all three players pass without bidding, the deal passes to the left and there is no score for the hand. (*Variant:* The German variant, Tapp-Tarok, is played

like regular Tarok, except that when all pass, the forehand is awarded a score of 25 points.)

The Widow. If the winning bid was threesome, the player who made that bid picks up the top three cards of the widow. If these cards do not suit him, he may expose them on the table and then pick up the other three. If he then decides to play with these cards, the game counts double. If he rejects these three cards, and decides to play with the first cards of the widow, the game counts triple. But once he decides on the three cards he wants, he discards any three cards (except kings) from his hand face down. (If a trump is discarded, the fact must be announced.) At the end of the play, the discards belong to the winner of bid, while the other three cards of the widow belong to his two opponents who play as a partnership against him.

After seeing the widow cards, the bidder may elect to play for game or for consolation. For game, he tries to win 36 or more points in play; for consolation, he tries to avoid winning more than 35.

If the winning bid is solo, the widow is set aside without being exposed and at the end of the play is added to the tricks of the opponents.

Melds. Before the opening lead, but after the bidder has discarded (in a threesome bid), any player holding a meld must declare it. There are two possible melds: skus (joker), mond (XXI), and pagat (I); and four kings. Each of these melds counts 50 in a threesome, 100 in a solo.

The Play. Regardless of the bidder, the forehand makes the opening lead, which may be any card he desires. After any lead, each of the other hands must follow suit if able. If unable to follow suit a player must trump. If unable either to follow suit or to trump, a player may play any card. A trick is won by the highest trump, or, if it contains no trump, by the highest card of the suit led. The winner of a trick leads to the next.

Scoring. The bidder wins his game if he takes 36 or more point tricks, together with his discard; or, if the game was consolation, if he takes no more than 35. If the bidder wins his game, he scores double the number of points he took over 35, plus 50 for threesome or 100 for solo. *Example:* If he took 44 points, he scores 68 or 118, as the case may be.

If the bidder fails to make his game, each

opponent (this includes the dealer when sitting out) receives the value of the bid (threesome 50, solo 100) plus double the number of all points taken by two opponents over 35.

If any player wins the last trick with pagat (trump I), he scores a bonus equal to the value of the game (threesome 50, solo 100). The bidder may, before the opening lead, announce *ultimo,* that is, that he will try to win the last trick with the pagat. If he succeeds, he scores a bonus of twice the game value; if he fails, he loses this amount. Success or failure of ultimo has no effect on winning or losing the game (taking more than 35 points in tricks). If ultimo is announced, and the bidder loses his pagat on an earlier trick, he is nevertheless credited with its 5 points if he wins last trick; if he plays the pagat unnecessarily, the 5 points go to the opponents regardless of who captured the pagat.

After the announcement of ultimo, either of the two opponents to the bidder may declare *contra-ultimo,* that is, that he will try to win pagat from the bidder. If he succeeds, the opponents win a bonus of quadruple its game value; if he fails, the bidder collects this amount.

The score may be kept on paper or each deal may be settled as a separate game. In the latter case, melds should be settled as soon as they are shown (before the actual play); any meld collects its value from both other players (and the dealer if he is sitting out the game).

PREFERENCE

This is an interesting game for three people.

Requirements

1. Three players; four may play but the dealer takes no cards and does not participate in the payoffs.

2. A 32-card deck is used, made up by stripping out all cards below the seven from a standard 52-card deck.

3. Cards rank as follows: ace (high), king, queen, jack, ten, nine, eight, seven (low). Hearts are the highest-ranking suit, known as "preference," then diamonds, clubs and spades (lowest).

4. Each player antes an equal amount of chips into the pot.

The Deal. It does not matter who deals the first hand. The turn to deal passes to the left in subsequent hands. The cards are dealt three at a time to each player in the first round of dealing; then two cards are dealt as a widow face down. The deal is then continued to each player, four cards at a time, and then three until each has a hand of ten cards.

The Bidding. The player at dealer's left has first chance to bid. He names a suit and in so doing obligates himself to take at least six of the ten tricks in play against the others. If he does not name a suit, he must pass. The bidding turn goes to the left, with each player either bidding a suit or passing. Each player gets only one bid. No one mentions the number of tricks that he will take in play, but merely bids a suit. A player must name a higher-ranking suit than that named by a previous player. The one who names the highest-ranking suit is the winning bidder. The winner in the first round of bidding may not use the widow for play.

If all players pass in the first round, there is a second round of bidding. In this round players simply chip to the pot without making a bid, or they pass. Each player gets only one turn to chip. The player who puts in the most chips has the right to name trump for the deal and may also use the widow, taking it into his hand and discarding any two cards, so that his hand is at ten cards again.

The Play. The player to the left of the highest bidder leads to the first trick. Each player in turn to the left must follow suit if able to do so. If he cannot follow suit, he may play a trump, if he chooses. If he cannot follow suit and does not choose to trump, he may throw off any card. Highest card of the led suit wins a trick. But the highest trump in a trick wins it. The winner of a trick leads to the next until all ten tricks have been played. The bidder must win at least six tricks to fulfill his contract.

The Payoff. Before the game, players set a value for winning tricks according to the rank of the trump suit. If a player fulfills his bid, he takes a certain number of chips out of the pot, according to the schedule set by the players beforehand; for example, taking all ten tricks with hearts as trumps would entitle the successful player to the entire pot. If a player fails in his contract, he pays a certain penalty (agreed on beforehand) into the pot.

THREE-IN-ONE

This game in various versions is known as Tripoli, Tripoley, and Pochen.

Requirements

1. Four to six players, each playing for himself.

2. A standard 52-card deck for play; another deck to make the layout shown here.

Forming the Pot. Each player places one chip next to ace, jack, and ten, and two chips next to king-queen combination (known as the *marriage*). Also one chip is placed on the sequence (seven, eight, nine). Thus, each player must ante six chips before the start of each game.

Beginning of the Game. The selection of the dealer, seating positions, changing seats, shuffle, and cut are as provided under the General Rules for Card Games, chapter 1.

The Deal. Any player may be selected as the first dealer. He deals cards to all players, including himself, one at a time per round in rotation to the left. But, not all cards should be dealt out, enough being left over to form a "widow," or "dead hand," which is not to be used in play. (A minimum of four cards should be in this dead hand.)

The Play. Play is divided into three stages as follows:

1. In the first stage, players who hold any of the cards or the marriage or the sequence collect all the chips bet on them. To collect on the marriage, the player must hold both the king and queen in his hand, while to take chips on the sequence, he holds all three cards in his hand.

2. In stage two, each player must put a chip in the pot. The players then select the best five cards of their hands and play a round of closed poker, betting, raising, etc. The best hand at the showdown wins the pot,

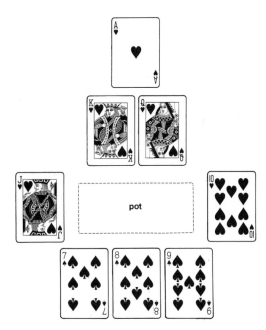

The layout for Three-in-One.

as in the General Rules of Poker (see page 7).

3. In the final stage, the players each ante a chip in the pot again and play a game of Michigan (see page 327). Winner takes the pot.

Final Settlement. All chips left on any cards of the layout are carried over to the next deal, but each player must again place chips on the layout. The turn to deal passes to the left.

When the game breaks up and there are still chips left in any of the layouts, a round of cold hands in poker (as described on page 7) is dealt out. The winner takes all the chips on the board.

FIVE-IN-ONE

This game, also called Variety, is actually a sort of a combination of several games elsewhere described in this book.

Requirements

1. Any number may play, but no less than three.

2. Two regular 52-card decks are shuffled

together and used for any number of players up to ten. For more than that it is better to use three decks.

Beginning of the Game. The selection of the dealer, seating positions, changing seats, shuffle, and cut are as provided under the General Rules for Card Games, chapter 1.

The Play. Dealer is decided by cut, low card dealing. There are five stages to the play, as follows:

1. After shuffling the cards and having them cut, dealer gives each player including himself five cards, face down. Each in turn announces "Red" or "Black" and turns up his cards. If a majority of his cards are of the same color as he called, he collects a chip from the dealer; if not, he pays a chip to the dealer. Dealer's hand is not played in this.

2. All hands including dealer's are then compared, and the best poker hand wins a chip from each other player (see page 7, General Rules of Poker, for rank of hands).

3. The hands are left turned up, and a game of Bango is now played, as described on page 323, except that players do not chip in for a pot and the winner collects a chip from each of the others. Dealer plays in this also.

4. Next a game of Put and Take is played, as described on page 321, players who lose putting chips into the pot and winners drawing from the pot. Dealer's hand is not played. But dealer collects all chips left in the pot or pays out any chips coming to the player.

5. The next step is for dealer alone. He turns up the first ten cards from the remainder of the deck, counting as he turns up each card; one for the first, two for the second, etc. If the denomination of the card turned is the same as dealer's count at that point, dealer collects one chip from each other player. He pays out nothing, though, if he fails to match his count and the denomination of a card. This stage is known as *consolation*.

The turn to deal passes to the left after each five stages of play.

GRAND

This is really three games in one, the players having the option in any deal of playing Whist, Hearts, or Euchre. Consequently, a player must know all three games.

Requirements

1. Four players, two against two in partnership.

2. A regular 52-card deck is used. The cards rank according to the game played.

The Object of Game. A time limit or a certain number of deals are set. The object is to be the first side to reach game of 100 points before the expiration of this period or to be the closest to 100 points if neither side has reached game.

Beginning of the Game. The selection of the dealer, seating positions, changing seats, shuffle, and cut are as provided under the General Rules for Card Games, chapter 1.

The Deal. Each player receives a hand of 13 cards dealt as in Whist.

The Bidding. Beginning at dealer's left each player receives one chance to make a bid or pass. He mentally decides whether he wishes to play at Whist, Euchre, or Hearts. He makes a numerical bid but does not name the game. The lowest bid is five. If everyone passes to dealer, he must make a bid of five. Highest numerical bidder names the game to be played.

When Whist Is Named. If the play is at Whist, the highest bidder must specify whether it is to be Partnership Whist. In straight Whist, the bidder names the trump. Each trick over book counts 5 points, and a grand slam earns a bonus of 30 points, so that it is worth 65 points altogether. There is no score for honors.

If bidder names Grand as the game to be played, the play is at no-trump. Each trick over book counts 9, and the bonus for grand slam is 40, so that it is worth 103 points altogether. Making a grand slam wins game without further deals, regardless of the state of the making side's score.

If the bidding side in either game fails to fulfill its bid, it is set back, that is, the amount of its bid is subtracted from its previous score. Opponents score for any tricks above book that they make.

Any infraction of the Whist rules is an irregularity and the penalty is as follows: Offender's side is set back if it took the bid or cannot defeat the contract if opponents took the bid.

When Euchre Is Named. If the bidder announces Euchre, he names trump, and each player must discard eight cards, leaving a hand of five. No player may keep a trump lower than the eight. The odd trick ("point") counts 5; four tricks, 10; all five tricks ("march") made by partners, 20; all five made by a lone hand, 25. If the bid is 25, the bidder must play a lone hand. A lone hand must discard one card, and he gets his partner's best in exchange. Opponents may do likewise.

If the bidding side is successful, it scores for all tricks it wins. If it fails, the side is set back the amount of its bid plus 20. A lone hand that is defeated at a bid of 20 is set back 40 (20 + 20).

Irregularities are as in regular Partnership Euchre, and the penalty is that offender's side is set back if it took the bid or cannot defeat the contract if opponents took the bid. A player who holds a lower trump than an eight or holds more than five cards has committed an irregularity. The penalty is as described above.

The Play at Hearts. The highest bidder may announce "Hearts" only if he has not bid more than 50. If neither he nor partner takes in a heart, they score 50, and opponents are set back 13. If bidder's side takes in any hearts, it scores nothing and is set back the amount of the bid plus 1 for each heart. Opponents are also set back 1 point for each heart they take.

If dealer's side has a score of 70 or more, the player at the dealer's left may decide the play at Hearts by simply leading a heart and announcing "Hearts." Only this player may decide the play at hearts and only when opponents—dealer's side—have a score of 70 or more. If the player at dealer's left makes no bid when dealer's side is below 70 in the score, it is considered a conventional indication that he is prepared to play at Hearts but wishes to give partner a chance to put in a higher bid.

Irregularities are as in regular Partnership Hearts, and the penalty is that offender's side is considered to have taken in all the hearts.

Final Settlement. Setbacks are checked on the tally sheet. The lesser number of setbacks are subtracted from the greater number, and the difference is multiplied by ten and credited to the side with the fewer setbacks. The side closer to 100 at the end of play is credited with the difference between opponent's score and 100. Setbacks and final score difference are then compared to decide which side has the winning margin. *Example:* Side A finishes with 90 points, side B with 70 points. Side A is credited with 30 points (100 − 70). But Side A has eight setbacks. Side B has six. Side B therefore is credited with 20 points (8 − 6 × 10). Side A has a net winning margin of 10 points (30 − 20).

YUKON

This game was supposed to have been a great favorite with the gold rushers of the old Klondike days. It still has something of a following.

Requirements

1. It may be played by two or three but is best for four playing in opposing partnerships.

2. A regular 52-card deck is used. One deuce is removed if three play.

3. The four jacks are known as *yukons* and rank as the highest cards of the deck. The jack of spades is the *grand yukon* and ranks higher than the other three jacks, which are equal in rank. Below the yukons the other cards rank as follows: ace, king, queen, ten, nine, eight, seven, six, five, four, three, two (low). The ace of spades is known as the *yukon digger*.

The Deal. Players cut for deal, and the highest cut deals. Each player receives a hand of five cards, dealt one at a time per round, beginning at dealer's left and going in rotation to the left. The remainder of the deck, known as the *stock,* is placed face down in the middle of the table.

The turn to deal in subsequent hands passes to the left.

The Play. Player at dealer's left leads a card to the first trick. Each player in turn must follow suit if he is able to. If a player cannot follow suit, he must then play a yukon. (There are never any trumps in this game.)

If any player leads a yukon, each player in turn must follow to the suit of the yukon if he is able to. If he cannot follow suit to a yukon, he must play a yukon if he holds one. Highest card of a suit led wins the trick except when a yukon is played. A yukon wins a trick, and if more than one yukon is played, the first one played wins. But the grand yukon wins any trick, no matter in which order it is played.

The winner of one trick leads to the next. But before doing so, he draws the top card of the stock into his hand without showing it to the others. Each other player in turn draws a card from the top of the stock. After the stock is exhausted, the hands are played out until there are no more cards.

Scoring. Players then score for any of the following counting cards they won in tricks as follows; grand yukon, 15 points; each other yukon, 10; each ten, 10; each ace, 5; each king, 3; each queen, 2. The winner is the first to score a total of 250 points. The deal in which the 250 is scored must be played out to the end. If both sides have 250 or more, the higher score wins; but if the scores are equal, the side winning the ace of spades is the winner.

CRAZY EIGHTS

This game is completely different from the game described on page 331.

Requirements

1. From two to eight players; four to eight players make the best game.

2. A regular pack of 52.

Beginning of the Game. The selection of the dealer, seating positions, changing seats, shuffle, and cut are as provided under the General Rules for Card Games, chapter 1.

The Deal. Each player is dealt five cards, one at a time. Then eight cards are placed face up in the center of the table in two horizontal rows of four cards.

Object of the Game. To get rid of the five cards by matching cards in the center. Play ends when a player gets rid of his five cards. If player fails to get rid of his five cards, high and low man in points win (two winners).

Point Scoring. Points are scored as follows: aces count 15 points; picture cards, 10 points; all other cards, face value. (*Example:* Two counts 2 points, three 3 points, etc.)

When you get rid of all cards, you shout "Crazy Eights," and win both high and low.

The Play. The turn to play rotates to the left (clockwise) beginning with the player to the left of the dealer. The play consists of placing one card face up on one of the eight cards turned up in the center of the table. Each card played must match the card in rank. If unable to play in turn, the player says "Pass" and the turn reverts to the next player. This continues until one player gets rid of all his cards and shouts "Crazy Eights." If none of the players gets rid of his five cards, the players with the highest points and the lowest points are declared the winners and share the pot.

SPECULATION

Requirements

1. From two to nine players.

2. A standard 52-card deck.

3. Rank of cards is as follows: ace (high), king, queen, jack, ten, and so on down to two (low).

4. Each player contributes equally to the pot.

Beginning of the Game. The selection of the dealer, seating positions, changing seats, shuffle, and cut are as provided under the General Rules for Card Games, chapter 1.

The Deal. After dealer is decided by cutting (ace is low), he gives three cards, face down and one at a time, to each player, in rotation to the left, beginning at the dealer's left. After the deal is completed, the next card from the deck is turned face up; this is trump.

The Play. If the card turned face up is an ace, the dealer takes the pot immediately. If it is a king, queen, or jack, he offers it for sale to the highest bidder; but he need not accept any offer unless he so desires. If he sells, he passes it to the buyer; if he does not sell, he retains it. Then all the cards are faced up, and the holder of the highest trump takes the pot.

If the faced-up trump is a numeral card, the dealer offers it for sale, as above, before any player looks at his hand. Whether it is sold or not, it must be left face up on the table. The player to the dealer's left then faces up his top card; and this continues in rotation to the left, around and around, until a higher trump than the faced one is turned. The purchaser of the original trump does not face any cards until the trump is beaten. If a better trump shows, it is offered for sale, as above; and the rest of the unfaced cards in the hands are turned face up one by one, until a better trump shows, or all have been exposed. The holder of the best trump at the end takes the pot.

CHAPTER 21

Solitaire and Patience Games

Every person who knows one card from another has a favorite solitaire, or perhaps several favorite solitaires, to which he turns from time to time for relaxation. In this section I have chosen a representative and interesting collection of the innumerable varieties of games played, listed by titles that are generally most familiar. Many of the games are known by several names, but a player looking for some particular game should be able to identify it easily by its characteristic layout.

Scarne's Notes on Solitaires

Though solitaires are naturally intended primarily for play by an individual, many can be adapted for play by two or more persons. Outstanding examples, of course, are Russian Bank and Spite and Malice, both of which are really sorts of double solitaire. Certain technical terms have become conventional in describing the play in all solitaires; these terms will be explained in this general description of the features common to most of the games in this chapter.

The Cards. A standard 52-card deck is used in most solitaires. But two decks shuffled together are also used in the games toward the end of the chapter.

Sequence. The cards run in sequence for play in the following order: ace (low), two, three, four, five, six, seven, eight, nine, ten, jack, queen, king (high). Sequences may run in ascending order, for example, three, four,

five, six, etc.; or they may run in descending order, for example, queen, jack, ten, nine, eight, etc. Suits have no comparative rank. Hearts and diamonds form one *color*, spades and clubs form another.

The Layout Tableau. Cards are usually arranged in some plan or pattern according to the rules of the game. Most often this pattern is laid out before the start of play, but sometimes it is developed during play. The pattern is referred to as a *tableau*.

Foundation. Face-up cards that are not part of the tableau, upon which cards may be played in ascending or descending sequences, are referred to as *foundation cards* or simply *foundations*. The sequences built on them are *foundation piles*. The main object in most solitaires is to play cards onto the foundation piles.

Space. The unoccupied place where a card may legally be played in the tableau is usually referred to as a *space*.

File. A vertical row of built-up cards in the tableau, overlapping each other but leaving the denomination and suit of the partially covered cards visible, is called the *file*.

The Play

Stock. The remainder of the deck, or some part of it, is referred to as the *stock*. The stock, also called in some situations the *hand,* is used in the play according to the rules for the game.

Discard Pile. When cards, at the time they are turned up in a dealing, are not available for play, they become part of a *discard pile* or *talon*. This pile is also referred to by some as a *trash pile* or *waste pile*, especially when the cards are not dealt again. Sometimes these cards are dealt again for further play, sometimes they are not.

Available Cards. Cards that may be played onto the tableau, a foundation pile, or a space are *available, exposed,* or *playable.*

Released Cards. Cards that have become playable, owing to the fact that they have become exposed by having other cards removed, are known as *released cards.*

Building. Playing cards in a legal sequence is referred to as *building.* Playing in ascending sequence is *building up.* Playing in descending sequence is *building down.* Playing cards of the same suit is *building in suit.* Playing cards in alternate colors is *building in alternate colors.*

SINGLE-DECK SOLITAIRE

Simple Addition

Grouped under this name are several solitaires of elementary character, alike in object and procedure.

Play. Deal a tableau as directed below. Remove cards from the tableau in groups and discard. The groups must be specified face cards, or cards that make a specified total. Aces count 1 and, where they have any numerical value, the jacks count 11, queens 12, and kings 13. Fill spaces in the tableau by cards from the hand. The game is won if entire pack is discarded or dealt into the tableau.

Elevens. The tableau is nine cards in three rows of three. Discard jacks, queens, kings in trios of one each rank, regardless of suits. Discard all other cards in pairs totaling 11.

Tens. The tableau is 13 cards in any convenient array. Discard tens, jacks, queens, and kings in quartets of one suit. Discard all other cards in pairs totaling 10.

Fifteens. The tableau is 16 cards in four rows of four. Discard tens, jacks, queens, and kings in quartets of four of one suit. Discard all other cards in groups of any number of cards totaling 15.

Block Solitaire

Some elementary solitaires of the Simple Addition type are played in a slightly different way.

Play. Deal a tableau as directed below. Continue dealing cards to cover tableau cards that total as specified. The game is won if the entire block is dealt upon tableau cards.

Elevens. The tableau is 12 cards in three rows of four. If face cards appear in the layout, remove them and place at the bottom of the pack. Fill the spaces, and continue removing face cards until all 12 cards of the layout are of lower rank than jacks. If no face cards have been removed from the original layout, place the first face card turned up in later dealing on the bottom. Cover all pairs totaling 11 with 2 cards face-up from the pack.

Baroness

This game, also called Thirteens, is Simple Addition with a difference in the manner of play. Deal a row of five cards. Discard any kings or pairs that total 13. Deal five more cards on the first five, or in the spaces left by their removal. Discard as before. Continue until the complete pack is dealt into one row of five packets. There will be two cards at the end, which may be spread separately from the piles and which are both available. Each new row of five buries the cards below the piles until they are released by play of the top cards. The game is won if the entire pack is discarded.

Fourteen Puzzle

This version of Simple Addition, also called Take Fourteen, is radically different from other members of the family. It allows fair scope for skill and does not so frequently present an unbreakable block. Deal the entire pack into 12 piles, face up. Put the four extra cards on the first four piles. Since all piles may and should be examined, they should be spread downward in overlapping formation. Top cards of all piles are available. Remove available cards in pairs totaling 14. The game is won if all the cards can be so paired and removed.

Pyramid

Pyramid is the most popular member of the Simple Addition family. It is widely played and is the subject of elaborate record-keeping on the part of some devoted followers.

Layout. Deal 28 cards in the form of a pyramid (see diagram). This is composed of successive rows of one to seven cards. Each card is overlapped by two cards of the row below. A card in the pyramid is available if not covered by any other. At the outset, the seven cards of the bottom row are available. The play of two adjacent cards releases one card in the sixth row, and so on.

Play. From available cards, remove and discard all kings singly, and all cards in pairs that total 13.

Turn up cards from the hand singly, plac-ing unplayable cards face up on a single waste pile. The top card of this pile and the top card in the hand are available. Note that a card turned up from the hand may be matched with a card on the waste pile. To win the game, not only the pyramid but also the waste pile must be cleared away and dis-carded.

Competitive Scoring. This is a method of playing Pyramid against "par" or against an-other player. A match is six games. In each game, two redeals are permitted. If the player clears away the pyramid on the first deal, he scores 50, less the number of cards remaining in the hand; he may use the redeals to deplete this number. If the pyramid is cleared away in the second deal, the score is 35, less the residue of the hand after the third deal. If the pyramid is cleared away in the third deal, the score is 20, less the cards in hand. If the

The layout for Pyramid.

The layout for Monte Carlo.

pyramid is not cleared away in three deals, the score is minus the total of cards left in the pyramid and hand.

Par is a net score of zero in six games, and any net plus may be considered a win. Two or more players in competition compare their net scores for a series of six games. Since the order of the cards in hand is known after the first deal, there is scope for some planning of the play in the redeals.

Nestor

The layout in this game, which is also called Matrimony, is simple but spectacular; and play is uncomplicated.

Layout. Deal six rows of eight cards each, with rows overlapping. Do not place two cards of the same rank in the same columns. When a card is turned from the pack, and a card of the same rank already lies in the column to which the next card must be dealt, place the card on the bottom of the pack. The tableau uses all the cards but four. Place these four face down in a pile to form the stock.

Play. The bottom card of each column of the tableau is available; remove available cards by pairs in rank, regardless of suit, and discard. When play is blocked, turn up the top card of the stock. Use it if you can; otherwise, discard it and turn up the next stock card. The game is won if the entire tableau is discarded by pairs.

Monte Carlo

The shifting tableau makes a kaleidoscopic game, with some opportunity for skill. This game is also called Weddings, Double, or Quits.

Layout. Deal five rows of five cards each, making a rectangular tableau.

Play. Two cards of the same rank may be removed from the tableau if they are adjacent vertically, horizontally, or diagonally. After all possible pairs are removed, the remaining cards must be consolidated. Back them up, preserving their order in which they were dealt, until the tableau rows are solid from the top down. If you tend to make errors in backing up, pick up the cards in the same order as dealt, left to right, and from top row down, then deal them again in solid rows of five. After consolidating, deal additional cards in regular order to fill out the tableau to five rows of five. Again remove adjacent pairs. Continue in the same way. The game is won if the entire pack is discarded by pairs.

Decade

Layout. Deal cards in a row singly, face up.

Play. Discard any three adjacent cards that add up to 10, 20, or 30. Count jacks, queens,

and kings as 10 each. The game is won if all cards but one are discarded.

Betrothal

This Marriage Solitaire, also called Royal Marriage and Matrimony, is rarely consummated. You may consider it a victory to bring the principals within eight cards of each other.

Layout. Place the queen of hearts on the table at left and place the king of hearts on bottom of the pack.

Play. Deal cards in a row to the right of the queen. Whenever two cards of the same suit or same rank are separated by one or two cards in this tableau, throw out the intervening cards. The game is won if, after the entire pack is dealt out, the king and queen of hearts are side by side, other cards having been discarded.

Accordion

Also called Idle Year and Tower of Babel, this game is the best and certainly the most popular game of the family that includes Decade and Betrothal.

Layout. Deal cards in a row. Whenever a card is of the same suit or same rank as the next at its left, or the third at its left, the right-hand card (or pile) may be moved upon the other. If a card matches both the next and the third-next cards, the player may make either move. After each move, look to see if others are now possible.

Game is won if the entire pack is consolidated in one pile.

Golf

Layout. Deal five rows of seven cards each, overlapping. Deal one card below this tableau to start the waste pile.

Play. Bottom cards of the tableau columns are available. The object is to clear away the tableau by building all the cards upon the waste pile. Building is in sequence, up or down, regardless of suit. Sequence of rank is not circular; only a two may be built on an ace, and nothing may be built on a king.

Turn up cards from the hand singly and place them on the waste pile, using each to take off as many cards from the tableau as possible or expedient. The game is won if the entire tableau is cleared away.

Competitive Play. One game of Golf is treated as a "hole." The number of "strokes"

The layout for Accordion.

taken by the player to make this hole is the number of cards left in the tableau after play is blocked. A hole may be made in zero or less than zero; if the game is won, the number of undealt cards remaining in the hand is a minus score.

One player may compete against "par." Play nine holes and total the scores. You beat par if your total is 36 or less.

Two players may compete for lowest total over nine holes. Another plan is to play hole by hole, allowing one point to the winner of each, or a half-point to each of two tieing winners. The player who collects three match points first wins.

Hit or Miss

Many a student of card probabilities has been attracted to the problem of determining the chance of winning this game, which is also called Treize, Roll Call, Talkative, and Harvest.

Layout and Play. Deal cards face up singly into one pile. Count the cards from 1 to 13, then repeat. A card is *hit* if it is of same rank as the ordinal number called. Jack ranks 11, queen 12, and king 13. Discard all cards that are hit. Do not alter the sequence of counting because of a hit. *Example:* If a six is hit, count the next card "seven."

Each time the hand is exhausted, pick up the pile of unhit cards, redeal, and continue the count from where it was stopped. If pack is gone through twice in succession, without a hit, the game is lost. To win, every card in the pack must be hit.

Idiot's Delight

The attraction of this solitaire, which is also called Aces Up, is that the percentage of wins is higher than in most of the other tableau-

The layout for Golf.

depleting games. Aces rank high, above the kings.

Layout. Deal four cards in a row.

Play. Discard any card lower than another card of the same suit. Continue in the same way, dealing in rows of four upon four fixed piles or spaces, and discarding whenever possible. A space left in the tableau by removal of an entire pile may be filled by the top card from any other pile. Of course, the selection should be made if possible so as to release additional cards for discard. Spaces must be filled before a new row of four cards is dealt, if there are enough cards in the tableau for this purpose. Since aces are high, they may be moved only into spaces. The game is won if, after the entire pack is dealt, only the four aces remain in the tableau, the rest having been discarded.

Royal Flush

The royal flush comprises an ace, king, queen, jack, and ten of the same suit.

Layout. Deal the entire pack into five piles face down (put the two extra cards on the first two piles).

Play. Turn the first pile face up. If the top card is a ten or higher, it fixes the suit of the royal flush. If not, remove cards one at a time from this pile until you come to a ten or higher card. If there is none in the first pile, turn up the second and continue the search in the same way.

Having fixed the suit of the royal flush, turn up each pile and discard cards from the top until a card of the flush appears. If there is none, the entire pile is discarded. Eventually each of the remaining piles will be topped by a card of the flush. Pick up the piles in reverse order, so that the last dealt will be at the top of the new hand. Deal the cards into four piles face down as far as they go. Turn up the piles and discard cards from the top until one of the flush cards appears. Continue in the same way, discarding cards that cover the uppermost flush card in each pile. Reduce by one the number of piles dealt each time. The game is won if, when only one pile remains, it comprises the five cards of the royal flush and no others.

Perpetual Motion

Layout. Deal four cards face up in a row. If two or more are of the same rank, move

the others upon the one at the left.

Play. Continue dealing the whole pack by rows of four upon the previous piles and spaces. Move cards from right to left whenever they can be matched by rank. These moves are made only with individual cards, not with piles.

When the hand is exhausted, pick up piles in the same order as dealt, turn them over to form a new hand, and deal again by fours. Whenever four cards of the same rank appear in a row, one at the top of each pile, discard them from the pack. The game is won if all 13 fours of a kind are so discarded. Continue redealing the pack without limit until the game is won or reaches an impasse. When only 12 or eight cards are left, note the order of the cards before dealing and examine the pack before each subsequent deal to see if this same order has recurred. Once an order recurs identically, the game is blocked.

Clock

While purely mechanical, Clock, which is also known as Travelers, Hidden Cards, and Four-of-a-Kind, has the merit of moving fast; you are not kept long in suspense as to the outcome.

Layout. Deal 13 piles of four cards each, face down. Any method of dealing is permitted; the simplest is to count off four cards at a time from the top of the pack. Place 12 of the piles in a circle, representing the numbers on a clock. Put the thirteenth pile in the center (see diagram).

Play. Turn up the top card of the thirteenth or king pile. Place this card face up underneath the pile of its number. For example, if the card is a queen, put it under the pile in the position of twelve o'clock. If it is a jack, put it under the pile for eleven o'clock, and so on.

Having put a card face up underneath a pile, turn up top card of that same pile and continue play. Should a card turn up on the pile of its own number, as a six on the pile at six o'clock, simply put it under and turn up the next card. If there is no next card—the pile now comprising all four cards of the pile number—take instead the top card of the next higher pile. Turn of the fourth king stops the play. The game is won if all 13 piles are changed to the proper fours of a kind. If the fourth king is turned up while any cards remain face down, the game is blocked.

The layout for Clock.

Eight-Day Clock

As the name implies, this game is a more protracted way than simple Clock of finding out whether the pack happened to be shuffled into a favorable order.

Layout. Deal 13 piles of four, arranged as for Clock, but with all cards face up.

Play. Begin with the first pile (starting at one o'clock) whose top number card is not the same as its number. Thus if the top of pile one is not an ace, begin there. Lift off the top card and put it under the next pile. Move the top card from that pile to the next, and so on. Go clockwise around the circle of piles, but include pile thirteen after twelve and before one. In making these transfers, however, skip any pile whose top card is the same as its number. The progressive changes will gradually increase the number of such piles and decrease those remaining in the cycle of shifts. If all the piles become topped with cards of their own number, stop and discard all these 13 top cards.

The last card removed before such a discard must be held in abeyance. Resume play by putting it under the pile of its own number, or the first thereafter that is not topped by a card of the same number as the pile.

The game is won if three sequences of ace to king are discarded. A block will result if at any time the circuit of "live" piles does not contain all the cards necessary to complete a sequence. For example, suppose that the transfers have become narrowed down to a circuit of three piles, the two, seven, and twelve piles. Spread these piles for examination. If together they cannot furnish a deuce, a seven, and a queen, further play is useless.

Auld Lang Syne

Layout. Remove the four aces from the pack and place them in a row. These foundations are built in sequence up to kings, regardless of suits.

Play. Deal a row of four cards below the foundation, forming the reserve. Top cards of reserve piles are available for play on foundations. Spaces in the reserve are not filled except by the deal. Continue to deal in groups of four cards, one on each pile or space. Pause between deals to play up what you can.

Sir Tommy

A derivative of Auld Lang Syne, this game is also known as Old Patience, Try Again, and Tim O'Shanter. It offers a choice in placing cards from the hand.

Foundations. The four aces, as they become available, are placed in a row and built up to kings, regardless of suits.

Play. Deal four cards, one by one, placing each on any of four waste piles below the foundations. Play up what you can. Continue dealing cards one by one and placing them as desired on the four piles. Pause to play up to

Layout for Auld Lang Syne.

the foundations only after each group of four cards has been placed. Top cards of waste piles are available for play on foundations. As many or as few cards may be placed on one pile as desired.

Puss in Corner

This game is so called because the waste piles are traditionally placed outside the corners of the foundations, which are placed in a rectangle.

Foundations. Remove the four aces from the pack and place them in a row. Each is to be built up to the king in its own color, either red or black.

Play. Follow the rules for the play of Sir Tommy.

Redeal. One redeal is permitted. After the hand is exhausted and play is at a standstill, pick up the four waste piles in the same order they were dealt, turn them face down, and deal again.

Calculation

Calculation stands at the top of the list of games that give opportunity for skill. Some devotees go so far as to say that two games out of three can be won by patience and application. While this may be an exaggeration, certainly the experienced player wins four or five times as often as the beginner.

Foundations. Remove from the pack any ace, deuce, three, and four, regardless of suits. Place these four cards in a row to form the foundations. Each is built up in arithmetical series as follows, without regard to suits:

A, 2, 3, 4, 5, 6, 7, 8, 9, 10, J, Q, K
2, 4, 6, 8, 10, Q, A, 3, 5, 7, 9, J, K
3, 6, 9, Q, 2, 5, 8, J, A, 4, 7, 10, K
4, 8, Q, 3, 7, J, 2, 6, 10, A, 5, 9, K

Play. Turn up cards from the hand singly and place unplayable cards on any of four waste piles below the foundations. These piles should be spread downward so that all cards can be read. The top card of each waste pile, as well as the card in hand, is available for play on foundations.

Four Kings

This is a way of playing Calculation so as to remove most of the choice; hence, most of the opportunity for skill is gone.

Layout for Quadrille.

Layout. Place in a row any ace, deuce, three, and four, regardless of suits. These are index cards. In a row below them place any deuce, four, six, and eight, regardless of suits. These are foundations.

The foundations are built up in arithmetical series. The separate index row serves as a reminder of the arithmetical difference in each series.

Play. Turn up cards singly, placing unplayable cards face up on a single waste pile. The top card of this pile, and the card in hand, are available for play on foundations.

Redeal. Two redeals are permitted.

Quadrille

Foundations. The fives and sixes, as they become available, are moved into a circle (see diagram). The sixes are built up in suit to jacks; the fives are built down in suit to kings, which come after aces.

The queens, as they become available, are placed in the center of the circle. These cards are dead, and they are used merely to complete the layout picture.

Play. Turn cards up from the pack singly, placing unplayable cards face up on a single waste pile. The top card of this pile, as well as the card in hand, is available for play on foundations.

Redeal. Two redeals are permitted.

Thirteen Down

The face-down stock is found in very few solitaires, though face-down cards in the tableau are common.

Layout. Count off 13 cards face down, and leave them face down in a pile to form the stock. Deal a row of four cards to left of the stock and four more to the right, forming the wings of the reserve. Deal one card above the stock, as the first foundation.

Foundations. The other three cards of same rank as the first foundation are moved into a row with it, as they become available. The foundations are built up in suit until each pile is 13 cards.

Play. Reserve cards are available for play on foundations. Each space in the wings must at once be filled by the top card of the stock, turned face up. After 12 cards have been played off the stock, the thirteenth may be turned face up, and it then is available for play on a foundation as well as into a space. After the stock is exhausted, reserve spaces may be filled from the hand or the waste pile as the player chooses.

Waste Pile. Turn up cards from the hand one by one, placing unplayable cards face up on a single waste pile. The top of this pile, as

Layout for Queen's Audience.

Layout for Scorpion.

well as the card in hand, is available for play on foundations.

Redeals. Two redeals are permitted.

Queen's Audience

Layout. Deal 16 cards in the form of a square. This is the *antechamber* (reserve). The enclosed area is the *audience chamber* (see diagram).

Foundations. The four jacks are moved into the audience chamber as soon as possible, and then built down in suit to deuces. An available jack may be moved in, however, only if the ace of the same suit is also available. The two cards are placed in a pile, jack uppermost, and the ace is thus discarded.

The kings and queens are similarly discarded, but they may be removed only in couples of the same suit as they become available. Pile all the kings and queens together in the audience chamber, keeping a queen uppermost.

Play. All cards in the antechamber are available for play on foundations. Turn up cards from the hand singly, filling each space in the antechamber at once and placing unplayable cards face up in a single waste pile.

The top card of this pile, as well as the card in hand, is available for play on foundations.

The ace–jack and king–queen couples may be moved into the audience chamber whenever the two cards of a suit are simultaneously available in the antechamber, on top of the waste pile, or from a card turned from the hand.

Scorpion

Layout. Deal seven cards in a row, four face down and three face up. Deal two more rows in the same way; then four more rows with all the cards face up. Overlap the rows to form piles of cards spread downward. The 49 cards so dealt make the tableau. Leave the three remaining cards face down, as a reserve.

Play. All building is confined to the tableau, there being no separate foundations. The object of play is to reduce the tableau to four piles, one of each suit, with the cards of each suit in sequence, the king at the bottom of the pile.

On the top card of each pile may be placed the next-lower card of the same suit; nothing may be built on an ace. Any card in the tableau, no matter how deeply buried, may be moved to make a build; but all the cards above it must be moved with it as a unit.

On clearing a face-down card, turn it face up; it then becomes available. A space made by clearing away an entire pile may be filled only by a king. Any king in sight is available

for this purpose, all covering cards being moved with it as a unit.

After play comes to a standstill, deal the three reserve cards, one on the top of each of the three piles to the farthest left. Then resume play; if the game becomes blocked again it is lost.

KLONDIKE

It is perhaps a tribute to the indomitable human spirit that this most popular of all solitaires is at the same time one of the most difficult to win.

Layout. Deal a row of seven cards, the first face up and the rest face down. Deal a row of six cards upon the first, beginning with one card face up on the second pile and then the rest face down on the piles to the right. Continue with successive rows of five, four, three, two, and one, beginning each time with one card face up, on the pile at the right of that on which the previous row was begun. The completed tableau comprises seven piles increasing in number from one to seven cards, with the top card of each pile face up and the rest face down (see diagram).

Foundations. The four aces, as they become available, are moved into a row above the tableau and built up in suit to kings.

Tableau. The face-up cards on the tableau may be built down in alternating colors. Tableau cards may be built on each other, but all face-up cards on a pile must be moved as a unit. Whenever such a transfer is made, the exposed face-down card on one pile is turned up and becomes available.

Top cards of tableau piles are always available for play on foundations. Aces must be moved up as soon as available, but any higher card may be kept on the tableau for building purposes, if the player wishes, rather than built on a foundation. A space in the tableau, formed by the removal of an entire pile, may be filled only by a king or by a build with a king at the bottom.

Waste Pile. Turn up cards from the hand one by one, placing unplayable cards face up on a single waste pile. The top card of this pile, as well as the card in hand, is available for play on foundations or the tableau.

Agnes

This is one of many variations of Klondike designed to increase the chances of winning.

Follow the rules of Klondike except: After dealing the tableau, deal the next card above it to form the first foundation. The other three cards of same rank are moved beside it as they become available. Build foundations up in suit until each pile is 13 cards. For example, if the foundation is an eight, build; eight, nine, ten, jack, queen, king, ace, two, three, four, five, six, seven. Below the tableau deal a row of seven cards forming the reserve. All reserve cards are available for play on foundations or the tableau. Do not fill spaces in the reserve, except by subsequent deals. Deal a second and then a third row of seven cards upon the piles and spaces of the reserve, pausing each time to make what plays you can. Only the top card of each reserve pile is available. After the third such deal, turn the last two cards of the pack face up, separate from the reserve. These two cards are also available.

Thumb and Pouch

When the "Chinaman" takes all your money at Klondike, you can win it back at Thumb and Pouch. Follow all the rules of Klondike except: In tableau building, a card may be laid on a next-higher card of any suit but its own. Face-up cards may be moved one at a time, in part, or in whole. A space may be filled by any available card or group.

Whitehead

A blend of Klondike and Spiderette, Whitehead is only a little easier to win than either of its very difficult progenitors. Follow the rules of Klondike except: Deal all the cards in the tableau face up. Tableau building is in the same color, either red and black. Any available card or group may be put in a space. Available for removal from one pile to another, or into a space, is the top card of the pile together with any or all immediately

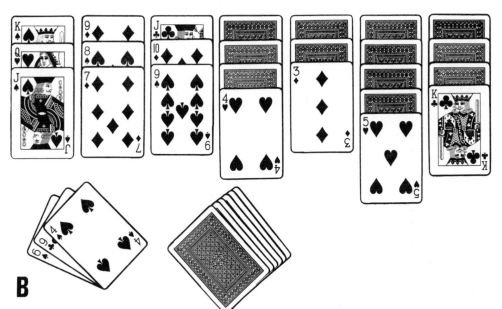

Layout for Klondike.

below it that are in unbroken sequence in the same suit. For example, if the six of hearts is on the seven of hearts, both may be moved together. But if the six of hearts is on the seven of diamonds, the upper card must be moved alone.

Westcliff

This game is a blend of Klondike and Forty Thieves, and fairly easy to win.

Layout. Deal a row of ten cards face down. Deal a second row upon the first. Deal a third row face up. This forms the tableau.

Foundations. The four aces, as they become available, are moved to a row above the tableau and built up in suit to kings.

Tableau. Available tableau cards may be built down in alternating colors. Any or all face-up cards on a tableau pile may be removed to another pile, if the sequence and alteration is correct. When all face-up cards are removed, the exposed face-down card is turned up and becomes available. A space in the tableau, formed by removal of an entire pile, may be filled by any available card or group from tableau, waste pile, or hand. Top cards of tableau piles are available for play on foundations.

Waste Pile. Turn up cards from the hand singly, placing unplayable cards face up on a single waste pile. The top card of this pile, as well as the card in hand, is available for play on foundations or the tableau.

Aces Up

Another variation of Klondike, this is easier to win because cards from the hand become available in groups, and fewer cards are buried in the layout.

Layout. Deal a row of seven cards face down. Deal a second row face down upon the first. Then deal a row face up on the piles, making 21 cards in all.

Foundations. The four aces, as they become available, are moved to a row above the tableau and built up in suit to kings.

Tableau. The face-up cards on the tableau may be built down in alternating colors. The top card of each pile is always available. A group of cards on top of a pile, in correct sequence and alternation, may be moved in whole or in part. If all the face-up cards are removed from a pile, turn up the top face-down card, which then becomes available.

Top cards of the piles are always available for play on foundations. Aces must be moved up as soon as available, but any higher card may be kept on the tableau for building purposes, if the player wishes. A space in the tableau, formed by removal of an entire pile,

may be filled only by a king or by a group of cards with a king at the bottom.

Hand. Whenever play comes to a standstill, deal seven more cards from the hand, one on each tableau pile. Tableau spaces need not be filled before the deal. The last three cards of the pack go on the first three piles.

Spiderette

Patterned after the two-pack game Spider (see page 415), Spiderette is much more difficult to win.

Layout: Deal 28 cards in seven piles, in the same manner as for Klondike (see diagram, page 399).

Play. All building is done on tableau piles. Cards may be built down, regardless of suit, each sequence ending at the ace. Top cards of tableau piles are always available. A group of cards on top of a pile, in correct sequence and all of the same suit, may be moved in whole or in part. When all of the face-up cards on a pile are removed, turn up the face-down card, which then becomes available. A space, formed by removal of an entire pack, may be filled by any available card or group.

When all 13 cards of a suit are assembled in correct sequence on top of a pile, they may be discarded. The game is won if all four suits are so assembled and discarded. Whenever play comes to a standstill, deal an additional row of seven cards, one on each pile, and resume play. All spaces must be filled before a new row is dealt. The last three cards of the pack are dealt on the first three tableau piles.

Will o' the Wisp

The major difficulty of Spiderette lies in the large number of buried cards, 21. Will o' the Wisp reduces the number to 14, but earns its name because it is by no means so easy to win as it looks on paper. Follow all rules of Spiderette except: Lay out seven piles of three cards each, two face down and one face up.

Four Seasons

Layout. Deal five cards face up in the form of a cross, forming the tableau. Deal the next card into one of the corner spaces, as the first foundation.

Foundations. The other three cards of same rank as the foundation are moved to the other corner spaces as they become available. The foundations are built up in suit until each pile is 13 cards, aces following kings.

Tableau. Tableau cards may be built on each other, downward, regardless of suit. Only one card at a time may be moved from the top of a pile. Spaces may be filled by available cards from the tableau, the waste pile, or the hand. Top cards of tableau piles are available for play on foundations.

Waste Pile. Turn cards up from the hand one by one, placing unplayable cards face up on a single waste pile. The top card of the pile, as well as the card in hand, is available for play on foundations or the tableau.

Simplicity

This variation of Four Seasons was probably invented to give emotional relief to frustrated devotees of Four Seasons. Follow all rules of Four Seasons except that, for the tableau, deal two rows of six cards each. Deal the next card in a row above for the first foundation. On the tableau, build down in alternating colors.

Fortune's Favor

Foundations. Remove the four aces from the pack and put them in a row, to be built in suit to kings.

Tableau. Below the aces, deal two rows of six cards each for the tableau. These cards may be built on each other, down, in suit; but only one card at a time can be moved in the tableau, and never into a space. Spaces must be filled from the waste pile, if any, or from the hand. Top cards of tableau piles are available for play on foundations.

Waste Pile. Turn cards up from the hand one by one, placing unplayable cards face up on a single waste pile. the top card of this pile, as well as the card in hand, is available for play on foundations or the tableau.

Redeal. One redeal is permitted.

Canfield

This solitaire takes its name from the celebrated gaming house of Saratoga Springs, New York.

Layout. Count off 13 cards face down from the pack, square them up, and place them up at the left to form the stock (face

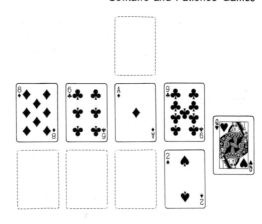

Layout for Canfield.

up). Deal one card above and to right of the stock for the first foundation. In a row to right of the stock deal four cards, forming the tableau (see diagram).

Foundations. The other three cards of same rank as the first foundation are moved to the row with it, as they become available. The foundations are to be built up on suit until each pile is 13 cards.

Play. Tableau cards may be built on each other, downward, in alternate colors. An entire pile must be moved as a unit in building. (Some players also allow one card at a time to be removed from the top of one pile to another.) Top cards of the piles are available for play on foundations, but never into spaces.

Spaces must be filled at once from the stock. The top card of the stock also is available for play on foundations or on tableau piles. After the stock is exhausted, tableau spaces may be filled from the waste pile or the hand, and the player may keep them open until he wishes to use them.

Waste Pile. Turn cards up from the hand in groups of three, counted off without altering the order within the group. Place them face up on a single waste pile. The top card of this pile is available for play on foundations or the tableau. Redealing by threes may be continued without limit until the game is won, or comes to a standstill.

Selective Canfield

The object of this variation is to let the player console himself that he might have won had he made a correct choice at the outset—if that is any consolation. Follow all rules of

Canfield except: After laying down the stock, deal five cards in a row. Choose one of them for the first foundation. The others remain to form the tableau.

Chameleon

This is a game much like Canfield, even to the degree of difficulty in winning.

Layout. Count off 12 cards face down from the pack, square them up, and place them face up at the left to form stock. Deal one card above the stock for the first foundation. In a row to the right of the stock deal three cards, forming the tableau.

Foundations. The other three cards of same ranks as the first foundation are moved to the row with it, as they become available. The foundations are built up in suit to 13 cards.

Play. Tableau cards may be built on each other, downward, regardless of suit. Any or all cards of a pile may be moved as a unit in building. Top cards of tableau piles are available to be placed on foundations. Spaces must be filled at once from the top of the stock. The top card of the stock is available for play on foundations or the tableau. After the stock is exhausted, the space it occupied becomes a fourth tableau space, and spaces may be filled from the hand or the waste pile.

Waste Pile. Turn cards up from the hand, one by one, placing unplayable cards face up on a single waste pile. The top card of this pile, as well as the card in hand, is available for play on foundations or the tableau.

Storehouse

Foundations. Remove the four deuces from the pack and place them in a row, to be built up in suit to aces.

Layout. Count off 13 cards face down from the pack, square them up, and place them face up to the left, forming the stock. To right of the stock deal a row of four cards, forming the tableau. (See diagram for Canfield, page 401.)

Play. Tableau cards may be built on each other, down, in suit. An entire pile is moved as a building unit. The top cards of the piles are available for building foundations. Spaces must be filled at once from the stock. The top card of the stock is also available for playing on foundations or tableau piles. After the

stock is exhausted, spaces may be filled from the hand or the waste pile.

Waste Pile. Turn cards up from the hand, one at a time, placing unplayable cards face up on a single waste pile. The top card of this pile, as well as the card in hand, is available for play on foundations or the tableau.

Redeal. Two redeals are permitted.

Gate

This is an interesting tableau–reserve combination, easier to win than might be thought. It is well to release reserve cards as soon as possible.

Layout. Deal two columns of five cards each, forming the "posts" of the "gate" (reserve). Between them deal two rows of four cards each, forming the "rails" (tableau). (See diagram.)

Foundations. The four aces, as they become available, are moved to a row above the gate and built up in suit to kings.

Play. Only the bottom card of each post is available. All cards in the rails are available. These cards (tableau) may be built on each other, downward, in alternate color. From a rail pile, one card at a time from the top (or the pile as a whole) may be moved to other piles. The top cards are available for play on foundations. A space in the rails may be filled only from the posts. Available post cards may also be moved to foundations or built on tableau piles.

Waste Pile. Turn up cards from the hand one at a time, placing unplayable cards face up on a single waste pile. The top card of this pile, as well as the card in hand, is available for play on foundations or the tableau.

Beleaguered Castle

Foundations. Remove the four aces from the pack and place them in a column, to be built up in suit to kings.

Layout. Deal the rest of the pack into two wings of a tableau, one on each side of the foundations (see diagram). Each wing is made up of four rows of six cards each, the cards in each row overlapping. The customary method is to deal by columns. First deal a column of four cards far to the left to start the left wing. Then deal a column just to the right of the aces to start the right wing. Continue dealing to the wings alternately, a

Layout for Gate.

column at a time, each column overlapping the previous column at the left.

Play. Only one card at a time at the open end of each row is available. The open end is that having the uncovered card. Available cards may be played on foundations or may be built on each other, downward, without regard to suit. A space made by removal of an entire row may be filled by any available card.

Citadel

This is a variation of Beleaguered Castle which may seem easier to some players. Follow all rules for Beleaguered Castle, except: Do not place the aces at the outset, but deal them to the center column in the course of laying out the tableau. Any deuce turned up in dealing may be built on its ace already in

Layout for Beleaguered Castle.

the center; and so on. A card turned from the pack in dealing may be played to the center if the foundation is ready for it; but a card once laid on the tableau may not be touched again until the deal is complete. When a card is so played to the center, do not replace it by the next card of the pack, but skip the place in the tableau where it would have gone. The completed tableau rows will thus not be of uniform length.

Streets and Alleys

This is Beleaguered Castle made more difficult, but it is unlikely that you will find the parent game too easy. Follow all rules for Beleaguered Castle except: Do not place the aces at the outset; move them into position as they become available. Deal an extra column of cards to the left wing of the tableau, making four rows of seven (see diagram for Beleaguered Castle).

Fortress

This game is perhaps the most popular of those in which the whole pack is laid out.

Layout. Deal the entire pack in two wings of a tableau, each wing consisting of five rows with the cards of each row overlapping. The top two rows are six cards, the other, five. The customary method of dealing is by col-

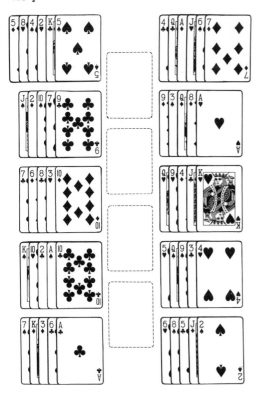

Layout for Fortress.

umns (see diagram). After completing five columns in each wing, place the last two cards on the ends of the two rop rows.

Foundations. The four aces, as they become available, are the foundations that are moved to a column between the wings, to be built up in suit to kings.

Play. Only one card at a time may be moved from the open ends of the rows. End cards are available for play on foundations, or to be built on each other in suit, either up or down.

Chessboard

The layout for Fortress too frequently shows no possible move. Such an impasse can usually be circumvented in Chessboard. Follow rules for Fortress except: After dealing the layout, choose any available card (it may be one made available by building) for the first foundation. The three other cards of the same rank are moved to the center, as they become available. Build each foundation up in suit until the suit is complete.

La Belle Lucie

Layout. Deal the entire pack into 17 fans of three cards each with one card left over (see diagram). The simplest method of dealing is to count off three cards at a time from the top of the pack and turn them face up, overlapped.

Foundations. The four aces, as they become available, are placed in a row and built up in suit to kings.

Play. Only one card at a time may be moved from the top of a fan. Top cards are available for building on foundations, or building on each other, down, in suit. A space formed by removal of an entire fan is never filled.

Redeal. Two redeals are permitted. To redeal, pick up all the cards exclusive of piles (foundations) and shuffle them thoroughly. Then deal again in fans of three, with any one or two odd cards at the end in a separate pile.

Draw. After the last redeal, any one card below the top of a fan may be drawn out and used on foundations or fan builds.

Trefoil

This is La Belle Lucie made easier. Follow all rules of La Belle Lucie except: Remove the aces from the pack in advance and place them in a foundation row. The layout comprises 16 fans of three cards each.

Flower Garden

Layout. Deal six rows of six cards each, forming the "garden" (tableau). Each row should overlap the one above. Spread the remaining sixteen cards of the pack below the garden to form the "bouquet" (reserve).

Foundations. The four aces, as they become available, are moved to a row above the garden and built up in suit to kings.

Play. Every card of the bouquet is available for building on foundations or on garden piles. The bottom card of each column of the garden is available for building on foundations or on another pile. Garden cards are moved singly and may be built downward, regardless of suit. A space in the garden, formed by removal of an entire pile, may be filled by any available card.

Layout for La Belle Lucie.

Shamrocks

Layout. Deal the entire pack in 17 fans of three cards each, with one card left over. If any king lies over a lower card of the same suit in the same fan, put it under that card.

Foundations. The four aces, as they become available, are moved into a foundation row and built up in suit to kings.

Play. Only one card at a time may be moved from the top of a fan. Top cards are available for building on foundations. They may also be built on each other, downward, regardless of suits, with the proviso that no fan may comprise more than three cards. Thus, the layout is blocked if no ace is on top of a fan and no build can be made on the single card. A space formed by removal of an entire packet (fan) is never filled.

King Albert

King Albert is a building game of a conventional type.

Layout. Deal a row of nine cards. Deal a row of eight overlapping the first, omitting the first card. Add a row of seven, omitting the first two piles at the left. Continue in the same way with rows decreasing by one each time, so as to form nine columns of cards that decrease from nine to one. These 45 cards form the tableau. Spread the remaining seven down below the tableau to form the reserve.

Foundations. The aces, as they become available, are placed in a row above the tableau and built up in suit to kings.

Play. All reserve cards are available for building on foundations or the tableau. The bottom card of each tableau column is available, to be built on foundations or on another tableau pile. Tableau piles may be built downward in alternating colors.

A space in the tableau, formed by removal of an entire column, may be filled by any available card.

Baker's Dozen

Layout. Deal entire pack into four rows of 13 cards each, with the rows overlapping. If there is a king in the bottom row, transfer it to the top of its column. If any buried king lies over the lower card of the same suit, move it under that card. (A simpler rule is to move all kings to the top of their columns. The game is none too easy, even then.)

Foundations. The four aces, as they become available, are moved to a row above the tableau and built up in suit to kings.

Play. The bottom cards of the tableau columns are available to be played on foundations, and may be built on each other downward, regardless of suit. A space formed by removal of an entire column is never filled.

Good Measure

This is a variant of Baker's Dozen and is about as difficult. Follow all the rules for Baker's Dozen except: Remove any two aces from the pack and put them in the foundation row. The other two aces are placed with the first two, as they become available. Deal the tableau in five rows of ten cards each. Before starting play, move all kings to the top of their columns.

Perseverance

This is a more difficult variant of Baker's Dozen.

Foundations. Remove the four aces and place them in a row, to be built in suit up to kings.

Layout. Deal the rest of the pack into 12 piles of four cards each.

Play. The top cards of the piles are available for building on foundations or on each other. On the piles, build down in suit. A group at the top, in correct sequence and suit, may be moved as a unit.

Redeal. Two redeals are permitted. When play comes to a standstill, pick up the piles in reverse of the order in which they were dealt, and deal again into 12 piles as far as the cards go.

Little Spider

Layout. Deal two rows of four cards each to form the tableau, leaving space between them for a row of foundations. Make any plays, then deal eight cards, one on each pile or space of the tableau. This deal is repeated. After each eight-card deal, pause and play up what you can as described below. Do not fill spaces in the tableau except in the course of dealing a group of eight cards. The last four

cards of the pack are dealt on the upper row.

Foundations. Two aces of one color and two kings of the other color, as they become available, are moved into a row between the tableau rows. The player has a free choice of colors. The foundation aces are built up in suit to kings, and the foundation kings are built down in suit to aces.

Play. The top cards of tableau piles are available. Any available foundation card may be moved into place from either tableau row. From the upper row, until the whole pack is dealt, a card may be built only on the foundation directly above the tableau pile.

Once the pack is completely dealt, top cards in the lower row as well as the upper may be played to any foundation, and top tableau cards may be built on each other in sequence up or down, regardless of suit. The sequence is circular, making ace and king adjacent in rank. A space formed by removal of an entire pile may not be filled.

Grandfather's Clock

Foundations. Remove from the pack and place in a circle the following 12 cards: two of hearts, three of spades, four of diamonds, five of clubs, six of hearts, seven of spades, eight of diamonds, nine of clubs, ten of hearts, jack of spades, queen of diamonds, king of clubs.

The cards should correspond to the hours on a clock, with the nine at 12 o'clock and the rest in sequence. Each foundation is to be built up in suit until it reaches the number appropriate to its position in the clock. Sequence is circular (ace after king). The ten, jack, queen, and king foundations will each require four cards, while the rest will require three.

Layout. Deal the rest of the pack in five rows of eight cards each, the rows overlapping. This is the tableau.

Play. The bottom cards of the tableau columns are available for building on the foundations and may also be built on each other downward, regardless of suit. A space formed by removal of an entire column may be filled by any available card.

Bisley

Foundations. Remove the four aces from the pack and place them in a row at the left. These foundations are to be built up in suit. The four kings, as they become available, are

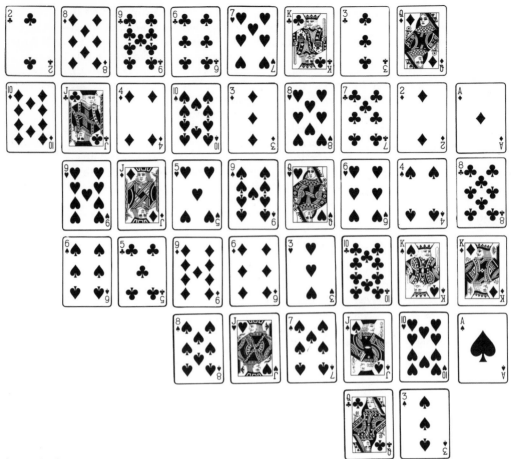

Layout for Pendulum.

moved into a row above the aces and built down in suit. When all the cards of a suit have been built on the ace and king together, the two piles are put together.

Layout. Deal nine cards in a row to right of the aces. Deal three more rows of 13 cards each below the first. The rows may be dealt overlapping, the aces being pushed up to be clear of the second row of the tableau.

Play. The bottom cards of the tableau columns are available for play on foundations. They may also be built on each other in suit, up or down. A space formed by removal of an entire column is never filled.

Pendulum

Foundations. Remove the four aces from the pack and place them in a column at the right. These foundations are to be built up in suit by any interval the player chooses after surveying the tableau. For example, if the

choice is to build upward by five, the sequence is: A, 6, J, 3, 8, K, 5, 10, 2, 7, Q, 4, 9. Add the number to the previous card of the series, then subtract 13 if the sum exceeds 13. Whatever interval is chosen must be followed on all four foundations.

Layout. Deal the rest of the pack into six rows of eight cards each, all cards separate (see diagram).

Play. The bottom cards of tableau columns are available to be played on foundations or the tableau.

An available card may be placed upon the card just above it in the column, if the upper card is of the same suit and next-higher in the chosen sequence. If, for example, the interval is five upward, the three of clubs may be moved upon the eight of clubs. Should several adjacent cards at the bottom of a pile be in suit and in upward sequence, going up the column, all may be stacked on the uppermost card of the sequence. Any available card,

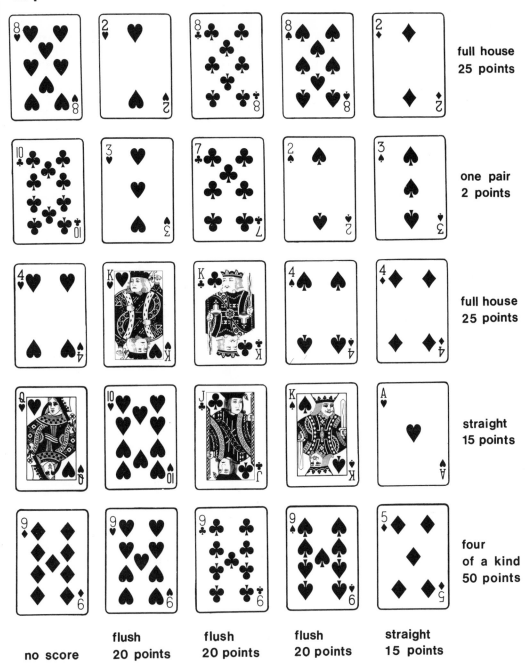

	full house 25 points
	one pair 2 points
	full house 25 points
	straight 15 points
	four of a kind 50 points

| no score | flush
20 points | flush
20 points | flush
20 points | straight
15 points |

Layout for Poker Solitaire.

regardless of column, may be moved upon either of the cards at the two upper corners of the tableau, if suit and sequence are correct.

A space formed by removal of an entire column may be filled only by a card which is last in the chosen sequence. For example, if the interval is five upward, only a nine may be put in a space. The card goes in the top row of the tableau. Spaces must be filled, if posssible, but the operation of the pendulum is not altered by a space in the top row.

The Pendulum. When play comes to a standstill, "swing the pendulum." The first swing must be to the right; and thereafter to the left and the right, alternately. The pendulum consists of moving all cards in rows containing spaces, except the top row, to the right or left side of the tableau, without changing the order of the cards in the row. The spaces thus being massed toward one lower corner of the tableau, new cards above them become available. The pendulum may be swung without limit until the game is won or becomes blocked.

Poker Solitaire

Layout. Deal 25 cards into a tableau of five rows of five cards each.

Play. Place each card to best advantage, so long as it remains within the confines of the tableau. (An alternate rule is that each card must be placed adjacent horizontally, vertically, or diagonally to some card previously dealt.)

Score the five cards in each row and column of the tableau as a Poker hand. Two methods of scoring are prevalent, as follows:

Hand	English	American
Royal flush	30	100
Straight flush	30	75
Four of a kind	16	50
Full house	10	25
Flush	5	20
Straight	12	15
Three of a kind	6	10
Two pairs	3	5
One pair	1	2

The English system takes account of the peculiarities of the solitaire. Trying for a straight is hazardous, as there is likely to be no score at all if it fails. Trying for a full house is sure to give a score, at least for one or two pairs or a triplet.

The object is to place the cards so as to make the highest possible score.

Cribbage Solitaire—I

This game is one to amuse a Cribbage player with no opponent.

Layout. Deal six cards face down to make the hand, and two face down to start the crib.

Play. Look at the hand and lay away two cards to the crib. Turn up the next card of the pack for the starter. Score the hand, then turn up and score the crib. Follow Cribbage rules in scoring.

Put the starter on the bottom of the pack and discard the other eight cards. Deal again in the same way. Continue dealing and discarding until only four cards remain in the pack. Turn these up and score them as a hand without a starter.

The object is to make the highest possible total on running once through the pack. By tradition, a score of 121 is considered to be a "win."

Cribbage Solitaire—II

This is another game on the Cribbage principle, limited, however, by one deal.

Layout. Deal 16 cards one by one in a tableau of four rows of four cards. Each card may be placed to best advantage with the proviso that it must be adjacent horizontally, vertically, or diagonally to some card previously dealt.

Play. Turn the seventeenth card of the pack face up as the starter. Score each row and each column in the tableau as a Cribbage hand, together with the starter in every case.

The object is to place the cards as dealt so as to make the highest possible total score. A total of 61 or more may be considered a "win."

Cribbage Solitaire—III

Deal cards one by one in a row, not overlapping. Look for any of the following scoring combinations in two or three adjacent cards:

One pair	2
Three of a kind	6
Three of same suit	3
Three in sequence	3
Three in suit and sequence	6
Two or three cards totalling 15	2

Note that, as in Cribbage, a sequence is valid even though the cards do not lie in sequential order. For example, seven-five-six is a sequence if the cards are adjacent.

Score each combination, then move any one of the cards involved upon any other. The choice here should be exercised so as to make additional scoring combinations, when possible. For example, with nine-seven-five-six, score the sequence; then move the six on the seven and score the 15, nine-six.

A combination must be scored and consolidated at once, before another card is dealt, with one exception: When a pair appears, a third card may be dealt, to try for three of a kind.

The object is to make the highest possible total score on running once through the pack. A total of 16 or more is a "win."

TWO-DECK SOLITAIRE

Patriarchs

Foundations. Remove the aces and kings from one pack. Put the aces in a column at the left, to be built up in suit to kings. Put the kings in a column at the right, to be built down in suit to aces.

Reserve. Between the columns of foundations, deal three rows of three cards each, forming the reserve. All cards of the reserve are available for play on foundations. Spaces must be filled at once from the waste pile, or from the hand.

Waste Pile. Turn up cards from the hand one by one, placing unplayable cards face up on a single waste pile. The top card of this pile, as well as the card in hand, is available for play on foundations.

Reversal. When the top cards of the two foundations of the same suit are in sequence, any or all cards of one pile may be reversed upon the other, except for the ace or king at the bottom.

Redeal. One redeal is permitted.

Contra-Dance

The traditional layout of the 16 foundations is in a circle, but the game is just as good with the more convenient arrangements here suggested.

Foundations. Remove all sixes and fives from the two packs and place them in two rows, the fives above and the sixes below. The sixes are to be built up in suit to queens; the fives are to be built down in suit to kings (following after aces).

Play. Turn cards from the hand, one by one, placing unplayable cards face up on a single waste pile. The top card of this pile, as well as the card in hand, is available for play on foundations.

Redeal. One redeal is permitted.

Sultan of Turkey

The intended final picture shows the lone monarch surrounded by his harem. Only an

exceptional run of cards can deprive you of this elegant view.

Layout. Remove the eight kings and one ace of hearts from the packs. Place them in three rows of three with a king of hearts in the center and the ace below it. These are the foundations. Deal a column of four cards on each side of the foundations, forming the "divan," or reserve.

Foundations. Do not build on the central king of hearts. All other kings are to be built up in suit to queens. The ace of hearts is to be built up in suit to the queen.

Play. All cards of the divan are available for play on foundations. A space in the divan must be filled at once from the waste pile, if any, or the hand.

Waste Pile. Turn cards from the hand one by one, placing unplayable cards face up on a single waste pile. The top card of this pile, as well as the card in hand, is available for play on foundations.

Redeal. Two redeals are permitted.

Windmill

Layout. Place any one ace in the center of the table. Deal two cards in column above it and two in column below; deal two in a row to left of the ace and two in a row at the right. These eight cards are the reserve.

Foundations. The center ace is to be built up, regardless of suit, until the pile contains 52 cards. Sequence is circular. The first four kings of any suits that become available are moved into the spaces between the arms of the cross. These four foundations are built down to aces, regardless of suit.

Play. All eight cards of the reserve are available for play on foundations. The top card of a king foundation may be transferred to the ace foundation, but only one such card may be moved from a given pile at a time. After such a transfer, the next card built on the ace foundation must come from the reserve, the waste pile, the hand, or another king foundation. The king itself also may be moved from a king foundation to the center pile. Each space in the reserve must be filled at once from the waste pile, if any, or from the hand.

Waste Pile. Turn up cards from the hand one at a time, placing unplayable cards face up on a single waste pile. The top card of this pile, as well as the card in hand, is available for play on foundations.

The Fan

Layout. Count off 12 cards face down, square up the pile, and place it face up at the left to form the stock. To the right of it deal a row of 12 cards, overlapping, to form the reserve, or "fan." Below the stock deal one card, the first foundation. The other foundations will go in a row beside the first. Below the space reserved for them, deal a row of four cards, forming the tableau.

Foundations. The other seven cards of the same rank as the first foundation are moved into the foundation row as they become available. All foundations are built in sequence, regardless of suits, until each pile contains 13 cards. The player has the option, after inspecting the reserve, of electing to build up or down. His decision, which may be delayed until the first card is placed on a foundation, applies to all eight piles.

Play. Available for play on foundations are the top card of the stock, the top card (right end of the fan) of the reserve, all cards of the tableau, the top card of the waste pile, and cards turned from the hand.

A space in the tableau must be filled from the hand or from the waste pile.

Waste Pile. Turn up cards from the hand one at a time, placing unplayable cards face up on a single waste pile.

Redeal. Two redeals are permitted.

Precedence

Foundations. Remove any one king from the pack and place it at the left. In the same row are also to be placed a queen, jack, ten, nine, eight, seven, and six, regardless of suit, as they become available. These foundations are built down, regardless of suits, until each pile consists of 13 cards. The top cards will then rank in order from ace down to seven.

Play. Turn up cards from the hand one by one, placing unplayable cards face up on a single waste pile. The top card of this pile, as

well as the card in hand, is available for play on foundations.

Place foundations as quickly as possible in a row with the kings as they become available; but observe the rule that no base card may be placed until all the others of higher rank have been placed. For example, no jack may be moved into the foundation row to start the third pile until a queen has been placed to start the second. Building on foundations already placed is permissible at all times.

Salic Law

This venerable game, in which the queens are discarded, no doubt took its name from the provision of Frankish law denying daughters the right to inherit land.

Layout. Remove one king from the pack and place it at the left. Deal cards face up on this king, overlapping downward in a column, until another king appears. Place the second king at the right of the first, and deal cards upon it until the third king appears. Continue in the same way to deal out the whole pack upon the eight kings, which should be arranged in a row.

During the deal, separate all aces and queens. Place the aces in a row above the kings, and the queens in a row above the aces. (The queen row is solely for pictorial effect; they can be discarded.)

Foundations. Aces are foundations, to be built up, regardless of suit, to jacks.

Building. Building on foundations may begin as soon as the first ace is placed. Cards as turned from the hand in dealing are available, together with the top cards of all king piles (bottom cards of the columns). If all the cards dealt on a king are played off, the uncovered king is the equivalent of a space. Any available card may be placed on it. But spaces may not be utilized until after the deal is finished. If play on foundations and the tableau comes to a standstill at any time after the last card is dealt, the game is lost.

Faerie Queen

This variant of Salic Law gives somewhat more opportunity for skill. Follow all the rules of Salic Law except: Do not discard the queens from the play. The ace foundations are to be built up to queens. After the deal is

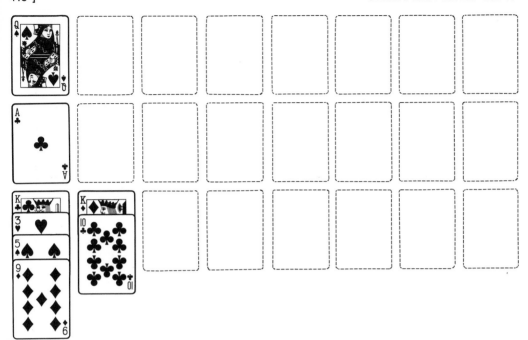

Layout for Salic Law.

finished, available cards may be built on each other downward, regardless of suit.

Intrigue

A variant of Salic Law, this was probably devised by someone who wanted to win every time. Follow all rules of Salic Law except: Use queens for base cards instead of kings. During the deal, throw out fives and sixes instead of aces and queens. The sixes are to be built up, regardless of suit, to jacks; the fives are to be built down, regardless of suit, to kings, following after aces.

Some competition can be put into this game by adopting this rule: Each queen placed in the base row permits the placing of a five and six in column above it. Should a foundation card appear at a time when there is no queen to receive it, it must be dealt on the pile. For a really difficult game, adopt the rule that each foundation card must be put in column above a queen of its own suit. Lacking such a queen in the base row, a foundation must be dealt on a pile.

Colorado

Layout. Deal two rows of ten cards each, forming the tableau.

Foundations. One ace and one king of each suit, as they become available, are placed in a row above the tableau. The aces are built in suit up to kings, and the kings down in suit to aces.

Play. Top cards of tableau piles are available for play to foundations. A tableau card may not be moved for any other purpose. A space in the tableau must be filled at once by a card from the hand. Several cards may be played from the tableau, when each leaves a space, provided that 11 spaces are then duly filled. But no play from a pile of two or more cards is permitted while there is an open space anywhere.

Turn cards up from the hand one by one, placing each on a foundation or on any one of the 20 tableau piles. These are in effect waste piles. Once a card is turned from the hand, it must be placed before another play is made. The reason for the stringent rule is that the game is too easy if the player looks at the card in hand before deciding whether to make a space for it or lay it on a pile.

La Nivernaise

Layout. Deal two columns of four cards each, leaving space between for four additional columns. These eight cards form the

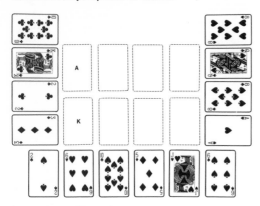

Layout for La Nivernoise.

"flanks." If no ace or king is dealt, shuffle and deal again. The game is hopeless without an immediate space in the flanks. Below the flanks, lay out a row of six piles of four cards each, forming the "line" (see diagram). Count off each group of four face down, square up the pile, and turn it face up, so that only the top card can be read.

Foundations. One ace and one king of each suit, as they become available, are moved into two rows between the flanks. The aces are built up in suit to kings, and the kings down to aces.

Play. All cards in the flanks, and the top of every line pile, are available for play on foundations. Only as many cards in the line piles, from the top, may be examined as there are spaces in the flanks.

A space in the flanks may be filled by any available card from the line, but a space need not be filled until the player chooses. As a rule, at least one space should be kept open at all times, to be filled only when cards are released that will reopen the space.

A space in the line, formed by removal of an entire pile, must be filled at once by a group of four cards counted out face down from the hand and then turned face up.

Hand. When play comes to a standstill, add four more cards to each pile on the line from the hand. These cards must be counted off face down and turned up when squared, in deference to the rule as to examination of piles. In the last round of dealing, however, when there may not be enough cards left to give each pile four cards, deal by rows so far as the cards will go, leaving them spread for examination.

Reversal. When the top cards of the two foundations of the same suit are in sequence, one card may be transferred from one pile to the other.

Redeal. Two redeals are permitted. To redeal, pick up the line piles in reverse order, so that the pile at the right will be at the top of the new hand.

Tournament

The rule of La Nivernaise as to the examination of piles is difficult to follow without unintentional peeking. Follow the rules of La Nivernaise except: Deal the line by rows, overlapping the cards, so that all can be read. When two foundations of the same suit are built to cards in sequence, any or all of them on one pile may be reversed upon the other, including the bottom cards.

Blockade

Foundations. Move the eight aces, as they become available, in a row above the tableau, to be built up in suit to kings.

Play. Deal a row of 12 cards face up, starting the tableau. Play up what you can. Tableau cards may be built down in suit. The top card of a tableau pile is always available for play on foundations or on another pile. A group of cards on top of a pile, in correct sequence and suit, may be moved in whole or in part.

A space may be filled by any available card or group from the tableau, or by a card from the hand. At least one card must lie on each of the 12 spaces of the tableau before an additional row is dealt. Whenever play comes to a standstill, deal a new row of twelve cards, one on each pile.

Miss Milligan

History does not record who Miss Milligan was, but if she invented this game, she deserves praise for a pleasing blend of Klondike and Spider.

Foundations. The eight aces, as they become available, are placed in a row above the tableau and are built up in suit to kings.

Layout. Deal a row of eight cards. If any aces and other playable cards appear, put them up. Do not fill spaces in this first row. Continue dealing eight cards at a time, overlapping the previous cards or filling in the spaces. Do not leave any gaps in the columns,

Layout for Spider.

and do not bother to align rows. Just be sure to add one more card at the bottom of each column during the deal. Between deals, make what plays you can.

Play. The bottom cards of the columns are available for play on the foundations or on each other. They may be built downward in sequence in alternating colors.

A space left by the removal of an entire column may be filled only by an available king or by an available build with a king at the bottom. After the entire pack is dealt, one available card or group may be lifted up and set aside. If these cards are eventually built correctly back on he tableau, or are all played off on foundations, the privilege of "weaving" continues with another card or group.

Spider

The devotees of Spider, who are legion, claim it as the king of all solitaires.

Layout. Deal a row of ten cards face down. Add three more rows face down on the first. Deal four more cards face down, one on each of the first four piles. This makes in all 44 cards face down. Now deal a row of ten face up on the piles. (Because of space limitations, the diagram shows two rows of five cards instead of the normal layout of one row of ten cards.)

Play. All operations are carried out on the ten piles, which are at once the tableau and foundations. The top card of each pile is available. Cards may be built on each other, downward, regardless of suit. The sequence ends with the ace. The king may not be built on it.

A group on top of a pile, in correct sequence and also in suit, may be moved in whole or in part. Hence there is a premium upon making the "natural" builds in suit,

when possible. On removing the last face-up card from a pile, turn up the top face-down card, which then becomes available.

A space made by removal of an entire pile may be filled by an available card or group. Kings may be moved only into these spaces.

The object of play is to assemble an entire suit of 13 cards in ascending sequence from ace to king, from top card to bottom. Whenever a suit is so assembled and is available, it may be lifted off and discarded from the tableau. The game is won if all eight suits are so assembled and discarded.

An assembled suit need not be discarded until the player chooses. There may be an advantage in breaking it up to help straighten other suits.

Dealing. After play on the original layout has come to a standstill, deal ten more cards, one on each pile. Continue in the same way, dealing a new row of ten cards and then pausing to play. Every space in the tableau must be filled before a new row is dealt.

Forty Thieves

This game is probably the most widely known of two-pack solitaires. It is known as Napoleon at St. Helena, St. Helena, and Big Forty.

Layout. Deal four rows of ten cards each face up, each row overlapping the one above. This is the tableau.

Foundations. The eight aces, as they become available, are moved to a row above the tableau and are built up in suit to kings.

Play. The bottom card of each column of the tableau is available, to be played on foundations or built on other piles. One card only may be moved at a time. Tableau cards may be built down in suit. A space made by removal of an entire pile may be filled by any available card from the tableau, the top of the waste pile, or the hand.

Waste Pile. Turn cards from the hand one by one, placing unplayable cards face up on a single waste pile, which may be spread so that all cards can be read. The top card of the waste pile, as well as the card in hand, is available for play on foundations of the tableau.

Limited

Follow the rules of Forty Thieves except: Deal the tableau in three rows of 12 cards each.

Lucas

Follow the rules of Forty Thieves except: Put the eight aces in the foundation row first. Then deal the tableau in three rows of 13 cards each.

Maria

Follow the rules of Forty Thieves except: Deal the tableau in four rows of nine cards each. On the tableau piles, build down in alternate color.

Number Ten

Follow the rules of Forty Thieves except: Deal the first two rows of the tableau face down, the top two rows face up. On the tableau piles, build down in alternate color.

Rank and File

Follow the rules of Forty Thieves except: Deal the first three rows of the tableau face down, the last row face up. On the tableau, build down in alternating colors.

Indian

Follow the rules of Forty Thieves except: Deal only three rows in the tableau, the first face down and the others face up. In building on the tableau, a card may be placed on the next highest card of any suit but its own.

Emperor

Follow the rules of Forty Thieves except: Deal the first three rows face down, the last row face up. On the tableau piles, build down in alternate color. All face-up cards on a pile may be moved as a unit. Cards on foundation piles may be removed and built on the tableau.

Midshipman

Follow the rules of Emperor except: Deal only 36 cards in four rows, the first two rows face down and the last two rows face up.

Octave

Follow the rules of Forty Thieves except: Deal only 24 cards in three rows, the first two rows face down and the last row face up. Below the tableau lay out a reserve of eight cards. On the tableau, build down in alternat-

ing colors. Reserve cards are available for tableau or foundation building, and spaces are filled from the hand. Cards may be turned from the hand so long as each can be built on foundations or the tableau, or placed in a reserve space. The game is lost if a card is turned that cannot be used.

Busy Aces

Layout. Deal two rows of six cards each, forming the tableau. These cards may be built on each other, downward, in suit. Spaces may be filled from waste pile or the hand. Top cards of tableau piles are available for play on foundations.

Play. The eight aces, as they become available, are placed in a row above the tableau and built up in suit to kings.

Waste Pile. Turn up cards from the hand one by one, placing unplayable cards face up on a single waste pile. The top card of this pile, as well as the card in hand, is available for play upon foundations or the tableau.

Rouge et Noir

Like Busy Aces, Rouge et Noir is a basic type from which many solitaires have been elaborated. The alternate color rule of building makes it much easier to win than Busy Aces.

Foundations. Remove the eight aces from the pack and place them in a row, to be built up in alternate colors to kings.

Tableau. Below the foundations deal a row of eight cards, forming the tableau. These cards may be built on each other downward in alternate color. Only one card at a time may be moved in building. The top card of a tableau pile is always available for play on another pile or on foundations. Spaces in the tableau may be filled only from the waste pile, if any, or the hand.

Waste Pile. Turn up cards from the hand one by one, placing unplayable cards face up on a single waste pile. The top card of this pile, as well as the card in hand, is available for play on foundations or the tableau.

Redeal. One redeal is permitted. You may find that the redeal makes the game too easy for your taste. An alternative is to bar it, but allow tableau piles as a whole to be moved in building.

Congress

Congress is one of the relatively few games in which foundation building is in suit, but tableau building disregards suit.

Layout. Deal two columns of four cards each, leaving room between the columns for two more columns. These eight cards start the tableau.

Foundations. The eight aces, as they become available, are moved into two columns in the center and built up in suit to kings.

Play. Cards in the tableau may be built downward, regardless of suit. The top card of a tableau pile is available for building on another pile or on foundations. Only one card at a time may be moved. Spaces in the tableau must be filled at once from the waste pile or the hand.

Waste Pile. Turn up cards from the hand one at a time, placing unplayable cards face up on a single waste pile. The top card of this pile, as well as the card in hand, is available for play on foundations or the tableau.

Harp

Harp is Klondike played with two packs. It would be too easy if whole builds could be moved bodily, so the rule makes only the top card available.

Layout. Lay one card face up and beside it a row of eight cards face down. Deal the next card face up on the second pile, then deal seven more face down, one on each remaining pile. Continue in the same way so as to make nine piles, increasing in number from one to nine cards, with the top card of each pile face up and the rest face down.

Foundations. The eight aces, as they become available, are placed in a row above the tableau and built up in suit to kings.

Play. Cards may be built on the tableau, downward, in alternating color. Only the top card of each tableau pile is available for building on the foundations or the tableau. If the last face-up card is removed from a pile, turn up the top face-down card, which then becomes available.

A space in the tableau may be filled only by an available king; but for this purpose a group of cards on top of a pile, in proper sequence and alternation, with a king at the bottom, may be moved as a unit.

Waste Pile. Turn up cards from the hand one by one, placing unplayable cards face up on one waste pile. The top card of the waste pile, as well as the card in hand, is available for play on foundations or the tableau.

Redeal. There is no limit on redealing until the game is won or blocked.

House in the Wood

This is La Belle Lucie with two packs, but what a difference! The one-pack deal is blocked nine times out of ten by an unlucky third deal. Though restricted to one deal, this game is and can be won nine times out ten, assuming you don't destroy it with your own hand.

Layout. Deal the cards face up in 34 fans of three cards each and one fan of two. (See La Belle Lucie, page 406, for diagram.)

Foundations. All aces are foundations, to be put in a row as they become available, and to be built up in suit to kings.

Play. Only the top card of each fan is available. Available cards may be built on foundations or upon each other, in suit, up or down. Only a queen may go on a king and only a deuce on an ace. If all cards of a fan are removed, it is not replaced. There is no redeal.

House on the Hill

Follow the rules for House in the Wood except as regarding foundations. Here the foundations are one ace and one king of each suit, placed as they become available. Aces are built up in suit to kings, and king foundations are built down in suit to aces.

Intelligence

This is a European variation of La Belle Lucie, generally called Patience Intelligent in tribute to its opportunity for skill.

Layout. Deal 18 fans of three cards each. (See La Belle Lucie, page 406, for diagram.) If any aces are turned up in dealing, place them at once in the foundation row and replace them with the next cards.

MULTIPLE SOLITAIRE

Any solitaire may be played as a competitive game among two or more persons. Following

are the three chief methods.

Comparative Scoring. Each player has his

own pack or packs, and plays his own game. After each player has finished by winning his game or coming to a standstill, the scores are compared. The score is usually the number of cards built on foundations, but it may be some other quantity if the game is not one of foundation building. It may be agreed that a competition will comprise a certain number of games. Special systems of this kind are described in connection with Golf and Pyramid.

Common Foundations. The comparative scoring method may be combined with the idea of playing on common foundations. Each player has his pack or packs, and his own layout; but the foundations are common to all, and are built on by all the players. After the game comes to a standstill, the foundation piles are sorted out and the number of cards belonging to each player is counted. Widely popular is multiple Klondike using this system.

Identical Cards. Cribbage Squares, Poker Squares, and like games lend themselves to a very effective test of skill among a number of players. Each has his own pack. One player, appointed as "caller," shuffles his pack and then turns cards up, one by one, announcing the suit and rank of each. Each other player, having sorted his pack into suits for convenience, picks out the called card and puts the card into position as he pleases in his own tableau. Thus, all the tableaux comprise the same 16 or 21 cards, and the player with the highest count wins.

Russian Bank

This popular pastime for two players is often called Crapette, but is really a double solitaire. Each player uses a deck with a differently colored or differently designed back, so that there will be no confusion when the cards are separated after the game. Each shuffles his deck and has his opponent cut it before play begins.

Layout. Each player then lays out four cards face up, at his right and in a line toward his opponent. These eight cards (four by each player) constitute the tableau. Each then counts off the next 13 cards from the deck (some make it 12) and places these cards face down at his right. He may place them at his left if he chooses. This is the player's stock.

The top card of the stock is turned face up.

Layout for Russian Bank.

It does not matter whether the cards for the tableau or the stock are dealt first, but both players should follow the same procedure. The remaining cards of the deck are placed face down in front of each player. These packets are the hands from which cards will be dealt, as described later. A space is left between the tableau cards where the eight aces, which make the foundation, will go. Any aces that turn up in forming the layout are immediately placed into the foundation spaces.

Object of the Game. To build as many of one's 52 cards on the foundations, tableau, or opponent's stock as possible according to the rules of play.

The Play. Players may cut the cards before the layout is made to decide which player makes the first play—low cut having the privilege. An alternate method (more popular) is to have the player whose first tableau card is of lower rank than his opponent's make the first play. If these are equal, then the next tableau card decides it, etc. The first plays must be to build any available cards from the tableau or the stock on the foundations, also known as *center piles*.

Aces begin a foundation pile and are built up in ascending sequence in the same suit. Cards must be played to foundations when they become available. This play takes precedence over all others. Many players follow the rule that a card from the tableau must be played to the foundation, even if it necessitates moving an available card on top of it to some other place where it is playable. A card once built on a foundation may not be removed from there under any circumstances.

After having made all possible plays to the foundation, a player may make plays in the tableau if he wishes. But he is not required to do so. Only the top card in any tableau is available for play. However, available cards may be moved from one tableau pile to another. Available cards in the tableau are built in descending sequence, alternating in color.

A player may use an available card from his opponent's stock to make builds to the tableau in his turn of play. Cards must be built on the tableau in such a manner that all cards in the tableau are visible.

The top card of the stock is always available for play. If it can be built on a foundation pile, it must be played there before any other play can be made. An available card from the stock may be built on any tableau pile in descending sequence and alternating color. It may be played on an available card in the opponent's stock in a sequence going either way so long as it is in the same suit. These plays are known as *feeding* or *loading*.

When an available card is played from the stock, the next card underneath it becomes available. If it is face down, it is turned up.

Beside the feeding plays from the stock, a player may also feed cards to his opponent from the tableau or from his own hand. But he may not feed cards to his own stock. And no cards may be fed from the foundations. If a player in his turn does not wish to make any plays from his stock or the tableau, he turns up the top card of his hand, placing it face up to one side into a discard pile.

The top card of the stock is always available for play. If it can be played to any of the foundations, it *must* go there before any other play may be made. When an available card from stock is used in play, the card under-

neath it (if any) becomes available for play.

If a card turned up from the hand is not used for play, and is discarded, the turn to play goes to opponent. If a player uses the last card of his hand, he turns over the discard pile and this becomes his hand from which he will turn a new pile. If a player does not use the last card of his hand, he must leave it face up on the discard pile, and it is not available for play by him when his turn to play next comes. He turns over the entire pile for use as a new hand.

A card from the hand must be turned up in such a manner that opponent can see it easily. If a player turns a card from his hand, he must play it if possible or put it into the discard pile.

When a space appears in the tableau, it must be filled by a card from the stock or by an available card in the tableau. Some make it a rule that it must be filled first from the stock if possible. If no cards are available in the stock, a space may be filled from the discard pile or the hand. But some forbid the use of a card from the discard pile.

If a player makes any other play or touches any other card when a card is available for play to the foundations, his opponent may call "Stop," and the turn to play ends for the offender. The card in error is returned to its original position. But if the error involves a card in the discard pile, opponent of the offender may play that card to the foundations if he chooses.

Scoring. The game ends when a player disposes of all of the cards in his hand, stock, and discard pile. He scores 1 point for each card left in opponent's hand or discard pile and 2 points for each card left in his opponent's stock. It is customary to score a 30-point premium, additionally. When the game ends, the opponent may not play off any cards. If neither player gets rid of all his cards, one of two methods may be used in scoring. The player with the lowest count scores the difference between his count and opponent's. There is no additional premium. Or, the game is a draw.

Additional Rules. If too many cards are placed in the stock or tableau, the error cannot be rectified after the first card has been turned for play in the stock or from the hand.

Aside from the stop penalty of losing one's turn, there is no other penalty for making an incorrect play. If the incorrect play is detected by opponent, it must be corrected while it is still the offender's turn to play. Otherwise, it stands.

If a player looks at any but the top card of a stock or hand, he may play the top card if it is available. But he may make no further plays in that turn.

A player may look back through his stock or the face-up cards of his stock only if opponent permits it. In either case, the opponent may also see those cards.

Single-Deck Russian Bank

Object of the Game. The object of this game is to build on the tableau piles or the opponent's stock.

The Layout and Play. Players cut, low card dealing. Beginning with nondealer, each receives 26 cards, two at a time, then three at a time after that, all face down. Nondealer lays out his first four cards in a row, face up, to form the first part of the tableau. Cards available for builds in the tableau are played on each other in sequence and in the same suit.

Cards may be built in sequence, either ascending or descending; but once a player has started building a sequence in one direction, he must continue to build in the same direction. Sequences are continuous; that is, an ace may be built on a king or a king on an ace.

The spaces created in the tableau by building cards are filled by cards which the nondealer turns from his hand one at a time. If any other builds are thus created, the nondealer may make them. So long as spaces are created or builds are made, the nondealer may continue to turn available cards from his hand. When he turns a card that cannot be used in play, he leaves it face up in the discard pile.

It is then dealer's turn to play. He turns up four cards to complete the tableau to eight cards. He then makes plays exactly as described for the nondealer, but using all available cards in the eight piles of the tableau. When he can no longer play according to the rules, he turns a card face up into his discard pile. Players thus alternate.

A player may build on his opponent's discard pile in suit and in ascending or descending sequence. But cards from the tableau may not be used for this purpose. If an entire pile can be moved from one part of the tableau to continue a sequence in the same suit and in the same direction in another pile, it is per-

missible to do so. A space may be thus created. Spaces in the tableau must otherwise be filled by cards from the hand or discard pile. When the top card of the discard pile is used in play, the one under it becomes available for play.

When a player has no more cards in his hand, he turns over his discard pile to deal a new hand from it. When either player gets rid of all his cards, or when neither can continue according to the rules, the game ends. There are no stop penalties in this game.

Scoring. This is the same as in Russian Bank with two decks, except that there is no score for cards left in the stock.

Spite and Malice

This is one of the most popular two-hand games played in the United States, and for a good reason. Spite and Malice is a game of recent vintage, and is especially popular as a husband-versus-wife game in many parts of the United States. It has supplemented Russian Bank, which in some ways it resembles. Interest in the game continues to the very end. It is almost impossible for one player to be so far behind that he must abandon hope of winning. The opponent may be down practically to his last card, while you have scarcely started, and you can still run out the game on him. In mechanics, Spite and Malice is very similar to the principal solitaire games, and is quickly learned by anyone who plays solitaire.

Two standard 52-card decks plus four jokers are needed for Spite and Malice. The decks should be of different back designs or colors. The rank of cards is king (high), queen, jack, ten, and so on, down to ace (low).

Object of the Game. To play off one's payoff pile.

The Play. One deck (without the jokers) is shuffled and divided into two equal packs (26 cards each). These are *payoff piles* for the two players. Each player selects a pile and turns over the top card. The highest designates the *lead player*. Should both cards be of the same rank, the cards are reshuffled and a new top card is turned over.

The second deck (with the four jokers) is shuffled by the lead player's opponent, who deals a five-card hand to each player (one at a time, face down) and places the remaining cards in the center of the table as the stock.

To start the play, each available ace must be played immediately to form a center stack. There may be any number of center stacks. Each available two must be played, if possible, on an ace in a center stack. Center stacks are built up in ascending order, regardless of suit—any deuce on any ace, any three on any two, etc. Both players play to the center stacks.

Each player may have four *side stacks*. These are discard piles. A player may play only to his own side stacks and only from his hand. Any card may start a side stack. Side stacks are built downward, regardless of suit (any five on any six), or with like cards (any queen on any queen).

The top card of a payoff pile may be played only to the center. When it is played, the next card is turned up. A card from the hand or from the top of a side stack may be played to the center. A card from the hand may be played to a side stack, but only one such card in a turn. A player may make as many legal plays to center stacks as he wishes; but when he plays to a side stack, his turn ends and his opponent's turn begins. Cards may not be moved from one side stack to another, or moved to fill a space. A player may also end his turn by saying so, when he cannot—or does not—wish to play.

Each joker is wild and may be played in place of any card except an ace. If a joker becomes available at the top of a side stack, it may be played to the center. At the beginning of each turn, a player draws enough cards from the stock to restore his hand to five cards. When any center stack is built up through the king, it is shuffled back into the stock.

Scoring. The player who first gets rid of all the cards in his payoff pile wins, his margin being the number of cards in his opponent's payoff pile. If there are cards left in both payoff piles, and neither player can or will play, the winner is the player who has fewer cards in his payoff pile and he wins the difference; but it is never legal to count the cards in a payoff pile during play.

Spite and Malice for Three or Four Players

This game is played the same as two-hand Spite and Malice, except for the following:

1. Three decks of cards are used. One standard deck of 52 cards is shuffled and divided into three 17-card packets in the three-

hand game (the one card left over is mixed in with the stock); or it is divided into four 13-card packets in a four-hand game. These packets are the payoff piles. Each player turns up the top card of his payoff pile and the high card becomes the lead player. Play always proceeds in a clockwise rotation.

2. The two decks of 52 cards plus six jokers are shuffled together and then five cards are dealt to each player (one at a time face down). The remainder of the combined pack is placed in the center of the table as the stock.

3. The game ends when any player gets rid of his payoff pile. Each player pays to or collects from all other players the difference in the number of cards left in their respective payoff piles.

Pishe Pasha

This is a simple and fascinating two-hand card game played double-solitaire style. It is found in most towns and cities in the United States with a high concentration of foreign-born Jews. Two standard 52-card decks are used in Pishe Pasha.

The Object of the Game. To be the first player to get rid of all cards in his stock and discard pile by laying them off on the opponent's discard pile and/or onto the four foundation piles.

Foundations. The four aces are the foundations. Each ace, as it becomes available, must be immediately placed in one of the reserved spaces between each player's cards (stock and discard piles). The foundations are built up in a suit and sequence. *Example:* On the ace of diamonds must be played the two of diamonds, then the three of diamonds, and so on, up to the king of diamonds. A card once played on a foundation may not thereafter be removed.

The Deal. Either player shuffles the cards and becomes the first dealer. The opponent cuts the cards. The dealer, starting with his opponent, deals each player 26 cards; the first round is dealt two at a time, and the subsequent eight rounds are dealt three at a time. Each player squares his 26 cards face down in a pile at his left, forming his stock.

The Play. The nondealer starts the play by turning the top card of his stock face up and placing it next to his stock to form his discard pile. If the card is an ace he places it in one of the foundation's reserved spaces. The nondealer then turns up another card from the stock and starts his discard pile. The dealer then turns up the top card of his stock and may do one of two things:

1. He can, if able, place his card on the foundation.

2. He can, if able, place the card on his opponent's discard pile. A card, regardless of suit, may be placed on the opponent's discard pile if it is in sequence, the sequence going up or down. *Example:* If the top card of the opponent's discard pile shows a ten of any suit, a player may add (lay off) either a jack or a nine. Having added a jack, the player may continue with a queen or a ten, etc.

When the stock is exhausted, the discard pile (if any) is turned face down to form a new stock, and so on. Cards are turned up from the player's stock one by one; so long as each can be played on either the foundation or the opponent's discard pile, the player's turn continues. On turning an unplayable card, the player must put it face up on his discard pile and his turn of play ends. Having played a card from the stock, the player may complete whatever additional moves the play makes possible from his discard pile before turning the next card from the stock.

End of Game. When a player gets rid of his last card of his stock and discard pile, he calls "Game" and is declared the winner. He scores 1 point for each card left in his opponent's stock and discard pile. *Example:* The opponent's stock holds ten cards and the

opponent's discard pile holds 11 cards. The winner scores 21 points for game.

Additional Rules. Whenever a card becomes available that can be played on a foundation, it must be played immediately.

When a card is playable both on foundations and on the opponent's discard pile, the card must be played to the foundation.

When a player violates a rule of play, his opponent may say "Stop." And, on demonstration of the error, he may compel the violator to correct his error—or take over the turn of play.

Pounce

This is a round game for three players or more. The object of the game is to be the first to get rid of his stock. Each plays with his own deck of cards, each starting a game of Canfield or any other solitaire in which aces are foundation cards. Each player makes his own tableau. All play at once, not waiting for turns. But all foundations are placed in the center, and a player may play on any foundation in the center.

The first player to get rid of all the cards in his stock is the winner, regardless of how many cards he has managed to play to the foundations. (*Variation:* Some play that all the cards must be played up to the foundation to win.)

Players may run through their hands as often as they like.

CHAPTER 22

Cheating at Card Games

Though I should have preferred sparing you the reading of this chapter, we had better face facts about playing cards for money. And one of these facts is that more cheating takes place at illegally operated card games than at all other forms of gambling. The main reason, of course, is that the average card player knows little or nothing about card-cheating techniques and hence is easily victimized.

My observations of a lifetime have convinced me that more cheating takes place at private, or so-called friendly, card games than at all other forms of gambling combined. The main reason, of course, is that cheating in private games is much easier. Ten out of every 100 male and female card players will cheat in private games when they have the opportunity and think they can get away with it. Many of these cheaters are highly respected in their communities: businessmen, sportsmen, politicians, civic leaders, and just plain housewives. Although most of these people are otherwise honest, they think nothing of trying to steal your last dime in a card game. Private card gambling seems to bring out the worst in many people.

The one in ten ratio varies from game to game and town to town, depending on the ability of the players to detect cheating. A knowledge of cheating methods and the ability to detect them is your only protection against dishonest players in private games. It is for this reason that the most ethical, fastidiously honest card games are those in which the players are top-notch gamblers,

gambling operators, gambling-house employees, and cardsharps. When they play together the game is nearly always honest. It has to be, because they play in an atmosphere of total and icy distrust, and their exhaustive knowledge of the mechanics of cheating makes using this knowledge much too dangerous. They do not cheat because they dare not.

In a big-time money card game patronized by men and women who know little or nothing about cheating techniques, the odds are two to one that a card cheater is at work. Even bridge tournaments, where little or no money is at stake, are infested with bridge cheats. More than 500 bridge tournaments are played annually in this country and few, if any, are completed without one or more incidents in which a team appeals to the tournament directors for redress from some unfair practice allegedly committed by an opposing team. And much more tournament cheating goes undetected by the players. I know because I have seen it.

Some writers of books on card games contend that explanations of card-cheating methods have no legitimate place in the proper study of card games. They claim that the friendly card game is no place for suspicion and distrust. Let us say an opponent fails to offer you the deck for the cut and you call his attention to this omission; let us say that in playing Gin Rummy he has a peculiar habit of peeking at the second card of the stack when picking off the first card and you ask him to avoid this eccentricity. He is offended.

A beautiful friendship ends. This, these writers say, is to be avoided. This is rubbish. There is no more excuse for illegal play at any money card game than for dishonest practice in any other human activity. If a player can't abide by the rules of the game, he deserves any embarrassment it causes him. He should obey the rules or get out of the game, and let's not allow any false consideration of personal friendship to obscure the issue.

Three Kinds of Card Cheats

There are three kinds of card cheats: the amateur, the semiprofessional, and the professional. I call the amateur that not because he doesn't win money cheating but because he is a brazen and unskilled cheat. The semipro is one who earns part of his living by cheating but lacks the manipulative skill of the real cardsharp, and who, when he is working single-o, has to depend upon marked cards and other gaffed gambling equipment. The professional cardsharp is the skilled sleight-of-hand expert who has spent many hours in practice to gain the necessary proficiency in crooked card manipulation. He is called a *card mechanic,* and he usually travels a lot, seldom staying in one spot too long.

Cheats working together are known as a *card mob.* The mob is usually made up of a card mechanic, a bankroll man who supplies the necessary money to finance the operation, a couple of shills, and several steerers. The latter are often good-looking girls who pick up victims on the pretense of taking them to their hotel rooms, and steer them instead into the crooked game.

The semipro who works with a cardsharp helps by directing attention away from the cards at the moment the sharper makes his crooked move, by signaling the value of his hand, by making the right kind of cut when given the deck by the sharper, etc.

The honest player's best protection against these crooks is to learn enough about their methods so that he can spot the most common cheating moves when they occur. The crooked angles, ruses, subterfuges, sleights, and mechanical methods are so many and so varied that a detailed description of them all would more than fill this book. The most common methods can, however, be spotted when you know what to look for. Most of them require unnatural moves or actions on the part of the cheat. You may never be able to catch the expert cardsharp's bottom or second deal at the split second that it is made, but there is a way of recognizing the expert card mechanic for what he is by the way in which he holds the deck (see Mechanic's Grip, page 426).

I shall try in the succeeding pages to give you the information you need to protect yourself.

The Amateur Cheat

It is sometimes difficult to distinguish between the amateur cheat and the thoroughgoing, no-holds-barred, but honest player. I used to play Gin Rummy with an elderly lady who had a habit, after the cards had been cut for her deal, of glancing down and noting the bottom card of the deck as she squared it. Harmless? She peeked at a card that would never get into the play of the hand. Harmless? Well. . . . Her knowledge that the card is dead is useful information in planning her play; it is pertinent information not available to me.

She is a cheat. And she is the most dangerous kind—the amateur cheat. The amateur is usually a friend whom you don't think of suspecting and who for that reason can get away with murder. The good-natured, trusting American card chumps collectively lose billions of dollars annually to friends and acquaintances whose card-playing tactics are less than honest.

For every dozen crooked moves made by the agate-eyed professional card sharp, the amateur will blandly and brazenly attempt a hundred swindles. At Poker the amateur cheat will connive with a confederate and each will give the other some sort of a signal when he has a good hand and wants a raise. At Gin Rummy, Pinochle, or Canasta, the amateur cheat will add an extra five or ten points on the count of the hand. Trapped in a recount—any embarrassment? No! Aren't we all entitled to a certain percentage of error?

At Black Jack, when the dealer is busy, the amateur cheat will call a phony count on his cards, collect his cash and account the feat an act of skill with not the slightest objection from his conscience.

At Bridge he will deliberately drop a card to the floor and while leaning down to retrieve it try to get a peek at an opponent's hand. He likes to think of this maneuver as bridge strategy.

What do you do when you suspect a friend or acquaintance of cheating? It can develop very easily into a sticky situation because it is possible that an honest player may unconsciously do some of the things that cheaters do, and your suspicion may be unjustified. There is no need to raise a hue and cry. Your best bet is to demand quietly and graciously that the rules of the game be strictly followed. This should in most cases remedy what is wrong or looks wrong. If not, then make some polite excuse and leave the game. This will give no offense and do no harm to anyone's sensibilities or reputation or to your pocketbook. Rules are made to be followed—or broken revealingly—by players. A friend told me once, "John, I play Poker with a good friend. He never offers me the cards for the cut. I'm afraid to insist on the cut because he may think I'm accusing him, and I value our good relationship. What shall I do?"

I asked him who was the winner between them, and he said his friend was a few hundred dollars ahead. "I don't know whether your Poker game is lousy or whether you're being cheated," I told him. "I've never seen you and your friend play, but I know that if the cards were always cut you would not be suspicious of your friend—and suspicion is a lot worse than losing a few hundred dollars."

You must decide such things for yourself. As for me, I play by the rules, and I play no more with the old lady who peeks at the bottom card.

Professional Card Cheats

The underworld has many names for various types of card cheats. In the western part of the United States, Nevada included, a professional card cheat who travels over the country seeking card games where he can ply his trade is called a *crossroader*. A cheat who specializes in palming cards is referred to in the trade as a *hand-mucker*, or *holdout man;* one who deals from the bottom of the deck is a *base*, or *subway, dealer*.

The surreptitious manipulation of cards by card mechanics, hand-muckers, holdout men, crossroaders, card sharks, base dealers, or other card cheats requires considerable skill and practice, plus the nerve of a thief. A topnotch card mechanic must be considerably more adept with a deck of cards than a first-rate magician. The magician is free to use a great deal of conversation and misdirection to

fool his audience, but the card cheat is limited by the game's regulations. As a matter of fact, most present-day magicians—including most of those who advertise their acts as exposés of crooked gambling tricks—know little about the operation of the modern card sharper. They themselves are as easily fleeced by a good card mechanic as the average layman. Much of the sleight of hand and nearly all of the mechanical gadgets they expose were discarded by the cheats decades ago.

There is a popular delusion that card cheats and magicians can take a well-mixed deck of cards, riffle and shuffle the pack several times, and then deal each player in the game a good hand—in Poker, for example, four jacks to one player, four kings to another, and four aces to himself. The truth of the matter is that no cardsharp or magician can take a deck honestly shuffled by someone else, shuffle it two or three times, and arrange more than a couple of cards in two different hands without previous sight of or prearrangement of the deck. Whenever you see any sleight-of-hand expert claim to do this and deal out a perfect Bridge hand of 13 cards of one suit, or four or five pat Poker hands, you can be sure that the cards were previously stacked. Actually the cheat doesn't need to do anything so spectacular. It doesn't matter whether the game is Draw Poker or Gin Rummy in some gin mill or the most recondite Contract Bridge at a Park Avenue club— a cheater can take all the chumps in the game simply by knowing the approximate location of very few cards. If he knows the exact position of only one of the 52 cards, he will eventually win all the money in sight.

Never overestimate a card cheat. Don't expect him to work miracles. Just expect him to win the money. If luck favors him, he may not make a crooked move all night, or he may make only one crooked move in the whole card session. But that one move always comes at just the right time to get the money. In most games the move can even be executed clumsily and get by; the average player almost never spots it because he seldom suspects the people with whom he plays and because, even if he did, he lacks the necessary knowledge to know what to look for and wouldn't recognize it if he did happen to be looking in the right place at the right time.

Believe it or not, most sharpers are poor card players on the square (playing honestly). A good card mechanic spends so much of his time practicing cheating moves and concentrating, in play, on watching for the right opportunity to use his skill that he seldom develops a good sense of card strategy. During one of my gambling lectures at a Chicago club some years ago, a member of the audience asked me, "Isn't the old rule, 'Never play cards with strangers,' about the best protection one can have against cheaters?"

"That rule," I replied, "gives the average player about as much protection as a broken umbrella in a rainstorm." The card cheat has had the answer to it for years. Suppose that Harry, the card mechanic, discovers there's a big and neighborly Poker game every Friday night in the back room at Joe's cigar store. He also learns, for instance, the name of a doctor who is one of the players. Harry simply puts in a phone call and makes an appointment to have a physical checkup. During the examination Harry steers the conversation around to Poker and manages to get an invitation to the game. It's easy; he's done it a good many times before. And when Doc introduces him to the other players as one of his patients, no one thinks of him as a stranger; he's already one of the boys.

I repeat: The best protection against card cheats is a knowledge of how they operate and some ability at recognizing their slick sleight-of-hand and other crooked ruses. Most cheating moves, fortunately, have one or more giveaway signals, usually an unnatural action, either in preparation for the move or in executing it. If after learning how to spot these clues to trickery you still think you are being cheated at cards, your best bet is to take up some noncard game, preferably a game that can't be cheated. Since I invented it, naturally I hope you'll pick Teeko.

The Mechanic's Grip

Most cardsharps announce the fact that they are mechanics long before they make a crooked move. They do it as soon as they begin to deal. The giveaway is the peculiar manner in which they hold the deck, known as the *mechanic's grip.*

This cheat holds the deck in either the right or left hand (we will assume from here on that it's the right hand). Three fingers are on the edge of the long side of the deck and the

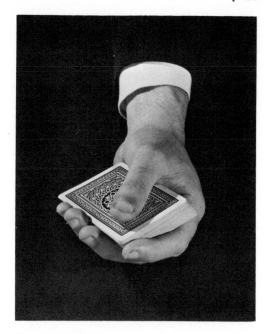

The mechanic's grip.

index finger at the outer right corner. Some mechanics keep two fingers on the side of the deck and two at the outer corner.

Many professional dealers in gambling houses also hold the deck in this manner but for a different reason: They do it to prevent players from glimpsing the bottom card. But when you spot a player using the mechanic's grip in a private, friendly game, find yourself another game. The odds are that the player who holds the deck this way is doing so because peeking at the top card, second dealing, bottom dealing, and other cheating moves require this grip. The index-finger position at the outer corner of the deck acts as a stop when the cheat is second dealing and peeking and also helps conceal a card when it comes from the bottom of the deck. It is possible that an honest, even innocent, player, might accidentally hold the deck this way, but it is highly unlikely because it takes practice to hold the cards in this manner while dealing. The only reason anyone would practice this grip is because he intends to cheat. There's one exception: magicians also use the mechanic's grip, but not many of them play cards for money, for the same reason Harry Houdini always gave: "If I win I am accused of cheating; if I lose they think I am a lousy magician."

Palming

Palming cards, called by cheaters *holding out,* is in all probability the cheating method most commonly practiced and most commonly suspected and detected. It can be learned by almost anybody, but doing it well requires some native talent and assiduous practice.

Palming is risky in fast company, but among half-smart card players it can be put to fairly profitable use in almost any kind of game. It is done as follows: When the cards are being thrown in for a new deal—it works for any game involving a deal, Poker, Rummy, Black Jack, Euchre, Cribbage, Pinochle—the cheater secretes the cards he wants in the hollow formed by the palm of his hand. He may hold the hand folded nonchalantly over his arm, or he may conceal the cards under his knee or armpit. The move is normally screened by the cheater's reaching into his shirt pocket for a match or hitching his chair closer to or farther from the table.

Having been dealt his new hand, the cheater substitutes his palmed—or, to be precise about it, armpitted or kneed—cards for an equal number out of hand, making use of the palm. Then, biding his time, he gets rid of the cards he's holding out by chucking them back at the end of the deal or palming them into the discards. Keep a respectful eye on the player who keeps his hand rigidly flat with the fingers close together.

The Pickup Stack

The pickup stack is the method cheats most often use for stacking cards. Its cleverness lies in its simplicity. It requires no special skill and it rarely fails. Suppose you are a cheater in a five-handed Stud Poker game. The next deal is yours, and two hands were exposed in the hand just completed. In each hand you spot one card you'd like to get for yourself the next time around. Let's say they are two aces.

You simply stack the deck in such a way that you deal the two aces to yourself. You do it in full view, and it's ridiculously easy. As dealer, you pick up the cards, taking them a hand at a time. You pick up the cards lying above the first ace, then use these cards to scoop up the remainder of the hand. Place these cards on top of the deck. This puts the

ace fifth from the top. Repeat the action with the remaining hand. That's all there is to it. The deck is stacked, ready for the deal and you will get the fifth and tenth cards—the two aces—back to back. If you have a fair memory and can remember the other cards and their order in the first hand you picked up, you will also know your opponent's hole cards, which can be an equally lucrative advantage.

Yes, you must shuffle before the deal, but that's not difficult either, you only need to riffle and let the top ten or so cards fall last, thus keeping them on top. As for the cut, the cheat has many ways of taking care of that without even resorting to sleight of hand. He may simply deal without offering the cards to be cut, he may cut and then pick up the two packs incorrectly, or he may have a confederate on his right who refuses the cut, saying "Run them." That's darned near all there is to stacking as it is generally practiced by the amateur or semiprofessional cheat. When the cut is omitted, insist that some other player or yourself be allowed to cut. The dealer may feel insulted but he can't object; the rules give you this right.

The Riffle Stack

The riffle stack is the most difficult of card-stacking methods, but the sharper who has perfected it is capable of fleecing the most seasoned players. If, at Poker, Bridge, Black Jack, or one of the Rummies, you think you detect an opponent using this cheating method, beware: You are up against a practiced, unscrupulous, and perhaps even dangerous card mechanic.

The sharper, let us say, has three kings on top of the deck. He cuts the deck into two blocks and shuffles them together. It looks like an ordinary standard shuffle, but during the action he puts just the right number of cards between the kings so that in the deal, which will be on the level, his opponents get cards at random and he gets the kings. It may take him four or five riffles to arrange the kings as he wants them, but if the riffle is his specialty, he can and will do it in two or three riffles. He gets the same result as in the pickup stack, but this sleight-of-hand method will take the smart boys who would spot the pickup.

Cleverly executed, this stack is almost detection-proof, but there is one way of spotting it, and then, if you can't correct the matter by forcing the cheat out of the game, the only safe thing to do is force yourself out. Most riffle-stack sharpers riffle the first cards fast and slow up perceptibly near the top where they must count the cards as they riffle. They also watch the deck carefully as they count the cards into place. Riffling in this fast-slow tempo and watching the deck too intently during the shuffle are the danger signals. The player may not be a riffle-stack expert, but he's acting like one. Look out.

The Crooked Overhand Shuffle Stack

This is the semiprofessional sharper's best friend. It is used in clipping chumps from New York to California more extensively perhaps than any other stacking method. It involves less skill than the riffle stack and comes in handy oftener than the pickup stack.

The sharper puts the cards to be stacked on the bottom of the deck. During his shuffle he milks the deck, pulling down one card from the bottom and one card from the top at the same time. On these two cards he shuffles off two cards less than the number of players in the game. He repeats this maneuver once for each card he wants to stack. He lets the next card project slightly from the deck, shuffles the remaining cards on top. He is now set for the deal. The wanted cards are spaced out so that they will fall to the dealer, or perhaps to a confederate, during the deal. The cut is then canceled or avoided as explained in the section on the pickup stack.

The giveaway signal here is the unusual sound of the shuffle caused by having to run off so many cards singly. A second clue is the fact that this shuffling sound is interrupted slightly at regular rhythmic intervals each time another bottom card is pulled down. The smart card player keeps his ears open as well as his eyes.

False Shuffles

The ability to appear to be shuffling a deck while keeping some or all of the cards in their original positions is an absolutely essential weapon in the arsenal of the accomplished cardsharp. The most popular and most deceptive of the false shuffles is the pull-through, a dazzling and completely crooked shuffle which doesn't alter the position of a single card.

When a hand of cards has been completed the cheat scoops up the tabled cards, taking special care not to disturb certain melds or discards which he wants and which he places on either the top or bottom of the pack. This shuffle is also used when a cold (stacked) deck has been switched into the game which must be shuffled without disturbing its prearrangement.

The deck is cut into two blocks and their ends riffled together quite honestly. The move comes during the split second that the cards are pushed together and reassembled into a single pack. The cheat pushes the two blocks of interwoven cards into each other at an angle, an action that is covered by the manner in which he holds his hands. Then, without any hesitation, he gives the cards a fast cut—or that is what seems to happen. Actually, he takes a new grip on the cards, grabs the right-hand block with the left fingers, the left-hand block with the right fingers, pulls the interwoven blocks through each other, slaps the block originally on top back on top, and squares the deck fairly as he should have done but didn't do immediately after the riffle. The pull-through action is done so smoothly and so fast that as far as the average chump is concerned it is quicker than the eye can follow.

Although the cards were fairly riffled and the action had the appearance and sound of a legitimate shuffle, not a single card has changed position. You have only one small clue here—that fast "cut" following so closely on the heels of the shuffle.

Nullifying the Cut

The greatest obstacle the card cheat has to overcome is the cut. If the rules did not ask for a cut, gambling with cards would have long ago become obsolete and playing cards would now be used only for Solitaire. Stacking and false shuffling are moves not too difficult for the average sharper to master, but shifting the cut (secretly returning the cut deck to its original order) successfully under the pressure of the game and under the watchful and observant eyes of experienced card players requires the skill of a master cheater. Since most card players are chumps

One-hand shift. The lower half of the deck is being pushed up by the fingers. When it touches the thumb, the top half drops down and the lower half takes its place on top. Done under cover, it cancels the cut.

who can't spot crooked card moves even when sloppily executed, average cheaters still manage to get away with it. Other cheats manage to avoid the cut altogether as explained in the section on the pickup stack.

Ordinarily, when the deck is cut, the dealer pushes it toward you and says "Cut, Mac?" You take a block of cards off the top, put them on the table, and the dealer completes the cut. He picks up the bottom block and places it on the top block you cut off. This buries the cards the cheater is trying to control; he must undo the cut and return the deck to its precut position. It must be done swiftly and without causing any suspicion.

Crimping is most often used for this purpose because it is much easier than shifting the cut and is almost impossible for the untrained or unsuspecting eye to detect. It has the further advantage that it is the honest chump himself who unknowingly does some of the work. Actually, a crimp is a bend placed in one or more cards. When such cards are in the middle of the deck, the crimp causes a small break or opening in the deck's edge which can be felt and cut to. Don't look for an obvious crimp from a pro. His crimp is so slight that the eye can hardly detect it, if at all, but his educated fingers can always feel it. Even when the sucker cuts the deck he is more likely than not to break at the crimp. Also, the crimp is almost always so placed that the break appears in the edge of the deck nearest the cheater and away from the other players.

A crimp so slight that it can barely be seen is still sufficient to cause the pack to break

five times out of ten exactly as the cheater wants, even when the unsuspecting chump does the cutting. The cheat also assists the victim to cut at the proper place by putting the crimp in the middle of the deck, which is where most players naturally cut. The bigger the crimp, of course, the greater the chance that the sucker will cut to it. Some stumble-bum cheats even make crimps so big that a tunnel appears in the center of the deck. When the cheater must have an absolutely sure-fire foolproof crimp, he simply has a confederate sitting on his right who obligingly cuts to the crimp every time it is needed.

The cheater uses the crimp this way: He stacks his wanted cards as previously explained, has them where he wants them, and must keep them there. An honest cut would bury them in the deck, so the sharper simply gives half the deck a fast crimp during another false shuffle or cut, leaves the crimped half on the bottom, and offers the pack to be cut. If the unsuspecting player cuts in his usual fashion, the cards break at the crimp. When the dealer completes the cut, the cards he is interested in automatically return to their original position and at least one player is happy.

Shifting the Cut

This is a sleight-of-hand maneuver which secretly restores the deck to its original order after the cut. It offers no particular challenge to the magician or exhibition card manipulator, who can employ various types of misdirection to cover it. But it is tough to accomplish without being detected at the card table, where a single slip is disastrous. In fact, there isn't a sharper living who can execute

The pass. The lower half of the deck moves up to the top as the upper half is pulled out of the way, restoring the original order of the deck.

the move successfully without a coverup, that is, without hiding the move in one way or another.

The crimp and the shift are used together after an honest cut. Before offering the cards to be cut, the sharper crimps the inner half of the deck, usually bending all the cards slightly downward. Because of the deck's thickness the bottom cards are bent somewhat more than those on top, and when the deck has been honestly cut, a small break appears in the middle of the deck at the narrow end nearest the cheat. When he picks up the deck his practiced fingers locate the break, and the cards are shifted back to their original position. There are many cut shifts, the most common of which are as follows:

One-Handed Cut Shift. Here the two portions of the deck are shifted back to their original positions with one hand only. It is deceptive because the chumps don't suspect that such a complex maneuver can be done with one hand and do not, therefore, watch closely when the deck is held this way. Since the other hand is away from the deck, some other type of cover must be used. The usual practice is to reach across the body with the free hand to take a cigar or cigarette from an ash tray which has been purposely left at that side. The reaching arm covers the hand holding the deck for a brief moment and the shift takes place unseen.

One-Handed Table Cut Shift. After an honest cut, while the two blocks of cards are still on the table, the cheater completes, or rather pretends to complete, the cut. He picks up the cards originally on the bottom and appears to place them on the top block. Actually the bottom block passes above and a bit beyond the top block, comes quickly back and slides in under the top block. This is a very deceptive shift provided that it is done with lightning speed and a single, unhesitating sweep of the hand.

Two-Handed Cut Shift. Magicians, who call this *the pass,* have used this shift for many years; it is still used by some sharpers. After the cards have been cut by another player, the cheat replaces the lower block on the upper one, but not squarely; it projects slightly at the inner end, leaving what is called a *step.* He scoops up the cards and inserts his little finger into the deck at the step. In the act of apparently squaring the deck and under cover of the hand above the deck, the lower half of the deck is pivoted upward. It pushes against the upper half, which swings aside as though hinged, and is deposited again on top, where it was before the cut was made. This is accomplished in a split second.

False Cuts

Like the false shuffle, a false cut, when well executed, appears to transpose the two halves of the deck but actually leaves them just as they were. When the other players are in the habit of letting the dealer do his own cutting, he executes the false cut. Otherwise, a confederate at his right does the dirty work. This last is the most effective method because suspicion is much less likely to fall on a nondealer. In games involving more than two players, particularly Poker, most cheating is done by two cheats who pretend to be strangers to each other. The partnership in crime is more dangerous to your bankroll than any other kind of cheating.

False cuts are employed not only when the cheat is the dealer but also when it is your deal. How? Most players are honest and awkward. When they shuffle, they often fail to mix the bottom cards of the deck thoroughly. The cheater detects something down there he wants, or he may glimpse the bottom card during the shuffle and see that it could be useful. Or, perhaps, after your shuffle, he secretly puts some palmed cards on the deck and false-cuts so that they stay there.

The Running False Cut. Instead of a single cut, the sharper makes a fast series of single cuts using both hands. He pulls a small block of cards off the bottom, slaps it on top and leaves a step. He repeats the action with the opposite hand, and continues until the block originally on top has gone down through the deck and, on the last cut, comes back once more to the top. It looks good, but nothing was changed; all the cards are in their original order. Many honest players make running cuts like this—but eye anyone closely who does so. Watch for a step in the deck, although the whole action is done so fast your chance of spotting it is slim.

Your best bet is to wait until after the dealer has completed his fancy cut, then ask for the deck, as is your right, reshuffle and offer it to the dealer to be cut. This will totally upset all his careful preparation and expert card manipulation. He can't very well object because that would be suspicious in itself.

The Prearranged or Cold Deck

A cold deck is any deck that has been stacked (prearranged) either before the game or during the game by a cheat who leaves the room for that purpose. It is switched (exchanged) during the play for the deck in use either on the cheat's or player's deal. If the room temperature is low, an experienced player might detect a prearranged deck which has just been switched in because it has not been warmed by the heat of the player's hands—hence the name "cold deck." Cheats sometimes warm the arranged deck before switching it into the game.

The cold deck is useful in any card game. It must, of course, be an exact duplicate of the deck in play. The object of the swindle, in case there are any men from Mars reading this, is to insure the crook a killing hand and send the chumps home broke.

The cold deck was the favorite cheating device used by the transatlantic card mobs some years ago. In a Poker game the boys would switch in on the chump's deal and let him deal himself a straight flush or four of a kind. The rest of the mob would also get good hands; one, perhaps a straight flush, would be just a shade higher than the chump's. Beating a mark for $25,000 on one cold-deck hand used to be a common occurrence on the liners.

Deck Switching. The most usual methods of replacing the original deck with a stacked deck are these:

1. The cheat leaves the shuffled deck on the edge of the table just as the waiter arrives with a previously ordered tray of sandwiches or drinks. The waiter holds the cold deck beneath the tray, which he rests on the table for a moment above the square deck. When he leaves, the cold deck remains behind and the shuffled deck goes with him. Or the tray may simply cover the shuffled deck for a moment as the cheat makes the switch under it.

2. A special mechanical deck-switching machine strapped to the cheater's body may be used, although its proper handling requires some skill. Not many present-day crooks use this gadget because, if discovered, its possession is prima facie evidence of guilt. A player using a mechanic's grip or a two-handed false cut may possibly be innocent; if not, he can at least try to talk himself out of trouble, since there is no tangible evidence of his guilt. A man caught with a holdout machine can, at best, try to get out of town in one piece.

3. The commonest and cleanest cold-deck switch consists of pure sleight of hand. The sharper surreptitiously spreads his handkerchief on his lap, slips the cold deck from his pocket and holds it in his left hand below the table. When he takes the deck after the cut he pulls it back toward himself and appears to catch it with his left hand just as it clears the edge of the table. Actually the deck drops neatly into his lap and his left hand comes up at the same time with the cold deck. A spot of misdirection by another member of the mob (a paroxysm of sneezing, a spilled drink, or the punchline of a joke) may be used to take attention away from the action. After the deal, the discarded deck is gathered up in the handkerchief and replaced in the pocket.

4. The best results are obtained by switching the cold deck in on the chump's deal. One method is this: When the sucker has shuffled and offers the deck to be cut by the player (a cheat) on his right, another cheat at his left asks the victim to change a large bill. While he is busy being helpful and making change, the cheat who should be cutting the deck is switching it. He takes his handkerchief out, blows into it and lets it cover the shuffled deck momentarily on the way back to his pocket. As the shuffled deck leaves the table under the handkerchief, the cheat's left hand replaces it with the cold deck. And when the mark turns back to take the deck for the deal the cheat executes a false cut to put him at his ease. The mark is now ready to deal himself to the cleaners.

Second Dealing

One of the most common cheating moves used by both the top-notch card mechanic and the would-be cardsharp is the second deal. This consists, as the names implies, of dealing the second card from the top rather than the first one. Any good second dealer will clip the best of players in any card game. The underworld calls a second dealer a *number two man*.

Dealing seconds is the move most often used when the cheats have had no opportunity to stack the cards. This time the cheating is done during the deal rather than earlier. The time-honored mechanic's grip is again used. When the left hand holds the pack, the

The one-hand hop. Scarne demonstrates this move with the deck face up (left). When an opponent cuts off the upper half of the deck (topped by the ace of spades here) Scarne apparently places the lower half (five of diamonds) on it, completing the cut. Actually, the fingers of the right hand (right) pull the top half of the deck up into the palm, and when both hands square cards, the original bottom half goes back on the bottom.

thumb pushes the top card over the side of the deck in the usual fashion so that it can be taken by the right hand. But when the right hand comes up to take it the right thumb strikes against the exposed corner of the second card and pulls it out enough so that it can be gripped and taken by the right thumb and forefinger. As the second card leaves the pack, the right thumb pulls the top card back to its starting position, the curled index finger of the mechanic's grip acting as a stop for the swinging top card. When expertly done, the sleight is a split-second, beautifully coordinated move that is exceedingly difficult to detect even by the most observant players, and it will deceive the average player if done merely competently.

When playing Black Jack or Stud Poker some cheats deal with one hand only, turning the deck over as the card is dealt so that it comes out face up. Don't let this one-hand action convince you that everything must be on the up and up; a good mechanic can and does deal seconds with one hand just as neatly as with two.

Second dealing isn't worth a plugged nickel unless the cheat knows what the top card is and wants to save it for himself or a confederate, or, in Black Jack, give it to the player who doesn't want it. It is, for this reason, mostly employed with marked cards, although it is also used with the peek, which is explained below. If you suspect a second dealer is at work, look for the mechanic's grip; they nearly all use it.

The Peek

Peeking is the art of secretly glimpsing the top card of the deck. This is one of the most useful and valuable dodges in the cheat's repertoire. When the peek is used in conjunction with the second deal, a good peeker is poison in any card game. It is especially useful in Black Jack and Stud Poker.

The move, a simple one, consists of exerting pressure on the top card with the thumb and pushing it against the fingers on the opposite outer corner of the deck. This causes the card to buckle or bend upward near the index corner just enough so that the cheat can look into the opening thus formed and glimpse the index. He gives it a careless glance at the right moment, releases the pressure of his thumb, and the top card flattens out again.

Some cheats peek while dealing one-handed. Others pretend to look at the face-down card in their Black Jack or Stud Poker hand and peek at the top card at the same time. Eye with suspicion the player who uses the mechanic's grip and looks too often at his face-down card.

Peeking on the Draw. Both the bungler and the expert cheat use this one, particularly in Gin and other Rummy games, and in other card games when drawing from the stock. The cheat reaches out to take the top card of the stock and his thumb lifts up two cards at the inner edge. He spots the second card, lets it down again onto the deck, and takes off the top one. The giveaway is that he isn't casual enough; he hesitates briefly as he makes the peek.

The Bottom Deal

A bottom dealer—the boys in the know refer to him as a base dealer or subway dealer—like the second dealer, uses the mechanic's grip. His left thumb pushes the top card over as the right hand comes up to take it, but the right hand has other instructions. Instead, its forefinger moves in under the deck at the outer right corner and pulls out the bottom card while the left thumb is engaged in pulling back the top card. The index finger of the left hand in the mechanic's grip position covers much of the front edge of the deck, making it difficult for an observer to see whether the card comes from top or bottom. The movement, naturally, must be fast and smooth and must follow the same rhythm as when the top card is taken legitimately.

The subway dealer saves time because he doesn't have to fuss around stacking cards. He or his confederate usually picks up the cards after the previous hand and places the previous deal's winning hand or some useful discards on the bottom of the deck. He retains them there during a phony shuffle and deals them off the bottom as needed. This is easier said than done—much easier. It takes years of practice to become a good bottom dealer, and the chances that you will find yourself in a game with a cheater who can bottom-deal cards from a full deck noiselessly and without detection are roughly about 100,000 to 1. There is another character,

The famous Scarne cut. Pull a block of cards (top) from the center of the pack. Place them on top of the pack (center) and square it up. Then pull a block of cards from the bottom of the pack (bottom), place them on top. Repeat these three steps several times if you like. Finally, square up the pack and cut it in the regular manner.

however, whom you might meet oftener. Since it is easier to deal a respectable bottom from half a deck of cards, there are mechanics who have the nerve to pick up the bottom half of the deck after the cut, skip putting them on the top half, and begin dealing. When this happens, ask that the cut be completed in the usual manner; then keep your ears open. If he attempts a bottom deal with a full deck you may hear it—when badly executed, it is noisy.

There's a foolproof defense against the bottom dealer—the *Scarne cut*. This is guaranteed to lose the cheat's carefully iced cards in the deck and make him an honest man.

The Scarne Cut

This is a cut I invented during World War II as a defensive weapon for the men in the armed forces. It will protect you against all the moves above except the peek and second-deal combination and a cold deck which is switched in after the cut. Top Army brass have told me that it saved GI Joe millions of dollars.

1. Pull a block of cards from the center of the pack.

Bottom dealing.

2. Place them on top of the pack and square it up.

3. Pull a block of cards from the bottom of the pack, place them on top.

4. Repeat steps 1, 2, and 3 again, several times if you like.

5. Finally, square up the pack and cut it in the regular manner.

The illustrations here picture the Scarne cut in action. Use it and you won't need to worry about nearly all bottom deals, stacked decks, crimps, false shuffles, and false cuts. At the very least, it will give any cheat enough headaches to reduce his cheating down close to the vanishing point. It may frighten him out of the game entirely or even into playing honestly.

Belly Strippers

Decks in which the cards have been trimmed so that they are not quite rectangular are known as *strippers* because the wider cards can be stripped out. The most highly prized form of strippers, those that get the money fast for the semiprofessional cheat, are known as *high and low belly strippers* (also called *humps*). A deck of this type is so gaffed that the cheat can cut to a high or low card at will.

The crooked gambling-supply-house dealer makes such a deck by removing the 28 high cards, eights and above. Using special card shears, he trims about 1/32 inch off both long sides of each high card, then rounds the corners again. The long sides of the low cards, seven and below, are trimmed in a curve so that they are slightly wider than the high cards at the center and slightly narrower at the ends. After the deck is shuffled, the cheat merely has to grasp the cards at the center when he cuts and the bottom card of

the cutoff portion will always be a high card. If he grips the deck near the ends he always cuts to a low card. What could be simpler?

In any game that involves cutting to a high or low card, such as Banker and Broker, belly strippers are lethal. They are also useful in Pinochle or Gin Rummy; the sucker is cheated on his own deal and it is all done with a simple cut. In Gin Rummy the deck is usually trimmed to favor a four- or three-card meld—let's say four kings and three queens. These seven cards are shaved like the high cards above; the remaining 45 cards are shaved like the low cards. When the cheat cuts the shuffled deck for his opponent's deal he simply grips the deck at the end with his left hand and holds it at the center with his right. The two hands pull in opposite directions and the four kings and three queens are stripped neatly out of the deck and slapped on top. Done quickly, this appears to be nothing more than an ordinary cut.

When the chump deals, the cheat gets four of these cards, the victim gets the other three, and, since the cheat knows what they are, the mark's chance of winning is zero. Strippers are also gaffed on the short sides of the deck and are called *end strippers*.

The catalogs list these decks at a low $5 apiece or a dozen for $33.50. "We furnish," they say, "special strippers made to strip any card or combinations of cards you desire. When ordering state what cards you want to strip." At $5.50 per deck they will also make up a deck of combination strippers which will strip one combination from the side and a different one from the end.

To detect strippers simply grasp the deck at the center with your left hand and at the end with your right hand. Then pull in opposite directions. If the deck is stripped, the cards will strip out from various sections. Try the same test on the short ends.

Marked Cards

About one out of every hundred decks of playing cards sold in this country are doctored at some time or other so that some or all of the 52 cards may be read from the back. Gamblers call marked cards *readers,* cheats refer to them as *paper,* and to the average player's bankroll they are poison. They are the most widely used mechanical cheating device and are used by amateurs, semiprofessionals, and top-notch pros because

Belly strippers. High-valued cards (left) are trimmed narrow, low cards (right) are wide at the middle.

they require no manipulative skill, are sure-fire money winners, and are almost never detected by the average easygoing, unsuspicious card player.

My survey results show that not more than two average card players out of a hundred know how or where to look for the markings. Some years ago, I invited six card-playing couples to my home and tried an experiment. I gave them a dozen decks of cards still sealed in their original wrappers. "You have all been playing cards for the past twenty years," I said. "Some of you have lost considerable sums of money at cards on your winter vacations in Florida. These packs—four Bridge, four Poker, and four Pinochle—were made by twelve different manufacturers, and each has a different back design. One deck is marked and can be read from the back. I'll bet that in an hour's examination none of you can find it."

This was a challenge they couldn't resist and they went to work to prove that they could spot marked cards when they saw them. They even examined the card cases before opening the decks, looking for signs of tampering with the government seal. (Card decks no longer have such seals.) After taking the decks from the cases they did the same with the glassine paper in which the decks were wrapped. They found nothing. Then they began examining the backs of the cards. It was an arduous task but they stuck to it for the full hour; none of them wanted to admit that he couldn't spot a marked deck, even having been told the marks were there.

"Okay," one of them said finally. "We give up. Which one is it?" "I have a confession to make," I said then. "I lied when I told you that one deck is marked."

One man, deck in hand, nearly threw it at me. "That," he growled, "is a dirty trick if I ever saw one. We spend an hour looking for something that isn't there. Is this supposed to be funny or something?"

"Well," I said, "it proves something. As a matter of fact, all twelve decks are marked."

Since I had lied once, they wanted proof of this statement. I spent the next half hour reading the backs of cards from all twelve decks before my friends were completely convinced. They all agreed then that they would be smart to stay out of any big-money card games until they had learned how to spot marked cards. Like millions and millions of players who play regularly and who often lose

more than they can afford, all my friends had heard of marked cards but hadn't the slightest notion of what to look for or how to examine a deck properly.

Marked cards are commonplace because they are easy to obtain. Anyone can visit one of the gambling-supply houses, which are located in most big cities, and purchase many varieties of marked cards at $4 to $5 per deck. Marked decks can also be obtained cheaper (about $3 per deck) at many trick and novelty stores whose proprietors sell them "for magic purposes only."

It's even possible that you might buy a marked deck without knowing it from a retailer whom you know and trust because some cheat has slipped him a few bucks. On one occasion, some years ago, during the racing season at Saratoga, it was difficult to buy anything else. A card mob had jimmied its way into a warehouse and substituted a whole case of marked cards for a case which had been shipped in by a legitimate distributor. As soon as the cards were jobbed and retailed the mob went to work. Nearly every game in town had a marked deck in it, and the chumps were cheated with cards they had purchased themselves. The mob, naturally, made a tidy profit on this wholesale switching operation.

The average player has several misconceptions about marked cards. He believes, for instance, that the markings show both rank and suit. This is true only of Bridge and Pinochle decks, where the suit is important. Usually only the numerical value is indicated; but that is all the cheat needs. If he can identify the value of each card as it comes off the top of the deck or always know what the value of his opponents' hole cards are in Stud Poker, the chumps might just as well be playing with their cards face up. That isn't a card game; it's a swindle.

The ordinary player also thinks the cards are marked when they are printed. They aren't; reputable card manufacturers are not on the side of the cheats. But their cards do get marked later. The gambling-supply house or the cheat himself buys honest decks of standard brands. They heat and soften the adhesive and remove the glassine wrapping. Then the cards are marked by hand with special matching inks. Finally, the glassine wrapper is replaced and neatly repasted, the deck reinserted in its case, and then the seal glued on again.

Markings may be *light work* or *strong work,* that is, marked with fine lines or with easier-to-see heavier lines. Light work is used by professional cheats against smart or alert opponents; against the chumps the strong work goes in because it is easier to read from across the table, five or six feet away. Cards are marked near both ends, so that they can be read no matter which end is exposed in the hand. Although individual systems vary, all card markings fall into eight kinds of work:

Edge Work. On cards having white margins on the backs, the line between the margin and back design is thickened slightly at certain points. A mark high up indicates an ace, a little lower down a king, etc.

Line Work. Additional small spots, curlicues, or lines are added to the back design.

Cutout. A chemical preparation bleaches out or a sharp knife scrapes off a minute area of ink from the design, thus adding white areas that weren't there orginally.

Blockout. Parts of the design are blocked out with white ink, or some configuration in the design is exaggerated slightly. This is especially useful on cards whose back designs are claimed to be markproof—those with overall designs and no white border. An example of this is the bee card, whose back design is a simple overall pattern of diamond shapes. Certain diamonds are made smaller or larger by blocking out.

Shading. White areas of the card are delicately shaded with a dilute solution of the marking ink. A good marked-card man can read it from across the table.

Trims. A marking method used on cards whose back designs have white margins. The shark removes the cards he wants to be able to recognize (say the high cards) and trims a thin 1/32-inch slice off one side edge of the card so that the white margin is narrower than on the opposite edge. So that the remaining cards in the deck will be the same size and the margins will remain equal, he then trims 1/64-inch off both side edges. The net effect is that the back design on some cards seems to have been misprinted slightly off center. This can also be done on some cards which have overall back designs. Again the pattern is off center and does not run off the edge of the card in the same way on both sides. The simplest detection method is to place a suspected card on an honest card from another deck. The trimmed card will be smaller.

Pictures. A good rule to paste in your hat is never to play for money with one-way cards, that is, cards whose backs bear pictures or designs that are not symmetrical from top to bottom. During play, a cheat can arrange such a deck so that high cards are right side up, low cards upside down. I know it sounds obvious, but card cheats know from experience that the obvious device is sometimes the one least likely to be suspected. Most players dismiss this idea, if it does occur to them, as too obvious and primitive a device to be used. Therefore the cheat, well aware of this, sometimes uses it; and a quick shuffle, after turning half the pack end for end, will destroy the arrangement and the evidence if anyone shows any sign of suspicion.

How to Detect Marked Cards. There is one detection method that can be used on all marked cards—the Scarne riffle test. Remember the animated cartoon books you used as a kid in which the pictures moved as the pages were riffled? Hold the deck face down, riffle the cards and watch the backs. Do it several times watching different parts of the back. An honest design will stand still, but with marked cards the back pattern will move in the area where the marking has been done.

Marking Cards During Play. When the skilled cheat has no good opportunity to switch a marked deck into play, he uses a type of mark which can be applied during the game. The markings are more easily detected by a smart player and the cheat takes more risk, but it is a mighty common practice in high-stake games where knowing the value of one or two cards is highly important.

Nailing. The cheat digs his thumbnail into the side edge of the card and leaves a small identifying indentation which, like all expert markings can be seen at some distance when you know what to look for. The mark is placed on both side edges so that it can be spotted no matter which way the card is held, and turning the card end for end does not change the mark's location in relation to the end of the card.

In Stud Poker, for example, only high cards are marked, the others being less important. A nail mark near the upper end of the card indicates an ace, a quarter of the way down it signals a king, halfway down it means queen, and so on. In Black Jack the cheat marks the low cards, since they are more important.

Waving. Essentially the same gaff, except

that the cheat places one finger on one side of the card at the edge, two underneath, and applies pressure. This puts a bend or wave in the card's edge, and the location (top, middle, or bottom) supplies the needed information. *Detection:* Square the pack and examine edges. Nail marks and waving will stand out like a well-stacked blonde.

Daubing. A gaff similar to shading, except that the mark can be applied during play. The cheat carries a small flat container of a waxy paste called *daub.* Pressing the tip of a finger on this and then on the card leaves a light smudge, usually a yellowish brown, which can be mistaken for a nicotine stain. Its location on the card back supplies the information.

Pegging. A very old marking method which is sometimes still used. Here the cheater uses the principle of braille and is able to feel rather than see the marks. The sharper who pegs shows up at the game with a Band-aid on his thumb or finger. This hides a sharpened thumbtack whose point penetrates the bandage and with which the cheat pricks the cards, usually only aces and kings in the right places. A prick applied to the face of a card raises a small bump on the card's back. When the cheat deals, the thumb of the hand holding the deck feels the bump and he seconds deals, retaining the high card for himself or a confederate. Your tactile sense is just as sensitive; run a finger over the card backs now and then to satisfy yourself that the cards aren't pegged; when any player has a bandaged finger be sure to do it.

Sanding. Another method of edge marking, also requiring a bandage. There is a slit in the bandage and beneath it a piece of fine sandpaper. The cheat pulls the card's edge along the slit. Card edges become grayed with use and the sandpaper cleans the dirt off, supplying a white edge that stands out clearly.

How to Spot a Marked-Card Cheat. Suspect the player who concentrates too much on the backs of the cards in your hand, the back of the hole card in Stud, the top card of the deck in Black Jack, the top card of the stock in Gin, or the important card in any game. There's nothing wrong with a natural, healthy interest in the cards, but an undue interest in their back designs may be your tip to take a scholarly interest in the deck yourself. As a general rule be leery of the player who wins continuously against all the probabilities. Any player who wins and wins and wins

The Scarne marked-card riffle test. Riffle the cards as above and watch for the "moving pictures" on the backs.

keeps on winning has something more than luck working for him.

After you have convinced yourself that you have been victimized by marked cards—then what? That's hard to answer. It depends on whether or not you outweigh and can outpunch the cheat. If you believe you can handle him you can try asking for your money back—but be careful. Any cheat caught red-handed is dangerous. Move with caution. I have described the most used card-cheating devices, but there are still a good many others. For information on such things as dealing from the middle, slick ace cards, sorts, check cop, shiners, locaters, hold-out machines, etc., see *Scarne on Cards.*

How to Shuffle Cards

At least 50 percent of amateur card fanciers make this mistake after a shuffle: They take the pack up into their hands to square it before offering it for the cut. Why, after taking such fastidious pains to conceal that bottom card, must they expose it thus to a hawk-eyed opponent? Because, make no mistake about it, the opponent will take advantage of that card. He'll know where it is after the cut. He can cut the pack in such a way as to force it into the deal (placing it high in the pack) or keep it out. In either case, a significant percentage swings in his favor. Square the cards flat against the table.

It must be a matter of record that I'm a card manipulator by trade. I know how to shuffle, and I'm going to take the liberty of assuming you'd like to be taught by a professional. Nothing fancy about it; it won't take

The steps in the Scarne shuffle.

much time; and, while I don't guarantee to transform you into a magician, I think that the next five minutes we spend together will insure you against ever being embarrassed by shuffling badly.

First, hold the pack as I show you in the illustration, Figure A. Pull about half the cards off the top of the pack with your right hand, leaving the other half in your left, then putting both halves end to end.

Second, keep your hold on the cards as in Figure B, and riffle the halves together by running your thumbs up the sides of the cards. Hold the blocks firm by setting the fingers on the opposite edge of the cards.

Third, after the cards have riffled together, loosen your hold, and slide them into a single block as in Figure C. Never take the cards off the table, either for the riffle or in the act of squaring the pack.

Fourth, get into the habit of cutting the cards just for insurance at least once during the shuffle by pulling out the bottom half and

slapping it onto the top between riffles—good protection against locaters.

The G.I.'s used to call this the Scarne shuffle. It's foolproof, crookproof, and tidy as a con man's tuxedo . . . and it'll save you money if you never play anything but Solitaire. It just saves wear and tear on a pack of playing cards. But a couple of last warnings against your most insidious enemy: You're not playing for paid admissions; so you don't have to expose yourself to kibitzers. If you can do so without awkwardness, try to sit with your back to a wall so as to cut down your audience. Many a hand is betrayed to an opponent by a spectator's sigh or chuckle or sharp inhalation of breath or such a fool crack as: "What a lucky pick!"

Before each game—whether Stud, Draw, Gin, Pitch, Cribbage, Pinochle, or any other game—do yourself the justice of counting the cards, just to be sure the whole pack's there and nothing is missing by any accident. And don't play when you're disturbed. Most of us are convinced we play a pretty in-and-out game; we tend to be champs one day and chumps the next; and we attribute it all to the run of the cards.

When you play cards, give the game all you've got, or get out; not only is that the one way on earth to win at cards; it's the only way you and the rest of the players can get any fun at all out of what ought to be fun. You can't play a good hand well if your mind's on that redhead down the street or the horses or your boss's ulcers or your wife's operation. When you don't remember the last upcard your opponent picked and you throw him the like-ranked card which gives him Gin, it's time to push back your chair and say "Boys, I just remembered I have a previous engagement."

Do as the professionals do. When they make a few bad plays in a row, they just mutter "That's all for today, gents"; and they mean it. They mean today is, for certain reasons, written off; they mean they'll be back tomorrow, which is another day. By all means, when you're in this kind of losing streak, don't let yourself get panicky. The more reckless you feel, the more desperate is the necessity that you get away from that table at once. An excited player, a player plunging to recoup losses, is a player at his worst. Learn to recognize him. That player has been and will again be—unless you learn how to deal with him—your own worst enemy. And one more thing. The player who resorts to systems is just adding method to his madness—he is systematically ensuring his losses. There is no such animal as an unbeatable system. Only the chump believes in one.

CHAPTER 23

Tile Games

Of the many so-called "tile" games (games played with rectangular shapes of wood or bone) that were popular since the beginning of time, only Dominoes and Mah Jongg are still played today to any degree.

DOMINOES

Dominoes in one form or other is played in most countries of the world. Its biggest popularity is in Latin American countries where gambling with Dominoes is second only to cards. The biggest sum of money this author has ever known to have changed hands in a Domino session was $54,000. It involved two players and took place in Curaçao, Netherlands Antilles.

Dominoes is a fascinating game whose origin has never been definitely established. It has been widely claimed that the game was invented by the Chinese and reached Europe in the fourteenth century, but this claim has little foundation in fact. Dominoes has been traced back only as far as the eighteenth century in Italy, where it had great popularity among the idle courtiers of Venice and Naples. The game as it now is played was, I am sure, an Italian creation.

The Domino Set. The standard Domino set is comprised of 28 pieces called *dominoes,* and sometimes *stones* or *bones.* They are oblong pieces of bone, stone, ivory, wood, plastic, etc. Each domino is divided by a line across its center separating the two ends. Its face looks like the two uppermost faces of a pair of dice, and each half bears the spots from one through six or is blank (without spots). The dominoes rank in value from the double six or 6–6 (12 points, high), to the double blank (0 points, low). All dominoes are valued at their sum total: 6–5 is 11 points, 4–3 is 7 points, etc.

If you examine a standard double-six Domino set, you will see that there are seven "double" dominoes, one for each double number from blanks up to sixes. The six dominoes that possess two identical numbers, plus the one bearing a double blank, are called *doubles* and sometimes *spinners.* The other 21 dominoes (known as *mixed numbers*) all belong to two *suits:* the 4–2 belongs to both the 4 suit and the 2 suit; the 6–3 belongs to the 6 suit and the 3 suit, etc. The spots on all 28 dominoes, added together, total 168.

All Domino games are based on the principle of matching or following suit, which means that each domino played must belong to the same suit and match one of the open ends of the *layout.* The layout consists of the played dominoes which are resting on the table.

Most Domino experts hold as many dominoes as possible in one hand and leave the others remaining on the table. The illustration above shows a hand holding six dominoes and the seventh resting on the table.

Standard Partnership Block Game

Dominoes is played in many different ways, but if one first learns the Standard Partnership Block Game the others can be mastered very quickly. This is the most interesting and the most popular form of Dominoes throughout the world. Also, this four-handed game lends itself to more skillful play than do the two- or three-handed variants.

Requirements

1. Four players, two against two as partners.

2. A standard set of dominoes.

The Object of the Game. A game consists of an undetermined number of hands or deals, and the partnership that first obtains a score of 200 points or more wins the game.

Selecting Partners and Seating Positions. Players team up as partners either by mutual agreement, or by lot. If by mutual agreement, the partners take seats facing each other. If by lot, the players first sit at any of the four places around the table and decide the partnerships as follows:

1. All 28 dominoes are placed face down on the table and mixed in a haphazard manner. The four players all join in the mixing, all at the same time.

2. Starting with the first player (selected by mutual consent), each player in turn (moving clockwise) draws one of the face-down dominoes and turns it face up. The two players who draw the two low-scoring dominoes become partners, as do the two players who draw the two high-scoring dominoes. If dominoes of the same scoring value are drawn, additional draws are made until two low and two high dominoes have been drawn. When the partners have been teamed up, they then take seats facing each other.

3. The player who drew the highest scoring domino becomes the first dealer.

All 28 dominoes are now mixed face down by the dealer. After this mixing, each player, beginning with the player on the dealer's left (and continuing clockwise), selects seven dominoes from the shuffled face-down dominoes. The dealer takes the last seven remaining dominoes. (In Latin-American countries, the play moves counterclockwise, to the dealer's right.)

Each player may (*a*) hold his seven dominoes in his cupped hand so that his opponents cannot see their faces, (*b*) place them on the table standing edgewise, the faces towards himself and hidden from the other players, or (*c*) make use of a domino rack, which holds the dominoes in full view of the player and hidden from the other players.

The Play of the Hand. The starting domino of the first deal (hand) must be the double six. The player holding it starts the play by placing the double six, face up on the center of the table, crosswise (vertically in relation to himself). In fact, whenever any double is played, it must be placed crosswise on the layout.

Then each player, starting with the player on the starter's left (and continuing clockwise) must if possible play (add) a domino that matches one of the two open ends of the layout. *Example:* Since the starter played a double six, the next player must play a 6-spot. For instance, he could play the 6–2 by placing its 6 end against the center line of the 6–6. The third player can then play to either open end of the layout; he can match either the double six or the 2-spot. If he plays, the

6–3, he puts its 6 end against the center line of the 6–6 domino. The fourth player can play either a 3-spot or a 2-spot. If he plays a 2–4, he puts it next to the 2–6 domino, the 2 ends touching. Dominoes are usually placed end to end against an open end. However, when necessary to keep the layout from running off the table, dominoes are placed at right angles to an open end.

If a player, at his turn of play, has no end-matching domino, he says "Pass" and waits for his next turn to play. This procedure continues from player to player until (a) one player goes *domino* by getting rid of all his pieces, or (b) the game ends because no player is able to match an open end of the layout. This is called a *block game* or a *closed hand,* and the team holding the least number of domino points is declared the winner of the hand.

After the first hand ends, each succeeding hand is started by the player who dominoed in the previous hand. In a block game, the player of the winning partnership who held the least number of penalty points is the next starter. In either case, the starting player of each hand (after the first) may start with any one of his seven dominoes, be it a double or a mixed number. Should he start a mixed number, he must place it in a vertical position with the highest number facing himself. Should both sides in a block game have identical total scores, the hand is declared a tie or "no game" and the same starter starts again. Should this occur in the first hand, the holder of the double six opens.

The player sitting to the left of the winner of the previous hand becomes the next dealer. After the dealer has completed the shuffling of the dominoes, each player (begining with the winner and continuing clockwise) selects seven dominoes. The dealer takes the last seven remaining dominoes.

How to Score a Hand. When a player gets rid of his seventh (last) domino, he calls "Domino" and wins the hand. In all partnership games his partner automatically goes out too. The points on the dominoes both opponents still hold are added and score for the winning side. *Example:* Partners A and B and playing against C and D. A and B win by going domino and partnership C and D still hold dominoes whose point values add to 39. This score is credited on the score sheet to partnership A and B.

In case of a block game, when no player is able to match a domino to an open end of the layout, the hand ends and the partnership holding the least number of domino points is declared the winner. This side is credited with the total number of points held by the losing partnership. *Example:* Partners A and B are caught with 40 points in hand, partners C and D with 43 points. A and B win and are credited with the loser's 43 points.

If a block game occurs and each partnership has the same number of penalty points, the hand is declared, as previously stated, "no game" and there is no winner.

SAMPLE SCORING OF A STANDARD DOMINO PARTNERSHIP BLOCK GAME

They	We
36–36	11–11
41–77	26–37
84–161	28–65
53–214	62–127
	14–141
	29–170
Total game scores: 214	170

In the above sample game They, the winners, scored 214 points; We, the losers, scored 170. The partnership score for each hand won is written down in the left-hand column and the cumulative score in the right-hand column. You will note that, in the right-hand column, the score for each winning hand is added to the previous total and brought down as a new total. This makes known to both sides at all times just what the total score is and how far each side is from game.

End of Game. The game ends at the completion of a hand when one or both sides has scored 200 or more points. The partnership with the higher score wins the game and is credited with the difference in points between the two scores.

Additional Domino Rules

1. If a player in a two- or three-hand game draws too few dominoes at the beginning, he must fill his hand from the discard pile as soon as the error is discovered. If he draws too many dominoes he must keep them all.

2. If a domino is played that does not match, the offending player must correct the error on demand before any other player plays; but if the error is not noticed until after another player has played, it stands.

3. If a player in a two- or three-hand game *overdraws* (takes) one or more dominoes

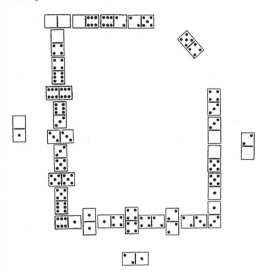

Standard Partnership Dominoes. Holder of 5–4 domino and (his partner) holder of 2–1 domino are credited with three points. Holder of 1–0 domino and (his partner) of 2–0 domino are the losers.

from the discard pile when he has one in his hand that could be played, he must announce the fact that he has overdrawn and he is penalized 10 points. Should he fail to announce an overdraw, the penalty is 20 points.

4. If a domino is exposed in drawing or before the game starts, the dominoes must be shuffled again.

5. A domino is considered played when a player takes his hand off the domino.

6. Each hand must be played out to a finish. A player is not permitted to concede a loss and throw in his dominoes.

7. In a three- or four-handed game, no indication of any sort by word or deed may be given that will impart information to other players.

8. If a player makes a move to play on a particular domino he must make the play if the domino is available for play.

Strategy of Dominoes. To play a good game of Dominoes requires that you give some study to your hand. In many hands you will have but one play, so there is nothing you can do about it. However, you will often have the choice of two or more plays, which will afford you the opportunity to use your skill.

Some study of simple arithmetic as it is related to dominoes will be time well spent. Please keep in mind the fact that dominoes is

a pastime, and you must not make work out of play. However, if you learn a bit of the game's strategy, it will add a lot of zest to your game.

At the beginning of the chapter you were told that when the spots on each of the 28 dominoes are added together, they total 168. Should we divide 28 into 168, we get an average of 6 spots to a domino. It is very important to keep this in mind; one should give some thought to this factor if he wants to become proficient at the game, as the entire strategy of the game is based on this factor.

If you play (*set*) a double four, for instance, have a 4–2 or a 4-something to match its end. If you can't set a double, play a domino that will indicate to your partner that you have a match for one or both ends. If you set a 5–1, be sure you have a 5-spot of some sort and/or a 1-spot of some kind.

Should your partner make a play that indicates to you what number he wishes you to set, try not to *cover* it (change an end number). Try to keep the same number alive, that is, unless you are strong in one particular suit and you believe you can go out in the next few plays. Should your partner set a double, don't play on it unless you are forced to do so, for that is his number and you should steer clear of it. Either of the above plays may not be possible at times. But later on you may have the opportunity to give your partner back his original played end number; or, if the situation develops, you may follow through with your own open-end strategy and try to go out.

If your hand appears weak after several plays, try to get rid of your high-scoring dominoes. If your hand appears strong, forget the value of your dominoes and play to go out; but by all means try to force your opponent to pass. Always try to help your partner go out, always try to compel your opponent on your left to pass, and always watch the dominoes being played to figure out what dominoes your opponents hold. There are times when you must dispose of high-scoring dominoes to cut down the penalty points in your hand; and this requires a study of the domino layout to decide which domino you should play.

As a rule, when your opponent sets a double, your play is to cover the double as soon as you can for the obvious reason that most of the time he has at least another play on it. Remember, there is nothing difficult about playing Dominoes well—just a little patience and some study is all that is needed to become a good Domino player. *Note:* Most of the tips given above apply to the two- and three-hand Domino Draw Games.

Block Dominoes or The Block Game

It is played like the Standard Partnership Block Game, except for the following:

1. While it can be played two-hand, it is best with three or five players, each playing for himself. (When played with four players, the game is frequently called Fours.)

2. With two and three players, take seven dominoes each; with four or five, each takes five.

3. If no one can go domino and there is a block game, whoever has the lowest number of spots wins and adds to his count the number held by his opponents. If there are two players with the same number of spots, there is no count or no game.

4. The number of points required to win the game is 100, but it may be made less by agreement.

Standard Three-Hand Draw Domino Game

The rules of the Standard Partnership Block Game prevail except as follows:

1. Each player plays for himself.

2. Each player draws one domino, and the player drawing the highest becomes the first starter. In turn, thereafter, the starter position moves to the left.

3. Each player draws seven dominoes.

4. The remaining seven dominoes form a discard pile. They are pushed to the left of the starter and their position helps players remember who is to start the next hand.

5. The starter of a hand may play any domino to start.

6. When a player cannot play (match an open end of the layout), he keeps drawing from the discard pile (often called the *boneyard*) until he gets a domino that can be played, or until only one domino remains in the discard pile. If all but the last domino have been drawn from the discard pile, and the player or any player cannot play, the hand ends; the player having the lowest total count in penalty points wins the hand and receives the total penalty count from his opponents.

7. A player who dominoes (goes out) scores the total of the points left in the hands of both opponents. The same scoring holds true as for the winner of a block game.

8. Game may be played for 100, 150, or 200 points. The winner receives the difference in points from both players. *Note:* A fascinating three-hand variation, played without a discard pile, is as follows: At the start of the game the double blank domino is removed from play and each player draws nine dominoes. Thereafter, the play is as above without a discard pile.

Standard Two-Hand Draw Domino Game

The rules for the Standard Partnership Block Game prevail except for the following:

1. The player drawing the highest domino becomes the first starter. Thereafter the turn to start alternates from player to player.

2. Each player draws seven dominoes.

3. The remaining 14 dominoes form a discard pile. They are pushed to the left of the starter.

4. The starter of a hand may play any domino to start the hand.

5. When a player cannot play (match an open end of the layout) he keeps drawing from the discard pile until he gets a domino that can be played, or until only two dominoes remain in the discard pile. If all but two dominoes have been drawn from the discard pile and a player cannot play, he passes until he can play. When neither player can play, the hand ends and the player having the lowest total count in penalty points wins the hand and receives the total penalty count from his opponent.

6. A player who dominoes (goes out) scores the total of the domino points left in the hand of his opponent.

7. Game may be played for 100, 150, or 200 points. The winner receives the difference in points between the two scores.

Additional Domino Rules for Two or Three Players. Irregularities are handled the same as on page 442, except for the following:

If a domino is played that does not match, the offending player must correct the error on demand before any other player plays; but if the error is not noticed until after another player has played, it stands and the offender is penalized 25 points.

Latin American Match Dominoes

This variation is recommended to Domino fans who prefer a faster and easier game than those described. It is the favorite lunch-hour pastime of millions of Domino fans in the Caribbean Islands and in Latin America. The rules for Standard Partnership Block Dominoes apply with the following exceptions:

1. Each hand played is counted as a full game, and the winner records a win on his score sheet simply by drawing a short vertical stroke. Each time he wins a game he adds another stroke. The strokes are kept in groups of five to make counting them easier.

2. Penalty points held by the losing partnership are not counted or scored.

3. The player who holds the double six *always* starts the game.

4. A match ends when a partnership scores 10 strokes (games) and the winners collect the previously agreed-upon stake. But the winning partnership must score 10 strokes *before* the opposition has scored 5 strokes. If a partnership's score shows 6, 7, 8, or 9 strokes and the opposition reaches a score of 5 strokes, both scores are canceled out and the match ends. The next game begins a new match.

All Fives

All Fives also known as The Five Game, Sniff, and Muggins is the most popular form of Dominoes in the United States. (When this game is played as a partnership game, it is usually called Five-Up.) The rules for Standard Partnership, Standard Three-Hand, and Standard Two-Hand apply, except as follows:

1. The object of the game is to score exactly 61 points, which are scored not only by winning hands but also by scoring points during play. The scoring is based on multiples of five.

2. The scoring during play is accomplished as follows:

    (*a*) The total of the numbers on all open ends is noted after each play, and if the total adds up to five it counts 1 point; ten counts 2 points; 15 counts 3 points; and 20 counts 4 points; and so on. To score during play you must play a domino which added to or subtracted from the total of all the open ends will total

five or a multiple of five. If the total is six, add four to make it ten and score 2 points (ten divided by five is two); or take off one and make the total five, scoring 1 point.

    (*b*) The scoring of the hand is figured as follows: For instance, if a player or partnership wins the hand by 36 points, he or they score 7 points only (36 divided by five equals seven—forget the fraction).

3. Each player draws five dominoes be it a two-, three- or four-hand game. The remaining dominoes become the discard pile.

4. The starter of each hand may play any domino he wants. The first double played is open to play on all four sides, no matter when it is added to the layout.

5. The best and most popular way to score a game is by making use of a Cribbage board (see Chapter 11). However, although 61 points is game, the game is not finished until the last hand is completed. If you do not possess a Cribbage board, use the stroke scoring as in Latin American Match Dominoes. The score is kept in groups of five. This makes it easier to count the strokes.

6. If a player fails to announce that he has scored, any other player may call "Fives" and take the score himself.

7. A player cannot claim a score he has overlooked or failed to take after the next player has played.

All Threes

This game is similar to All Fives; but the object of play is to make the sum of the end values on the layout three, or a multiple of three. The game is 60.

Fives and Threes

This game is played like All Fives except for the following:

1. Multiples of both three and five are good for points on the table, and points are awarded on the basis of 1 point for each spot. Thus, ten spots would be good for 10 points as a multiple of five; nine spots would be good for 9 points as a multiple of three; 15 spots would be good for 30 points as a multiple of both five and three.

2. Points in the hand score are also awarded on the basis of 1 point for each spot, regardless of the number.

3. Game is 100 points.

All Sevens

All Sevens is played the same as the Standard Two-Hand Draw Game except for the following:

1. The end number must not be matched. Rather, the end number and the number set must add up to seven. A six is played on a one, a five on a two, etc. Doubles count single. *Example:* A 2–2 calls for a 5-spot, not a 3-spot.

2. There are four "wild" dominoes: 0–0, 6–1, 5–2, and 4–3. The wild dominoes can be played at any time, anywhere.

3. Nothing can be played on a blank but a wild domino.

Seven-Toed Pete

This is played the same as All Fives except for the following:

1. The lead play must be a double or a scoring domino. The scoring dominoes are: 6–4, 5–0, 4–1, 3–2. If the lead player is unable to lead, the lead passes to the left.

2. When a player plays a double or makes a score, he is entitled to play another piece, and he may continue to play as long as he is thus able.

3. When a player plays his last domino, he must score with it if he can. If he cannot score his last piece, the round is closed and the hand score is taken. If he can score, the play is still open, although this player may not draw from the stock (if there is any) until the next time round.

4. The scoring dominoes do not in themselves make a score except in the lead play. End multiples of five score.

Domino Pool

In this variation, the rules of Block Dominoes are followed except for the following:

1. A pool or pot is formed by equal antes, and the winner takes the pot. If (in a block game) two or more tie for lowest hand, they divide the pot equally.

Sebastopol or the Fortress

This is Block Dominoes for four players, each taking seven dominoes. The double six is set by the player holding it. The double six is open four ways and the next four plays, in turn, must be on it—no branches may be extended until all four sides have sprouted. After the central "fortress" is completed, the game proceeds as in Block Dominoes.

Diamond

Each of six to nine players takes three dominoes each. The player having the highest double sets it. The layout has only one open end, and each player must play on the last previously played domino. Anyone playing a double (including the starter) may play a second time if able. The winner is the first player to go out, or the player with the least number of penalty points in his hand after a block game is effected. Players usually ante before the draw and the winner takes the pool.

Bergen Game

The Bergen Game is played the same as the Standard Partnership and the Standard Two- and Three-Hand Draw Games except for the following:

1. If there are two or three players, each takes six dominoes; if there are four players (partnership) each draws five dominoes. The remaining dominoes become the discard pile.

2. The holder of the lowest double starts each new hand. Starting the lowest double is called "double heading" and scores 2 points for the starter. Should no one hold a double, the lowest-ranking mixed-number domino is led. There are no points for such a play.

3. The object of the game is to make as many *double headers* and *triple headers* as possible.

A double header is made by playing a mixed-number domino to an open end of the layout so that the two open ends possess the same numbers. This counts 2 points.

A triple header is made by playing a double to an open end of the layout so that the two open ends possess three same numbers. A triple header counts 3 points.

4. *Game.* When there are three or four players, game is 10 points; when there are two players, game is 15 points.

5. (*a*) A player who calls "Domino" goes out, wins the hand, and scores 2 points.

   (*b*) If there are two dominoes left in the discard pile, and no one can match either open end of the layout, the hand ends in a closed hand and the player holding no doubles wins the hand.

(*c*) If no doubles remain in any hand, the player with the least number of penalty points wins.

(*d*) If there is more than one double in each hand, the player with the least number or doubles wins regardless of the penalty count.

(*e*) If two or more players tie in doubles, the holder of the least number of penalty points wins.

Tiddley-Wink

This is a Block Game except that six to nine players take three dominoes each. The player having the highest double sets it. The layout has only one open end, and each player must play on the last previously played domino. Anyone playing a doublet (including the set) may play a second time, if able. The first player to go out wins; if play comes to a stop before that, the lightest (lowest spot count) hand wins. Players usually ante before the draw and the winner takes the pot.

Forty-Two

Forty-Two, or Domino Rounce as it sometimes is called, is not played like other domino games that revolve around the domino layout. The object of the game is to take in (win) tricks and to capture point-scoring dominoes in tricks. Each trick is worth 1 point, while every domino whose spots total five or ten is a point-scoring domino and is worth the total of its spots. The rules for the Standard Partnership Block Game prevail except as follows:

1. There are four players, two against two, as partners.

2. Each player draws seven dominoes.

3. The players study their dominoes and the bidding follows.

The player holding the 1–0 mixed domino bids first. Each player in turn may make one bid and no more. However, a player may pass instead of bidding. The lowest allowable bid is 30 and each successive bid must be higher than the previous one.

4. *The Play.* The highest bidder leads a domino, which becomes a trump suit. If he leads a mixed number he must specify which

number he intends as trump. There are eight suits: blanks, doubles, and the numbers from one through six. A lead calls for each other player to follow suit if able; the domino of the suit led having the highest value wins the trick, unless a trump domino has been played. The winner of the trick takes in the four dominoes which constitute the trick. When a trump is not led, the highest single mixed number determines its suit. Doubles take any trick of their suit.

5. *Scoring.* Each trick counts 1 point. The 5–5 and 6–4 dominoes are valued at 10 points each; the 5–0, 4–1, and 3–2 dominoes are valued at 5 points each. This adds up to a total of 35 and, with the 7 points in scored tricks, the highest possible total score is 42.

6. After the seven tricks have been played, each side totals the points in trick and scoring dominoes. If the bidding side makes more points than it bid, it scores the bid plus the amount of its total score. If the bidding side fails to make its bid, it scores nothing and its opponents score their total won in points plus the sum total of the bid.

Bingo

This game is based on the card game of Sixty-Six (see page 205).

Requirements

1. Two players.

2. Rank of pieces is the same as in the Partnership Draw Game, except that blanks count as 7-spots. The double blank, which is called *bingo* and counts for 14 spots, is the highest domino, and takes the double of trumps. When blanks are trump, bingo counts 28.

The Play. Play is started by each player drawing for the lead; he who draws the highest piece is the leader. Then each player draws his seven dominoes, after which the leader turns up another piece, the highest spot on which is trump. This trump domino is left face up. The leader leads first; but, after that, the winner of a trick leads to the next trick. In addition, the winner of a trick draws one domino from the discard pile, and the opponent then draws a piece, so that until the discard pile is exhausted both hands are maintained at seven dominoes.

A trick containing a trump is won by the higher trump. A trick containing no trump is won by the piece having the higher spot count, or by the leader if both are of the same count. Until the discard pile is exhausted, the second player to a trick may play any piece— he need not follow suit. But, when the discard pile is exhausted (the trump domino going to the player who did not win the last trick of the early play), the rules of final play come into effect and dictate that each lead then requires the opponent to follow suit if able. He must follow to a trump with a trump, or follow to a nontrump in the order of precedence: the higher suit, the lower suit, a trump. Only if unable to follow to either suit and unable to trump, may he discard.

Closing. At any time during the early play, a player who believes he can reach 70 points and who has gained the lead can *close*. Closure is signified by turning the trump domino down. Thereafter, no more pieces are drawn from the discard pile, and the rules of final play come into force.

Scoring. The game consists of 7 points, which are made in the following manner: The player who first counts 70 scores 1 point toward game; if he makes 70 before his opponent has counted 30, he scores 2 points; if he makes 70 before his adversary has won a trick, he scores 3 points. If bingo captures the double of trumps, it scores at once 1 point for the winner of the trick.

The pieces count as follows to the winner of the trick containing them: The double of trumps always counts 28; the other doubles and all the other trumps count according to their spots; the 6–4 and 3-blank are always good for ten each, whether trumps or not; the other pieces have no value.

If at any time a player has two doubles in his hand, he can do the following: When it is his turn to lead, play one double, show the other, and announce 20 points, which are added to his count as soon as he has won a trick. If he holds three doubles, he counts 40; for four doubles, 50; for five doubles, 60; for six doubles, 70 points. If bingo is among the doubles held, it adds 10 more points to the count.

Cyprus

While all the Domino games thus described have been played with a double-six Domino set, some of them can be adapted to using a double-nine set (55 pieces). One of the most popular double-nine games is Cyprus, which is played like Sebastopol (see page 446), except for the following:

1. From four to ten play, with number of

pieces drawn depending on the number of players as follows:

Players	Pieces Drawn
4	13
5	11
6	9
7	7
8 or 9	6
10	5

2. The holder of the double nine plays first. If no one has the double nine, the dominoes are reshuffled and redrawn. This continues until someone receives the double nine.

3. In clockwise rotation, the players may play nines to form a star or fortress. But only after the central fortress has been completed as in the diagram, can the ends of the nines already played be matched. The game then proceeds as in the ordinary Block Game.

The Matador Game

This double-nine Domino set game is played like All Sevens except that the sum of the two adjacent ends (the end of the piece played and the end of the piece in the layout) must add up to ten unless one of the special *matadors* (wild dominoes) is used. A one is added to a nine, a two to an eight, a three to a seven, etc. Doublets are placed endwise and count as a single (i.e., 4–4 calls for a 6-spot, not a 1-spot). Nothing can be played on a blank but a matador, of which there are six: 0–0, 5–5, 6–4, 7–3, 8–2, 9–1. Matadors are wild and can be played at any time, anywhere. Play progresses as follows:

1. If there are three to six players, each draws seven dominoes. If there are more, then each player draws five.

2. The leader plays a double, if he has one; if not, he plays his highest domino. *Example:* If a double eight is led, it must be joined at either side with a two by the next player. If he does not have a two, he must play a matador or draw from the discard pile until he obtains a two. If he played a 2–5, the end spots of the layout would then be eight or five. The next player must play a two to the eight, or a five to the five. Play proceeds in a clockwise direction.

3. When a player cannot make the required ten, and does not wish to play a matador or does not have one, he must draw until he can play or until only two dominoes are left in the pool; then, if he has failed to

draw a playable domino, he must play a matador if he has one.

4. When one player has drawn all but the last two dominoes from the discard pile, and can neither make a ten, nor play a matador, he must pass. If no other player can play, the game is blocked and the player holding the lowest number of spots scores the spots held in his opponents' hands.

5. A player who goes domino scores all the spots held in his opponents' hands.

6. A game is 200 points.

MAH-JONGG

This game is a Chinese development of Dominoes, with similarities to Rummy. In China, it is played in various ways in different provinces. An American businessman and traveler in China, Joseph P. Babcock, made a study of the game, devised a set of rules for Occidental play, and added Arabic numerals to the tiles. In 1920 he began to import sets under the trademark of Mah-Jongg. It became a major craze until 1926, then faded, but still has many enthusiasts.

Equipment. The Mah-Jongg set contains 144 tiles comprised of 108 *suit* tiles, 28 *honors*, and 8 *flowers* (also called *seasons*).

Suits. The three suits are *bamboo* (also called *bams* or *sticks*), *circles* (also called *dots*), and *characters* (also called *cracks* or *actors*). Each suit contains four each of the tiles numbered 1 through 9.

Honors. There are four duplicates each of

red dragon, green dragon, white dragon, East wind, West wind, North wind, and South wind.

Flowers. These are all individually marked, but are assigned in pairs to the four winds.

Additional equipment includes two dice, a number of tokens or colored sticks used for scorekeeping, and four racks—one for each player, to hold his tiles upright.

Players and Positions. The game is played by four, each playing for himself.

One player is chosen by throwing the dice to be East, and he has the choice of seats. The others sit where they please and are designated as West, North, and South depending on the position of East. The East player wins or loses double. If he wins he keeps his position. If he loses, the player at his left becomes East, and all the others move around to the left.

Mah-Jongg tiles (top to bottom): Bamboos (sticks), circles (dots), characters (cracks on actors), flowers (seasons), winds and dragons (bottom line). The modern game also has eight big jokers.

Winds. East wind prevails during the first deal, South wind in the second, West wind in the third, North wind in the fourth. A player who obtains a set of tiles of the prevailing wind scores more for it than for another wind. After a round of winds—four deals—the players cast again for positions at the table.

The Wall. All the players assist in shuffling the tiles which are face down on the table. Each player then draws 36 tiles at random and builds a wall before himself, two tiles high and eighteen long, all tiles face down. Each pile of two tiles is a *stack*. Then the four walls are pushed together with the aid of the racks to form a hollow square. Each player sets a rack before himself, East's being of a different color than the others.

Breaking the Wall. East casts the two dice, adds the two numbers, and counts up to this total, beginning with the East wall as 1 and going clockwise. The wall on which the count ends is the first wall to be broken. The player at that position throws the dice again and adds his total to the previous total to determine which stack of the wall shall be taken first.

The player begins at the right end of his wall and counts to the left the number of stacks indicated. If the total is more than 18, he counts around the corner on to the wall at his left. The indicated stack is lifted out and both tiles are placed face down on the wall, the undermost next to the break, the upper tile at its right. These are called *loose* tiles and, whenever both have been taken, the next stack on the right of the break is set on the wall as loose tiles.

Drawing the Hands. Beginning with East, each player in turn takes two adjacent stacks (four tiles) from the left side of the break until he has 12 tiles. Each in turn then takes one more tile (a total of 13); finally, East takes one extra tile (a total of 14).

Object of Play. To obtain sets of tiles which are of three kinds:

Chow. A set of three tiles in numerical order (a sequence) of the same suit.

Pung. A set of three identical tiles (same suit and rank), or three dragons of the same color, or three winds of the same direction.

Kong. A pung plus the fourth like tile. This fourth tile is not counted among the 14 which make up a complete hand (four sets or three and a pair). A player who finds a kong in his original hand may *ground* it (place it face up

on the table), and draw a loose tile to fill his hand. The two end tiles then are turned face down to show that it counts as a *concealed* set (obtained entirely by drawing from the wall).

Flowers are not counted as part of the original hand of 13 tiles. Any flowers drawn either in the original hand or later must be grounded and replaced by drawing loose tiles. The loose tiles are drawn in rotation beginning with East.

The Play. East plays first, by discarding one tile and reducing his hand to 13. From then on, all hands are maintained at 13 tiles, counting unmatched tiles, chows, and pungs; but flowers and the fourth tiles of kongs are not counted.

The turn to play moves counterclockwise, except when interrupted by the claim of a discard out of turn (see below). In turn, each player either draws one tile from the wall (to the left of the break), or takes the last discard. He ends his turn by discarding one tile. Discarded tiles are placed face up within the enclosure formed by the walls. Grounded sets are put between the wall and owner's rack.

Discards. A discard may be used if it can be grounded at once as part of a set, but it must be claimed before the next player draws.

Any player who can use the discard can claim it whether or not it is his turn to play. If two or mor players claim the same discard, precedence is according to the purpose for which it is wanted: (*a*) to complete a hand, (*b*) to make pung or kong, (*c*) to make chow.

If two hands claim for the same purpose, the one whose turn would come first has precedence.

The player who obtains the discard grounds it with the set in which it is used, discards, and the turn then passes to his right neighbor. Intervening hands, between discarder and claimer, lose their turns.

Grounding Sets. After play starts, a concealed kong can be grounded only after the player has drawn from either the wall or the table, and before he discards. A kong in the hand, not grounded before some player ends the deal by completing a hand, counts only as a concealed pung.

A player who holds a concealed pung and draws a fourth tile from the table may ground only three tiles, and must hold the fourth in his hand. But if it is still in his hand when the deal ends, the set counts only as a pung.

A player who holds or draws from the wall a fourth tile for his grounded pung may add it to the set to make a kong, and then draw a loose tile. But he cannot claim a discard and add it to an already grounded pung.

Woo or Mah-Jongg. When he completes his hand, four sets and a pair, a player may *woo* or *mah-jongg* by showing his whole hand. He wins the deal, ending play.

The tile needed to complete the hand may be obtained by drawing from the wall, by claiming a discard, or by *robbing a king*. This consists in claiming the fourth tile that another player has just added to a grounded pung; it can only be done to woo.

The last 14 tiles may not be drawn from the wall. If all the rest are drawn, play continues only as long as successive discards are used. If play ends and no player has wooed, the deal is a draw, without score, and East keeps his position for the next deal.

Scoring. The value of the winning hand is computed first, and each other player pays this amount to the winner. If East is winner, he collects double.

The values of the other three hands are then computed, and each player settles with each other according to the difference of their scores. If East is one of the three, he pays or collects double. The basic value of each hand is found by adding th points for sets, and this total is doubled one or more times for special sets.

BASIC VALUES FOR ALL HANDS

Sets	From Table	Concealed
Pung of simples (suit ranks 2 through 8)	2	4
Pung of terminals (suit ranks 1 and 9)	2	4
Pung of honors (winds or dragons)	4	8
Kong of simples	8	16
Kong of terminals	16	32
Kong of honors	16	32
Pair of dragons	2	2
Pair of prevailing wind	2	2
Pair of player's own wind	2	2
Pair of player's own wind (when prevailing)	4	4
Each flower	4	

DOUBLES FOR ALL HANDS

Multiply the basic value by the factor given.

	Factor
Each pung or kong of dragons	2
Pung or kong of prevailing wind	2

	Factor
Pung or kong of player's own wind	2
Player's own flower	2
All four flowers (includes the double for the player's own flower)	16

BONUSES FOR WOO HAND ONLY

	Add to Basic Value
For going woo	20
For drawing from the wall	2
For filling the only place to complete the hand	2

	Factor
Winning with last tile of the wall or a subsequent discard	2
Winning with a loose tile drawn after a kong	2
No chows	2
All chows and a worthless pair	2
All one suit, with honors	2
All terminals, with honors	2
All one suit, without honors	8
All terminals, without honors	Limit
All honors, without suits	Limit

Limit Hands. Players should agree in advance on the *limit* any player may collect or be required to pay. In the American game this is usually 500 (for East, 1,000).

Additional Rules

Imperfect Set. If the set is found to be incomplete, the current deal is void unless a player has wooed, but scores of previous deals stand.

Exposed Tile. If a tile is exposed in building the wall the tiles must be reshuffled. If a tile is exposed when drawing another, it must be shuffled with six adjacent stacks and that section of the wall rebuilt.

Incorrect Set. If a player grounds tiles that do not form a correct set, he may retract or correct the set before the next hand has discarded; otherwise, he must play with a *foul* hand (too few tiles).

Foul Hands. A hand that is foul or incorrect may not woo. A *long* hand (too many tiles) scores as zero. A short or foul hand may score its basic value, but no doubles (factors) may be applied.

Incorrect Claim. If a player takes or claims a discard that he cannot use, he may correct the error without penalty before the next hand has drawn. The discard is open to claim by the other players; otherwise, it is treated as an exposed tile and is reshuffled.

False Woo. If a call of woo or mah-jongg is found to be incorrect because the hand is incomplete (short or long), the play ends. If the offender is East, he must pay the limit to each other player; if another player offends, he must pay the limit to East and half the limit to the other two. There is no settlement between the other three players. East keeps his position if he was not the offender; but he loses it if he was the offender and the positions rotate.

Mah-Jongg Variations

Of many different ways of playing and scoring in Mah-Jongg, the most widely circulated method is that of the National Mah-Jongg League, Inc., 250 West 57th Street, New York, N.Y. 10019. While that League's official standard hands and rules change slightly each year, and such changes are sent to their members (membership is $1 a year), the principal differences from the procedure described in the foregoing pages are as follows:

In the so-called modern game, flowers are wild and there are eight *big jokers,* which are also wild. Any hand made without a big joker is paid double. Big jokers may be discarded at any time during the game and called the same as the previous discard. Big jokers may be used to replace any tiles in any hand. A big joker may be replaced in any exposure with a like tile or tiles by any player, whether picked from the wall or in a player's hand, when it is the player's turn. If a player declares mah-jongg or woo, and all jokers in exposures have been replaced and no jokers are in concealed part of hand, the player is paid double. This is called a *no-joker* hand.

After the hands have been drawn, but before play begins, there are one or two *Charlestons,* or passes of tiles. That is, each player passes three tiles to his right-hand neighbor; then (having received and seen the tiles passed to him), he passes three to the player opposite him; then, in the same manner, he passes three to his left-hand neighbor. By agreement of all players, there may then be a second Charleston with the first pass to the left, the second to the player opposite, and the third to the right. Sometimes a *blind pass* is permitted on the last pass of a second Charleston; that is, a player may pass along the three tiles passed to him, without looking at them. Flowers may be passed during any pass or Charleston, but big jokers may never be passed (except in the blind pass).

East does not receive or pay double. When a player picks his own Mah-Jongg tile, all players pay double the value of the hand. When a player woos on a discarded tile, the person who discarded the tile pays the winner double the value of the hand. All other players pay the single value.

No more than four may play in a game; but a fifth player, after looking at all four hands, and after the Charleston but before the first play, may write on a slip of paper the name of the player he bets on. He then pays in full if another player wins, but collects from the three losers in equal shares if his chosen player wins. In the same manner six may participate, there being two "bettors."

The game ends only when a player woos or mah-jonggs. The winning hand has a predetermined value, according to the schedule adopted for the game, and is not increased by doubles. The entire wall may be drawn and, if no one goes out, the game is void.

A hand may be played concealed or exposed. Any hand may be played concealed; but then a discard may be claimed only to woo. A hand becomes exposed when a discard is claimed to complete a kong, quint, or sextette; whereupon, the set must be exposed on top of the player's rack. (A discard may be claimed only to complete these sets or to go out.) Concealed and exposed hands score the same.

A typical list of hands and values follows:

Hand	*Points*
Kongs of North and South winds and an odd-numbered sextette; or kongs of East and West winds and an even-numbered sextette	10
Quints (sets of five like tiles) of North and South winds, or quints of East and West winds, and a kong of dragons	15
Quints of ones and fives, a kong of threes; or quints of fives and nines, a kong of sevens; all in the same suit	15
Two kongs of dragons plus two pungs of the same numeral but in different suits	15

Hand	*Points*
Quints of threes and nines, and a kong of sixes, or quints of fives and sevens, and a kong of sixes; or quints of sixes and eights, and a kong of sevens; or kongs of sevens and nines, and a kong of eights; all in different suits	10
Quints of ones and twos with a kong of threes, etc. (the kong representing the sum of the numerals of the quints, $1 + 2 = 3$, so that the sets may be twos, threes, and fives, etc.), all in different suits	10
Sextettes (sets of six like tiles) of North and South winds, plus one East and one West wind	25
Quints of the terminals, or of twos and eights, or of the same numeral, in different suits, plus a kong of dragons	25
Kongs of red, white, and green dragons, with a pair of North or South winds; or two kongs of dragons and a sextette of threes, sixes, or nines	25
Sextettes of the same number in different suits, plus two tiles of a third suit representing the square of this number (for example, two sextettes of sixes, a three, and a six, for 36)	25
Sextettes of the terminals, or of twos and eights, in different suits, and a pair of dragons	25
Sextettes of consecutive numbers plus two tiles of the suit representing the sum of these numbers (for example, sevens, eights, a one, and a five, or 15), in three different suits	25
Quints of red and green dragons and a kong of whites	25

If a player claims to be out when not having a valid combination, his hand becomes dead; the others continue without him, and he pays the winner at the end.

CHAPTER 24

Dice and Their Many Games

Dice have been fascinating people and deciding fates for over 2,000 years. Even the language of dice echoes history. When Caesar made the critical decision to take his victorious army across the Rubicon against the edict of Rome, he took his retort from the lexicon of the dice player: "Tacta alea est." *The die is cast.*

Primitive tribes all over the globe—the American Indian, the Aztec, and Maya, the South Sea Islander, the Eskimo, the African—have gambled with dice of many curious shapes and markings. Dice have been made from plum and peach stones; seeds; buffalo, caribou and moose bone; deer horn; pebbles; pottery; walnut shells; beaver and woodchuck teeth. In Greek and Roman times, most dice were made of bone and ivory; but others were of bronze, agate, rock crystal, onyx, jet, alabaster, marble, amber, and porcelain.

Almost all modern dice are made of cellulose or some other plastic material. The standard die is marked with a number of small dots (called *spots*) from one to six. The spots are arranged in conventional patterns and placed in conventional relative locations. Thus, the spots on the opposite sides must always total seven: one opposite six, two opposite five, and three opposite four. When the visible vertical sides are two and three and the top side is one, then six must be the bottom number while five and four must be on the opposite vertical sides. The combinations of the six spots (sides) plus the number of

dice in play determine the mathematical probabilities.

In most games played with dice, the dice are thrown (rolled, flipped, shot, tossed, or cast) from the hand or from a receptacle called a *dice cup* in such a way that they will turn at random. The spots that face upward when the dice come to rest are the deciding spots. The combination of the topmost surfaces of the dice decides, according to the rules of the game being played, whether the thrower (called the *shooter*) wins, loses, continues to throw, or loses possession of the dice.

There are two kinds of dice. *Perfect dice* or *casino dice,* made by hand and true to a tolerance of 1/5,000 of an inch, are used to play casino craps. Round-cornered imperfect dice, called "drugstore" or "candystore" dice, are fabricated automatically and are generally used as implements to play social and board games.

Modern casino dice are sawed from extruded rods of cellulose. The spots are drilled into the faces of the die approximately 17/1,000 of an inch. Then all recessions are filled with a paint the same weight as the cellulose that has been drilled out. The dice are then buffed and polished and, since no recessions remain, are known as *flush-spot dice.* Most casinos use red flush-spot dice which are transparent and come in sets of five. The standard size used in Nevada, the Caribbean, and most casinos the world over, is .750 of an inch. The dice edges are generally either square and known as *razor edge* or slightly turned and known as *feather edge*. Casino dice usually carry their own special monogram and coded serial number as a means of thwarting dice cheats. Perfect dice used in various other dice games range from a .250-inch celluloid or bone "peewee" die to an extra large size .770-inch. Perfect concave-spot dice, although still in use, are rarely seen in topnotch casinos. Drugstore dice are generally used for social and board games and are all round cornered. Pyramidal dice, pentahedral dice, and octahedral dice, with all sorts of face designs, are and have been used.

Dice in various forms are the oldest gambling instruments known to man, and countless games are and have been played with them. Craps, the most popular gambling house game, is played with two dice. In more social play there are Poker Dice and Scarney Dice, played with five dice; there are various counter and bar games, such as Twenty-Six, played with ten dice. In Backgammon and hundreds of "board games" two or more dice are thrown to determine the moves.

CRAPS

History's biggest and fastest-action gambling game, Craps is undoubtedly the most widely played dice game in the United States today. More money is won and lost at Craps every day than at any other form of casino gambling. It is of American Negro origin, as shown by the colorful slang still used in the game. (Dice are still often called "African Dominoes.") Around New Orleans, some time after 1800, the Negro tried his hand at the old English game of Hazard, which the English sometimes called Craps, or Crabs. But the intricacy of the rules led him to simplify the playing procedure so greatly that he ended up inventing the present game of Private Craps. This was the situation in 1907 when John H. Winn, a New York City dice maker by trade, became the first Craps bookmaker or banker in history. Winn invented the game of Open Craps—he did this by charging both right and wrong bettors a quarter for a $5 bet and 50 cents for a $10 bet. This innovation gave Winn plenty of action and other operators, noticing it, began to follow suit. Shortly afterward, Winn made Bank Craps a two-way action game by adding the Don't Pass line and charging 5 percent of the amount of any bet made against the house. Later, other gamblers eliminated the direct charge, substituted shorter house odds, and added more bets to the layout.

There are basically four ways to play Craps (a Craps game is usually referred to as "crap-shooting" or "shooting crap"), which are as follows:

Private Craps is a friendly social game that does not use a casino, Craps table, or banker. The only requisites for Private Craps are two or more persons with cash in their pockets and a pair of dice. It can be played on a street corner, in a back alley, private club, army barracks, living room—anywhere the players have room in which to roll the dice.

Bank Craps is the version of the game found in all Nevada Casinos and in most legalized establishments throughout the world. Bank Craps is played on a specially constructed dice table of size and form similar to a billiard table. (For a description, see The Casino Game: Bank Craps, page 458.) Three dealers and two house employees known as *boxmen* stand at the side of the table. One of the dealers, known as a *stickman,* handles the dice and stands opposite the boxmen. Although there are other different-shaped layouts, the actual difference is small. Players are not permitted to gamble against each other; all bets are made against the house. Chips or checks are used instead of cash when wagers are placed on the layout. The layout is fixed so that the house has a mathematical advantage on every bet.

Money Craps, Open Craps, or Fading Craps is a game played with cash in which players are permitted to bet on point numbers among themselves. A houseman, called a banker or bookie, is present to accept any bet within the house limit on all other bets and to point numbers that a player is unable to place with another player. For this privilege, the player must pay the banker a charge, usually 5 percent of the amount wagered.

New York Craps is a version of Bank Craps found in gambling houses in the Eastern part of the United States, the Bahamas, and in England. The game is played on a specially constructed dice table that is similar to a Las Vegas or Bank Craps table.

However, the table and layout are somewhat different and the house employees (dealers) are posted at each end of the table. A stickman stands at the center of the table and two boxmen sit opposite the stickman. The table is known as a *double-end dealer* and the dealers take a charge of 5 percent of the amount wagered on the point numbers (4, 5, 6, 8, 9, 10).

Scarne's Official Rules for Private Craps

Requirements

1. Two dice. Each is numbered from one to six in such a way that the spots on opposite sides add to seven.

2. A wall or backboard against which the dice are thrown.

Players

1. Any number may play.

2. The player throwing the dice is the shooter. Any player, by consent of the others, may start the game by becoming the shooter.

3. A new player may enter the game at any time, provided there is an opening in the circle. If no player objects at the time he takes his position, he becomes the shooter at his proper turn (even though he may take a position directly at the left of the shooter).

4. The dice pass around the circle of players to the left—clockwise.

5. Players may leave the game at any time (without regard to their wins or losses).

The Play

1. The dice are thrown and the two numbers that face upward when the dice come to rest, added together, are the deciding numbers.

2. If on the first roll, called the *come-out*, the shooter throws a *natural* (7 or 11), it is a winning decision called a *pass*. If it is a *craps* (2, 3, or 12) it is a losing decision called a *missout*. If 4, 5, 6, 8, 9, or 10, that number becomes the shooter's *point* and he continues throwing until he:

   (*a*) throws his point again, which effects a winning decision or pass; or

   (*b*) throws a seven which effects a losing decision or missout.

3. The shooter's first roll after a decision has been effected is a come-out.

4. When the shooter misses out on the point, the dice pass to the next player on his left and it becomes this player's turn to shoot.

5. The shooter, if he wishes, may pass the dice to the next player on the completion of any decision, without waiting to miss out on the point.

6. Any player may, if he likes, refuse to shoot his turn, and may pass to the next player.

7. When more than one pair of dice are employed, players may call for a *box-up* or change of dice at any time, the change taking place immediately after the next decision.

The Throw or Roll

1. The shooter shakes the dice in his closed hand and must try to throw them so that both dice hit and rebound from the backboard.

2. If only one die hits the board, the roll counts but the players may reprimand the shooter.

3. If this occurs a second time, the other players may designate someone else to complete the shooter's turn at throwing. If they wish, they may also bar him from shooting for the duration of the game.

4. If neither die hits the board, or if (when playing on a table or elevated surface) one or both dice fall off the playing surface, the roll is *no-dice*. It does not count and the dice must be thrown again.

5. If the dice hit any object or person after hitting the board, the roll counts. It is not no-dice.

6. If a die comes to rest cocked at an angle on a coin or any irregularity on the playing surface, and if there is a difference of opinion as to which number faces upward, a neutral player or any player or bystander designated by common consent shall stand at the shooter's position and decide which number counts. He does this by stating which surface of the die appears to be the top surface from that position.

7. If, after hitting the backboard, a die rolls out of sight under a bill or any other object on the playing surface, either a neutral player, a player designated by common consent, or a bystander shall take extreme care in trying to ascertain the top number.

8. The practice of knocking the dice with the hand or kicking the dice aside with a foot on the roll and then calling "Gate!" or "No dice!" (known as *gating*) is, of course, not permitted.

Betting

1. *Right Bet*. This is a wager that the dice will pass (win either by making a natural on the come-out or by throwing a point on the come-out and then repeating it before throw-

ing a seven). Players making right bets are *right bettors*.

2. *Wrong Bet*. This is a wager that the dice *don't pass*. Players making wrong bets are *wrong bettors*.

3. All bets must be made before the dice are thrown and cannot be made while they are rolling.

4. Any off-number bet (see paragraph 15) may be called off by the bettors concerned before a decision is affected.

5. *Center Bet*. Before the come-out, the shooter may (but is not required to) bet that he will pass. Players who cover this wager by betting an equal amount against the shooter, *fade* the shooter and are known as *faders*. These wagers, placed in the center of the playing surface, are center bets.

6. If only a part of the shooter's center bet is covered, the shooter may shoot for that amount or he may call the bet off by saying "No bet."

7. *Side Bet*. Any bet that is not a center bet is placed at one side of the playing surface and is known as a side bet. The shooter may make any side bet including the flat bet.

8. *Flat Bet*. This is a side bet, made before the come-out, that the dice pass or don't pass. It is the same as the center bet except that the shooter is not being faded and the bet is placed at the side.

9. *Point Bets*. After the shooter has thrown a point on the come-out, a bet made by a right bettor that the shooter makes his point is a *right point bet*. A bet by a wrong bettor that the shooter misses his point is a *wrong point bet*. A right bettor *takes the odds* on that point; the wrong bettor *lays the odds* on that point.

10. *Come Bet*. This is a bet that the dice will pass (win) the next roll, which is considered to be a come-out roll. *Example:* Suppose the shooter's point is 4 and he bets that he comes. If he throws a 7, he loses any bet he has made on the 4; but he wins the come bet because, on this bet, the roll is considered to be a come-out, and the 7 is a natural and wins. If he throws an 11, the point is still undecided but he wins the come bet. If he throws a 4, he wins the original point bet, but must continue throwing and make another 4 before throwing a 7 in order to win the come bet. If then he throws any other number (such as 6), it counts as a second point and he continues throwing in an attempt to make

either or both points before throwing a 7.

11. *Don't Come Bet*. This is a bet that the dice don't pass (lose) the next roll, which is considered to be a come-out roll.

12. *The Hard-Way Bet* or *Gag Bet*. This is a bet that a specified even number (which may be either the shooter's point or an off number) will or will not be thrown the *hard way*. The hard way means with two like numbers, such as making a 4 with a double two, a 6 with a double three, an 8 with a double four, or a 10 with a double five. If the number is thrown any other way, or a 7 is thrown, the bettor loses the hard-way bet.

13. *One-Roll Bet* or *Come-Out Bet*. This is a bet that the shooter does or does not throw (*a*) a certain number in any way, (*b*) a certain number in a certain way, or (*c*) any one of a group of numbers on the next roll. *Examples:* (*a*) a bet that the shooter will or won't throw a 7 with any of the specific-way combinations: 1–6, 2–5, 3–4; (*b*) a bet that the shooter will or won't throw a 7 with one specific combination, such as 3–4; (*c*) a bet that the shooter will or won't throw any of the numbers in a group such as 2, 3, and 12 (craps), the group 4 and 10, the group 11 and 3, etc.

14. *One-Number Bet*. This is a bet that a certain number or group of numbers will or will not be thrown before another number.

15. *Off-Number Bet*. This is a bet, made at odds, that the shooter will or will not throw a specified number other than his point (any of the numbers 4, 5, 6, 8, 9, or 10) before throwing 7.

16. *Proposition Bet*. This term applies in Private Craps to any bet not a Point or Off-Number Bet or a Flat Bet.

17. *Two-Number Bet*. This is a bet that one of a certain two (sometimes more) numbers will or will not be thrown before a 7.

18. *Two-Roll Bet* or *Three-Roll Bet*. This is a bet that a certain number or group of numbers will or will not be thrown in a specified number of rolls.

Strategy at Private Craps. There is little to skillful play in Private Craps other than knowing the correct odds concerned in the various bets, and not accepting sucker bets (bets that offer the player unfavorable odds). However, there is one unfavorable bet that even the best-informed players make and that is a right center bet, which has a 1.414 percent disadvantage, or odds of 251 to 244, against the shooter. Many Craps players, knowingly or unknowingly, seem to enjoy suffering this disadvantage. But if you continue to buck that 1.414 percent, you are bound to lose.

The following are several odds tables relating to Private Craps that, if memorized, will surely help to improve your Craps shooting knowledge.

ODDS AGAINST PASSING ON THE POINTS

The Points	Odds
4 can be made in three ways; 7 in six ways	2 to 1
5 can be made in four ways; 7 in six ways	3 to 2
6 can be made in five ways; 7 in six ways	6 to 5
8 can be made in five ways; 7 in six ways	6 to 5
9 can be made in four ways; 7 in six ways	3 to 2
10 can be made in three ways; 7 in six ways	2 to 1

ODDS AGAINST PASSING THE HARD WAY

The Points	Odds
4 can be made with 2–2 in one way	8 to 1
10 can be made with 5–5 in one way	8 to 1
6 can be made with 3–3 in one way	10 to 1
8 can be made with 4–4 in one way	10 to 1

ODDS ON ONE ROLL OR COME-OUT BETS

Numbers	Odds	Numbers	Odds
Any pair	35 to 1	6	6⅕ to 1
11	17 to 1	8	6⅕ to 1
Any crap	8 to 1	Any 7	5 to 1
5	8 to 1	1–2 (3)	17 to 1
9	8 to 1	3–4 (7)	17 to 1
4	11 to 1	5–2 (7)	17 to 1
10	11 to 1	6–1 (7)	17 to 1

The Casino Game: Bank Craps

Bank Craps not only has replaced Faro as the great American banking game in this country, but it also has outdistanced all the other casino games in popularity. One reason is that it offers the players a greater chance of participation. In Roulette and Chuck-A-Luck, the croupier spins the wheel or the cage; in Chemin-de-Fer and Blackjack, the dealer turns up the cards. But in Craps the player has the opportunity of trying to change his luck by throwing the dice himself. The thrill he gets when he matches his luck against that of the others is of a more personal kind than the one he gets when he simply waits and hopes that the ball will drop into his number or that the card he wants will turn up.

The basis of Bank Craps, from the shooter's point of view, is the same as the private game. That is, the shooter makes a bet that he'll pass or win. The shooter wins immediately if on the come-out he rolls a 7 or 11; he loses immediately if on the come-out he rolls a 2, 3, or 12. If on the come-out he doesn't roll a natural or a crap, and instead rolls either 4, 5, 6, 8, 9, or 10—whichever of these he rolls now becomes his "point" and he continues rolling until he either wins by rolling his point once again, or loses by rolling a 7. Remember that the shooter retains the dice as long as he continues to roll naturals and craps and *make points*. When he rolls a 7 while trying for a point, he loses the dice, and the shooter to his left becomes the next shooter. This person may decline to shoot the dice; then the person to his left becomes the next shooter, and so on. But, before you can consider yourself a Bank Craps player, you must know the different wagers and payoff odds that may be made at the dice table. And so let's take a look at the dice table itself.

The table is about the size of a standard pool or billiard table, with a ten-inch upright wooden rail running around the table's outside edges, forming a rectangular enclosure. The rail serves as a backboard, and also helps to prevent the rolling dice from falling off the table. The rail opposite to the boxmen's seat-

The Scarne Bank Crap layout created by the author and first introduced in the Curaçao Hilton Hotel Casino in the Netherlands Antilles. The center portion shows the letters C-E. They stand for Crap and Eleven.

ing position is fitted with a nine-inch by six-foot mirror. This is a protection device to help spot misspotted dice that a cheat may have introduced into the game. The mirror permits the boxmen to see five sides of each die while it is resting on the table layout.

Modern dice tables have grooves running around the top edges of the rail. The grooves are for the players to place their chips so that they do not clutter up the table's playing surface. The inside of the four-sided rail is lined with sponge rubber, embossed in various patterns to ensure that the dice rebound in a random manner. Gambling-house operators, well aware that there are nimble-fingered players who have spent years mastering the art of making honest dice roll in a predetermined manner, insist that everyone—including any shooter suspected of trying to control by sliding one or both dice across the center of the table—must throw the cubes so that they strike the rubber-covered backboard and bounce at random before coming to a stop.

The five men required to run a dice table include three dealers and two boxmen. The boxmen, the men who sit in-between the two dealers at the table's center, are the bosses. Their duty is to keep their eyes on everything—dice, money, chips, players, dealers, and so on. Two of the dealers stand on each side of them. After each dice decision, the dealers take in the losses and pay off the winnings. The third dealer, who stands opposite the boxmen, has charge of the dice. He calls out the dice numbers as they are made and helps with the proposition bets when placed. He is often referred to as the "stickman" because he retrieves the dice after each roll with a curved stick and holds them until such time as all previous bets have been settled and new bets are made. Whereupon, with the stick, he pushes the dice toward the shooter.

The table's surface is covered with a tight-fitting green baize cloth on which are printed two exact large-sized designs separated at the table's center by another large design allocated for various side bets. The purpose of the duplicate designs is to accommodate more players and to permit them to make their bets without leaning forward too far or leaving their places at the table. Because of these duplicate layout designs, the Craps table itself is called a *double-side dealer*. Each of these designs is divided into spaces, of different shapes and sizes, representing the various bets that can be placed against the house. This green baize table covering is known as a *Craps layout*. Although there are numerous differently shaped layouts, the actual difference is small. Some layouts may carry one or two wagers that others don't have; some may differ more or less in the odds offered. This last variation depends directly upon the players who patronize that particular casino—how much they know about dice odds and how much of a house percentage they will stand to buck. The smarter the patronage, the better the odds approach the correct ones; the less they know, the greater the house percentages.

All Craps layouts are clever exercises in mathematics, designed to give the player an exciting run for his money—and at the same time to give the house a mathematical edge on every bet shown on the layout. Unfortunately, the majority of Craps players know little or nothing about the house percentages they are fighting, and this lack of knowledge puts them in the chump, or sucker, category. The following odds and percentages will tell you how to stop being a chump and become as gambling-wise as the most seasoned dice gambler found in Las Vegas or anywhere else.

Before we begin our analysis of Bank Craps odds and percentages, you must remember that if you become a habitual crapshooter, you will lose, no matter how smart you bet. It makes no difference in the long run whether you make bets having less than 1 percent against you or whether you place bets that have a big 16 2/3 percent going against you. Over a long period of play, the house's percentage is bound to take both the smart dice player and the chump. The only difference is that the chump doesn't have even a fighting chance—he gives his money to the house.

Line Bets. There are two different types of line bets: the *pass line bet* and the *don't pass line bet*. Each bet can be made only before a come-out roll. After the come-out, they cannot be withdrawn. First to be discussed is the pass line bet.

Pass Line (also referred to on different layouts as "Pass," "Line," "Win," or "Do"). The player who wants to bet the house that the shooter will win—that the dice will pass—places his chip or chips, before the come-out, on the long narrow space of the layout printed with any of the following words: *Pass Line, Pass, Line, Win,* or *Do.*

This bet is without a doubt the most popular bet made by dice players in the Craps table, because it's the bet they first learned when shooting Private Craps. The house pays this bet off at even money (1 to 1) and enjoys a favorable edge of 1.414 percent, or about 7 cents on a $5 wager. Owing to the house's low percentage take, this is one of the wisest casino bets a player can make. But most Craps players are attracted by other bets that pay off at bigger odds; and because they don't know odds, they don't know they are fighting greater house percentages. Like all bets placed on the Craps layout, this wager can be made by any player whether he is the shooter or not; however, it cannot be withdrawn; it remains until it's won or lost.

Don't Pass Line (also referred to on different layouts as either "Don't" or "Lose"). The player who wants to bet that the shooter will lose—that the dice will not pass—places his chip or chips, before the come-out, on the small corner layout space marked with the words *Don't Pass, Don't,* or *Lose.* The house pays off at even money (1 to 1). If you were to make this bet in a private or noncommercial crap game, you'd have an advantage for, as I told you above, the shooter has a 1.414 percent disadvantage. Remember, however, that you are not playing in a private crap game—you're playing in a gambling casino. And casinos wouldn't stay in business long if they took a beating of 1.414 percent. The casino resorts, therefore, to a simple tactical maneuver: It bars either the double sixes (or the double aces) on the come-out roll. This means that if, on the come-out, the shooter throws a double six (6–6) or a double ace (1–1), as the case may be, your bet is a standoff; there is no action for the player or players who have placed bets on the spaces of the layout marked *Don't Pass, Don't,* or *Lose.* In a private or noncommercial game of Craps, the fader or wrong bettor would have won the bet; but at the Bank Craps table, it is no decision or "standoff" for the don't bettor. By barring the two sixes or the two aces and counting a standoff as a neutral roll in this bet, the house is taking away the 1.414 percent edge you would have had, and has replaced it with a house advantage of 1.402 percent or about 7 cents on a $5 wager. If a standoff is counted as a roll the house advan-

tage becomes 1.364 percent. So, for all practical reasons, it doesn't matter whether you bet the pass line or don't pass line; the house percentage remains about the same. However, because this wager has a standoff, players think erroneously that it has a much higher house percentage than it actually does—hence you'll seldom find many players betting the don't pass line. If the house bars the double aces instead of double sixes, as some do, it gets the same results as if it were barring two sixes. When some houses bar the ace-deuce (1–2) instead of the double six or double one (ace), the 4.385 percent in its favor has not merely doubled—as so many dice players think—it has more than tripled! When you see a layout that bars the ace-deuce, forget that the don't pass line exists.

Come and Don't Come. The player who wishes to bet on the come or don't come places his bet on the spaces of the layout marked *Come* or *Don't Come.* These bets are put there to help speed up the line action because, even if a shooter is trying for a point number, a bettor can put his money on the layout and bet as he would on the come-out. The come bet is essentially the same as the pass line bet, and the don't come bet mimics the don't pass bet, except that the come and don't come bets are made after the come-out. Both are paid off at even money, and the house percentages on these wagers are the same as on pass line bets and don't pass line bets. The house edge is 1.414 percent, or about 7 cents on a $5 wager, on the come; and 1.402 percent, or about 7 cents on a $5 wager, on the don't come.

If you put a chip on the space of the layout marked *Come,* then the first roll of the dice is the point number as far as you're concerned. For example, the shooter is trying to make his point, which happens to be 8. You make a come bet, and on the next roll the shooter throws a 5, your point number if 5. In every subsequent roll of the dice, your come bet stands until either a 5 is made and you win, or a 7 is made and you lose. This also holds true for the don't come bet and the don't pass bet—even to the bar on the two sixes or the two aces. Come or don't come bets, like line bets, cannot be withdrawn; they remain until they are won or lost.

Free Odds Bets. The smart dice player ("do bettor") can slice down the house's edge of 1.414 percent on the pass line bets and come bets to less than 1 percent by taking the odds that the shooter will make his point number. When you have made a pass line bet or come bet, and the shooter already has come out on a point or a new number, you're allowed to make a free second bet, limited to the amount of your wager on the pass line or come, that the shooter will make his point number. This is called "taking the free odds," meaning that the house will give you the true odds that the shooter won't make the point. The true or correct odds on each point number are as follows:

ODDS AGAINST MAKING THE POINT NUMBERS

The Point Numbers	Correct Odds	Correct Payoff Odds in Dollars
4 or 10	2 to 1	$2.00 to $1.00
5 or 9	3 to 2	$1.50 to $1.00
6 or 8	6 to 5	$1.20 to $1.00

Let's say that you have a $10 bet riding on the pass line, and on the come-out the shooter rolls a 4; the above chart reveals that the correct odds against the shooter making this point are 2 to 1. If you want to "take the odds," you place an additional $10 on the layout directly behind your $10 pass line wager. If the shooter makes the 4, the house pays you $20 for the second bet plus $10 for your original pass line bet.

When you have a bet riding on the pass line, it's always advantageous to take the free odds on the point, since this reduces the 1.414 percent the house originally had on the pass line bet to less than 1 percent (to be exact, .848 percent). However, if you are one of the few players who do bet the don't pass line, remember that the house will allow you to "lay the odds" on the point equal to your don't pass line bet or don't come bet. Suppose the point is 4 again and you have $10 riding on the don't pass line. Also, you want to lay the odds that the shooter will not make it, and you can put down any even amount up to $20. When you take the odds, on a pass bet, you are limited to the amount of your line bet. But when you lay the odds on a don't pass bet, you are limited to the amount that could give you winnings of not higher than your original bet. If the shooter fails to make the point, the house pays you $10 for each of your two winning bets. The house advantage on both these wagers also runs to less than 1 percent (to be exact, .832 percent).

The free odds bets made on the pass line, don't pass line, come, or don't come, may be taken down (removed) at any time before the bet is decided. One thing should be remembered, however: The lowest-valued chip in a luxury casino is a $1 chip and, for that reason, dealers cannot pay off on any part of a dollar. Therefore, when you're taking the free odds, make sure that your bet doesn't pay off in cents. For example, if your pass line bet is $1 and the point is 5, taking the free odds for $1 would hurt you rather than benefit you. The dice dealer would not pay you the $1.50 your bet should bring; rather, you would be paid one lone $1 chip—that's all. To receive the correct odds of 3 to 2, your pass line bet should be $2.

The only way to take full advantage of the free odds is to make your bet a minimum (or multiple) of ten ($10). Since the average pass line bettor usually bets only a buck or two, he cannot take full advantage of the free odds. Here's why: When you make your pass line bet, you don't know what the come-out number will be. If you bet $1, and the come-out is 4 or 10, you're all right because you can get the full 2-to-1 odds. If the come-out is 5, 6, 8, or 9, you're in trouble. You'd get $1 to $1, instead of $1.50 to $1, on the 5 or 9. You'd get even money, instead of $1.20 to $1, on the 6 or 8. Similarly, on every bet up to $10, you'd be blocked from getting full odds on one or another number. But, on a $10 bet, you can get 2 to 1, 3 to 2, or 6 to 5, depending on the come-out number. This is true of any multiple of ten, but not of any other number or multiple. You can figure it yourself. This does not mean that you have to bet $10. With a smaller bet you can still find free odds on some numbers, though not all.

If you happen to be in a situation like that just described and the Craps dealer tries to induce you to increase the amount of your pass line bet after the come-out by telling you that it is to your best advantage, since it will permit you to take full advantage of the free odds offered, *don't*. Acceptance is to take even money instead of odds that the shooter will make his point and the free odds bet is no longer free. Although "betting the line" and taking or laying the free odds as described is the smartest way of gambling at casino dice tables, it is strange how very, very few gamblers take full advantage of such a play. I have found that many players are just as unpredictable as the dice. During the thrill, action, and excitement of the game, they bet as their emotions, rather than their minds, dictate. They follow their intuition rather than their knowledge of the game, and seldom do the right thing at the right time.

Place Bets. Now we come to two spaces of the layout exactly similar in design, and with each situated nearest the dealer. Each design depicts six large boxed numbers that read *4, 5, 6, 8, 9, 10*. These are called *place numbers,* and are similar to the free odds bets previously discussed, such as taking or laying the odds that the shooter will or will not throw a given number or numbers before making a 7. Most gamblers don't bet the place numbers until after a come-out. However, place bets can be made at any time, and withdrawn

whenever desired.

The two major differences between a free odds bet and a place number bet are that, when you bet a place number, you don't have to make a line bet first; and, unlike the free odds bet, you may bet one or all six place numbers at any time before the next roll of the dice. But, for this privilege, the house charges you a percentage fee for each and every place bet you make.

The house extracts its percentage by paying off place bets at less than the correct odds, instead of charging a fee. The following chart gives you the house payoff odds, the correct odds, and the favorable house advantage in terms of percentage and money, on all the possible place bets that can be made at Bank Craps:

BANK'S FAVORABLE PERCENTAGES ON RIGHT AND WRONG PLACE BETS

House Payoff Odds	Correct Odds	Percentage in House's Favor	House Percentage on $5 Bet
House lays 9 to 5 on 4 or 10	10 to 5	6.666	About 33 cents
House lays 7 to 5 on 5 or 9	7½ to 5	4.000	About 20 cents
House lays 7 to 6 on 6 or 8	6 to 5	1.515	About 8 cents
Player lays 11 to 5 on 4 or 10	10 to 5	3.030	About 15 cents
Player lays 8 to 5 on 5 or 9	7½ to 5	2.500	About 12 cents
Player lays 5 to 4 on 6 or 8	6 to 5	1.818	About 9 cents

Obviously the best place bet is to take the 7 to 6 odds on the 6 or 8, since the house's favorable advantage is 1.515 percent, or about 8 cents on a $5 bet. However, most inexperienced players, as you'll learn later, insist on putting their money on the big 6 or big 8, which returns only even money, thus costing 9 1/11 percent, or about 46 cents on the same wager. This is a perfect example of foolish betting at the dice table.

Most luxury casinos on the Las Vegas Strip, in addition to permitting place bets, also allow players to "buy the numbers." In buying the numbers, the player is paid off at correct odds, such as 6 to 5 on 6 or 8; 3 to 2 on 5 or 9; and 2 to 1 on 4 or 10. However, for such services, the bank levies a direct charge of 5 percent payable in advance on the total sum wagered; this amounts to a charge of $1 on each $20 bet, which happens to be the minimum bet permitted at Strip casinos where bets of this type are allowed. Buying

the numbers is favored by dice gamblers hailing from New York, New Jersey, and other Eastern states, but it is only recommended on the 4 and 10.

A number of casinos in this country and the Caribbean Islands operate their Bank Craps tables by compelling players to buy the numbers. Place bets, come and don't come bets, and free back-line bets (see page 460) are not permitted. The most notable casino of this kind is the plush El Casino in Freeport, Grand Bahama. This type of game is known as New York Craps. There is one very peculiar fact about the direct 5 percent charge: In most games, the house's favorable percentage is greater than most players think, but the 5 percent charge at New York Craps is less than nearly all crap players and most casino operators suspect. Here are the correct percentages in favor of the house when the operator levies a 5 percent charge:

1. The do bettor pays $1, or 4.761 percent,

when taking $20 worth of odds on the numbers 4, 5, 6, 8, 9, and 10.

2. The don't bettor pays $1, or 2.439 percent, when laying odds of $40 to $20 on the numbers 4 or 10.

3. The don't bettor pays $1, or 3.225 percent, when laying odds of $30 to $20 on the numbers 5 or 9.

4. The don't bettor pays $1, or 4 percent, when laying odds of $24 to $20 on the numbers 6 or 8.

In Bank Craps games that permit a player to make a place bet or buy the numbers at 5 percent, it would be to a player's advantage to buy the 4 and 10 and place the 5, 9, 6, and 8.

It soon becomes clear that once you've learned the basic rules of Bank Craps, the bets that may be made on the Craps layout aren't at all difficult to understand. The trouble with the average player lies not in not knowing how to play the game, but in knowing little or nothing about odds and the house percentages he is out to beat. As a result, in a game where he has an opportunity to slice the house edge down to less than 1 percent, as explained in the foregoing, he insists on making all sorts of ridiculous side bets where at times he's bucking a house edge as high as 16 2/3 percent. Side bets are called "proposition bets" by casino operators. I call them by their right name: "sucker bets."

Let's analyze some of these ridiculous bets favored by many dice players, starting with field bets.

Field Bets. Many of the Craps players whom I have observed playing Bank Craps are suckers for field bets. The Craps stickman begins to sell the field bets by chanting constantly during the game: "Place your bet on the field. Nine, that's a field number. Ten, another field number." Then, occasionally, he adds that the field has seven winning numbers and only four losing numbers. The field usually bears the numbers 2, 3, 5, 9, 10, 11,

and 12. When the player puts the bet on the space of the layout marked *Field,* he is betting that one of the group of seven numbers listed there will be thrown on the next roll. The bank pays even money. Since the field shows seven numbers, and there are only four (4, 6, 7, and 8) that can make him lose, the non-thinker figures that his chances are excellent. He may even believe that he has the best of it, or at the very least, an even chance. But appearances are nearly always deceptive, especially in casino games. If we add together all the ways in which the winning and losing numbers can be thrown, we find that the above field numbers can be made in only 17 ways as against 19 ways for the losing numbers. The house, consequently, has an advantage of 5 5/9 percent, or about 28 cents on a $5 bet.

Other layouts are made with the 4 in place of the 5, so that the field bears the numbers 2, 3, 4, 9, 10, 11, and 12. Some layouts pay double on 2 and 12; others pay 3 to 1 on 2. In each case, the player's disadvantage is still 5 5/9 percent or about 28 cents on a $5 bet.

The lure of Craps is its fast action. But, because wagers on the field are either won or lost every time the dice are rolled, the action is so fast and furious that most players' bankrolls can't take it. With the 5 5/9 percent grinding away and taking 1/18 of every bet you make, the house can expect to eat up the amount of your wager in 18 rolls. To show what this means in dollars and cents, let us assume you place 180 field bets of $10 each, which you can do in an hour's time at many fast-action Craps tables, and let us assume that the law of averages works according to expectation. This hour of field betting would cost you exactly $100. It's a cinch that the field bettor who believes that his chances of winning are excellent has not looked at the following chart, which shows all the 36 possible combinations that can be made with two dice:

36 COMBINATIONS OR WAYS WITH TWO DICE

2 can be made in one way:	1–1					
3 can be made in two ways:	1–2	2–1				
4 can be made in three ways:	1–3	3–1	2–2			
5 can be made in four ways:	1–4	4–1	2–3	3–2		
6 can be made in five ways:	1–5	5–1	2–4	4–2	3–3	
7 can be made in six ways:	1–6	6–1	2–5	5–2	3–4	4–3
8 can be made in five ways:	2–6	6–2	3–5	5–3	4–4	
9 can be made in four ways:	3–6	6–3	4–5	5–4		
10 can be made in three ways:	4–6	6–4	5–5			
11 can be made in two ways:	6–5	5–6				
12 can be made in one way:	6–6					

When we know that there are 36 ways of making the 11 numbers, and also how many ways each number can be made, we can easily obtain the true odds and house percentages on most bets made at Bank Craps. The general rule for figuring dice percentages is simply this: The house's favorable percentage is the number of ways that the player is short divided by the total number of ways the event can happen. In the field above, the house has 19 ways to the player's 17. The player is short two ways. Divide 2 by 36 and you get a favorable house advantage of 5 5/9 percent.

The Big 6 and the Big 8. The player who places his bet on the spaces of the layout marked *Big 6* or *Big 8* is wagering that the number will be thrown before a 7. He can put his money on that space at any time. The bank pays even money, and most players labor under the impression that it is an even-money bet. The *6* and *8* spaces on most layouts are usually made large and are positioned where the players can reach them easily. Why any gambler should think that the bank would emphasize a bet that gives the house no percentage at all is a mystery.

We know from our combinations and ways table that, since either 6 or 8 can be made five ways and 7 in six ways, the correct odds are 6 to 5, or $1.20 to $1.00. The house's advantage is 9 1/11 percent, which amounts to about 45 cents on a $5 bet. The *6* and *8* spaces on most layouts have grown large and have come to be known as the big 6 and big 8 not because they are the best bet on the layout—but because the house has such a big edge. They are strictly sucker bets.

Smart-money gamblers wouldn't touch such a bet with a ten-foot pole—especially when they know they can *place* the 6 and 8 and get far better odds. Again, why many dice players insist on putting their money on the big 6 or big 8 and pay a whopping house percentage of 9 1/11 percent or 46 cents on a $5 bet, when they can just as easily place the 6 or 8 and pay a low house percentage of 1.515 percent or about 8 cents on a $5 bet, is to me another perfect example of foolish betting.

Hard-Way Bets. Another ridiculous type of side bet is to wager on one of four spaces in the center of the layout headed by the words *Hard Way*. This is to bet that the shooter will make a specified even number (4, 6, 8, or 10) with two double numbers (the hard way) before it is made the "easy way" (any other

way than a hard way) or before a 7 is made. Hard-way bets can be made at any time and withdrawn at any time.

Hard-way wagers can be found on all layouts and, once again, many dice players believe that the odds offered by the bank are fair enough. Some even think they are getting correct odds, a lack of logic that almost classes as not thinking at all!

The layout does not offer correct odds on any of these bets; further, in many cases, it offers even less than it appears to. This *misdirection,* as gamblers call it, is accomplished by wording the Craps layout so as to mislead players who forget that the two little words "for" and "to" do not mean the same thing. You will see how this deception operates in the following analysis of the hard-way wagers: The 4 (2 and 2) and 10 (5 and 5) pay 7 to 1; the 6 (3 and 3) and 8 (4 and 4) pay 9 to 1. The correct odds on a hard-way 4 or 10 are 8 to 1; and on a hard-way 6 or 8, the odds are 10 to 1. Thus, the house has a 9 1/11 percent, or about a 45-cent, edge against the player who bets $5 on the hard-way 6 or 8; and an 11 1/9 percent, or about a 56-cent, edge against him when he bets $5 on the hard-way 4 or 10.

Some of the smaller casinos pay only 6 to 1 on the hard 4 and hard 10, and 8 to 1 on the hard 6 and hard 8—only, it doesn't look that way. The following example shows how this misdirection is achieved: The Craps layout is made to read "7 for 1" above the hard 4 and hard 10, and "9 for 1" above the hard 6 and hard 8. The difference is this: When paying off at 7-*for*-1 odds, the house keeps the $1 you bet. Some of the larger casinos make use of this same gimmick to mislead players in believing they are getting larger odds by having their layout read "8 for 1" on the hard 4 and the hard 10, and "10 for 1" on the hard 6 and hard 8.

Many dice players with whom I've discussed the hard-way bets find it difficult to understand why the player gets 9-to-1 odds on the hard 6 and hard 8 and only 7-to-1 odds on the hard 4 and hard 10. These players believe that it is just as easy to make a double 3 as it is a double 5 and that the odds should therefore be the same against making either 6 or 10 the hard way. They see no reason why, if the house pays 9 to 1 against throwing a double 4 or a double 3, it shouldn't also pay 9 to 1 against throwing a double 5 or a double 2.

The fallacy in the average gambler's reasoning is that, when he makes the statement that it is just as easy to throw a double 3 or a double 4 as it is a double 2 or a double 5, he forgets that he is talking about the hard way. Suppose your point is 4 and you bet that you can make it the hard way with 2 and 2. There are, according to our table of combinations and ways, three ways to make 4: with 2 and 2, 1 and 3, and 3 and 1. If either 1 and 3 or 3 and 1 is thrown, you have made your point; but since you didn't make it the hard way, you lose the bet. You have one way to win and two ways to lose. In addition, you can also lose if you 7 out; and since there are six ways to make 7, there are altogether eight ways you can lose as against one way in which you can win. Consequently, the odds are 8 to 1. The same reasoning also applies to making the point 10 with 5 and 5.

Let's try the same process with points 6 and 8. The 6, according to the combinations and ways table, can be made in five ways. Betting on the 6 the hard way means that only one of these ways (3 and 3) wins and the other four lose. Add to those the losing six ways that 7 can be made, and you have 10 ways to lose against one way to win. The odds, therefore—strange as it may seem to players who don't think logically—are 10 to 1. The same reasoning applies to making 8 with 4 and 4. Once a shooter passes by making his point number, all remaining undecided bets on the layout must be called "on or off" before the next come-out throw. If the bettor wants the come-out throw to count, he says, "All bets go on the come-out." If he does not want the come-out throw to count, he calls, "All bets off on the come-out," which means the come-out throw does not count.

One-Roll Bets or Come-Out Bets. And now we come to the last of the foolish side bets that can be made on the Craps layout: the "one-roll" or "come-out" bets. Strange as it may appear, these bets are made by smart-money gamblers and chump players alike. Gamblers who like their action fast and sweet and those who like their odds big go for these bets the way Reds flock to riots. Like the field bet, these bets are wagered in one roll, or throw, of the dice. The player bets that a specific number will be made. The dice are rolled, and the bet is won or lost on that roll.

1. 12 (double 6) in one roll: The house pays 30 to 1. Since the correct odds are 35 to 1, the house has an edge of 13 8/9 percent or about 69 cents on a $5 wager. When the house pays 30 for 1, it has an edge of 16 2/3 percent, or about 83 cents on a $5 wager.

2. 2 (two aces) in one roll: The house odds and percentages are the same as for double 6.

3. 11 (5 and 6) in one roll: The house pays 15 to 1. Since the correct odds are 17 to 1, the house has an edge of 13 8/9 percent or about 56 cents on a $5 wager. When the house pays 15 for 1, it has an edge of 16 2/3 percent or about 83 cents on a $5 wager.

4. 3 (1 and 2) in one roll: The house odds and percentages are the same as for 11.

5. All 7's (3 and 4, 5 and 2, or 6 and 1) in one roll: The house pays either 5 for 1 or 4 to 1. Since the correct odds are 5 to 1, the house has an edge of 16 2/3 percent, or about 83 cents on a $5 wager, which makes this and the four bets described above the biggest sucker bets found on the Bank Craps layout.

6. Any craps (2, 3, or 12) in one roll: The house pays 8 for 1 or 7 to 1. Since the correct odds are 8 to 1, the house has an edge of 11 1/9 percent, or 56 cents on a $5 wager.

Insurance Bets. Many crapshooters have a habit of making two wagers simultaneously in an attempt to insure one or the other. *Example:* A player places a bet on the pass line, and tries to protect it against a craps on the first roll by making a come-out bet on all craps. He thinks that if he loses one bet he may win the other, thus cutting down or cancelling out his loss; actually, he stands to lose at least one of the bets and maybe both. Or he may attempt to insure a don't pass line bet after the come-out by taking odds on the point. Since every wager in Bank Craps must be considered as a separate and distinct wager, the only effect of insurance betting is simply to pay the house a toll on two bets rather than on one. Instead of insuring himself against loss, the player has merely increased the percentage against himself.

How to Gamble Sensibly at Bank Craps. As in any banking game, the house earns a percentage on every bet made at Bank Craps. This is not unreasonable because somebody has to pay for the casino rent, equipment, employees' salaries, etc. But just how much you pay for the privilege of shooting Craps in a casino is entirely up to you. Nobody can tell you how to win at Bank Craps because, if you gamble long enough and often enough, the house percentage will take its toll. But if you still insist on taking a fling at the dice tables, here are several rules to follow which can save you money.

1. Whenever you gamble at Bank Craps, set aside in advance the amount of money you are willing to lose. If you lose that amount, quit the game for the evening; do not borrow money, write a check, or obtain credit to continue gambling.

2. Also set for yourself a reasonable amount that you might expect to win, and if you succeed in winning that much, quit the game, no matter how lucky you feel. If you follow this rule you will retain your winnings more often, and you will have more winning plays because you are trying to win smaller amounts.

3. If you lost yesterday, do not gamble today with the object of recouping yesterday's losses. That is the most dangerous course any

gambler can follow. Trying to get even has sent more players to the poorhouse than anything else. Write off yesterday's losses and forget them.

4. Naturally, I expect that after reading this text on Bank Craps you will place your bets on the layout spaces which have the least percentage against you. If you follow this rule, your chances of winning are greatly increased.

5. Try to win the amount you hoped to win in the fastest time possible. Making bets back and forth all night merely gives the law of averages a chance to perform as expected in the long run and helps Old Man Percentage slowly but surely to eat up your chances of winning.

If the Bank Craps player follows the above rules, he will be gambling intelligently; by avoiding sucker bets, his winnings may be greater. And when he does lose, his losses won't hurt him too much.

THE CASINO'S PERCENTAGE ON BANK CRAPS BETS

Bet	Percentage in Bank's Favor	Bank's Take on $5 Bet
Win (pass)	1.414	$ .07*
Come	1.414	.07
Lose (don't pass) bar 6–6 or 1–1	1.402	.07
Don't come, bar 6–6 or 1–1	1.402	.07
Lose (don't pass), bar 1–2	4.385	.22
Don't come, bar 1–2	4.385	.22
Place Bets to Win		
Bank lays 9 to 5 on 4 or 10	6.666	.33
Bank lays 7 to 5 on 5 or 9	4.000	.20
Bank lays 7 to 6 on 6 or 8	1.515	.08
Box Number Bets to Win (5% Charge)		
Bank lays 10 to 5 on 4 or 10	4.761	.25
Bank lays 7½ to 5 on 5 or 9	4.761	.25
Bank lays 6 to 5 on 6 or 8	4.761	.25
Place Bets to Lose		
Bank takes 11 to 5 on 4 or 10	3.030	.15
Bank takes 8 to 5 on 5 or 9	2.500	.12
Bank takes 5 to 4 on 6 or 8	1.818	.09
Box Number Bets to Lose (5% Charge)		
Bank takes 10 to 5 on 4 or 10	2.439	.12
Bank takes 7½ to 5 on 5 or 9	3.225	.16
Bank takes 6 to 5 on 6 or 8	4.000	.20
Field Bets		
Field (2, 3, 4, 9, 10, 11, 12)	11.111	.56
Field (2, 3, 4, 9, 10, 11, 12, with double payoff on 2 and 12)	5.263	.26
Field (2, 3, 5, 9, 10, 11, 12)	5.555	.27
Big six	9.090	.45
Big eight	9.090	.45

Bet	Percentage in Bank's Favor	Bank's Take on $5 Bet
Win bet (pass or come line) plus free single point, odds bet to win	.848	.04
Lose (don't pass or don't come line) plus free single point, odds bet to lose	.832	.04
Win bet (pass line) plus free double point, odds bet to win	.606	.03
Lose (don't pass) plus free double point, odds bet to lose	.591	.03

* The bank's edge on a $5.00 wager has a plus factor which is omitted (except for the place-win bet on numbers 5 and 9, and in the box numbers 6 and 8 to lose).

Cheating at Dice

Most gambling casinos that cater to the masses are *on the square* (honest) and earn their profits by employing Old Man Percentage. The same cannot be said for thousands and thousands of private Craps games or for the countless dice games played in illegally run gambling joints. Nearly every private Craps game has either its Craps hustler (a player who offers short odds) or its dice cheat —two characters who are consistent winners in 90 percent of all friendly games.

Of course, dice specially made for cheating have been found in the tombs of ancient Egypt and the Orient, and in prehistoric graves of North and South America. Any die that is not a perfect cube will not act according to the correct odds and is called a "shape." *Shapes* are cubes that have been shaved down on one or more sides so that they are slightly brick-shaped and will tend to settle down most often on their larger surfaces. Shapes are the most common of all crooked dice and can be made either as *passers* or *missouts*.

Six-ace flats are the commonest variety of missouts, and have the six-ace sides shaved down. Thus, these sides turn up oftener than they would with square dice, and produce more sevens. The cheat bets the dice to lose.

Flat passers have had the six-ace sides cut down on one die and the three-four sides on the other, so that the points 4, 5, 9, and 10 appear more often than they should. Or the two-five sides are shaved on one die and the three-four sides on the other, so as to favor the points 5, 6, 8, and 9. The cheat bets the dice to win.

Two-way flats (fast sevens or four-way sevens) are shapes that have been shaved down on two different sides. When a few thousandths of an inch is taken off the six and three sides, for instance, the six-ace and three-four sides are rectangles having a greater area than the two-five sides. The numbers 6, 1, 3, and 4 will appear oftener than usual and, when both dice are cut down in the same way, these numbers will combine to form 7 more often than is normal. They are, therefore, missouts, and cheaters call them *fast sevens* or *four-way sevens*. The six-ace and two-five sides, or the three-four and two-five sides, when cut down, act the same.

Bevels are shapes having one or more sides sandpapered so that they are slightly rounded rather than flat. Such cubes tend to roll off the rounded sides and come to rest more often on the flat sides. Bevels can also be made as passers or missouts as weak or as strong as desired. Use the "wobble test" to detect beveled shapes. Hold one die in each hand and rub two sides together, trying different sides. When a beveled surface is rubbed against a flat surface or another beveled surface, the dice will wobble, or rock, back and forth.

Cut edges are dice whose edges are not all beveled at the customary 45-degree angle. The four edges on some sides are cut at a 60-degree angle. This gives some sides a larger area than others, and the dice tend to settle on the larger surfaces more often. To detect cut edges, hold the dice together and note the width of the separation line between them. If this varies when you try different sides, the edges have been cut.

Loaded Dice. The *gaff* (doctoring) on shapes is called *outside work;* on *loaded dice* it is *inside work.* Loads may caliper as perfect cubes, but extra weight just below the surface on some sides will make the opposite sides

A beveled die and the wobble test for bevels.

come up oftener than they should. Loads, contrary to what most people think, are not so heavily weighted that the same sides always appear; this behavior in a game would look very odd indeed. Like shapes, loads are percentage dice that throw certain combinations more often than they should.

Most Craps players know so little about crooked dice that they are cheated out of millions of dollars every year because they think that transparent dice cannot be loaded. Dice makers have never found this very difficult; they simply drill the recessed spots on two or three adjacent sides of the dice a little deeper than usual. Then they insert thin gold, platinum, or tungsen amalgam slugs, which are covered by opaque paint on the spots. In a well-made pair of transparent loads, the other spots are also drilled deeper and filled with paint. Then, when you look through the dice, all the spots seem to be recessed to the same depth. In addition, many players believe that the practice of throwing the cubes against a background is protection against crooked dice. This protects you only against controlled shots, not against shapes or loads.

There are a couple of good tests for loaded dice. The best method is to fill a tall glass with water, hold the suspected cube just above the surface and drop it gently into the water; do this several times holding the die with a different number up each time. Note whether the die settles evenly or whether it

The pivot test for a loaded die.

turns over as it goes down. If it turns, and if two or three numbers always show up and others never show, then the dice are loaded.

If there is no tall glass of water handy, try this: Hold the cube loosely between thumb and forefinger at diagonally opposite corners so that there is as little pressure as possible. Try all four combinations of diagonally opposite corners. If the cube is loaded and the weighted sides are on top, the die will pivot as the heavier sides swing around to the bottom. The feeling of movement of the die is unmistakable.

Tops and bottoms are dice with one or more faces duplicated on the opposite side of each die. Since certain numbers are omitted, this will tend to produce some numbers in disproportionate frequency and never to produce certain other numbers. For example, two dice marked respectively with duplicates of 3-4-5 and 1-5-6 can never produce combinations totaling 2, 3, 7, or 12, which are the only combinations with which one can lose in the game of Craps. Such dice are usually introduced into the game by sleight of hand and, as a rule, are used only by accomplished dice cheats. Since it is impossible to see more than three sides of a cube at any one time, tops and bottoms are unlikely to be detected by the inexperienced gambler.

The Slick Dice Cup. The average player believes that the use of a dice cup protects him against dice cheats. Nothing could be further from the truth. More cheating at Craps, Backgammon, Poker Dice, Buck Dice, High Dice, and other dice games takes place when a dice cup is in use than when the dice are thrown from the hand. Why? Because it's easier to cheat and less detectable when crooked dice and a dice cup are in use. All a cheat requires to take the unsuspecting player is a *slick dice cup* and a set of two, three, four, or five loaded dice, called *first flop dice*, depending on the game being played. The cheat places the loaded dice into the crooked dice cup and the dirty work begins.

The slick dice cup has a smooth slicked inner surface and when the cheat shakes the cup with an up and down and slightly rotary motion of his arm, the loaded dice instead of rattling at random inside the cup spin around the inside surface like wooden horses on a merry-go-round. The centrifugal force lines the dice up within the cup in a horizontal position. The last sideward shake just before they are thrown causes the loaded dice to topple over so that their loaded sides are down. When the cheat throws them, he holds the cup parallel with the playing surface, shoves it forward a bit and jerks it back quickly so that the dice all slide out without turning over and the cheat throws a desired number. When the other players throw using the same cup and dice, they shake and throw properly and the loaded dice do them no good. To avoid being cheated with a slick cup, use a *trip cup,* which contains obstructions in its inner surface that makes the dice tumble as they are thrown and prevents the shark from sliding them out. Some cups have a trip rim; others are lined with ribbed rubber.

If a trip cup is not available, you can insist that the dice be well shaken and that the cup be turned completely upside down on the throw so that the dice bounce on the playing surface and do not slide out. Don't hesitate to examine the dice.

Cheating with Honest Dice. There are still a great many gamblers who don't quite believe the stories about cheats who can make fair dice act like performing seals. "Can fair dice be controlled?" is a question I am often asked. The answer is "Yes," but only on certain playing surfaces. There are a good many dice cheats who have practiced long and hard and have perfected the ability to make honest dice behave as they want them to under certain conditions.

Following are five of the most effective controlled dice shots used to fleece even the most seasoned Craps players. Three of these, highly guarded dice-shark secrets, are the Backboard Control Shot, the Three-Cushion Controlled Dice Shot, and the Dice Table Control Shot. They appear here in print for the first time.

The Spin Shot or *Whip Shot.* Although difficult to perfect, this is the most common controlled dice shot. It works best on soft dirt. The dice are held with the desired numbers on top, rattled in the hand, but not actually shaken. A quick whiplike snap of the hand sends them spinning through the air like twin helicopters. When the dice land, the spinning motion keeps them from turning over and they settle down, the wanted numbers still on top. This shot can also be done on hard surfaces; some surfaces even help the dice to spin and slide without turning over. It can also be accomplished on the green baize surface of the bank—or open crap table—which is why casinos insist that the player hit the backboard or throw the dice over an elastic string which is sometimes stretched across the center of the table.

The Blanket Roll. This controlled percentage shot is also called the *soft roll* or *pad roll* shot, and makes use of a blanket, soft rug, or carpet. The dice are held with certain numbers on the two sides that face each other. The cheat gives the dice a phoney shake, *à la* the spin shot described above, and as his hand comes down to make the throw, the thumb pushes the dice, still together, out toward the ends of his fingers and he gently rolls them out across the blanket. The dice land together and roll end over end like a pair of cartwheels without turning sideways. If the sixes and aces are on the hubs of the wheels, they cannot appear uppermost, therefore a crap, 11, or a 7 with a six-ace cannot be made. This is a percentage shot that seldom fails.

The Backboard Control Shot. This modern percentage controlled shot makes use of blanket, soft rug, or carpet plus a 3-foot high vertical backboard lined with foam rubber. As a rule, throwing the dice against a backboard is a protective measure against dice cheats, but not with this controlled shot. Prior to the time of releasing the dice from the hand, the cheat gives the dice a phony shake, *à la* the spin shot. Then, instead of rolling the dice on the soft surface as in the blanket roll, he lets them fly against the backboard in such a way that both dice hit the backboard at the same time causing the dice to bounce off the backboard onto the soft surface. The momentum causes them to roll back end over end like a pair of cartwheels without turning sideways. If the one-six is one hub of the wheel and the two-five is the other, the only way the cheat can seven out is with a three and four.

Two types of shots to look out for: the blanket roll (top) and the whip shot (bottom).

The Three-Cushion Controlled Dice Shot. This highly secretive private dice-game controlled throw requires the use of a 3-foot high vertical backboard and two sideboards, each lined with foam rubber. Also needed are a smooth table surface, usually a piece of linoleum, onto which the dice fall and slide to a stop. This controlled shot is very effective because few gamblers believe it is possible to hit a sideboard, backboard, and sideboard and still control the dice. To execute this fantastic dice control shot, the cheat shakes the dice *à la* the spin shot and throws the dice against the right sideboard where they ricochet off the sideboard onto the backboard and onto the second sideboard where they drop onto the smooth playing surface, finally coming to rest with the desired numbers uppermost.

The Dice-Table Control Shot. This new casino dice table control shot is the most difficult dice throw to perfect because it requires perfect aim and timing that can be gained only by long and arduous practice on a regulation casino dice table. This dice throw has taken many a casino operator for a bundle. Prior to the publication of this book, it is doubtful that more than a handful of gamblers and casino operators have had the slightest idea that such a controlled shot ever existed. And I firmly believe that once this book hits the book stands, dice-table manufacturers will make certain that it can't work on their tables.

Most modern dice tables have a sponge rubber embossed zigzag pattern lining the inside of the four 10-inch upright rails that enclose the table's playing surface. However, a bottom inch of this lining, at the juncture of the table surface and the upright rails does not possess the embossed zigzag patterns—it is plain sponge rubber. And this is exactly the spot the dice cheat must hit to control this shot.

The pickup of the dice in order to execute this controlled shot is difficult to detect because only one die has to be maneuvered into position. Immediately after the dice have been offered to the cheater-shooter, he picks them up in such a manner that one die has the desired number uppermost. This die is held palm down between the thumb and the first two fingers of the cheat's right hand flat on the table surface. The cheat lets the dice fly out of his palm-down hand from the table surface giving the one die he wants to control a whiplike snap aiming at the juncture of the table surface and the sponge rubber sideboard. When the spinning die hits this spot of the sideboard (the bottom inch), it bounces off at an angle and drops into the center of the table without turning over, with the desired number remaining uppermost. If the cheat holds the die so that a five is always uppermost, "a hard-way 10" becomes an even bet. The same holds true for the point numbers 6, 8, or 9.

Protection Against Dice Cheats. At this point you are probably wondering if there is any simple sure-fire all-around method of making sure that the dice in the games you play are honest. I'm sorry, but the answer is "No!" Your best protection is to have the information given in this dice chapter in your head. If you are smartened up to all the methods and angles, you will have reduced your chance of being cheated with crooked cubes or a controlled dice throw to a minimum.

The only absolutely certain way of never being cheated at a dice game is not to play. But if this rule proves a little too tough to follow, you should at least take a good close look at the cubes and make sure of the following:

1. Each of the two dice in use total seven on all opposing sides.

2. All sides are level and not concave, rounded, or with raised spots.

3. All sides are equally polished.

4. The edges and corners are all straight, square, and preferably sharp rather than rounded. If rounded, see that all edges and corners are rounded equally.

5. The spots are all countersunk the same distance and the paint on all spots is the same distance from the cube's surface. Better still, use flush-spot dice.

6. The dice pass the pivot or water test for loads.

7. Whenever possible, use transparent dice.

8. If the dice cup in use is not a trip dice cup, insist that the dice be well shaken and the cup turned completely upside down on the throw so that the dice drop on the playing platform.

9. Never play dice on a blanket or soft surface and avoid turning dice against an upright backboard lined with sponge rubber.

If the dice meet the above requirements and you are able to protect yourself against the dice cheat's crooked control throws, your only worry as far as being cheated is concerned with the dice cheat whose trained fingers can switch a pair of crooked dice for an honest pair as quickly as you can say "Scarne on Dice."

I have described the most-used dice cheating devices and methods, but there are still a good many others. For information on such things as the slide shot, the Greek shot, the twist shot, how to switch dice, the dice cup switch, and (with two dice) the pin gaff, heavy paint work, busters, etc., see *Scarne on Dice,* a definitive 439-page book devoted solely to dice and dice games.

SCARNE'S RULES FOR OTHER DICE GAMES

There are many parlor games using dice; game manufacturers are constantly issuing board games based on current events, politics, real estate, or on other games such as football, baseball, hockey, boxing, etc., in which dice determine the moves of the counters. Since these games are so numerous and many of them are exceedingly short-lived, the rules given here are limited to the most popular dice games currently played in carnivals, bazaars, Monte Carlo nights, gaming clubs, bars, and homes.

Most of these games have been completely neglected by previous rule book compilers and many of them first appeared in print in *Scarne on Dice.* For the first time, each game was analyzed to find out whether the game was an even-up proposition and, if not, who had the advantage. In the banking games, the percentages in favor of the banker are given.

Both the names and rules of some of these games vary in different parts of the country. The commonest method of play is the one given here, except when it is either strategically or mathematically unsound, in which case the error has been corrected. Some players do not distinguish between similar games such as Indian Dice and Poker Dice, and they play one nearly the same as the other. In these cases I have set down the methods of play that are most dissimilar.

The great majority of dice games to be found in most of the Hoyle-type game books are hundred-year-and-more-old games that are seldom played today, probably because the rules given are nearly always incomplete.

Correct Odds in Dice Games Using Two,

Three, Four, or Five Dice. Dozens of different private and banking dice games are played today and their names and rules vary in different parts of the country. For example, some players do not distinguish between similar games such as Hazard and Chuck-A-Luck.

The great majority of these games make use of from two to five dice, and nearly all the hustler's sucker or proposition bets are made on throws of two, three, four, or five dice. They usually involve either the combined total or the appearance of one or more of several possible combinations of hands such as one pair, two pair, three of a kind, etc.

The following tables show the various combinations, the number of ways they can be made, and the odds against making them in one trial. These tables will enable the player to analyze most of the dice problems he will meet. Reference to the correct odds shown here will show whether a proposition bet is or is not a sucker bet. These odds will also enable the player to figure the house's favorable percentage in a banking game. The tables also give you the answer to odds problems that arise in other dice games.

TABLE OF COMBINATIONS AND WAYS

Two Dice

Specific Hands and Combinations	Number of Ways	Odds Against in One Trial
One pair	6	5 to 1
A specific pair	1	35 to 1

TABLE OF COMBINATIONS AND WAYS (cont.)

Two Dice

Specific Hands and Combinations	Number of Ways	Odds Against in One Trial
No pair	30	1 to 5
A specific no pair	2	17 to 1
Total combinations of all nonspecified hands	36	

Three Dice

Specific Hands and Combinations	Number of Ways	Odds Against in One Trial
Three of a kind	6	35.0 to 1
A specific three of a kind	1	215.0 to 1
One pair	90*	1.4 to 1
A specific pair	15	13.4 to 1
No pair	120	4.0 to 5
Total combinations of all nonspecified hands	216	

Four Dice

Specific Hands and Combinations	Number of Ways	Odds Against in One Trial
Four of a kind	6	215 to 1
A specific four of a kind	1	1,295 to 1
Three of a kind	120	9.8 to 1
A specific three of a kind	20	63.8 to 1
Two pairs	90	13.4 to 1
A specific two pairs	6	215 to 1
One pair	720	4 to 5
A specific one pair	120	9.8 to 1
No pair	360	7.6 to 1
Total combinations of all nonspecified hands	1,296	

Five Dice

Specific Hands and Combinations	Number of Ways	Odds Against in One Trial
Five of a kind	6	1,295 to 1
A specific five of a kind	1	7,775 to 1
Four of a kind	150	50.8 to 1
A specific four of a kind	25	310.0 to 1
Full house	300	24.9 to 1
A specific full house	10	776.6 to 1
Straight	240	31.4 to 1
A specific straight	120	63.8 to 1
Three of a kind	1,200	5.5 to 1

* Although there are actually only six one-pair combinations, from aces, to sixes, the figure 90 gives you the total number of ways of holding a pair plus one of the other 5 numbers on the third die. The same holds true for most of the hands shown in the following tables.

Five Dice (cont.)

Specific Hands and Combinations	Number of Ways	Odds Against in One Trial
A specific three of a kind	200	37.8 to 1
Two pairs	1,800	3.3 to 1
A specific two pairs	120	63.8 to 1
One pair	3,600	1.2 to 1
A specific one pair	600	11.9 to 1
No pair	480	15.2 to 1
Total combinations of all nonspecified hands	7,776	

Note: When straights do not count, the number of no pairs increases to 720.

Five Dice, Aces Wild

Specific Hands and Combinations	Number of Ways	Odds Against in One Trial
Five of a kind	156	48.8 to 1
A specific five of a kind (no aces)	31	249.8 to 1
Five aces	1	7,775 to 1
Four of a kind	1,300	4.9 to 1
A specific four of a kind (no aces)	260	28.9 to 1
Full house	500	14.5 to 1
A specific full house (no aces)	100	76.7 to 1
Straights	1,320	4.8 to 1
A specific straight	660	10.8 to 1
Three of a kind	2,400	2.2 to 1
A specific three of a kind (no aces)	480	15.2 to 1
Two pairs	900	7.6 to 1
A specific two pairs (no aces)	180	42.2 to 1
One pair	1,200	5.5 to 1
A specific pair (no aces)	240	31.4 to 1
Total combinations of nonspecified hands	7,776	

Note: The words in parentheses (no aces) mean that you cannot make such a hand. *Example:* No matter what numbers show on the dice, it is impossible to make a four-ace hand (with aces wild). If you threw four aces and a deuce, you would have five deuces; if you threw two aces and a pair of deuces, you would have four deuces, etc.

TABLES OF NUMBERS AND WAYS

Two Dice

Numbers	Ways	Odds Against in One Trial
2 (or 12)	1	35.0 to 1
3 (or 11)	2	17.0 to 1
4 (or 10)	3	11.0 to 1
5 (or 9)	4	8.0 to 1
6 (or 8)	5	6.2 to 1
7	6	5.0 to 1

Three Dice

Numbers	Ways	Odds Against in One Trial
3 (or 18)	1	215.0 to 1
4 (or 17)	3	71.0 to 1
5 (or 16)	6	35.0 to 1
6 (or 15)	10	20.6 to 1
7 (or 14)	15	13.4 to 1
8 (or 13)	21	9.3 to 1
9 (or 12)	25	7.6 to 1
10 (or 11)	27	6.6 to 1

Four Dice

Numbers	Ways	Odds Against in One Trial
4 (or 24)	1	1,295.0 to 1
5 (or 23)	4	323.0 to 1
6 (or 22)	10	128.6 to 1
7 (or 21)	20	63.8 to 1
8 (or 20)	35	36.0 to 1
9 (or 19)	56	22.1 to 1
10 (or 18)	88	13.7 to 1
11 (or 17)	96	12.5 to 1
12 (or 16)	125	9.3 to 1
13 (or 15)	140	8.3 to 1
14	146	7.8 to 1

Five Dice

Numbers	Ways	Odds Against in One Trial
5 (or 30)	1	7,775.0 to 1
6 (or 29)	5	1,554.2 to 1
7 (or 28)	15	517.4 to 1
8 (or 27)	35	221.1 to 1
9 (or 26)	70	110.0 to 1
10 (or 25)	126	60.7 to 1
11 (or 24)	205	36.9 to 1
12 (or 23)	305	24.4 to 1
13 (or 22)	420	17.5 to 1
14 (or 21)	540	13.4 to 1
15 (or 20)	651	10.9 to 1
16 (or 19)	735	9.5 to 1
17 (or 18)	780	8.9 to 1

Chuck-A-Luck

This is a very old dice game, originally called Sweat-Cloth in England, and known in this country, where it appeared about 1800, as Sweat. Later it came to be known as Chucker-Luck and finally as Chuck-Luck, Chuck-A-Luck, and simply Chuck. More recently it has been known as Bird Cage. Since the numbers on the back line of the Hazard layout (origi-

nally called Grand Hazard) are the same, these are called the *chuck numbers* and are paid off at the same odds. Thus, the two games are very closely related.

Rules. Three dice are tumbled in a wire cage called the *chuck cage* and the layout bears the numbers 1, 2, 3, 4, 5, 6. The players place their bets on the numbered spaces of the layout and, if the player's number appears on one die, the bank pays off even money; if his number appears on two dice, the bank pays 2 to 1; and if it appears on all three dice, the bank pays 3 to 1.

In the casinos today it is the occasional gambler and the women who give the cage its action. It is also found at outings and bazaars where, when it gets action, it is an outing hustler's dream. "Three winners," the dealer shouts, "and three losers every time." This come-on sounds good and is apparently believed by the nonthinkers who play the game; but it is considerably shy of the truth. Suppose we test the dealer's claim by putting one dollar on each of the six numbers and spin the cage. If the three dice show three different numbers, the house takes in $3 and pays out $3. So far it's even-up. Then, notice what happens whenever two dice show the same number. Suppose that two three's and a four are thrown. The bank pays $2 on the three and $1 on the four but collects $1 each on the one, two, five, and six. There are two winners and four losers and the house pays out $3 and collects $4 for a dollar profit. And, if three of a kind are thrown, there is one winner and five losers; the house pays out $3 and takes in $5 for a $2 profit.

To find out what this advantage, in favor for the house, amounts to in percentage, we consult our three-dice table. We find that 216

A Chuck-A-Luck cage with layout.

combinations can be made with three dice which, in the long run, will consist of 120 no pairs, 90 pairs, and six three of a kind. A continuation of our mathematical analysis gives us the percentage in favor of the house: 7 47/54 percent.

Some impatient Bird Cage operators apparently feel that even this percentage is not strong enough because they gaff the cage as well, using "electric dice" and an electromagnet in the table beneath the cage. Actually, electric dice are loaded in such a way that, when the magnet is on, they bring up either one of two opposite sides. The three chuck dice are all loaded alike and, when the juice is on, either a pair or three of a kind must appear. If the open sides are the six and ace, the dice will show three sixes, three aces, a pair of sixes, and an ace or a pair of aces and a six. The tipoff on the electric cage is the fact that the distance between the floor of the cage and the table in which the magnet is concealed is not as great as on a fair cage.

Hazard

There used to be two games of Hazard, the 700-year-old English Hazard, played with two dice from which Craps evolved; and a three-dice Hazard played with a layout and called Grand Hazard. Writers of game books have long confused them; even today they think that Grand Hazard is Chuck-A-Luck.

English Hazard

This game for two or more players became a mania in London's swank gaming establishments in the seventeenth and eighteenth centuries. In English Hazard, two dice are thrown from a cup by one of the players known as the *caster*. To start the game or hand, the caster places his bet in a marked circle in the center of the table. If any other player chooses to lay some money with the caster, he does likewise. If the caster agrees to this bet, he knocks the box or cup upon the table at the player's money with whom he intends to bet or mentions at whose money he is throwing against. After all bets have been covered, the caster throws the two dice from the cup to determine the *main point*. This has to be a 5, 6, 7, 8, or a 9; otherwise, it is *no main* and he throws again until one of the main points comes up. This done, he must throw the two dice until he throws a 4, 5, 6, 7, 8, 9, or 10, called a *chance point*. Then he continues to throw the two dice until he either duplicates the chance point thereby winning the bet, or throws the main point by which he loses the bet. When the caster throws to determine the chance point, he loses his bet immediately if he throws an *out;* a throw of 12 is out if the main point is 9, 8, 6, or 5. A throw of 2 or 3, known as *crabs,* is out regardless of the main point. There are winning throws for the caster, known as *nicks,* when he is throwing for the chance point. If he duplicates the main point (i.e., if the main is 6, and he throws a 6), he makes a nick and wins the bet. He also wins a nick, by throwing a 12 when the main point is a 6 or an 8. If he throws an 11, when the main point is a 7, he also scores a nick.

Grand Hazard

Today, in the United States, Craps has superseded the two-dice English Hazard. But the three-dice Grand Hazard is still played in bazaars and carnivals. The layout shown here and three dice are employed. The players place their money on the various spaces of the layout and the banker, behind the layout, drops the three dice through a Hazard chute which sometimes contains a series of inclined planes called steps down which the dice roll. Or they are thrown from a Hazard cup.

The game is one of the fastest for the players and one of the most profitable for the bank, because all bets are decided every time the three dice are thrown.

PERCENTAGE IN FAVOR OF THE BANK ON ALL BETS AT GRAND HAZARD

Bets	Correct Odds	When Bank Pays	The Percentage Is	When Bank Pays	The Percentage Is
Chuck numbers					
Singles		Even money	7⁴⁷⁄₅₄		
Doubles	2 to 1		7⁴⁷⁄₅₄		
Triples	3 to 1		7⁴⁷⁄₅₄		

Bets	Correct Odds	When Bank Pays	The Percentage Is	When Bank Pays	The Percentage Is
High / Low		Even money	$2\frac{7}{8}$		
Odd / Even		Even money	$2\frac{7}{8}$		
Raffle	215 to 1	180 for 1	$16\frac{2}{3}$		
Any raffle	35 to 1	30 for 1	$16\frac{2}{3}$		
4 / 17	71 to 1	60 for 1	$16\frac{2}{3}$	60 to 1	$15\frac{5}{18}$
5 / 16	35 to 1	30 for 1	$16\frac{2}{3}$	30 to 1	$13\frac{5}{9}$
6 / 15	$20\frac{5}{8}$ to 1	18 for 1	$16\frac{2}{3}$	18 to 1	$12\frac{1}{27}$
7 / 14	$13\frac{5}{8}$ to 1	12 for 1	$16\frac{2}{3}$	12 to 1	$9\frac{13}{19}$
8 / 13	$9\frac{6}{7}$ to 1	8 for 1	$22\frac{2}{3}$	8 to 1	$12\frac{1}{2}$
9 / 12	$7\frac{16}{25}$ to 1	6 for 1	$30\frac{5}{8}$	6 to 1	$18\frac{53}{64}$
10 / 11	7 to 1	6 for 1	25	6 to 1	$12\frac{1}{2}$

Note: The word *Raffle* as shown on the Grand Hazard and the chart simply means three-of-a-kind.

Crown and Anchor

This fast banking game, very popular among the British and Australians, is now being played by many Americans. Three dice are used, each of which carries six symbols: crown, anchor, heart, spade, diamond and club. A layout carries the same symbols.

The players place their bets on the symbols on the layout and the banker throws the three dice from a cup. The payoff is even money on singles, 2 to 1 on pairs, and 3 to 1 on three of a kind. This shows that the game is actually Chuck-A-Luck in disguise, and the advantage for the bank is the same 7 47/54 percentage as in Chuck.

Barbooth or Barbudi

This two-dice game of Greek origin is also

The Grand Hazard layout.

called Even-Up Craps. It is much played in the United States, chiefly by persons of Greek and Jewish ancestry; it is usually played in illegal gambling houses for high stakes. Unlike Craps, the shooter does not specify the amount of his wager; the player on his right, called the *fader,* bets any amount up to the maximum limit that the shooter will not win. The other players may make side bets on whether the shooter or the fader will win. The game provides no mathematical advantage for either the shooter or fader and is known as a dead even game. A house employee known as a *cutter* takes a charge of 2.5 percent of the amount of each winning bet. A bookmaker or banker is usually available to accept side bets for a charge of 5 percent, which is divided equally among the bookmaker and house cutter.

As many can play as can fit around a poker-sized table. Two small peewee (.375-inch) dice and two dice cups are used. The shooter and fader, beginning with the shooter, alternate throwing the dice until a decision has been achieved. If a shooter or fader throws 3–3, 5–5, 6–6, or 6–5, he wins. If he throws 1–2, 1–1, 2–2, or 4–4, he loses. All other throws are meaningless. If the shooter loses with a throw of 1–1, 2–2, or 4–4, or if the fader wins with a throw of 3–3, 5–5, or 6–6, then the dice pass to the fader who becomes the next shooter. If the shooter loses with a throw of 1–2 or the fader wins with a throw of 6–5, the shooter retains the dice.

Four-Five-Six or Three Dice Game

This is a popular gambling-house game in the Northwestern United States, in Western Canada, and in Alaska. Three dice and a dice cup are used. Each player puts the amount he desires to wager down in front of him and the operator, the banker, covers the bets and plays against each player in turn. The banker starts the game by throwing the dice from the cup once. If he throws any three of a kind (such as 1–1–1) or any pair plus 6 (such as 1–1–6) or 4–5–6, he wins all bets. If he throws 1–2–3 or any pair plus 1 (such as 2–2–1), he loses all bets. When any pair is thrown and the third die is a 2, 3, 4, or 5 (such as 1–1–2), the number on the third die becomes the shooter's point. All combinations except the ones stated are meaningless and, if they come up, the banker throws again. If the banker throws a point number, each other

player (in turn, to the banker's left) throws the dice to determine the outcome against the banker. If the player fails to score a winning or losing decision and throws a point, then the banker's point or the player's point, whichever is the highest, wins. A tie is a standoff or no decision. When a player does not get a pair and does not throw either 4–5–6 or 1–2–3, the roll is meaningless, and he must continue throwing the dice until he wins, loses, or ties. The banker's advantage lies in the fact that there are more winning than losing combinations and he has the first chance to throw them; the bank's advantage is 2 38/81 percent.

Indian Dice

One of the most popular bar and counter games in the United States is Indian Dice. Any number can play and five dice are used. The players throw one or more dice to determine the order of play. High man plays first, next highest second, and so on. Sixes are high, deuces are low, and aces are wild. That is, aces can be counted as any number desired. The first player may take as many as three throws but may stand pat after the first or second if he so desires. Following players may not take more throws than the first player.

After the first throw, the player may put aside any of the five dice and place the others in the cup for his second throw, or he may rethrow all five. He repeats this process of selection after the second throw, and may throw any or all of the five dice on the third time, including any of those which he set aside on his first throws. The object is to secure high poker hands which rank in the following order: five of a kind, four of a kind, full house, three of a kind, two pair, one pair. No pair and straights do not count. Whatever the dice show after the last throw is the final value of the hand. *Example:* The first player throws two fives and the other dice show two, three, and four. Unless he wants to throw all five again in the hope that he will throw something better than a pair, he places the two fives to one side and throws the remaining three dice in an attempt to better his hand similar to the draw in Poker. If he throws ace, three, four this time, and if the ace is wild, he places it with the two fives and has three of a kind. He then throws the last two dice in an attempt to get another five or a pair, which will give him a full house.

Each round is called a *leg*. If it is a two-hand game, the player winning two out of three legs wins the game. When there are more players, they are all entered in two legs. The lowest man in the first leg plays a two-hand game with the lowest man in the second leg and the loser pays the check. If two players tie for low man in any leg, they play it off in the same way. When played as a betting game for stakes, the high man in the first leg plays a two-hand game with the high man of the second leg. When played for drinks, low men play off, loser paying the check. If two or more men in any leg tie, they also play it off. The game is an even-up proposition, each player having an equal chance.

Counter Klondike

Five dice are used and are dropped through a chute that contains a series of inclined planes which trip the dice. The banker throws first and then each player throws in turn, trying to beat the banker's original throw. The bank takes all ties. The scoring is similar to Indian Dice: The combinations or hands made, in descending order of value, are: five of a kind, four of a kind, full house, three of a kind, two pairs, one pair. No pair and straights (numbers in sequence) have no value. The dice that do not help make one of these combinations do not count; for example, a pair of deuces with a six have the same value as a pair of deuces with any other number. The ace is high, the deuce is low.

Casino Klondike

This is similar to the counter game except that two dice cups and two sets of five dice each are used, together with a layout which offers the player three different types of bets: *Win, Lose,* and *To Beat Two Aces.* A bet on a Win space wins for the player if he beats the banker's throw; a bet on a Lose space wins if he scores less than the banker's throw; a bet on the space marked To Beat Two Aces wins if then he throws two pair or more.

The banker throws first on the Klondike space and lets his dice remain there. The player on his left throws next, using the second set of five dice, and the others follow in rotation from left to right. The bank pays even money on all bets and collects or pays off on each wager after each player's turn. The bank takes all ties.

On the win and lose bets, the bank's advantage obviously lies in the ties and it works out to 5.195 percent. On the to beat two aces bet, the percentage is twice as strong, 11.111 percent. The percentage makes cheating unnecessary and, in most casinos, the game is not gaffed. But fly-by-night operators sometimes make use of electric dice so that the dealer can throw high at will. For information on electric dice, see Chuck-A-Luck, page 474.

High Dice

This very popular and very fast counter game is also called Beat the Bank and Two Dice Klondike. It is also a very deceptive game because it looks as though it should be easy to beat, but is not.

A pair of dice are thrown from a cup. Banker and player each throw once, the banker first. The player must throw a higher number than the banker to win. The banker takes all ties.

The game is an even-up proposition except for those ties which constitute the house percentage. To calculate this, we simply need

The Klondike layout.

to find out how many ties the law of averages says can be expected to be thrown in the long run. The banker stands to throw the number 2 (with two aces) once out of the 36 throws. The player's chance of throwing two aces in succession is 1/36 times 1/36, or 1/1,296. A tie with two aces will be thrown once out of every 1,296 times in the long run. Since 3 can be thrown in two ways (1–2 and 2–1), the banker will throw it 2/36 of the time and the player will do the same. We multiply 2/36 by 2/36 and get 4/1,296, which means that a tie of 3 will be thrown four times in 1,296 throws. If we make this same calculation with each number from 2 through 12, we find that a player can expect to throw 146 ties out of 1,296 times; this gives a bank's advantage of 11.265 percent, which amounts to 56 cents on a $5 wager. If the banker pays the player when the latter throws two aces, there are 144 ties and the bank's percentage is reduced to 11.111 percent.

Under and Over 7

This is an old-time game that is still going strong. It gets a steady play because it is simple and easy to learn. Also, it is so deceptive in appearance that the average player looks at it, scratches his head, and can't understand why the operator of the game doesn't go broke in short order. The game is popular with the operators because they know that their chance of losing is nil, that it is one of the biggest sucker games ever to come down the pike, and that the percentage for

the house, although the player can't see it, is as strong as they come.

The game is usually operated by hustlers. Two dice, a dice cup, and the layout shown below are used, the design sometimes being simply drawn on the pavement with chalk or scratched on the ground. The player puts his money on any one of the three spaces and throws the dice. If he bets on *Under 7* and throws any of the numbers under seven, the bank pays him off at even money. The same is true of the *Over 7* space. If he puts his money on the *7* space, he is paid off at 5 for 1. No matter where you place your money, the bank's advantage is 16 2/3 percent.

Twenty-Six

In the 1950's this was a favorite counter game found in many stores and taverns throughout Midwestern United States. Customers would play for a fee, such as 25 cents, to win checks or tokens that could be cashed for drinks, cigarettes, or other merchandise. Federal and State antigambling crusades during the late fifties eliminated most of these games. However, many still are doing business.

Ten dice and a cup are used. The player selects any number from 1 through 6 as his point. He throws the ten dice 13 times and totals the number of times he has thrown his point number. The object is to throw 26 or more point numbers.

Most Twenty-Six operators use a score sheet giving specific rules and payoffs. Generally

Layout for Beat-the-Dealer.

these payoffs are: 4 to 1 if the player scores from 26 points to 32; 8 to 1 for a score of 33 or more; 4 to 1 for a score of 11 or less, and 2 to 1 for a score of exactly 13. All other counts lose. Basically, a player wins one game in slightly more than five games (5.04 games) played; this means a house advantage of 19.9 percent.

A common cheating technique used by dealers, to reduce the player's chance for a high score, is to hold out one of the dice now and then so that the players only use nine dice. Another cheating method, called "pushing the pencil," is worked by having the dealer "short" a player on the count by putting down fewer points on the score sheet.

Buck Dice

Any number can play and three dice are used. Each player throws the dice to determine the order of play; the player making highest score goes first, next highest second, and so on. The low man then throws one die and the number thrown becomes the point number. The high man begins throwing all three dice, and scores one point for each point number thrown. He continues to throw as long as he throws point numbers, which are added as he goes along. When he fails to throw a point number on any throw, the dice pass to the next player.

The object is to score exactly 15 points, called *buck* or game; each player, as he reaches this score, drops out of the game until only one player remains who is the loser and who foots the bill. If a player whose number is close to 15, on his next throw, reaches a total above 15, the throw does not count and he must throw again. Any three of a kind (not point numbers) is a *little buck* and counts 5 points. When the point number appears on all three dice, it's *big buck* or *the general*, which counts 15 points and eliminates the player no matter what score he has previously made.

In one popular variation, the additional rule is added that, when the shooter has 13 point numbers to his credit and 2 to go, only two dice are thrown; and when he has scored 14 and has only 1 to go, only one die is thrown.

The player shooting first has a slight advantage.

Hooligan

This is a popular bar game, played for drinks with low man paying, or played as a betting game. Any number may play and five dice are used with a cup. Score is kept on a sheet ruled into boxes that bear the numbers 1 through 6 and the letter *H* for *hooligan*. A hooligan is a straight, a throw of 1–2–3–4–5 or 2–3–4–5–6. Each player throws dice to determine order of play, high man going first, next highest second, and so on.

Each player takes three throws per turn, called a *frame*. After the first throw, he may select any number as his point. He then puts all dice bearing this point number to one side and throws the remaining dice a second time. If one or more point numbers appear on this throw, those dice are also put aside and a third throw is made with any dice that remain. If, after the first or second throws the player has thrown five point numbers, on his next throw he uses all five dice again. After the third throw, the point number is multiplied by the number of points thrown to get the score for that frame. If the player has thrown five threes, his score is 15, if seven sixes, his score is 42, etc.

If in coming out for any number (that is, on the first roll) a hooligan is thrown, the player is credited with 20 points for hooligan. If, however, a player has tried for all of the points with the exception of hooligan, he must then try for hooligan on the last frame and is allowed three throws. The player is not required to select a point number after the first throw; but he may, if he likes, pick up all five dice and throw again for a point; and he may do the same after the second throw.

On each succeeding turn, the player must shoot for a different point number than any played previously. Thus, at the end of seven turns, which constitutes a game, he will have shot for each of the point numbers: 1, 2, 3, 4, 5, 6, and hooligan. The scores for each frame are added and the player having the highest total score wins; or, when played for drinks, the low man or sometimes the two lowest men pay. *Example:* If the first player throws three deuces and a pair of threes, he may select either the deuce or the three as his point; or, if he likes, he may pick up all five dice and throw again, selecting his point from among the numbers thrown on his second throw, in which case none of the numbers can be scored which appeared on the first throw.

When three deuces and a pair of threes are thrown, the logical choice is to select the deuce as the point, place the three dice that show deuce to one side, and throw the remaining two dice for a second throw. If he should now throw two deuces for a total of 5, the player then throws all five dice for the third throw. If he should throw three deuces on this last throw he has made a total score of eight deuces or 16 points. If on the second throw one deuce is thrown, that die is placed to one side and the remaining die is thrown for the third and last throw. If a deuce is thrown for a third time, the player scores 10; if not, the player has made four deuces altogether for a score of 8 for that frame. On his next turn the deuce is dead and he must shoot for some other point.

Hooligan is also played as a banking game in which the player does not shoot against an opponent, but tries to reach as high a total as possible. The player usually pays a quarter to play and the operator pays off various amounts (usually in trade rather than cash) for high scores. Sometimes a score between 84 and 89 inclusive will get the player $1, a score between 90 and 93 is paid off at $2, and so on; but the payoff varies with different operators and in different places.

It is impossible to figure an exact house percentage on this game because different operators pay off differently, and because the players have a choice as to the order in which they select their points and the way they play them. The number of throws is also a variable factor. A perfect score is 335.

Poker Dice

This game is quite similar to Indian Dice (see page 476). It is usually played with five poker dice whose sides bear the playing card denominations: ace, king, queen, jack, ten, and nine. Of course, the usual spotted dice are sometimes used, ace being high, followed by 6, 5, 4, 3, and 2 in that order. The ace is also sometimes played wild. Any number can play and each player throws one die to determine the order of play, highest man going first, next highest second, and so on.

The object is to throw the highest poker hand in either one or two throws as desired. After the first throw, the player may stand pat or may draw (as in Draw Poker) by

throwing one, two, or three of the dice again. The object is to secure high poker hands which rank as follows: five of a kind, four of a kind, full house, straight (any five cards or numbers in numerical sequence), three of a kind, two pair, one pair. The extra die or dice not included in one of the above hands do not have any value. If a player throws four jacks for instance, the fifth die does not help to decide the winner in case of ties. Tying players throw off. In the two-hand game the best three hands out of five win.

Chicago or Rotation

This dice game probably derives from the similar pool game called Chicago. Any number can play, two dice are used, and any player may go first. On the first round each player throws once and tries to make a 2. If successful, he scores 2 points, if not he scores nothing. On the second round each player shoots for a 3 which, if made, scores 3 points. All of the eleven number combinations possible with two dice (2, 3, 4, 5, 6, 7, 8, 9, 10, 11, and 12) are played for in this manner, beginning with the lowest. The player having the highest total score after all numbers have been shot for is declared the winner.

Baseball

Baseball fans go for this one. Baseball is a two-person game with two dice and several counters to represent men. A diagram representing a baseball diamond and a nine-inning box score chart are drawn. Each player throws once, and high man has the choice of throwing first or second. The player up at bat (throwing the dice) throws until he has three outs counted against him, after which the number of runs he has made in that inning is entered on the box score and his opponent throws. The player with the highest number of runs at the end of nine innings is the winner.

Scoring. The numbers 3, 4, 5, 6, 7, or 8 are strikeouts or putouts except that when either 4 or 8 are thrown the hard way (with 2–2 or 4–4)), they are walks and put a man on first base. When 6 is thrown the hard way (3–3), it is a double play and two outs are scored against the shooter.

Number 9 is a one-base hit, called a single.

Number 10 is a two-base hit, called a double.

Number 11 is a three-base hit, called a triple.

Number 2 and number 12 are home runs.

If a runner is on first when a walk is scored, he advances to second base. A single advances all runners one base; a double, two bases, a triple, three bases; a home run brings all players in. A run is scored for each player crossing home plate.

Pig

Any number of players may play and one die is used. Each player throws to decide the order of play, low man going first, next highest second, and so on. The first player throws the die as many times as he desires, adding the numbers on the upper face of the die each time. If he throws an ace it cancels out whatever score he has made on that turn and he must pass the die to the next player. He may stop throwing and pass the die to the next player at any time, and if he does so before throwing an ace, he is credited with the sum of the numbers he has thrown on that turn.

As usually played, the player who first scores 100 points is the winner. Since this gives the player who throws first an advantage because, all else being equal, he has the best chance of reaching 100 first, the rule is sometimes made that each player must be allowed an equal number of turns. When a player reaches 100, those players who have not yet had a turn in that round are allowed to throw, and if any of them also go over 100, the highest man is declared the winner. The game is still not an even-up proposition because now the last player has the advantage, since he knows what the previous scores have been made and, unless he throws an ace, he can continue shooting until he makes a higher score and wins.

If all players are to have an equal chance, the game should be played in sets with as many games per set as there are players, and with the first throw of each game rotating in turn around the circle of players. In the first method of scoring, this will allow each player to go first once in each set; in the second scoring method, this will allow each player to go last once in each set.

Thirty-Six

Any number can play and one die is used. Each player puts a stake in the center forming a pool and each one throws the die to determine order of play, low man going first, next highest next, and so on. The players throw the die in turn and continue to throw, adding each number thrown to the previous one and calling out the totals. The object is to reach 36 or approach it as closely as possible without passing it. Players passing 36 are busted.

The player who comes closest to 36 wins. Ties divide the pool. Most players throw again at 32 or less; stop at 33 or more.

Aces

This game is also called Aces to the Center, Deuces to the Left, and Fives to the Right. This is one of the most fascinating of all dice games. It is very popular in the Far East, particularly the Philippines.

Any number can play, and each player must have a dice cup and five dice. Each player throws five dice; the player throwing the highest poker hand (ace is high and 6, 5, 4, 3, and 2 represent king, queen, jack, ten, and nine, respectively) takes any seat and is the first shooter; the player throwing the second highest hand sits on his left, and shoots second; and so on. Tying players shoot again.

The first shooter begins by throwing five dice. Each thrown die that shows an ace is placed in the center of the playing surface; all deuces are passed to the player on his left; all dice showing fives to the player on his right. The player continues to throw until he either fails to throw an ace, two, or five, or until he has no more dice left. It then becomes the turn of the next player on his left who has dice to throw. Players who have no dice left remain in the game because other dice may pass to them from the other players at any time. When all but one die have been placed in the center, the player throwing the last ace with the last die is declared the loser. When played for drinks, the loser pays the check. When played for a wager, the player throwing the last ace is declared the winner and takes the pot.

In this game, like Barbudi, it is almost impossible to cheat. Percentage dice such as shapes and loads would give the cheater no advantage because the dice pass from one player to another. On his own throw with the last die, a cheater might switch in a misspotted die that lacked an ace so that he could not throw an ace and lose. But, since the players on the left and right usually grab the die when a 2 or 5 is thrown, it would be almost impossible to switch it out again.

Help Your Neighbor

Again becoming popular, this is one of the oldest dice games in existence. Three dice and a cup are used. Each player throws three dice and the player who makes high score shoots first, the player with the next highest score sits at his left and shoots second, and so on. Tying players shoot again.

No more than six players can play. Each player has his own number, the first shooter being number 1, the second number 2, and so on. If there are only three players the first shooter takes the numbers 1 and 2, the second shooter has 3 and 4, and the third shooter takes 5 and 6. If there are only two players, the first takes the numbers 1, 2, and 3, and the second has 4, 5, and 6. If there are five players the 6 is dead; if there are four players, the 5 and 6 are dead. Each player gets one throw of the three dice; turn of play rotates clockwise.

Counters or chips (usually ten to each player) are used. Each player at his turn throws the three dice and each player whose number (or numbers) appears must place one counter in the center for each such number. For example, if there are six players and the first shooter throws a 3 and two 5's, the third player places one counter in the center and the fifth player puts out two counters. The player who gets rid of all his counters first is declared the winner and takes the pot. The player on the first shooter's left begins the following game.

Liar or Doubting Dice

Any number can play. Five dice are used with a dice cup. Each player throws five dice and the player throwing the highest poker hand (ace is high, and 6, 5, 4, 3, and 2 represent king, queen, jack, ten, and nine, respectively) takes any seat and is the first shooter; the player throwing the second highest hand sits at his left and shoots second; and so on. Tying players shoot again.

At the beginning of play, each player places before himself three betting units. The first shooter shakes the dice, turns the cup upside down, and lifts it, shielding the dice from view with his hand. He then announces the value of his hand but need not state the

truth. The player on his left must either accept the statement or call him a liar.

If the first shooter's statement is doubted and if he has at least as good a hand as he called, the doubter puts one betting unit into the pot. If the shooter has lied about his hand, he must pay one unit to the doubter and put one unit into the pot. It then becomes the doubter's turn to throw, and he plays against the player on his left; and so on, around the table.

If the first shooter's statement is accepted as true by the player at his left, it becomes the latter's turn to throw. He may use all the dice originally thrown or leave as many of them as he cares to and throw the others. As the first shooter did, he covers the dice he throws and must then announce that the five dice have a value that beats the hand which the first shooter announced and which was accepted. The first shooter then either accepts or doubts this statement, and this process continues until one of the two players has doubted a hand which the other player has actually thrown or bettered. The doubter then puts one of his units into the pot.

When a player has placed all three of his betting units into the pot, he drops out of the game and the other players continue until only one player is left who still retains one or more of his original three units. This player is declared the winner and takes the pot.

The player on the left of the first shooter begins the next game.

Martinetti

Any number can play this game, which is also called Ohio and Centennial. Three dice, a cup, individual markers for each player (usually coins of different denominations), and a layout numbered from 1 to 12, as shown below, are used. Each player throws the three dice and the player making high score shoots first. The player making second highest score sits on his left and shoots second, and so on. Tying players shoot again.

The first shooter then throws the three dice. If an ace is thrown, he places his marker on space number 1 on the layout. If he fails

| 1 | 2 | 3 | 4 | 5 | 6 | 7 | 8 | 9 | 10 | 11 | 12 |

Layout for Martinetti.

to throw an ace, the dice pass to the player on his left. If he throws an ace, he may also use a deuce on the same throw, and if he throws both an ace and deuce, he may use a three-spot and advance his marker to the second and third layout spaces accordingly. He may also use any two or three numbers thrown and add them together to form the number needed. *Example:* The numbers in a throw of 1–3–6 can be combined in various ways to produce the additional numbers 4, 7, 9, and 10.

Each player continues throwing as long as he continues to throw numbers he can use. If a player throws a total which he needs, but which he overlooks, any opponent who can use that number may, as soon as the shooter has passed the cup, call the number and make use of it by advancing his marker. If two players call the number at the same time, the one who is first on the shooter's left may use the number.

The player whose marker first travels from 1 to 12 and back from 12 to 1 again is declared the winner.

Everest

This game is played in the same manner as Martinetti, except for the following:

1. The numbers can be counted in any order desired and need not be consecutive.

2. Each die can be counted in only one combination on any throw.

3. Each player must have a double chart, showing the numbers from one through twelve in one column, and from twelve back to one in another; this is necessary because the player will be scoring in both series of numbers at the same time. *Example:* If a player throws 2–3–6 he can count a 2, a 3, and a 6; or, he can count 5 and 6, or 2 and 9, or 3 and 8, or 11. If the number or numbers on the dice are unusable, they may be disregarded. Remember that a player can count at any time any of the 24 numbers; thus a throw of 1–1–2 could give credit for the 1 and the 2 in the ascending series, and the 1 in the descending series.

4. The first player who scores all 24 numbers is the winner.

Par

This is one of the most interesting of dice games, played mostly in the Middle West.

Any number can play, but six or seven make the best game. Five dice and a cup are used.

Each player throws five dice and the player throwing the highest poker hand (ace is high and 6, 5, 4, 3, and 2 represent the king, queen, jack, ten, and nine, respectively) takes any seat and is the first shooter; the player throwing the second highest hand sits on his left and shoots second; and so on. Tying players shoot again.

The first shooter throws all five dice on his first throw. He may then use as many of the dice as he likes, but not more than four, and throw again. He may then continue throwing but must always, after the second throw, leave one additional die on the table each time. Or he may discontinue throwing on any throw.

The object of the game is to make the dice total 24 or more. If, after rolling the last die, the number is less than 24, the player must pay the betting unit times the difference between his score and 24 to each of the other players. *Example:* If his total is 20, he would pay each player four times the unit bet. If he gets an even 24, the player neither gains nor loses and the dice pass to the next player on his left. If he exceeds 24, the amount in excess of 24 becomes his point. *Example:* If the total is 27, three is his point. The player then throws all five dice one time and, for each three that he throws, he collects three times the unit bet from each of the other players.

Ship, Captain, Mate, and Crew

Also called Mariner, Battleship, Destroyer, and Seaman. Any number can play and five dice thrown from a cup are used. Each player throws a single die to determine the order of play, highest man going first, second highest second, and so on. Tying players throw again. The deal rotates to the left.

Each player in turn is allowed three throws and first tries to get a 6, 5, and 4 in that order; the 6 represents the ship, the 5 is the captain, and the 4 is the mate. If a 6 and 5 appear on the first throw the player puts those dice aside and rolls the remaining three dice trying to get a 4. If a 6 and 4 appear on the first roll, the 4 cannot be used until a 5 has been made and the player sets aside the 6 only and throws four dice on his next throw.

When the player has succeeded in getting a 6, 5, and 4 in that order, the points on the remaining two dice constitute his score, called the crew. If he has not used all of his three throws he may, if he likes, use any remaining throws of the two dice in an attempt to make them show a higher total. The player who has made ship, captain, and mate and whose two remaining dice show the highest score is the winner and takes the pot into which each player has contributed equal stakes. If the two high players tie, it is considered a tie for everyone and another round is thrown. The player to the left of the first shooter in the first round becomes the first shooter in the second round.

General

Puerto Rico's most popular dice game, played in bars, clubs, and homes throughout the island, is Generala or, in English, General. In bars it is usually played for drinks, low man paying; but I have also seen thousands of dollars change hands at a single General game session.

Any number may play, singly or in partnership. Five dice are used with a dice cup. Score is kept on a sheet ruled into boxes. The players' names are entered across the top, and down the left hand vertical column are the numbers 1, 2, 3, 4, 5, and 6 followed by the poker hands: straight, full house, four of a kind, and small general (five of a kind), as shown on page 485. The big general listing is not necessary.

Value of Poker Hands and Point Numbers

Five of a kind, known as the *big general* when made on the first throw, automatically wins the game, regardless of the score. Five of a kind made on the second or third throw is known as the *small general* and is valued at 60 points.

Four of a kind, made on the first throw, is valued at 45 points; on the second or third throw, 30 points.

A *full house,* made on the first throw, is valued at 35 points; on the second or third throw, 30 points.

A *straight* (1, 2, 3, 4, 5, or 2, 3, 4, 5, 6), made on the first throw, is valued at 25 points; on the second or third throw, 20 points. Aces (1) may be used as "wild" in making a straight, but they can only be used to equal a 2 or 6. They cannot be used to equal a 3, 4, or 5 to make a straight. This is the only time during the play of the game that aces may be wild.

The *point numbers* (1, 2, 3, 4, 5, and 6) are valued at their total spot value. *Examples:* Three sixes are 18 points; two fives are 10 points; four aces are 4 points; and so on.

The Play of the Game. Each player throws the five dice to determine the order of play, holder of lowest-valued hand going first, next lowest second, and so on. In determining partners, the two lowest and two highest hands are partners. The dice and cup pass to the left, clockwise. Each player may take either one, two, or three throws per turn, called a frame. A complete game consists of ten frames, unless some player throws a general.

First Throw of the Dice. The player shakes the five dice inside the cup and throws them onto the bar or table. If he throws a pat poker hand, such as four of a kind, full house, or straight, he enters his score on the sheet. If, however, he throws any other hand such as a pair, two pair, and so on, he has the following option: He may put aside one, two, three, or four dice and throw the leftovers; or, he may throw all five dice again. *Example:* If the player has thrown a total of two or three sixes, he may decide to hold the sixes and try to better the hand by throwing the remaining dice. This is similar to holding certain cards and drawing to improve the hand in Draw Poker.

Second Throw of the Dice. The same rules apply as in the first throw, except that a general becomes a small general and the value of the poker hands diminish.

Third Throw of the Dice. After the third throw, if a small general, four of a kind, full house, or straight has not been made, the player may select any number for his scoring point number. *Example:* His hand is made up of three aces, a five, and a six. Since the best score he can make with the ace (1) is 5 points, it is to his advantage to name the aces as his point and to enter 3 points alongside number 1 on the sheet. Or, if his hand shows a pair of twos, a pair of fours and a five, his best bet is to name the twos as his point number and score 2 + 2 = 4. He would then enter 4 points on the sheet in the 2 line. However, after a score has once been entered on the sheet, the player cannot shoot for that hand or point number again. On each succeeding turn of play, the player has one less hand or point number to shoot for so that, at the end of the game, the player will have shot and entered a score for each of the ten frames.

The following is a typical final score of General:

	A	B	C	D
1	0	0	4	3
2	4	6	6	4
3	9	9	6	6
4	8	8	12	12
5	20	10	15	20
6	12	0	18	18
Straight	25	25	20	25
Full house	35	30	30	30
Four of a kind	40	40	45	40
Small general	00	00	00	60
Total	153	128	156	218

Note: Player D with a total of 218 points is the winner of the game. If the game is played, for example, at 1 cent a point, player C owes D 62 cents (the difference between his final count of 156 and D's 218). Player B owes D 90 cents and Player A owes D 65 cents.

Yacht

Yacht is often called an English version of General. Its plan is similar. Five dice are thrown from a cup, each player in rotation may throw the dice three times in each round, and there are 12 rounds in all. After each round, a player may leave standing such dice as satisfy him and throw the rest. Various dice combinations are assigned scoring values: yacht (five of a kind) scores 50; big straight (2, 3, 4, 5, 6) scores 30; little straight (1, 2, 3, 4, 5) scores 30. Also, full house (three of one kind and two of another), four of a kind, and choice (any five dice) each scores the total number spots showing on the five dice thrown in that turn. Sixes scores as many times six as there as sixes among the five dice. Likewise the fives, fours, threes, twos, and aces. At the end of each turn, the player must designate his five dice to count in one of the 12 categories shown on the scorepad.

Hand	Maximum	A	B	C	D
Yacht	50				
Big straight	30				
Little straight	30				
Four of a kind	29				
Full house	28				
Choice	30				
Sixes	30				
Fives	25				
Fours	20				
Threes	15				
Deuces	10				
Aces	5				

In each turn a player must select a category not previously selected; therefore at the end of the game (12 rounds) he will have selected each category once. He may select a category even though it will score zero for that round. At the end of the 12 rounds the score is added and highest score wins.

Crag

This game is similar to Yacht, except that only three dice are used and in each turn a player may throw the dice only twice (or may stand on his first throw). Also there are 13 categories (rather than 12) in this game: *Crag* is a pair plus a third die that makes the total of the spots on all three dice, 13; this counts 50. *Thirteen* consists of any three dice whose spots total 13, and counts 26. Three-of-a-kind counts 25. *High straight* (4, 5, 6), *low straight* (1, 2, 3,), *even straight* (2, 4, 6) and *odd straight* (1, 3, 5) count 20 each. Sixes, fives, fours, threes, twos, and aces are counted in the same manner as in Yacht. Also a special score sheet is ruled off, as in Yacht.

Double Cameroon

This is another version of Yacht, but in this game ten dice are used. There is also another important difference: After the player's third throw in each turn, he must divide his ten dice into two groups of five and select a category for each. There are ten categories, thus each player has five turns in all. The categories are as follows: five of a kind, counts 50; *large cameroon* (2, 3, 4, 5, 6), counts 30; *little cameroon* (1, 2, 3, 4, 5), counts 21; full house, sixes, fives, fours, threes, twos, and aces each count the total number of spots on the five dice selected that match that category. A special score sheet is used, as in Yacht.

Going to Boston

This game, played with three dice, is also known as Yankee Grab and Newmarket. It can be played with any number of players, each of whom contributes equally to the pot and each of whom has three throws with the dice. Each player plays as follows:

On the first throw, the highest die must be set aside, and the two others retained for another roll. On the second roll, the higher die is kept and the lower is used for last roll. When two dice are equal, one must be used for the last roll. After the third throw, the player's total is the sum of the three dice.

Multiplication

This game is played in the same manner as Going to Boston, except that the last die thrown is the multiple of the sum of the two former ones. That is, if a 3 and 4 of the first two throws have been put aside, and the last thrown die is a 6, the player's total score is 6 times the sum of 3 and 4, or 42.

Hearts Due

In its original form, this game is played with six special dice, each with the letters H E A R T S on its respective faces. However, six regular dice may be used, 1 being H; 2, E; 3, A; 4, R; 5, T; and 6, S. The players take turns in making one roll with all six dice and score as follows:

H (1)	5
H–E (1–2)	10
H–E–A (1–2–3)	15
H–E–A–R (1–2–3–4)	20
H–E–A–R–T (1–2–3–4–5)	25
H–E–A–R–T–S (1–2–3–4–5–6)	35

When doubles, triples, etc., are thrown, only one of the letters or numbers counts. The exception to this is when three H's (1's) are rolled; then the entire score of the play is canceled and the player goes back to zero score.

SCARNEY DICE®

Several years ago I created Scarney Dice—with which over 40 exciting different dice games can be played. While these Scarney Dice games can be played with two or more standard dice by considering the 2 and 5 spots on each die to indicate the word "dead," they are considerably more enjoyable when played with the specially created Scarney Dice. Each die of these dice is marked with 1, 3, 4, and 6 spots, plus the word *dead* repeated on two opposite sides.

While there are over 40 different games, due to limited space only the rules of play for Straight Scarney Dice, Scarney 3000, Scarney Put and Take Dice, Scarney Duplicate Jackpots, Scarney 21 Up and Down, Scarney Bingo Dice, Scarney Black Jack, Scarney Chemin De Fer, Scarney Pie-Eyed Dice and their variants are listed in this chapter. For the other Scarney Dice games, see *Scarney Dice,* an 80-page book that contains the complete rules for the more than 40 Scarney Dice games.

Straight Scarney Dice

Requirements

1. Two or more players.
2. A dice cup.
3. A set of five Scarney Dice. Each die is marked with 1, 3, 4, and 6 spots, plus the word *dead* repeated on two opposite sides.

4. A set of multicolored chips.

Seating Positions and Turn of Play. The players seat themselves at any places around the table. Where they sit for the moment is irrelevant. To determine seating position and turn of play, each player shakes the five dice in the cup and throws them onto the playing surface. The player throwing the highest five-dice number total selects any seat he wants, the player throwing the next highest number total sits to his left, and so on. Dice showing the word *dead* count nothing (zero). Once the seating has been arranged, the holder of the highest number total starts the game and is referred to as the *shooter*. From then on, each shooter's turn of play moves to the left, clockwise, from player to player.

A complete game consists of seven frames. At the completion of each game, the right to start the next game passes to the player at the immediate left of the player who won the previous game.

Scarney Dice Bonuses. When a throw is made without a *dead* die showing, the shooter scores the total point value of all the numbers plus the point value of any one of the following Scarney Dice bonuses that may have been made:

1. *Big Scarney,* which is any five of a kind including five *dead* dice made on any one throw of any frame, wins the game and pot regardless of the scores.

2. *Any four of a kind* (numbers only), made on any one throw, receives a bonus of 40 points.

3. *Any Full House,* which is three of a kind and a pair (numbers only), made on any one throw, receives a bonus of 30 points.

4. *Little Scarney,* which is four *dead* dice, made on any one throw, receives a little Scarney bonus of 25 points. The four *dead* dice are put aside and are out of play.

5. *Any three of a kind* (numbers only), made on any one throw, receives a bonus of 20 points.

6. Any two pairs (numbers only), made on any one throw, receives a bonus of 10 points.

Bonus hands, which include one or two *dead* dice, do not count.

The Ante. Each player before the game gets started antes (puts) an agreed-upon equal number of chips into the center of the playing surface known as the *pot*. All players must ante in turn, starting with the first shooter and rotating clockwise.

The Play. The shooter places the five Scarney Dice into the cup and after a proper shake promptly throws them on the playing surface. If five *dead* dice or any five of a kind are made on any one throw, the shooter calls "Big Scarney," wins the game, and takes the pot regardless of the score. However, if one, two, or three *dead* dice (known as *craps*) are thrown, they are put aside and the remaining aces, threes, fours, and sixes (known as *live dice* or *numbers*), are put back into the cup and thrown again. In short, with the exception of big Scarney and little Scarney, every dice throw that shows one or more dead dice is a scoreless hand and the dead dice are put

aside and are out of play. The remaining numbers are put back into the dice cup and thrown again. When a throw is made without a dead die, it is referred to as a *live throw* or a *point score,* and the total points of all the thrown numbers plus any bonus that may have been made are credited to the shooter. Once a shooter has thrown a point score he may do one of these two things:

1. He may call "pass," or "stay," and enter the points on his score card as his frame score, and pass the dice and cup to the opponent on his left, or

2. He may call "hit," which means he wants to throw again to try to better his frame score. Should he make a point score on his next throw, the total of the thrown numbers plus the bonus points, if any, are added to his score for a new frame total. *Example:* The shooter on his first throw scores 17 points. He calls "hit," and throws a second time scoring 16 points plus a three of a kind bonus of 20 points for a total of 36 points. Adding these 36 points to the 17 points gives him a new frame total of 53 points. However, if the shooter throws one or more *dead* dice on his second throw, it cancels out the 17 points made on the first throw and the shooter has nothing (zero points). When the shooter has one or more live dice in play, he may *hit* and continue to throw until he *passes* and enters his scored points as his frame score. Or, he may continue to throw until he *craps out* (when all five dice are *dead*) and enters a zero as his frame score. And so it goes, to the left, clockwise, from player to player, until each player has completed seven frames and the game ends.

When a player has a single live die in play he may, if he likes, take the remaining die, put it in a cup, and call "Opposite." He then shakes and turns the cup mouth down onto the table and lifts the cup. When a player calls "Opposite," he accepts the die's *bottom* number as his point score rather than that of the top. *Example:* Opposite, when throwing a three, is four; a four is three; an ace is six; and a six is ace. A *dead* die is *dead,* be it opposite or not.

The Double-Down or Double-the-Score Option. Before the first throw of each frame and after a dead throw (scoreless hand), the shooter may double down if he cares to. The double-down option gives the shooter an opportunity to double the points, if any, of his

Scarney Dice.

next throw. Whenever a shooter elects to double down, he must ante one chip into the pot and call "Double down," before throwing the dice. If the shooter succeeds in throwing a point score, the total points thrown are doubled. When doubling down, only the point score total is doubled; Scarney Dice bonuses remain the same. *Example:* The shooter throws a point score of 15 points plus a three of a kind, 20 points bonus hand. He simply doubles the 15 points for a total of 30 points and adds the 20 points, getting a grand total of 50 points for the throw.

The above rule holds true except when the double down involves only one die; then only the numbers ace and six are doubled. The three and four are still scored at 3 and 4 points. When a player wants to double down on a single die's opposite side, he calls "Double the opposite."

Note: A player is only permitted to double down before the scoreless hand. A player is not permitted to double down when possessing a point score. To repeat, a player can only double down before the first throw of each frame or after throwing a dead or scoreless hand.

How to Score a Scarney Dice Game. After the first shooter's frame score has been entered on the score sheet, the player seated to the first shooter's left becomes the next shooter. And so it goes to the left, clockwise, from player to player until each player has shot seven frames and the game ends. Exception: When a player shoots big Scarney, this immediately ends the game regardless of the score. When a player craps out, zero (0) is entered on the score card as his frame score.

Score is kept on a score pad which allows for a single and cumulative game score. A game consists of seven frames for each player. A player with the highest score wins the game and takes the pot—except when big Scarney (any five of a kind including five *dead* dice) is made on any one throw of any frame; this automatically wins the game and takes the pot regardless of the scores. Should two or more players have identical high game scores, one or more extra frames are played by each of the high scorers until the tie is broken. The following is a sample score sheet of a Straight Scarney Dice game played by four players:

Frames	A	B	C	D
1st	10–10	33–33	9–9	0–0
2nd	12–22	6–39	52–61	26–26
3rd	9–31	6–45	18–79	45–71
4th	0–31	8–53	36–115	0–71
5th	0–31	0–53	27–142	32–103
6th	16–47	12–65	26–168	0–103
7th	0–47	32–97	0–168	0–103
Game scores	47	97	168	103

In the above game, player C, scoring 168 points, is the winner and takes the pot. The score for each player's frame is written down to the left of the dash, the cumulative score to the right. In the right-hand column the score for each frame is added to the previous total and brought down to a new total. Thus, each player always knows what the score is and how far ahead or behind he is.

Partnership Straight Scarney Dice

Partnership Scarney Dice is a game for four players, two against two, as partners. The rules for Scarney Straight Dice apply with the following exceptions and additional rules:

1. Each player throws five dice for partners; the holders of the two highest number totals (*dead* dice count nothing) are teamed up against the holders of the two lowest. If three- or four-way ties occur on the throws for partners, one or more extra throws must take place until the ties are broken. Partners seat themselves opposite each other, and the holder of the highest total number is the first shooter. From then on the turn of play moves to the left, clockwise, from player to player.

2. At the completion of a game (seven frames for each player), partners' game scores are added together and the side with the highest total score takes the pot. Winning partners divide the pot equally.

Note: Team play can be extended to six persons, three against three.

Scarney 3000®

Scarney 3000 rivals Straight Scarney Dice as a most exciting bar, club, and home dice

® Copyright © John Scarne Games, Inc. The design and name are trademarked and its contents copyrighted and no part of this game can be reproduced in any form without written permission from its owner and distributor: John Scarne Games, Inc., 4319 Meadowview Avenue, North Bergen, New Jersey 07047.

game. It is the favorite dice game of the members of the John Scarne Game Club of my hometown of Fairview, New Jersey. A game consists of an undetermined number of rounds of play, and the player who first obtains a score of 3000 points or more wins the game and receives the difference in points between his total and that of each of the losing players.

Requirements. Any number can play, each playing for himself. Five Scarney Dice, a dice cup, and pencil and paper to keep score are used to play the game.

Seating Positions and Turn of Play. They are the same as those prescribed under Straight Scarney Dice, page 486.

Point Values of the Dice. Any dice throw which contains one or two *dead* dice is a point-scoring throw and each *dead* die is valued at 50 points. A dice throw containing three, four, or five *dead* dice is a bonus hand (see Point Values of Bonus Hands). The only time the point numbers (1's, 3's, 4's, and 6's) have any value is in bonus hands. Otherwise they are known as "bust dice" and count nothing, zero points.

Point Values of Bonus Hands. Any dice throw containing three or more dice of the same number, aces, threes, fours, sixes, is considered a bonus hand when accompanied by one or two *dead* dice on the same throw, or if one or more *dead* dice appear on the next toss. Throwing a *dead* die with a bonus hand or on the next roll is known as "confirming the bonus."

Any dice throw containing three or more *dead* dice is also a bonus hand but needs no confirmation because *dead* dice are point-scoring dice.

Bonus hands are valued as shown in the table at the bottom of this page.

Rules for Bonus Hands.

1. If a dice throw contains a bonus hand plus one or two *dead* dice, the hand is confirmed and all points scored on the hand including 50 points for each *dead* die count.

2. If a dice throw reveals a potential bonus but does not include a *dead* die, the bonus hand is not confirmed and the player must put aside the bonus dice and throw the remaining dice or the five put-aside dice whichever the case may be. If this subsequent throw contains one or more *dead* dice, the bonus hand is confirmed and all points made on the hand count.

3. If the confirming throw does not contain a *dead* die but does contain another potential bonus, the player throws again in an attempt to confirm all points made on the hand.

4. If the confirming throw does not show a *dead* die, the potential bonus hand is busted and all previously made points for the hand plus the potential bonus points are canceled out. The player scores zero points for the hand and passes the dice and cup to the player on his left.

5. A bonus throw made up of *dead* dice does not require confirmation since they are point-scoring dice.

The Play. At each turn of play, unless a player throws a bust hand, he must throw the dice until he scores a minimum of 200 points. Then he can do one of two things: (1) he can "stand" (pass) and enter his score on the score sheet and pass the dice and cup to the player on his left, or (2) he can continue to throw the dice in an attempt to better his score. If, however, he throws a bust hand, his turn immediately ends, he scores nothing, and the turn of play passes to the player on his left.

The Play in Detail.

1. The shooter shakes the five dice inside the cup and throws them onto the table. If he fails to throw a *dead* die or a bonus hand, he calls, "Bust," and passes the dice and cup to the player on his left, his turn of play being ended.

2. If the shooter throws a hand whose point total is less than 200, such as *dead*–3–4–6–6,

Bonus Hands	Point Values	Bonus Hands	Point Values	Bonus Hands	Point Values
3 DEAD	200	4 DEAD	400	5 DEAD	3000
3 Aces (1's)	100	4 Aces (1's)	200	5 Aces (1's)	3000
3 Threes (3's)	300	4 Threes (3's)	600	5 Threes (3's)	3000
3 Fours (4's)	400	4 Fours (4's)	800	5 Fours (4's)	3000
3 Sixes (6's)	600	4 Sixes (6's)	1200	5 Sixes (6's)	3000

he counts aloud 50 points for the *dead* die and puts it aside with the *dead* side facing upwards.

3. He returns the non-scoring (3–4–6–6) dice back into the cup and throws these four dice again. The second throw shows *dead*–3–6–6, the shooter counts aloud 50 for the *dead* die, puts it aside with the previously scored *dead* die, and calls aloud his point total which is now 100.

4. He next places the three non-scoring dice (3–6–6) back into the cup and throws them again. This throw reveals two *dead* dice and a 6. The shooter adds the 100 points for the two *dead* dice to his 100 previously scored points and calls aloud 200. He then puts the two *dead* dice aside with the two previously put-aside dice.

5. Since the shooter has scored the required 200 points for a score to be valid, he may do one of two things: (1) he may call "Stand," and pass the cup and dice to the player on his left and enter the 200 points to his credit on the score sheet, or (2) he may call "Hit," and throw the remaining non-scoring die in an attempt to better his 200 point score. If, however, the shooter throws the non-scoring die and it fails to show *dead*, the hand is busted and the player scores nothing for the hand. But, if the throw produces a point-scoring *dead* die, its 50 point value is added to the previously scored 200 points, and he calls "250" aloud. The player then may as before stand or hit, and throw out the five put-aside dice and continue the same procedure of play as described above until he decides to stand or until he busts.

6. If during his turn of play, a player should throw a potential bonus hand, the rules as described under Rules for Bonus Hands apply.

7. The procedure of placing point-scoring dice aside and rethrowing the non-scoring dice continues until one of two things happen: either the player throws a bust hand and loses the dice as well as all points scored for the hand, or the player says, "I stand," and enters his scored points which must be 200 or more for each round of play. The dice and cup are then passed to the player on his left.

8. A player never enters his hand score until he decides to stand and his turn of play is finished.

End of Game. The game ends when a player scores 3000 or more points. By so doing, he wins the game and gets credit for the point difference between his score and that of each opponent.

Following is a sample score sheet of a Scarney 3000 game played by four persons. The score for each player's turn of play is written down to the left of the dash and the cumulative score to the right. This makes it known to each player at all times what the total score is and how far below or above the 3000-point game mark each player is. Bust hands are not entered on the score sheet.

A	B	C	D
200—200	200—200	450—450	600—600
450—650	200—400	200—650	800—1400
200—850	550—950	200—850	1900—3300
950—1800	200—1150	300—1150	
1050—2850		650—1800	
2850	1150	1800	3300

Player D, the winner of the game, with 3300 points is well over the 3000-point mark for game. Because the game was played for points, A owes D 450 points, the difference between his final game score of 2850 and D's 3300. B owes D 2150 points and C owes D 1500 points.

Note: For players who prefer a longer game, a 5000-point game is recommended.

Partnership Scarney 3000

This is four-handed Scarney 3000. Two players are teamed against the other two. The rules for Scarney 3000 apply with the following exceptions and additional rules.

1. Each player throws five dice for partners, holders of the two highest number totals (*dead* dice count nothing) are teamed against the holders of the two lowest. If three- or four-way ties occur on the throw for partners, one or more extra throws must take place until the ties are broken. Partners seat themselves opposite each other, and the holder of the highest number total starts the game by becoming the first shooter. From then on, each player's turn of play moves to the left, clockwise from player to player.

2. The score sheet heading is marked "They" and "We." Each player enters his hand score under his partnership heading and when a partnership's score totals 3000 or

more points, the game ends and each of the winning partners collects the total point difference between their total and that of the losing partnership.

Note: Team play can be extended to six persons, three against three.

Scarney Put-and-Take Dice

Scarney Put-and-Take Dice is without a doubt one of the best poker-style betting dice games in history. It combines the ante and pot-building flavor of Poker, the double-down psychology of Black Jack, and the thrill and chance uncertainty of dice throwing.

Requirements. Scarney Put-and-Take Dice can be played by as many players as can sit around the playing surface. Three Scarney dice, a dice cup, and a set of gaming chips are used to play the game. The main objective of the game is to throw *Scarney* (any three of a kind including three *dead* dice), which wins the game and takes the pot.

Selecting Seating Positions and Turn of Play. Each player shakes the three dice inside the cup and throws them onto the playing surface. The player throwing the highest total (*dead* dice count zero) takes any seat and is the first shooter. The player throwing the second highest sits on his left and shoots second, and so on. Tying players continue to throw until the ties are broken. Upon completion of a round, the right to start the next round goes to the player on the left of the previous winner.

The Ante. Each player, before the round (game) gets started, antes (puts) an agreed-upon equal number of chips in the center of the playing surface, known as the pot. Each player must ante in turn starting with the first shooter and rotating clockwise.

The Play. Each player's turn of play is governed by the following rules:

1. The shooter places the three dice in the cup and, after a proper shake, promptly throws them onto the playing surface.

2. When the thrown dice show two *dead* dice and a number, known as a *put,* the shooter must pass the dice to the player on his left and contribute to the pot an equal number of chips as there are spots on the third numbered die. *Examples:* The shooter throws two *dead* dice and a four; he must put

four chips into the pot. The shooter throws two *dead* dice and a six; he must put six chips into the pot; and so on.

3. When the thrown dice show a double (two identical numbers) and a single (different number or a *dead*), known as a *take,* the shooter takes from the pot an equal number of chips as spots shown on the single die and throws again. *Examples:* The shooter throws two threes and a *dead* die; since a *dead* die counts zero, no chips are taken from the pot. This is known as a *push* or *standoff* and the shooter throws again. The shooter throws two fours and a six; he removes six chips from the pot; and so on.

4. When the shooter throws three singles (three different numbers) or two singles and a *dead* die, such as 1–3–6, 3–4–6, 3–4–*dead,* and so on, the throw does not count and the shooter throws again. This is known as a *split, in-between, neutral,* or *no decision throw.*

5. When a shooter throws a three of a kind, including three *dead* dice (1–1–1, 3–3–3, 4–4–4, 6–6–6, or *dead-dead-dead*), he calls "Scarney," is declared the winner of the round, and takes the pot.

6. Before any throw of the dice the shooter may, if he cares to, call "Double down." The double-down option gives the shooter an opportunity on a possible hit to take double the number of chips from the pot as the take indicates. *Example:* The shooter's throw is 4–4–6. He simply doubles the 6 and takes 12 chips from the pot. If when doubling down, however, the shooter throws a put, he must put double the number of chips that the put indicates. *Example:* The shooter's put shows *dead-dead*–4. He simply doubles the 4 and puts eight chips into the pot.

7. To emphasize: A player continues to throw the dice until he throws a put and passes the dice to the player on his left; and so it goes, from player to player, until a player throws Scarney and wins the pot.

8. Should the number of chips in the pot be reduced to five or less, each player puts into the pot an amount equal to the original ante. Should a player throw a take on a double down and the number of chips in the pot is less than the take calls for, there is no redress; he simply takes the remaining chips in the pot and a new round gets underway.

Scarney Duplicate Jackpots

Scarney Duplicate Jackpots is one of the most thrilling and fastest-action dice games ever invented. The object of the game is to win the jackpot by throwing the same three-dice number total as did the previous shooter.

Requirements. Any number can play. It makes an excellent four-, five-, six-, or seven-person game. Three Scarney dice, a dice cup, and a set of gaming chips are used. *Dead* dice count zero.

Seating Positions and Turn of Play. To determine seating positions and turn of play, each player shakes the three dice in the cup and throws them onto the playing surface. The player throwing the highest three-dice number total (*dead* dice count zero) takes any seat and is the first shooter. The player throwing second highest sits on his left and shoots second; and so on. Tying players shoot again. Upon completion of a game, the right to start the next game goes to the winner of the game.

The Jackpot Ante. Each player, before the game gets started, antes (puts) an agreed-upon equal number of chips into the center of the playing surface known as the *jackpot*. All players must ante in turn, starting with the first shooter and rotating clockwise.

The Play. The first shooter places the three Scarney dice into the dice cup and, after a proper shake, throws them onto the playing surface. There is no action for the first shooter on his first throw. He merely calls the total of the three thrown dice and passes the dice cup and the three dice with the same numbers face up toward the player to his left whose turn it is to play. From then on, the rules governing each shooter's turn of play (one throw with three dice) are as follows:

1. If the shooter throws (matches) the exact same number total as the previous shooter (the player to the shooter's right) he calls "Scarney," wins the game, and takes the jackpot. *Example:* The previous shooter made a total of 13 points (3, 4, and 6). Upon completion of his throw he passed the cup and three dice—with the 13 points face up—to the next shooter. If the next shooter throws any three-dice combination totaling exactly

13 points, he calls "Scarney" and takes the jackpot.

2. If the shooter throws a lower number total than the previous shooter, he must put one chip into the jackpot for each point number below the previous shooter's total. *Examples:* The previous shooter's total was 15; the next shooter throws 10 and puts five chips into the jackpot. The previous shooter's total was 16; the next shooter throws 4 and puts 12 chips into the jackpot. The cup and dice, with the same numbers upward, are passed to the next player.

3. If the shooter throws a higher number total than the previous shooter, he simply passes the cup and dice with the total upward to the player on his left.

4. If the shooter throws three *dead* dice, called craps, zero points is his score; each player except the shooter must put five chips into the jackpot. The shooter then passes the dice and cup to the next player. And so it goes, to the left, clockwise, from player to player, until a shooter wins the game and jackpot by throwing the exact same number total as did the previous shooter on his right.

Scarney 21 Up and Down

Anyone can learn to play the game in a few minutes, yet it is an unending source of entertainment for children and adults alike. Scoring is the direct opposite of that in Straight Scarney Dice. With the exception of big Scarney, only *dead* dice count. That is, the object of the game is to win the pot by bringing the players' combined total of thrown *dead* dice to exactly 21—and then follow with a throw of numbers (no *dead* dice).

Requirements

1. Any number may play, singly or in partnership. Needed are five Scarney dice, a dice cup, and a set of gaming chips. Score is kept by oral count.

2. For seating positions and turn of play, see Straight Scarney Dice Rules of Play, page 486.

The Ante. Each player, before the game gets started, antes (puts) an agreed-upon equal number of chips into the center of the table, known as the pot. All players must ante in turn, starting with the first shooter and rotating clockwise.

The Play. The first shooter begins by throwing five dice. If one, two, three, or four *dead* dice (called crap or craps) are thrown, they are counted aloud and put aside. The remaining numbers (dice) are thrown again. The shooter continues throwing, each time adding aloud each crap (*dead* die) thrown to the previous total. The shooter continues to throw the remaining numbers until he fails to throw a *dead* die. Whereupon, the dice and cup pass to the player on his left.

If all five dice show *dead,* either on the second throw or after any number of throws, they are added to the score and all five dice are thrown again by the same shooter; any subsequent *dead* dice thrown are added to the running total. And so it goes, until the shooter fails to throw a *dead* die and his final total score is the second shooter's starting number. If the first shooter threw nine *dead* dice, the first *dead* die thrown by the second player is numbered 10, and so on. This continues until one player throws a *dead* die which brings the total to exactly 21; but the game does not end unless his next throw is comprised of numbers (no *dead* dice).

If a *dead* die appears on the next throw, the total is 22. If two *dead* dice appear, the total is 23 and the shooter continues throwing and adding *dead* dice to the total until no *dead* die is thrown. Whenever a player's starting number is 22 or more, all subsequent thrown *dead* dice are subtracted from the total until the shooter fails to throw a *dead* die. *Example:* If a player's starting number is 25 and he throws a total of 11 *dead* dice and then fails to throw a *dead* die, the total number is now 14. To emphasize: Whenever a player's starting total is 20 or less, all subsequent thrown *dead* dice are always added to his starting total. But when a player's starting total is 22 or more, all subsequent thrown *dead* dice are subtracted from his starting total. If a player's total reaches zero, his next thrown *dead* die is counted as 1, and the second *dead* die is 2, etc.

Chip Penalties. Whenever a player's *dead* dice total passes the magic 21 mark, he must put one chip into the pot for each *dead* die he throws below or above 21. *Examples:* The player's starting number is 19 and he throws 6 *dead* dice for a new total of 25. Since he is 4 over 21, he must put four chips into the

pot. The player's starting number is 23 and he throws 7 *dead* dice for a new total of 16. Since he is 5 under 21, he must put five chips into the pot. And so it goes, until the end of the game. *Note:* Some players prefer to pay only a one-chip penalty for passing the magic 21 mark instead of one chip for each thrown *dead* die below or above 21. For this ruling to be valid, it must be mutually agreed upon by all players before the start of the game.

The End of the Game. The game ends when a player hits 21 exactly and then throws *numbers* (fails to make a *dead* die on his next throw). When this occurs, the player calls "Game," is declared the winner, and collects the pot—except when big Scarney (any five of a kind including five *dead* dice) is made on any one (single) throw. Big Scarney automatically wins the game and takes the pot, regardless of the *dead* dice total. Upon the winning of the pot, the right to start the next round and throw first goes to the player to the left of the previous winner.

Scarney Bingo Dice

Scarney Bingo Dice combines the psychology of Bingo, the probabilities of Poker, and the constant fascination of dice throwing.

Requirements. Any number can play. Needed are three Scarney dice, a dice cup, a set of gaming chips, and a standard 52-card deck of playing cards. Each player throws the three dice; the player throwing the highest score (*dead* dice count zero) takes any seat and is the first dealer and shooter. The player throwing second highest sits on his left and shoots second, and so on. Upon the completion of the game, the right to start the next game goes to the player on the left of the previous winner.

Preparation to Start the Game. The player who is to shoot first shuffles the deck of cards and puts them face down on the table to his right. The player to his immediate right cuts the cards. Next, the player who is to shoot first deals 16 cards one-at-a-time face up onto the center of the table forming four rows of four cards each (vertically and horizontally). The rest of the deck is set aside.

Value of the Cards. Kings count 13 points; queens, 12; jacks, 11. All other cards have their face values: tens, 10; nines, 9; eights, 8;

sevens, 7; sixes, 6; fives, 5; fours, 4; threes, 3; twos, 2; and aces, 1. The suits (clubs, diamonds, hearts, and spades) have no value relative to each other and do not count.

The Ante. The player, before the game gets started, antes (puts) an agreed-upon equal number of chips aside known as the pot. All players must ante in turn, starting with the first shooter, and rotating clockwise.

The Play. Each player at his turn makes one throw of the three dice. When a thrown number or a combination of numbers (*dead dice count zero*) matches the value of one of the face-up cards, the player must turn it face down. A player can only turn one card face down at each turn of play. However, if two or more cards can be turned face down, the player may choose which card he will turn face down. *Example:* The shooter's three-dice throw shows a 3, 4, and 6. With such numbers, the player may turn face down any one of the following cards: 3, 4, 6, 7, 9, 10, or king (13), providing such cards are resting face up on the table. When a player throws a number total whose point value fails to match the point value of a face-up card, it is a no decision throw and he passes the dice and cup to the player on his left.

When a player throws Scarney (any three same-numbers or three *dead* dice), he can elect to turn face down any face-up card he wants; or he can refuse to turn a card face down and pass the dice and cup to the next player.

When a player turns face down the fourth or last face-up card of any vertical or horizontal row, he calls "Bingo," and receives one chip from each player. When a player goes bingo two ways by turning a card face down, he calls "Double Bingo," and receives a Double Bingo bonus of two chips from each player. When a player goes Double Bingo by turning a corner card face down, he calls "Double, Double Bingo," and collects a bonus of four chips from each player. The players continue to throw in turn until one player turns face down the sixteenth or last face-up card resting on the table. When this happens the player calls "Bango," wins the game, and rakes in the pot.

Scarney Speedy Bingo Dice

Scarney Speedy Bingo Dice is a very interesting variation of Scarney Bingo Dice and is recommended to players who desire a much quicker-ending game. The same rules of play as for Scarney Bingo Dice apply with the following exceptions and additional rules:

1. Any number can play. Four Scarney dice, a dice cup, a set of gaming chips, and a standard 52-card deck of playing cards are used.

2. Any four of a kind (four same-numbers or four *dead* dice) made on any one throw, known as *Bingo,* automatically wins the game and takes the pot regardless of the positions of face-down or face-up cards.

3. Three of a kind and three *dead* dice count only their point value.

Scarney Black Jack

Scarney Black Jack possesses the hit, stay, and double down features of the Casino card game of Black Jack; in addition, it offers the player a greater chance of participation with the throwing of the dice.

Requirements. Any number can play, usually as many as can sit around the playing surface. Two Scarney dice, a dice cup, and a set of gaming chips are used. The object of the game is to get a higher count (total value of thrown dice) than the banker-shooter, up to but not over 21. Should the player throw the dice and force his total over 21, he loses his bet and sacrifices any chance to beat or tie the banker-shooter.

Count Value of the Dice. Each *dead* die counts 10; each one (ace) counts 1 or 11 according to the discretion of the shooter; and each three, four, or six count their spot value.

Selecting the First Banker. To determine the first banker and seating positions, each player shakes the two dice in the cup and throws them onto the playing surface. The player throwing the highest total becomes the first banker and selects any seat he wants. The player with the next highest sits to his left and so on. Dice showing the word *dead* count 10. Once the seating has been arranged, each player, starting with the player to the banker's left, places the number of chips he wants to bet in front of him. The banker, who accepts all bets within the limit, shoots against each player in turn. The player shoots first and the banker second. And so it goes, to the left, clockwise, from player to player, around the table.

Rules Governing Shooter's Turn of Play.
The shooter places the two Scarney dice in the cup and, after a proper shake, throws them onto the playing surface.

1. When the shooter, on his initial throw, makes a *natural black jack* (a *dead* die and a one or ace), he calls "Black jack," and it becomes the banker-shooter's turn to play. If the banker-shooter also makes a natural black jack, it is a standoff or push. No one wins, no one loses. If the banker-shooter fails to throw a natural black jack on his first throw, the banker-shooter loses and pays the shooter at 2 to 1 odds.

2. When the shooter's first throw shows a count of 20 or less, the player may elect to hit (throw) or stand (not to throw). If he is satisfied with his count he says "Stand," or "Good," and passes the dice and cup to the banker-shooter.

3. If he is not satisfied with his count and elects to throw to try and better his count, he can do one of two things—he can either throw one die, called a *one shot,* or throw both dice, called a *two shot.* Examples: (*a*) The player's first throw shows a 4 and a 3 for a count of 7. The player decides to take a two shot; he says "Hit the 7" and again throws out the two dice, which show a 6 and 4 for a new count of 17. (*b*) The player hits the 7 with a one shot which shows a 10 count. He has a new count of 17. (*c*) The player is satisfied with his count. As mentioned before, he says "I'll stay," or "Good," and passes the dice and cup to the banker-shooter. (*d*) The player throws a number that forces his total over 21, which is called a *bust.* The banker-shooter collects the player's bet and pushes the cup and dice to the next player.

4. *The Double Down.* After his first throw, and at no other time, a player may elect to double his bet and make only one additional throw, which can be either a one shot or a two shot. This is known as a double down. The player must then double his original bet by putting up an amount equal to his original bet.

Rules Governing the Banker-Shooter's Turn of Play

1. The banker-shooter follows the same throwing rules described above for the shooter.

2. If the shooter made a natural black jack and the banker-shooter fails to do so, the banker-shooter pays the player 2 to 1 odds

for his bet. If the shooter and the banker-shooter each throw a natural black jack, it is called a standoff or push, in which case no one wins. It's a tie or standoff.

3. When the banker has a count of 16 or less, he must throw again.

4. When the banker has 17, 18, 19, or 20, he must stay—he cannot throw again.

5. When a banker has a count of 17 with an ace and a six—called "a soft 17"—it is an optional play. He can elect to stay or throw at his own discretion.

Final Settlement

1. When the banker's count goes over 21, he must pay the player still in the game.

2. When the banker's count is higher than the player's, he collects the player's bet.

3. When the banker's count is lower than the player's, the banker pays the player's bet at even money.

4. When the banker and the player have the same count, it's a standoff or push, and neither wins.

Rules Governing the Bank

1. After the first banker has been selected by the procedure set forth under "Selecting the First Banker," he shall bank five complete rounds (five turns of play for each player).

2. Upon completion of these five rounds, the bank shall pass to the player on the first banker's left, and each five rounds thereafter shall move to the left clockwise.

3. A banker deciding he no longer wants the bank may pass the bank to the player on his left before the completion of the five rounds—provided there are no uncompleted bets remaining on the board.

Scarney Chemin de Fer

As described in Chapter 16, Chemin de Fer is one of the most popular card games found in fashionable European casinos. Now, its dice counterpart, Scarney Chemin de Fer—a private banking game but possessing all the thrills and excitement found in its casino forerunner—can be played right in your own home or club. Unlike Baccarat, Chemin de Fer, or Black Jack, Scarney Chemin de Fer is an even-up game. There is no advantage for the bank or player.

Requirements. Five Scarney dice, a dice cup, and a set of gambling chips are used to play the game.

The Game. Scarney Chemin de Fer can be played by two, three, four or more players each playing against the banker. The object of the game is to beat the banker by making either one or two throws and hold a combination of dice totaling as close as possible to 9, or to a two-digit number ending in 9. *Dead* dice count zero (0) points. When the total of the dice is a two-digit number, only the last digit has any value. *Examples:* A count of 17 has a point value of 7, a count of 19 has a point value of 9, a count of 23 has a point value of 3, a count of 30 has a point value of 0, and so forth.

Selecting the First Banker. To determine the first banker and seating positions, each player shakes the five dice in the cup and throws them onto the playing surface. The player throwing the highest five-dice total becomes the first banker and selects any seat he wants. The player throwing the next highest sits to his left, and so on. Dice showing the word *dead* count nothing (zero). Once the seating has been arranged, the banker starts the game and each player's turn of play moves to the left, clockwise, from player to player.

The Banker's Turn of Play. Before the play begins, the banker establishes arbitrarily his own betting limits. *Example:* He may declare that while he's the banker, the bets are from one to five chips. Once the betting limit has been established and before the banker throws the dice, each player must place his chip bet directly in front of himself, toward the center of the table. Once the players' bets have been placed, the banker puts the five Scarney dice into the cup and after a proper shake throws them onto the playing surface, and adds their sum total and abides by the following rules:

1. If the banker on his first throw makes a 7, 8, or 9 for his point number, his turn of play ends. If the point is 9, it is called La Grande. If it is 8, it is called La Petite. If it is a 7, it is called a Natural. The banker's point is noted by each player—since this is the number he will try to beat.

2. If the banker on his first throw makes a 0, 1, 2, 3, 4, 5, or 6, as his point, called a Hit Number, he must draw (throw a second time). However, he is only permitted to throw the *dead* dice, if any, made on the first

throw. He cannot pick up and throw a numbered die—nor can he throw only some of the *dead* dice. He must throw all the *dead* dice made on the first throw on his second throw. *Examples:* The banker's first throw shows a 6, 4 and three *dead* dice for a count of 10 and a 0 (zero) point number. Because zero is a Hit Number, the banker must throw a second time and the throw must be made with the three *dead* dice. The banker has no option, he cannot throw one or two of the *dead* dice—he must throw all the *dead* dice made on the first throw, which in this instance are three.

3. If the banker makes five numbers (no *dead* dice) on his first throw, he cannot throw the second time because he has no *dead* dice to throw even though his count may be a Hit Number such as 0, 1, 2, 3, 4, 5, or 6.

Once the banker has made his point with either one or two throws, the point number is noted by each player. The banker, then, passes the dice and cup to the player on his left, who shall be referred to as the first player.

Player's Turn of Play. The first player places the five Scarney dice into the dice cup, and after a proper shake throws them onto the playing surface and follows the same rules as the banker-shooter to attain his point number.

1. If his point is lower than the banker's, the banker collects the bet from the first player.

2. If the first player's point is higher than the banker's, the banker pays the bet.

3. If the first player and the banker have the same point, it's a stand-off and neither wins.

Once the first player's turn of play ends, the second player's turn of play begins, and so it goes, clockwise, from player to player until each player has had his turn of play and a new round gets underway.

Rules Governing the Bank. The following rules govern the bank:

1. After the first banker has been selected by the procedure set forth under Selecting the First Banker, he shall bank five complete rounds (5 turns of play for each player).

2. Upon completion of these five rounds, the bank shall pass to the player on the first

banker's left and, each five rounds thereafter, shall move to the left clockwise.

3. A banker deciding he no longer wants the bank may pass the bank to the player on his left before the completion of the five rounds—provided there are no uncompleted plays remaining on the board.

Scarney Pie-Eyed Dice

This drinking fun game is only recommended for adults who have a sense of humor and are not allergic to drinking as well as to club memberships where dice throwing for drinks is permitted by law.

Any number can play (the more, the merrier) and five Scarney dice are used with a dice cup. Each player throws the five dice once to determine the order of play. The player who throws the highest total (*dead* dice count zero) goes first, next highest second, and so on. Tying players throw again.

Although the playing rules are extremely simple, you may get pie-eyed following them. Each player gets three throws. Each player in turn, for his first throw, shakes the five dice inside the cup and throws them onto the bar or table. If he throws one, two, three, or four *dead* dice, he puts them aside and throws the leftover numbered dice (1, 3, 4, 6) a second time. The same holds true for the third throw. The first player to throw five *dead* dice orders a drink—a double rye with celery tonic, vodka with chili sauce, or anything the bartender claims he can mix.

The next player to throw five *dead* dice must drink it, no excuses accepted, on penalty of being tossed out of the game. The third player to throw five *dead* dice foots the bill for the drink. The number of rounds depends upon the amount of punishment the players can take. *Note:* If you want to speed up your drinking, change the ordering, drinking, and playing rules to four *dead* dice instead of five. *Note:* Many players prefer to play Scarney Pie-Eyed Dice with two Scarney dice. A player makes one throw of the two dice at each turn of play. The first player to throw two *dead* dice orders the drink, the next player to throw two *dead* dice must drink it.

The third player to throw two *dead* dice pays for the drink.

Additional Rules for Scarney Dice Games. If you observe the Scarney Dice rules of play, you will have interesting and enjoyable games. You will also avoid arguments that might arise during play. Follow the rules of the game you are playing and insist that other contestants do the same.

1. If a die comes to rest cocked at an angle on a chip or any irregularity on the playing surface, and if there is a difference of opinion as to which side faces up, the player to the shooter's right shall stand at the shooter's position and shall decide the outcome by stating which top surface of the die appears to be upward from that position.

2. If playing on an elevated surface, and one or more dice fall off the playing surface, the throw is *no-dice*. It does not count and the dice must be thrown again.

3. If a throw is made and one or more dice still remain in the cup, the throw counts and the player must throw the remaining die or dice to complete the throw.

4. When a score is agreed upon and written down, it may not later be set aside. Proven mistakes in addition on the score sheet must be corrected. If the error is noted during a play of a frame, the frame must be completed before the error is able to be corrected.

5. A player during his turn of play, and at no other time, may ask the scorekeeper to call out the scores.

6. If a player shoots out of turn, and it is discovered before the next shooter's first throw, his turn of play does not count. The next turn of play reverts back to the player whose turn it would have been if no irregularity had occurred.

7. If a player fails to give the dice a proper shake; or if, after the shake, he looks into the cup before throwing; or if he acts in a way that causes an opponent to believe he is trying to control the dice roll; then the other players may reprimand the shooter and may call for a proper shake. If an irregularity occurs a second time, other players may call the throw dead and the offending player is barred from further play.

CHAPTER 25

Chess, Checkers, and Teeko

America's three favorite "think" games are Chess, Checkers, and Teeko. One dates back to before the birth of Christ, the other to the Middle Ages, while Teeko is the baby of the group having been introduced in the 1950's.

CHESS

Chess, the most universal of games, is probably the most sophisticated and profound; at the same time, it is one of the oldest. There have been many fanciful legends as to its origin, and scholars who have tried to track down its source disagree. The earliest evidence indicates that it originated in India sometime before the seventh or eighth century, and probably evolved from very ancient board games of movement like Parcheesi and Backgammon.

The present forms of the pieces, and some of the modern moves, date to about the fifteenth century. The literature of Chess, which began with collections of Chess problems in the Middle Ages, has grown until it surpasses that of any other game.

Requirements

1. Two players.
2. *The Board*. The board is a large square of 8 by 8 smaller squares, alternately colored light and dark. The board is placed so that each player has a white square in the corner at his right. (The light-colored squares are always called "white.") In printed diagrams, by convention, the white player is always at the bottom, and the black player is at the top.

3. *The Pieces*. Each player has 16 pieces of his own color: one King, one Queen, two Rooks, two Bishops, two Knights, and eight Pawns. At the beginning they are placed on the board as shown here.

The Powers of the Pieces. The six different kinds of pieces each move in a different way, as described below:

The *King* moves one square at a time in any direction, on the rank (sideways), on the file (forward or backward), and diagonally. The King may not move to any square that is attacked by an enemy piece.

The *Queen* is the most powerful piece,

The notation of the chessboard.

being able to move in any direction for any distance, so far as the line is unobstructed.

The *Rook* moves any distance along an unobstructed rank or file (forward, backward, or sideways).

The *Bishop* moves on diagonal lines only (forward and backward), so far as the line is unobstructed by a man of his color. If there is a hostile man in the way he may capture him.

The *Knight* moves by jumping from point to point, unlike all the other pieces that move on a line. Also, it cannot be obstructed by intervening pieces. The Knight makes an L-shaped move, going from one corner to the diagonally opposite corner of a rectangle measuring three squares by two.

The *Pawn* moves forward on the file (away from the player). On its first move only, it has a choice of moving forward either one or two squares. Thereafter, it may move only one square at a time.

Capturing. All pieces (except Pawns) capture in the same way that they move. If a piece can move to a square occupied by an enemy piece, the move captures it. The captured piece is removed from the board and replaced by the captor. Capturing is always optional.

The Pawn captures differently. It does not threaten the next square forward on the file; rather, it attacks the two squares forward on either side. It captures by moving one square diagonally. Advancing Pawns are open to capture by enemy Pawns on both adjacent files, and may not avoid this attack by moving forward two squares on the first move. Suppose a player advances his Pawn two squares, bringing it to rest beside an enemy Pawn. Had the Pawn advanced only one square, the enemy Pawn could have captured it. Under these circumstances the enemy may, if the player wishes, capture *en passant* (in passing) by taking the advancing Pawn and moving to the square that was passed. This en passant capture must be made immediately and not at any later turn.

Castling. Castling is a special move which a player may make only once during a game. It is a simultaneous move of two pieces: the King and a Rook. The move is legal only if neither piece has moved previously, if the squares between King and Rook are vacant, if the King is not in check, and if the squares the King must cross are not threatened by the enemy. The move is made by moving the King two squares toward the Rook, and then placing the Rook on the square jumped over by the King. The purpose of castling is usually to put the King in a safer place behind unmoved Pawns, or to "connect the Rooks" and bring them to central files on which they can exert pressure.

Queening. If a Pawn reaches the eighth rank (the far edge of the board), it is promoted; that is, it is removed from the board and any other piece may be substituted for it. It is usually exchanged for a Queen because this is the most powerful piece, but the player may choose a Rook, Bishop, or Knight, which is sometimes an advantage.

The Play. White always moves first, and then the moves alternate. The object of play is to capture the enemy King, although the King is never actually removed from the board. When a move threatens the King it is a *check,* and the attack must immediately be parried—by moving the King, capturing the attacking piece, or interposing a piece on the line of attack. When none of these defenses are possible, the King is *checkmated,* and the game ends. Most games end before a checkmate, one player resigning because he sees that he will eventually lose.

Drawn Games. A draw may result in any of the following ways:

Stalemate. When a player whose turn it is to move can make no legal move, even though not in check, the game is stalemated and considered drawn.

Lack of Force. When the pieces left on the board are too few and too weak to force checkmate, the game is drawn.

Perpetual Check. One player shows that he can continue to check the adverse king indefinitely.

Repetition. If the identical position of all pieces, white and black, recurs three times in a game, with the same player to move each time, this player may claim a draw.

Fifty-Move Rule. If during 50 consecutive moves no pawn has been moved and no capture has been made, either player may ask the other to demonstrate a forced win or to agree to a draw.

Agreement. The players may agree to a draw. In tournament play this is usually permitted only after Black's thirtieth move.

Additional Rules. Irregularities in Chess are handled as follows:

Touch and Move. If a player touches one of his own pieces, he must move it if he can legally do so. If he touches an adverse piece, he must capture it, if legally possible. If a player touches several pieces, his opponent may choose which is to be moved or which is to be captured, provided a legal move is available.

Adjusting. A player may touch his own pieces in order to adjust them, provided he gives notice in advance by announcing "I adjust."

Completed Move. A completed move, if legal, may not be retracted. A simple move is completed when the player removes his hand from the piece. A capturing move is completed when the adverse piece is taken from the board and the player removes his hand from the capturing piece. A promoting move is completed when the Pawn is taken from the board and the player removes his hand from the piece that replaces it.

Illegal Move. If a player makes an illegal move, and his opponent calls attention to the fact before touching any of his own pieces, the illegal move must be retracted, and the player must if possible make a legal move with the same piece. If the illegal move was a capture, the player must if possible make a legal capture of the same piece.

Erroneous Position. If during play it is proved that an illegal move was made and not retracted, or that the number or position of the men was altered illegally, the position just prior to the illegal move or alteration must be restored, and the game continued from that point. If during play or immediately afterward it is proved that the pieces were initially placed on the board incorrectly, or that the board was turned wrongly, the game is annulled.

Erroneous Checkmate. An erroneous announcement of checkmate, either on the move or in several moves, is void without penalty and the game must be continued.

Deportment. A player may not take advice from spectators, and may not refer to or have at the table any written notes other than the record of the game. A player should not comment on any of the moves to his opponent, or in any way annoy or distract his opponent. A player forfeits the game if he willfully upsets the board or disarranges the men, refuses to comply with a legal requirement, arrives more than an hour late for commencement or resumption of play, or exceeds the time limit.

Time Limit. In tournament play a time limit is used. Each player must make 30 moves in the first two hours of his own time, 45 moves in the first three hours, etc. (This is sometimes stepped up to 20 moves per hour.) In "rapid transit" play, only ten seconds is allowed for each move, and a referee who keeps time is used.

Values of the Pieces. The relative powers of the pieces are approximately in this ratio: Pawn, 1; Knight, 3; Bishop, 3; Rook, 5; Queen, 9. The Knight and Bishop are about equal, except that the latter sometimes has an edge depending on position. Two Bishops together are usually stronger than an opposing Bishop and Knight, and are even stronger against two Knights. The Bishop is less vulnerable to attack because it can operate at a distance, and in two directions. The Knight is more easily repelled because it must be brought closer to its targets. It is superior only in positions where lines are blocked, or in an ending against a single Bishop when its ability to reach squares of both colors is an advantage.

Minimum Force. If one side is reduced to only a King, the other can force checkmate if, besides his King, he has any of the following: one Queen, one Rook, two Bishops, or a Bishop and a Knight. Having either one Bishop, one Knight, or two Knights is not sufficient to force checkmate.

A Queen wins against a Rook and usually against a Rook and a Pawn, but can only draw against a Rook and a minor piece. (Bishops and Knights are *minor* pieces; Queens and Rooks are *major* pieces.) Two bishops can usually draw against a Queen, but a Bishop and a Knight or two Knights usually lose.

A Rook and a minor piece against a Rook can usually only draw, and a Rook against one minor piece can usually only draw.

A single Pawn cannot win unless it can be promoted. If the lone King can occupy the square in front of the Pawn before it has reached the seventh rank, the game is a draw.

Notation. Chess books in English usually use a descriptive notation in which the pieces are abbreviated to initials: K, Q, B, R, P. Kt was formerly used for Knight, but this is now usually N.

Each file is designated by the first-rank piece that originally stands on it, such as K-file and Q-file. For the other pieces, K or Q must be prefixed to show whether the file is on the King's or Queen's half of the board,

The chessmen (left) and how they are set up at the start of the game.

such as KB-file and QR-file.

The ranks are numbered 1 through 8, going away, in each case, from the player whose piece moves. White's ranks 1 and 2 are Black's ranks 8 and 7.

A square is identified by its file and rank, in that order. Because the ranks are numbered two ways, the color must be named; for example, White's KB6 is the same square as Black's KB3. The color is omitted in recording the moves because the reference is always to the color of the moving piece.

The initial of the piece moved is written first, followed by a hyphen, then the square moved to; for example, P-K4 means that a Pawn moves to King 4 (the fourth rank of the K-file). For a capturing move, the hyphen is replaced by the symbol x (meaning "takes"), followed by the initial of the piece captured, as PxP, BxN.

If N-KB3 is ambiguous because either Knight could make that move, the Knight is specified, as QN-KB3. Other symbols used are:

ch	Check
O-O	Castles on the King side
O-O-O	Castles on the Queen side
!	Best (indicates a good move)
?	Not the best move

Moves are numbered consecutively, each move comprised of one by White and one by Black. In linear form: 1 P-K4, P-K4; 2 N-KB3, N-QB3; B-N5, P-QR3, ...

In columnar form White's moves are in the left column, Black's in the right:

1 P-K4	P-K4
2 N-KB3	N-QB3
3 B-N5	P-QR3

Chess Strategy

The two opposing armies begin with an equality of force; they have the same number and kind of pieces. The loss during action of a single piece, even a Pawn, can lead to defeat. When a piece is threatened with capture this equality of force can be maintained by the counter capture of a piece of equal value. If the counter capture wins a piece of less value, the exchange has been lost and the winner has acquired a decided material advantage because the total value of his pieces gives him greater fighting power, which can be used to acquire further advantages.

But the force the pieces exert also depends upon their positions on the board. Advanced pieces, centrally located, with open lines along which they can attack, have great mobility; the total force they can bring to bear on the enemy is greater than for pieces far from the battle. The added fighting power acquired from superior position can even defeat an army that has greater material. These two objectives, material and positional superiority, are both vital and must be considered together.

Following are some of the positional advantages which you must keep always in mind and try to achieve.

Early Development. Development consists in moving the pieces (especially the major pieces on the first rank) forward where they can engage the enemy pieces in action. At the game's beginning only the player's Pawns and his Knights are free to move; they guard and exert pressure only on the third rank. Pawns, usually the KP and QP, must be moved in order to open up lines along which the Bishops, Rooks, and Queen can move forward to squares from which they can threaten more advanced ranks and attack enemy pieces.

A piece is said to be *developed* when it has left its original square, and development is considered to be complete when the Queen, Bishops, and Knights have moved forward and the King has moved (usually by castling) so that the Rooks are *connected,* that is, no pieces remain on the first rank between them.

The player who completes his development first has an advantage, because he has acquired more opportunities for attack. Any undue delay in development leads to trouble, and sometimes to quick defeat.

It is preferable to develop a piece to a square on which it will not impede the development of any other piece. An effort should be made to post each piece at once on its most effective square, usually the most advanced square from which it cannot easily be driven off. As a general rule, avoid moving any piece more than once during the development because this loses time.

Control of the Center. As the pieces develop they must also exert their force on the four *center squares* of the board (the fourth and fifth squares on both the King's and Queen's files). A piece or Pawn does not need to occupy one or more of these squares; more often it threatens these squares so that the adversary is prevented from posting and maintaining a piece there. A Pawn, being a short-range piece, must at least reach the *secondary center* (the eight squares surrounding the four center squares) in order to exert its pressure on the center.

Controlling or guarding the center is important throughout the game because long-range pieces have maximum range and mobility when posted there, and because such control tends to split the opposing army into two wings and to obstruct its communications.

Outpost Knight. Queens, Rooks, and Bishops can attack on open lines from a distance, but the Knight must engage the enemy at close quarters and his most effective position is on an advanced square, especially in the center. A Knight posted safely on the enemy fourth or third rank threatens so many surrounding squares that he is a constant danger.

Open Files. A file is *open* when there are no Pawns on it, and *half-open* for a player when his own Pawn is no longer on it. Such files provide avenues along which the Rooks can operate: attacking, aiding in the defense, or moving out and then attacking along the rank. A Rook is a heavy gun whose long-range threats are serious. A player must often oppose an enemy Rook on an open file with his own Rook, neutralizing its power by threatening to exchange. If the player cannot ward off an attack that penetrates his own forces deeply, he may find his King in sudden danger.

Diagonals. These are the avenues along which the Bishops exert their force, either for attack or for defense. Pawns and minor pieces that obstruct a diagonal limit a Bishop's range and mobility. Long open diagonals invite attack and are positional weaknesses to be avoided.

Pawn Skeleton Formation. Pawns are problems. They must advance to open the way for other pieces, but Pawn advances also weaken the protection they can give to the squares of their home territory. Pawn advances are irrevocable—both the immediate and long-range effects must be carefully considered. Pawns must protect each other and stay connected in a skeletal formation that is not easily broken. Premature advances may leave *holes* which enemy outposts can fill; *doubled Pawns* (two of the same color on the same file) weaken their defensive formation.

Mobility. Like cavalry, pieces must maintain as much freedom to move as possible. When they are constricted and their avenues of attack blocked, either by other pieces or their own, the firepower of the pieces is diminished. Immobility can cause a player to lose fairly rapidly.

Skirmishes. Both material and positional advantages accrue from winning local engagements such as advancing an unopposed piece to a strong post, forcing a major piece to withdraw by an attack with a less valuable piece, and the successful capture of an enemy piece by massing more attackers against it than there are defenders that can be brought into position to guard it. Each player must watch continually for the development of such skirmishes, and must try to have a superior force near enough to fight it successfully.

Tactics. Tactical threats, which are often easily countered, are continually employed. The attacker uses them to improve his own position, and at the same time to weaken that of the enemy by forcing him to limit his replies to defensive moves.

The Pin. A piece is *pinned* when it is attacked but cannot move without exposing its own King to check, an illegal move. It is also said to be pinned if it cannot move because it protects another more valuable piece on the same line of attack. A pinned piece has lost its mobility, as well as the protection it may have been giving any other piece by guarding it. The pinned piece is in immediate danger when the attack is made by a less valuable piece, or when more pieces can join in the attack than there are friendly pieces that can come to its defense.

Discovered Check. Checks of any sort harass the defender because his choice of replies is limited. Especially dangerous is a *discovered check,* which occurs when an attacker moves an intervening piece off the line of a Queen, Rook, or Bishop, and unmasks its attack on the King. The unmasking piece may capture a guarded enemy piece without being recaptured because the King must first move out of check, which gives the capturing piece a free move to take him out of danger. Or the unmasking piece may, on its first move, reach a square from which it can attack a more valuable piece and then capture it on its next move.

Double Check. A discovered check can become a *double check* when the unmasking piece also delivers a check. The King's only legal reply is to move, and if he cannot move he is checkmated.

Fork. A *fork* is a simultaneous attack on two or more pieces. It is always difficult to counter, and one piece is usually lost, as when a Pawn forks two Knights. Knight forks attacking the Rooks, or the Queen and a Rook, can be expensive; any fork, one prong of which checks the King, can be dangerous.

Anyone can learn the mechanics of Chess which are outlined here, and it can be a fascinating game even for the beginner. But the more he plays, the more he realizes what vast possibilities and what infinite variety the game contains. No matter how much experience a player gains, no matter how deeply he

studies the strategy and tactics inherent in those 64 squares and 16 pieces, he will find that there is always more to learn. No man has mastered the game completely. That is the challenge which has made it the most universally played and perennial of games.

Famous Openings. A *gambit* means the sacrifice of a pawn or a piece, or several successively, for an advantage in position. Among famous chess openings and responses are:

Alekhine's Defense: 1 P-K4, N-KB3; 2 P-K5, N-Q4; 3 P-QB4, N-N3; 4 P-Q4, P-Q3

Caro-Kann Defense: 1 P-K4, P-QB3; 2 P-Q4, P-Q4

Falkbeer Counter Gambit: 1 P-K4, P-K4; 2 P-KB4, P-Q4; 3 KPxP, P-K5

French Defense: 1 P-K4, P-K3; 2 P-Q4, P-Q4

Giuco Piano: 1 P-K4, P-K4; 2 N-KB3, N-QB3; 3 B-B4, B-B4

Queen's Gambit: 1 P-Q4, P-Q4; 2 P-QB4, PxP

Queen's Pawn's Game: 1 P-Q4, P-Q4

Reti's Opening: 1 N-KB3, P-Q4 or N-KB3

Ruy Lopez: 1 P-K4, P-K4; 2 N-KB3, N-QB3; 3 B-N5

Sicilian Defense: 1 P-K4, P-QB4

There are classic games among chess players. Here's one that I selected to show how a game is played to completion:

	White	*Black*
1	P-K4	P-K4
2	N-KB3	N-QB3
3	B-B4	B-B4
4	P-QN4	BxP
5	P-B3	B-R4
6	P-Q4	PxP
7	O-O	P-Q6
8	Q-N3	Q-B3
9	P-K5	Q-N3
10	R-K1	KN-K2
11	B-R3	P-N4?
12	QxP	R-QN1
13	Q-R4	B-N3
14	QN-Q2	B-N2
15	N-K4	Q-B4
16	BxP	Q-R4
17	N-B6ch!	PxN
18	PxP	R-N1
19	QR-Q11	QxN?
20	RxNch!	NxR
21	QxPch!!	KxQ
22	B-B5ch	K-K1
23	B-Q7ch	K-Q1
24	BxN mate	

The beginner, of course, must first learn by playing; but his ability will improve faster if he also spends some time with one or more of the guidebooks for beginners that outline the basic principles of strategy and tactics. There are now many good ones available.

CHECKERS

The origin of the game of Checkers, like that of Chess, is lost in history. But from fleeting references found in ancient manuscripts, together with discoveries unearthed in scientific excavations, modern man has been able to trace Checkers back to about 6000 B.C. History also reveals that the game was known and played in Egypt at least as early as that date, if not earlier. The game in much its present form was an amusement among the Moors at the time of the conquest of the city of Granada. The extreme age of the game may be appreciated when it is remembered that playing cards were first traced to China in the eleventh century.

Checkers bears different names in almost every country of the world. For instance, Checkers is known as Draughts in Great Britain, Dama in Italy, La Jeu de Dames in France, Aracaby in Poland, and das Damenspiel in Germany. The first book on Checkers ever printed rests in the Royal Library of Madrid, Spain. This book first made its appearance in the city of Valencia, Spain, in A.D. 1547. The first Checkers book published in English was written by mathematician William Payne of London, England, in 1756.

Checkers is an ancient and honorable game, contributing to the education and pleasure of millions and millions of players of all ages throughout the world. It holds unflag-ging interest for the most constant player and yet it affords the highest type of mental recreation. The following rules and instructions are based on American or English Checkers.

The Standard Game (employing Go-As-You-Please opening). Checkers is a game of skill played between two players. It is played upon a checkered board made up of 64 squares of light and dark colors with pieces called *checkers* or *checker men*. The men are in the form of thick discs and have a diameter of between 1 1/4 inches and 1 1/2 inches. Each player possesses 12 checker men of opposite colors and the game is played on the 32 dark squares of the board only. The board is so placed that the *single corner* is situated on the left side of each player, and the *double corner* is on the right.

The Object of the Game. The object of the game is twofold: To win the game by capturing all of your opponent's pieces so that he has none to move; or, to confine your opponent's pieces so that he cannot move any of them. When the respective pieces of each player are so reduced, however, that neither of these two goals can be attained, the game is considered drawn.

The Moves. The pieces never leave the black (dark) squares, so that they always move in a diagonal direction. At the begin-

 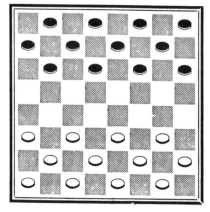

The numbered checkerboard (left) and where the pieces (men) are placed at the beginning of the game. Note that the white squares are used in the diagram although it is customary to use the black squares when playing. Do not let this confuse you, as it is done only for the sake of clarity.

ning of the game, the pieces only move one square at a time either to the right or to the left and always forward; the pieces can move only on squares that are unoccupied. A single man, upon reaching the final row, known as the *king row,* is crowned with another piece and is known as a *King.* This piece can move and capture both forward or backward in a diagonal direction. If an opponent's piece rests upon a square to which a man might be moved and there is a vacant square beyond, the man must jump over the opponent's piece onto the unoccupied square at the same time capturing (removing from the board) the piece that was jumped over.

Single, double, triple, quadruple, and even quintuple jumps are possible, in which case the jumping process is continued until captures are no longer possible. However, a single man must *pause* (complete his move) when reaching or jumping into the king row.

"Move on the black squares and jump whenever possible" is an old saying which briefly summarizes the mechanics of the game. It should be noted that in the conventional representations of the checkerboard in textbooks, the colors of the squares are reversed to make the men and numbers clearer.

The Numbered Board. The best form of practice at Checkers is to play alone; hours of enjoyment and heightened skill will reward your efforts when you play solitaire Checkers. For a player to become an expert checkerist, or even a respectable amateur, he should memorize the position of the squares shown on the numbered board detailed in illustration 1. In this way, you can follow each move detailed in this section, enabling you to take the first steps in improving your game. Many checkerists know the numbered checkerboard so well that they can take an unnumbered board and call out the number of any square as fast as you can place your finger on it.

Ten Points Every Winning Checkerist Should Know

1. Learn the rules of the game so thoroughly that you can call them instantly and correctly.

2. Always try to take possession of the center of the board, especially squares 14 and 19. These are "key" squares and their occupation or control leads to a superior game.

3. The *bridge* is formed by checkers resting on squares 1 and 3 when playing Black,

and on squares 30 and 32 when playing White. Try to break your opponent's bridge and protect your own.

4. Attack your opponent's double corner, and weaken it by the exchange of checkers whenever possible. In many instances a well-filled double corner is better than a bridge. The double corners are depicted on the numbered board as the four squares 9, 6, 5, and 1; or 24, 27, 28, and 32. Sometimes double corners are considered to be the six squares 9, 6, 5, 1, 14, and 10; or 24, 27, 28, 32, 19, and 23.

5. Never make a move without a definite purpose in mind and the knowledge that it is a good move. In addition, always try to analyze the reason for every move played against you.

6. Observe games between good players whenever possible. And, when such players are experts, record their moves for later study.

7. Don't discuss or criticize a move or a position on the board during the play of the game. Use this time to study the board.

8. Due to the fact that Checkers requires deep concentration, many winning moves are often overlooked. Therefore, it is suggested that, even though a player knows he is in an obvious losing position, there is no reason for him to be sure that his opponent recognizes it also. In view of this fact, one should not point out winning or losing positions while a game is in progress.

9. All the moves in Checker games have a reason behind them. Therefore, should an opponent deviate from a play you know, study the position carefully for a possible trap.

10. Memorize all checker playing charts that you can get your hands on, evolve other transpositions yourself, acquire a library of Checker books, and attend as many tournaments and exhibition matches as possible.

Tournament Checkers

There are three forms of Checker openings employed in tournaments: The go-as-you-please style opening, as discussed in the foregoing text, the two-move restriction, and the three-move restriction.

Go-As-You-Please. The go-as-you-please style of opening is the one played by the millions of Checker players the world over; as one might infer, it is a freelance one. Black moves first and plays any one of seven moves

FIRST POSITION

SECOND POSITION

THIRD POSITION

FOURTH POSITION

FIFTH POSITION

SIXTH POSITION

SEVENTH POSITION

EIGHT POSITION

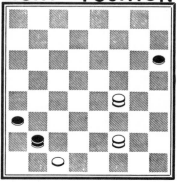

The basic positions in Checkers.

to open the game, White does likewise, and the game continues without restriction of any sort. This was the style in vogue with the experts prior to about 1895. As Checkers grew more popular and the population increased, the experts became more proficient. Due to improved Checker competition, the old Checker masters began drawing most of their games. For instance, in one 40-game championship match played between two masters, 37 out of the 40 games played were repeats, move for move.

Two-Move Restriction. This style of tournament opening was first introduced in Great Britain about 1890. The idea was to give the opening game in Checkers greater scope in play and to avoid the same opening moves. In this type of play, a deck of 43 cards is used. There are seven possible opening moves for Black and seven possible replies for White, a total of 49 possible opening combinations of play on the first two moves. However, six of these 49 combinations have been shown to be extremely weak for one side; they were therefore omitted from the deck of cards, leaving 43 official openings in the two-move ballot. The cards are shuffled and cut and the top card is turned face up to determine the opening to be played. After the first game is finished, players switch and play the opposite-colored checkers; then the second card of the deck is turned face up, etc.

Three-Move Restriction. The two-move restriction, like the free-style opening, soon lost its virginity. The various openings were studied and played to a state of near perfection. Draws were many and wins were few in tournament play. Even with this style of opening, about 90 percent of the Checker games played between experts end in drawn games. Then came a movement to adopt a three-move-restriction type of opening. It was found that by adding an extra move, no less than 137 different playable openings could be used to baffle the experts. About 1935, the three-move restriction in Checkers was adopted in the United States and, since that time, it has been the official style of opening play for all national and state Checker association tournaments, as well as in local club matches.

Having the Move. *Having the move* has been overemphasized. It has been constantly pointed out that a player at any stage of the game can compute whether he has the move or not. What these authors fail to state is that the move rarely plays an important part in the

opening or the middle game. Near the end game, when the move and its changes become an important part of the partial Checker setup, any fair Checker player does not have to start counting pieces or four columns of the board (as explained below) to learn who's got the move. He can tell by looking at the board and analyzing the possible movement of his men. During my lifetime, I have never met one Checker expert who calculated any form of strategy by a count, for the obvious reason that the move may have no bearing whatsoever on the outcome of the game. When the move does become an important factor, more often than not it involves a great many other factors which certainly cannot be solved theoretically or by proceeding merely on the count factor.

However, for what it's worth, the most easily understood explanation of what is meant by having the move is to place a black piece on square 3 and a white piece on square 30. Black to play will win, because he has the move. Proceed, 3–7, 30–26, 7–10; if White moves 26–23, Black wins by 10–15; if White moves 26–22, Black moves 10–14 and wins by having the *opposition*. In other words "He has the move who has the last move." In order to calculate the move, the board is supposed to be divided into two *systems*. One system consists of the four columns that end in Black's king row with the squares 1, 2, 3, and 4. The other system consists of the four columns that end in White's king row with the squares 29, 30, 31, and 32. In order to determine who has the move (at your turn of play), add together all the pieces both black and white, in your own system. If the sum is odd, you have the move; if even, your opponent has the move. This applies only when the pieces of each opponent are equal. To alter the move, an exchange of odd pieces is required, such as one for one, or three for three; but one of the capturing pieces must also be taken for this rule to apply. To determine who has the move when the pieces are unequal (such as three Kings to two, or four Kings to three), imagine that the board is equally divided, vertically. Now count as before; if the total is odd, you have the move (at your turn of play) only on the half of the board in which your double corner lies. If the total is even, you have the move only on that half of the board in which your single corner is situated. Don't make the move an important factor in your play, for it is secondary to the more important principle of building tenable formations and positions. Learn the strategy of the opening, middle, and end game first; then the problem of the move and its changes will unfold by themselves. Don't count—just compute and analyze each and every play.

Checker Strategy. Many books have been written on Checkers and thousands of game problems have been analyzed, without exhausting Checkers. Here, space permits us to state only what I consider the pointers most useful to the average Checker player. In 1945, Willie Ryan, then America's Checker champion, said to this author "Checkers is an easy game to come out on top. All you have to do is to avoid losing a Checker and you are sure to win." Then he added "However, the average checkerist can be depended on to lose a checker after his first six moves of the game." For instance, Black opens 11–15 and White answers 22–17. Black plays 12–16, hoping to go on to 20, but White plays 24–19, forcing Black to play 15–24 and White to play 28–19–12 and Black has lost a piece. Another way to duplicate the same thing is 9–14, 22–17, 12–16, 23–18, 14–23, 26–19–12. The first thing the student has to do is to learn to avoid such simple two-for-one shots, of which there are many. The loss of a single piece by an opponent is normally all a good player needs to win the game. He can swap piece for piece and so end up with one to none.

How the student plays his end game and middle game is important; but a bad beginning usually ends with a losing game, so let's analyze Black's and White's opening moves. By glancing at your checkerboard, you will note that Black has seven possible opening moves, and White has seven possible replies. The question now arises: What is Black's best opening play, and what is White's best reply to each of Black's seven possible opening moves? The answer to these basic questions varies often with players as well as experts. However, I give my preference in all seven moves and countermoves.

Black's Opening Moves		White's Reply
1.	11–15	22–18
2.	9–14	22–18
3.	11–16	22–18

Black's Opening Moves		White's Reply
4.	10–15	21–17
5.	10–14	22–18
6.	12–16	24–20
7.	9–13	22–18

Knowing the best opening moves will not make the student a good player, but a job started properly usually follows through in the same manner. The best way for a person to learn the manner in which various openings are followed up is to play over illustrative problems and, in doing so, he should set and play the board from the winning side.

Basic Positions in Checkers. Although Checkers does not have a definite theory and is minus a practical application of set principles, still the game possesses a number of fundamental positions or so-called "elementary settings." It is upon these familiar setups and end-game maneuvers that most games are won among experienced players. That is, more games are won by the knowledge of these positions than through any other Checker strategy. One can well appreciate the wisdom of this statement when he learns that the First Position may come up in approximately 35,000 different ways, and that more games are won by this simple two-by-two ending than by any other single position found on the checkerboard. Perhaps this is why it has been appropriately named the First Position.

The end game usually resolves itself into one of several basic positions but space permits me to give only the most important of such positions. These positions are those in which there is a win or draw for Black or White owing to the position occupied by the opposing pieces, although they may be equal in number. Every fair-to-middling Checker player must be familiar with most of these positions—lacking such knowledge, he may abandon many a game as drawn that he could win, and will lose many a game that he could draw. The basic positions that follow are found in most books on Checkers; but the player must be able to recognize on the checkerboard any position that resembles them or that can be maneuvered up to them. The expert strives to exchange his men so as to bring about one of these positions; after this he knows that he has a sure win, although his less-skilled opponent may be unaware of the fact.

First Position

Solution: 18–23, 32–28, 23–27, 28–32, 19–23, 32–28, 27–32, 28–24, 32–28, 24–20, 23–19!, 20–24, 19–15, 24–27, 15–18, 3–8, 18–15, 8–12, 15–18, 12–16, 28–32, 27–24, 18–15, 24–28A, 15–11!, 16–19, 32–27, 28–32, 27–31, 32–28, 11–16, 19–24, 16–19, and White wins.

A. Against Black's 16–20, White answers 15–18 and the play continues as follows: 24–19, 32–28!, 19–16, 18–23, 16–12, 23–19, 12–8, 28–32, 8–11, 32–27, 11–8, 27–23, and White wins.

Second Position

Solution: 32–28, 25–22, 28–24, 22–18, 24–19, 18–22A, 19–15, 22–17, 15–18, 17–13, 18–22, 13–9, 30–26, 9–6, 26–23, 6–10, 23–18, 10–6, 18–14, 6–1, 14–9, 1–5, 9–6, 5–1, 6–2, 1–5, 2–6, 5–1, 6–10, 1–5, 10–15, 5–9, 15–19, 9–14, 27–23, 14–10, 23–18, 10–6, 18–14, 6–1, 14–9, 1–5, 9–6, 5–1, 6–2, 1–5, 2–6, 5–1, 6–10, 1–5, 10–14, 5–1, 14–18, 1–6, 18–23, 6–10, 23–27, 10–14, 19–23, 14–9, 23–18, 9–6, 18–14, 6–1, 14–9, 1–5, 22–17, 5–14, 17–10, 21–25, 10–15, 25–30, 15–19, 30–26, 27–32, 26–22, 19–24, 20–27, 32–23, 22–17, 23–18, 17–13, 18–14, and White wins.

A. Against Black's 18–4, White answers 27–23, the play runs back into the above play, and White wins.

Third Position

Solution: 13–9, 22–18, 9–6, 18–22A, 6–1B, 22–18, 21–25, 18–15, 1–6!, 14–17, 6–2!, 17–14, 25–22!, 15–10, 22–26, 14–18, 5–9, 10–6, 9–13, 6–10, 26–31!, 10–14, 31–27, 18–22, 27–23, 22–25, 2–7, 25–22, 7–11, 22–25, 11–15, 25–22, 23–27, 22–26, 27–24, 26–22, 24–20, 22–26, 20–16, 26–22, 16–12!, 22–26, 12–8, 26–22, 8–3, 14–9, 15–10, and Black wins.

A. Against 18–15, Black answers 21–25 and the play runs back into the above play after a few moves. However, if White plays 18–15 and Black replies with 6–1, then White gets a draw by 15–10, 21–25, 14–17, 25–30, 17–14, 30–26, 14–17, etc., with a perpetual draw (a deadlocked position where the moves made by both sides are repetitions, finally resulting in an agreed-upon draw).

B. Now that White has gone back to square 22, this is Black's only move to win. If

Black plays 6–2, then White again draws with 14–10, 5–9, 10–6, 9–13, 6–10, 21–17, 22–18, with a perpetual draw.

Fourth Position

Solution: Black to play: 24–20, 31–27, 23–19, 27–31, 19–24, 32–27, 22–18, 27–32, 18–23, 31–26, 23–18, 26–31. Drawn. Black cannot force an exchange or advance because the move is against him.

White to play: 32–28, 24–20, 28–32, 22–18, 31–27, 23–19, 27–31, 19–24, 32–27, 24–28, 27–32, 18–23, 31–27, 23–26, 30–23, 28–24, 27–31, 24–27, 31–24, 20–18, and Black wins.

Fifth Position

Solution: 26–23, 14–17, 23–26, 17–21, 26–23, 15–10, 23–26, 21–17, 22–18, 10–6, 18–22, 17–14, 26–30, 6–2, 30–26. Drawn (perpetual back and forth). Black cannot move the black piece on square 13. This is a very unusual position where White, with one piece short, can effect a draw by his positional advantage.

Sixth Position

Solution: Black to play: 9–5, 15–18, 5–9, 10–14, 9–6, 19–23, 27–24, 18–15. The same position but White to play.

White to play: 15–18, 27–32, 19–24, 9–5 (if 32–28, reply 18–15), 10–14, 32–28 (if 5–1, reply 24–27), 24–27, 5–1 (if 28–32, reply 27–23), 14–9, and Black is forced into a swap leaving White with two against one.

Seventh Position

Solution: 10–15, 1–16, 15–19, 6–10, 19–23, 10–14, 11–15, 14–9, 23–27, 9–14, 27–32, 14–9, 15–11, 9–14, 12–16, 14–18, 16–19, 18–22, 19–23, 28–24, 11–15, 20–16, 32–28, 24–20, 28–24, 16–12, 15–11. Black now has an easy win, as he holds the two white pieces hemmed and can trap the remaining white piece after getting a third King.

Eighth Position

Solution: 27–31, 25–29, 31–26, 29–25, 19–24, 12–16, 24–27, 16–20, 27–32, 25–29, 26–22, 20–24, 22–26, 29–25, 26–31, 24–28, 31–26, and White wins.

The Standard Checker Laws

The first Checker laws were formulated by World's Champion Andrew Anderson in 1852. With only a few additions and minor changes, these laws are still in effect today.

1. *The Standard Board.* The Standard Board must be of light and dark squares, not less than 14 1/2 inches, nor more than 16 inches across said squares. The board shall be placed for play so that the bottom corner square on the left hand shall be black.

2. *The Standard Men.* The Standard Men, technically described as Black and White, must be light and dark (say red and white preferably, or black and white), turned, and round, and not less than 1 1/4 inches in diameter, nor more than 1 1/2 inches in diameter.

3. *Placing the Men.* The men shall be placed on the black squares. The black men shall invariably be placed upon the real or supposed first 12 squares of the board; the white men upon the last 12 squares.

4. *Order of Play.* Each player shall play alternately with black and white men; lots shall be cast for the choice of color only for the first game of a match. Thereafter, the players change color so that both players have the same chance to play first, since the first move shall invariably be made by the player having the black men.

5. *Time Limit for Moving.* At the end of 5 minutes (if the move has not previously been made), "time" must be called in a distinct voice by the person appointed for the purpose; and if the move be not completed on the expiration of another minute, the game shall be adjudged a loss through improper delay. When there is only one way of taking one or more pieces, "time" shall be called at the end of 1 minute and, if the move be not completed at the expiration of another minute, the game shall be adjudged as lost through improper delay.

I recommend changing the old standard five-minute time limit to a fixed number of moves per hour, as in chess, allowing the time to be used as desired. It would be a big step forward if time clocks were officially used in all Checker tournaments and matches. This would put an end to all delaying tactics and make for a more disciplined game.

6. *Arranging the Men During a Game.* Either player is entitled, on giving notice, to arrange his own or his opponent's pieces properly on the squares. After the move has been made, however, if either player touches or arranges any piece without giving notice, he shall be cautioned for the first offense, and shall forfeit the game for any subsequent act of the kind.

7. *Touch and Move.* After the pieces have been arranged, if the person whose turn it is to play touches or grasps a piece, he must either play it or forfeit the game. When the piece is not playable, he is cautioned for a first offense and forfeits the game for a second. If a piece is moved over the angle of the square on which it is stationed, the play must be completed in that direction.

8. *Capturing Play.* A capturing play, as well as an ordinary one, is completed whenever the hand of the player is withdrawn from the piece played, even though one or more pieces could have been taken. When taking, if a player removes one of his own pieces, he cannot replace it; but his opponent can either play or insist upon his replacing it. A single piece capturing an opposing piece or pieces and landing into the opposing king row constitutes a completed move and becomes a King. It then becomes the opponent's turn to play.

9. *False or Improper Moves.* Either player making a false or improper move instantly forfeits the game to his opponent, without another move being made.

10. *The Huff or Blow.* Some years ago, a player had the option of removing his opponent's piece from the board when he failed to make a possible jump. In tournament games this ruling has been abolished, much to my dismay. In my opinion, if a player is careless enough to overlook a jump, he deserves to lose the piece, the game, or possibly the match. Today, however, if a player fails to jump, his opponent has the right to point out his opponent's possible jump and insist he make the capture.

11. *Crowning the Men.* When a single piece first reaches any of the squares on the extreme opposite end of the board (the opponent's king row), it becomes a King; it must be *crowned* by placing a same-colored piece on top of it, before another move is made by either player. It can then be moved backward or forward, one square at a time, as the limits of the board permit. The King must be crowned by the player having the opposite-colored pieces.

12. *Drawn Games.* A game is drawn when neither of the players can force a win. If one player appears stronger than the other, that party is required to complete the win or show a decided advantage to the satisfaction of the opponent within 40 of his own moves—to be counted from the point at which notice was

given—failing which he must relinquish the game as drawn.

13. *Conduct of the Players and Spectators.* Anything tending to distract or annoy a player is strictly forbidden, such as making signs or sounds, pointing or hovering over the board, or unnecessarily delaying to move a piece touched. Spectators should not smoke or talk near the players. A player may smoke if agreeable to his opponent. Any player acting in a distracting or annoying manner, after having been warned, shall forfeit the game. While play is pending, neither player shall leave the room without sufficient reason or without having the other's consent or company. Any spectator giving warning or comment in any manner on a game, whether playing or pending, shall be ordered from the room during the match—play to be discontinued until such offending party retires.

14. *Match Games.* A match between equals, wins and draws to count, shall consist of an even number of games, so that each player may have the first move of the game the same number of times.

15. *Tourney and Team Matches.* Tourney and team matches should consist of an equal number of games between each pair of players, regardless of the number of players in the tourney, or on each team.

16. *Excessive Tie Scores.* Tourneys played under the straight "knockout" style of play should consist of as many additional sets of two games as are found necessary to eliminate one of the contestants. This is done to prevent excessive tie scores. In the double knockout style of play, a player must lose two full lives (games) before being eliminated from play. This may consist of two lost games or one lost game and two drawn games. If a player has drawn three games, putting him a life and a half (1 1/2 games) down, I feel that he should lose one game before being ousted. I don't believe a player should be eliminated by drawn games alone—he should be defeated at least once.

17. *Enforcement of the Laws.* Either player committing a breach of any of the foregoing laws must submit to the prescribed penalty; and his opponent is equally bound to exact the same.

18. *Unforeseen Disputes.* Should any dispute arise not satisfactorily determined by the preceding laws, a written statement of the facts shall be submitted to a disinterested arbiter having a knowledge of the game, whose decision shall be final.

The Losing Game

Also called Giveaway Checkers, this variant is played under the same rules as regular Checkers, except that each player attempts to force his opponent to capture his pieces; the first player to lose them all wins the game. Thus, opening play is almost completely concerned with luring or forcing a white piece to square 12 or a black piece to square 21. A piece on this advanced square costs its owner the game, since the opponent can at leisure dispose his men so that, after the piece is released and forced to jump to the king row, the new King will devastate the board. Incidentally, it is not possible in the Losing Game to have a draw, except when a block is counted as such.

Italian Checkers

This game was played in Italy at the end of the sixteenth century, and differs from regular Checkers as follows:

1. A single piece cannot take a King.

2. A player must take when possible, or lose the game. If he has a choice of captures, he is forced to take the greater number; if the number is equal, then he must take the more powerful pieces (e.g., he is compelled to take a King in preference to a single piece).

3. The double corner is placed at the player's left.

Spanish Checkers

This game is played like the Italian Checkers game with the following difference: The King moves any distance along an open diagonal, and captures by jumping to the adjacent vacant square beyond an adverse piece, any distance away.

Continental Checkers or Polish Checkers

This game is played on a board 10 by 10, and each side has 20 pieces, set initially on the first four ranks. The rules are as follows:

1. A single piece moves one square diagonally forward; but a single piece captures by the short jump both diagonally forward or backward.

2. A King can move diagonally any number of unoccupied squares and may land any number of vacant squares beyond a captured piece.

3. Capturing is compulsory; if a player has a choice of captures, he must choose the one in which the greatest number of captures are made. If equal numbers are involved, then the more-powerful pieces must be taken.

4. Captured pieces are only lifted at the end of the move and a dead piece forms an impassable barrier.

5. A single piece is only promoted to a King when it remains on the opponent's back line or king row. If, on reaching the king row, more captures are possible, they must be made and the move completed; the single piece remains unpromoted until he again reaches the king row and remains there at the end of the move. (By the way, in all the European variants, I use the term King as in American Checkers, but the actual term is *Queen, Woman,* or *Dame.*)

Damenspiel

Damenspiel, or German Checkers, follows the rules of Polish Checkers except that it is played on a board 8 by 8 with 12 pieces on each side, arranged as in American Checkers.

Shashki

Shashki, or Russian Checkers, follows the rules of Damenspiel except for the following:

1. Choice of capture is not compulsory.

2. When a single piece reaches the back line or king row, it becomes at once a King and continues to function as one.

Turkish Checkers

This game is played on a board 8 by 8; and 16 pieces on each side are arranged on the second and third ranks, leaving the king rows vacant. The rules are as follows:

1. A single piece moves one square forward or sideways, but not diagonally; on reaching the backline, it becomes a King.

2. A single piece captures by short jumps forward or sideways and may take more than one piece in a turn of play.

3. A King can move forward, backward, or sideways, any number of vacant squares. The King can place himself on any vacant square beyond the captured piece to make further captures.

4. Captured pieces are removed as taken and a turn continues until the piece can make no more captures.

5. Capturing is compulsory and, with a choice of captures, the player must take the maximum number of adverse pieces.

6. The first player to capture or immobilize all his opponent's pieces, or to reduce the adversary to a single man against a King, wins the game.

Reversi

This Checker-like game is played on a board of 64 squares, eight to each side. (A standard

 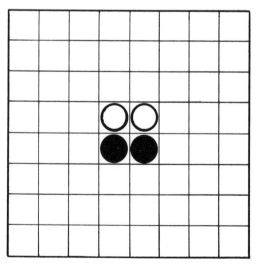

In Reversi, the oblique opening (left) and square opening (right).

checkerboard, 8 by 8, will do.) Each player has 32 men or pieces, each piece being black on one side and white on the other.

White begins by placing a piece white side up on one of the four central squares on the empty board. Black replies by placing his first piece black side up on another of these squares. The central four squares must be filled first and then the players play alternately, each piece being placed on a square adjacent to one occupied by an opponent's piece. Any enemy pieces directly intervening between this piece and another of the player's own color, orthogonally or diagonally, are captured and turned over to show the player's color uppermost. That is, the player's object is to have another of his own pieces in a direct line, horizontally, vertically, or diagonally, on the other side of the opponent's piece or pieces on the line. If a black piece, for instance, is set beside a white piece, it doesn't matter how many white pieces are beyond in the line, provided there is a black piece at the other end of the line. When a player succeeds in doing this, he turns over all the intervening men of his opponent, transferring them to his own color. A piece may change owners several times in a game. When all the squares of the board are covered with the pieces, the player with the most of his color showing wins the game.

TEEKO®

Teeko is the first really new all-skill board game since the invention of Checkers 8,000 years ago. One of the greatest gratifications of my life was the invention and perfection of Teeko, a game I labored 27 years to perfect. I firmly believe that Teeko will some day replace Checkers as the number one all-skill board game throughout the world. My three main reasons follow: (1) For sheer fun and enjoyment, Teeko leaves Checkers far behind because it can be played in 21 different ways (Standard Teeko is just one of these ways), each of which has 16 different methods for starting a game. Checkers, on the other hand, can only be played in one way. (2) Teeko was the first all-skill board game invented with a point scoring system, a feature that, in turn, leads to many different ways of scoring a game or match. In addition, this point scoring feature permits Teeko to be played by two, three, or four persons at the same time. Checkers lacks this feature. (3) Memory plays a smaller role in Teeko ability than in Checkers, simply because the opening, middle, and end game in Teeko have a far greater range than in Checkers.

Due to space limitation, only the playing rules for Standard Teeko (one of 21 different Teeko games) are listed in these pages. If you wish to study the complete strategy of winning play for Standard Teeko, it is suggested that you read *Scarne on Teeko,* a 137-page book devoted exclusively to the game of Teeko. This book also contains the official rules of play and the strategy of winning play for 21 Teeko variants.

Official Rules for Standard Teeko

Requirements. Standard Teeko, also known as Teeko 44 Positions, can be played by two people only. Although the game may involve two, three, or four players, only two persons can be in play against each other simultaneously. Only a Standard Teeko game board and eight Standard Teeko pawns are required to play the game. A Teeko score pad and pencil are necessary to keep score.

The Standard Teeko Game Board. The Standard Teeko game board is 16 1/2 inches by 16 1/2 inches, and is made up of 25 solid blue circles, 1 1/2 inches in diameter, outlined by white circles. Adjacent circles are connected by fine red lines: vertical, diagonal, and horizontal.

The Standard Teeko Pawns. The Standard Teeko pawns are eight in number: four black and four red. Each is a disc 1 1/2 inches in diameter and 1/2 inch thick. The four pawns of each color group are marked with white spots numbered from 1 to 4.

The Object of the Game. The object of the game is to form a winning position on the game board from either of the two following group configurations:

Group 1. Four in a Row: To try to win the game and score the greatest possible number of points by arranging four pawns of the same color on four connecting circles of the Teeko game board in any numerical order in such a manner as to form a *four-in-a-row* winning position running vertically, horizontally, or diagonally. There are 28 possible four-in-a-row winning positions on the game board.

**Four in a Row
A Vertical Winning Position**

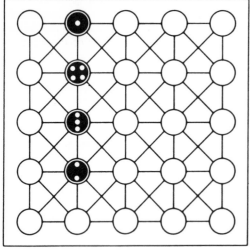

**TEEKO has 10 of the
above winning positions**

**Four in a Row
A Horizontal Winning Position**

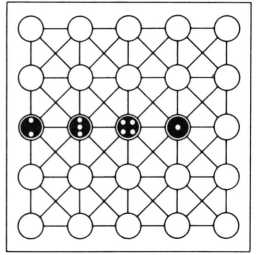

**TEEKO has 10 of the
above winning positions**

**Four in a Row
A Diagonal Winning Position**

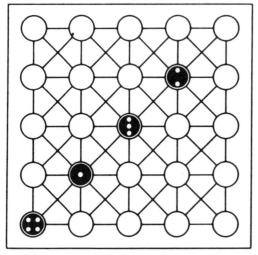

**TEEKO has 8 of the
above winning positions**

**A Small Square
winning position**

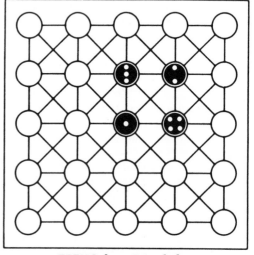

**TEEKO has 16 of the
above winning positions**

In Standard Teeko, the winning positions.

Group 2. Small Square: To try to win the game and score the greatest possible number of points by arranging four pawns of the same color on four connecting circles of the game board in any numerical order in such a manner as to form a *small-square* winning position. There are 16 possible small-square winning positions on the game board for a total of 44 possible winning positions in Standard Teeko.

The Start of the Game: Choosing the Teeko Pawns. The players choose their pawns, and each player must take four Teeko pawns of the same color. Colors are chosen by mutual consent or as follows: Either player by consent of the other takes a black and a red Teeko pawn. Placing both hands behind his back he puts one pawn in each hand. Making two closed fists he brings both hands forward. His opponent touches either fist. If it contains a red pawn, the guesser takes the red pawns; if black, he takes the black pawns. His opponent takes the four remaining pawns. The holder of the red pawns may choose any seat. His opponent sits opposite him. The first move in every game is always made by the person holding the black pawns. Thereafter, each player plays alternately: Black, then Red, Black, then Red, etc. In the second game the player who had the red pawns now takes the black and so moves first. Hereafter, to simplify matters, the player making the first move in each succeeding game shall be referred to as "Black" and his opponent as "Red."

Placing the Pawns on the Game Board: The Regular Drop Move. The placing of the Teeko pawns on the circles of the game board is part of the strategy of the game and is accomplished by the use of the *regular drop move* or the go-as-you-please type of drop move. This simply means that a player, at his turn of play, has the choice of selecting any one of the pawns he holds and placing it on any one of the unoccupied circles of the game board (with the exception that Black's first regular drop move cannot place a pawn on the center of the board). Players must make their regular drop moves one at a time, alternately. To illustrate, a detailed description of how the regular drop moves are employed in the placing of the pawns on the game board follows:

1. Black, the starting player, places his first Teeko pawn, which may be any one of the four numbered pawns, on any circle of the game board with this exception: Black is not permitted to place his first pawn on the center circle of the game board. The placing of a pawn on a circle of the game board is known as a regular drop move.

2. Red places any one of his four Teeko pawns on any one of the 24 remaining unoccupied circles.

3. Black places any one of his three pawns on any one of the 23 remaining unoccupied circles.

4. Red places any of his three pawns on any one of the 22 remaining unoccupied circles.

5. Black places either of his two pawns on any one of the 21 remaining unoccupied circles.

6. Red places either of his two pawns on any one of the 20 remaining unoccupied circles.

7. Black places his fourth and last pawn on any one of the 19 remaining unoccupied circles.

8. Red places his fourth and last pawn on any one of the 18 remaining unoccupied circles.

If a player succeeds in placing his fourth and last pawn in either a four-in-a-row winning position or a small-square winning position, he calls, "Teeko" or "Teeko-Teeko," and wins the game. The game score is determined by the spot value of the last (fourth) played pawn, which completes a winning position, and by the circle of the game board on which it rests. A pawn that completes a winning position and ends the game is known as the *winning pawn.*

If a winning position has not been achieved with the placing of the eight Teeko pawns on the circles of the game board, the game continues as follows.

Continuation of the Game. Line Moves. If in a Standard Teeko game a four-in-a-row or a small-square winning position has not been achieved by either of the two players in the initial placing of their four pawns on the circles of the game board, the game continues in this fashion: Black, who moves first, must move one of his four pawns forward, backward, sideways, or diagonally from the circle on which it is resting onto an adjacent unoccupied circle. This is known as a *line move* and is done by sliding the pawn over one of the red lines connecting any two circles as shown on the game board. Black having completed his first move, it becomes Red's turn to move. This method of moving is continued alternately until one player succeeds in forming either a winning four-in-a-row position or a small-square position. When this occurs, the winning player calls "Teeko" or "Teeko-Teeko," ending the game. The game score is determined by the spot value of the last (fourth) played pawn which completes a winning position and the circle of the game board on which it rests.

How to Score a Teeko Game. The last-played pawn, which completes a winning position and ends the game, is called the *winning pawn*. The numerical spot value of the winning pawn and the circle on the game board where it comes to rest determines the number of points credited to the winning player, which may be 1, 2, 3, 4, 5, 6, 7, or 8 points. This holds true whether the winning position is completed by making use of a regular drop move, a point drop move, or a line move.

The scoring is as follows:

1. *Teeko:* If the winning pawn is played onto any one of 20 circles of the game board (center and corner circles excluded) the player calls "Teeko," and scores the numerical spot value of the winning pawn. *Examples:* If the winning pawn is a 1-spot, the player scores 1 point for the game. If it is a 2-spot, the player scores 2 points; a 3-spot, 3 points; a 4-spot, 4 points.

2. *Teeko-Teeko:* If the winning pawn is played onto the center circle or onto one of the four corner circles of the game board, called *bonus circles,* the player calls "Teeko-Teeko," and scores the numerical spot value of the winning pawn plus a Teeko game bonus of 4 points. *Examples:* If the winning pawn is a 1-spot, the player scores 1 point plus a 4-point game bonus for a total game score of 5 points. If the winning pawn is a two-spot, the player scores 2 points plus a 4-point game bonus for a total game score of 6 points. If it is a three-spot, 3 points plus 4 points or 7 points. If it is a 4-spot, score 4 points plus 4 points, or 8 points.

A corner-circle Teeko-Teeko small-square winning position can only be completed with a regular or point drop move—not with a line move.

Teeko's 16 Game Openings. The author has developed 16 game-opening methods for the initial placing of the eight Teeko pawns on the circles of the game board. Most of these game openings are achieved by making use of the regular drop move, combined with a new basic game-starting principle called the *point drop move*. This point drop move is the direct opposite of the regular drop move. When making use of the regular drop move in the placing of the pawns on the circles of the game board, each player at his turn of play places one of his pawns on any unoccupied circle of the game board. When a point drop move is to be used, each player at his opponent's turn of play must determine on which circle of the board his opponent must place his pawn. He does this by touching any unoccupied circle with his index finger. This action being completed, his opponent must abide by this decision and place one of his pawns on the circle indicated.

The point drop move rule is as follows. A player at his proper turn of play says the word "Point." The expression *point* signifies that the player is asking his opponent to point or touch an unoccupied circle of the game board on which he wants the player to place his pawn. The player's opponent on hearing the player say "Point" must touch with his index finger any unoccupied circle that he desires. This action being completed, the player (whose turn it is to play) must abide by this decision and place one of his Teeko pawns on the circle touched by his opponent.

The strategy involved in the use of the point drop move is in direct contrast to that of a regular drop move. Using the point drop move tends to form one of the countless millions of loose spread-out initial eight-pawn setups (opposite from the tighter setups achieved when using only the regular drop move). These looser setups are accomplished by directing one or more of the opponent's pawns to a circle or circles of the Teeko board so that they will be as far removed as possible from the others; this causes the opponent's pawns to be in as unfavorable a setup as possible for achieving a win.

The point drop move in combination with the regular drop move is used in the 16 different game opening styles that follow. These opening game variations strike a mean that falls somewhere between a tight center opening game and a spread-out loose one.

If a winning position as stipulated by the rules of Standard Teeko has not been achieved by either of the two players with the initial placing of their eight pawns on the circles of the game board, the game is played to a finish by making use of one or more line moves.

Following are Teeko's 16 different game openings.

1. *Point the First Drop Move.* This means that each player's first drop move must be made with the point drop move; his second, third, and fourth drop moves are made with the regular drop move.

2. *Point the Second Drop Move.* This means that each player's second drop move must be made with the point drop move; his first, third and, fourth drop moves are made with the regular drop move.

In a similar manner the 13 other game openings are played. In each case the name of the opening tells which moves must be played as point drop moves.

3. *Point the Third Drop Move.* This means that each player's third drop move must be made with the point drop move and his first, second and fourth drop moves with the regular drop move.

4. *Point the Last Drop Move.* This means that each player's fourth drop move must be made with the point drop move and his first, second and third drop moves with the regular drop move.

5. *Point the First Two Drop Moves.*

6. *Point the First and Third Drop Moves.*

7. *Point the First and Last Drop Moves.*

8. *Point the Second and Third Drop Moves.*

9. *Point the Second and Last Drop Moves.*

10. *Point the Last Two Drop Moves.*

11. *Point the First Three Drop Moves.*

12. *Point the First, Second, and Last Drop Moves.*

13. *Point the First, Third, and Last Drop Moves.*

14. *Point the Last Three Drop Moves.*

15. *Point All Four Drop Moves.*

16. *Point No Drop Moves.*

Loser's Choice

Playing Loser's Choice usually means playing a different drop-move game opening for each subsequent game. Prior to the start of the Teeko session, the player who is holding the red pawns has the right to name any one of the 16 different drop-move game openings for the first game. Thereafter, the loser of each game has the right to name the drop-move game opening for the following game, and so on.

Let's say you have been playing Standard Teeko with the four regular drop-move game openings, and the loser wishes to change the next game opening to point the first drop move. The loser simply says "Point the first drop move." This means that each player's first drop move must be made with a point drop move and the remaining three drop moves must be made in regular drop-move fashion. Perhaps the loser of the previous game calls "Point the last drop move." This means that the first three drop moves must be made using the regular drop moves and the last (fourth) drop move must be made using the point drop move. You'll find Loser's Choice is a fascinating variation that will appeal to all as a change of pace.

Teeko Match Play

Match Play is an enjoyable way to score a series of Teeko games. A match consists of one or more games and terminates at the end of any game in which a final score of 10 or more points is attained by either player.

How to Score a Teeko Match

1. Winner of the match scores the point difference between both players' match totals.

2. Winner of the match receives a match bonus of 10 points for winning.

3. Should a player score 10 points or more before his opponent scores any points at all, winner gets a 10-point match bonus plus a 10-point shutout bonus—plus the points scored. Following is a sample scoring of a Teeko match:

	Player A		Player B	
	Points	*Total*	*Points*	*Total*
First game			4	4
Second game			1	5
Third game	3	3		
Fourth game			4	9
Fifth game			8	17
Players' match scores		3		17
Match bonus				10
				27
				− 3 (A's Score)
			B wins by 24 points	

In the above sample match, B won four games including an 8-point Teeko-Teeko for the last game—making a match score of 17 points. Player A won one game totaling 3 points. B's 17 points puts him over the 10-point match mark, which ends the game and makes him the winner. B also gets a 10-point match bonus for winning the match. B's total match score is 27 points, A's 3. So, B's total point winnings for the match are the point difference in score, or 24 points. At a penny a point, B collects 24 cents from A.

Three-Handed Teeko Match Play

This is a two-handed Teeko match variation for three players. Although three players take part, only two are in play against each other simultaneously. The rules for Teeko Match Play apply with the following exceptions and additional rules.

To determine which two shall start, any player, by consent of the others, places three pawns of the same color face down on the table and moves them around to mix them. Each of his opponents takes one and he takes the last. Low man, the player who picked the pawn with the lowest point value, sits out the first game. The others play a two-handed Teeko game. The player who picked the highest numbered pawn takes the black pawns and makes the first move of the game. The opponent takes the red pawns.

The score of the first game is credited to the winner on the score sheet and the loser drops out. The winner proceeds to play the next game against the third player. So it goes, loser giving way to nonplayer, game by game, until one of the three scores 10 points or more and ends the match. After the first game has been completed, and the nonplayer sits down to play his game, he must play the colored pawns destined for the seat he is occupying. The winner is paid off in the amount of his credit over each opponent. To receive a shutout bonus, both of his opponents must score zero. Following is a sample scoring of a three-person Teeko match:

	Player A		Player B		Player C	
	Points	Total	Points	Total	Points	Total
First game	3	3				
Second game			8	8		
Third game					6	6
Fourth game					3	9
Fifth game					4	13
Players' match scores		3		8		13
Match bonus						10
Players' total match scores		3		8		23

The game credits plus the match bonus bring C's total to 23 points, A's to 3, and B's to 8. Player C, the winner, collects the following point difference from each player: 20 points from A and 15 points from B. At a penny a point, C collects 20 cents from A and 15 cents from B.

Standard Teeko Strategy

The best form of practice at Teeko is to play alone. Many hours of enjoyment and heightened skill will reward your efforts when you play solitaire Teeko. For a player to become an expert Teekoist, or even a respectable amateur, he first should memorize the position of the circles shown on the numbered Teeko board (see the illustration on page 520). Next, the player should familiar-ize himself with Standard Teeko's 44 winning positions. Of these 44, 28 are positions of four in a row, and 16 are small-square positions. As you study Teeko, place your four pawns on the circles of the game board in the various winning positions. Follow this procedure with each of the 44 winning positions—get accustomed to their design on the game board. Continue this kind of practice until you are thoroughly acquainted with the configurations of the 44 winning positions on the game board.

Now put a pawn on the board. Study its position. Decide on which circle you should place the second pawn—then the third—finally, the fourth. Next, practice placing the black and the red pawns alternately on the board. Make Black's move first, then Red's, and continue this practice until you are acquainted with the best possible kinds of regular drop moves on the game board. It is important to remember that a player must think with the placing of each pawn on the game board, as this is a vital part of the game; games can be won or lost with the bad placement of just one pawn.

Teeko's starting game has no definite break where one can be said to be leaving the starting game and entering the middle game. In order not to confuse this text, we will consider that, if a winning position has not been achieved by either player and Black has made his third line move, the starting game ends and the middle game commences. The opening phase of Standard Teeko with its regular drop moves is characterized by each player trying to win the game by dropping (placing) his four pawns on the game board in a winning setup; or, failing that, to maneuver to achieve as strong an offensive position on the board as possible.

Black, who has the first drop move, will strive to win the game in his first four regular drop moves or at least to obtain the initiative with a strong placement position. Red will attempt to prevent Black from winning and will try to win by taking the initiative himself, attempting to neutralize Black's offensive position and preparing his own counter offensive.

The player must bear in mind that there are untold millions of different possible setups of the eight pawns on the circles of the game board. Some of these setups are weak, some are strong, some are surefire winners, and some are surefire losers for either player. Therefore, in order to play a good game of Teeko, it is necessary to place your pawns on the board in as advantageous a setup as possible. The sequence in which the numbered pawns are dropped on the game board can, at times, make the difference between winning or losing the game by a lesser or greater number of points. Most beginners drop their pawns on the circles of the board in a 1, 2, 3, 4, sequence. The importance of such a maneuver depends entirely upon the ability of the player and his opponent.

To aid the player in improving his starting game as quickly as possible, eight of my favorite Standard Teeko regular drop move traps and their solutions follow. Some of these traps can be maneuvered into a winning position with the regular drop of the fourth pawn on the game board, others require one, two, or more line moves. But, before referring

to the solution for the proper move, always try to analyze the reason for the move or moves given. Follow this procedure with each regular drop move and line move you make and then compare your result with the play-by-play solution given below each trap. For the explanation of the letters and numerals listed in the following pages, see page 520.

Regular Drop-Move Traps in Standard Teeko

1. *Sucker Drop Trap.* Place B1 on C8; B2 on C13; R2 on C9; R1 on C14. Black moves first. *Solution:* Black drops B3 on C18; Red drops R3 on C23; Black drops B4 on C3, calls "Teeko," and wins the game by 4 points.

2. *Two-Way Square Drop Trap.* Place B2 on C4; B1 on C5; B4 on C10; R4 on C9; R2 on C14; R3 on C19. Black moves first. *Solution:* Black drops B3 on C24; Red drops R1 on C18; Black moves B2 to C8; Red moves R4 to C13, calls "Teeko-Teeko," and wins the game by 8 points.

3. *Two-Way Drop Trap.* Place B1 on C6; B2 on C7; B3 on C16; R3 on C8; R2 on C17; R1 on C21. Black moves first. *Solution:* Black drops B4 on C11; Red drops R4 on C1; Black moves B3 to C12, calls "Teeko," and wins the game by 3 points.

4. *Diagonal Sucker Drop Trap.* Place B1 on C7; B4 on C13; R2 on C8; R1 on C9. Black moves first. *Solution:* Black drops B2 on C19; Red drops R3 on C25; Black drops B3 on C1, calls "Teeko-Teeko," and wins the game by 7 points.

5. *Sneaky Side Drop Trap.* Place B3 on C5; B1 on C10; B2 on C15; B4 on C19; R1 on C9; R2 on C14; R4 on C20. Red moves first. *Solution:* Red drops R3 on C4; Black moves B4 to C13; Red moves R4 to C19, calls "Teeko," and wins the game by 4 points.

6. *Switcher Three-Way Drop Trap.* Place B1 on C9; B2 on C10; B3 on C13; R3 on C14; R2 on C18; R1 on C22. Black moves first. *Solution:* Black drops B4 on C17; Red drops R4 on C5; Black moves B4 to C12; Red moves R3 to C8; Black moves B1 to C14; Red moves R2 to C19; Black moves B2 to C15, calls "Teeko," and wins the game by 2 points.

7. *Two-Way Drop Trap.* Place B3 on C9; B2 on C15; B1 on C19; R2 on C8; R1 on C13; R3 on C21. Black moves first. *Solution:* Black drops B4 on C14; Red drops R4 on C20; Black moves B2 to C10; Red moves R2 to C4; Black moves B1 to C15, calls "Teeko," and wins the game by 1 point.

8. *Diagonal Switcher Drop Trap.* Place B3 on C7; B1 on C8; B4 on C14; B2 on C20; R1 on C5; R4 on C12; R2 on C17. Red moves first. *Solution:* Red drops R3 on C2; Black moves B1 to C13; Red moves R2 to C18; Black moves B4 to C19; Red moves R2 to C24; Black moves B2 to C25, calls "Teeko-Teeko," and wins the game by 6 points.

All previously discussed regular drop-move traps apply to the point drop openings, but these traps appear in disguise and their formation is very deceptive in this loose phase of the game. Therefore, as author-inventor, I feel it advisable to list some of the workings of these traps in a loose, spreadout position typical of the average point drop openings. Following are my five such traps selected from the many thousands of possible traps found in this phase of the game. These traps are elementary in nature and can be formed into a winning position in two, three, or four moves. There is just enough difference to bring home to the player the working of most traps found while the eight-pawn setup is in a loose position. Some of the traps listed here have more than one correct solution; but, to save space, only one winning solution is given. However, if you score a win by another method of play, it must score the same number of points. Each of these drop-move traps that follow has been achieved by employing a point drop opening.

Line-Move Traps with Point Drop Openings in Standard Teeko

Line-Move Trap No. 1. Place B1 on C1; B2 on C6; B3 on C11; B4 on C5; R1 on C25; R2 on C20; R3 on C15; R4 on C21. Black moves first. *Solution:* Black moves B4 to C9; Red moves R3 to C14; Black moves B4 to C8; Red moves R3 to C13; Black moves B3 to C7; Red moves R3 to C19; Black moves B4 to C2, calls "Teeko," and wins the game by 4 points.

Line-Move Trap No. 2. Place B1 on C7; B2 on C9; B3 on C10; B4 on C17; R1 on C8; R2 on C11; R3 on C12; R4 on C21. Black moves first. *Solution:* Black moves B1 to C13; Red moves R1 to C4; Black moves B3 to C5, calls "Teeko-Teeko," and wins the game by 7 points.

Line-Move Trap No. 3. Place B1 on C8; B2 on C13; B3 on C15; B4 on C18; R1 on C9; R2 on C14; R3 on C19; R4 on C21. Black moves first. *Solution:* Black moves B3 to C20; Red moves R4 to C17; Black moves B3 to C24; Red moves R3 to C23; Black moves B4 to C19; Red moves R2 to C20; Black moves B3 to C25; Red moves R4 to C12; Black moves B1 to C7, calls "Teeko," and wins the game by 1 point.

Line-Move Trap No. 4. Place B1 on C9; B2 on C12; B3 on C19; B4 on C25; R1 on C1; R2 on C2; R3 on C11; R4 on C17. Red moves first. *Solution:* Red moves R2 to C6; Black moves B2 to C16; Red moves R4 to C12; Black moves B1 to C8; Red moves R1 to C7, calls "Teeko," and wins the game by 1 point.

Line-Move Trap No. 5. Place B1 on C5; B2 on C13; B3 on C15; B4 on C25; R1 on C1; R2 on C2; R3 on C7; R4 on C17. Black moves first. *Solution:* Black moves B2 to C12; Red moves R4 to C11; Black moves B2 to C6; Red moves R3 to C12; Black moves B2 to C7; Red moves R2 to C6; Black moves B2 to C13; Red moves R3 to C16, calls "Teeko," and wins the game by 3 points.

The Numbered Teeko Board. To aid the reader to understand more readily the structure and formation of the pawn setups on the Teeko game board, which are given in this book, the lettered and numbered illustration of a Teeko game board is reproduced. No Teeko game board is made with letters and numbers on it; but, before the reader attempts the study of Teeko, he should memorize the position of the lettered and numbered circles as shown in the illustration below. In this way, he can follow each move or step detailed in this Teeko description. You will note that in each of the 25 circles of the illustrated game board, the letter C and the numerals 1 to 25 appear. The letter C followed by a

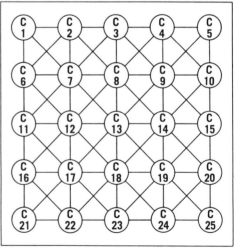

Reproduction of a numbered and lettered Teeko Game board.

number represents an identical circle on your own game board.

To properly use the illustration, an abbreviated description of the color and numbered values of the game pawns is also necessary. The letter B represents a black pawn, the letter R a red pawn. *Examples:* B1 represents the black pawn numbered 1; B2, the black pawn numbered 2; B3, the black pawn numbered 3; and B4, the black pawn numbered 4. R1 represents the red pawn numbered 1; R2, the red pawn numbered 2; R3, the red pawn numbered 3; and R4, the red pawn numbered 4.

Additional Teeko Rules. If you observe the Teeko rules of play, you will have more interesting and enjoyable games. The rules that govern irregularities are designed to define the offense and to provide an adequate remedy in all cases where a player accidentally, carelessly, or inadvertently violates a rule of the game and gains an unintentional but nevertheless unfair advantage. The right to penalize an offense or irregularity is forfeited if the offended player (*a*) waives the penalty, or (*b*) calls attention to an opponent's irregularity after he (the offended player) has made either a drop move or a line move. The general rules governing irregularities follow.

Placing a Pawn on the Game Board. During the starting game: Once a pawn has been placed on a circle, regardless of whether or not the player is still holding it, it shall be considered a completed move and the circle it touches is its final destination. The player is not permitted to remove it from that circle and place it on another circle. Any infraction of the above rule forfeits the game for the offender, and his opponent is credited with 8 points.

Compulsory Moves. The following are the so-called compulsory moves:

1. Once the eight Teeko pawns have been placed on the circles of the game board, and a player at his turn of play touches one of his own pawns, he must move that pawn. Should he indicate, by moving his pawn, a particular direction or to a specific circle, the play must be completed in that direction or to that circle.

2. If the player merely touches a pawn without indicating any direction, he must move that pawn; however, he may move it to any unoccupied adjacent circle.

3. A pawn, once moved to an unoccupied adjacent circle, cannot be taken back. The move is considered completed, whether or not the player still holds a hand on the pawn.

4. Once a player names the style of game next to be played, or the kind of drop-move game opening at his proper turn of call, he cannot change his mind and name another.

5. Once a player points to a circle while directing his opponent's point drop move, he cannot change his mind and point to another circle.

Any violation of the above rules forfeits the game for the offender and his opponent is credited with 8 points.

Time Limit for Moving. If a player fails to move within 3 minutes, time shall be called by the opponent. After subsequent failure to move in one more minute from the time notice is given, the game shall be adjudged lost through improper delay and the offender's opponent shall be credited with 8 points.

False or Improper Move. Either player making an improper move shall instantly forfeit the game, and the offender's opponent shall be credited with 8 points. Examples of improper moves are moving out of turn, moving an opponent's pawns, etc.

Conceding Defeat. A player cannot concede defeat until the game is completed. Infractions of this rule shall forfeit the game for the offender and his opponent shall be credited with 8 points.

No-Game. If one or both players are continuously moving one or more pawns back and forth from two or more circles in such a manner as to indicate deadlock or stalemate, either player may call "No-game." If the same position exists after ten moves (five for each player) from the time no-game is called, the game shall be declared a no-game (drawn game), which neither player wins or loses. No-games are almost nonexistent in Teeko.

Adjustment of the Pawns. A player may adjust one or more of his pawns on their respective circles of the board, after giving notice of his intention to do so. He may ask his opponent to adjust one or more pawns by saying "Please adjust your pawns." The opponent must comply with the request. Infractions of this rule shall forfeit the game for the offender and his opponent be credited with 8 points.

Selecting the Seating Positions. Prior to the start of the first match game, the player who is holding the red pawns has the privilege of choosing his seat. Holder of black pawns must sit opposite him.

CHAPTER 26

Games Requiring
Special Equipment

True, the board games of Chess, Checkers and Teeko require special game boards and counters or pieces, but these games have become standard part of the household equipment and there are few homes in North America or Great Britain that don't have at least one of these three game boards in it.

The games in this chapter are popular in various parts of the world and are becoming more international as the years go by. Actually some of these games are very old, others are fairly new.

BACKGAMMON

Backgammon, one of the world's most ancient games, has been played for thousands of years in all parts of the world. It was played in Egypt, Greece, and Rome, and probably derives from the even earlier oriental game of Pachisi (Parcheesi), in which the movements of counters on a board are governed by the throw of dice. It was played throughout the Middle Ages in Europe as Tables until Chess became the more popular game in the fifteenth century. In the early seventeenth century improvements in the game gave it a tremendous revival and it swept Europe under various names: Backgammon in England, Gammon in Scotland, Tric-trac in France, Puff in Germany, Tarola Reale in Italy. Another craze for the game occurred just before World War I, and it is still widely played in the Middle East as Tric-trac. Incidentally, the word Backgammon has been ascribed to the Welsh words *back* and *gammon* (little battle), and also to the Saxon *bac* and *gamen* (back game).

Requirements
1. Two players; three or more sometimes participate in the stakes (see Chouette, page 527).

2. *The Board.* A rectangular board is di-

WHITE

BLACK

The Backgammon board and the location of the men or stones at the start of the game.

vided into two halves by a vertical *bar*. One half is called the *inner* (or home) *table;* the other the *outer table.* (Traditionally the inner table is the one nearest the light.) The players, designated *Black* and *White,* face each other. Twelve alternately colored triangles, called *points,* project from each side of the board toward the center. The players sit on opposite sides of the board.

3. *Pieces.* Each player has 15 checkerlike pieces (often called *men* or *stones*) of contrasting colors, usually black and white. Their starting positions are shown in the illustration. The movement of White's pieces is from Black's inner table clockwise to White's home table. Black's pieces travel in the opposite direction.

4. *Dice.* Each player has a dice cup and two dice.

5. *Doubling Cube.* A large die whose faces are numbered: 2, 4, 8, 16, 32, 64.

Notation. Each point is numbered as in the diagram although the numbers do not appear on the board. The initials B and W indicate which side of the board the point is on. A move lists the point moved from and the point moved to. *Example:* White, B12–W6, B1–B3 means: White moves one stone from Black's 12 point to White's 6 point, and one stone from Black's 1 point to Black's 3 point. If more than one stone makes the same move, the number of stones being moved is added in parentheses as: B1–B3 (2).

Start of the Game. Each player throws one die from his cup and the player throwing the highest number has the choice of seat and color of men. If both players throw the same number they throw again. The player throwing the highest number is the winner and plays first by using the numbers on both his own and his opponent's dice. Thereafter, the turn of play alternates and each player throws both his own dice.

The Play. The object of the game is for each player to move his 15 men toward the inner table on his own side of the board, and then *bear* them off the board. White moves clockwise, Black moves counterclockwise. The first player to bear all his men off wins the game.

The numbers on the two dice, taken separately, show the number of points over which the men may be moved. When one man has been moved the number of points indicated by one die, the other number may be used either to move the same man further or to move another man. When a player throws a doublet (both numbers the same) it counts double. A 6–6, for instance, counts as four sixes, a total of 24 points, not 12. Since a doublet consists of four numbers, the player may move as many as four men, or stones.

The player must attempt to use both (or all four) numbers if he can. If he can use only one number, he must try to use the higher (or as many as can be used of a doublet). If none of the numbers thrown are usable, the play passes to his opponent.

The Moves. A point is open to a player when it is not occupied by two or more of his opponent's men. A player who has two or more men on one point has *made* that point and his opponent's men may not land on it. A man may pass over a closed point in using the total of both numbers on the dice provided each number could be played separately.

A single man on a point is a *blot.* When a man of the opposite color lands on that point the blot is *hit,* and the man originally there is taken off and placed on the bar. A man *on the bar* may *enter* again when a number is thrown that will place the man on an unoccupied point of his opponent's home table. All men on the bar must be reentered before any other moves may be made. When a player has two or more men on a point it is said to be *blocked,* and an opponent's man may not come to rest on the point although it can move past the blocked point. If a player blocks six adjacent points and has one or more of his opponent's men behind it, he has made a *prime.* If he blocks all six points of his home table when his opponent still has one or more men on the bar, he is said to have *shut-out.*

Bearing Off Men. Once a player has advanced all 15 of his stones or men to his own inner table, he may start *bearing off,* which consists in removing men from the board. The first player to bear off all his 15 men wins. A man may be borne off any point whose number shows on either die. *Example:* If White rolls 4–3, he may remove a stone from W4 and another from W3. Instead of bearing off he may also use the numbers to move inside his inner table.

When a number rolled is higher than the highest point on which a player has any men, he bears off from the next highest number. If, after having started to bear off, a man is hit, it goes to the bar and must enter, and come around again to the inner table, before the player can continue bearing off.

Scoring. The first player to bear off all his men wins the game. If the loser has borne off at least one man, and has no man left in the winner's inner table, he loses a *single* game. If he has not borne off a single man, he loses double (*gammon*). If, in addition, he has a man left in his opponent's inner table or on the bar, he loses triple (*backgammon*).

Doubling. Backgammon is played for an agreed base stake which may be increased by *doubling* during play, and by *gammon* and *backgammon* (as above). An automatic double occurs when equal numbers are thrown on the first roll, and both players roll again. (Automatic doubles may be waived by agreement, and, if not, are usually limited by agreement to one or two per game.)

Either player has the right to offer the first voluntary double before casting, and this right alternates thereafter. The opponent must agree to play at the double stake, or forfeit the game and the stake. If he accepts the double, the game continues at the increased stake. The player who offered the double may not immediately double again. The privilege of making the next double falls to his opponent and if he doubles, the first player either resigns and pays the double stakes or accepts and the game continues with stakes that are four times the original amount. There is no limit to the number of doubles that may be made but the option of offering doubles alternates between players. These doubles are cumulative and in addition to increases from gammon or backgammon.

Additional Rules. The following additional rules will cover most irregularities that may occur:

1. After the game has started, if it is seen that some of the men have been set up in the wrong position, the game must be started again.

2. The dice must be thrown from the box onto the player's right-hand table. If the dice are thrown out of the right-hand table, or if they are tilted and do not rest flat on the surface, or if either die is touched by either player during the throw or before the player has called the numbers showing, the throw is faulty and must be thrown again.

3. A player must not throw his dice until his opponent's play has been completed.

4. After a player has moved a man and taken his hand from the piece, he cannot change his play.

5. If a player moves incorrectly, his opponent can demand that the error be corrected provided he does so before he has made his own throw.

Backgammon Opening-Move Strategy. There are really three distinct styles of playing Backgammon:

1. *The Running Game.* It is usually adopted by a player when he gets several high throws at the outset of the game and everything is subordinated to full speed ahead and no concern about his opponent's moves.

2. *The Block Game.* The object of this strategy is to block as many points in a row as possible to impede opponent's progress. This is purely a defensive game.

3. *The Back Game.* With this type of strategy, a player, instead of trying to rush his men forward, concentrates upon doing everything possible to delay his own forward progress, which he does by endeavoring to have his own men set home and reentered in his opponent's inner table, making points, so that later they may hit the opponent's blots.

Actually, there are two kinds of Backgammon players, those who depend entirely on the element of chance to win and those who put their trust in the fascinating factor of skill. While skill plays a very important part in winning Backgammon, still the element of luck is always present. Therefore of paramount importance to a winning player is an accurate knowledge of the odds in the various dice throws that arise during play. For instance, suppose you wanted to calculate your opponent's chances of a 2 or a 3 compared to the probability of his throwing a 6 or a 7. This can be figured out as follows: The total number of different combinations that can be made with two dice is 36 (see Combination or Ways Table, page 524). A single 2 can be made on the dice in 12 different ways. It can be made as a double, and it can be made with any of the other five numbers on the dice. *Examples:* 1–1, 2–6, 6–2, 2–5, 5–2, 2–4, 4–2, 2–3, 3–2, 2–2, 2–1, and 1–2. Hence the chances of throwing a 2 in one throw of the dice is 23 to 12, or less than 2 to 1 against. It is obvious of course that a double can be thrown only one way, but there are two ways to throw any other number, such as 4–2, or 2–4.

The player with a special knowledge of two-dice mathematics need only apply it with intelligence to have a decisive advantage over his opponent whose plays are contrary to the mathematical chances. It takes a knowledgeable player to tell whether or not he is facing a worthy opponent on the first few throws of the dice. A player who fails to play his opening moves correctly cannot be expected to play a good game. To aid such a player, the following examples depict all the first throws with two dice and the best way to play each to gain the best advantage. The various parts of the board and the different points mentioned that follow may be readily located by looking at the diagram on page 522. It also shows the setup for the start of the game.

The best doubles plays to make at start of game are as follows:

1. A 6 and 6 throw: Move two men from your opponent's 1 point to his bar point. Move two men from your opponent's 12 point to your bar point (a very strong throw). Another strong play is to move three men to your bar and one man to your opponent's bar point.

2. A 5 and 5 throw: Two men from your opponent's 12 point to your 3 point.

3. A 4 and 4 throw. Move two back men from your opponent's 1 point to his 5 point and two men from your opponent's 12 point to your own 9 point.

4. A 3 and 3 throw: There are two excellent ways of playing this throw which are as follows: Move two men from your 6 to your 3 point, and two men from your 8 to your 5 point. Move two men from your opponent's 12 point to your 7 or bar point.

5. A 2 and 2 throw: Move two men from your opponent's 1 point to his 5 point.

6. A 1 and 1 throw: The best opening throw of two dice: Move two men from your 8 to your bar point, and two men from your 6 to your 5 point.

The best regular throws and plays at start of game are as follows:

1. A 6 and 5 throw: Move one man from your opponent's 1 to his 12 point.

2. A 6 and 4 throw: Move one man from your opponent's 1 to his bar point, and one man from opponent's 12 to your 9 point. This is a weak throw.

3. A 6 and 3 throw: Move one man from your opponent's 1 point to his bar point and one from opponent's 12 to your 10 point.

4. A 6 and 2 throw: Move two men from your opponent's 1 point to his bar and 3 point.

5. A 6 and 1 throw: Move one man from your opponent's 12 point to your bar point and one man from your 8 to your bar point.

A strong throw.

6. A 5 and 4 throw: Move one man from your opponent's 1 point to his 5 and one man from his 12 to your 8 point.

7. A 5 and 3 throw: Move two men from your opponent's 12 point, one to your 10, and one to your 8 point.

8. A 5 and 2 throw: Move two men from your opponent's 12 point, one to your 11, and one to your 8 point.

9. A 5 and 1 throw: Move one man from your opponent's 1 point, one to his bar point. A weak throw.

10. A 4 and 3 throw: Move two men from your opponent's 1 point, one to his 4 point and one to his 5 point.

11. A 4 and 2 throw: Move one man from your 8 and one from your 6 to your 4 point.

12. A 4 and 1 throw: Move two men from opponent's 1 point, one to opponent's 2 point and one to opponent's 5 point.

13. A 3 and 2 throw: Move one man from opponent's 1 to opponent's 4 point and one from opponent's 12 to opponent's 11 point.

14. A 3 and 1 throw. Move two men, one from your 8 and one from your 6, to your 5 point.

15. A 2 and 1 throw: Move one man from opponent's 1 point to opponent's 2 point and one man from opponent's 12 to your 11 point. The weakest throw of the dice.

Backgammon Strategy. Now that we have discussed opening-move strategy, we continue with the following abbreviated tips, hints, and strategy that are essential to good Backgammon playing.

1. The most important strategy of Backgammon is to start the two men on the opponent's table as soon as possible to prevent their being blocked. These two men are the weakest members of your forces and you should bring them to safety without any delay. Once you form this habit you will have improved your game many times.

A good double early in the game will prevent these men from being blocked; even a small double will help in this direction. Also, if your two furthermost men are on your opponent's 5 point, it will slow the progress of your opponent's men as they arrive at his home table. If you advance these two men to your opponent's bar point, it is also a valuable advantage, but at the start of the game it is wise to hold them on the 5 point just in case you decide to switch to a back game.

2. Avoid taking unnecessary chances. This follows next in importance to advancing your

outposts. The beginner usually attempts an overbold game, taking all kinds of chances to make point. This is a very bad habit, for the reckless type of play generally ends in a lost game.

3. The primary objective of a strong opening is to obtain the advantageous points that will slow up the advance of your opponent's two men in your home table. The most important point to secure first is your 5 point, then your bar point, which furnishes you a powerful blockade on your opponent's two outposts. While some players prefer the bar point before the 5 point, all agree that the bar point and the 5 point are the two strongest points to secure. Next in order comes your opponent's 5 point, which permits the escape of your two outposts.

4. Another important factor to keep in mind is not to crowd your men on your points. Getting a long string of 6 or more men on any point limits your position and places a number of your men out of play. Also, avoid playing your men on to the low points in your home table, as these men also are out of action, and the position puts you at a disadvantage.

5. Never take up a blot in your home table, unless certain that you can block that point. Remember that the men reaching your home table have theoretically traveled all around the board, and their value is much greater than your opponent's two men in your home table. If your opponent's men are hit in your home table, they are only set back a few points, whereas if your men are hit in your home table, they must retravel 19 points to again reach the point where they were hit.

6. Do not expose a man to being hit unless the risk means a greater risk for your opponent if he takes advantage of it.

7. Another vital tactic that is important to learn is that of shutting out your opponent by closing your home table. This basically consists of blocking all the points in your home table so that if you hit an opponent's blot on some other part of the board, he will be unable to restart that man and must rest idle while you continue to play.

8. When forced to leave a blot, always attempt to keep as far away as possible from your opponent's men. A blot seven points away from your adversary can only be hit with a combination throw, and the chances of doing this are about 5 to 1 at that distance. If you are forced to leave a blot within 6 points of your opponent, leave it as near as possible,

one point away being safest. Also, when leaving a blot, try to choose a point which is more likely to be covered next throw.

9. When the numbers thrown on the dice are not available to make points, be sure to use them to make preparations for securing points. If your opponent is a safe distance away, spread these builders so that the following throw will permit you to make another point.

10. The expert Backgammon player always knows at all times exactly how far ahead or behind he is of his adversary. The best way to determine your comparative strength or weakness is as follows: First, pair any men you and your opponent have on opposite points, then calculate how many points your unpaired men are from the home table. Then by making the same calculation with your adversary's unpaired men and comparing the total you can estimate which player is ahead. Once your position is known, you will know just when you must change your tactics or resort to a back game.

11. If your adversary is ahead of you when bearing off, never play up from your 4 or 3 points while still having a large number of men on your 6 point. *Example:* Suppose that your 6 point is loaded with six men and you obtain a small throw of a three and a two; it would be wiser to move up two men from your 6 point, rather than play the men up from the lower points. The two men played forward from the 6 point would leave only four men on that point, and a lucky throw of double sixes would clear these men from the board and give you a possible chance of overtaking your opponent. If you had played up the low throw from the 4 or 5 points, the double sixes would still leave two men on your 6 point, and the chances of hitting two more sixes in the next few throws would be highly improbable.

12. After sending one or two of your opponent's men to the bar and having three or more points blocked in your home table, do not fail to spread your oncoming men so that you can make a new point in your home table or be ready to rehit his men as they reenter.

13. Guard against decoy blots left by your opponent, especially if he is an experienced player. Make doubly sure that the blots are forced or attempted at a great risk, and before hitting same, make certain that his home table is not closed so that if your men are rehit they will be locked out on the bar.

14. If your adversary has locked your two

outposts in his home table on his one point and has already brought all his men into his home table and is bearing off his men, the only chance of victory you have is to hold these men in position in the hopes of forcing him to leave a blot as he bears his men. If he should open another point in the midst of his men, endeavor to split up your two men, leaving two blots which form a greater menace to him, as you still have the opportunity of hitting him with the favorable throw and you are putting him in a position where an unfavorable throw on his part may force him to hit one of these blots which then may reenter and send his man or men back to start over. If you can establish your two outposts on the 5 point in your opponent's home table, you are quite safe from any effective block of these two men, and your outside men can then be advanced with more effective action.

15. As the game nears the end and the contest is tight, the men must be advanced to the home table in the fastest manner possible. One way of doing this is to make plays that will carry a man from one table to another. *Example:* If you have a man on your opponent's 10 point and a three is thrown, move this man across the table to your 12 point; a play that takes the man into your outer table. If you had a man on your 12 point and six is thrown, the play would be to move this man into your home table. Playing your men so that they can go from one table to another permits you to gain the maximum amount of speed in bringing them home.

16. In throwing off, when your home table is closed and your opponent has men on the bar, the safest procedure is to move your men up in your home table rather than to take men off for the throws. This opens up the high points in your home table, so that your adversary can enter on these points, which removes the danger of his hitting you on reentry.

17. In throwing off, when your opponent still has a man or men in your home table, try and keep an even number of men upon the points nearest the bar to avoid an unnecessary blot.

18. In throwing off, after your opponent has passed your men, try to bear off with the fastest possible speed. Remove as many men as possible with each throw, and when certain throws compel you to move up, try to cover the vacant points. A home board with all points covered is more quickly cleared in bearing.

Chouette

This variant of Backgammon is played by three or more players although it is still a two-handed game. The players cast dice for precedence, and the one throwing the highest number becomes the *man in the box;* second highest is *captain* for all the others, and they rank below the captain in accordance with the numbers they throw. Players who tie throw again to determine their rank.

The play is between the man in the box and the captain. Other players may advise the captain, but in case of disagreement he himself has the final decision as to how a move shall be made. If he wishes to double and any of his partners do not want to take the risk, they resign and forfeit their stakes to him. He continues the game on his own responsibility assuming all risk. The man in the box then decides whether to accept the double or resign.

If the man in the box doubles, each opponent must accept individually or pay the current stakes and resign. If the opponent of the man in the box resigns, the next highest player in standing who accepts the double takes his place at the board as the new captain.

If the player in the box wins the game, he stays in the box, and the next member of the team in order replaces the losing captain. If the man in the box loses (including loss by refusal of a double), he becomes the lowest-ranking member of the team. His place in the box is taken by the winning captain, and the next player in order moves up to captain. When a game ends, the player in the box collects from or pays to each remaining active member of the team the full value of the stake at that time.

Partnership Backgammon

Backgammon can be played, like many other two-player games, in partnership—two players versus two, or three against three. In the two-against-two partnership game, one member of each team plays against a member of the other, their Backgammon boards arranged so that rolls of the dice can be seen by all four players. On each side, one player plays Black, while the other partner plays White. The members of only one team roll the dice; one casts for Black and his throws are used by the Black players on both sides, the other rolls for White and his casts are used by both White players. When any player has borne off all his pieces, his team wins the contest.

Dutch Backgammon

This game is played in the same way as Backgammon except that all the men or stones start on the bar, and each player must enter all his 15 men before advancing any of them. He may not hit a blot until he has moved at least one man around to his own inner table.

Turkish Backgammon

In this variation, which is also called Moultezim, the play is the same as in regular Backgammon except for the following:

1. All 15 of White's men start on Black's 12 point and Black's 15 men start on White's 12 point. Black must move all of his men the full 24 points around the board: first to the right from White's 12 point in the White outer board, into White's inner board, then into his own inner board, and off to the left (instead of the right as in regular Backgammon). White also moves in a counterclockwise direction: from the outer board and into the White inner board and off to the right, the same as in the regular game.

2. Both players must get to their own outer boards with their first men before moving a second one from the starting point.

3. One man on any spot is a point.

4. Men are not hit or sent home; there are no blots. Therefore since you cannot stop on top of any man, the most important point of strategy in Moultezim is to create a prime in order to block your opponent. However, the rules of the game do not permit a player to create a prime commencing at the starting point of his opponent; that is, on this section of the board a player must leave one point open.

Greek Backgammon

Greek Backgammon, commonly called Plakato, is played like regular Backgammon except for the following:

1. All 15 of White's men are on the Black one point, and all of Black's men are on the White one point. All the men must move the full 24 points, in the same direction as they do in regular Backgammon.

2. A player can stop on an opponent's man but he cannot remove the piece from the board. That is, the player can leave his man on his opponent's point and the opponent cannot move his man until the player moves his man off.

Gioul

This Middle East variation is played like regular Backgammon except for the following:

1. The men are arranged on the board and move in the same direction as in Greek Backgammon.

2. As in the case of Turkish Backgammon, the men are not sent home.

3. One man stopping anywhere is considered a point, while six men in a row constitute a prime.

4. When a player rolls a double, he plays it as in regular Backgammon, but in Gioul, he continues playing the succeeding doubles all the way to double sixes. *Examples:* If double ones are cast, the player first plays the double ones, followed by double twos, double threes, double fours, double fives, and double sixes. If double fours are rolled, the player plays the double fours, followed by double fives and double sixes. All moves are made before the opponent makes his next roll.

5. If a player cannot complete all of his doubles, he forfeits the rest to his opponent. *Example:* Suppose double fours are rolled and the player is able to play the double fours but he cannot play the double fives, or can only play one five, his opponent will then complete playing the fives and also play the double sixes. If, in turn, the opponent is unable to finish the doubles, the play of that toss is then considered finished and the opponent makes a new roll.

Acey Deucey

An elaboration of Dutch Backgammon which is a favorite of the United States Navy, Marine Corps, and merchant marine. It is a game for two players and uses a pair of dice which are usually thrown from the hand, although a cup is used in tournament play. Thirty counters, or men, are used, 15 of each color, and an Acey Deucey mat or a Backgammon board is used.

Each player *peewees* a die, that is, each rolls a die, and the player throwing the highest number has the first move. If both throw the same number, the throw is made again. If Black moves first and enters his men on the spaces 1 to 6, White must enter his men on the spaces directly opposite—24 to 19. Black moves to his right and around the table toward White's starting spaces (counterclockwise), and White moves in the opposite (clockwise) direction toward Black's starting spaces. Black may, if he likes, enter his men on spaces 12 to 7 and move in the opposite (clockwise) direction, in which case White must enter on spaces 8 to 13. The players always move in opposite directions.

Each player's object is to enter and move his 15 men through one complete circuit of the board and take them off before his opponent succeeds in doing the same. Men are entered on the board and moved according to the numbers appearing on the dice, either number being played first and each number being played separately. If a player throws "fifty deuce" (5–2) he may enter one man on the 5 space and move it ahead two spaces or he may put two men in play, one on the 5 space and one on the 2 space. The same rule applies to the movement of the men, both numbers thrown being used to move one man or each number being used to move different men. As in checkers, once the player has moved and lifted his fingers from the man, the move may not be retracted.

Any number of men of the same color may occupy the same space. Two or more men of the same color on one space make that space dead for opposing men, who may not land on it. If a man lands on a space occupied by a single opposing man the latter is *booted,* or *kicked,* and must be removed from the board and reentered on the starting spaces. It may be reentered at any time.

A pair of men on the space do not constitute a block past which the opposing pieces may not move but merely prevents opposing men from landing on that space. If Black has a man on space 1, White has a pair each on spaces 5 and 3, and Black throws 4–2, Black may not move his man the total of six spaces because each number thrown must be used separately. He cannot use either the 4 or the 2 because these moves would bring him to spaces 5 and 3, which are occupied by opposing pairs. If he threw 4–3, however, he could move his man three spaces and then four spaces.

Doubles. When a pair of like numbers (two threes, two fours, etc.) are thrown, the player moves his men double the amount thrown. If two fours are thrown he makes four moves of four spaces each.

Acey Deucey. When ace-deuce is thrown the player moves one man three spaces, or one man one space and another, two spaces. Then he selects any double number he desires and moves accordingly. If he selects double fives he makes four moves of five spaces each. After these moves are completed he takes an additional throw of the dice. If the player cannot use any part of his acey-deucey throw or cannot select a double that he can use entirely, he uses whatever part he can and loses the balance including the right to make an additional throw.

Taking Off. When all 15 men have moved around the board and are within the last six spaces, they are taken from the board according to the throw of the dice. They may also be moved forward within the last six spaces toward the last space on the board. This is often done in order to pair men and prevent booting when an opponent still has a man to enter. If a man is booted when men are being taken off, he must be reentered in the starting spaces and moved around the board again until he reaches the last six spaces before the taking-off process may be resumed.

When there are no men on the space whose number is thrown and when all the men remaining are so close to the last space on the board that they cannot move the number of spaces indicated by the throw, a man on the next highest space to the number thrown is taken off. For example, if there is a man on the opponent's first space and three on his third space and a throw of 5–6 is made, since none of the men can be moved that many spaces, two of the men on the next highest (third) space are taken off. If one player covers six adjacent spaces with pairs it is known as a *Hindenburg Line* and completely blocks his opponent from moving past that section of the board until the arrangement is broken up.

Stakes. Players usually play for a specified amount per game or for so much a man. In the latter case the player who first takes off all his men wins the game and collects from his opponent as many units as the opponent has men left that have not been taken off. If the stakes are a nickel a man and the losing player has five men left, he loses 25 cents.

Ten Things Every Winning Acey-Deucey Player Must Know

1. Learn the rules so thoroughly that you can recall them instantly and correctly.

2. The best form of practice is to play

alone. Many hours of enjoyment and heightened skill will be your reward.

3. Take your time and study each play thoroughly before making it.

4. Pay attention to your own game and try not to discuss your or your opponent's plays during the game.

5. Never touch a man (piece) until you are certain you are going to play it.

6. Don't take too great risks during the game, because a good sound game is generally a cautious one.

7. Try and play with better players, as this is one of the best means of improving your game.

8. Do not rattle the dice or draw on the table when it is your opponent's turn to play—instead use that time to analyze the men on the board.

9. When moving a man, don't play hunches —play the odds.

10. Lose with good grace and sportsmanship, and remember that the main purpose of the game is entertainment.

European Acey Deucey

While the pieces are set on the board as for regular Backgammon, this variant differs as follows:

1. On a roll of acey-deucey (1–2), the stakes are doubled and the player may use the roll of 1–2, name any doublet he wishes, move this doublet and also the complementary doublet, and roll again. (The complement of a number is its difference from 7. Thus, having named 3–3, the player next uses 4–4.) Of course, if the player is unable to use any portion of the roll, he loses the rest of the acey-deucey privilege. *Example:* A player rolls 1–2, moves, names 5–5, moves, but can then move only three 2's. He loses the fourth 2 and does not roll again.

2. To bear off, the player must roll the exact number of the point on which he has men. *Example:* The player rolls 6–2, having men on all points but 6 point and 2 point. He has no move. But with any pieces outside his own table, he may move the men inside his

home table. With all in the home table, however, only bearing off is permitted.

Russian Backgammon

In this variation, no men are placed upon the board at the start, but each player enters his men by throws of the dice—both players enter in the same home table and both move in the same direction around the board to the opposite table. Bearing off is the same as in Backgammon. After having entered two or more men, a player is at liberty either to continue entering his men with any subsequent throws, or to move the men already entered. When a blot is hit, the owner must reenter it before he makes any other move. But at any other time a player must move men already entered to use his full roll, even if unable to enter any additional of the original 15 off the board. Except on a player's first roll of the game, doublets are used twice over; he can not only play the upper faces of the dice twice over, but the bottom (opposite) faces also, and can throw again before his opponent. After each thrown doublet the player continues to throw until he fails to throw a doublet, in which case he plays the numbers thrown and the throw passes to his opponent.

Tabard Backgammon

This variant is played like regular Backgammon except that all of Black's pieces are set up in White's inner and outer tables, while all of White's men are set up opposite these in Black's inner and outer tables. There are the same number of pieces that there are on the same points as in the regular game and the play from there on is identical.

Snake

In this variation, which is played primarily as a basic practice game, Black pieces are set up as usual (five on B6, three on B8, five on W12, and two on W1), but White has only six men on the board, two each on B1, B2, and B3, the other nine being on the bar. All other rules are as in regular Backgammon.

PARCHEESI

Parcheesi (also spelled Pachisi, Parchisi, Parchesi) is a variation of Backgammon originating in India and it is the national game of that country. The Indian Emperor Akbar, I am told, played Parcheesi in a truly regal fashion on courts constructed of inlaid marble. In the center of the court was a dais four feet high on which the Emperor and his courtiers sat, while 16 young, beautiful slave girls from the harem, wearing appropriate colors, moved about the squares as directed by the throws of cowrie shells. While the rules have not changed since the emperor's day, the equipment surely has: dice have replaced the cowrie shells, a small board is used rather than huge marble courts, and unfortunately, counters have taken the place of the girls.

Requirements

1. Two to four players.

2. A Parcheesi board, plus 16 counters in four colors (four of each color) and one pair of dice and a dice cup for each player.

Object of the Game. Each player attempts to get four counters into the inner center of the board before any other player can do so.

The Play. After the seating has been arranged and the color of the counters selected, a single die is cast by each player and high throw wins the first move. If there is a tie, the die is cast again until the tie is broken. The players take turns, in a clockwise direction.

On each of his turns, a player throws the two dice from the dice cup. In order to move a counter from the home circle, a five must appear on at least one of the dice (not as the sum of the dice). When a five is cast, a player may move one counter onto the colored space just next to his home base. If double fives are rolled, two pieces may be moved out at the same time; or one counter may be moved out, and then it may be moved five spaces forward or some other man, already out, may be moved five spaces forward. At any time during the game a player who casts a doublet moves his counters the proper number of spaces forward and throws the dice again. (*Variation:* Some play that if a player throws three consecutive doublets, he must return his counter that is farthest around the board to the home circle. He must also pass the turn to the player on his left.)

The dice are played as two separate counts, as in Backgammon. That is, if a player casts a three and a four, he may move one counter three spaces and another four spaces, or he may move one piece seven spaces. But, no more than two pieces may be located on one space at the same time. Two counters of the same color on the same space block passage

past that point to any piece coming up behind. A player may move two counters per turn, and should he throw a doublet, he may move two counters into a side-by-side blocking position. Where a block occurs ahead and the number on the dice would carry any player's piece up to, or beyond the block, that player may not move his counter forward even one space. *Example:* If a block lies on a space five units ahead and the roll of the dice yields five or more, the player may not move the counter at all. Remember that a player may not jump over his own block or an opponent's until he or his opponent moves one or both of the men out of a blocking position.

Where one counter is located on a space, an opposing piece landing squarely on that space sends the first man back to his home circle. That is, if an opponent's man lies five spaces ahead and a player rolls a five on one die—or a combination on both dice add up to exactly five—he moves up his counter, replacing the opposing man and sending him back to his home circle. A counter sent home in this way cannot reenter the game until the player throws a five—as at the start of play. There are safe bases located about the board—generally blue-colored spaces. A counter located on one of these spaces cannot be sent home, regardless of whether an opponent lands a piece next to his.

After going around the rest of the board, a player's counters enter the center of the board through the avenue just to the left of his home circle. Once inside this avenue, a player's men cannot be attacked by an opponent's men. Pieces are moved in the avenue in the same manner as they are around the rest of the board. But, no counter can enter the inner circle unless the exact number of spaces necessary to do so appears on one of the dice or as the sum of both dice. Therefore, a piece lying four spaces from the inner circle can move into the circle only if a four or some combination adding up to four is rolled. If a three is thrown, the piece can be moved up to the first space of the avenue. However, the only way this counter can enter the inner circle is if a one comes up on a die on a subsequent turn; a two or some higher number does not permit a move into the inner circle. Of course, as previously stated, the first player to move all his counters into the inner circle wins the game.

MILL

This ancient game, which is also known by such names as Nine Men's Morris, Morelles, Muhle, and Morris, is still one of Europe's most popular board games.

Requirements

1. Two players.

2. A board such as illustrated here. There are 24 points arranged in 16 lines of three points each. (The diagonal lines, such as 1–4–7, are usually omitted in the modern game.)

3. Eighteen counters in two contrasting colors, nine for each player. Ordinary poker chips or checkers will serve.

The Play. A draw of lots or toss of a coin determines who plays first. Play then alternates. Each player places one counter in turn upon any of the 24 points of the board. When all 18 pieces have been placed, play continues by alternate moves. A piece may move to an adjacent vacant point on the same line.

The object, both in laying pieces on the board and in moving them, is to get three pieces of one's own color in a horizontal or vertical (not diagonal) line. Such an arrangement is called a *mill*. On making a mill, the player may remove any one adverse piece from the board provided that it is not part of a mill, unless there are no others on the lay-out. Once a piece is removed from the board, it is dead and never returns into play.

A mill may be *opened* by moving a piece off the line; *closing* it by moving the piece back counts as a separate mill, and entitles the player to remove another adverse piece. *Example:* Black has a mill on 1–2–3. If he is able to move 3–15; then 15–3, he is entitled to remove a White counter.

The player who is first reduced to two pieces, or who is first to be unable to move in his turn, loses the game. (An optional rule is that when a player is reduced to three pieces he may move "wild" from any point to any point, regardless of the lines.)

Strategy of Mill. If White, playing first, takes one of the best points, as 5, Black can prevent the formation of a mill only by playing on an adjacent point, as 2, 4, 6, or 8. But more enterprising is to take another of the four key points, as 14, because White will lose by block if he immediately plays for a *fork* (a simultaneous attack on two enemy pieces), thus:

White	Black
5	14
8	2
7	9
12	16
11	10
4	6
19	

Whatever piece White removes, Black replaces, then White has to block at 21 and

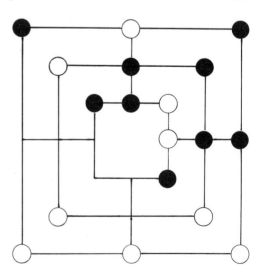

The Mill board (left). The illustration at the right shows that black has a double mill (2-5 and 5-2).

Black at 20. Now all of White's eight pieces are immobile, being held by Black's seven. Wherever White puts his last piece, Black can play adjacent and then run down this only free enemy. Thus even if the player who forces an early mill does not run into a complete block, his extra piece by no means assures victory. In the following game, for instance, Black after becoming a piece up made a mistake and actually lost, but with the best of play he could do no more than draw. Thus:

White	Black
5	14
21	11
2	8
17	23
12	13
15	9
7	18 (7)
7	16
1	3
1–10	14–21
15–14	23–22
5–41	8–5
7–8	etc.

White now maintains his pieces on 8, 14, and 17, keeping the Black mill closed, and his other five pieces can meet all threats exerted by Black's six, without suffering paralysis. It seems as though the loss of a piece is an advantage to White in that it gives him room to maneuver. But it does not follow that a mill made by force in laying down the pieces is useless. On the contrary, it will usually bring victory if delayed just long enough so that the opponent runs out of pieces before he can blockade it. For instance:

White	Black
5	14
20	11

White	Black
1	18
7	23?

Black's last move is a mistake. His policy of scattering his pieces to occupy many lines is correct—probably the game is intrinsically a draw if this policy is accurately carried out by both players—but here he should play 2 or 8 to intercept the White constellation. There follows:

White	Black
6	4
19	21
8	2
9 (2)	2
15	13
7–12	any
12–7 (2)	

White wins as he now has two mills.

If each side makes one mill, the game is usually won by the first to open. The play is likely to be a matter of alternate captures, hence the name Mill (German *Muhle*, grinder)—the forces are ground down slowly but surely. But the player behind at the outset can sometimes overtake his opponent by collateral threats, especially the formation of a second mill. The ideal to be striven for is the *doublemill*, which grinds down the enemy in a hurry. *Example:* White pieces on 1, 2, 3, 4, 6. By moving 2–5 and 5–2, White closes a mill at each turn.

As has been mentioned previously, the game is probably a draw with the best play on both sides. The drawing policy is to scatter the pieces so as to intercept on all possible lines. This is also the way to lure the opponent in traps, such as self-destruction through forcing the play too soon.

GO OR WEI-CHI

Go, or Wei-Chi, the great Chinese game of skill, is played by millions of people throughout the Orient and is considered by most Oriental game experts as the world's greatest strategic skill game, far surpassing Chess in scope. Go, if we are to believe Chinese history, was invented by Emperor Shun (2255–2206 B.C.) to help develop the mental faculties of his son, Shokin. A second version ascribes the invention of Wei-Chi to U, a subject of Emperor Kieh Kwei, who lived several hundred years later. Anyone's guess is as good as mine. However, I would venture to say that the second version is more likely to be the truth. Emperors, even in the old days B.C., had enough problems ruling a country without devoting years to inventing a great skill game.

History further records that in the tenth century B.C., Wei-Chi was well known, because it is mentioned in a number of poems and allegories found in Chinese literature dating from the period.

The first books devoted entirely to Wei-Chi were written during the T'ang dynasty sometime in the years 618–906. In the year 754, the Chinese Emperor Hinan Tsung presented a Wei-Chi game set to the Japanese Emperor Koken Tenno through the latter's representative, Kididaijin. The Japanese named it *Igo*, spelled phonetically Go. This name has been generally used by the few thousand people in America, Europe, and South America who play the game. Go is definitely a modern military game. Its object is territorial conquest and the capture of opponent's stones by encirclement. The stones with which the game is played do not have a single capture objective as in Chess, but an overall objective that is made up of many captures, and the final result hinges on the strategic disposition of a large number of stones and on the proper timing of their activities. The different ways the stones are played on to the board seem to give rise to a greater variety of combinations than might be found in Chess, and unlike Chess, all men in Go are alike in shape. An average game of Go lasts about as long as the average game of Chess.

Requirements

1. Two players.

2. Each player has a set of stones (181 in number). One set is colored black and the other white, a total of 362 stones. The stones have the shape of convex lenses about 7/8

of an inch in diameter and 1/8 to 1/2 inch in thickness.

3. The board: Go is played on a rectangular board (Go-Ban) on which 19 equidistant lines are drawn parallel to one edge and 19 at right angles to them, as shown here. These lines are about 15/16 inch apart from each other in one direction and 7/8 inch in the other. A margin of about 1/2 inch runs around all the board's four edges. The board is placed between both players with its narrow sides running vertically. A Go set may be improvised by using small poker chips or buttons as stones and drawing 19 by 19 lines on a cardboard. The distance between lines should be slightly larger than the diameter of the poker chips or buttons in use.

To aid the reader to understand at a glance the structure and formation of the stone setups on the Go game board that follow, a lettered and numbered Go game board is shown below. The vertical lines are named A, B, C, etc., to T, omitting the I, beginning from the left of the player of the Black stones. The horizontal lines are numbered from 1 to 19, beginning from the side of the same player. A point of intersection called a point is simply defined by listing the letter and numbers of the lines concerned.

The determination of positions on the board is simplified by little dots on the intersections of the fourth, tenth, and sixteenth lines with lines D, K, and Q. These nine points are called *handicap points,* or *stars.* This is one of the inherent advantages of

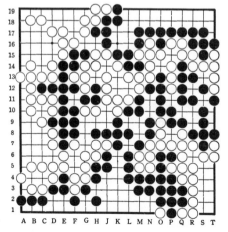

The Go board. Note the little dots on the intersections of the forth, tenth, and sixteenth lines with lines D, K, and Q. These nine points are called "tars" or "handicap points."

the structure of Go because these handicap points help compensate for any disparity in the contestant's degree of skill by permitting the weaker player to place one or more stones on the handicap points before the play begins.

The Object of the Game. The object of the game is for a player to place his stones on the board so as to completely surround more unoccupied territory and opponent stones than does his opponent. When the game ends, each player scores the number of points (intersections of two lines) situated in his territory, minus the number of stones he has lost to his opponent. The player with the higher score wins the game and scores the point difference between his score and that of his opponent. Should both players have identical scores, the game is a tie.

The Rules of Play

1. The board is vacant to start the game. Each player takes 181 stones of one color. The players, called Black and White, have the privilege of moving alternately, with Black always making the first move in the starting of the game. A move consists of placing a stone on any unoccupied point, with the two exceptions noted in rule 3. Once placed, a stone is never again moved during the game, unless it is captured by the opponent.

A play consists of placing a stone not on the square formed by the lines on the board but on the points of intersection of these lines. There are 361 points on the board.

2. The idea is for a player to place his stones so that they form connected groups— also called *chains*—which surround as many unoccupied points and opponent's stones as possible. If all of the intersections (points) adjacent to a stone or a group of stones are occupied by stones of the opposite color, that stone or group of stones is captured and removed from the board immediately. (Such adjacent points are referred to as *breathing spaces*.)

3. A player is not permitted to make a move which results in the repetition of a position reached previously, nor is he permitted to play on any point which is completely surrounded by the opponent's stones unless the play results in the capture of all or part of the surrounded stones, because it is against the rules of the game for any stone to remain on the board if it is completely surrounded by stones of the opposite color. A point which is completely surrounded by stones of the opposite color is called an *eye*. If a group of stones contains two separate eyes, it is always

safe from capture, regardless of the enemy stones surrounding the group, because it is not possible for the opponent to occupy either of two eyes.

4. The game is over when both players decide there are no plays left on the board that can benefit either player. However, if there is a difference of opinion as to whether additional points or stones can be captured and one of the players insists upon continuing the game, the opponent may pass his turn of play. When both players pass consecutively, the game ends.

In Chess a game is drawn when the same position is repeated three times. However, Go rule 3 prevents a repetitive move from resulting in a draw. To illustrate, the drawing on this page shows in figure A a White stone surrounded on three sides by Black stones and in check. Black can capture this single stone, and the developed position will be as shown in figure B. The result achieved is that a Black stone is now in check. If, as in figure C, White now captures this Black stone, we are back to the position we started in figure A. This play could go on indefinitely—which the Japanese call *KO*, which means eternity. KO situations occur often in Go, but do not end the game in a draw because of the following rule of play. In a KO situation, after one player has captured an enemy stone, his opponent is not permitted to recapture until he has made one or more plays elsewhere on the board. This rule not only prevents drawn games but adds excitement and strategy to the

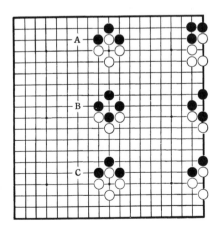

The rules of play in Go illustrated.

game, because in their efforts to win a vital KO the players continuously analyze the board for plays which they believe their opponents will be forced to protect, and at times these diverting tactics become more important than the KO itself. In the elementary KO situation on page 535, there is only one stone at stake but in many games the outcome of a KO maneuver often determines the outcome of the game.

5. When the game ends, all stones left in enemy territory are considered dead and are removed from the board. The White player then places his captured Black stones on the vacant points in Black's territory. The Black player places his captured White stones on the vacant points in White's territory. Last, the total number of *vacant* points in each territory are counted. The player with the higher count is declared the winner and scores the point difference between his winning score and his opponent's losing score.

Go Strategy. Playing first gives Black an advantage much greater than it may appear, and in games between experts, it is often decisive. Many Japanese Go masters to whom I have spoken go as far as to insist that Black's victory is absolutely certain by moving first. I do not agree that the first move is that crucial, but it certainly is advantageous. However, it is best to change colors at the start of each game and balance the play.

The two opposing arrays of stones as they develop during play are much like soldiers on a battlefield; if a segment is cut off from their main force, they are extremely vulnerable to attack and capture by the opposing force.

The opening is undoubtedly the most difficult phase of a Go game. Even the most proficient experts with years of playing experience cannot pass final judgment on some opening maneuvers. In the opening stages of Go, each player must not only visualize or sketch out the territories he will play for, but in addition each player must deploy his stones in such a manner that they will be capable of defending against enemy attack and at the same time be capable of attacking the enemy stones.

Most beginners make the mistake of attacking the opponent without adequate preparation. They try to surround hostile groups wherever they are forming instead of selecting

a battle group on which they have at least an even chance of emerging unscathed. Such a result cannot be expected if they try to attack a strong chain with a few scattered stones.

In the illustration above, if White plays as indicated in the middle figure, the four Black stones will be cut into two separate groups, either of which can be attacked by White. On the other hand, if Black plays as indicated in the figure on the right, all his stones are connected into a single chain, and the White stones on either side of the Black chain are in grave danger. Although stones are not actually connected until they occupy adjacent intersections, there are many loose plays which in effect connect the stones involved because it is impossible for the opponent to prevent their connections. The illustration above is a good example of such a play. Note White cannot stop the connection of Black's stones.

With even the advantage of Black playing first, both players have equal chances to capture territory with their subsequent plays. It should then be assumed that each player will seek to capture the largest territories possible at the beginning of the game. What is the best way to accomplish this? The illustration on the facing page graphically demonstrates this point. You will note that each of the Black groups has surrounded nine points of territory. Although these three Black groups have captured the same amount of territory, they did not do so with the same number of stones. The corner group contains only seven stones and its investment ratio to gain is 7 to 9. The Black group on the top side of the board is made up of nine stones, or just as many as the captured points. In the center of the board, 12 stones were required to capture nine points of territory. The basic strategy of the opening game is based almost entirely upon results evident in this illustration. Territory is easiest to capture in the corners of the board because

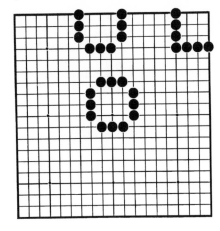

Space limitation has forced me to confine myself to a rather sketchy treatment of Go. But I hope that even the few examples of combinatory and positional play which I have chosen may enable the reader to get a good glimpse of the scope and beauty of the game of Go.

Partnership Go

Four players play as partners. Black plays first, then White, then Black, then White, etc. There can be no discussion between partners during the game. Partners are determined by mutual consent. All the rules for two-handed Go apply to this four-handed variant.

the two edges of the board provide half of the protection required for such territories. The center of the board is the most difficult area in which to capture territory because it is open on all sides and requires the maximum amount of stones to complete a capture of territory. Naturally, there are factors other than the mere capture of points to be considered, and a "tendency toward the center" is one of them. But, the principle expounded in this diagram above is basically true and it has been followed in about 95 percent of all games ever played.

A tactical method called a *shicho*, or *ladder*, more characteristic of the middle game than of the opening or end game, is the cutting of an enemy group in two where two of its men are joined diagonally rather than connected in a straight line. In executing such a cut, a player must be careful not to lose through a shicho the stone which he used for the purpose. Also this stone should have a fair chance of connecting up with other stones of the same color which can be used for an attack against the part of a hostile chain that has been cut off from the main body.

Go Moku or Go Bang

This is a very simple game played on the Go board which is particularly popular among Oriental women and children who prefer a more simplified and quicker-ending game to the more exacting drawn-out battle characteristic of Go. As in Go, the board is vacant at the start and the players play a stone alternately on any intersection of lines. The object is to get five stones adjoining in a straight line, either horizontally or vertically or diagonally. Black moves first, and as in Go a stone remains on the point on which it was first placed. If a player succeeds in placing four stones in a line open on both ends, he wins because the opponent can block only one end, and then the fifth stone is placed on the other end. This winning position can always be achieved if a player can place a stone on a point so that he forms two lines of three stones each, one of which can be maneuvered into an open four in a line. The first move is such an advantage in Go Moku that I recommend that Black (in his first move) should not be permitted to place a stone on a point that forms two open threes simultaneously.

HASAMI SHOGI

This very popular Japanese game, generally called just Shogi, is played on a board of nine

by nine squares and each player has 18 pieces of his own color. They are placed on the two back rows. The rules generally followed for Shogi are as follows:

1. No diagonal moves are permitted.

2. A piece cannot land on a square occupied by another piece.

3. A piece can jump over an adjacent piece to land on a vacant square beyond. It cannot, however, jump over a vacant square and an occupied square in the same move.

4. When a player traps an opposing piece between two of his pieces on a rank or file (*custodian capture*), it is removed from the board.

5. A piece may move between two enemy pieces safely.

6. A player wins the game when he has five men in a row on a file, rank, or diagonally, excluding the two home rows.

HALMA

This game was invented about 1880 in England and immediately became popular in that country and Europe.

Requirements

1. Two to four players, each playing for himself.

2. The board is a square of 16 by 16 small checkered squares. At each corner heavy lines mark an enclosure of 13 squares, and in two diagonally opposite corners additional lines increase the enclosure to 19 squares.

3. The pieces are counters like checkermen, though smaller in order to fit the smaller square of the Halma board. Each player is given 13 pieces (in a four-hand game) or 19 pieces (in a two-hand game) in distinctive colors.

The Object of the Game. Each player tries to move all of his pieces across the board to the corner enclosure diagonally opposite that from which he started. The first player to do so wins the game.

The Play. A draw of lots determines who

plays first. Players take alternate turns. With three or more players, the turns move in a clockwise direction from the left of the person who goes first. A player may move only one of his pieces on each turn. A move may be made by either a step or a hop, but never a combination of the two. The step is a move to an adjacent square in any direction, vertical, horizontal, or diagonal—forward or backward. A hop move—like a jump in Checkers—may be made in any direction over an adjacent piece to a vacant square just beyond the same line. As in Checkers, the hopping move once started may be continued as long as the piece finds others to jump. But in Halma, a piece may hop over friendly as well as enemy pieces and the pieces jumped are not captured. No pieces are ever removed from the board. Furthermore, it is not compulsory to jump when able; having started a series of hops, the piece may come to rest at any time the player wishes, though additional hops would be possible.

The Halma board (left) and Chinese Checker board (right).

Strategy in Halma. The best way to move the pieces across the board is to form "ladders" from the starting base to the goal, and to advance rearmost pieces as frequently as possible by hops up the ladder. When enemy forces meet in the center of the board, every effort should be made to block, or at least to avoid helping the opponent.

Chinese Checkers

Chinese Checkers is a modern version of Halma.

Requirements

1. Two to six players, each playing for himself.

2. A Chinese Checker board, which is in the form of a six-pointed star.

3. Ninety marbles in six colors; 15 of each color.

Object of the Game. Each player attempts to move all his pieces from one of the six points of the star into the opposite point of the star before any opponent can do so.

The Play. If two are playing, they take seats opposite one another and each player positions 15 marbles of a single color in the point of the star in front of him—opposite his opponent's point. If three or more play, ten marbles are used instead of 15; these are grouped within any point of the star a player selects.

All rules are as in Halma, but due to the hexagonal arrangement, a step can be made in any of six directions, as compared with eight in Halma.

MANCALA

This game (*Mankala'h* in Egypt, *Pallanguli* in India and Ceylon, *Kalah* in Syria, *Wari* in Africa, *Awari* in Guiana and the Caribbean) may be the world's oldest game since it can be played using shells or pebbles as counters and in hollows scooped into the earth. Although it is played by primitive peoples throughout the world it is a wholly mathematical game (somewhat similar to but much more complicated than the Match Game), and its more complex versions have been ranked with Chess as an intellectual exercise.

Mancala was being played in Egypt before 1400 B.C.; stone boards have been found at Memphis, Thebes, and Luxor. Sometimes called the African national game, it is played throughout that continent under a great many different tribal names. While the boards and the number of pieces used vary, the so-called two-rank Mancala board which contains two parallel rows of six holes (called *pits*) is the most commonly used. There are usually two larger holes (called scoring pits) at each end of the board.

Mancala boards have recently been put on the market in the United States, and I give here only one of the commonest and simplest methods of play.

Requirements

1. Two players.

2. A two-rank Mancala board.

3. 36 or 72 counters, called *pebbles*, or *seeds*.

The Play. The two players sit behind the two ranks of six pits on the board between them. Each pit contains three (for beginners)

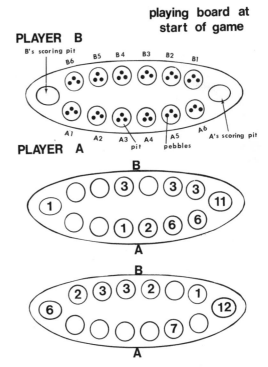

The Mancala board (top) set up for start of game. Each player in turn picks up all in one of his own pits and sows them to the right. Game ends when one player's pits are empty. Player with the most pebbles wins. In the sample game (center), A11, A1-B6-A3, A2, A1. After move A1 (bottom), B4, B6, B1-A4-B3-A6-B2. The latter is B's winning move.

or six (for experienced players) pebbles. Object of the game is to accumulate as many pebbles as possible in the scoring pit (mancala) to each player's right. Each player in turn picks up all the pebbles in any one of his own six pits and sows them, one in each pit, around the board to the right, including, if there are enough, his own mancala and on into his opponent's pits (but not his opponent's mancala). If the player's last counter lands in his own scoring pit, he gets another turn, and if it lands in an empty pit on his own side, he captures all his opponent's counters in the opposite pit and puts them in his mancala together with the capturing pebble. The game is over when all six pits on one side or another are empty. It is not always an advantage for a player to go "out," since all pebbles in the pits on the opposite side go into the opponent's scoring pit. The score is determined by who has the most pebbles. That is, the difference between the two amounts is the number of points won. Forty points is usually the deciding score for a series of games.

Mancala Strategy. A sophisticated player learns not to accept all short-term advantages, however tempting. Thus, in the game illustrated, player A began by moving the three pebbles in his pit A4, ending in his mancala and thus earning another move, which he used to play from pit A4 and thereby capturing B's men. By similar maneuvers and captures, A, by the fourth turn, has become pebble proud, with eleven in his mancala to a pathetic one in B's (see diagram). But A is dangerously concentrated in the two pits A5 and A6. B, seeding six pebbles on his own side, forces A to start distributing his hoard around the board. By the eighth turn (see diagram) A still has 12 in his scoring pit to five in B's; but B moves the five pebbles in B2 and then has only to move the single pebble in his pit B1 to capture A's seven remaining pebbles—ending the game and winning it by a score of 24 to 12. Thus B receives 12 points —toward the total score of 40—for his victory.

FOX AND GEESE

This old English game, which dates back to about 1450, can be played with one or more players. Let's first look at a two-player version.

Requirements
1. Two players.
2. A Fox and Geese board such as illustrated here. (Disregard letters and numbers shown on edge of illustration as they apply only to Peg Solitaire.)

3. Seventeen white marbles (the geese) and one black marble (the fox).

The Play. A draw of lots determines which player is the fox and who is the geese. The player who is the geese arranges his 17 white marbles on the board as shown, and the fox is placed on any vacant point. The player representing the fox makes the first move and from then on the moves alternate. The fox can move in any direction along a line to the next

The Fox and Geese board set for the two-player game (left) and the solitaire version (right).

contiguous point, but the geese may move only sideways or forward—not backward. If the fox jumps over a goose, as in Checkers, and lands on an empty point beyond, the goose is killed and is removed from the board. Two or more geese can be killed in one move by a series of short jumps by the fox. The geese cannot jump over the fox, but they try to crowd him into a corner and make it impossible for him to move. If the fox is immobilized he loses the game, but if he can remove the geese from the board before they can trap him he wins.

Peg Solitaire. This game is played with a Fox and Geese board, but 32 marbles are used. Color of marbles is unimportant. To record solution of Peg Solitaire game, see Fox and Geese game illustrated on page 540.

The Play. The marbles are so arranged that the center spot (D4) is left blank. Then at each turn of play one marble must jump over an adjacent marble into a vacant hole beyond. The marble passed over is removed. All jumps must be vertical or horizontal—never diagonal. The object of the game is to remove all the marbles from the board except one, and this should be left in the central hole.

Here's one way that it can be done:

1.	D2 Into D4 remove D3			17.	C2 into C4 remove C3	
2.	F3	D3	E3	18.	A3	C3	B3
3.	E1	E3	E2	19.	D3	B3	C3
4.	E4	E2	E3	20.	A5	A3	A4
5.	C1	E1	D1	21.	A3	C3	B3
6.	E1	E3	E2	22.	D5	D3	D4
7.	E6	E4	E5	23.	D3	B3	C3
8.	G5	E5	F5	24.	B3	B5	B4
9.	D5	F5	E5	25.	B5	D5	C5
10.	G3	G5	G4	26.	D5	F5	E5
11.	G5	E5	F5	27.	F4	D4	E4
12.	B5	D5	C5	28.	C4	E4	D4
13.	C7	C5	C6	29.	E3	E5	E4
14.	C4	C6	C5	30.	F5	D5	E5
15.	E7	C7	D7	31.	D6	D4	D5
16.	C7	C5	C6				

This sequence of moves leaves the last marble in the center, D4. Other problems can be set and solved in similar ways.

SOLITAIRE

In the eighteenth century, the French game of Solitaire, known as Pegboard, was invented, according to legend, by a French count while a prisoner in the Bastille during the French revolution. It is a form of patience for one player similar to Fox and Geese.

Requirements

1. One player.
2. A square board with 37 holes, arranged as shown. In each hole is placed a peg.

The Play. One peg of the 37 is removed. Then one peg at a time is jumped over another into a vacant hole, the peg so jumped being removed from the board. As in the Fox and Geese solitaire game, all jumps must be vertical or horizontal—never diagonal.

Many problems may be created and worked out with a Pegboard. Here are two simple ones:

First Problem. Peg 1 being removed, to leave the last peg in hole 37.

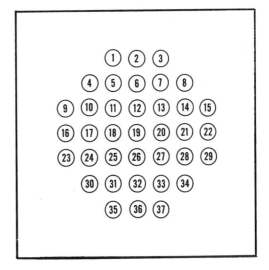

The Solitaire board and its numbers.

3–1	20–7	18–20
12–2	9–11	20–33
13–3	16–18	33–31
15–13	23–25	2–12
4–6	22–20	8–6
18–5	29–27	6–19
1–11	18–31	19–32
31–18	31–33	36–26
18–5	34–32	30–32
20–7	20–33	26–36
3–13	37–27	35–37
33–20	5–18	

Second Problem. Peg 19 being removed, to leave only hole 19 and all outer holes occupied.

6–19	26–24	29–27
4–6	35–25	14–28
18–5	24–26	27–29
6–4	27–25	19–21
9–11	33–31	7–20
24–10	25–35	21–19
11–9		

SCARNEY®

Scarney, an all-skill solitaire board game invention of the author, can be played in more than 25 different ways. However, due to limited space, only the rules of play for Scarney Solitaire, Scarney Singles, Scarney Doubles, and High-Low Scarney appear in these pages. Scarney Solitaire and Scarney Singles, types of a Checkers solitaire game, are based on several new skill board game principles including the newly discovered "Kaleidoscopic Principle." An unusual scientific aspect of all three Scarney games that follow is that at each turn of play, the possible number of playable moves fluctuates. They may increase, decrease, remain the same, or dwindle to zero. Because of this mathematical development, plus the millions of different starting positions, Scarney can never become a game of routine mechanical skill or memory like other board games. For detailed information and strategy of winning play for all 25 Scarney Variants, see *Scarney,* an 88-page book that I wrote several years ago.

Scarney Solitaire

"What solitaire players the world over need badly is a great skill game." I have said this for many years; and now it seems, Scarney Solitaire has filled the bill. It is truly the most fantastically perplexing one-person skill game in history. Anyone can learn to play it in a few minutes, yet it holds an unflagging interest and challenge for the most constant player.

The object of Scarney Solitaire is to try to attain the highest possible point score as shown under each of the four point rating tables that follow. (1) Scarney Solitaire Game Point Ratings, page 544. (2) Scarney Solitaire Match Point Ratings, page 544.

Requirements

1. One player.

2. A Scarney game board.

3. Sixteen numbered discs called *pawns.* There are four black, four red, four yellow, and four green. The four pawns of each color group are marked with one to four spots representing their point values.

The Start of the Game. The solitaire player makes up his own starting position by utilizing the following rules:

1. The solitaire player places the 16 pawns face down on the open Scarney game board.

2. The player by making use of both hands shuffles the face-down pawns around in a circular haphazard mixing fashion.

3. After the face-down pawns have been shuffled, the player places both hands around the pawns and squeezes them together causing the pawns to form two vertical rows.

4. The player then separates the 16 face-down pawns into two groups of eight pawns each. This is done by pushing the eight face-down pawns nearest the top edge of the board onto the top half of the board and the eight face-down pawns nearest the bottom of the board onto the bottom half of the board.

5. The player then places the eight face-down pawns resting on the top half of the board on the eight circles forming the two top horizontal rows of the board in any color pawn arrangement desired. Next, he places the eight face-down pawns resting on the bottom half of the board on the eight circles forming the two bottom horizontal rows of

the board in any color pawn arrangement desired.

6. Once the 16 face-down pawns have been properly placed on the circles of the board, they are then turned face up on their respective circles, thus revealing their spot values. A pawn once properly placed on a circle, be it resting face down or face up, cannot be removed and placed on another circle.

The Play of the Game. After the 16 pawns have been turned face up on the circles of the board, and the player has studied the 16-pawn setup, he, for his first move, must pick up and remove from the board any one of eight pawns that has either a one- or two-spot value. The removed one- or two-spot pawn is placed aside and later credited to the player's score. This is known as a *take-off move* and only one such move is permitted during a game and it must be the first move of the game.

The player's following moves until the completion of the game must all be *jump moves*. A jump move is a move that permits a player to pick up a pawn from any one circle of the board and jump over a different colored pawn resting on an adjacent circle onto a vacant circle adjacent to the jumped pawn. The jumped pawn is then removed from the board and placed aside and later scored. To emphasize, a black colored pawn is not allowed to jump over another black colored pawn, nor can a red jump a red, nor a yellow jump a yellow, nor can a green jump a green pawn. A jump move in Scarney Solitaire is similar to a jump or capture move in regular Checkers, except that in Scarney Solitaire the jump move can only be made horizontally or vertically (in a sideways, or in a forward or backward direction) as indicated by the connecting red lines shown on the game board. A diagonal jump move as in regular Checkers is not permitted. A player is permitted to jump and capture only one pawn at a time. Multiple jump moves are not permitted. As a pawn is jumped, it is removed from the board and credited to the player's game score. And so it goes, jump and capture, until the end of the game.

How to Score. A game is completed when one pawn is left on the board or the remaining pawns on the board are resting on circles of the board in such a position that a jump move is not possible. When this occurs the player adds the point values of the pawns he has removed from the board and that total

becomes his game score.

To determine a player's game score without adding the point values of his captured pawns, simply add the point value of the pawns remaining on the board at the end of the game and subtract this total from 40. The difference is the total number of points scored by the player. Should the player score a bonus of one kind or another (see below), the point value of the bonus is added to the game score and the result is the player's total game score.

Scarney Solitaire Game Bonuses

Single-Pawn Bonuses—Red, Green, and Yellow. When the game is ended and there is only one pawn remaining on the game board, be it red, green, or yellow, the player scores the total point value of all the pawns he removed from the game board; in addition he receives a *single-pawn bonus* of 10 points for each spot on the remaining pawn. *Example:* If the lone remaining pawn is a one-spot, the single-pawn bonus is 10 points, a two-spot 20 points, a three-spot 30 points, a four-spot 40 points. To further illustrate, a lone red 3 spot is left on the game board. Player scores 37 points for game plus a Single Pawn Bonus of 30 points for a total game score of 67 points.

Black Single-Pawn Bonuses. When the game is ended and there is only one black pawn remaining on the board, the single-pawn bonus is valued at 20 points for each spot on the pawn. *Example:* If the lone black pawn is a one-spot, the single-pawn bonus is 20 points, a two-spot 40 points, a three-spot 60 points, a four-spot 80 points. To further illustrate: the lone black 3 spot is left on the game board. Player scores 37 points for the game plus a single black pawn bonus of 60 points for a total game score of 97 points.

Color and Corner Bonuses (Red, Green, and Yellow). When a game is completed and there are only two, three, or four remaining pawns on the game board all of the same color (except black)—all reds, all greens, or all yellows—the player scores the total point value of all the pawns he removed from the board and in addition he receives a *color bonus* of 10 points for each same-colored pawn (red, green, or yellow) remaining on the board. *Example:* Three green pawns whose spot values are 1, 2, and 3 are left on the board. Player scores 34 points for game plus a three-pawn color bonus of 30 points for a total game score of 64 points. If one or more of the two, three, or four remaining same-colored pawns (red, green, or yellow) are resting on corner circles of the game board, the bonus for each corner pawn is doubled to 20 points and is known as a *color corner bonus. Example:* Three green pawns whose spot values are 1, 2, and 3 are left on the board. Two of these three pawns are on corner circles. Game score 34 points, color corner bonus 40 points, and color bonus 10 points. Total game score: 84 points.

Black Color and Corner Bonuses. When a game is ended and there are only two, three, or four remaining pawns on the game board and they are all black, the player receives a color bonus of 20 points for each black pawn resting on the board. *Example:* Three black pawns whose spot values are 1, 2, and 3 are left on the game board. Player scores 34 points for game plus a three-pawn color bonus of 60 points for a total game score of 94 points. If, however, one or more of the remaining two, three, or four black pawns are resting on corner circles of the game board, the bonus is doubled to 40 points for each corner pawn and is known as a *black corner bonus.*

Number and Corner Bonuses. When a game is completed and there are only two, three, or four remaining pawns on the game board all of the same spot values—all one-spots, all two-spots, all three-spots, or all four-spots, the player receives a *number bonus* of 10 points for each different-colored pawn (black, red, green, or yellow). *Example:* Four different-colored pawns—all four-spots—are left on the board. Player scores 24 points for game plus a four-pawn number bonus of 40 points for a total game score of 64 points. However, if one or more of the two, three, or four remaining same-numbered pawns are resting on the corner circles of the game board, the bonus for each corner pawn is doubled to 20 points and is known as a *number corner bonus.*

Scarney Solitaire Game Point Ratings. Upon completion of the game, rate your skill by comparing your game score with the ratings given below. The game and match ratings that follow are based on the strict adherence to the Scarney Solitaire Rules of Play as described in the foregoing text with special emphasis on an honest shuffle and placement of the 16 pawns on the circles of the game board.

Game Score	Rating
150 or more points	Perfect game
125 to 149 points	Excellent game

Game Score	Rating
95 to 124 points	Par game
75 to 94 points	Good game
55 to 74 points	Fair game
35 to 54 points	Average game
30 to 34 points	Poor game
20 to 29 points	Try again!
19 or fewer points	You need practice!

Scarney Solitaire Match Point Ratings. All the rules of Scarney Solitaire are in force except that five games constitute a match. Write down your game scores for each of the five games, then add them and compare the total with the ratings given below:

Match Score	Rating
700 or more points	Perfect match
625 to 699 points	Excellent match
475 to 624 points	Par match
375 to 474 points	Good match
275 to 374 points	Fair match
175 to 274 points	Average match
150 to 174 points	Poor match
100 to 149 points	Try again!
99 or fewer points	You need practice!

Scarney Solitaire Strategy. To aid the player in improving his Scarney Solitaire game as readily as possible, four sample end games and their solutions follow. The game score for each of the four end games that follow is the point difference between 40 (total spot value of all 16 pawns) and the total spot value of the pawn or pawns left on the board at the end of the game. *Example:* An end game is completed and five pawns totaling 17 points remain on the board—game score is 23 points. Should a single, corner, color, or number bonus be scored, its bonus point value is added to the game score and the result is the player's total game score. Some of these end games may be played correctly in more than one way; however, the total game scores are the same.

For explanation of letters and numerals in each of the four end games that follow, see page 551. For the progression of the placement of the pawns on the circles of the board and the subsequent jump moves listed under the solution in each of the following four end games, read down the first column, then down the second column, and last, down the third column.

1. *A Six-Pawn End Game*

Total Game Score 36 Points

The Placement of the Pawns

Y4 on C2	B2 on C10	B1 on C14
Y3 on C5	G3 on C11	R4 on C15

The Solution

G3 jumps B2	G3 jumps Y4
G3 jumps Y3	B1 jumps R4,
	ends game

Two pawns, G3 and B1, are left on the board. Total game score 36 points.

2. *A Seven-Pawn End Game*
Total Game Score 63 Points

The Placement of the Pawns

G3 on C1	B3 on C8	G4 on C12
R1 on C3	R4 on C9	
Y4 on C6	B4 on C10	

The Solution

G4 jumps B3 G4 jumps R1 G4 jumps R4,
R4 jumps B4 G4 jumps Y4   ends game

Two same-colored pawns, G3 and G4, are left on the board. Game score 33 points. Color corner bonus 20 points. Color bonus 10 points. Total game score 63 points.

3. *An Eight-Pawn End Game*
Total Game Score 63 Points

The Placement of the Pawns

G3 on C2	G4 on C7	B2 on C15
Y1 on C3	R4 on C11	R1 on C16
B4 on C6	Y2 on C12	

The Solution

Y2 jumps R4 G4 jumps B4 G3 jumps Y1
R1 jumps B2 R1 jumps Y2 G4 jumps R1,
                           ends game

Two same-colored pawns, G3 and G4, are left on the board. Game score 33 points. Color corner bonus 20 points. Color bonus 10 points. Total game score 63 points.

4. *A Twelve-Pawn End Game*
Total Game Score 116 Points

The Placement of the Pawns

G4 on C1	R4 on C7	Y2 on C13
G2 on C3	G3 on C8	B4 on C14
R3 on C4	R2 on C11	Y4 on C15
B1 on C5	Y3 on C12	G1 on C16

The Solution

Y3 jumps R2 R3 jumps G2 G4 jumps B1
G3 jumps R4 G1 jumps Y4 Y2 jumps G4
B1 jumps G3 Y2 jumps G1 B4 jumps Y2,

B4 jumps Y3 G4 jumps R3   ends game

The lone B4 is left on the board. Game score 36 points. Black single-pawn bonus 80 points. Total game score 116 points.

Scarney Singles

Scarney Singles can be played by two, three, four, or more players, each taking turns in playing a game by himself. It is played like Scarney Solitaire except that one of the contestants aids the active player in placing the 16 pawns on the circles of the game board. A game set called a match is comprised of five games for each player. The player who scores the highest number of points for the five-game set is the winner of the match and scores the point difference between his total match score and that of each of his opponents. Should two or more players have identical high match scores—one or more extra games are played by each of the high scorers until the tie is broken.

Selecting the First Active Player

1. Each of the players by mutual agreement seats himself at a designated place around the table where he must remain for the duration of the match, when a new seating arrangement may take place. The last player to be seated places the 16 pawns face down on the open game board and moves them about in a mixing fashion.

2. After the mixing has been completed the player seated to the immediate left of the person who mixed the pawns picks any one of the 16 face down pawns, the player seated to the first picker's left picks any one of the 15 face down pawns, and so it goes from player to player around the table in a clockwise fashion until each player has picked a pawn, the person who mixed the pawns picking last.

3. The picked pawns are then turned face up revealing their spot values and the player who picked the highest numbered pawn becomes the *first active player*. Only the highest numbered pawn counts. In case two or more players are tied for high, the tied high players pick again until the tie is broken. From then on, each player's active turn of play moves to the left from player to player.

The Start of the Game

1. The active player takes 8 pawns comprised of any two colors, say the 4 black and the 4 red pawns; and the player seated to his immediate right, who shall be referred to as

his "opponent," takes the remaining 8 pawns which in this instance are the 4 green and the 4 yellow. The first move in the placing of the 16 pawns on the game board is made by the active player; he takes any one of the eight pawns he is holding and places it face up on any one of the 16 vacant circles of the game board. Opponent then takes any one of the eight pawns he is holding and places it face up on any one of the 15 remaining vacant circles of the game board. Then the active player takes any one of his seven remaining pawns and places it on any one of the 14 remaining vacant circles of the game board. Next, opponent takes any one of his seven remaining pawns and places it on any one of the 13 remaining circles of the game board and so it goes until the 16 pawns have been placed on the game board.

2. In play, the active player must remove from the game board any one of eight pawns possessing either one or two spots on its face. The removed one- or two-spot pawn is placed aside and later credited to the active player's game score. This is known as a *take-off move* and only one such move is permitted per game and it must be the player's first move of the game.

3. The active player's following moves until the completion of the game must all be jump moves (see page 543). A player is permitted to jump and capture only one pawn at a time. Multiple jump moves are not permitted. As a pawn is jumped, it is removed from the board and credited to the player's game score. And so it goes, jump and capture, until the end of the game.

4. A game is completed when one pawn is left on the board or the remaining pawns on the board are resting on circles on the board in such a position that a jump move is not possible. When this occurs, the active player calls "Scarney," and such a call officially ends the game, even though there may still be one or more possible jump moves left on the board which the active player failed to take advantage of. Immediately after the active player has called "Scarney," he adds the point values of the pawns he has removed from the game board and the total becomes his game score. To determine a player's game score without adding up the point values of the captured pawns, simply add the point value of the pawns remaining on the board at the end of the game and subtract this total from 40. The difference is the total number of

points scored by the player. Should the active player score a bonus of one kind or another, he adds the point value of the scored bonus to his game score and the result becomes his total game score. See Scarney Solitaire Game Bonuses (page 544) which hold good in this game, too.

After the first active player's total game score has been computed, written down and entered on the score sheet, the player seated to the previous active player's left plays the next game as the active player, and the player to his right (previous active player) becomes the opponent and aids the active player in placing the 16 pawns on the game board. And so it goes to the left, clockwise, from player to player until each player has played five games and the match ends.

How to Score a Scarney Singles Match. The match ends upon the completion of five games for each player; the player with the highest score wins the match and gets a *match bonus* of 100 points. The winner is credited with the point difference between his total match score and that of each of the losers. Following is a sample sheet of a Scarney Singles match played by three players:

Game	Player A	Player B	Player C
One	32–32	19–19	6–6
Two	24–56	77–96	34–40
Three	13–69	29–125	27–67
Four	38–107	53–178	110–177
Five	21–128	30–208	36–213
Player's match scores	128 points	208 points	213 points
Match bonus	—	—	100 points
Total match scores	128 points	208 points	313 points

In the above sample match player C, the winner, scored 313 points, B 208 points, and A 128 points. As it totals out, Player C collects 105 points from B and 185 points from A.

Scarney Doubles

A Scarney Doubles match consists of three or more games and terminates at the end of any game in which a total score of 100 points or more is attained by one or both players. In either case the player with the higher score wins the match and scores the point difference between his total match score and that of his opponent. Should both players have identical match scores, an extra game or games is played until the tie is broken. It is played as Scarney Singles except that there are two players, each playing against the other simultaneously.

The Play. After the 16 pawns have been placed on the circles of the board, beginning with the nonstarter (player who placed the last, sixteenth, pawn on the game board), the turn of play passes alternately from player to player until the completion of the game.

A description of the Scarney Doubles game moves and method of play follows:

1. The nonstarter, for his first move, must pick up and remove from the board any one of eight pawns that has either a one- or two-spot value. The removed pawn is placed aside and later credited to the nonstarter's game score. This is a compulsory first move for each player and is known as a *take-off move.*

2. The nonstarter's opponent then picks up and removes from the board any of the seven remaining pawns that has either a one- or two-spot value. The take-off pawn is placed aside and later credited to the nonstarter's game score.

3. Next, beginning with the nonstarter and continuing alternately, each player's following move or moves must all be jump moves. But, a player is not permitted to jump a pawn with the same-colored pawn. *Examples:* A black pawn cannot jump over another black pawn, nor can a red jump a red, a yellow jump a yellow, nor a green jump a green.

4. A player at his turn of play is permitted to jump and capture only one pawn. As a pawn is jumped, it is removed from the board and credited to the player's score, and that ends his turn of play. And so goes the jump move from player to player until the end of the game.

How to Score a Scarney Doubles Game. A game is ended when one pawn is left on the game board, or the remaining pawns on the board are resting on circles of the board in such a position that a jump move is not possible. When such a situation is reached, the player who made the last jump move calls "Scarney" and officially ends the game. He then sweeps the remaining pawn or pawns from the board and adds the point values of these pawns from the board to those he has already removed from the board. Upon completion of the game each player adds the point values of the pawns in his possession and that total becomes his game score. At the end of each game the score for each player is

computed, written down, and added to any score made earlier in the match.

How to Score a Scarney Doubles Match. The match terminates at the end of any game in which a total of 100 or more points is scored by one or both players. The player with the higher score wins the match and receives a 100-point match bonus plus the point difference between both match scores.

Sample Scoring of a Scarney Doubles Match

Game	Player A	Player B
One	11–11	29–29
Two	8–19	32–61
Three	27–46	13–74
Four	20–66	22–96
Five	15–81	25–121
Player's match scores	81 points	121 points
Match bonus	—	100 points
Total match scores	81 points	221 points
Minus player A's score		− 81 points
Player B wins the match by		140 points

At the end of the fifth game Player B's score totaled 121 points. Since 100 points or more ends the match, B is the winner. In addition B gets a 100 point bonus for winning the match, giving him a match total of 221 points. Player B gets credit for the 140 points difference between his total match score of 221 points and A's 81. You will note that each player's individual game score is written down in the left hand column and the cumulative score in the right hand column. This makes it known to each player at all times how many points each needs to win the match.

Scarney Doubles Strategy. Following are a few essential bits of strategy that if put to use will save the beginner many an early loss and also help him better his Scarney Doubles game. For instance, the beginner, when placing his eight pawns on the circles of the board, should at all times place at least one possible take-off pawn (a one- or two-spot) on one of the four center circles of the board to be utilized as his take-off move. However, before making the play the beginner should try to make sure that after his move there will remain on the board at least one possible jump move which can land onto the circle vacated by his take-off move.

If the beginner is the nonstarter of the game and he makes his take-off move from the circle situated on the board's edge, he must try to leave two possible jump moves which will land onto the circle vacated by his take-off move—while at the same time taking into consideration that his opponent may or may not make his take-off move from a circle adjacent to the circle which the beginner's take-off move vacated.

The beginner's best overall game strategy is to try to capture as many high-valued pawns as possible while trying at the same time to go Scarney as quickly as possible. To aid the beginner in this direction, it is suggested that at each turn of play and before making his move, he should try to analyze the number of possible jump moves left on the board. This is done by mentally counting the number of possible jump moves that will remain on the board should he make a certain jump move. Should the total number of possible jump moves be an odd number (1, 3, 5), pass the move by and try to find one that totals an even number (2, 4, 6) of possible jump moves. If you cannot find such a move, your next-best bet is to try to play into as complicated a position as possible.

Scarney Doubles requires deep concentration and sometimes one might inadvertently overlook many simple winning plays. Therefore, it is suggested that even though a player believes he is in a losing position, there is no reason for him to be certain his opponent recognizes it also. In face of this fact, one should not discuss or point out winning or losing positions on the Scarney board while a game is in progress. Very often a losing position can be maneuvered into a winning one on the following play and the player can bring victory out of defeat.

High-Low Scarney

High-Low Scarney, the world's greatest mathematical game of skill, another invention of the author, is played unlike any other game. Anyone can learn to play the game in a few minutes; yet a mathematical wizard will have more success mastering the game of Chess. High-Low Scarney is truly history's greatest mathematical skill game.

A High-Low Scarney match consists of a series of games and terminates at the end of any game in which a total score of 100 points or more is attained by one player.

The object of the game is twofold: (1) To try to win the game by removing the 15th pawn from the game board and leave either a three- or four-spot pawn remaining on the

board; or (2) To try to force your opponent to lose the game by compelling him to remove the 15th pawn from the board and leave either a one- or two-spot pawn remaining on the board.

Requirements

1. Two players, each playing against the other simultaneously.

2. A Scarney Game Board.

3. Sixteen numbered discs called "pawns." There are four black, four red, four yellow and four green. The four pawns of each color group are marked with one to four spots representing point values.

The Start of the Game. To determine the selection of the pawns and to choose the player who makes the first move, either player, by mutual consent, places two pawns of the same color face down on the table and moves them around in a mixing fashion. His opponent picks one and he the other.

The player who picked the high-numbered pawn takes eight pawns of two colors—say, four blacks and four reds, four greens and four yellows, or four blacks and four greens. His opponent takes the remaining eight pawns. The player who picked the higher-numbered pawn plays first and is referred to as the starter. Thereafter, the loser of the previous game becomes the starter and has the right to select the first eight pawns.

The First Play of the Game. The starter takes any one of the eight pawns he is holding and places it face up on any one of the 16 vacant circles of the game board. His opponent then takes any one of the eight pawns he is holding and places it face up on any one of the 15 remaining vacant circles of the game board.

The above method of placing the remaining pawns held by the players continues alternately until all 16 pawns have been placed on the game board. The method of placing the pawns on the game board is part of the strategy of High-Low.

The High-Low Scarney Game Moves. Each of the two players, beginning with the starter, takes turns in removing either one, two, or three same-colored pawns from the board. A detailed description of each of these three High-Low moves follows:

1. *A Single-Pawn Move.* The player may remove from the board any one pawn resting on any one of the 16 circles of the game board.

2. *A Two-Pawn Move.* The player may

remove from the board any two same-colored pawns from any vertical or horizontal row provided that the two pawns are not separated from one another by one or two different-colored pawns. An unoccupied circle or circles of the same row that separate the two same-colored pawns from one another does not prevent the removal of the pawns.

3. *A Three-Pawn Move.* The player may remove from the board any three same-colored pawns from any vertical or horizontal row, provided that the pawns are not separated from one another by a different-colored pawn. An unoccupied circle of the same row that separates three same-colored pawns does not prevent their removal from the board.

Note: When three or four same-colored pawns are resting on circles of a row, the player, when using a two-pawn move, has the privilege of removing any two pawns from the group of three or four same-colored pawns. They do not have to be resting on adjacent circles of the board. The same rule applies when using a three-pawn move when four same-colored pawns are situated in a row.

The Final Play of the Game. The players move alternately by using either a one-, two-, or three-pawn move until only one pawn remains on the game board, thus ending the game. The last pawn (sixteenth) always remains on the board, and it is this pawn that determines the winner and loser of the game. If the player who made the last move of game leaves a three- or four-spot pawn on the game board, he calls "Scarney" and is declared the winner. If the player leaves a one- or two-spot on the game board, his opponent calls "Scarney" and is declared the winner of the game.

How to Score a High-Low Scarney Game

1. Only the winner of the game receives point credits for the pawns he removed from the board. The pawns removed from the board by the loser of the game are disregarded. They are lost and hence are valueless.

2. If the player who made the last move of the game (remover of the fifteenth pawn) leaves either a three- or four-spot pawn remaining on the board, he calls "Scarney" and is declared the winner of the game and is credited with the total number values of the pawns he removed from the board, and that total becomes his game score. However, if the last remaining three- or four-spot pawn is black, the winner's game score is doubled. *Example:* If the winner removed nine pawns

from the board and the sum of their number values is 21, the winner's game score is 21 points. If the last remaining three- or four-spot pawn is black, the winner simply doubles the 21 points and gets a total game score of 42 points.

3. If the player who made the last move of the game (remover of the fifteenth pawn) leaves either a one- or two-spot pawn remaining on the board, he loses the game. His opponent calls "Scarney" and is declared the winner of the game and is credited with the total number values of the pawns he removed from the board and that total becomes his game score. However, if the last remaining one- or two-spot pawn is black, the winner's game score is doubled. *Example:* If the winner removed seven pawns from the board and the sum of their number values is 16, the winner's game score is 16 points. If the last remaining one- or two-spot pawn is black, the winner simply doubles the 16 points and gets a total game score of 32 points.

4. The last pawn (sixteenth), which determines the winner or loser of the game, remains on the game board and does not enter into the scoring.

How to Score a High-Low Scarney Match

1. The match terminates at the end of any game in which a total of 100 or more points is scored by either player.

2. At the completion of each game the winner enters his score on the sheet.

3. At the end of the match an extra 20 points known as a game bonus is added to each player's score for each game won.

4. Winner of the match gets a match bonus of 100 points for winning.

5. Should a player score 100 points or more before his opponent scores any points at all, the winner gets a 100 point shutout bonus.

6. Winner of the match scores the point difference between his total match score and that of his opponent.

Following is a sample score sheet of a High-Low Scarney Match. You will note that each player's individual game score is written down in the left hand column and the cumulative score in the right.

	A		B
	—		21—21
	22—22		—
	—		44—65
	—		26—91
	—		23—114
Players' Match Scores	22 points		114 points

	A	*B*
Game Bonuses	20 points	80 points
Match Bonus	—	100 points
Total Match Scores	42 points	294 points
Minus A's Match Score		−42 points
B wins the match by		252 points

In the above sample match B won five games scoring a total of 114 points. A won one totaling 22 points. B's 114 points put him over the 100 point match mark which ends the match and makes him the winner. B gets four game bonuses, a total of 80 points at 20 points each. A gets one 20 point game bonus. B also receives the 100 points match bonus for winning the match. B's total match score is 294, A's 42. B's point winnings for the match are the point difference in scores or 252 points.

High-Low Scarney Strategy. Most beginners tend to take pawns off the game board blindly without giving any thought to their moves until but five or six pawns remain on the game board. Then they stop and begin to study the end-game setup of these last few pawns. But as the player gains proficiency he will learn that considerable strategy can be employed even with the placing of the pawns on the game board.

Some players favor placing the same-colored three- and four-spot pawns on adjacent circles of the board. Others do the same with one- and two-spot pawns, and others favor placing as many same colored pawns on the same row as their opponent will permit by his strategy. And, some prefer a mixture of different-colored pawns on adjacent circles. How important this strategy becomes to the winning or losing of the game depends entirely upon the player's own ability. High-Low experts start planning their strategy with the placing of the first pawn on the board. Undoubtedly, this demonstration of skill is too far advanced for the average High-Low player. However, there are a few essential bits of strategy that all grades of High-Low players should be familiar with, and they are as follows:

It is assumed the player has learned the workings of a number of end-game traps (there are seven end-game traps described in the following pages).

When the removal of the pawns takes place, the player should, if possible, try to remove all the other pawns and leave a known winning end-game trap for himself. Or, he may spot a possible winning trap placed on the board by his opponent. Or, he may add some pawns to such a partial setup made by his opponent and form a possible winning end-game trap. Under such conditions the strategy when removing the pawns would be to try to leave this setup as an end-game trap on the board. When the removal of the pawns takes place, the player should, if possible, try to remove all the other pawns and leave a known winning end-game trap for himself.

Usually the opponent will break up this end-game trap possibility by removing pawns from it. For that reason a player should try to form several different end-game traps on the board during the placing of the pawns. Then should one trap be broken up by the opponent while removing pawns from the board, the player has the possibility of having another end-game trap remain intact. Naturally, if all the traps are broken up by the opponent, the player must then try to play into a winning end-game trap with the remaining pawns. Therefore, the player must be on the lookout for every possible setup that can be formed into a winning end-game trap during all phases of the game.

For obvious reasons the point scoring result for the end-game traps that follow have been omitted. Some of these traps may be played correctly in more than one way; the result and the total point value of pawns removed from the board by the winner should be the same. As you play these traps on your game board, give the board a quarter turn and study them from all angles so they will be recognizable should they occur during play. For explanation of letters and numerals that follow, see page 551.

Seven High-Low End-Game Traps

1. *A Four-Pawn End-Game Trap.* Place R3 on C2, R4 on C4, G4 on C5, and G2 on C9. Player A moves first and B loses the game. *Solution:* Player A removes G4, B removes R3 and R4, and loses the game by leaving G2 on the board.

2. *A Five-Pawn End-Game Trap.* Place B1 on C2, R3 on C10, G4 on C5, G2 on C7, and G3 on C8. Player A moves first and wins the game. *Solution:* Player A removes G4 and G2, B removes G3, A removes B1, and wins the game by leaving R3 on the board.

3. *A Six-Pawn End-Game Trap.* Place B4 on C2, R2 on C4, R3 on C5, R4 on C8, B3 on C10, and R1 on C16. Player A moves first and wins the game. *Solution:* Player A removes R2 and R1, B removes B4 and B3, A

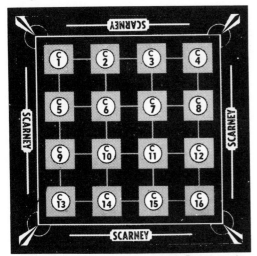

The numbered Scarney game board. But remember in actual play no Scarney game boards are numbered.

removes R4, and wins the game by leaving R3 on the board.

4. *A Seven-Pawn End-Game Trap.* Place B1 on C5, Y4 on C7, B2 on C8, Y3 on C11, R2 on C12, G2 on C14, and R1 on C16. Player A moves first and B loses the game. *Solution:* Player A removes Y4 and Y3, B removes B1 and B2, A removes R2, B removes G2, and loses the game by leaving R1 on the board.

5. *An Eight-Pawn End-Game Trap.* Place R1 on C5, R4 on C6, R3 on C7, R2 on C8, G2 on C13, G3 on C14, G1 on C15, and G4 on C16. Player A moves first and wins the game. *Solution:* Player A removes G2, G1, and G4, B removes R4, R3, and R2, A re-

moves R1, and wins the game by leaving G3 on the board.

6. *A Nine-Pawn End-Game Trap.* Place G3 on C1, R1 on C3, G4 on C5, R3 on C6, R4 on C7, Y4 on C8, R2 on C11, Y3 on C12, and B4 on C14. Player A moves first and wins the game. *Solution:* Player A removes R1, R4, and R2, B removes Y4 and Y3, A removes G4, B removes B4, A removes G3, and wins the game by leaving R3 on the board.

7. *A Ten-Pawn End-Game Trap.* Place G2 on C1, G1 on C2, R4 on C3, G3 on C5, B3 on C6, Y3 on C7, G4 on C9, R2 on C10, Y4 on C12, and B4 on C16. Player A moves first and wins the game. *Solution:* Player A removes G2, G3, and G4, B removes B4, A removes Y4, B removes B3, A removes R2, B removes R4, A removes G1, and wins the game by leaving Y3 on the board.

The Numbered Scarney Game Board. To aid the reader to understand more readily the structure and formation on the game board of the pawn setups which are given in this book, the lettered and numbered illustration of a game board shown here is necessary. You will note that on each of the 16 circles of the illustrated game board, the letter C and numerals from 1 to 16 appear, representing an identical circle on your game board. The letter B represents a black pawn, R a red pawn, Y a yellow pawn, and G a green pawn. *Examples:* B4 represents the black 4-spot pawn. R3 represents the red pawn numbered 3. Y2 represents the yellow pawn numbered 2. G1 represents the green pawn numbered 1. And so on.

FOLLOW THE ARROW®

This is a game I invented a few years ago in which the board rather than the playing pieces determines the direction of the movement of the pawns and combines the fun of a track-type game and checkers.

Requirements

1. Two players. Although only two persons play against each other simultaneously, the game may involve two, three, or four players.

2. A Follow the Arrow game board.

3. Five black and five red Follow the Arrow pawns. The five pawns of each color group are marked with spots numbered 1, 2, 3, 4, and 5.

The Object of the Game. The object of Follow the Arrow is for a player to try to win the game by being the first to move his five pawns across the board from his start position to his opponent's start position. When this is accomplished, the game ends and the winning player is credited with the result of the point value of all of his opponent's pawns that have failed to reach his (winner's) start position multiplied by the numbered value of the winner's fifth and last pawn to reach the loser's start position.

The Follow-the-Arrow game board with pawns.

To Start the Game. The selection of the five black and red pawns is made as follows: Either player, with the consent of the other, takes a black and a red pawn. Holding both hands behind his back, he places one pawn in each hand. Making two closed fists, he brings both hands forward. His opponent touches either fist. If it contains a red pawn, the guesser takes the red pawns; if black, the black pawns. His opponent takes the five pawns of the other color. The open game board is placed between the two players with the horizontal row comprised of the black circles marked S-T-A-R-T directly in front of the player holding the black pawns and the horizontal row comprised of the red circles marked S-T-A-R-T directly in front of the player holding the red pawns. Each player in each succeeding game retains the same-colored pawns with which he began.

Placing the Black and Red Pawns on the Game Board. The holder of the black pawns is the first to place his five pawns on the board. He must place them on the five black circles marked S-T-A-R-T of the bottom horizontal row nearest him and he may place the

five pawns in any numerical order desired. This accomplished, the holder of the red pawns places his five pawns in any numerical order he desires on the five red circles marked S-T-A-R-T of the bottom horizontal row nearest him. Once the holder of the red pawns has placed his first pawn on a circle of his start position, the holder of the black pawns (first player to move) cannot make any change in the numbered arrangement of the black pawns. Thereafter the players in each succeeding game alternate in first placing their pawns on the game board and in making the first move of the game.

How to Move. Once they have placed their pawns on the board in the official start position, the players, starting with the player who placed his five pawns on his start position first, take turns in moving either forward or sideways by making use of either a line or jump move until the completion of the game. A backward line or jump move toward a player's own start position is prohibited. In other words, a pawn cannot move (retreat) toward its original starting position, nor is a side jump permitted on either of the players' starting positions.

Detailed explanation of a Line and Jump Move follows:

1. Line Move. At his turn of play, a player may move either one of his five pawns forward or sideways from the circle on which it is resting to an unoccupied adjacent circle provided an arrow points from the circle on which the pawn is resting to the adjacent unoccupied circle. A forward or side line move is permitted on each of the thirty circles of the game board, rules and arrows permitting. However, a backward line move toward a player's own start position is not permitted. Or the player may make use of a Jump Move.

2. A Jump Move is a move that permits a player to pick up one of his pawns and, in a forward or sideways direction, jump over an opponent's pawn resting on an adjacent circle onto an unoccupied circle adjacent to the jumped pawn. This move is similar to a jump move in checkers; however, the jumped pawn or pawns remain on the circles of the board. They are not removed from the board as in checkers. This jump move is legal provided an arrow points from the circle on which the pawn is resting to the adjacent circle occupied by the opponent's pawn—the position of the arrows or lack of an arrow on the circle where the opponent's pawn or pawns to be jumped are resting are ignored when jumping. The same holds true for the circles on which the jumping pawn lands. A two, three or four pawn jump move is permitted in Follow the Arrow. Again I repeat, a backward jump move toward a player's own start position is not permitted, nor is a side jump move permitted on either of the players' starting positions.

When it is possible for a player to make a legal jump move, his opponent may do one of three things: (1) call "Jump"; (2) remain silent; or (3) call "Pass." (A pass call indicates a player relinquishes his privilege of calling jump.) When the opponent calls "Jump" he must also point out the possible jump move. When this situation occurs, the player is compelled to make a forced jump as directed by his opponent. This rule holds true except when there are two or three different directions in which he may jump. In that case, although the player still must make a jump move, he has the right to select his own jump move. If a legal multiple jump move of two, three, or four pawns is possible, the player has the privilege of jumping one or as many pawns as he desires.

If a player at his turn of play has one or more possible jump moves and his opponent has either remained silent or called "Pass," his opponent knowingly or unknowingly has signified that he gives up his privilege of compelling his opponent to make a forced jump move. The player under such conditions is now free to do as he wishes; he may make use of either a jump or line move.

To help speed up the game and avoid unnecessary arguments that may arise over the jump call, the following rule should be enforced. A player must call "Jump" immediately after completing his move and while his fingers still rest on his played pawn.

Point Scoring for Standard Follow the Arrow. A game is completed when one of the players succeeds in moving his five pawns onto the five circles of his opponent's start position. When the player moves his fifth and last pawn onto the opponent's start position, he calls either "Single game," "Double game," "Triple game," "Quadruple game," or "Quintuple game," according to the number on this pawn, and by so doing is declared the winner of the game. He receives point credits as described below.

1. If the winner of a game succeeds in moving his fifth and last pawn onto his opponent's start position—and if this numbered pawn is a one-spot—he calls "Single game." This officially ends the game, and he receives the total point credits of all the loser's pawns that have failed to reach his (the winner's) start position. *Example:* If only one of the loser's pawns has failed to reach the winner's start position, the winner receives its numerical value—if it is a one-spot 1 point, a two-spot 2 points, etc.

If two or more of the loser's pawns have failed to reach the winner's start position, the winner is credited with their total numerical value. *Example:* If the loser's numbered pawns 1, 2, and 4 have failed to reach the winner's start position, the winner receives credit for 7 points—and so on.

2. If the winner of a game succeeds in moving his fifth and last pawn onto his opponent's start position—and if this pawn is a two-spot—he calls "Double game." This call officially ends the game, and the winner receives double (two times) the total point credits of all the loser's pawns that have failed to reach his (the winner's) start position. And, similarly, for the three-spot he wins a triple game; for the four-spot a quadruple game; for the five-spot a quintuple game.

ROULETTE

Roulette, the glamour casino game that made Monte Carlo the world's most famous casino, is said by some historians to have been invented in 1655 by the French scientist Blaise Pascal during his monastic retreat, and first played in a makeshift casino in Paris. Other historians say it was invented by a French monk to help break the monotony of monastery life. Still others say it originated in an old Chinese game whose object was to arrange 37 statuettes of animals into a "magic square" of 666 (the sum of all the numbers on the Roulette wheel), but they fail to describe the method of play. They add that the game was later played in Tibet and eventually by French Dominican monks, one of whom transposed the statuettes into numbers from 0 to 36 and arranged them haphazardly along the rim of a revolving wheel. Since the early French wheels of the 1800's had both the 0 and 00, this theory does not sound plausible.

Roulette is the most popular casino game found in European and Latin American casinos and for a very good reason. The Roulette wheels found in Monte Carlo, Deauville, San Remo, London, and other European and Latin American casinos have 36 numbers (1 to 36) and a single zero (0). When zero appears, all bets paid off at even money such as red, black, odd, or even are "imprisoned" and their ultimate fate is determined by the next spin of the wheel. They are either lost or are returned to the winning player. The player loses half of his wager on red, black, odd, or even, when the zero appears. The bank's favorable percentage, in this case on red, black, odd, or even, is 1 13/37 percent, and on all other types of bets it is 2 26/37 percent.

The American-style roulette wheel with its single 0 and double 00 has a bank's favorable percentage of 5 5/19 percent and more—and this is the reason Roulette runs third in popularity in American and Caribbean casinos (Craps and Black Jack outrun it in popularity).

Roulette combines a number of elements that make it the ideal casino game. To begin with, it's very easy to play. Second, it's a game where big winnings build up quickly, and two straight number hits, each of which pay off at odds of 35 to 1, are equivalent to

the winnings of seventy constant Pass or Don't Pass Line bets at the Bank Craps table. It is a game where a person's favorite lucky number is a very real, very romantic factor. It is the casino's number-one spectator sport—when a high bettor gets hot, a crowd forms, tension fills the air, and everybody is as excited as the hot bettor himself. All these factors are what make the game of Roulette so fascinating.

Roulette is a game that every American feels he has to try at least once when he visits a casino in Nevada, the Caribbean, or elsewhere. To most players its appealing quality is that it is a relaxing game—that is, unless one happens to be a Roulette addict who spends the time in between spins placing wagers all over the betting layout. Roulette is undoubtedly the most cultured of all casino games. Contrary to the views expressed by most of our present-day gambling writers, it gives the average gambler as good an overall run for his money as Bank Craps or Black Jack. In addition, Roulette offers as wide a variety of bets as any other casino game, including Bank Craps, yet the slower pace and simpler rules of play make it a much easier game for the average gambler to enjoy. To this, add the fact that it offers the gambler whose budget is modest an opportunity to gamble for a long while with a small investment.

So that you'll understand everything about the structure, science, and rules of play concerning Roulette, let's walk over to a table situated in a Las Vegas Strip casino and allow me to explain the game to you. You'll notice that the table is composed of two sections—the wheel and the player's betting spaces—better known as the Roulette layout. The only moving part of the wheel consists of a solid wooden disk, slightly convex in shape. Around its bottom rim are metal partitions known as separators, and the compartments between these are called pockets. These pockets are metal, painted alternately red and black, except for two pockets that are green. Each of the red and black pockets bears a number from 1 to 36 in gold. The green pockets carry the signs 0 and 00, also in gold. With these two exceptions, the odd and even numbers and the high and low numbers run alternately, but not consecutively. Each number, color, and sign on the wheel has its counterpart on the betting layout.

The standard American Roulette table employs five, six, or seven sets of 300 chips; and there is one set for each player. Chips are valued at 10 cents, 25 cents, 50 cents, $1, $5, $25, and $100. The values of the lower chip denominations, from 10 cents to $1 (unlike other casino chips) are not marked on them. The player must buy a minimum stack of 20 chips from the croupier (dealer), specifying the value he wishes to place on each chip and paying for them accordingly. The player then receives chips of a color different from those of the other players. He must cash them in when he leaves the table.

The maximum amounts permitted to be wagered on different spaces of the betting layout vary in Nevada and Caribbean casinos. However, the minimum bet allowed usually involves four minimum-value chips. For example, when playing 25-cent chips the player must bet a minimum of four chips on each spin of the wheel, although the four chips can be spread over the numbers on the layout as he desires, excluding bets that pay off at even money and 2 to 1, such as wagers placed on black, red, odd, and even numbers, dozens (first 12, second 12, third 12), and vertical columns of the layout (each column containing 12 numbers). A minimum of four chips or a bet valued at $1 is required on all even-money or 2 to 1 bets. Many Strip casinos in Las Vegas permit a maximum of $100 bet on a single or straight number, with even that limit upped to $500 in special cases. Puerto Rico's casinos, whose wagers are standardized by law, permit a maximum of only $10 on all betting spaces of the layout with the exception of even-money and 2 to 1 wagers, where the limit is $180.

To play the game, each player places his bets on the layout in any manner permitted by the rules. The croupier starts the wheel spinning in a counterclockwise direction, then flips the ball onto the wheel's back track so that it travels clockwise. Players may continue placing bets while wheel and ball are in motion until the croupier calls "No more bets!" He does this as the ball slows down and is about to fall off the back track.

When the ball comes to rest in one of the pockets on the wheel, the croupier announces the winning color and number as he points with his index finger to the corresponding number on the betting layout. He then rakes in the losses and pays off the winners. It's as simple as that. To avoid confusion as to the winning number, the author has recommended to a number of casino operators that the croupier, rather than point to the winning number, should be supplied with a marker to place on the winning number.

You can bet on a single number (including 0 and 00), a combination of numbers, the colors red, black, or green, or the odd or even numbers. The 0 and 00 are usually referred to as "house numbers" for the obvious reason that when the ball drops into either of these pockets the house wins all bets—except those that were wagered on 0 and 00. On the betting layout (see next page), there are an equal number of red, black, odd, and even numbers—18 of each. A win of this type pays the winner even money (1 to 1). If we do not consider the house numbers 0 and 00, the probability of red, black, odd, or even winning would be 50–50. However, the 0 and 00 must be considered, and here is where the house percentage comes into the picture. All wagers placed at the Roulette table with the exception of the five-number bet (explained later) amounts to a house advantage of 5 5/19 percent.

Here is how it is calculated: The player places his bet on a space of the layout marked black, red, odd, or even. He is betting that one of 18 numbers will win. There are, however, 18 numbers, plus the 0 and 00, for a total of 20 numbers, that will lose for him. Therefore, the house's average gain will be 2 wins out of every 38 spins, so that its advantage is 2/38 of 100, 5 5/19 percent, an average cost to the player of 5 5/19 cents of each dollar wagered.

Let's follow this reasoning a step further: Suppose you placed a chip bet on each of the 38 numbers (which includes the house numbers of 0 and 00). You would be sure to win because you covered all the numbers. But since you bet 38 chips, and received only 36 chips in winnings, you have lost two chips, or 2/38 of 100, or 5 5/19 percent—an average money cost to you of 5 5/19 cents with each dollar bet. Since Roulette layouts in America or the Caribbean do not vary as to bets permitted, odds offered, and percentages against the player, the following text covers all the bets permitted on any layout and the house's percentage advantage on each.

Straight Bet, or Single-Number Bet. The player places his chip (or chips) squarely on one number on the Roulette betting layout, making certain that the chip does not touch

LINE
six numbers
(chip on dividing line
at side)
pays 5 to 1
5 5/19%

SQUARE
four numbers
(chip in center)
pays 8 to 1
5 5/19%

LINE
five numbers
(1, 2, 3, 0, and 00)
pays 6 to 1
7 7/19%

HIGH (19 to 36)
or LOW (1 to 18)
pays even
5 5/19%

SPLIT
two adjoining numbers
(including 0 and 00)
pays 17 to 1
5 5/19%

ODD or EVEN
BLACK or RED
pays even
5 5/19%

STRAIGHT
any single number
(including 0 and 00)
pays 35 to 1
5 5/19%

DOZEN
1 to 12, 13 to 24
or 25 to 36
pays 2 to 1
5 5/19%

STREET
three numbers
(chip on line at side)
pays 11 to 1
5 5/19%

COLUMN
1 to 34,
2 to 35
or 3 to 36
pays 2 to 1
5 5/19%

Players indicate the bet or bets they make by the placement of chips on the layout as shown here.

any of the lines enclosing the number. This indicates that the player is betting that on the next spin of the wheel the little ivory ball will come to rest in the pocket of his number on the Roulette wheel. The house pays off at 35 to 1, pushing you a stack of 20 and a stack of 15 chips for each chip successfully wagered, leaving your original wager on the layout as your next bet. Since the odds against are 37 to 1, the house's advantage is 5 5/19 percent.

The Signs 0 and 00. These can be played the same as any one of the 36 numbers. The house's favorable percentage is the same as on a single-number bet: 5 5/19 percent.

Split Bet, or Two-Number Bet. The player places his chip directly on any horizontal or vertical line separating any two numbers on the betting layout. If the winning number is one of the two wagered on, the player wins and is paid off at 17 to 1 odds. Since the odds against are 18 to 1, the house's favorable advantage is 5 5/19 percent.

Street Bet, or Three-Number Bet. The player places his chip on the outside vertical line of the betting layout. This indicates that he is betting the three numbers opposite the chip, across the layout. If the winning number is one of these three, the player wins and is paid off at odds of 11 to 1. Since the odds against are 11 2/3 to 1, the house's favorable advantage is 5 5/19 percent.

Square Bet, Quarter Bet, Corner Bet, or

Four-Number Bet. The player places his chip on the intersection of the lines touching any four numbers. If one of these four numbers wins, the player is paid off at 8 to 1 odds. Since the odds against are 8 1/2 to 1, the house's favorable edge is 5 5/19 percent.

Line Bet, or Five-Number Bet. The player places his chip on the line separating the 1, 2, 3 from the 0 and 00 spaces at a corner intersection. This indicates that he is betting that one of the five numbers 1, 2, 3, 0, or 00 will win. If one of these five numbers wins, the player is paid off at odds of 6 to 1. Since the odds against are 6 3/5 to 1, the house's favorable advantage is 7 17/19 percent. Note that the house percentage differs from the 5 5/19 percent that is the bank's edge on all other Roulette bets. From the player's viewpoint, therefore, it is a bet to avoid because it has an additional disadvantage of 2 12/19 percent against the player as compared to all other Roulette bets.

Line Bet, or Six-Number Bet. The player places his chip on the intersection of the vertical sideline and a horizontal line between two "streets." This indicates he is betting the three numbers above and the three numbers below the line on which the chip is resting. If any of these six numbers wins, the player is paid off at odds of 5 to 1. Since the odds against are 5 1/3 to 1, the house's favorable advantage is 5 5/19 percent.

Column Bet, or Twelve-Number Bet. The player places his chip on one of the three blank spaces at the bottom of the layout. (Some layouts have three squares marked "1st," "2nd," "3rd.") This indicates that the player is betting the twelve vertical numbers above the space wagered on. If one of these twelve numbers wins, the player is paid off at 2 to 1 odds. Since the odds against are 2 1/6 to 1, the house's favorable advantage is 5 5/19 percent.

Dozens, or Twelve-Number Bet. The player places his chip on one of the spaces of the betting layout marked "1st 12," "2nd 12," or "3rd 12." The 1st 12 indicates that the player is betting on the numbers 1 to 12 inclusive; the 2nd 12, the numbers 13 to 24 inclusive; and the 3rd 12, the numbers 25 to 36 inclusive. If one of the 12 numbers wagered on wins, the player is paid off at 2 to 1 odds, like the column bet described above. The correct odds are 2 1/6 to 1. The house's advantage is 5 5/19 percent.

Low-Number Bet (1 to 18). The player places his chip on the betting layout marked 1 to 18, which indicates that he is betting on the numbers 1 to 18 inclusive. If one of these numbers wins, the player is paid off at even money (1 to 1). The correct odds are 1 1/9 to 1. The house's advantage is 5 5/19 percent.

High-Number Bet (19 to 36). The player places his chip on the space of the betting layout marked 19 to 36, which indicates that he is betting on the numbers 19 to 36 inclusive. If one of these 18 numbers wins, the player is paid off at even money (1 to 1). The correct odds are 1 1/9 to 1. The house's advantage is 5 5/19 percent.

Black-Color Bet. The player places his chip on a space of the layout marked "Black." (Some layouts have a large black diamond-shaped design containing the word "Black.") The player is betting on the 18 black-colored numbers. If one of these numbers wins, the player is paid off at even money (1 to 1). The correct odds are 1 1/9 to 1. The house's advantage is 5 5/19 percent.

Red-Color Bet. This is the same as a black-color bet except that the player places his chip on the space marked "Red," or on the red diamond, and is betting on the 18 red-colored numbers. If one of these numbers wins, the player is paid off at even money (1 to 1). The correct odds are 1 1/9 to 1. The house's advantage is 5 5/19 percent.

Odd-Number Bet. The player places his chip on the space of the layout marked "Odd." The player is betting on the 18 odd numbers. If one of the odd numbers wins, the player is paid off at even money (1 to 1). The correct odds are 1 1/9 to 1. The house's advantage is 5 5/19 percent.

Even-Number Bet. This is the same as the odd-number bet, except that the player is betting on the 18 even numbers. If one of the numbers wins, the player is paid off at even money (1 to 1). The correct odds are 1 1/9 to 1. The house's advantage is 5 5/19 percent.

Roulette Systems

Roulette is the casino game that has invited more systems "to break the bank" than all other casino games combined. So many systems have been created by mathematicians and scientists in an effort to beat the bank at Roulette that most casino operators sometimes call it the "egghead's game." Professional male gamblers call it a "woman's game."

The most popular Roulette system used by Roulette players is the D'Alembert System. It is based on what its proponents called the "Law of Equilibrium." This is nothing more than the doctrine of the Maturity of Chances, which mathematicians call the "Gambler's Fallacy." The theory is that any two opposite chances, such as red or black, odd or even, must sooner or later win an equal number of times. If red, for instance, dominates for a series of spins, it is only a question of time until black will have its turn. The D'Alembert System player, therefore, after every losing bet, adds an additional chip or two to his bet on the next spin, and after every winning bet reduces the bet by one or more chips. These players misinterpret the theory of probability. They think that these opposite chances will even up in a short run, whereas the probability theory gives only an approximate statement of what can be expected to happen in a very long run. The bank's favorable advantage of the 0 and 00 will, in the long run, break all players.

Thousands of Roulette players refuse to believe this. Many of them haunt the casinos day after day, endlessly recording statistics, clocking how often certain numbers, colors, or combinations have or have not appeared in the last few hours, nights, or even weeks. No casino operator is ever worried that these players will come up with a workable system. In fact, on request, at many casinos, the management will supply the addict with a chart on which the Roulette numbers are printed so that he can save time, paper, and pencil by merely checking off the winning numbers instead of having to write them down.

Some addicts compile all data for a different reason. They compare their statistics with all sorts of probability calculations, hoping to find some indication that the wheel is biased. A wheel very seldom goes haywire of its own accord, and I can't think of any fault a wheel could develop by itself that would not be spotted by the management in very short order.

The latest Roulette system making the rounds is called the "Cancellation System." It consists of writing down a column of figures in serial order, beginning with 1. Suppose we use the sequence 1, 2, 3, 4, 5, 6, 7, 8, 9, 10. The player begins by betting the total of the top and bottom figures—in this instance, 11 chips. If he wins, he crosses out the top and bottom figures—and then bets the total of the new top and bottom figures—in this instance,

9 plus 2, or 11. If the player loses, he adds the amount lost at the bottom of the column and then bets the total of the new top and bottom figures. In this instance, he would bet 11 plus 2 or 13 chips. This procedure of betting and crossing out and adding numbers continues until all the numbers in the column have been crossed out.

As in most systems, the player must increase the amount of his bet after each loss. In the Cancellation System the player sticks to bets that pay even money, and the theory is that since he crosses out two numbers of his series when he wins and adds only one number when he loses, he must eventually cross out all numbers. When this happens, he will have won 55 betting units.

On paper it looks good; however, the Cancellation System, like all other so-called systems, sooner or later is interrupted by the fact that the player goes broke. In this system the player increases his bets to the point where he is stopped by the house limit. But when a long losing streak hits the player, he finds himself so far in the hole that he has reached the limit of his own bankroll, or he discovers that the constantly increasing size of his bets has put him in the position of having to risk a large amount of money to try to recoup his losses. At his point, afraid to risk a large bet, he quits a loser, saying, "Well, it wasn't supposed to happen that way. I wonder what went wrong with the system."

Another catch is that if the table is busy, the croupier views the system player who places a long series of small bets with distaste. The player is giving him a lot of work, and he is very likely to make it clear that he doesn't want your business. "Look, man," he'll say, "play your system down the street. We're busy now."

It doesn't matter what system you make use of, in the long run you can't overcome the house advantage of the single and double zero that the Roulette bank has stacked against you. This house advantage is the only surefire system that works as expected.

Don't Be Cheated by Short Payoffs. It's easy to learn how to play Roulette, and yet surprisingly few players know exactly how many chips they should receive when they win on a combination of several bets, particularly if the wager involves single, double, or four-number wagers. When a croupier pushes over several stacks of chips, only about five out of a hundred players have any idea of whether or not the payoff is correct. I have seen a good many players shorted on chips in many of our top casinos. It is often an honest mistake on the croupier's part, but whether it is or not, if you are going to play Roulette you'd be smart to learn how to calculate your winnings. Why should you pay an extra charge by being short-changed when it is so easy to be sure?

Here is a mathematical shortcut the reader can use to calculate mentally the number of chips to be paid off on single-number bets on which the odds are 35 to 1. For any even number of chips, simply divide by 2, multiply by 7, and tack a zero onto your answer. *Example:* You bet 16 chips on a single number and win. Divide 16 by 2, multiply by 7, and add a zero, which gives you 560—the correct number of chips due you.

If you wager an odd number of chips, you make the same calculation except you subtract 1 before you start and add 35 at the end. *Example:* You wagered 15 chips. Subtract 1, getting 14, divide by 2, getting 7, multiply by 7, getting 49, add a zero, getting 490, and add 35 for a final answer of 525. If you want to avoid mental calculation, give the following chart a little study and memorize the payoffs on the more complicated bets. Here are all the correct payoffs on straight, split, street, quarter, and line bets when wagering 1 to 20 chips. Simple multiplication will enable you to extend the chart to payoffs on more than 30 chips.

ROULETTE PAY CARD

Straight	Split	Street	Quarter	Line
35 to 1	*17 to 1*	*11 to 1*	*8 to 1*	*5 to 1*
1 35	1 17	1 11	1 8	1 5
2 70	2 34	2 22	2 16	2 10
3 105	3 51	3 33	3 24	3 15
4 140	4 68	4 44	4 32	4 20
5 175	5 85	5 55	5 40	5 25
6 210	6 102	6 66	6 48	6 30
7 245	7 119	7 77	7 56	7 35
8 280	8 136	8 88	8 64	8 40
9 315	9 153	9 99	9 72	9 45
10 350	10 170	10 110	10 80	10 50
11 385	11 187	11 121	11 88	11 55
12 420	12 204	12 132	12 96	12 60
13 455	13 221	13 143	13 104	13 65

Straight	Split	Street	Quarter	Line
35 to 1	*17 to 1*	*11 to 1*	*8 to 1*	*5 to 1*
14 490	14 238	14 154	14 112	14 70
15 525	15 255	15 165	15 120	15 75
16 560	16 272	16 176	16 128	16 80
17 595	17 289	17 187	17 136	17 85
18 630	18 306	18 198	18 144	18 90
19 665	19 323	19 209	19 152	19 95
20 700	20 340	20 220	20 160	20 100

Curiously enough, there are many more methods used by cheats to beat a roulette game than there are cheating methods to beat the player. Roulette mobs have on several occasions secretly visited Monte Carlo during the night, gaffed the wheels, and then won considerable amounts from the house before the casino discovered what had happened. This has also happened in a good many other casinos. The methods they use to gaff the wheel are rather easy to install but I won't discuss them here because I'm not trying to smarten up any cheats. Also, this cheating doesn't affect the honest players at the table; only the cheats who know about the gaff gain by it, and it's only the house that loses.

How to Gamble Sensibly at Roulette. The best way to avoid losing at Roulette is to stop playing the game, but since it is such a favorite with so many millions of people, I doubt that very many of them will take this advice. And I can't give a best bet at the game because, unlike all other casino games, all but one of the bets have the same 5 5/19 percent against the player. The best I can do to save you some money is to suggest that you avoid the five-number combination bets with their 7 17/19 percent advantage for the bank.

You may be lucky and win at Roulette over a short period, but your chances of beating the wheel if you play continuously through several long sessions are dubious.

If you intend to play for several sessions, budget yourself. Divide the amount of money you can afford to lose by the number of times you expect to play, and don't exceed that loss limit in any session. If you should at any time find yourself ahead of the game by a good sum, pack the game in. Tomorrow is another day. This advice will at least prevent you from becoming a roulette degenerate.

PUT AND TAKE TOP GAME

The Put and Take Top game had its biggest fad in the late 1930's and early 1940's, when it was second only to Poker as a private gambling game. However, due to its cheating

Gaffed Put-and-Take Top. Arrow indicates edge which has been rounded.

factors, the Put and Take Top fad did not last too long. But, there seems to be a resurgence of Put and Take Top and for that reason, I have included it in this book. The rules of the game are as follows:

Any number can play. It requires a Put and Take Top. The top is eight-sided and the sides are usually marked P–1, T–1, P–3, T–3, P–4, T–4, P–All, T–All.

Each player puts a stake into the pot and each player takes turns in spinning the top once. If a P–1 appears, the player puts one unit into the pot; if T–1 appears he takes one unit out of the pot. If a P–3 appears he puts 3 units into the pot; if T–3 appears he takes 3 units out of the pot. The same procedure

holds true for P–4 and T–4. If T–All appears, he takes all the money in the pot. If P–All appears, he must put in an amount equal to that in the pot.

Cheating with Put and Take Tops. Most tops are gaffed (fixed crookedly) with edge work, the edges being rounded on some sides and sharp on others. The top will tend to roll off the sides with the rounded edges and stop on the sides whose edges are sharp. Some tops have alternate edges beveled so that when the victim spins the top clockwise with his right hand (the normal manner), it always lands put.

The cheat spins the top counterclockwise and always takes. Some gaffed tops have a central spindle which projects farther on one end of the top than the other. It is so beveled that take numbers always come up when the cheat is spinning. When he passes the top to the next player, he pushes the spindle down through the top so that the end that projected farthest becomes the short end and what was the upper side of the top becomes the bottom. This end for end reversal is the same as reversing the direction of the spin and the victim finds that he can only throw put numbers. Put and Take Tops can be tested by changing the direction of the spin to see if it has any effect on the result. Not playing with strangers, and that includes anyone you haven't known since you were knee high to a pup, is also a help.

TIDDLY-WINK

No encyclopedia of games would be complete without mention of several children's favorites that require special equipment. One of the most popular child's game is Tiddly-Wink.

Requirement
1. Any number of players.
2. Small plastic discs. Each player has the same number.

3. Cup or container to catch small discs.

The Play. After determining the rotation of play by tossing a coin, each player tries to get the small discs into a cup by snapping them with the pressure of the larger disc against their edges. The player scores one for each disc snapped into the container and the player who receives the agreed score first is the winner.

JACKSTRAWS

Jackstraws, which is also known as Four-Five-Six, Pick Up Sticks, and Wood Pile, is another old-time children's favorite.

Requirements
1. Any number of players.
2. Set of jackstraws; each straw or stick

resembles a knitting needle, 6 to 8 inches long and tapering at both ends. The colors of the sticks indicate their scoring values (generally): green 3; red 5; blue 10; and black 20.

The Play. The first player, chosen by tossing a coin or lots, holds the straws over the center of the table, the bottom ends touching it, and releases them so that they fall into a pile. He then removes as many sticks as he can without causing any other straw to move. When another straw moves, the player must replace the stick he was removing, and the play passes to the player next on the left. Fingers must be used, until the black jackstraw is removed, in which case it may be employed, only by its owner, to help lift off the other sticks. Play continues until all the straws have been removed. The player with the highest point total is the winner.

Variation: Each player, in turn, removes all the straws from the pile that he can before he misses. When he does, the pile of sticks is released at the table again, and the next player plays.

OTHER BOARD GAMES

There are many copyrighted board games on the market. I have not included these games in this encyclopedia because all have fairly clear instructions accompanying the boards.

CHAPTER 27

Lottery and Guessing Games

Since their first appearance, lotteries have been and still are the number-one gambling activity for the greatest number of people the world over. Government lotteries or government-supervised lotteries are conducted today in more than 50 countries, including the Latin-American countries, Ireland, England, France, West Germany, Italy, Spain, Turkey, Russia, Poland, China, Thailand, Australia, and several states in the United States. These lotteries vary as to methods of determining winners, ticket prices, and amounts of prize awards; but, essentially, they all consist of either the chance selection of tickets and numbers or the prediction and selection of the results of sporting events.

Lotteries are ancient. The casting of lots to divide up the land is mentioned numerous times in the Bible. St. John, writing of the crucifixion of Jesus, mentions the prophecy concerning His garment when he says, "They said therefore among themselves, Let us not rend it, but cast lots for it, whose it shall be: that the scripture might be fulfilled, which

saith, They parted my raiment among them, and for my vesture they did cast lots. These things therefore the soldiers did."

Door-prize drawings, a form of lottery, are at least a couple of thousand years old. This type of drawing was an entertainment feature of the dinner parties given by many of the Roman emperors. Nero gave his guests presents by letting them draw for such prizes as a slave or a fashionable villa. Helogabalus added a touch of humor by mixing among the valuable prizes such odd and worthless ones as six dead flies, several ostriches, or a dead dog. Augustus Caesar sometimes sold his guests tickets and gave out articles of very unequal value; it was he who sponsored the first known public lottery in order to raise funds to repair the city of Rome.

While there are myriad types of lotteries around the world, only a very few of them may properly be classed as games. In this chapter I have selected the best known of them, in addition to several so-called "guessing games."

LOTTO

The Italian parlor game of Lotto, the fore-runner of Bingo, is patterned after *Lo Giuoco del Lotto del Italia* (The Italian National Lottery), which has been in almost constant weekly operation since it began in 1530.

The parlor game of Lotto requires a number of special *Lotto cards,* which contain

nine vertical rows and three to five horizontal rows. On each horizontal row five figures and four blanks appear, while the vertical rows represent, respectively, numbers from one through ten, 11 through 20, 21 through 30, etc., to 81 through 90. Each number appears in its appropriate vertical row, and no number is duplicated on a card. As a rule, one card is issued to each player.

There are also 90 small balls with flattened surfaces or disks which are numbered from one to 90. These are placed in a bag or similar container and, after being thoroughly shaken, they are withdrawn at random, one by one. As each ball or disk is withdrawn, its number is announced and each player marks wherever that number appears on his card with a marker —a grain, a bean, or a pasteboard marker. The player first covering all the numbers in any horizontal row calls out "Lotto" and wins. Generally, the announcer of the game, who has a chart of the numbers called, requests that the player or some observer call back the numbers, so that the announcer can make sure that *lotto* has in fact been made. For an incorrect call there is no penalty. The game just continues until there is a legal winner. If two or more players go lotto on the same number, the prize is divided equally.

The prize is usually a purse made up of an equal ante from all players, less the house percentage, if any, taken by the proprietor of the game. Frequently, in games not played in the home, a player may have more than one card by contributing in full for each.

Standard Keno

Keno is played in the same manner as Lotto except that the numbered balls are rolled one by one out of the spout of the container, called the *Keno goose*. While the original Keno cards always had five horizontal rows, the modern game is generally played with three-row cards.

Bingo

The modern American form of Lotto is Bingo. Actually, it is the favorite weekly pastime of millions of American women living in cities, towns, and hamlets throughout the United States. Bingo, in one form or another, is played in most countries of Latin America, Europe, Africa, and Asia.

Bingo's great popularity is due primarily to two factors: (1) the game is simple to play, and (2) every game must produce one or more winners. Since a series of games is usually played in one session, the game supplies hours of fun and tension. Only a game like Bingo could produce the phenomenon of a hall full of several hundred men and women

(mostly women) who seldom make a sound except for cries of jubilation or disappointment at the end of each game.

Bingo is a weekly habit for millions of Americans. None of the players loses a great sum. At an average cost of $4 per session (actually, only $2 over the long run, because half of the money wagered is returned in prizes), millions of women—mostly middle-aged and elderly ladies who have few, if any, outlets for their gambling urge—buy hours of sociability, excitement, and fun playing a game that also provides considerable sums for worthy causes and community projects. As it is played today, Bingo is a form of lottery because the game calls for the sale and distribution of printed cards. However, unlike lotteries, Bingo cards cannot be purchased outside the Bingo premises; each player must be present to cover the drawn numbers on her Bingo card with markers while the game is taking place.

Modern Bingo equipment is composed of Bingo cards, made of either cardboard or paper, with a playing surface that bears a printed design of five rows of five squares

A typical Bingo card.

each—25 squares in all. The letters *B-I-N-G-O* appear above this design, each letter above one of the vertical columns. All the squares contain numbers except the center square, which is considered a free play. The following arrangement of numbers is standard, and appears on most Bingo cards:

The first column, or vertical row, on the left under the letter *B* contains any five numbers from the group 1 through 15. Under *I* there are any five numbers from the group 16 through 30. Under *N*, the center vertical row, there are only four numbers from the group 31 through 45. The middle square of this row is the center square of the card, and it is either blank or bears a printed 0 or *X* or the words FREE PLAY. Under *G* in the fourth vertical row are any five numbers from the group 46 through 60, and under *O* in the fifth column are any five numbers from the group 61 through 75.

In many Bingo parlors one, two, or three Bingo cards are pasted on a larger heavy cardboard called a *lapboard*. This prevents the players from taking the cards home as souvenirs, and the board serves as a table. In fact, the latest Bingo innovation is the fingertip Bingo card, which requires no markers. Slides can be moved to cover each of the card's 25 squares.

The most popular device for selecting numbers is the Bingo bowl, often called the *Bingo cage*, a spherical wire-mesh cage, about 9 1/2 inches in diameter, into which the Bingo balls are placed. It is mounted on a wooden or metal base, and has a crank-turning, ball-selecting device. There are 75 bingo balls, each of which bears one of the letters of the word "Bingo" and a number. The letter-*B* balls bear numbers from the one through 15 group, the letter-*I* balls bear numbers from the 16 through 30 group, and so on. They have the same grouping arrangement as on the cards.

When the operator turns the crank, the wire cage revolves and the players can see the balls being mixed. When he stops turning the crank, an opening at the bottom of the cage releases one ball. Another popular device for mixing and selecting the balls is the *Bingo blower*, which consists of a glass enclosure into which 75 lettered and numbered Ping-Pong balls are placed. An electric air compressor sends a stream of air into the glass case, agitating and mixing the balls until one ball falls into a small pocket and then drops out of the enclosure.

An announcer, known as the *caller*, calls the letter and number of the released ball over the loudspeaker. If, for example, *B*5 is drawn, players whose cards bear a 5 in the *B* column place a cardboard or plastic marker over it. This is called *covering the number*. The caller then places the drawn ball on a *master board*, which is often connected to an electrically operated panel that lights up the number on a large flashboard so that it can be seen as well as heard. The master board is also used as a check on the drawn numbers. As soon as any player succeeds in covering five numbers in a straight line on his card, vertically, horizontally, or diagonally, he shouts "Bingo!" A floorman or floorwoman goes to the player and reads the covered numbers on the player's card aloud to the caller or a tallyman for verification. If the caller confirms that these five numbers have been drawn, the player is declared the winner of the game and receives the prize.

In many Bingo parlors the jackpot game is a two-way play. Some parlors have added three- and four-way plays, although the jackpot is the important factor. The player who first covers a straight-line combination wins a prize, but the big prize or jackpot goes to the player who first covers his entire board. This is called a *coverall* or *blackout*. If two or more players get a winning position at the same time, the prize money is divided equally.

Many Bingo parlors also feature a four-way play or round robin, in which there are four winning positions:

1. The covering of five numbers in a straight line in any direction.
2. The covering of the four numbers at the four corners of the card.
3. The covering of eight numbers that surround the center "freeplay" square.
4. The covering of all the numbers on the card.

Some Bingo parlors consider as winning plays the covering of two or three straight lines when they cross or intersect so as to form the letters *X, U, L, H,* or *T*. Some parlors give a double bonus for specific straight-line positions of five numbers, such as the top line, the bottom line, and so on.

Recently some Bingo operators have added an extra ball that is distinctively colored and bears no letter or number. It acts as a wild number. In some games, when this ball is drawn, a player can cover any number on his card at any time during the game; sometimes, it can be used only to cover the last number completing the winning position.

At the end of each game, after the awarding of the prize or prizes, all players clear their card or cards of markers and either retain them or exchange them for the next game. They may also purchase additional cards.

Bingo operators have also created a number of special features to stimulate business, such as early-bird tickets, which are sold at a special discount to induce players to come to the parlor early. Sometimes intermission tickets are also sold at a discount in the hope of continuing the Bingo action throughout the intermission period. There are also junior-jackpot tickets that pay off a smaller jackpot. Actually, all these specials have the same purpose: to relieve the Bingo player of more cash.

The admission ticket to a Bingo parlor usually costs from $1 to $3, and the player gets one card called an "all-night board." Additional single-game cards usually cost 25 or 50 cents each. Most players play more than one card at a time, and it is not uncommon to see a player playing as many as 21 cards at once. If you think that playing 21 cards simultaneously is a relaxing way to spend an evening, just try it. I have—and you can't relax for a second. It's hard work, but the Bingo players love it.

Many Bingo parlors in states where Bingo is not legal have a special jackpot that must be won in a specified number of drawn balls. For example, a jackpot coverall winner must be declared within the first 50 numbers drawn. If there should be no winner at one session, an additional $200 or more is added to the jackpot the following week. Jackpots of this kind, starting with $500, have been known to reach $10,000 and more before being won.

After clocking a great many Bingo players in different parts of the country, I found that in Bingo halls in New York and New Jersey, where the limit jackpot payoff is $250, the average player spends $4 per session. Some players spend as much as $7 per session; very few spend as little as the $1 or $2 admission fee. An avid Bingo player from my neck of the woods summed it up this way: "A person would look awfully cheap sitting through several hours of Bingo playing with just the one admission card."

The Bingo player will be interested to learn that his chances of hitting the coverall jackpot in 55 or less drawn numbers is approximately 1 in 10,000. In a hall crowded with several hundred players, where the complete set of 3,000 Bingo cards is in use (Bingo cards are usually printed in sets of 3,000), the chances of *someone* hitting the jackpot coverall in 55 or less drawn numbers is approximately 1 in 3 (3,000 in 10,000).

Here, in tabular form, are the chances a one-card holder has of making a coverall in 50, 51, 52, 53, 54, or 55 drawn numbers:

Total Numbers Drawn	Chances of Making a Coverall with One Card
50 or less	1 in 212,085
51 or less	1 in 112,284
52 or less	1 in 60,458
53 or less	1 in 33,081
54 or less	1 in 18,379
55 or less	1 in 10,359

Most Bingoists take from six to ten cards at a time because this increases the odds in their favor. It does, if the price of the extra cards is less than the price of the original admission card. If the price of the original card is $1 and the price of extra cards is 25 cents, here's how it breaks down: Let's say there are 300 original admission cards at $1 each, of which you have one. Your chances of winning the Bingo prize is 299 to 1. If you buy 4 extra cards at 25 cents each, you have 5 chances in 204. This is obviously better than 1 in 299; but you paid a total of $2, twice as much as your neighbor who only has one card. Therefore, to get your odds to the equivalent of your neighbor's divide by 2. For your dollar you have 2 1/2 chances in 203 to your neighbor's 1 in 203. However, if the price of the extra cards is the same as that for the original card, you may get more excitement with the extra card, but no better odds. Since the total prize awards for each game remain the same, whether 300 or 500 cards are sold, it is the Bingo operator who really profits when extra cards are sold.

Cheating at Bingo. As a rule, when run by charitable organizations, Bingo is relatively free of the crookedness that accompanies many other forms of games. A few professional operators who run Bingo games at fairgrounds, amusement centers, and other public places are not always satisfied with their percentage take; these operators may cheat the players of the big jackpot prizes they have advertised.

It's a simple dodge. The operators plant a confederate (house player) in the crowd who wins the big prize and later returns it, receiving only a fee for his day's or night's work. He wins because he is given a couple of Bingo boards whose numbers have been recorded on a sheet of paper that the announcer keeps within view. Sometimes identifying markers are placed near the numbers on the master board that correspond with those on the house player's cards. Then, as he draws the balls from the cage, the announcer miscalls one or more numbers. If, for example, he sees that the house player needs B8 and G47 to go Bingo, he pretends to read these two numbers from the next two balls drawn. The house player shouts "Bingo!" The announcer goes through the motions of confirming the numbers as the usher checks the player's card; then the announcer nonchalantly replaces the miscalled balls in the Bingo cage. The confederate collects the jackpot, and the other players are none the wiser.

Another method employed by crooked Bingo announcers to steal the jackpot is accomplished as follows: The announcer's confederate takes a front seat as close as possible to the announcer, making sure that no other player will be between them. To help facilitate the scheme, the confederate plays ten or more Bingo cards. The announcer continues drawing and calling numbers until the confederate cues him by lifting and turning his head. This is the signal that informs the announcer that the confederate requires one number to hit the jackpot. Once contact is made between the announcer and confederate, the confederate inaudibly calls the desired number. This is strictly a lip expression. The announcer, accustomed to the confederate's lip movement, gets the message and miscalls the next drawn number by calling the signaled number. The confederate then shouts "Bingo!" and the suckers are left holding the bag.

Bingo players can protect themselves from the above methods of cheating by selecting one player to sit beside the announcer and to check the numbers on the balls as they are drawn. A random choice of player could easily be made by having the announcer, with his back to the audience, throw out a Ping-Pong ball; the person catching it is the one to act as checker. This checking would be necessary only when the Big Special or Big Jackpot is being played. If you suggest this procedure

to your Bingo operator, and he welcomes your recommendation, he's honest. If he doesn't, then you would be wise to find yourself another Bingo parlor.

Race-Horse Keno

Race-Horse Keno or Nevada Keno is the most popular type today. Visit any Keno parlor in Nevada, night or day, and you'll find dozens of Keno players in action. The great popularity of these parlors among gamblers is due primarily to two factors: (1) the game is played somewhat like the very well-known and popular Bingo, and (2) there are continuous casino advertisements in newspapers and on billboards in Nevada of the $25,000 Keno jackpots that build fascinating dreams of hitting these gigantic jackpots. All one has to do to win one of these $25,000 Keno jackpots is to plunk down a couple of bucks and pick from eight to 15 lucky numbers out of a total of 20 numbers selected at random out of 80.

As played in Nevada casinos, Keno differs from regular Keno in several ways. Standard Keno, like Bingo, requires large numbers of players for the successful operation of the game. The purchase price of a Keno or Bingo ticket is the same for all players; these game sessions, lasting only a few hours, are usually run once a week. On the other hand, Keno, Nevada style, can be played by one or more players; each player selects from one to 15

A typical Keno card.

numbers and can wager any amount he likes on his selection, providing it is within the house maximum betting limit. Keno parlors in Nevada operate 24 hours a day, with a new game being dealt every few minutes.

Most Nevada parlors seat 60 or more players. They contain several tables loaded with Keno tickets, and the players are supplied with either black crayons or ink and brushes. Each ticket bears the numbers one to 80 and, on his ticket, the player marks the number or numbers he wishes to play. A great number of different bets can be made at Keno because the players can select various combinations of numbers. A *1-spot ticket* is one on which a player has marked, and is betting on, a single number. If that number appears in the 20 drawn numbers, the player wins. When he marks two numbers, it is a 2-spot ticket, and he wins if both numbers appear among the 20 that are drawn. He may mark and bet on groups of as many as 15 numbers; that is known as a *15-spot ticket*. But the most popular ticket is the 10-spot ticket.

The play of the game is as follows: Once the player has marked his ticket, he presents his cash (which usually averages from 60 cents to $3) and the marked ticket at the Keno counter, where the clerk makes two duplicates by punching out the player's numbers on a house ticket, and adds the amount wagered and the number of the game to be next played. The clerk gives the player one copy, and retains the original and the other copy.

When it is time for the drawing to begin, an announcement is made over the loudspeaker, and everyone gathers to watch. The Keno blower, which is elevated behind the Keno counter, contains 80 Ping-Pong balls numbered one through 80. The operator starts the Keno blower, and the Ping-Pong balls can be seen as they are being thoroughly mixed by a constant stream of compressed air. Then, one by one, they are drawn. As each ball is drawn, its number is called and flashed on the electrically lighted Keno boards for the players to check against their tickets. When the twentieth ball has been drawn, the game ends. With bated breath, each player compares his ticket with the drawn numbers, and the winners go to the Keno counter to collect. Minutes later, a new game is played.

KENO INSTRUCTIONS

1-spot ticket	$1—$2—$5—$10
Catch 1 number	Pays $3.20 for $1
2-spot ticket	
Catch 2 numbers	Pays 13 for 1
3-spot ticket	
Catch 2 numbers	Money back
Catch 3 numbers	Pays 47 for 1
4-spot ticket	
Catch 2 numbers	Money back
Catch 3 numbers	Pays 47 for 1
Catch 4 numbers	Pays 118 for 1
5-spot ticket	
Catch 3 numbers	Pays 3 for 1
Catch 4 numbers	Pays 26 for 1
Catch 5 numbers	Pays 332 for 1

The 1-spot ticket is the simplest form of Keno betting. If you select the one number and wager $1 and win, you receive $3.20 ($2.20 plus your $1), which means the odds you received were 2.2 to 1. What most women Keno players don't stop to consider is that although only 1 number out of 20 has to be picked, those 20 are selected at random out of 80. In other words, there are 80 numbers on your ticket, and 20 of the numbers are drawn—so your chance of winning is 20 in 80, or 1 out of 4. So it costs $4 to win $3.20; the house take on four $1 bets on a 1-spot ticket is 80 cents, or 20 percent. This makes the 1-spot ticket one of the sucker bets in the casino.

If you play a 2-spot ticket for $1 and win, you receive $13, when the correct payoff should be about $16.60—this time the house bite is 21.8 percent. This makes the 2-spot ticket a worse bet than the 1-spot ticket. The 3-spot, 4-spot, 5-spot, 6-spot, 7-spot, 8-spot, 9-spot, 10-spot, 11-spot, 12-spot, 13-spot, 14-spot, and 15-spot tickets, as well as similar tickets such as 12-spot high-low ticket, 10-spot group of 5, deuce ways group of 2, 9-spot groups of 3, and others, average about 23 percent against the player. Of the millions of dollars wagered at Keno, about 60 percent is bet on the 10-spot ticket. A $2.50 bet on a 10-spot ticket can net you a $25,000 Jackpot:

10-spot ticket	
Catch 5 numbers	Pays 2 for 1
Catch 6 numbers	Pays 18 for 1
Catch 7 numbers	Pays 180 for 1
Catch 8 numbers	Pays 1,300 for 1
Catch 9 numbers	Pays 2,600 for 1
Catch 10 numbers	Pays 10,000 for 1

What are your chances of betting $2.50 on a 10-spot ticket and hitting the $25,000 jackpot? Your chance of accomplishing this feat is about one in nine million. Yet, daily, hundreds of Keno players are hoping to achieve this miracle. But there are other winning payoffs that are not quite so improbable. Picking nine numbers will bring a payoff of 2,600 for 1; here the chance is about 1 in 163,000. Picking eight numbers pays off at odds of 1,300 for 1; here the chance is about 7,000 to 1. And so on down the line, to picking five numbers, which pays off at even money, with about one chance in 20 of happening. If four or fewer numbers are picked there is no payoff.

The following table shows the percentages in favor of the house on all tickets from the 1-spot ticket through the 15-spot ticket, calculated on the payoff price as in most Keno parlors in Nevada.

Ticket	*House* Percentage	Ticket	*House* Percentage
1-spot	20.0	9-spot	21.2
2-spot	21.08	10-spot	20.7
3-spot	26.4	11-spot	25.6
4-spot	24.7	12-spot	18.9
5-spot	21.5	13-spot	20.1
6-spot	21.3	14-spot	23.1
7-spot	21.1	15-spot	23.8
8-spot	20.2		

However, each casino has a $25,000 maximum payoff limit on each game to aggregate players. Thus, if two outstandingly lucky players were to hit the $25,000 jackpot, they would have to share the remains of the $25,000 jackpot after the smaller winners were paid.

A final bit of advice to Keno players: Don't gamble your money away expecting to win a $25,000 Keno jackpot—this is nine times more difficult than winning the $50,000 top prize in the New York or New Jersey state lotteries in which, by the way, the odds happen to be one in a million to win.

Moko®

Moko is the lottery game that I invented several years ago. It combines the principles

of Lotto, Standard Keno, and Bingo, plus several entirely new game principles. However, unlike any of the above-mentioned games, Moko is played using only 20 numbers, one through 20. Every card given to the players has all 20 numbers on it: one through 20, and only one through 20, not a number more. All the player must do to win is guess whether the number, when called, will be a *left, center,* or *right* column number.

Requirements

1. Moko makes use of two Keno-type blowers, electrically operated, which are situated in front of the caller.

2. Fifty balls the size of Keno balls are used. Twenty of the balls are numbered from 1 to 20 inclusive and are placed in the Moko blower to the right. The other Moko blower will contain 30 Keno-sized Moko balls, ten of which are marked *Left,* ten of which are marked *Center,* and ten of which are marked *Right.*

3. Electrically lighted tally boards situated throughout the casino and in adjacent restaurants are used to record the numbered balls and their positions (left, right, or center) as they are drawn.

4. Moko tickets. Each ticket bears the numbers 1 through 20 in each of three vertical rows, one row headed by the word Left, one by the word Center, and the other by the word Right. These Moko tickets are placed on several tables in well-trafficked areas.

5. Black crayons are provided for the players' use in marking the players' selections.

6. Moko receipt tickets. The tickets are imprinted with the name of the casino and the number of the game being played; space is provided for the date and for the amount wagered. They also bear the numbers 1 through 20 triplicated in three vertical rows, one row headed by the word Left, one by the word Center, and the other by the word Right.

7. Paper punches are used by the operator to punch out on the receipt tickets the numbers wagered on.

The Play

1. Moko can be dealt to one or more players. Each player may wager $.60, $1.20, or $3.00 on a single ticket and may purchase as many single tickets as the rules permit.

2. The player marks on the Moko ticket the number or numbers he wishes to play Left, Center, or Right. He also may insure a number by marking it Left, Center, and Right. He may bet on how one selected number will fall, how several selected numbers

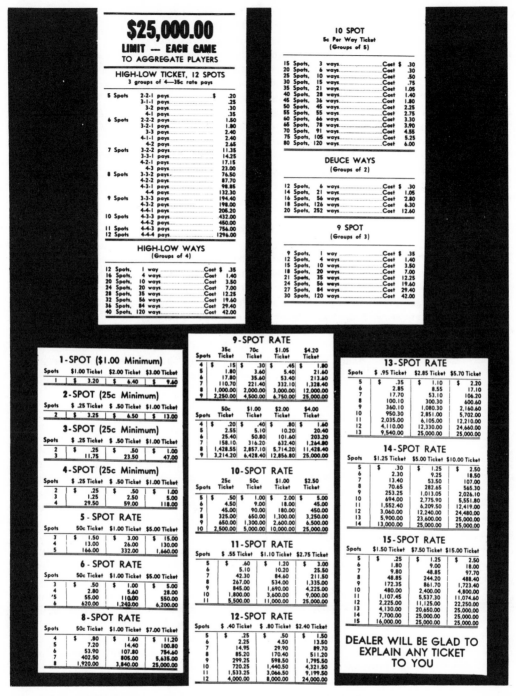

Keno charts which players receive listing the various wagers that may be made.

will fall, or on how a maximum of 15 selected numbers will fall if he so desires. He also indicates the sum he is wagering on the ticket.

3. The player presents his cash and his marked ticket at the Moko counter where the operator makes two receipt tickets by punching out the selected numbers on two house tickets. The dealer gives the player one copy and retains the player's marked ticket and the other house copy. These are checked after the game has been played and are paid off if the ticket wins.

4. The dealer announces the start of the

game. Both Moko blowers are electrically operated, constantly mixing the balls in each blower. Then one ball is released from the drum that contains the numbers one through 20. For example, as the ball numbered 5 is released from this blower, the dealer calls "Number five." The dealer then releases a ball from the drum containing the 30 balls marked Left, Center, and Right. If the ball is marked Right, the dealer immediately announces "Right, number five." This information is flashed on the electrically lighted tally board throughout the casino and restaurants.

The numbered ball remains out of play, the ball indicating Left, Center, or Right is returned to its proper Moko blower. When all 20 numbers have been released from the drum and their positions have been called out and recorded on the tally board, the game ends.

5. Winning tickets are then taken to the Moko counter to be verified and they are paid off according to how many winning numbers are played and the amount wagered on the ticket.

CHINESE FAN TAN

In Chapter 16 I explained Chinese Fan Tan as it was played in the early days in the Western United States. However, this game dates back hundreds of years in China. Both games are very similar with the only differences being as follows:

1. The layout consists of a marked table, numbered in its corners *1, 2, 3,* and *4.*

2. Instead of using cards, the banker, after the bets are completed, takes a random handful of beans or small counters of some kind from a bowl, and places them in the center of the table. He then counts them off, four at a time, with a little stick. All completed fours are disregarded; the numbers of counters left at the end determines the winner. If the counters run out in even fours, bets on *4* win; otherwise, the remainder *3, 2,* or *1* wins.

MONEY POKER

Money Poker, also known as Liar Poker or Dollar Poker, is a fascinating guessing game played with one-dollar bills. It is most popular in bars, cafes, and clubs where it is usually played for the dollars used to play the game.

Requirements

1. Two to nine players. Five or six make for the best game.

2. Five or more one-dollar bills for each player, although only one bill is used by each player to play the game. A dollar bill, as you probably know, possesses a two-letter eight-digit serial number on its face. The playing of Money Poker is based on these eight digits. The two letters are disregarded.

Rank of the Serial Numbers. 0 or zero (high), 9, 8, 7, 6, 5, 4, 3, 2, and 1 (low).

The Object of the Game. To bid (call aloud) a specific amount of digits that you believe are on the combined dollar bills held by all contestants. If the player who bids highest makes his bid, he is the winner and collects the dollar bills in play from each player. If he fails to make his bid, he must pay each player a dollar.

Start of the Game. The first dealer is decided by mutual consent. The dealer collects five one-dollar bills from each player and shuffles (mixes) them up with their serial numbers face down. Then the dealer, starting with the leader (player on his left), deals each player including himself five face-down bills, one-at-a-time, in a clockwise fashion. Then each player studies his five bills and selects any one he wishes. The remaining four bills are put aside for future use. Caution is used by each player not to expose the serial number of the bill in play to the other players. This is usually accomplished by folding the bill in such a way that the serial number is visible only to the owner.

How to Score the Game. I recommend that the maximum amount of numbers that can be scored from each dollar be three. To illustrate, suppose a player's bill shows five sixes. Only three of these sixes are counted toward the bid. The other two sixes do not count in the scoring. The reason for this three-number maximum count in the scoring is to nullify the advantage gained by a dishonest player when he introduces a bill into the game which possesses four, five, six, seven, or eight of the same number. However, if you are the trusting kind and want to count all the numbers on each bill, go ahead and do so—but if you get rooked don't say I didn't warn you.

The Bidding. The leader has the first privilege of play. After studying the serial number of his bill, he must do one of two things:

1. He may bid any number he wants. Or,
2. he may pass, which indicates he passes his privilege of bidding for the present. However, he may reenter the bidding at any time that it is his turn to play.

After the leader has decided, each player in turn, starting with the player on the leader's left and moving clockwise, must do the same (bid or pass). This procedure is followed until the end of the game. Each successive bid must be higher than the previous one, either in the amount or in the same amount of a higher-ranking number. *Example:* The leader bids two fives. The next bidder's lowest progressive bid must be two sixes, two sevens, two eights, two nines, two 0's (zeros), or three ones, three twos, three threes, three fours, three fives. When a player bids and all the other players pass, he (being the highest bidder) gets the bid. On the showdown, should he fulfill his bid, he is the winner. If he fails to fulfill his bid, he is the loser.

Players at the showdown usually take each other's word as to the amount of numbers they hold and do not bother to verify. However, if a player so desires, he may ask each and every player to show his bill to verify the called count.

End of the Game. Once the bidding has ceased and the high bid of the last bidder has been established, the bidder calls out the amount of the bid number shown on his dollar. Let's say his bid was nine eights and his dollar shows three eights. He calls "three," and the player to his left calls "two" (indicating that his dollar possesses two eights). And so it goes, from player to player. Should the sum total of eights held by all the players total nine or more, the bidder wins and collects one dollar (the dollars in play) from each player. Should the number of eights total eight or less, the bidder loses and he must pay each player one dollar and that game is ended.

Start of a New Game. Each player selects one of his four remaining bills and the second game begins. If the previous bidder made his bid, the player to his left must bid first. But, if the previous bidder failed to make his bid, he must bid first.

The same procedure is followed game by game until each player's five one-dollar bills have been played. Then a new shuffle of five one-dollar bills from each player takes place and a new series of five games is played.

THE TOSSING GAME

This game is also called the Penny Game, Two Up, and the Penny Tossing Game. Actually, American sailors learned to play the game in Australia under the name of Two Up and introduced it in the United States where it became known as the Tossing Game, the Penny Tossing Game, and the Penny Game. Some highly substantial bookmakers who used to be Craps specialists have switched to the Tossing Game since most law-enforcement agencies pay no heed when they hear of a Penny Tossing Game taking place in their community. A professional Craps game, on the other hand, is not tolerated.

There is a private variety, of course, in which some fanciers get together—maybe in a lot or back alley—and work their own money against each other without benefit of book or take.

The professional game is divided into two kinds.

The first is the take-off game, in which the operator takes a cut from the shooter (the player tossing the pennies) when the shooter makes a pass and wins. This is the cut familiar to any Craps player.

The second professional variety is the book game. Its distinguishing feature is the presence of a bookmaker who accepts bets from players and charges 5 percent of the bet for his banking services. Believe it or not, this is the more prevalent of the two kinds of play. The book game has to have the same kind of employees as are needed to run a Craps game. To wit:

A *cutter,* who takes the house charge out of a player's profits for making a winning decision.

The *bookmaker,* who accepts all bets up to the limit, generally $300, and charges 5 percent.

Luggers, who are chauffeurs who drive or direct players to the joint.

Lookouts, who are there to prevent or minimize thievery among the players and to see that the book pays off and collects correct amounts from winners and losers.

The Penny Game gambling house is no plush establishment. Generally, it is a stripped-down, purely functional old barn or garage just off some main-traveled highway. It is patronized almost exclusively by professional or habitual—which is not quite the same thing—gamblers.

Requirements

1. Ten or more one-cent pieces, of which two at a time only are in use.

2. A little paddle 3 inches long and 1 inch wide.

Players

1. Any number may play.

2. The player whose turn it is to play is the *shooter.*

3. The player or players covering the shooter's bet are the *fader* or *faders,* and what they do is *fade* the bet.

4. The players stand forming a circle.

5. By mutual consent, or by any method in local usage, any player may start the game by becoming the first shooter.

The Play

1. The shooter puts any amount he elects in the center of the playing circle and says, "I shoot *X* dollars." One or more players fade him by covering part or all of the bet.

2. The shooter selects two pennies from the supply of ten or more, and puts them tail-side up on the little stick or paddle.

3. The shooter tosses the pennies into the air so that they spin to the satisfaction of the observing cutter or operator.

Note well: If the pennies sail or slide or otherwise fail to spin uncontrollably, the cutter calls, before they land, "No toss!" This is final. The toss is void. Its result cannot and does not count.

(a) If the pennies fall so that the two heads face up the shooter has won; he has passed, or made a pass.

(b) If they fall so that the two tails face up, the shooter has lost (made a miss-out), and the player to his left becomes the next shooter.

(c) If the pennies fall so that a head and a tail face up, the shooter has made a no decision, and the shooter keeps tossing until he wins or loses.

(d) As long as a shooter tosses passes or no decisions, he keeps shooting; when he loses, the stick and the right to shoot move to the player at his immediate left; and the play rotates clockwise.

4. Right and wrong bets are made among the other players. A right bet is that the shooter will toss a pass and win. A wrong bet is that he will toss tails, miss out, and lose.

5. If a shooter or any other player can't get a bet from the rest of the company, they are accommodated by the bookmaker for a 5 percent commission on the amount they propose to bet. The bookmaker's action is both ways; he will accept right and wrong bets.

6. Most games employing a cutter levy a charge of 25 cents or 50 cents on each pass made by the shooter. The cut comes out of his winnings. The wrong bettor is often compelled to pay a cut.

Variation of the Penny Game. To speed the game, some operators and cutters use three pennies for the toss instead of two. This makes every toss a winning or losing decision, since of course at least two heads or two tails must face up on each toss. To avoid ambiguity, let me add that three heads win and three tails lose.

The Financial Section

1. The game is dead even; there is no mathematical advantage for shooter or fader.

2. But, if you like to play the book, you might want to bear in mind that its edge is really 4 16/21 percent rather than the 5 percent it charges.

This would seem to be the crookproof gambling game; every move is away out in the open under a strong light, watched by 20 or 30 intelligent and experienced realists. But the assumption that here at last is a game whose only defect is that it's illegal would be a pathetic assumption. Double-headed and double-tailed pennies, which any competent machinist can produce, have been switched into and out of games by gamblers skilled in sleight of hand. And many a player, once caught in the meshes of this oddly fascinating game, has put in hours practicing the control of the tossed pennies. The principle is, of course, merely an extension of the game of mumbly-peg that every kid plays in soft earth with a jackknife—a matter of controlling the arc and spin of a thrown object. Some fanatics have actually succeeded in mastering this bizarre skill; they will never make perfect scores, but by passing just a little oftener than average they have a cold lock on the game.

This sets up about the only clue I can give you. When the Penny Game is played on a hard surface, the pennies must bounce after they hit the floor, and then roll and wobble and topple. On this kind of playing surface the controlled toss is utterly useless. For advice:

1. Don't play on a soft surface like earth, a billiard table, or any padded gambling table.

2. Don't play unless you can hear those pennies ring when they hit the ground.

If you're losing a little too often to one special player, make it your or the house's business to pick up one of his tosses before he does and have the pennies examined. A penny with two tails is quite a curio, but is a possibility.

MORA

Mora, also known as Fingers, is a popular guessing game with Americans of Italian extraction. Mora is probably the oldest guessing game in history and the reason is that no equipment whatsoever is required to play the game. The game is usually played for refreshments.

Mora Two-Handed

Requirements. Two players. Although the game may involve three or more players, only two of these may be in play against each other simultaneously.

The Object of the Game. A Mora match consists of a series of mutually agreed-upon total number of games, which may be three, five, ten, or 15, and terminates at the end of a game in which the agreed-upon total number of games has been won by a player.

How to Score a Game. A game is won by calling correctly the combined total of open fingers of each player's right hand. A player has the privilege of throwing as many open fingers as his hand permits, which may be one, two, three, four, five, or a closed fist which counts zero. The thumb is considered as a finger.

If both players fail to call the correct total, it is a no-game (a game that does not count) and the players throw again. Should both players call the correct total it is also a no-game and the players throw again.

The Actual Play of a Game. The two players face each other, the right fist of each resting on his chest. They eye each other for a moment in an attempt to try to figure or guess how many open fingers his opponent will throw. Then, they raise their right fists which indicates that they are ready to throw (play). Both right fists are snapped downward and the played fingers opened en route. The instant the fists start their downward movement each player calls a number which he hopes will match the total number of open fingers of both player's hands. *Example:* Player A calls "five," and shows two open fingers. Player B calls "Mora," or "Ten," and shows five open fingers. Since seven was the correct total of open fingers, and since player A called five and player B called ten, the game does not count—it's a no-game. Another game follows immediately. And so it goes, from game to game, until a player wins the match by scoring the agreed-upon number of games that constitute the match.

As the games are won and lost each player keeps a mental count. *Example:* Player A wins the first game and calls aloud "One up." B wins the second game and calls "One and one." A wins the third game and calls "Two for me, one for you." And so it goes, from game to game, until a player wins the match which may be three, five, ten, or 15 games.

Mora for Three Players

Mora, though primarily for two players, makes an enjoyable game for three players. Although three players take part, only two are in play against each other simultaneously. To determine which two shall start, a player is designated as the count-starter. Then each of the three players throw out their desired number of open fingers without announcing a total. The open fingers of the three players are totaled, and a progressive count begins with the count-starter as number one, the player on his left as number two, the third player as number three, and then the starter as number four. And so it goes, from player to player, until the progressive count matches the total number of the open fingers. When this occurs, the player that the count stops at becomes the nonplayer in the first game. After the first game is played, the winner is credited with one game and he plays the next game with the nonplayer. The loser of the first game now becomes the nonplayer. So it goes, loser giving way to nonplayer, game by game, until one of the players scores the required number of winning games that make up the match.

Partnership Mora

This is four-handed Mora. Two players are teamed against the other two. Two games of Mora are played simultaneously and the partners score as one.

The rules for Mora Two-Handed apply. The only variation is in the scoring and who plays whom and when. Partners are usually decided by mutual consent and engage their opponents as follows:

A and B are partners, playing against C and D. A plays the first game against his opponent C, and his partner B plays against opponent D. After the first game (one for each two players) is played, A plays D and his partner B plays C. This alternation continues with each game until the match ends.

THE MATCH GAME

The Match Game is deceptively simple. Its rules of play are few and easily learned, but it is much more than just a game of chance. It contains mathematical and psychological factors which introduce a skill element and make it one of the most fascinating of all guessing games in the world of gambling.

Requirements. A set of three paper or wooden matches for each player. Two, three, four, five, six, or more persons can play at one time. The game is best suited to six-handed competition.

Object of the Game. Each player tries to guess the sum total of the matches held by all the players. The one who guesses the correct total is declared the winner of the game or *hand* or *leg* (one game of a series) and is eliminated. Ties are no-games. The remaining players continue playing until only one player is left; and he is the loser of the game.

Selecting the First Player or Caller. Before beginning the game, each player hides his three matches from his opponent or opponents (behind his back or under a table). He puts one, two, three, or no matches into his right hand, closes his fist tightly, and brings it into view.

Any player, by mutual consent, calls out his guess as to the sum total of the matches held by all the players, including himself. Then the player on his immediate left makes the second call, followed by calls from the others in turn, proceeding clockwise. No player is permitted to call a total which has already been called.

After the last player has called his guess, the first caller opens his hand, showing his matches; then the other players, in turn, do the same. The exposed matches are counted. Since the person who makes the last guess has the best chance to win because he can base his guess on information derived from the other player's calls, the player whose guess is closest to the total gets the advantage of becoming the last player in the game or hand about to be played. The player who makes the next closest call becomes the next to last player, and so on. The player whose guess is furthest from the correct total starts the game by making the first call.

With the start of each new hand or game the first call passes to the left so that each player has an opportunity to be last caller and has an equal number of chances to win.

The Two-Handed Match Game

The first player tries to guess how many matches his opponent is holding, adds this to the number he himself holds, and calls the total, which may be any number from zero to six. His opponent follows suit, but may not call a total that has previously been called.

If neither player guesses the correct total, it is a no-game or a standoff. Neither player wins or loses, and the play continues until one player makes a correct call. Players alternate in making the first call, even after a no-game.

The player who first makes two correct calls out of three wins the game.

Two-Handed Strategy. Many people, at first, think that the Match Game is purely one of chance; but any beginner who sits down to play against an expert soon discovers that he is losing far too often and that something more than chance is involved. There are two additional factors: a knowledge of the game's mathematics, and skill in judging the psychology of the other players. The best two-handed playing strategy is based on the following mathematical analysis of the game.

Each of the two players may hold zero, one, two, or three matches. In order to win, the first player must add to the number of matches he himself holds a correct guess as to the number his opponent holds. Since his opponent may hold zero, one, two, or three matches, the first player has one chance in four of making a correct guess—a 25 percent chance to win the hand. In a two-handed game the first player's chance of winning the hand is always the same: 1 out of 4, or 25 percent. But the second player's chances vary, depending on the first call, from 25 percent to as much as 75 percent.

The second player has a better chance of winning most of the time because six of the seven possible calls (zero, one, two, three, four, five, six) that the first player can make reveal information which enables the second caller to infer, rather than to guess blindly, the number his opponent holds.

A first call of "None" tells the second player that his opponent probably holds no matches and is guessing that the second player also holds none. If the first player calls "Six," his opponent can infer that he holds three matches and is guessing that the second player holds three. In the two cases above, the first caller has one chance in four, or a 25 percent chance to win. But since he will miss three times out of four, or 75 percent of the time, his opponent will win three out of every four times—a favorable chance of 75 percent.

A first call of either "One" or "Five" is slightly less informative. A call of "One" indicates that the first player is probably holding none or one, and a call of "Five" indicates that he is probably holding two or three. This gives the second player an even chance of guessing correctly the number of matches the first player is holding and his chance of winning, therefore, is 37 1/2 percent. The chance that neither player will make a correct guess and the game will be a standoff is also 37 1/2 percent. A first call of "Two" or "Four" reveals still less. A call of "Two" indicates that the first player may be holding zero, one, or two. A call of "Four" indicates that the first player may be holding one, two, or three. The second player has four chances in seven of winning. The odds favor him at four to three and his chances of winning are 33 1/3 percent. His chance that it will be no game are 41 2/3 percent. A call of "Three" indicates that the first player may be holding zero, one, two, or three matches. From a mathematical standpoint this call is, therefore, the first player's best strategy. But, because of psychological factors, the expert seldom sticks to a first call of "Three." He studies his opponent's playing characteristics for faults. If he sees that his opponent prefers a hold of three more often than zero, or if he often repeats previous holds on the next play, etc., the expert may change his strategy accordingly.

The Second Call. Having heard the first player's call, the second player uses whatever information that has been given him as the basis for his own call. If the first player calls "None," he probably holds no matches and the correct total is the number the second player holds. If the first call is "Six," the first caller probably has three matches, and the second player simply adds three to what he himself holds. In both cases the second player has a 3 to 1 chance against the first player of winning the hand.

ODDS AND CHANCES IN TWO-HANDED MATCH GAME

| | Chance to Win | | | Odds in Favor |
| | 1st | 2nd | Chance of | of 2nd |
First Call	Player	Player	No-Game	Player
None or 6	25%	75%		3 to 1
1 or 5	25%	37½ %	37½ %	3 to 2
2 or 4	25%	33⅓ %	41⅔ %	4 to 3
3	25%	25%	50%	1 to 1

The Miscall. Because the second player has a mathematical advantage, the first player sometimes purposely makes a miscall by guessing a total which can't possibly win for him. His object is to make the first call revert to his opponent. For instance, when the first caller holds one match, he calls "None." He cannot win the hand; he will either lose or the hand will be a no-game. If the second player does hold no matches and supposes that his opponent's call of "None" means that his opponent is holding none, he cannot call "None" because the rules prevent this, so he calls "One" and is surprised to find this call wins.

Here are all the possible miscalls the first player can make in a two-handed game.

1st Player Holds:	His Possible Miscalls:
0 matches	4, 5, or 6
1 match	0, 5, or 6
2 matches	0, 1, or 6
3 matches	0, 1, or 2

The miscall, when used wisely, is a valuable asset to Match Game strategy, and can be compared to the bluff in Poker.

Three or More Players. When there are three or more players in the game, the rules of play are the same as for two players, with one exception: The game is now an elimination contest. As each player wins a hand by guessing the correct total, he drops out of the game; he is safe and cannot become the final loser. For example: There are six players: A, B, C, D, E, and F. B guesses the first hand correctly, and is eliminated. A, C, D, E, and F play the next hand, D wins and is eliminated. This elimination process continues until only two players remain. They continue the play, and the winner of two out of three hands is eliminated. The sole remaining player is declared the loser of the game, and he must pay the amount of the stake originally agreed upon (5 cents, 25 cents, $1, etc.) to each of the other players; or, as is the custom at the Artists and Writers Restaurant (it is at this famous New York City restaurant that my good friend the late John Lardner, famed sportswriter, first taught me the game), he buys a round of drinks.

Three-Handed Strategy. The last caller again has a mathematical advantage, although it is not quite as strong as in the two-handed game. The first caller knows that the total number of matches his opponents may hold ranges from none to six.

The number of ways each of these totals can be made are as follows:

Zero or 6	Each can be made 1 way
1 or 5	Each can be made 2 ways
2 or 4	Each can be made 3 ways
3	Can be made 4 ways
	A combined total of 16 ways

The first player's call, of course, is the sum of what he guesses his opponents hold plus the number of matches he himself holds. The first caller's best chance to win, therefore, is to add three to the number of matches he himself holds and call the total. This gives him one chance in four of winning, or 25 percent.

The second player reverses the strategy of the first player by subtracting three from the first player's call. *Example:* The first player calls "Six." The second player subtracts three and infers that the first player holds three matches. The second player now has a 25 percent chance of guessing the number held by the third player. He makes a guess as to the third player's hold, adds the number he calculated the first player may be holding, adds the number he himself holds, and announces the total. On the occasions when this total has already been called by the first player, the second player's next best bet is to add or subtract one to the number already called, and announce this total.

If the second player calls three more or three less than the first call, he gives the third player too much valuable information. *Example:* The first player calls "Six." If the second player calls "Nine," he is telling the third player that he holds three; if he calls "Three," the third player can assume he holds none. Whenever the second player makes a lower call than the first player, the third player can assume the second is holding either zero or one. If the second player calls two or three more than the first player, the third player can assume that the second holds three.

To summarize: When three experts are playing, the first caller has a 25 percent chance of winning the hand, the second has a 25 percent chance, and the third and last has a 33 1/3 percent chance. The remaining 16 2/3 percent chance is the percentage in favor of a no-game result.

Four, Five, Six, or More Players. When

there are four or more players, the last caller's advantage is diminished somewhat because the more players there are, the greater are the chances that the number the last player wants to call has already been called. Often the next nearest number above or below has also been called. All the last player can do in this case is to call the closest number that has not yet been called.

The best strategy in a game with four or more players is to play the averages. Assume that the average number held by each player is one and one-half matches. *Example:* In a five-handed game in which you call first, you guess that each of the other four players holds one and one-half matches, a total of six. Add the number you hold to this six-count, and call the total. If you hold none, you call "Six." Holding one, you call "Seven."

Holding two, you call "Eight." Holding three, you call "Nine."

When you have an odd number of opponents and assume that each holds an average of one and one-half matches, your total will contain the fraction one-half. Here you either add or subtract one-half. *Example:* When there are five opponents, you arrive at a total of seven and one-half. Add or subtract one-half for the total of either seven or eight. Then add the number of matches you hold.

In a five-or-more-handed game, if the calls made by the preceding players add to a total considerably above or below the total obtained by allowing them each an average of one and one-half matches, the remaining players or player should increase or decrease the one-and-one-half-match average to conform to the information he has gathered from the preceding calls.

THE NUMBERS GAME

Although playing the Numbers is more of a lottery than a guessing game, I can't resist the temptation to get it in print since it's the most popular illegal form of lottery betting in the United States. My own sample findings of what makes the Numbers so attractive to players show that: (1) players are natural suckers for big odds (the-500-for-1 Numbers odds are tempting to most players); (2) Numbers players can select their own numbers and bet their money on their favorite lucky numbers (and what person doesn't have at least one lucky number?); (3) you can make small bets: 25 cents, 50 cents, and sometimes even pennies. In addition, the action is daily, and the players get the Numbers result the same night from the racing section of most metropolitan newspapers. All of these factors combined make them feel that the Numbers game is honest.

Playing the Numbers was once referred to as a poor person's way of expressing his or her gambling instinct, since its participants used to bet pennies on the illusive three digits. Things are different today. Of the millions who play the Numbers, it is doubtful if one out of a hundred wagers less than 25 cents on a number. The daily average bet on the Numbers for players living in metropolitan areas of the United States ranges from $1 to $2. Many players, however, bet $10 to $20 or more on a single three-digit number; and a few high-rollers think nothing of betting $100 or more on a "hot number," especially one they dreamed of the night before.

Most people today wouldn't bet money on a fortune teller's prediction based on a layout of cards, or on tea leaves, or on the juggling of some astrological figures; but most Numbers players believe that the sight or mention of any three-digit number is a psychic sign and that some supernatural force has brought it to their attention. Millions of dollars are bet by Numbers players every day on what they consider to be their lucky number for the day: their street address, the last three digits of their birth year, the sales total of a purchase, or the license number of a passing car.

The favorite reading matter of millions of players is (1) the newspapers that report the winning numbers, and (2) dream books and numerology pamphlets that give interpretations of dreams, daily happenings, birthdays, and so on, in terms of three-digit numbers. *Know Your Dream, Lucky Star, King Tut,* and *Gypsy Queen* are among the best sellers in New York City.

The system is simple: If you dreamed last night that you took a trip on a bus, look under *Travel.* You are told that "traveling means you will change jobs (213)." If you dreamed of visiting a lawyer, this means "you will suffer from a cold (165)." Dreaming of money: "Your luck will change (381)." Dancing girls denote "happiness, and you will come into money (814)." A doctor denotes pregnancy (119) for a woman and illness for a man (415). Oddly enough, although many of these books are published by the same company, they all give different interpretations and numbers.

Let's take a good look at the Numbers game. Although it's illegal in every state, city, or hamlet—if you know your way around, it won't be difficult to find a Numbers runner who'll accept your bet. The winning number is usually based upon the last digits—three in all—of the daily mutual betting handle at a major metropolitan racetrack. Let's say that Monday's mutual betting handle for nine races at New York's Aqueduct Racetrack was $2,586,123. Monday's winning number is 123. If you have been lucky enough to bet $1 on that number, you are a winner; and since such a bet pays off at odds of 500 for 1, you receive $500 in return. Some banks, however, pay off at 450-to-1 odds; others pay off at 600-for-1 odds.

Another bet permitted at the Numbers game is known as "boxing." When you write your number on the betting slip, you may box it by drawing a square around it. This indicates that you are betting on all possible combinations of the chosen number, and it is known as a six-way combination bet. If you select number 125 and box it, you are betting on 125, 152, 215, 251, 512, and 521. Of course, this reduces the payoff to one-sixth. If the bank pays 500 for 1 on a straight bet, a six-way payoff should be 83 1/3 for 1; but the operators round the number to 80, and the payoff is 80 for 1.

Any straight or head number that contains two identical digits (such as 121, 323, 556) is known as a three-way combination because only three different combinations can be made with it. If you box number 121, for instance, you are betting on 121, 112, and 211. Since most banks pay only 80 for 1, the same as on a six-way combination, it is sheer lunacy to box numbers of this sort. Incidentally, most banks insist that the player also bet on a straight number with each combination or box-number bet.

What chance does that lucky number of yours have of hitting and paying off? No complicated mathematics are needed to figure this answer. There are 1,000 numbers from 000 to 999, and one of them wins. You have 1 chance in 1,000, which means that the odds are 999 to 1 against you. Every player has an equal chance, and the odds remain the same for any number selection, even if it is a repeat of yesterday's winning number or one that hasn't appeared in years.

Most banks pay off at less than the usual odds on "cut and disaster numbers." These are numbers that get too much play because too many players believe they are lucky numbers. Some banks issue a cut-number sheet listing nearly 200 cut numbers. In some sections of New Jersey any three-digit number whose middle digit is a 1, such as 010, 015, 116, 217, and so on, is a cut number and is paid off at 400-for-1 odds. Should a newspaper carry an illustration on its front page showing a cracked-up automobile whose license number reads XY 151, the number 151 is a catastrophe number as far as the Numbers operators are concerned and winners get paid off at odds of 400 for 1.

The Numbers operators give various reasons as to why they cut as many as 200 numbers, but true or false, cutting numbers reduce the player's winnings considerably.

If the correct odds on hitting three numbers are 999 to 1 and the bank pays only 500 for 1, and in the case of cut numbers 400 for 1, it should be obvious by now that the only people who consistently make a profit at the Numbers are the operators, their employees, and the politicians and cops that sell protection.

There's not much point in advising a Numbers player to forget about his favorite game, and gamble, if he must, at some game whose unfavorable percentage isn't so high. The many players I know just don't listen to such advice. If you want to play because it's fun, and are willing to pay the price, that's your business. But if you play because you figure to come out ahead, you can forget it. If you have read this far, in this book, you know that bucking a house edge of from 50 to 60 percent is a sure way to a pauper's grave.

CHAPTER 28

Parlor Games for All

Parlor games are sometimes genuine games and sometimes no more than tricks and stunts. In this chapter I have tried to select a few of the more popular so-called "parlor games" that require some skill, but are fun to play.

CATEGORIES

Any number may play this game, which is also called *Guggenheim*. Each player is given paper and pencil. Each player names one category and everyone lists these categories in a column on the left of his paper. Nominations may be vetoed by a majority vote so that one player may not gain an advantage by naming a category of which he may have special knowledge.

The players then agree on a key word, usually of five letters, which has no repeated letters and no uncommon letters such as J, Q, X, Z. The letters of this word are written at the head of columns to the right of the category list.

A time limit is agreed upon, say 15 minutes, and at the signal to start each player tries to write a word in each row and column —a word which belongs to the category on the row and which has the initial letter heading that column. A completely filled in paper having five categories and the key word SPORT might look like this:

	S	*P*	*O*	*R*	*T*
Mammals:	Seal	Panda	Oryx	Rabbit	Tiger
Occupations:	Sailor	Printer	Organist	Riveter	Typist
Rivers:	Swanee	Po	Orinoco	Rappahannock	Tiber
Painters:	Sargent	Picasso	Orozco	Renoir	Turner
Foods:	Steak	Pancake	Olive	Rhubarb	Tapioca

When time is called all players must stop writing, and the lists are then compared and scored. A word which was not written by any other player receives the maximum score, one point less than the number of players. For instance, with five players, if no one else wrote *panda* the player scores 4 for this word. One point is deducted from the maximum score for each additional player who wrote the same word, so that if two players wrote *panda,* each player scores 3 for the word. If all the players wrote the same word in any space it scores nothing. And if a player left a blank space it also scores nothing, although some players rule that one point must be deducted for each blank. The player with the highest total score wins the round.

Change the key word and perhaps the categories as well for succeeding rounds.

The game may be as easy or as difficult as the players like depending on whether the categories selected are broad or restricted. Experienced players usually prefer to restrict a broad category like rivers to something like American or European rivers, and foods might be limited to fruit.

Some rules as to the admissibility of words should be agreed on in advance to avoid arguments that may otherwise arise. Players often agree that:

1. If the writer can give no identifying information about it, a word, when challenged, does not score.

2. Compound words score one point less than simple words—Rio Grande being worth less than Rhone.

3. In categories calling for names of persons, the initial applies only to the surname. In a category characters from Mark Twain, Tom Sawyer would be valid under the initial S, but not under T.

4. Only the American spelling of foreign geographic names is valid.

5. Questions as to whether a word fits a category properly are decided by majority vote. If a word itself is challenged, its validity is decided by a dictionary.

ANAGRAMS

Requirements

1. Any number up to eight, but five or six players are best.

2. A set of anagram tiles or a pack of anagram cards is needed. Most sets contain about 200 units, but it is a better game if two sets are used. Each unit bears a letter on one face, and the letters supplied are roughly in proportion to the frequency of their use in English (no more than two J's, Q's, X's, and Z's, for example).

The Play. Tiles are scattered face down on the table and a space cleared in the center for play. Cards, after shuffling, are stacked in one pile face down in the center.

Any player begins play by turning one tile (or card) face up and putting it in the center. Thereafter each player in turn to the left turns up a tile. A time limit is sometimes used (anything from 15 seconds to 1 minute by agreement), sometimes not, in which case the turn to play need not rotate and any player may turn a tile to keep the game moving provided the others agree that they are ready to see a new tile.

The object is to form good English words from the face-up letters in the center. Whoever sees letters that will form a word calls the word, takes the letters from the center, and builds the word before himself. The first player who makes five or ten words (as agreed) wins the game.

A player may capture a word from another player by adding one or more letters from the center to form a new word. A player may also add to and transform his own words in order to make them harder to capture.

Words must be good English and at least four letters long. Plurals made by adding S to three-letter words do not count. A dictionary should be at hand to settle arguments as to the validity of words.

Other rules, on which the players should agree in advance, are:

1. Some essential change in form or meaning of a word must be made in order to capture it; adding S to make a plural or D to change the tense is not enough. Adding prefixes or suffixes which do not change the word root are also sometimes not permitted, although the owner of a word may make such additions in order to protect it.

2. If two or more players call new words at the same time, or try to capture the same word, the longest new word has priority. If both words are the same length, the first to speak has precedence, and the host decides who spoke first.

3. If a player calls a word for which the necessary letters are not available (including any word he intended to capture), his call is a foul, and, as penalty, he must return his last word to the stock.

4. Any player may challenge the validity

of a word claimed by another. The host or the dictionary decides. If the challenger is correct, the challenged player loses not only the word claimed, but the last previous word he made; if the challenger is incorrect, he must return his last word to the table. Returned words are shuffled face down into the stock.

When players take too much time to figure out capturing possibilities and the game moves too slowly, it is best to specify a maximum interval (such as 1 minute) between the turn of a tile and the next turn of a tile.

GHOSTS

Any number may play. One player names a letter, the next in turn adds another letter, and so on, the letters being visualized as written in the order named. Players must avoid completing any English word of more than three letters, but must be prepared, when challenged, to give a word which contains all the letters thus far named.

Instead of calling a letter, any player on his turn may challenge the last previous player to give such a word. If the challenged player cannot do this, he loses; if he gives an acceptable word, the challenger loses. A round ends when a player completes a word, or when a challenge is decided.

A player who ends a round, either by completing a word, or by losing after a challenge, becomes "one-third of a ghost." A second loss makes him "two-thirds of a ghost." A third loss makes him a "full ghost." Full ghosts may not continue to call letters, but they may talk to other ghosts and to the players. But if any player makes the mistake of talking to a full ghost he becomes a full ghost himself. The full ghosts try to make the players forget this rule.

The sole survivor wins the game. Remember that only the player whose turn it is to call has the right to challenge; otherwise there are too many challenges, bluffing successfully becomes almost impossible, and much of the fun is lost.

Two-Way Ghosts or Heads and Tails Ghosts

This is Ghosts plus a rule that allows a player to add his letter either after or before the sequence he receives. For instance, he can avoid having to add a T to PERFEC, which would cost him a life, by prefixing an M, with IMPERFECT in mind.

WORD CHAIN OR WORD DOMINOES

The first player names a category (animal, flower, country, and the like), then gives a word that fits it. The player at his left must supply a word in the same category which starts with the last letter of the preceding word. *Example:* If the category is animals and the first word is buffalo, the succeeding players might give: ostrich, hippopotamus, skunk, and so on.

A player who cannot supply a name is out of the game, provided the next following player can do so, or, if no following player can do so, if the player who gave the preceding word can. If this player cannot, he must substitute another word for the one he first gave. The survivor wins.

WORD SQUARES OR STOCK EXCHANGE

Any number may play. Each has pencil and paper, and draws a diagram of 25 squares, 5 by 5. Any player starts and the turn moves to the left around the room. Each player, at his turn, calls a letter of the alphabet, and each player writes that letter on his diagram in any space he likes. Once written it must not be moved.

The object is to form words of three or more letters horizontally and vertically on the diagram (diagonals do not count). The game ends when 25 letters have been called, filling all the spaces on the diagrams.

A word of five letters scores 10; of four letters, 5; of three letters, 2. The player scoring the highest total wins.

Poker Squares

Any number may play. Each has pencil and paper, and draws a diagram of 25 squares, 5 by 5, as in Word Squares. In addition, a standard 52-card deck is needed.

After the cards have been shuffled, one player picks a card from the deck. Each player then must write this card into one square on his diagram. *Example:* If the ten of hearts is drawn, the players must mark "H10" in one of the squares in the diagram. This must be done before the next card is drawn and called, and its location may not be changed.

The object of the game is to form the best possible Poker hands (see page 9) along the horizontal and vertical lines; the diagonal lines do not count. When 25 cards have been turned up and written in, the game ends and best hand is decided.

TWENTY QUESTIONS

One person is chosen to be "It" or the Guesser. He leaves the room while the other players choose a word. Then the Guesser returns, and tries to discover what has been chosen by asking not more than 20 questions, all of which must be answered truthfully. If he succeeds within 20 questions, he joins the others, and a new Guesser is chosen.

The game can have various degrees of difficulty. Some players allow any word to be chosen, some players agree that only concrete objects, or events, or persons, may be chosen; others allow any word, even abstract ones, also phrases, sentences, fictional characters, literary quotations, and the like.

The Guesser usually begins by trying to determine the category, as "Is it animal?" "Is it vegetable?" "Is it mineral?" Additional questions attempt to narrow this down. The Guesser is supposed to ask only questions which can be answered "yes" or "no," but sometimes when a chosen object is complex, the answer, to be truthful, may have to be "partly."

Botticelli

This is a rarefied form of Twenty Questions. The best player is the one who knows the most about famous and infamous people and fictional characters.

The Play. Draw lots or cut for high (or low) card to select one player to be It. Unlike most question and answer games, the player who is It has the roughest assignment.

The person who is It decides who he is, and can select any character from life or fiction, living or dead.

He announces the initial of his surname.

(If he decides to be Botticelli, he says, "I am a B.")

The other players, in order from left to right, try to guess his name in the following fashion. The first player might ask, "Are you a movie actor who played tough-guy roles?" And It has to figure out who is meant and reply in this case, "No, I am not Humphrey Bogart." Or the question might be: "Are you a Shakespearian actor who was a murderer?" It has to come up, in this instance, with the reply, "No, I am not John Wilkes Booth." Another question might be: "Are you a French general whose most famous battle was the one he lost?" The answer here is, "No, I am not Napoleon Buonaparte."

The questioner must think of someone whose name begins with a B and supply enough of a description so that It has a decent chance of guessing it. If the questioner cannot think of anyone whose name begins with B, he must say "I pass" and let the next player take his turn.

If It cannot guess who the questioner has in mind he gives up. If It gives up, but claims he wasn't given enough clues, the fairness of the question is decided by a vote of the other players. Then the questioner is allowed one question of the type used in Twenty Questions, such as "Are you living or dead?" or "Are you real or fictional?" or "Did you live in the nineteenth century?" or "Are you a painter?" It must answer with a simple yes or no.

These questions finally narrow down the place, occupation, etc., until someone in his turn eventually asks, "Are you Botticelli?," receives an answer of "Yes," and wins the game.

Experts at this game can sometimes be very tricky. Such as deciding to be Michelangelo and saying, "I am a B," which throws everyone off because most people have forgotten that Michelangelo's surname was Buonarroti! Botticelli, as you can see, is no game for children.

Optional Rules

1. If the game proceeds too slowly, it may be wise to appoint a referee who keeps time and insists that each questioner must not take more than 1 minute to come up with a question, and allows It not more than 2 minutes to answer.

2. It can also decide to be a famous animal such as Lassie, Mickey Mouse, or Black Beauty, or Flush, or Jemima Puddleduck, or Uncle Wiggley.

CHARADES

The players are divided into two teams and they alternate as actors and audience. In another room the actors select a word of three or more syllables and plan a pantomime in which each syllable is to be acted out. *Taxpayer,* for instance, might be divided as *tax-pay-her.* Then the actors act out a scene for each syllable, with a final scene which tries to convey the whole word. Try to include all the actors in each scene.

The audience team tries to guess the word, and is timed from the beginning of each pantomime. The team which succeeds in guessing words in the least amount of time wins.

The Game

A modern and lively version of Charades. The players are divided into two equal teams and a captain is chosen for each. They alternate as actors and audience. Each player on the audience team writes a phrase or a sentence on a slip of paper. The captain of the audience team gives one slip to each actor, who must not show it to any other actor. Then, in pantomime, each actor must act out the words on his slip in such a way that his fellow actors can guess them.

The actor may try to act out the whole meaning at once, or break it up into words or syllables and act them separately. The captain of the audience times each actor from the moment he starts until the other actors have guessed the complete message. The team of actors that guesses all the messages in the least total time wins the game.

There are many different variations as to the rules. Some players allow any sentence, word, or phrase to be used. Others impose limitations, requiring that the sentence must be a well-known quote from history, fable, or literature such as "Don't shoot until you see the whites of their eyes!" Others limit the message to single words or short well-known phrases.

Although the actor may not speak, certain prearranged signals are usually agreed on as permissible. Signals such as these:

Arms clasped over chest: The whole message will be acted out.

Chopping motion: I will cut the word into syllables.

Holding up two fingers, then closing fist: Next two words (or syllables) will be combined.

Beckoning: "You're warm!"

Pushing away: "You're cold!"

Twisting motion: Another form of the same word.

Counting on fingers: Make it plural.

Looking back: Make it past tense.

Hand over eyes, peering ahead: Make it future tense.

Finger on nose: That's right.

Props are usually barred, although some players allow an actor to use any prop he can find in the room.

Members of the guessing team may call out all the ideas the pantomime suggests, and the actor may point to the player who comes closest and signal that he is "hot."

When the acting team has conveyed all its messages, the audience players become actors and try to get across their messages in less time.

TIT-TAT-TOE

This simple game, also called Noughts and Crosses in Great Britain, is played on diagrams consisting of intersecting parallel lines. The opening player places an X in any posi-

The layout for Tit-Tat-Toe.

tion on the board. His opponent then adds an O, and the players make their marks alternately until one of them has three of his symbols in a straight line. This wins the

game. If neither player can make a line the game is drawn. Since it is an advantage to go first, the players alternate in having first move in successive games.

Gomuku

This form of Tit-Tat-Toe is very popular in Japan and it is played on a grid or diagram consisting of 19 horizontal and 19 vertical lines. One player chooses to use O's, and the other player selects X's. They take turns marking O's or X's on the intersections of the lines. The first player to obtain five O's or X's in a straight line is declared the winner.

DOTS AND SQUARES

A square of dots is drawn and laid out in rows. There should be from 10 to 15 rows of dots in each direction. The players take turns drawing lines horizontally or vertically to connect any two dots. The object of the game is to complete a square or unit, and to prevent one's opponent from completing any square or unit. Each time a player succeeds in drawing the fourth line of a square, he may put his initials in it. Whenever a player completes a square, he draws another line. Frequently, when the diagram becomes fairly well covered with lines, he may find that he is able to complete several squares in one turn. When all the lines have been drawn, the player with the most squares or units filled in and initialed is the winner.

Triangles

This game is played as Dots and Squares except that drawn units of the diagram are triangular rather than a square. The diagram is prepared by placing dots on the paper, to mark the vertices of equilateral triangles (but precision is not important). The diagram it-

self is by custom a large triangle, but to make available more units, it can be made rectangular. A player wins a unit by adding its third side.

Spiderweb

This is another game for two players who each mark dots alternately on a piece of paper. The exact number of dots that will be marked should be agreed on before the start of the game (50 to 80 is a good amount). The players may place their dots any place they wish on the paper. After all the dots are marked, each player in turn connects any two of them by a straight line. However, no line must ever cross another. If three dots chance to be collinear, they may not be connected by a single line segment, but may be connected by two separate segments. It is a good idea to agree in advance as to which sets of three or more points are collinear and which are not. This will prevent arguments. The winner is the player who places the last connecting line that does not cross another.

BATTLESHIPS OR SALVO

Requirements

1. Two players or teams may be formed, playing against each other by consultation.

2. Pencils and paper. Each side constructs two diagrams of 100 cells, 10 by 10. It is easiest to use graph paper. The rows and columns of each diagram are marked with the

numbers 1 to 10 and letters A to J as shown in the illustration. One diagram is labeled "My Zone" and the other "Opponent's Zone."

Out of sight of his opponent, each player positions four warships on his own zone, each being a line of blacked squares along any row, column, or diagonal. The ships may be

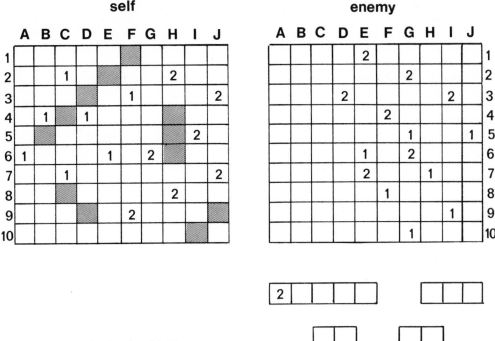

The diagrams set up for the play of Battleships.

placed anywhere but must not touch along the sides or at the corners. The fleet consists of one battleship (five squares), one cruiser (three squares), and two destroyers (two squares each).

The Play. Toss a coin to decide who fires first. This player fires a salvo of seven shots by writing the figure 1 (for first salvo) in any seven cells of "the enemy zone." He announces where these shots have landed by naming the cells (row number and column letter), and his opponent writes the figure 1 in the named cells on his "my zone" diagram.

The opponent then states whether any hits were made on his ships, and if so, what type of ship and the number of hits, but he does not say which shots were hits.

The second player next takes his turn and fires seven shots as his salvo number 1. The play continues alternately and the salvos are numbered serially. The player who sinks his

enemy's entire fleet by hitting every cell of every ship wins the battle.

The loss of ships reduces the number of shots that a player can fire in succeeding salvos; losing the battleship costs him three shots; the cruiser, two shots; and each destroyer, one shot.

On his paper below the main diagrams, each player has outlined a fleet of enemy ships, and he records each of his hits by writing the salvo numbers in the appropriate squares. The numbers of these hits supply clues as to the location of your enemy's battleship, cruiser, and destroyers.

Strategy. Don't scatter the shots of your first salvos; confine them to not more than a quarter of the board so that if you make a hit you'll know where to concentrate your fire. Try to reduce the enemy's firepower as quickly as possible by locating and sinking his largest ships first.

COOTIE

This game has many other names including Bug, Beetle, and Humbug.

Requirements
1. Two to eight players.
2. One die.

3. Paper and pencil.

The Cootie. The legendary cootie has six parts, one for each number on the die. They are: 1, a body; 2, a head; 3, legs; 4, eyes; 5, a tail; 6, feelers on his head.

The Play. The players take turns in rolling the die, one roll for each turn. No one can make any progress until he has rolled a one, and a player who rolls any other number at his first turn must pass the die to the next player and wait for his second turn, and then possibly for several more turns. When he finally rolls a one, he draws an ellipse on a piece of paper to represent the body, and then he gets a second roll on this turn. Now his problem is easier, for he can use a two for head, a five for tail, or three for leg, all of these being parts that connect directly with the body; a four for eye or a six for feeler will do him no good, since they cannot be added until the head is in place.

After he has drawn the head, he can use a four or a six. Thus each player takes his turn and each time that he rolls the number of a part that he can use he draws this part and takes another roll. He needs in all 13 parts; a body, a head, a tail, two eyes, two feelers, and six legs. The game is ended when any player has completed his cootie. This player scores 13 points and others 1 point for each part completed.

HANGMAN

This game is a favorite for two players. One player, called the *hangman,* draws on paper a gallows, or upside down L. Then, he thinks of a word containing five or more letters and writes down as many dashes as the word has letters below the gallows. The opponent tries to guess the word by calling out one letter at a time. If this letter appears in the word one or more times, the hangman writes it in the proper blanks. If it does not, he draws the noose and his opponent is on his way to be hanged. A player has seven incorrect guesses (one for the noose, one for the head, one for the body, one for each arm and leg) before being hanged. If the opponent guesses the word correctly before the entire figure can be drawn, he is the winner and becomes the new hangman. If not, the hangman is the winner and he takes another turn.

The diagram used in the Hangman.

S _ _ A R _ _ E

RAT-FINK

This is a popular new parlor game which is good for children and adults:

Requirements

1. Two to ten players, but five to eight make the best game.

2. A standard 52-card deck from which four of a kind are taken for each player in the game. For example, in a six-person game, four twos, four threes, four fours, four fives, four sixes, four sevens would be used. The remainder of the deck is put to one side and is not used.

3. Ordinary teaspoons, one less than the number of players in the game, which are placed in the center of the playing area.

Object of the Game. To avoid receiving letters which will spell out Rat-Fink, thereby making you a loser of the game. When all the players except one have received letters spelling out Rat-Fink, the remaining player is declared the winner.

The Play. The players sit around in a circle, either at a table or on the floor, the spoons being placed in a row in the center of the circle. The cards used in the game (four of a kind for each player) are thoroughly shuffled and cut. (For selection of dealer, shuffle, and cut, see General Rules, page 1.)

The dealer deals one card at a time (starting with the player to his left) face down on the table in front of each player. He continues dealing until each player has four face-down cards in front of him. The players cannot pick up their cards until the signal from the dealer. When the dealer shouts "Now" or "Pick-up" the players quickly pick up their cards and assemble them into melds, the object being to get four of a kind. Then, the dealer shouts "Pass to your right," and each player passes one card (the card he considers least valuable to his hand) to the player on his right. This passing on command by the dealer is continued at a rapid pace until one of the players holds four of a kind.

When this happens, that player takes one of the center spoons. He may do this with a flourish or he may try to do this in a manner which will be unnoticed by the other players, however he chooses. Once a player has taken a spoon, it is a signal to the others to grab a spoon as quickly as possible. Since there is one spoon less than the number of players,

it is obvious that one player will be left without a spoon.

For failing to have a spoon at the completion of a round of play, the spoonless player is given a letter. First R, the next time around A, etc., until he receives all the letters of the word Rat-Fink. Obtaining this title, he becomes the loser, but continues to play until there is only one player who has not obtained the title Rat-Fink. This player is declared the winner.

Strategy. This game contains an aspect of Poker, namely bluffing. The winner of a particular round (the player to take the first spoon) is not compelled to show his hand. He may have had four of a kind when he took the first spoon or he may have been bluffing. If no one challenges him, he gets away with his bluff and it is all the better for him. However, he can be challenged by any player. When this occurs, he must show his hand. If he truly held four of a kind, the player who challenged him is penalized two letters. If the challenger was correct in calling his bluff, the player who bluffed is penalized two letters.

The Stakes. If the game is played just for fun as at a party, each player becoming a Rat-Fink performs for the amusement of the others by singing a song, reciting a poem, or performing some kind of stunt designated by the winner. To bet at the game, each player would ante a specified amount into the pot before the start of the game. Upon completion of the game, winner takes all.

Glossary of Game Terms

Abandon the deal. Discontinue the play and throw the cards together to be shuffled.

Above the line (*Bridge*). The place on the score sheet where premiums are scored.

Absolute (*Alsos*). A declaration to win 82 points at trump or 62 at no trump.

Ace. The one-spot in a pack; the one-spot on a die; one dollar.

Acey Deucey (*Backgammon*). The roll of 2–1 with two dice.

Ace high (*Poker*). A hand with an ace but no pair or better.

Ace pots (*Poker*). Draw poker in which no player may open without a pair of aces or better.

Aces. (Casino) The count of 1 point for each ace won. (*Craps*) A cast of 1–1.

Aces up (*Poker*). A hand of two pairs including aces.

Accept. Declaration by dealer or another player that he accepts the turn-up as trump, or accedes to a proposal.

À cheval. Placing a bet on a line of a banking layout, so as to bet on both sides at once.

Action. Betting; opportunity to bet.

Active player. (*Poker*) A player still in competition for the pot; one who has not dropped or passed or folded by throwing his hand into the discard pile. (*Skat*) One who receives cards in the current deal.

Actors (*Mah-Jongg*). The suit of characters.

Ada from Decatur (*Craps*). The roll of 8.

Adjusted score (*Duplicate Bridge*). An arbitrary score assigned by the referee, when regular play is not feasible.

Adversary. Any opponent; one playing against the highest bidder.

Advertise. (*Poker*) Make a bluff intended to be exposed. (*Gin*) Discard a card to induce an opponent to discard another of the same or near rank.

African dominoes. Another name for dice.

Against (*Skat*). Same as *without*.

Age. (1) Player first to receive cards in a deal. (2) (*Poker*) The right to bet last after the draw.

All the trumps (*Alsos*). A declaration to win all the trumps.

Alone (*Euchre*). A bid to play without help of a partner.

Alternates (*Solitaire*). A card in the game.

Alternate straight. Same as *skip straight*.

Anchor (*Duplicate Bridge*). In pivot or progressive play, one who retains his seat throughout the contest.

Angle. A situation favorable to a bet.

Angling (*Poker*). Proposing to another player an agreement, private and outside the rules; for example, that the pot be split evenly regardless of which player wins it, or that the players refrain from raising against each other.

Announce. (1) Name the trump suit. (2) Show melds. (3) Predict schneider or schwarz.

Ante. (1) A bet made before the deal or before drawing cards. (2) Contribution to a pot which, at the start, belongs equally to all players.

Appres (*Trente et Quarante*). Dealer's announcement that bets are off because of a refait (tie).

Approach bid (*Bridge*). Bid made for information of partner rather than with intention to play the named declaration.

Ask. (*Skat*) Inquiry by the eldest hand whether the next hand wishes to compete in the bidding. (*Whist*) Signal partner to lead trumps. (*Scarney, Canasta*) Inquire "May I go out, partner?"

Asking bid (*Contract Bridge*). Bid that systematically asks partner to make a control-showing response.

Assist. (*Euchre*) Order partner to take up the trump. (*Bridge*) Increase partner's bid; raise.

Auction. The period of the bidding.

Authorized opponent (*Bridge*). One solely entitled to assess a penalty.

Auxiliary cards (*Solitaire*). Same as *reserve cards*.

Available card (*Solitaire*). One which may be transferred elsewhere in the layout.

Avondale schedule. The recommended table for scoring of Five Hundred.

Back door (*Bezique*). A sequence in a plain suit.

Backer. (1) Nonplayer who finances an active player. (2) Banker.

Back game (*Backgammon*). The strategy of not advancing runners early, but of using them to catch adverse blots when opponent is well advanced.

Backgammon (*Backgammon*). The winning of a game when the loser has one or more stones on the bar or in the adverse home table.

Back in (*Poker*). Come into the betting after checking.

Back to back (*Stud Poker*). Said of the hole card and first upcard when they are a pair.

Backward pawn (*Chess*). One that is subject to attack from an enemy pawn if advanced, especially if the advance is difficult to enforce without loss.

Bait. (1) Same as *Bete*. (2) (*Rummy*) A discard intended to influence an opponent's later discard.

Balanced hand. A hand with no void, singleton, or very long suit.

Balking cards (*Cribbage*). Cards unlikely to produce a score, given to the opponent's crib.

Bam (*Mah-Jongg*). A card of the Bamboo suit.

Bamboos (*Mah-Jongg*). One of the three suits.

Banco (*Chemin-de-Fer*). A bet equal to the entire bank.

Bank. Gambling house; dealer in a gambling game.

Bank Craps. The game of Craps as played in a gambling house, all bets being laid against the house.

Banker. (1) Dealer in a gambling house. (2) The person (usually a player) who sells and redeems chips.

Bar. (1) (*Bank Craps*) Rule out a decision on a certain number, as to bar double aces. (2) (*Craps*) Back line. (3) (*Backgammon*) Dividing line between the inner and outer tables.

Bar point (*Backgammon*). Either seven-point.

Barred. (1) Estopped from bidding by a legal penalty, as in Bridge. (2) (*Checkers*) Not permitted (as a move) in tournament play. (3)

(*Craps*) Not affecting the bet.

Base (*Canasta*). The number of natural cards required in a canasta.

Base count, basic (*Canasta*). The total of all bonuses.

Base value. (1) (*Skat*) A constant factor in computing the value of a game. (2) (*Bridge*) Value of an odd trick.

Bate. Same as *bete*.

Bear off (*Backgammon*). To remove stones from the house board in the last stages of a game.

Beat the board (*Stud Poker*). Have a higher Poker combination than the cards of any other player.

Beg (*All Fours*). A proposal by eldest hand to dealer that three additional cards be dealt to each hand and that a new card be turned up for trump.

Bela, or bella (*Klaberjass, Alsos*). The king and queen of trumps.

Below the line (*Bridge*). The place on the score sheet where the trick score is entered.

Best bower (*Euchre*). The Joker, when it is the highest trump.

Best card. Highest card of a suit remaining unplayed; master card.

Bet. Any wager on the outcome of play or of a game, such as that the bettor holds the winning hand.

Bet blind (*Poker*). Bet without looking at the hand.

Bete. (1) Beaten; having failed to make contract. (2) A forfeit paid by a loser or by a transgressor of a rule or correct procedure.

Bet the pot. Bet as many chips as there are in the pot at the moment.

Betting interval. Period during which each active player in turn has the right to bet or to drop out.

Bezique (*Bezique*). The queen of spades and jack of diamonds.

Bicycle (*Poker*). The lowest hand at Lowball.

Bid. An offer to contract to win a certain number of tricks or points in play; to make a bid.

Biddable suit (*Bridge*). A player's holding in a suit that meets the systemic requirements for a bid.

Bidder. (1) Any player who makes a bid. (2) The player who makes the highest bid and assumes the contract.

Bidding. The auction; the period during which bids are made; competing in the auction.

Bid-over. Overcall; bid higher than the last previous bid.

Big casino (*Casino*). The ten of diamonds.

Big Dick (*Craps*). The roll of ten.

Big Dog (*Poker*). A hand consisting of ace-high and nine-low but no pair.

Big eight (*Craps*). (1) A bet that neither 8 nor 7 will be cast in the next two rolls. (2) A bet that 8 will be cast before 7.

Big six (*Craps*). (1) A bet that neither 6 nor 7 will be cast in the next two rolls. (2) A bet that 6 will be cast before 7.

Big Tiger (*Poker*). A hand consisting of king-high and eight-low but no pair. Same as *big cat*.

Bishop. A chess piece.

Black. Conventional designation of one of the players in a two-hand board game.

Blackjack (*Black Jack*). Ace and any 10-point card.

Black lady (*Hearts*). The queen of spades. Same as *black Maria*.

Blackwood convention (*Contract Bridge*). A system of cue-bidding to reach slams, invented by Easley Blackwood.

Blank. (1) Void; holding no cards of a suit. (2) To discard all cards of a suit, or all low cards from a high hand.

Blank a suit. Discard all cards held in that suit.

Blank suit. Absence of any cards of that suit from the hand.

Blind. (1) A compulsory bet or ante made before the cards are dealt. (2) Same as *the widow*.

Blind lead. One made before certain cards are disclosed.

Blitz (*Gin*). Same as *shutout*.

Block. A situation in which the player in turn is unable to play, or no player is able to play.

Blocking a suit. So playing that a partner with the longer of two partnership holdings in a suit cannot obtain the lead in that suit.

Blot (*Backgammon*). A single stone on a point.

Blue Peter (*Whist*). The asking signal for a trump lead.

Bluff. A bet on a hand that the player actually does not believe is best.

Board. (1) The field of squares or lines on which certain games are played. (2) (*Duplicate Bridge*) A deal. (3) (*Stud Poker*) The exposed cards of all active players.

Bobtail (*Poker*). Same as *four flush* or *double-ended straight*.

Bold stand (*Loo*). A deal in which the pool contains only the dealer's ante and all must play. Also called a *single*.

Bone. Dominoes; dice.

Boneyard (*Dominoes*). The reserve of dominoes from which a player must draw when unable to play from his hand.

Bonus. A score given for holding certain cards or completing a high contract.

Bonus circles (*Teeko*). The center circle and each of the four corner circles of the game board.

Booby prize. Prize for lowest score.

Booby table. In progressive play, the table of highest number, to which losers move from table No. 1.

Boodle card (*Stop family*). Extra cards placed

in a layout on which bets are laid.

Book (*Bridge, Whist*). The number of tricks a side must win before it can score by winning subsequent tricks; usually, six tricks.

Boost. To raise a bet.

Borderline bid (*Bridge*). A bid on a hand that barely meets the systematic requirements.

Borrow. Take extra cards from one's previous melds to complete new melds.

Bower. A jack, as in Euchre.

Box (1) (*Gin*) The score for winning a deal. (2) An apparatus from which cards are dealt, as in Faro.

Box cars (*Craps*). The roll 6–6.

Box numbers (*Craps*). Spaces in the layout on which a bet may be placed that any given number will be cast before 7.

Box-up (*Craps*). Shuffle a batch of dice preparatory to selecting a pair.

Bracket. In a knockout tournament, a group of two, four, eight, etc., contestants scheduled together for a series of elimination matches.

Break. (1) To divide in a specified way, as evenly or unevenly—said of the cards held by one's opponents. (2) (*Rummy*) The point at which the stock contains too few cards for everyone to have another draw. (3) (*Rummy*) The act of making the first meld.

Break the bank. Exhaust the quota of funds supplied to the dealer in a house. (Note: The term does not imply that all funds available to the house have been won.)

Break even (*Faro*). (1) Bet on a card an equal number of times to win and lose. (2) Win or lose nothing on net. (3) (Of outstanding cards) found equally divided between the opponents.

Breaks. (1) Chance occurrences. (2) Division of crucial unplayed cards between two hands. (3) Luck.

Breathe (*Poker*). Same as check.

Brelan (*Bezique*). Three of a kind.

Brelan carré (*Bezique*). Four of a kind.

Bridge (*Euchre*). A score of 4 when opponents have not more than 2.

Brisque (*Bezique*). Any ace or ten.

Buck (*Poker*). A token used as a reminder of the order of precedence in dealing, exercising any privilege or duty, etc.

Buck the game. Bet against the house.

Buck the tiger (*Faro*). Play against the bank.

Bug (*Poker*). The joker, when it may be used only as an ace or as a wild card in filling a flush, a straight, or a low hand.

Build. (*Casino*) Combine two or more cards to be taken in later. (*Solitaire*) Transfer cards among the tableau cards and foundations.

Builders (*Backgammon*). Stones in advantageous position to make valuable points, especially stones in one's own outer table.

Bumper (*Whist*). A rubber won by two games to none.

Bunch. (1) Abandon the deal; gather cards preparatory to shuffling. (2) (*Auction Pitch*) An offer to play a contract of 2 or to have a new deal, at the opponent's option.

Buried card (*Rummy, Solitaire*). A card not immediately available.

Burn a card. Expose and bury it, or place it on the bottom of the pack.

Bury a card. (1) Place it in the middle of the pack or among the discards, so that it cannot be readily located. (2) (*Pinochle*) Lay aside, for future counting.

Business double (*Bridge*). One made for the purpose of exacting increased penalties.

Bust. (1) A very poor hand. (2) (*Black Jack*) Go over 21 and lose one's bet immediately. (3) (*Oh Hell*) Take too many or too few tricks.

Buy. Draw from the widow or stock; cards so received.

Buy-in (*Poker*). Same as *stack*.

Buy the contract. Win the right to name the trump or game by making the highest bid.

Buy the pot (*Poker*). Put in the pot as many chips as are already there, to buy a privilege.

By gards (*Whist*). Won in tricks.

Bye. A round of a tournament in which a contestant is not scheduled to play.

By me. A declaration meaning "Pass."

Call. (1) Declare; bid or pass. (2) (*Bridge*) Any pass, double, redouble or bid. (3) (*Poker*) Make a bet exactly equal to the last previous bet.

Call solo (*Six-bid Solo*). A bid to win all the points in play, the bidder being privileged to call any card not in his hand and receive it in exchange for a discard.

Call the turn (*Faro*). Predict correctly the order of the last three cards in the box.

Can (*Faro*). The Faro box.

Canasta. A meld of seven or more cards. Natural canasta, one using no wild cards, as distinct from mixed canasta.

Capot (*Piquet*). Winning of all the tricks by one player; the score therefor.

Captain. The team member who has final decision, as in Chouette and in certain partnership bidding systems.

Capture. Remove an enemy piece from the game board.

Cards. (1) Playing cards; dominoes or other implements of play. (2) (*Casino*) The count of 3 points for winning 27 or more cards. (3) (*Whist*) The number of tricks won over six.

Carolina (*Craps*). The roll of nine. Also *Nina from Carolina*.

Carte (*Baccarat*). Player's request for an additional card.

Carte blanche. A hand without a face card.

Case (*Faro*). An abacus or counting rack used to record the cards as they show.

Case card. (1) The last card of a rank remaining in play. (2) (*Faro*) The last of its rank left in the box.

Casekeeper. The house man who keeps track of the cards that have already been exposed.

Cash. Lead and win tricks with established cards.

Cash points (*Casino*). The scores for big and little casino and aces.

Caster (*Craps*). The player who throws the dice.

Castle. A chess piece; also rook.

Castling (*Chess*). A certain compound move of the king and one rook.

Catch. Find valuable cards in the widow or draw from the stock.

Cat-hop (*Faro*). Two cards of the same rank among the last three.

Center (1) (*Chess*) The central squares, specifically d5, d4, e5, and e4. (2) (*Solitaire*) The foundation piles. (3) (*Craps*) That part of the playing area where the dice are cast.

Center wedge (*Teeko*). To play four same-colored pawns toward the center of the board and disperse and separate the four opposite-colored pawns.

Characters (*Mah-Jongg*). One of the three suits; also *cracks*.

Charleston (*Mah-Jongg*). The passing of unwanted tiles to other players.

Check. (1) A Poker chip; any token. (2) (*Poker*) A declaration that a player elects to remain in the pot without betting, or by making the minimum bet when it is one chip. (3) (*Chess*) A threat to capture the enemy king.

Checker. A piece in Checkers; any disk used in a board game; draughtsman.

Checkerboard. The field of light and dark squares used in Checkers; any similar board.

Checkmate (*Chess*). Capture of the adverse king, the object of play. Also *mate*.

Chessboard. The field of light and dark squares used in Chess; any similar board.

Chicane. Void of trumps.

Chico (*Solo*). A bid to play without use of the widow, naming any suit but hearts as trumps.

Chip. A token used in place of money; place chips in the pot.

Chouette. A method by which three or more players can participate in a two-hand game.

Chow (*Mah-Jongg*). A set of three tiles in suit and sequence; to ground such a set.

Cinch (*Cinch*). Play a trump higher than the five, to prevent an opponent from winning with a pedro.

Cinch hand. (1) (*Stud Poker*) One that no other player can beat in the showdown, regardless of his hole card. (2) Any hand sure to win.

Circles (*Mah-Jongg*) One of the three suits; also *dots*.

Clear. (1) Establish a card or suit by forcing out adverse higher cards or stoppers. (2) (*Hearts,* etc.) Having taken no hearts or other minus cards.

Cleared hand (*Mah-Jongg*). One in which all the suit tiles are of one suit.

Close (*Whiskey Poker*). A call limiting each other player to one more turn, after which there is a showdown. (*Sixty-Six*) End the period in which cards may be drawn from the stock.

Close cards (*Cribbage*). Those near in rank. Also same as *near cards*.

Closed point (*Backgammon*). One that is occupied by two or more adverse stones.

Close the board (*Backgammon*). Establish a shutout.

Club stakes. The limitations of betting and rate per point that apply to play in a club, in the absence of any special agreement among the players.

Cockeyes (*Craps*). The roll of 3.

Coffeehousing. Attempting to mislead opponents as to one's cards by speech and manner.

Cold deck. Prearranged pack switched for the fairly shuffled pack in a crooked game.

Cold hands (*Poker*). Hands dealt face up, as for the determination of the winner of extra chips in dividing the pot.

Color. Suit; also, red or black.

Column (*Solitaire*). A line of cards extending away from the player.

Combination. (*Cribbage*) Group of cards of scoring value; any group of cards. (*Rummy*) Two cards that can become a meld by addition of a matching third card. (*Chess*) A precisely calculated series of moves and alternatives.

Combine. (1) (*Casino*) Take in cards by pairing. (2) (*Solitaire*) Consolidate piles; build. (3) Combination.

Come bet (*Craps*). A bet that the dice will win, treating the next roll as the first of a series.

Come-on. (*Bridge*) Signal to partner to lead or continue a suit; echo. (*Gin*) A discard selected for purpose of advertising.

Come-out (*Craps*). To make the first roll of a series.

Comet (*Stops*). A wild card, sometimes the nine of diamonds.

Comfort station (*Backgammon*). Either 12-point.

Command. The best card of a suit; master card; control.

Compass game (*Duplicate Play*). A tournament comprising separate contests among North-South pairs and East-West pairs.

Completed trick. One to which every hand has played a card.

Complete hand. (*Draw Poker*) The five cards held by a player after the draw. (*Rummy*) One entirely formed in sets, with no odd cards.

Concealed. (*Mah-Jongg*) Still on the player's rack, not grounded. (*Canasta*) Going out without having previously melded.

Condition. A meld that has extra value, as in Panguingue.

Condone. Waive penalty for an irregularity.

Contract. The obligation to win a certain minimum number of tricks or points.

Contractor. The high bidder.

Conventions. Advance agreement between partners on how to exchange information by bids and plays.

Copper (*Faro*). A token placed on a bet indicating that it is a bet on a card to lose.

Count. (1) Score; determine or total the score. (2) Numerical total of certain cards, as deadwood in Gin, cards played in Cribbage. (3) Base values.

Counter. (1) A token used in place of money; chip. (2) A piece used in a board game; checker. (3) (*Chess*) In the name of an opening, a Black choice of moves. (4) Counting card or bone.

Counting card. One that has intrinsic scoring value when taken in a trick.

Count minimum (*Canasta*). The requirement in point values for a valid initial meld (50, 90, or 120, according to the side's accumulated score).

Count out. Go game, especially by accumulation of points during play of a hand.

Coup. (1) A brilliant play. (2) A winning play or bet.

Court card. Same as *face card*.

Cover. Play a card higher than the highest previously played to the trick.

Crack. Discard a card wanted by an opponent; meld when there is possible advantage in keeping the cards in the hand; unload.

Cracks, craks (*Mah-Jongg*). The suit characters.

Crap (*Craps*). Cast of 1–1, 1–2, or 6–6 (2, 3, or 12).

Crap out (*Craps*). Throw a 7 when trying for a point.

Crazy joker (*Poker*). The joker when used as a completely wild card.

Crib (*Cribbage*). The extra hand formed by the players' discards, belonging to the dealer.

Cribbage board. A device for scoring.

Cross-ruff (*Bridge, Whist*). Alternate trumping of each other's plain-suit leads by the two hands of a partnership.

Cross the suit (*Euchre*). Name as trump a suit of color opposite from that of the rejected turn-up card.

Croupier. A banking-house employee who collects and pays bets, and sometimes also deals.

Crown (*Checkers*). Promote from a single man to a king; place a checker on another to show that it has become a king.

Cue bid (*Contract Bridge*). One that systematically shows control of a suit, especially by possession of the ace or a void.

Cumulative scoring (*Bridge*). A method of scoring in duplicate play, by determining the net total of the plus and minus scores made on all the boards played by a partnership.

Cup. Receptacle in which dice are shaken before casting.

Cut. (1) Divide the pack into two piles and reverse their order. (2) Same as *draw*.

Cut in. Enter a game by drawing cards for precedence.

Cut the pot. Take a percentage from the pot.

Cutthroat. Three-handed; applied also to any game in which each plays for himself.

Dead (*Stud Poker*). An expression meaning no cards of a rank are available, e.g., "The aces are *dead*." This means all aces are exposed on the table or were exposed by players who dropped out.

Dead card. One which cannot be used in play.

Dead hand. One barred from further participation.

Dead man's hand. A Poker hand, two aces and two eights, said to have been held by Wild Bill Hickok when he was shot and killed.

Deadwood. (*Poker*) The discard pile. (*Rummy*) Unmatched cards in a hand.

Deal. (1) Distribute cards to the players; the turn to deal. (2) The period from one deal to the next, including all incidents of making the trump, bidding, melding, discarding, playing, showing, and scoring. (3) The cards dealt to the players respectively; a layout of the hands of all players.

Dealer. (1) The player who distributes the cards in preparation for play. (2) Banker.

Dealer's choice. Any Poker game in which the dealer has the right to name the variant to be played in that deal.

Deal off. Make the first deal in the last round, after which the session ends.

Deal out. Omit giving a card or cards to a hand in regular turn during the deal.

Deck. All the playing cards with which a game is played; also called *pack*.

Deckhead. A card turned for trump; turn-up.

Declaration. Call; bid; naming of a trump suit or game; the trump suit or game as named in a bid.

Declare. (1) Call; bid; name the trump. (2) Announce; meld.

Declare out. Same as *count out*.

Declarer. (1) Same as *bidder*. (2) (*Bridge*) The player who plays both his hand and the dummy. That is, the partner who plays the contract, the one who first bid the trump suit or no trump.

Defender (*Contract Bridge*). An opponent of declarer.

Defense bid (*Bridge*). (1) One made by an opponent of the opening bidder. (2) One made to prevent opponents from winning the contract cheaply.

Defensive strength (*Bridge*). Cards that are expected to win tricks against an adverse contract.

Demand bid (*Bridge*). One that systematically requires partner to keep the auction open or to make a responsive bid.

Denial bid (*Bridge*). One showing lack of support for partner's declaration.

Denomination. (1) Rank. (2) (*Contract Bridge*) The suit or no-trump as named in a bid.

Deuce. Any two-spot.

Development (*Chess*). The initial phase of a game, particularly the moving of other pieces off the first rank and castling so as to "unite the rooks."

Dice. Cubes having faces numbered from 1 to 6, used in many games (singular, *die*).

Dis (*Pinochle*). The lowest trump. Also, *dix*.

Discard. (1) Lay aside excess cards in exchange for others from the stock or the widow; a discarded card or cards. (2) Play a plain-suit card not of the same suit as the lead.

Discard pile. (*Rummy*) Cards previously discarded. (*Solitaire*) Same as talon or waste pile.

Discouraging card (*Bridge*). Any played card that indicates no desire to have the suit led or continued.

Distribution. Division of cards among the hands, especially as to the number of each suit held by each hand.

Dominoes. Tiles used in many games; the usual set contains tiles marked with each possible combination of 0, 1, 2, 3, 4, 5, 6, taken two at a time and including repetitions (28 tiles).

Domino game. (1) Any game with dominoes. (2) Any card game in which the hands are replenished, after each trick, by drawing from the stock, as Gin Rummy.

Don't come (*Craps*). The proposition that the shooter will lose, counting his next roll as the first of a series.

Don't pass line (*Craps*). The part of the betting layout on which is placed a bet that the shooter will not pass.

Double (*Bridge*). A call which has the effect of increasing the trick values and penalties in case the last preceding bid becomes the contract.

Double bete (*Pinochle*). The penalty suffered by a bidder who has elected to play the hand and has lost.

Double check (*Chess*). Check by each of two pieces simultaneously.

Double dummy (*Whist*). A game or situation in which a player knows the location of all cards.

Double-ended straight (*Poker*). Four cards in sequence that can be filled to a straight by the draw of a card of next-higher or next-lower rank.

Double pairs royal (*Cribbage*). Four of a kind.

Double run (*Cribbage*). A hand comprising a run of three cards with one rank duplicated.

Doublet. (*Dice*) A cast of like numbers on two dice. (*Dominoes*) A bone having the same number on both ends.

Doubleton (*Bridge*). An original holding of two cards in a suit.

Doublets (*Backgammon*). The roll of the same number on both dice.

Double up. Bet twice as much as was previously bet and lost.

Down. Defeated; having failed to make a contract; set back.

Drag down (*Craps*). Remove all or part of one's winnings from the pool.

Draughtsman. Checker piece; any piece of disk shape used in a board game.

Draw. (1) Pull cards from a pack spread face down to determine seats, first deal, etc. (2) Receive cards from the stock to replace discards.

Draw game. One abandoned without victory for any player, as in Chess, Gin Rummy, etc.

Driver's seat, in the (*Poker*). Said of a player who holds what is sure to be the best hand.

Drop. Withdraw from the current deal; discard one's hand, rather than put enough chips in the pot to remain an active player.

Drop move trap (*Teeko*). To form a winning or a possible winning position with the placing of a player's four pawns on the game board.

Duck (*Bridge*). Fail to cover when able.

Dummy (*Bridge*). Declarer's partner; the hand laid down by him and played by declarer.

Duplicate. A form of Bridge or Whist play in which all contestants play the same series of deals, which are kept in original form by use of duplicate boards.

Dutch straight (*Poker*). Same as *Skip straight*.

Eagles. The United States name of the fifth suit, green in color, at one time added to the standard deck.

Easy aces (*Auction Bridge*). The condition when each side holds two aces.

Echo (*Whist*). The play, for signaling purposes, of a higher card before a lower card of the same suit.

Edge. Same as *age*.

Eighty kings (*Pinochle*). A meld of four kings, one of each suit.

Eldest hand. The player at the left of the dealer.

Encouraging card. One played that indicates a desire to have the suit led or continued or indicates strength in it.

End (*Dominoes*). The number on one half of a bone.

Endbet. A bet in the last betting interval.

End game. (*Chess*) The period of a game after queens are exchanged, or when the immediate goal is to promote a pawn. (*Checkers*) The period of a game after one or more kings have been crowned.

Endhand (*Skat*). The active player who is third in order of bidding.

Endhole. Extra hole at one end of a Cribbage board; game hole.

End play. Any of several stratagems (especially, *throw-in*) that can usually be executed only in the last few tricks of the play.

En passant (*Chess*). A manner of capture by a pawn.

Enter (*Backgammon*). Move a stone, after it has been hit, from the bar to the adverse home table.

Entry. A card with which a hand can eventually win a trick and so gain the lead.

Equals. Cards in sequence or which have become sequential through the play of the cards of intervening rank.

Established. Make cards the best by forcing out adverse higher cards; clear.

Established suit. One that can be cashed in its entirety without loss of a trick.

Euchre (*Euchre*). Failure of the maker to win the number of tricks contracted for.

Exchange (*Chess, Checkers*). Capture and countercapture of pieces.

Exit. Get out of the lead; compel another hand to win a trick.

Exposed card. One played in error, inadvertently dropped, or otherwise shown not in a legitimate manner, and therefore (in most games) subject to penalty.

Exposed hand. (*Solo*) A hand laid down in open play for a greater score. (*Bridge*) The dummy hand.

Eye (*Go*). An open point entirely enclosed by stones on one color.

Face card. Any king, queen, or jack. (The ace is not a face card.)

Faced. Lying with its face exposed.

Fade (*Craps*). Bet against the shooter's center bet.

False card. One selected for play, when there is a choice, to mislead opponents as to the contents of the hand.

False openers (*Poker*). A hand with which a pot has been opened, but which is not as good as the rules require.

Fan (*Solitaire*). Cards spread face up, fan-fashion.

Fatten. (*Poker*) Same as *sweeten*. (*Pinochle*) Same as *smear*.

Fat trick. One rich in counting cards.

Feed the kitty. Set aside a percentage of each pot to defray expenses.

Field (*Craps*). A group of numbers, usually 2, 3, 5, 9, 10, 11, 12.

Fifteen (*Cribbage*). A combination of cards totaling 15 in pip values; the score of 2 for such a combination.

File. A line of squares perpendicular to the sides at which the players are seated.

Fill (*Poker*). Draw cards that improve the original holding.

Finesse. An attempt to make a card serve as an equal to a higher-ranking card held by an opponent.

First hand. (1) The leader to a trick. (2) The first player in turn to *call*.

Fish. Draw cards from the stock.

Five fingers. The five of trumps.

Five of a kind. The highest-ranking hand in Poker, composed wholly of cards of the same rank plus wild cards designated to be of that rank.

Five-point cards (*Canasta*). Any seven, six, five, four, or black three, each valued at 5 points.

Flag flying (*Bridge*). Assuming a losing contract to prevent the opponents from winning a game.

Flash. Expose a card, as in dealing.

Flat bet (*Craps*). A bet that the shooter will or will not pass, made between players other than the shooter.

Flowers (*Mah-Jongg*). Certain special tiles, used like wild cards in modern Mah-Jongg.

Flush. (*Poker, Cribbage*) A hand with all cards of one suit. (*Pinochle*) A meld of the A, K, Q, J, 10 of trumps.

Fold (*Stud Poker*). Withdraw from the current deal, as signified by turning one's cards face down.

Follow suit. Play a card of the same suit as the lead.

Foot. The bottom portion of the stock, when it is divided in two parts for easier handling.

Force. (1) Compel a player to trump if he wishes to win the trick. (2) (*Contract Bridge*) By a conventional call, demand that partner bid. (3) (*Rummy*) Discard a card that the next player is required to take.

Forcing bid (*Contract Bridge*). Demand bid.

Forehand (*Skat*). The active player who is first in order of bidding; eldest hand.

Fork (*Chess*). Simultaneous attack on two pieces or squares.

Forty jacks (*Pinochle*). A meld of four jacks, one of each suit.

Foul hand (*Poker*). One of more or less than the legal number of cards.

Foundation (*Solitaire*). A card on which a whole suit or sequence must be built up.

Four flush (*Poker*). Four cards of the same suit.

Four of a kind. Four cards of the same rank, as four aces.

Fourth-best (*Whist*). The fourth-highest card of a suit held by a hand.

Freak (*Bridge*). A hand of extraordinary pattern. (*Poker*) A wild card.

Free bid (*Bridge*). One made voluntarily, not under any systemic compulsion.

Free double (*Bridge*). The double of an adverse contract which is sufficient for game if made undoubled.

Free ride (*Poker*). Playing in a pot without having to ante or bet.

Freeze or Freeze the pack (*Canasta*). Discard a wild card, making it more difficult to take the discard pile.

Freezeout. Any variant of a game in which a player must drop out when his original stake is exhausted.

Frog (*Skat*). The bid of lowest value.

Front line (*Craps*). Pass line; part of the betting layout on which are placed bets to win.

Full house (*Poker*). A hand comprising three of a kind and a pair. Also called *full hand*.

Gain the lead. Get entry or opportunity to lead by winning a trick.

Gambit (*Chess*). Loss of a pawn or piece to gain a compensating advantage.

Game. (1) A pastime in general, as Poker, Chess. (2) A variant of a basic game, as Seven-Card Stud Poker. (3) A bid or declaration, as club solo, grand tournee, in Skat. (4) A period in a session of play, from which emerges a winner, as a game of Chess. (5) The number of points, accumulation of which wins a game, as the game of 100 in Piquet. (6) Fulfillment of contract; the number of points necessary to fulfill contract; e.g., the player makes game at Skat by winning 61 or more points. (7) (*All Fours*) The ten of trumps; a point awarded for winning a majority of the count in counting cards. (8) A style or system of play, as the forward game in Backgammon.

Gammon (*Backgammon*). Loss of a game, when the loser has borne off no stones but has advanced all his stones beyond the adverse home table.

Gate (*Monte Bank*). The payoff card.

Gift (*All Fours*). The point scored by eldest hand when he begs and dealer rejects.

Gin (*Gin*). A hand completely formed in sets, with no deadwood.

Gin hand (*Gin*). One with no unmatched cards.

Go (*Cribbage*). A call signifying that the player cannot play another card without exceeding 31; the score of 1 point to opponent when "Go" is called.

Go down (*Rummy*). Meld, especially when the act terminates play.

Go Gin (*Rummy*). Lay down a gin hand; go rummy.

Go in. Ante, or stay in, before any betting interval but the last.

Go out. (1) Get rid of all cards in the hand, as in Rummy, Michigan. (2) Reach the cumulative total of points necessary for game, as in All Fours, Cribbage; count out.

Go over. Bid higher.

Go rummy (*Rummy*). Lay down a hand with no unmatched cards, not previously having melded.

Goulash (*Bridge*). A deal of unshuffled cards, three or more at a time, to produce unusual hands.

Grand (*Skat*). A declaration in which only the jacks are trumps. Also, *grando.*

Grand coup (*Bridge*). A stratagem of play; the trumping of partner's winning plain card in order to shorten a trump holding to advantage.

Grand slam (*Bridge*). The winning of all 13 tricks by one side.

Grounded (*Mah-Jongg*). Melded face up on the table.

Group (*Rummy*). Cards forming a valid meld; especially three or four of a kind, as distinguished from a sequence.

Guard. (1) A low card accompanying a high card, saving the latter from having to be played on adverse higher cards, as Q-x-x, the low cards falling on the ace and king if led. (2) (*Chess*) To defend one piece with another; a piece that defends another.

Guckser (*Skat*). A declaration in which jacks are trumps and the bidder picks up the skat. Also *gucki.*

Hand. (1) The cards originally dealt to a player; any portion thereof remaining unplayed. (2) Same as *deal.* (3) A player (holder of a hand). (4) (*Solitaire*) Stock; remainder of the pack after the layout is dealt.

Handplay. A game in which the high bidder does not pick up the widow.

Hard (*Black Jack*). Hand not including an ace.

Hard way (*Craps*). With the same number on both dice, as the number 8 made by rolling 4–4.

Head a trick. Play a card higher than any previously played to the trick.

Head-to-head. Indicating that only two players are engaged in a card game, one against the other.

Heavy (*Dominoes*). Having a relatively high number of pips.

Hedge. Bet against a contingency formerly bet on, to reduce or limit possible losses.

Heeled bets (*Faro*). Bets on one card to win and another to lose.

Help. (1) Raise, assist. (2) Hold helpful cards (in support of partner).

High (*All Fours*). The ace of trumps, or the highest trump dealt; the score for holding such card.

High-Low. (*Bridge*) Same as *echo.* (*Poker*) Designating a pot that the high and low hands divide.

Hinterhand. Same as *endhand.*

His heels (*Cribbage*). A jack turned as starter; the score of 2 to the dealer for this turn-up.

His nobs (*Cribbage*). A jack of the same suit as the starter, in hand or crib; the score of 1 point for such jack.

Hit. (*Gin*) Discard a card that the next player can use. (*Black Jack*) Deal another card to a player.

Hit me (*Black Jack*). Player's request for an additional card.

Hoc. The last card in a deal of Faro.

Holding. The cards in one's hand.

Hold up (*Bridge*). Refuse to win a trick with.

Hole card (*Stud Poker*). The first card received by a player, which is dealt face down.

Home. Up to average expectation in total score, as in Cribbage.

Honors. (1) High cards, especially if they have scoring value. (2) (*Bridge*) The five highest trumps, or, if there is no trump, the four aces.

Honor tricks (*Bridge*). High cards, in hand evaluation.

Howell settlement (*Hearts*). A method of scoring.

Hundred aces (*Pinochle*). A meld of four aces, one of each suit.

Immortal hand. Same as *cinch hand.*

Imperfect pack. One from which cards are missing, in which a card is incorrectly duplicated, or which has become so worn that some cards are identifiable from the back.

Improve. Draw cards that increase the value of the hand.

Index. The small number and suit symbol printed near the corner of a card, used to read the card when it is held in a fan with others. The index value of a card is its number, face cards counting 10 each.

Information. Disclosure of holdings, intentions, and desires between partners through the legitimate channel of bidding or play.

Informatory double (*Bridge*). A systemic double made primarily to give information to partner.

In the hole. Minus score, so-called from the practice of marking a score as minus by drawing a ring around it.

Initial bid. Same as *opening bid.*

Initial meld (*Canasta*). The first made by a side.

In the mitt (*Pinochle*). Received in the deal, as a hundred aces in the original hand.

Inner table (*Backgammon*). That half of the board toward which the stones enter and from which they bear off.

Inside corner (*Faro*). A bet on three cards, so-called from the placement of the bet on the layout.

Inside straight (*Poker*). Four cards needing a card of interior rank to make a straight, as nine, eight, six, five.

Insufficient bid. One that is not legally high

enough to overcall the last previous bid.

Insurance (*Black Jack*). A bet that dealer will not get a natural, when he has an ace showing.

Intermediates (*Bridge*). Cards such as nines and tens, not high enough to be valued but affecting the strength of the hand.

Interpose (*Chess*). Move a piece on the line to avert a check from an enemy queen, rook, or bishop.

Interval of betting. Period during which bets are made and players may drop.

Irregularity. Any departure from a law of correct procedure.

Isolated pawn (*Chess*). One that cannot be protected by another, there being no friendly pawn on either adjacent file.

Jack. (*All Fours*) The score for winning the jack of trumps in play. (*Hearts*) A pool not won because no hand is clear, and therefore held intact for the next deal.

Jackpot (*Poker*). A deal in which everyone antes; usually, in such a deal a pair of jacks or better is required to open.

Jack up. Raise or boost.

Jambone (*Railroad Euchre*). A bid to play alone and with the entire hand faced on the table.

Jamboree (*Railroad Euchre*). A hand holding the five highest trumps, which is shown and scored without play.

Jass, Jasz. The jack of trumps, in Klaberjass.

Jink it (*Spoil Five*). Play for all five tricks.

Joker. An extra card furnished with the standard pack, and used in some games as the highest trump or as a wild card.

Jump bid (*Bridge*). A bid of more tricks than are legally necessary to overcall a bid.

Jump overcall (*Bridge*). An overcall at a level higher than necessary to top the preceding bid, either strong (forcing) or weak (preemptive).

Jump raise (*Bridge*). A raise of partner's suit to higher than the next level.

Jump shift (*Bridge*). A bid of a new suit at a level higher than necessary to top partner's bid.

Junior. Same as *younger*.

Kibitzer. A nonplaying spectator.

Kicker (*Draw Poker*). An extra card kept with a pair for a two-card draw.

Kilter (*Poker*). A hand nine-high with no pair, straight, or flush.

King. (*Chess*) A piece, the protection of which is the object of play. (*Checkers*) A piece that has reached the farthest rank from its initial position and has been crowned.

King row (*Checkers*). Either row adjacent to the Black or White side of the board, where adverse pieces crown.

Kitty. (1) A percentage taken out of the stakes to pay expenses or admission fees. (2) A pool to which bets are paid and from which royalties are collected; a pool that shares like a player in winnings and losses of certain Pinochle bids. (3) Same as *widow*.

Knave. The jack of a suit.

Knock. (*Rummy, Gin*) Signify termination of play by laying down one's hand. (*Poker*) Signify disinclination to cut the pack, or to bet, by rapping on the table.

Kong (*Mah-Jongg*). A set of four identical tiles.

Laps. The carrying forward of excess points from one game to the next.

Last. (*Cribbage*) The point for playing the last card. (*Pinochle*) The score for winning last trick. (*Casino*) Obligatory warning by dealer that the last eight cards of the pack are reached.

Lay away. (*Pinochle, Skat*) Discard after taking up the widow. (*Cribbage*) Give cards to the crib.

Lay down (*Rummy*). (1) Meld a set. (2) Knock.

Laydown. A cinch hand.

Lay odds. Offer a bet of a larger amount against a smaller amount.

Lay the odds (*Craps*). Bet that the shooter will not make his point; or against any contingency that is apparently unlikely to occur.

Lay off. (*Rummy, Gin*). (1) Meld separate cards by adding them to sets already on the table. (2) Bet money previously accepted as the bet of another person.

Layout. (1) A table marked with compartments for bets on various propositions in a banking game. (2) The array of cards first dealt to begin a Solitaire game. (3) (*Dominoes*) The array of all bones played on the table.

Lead. Play first to a trick; the card so played.

Leader. A player on the dealer's immediate left.

Least (*Schafskopf*). The game played if all players pass, the object being to take as few counting cards as possible.

Left bower (*Euchre*). The other jack of same color as the jack of the trump suit.

Left Pedro (*Cinch*). The five of the other suit of same color as the trump.

Light. (1) In debt to the pot. (2) (*Dominoes*) Having relatively few pips.

Limit (*Poker*). The maximum amount by which any player may increase the previous bet.

Limit hand (*Mah-Jongg*). A complete hand that collects the limit in stakes.

Line. (*Craps*) The pass line; the section of the layout on which is placed a bet that the shooter will pass. (*Gin*) The score for a box. (*Chess, Mill*) Squares or points in a line on the board.

Line move (*Teeko*). To move a pawn either forward, backward, sideways, or diagonally from the circle on which it is resting onto an adjacent unoccupied circle.

Line score (*Gin*). Same as *box* score.

Little casino (*Casino*). The two of spades.

Little Dick (*Craps*). The roll of four. Same as *Little Joe*.

Little Dog (*Poker*). A hand consisting of seven-high and deuce-low but no pair.

Little Phoebe (*Craps*). The roll of five.

Little slam (*Bridge*). Same as *small slam*.

Little Tiger (*Poker*). A hand consisting of eight-high and three-low but no pair.

Live card. One still in the hands or stock or otherwise available; one that is not dead.

Lock. A sure thing; cinch.

Lone hand (*Euchre*). One that plays without help of partner.

Lone player. One who elects to play without help of his partner's hand; solo player.

Long card. One left in a hand after all opponents are exhausted of the suit.

Long game. A game in which all cards are dealt originally, as Bridge.

Long suit (*Bridge*). A holding of more than four cards in a suit; the longest holding in any suit in a hand.

Look. Same as *call.*

Lookout (*Faro*). Houseman who watches, deals, and pays bets.

Loose card (*Whist, Rummy*). One that can be discarded as useless.

Loose tile (*Mah-Jongg*). One placed on the wall, to be drawn in replacement of a flower or the fourth of a kong.

Losing card. One that cannot be expected to win a trick. Same as *loser.*

Love. A score of zero.

Low (*All Fours*). (1) The deuce of trumps or the lowest trump dealt; the score for winning it. (2) One's lowest card that can legally be played.

Lurch. The winning of a game when the opponent has not yet passed the halfway mark.

Main (*Craps*). The pass line. Also a bet in Hazard.

Major. The nondealer in two-handed play.

Major piece (*Chess*). A queen or rook.

Major suit (*Bridge*). Spades or hearts.

Major tenace (*Bridge*). The A–Q of a suit, or equivalent combination when some of the high cards are dead.

Make. (1) The contract; the denomination or game named in the contract. (2) To name the trump suit or game. (3) To fulfill the contract.

Make good (*Poker*). Add enough chips to meet the previous bet.

Make a point. (*Craps*) Roll the point number be-

fore 7. (*Backgammon*) Occupy a point with two or more stones.

Maker. Player who names the trump suit or game.

Make up. Gather and shuffle the pack for the next deal.

Man. Same as *piece, pawn,* or *stone.*

March (*Euchre*). The winning of all five tricks by one player or one side; the score for winning all the tricks.

Marker. (1) Token or chip used in place of money, especialy at Faro. (2) Device for keeping record of the score. (3) Scorekeeper. (4) Promissory note.

Marriage (*Pinochle, Bezique*). A meld of the king and queen of a suit.

Master card. The highest card of a suit remaining live or unplayed.

Matador. (1) (*Skat*) Each high trump held in an unbroken sequence with the highest. (2) Any high trump. (3) (*Domino Matador*) Any of the bones 0–0, 6–1, 5–2, 4–3.

Matched, matching. Corresponding in kind, said of cards or bones that may legally be melded (Rummy) or played (Dominoes) or built (Solitaire).

Matched card. (1) One that forms part of a valid set. (2) (*Rummy*) Matched set, three or more cards forming a valid meld, as three aces or 8-7-6 of hearts.

Matched set (*Rummy*). Same as *set.*

Match-point scoring (*Bridge*). A method of scoring in duplicate play.

Mate. Same as *checkmate.*

Meet a bet. Same as *call;* add enough chips so as to make a total contribution equal to the maximum made by any previous player.

Meld. A combination, set, or group of cards of value in scoring or in getting rid of one's cards; to show or announce such a combination.

Menel (*Klaberjass*). The nine of trumps.

Middlehand. (1) A player at right of the dealer, in three-handed play; second active player in order. (2) (*Skat*) The active player who is second in order of bidding.

Middle straight. Same as *inside straight.*

Mid-game. In a board game, the period of play that follows completion of the opening.

Milking. A method of shuffling by drawing cards simultaneously from top and bottom of the pack and piling them on the table.

Minor. The dealer in two-handed play.

Minor meld (*Canasta*). Any meld less than a canasta.

Minor piece (*Chess*). A bishop or knight.

Minor suit (*Bridge*). Diamonds or clubs.

Minor tenace (*Bridge*). The K–J of a suit, or equivalent combination when some of the high cards are dead.

Misdeal. Any departure from the laws of correct procedure in dealing.

Misere, or misery. Same as *nullo*.

Miss. (1) Fail to draw a helpful card (antonym of fill or improve); fail to cast a desired number with dice. (2) Fail to pass. Also *miss-out* (Craps), (3) (*Backgammon*) Fail to cast a number that will allow entry. (4) (*Loo*) The widow.

Mixed canasta (*Canasta*). A meld of seven or more of a kind, including wild cards.

Mixed pair. In tournament play, a partnership of a man and a woman.

Mouth bet. A bet offered without actually putting chips in the pot.

Move. (1) In a board game, one play; the turn to play. (2) (*Checkers*) Advantage in the opposition of the pieces, determinable by a precise formula.

Muggins (*Cribbage*). The right of a player to take points overlooked by his opponent.

Multipliers (*Skat*). Factors by which the base value of the trump suit is multiplied to determine the value of a game.

Natural. (1) Without use of a wild card. (2) (*Craps*) The cast of 7 or 11 on the shooter's first roll. (3) (*Black Jack*) The combination of an ace and a ten or face card, counting 21. (4) (*Baccarat*) Point of 8 or 9 in two cards. (5) (*Solitaire*) A build in suit, when builds not in suit are allowed.

Natural canasta (*Canasta*). A meld of seven or more cards, none wild.

Natural card. Any that is not wild.

Natural points. Those which must be scored on every deal, as big casino, little casino, high, low.

Near card (*Cribbage*). A card consecutive with another card, or nearly so.

Negative double. Same as *informatory double*.

Nonvulnerable (*Bridge*). Not having scored a game.

Notation. A system of recording the moves or plays of a game.

No-trump. A declaration that offers to play the hand without a trump suit.

N-S, E-W. Compass points, used to designate the four players in a game, as Bridge. (Note: Compass designations are often used also in three-handed and two-handed games.)

Null, Nullo. (1) A bid to win not a single trick, or not more than a specified number of tricks. (2) A noncounting card.

Numerical overcalling. Sufficiency of bids determined by the scoring values rather than by the number of odd tricks.

Odd trick (*Bridge*). Any won by declarer in excess of six.

Off, offside (*Bridge*). Not in position to be captured by a finesse.

Off card (*Rummy*). One that is neither matched nor part of a combination.

Offensive strength (*Bridge*). Cards that are expected to win tricks at one's own contract.

Official (*Pinochle*). Validated by the winning of a trick—said of the score for a meld.

Off number (*Craps*). One that is neither a crap, a natural, nor the shooter's point.

On the bar (*Backgammon*). Awaiting entry, said of a blot that has been hit.

Once around. Game fixed at 61, when scored on a Cribbage board.

One-end straight (*Poker*). A sequence of four cards either ace-high or ace-low.

One-eyes. Face cards on which the face shows only one eye: jacks of spades and hearts, king of diamonds.

One-over-one (*Bridge*). A response of a new suit at same level after an opening bid of one in a suit.

Open. (1) Make the first declaration or the first bid. (2) (*Poker*) Make the first bet, especially in a jackpot. (3) A declaration that offers to play with the entire hand faced on the table. (4) (*Stud Poker*) Face up on the table. (5) Make the first lead of a suit.

Open bet (*Faro*). A bet on a card to win.

Open craps. A game in which players may bet among themselves as well as with the house or banker.

Open-end (*Dominoes*). A branch of the layout on which it is legal to play.

Open-ender. Same as *double-ended straight*.

Openers (*Poker*). A holding that entitles a player to open the pot.

Opening. In a board game, the first phase of play; an established line or variation of early play.

Opening bid. The first bid of the auction. Same as *original bid*.

Opening game (*Teeko*). The placing of the four pawns on the game board plus three additional line moves for each player constitute the opening game.

Opening lead. The first lead of a deal.

Open play. Exposure of his hand by the high bidder, to earn increased score if he makes contract.

Open point (*Backgammon*). One that is not occupied by two or more adverse stones.

Opponent. (1) A player of the other side. (2) An adversary of the high bidder or contractor, especially when two or more adversaries combine against him.

Opposition (*Chess*). Relation of the kings such that one can prevent the other from reaching a desired square.

Order up (*Euchre*). A declaration by an opponent of dealer, accepting the turn-up card for trump.

Original hand. A hand as dealt, before alteration by discard, draw, play, etc.

Outer table (*Backgammon*). The other half of the board from the inner table.

Ouvert. Same as *open*.

Overbid (*Skat*). (1) A bid of more than the value of the game named by the bidder. (2) Same as *overcall*. (3) A bid for more than the player can expect to win.

Overcall. (1) A bid or declaration legally sufficient to supersede the last previous bid. (2) (*Bridge*) Such a bid when made by a defender. (3) To make such a declaration.

Overhand shuffle. A shuffle executed by holding the pack in one hand and dropping packets from the top into the other hand.

Overruff, overtrump. Play a trump higher than one previously played to a trick.

Overs. (1) Chips left on the table after a hand by reason of someone's neglecting to take his share or contributing more than his share. (2) (*Casino*) The count of one point for each card over 30 taken in.

Overtrick (*Bridge*). Any trick won by declarer in excess of his contract.

Pack. (1) The full deck of cards. (2) (*Canasta*) The discard pile.

Packet. A portion of the pack, especially in shuffling and cutting.

Paint. (*Hearts*) Discard a heart on a trick won by another player. (*Low Poker*) Deal a face card to a player drawing to low cards.

Pair. (1) Two cards of the same rank. (2) A partnership of two players. (3) (*Roulette*) A bet on the even numbers.

Pair royal (*Cribbage*). Three of a kind.

Pam (*Loo*). The jack of clubs.

Part score (*Bridge*). A trick-score total of less than game. Same as *partial*.

Partner. Another player with whom one shares a common score, and with whom one therefore cooperates in the bidding and play.

Pass. (1) A declaration signifying that the player does not wish to make a bid, or that he withdraws from the current deal. (2) (*Hearts*) The cards exchanged among the original hands after the deal. (3) (*Craps*) Win as caster, by rolling a natural or repeating point before 7.

Passe (*Roulette*). The numbers 19 to 36 inclusive.

Passed pawn (*Chess*). One not opposed by an adverse pawn on the same or either adjacent file.

Pass line (*Craps*). A space in the layout for bets that the caster will pass.

Pass and out. (*Poker*). The rule that a player who once passes must drop out of the deal.

Pass out a deal. Abandon the deal after all players pass.

Pat. (*Poker*) Without drawing. (*Chess*) A drawn game.

Pat hand (*Draw Poker*). One which makes no discard and no draw; a player who draws no cards.

Pattern (*Whist*). A group of four integers, as 4-4-3-2, expressing the way in which a given suit is divided among the four hands or a given hand is divided into suits.

Pawn. A piece in Chess or Teeko.

Pedro (*Cinch*). The five of trumps, or the other five of the same color.

Peg (*Cribbage*). A marker used for scoring on a cribbage board; win points, especially during the play.

Penalty card (*Contract Bridge*). An exposed card that must be played at first legal opportunity.

Penalty double. Same as *business double*.

Penny ante. A game in which the ante or limit is in pennies; broadly, any game played for insignificant stakes.

Percentage. Advisability, based on sagacious judgment; more purely, probability expressed in hundredths; also, an advantage accruing to the bank, or the house, or a player who has a better chance mathematically of winning than his opponent.

Perpetual check (*Chess*). Unremitting attack on a king, without checkmate, leading to a draw.

Perpetual draw (*Checkers*). Drawn game achieved by repetition of the same series of moves, deviation from which is impossible or fatal to the opponent.

Pianola hand (*Bridge*). One that is very easy to play.

Pic (*Piquet*). The bonus of 30 for scoring 30 in declarations and play before opponent scores a point.

Picture card. Same as *face card*.

Piece. (1) (*Chess*) This term is often restricted to pieces other than the pawns. (2) Objects moved on game board.

Pigeon (*Poker*). A card drawn that greatly improves the hand.

Pin (*Chess*). Immobilization of a piece through the fact that a move of the piece off a line would expose its own king to check.

Pinochle (*Pinochle*). A meld of the queen of spades and jack of diamonds.

Pip. Any of the large suit symbols printed on the face of a card (excluding index marks). Pip value is the numerical or index value of the card.

Pique (*Piquet*). The winning of 30 points before opponent scores a point; the bonus of 30 points therefore. Also *pic*.

Pitch (*Auction Pitch*). The opening lead, which fixes the trump suit.

Pivot. A schedule for four players whereby each plays with every other as his partner; the player who remains in the same seat while the others progress.

Places open (*Pinochle*). Outstanding cards that will improve a hand.

Plain suit. Any card that is not trumps.

Play back, or play behind (*Poker*). Guarantee a table stake beyond the stack one has on the table; the effect is the same as though the additional chips were also on the table, but some house rules do not permit such guarantees to be honored.

Played card. One gathered in a trick; one legally construed to be played.

Player. (1) A participant in a game. (2) (*Skat*) The highest bidder, who then plays alone against the two others in partnership. (3) A card that can legally be played.

Playing to the score. Modifying normal strategy of bidding or play when one side is close to game.

Play off (*Cribbage*). Play a card of rank far enough from that of previous cards so that opponent cannot make a run.

Play on (*Cribbage*). Play a card that may enable opponent to make a run.

Play over. Same as *cover*.

Plus values (*Bridge*). Elements of strength in a hand not directly countable under an arithmetic system of hand valuation.

Point. (1) A unit of scoring. (2) (*Piquet,* etc.) The score for holding the longest or highest suit. (3) (*Baccarat*) The digit signifying the numerical total of one's cards. (4) (*Craps*) Cast of 4, 5, 6, 8, 9, or 10 on the shooter's first roll. (5) (*Backgammon*) Any of the 24 marks on the board, usually elongated triangles.

Point bet (*Craps*). A bet that the shooter will make his point.

Point count (*Bridge*). A method of evaluating one's hand by assigning a relative number of points to each high card held.

Point drop move (*Teeko*). A move where the player asks his opponent to point or touch an unoccupied circle on the game board on which he wants the player to place his pawn.

Point value. The assigned value, for scoring purposes, of a counting card.

Pone. The player at dealer's right; in two-hand play, the nondealer.

Position. (1) (*Checkers*) One of the end-game studies deemed to be of basic and far-reaching importance, as first position. (2) The relative seating of the players, a factor of tactical importance.

Positive double. Same as *business double*.

Post-mortem. Discussion of the merits of the bidding and play of a deal.

Pot. The aggregate of chips or money at stake in a deal, consisting usually of contributions from each active player. Same as *pool*.

Predict (*Skat*). Announce intention to make schneider or schwarz.

Preempt (*Bridge*). A high opening bid, made to shut out adverse competition.

Premiums. (1) Same as *royalties*. (2) (*Bridge*) All scores other than for odd tricks.

Prime (*Backgammon*). The making of six consecutive points.

Primiera (*Scopa*). A scoring combination, one card of each suit.

Prison, in (*Roulette*). Said of bets not settled by the current coup, but held in abeyance for the next coup.

Prize pack, or pile (*Canasta*). The discard pile when frozen.

Progression. Movement of players or of boards from table to table in progressive or duplicate play.

Progressive. A form of tournament play in which players progress according to their scores, the cards being dealt at random at every table.

Promotion. The replacement of a piece by one of greater power, as in queening (Chess) and crowning (Checkers).

Proposal (*Ecarte*). Request by nondealer that additional cards be dealt.

Protection. (1) Cards by which others are guarded. (2) To cinch. (3) (*Chess*) Guard of one piece by another. (4) (*Contract Bridge*) A bid made in the belief that partner has passed with a strong hand.

Psychic bid (*Bridge*). One made without the cards to support it, for the purpose of misleading the opponents.

Pull down. Same as *drag down*.

Pung (*Mah-Jongg*). A meld of three of a kind.

Punter. One who plays against the bank.

Pure canasta. Same as *natural canasta*.

Push. To pass unwanted cards to the player to one's left.

Quart (*Piquet*). A sequence of four cards in the same suit.

Quatorze (*Piquet*). Four of a kind (tens or higher), counting 14.

Queen (*Chess*). The most powerful piece.

Queening (*Chess*). Replacement of a pawn that has reached the eighth rank by a queen.

Quick tricks. Same as *honor tricks*.

Quint. (*Piquet*) A sequence of five cards in the same suit. (*Mah-Jongg*) A set of five like tiles (including wild flowers and jokers).

Quitted trick. One that has been turned face down.

Quong (*Mah-Jongg*). Same as *kong*.

Raffle. Three like numbers cast on three dice.

Rail (*Craps*). Raised edge of the table against which the dice must be cast.

Raise. (*Poker*) Put more chips in the pot than are necessary to meet the previous bet. (*Bridge*) Bid an increased number of tricks in a declaration previously bid by partners.

Rake-off. The percentage of the stakes taken by the house or club, usually by means of a kitty.

Ramsch (*Skat*). A nullo game which is played if all players pass.

Rangdoodles. Variant of *roodles*.

Rank. (1) The original position of a card in its suit, determining which card wins or bests another; the precedence of suits in bidding or showing. (2) (*Chess*) A horizontal row of squares.

Rearhind. Same as *endhand*.

Rebid (*Bridge*). A bid made by a player who had previously bid.

Rebiddable suit (*Bridge*). Any five-card suit headed by at least three high-card points: (Q J or K x x x x), or any suit of 6 or more cards.

Redeal. A new deal by the same dealer, usually after a misdeal.

Redouble (*Bridge*). A call which has the effect of further increasing the trick values and penalties in case the last preceding bid, doubled, becomes the contract.

Reduce (*Rummy*). Lower the count of one's deadwood by discarding high cards; *reducer,* a low card.

Reentry. A card with which a hand can gain the lead after having lost it.

Refait (*Trente et Quarante*). A tie in totals of cards dealt to the two rows.

Refusal. (*Ecarte*) Rejection by dealer of a proposal. (*All Fours*) Acceptance by dealer of a beg (hence a refusal to let eldest hand score gift).

Regular drop move (*Teeko*). To place a pawn on any one of the unoccupied circles of the game board at the start of the game. The drop-move phase of the game is completed when all eight pawns are on the game board or a player has achieved a win with the dropping of his four pawns.

Reject (*Skat*). Nullo; a game to take as few points as possible.

Released card (*Solitaire*). One made available by the removal of covering cards.

Renege. Same as *revoke*.

Renounce. Play a card not of the suit led.

Repique (*Piquet*). The winning of 30 points in hand, without play, before the opponent scores a point; the bonus of 60 points therefore. Also, *repic*.

Replay double. A form of duplicate bridge between two pairs.

Requirement. The minimum holdings deemed systematically necessary for a bet, bid, or declaration as in Bridge.

Reraise. An amount of money put into the pot to equal the previous bet and raise, plus an additional bet.

Reserve (*Solitaire*). A part of the layout, cards available to be built elsewhere but not themselves to be built on until moved.

Response. (1) A bid made in reply to a bid by partner. (2) (*Bridge*) A card selected to be played to partner's lead so as to give him information.

Restriction play (*Checkers*). Selection by chance of the opening to be played.

Revoke. Fail to follow suit when able; fail to play a card as required by a law of correct procedure.

Revolution (*Skat*). A variant of null ouvert in which the opponents may pool their cards and redistribute their hands as they see fit.

Riffle. A manner of shuffling.

Right bet (*Craps*). A bet that the shooter will pass; or, depending on usage, that he will make his point, or that the dice will win on a series of rolls beginning with the next.

Right bower (*Euchre*). The jack of trumps.

Right Pedro (*Cinch*). The five of trumps.

Rob a king (*Mah-Jongg*). Claim a fourth tile just added to a pung by another player, to complete one's hand.

Rob the Pack (*Cinch*). Select any desired cards from the stock (the privilege of the dealer).

Robbing. Exchanging a card in the hand for the card turned up for trump.

Roll (*Craps*). A cast of the dice; the total of the numbers on the uppermost faces.

Roller (*Craps*). One who rolls dice; shooter.

Roodles (*Poker*). Any special pot with increased ante or stakes.

Rook (*Chess*). A chess piece.

Rope (*Rummy*). A set in sequence.

Rotation. The progress of the turn to deal, bid, play, etc., which is from player to player to the left, clockwise. (Note: Clockwise rotation is standard for all American and English games. Many games originating in Italy, Spain, China, and elsewhere are traditionally counterclockwise.)

Rough (*Poker*). Relatively bad.

Round. Any division of the dealing, bidding or play, in which each hand participates once, e.g., the series of deals from one player's turn to his next turn; the series of bids from one player's turn to the next; a trick.

Round game. One in which there are no partnerships.

Round house (*Pinochle*). A meld comprising a king and a queen of each suit. Same as *round trip*.

Round-the-corner. Circular sequence of rank, the highest card being deemed adjacent to the lowest, as Q, K, A, 2, 3, a round-the-corner straight in Poker.

Row. A horizontal line of cards (Solitaire) or squares on a board, as in Checkers.

Royal flush (*Poker*). An ace-high straight flush.

Royal marriage (*Pinochle*). A meld of the king and queen of trumps.

Royal sequence (*Pinochle*). Same as *flush*.

Royalties. Payments collected by a player who holds any of certain high hands, in addition to whatever he wins in regular play.

Rubber. The winning of the first two out of three games by one side, or of a series of deals in Four-Suit Bridge.

Rubber Bridge (*Bridge*). A form of play in which rubbers are scored (as opposed to duplicate play).

Rubber points (*Whist*). Points given for winning a rubber.

Rubicon (*Piquet*). Failure of the loser of a game to reach 100 points.

Ruff. Play a trump on a plain-suit lead.

Rule of eleven (*Bridge*). The fact that when a player leads the fourth-best of a suit the difference of its rank from 11 is the number of higher cards of the suit in the other three hands.

Rule of the fourth-best (*Bridge*) (1) The conventional practice of leading the fourth-best of a long suit. (2) The fact that such a lead shows that if the leader has more than four cards, the additional cards are lower in rank than the lead.

Rummy (*Rummy*). Get rid of the last card in the hand; lay down a hand completely formed in sets, also call attention to a play overlooked by an opponent.

Run. A sequence of three or more cards of the same suit, as in Cribbage, Rummy.

Run the cards (*All Fours*). Deal additional cards and make a new turn-up, when a beg is accepted.

Runner (*Backgammon*). A stone in the adverse home table.

Running game (*Backgammon*). The strategy of bringing all stones into the home board as quickly as possible; the period of a game after the two forces have completely passed each other.

Runt (*Poker*). A hand ranking lower than one pair.

Sacrifice. (1) Voluntary loss of one or more pieces for positional advantage, in a board game. (2) Make a sacrifice bid.

Sacrifice bid (*Bridge*). One made without the expectation that the opponents' contract will be fulfilled, for the purpose of saving greater loss.

Safe discard (*Rummy*). One that the next player surely or probably cannot use or pick up.

Sandbagging. (1) When two players who have a third player sandwiched between them keep raising and reraising with no consideration for the third player. (2) When a player checks and then raises after another player has bet.

Schmeiss (*Klaberjass*). A declaration which is a proposal to accept the turn-up card for trump or abandon the deal.

Schmier. Same as *smear*.

Schneider. (*Skat*) Failure of one side to win 31 or more points in a play. (*Gin*) Same as a *shutout*.

Schwarz (*Skat*). The winning of all the tricks by one player or one side.

Score. (1) Counting value of specific cards or tricks. (2) The accumulated total of points won by each player. (3) Scoresheet. (4) Mark or record the score.

Seasons (*Mah-Jongg*). Four special tiles.

Second hand. Second in turn to call or play.

Second turn (*Skat*). Turn-up of the second skat card for trump.

See (*Poker*). Meet a bet; call.

Senior. Eldest hand; adversary who leads to the first trick.

Septet (*Piquet*). A sequence of seven cards.

Sequence. Two or more cards of adjacent rank, as 8, 9, 10; in Rummy, such cards in the same suit.

Serve. Deal cards, especially in replacing discards.

Set. (1) Defeat the contract; defeated. (2) (*Rummy*) A valid meld; three or more cards of the same rank, or of the same suit in sequence. (3) (*Dominoes*) The first bone played.

Set back. Scoring in which the value of a bid is deducted from the contractor's score if he fails to make it.

Set match (*Bridge*). Play with unchanging partnerships.

Settanta (*Scopa*). The count of 1 point for winning the highest group of four cards.

Seven out (*Craps*). Lose, as caster, by rolling 7 before repeating point.

Sextette. (*Piquet*) A sequence of six cards. (*Mah-Jongg*) A set of six like tiles, including wild flowers.

Shoe. A dealing box used in Chemin-de-Fer, Baccarat, and other house gambling games.

Shooter (*Craps*). Caster; one whose turn it is to roll the dice.

Short game. Any game in which not all the cards of pack are put into play during a deal, as Euchre.

Short minor (*Bridge*). An opening bid in a three-card minor suit, used to avoid complications in later bidding on balanced hands too weak to be opened at 1 no trump.

Short suit (*Bridge*). A holding of fewer than four cards in a suit.

Shot (*Checkers*). An exchange of captures precipitated to gain an advantage.

Show. (1) Meld; expose. (2) (*Cribbage*) Count the hand.

Showdown (*Poker*). The facing of all active hands to determine the winner of a pot.

Shuffle. Mix cards, bones, or tiles together preparatory to dealing or drawing the hands.

Shutout. (1) (*Gin*) Failure of the loser of a game to score a single point. *Shut out,* defeated with zero score. (2) (*Bridge*) A high bid made to prevent the opponents from bidding cheaply. (3) (*Backgammon*) A prime in the home table, preventing adverse stones from entering.

Shutout bid. Same as *preemptive bid.*

Side. A competing unit; two or more persons playing for a common score and therefore cooperating in the play of a game.

Side bets (*Dice*). Bets among players other than the caster.

Side card. (1) Any of a plain suit. (2) (*Poker*) The highest card in the hand outside of a pair or two pairs, referred to in deciding higher hand between two that hold one or two pairs of the same rank.

Side money. A bet in a side pot.

Side pot (*Table-Stakes Poker*). One separate from the main pot, made by continued betting after one player has put all his chips in the main pot.

Side strength. High cards in plain suits.

Side suit. Same as *plain suit.*

Sight. The right to compete for the main pot in the showdown.

Signal (*Bridge*). Any convention of play whereby one partner properly informs the other of his holdings or desires.

Sign-off (*Bridge*). A bid that asks partner to pass or to close the auction as soon as possible.

Simple game (*Skat*). The lowest declaration that may be bid.

Simple honors (*Auction Bridge*). The holding of three honors by one side; the score therefor.

Simples (*Mah-Jongg*). Suit tiles of ranks 2 to 8 inclusive.

Single. (1) A pool containing no chips left over from a previous deal. (2) A game won at the minimum stake.

Single Bète (*Pinochle*). A forfeit paid by a bidder who concedes loss of the hand without play.

Single corner (*Checkers*). A corner of the board where a playing square abuts two sides.

Singleton (*Bridge*). An original holding of one card in a suit.

Sink (*Piquet*). Omit announcement of a scoring combination (for possible advantage in play).

Sixie from Dixie (*Craps*). A roll of six.

Sixty days (*Craps*). A point of six.

Sixty queens (*Pinochle*). A meld of four queens, one of each suit.

Skat (*Skat*). The widow.

Skeet (*Poker*). A special hand, consisting of 2, 5, 9 and two other cards lower than 9, but no pair.

Skinning. Dealing cards by sliding them off the top of the pack without lifting them.

Skip bid. Same as *jump bid.*

Skip straight (*Poker*). A special hand, consisting of a sequence of odd or even cards, as J, 9, 7, 5, 3.

Skunked. (1) Beaten without having scored a point. (2) (*Cribbage*) Beaten without having scored at least 61 points.

Slam. The winning of all the tricks by one side.

Sleeper. A dead or unclaimed bet left in the layout.

Slot. Dealer's position in a game conducted by a gambling house.

Sluff, slough. Same as *discard.*

Small slam (*Bridge*). The winning of 12 tricks by one side.

Smear. Discard a counting card on a trick won by a partner. Same as *schmier.*

Smoke out (*Hearts*). Force out the queen of spades by repeated leads of the suit.

Smooth (*Poker*). Relatively good.

Smother play (*Bridge*). The pickup of a guarded high trump by a less-guarded master trump.

Smothered mate (*Chess*). Checkmate by a knight, all squares adjacent to the king being blocked by his own pieces.

Smudge (*Auction Pitch*). A bid to win all four points.

Snake-eyes (*Craps*). A roll of 1-1.

Sneak (*Whist*). The lead of a plain-suit singleton.

Soda (*Faro*). The first card.

Soft (*Black Jack*). A hand including an ace that may be counted as 1 or 11.

Solid suit. (1) A suit holding composed all of winning cards. (2) (*Bridge*) A suit that can be established by straight leads, as Q-J-10-9-8.

Solo. (1) A bid to play without a partner. (2) A bid or game in which the high bidder does not pick up the widow.

Space. (*Solitaire*) A vacancy in the tableau created by the removal of all cards of one pile. (*Go*) Vacant points collectively.

Spade over (*Casino*). The score of 1 point for each spade won over eight.

Spit (*Poker*). A card placed on the center of the table face up which may be used by any player to help form a hand.

Split. (*Faro*) The turn of two cards of the same rank. (*Rummy*) Discard a card from a combination or set. (*Bridge*) Play, second hand, one of equal honors, as K-Q or Q-J.

Split a pair (*Black Jack*). Divide two equal cards originally received, to make two separate hands.

Splitting openers (*Draw Poker*). In a jackpot, discarding part of the combination that qualified the hand to open (in an effort to better the chances of improvement).

Spot card. Any of rank 10, 9, 8, 7, 6, 5, 4, 3, 2.

Spread. (1) Open; show. (2) A contract that can be fulfilled without playing. (3) Any meld.

Squeeze. (1) Look at one's cards by slightly separating them at one corner to see the indexes. (2) (*Bridge*) Compel other hands to discard; an end-play dependent upon compelling adverse discards.

Stack. Pile of chips; quota of chips assigned to each player.

Stalemate (*Chess*). Drawn game in which the player in turn has no legal move but is not checkmated.

Stand. (1) Accept the turned card for trump, as in All Fours. (2) Accept the cards already dealt without drawing, discarding, or redealing, as in Ecarté, Black Jack. (3) Stay in the game during the current deal, as in Loo.

Stand pat. Decline to draw additional cards; play with one's original hand.

Stand pat (*Draw Poker*). Draw no cards.

Standard Pack. (*Bridge*) 52 cards; 13 of each suit; spades, hearts, diamonds, clubs; in each suit A, K, Q, J, 10, 9, 8, 7, 6, 5, 4, 3, 2. (*Piquet, Skat*) 32 cards; the Bridge pack with all sixes and lower cards discarded. (*Pinochle*) 48 cards; equivalent to two Bridge packs with all eights and lower cards discarded.

Standoff. A tie or draw; cancellation of a bet by an indecisive result.

Starter (*Cribbage*). The card cut by nondealer and turned up by dealer prior to the play.

Stay (*Poker*). Remain in the pot without raising; meet a bet; call; see.

Steal a pot (*Poker*). To win a pot by bluffing or by the failure of another player to press his advantages with a higher-ranking hand.

Stich (*Pinochle*). The last trick.

Sticks (*Mah-Jongg*). The suit of bamboos.

Stiff card. Same as *long card*.

Stiff pack. The one not dealt or to be dealt, when two packs are used alternately.

Stock. An undealt portion of the pack, which may be used later in the same deal.

Stone. Any of the pieces used in playing Backgammon, Go, and other board games.

Stop. (*Stops*) Interruption of play caused by absence of the next card in sequence; the card so missing. (*Russian Bank*) A call upon opponent to cease play because of an irregularity in order of play.

Stop card (*Canasta*). A card, such as a black three, that cannot be taken as the top discard.

Stopper. A holding by which a hand can eventually win a trick in a suit led by an adversary.

Straddle (*Poker*). Raise the previous player's blind or the previous player's straddle, by doubling it.

Straight (*Poker*). A hand of five cards in sequence, but not all in the same suit.

Straight flush (*Poker*). A hand of five cards in sequence in the same suit.

String. A wire or cord stretched across and a few inches above a crap table; the dice are thrown over it.

Stringer. Same as *sequence*.

Strip. (1) Remove low cards from the pack to reduce the number of cards in it. (2) (*Bridge*) Play so as to render opponent(s) void in a suit, preparatory to an end play.

Stripped deck. One from which some cards are permanently discarded for a particular game.

Substitution. An exchange of cards. The player discards a card and is dealt one in return. Player usually pays a fee for a substitution.

Sufficient bid. One high enough legally to supersede the last previous bid.

Suit. (1) Any of the four sets of thirteen cards each in the standard pack: spades, hearts, diamonds, clubs. (2) Any of the three sets of 36 tiles each in Mah-Jongg: bamboos, dots, characters. (3) Any of the groups of seven Domino bones having the same number on one end.

Suitable card (*Solitaire*). One that may be built on another or put in a space.

Suit stopper (*Bridge*). High card which will stop opponents from running a suit.

Sweep (*Casino*). The taking in of all cards on the table; the score of 1 point therefor.

Sweepstake (*Hearts*). A method of settlement; the pot is won only by a player who is clear.

Sweeten (*Poker*). Ante again to a jackpot not opened on the previous deal.

Swing or swinging. To announce both low and high in high-low poker.

System. (1) (*Bridge*) A series of agreements between partners as to tactical procedure in various bidding situations. (2) (*Checkers*) One of the two groups of 16 playing squares on four alternate files. (3) A schedule of bets successively to be placed at Roulette, Faro, or other betting games.

Table. (1) The plane surface on which a game is played. (2) The group of players who compete together, including both active and inactive. (3) One of the quarters of a Backgammon board.

Tableau (*Solitaire*). That part of the layout, excluding foundations, on which builds are made. In some games, the entire layout.

Table stakes (*Poker*). A method of placing a limit on betting.

Take (*Klaberjass*). Accept the turned card for trump; such acceptance.

Take-all (*Hearts*). The winning of all the counting cards by one player.

Take a hole (*Pinochle*). Concede bet without playing.

Take-in (*Casino*). Capture cards from the table with a card from the hand.

Take the lead (*Stud Poker*). Make the first bet in a round.

Take odds. Bet a smaller amount against a larger amount.

Takeout. (*Bridge*) The bid of a different declaration from that bid by a partner. (*Poker*) Same as *stack*.

Takeout double. Same as *informatory double*.

Take up. (*Euchre*) Accept the turn-up for trump, said only of the dealer. (*Rummy*) Draw from the discard pile, especially when additional cards are thereby obtained.

Tally. Score sheet, especially as used in progressive play.

Talon (*Solitaire*). Waste pile; cards laid aside as unplayable on being turned up from the stock or hand.

Tap. (1) Rap on the table to signify a pass or a waiver of the cut. (2) (*Table Stakes Poker*) Bet the whole amount of chips in front of a player.

Tenace (*Bridge*). A holding of two cards in a suit, lacking one or more cards of intervening rank, as A, J. Perfect tenace lacks one intervening card; imperfect tenace lacks two or more. Major tenace is A, Q; minor tenace is K, J.

Ten-point card (*Canasta*). Any K, Q, J, 10, 9, or 8, each valued at 10 points.

Tenth card. Any of pip value 10, as a face card at *Cribbage*.

Terminals (*Mah-Jongg*). Suit tiles of ranks 1 and 9.

Third hand. Third in turn to call or play.

Threat. A specific move, play, or series of plays that impends in a given position, where the

first concern of the defending side must be to parry this threat.

Three of a kind. Three cards of the same rank, as three aces.

Threes. Same as *three of a kind*.

Throw-in. The stratagem of forcing an opponent into the lead, in order to compel him to lead to his disadvantage.

Throw off. Discard, smear.

Tierce (*Piquet*). A sequence of three cards of the same suit.

Tiles. Pieces used in Mah-Jongg.

Tops. Highest cards of a suit.

Total-point scoring (*Bridge*). A method of scoring in duplicate play.

Touching. Adjacent rank; cards in sequence.

Tournée (*Skat*). A declaration which offers to turn up a card from the skat to fix the trump suit.

Trail (*Casino*). Play a card to the table without building or taking in.

Transversale (*Roulette*). A bet on three numbers.

Trash. Useless cards.

Trey. Any three-spot.

Trick. A round of cards during the play, one card being contributed by each active hand; the packet of such cards when gathered.

Trick score (*Bridge*). Points made by declarer for odd tricks; the part of the score sheet where such points are entered.

Triplets. Three of a kind.

Trump. (1) A privileged card or suit, the privilege being that in the current deal every such card ranks higher than any plain card. (2) Play a trump on the lead of a plain suit.

Trump card. Any of the trump suit, or one arbitrarily designated as a trump by the rules of the game.

Trump echo (*Bridge*). Playing a high trump card before a lower one to show his partner he started play with three of the declarer's trumps.

Trump suit. One selected under the rules of the game to have the special privilege that every card in this suit ranks higher than any non-trump card in trick-winning.

Turn. (1) A player's opportunity, in due rotation, to deal, declare, play, etc. (2) (*Faro*) A play that decides how certain bets shall be settled.

Turn it down (*Euchre*). Reject the turn-up card as trump.

Twice around. Game fixed at 121, when scored on a Cribbage board.

Two pairs (*Poker*). A hand comprising a pair of one rank, a pair of a second rank, and a fifth card unmatched.

Two-suiter (*Bridge*). A hand containing five or more cards in each of two suits.

Unbalanced hand (*Bridge*). One that contains a singleton or void.

Unblock (*Bridge*). Avoid or resolve a blocked suit, by cashing or discarding high cards.

Under the gun (*Poker*). Said of the first player in turn to bet.

Undercut (*Gin*). Show a hand that counts the same or less than the opponent's after he has knocked.

Underknock

Underplay. Lead or follow suit with a lower card when holding a higher card; hold up; refuse to cover.

Undertrick (*Bridge*). Any by which declarer falls short of making his contract.

Unlimited poker. Agreement that there will be no limit on the size of a bet and the number of raises.

Unload. Get rid of the dangerous cards in one's hand.

Unmatched card (*Rummy*). Any that is not part of a set; deadwood.

Up (*Poker*). A term used, as in "aces up," to designate the higher pair in a two-pair hand.

Upcard. (*Stud Poker*) One properly dealt face up. (*Gin*) The first card turned up from the stock after the deal; the uppermost card of the discard pile.

Uppercut (*Bridge*). Play a high trump to force out a higher trump in an opponent's hand.

Valle cards (*Pan*). Threes, fives, and sevens, so called because there is a special bonus for groups of these cards.

Value of cards. (1) The arbitrary count assigned to each card, for scoring purposes. Also *point value*. (2) The strength or worth of various holdings, estimated for purposes of bidding, declaring, etc.

Vigorish. The fee or percentage accruing to the banker of a game.

Void. A holding of no cards in a suit.

Volat (*Alsos*). A declaration to win nine tricks.

Vole. Winning of all the tricks by one player.

Vulnerable (*Contract Bridge*). Said of a side having won a game toward rubber.

Wall (*Mah-Jongg*). The array of tiles arranged after shuffling.

Wall game (*Mah-Jongg*). Void game, by exhaustion of the wall without any declaration of a complete hand.

Waste pile (*Solitaire*). A pile in which cards turned from the stock are laid face up, if they cannot at the moment be played elsewhere.

Wedge (*Teeko*). A strategic play designed to spread the opponent's pieces over different sections of the game board.

Whangdoodles. Variant of *roodles*.

Wheel. (1) Same as *bicycle*. (2) (*Roulette*) The spinning bowl into which the ball is tossed.

Whipsawed (*Faro*). Condition of one who loses two bets on the same turn.

Wide cards (*Cribbage*). Two cards separated in rank by two or more cards.

Widow. Extra cards dealt at the same time as the hands, and which usually become the property of the highest bidder. Also called the *blind*, the *skat*.

Wild card. One that may be specified by the holder to be of any rank and suit.

Wild discard (*Gin*). Dangerous discard; one that may be used by the next player. (Note: seldom used to mean the discard of a wild card.)

Winds (*Mah-Jongg*). (1) The 16 winds tiles. (2) The four compass positions around the table; hence, the four players. *Prevailing wind:* that in which a set of tiles earns a special bonus.

Winner. A card that wins a trick; one that may be expected to win a trick.

Winning on the drop (*Teeko*). To win the game by placing the four pawns on the game board in a winning position before the actual moving of a pawn from one circle to another.

Winning pawn (*Teeko*). The last (fourth) played pawn which ends the game by completing a winning position—by making use of a regular drop move, a point drop move, or a line move.

With (*Skat*). Holding the specified number of top trumps in unbroken sequence from the jack of clubs down.

Without. (*Skat*) Lacking the specified number of matadors, as "without two." (*Bridge*) A call meaning no trumps.

Woo (*Mah-Jongg*). Declare a complete hand and so end the play.

Wrong bet (*Craps*). One that the shooter will not pass; see also *right bet*.

Yarborough (*Whist*). A hand containing no card higher than a nine.

Younger hand. In two-hand play, the one who does not make the opening lead.

Index

73 74 75 76 77 10 9 8 7 6 5 4 3 2